Cognition, Teaching, and Assessment

Cognition, Teaching, and Assessment

Michael Pressley
University at Albany
State University of New York

with **Christine McCormick**
University of South Carolina

HarperCollins*CollegePublishers*

Executive Editor: Christopher Jennison
Project Coordination: Ruttle, Shaw & Wetherill, Inc.
Design Manager and Text Designer: Mary Archondes
Cover Designer: Kay Petronio
Art Studio: FineLine Inc.
Electronic Production Manager: Valerie A. Sawyer
Desktop Administrator: Sarah Johnson
Manufacturing Manager: Helene G. Landers
Electronic Page Makeup: RR Donnelley Barbados
Printer and Binder: RR Donnelley & Sons Company
Cover Printer: The Lehigh Press, Inc.

Cognition, Teaching, and Assessment

Library of Congress Cataloging-in-Publication Data

Pressley, Michael.
       Cognition, teaching, and assessment / Michael Pressley, Christine McCormick.
          p.   cm.
       An abridgement of: Advanced educational psychology for educators, researchers, and policymakers.
       Includes bibliographical references and index.
       ISBN 0-673-99400-7
       1. Cognition.   2. Cognitive learning.   3. Learning, Psychology of.   4. Teaching.
5. Educational psychology.   6. Educational tests and measurements.   I. McCormick, Christine.
II. Pressley, Michael. Advanced educational psychology for educators, researchers, and policymakers.   III. Title.
LB1062.P74 1995
370.15′2—dc20   94-26477
     98 9 8 7 6 5 4 3   CIP

*Dedicated to those who aspire to improve education
in the United States, Canada,
and throughout the world*

Contents

Preface

For some time I have had a vision of educational psychology and research texts that focus on the field as it is right now, as it is defined by the educational research community. This book is part of the fulfillment of that vision. It is organized around the theme of promoting good information processing: the construction and constructive use of strategic knowledge, metacognitive abilities, important world and cultural knowledge, and motivation. The good information processing framework is informed by traditional and contemporary literature in educational psychology, a variety of theoretical perspectives, current thinking in curriculum and instruction, and both conventional and reform-minded thinking about assessment and individual differences. Good information processing requires coverage of all of these topics. Throughout the book the case is made that through modeling, explaining, and dialoguing, educators can stimulate the development of good information processing in their students.

My intent in *Cognition, Teaching, and Assessment,* is an introduction to educational research for graduate students, and in some cases advanced undergraduates. As I wrote the book, I envisioned it being used as the primary text in master's level courses in educational psychology or educational research, or as an introduction to educational psychology or educational research, either in a graduate sequence or as an advanced course in an undergraduate psychology program. Because of its broad coverage of research, however, it is appropriate for any course

devoted to presentation of education in the 1990s as defined by psychologically-oriented theories and studies. Readers of *Cognition, Teaching, and Assessment* will discover a variety of strategies-oriented interventions, from basic strategies to enhance memory, to reciprocal teaching to improve reading comprehension, to the most up-to-date strategic approaches to mathematics. Readers are also exposed to the full range of ways that knowledge is represented in the mind, with detailed coverage of the effects of knowledge on teaching, learning, and problem-solving. The social foundations of education also receive extensive coverage, including detailed discussions of contemporary perspectives on motivation; sociocultural approaches to cognitive development, such as Vygotsky's theory; and the social-dialogical foundations of thoughtfulness in classrooms. Traditional positions on social development in educational settings, such as social learning theory, are considered prominently as well, with clear relating of the traditional and more recent theories. There is ample coverage of both the laboratory problems that educational psychologists and researchers have addressed (e.g., distributed learning effects, mnemonics) and applied issues (e.g., the nature of effective schools). The most up-to-date research-based practices in mathematics, science, reading, and writing education are covered in the context of the theories and research inspiring them. Assessment is presented as it has traditionally been conceived, with detailed coverage of the most important psychometric concepts, and as it is being reconceived, with coverage of all the most important emergent approaches in assessment, including dynamic assessment, performance assessment, and portfolios. The book concludes with analysis of the important categories of individual difference in education—retardation, learning disabilities, and giftedness—but also differences across the life span (i.e., cognitive changes between early and later adulthood). The final chapter complements coverage throughout the book of potential gender and cultural differences in thinking and learning.

As part of the development of this book, it was tried out on students in my courses at the University of Maryland and University at Albany, State University of New York. The complete book in prepublication form has been used for more than a year by my students. The consistent feedback I have received from students is that reading this text transforms them from students with only a vague notion of the nature of educational research to informed readers of the literature. When students complete this text, they understand how articles in basic research journals, such as *Journal of Educational Psychology* and *American Educational Research Journal*, as well as practitioner journals, such as *Educational Leadership* and *Phi Delta Kappan*, fit into the overall context of educational research and educational reform. Such feedback is my reason for confidence that *Cognition, Teaching, and Assessment* fulfills my vision of a sophisticated introduction to educational psychology and research as it exists today.

Cognition, Teaching, and Assessment is part of a series of textbooks in educational psychology and research. *Advanced Educational Psychology for Educators, Researchers, and Policymakers* is aimed at advanced graduate students, practicing educational researchers, and policymakers who have a need for state-of-the-science information about educational psychology. *Cognition, Teaching, and Assessment* is an abridgement of the *Advanced* book. The main difference between the *Advanced* text and *Cognition, Teaching, and Assessment* is that this volume focuses more on what is now believed and known about education. Although this volume also orients its readers to where the field is moving, the *Advanced* book does so much more completely. For students who have read *Cognition, Teaching, and Learning* and who are looking for additional guidance with respect to potential research directions for their thesis work and be-

yond, the *Advanced* volume can take them there. For students taking an educational psychology course at the undergraduate level an entirely different volume has been prepared and will be available in the fall of 1995. The third book in the series, *Educational Psychology: Learning, Instruction, and Assessment*, is an entirely new way to introduce students to educational psychology and research. It showcases the best new theory and research, specifically developing the case that such research is relevant to the modern teacher. Thus, the most important ideas in this text are available in an advanced, an intermediate, and an introductory form. This volume is the intermediate text.

I could never have put together the trio of books alone. The project began with my drafting of the *Advanced* text. At that point I asked Chris McCormick, my friend and colleague of 20 years, to react to it and consider becoming the lead author for the undergraduate text. Chris provided many insights about the advanced book, and as the introductory volume was born and developed, the content of the advanced, intermediate, and introductory books affected one another. So many of the ideas in the *Advanced* text and this abridgement were influenced by Chris that the authorships to *Advanced Educational Psychology for Educators, Researchers, and Policymakers* and *Cognition, Teaching, and Assessment* properly reflect her contributions as coauthor. Chris McCormick's brilliant reformulation of the ideas in the *Advanced* text and *Cognition, Teaching, and Assessment*, and her addition of important topics covered at the undergraduate level but not in graduate courses, became *Educational Psychology: Learning, Instruction, and Assessment*, so that the introductory book will appear with McCormick and Pressley as authors in that order. Chris and I believe that the instructor who has read *Cognition, Teaching, and Assessment* will be especially well prepared to use *Educational Psychology: Learning, Instruction, and Assessment*, although the introductory book is also accessible as a stand-alone resource. One motivation for developing the trio of books came from our awareness that many graduate students are asked to teach introductory courses in educational psychology. If they have read this text in their graduate education, they will be ready to teach with *Educational Psychology: Learning, Instruction, and Assessment*.

There are so many people to thank. Joel Levin was a fine senior colleague to both Chris and me in the early years of our careers; he instilled in us the commitment always to be moving the field forward by knowing its past and thinking hard about its future, a commitment reflected in the pages of this book. I am especially grateful to Alan Wigfield, Jim Brynes, Cathy Wentzel, Bill Halliday, and Vicky Kouba, who read preliminary drafts of parts of the manuscript. The reviewers for HarperCollins were terrific: Paul van den Broek, University of Minnesota; Alice Corkill, University of Nevada, Las Vegas; Victoria Chou Hare, The University of Illinois at Chicago; Mary Lundeberg, University of Wisconsin, River Falls; Debra Mathinos, Bucknell University; and Brent Wilson, University of Colorado, Denver. Many graduate students in my classes, who experienced drafts of the book as a course text, convinced me that the book worked and provided input that helped to make it work better. Chris Jennison, and his colleague Shadla Grooms, made it a pleasure to work with HarperCollins, as did everyone in the New York office who contributed to the three-book project. Tom Conville and his associates at Ruttle, Shaw & Wetherill, Inc. did a professional job of getting the text ready for production. My wife, Donna, was a good sport about all those nights when I was word processing at 3 A.M. Tim Pressley provided a constant reminder to Dad about how important it is to educate well the next generation of educators and educational researchers. When the book began, he was discovering the worlds of letters and numbers with his friends on *Sesame Street;* as the book goes to press, he is becoming an avid reader, promising that someday he will read one of Dad's books.

My own students, especially former undergraduate and graduate students who have worked with me (many of whom are now tenured professors) did much to shape my thinking about many of the issues covered in this text. Their impact on me is partially reflected by citations in the text to articles they have published on these issues. Thanks especially to Janice Almasi, Margaret Brigham, Rachel Brown, Susan Bryant, Jacqueline Burkell, Teresa Cariglia-Bull, Thommie DePinto, Patricia DeVolder (now deceased), Pamela El-Dinary, Darlene Elliott-Faust, Linda Lysynchuk, Marilyn Marks, Jacqueline A. McGoldrick, Jennifer Mistretta, Margaret Oatout, Robyn Russow, Julia O'Sullivan, Brynah Schneider, Barbara L. Snyder, Sonya Symons, Peggy Van Meter, Ruth Wharton-McDonald, Teena Willoughby, Vera E. Woloshyn, Eileen Wood, and Linda Yokoi. I hope that our interactions have been as good for your heads as they were for mine.

I expect that this book will be revised eventually, to reflect educational psychology as it evolves. If you have reactions to *Cognition, Teaching, and Assessment* that might inform the next edition, I now hang my professional hat at the Department of Educational Psychology and Statistics, University at Albany, Albany, NY 12222. I would love to hear from you.

Michael Pressley

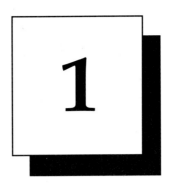

Introduction: Good Thinking, Good Teaching, and Alternative Ways of Studying Good Thinking and Good Teaching

This chapter includes an introduction to the good information processing model, which specifies that good thinking depends largely on strategic processes, nonstrategic knowledge, metacognitive knowledge, and motivational beliefs. This model is general enough to be relevant to all of the topics covered in this book and will be referred to in every chapter. The chapter also introduces some of the teaching processes and models that will be covered at various points in the book. Finally, the different types of research methods used by educational researchers are reviewed briefly, with the case made that diversity in methods is a strength of contemporary educational psychology.

It would be easy to write a pessimistic book about education. There is a sense of crisis covered continuously in the popular media, with many arguing (e.g., Hudson Institute, 1987) that American schools are not producing people who will be able to survive in an ever more technological world, a world requiring higher levels of literacy and numeracy than ever before. Given this context, it may be surprising to some that this book is an optimistic book about education. A main message that will be presented here is that a great deal is now known about how to create better readers, thinkers, and citizens. An important purpose of this book is to develop an understanding in the next generation of teachers, educational researchers, and policymakers that psychological theory and research has succeeded in identifying ways to improve student learning.

A contemporary text in educational psychology must be rich in theory and theoretically inspired research. Thus, there is particular emphasis in this text on the contemporary theory and research relevant to complex human learning, curriculum, and instruction. The content of this book was selected to empower the reader with a great deal of information about potent educational treatments and why they work.

As optimistic as this book is about the state of current knowledge, however, another important theme is that there is much more to find out. Thus, perhaps some readers will be sufficiently intrigued by educational psychology as a field of scholarly inquiry to consider careers in educational research. The case will be made throughout this book that the academic study of educational problems can be intellectually rigorous and fulfilling. Learning what is presented in this book can be an important first step in becoming an educational researcher.

An important theme in this book is that many students can become good thinkers and that education can do much to ensure that the next generation is a whole lot smarter than current students. Thus, this book begins with a description of good thinking (e.g., Pressley, Borkowski, & Schneider, 1989), a description that will be encountered throughout the book because much of educational research is aimed at promoting good thinking.

WHAT IS GOOD THINKING LIKE?

When we were young, we loved reading detective books. The best thinkers we knew were inhabitants of such novels. We particularly devoured *Hardy Boys* books. A few years ago, now well armed with background in educational psychology, we revisited some of the detective books of childhood, interested in whether the Hardy boys were really as intellectually capable as we thought they were during our youth. When the Hardy boys' **cognition** (i.e., their thinking) is analyzed in light of what is now known about good thinking (Pressley, Snyder, & Cariglia-Bull, 1987), it is clear that the Hardy boys were exceptionally smart (see especially Dixon, 1972).

First, the Hardy boys had an incredibly rich repertoire of **strategies** for solving crimes. Sometimes the boys would try to put themselves in the place of the criminal as they analyzed a crime. The boys had a host of specific tactics for lifting fingerprints from difficult places and for making certain that all of the physical evidence at the scene of a crime was collected. The boys recognized the importance of remembering important details, with the books including specific instances of them using cognitive strategies such as rehearsal and imagery to encode important information about a crime. One of our favorite strategies was their approach to remembering a physical description of a person, always beginning at the top of the head and working down to the shoes. The boys also knew that their memories were fallible—that there are memory errors reflecting prior knowledge and biases rather than what really happened—and thus the boys used photography to record crime scenes, made drawings when a camera was not available, and were extensive note-takers.

The Hardy boys possessed extensive **metacognition,** which is knowledge about and awareness of one's thinking (e.g., Flavell, 1985). In particular, they knew when and where to use the strategies they had acquired (i.e., they possessed extensive **metacognitive knowledge about strategies**). Thus, when first arriving at a crime, the boys knew it appropriate to use particular strategies to preserve the crime scene (e.g., cordoning it off). They also knew when to execute systematic search strategies and recording of information. Metacognitive knowledge about strategies is sometimes verbalizable (i.e., the person can say exactly when it is appropriate to use a particular strategy) and sometimes tacit (e.g., a person carries out the strategy on appropriate occasions, but cannot tell another person when and where the strategy works). Metacognitive knowledge is absolutely critical to the regulation of strategies, with knowledge of when and where particular strategies are appropriate guiding their application in the future (e.g., O'Sullivan & Pressley, 1984).

Often, understanding of when and where strategies are useful occurs as a function of the learner **monitoring** that performance is better with a strategy that is currently being deployed compared with when comparable learning tasks have been attempted without the strategy in question (Ghatala, 1986; Pressley, Borkowski, & O'Sullivan, 1984, 1985; Pressley, Levin, & Ghatala, 1984). The Hardy boys often justified use of a strategy by recalling successful use of it in a previous, similar case.

Strategies are used in conjunction with **nonstrategic knowledge** (e.g., Alexander & Judy, 1988), which for the Hardy Boys included knowledge of the law, criminals' behaviors, criminals' language, physical evidence, and drugs. For example, because a criminal investigator knows that glass is a particularly good source of fingerprints, the boys took special care to make certain that glass at a crime scene was undisturbed until it could be examined systematically.

No one could read the *Hardy boys* mysteries without being struck by the boys' **motivation.** They were **motivated** to acquire more sleuthing strategies and knowledge needed by a detective. These boys were always looking for crimes to solve and were determined to go about their investigations in a systematic way. They were also motivated to figure out how to adapt what they already knew to new challenges they confronted.

Good information processing requires a generally **healthy, normally functioning brain.** For instance, a tremendous amount of knowledge must be stored in long-term memory structures. Loss of long-term structures because of disease or injury results in loss of knowledge and a reduction in the competencies dependent on long-term knowledge.

An intact brain also permits **short-term memory,** variously referred to as consciousness, working memory, or short-term storage (see Baddeley, 1986; McCarthy & Warrington, 1990, especially Chapter 13), with some regions of the brain more active in consciousness than other areas. When someone holds a telephone number in memory while searching for a scratch pad, thinking goes on in short-term memory. Short-term memory is active as an author juggles bits and pieces of meaning he or she is trying to combine into sentences and paragraphs. Close your eyes and try to keep in "view" the room you are sitting in; your image is in consciousness. Short-term storage is exactly what the name implies, however— short term. If a person does not continue to rehearse a phone number, the number will fade from consciousness. If a person is distracted while writing, he or she will lose some of the meaning elements being juggled. An image of a room remains vivid only because of conscious effort to maintain the vision in the mind's eye.

Short-term storage is limited with respect to the amount of information that can be attended to consciously at any one moment. Only so many numbers can be rehearsed at once. Only so many bits of information can be considered before new pieces of information literally seem to push out some of the information already in short-term memory. People usually cannot envision the room they are sitting in and another room at the same time—they manage to hold two such complex images in mind at the same time only by shifting attention back and forth from one image to the other.

An important individual difference between people is their short-term capacity (Baddeley, 1986). That is, even among people with healthy brains, some can hold more things in memory and operate on more bits of information simultaneously than can others (Dempster, 1985). Suffice to advance here the conclusion that good thinkers have sufficient short-term capacity to carry out relatively complex tasks— a capacity that is at least partially due to an intact central nervous system.

In short, the Hardy boys possessed many characteristics of good thinking—strategies, metacognition, other knowledge, motivation, and healthy nervous systems—with these characteristics interacting to promote highly intelligent behavior and thinking. A view presented in this textbook is that developing thinking like that of the Hardy boys is a high ideal: Good schools teach important strategies, make certain students acquire metacognitive understandings about when and where to use strategies, convey a great deal of important knowledge about the world in general, stimulate academic motivation, and encourage lifestyles that will protect a vulnerable central nervous system. The case will be made throughout the book that good thinking—called good information processing in this book—can be developed in contemporary school settings (Figure 1.1).

Understanding good information processing is so central to educational psychology in our view that Chapters 2 through 6 are concerned with the main components of good information processing just overviewed: Chapter 2 will provide detailed coverage of strategies and metacognition; Chapters 3 and 4 will discuss the role of nonstrategic knowledge in thinking; Chapter 5 will be concerned with motiva-

tion; and Chapter 6 will review the biological foundations of good information processing.

Other Characteristics of Good Information Processing

In this section, some additional characteristics of good information processors are reviewed.

Good Information Processors have Well-Developed Language Flexible, **well-developed language** unambiguously supports sophisticated thinking. The criticality of language as supportive of thinking has been especially apparent with the renaissance of Soviet models of thinking (Bakhtin, 1981, or see Morson & Emerson, 1990, and Todorov, 1984; Vygotsky, 1962; see Chapter 8, this book), which emphasize the development of inner speech as an important determinant of skill in thinking (see Rogoff, 1990; Wertsch, 1991).

Good Information Processors Live in Richly Stimulating Environments A great deal is learned by the healthy brain as a function of experience. Even acquisitions such as language, which human biology virtually guarantees provided that there is some exposure to language (e.g., Anastasiow, 1990; Gleitman, 1986), are sensitive to environmental stimulation. Thus, when children are raised in isolation, language does not develop normally (e.g., see Puckering & Rutter, 1987, for a review). When raised by animals, such as the Wild Boy of Aveyron (Itard, 1801), human language does not develop at all. Other conditions that are associated with less severe deprivation have less severe effects on language development, although there are, nonetheless, detectable, pejorative effects. For instance, language acquisition is affected negatively by being reared in socially disadvantaged homes, as a twin, or in a large family—that is, whenever there are environmental pressures that reduce the amount that parents can play and verbally interact with their children (Puckering & Rutter, 1987).

Good Information Processors' Attitudes and Emotions Support Their Cognition Good thinkers are **appropriately confident.** They welcome challenges that are well matched to the skills and knowledge they possess. They recognize when they are equal to tasks as well as when academic tasks might be beyond them or when they need assistance to complete a task.

Figure 1.1 Sherlock Holmes knew many strategies for findings clues, possessed extinsive metacognitive about when and where to use the strategies he knew, was extremely knowledgeable about the world in general, and was extremely motivated to solve crimes. What other characteristics made Holmes a good information processor?

Good thinkers have **well-controlled emotions.** Anxiety does not overwhelm the good thinker. Good thinkers do not get so excited or agitated when confronting a problem that their thinking is clouded (Hembree, 1988; Tobias, 1979, 1985).

Good Information Processors Are Appropriately Attentive and Reflective Good thinkers have **attentional focus**—they are able to maintain attention even in the face of distraction (e.g., Aks & Coren, 1990; Kuhl, 1985). Good information processors **inhibit inappropriate responses** (Bjorklund & Harnishfeger, 1990; Dempster, 1992) and are appropriately **reflective**—thinking through problems rather than reacting impulsively. Even so, they are not reflective to the point that reflection is paralyzing (e.g., Duemler & Mayer, 1988), always reconsidering rather than acting (Baron, 1985, 1988, 1990a).

Good Information Processors Do Much to Create Their Own Enriching Environments Good thinkers **contribute to their own education and development** by placing themselves in situations that present such information (see Bandura, 1986; Ford, 1987; Lerner & Busch-Rossnagel, 1981; Scarr, 1992; Scarr & McCartney, 1983). How did the 15-year-old down the block come to know so much more about the inner workings of the microcomputer than her parents do? That girl spent many hours with her mother's computer, invested most of her allowance for the past 5 years on computer magazines, read the magazines from cover to cover, figured out how to apply some of what is presented in magazine articles to her own computing, and hung out with other kids at school who are also interested in computing. Good thinkers elect to do things that are enriching, and they seek out company that is intellectually engaging.

Just as important, other intellectually engaging people seek out the good thinker because the good information processor is stimulating for them to be with. Good thinkers find one another, often with the explicit goal of engaging in activities that will further increase the competence of all involved in the interaction.

Summary

No one characteristic makes a person a good information processor, but rather good thinking is the product of a number of factors in interaction, feeding on one another. For instance, by using efficient comprehension and learning strategies, more nonstrategic knowledge is acquired, which, in turn, can reduce the need to engage in strategic processing in the future. With greater knowledge, confidence increases so that what one knows can be applied with less concern for correctness.

This introduction to the complexities of good information processing sets the stage for the rest of the book, which is concerned largely with encouraging the competencies that interactively produce effective cognition. As most readers have probably inferred, much student thinking is not exceptionally skilled, however.

Not-So-Good Thinking

The same categories used to describe good thinking can also be applied to poor thinking. We encourage readers to compare the descriptions that follow with the thinking of the Hardy boys. The contrast is striking.

Children who experience academic difficulties are a diverse lot. Some do not have normally functioning brains, although the specific disorder is often difficult or impossible to pinpoint. Brain abnormalities can be reflected in a variety of ways, including language deficiencies, limited short-term capacity, lack of attentional focus, or impulsivity (Gaddes, 1985)—although, of course, language, short-term memory, attentional, and impulsivity problems can occur even in otherwise normal, healthy children, with these tendencies alone enough to undermine effective thinking and problem solving. Weaker students use fewer strategies than normal students, and they know less about when and where it is appropriate to use the strategies they do know (e.g., Forrest-Pressley & Waller, 1984; Schneider & Pressley, 1989, Chapters 4 and 5). Anxiety about academics is common in poor learners (Kasik, Sabatino, & Spoentgen, 1987; Perlmutter, 1987). Poor learners often hold beliefs that undermine their motivation to try (e.g., thinking that their learning problems are due to immutable ability factors; e.g., Pearl, 1982). Because poor learners acquire less from each lesson than classmates, often many aspects of their knowledge base are deficient relative to peers. Some poor learners have more difficulty than other children in applying what they know to academic work. Interactions between these component deficiencies compound difficulties (e.g., failing to use strategies decreases how much is learned, which decreases nonstrategic knowledge).

Even more mature students who are relatively successful (e.g., they are attending college) are not good thinkers all of the time. Pressley, El-Dinary, and Brown (1992) reviewed studies documenting the following inefficiencies in many university students' studying and restudying: They read and reread rather than identifying more and less important information and focusing on the important content. They frequently believe they are ready for tests when they are not. University students can completely miss the main point of a reading and nonetheless believe they understand the text completely. When searching for material, they often search ineffectively and fail to find what they are seeking. Often they possess prior knowledge that could be related to new content, but they fail to relate it.

Even university students who, relative to peers, process academic content well are not all that thorough. For instance, Wade, Trathen, and Schraw (1990) observed college students attempting to learn factual text. Only about 10% of them used a diverse repertoire of strategies in attempting to understand text. About a third of their sample relied on rote learning strategies—that is, they simply tried to "pound it in." Even the most strategic students in the Wade et al. (1990) study failed to learn much of what they studied.

Summary

Good information processing involves coordination of strategies and nonstrategic knowledge. Good thinkers are more aware of what they know and do not know than are weaker thinkers, and they are more likely to be aware of strategies that can improve their learning and performances (e.g., Leal, 1987). In addition, good information processors are highly motivated to use their intellectual resources to tackle important academic challenges. Although it is possible to identify instances of good thinking, it is anything but universal. How magnificent an accomplishment good thinking is will become clearer as you proceed through the book.

One frequent reaction of students new to cognition or educational psychology is that the conclusion just offered—that good thinking is an interaction of a number of factors—is so obvious that it is surprising that it could be offered as a scholarly insight. In fact, many cognitive psychologists have focused (and, in some cases, still do) on one or a few of the factors that constitute good information processing. That many believe that good thinking reflects predominantly a single factor—such as strategies or knowledge or motivation—makes our claim nontrivial: Good thinking depends on a number of factors in interaction.

THE DEVELOPMENT OF GOOD THINKING THROUGH INSTRUCTION

As complex as good thinking is, it can be developed through instruction. The perspectives on instruction offered in this book are decidedly catholic ones, emphasizing a variety of approaches to teaching. School involves learning many different types of information, and no one or two instructional approaches are appropriate for all contents. One approach, direct explanation, finds a great deal of favor throughout the book, however, largely because of the many research studies documenting its efficacy and because it works well with many other educational interventions (e.g., in homogeneous and heterogeneous classrooms, with cooperative learning, and in all of the content areas).

Direct Explanation

When teachers provide explicit and detailed information about academic processes or concepts, they are engaging in **direct explanation** (e.g., Roehler & Duffy, 1984). Consider the teacher who directly explains to students how to write short essays using a plan-translate-revise strategy. The teacher explains and models alternative ways of planning an essay, including searching one's own mind for information that might be included, brainstorming with others, and seeking information from library resources. The teacher might also cover ways of organizing the many ideas that are generated, perhaps teaching methods of outlining an essay before writing it. Translation of the outline into a draft consists of taking the rough outline and putting it into phrases and sentences. Once a good first draft is achieved via planning and translation, it is time for revision, which, in turn, may require more planning and seeking of additional information to put into the essay, followed by construction of new phrases and sentences that mesh with what is already in the draft. Much of this information is conveyed during direct explanation teaching by the teacher talking through examples of good writing. That is, the teacher shows how these examples were constructed using planning, translating, and revising.

In addition to teaching the steps of the strategy, the direct explanation teacher also provides substantial information about when and where to use the strategy as well as how to coordinate the steps of the strategy with one another. Providing such information is intended to increase transfer of the writing strategy to new situations where it could be employed gainfully (O'Sullivan & Pressley, 1984). The direct explanation teacher in particular emphasizes the utility of the strategy being taught, focusing on how the student's writing can be improved through use of the strategy. The idea is to get students to attribute their successes and failures to whether they are making use of the knowledge they possess (e.g., Clifford, 1984; see Chapter 5, this book).

An important assumption of the direct explanation teacher is that children are quite capable of learning many academic competencies rapidly, although it is also recognized that general use of the competencies requires extensive discussion, practice, trial, and error. A critical part of all of this is the teacher actually modeling use of the strategies explained—and doing so in an authentic way that includes struggling some with the task and having to work at it in order to use new strategies effectively. Exposure to such coping models deepens student understanding that constructive effort is required to respond to instructional explanations. That is, struggling with tasks is what academically talented people do, at least at first.

Direct explanation is a constructivist approach (e.g., Pressley, Harris, & Marks, 1992): Students do not passively learn from explanations but rather actively learn from them. They do not completely understand what the teacher is saying or doing, but the teacher's explanation and modeling is a starting point for the student. As the student struggles with the process the teacher modeled, he or she adapts it to the particular tasks at hand and modifies it in ways that are sensible to him or her. If a classroom of children hears and watches a demonstration (e.g., of multiplication of fractions) and then practices what was taught in the lesson, there will be much struggling, adaptation, and reflection on the part of the students, with the result that at the end of the instructional day, all will have somewhat different understandings of multiplication of fractions. Many days of re-explanations and remodeling are often required before students begin to construct under-

Figure 1.2 One explanation is never enough, with this teacher closely monitoring the student to infer what the student understood and failed to understand. She will respond to the student by providing re-explanations and addtitional modeling targeted at the student's needs and current understanding of what is being taught.

standings that are conventional enough to allow them to meet the demands of the curriculum (e.g., actually be able to multiply fractions successfully and consistently, with an understanding of both the procedures and why the procedures work). Direct explanations by teachers are the start of active exploration by pupils (Pressley, Harris, & Marks, 1992) (Figure 1.2).

Other Approaches to Instruction

Every one of the alternative methods to instruction that are covered in this section can be coordinated with direct explanation and the constructive learning that is stimulated by such explanations. In fact, some of the alternatives covered here, such as observational learning and scaffolding, are components of direct explanation. Even so, each of the models reviewed here is sometimes regarded as a unique approach to teaching. Our view is that good teachers interconnect various types of teaching.

Guided Participation Guided participation involves extensive and explicit teacher direction of student processing. Teachers cue students step-by-step about how they should accomplish a task (e.g., solving a problem, writing a letter). The assumption of **guided participation teaching** is that students will eventually internalize the steps they are cued to use, if they go through them enough times. Anyone who has taken golf lessons knows about this approach to teaching, with the pro carefully directing every millimeter of the beginner's swing (or at least trying to).

An interesting example was provided by Hansen and Pearson (1983), who taught a set of reading strategies to grade-4 students. One process Hansen and Pearson wanted students to learn was to compare what is in text with one's own life. Thus, students were cued to do this before each new text was read. The students were also questioned about the text they were reading, questions that required relating personal knowledge to the content of the text and making predictions based on personal knowledge about what might happen next in the text. This type of instruction went on for 10 weeks with some evidence, in the form of improved comprehension, that the processes cued during guided participation did come to be owned by the students. In contrast to guided participation, the approach covered next emphasizes student decision making.

Discovery Teaching and Guided Discovery   Proponents of discovery and guided discovery approaches to teaching sometimes contrast their teaching with direct explanation instruction. Discovery learning de-emphasizes instruction (Ausubel, 1961; Gagné, 1965; Wittrock, 1966), with Piaget's theory of intellectual development largely stimulating discovery-based approaches to instruction (see Brainerd, 1978a; 1987b; Chapter 7, this book). Discovery is facilitated by presenting tasks to students that offer rich opportunities for discovery. Teacher input is often limited to answering student-generated questions about the task (see Suchman, 1960).

Discovery learning is believed by its supporters to promote academic motivation by cultivating natural curiosity, producing more complete understanding of discovered strategies than would teacher explanation of the same strategies, and thus increasing the likelihood that students will know when and where to apply the processes they are learning and will be motivated to do so (e.g., Piaget, 1970).

Even though there are impressive demonstrations of children's invention of strategies (e.g., Groen & Resnick, 1977; Svenson & Hedonborg, 1979;

Woods, Resnick, & Groen, 1975), there are also difficulties with discovery learning. Not all children discover the many strategies that they need to know to negotiate the academic demands of school. For many students, discovery is inefficient at best, requiring far longer than it would to teach the same strategies to children using direct explanation. Perhaps the "glitch" with discovery that has commanded the greatest attention, however, is that learners often discover errant strategies. For example, van Lehn (1990) documented more than 100 subtraction strategies discovered by learners that are in fact incorrect. For instance, sometimes students "borrow" from columns when it is not necessary, do not write zeroes in their answers (e.g., generating an answer of 2 9 instead of 209), or subtract only from some of the columns.

That pure discovery sometimes produces less learning, less efficient learning, or less "correct" learning than might be desired (Shulman & Keislar, 1966; Wittrock, 1966) stimulated some educators and theorists who favor discovery to modify the approach. Guided discovery teaching is more explicit than pure discovery teaching, typically involving the teacher posing questions to students, questions intended to lead students to understand ways that a problem could be solved. The questions lead the students to "discover" strategies. Not surprisingly, guided discovery does produce more certain and more efficient learning of strategies and ideas than does simple discovery (Collins & Stevens, 1982; Gagné & Brown, 1961; Kersh, 1958).

Scaffolding   Of course, there are intermediate positions between discovery learning and guided participation. One considered already is guided discovery. Another is scaffolding, which involves provision of help to students on an as-needed basis.

A number of theorists take as their main tenet that mature thought in children is developed in adult-child interactions (e.g., Bakhtin—see especially Todorov, 1984; Feurstein, 1980; Vygotsky, 1962, 1978; see Chapter 8, this book). Adults both model good thinking and provide subtle hints and prompts to children when their offspring (or students) cannot manage on their own. Thus, adults direct children's attention to important dimensions of problems they are attempting to solve when the children do not attend to those dimensions in the absence of direction. Sometimes the adult suggests a strategy to the child.

The theory is that eventually children adopt as their own the thinking processes and patterns adults have modeled and assisted children in using.

The children are said to **internalize** the processes that previously were **scaffolded** (Wood, Bruner, & Ross, 1976) for them by adults. The metaphor of scaffolding is appropriate because scaffolding is an external structure that supports another structure under construction; as the new structure is completed and capable of standing on its own, the scaffolding is removed. So it is with scaffolded adult-child academic interactions, with the scaffolding adult providing only enough support for the child to acccomplish an academic task—not too much or too little. The adult monitors carefully when enough instructional input has been provided to permit the child to make progress toward an academic goal. If a child catches on quickly, the adult's responsive instruction will be less detailed than if the child experiences difficulties applying the strategy and internalizing it.

One way to understand scaffolding is to compare it with direct explanation: (1) Direct explanations flow more from the teacher to the students, whereas scaffolded instruction is a result of continuous and mutually responsive interactions between students and teachers. (2) Direct explanations of entire processes are often presented early in instruction, with direct re-explanations provided by the adult on an as-needed basis as the child and adult attempt the academic task collaboratively. In contrast, more is left for the child to infer during scaffolding, although the scaffolding teacher attempts to lead the child to important understandings about the task being attempted and how the task might be accomplished.

Much more will be presented about both scaffolding and direct explanations later in this book, particularly in Chapter 8, with it then possible to relate both scaffolding and direct explanation to larger theoretical frameworks than can be presented in this introductory chapter. Suffice to point out here that scaffolding, and direct explanation teaching that includes scaffolding, permits many more students to discover ideas than does a pure discovery approach. Such supportive instruction will be encountered often in this book.

Modeling and Observational Learning   Humans learn a great deal from watching others—that is, the behaviors **modeled** by others are often learned by those observing the models. This is the main claim of **observational learning theory,** one that can hardly be disputed in the 1990s (see Bandura, 1977b or 1986). Particularly relevant here, there have been many demonstrations by educational psychologists that students can learn intellectual content and processes from observing others (Rosenthal & Zimmerman, 1978). Much observational learning research documented that people also can learn from **symbolic models,** such as characters on television (see Bandura, 1969, 1977b; also Chapter 7, this book).

Observational learning is constructivist, not passive (see Moshman, 1982). What is learned from watching is not an exact copy but an interpretation. The young boy who learns how to "bat" by seeing it on television "plays" with that perception—for example, tapping the plate in different ways with the bat when he steps into the batter's box, trying alternative stances, and experimenting with holding the bat far back versus nearer the shoulder. Even with no one around, the youngster who has intently observed batters on television for three or four innings will "play" at batting, with the play stimulated by the batting that was observed. The batting that is ultimately learned, however, is a construction of the child—often resembling very little the stance or actions of a major leaguer.

Textbooks That Teach   The characters in books and stories can also serve as symbolic models to students, and a variety of materials are being created that are explicitly intended to teach particular content through such symbolic modeling. A well-known example is a series of novels by Matt Lipman, his *Philosophy for Children* (1985) program. The child characters in these novels do a lot of thinking aloud about important philosophical problems. As these characters discuss concepts such as truth, fairness, and freedom, they provide models of sound, thorough thinking. The characters in these books specify concepts well, make appropriate generalizations from data, infer cause-and-effect relations, monitor the reasonableness of their arguments, and shun ambiguities and vague thinking. Because the novels are used in conjunction with classroom discussion, additional observational learning opportunities occur as classmates attempt to reason about some of the philosophical problems posed in the novels. *Philosophy for Children* and other materials intended to stimulate critical thinking skills will be taken up in Chapter 11.

Classrooms are filled with all sorts of textbooks. Increasingly, these are designed by psychologists and those informed by psychological theory and research. Although published materials have played a role in instruction for a long time, it seems likely that if anything their role in teaching is going to increase. Many publishers are investing millions of dollars to redesign their materials so the texts reflect the theory and understandings from research featured in this book (see, in particular, Chapter 14).

Educational Technology Much new media and technology are designed to teach various types of information in classrooms. Particularly notable are interactive videodisks and microcomputer programs, both of which have the capacity to "explain" many types of information to learners, elicit participation of students, and provide feedback concerning the adequacy of student responses (e.g., see Chapters 12 and 13). These can open up new worlds that, at their best, are not only richly informative, but also stimulate student construction of understanding by patiently providing hints and clues (i.e., scaffolding the student).

Concluding Comment on the Nature of Instruction That Encourages Good Thinking

These various ways of teaching will be encountered again in later chapters. In some cases, strong claims will be presented about the potential efficacy of particular forms of instruction for particular purposes (e.g., many contemporary mathematics educators are enamored with variations on guided discovery). What must be emphasized, however, is that although these approaches to teaching can be placed in categories and operationalized in research studies, the various teaching methods typically are combined by skilled teachers rather than used exclusively.

For example, after the teacher explains a procedure, often through modeling, students are encouraged to try it on their own, with the teacher offering guidance and support as needed. Instructional books and other media sometimes are used during direct explanations or to supplement them. There are occasions when a direct explainer sets up classroom situations to promote discovery, with the effective teacher gently nudging students who might not be making good progress in the discovery process. Exceptionally capable teachers combine a variety of types of teaching to encourage the learning of strategies, nonstrategic knowledge, and metacognition that constitutes good thinking, with all of this occurring in an environment that encourages academic motivation.

In presenting this claim about exceptionally good teaching, however, we also recognize that most teachers do not teach the many strategies that can improve academic performance and learning (e.g., Moely, Hart, Leal, Santulli, Rao, Johnson, & Hamilton, 1992), let alone do all that could be done to improve students' motivation to be cognitively active (e.g., Brophy, 1987). That such teaching is not now common is one of the reasons we wrote this book. A first step for such instruction to become more common is for the next generation of educators to understand the various teaching and thinking models summarized in this book. The explosion of theory and research on effective teaching and learning summarized in this book permits a much more realistic portrait of effective classroom instruction than was possible only a few years ago.

Consider the Hardy boys again. The prime mover in their education as detectives was their father, Fenton Hardy, famous detective. A good deal of direct explanation occurred in the father-sons triad as well as substantial scaffolding by the father as the boys worked on cases. The boys were also extremely well read, and there are plenty of instances of discovery learning in the books. In short, the Hardy boys' education was accomplished through diverse mechanisms. Fenton Hardy provided good instruction, but the boys also did much to create their own instruction, consistently placing themselves in settings where new detective skills could be acquired and practiced. Throughout this book, the argument will be made that learning and instruction requires many different types of inputs.

Just as the Hardy boys cultivated methods for investigating crimes, so too have researchers cultivated methods for investigating education. It is essential that readers of this book understand, at least at a general level, the nature of the scholarly detective work that is research, with the next section presenting a brief overview of some of the most important paradigms and distinctions in educational scholarship.

METHODS OF EDUCATIONAL RESEARCH

Diverse methods are used in educational research, for different types of questions require different methods, and some situations permit some methods but not others. Thus, although experimentation permits powerful conclusions with respect to causes and effects, true experiments require random assignment of participants to conditions. If an investigator is interested in the effects of social class, race, or gender on educational achievement, it is impossible to assign students randomly to socioeconomic or biologically determined categories. Nonmanipulative designs are essential when the investigator is interested in such variables.

Personal preferences and beliefs of investigators also affect the methods used in an investigation. For example, some educational scientists have much greater faith in observations that can be quantified and statistically analyzed, whereas other educational researchers are suspicious that with quantification comes reductions in data that distort conclusions. Many concerned about distortions produced by quantitative methods are now opting to conduct qualitative investigations, which rely more on the human investigator to use his or her interpretive skills to bring order to data that are collected. Others, including us, are convinced that research programs are most likely to be fully revealing about important educational phenomena if both qualitative and quantitative approaches are combined. Presented in this section are brief summaries and commentaries about research methods that are encountered frequently in the educational research literatures.

Quantitative Methods in Educational Research

There are three main classes of quantitative studies: (1) manipulative investigations involving researcher control of variation (e.g., assignment to one educational treatment or another), (2) nonmanipulative studies involving the systematic analysis of naturally occurring variation between people (e.g., aptitudes) or settings (e.g., type of school), and (3) studies involving interactions between naturally occurring variables and manipulated variables (e.g., aptitude by treatment interactions).

Manipulative Investigations One of the most typical designs in educational research is the comparison of a new or preferred educational intervention with conventional instruction or some other alternative (Campbell & Stanley, 1966). What all experiments have in common is that participants are assigned randomly to treatments. That is, before the

experiment begins, each subject has an equal chance of being assigned to the experimental or control condition. Such random assignment is the most likely approach to produce nonbiased groups at the start of the study (i.e., on average, at the start of the study, the participants assigned to the treatment and control conditions will not differ significantly).

For each cell in an experiment—and there are two cells when a single experimental condition is contrasted with a single control condition—one statistic is particularly important. The mean for the cell is the arithmetic average of all scores for measurements taken in the study. If, at the end of an experiment, the means between the experimental and control conditions for important measurements differ—and they did not differ before the experiment began—the conclusion can be drawn that the experimental treatment *caused* the difference in performance. Such differences can be small, medium, or large, with statistical methods now available for determining the size of an experimental effect. Calculation of effect sizes flags which treatments have large payoffs and which ones have small impact.

One persistent criticism of drawing cause-and-effect conclusions from instructional experiments is that the introduction of new instruction is inevitably confounded with other factors. Perhaps the improvements are simply a reaction to novel teaching, perhaps owing to the concomitant increases in student arousal, motivation, or interest that accompany changes in instruction (e.g., Smith & Glass, 1987). Sometimes there are concerns that teachers' expectations change when new instruction is introduced, with shifts in expectations potentially affecting student motivation (i.e., the "Pygmalion" effect; Rosenthal & Jacobson, 1968; see Chapter 11, this book.) When students are aware that the goal of the study is to evaluate the effectiveness of the new instruction, they may want to do all possible to make obvious the efficacy of the treatment (i.e., the "Hawthorne" effect; Campbell & Stanley, 1966). (As the discussion about Hawthorne effects continues in what follows, readers should recognize that many attempts to produce Hawthorne effects have come up empty, suggesting such effects are perhaps not as much of a worry as researchers once feared they were; see Adair, Sharpe, & Huynh, 1989.)

There is a powerful way to evaluate the likelihood that the effects produced by an instructional innovation are due to general motivational factors, including Pygmalion and Hawthorne motivations.

Motivation should have broad effects on learning. In contrast, educational treatments are expected to have more specific effects. For example, Russow and Pressley (1993) have been studying the effects of graphing calculators on student learning of mathematics. They hypothesized that students' conceptual understanding of how graphs relate to functions should improve with the calculators, but they could conceive of no reason that simple calculation skills should be affected by use of the calculator unless the calculators were simply motivating or arousing. In fact, use of the calculators improved only conceptual understanding. When an intervention produces **discriminated effects** in a predictable fashion, as it did in Russow and Pressley's study of graphing calculators, there is powerful evidence that the specific intervention is producing the effects—that the benefits are not due to general shifts in motivation that might accompany instructional innovations.

Up until this point, only studies in which one experimental condition is contrasted with a control have been considered. Experiments are not limited only to two conditions, however. For example, if there are three possible instructional innovations, it sometimes makes sense to run a study that is a horse race, comparing directly the three innovations with each other and comparing each of the three innovations with a control condition. Sometimes an investigator is interested in studying several different variables, each of which can be manipulated. Perhaps the investigator believes that both nutritional supplements and preschool-instructional enrichment promote the learning and thinking of young children. A factorial study can be conducted in that case—for example, one involving cells with and without nutritional supplement as well as cells with and without preschool enrichment: Such a study can be set up as a two (levels of nutrition) by two (levels of instruction) factorial design: In one cell, children receive nutritional and instructional enrichment; in a second, children receive only the nutritional supplement; in a third, participants are given instructional enrichment; and in the fourth (control) condition, children receive neither the nutritional nor the instructional enrichment. Such a design permits evaluation of whether nutrition, instruction, or nutrition and instruction combined produces differences in children's performances.

In principle, any number of factors can be manipulated in an experimental study (e.g., $2 \times 2 \times 2$ $\times 2$ designs are common, as are $3 \times 2 \times 2$ setups). Practically, however, large multifactorial studies are unwieldy, with the number of subjects required in a 16-cell (i.e., such as a $2 \times 2 \times 2 \times 2$) or larger design often so great as to make the study too expensive in terms of experimenter time and other resources.

One rule of thumb among quantitatively oriented researchers is that when it is possible to evaluate an intervention in a true experiment, do a true experiment. True experiments produce data that are more clearly interpretable with respect to issues of causality than any alternative approach. Still, there are many occasions when manipulation is not possible, but it is important to understand the intervention or variable in question. Carefully conducted nonmanipulative studies often can provide information in such situations.

Nonmanipulative Studies   This section considers some of the fundamental types of nonmanipulative studies.

Diagnoses of Differences in a Population.   The discovery of ways to categorize people is essential for science. For example, in the late 19th and early 20th centuries psychologists devised tests to classify people as more and less intelligent, due to the increased understanding that human differences are heritable. In this generation, the medical profession has discovered the importance of categorizing people in terms of cholesterol level, dietary habits, and blood pressure status, largely because of new understandings of heart disease and its relation to diet and lifestyle. New methods of brain imaging are revealing differences in brain activity among people, permitting classifications based on neurophysiological structures and functions not possible previously.

Sometimes studies are conducted to determine the nature of cognitive processing differences in a population. Thus, some psychologists have been interested in the ways people differ with respect to memorization strategies, comprehension processes, and problem-solving tactics. Thus, there are studies demonstrating that people presented list-learning tasks (i.e., presented a long list of items with the requirement that the items be remembered later) can be classified as rehearsers, elaborative rehearsers, and imagery users. There are active and passive readers. Some problem solvers are planful and others impulsive. There will be many classifications based on processing covered in this book.

Relating Differences Among People to Differences in Performance. Researchers are typically interested in how differences in people (e.g., younger and older children, males and females) are predictive of important outcomes. Intelligence testing was important only because it promised to predict life success, and, indeed, at least predicts success in school. Cardiovascular and blood chemistry differences are important because they are predictive of long-term health. Contemporary neurophysiologists expect to be able to link brain activity differences to many performance differences. Information processing differences have consistently predicted performance: List learners who rehearse do not remember lists as well as people who integrate list items into memorable mental images. Active readers comprehend better than passive processors. Planfulness in problem solving predicts success at problem solving. (And, of course, it is because processing differences are so predictive of performance that much of the emphasis in this book is on promoting processing that facilitates learning, thinking, and performance.)

Individual differences in cognitive processing often can be exploited in the service of theory testing. For example, suppose that a psychologist holds the position that construction of mental images during reading should improve understanding of the relations in text (i.e., imagery construction causes text comprehension in part). If that is true, people who naturally construct mental images while they read should comprehend what they read better. In fact, they do (Sadoski, 1983, 1985; see Chapters 3 and 14, this book). Such a **correlation** between natural use of imagery and performance provides initial evidence relevant to the causal theory—if there had been no correlation between natural use of imagery and performance, the theory that imagery produces comprehension would be in big trouble. That is, causality implies correlation. Nonetheless, that there is a correlation does not cinch the case for the causal theory because there can be correlation without causation. That is, correlation does not imply causation. For example, perhaps it is the case that people who naturally use imagery are more intelligent or in general deeper thinkers. If so, their greater comprehension could be due to greater intelligence or deeper thinking rather than their use of imagery.

In short, studies examining potential correlations between individual differences with performance can be used to separate unlikely from plausi-ble causal hypotheses (Underwood, 1975). Because nonmanipulative studies are often cheaper and easier to conduct than manipulative investigations, it often makes good sense to use nonmanipulative studies to decide which hypotheses deserve the precious resources required to conduct manipulative evaluations.

There is also a larger reason to conduct correlational studies: They capture nature as expressed through natural variation better than do manipulations. If we knew only that instructing people to construct images improves their comprehension and memory of stories (which is all that we would know if imagery were manipulated only in experiments involving text processing), that would be knowledge removed from nature: What would not be known is whether anyone ever elects to use imagery to comprehend text on their own. Although some researchers choose to identify themselves as experimenters *or* differential psychologists (i.e., psychologists interested in naturally occurring differences), the best thinkers about social science methods recognize that top drawer research programs include complementary nonmanipulative and manipulative studies (e.g., Cronbach, 1957; Underwood, 1975). Such programs are revealing about what people are and do as well as about what people could be and do.

Diagnoses of Differences in Educational Settings. A great deal of effort has been expended in examining schooling environments for differences that can affect student processing, with some success. For example, some classrooms encourage competition and others cooperative learning. Some involve substantial questioning and others less questioning. Some include real conversations about subject matter, whereas others appear more like teacher drilling, with many teacher questions requiring student responses that the teacher evaluates (e.g., Mehan, 1979).

Relating Differences Between Settings to Differences in Performance. Sometimes researchers want to evaluate interventions but cannot randomly assign people to conditions. Often in education, such treatment differences boil down to differences in settings. For example, it is impossible to assign students randomly to public and private schools. Often it is difficult to assign students to classrooms emphasizing some particular form of instruction compared with another form (e.g., the whole language approach to beginning reading versus a more conventional approach, competition versus cooperation). What researchers typically do is to make comparisons between these different settings or interventions (i.e., they conduct a **quasiexperiment;** Cook & Campbell, 1979). Often the researcher will go to a great deal of effort to ensure that the subjects in the settings compared are as equal as possible except for the setting difference (e.g., studying public and private schools serving the same neighborhoods, checking the reading or intelligence scores at the beginning of the year of students enrolled in whole language and the more conventional comparison classrooms). The more certain it is that the participants in the cells of a quasiexperiment are equivalent except for the difference in the treatment (setting) in question, the more willing researchers are to interpret differences produced in quasiexperimental studies as informative about causality. In general, our perspective is that if a true experiment is possible, it is much preferable to a quasiexperimental evaluation. Still, if a quasiexperiment is the best that is possible, and the issue is important, conduct a quasiexperimental evaluation. The cause-and-effect conclusion is not airtight in a quasiexperiment if a difference is found as a function of setting, but if other factors that might cause the difference can be ruled out because they were known to be equivalent in the two conditions, the case in favor of a causal relationship strengthens. A number of quasiexperiments informed the conclusions presented in this book.

One important approach in psychology to evaluating setting effects is the **cross-cultural study:** Sometimes cultures vary systematically with respect to critical educational variables (e.g., cultures that do not formally school their children differ from Western cultures that do). Cross-cultural researchers interested in education attempt to link such cultural differences to differences in performances between the cultures in question (Figure 1.3). There are a few exceptionally important cross-cultural efforts in educational psychology that are covered in the chapters that follow.

Concluding Comment.   People differ in various ways, some reflecting biological differences (e.g., sex, age) and others reflecting differences in the settings they experience (e.g., culture, educational treatments adopted by the schools they attend). Whether

Figure 1.3 The cross-cultural study of mathematics achievement has been of great interest to educational psychologists. Because Japanese students excel in mathematics compared with American students, American researchers have analyzed carefully factors that might contribute to high mathematics achievement in Japan. Potentially critical differences between the cultures will be taken up in Chapter 13.

there is systematic variation in various educational outcomes as a function of biological and socially mediated differences is often studied by educational researchers. When nontrivial relationships between human differences and performance are detected, there is said to be a **correlation** between the difference and the outcome. Often the statistic used to summarize relationships between individual differences and outcomes is a **correlation coefficient,** which can range from −1.00 to +1.00. The greater the absolute value of the correlation coefficient, the more certain it is that the individual difference dimension is predictive of the outcome in question (i.e., a zero implies no relationship between the dimension of difference and the outcome, whereas either a −1.00 or a +1.00 implies perfect covariation between the dimension of difference and the outcome). When the correlation is positive, it means that high values on the individual differences dimension are associated with high values on the outcome dimensions. When the correlation is negative, it means that high values on the differences dimension are associated with low values on the outcomes dimension, and low values on the differences dimension are associated with high values on the outcomes dimension. There is no reason for making much of the sign of a correlation, however, for the sign can be reversed simply by reversing the ends of either the individual differences scale or the outcome scale. Thus, the positive correlation between a person's height from the floor and his or her basketball ability can be transformed into a negative correlation by construing height as distance of the head from the ceiling.

Combining Manipulative and Nonmanipulative Approaches in the Same Study: The Case of Aptitude by Treatment Designs Sly and the Family Stone made famous the line, "Different strokes for different folks." That is in fact the hypothesis inspiring studies of aptitude by treatment interactions (ATIs): Some types of individuals might benefit from one form of treatment, and others benefit from another type of treatment (Cronbach & Snow, 1977). It is easy to generate aptitude by treatment hypotheses. For example, it seems eminently sensible that people who are good at verbal processing should benefit from strategies requiring verbal fluency, and those who are more competent at spatial processing should benefit more from imagery strategies. The way to find out is first to identify students who are verbally facile and others who are spatially adept. Assign both types of students to perform a common task, with half of all students (of both types) using a verbally loaded approach and half using an imagery-loaded approach. The expectation is that performance with the verbally loaded approach would be greater than with the imagery approach for verbally facile students, with the outcome reversed for the spatially talented students.

Such hypotheses are easier to advance than to support with data, however, with Cronbach and Snow's (1977) book on ATIs filled with examples of ATI hypotheses that have not been confirmed or replicated (i.e., even though observed in one study,

not obtained in follow-up research). The nonconfirmed ATIs include ones about differential susceptibility to treatment effects based on verbal and spatial processing competencies.

Studies of Potential Generalization of Findings From One Population to Another Often a researcher will conduct an experiment and establish an effect. Then additional studies will be conducted with different populations to study the generality of an outcome. The hypothesis often is one that could be construed as an ATI (i.e., a belief that an instructional treatment might affect different populations differently), but rather than studying students with differing aptitudes in the same study as occurs in ATI investigations, separate evaluations are made for each population.

Summary There are many different types of nonmanipulative studies. Their common denominator is that there is some dimension of difference that cannot be manipulated. What was covered in this subsection were quantitative, nonmanipulative studies because the preponderance of nonmanipulative studies in educational psychology have involved formal quantitative analyses.

Qualitative Methods in the Social Sciences

There are entire books presenting and debating the differences between quantitative and qualitative approaches (e.g., Guba, 1990). A common theme in such commentaries is that the qualitative and quantitative approaches are incompatible, with incompatibility often argued based on philosophical underpinnings of the two approaches (see Howe, 1988): Quantitative approaches take as their ideal the classic scientific method, whereas qualitative researchers are more interested in interpretations, with the perceptions of participants in a setting valued as data. Although quantitative researchers do all possible to obtain objectivity, qualitative researchers are more comfortable with subjectivity. An especially important characteristic of quantitative researchers is that they are often interested in testing theories using experiments, statistical correlations, and other quantitative analyses. In contrast, qualitative researchers are frequently interested in constructing theories based on observations and interviews (i.e., qualitative researchers are attempting to develop a **grounded theory;** e.g., Glaser & Strauss, 1967).

Development of a Grounded Theory Strauss and Corbin (1990) summarized how grounded theories can be constructed. We describe here some highlights of their perspective, although in doing so import some ideas and emphases of others (in particular, Lincoln & Guba, 1985).

Construction of a grounded theory begins with collection of data. Thus, the researcher may spend a great deal of time observing behaviors in a setting of interest (e.g., many visits to first-grade reading groups for a researcher interested in constructing a theory of the grade-1 reading group). Alternatively the researcher may engage in many unstructured interviews (e.g., interviewing grade-1 teachers about what goes on in their reading groups). In some cases, the observations may be made by the participants themselves, perhaps in the form of diaries (e.g., grade-1 teachers keeping daily journals about reading group). Of course, there is also the possibility of combining methods of data collection, with many qualitative studies combining observational and interview data.

The task then is to induce regularities from the database. Thus, the researcher goes through the data systematically looking for meaningful clusters and patterns—behaviors that seem to go together logically. For example, if the teacher has students sometimes pair and read to each other, encourages students to ask one another about difficult words, and often encourages several students to read the same library book and engage in discussion, a meaningful cluster would be suggested. It is then necessary to name the cluster, to come up with a category name for the behaviors included in the cluster. In this case, perhaps "cooperative reading" would be a reasonable name.

Such an analysis of extensive observations and interviews is likely to result in a number of categories. The next objective is to attempt to identify evidentiary support for the categories. The investigator, however, is always open to—and actually looking for—data inconsistent with an emerging category. This can be done by reviewing previous data. We note that qualitative researchers often begin their data analyses early in the data collection, so that as tentative categories emerge, there is opportunity to look for support or nonsupport of categories with every new data collection opportunity. Analyses and data collection are seen as interwoven enterprises by the qualitative researcher.

One especially important check is to take the emerging categories back to those being observed and interviewed for them to indicate whether they find the categories that are emerging to be credible. (This is referred to by Lincoln and Guba, 1985, as **member checking.**) Often the subjects of the investigation can provide important elaboration of the categories at that point, citing potential refinements and extensions of the categories. As a result of member checking, the researcher may change categories or their names, consistent with the general qualitative emphasis on fluid interaction between data collection, data analyses, and construction of conclusions.

Eventually, there is a stable set of categories based on data collected to date. The task now is to begin to organize these categories in relation to one another. For example, the category of "teacher modeling" seems to subsume some of the other categories of behaviors that might have been observed during grade-1 reading groups, such as "thinking aloud about how to decode a word," "behaviorally acting out reading processes," and "behaviorally acting out deciding to read leisure material (e.g., 'I think during recess I will read the newspaper,' and 'Tonight I'm going to visit the library')." Thus, the category "teacher modeling" is higher in an organizational chart than the three categories it subsumes. Each of the categories that are placed in the hierarchical arrangement of concepts is then defined in terms of its properties and dimensions. For example, for the category "teacher modeling," one property of it is "abstractness," with this property measured on a dimension of "concrete to abstract." Other properties of teacher modeling might be "authenticity," "duration," and "timing in the lesson." Can you suggest potential dimensions for these properties?

Once the categories have been identified, placed in hierarchical arrangement, and dimensionalized, with these categorizations, arrangements, and dimensionalizations challenged by checking against the data, the researcher can begin to believe that the data on hand are understood about as well as they are going to be understood.

It is now time to collect new data. For the grade-1 reading group example, it would be time to observe some more groups, adjusting the categories and their arrangements in light of new observations, interviews, and so on. It would make sense to continue collecting data until no new categories are emerging from new observations, no new properties of categories are being identified, and no additional adjustments are being made to the hierarchical arrangement of the categories. This may take a while.

Once in possession of a great deal of data, it is possible to begin hypothesizing causal relationships between the categories of information that have been arranged as related to one another. There is a desire to know what causes each category as well as how categories affect one another. Thus, some reflection on the teacher interviews may make clear that teacher modeling is caused by contemporary teacher education practices (e.g., some teachers indicated they were running reading groups as they had learned to run them in college) or tradition (e.g., some teachers claimed they were running reading groups consistent with what they had experienced as children) or in-service resources (e.g., some teachers reported that there had been many in-services on teacher modeling of cognitive processes, especially during reading). Teacher modeling is not only caused, but also in turn causes reactions. Thus, perhaps students are observed modeling reading processes to one another, or the processes modeled by a teacher seem to be prominent in student responses on the day they are modeled. The various causal possibilities, actions and reactions, are evaluated against all of the available data as completely as possible. Those that are supported by the data are retained; those that are not are deleted.

Often, there will be extensive **conditional information** placed in the model. For example, teacher modeling may be indicated as occurring more often when the teacher believes students do not understand the processing they are being asked to learn and may be indicated as less frequent once the teacher observes students using the processes under instruction. Strauss and Corbin (1990, Chapter 10) argue that such conditional information can be quite extensive and complex, so that what goes on in grade-1 reading might be affected by conditions in the classroom, the school, the community in which the school is located, the nation, or even the world. For example, teachers might be more likely to emphasize modern cognitive processing views of reading, which specify that teachers should model effective reading for students, when the school is located in a community supporting education at the cutting edge. The pressure to teach in this fashion may also reflect the pressure of statewide assessments requiring students to demonstrate the cog-

nitive processes that teachers can model as exemplary reading. Of course, we could go on suggesting a number of external factors. Such factors would emerge in the grounded theory only if the data suggested them. Thus, our example of state assessment pressure was mentioned because in our own work on process models of instruction, teachers frequently mention that their teaching is adjusting because of pressures from the state level. It is realistic to expect that data may provide insights into causality that operate at a number of levels, that there will be evidence in the data that forces far removed from classrooms being observed are affecting what goes on in those classrooms.

As relations and conditional information emerge, it is important to check them against the data, always seeking support and making changes in light of discrepancies with data. More member checking should occur as well. This activity continues until no new categories or relations between categories emerge, until the point of **theoretical saturation.** Strauss and Corbin (1990) are emphatic that researchers must continue to analyze the data until this point is reached because to do otherwise results in an incomplete grounded theory.

Eventually the data must be reported in a way that they are consumable by the public or at least by other researchers. What is required is for the researcher to identify a key category or categories and to tell the story, in sufficient analytical detail to reflect the richness of the analysis done but in a fashion that makes the findings comprehensible. This emerging story should be member checked as well, until there is eventually a tale that seems reasonable to researchers and participants.

Why Do Qualitative Analyses? Our view is that analyses of many issues have been substantially enriched by qualitative analyses. How students and teachers interpret educational interventions probably often affects how those interventions impact on students and teachers. When interpretations make a difference, it is important to know what those interpretations are. Students and teachers often have extensive knowledge about why the classroom day is organized as it is, so that analyses tapping those understandings are going to be more complete than analyses that ignore teacher rationales for their behaviors (which was the predominant approach of quantitative, observational studies of teaching that predominated in teaching research in the 1960s, 1970s, and into the 1980s).

One exceptionally important value of qualitative analyses is that they can provide a theory worth testing. Thus, in recent years we have spent time constructing a theory of how reading comprehension instruction is carried out when it is done well, a grounded theory based on observations and interviews in schools providing effective comprehension instruction to their students (see Pressley, El-Dinary, Gaskins, et al., 1992; Chapter 14, this book). What that work provided to us is a theory of comprehension instruction that is being evaluated in much more quantitative studies. Those quantitative studies never could have been designed without the knowledge gained in the qualitative investigations.

Arguments against doing qualitative analyses are increasingly rejected by the researcher community, especially as researchers have come to realize that much of quantitative research involves qualitative decisions (Howe, 1988; Huberman, 1987). Every quantitative study involves deciding which variables to include and how to measure them, which are matters of interpretation. There are decisions about which statistical tests and criteria to apply, which again involves substantial subjectivity, especially because a number of assumptions are made about the data and the situation studied to make analyses judgments. The way the questions are framed in the introduction of the study, the hypotheses that are tested, and the story told in the discussion section of a quantitative article are also researcher interpretations.

Sometimes it is possible to quantify "qualitative" data. For example, there is nothing wrong with reporting proportions of participants who provide a particular rationale—supplementing observations and informal interviews with more formal and more quantifiable measurement (e.g., Pressley, Schuder, SAIL Faculty and Administration, Bergman, & El-Dinary, 1992). We are decidedly pragmatic, believing researchers should do whatever they can to inform important issues, consistent with the thinking of others who have wrestled the qualitative-quantitative debate to a stalemate (e.g., Howe, 1988). We do not make a big deal in this book about when the focus is on quantitative versus qualitative data, comfortable with the value of both types of research in thorough analyses of educational phenomena, consistent with the perspective of other leading researchers whom we respect (e.g., Rizzo, Corsaro, & Bates, 1992; Stanovich, 1990).

We both noticed years ago that the Hardy boys sometimes took precise measurements and made decisions based on objective evidence and other times spent time trying to make sense of a situation (i.e., organize it into related categories), with the personal interpretations of witnesses often helpful in the boys' theory construction processes. The Hardy boys' problems were much easier than most educational research problems—they always cracked the case in a few hundred pages, whereas years and thousands of pages can go by before there even begins to be a resolution of a mystery tackled by educational researchers. The Hardy boys would not have solved their cases if they had slept in a methodological Procrustean bed, however, either one emphasizing objectivity or another interpretation; neither should 21st century educational researchers, if they want to have a chance of solving the exceptionally challenging problems confronting education today.

WHAT'S AHEAD?

What follows is a summary of what we perceive to be the best theory and research on the development of good thinking and good instruction. Much of this work has been generated under the general rubric of cognitive psychology or cognitive psychology pertaining to education (e.g., as research in cognition and instruction), although certainly not all of it has. Indeed, some of the best and most interesting research has been produced by those who identify more strongly with particular fields of curriculum and instruction than with cognitive or educational psychology. This is not a book that much respects intellectual boundaries but rather picks and chooses research and theory from a variety of disciplines and subdisciplines that make contact with education and scholarship relevant to education.

There is definitely a mix of theory and research in what follows. In general, theories that enjoy some support in research are favored over those that are not tested or have failed to be supported when tested. There is also a mix of basic and applied research. We firmly believe that basic research can inform education, with many connections made between basic research and applications in this book. The more obvious the connection of a piece of basic research to educational practice, the more likely it is that the work appears here. Thus, there are some classic findings from cognitive psychology that do not appear here or are touched on briefly because they are only tangential to educational issues.

One of the most important criteria in deciding what to include was to rely on hearsay. We attend many education conferences, visit many schools, and talk with many educators and professionals concerned with education. Much of what appears in these pages is what these professionals are talking about. Many of the issues taken up are ones important to educators and to researchers concerned with education. We attempt to confront head-on many of the problems that are pestering educators and educational researchers the most.

As will become apparent in what follows, good thinking in general is a commodity that is anything but commonplace, the product of years of high-quality education and experiences. Thus, although we are optimistic throughout the book that education could be improved based on research insights, we are also realistic throughout this book that there are no quick fixes, only fixes that are tantamount to years of effective education, education that can be informed profitably by the work summarized in this book. The next four chapters elaborate the theory of good thinking summarized in the first half of this chapter—the good information processing model—relying greatly on research findings to do so.

Part

1

Good Information Processing

2

Strategies and Metacognitive Regulation of Strategies: Basic Theory and Research

Strategic processes are introduced in this chapter. The natural development of strategies takes place over the entire lifespan. The certainty of people acquiring strategies is increased substantially by explicit instruction of strategies and teaching aimed at assuring learners know when and where to use strategies. The chapter also includes a discussion of how strategies resemble the operations carried out in an important artificial intelligence program, ACT*.

In Chapter 1, we established the broad outlines of the argument that sophisticated thinking involves complex interactions and interdependencies between strategies, metacognition, nonstrategic knowledge, motivation, a normally functioning brain, and other factors. This chapter is the first of five that specifically will elucidate these various components and provide detailed discussion about how the components interrelate to produce sophisticated thinking.

This chapter is about strategies and their metacognitive regulation, including how a strategies-based approach to cognition relates to other models of cognition and learning. What is featured is basic research, much of it conducted with respect to memory tasks—for example, list learning (e.g., giving a learner ten objects to remember with recall of the list required at a later time) and associative learning (e.g., giving learners pairs of items such as "turkey and key" and requiring them to remember one given the other item). Admittedly, these tasks are not as **ecologically valid** (Bracht & Glass, 1968) as other tasks that will be considered in later chapters (i.e., they are not as representative of actual school-based learning problems). Use of such tasks in research, however, permits experimental control that is not always possible with more complicated tasks. Many important insights about learning and thinking emerged from research with such artificial tasks.

WHAT IS A STRATEGY?

Consider first a formal definition of strategies:

> [Strategies] . . . are composed of cognitive operations over and above the processes that are a natural consequence of carrying out [a] task, ranging from one such operation to a sequence of interdependent operations. Strategies achieve cognitive purposes (e.g., memorizing) and are potentially conscious and controllable activities (Pressley, Forrest-Pressley, Elliott-Faust, & Miller, 1985, p. 4).

This stilted definition can be understood with an example. Suppose you must read an article for a class. What are the cognitive operations and processes that you must carry out—that are a natural consequence of reading the article? You must decode the words. In general, you do so by reading the article from front to back. These are not strategic activities according to the definition presented here because decoding of the words in order is pretty much obligatory to "read" the article. Are there things that you could do that would be over and above front-to-back reading? In fact, there are many strategies that could be employed to understand and remember the text better. Before reading, you could skim the title, pictures, and headings to get a sense of the topical coverage. This might lead you to make predictions about the content of the article. Once front-to-back reading began, you might monitor carefully whether the meanings you anticipated actually occurred in the text. As reading progressed, you might also attend to whether what is being read makes sense. If it fails to make sense, you might reread. Finally, after concluding one pass through the text, you might self-test your recall of what was presented in the article. Then you might look through the article and construct a summary, noting which parts of the article were not remembered during the self-test.

There are a host of processes that you could execute that are over and above simple reading from front to back. These are strategies. Often these strategies are executed consciously and intentionally. Sometimes, however, good readers probably carry out at least some of these processes without conscious attention to whether they are doing so. An important point, however, is that even those readers who carry out such processes automatically could control them if they chose to do so. Strategies must be controllable. Strategies are different from processes that are so automatic that they are not controllable. For instance, when reading a passage about Queen Elizabeth, many readers would automatically infer the passage was about the queen of England. Such automatic inferential activity is not strategic because it is generally not controllable—you just cannot help but think of England when you think of Queen Elizabeth.

Finally the reading comprehension strategies just mentioned are aimed at achieving important purposes. They facilitate understanding and memory of text. There are an infinite number of cognitive operations that can be performed on any text that would not facilitate important cognitive goals (e.g., the reader could begin at the end and read backwards, the reader could count the number of words including the letter "d"). Only operations that enhance important cognitive purposes earn the label strategy. There will be several occasions in this book when the discussion will return to reading comprehension, but for now, the concern will be with more basic tasks and basic research.

MEMORY STRATEGIES

A number of issues pertinent to educational psychology were at the heart of the research on memory strategies that was conducted in the last 30 years. This section is organized around some of the most important of these.

Development of Strategy Use in Children

A strategy investigated in many of the most prominent studies of children's memory was **rehearsal** of lists of items. Consider a typical **serial recall task.** A number of items are presented to learners in a particular order, perhaps in the form of picture cards, one picture to a card. A child might be presented a straight row of such cards, with the faces turned down. The researcher informs the child that the task is to remember the objects pictured on the cards in the order of presentation. Proceeding left to right, each card then is turned over by the researcher for a few seconds, so the child could see the object on it (e.g., Flavell, Beach, & Chinsky, 1966).

A good strategy that can be applied to this task is **cumulative rehearsal–fast finish** (Barclay, 1979; Butterfield & Belmont, 1977). This involves saying the list items over and over in order as they are revealed. The "fast finish" is a test-taking strategy: When asked to recall the items on the list, the learner using fast finish immediately "dumps out" the last item or two that was presented and then recalls the earlier items in order. That is, the learner recognizes that the last two items still are in some type of shorter-term memory and can be recalled effortlessly if recalled first at the time of testing.

Use of the cumulative rehearsal–fast finish strategy develops slowly (see Schneider & Pressley, 1989, for a detailed review of the relevant literature). Preschoolers and early elementary-age students do not use it. Their most typical strategy is simply to say the name of the picture that is currently being displayed. This is a labeling strategy (Flavell et al., 1966). Cumulative rehearsal alone (without fast finishing), however, is commonly observed by the end of the grade-school years in Western cultures (e.g.,

Flavell et al., 1966; Ornstein, Naus, & Liberty, 1975). The fast-finish component is not observed until late adolescence (Barclay, 1979).

An important question in research on rehearsal strategies was whether their increased use was because of organic factors that are indexed by age (i.e., brain maturation that is roughly indicated by age) or due to experience. The work that was conducted in Western and industrialized nations was not revealing on this point, for biological development and number of years of schooling experience are inevitably confounded in the West (i.e., most 7-year-olds have had between 2 and 3 years of formal schooling; most 10-year-olds have had between 5 and 6 years of school). Researchers were able to disentangle the contributions of development and formal schooling to improvements in strategy use, however, because the confounding between age and number of years in school is not nearly as certain in some other cultures as it is in North America. Western-schooled students in such cultures (i.e., those attending Western-type schools in their home countries) were compared with other members of the culture who had not received Western schooling. Schooling made a difference. Use of strategies (and hence performance) on basic memory tasks was related to school experience in these cultures. Students who had experienced several years of Western-style schooling memorized much like students in the West with comparable education; students in the culture who had not attended Western-type schools did not resemble Western students nearly as much in the ways they used to try to remember information (Sharp, Cole, & Lave, 1979; Stevenson, Parker, Wilkinson, Bonnevaux, & Gonzales, 1978; Wagner, 1974, 1978). The same basic research strategy has also been used to establish that nonmemory reasoning abilities that are common in the West are due largely to Western-style schooling (Artman & Cahan, 1993).

Many readers are probably feeling somewhat dissatisfied with the research reviewed in this section. After all, rehearsal during list learning is artificial, even though people sometimes do rehearse text content that they need to remember, with learning gains produced by such rehearsal (e.g., Muth, Glynn, Britton, & Graves, 1988). Researchers also experienced such dissatisfaction, believing that much more interesting strategies might be observed if more naturalistic memory tasks were studied in more naturalistic settings. What resulted from this was movement away from the study of basic strategies such as rehearsal to more ecologically valid strategies, with such work especially revealing about the strategic competencies of even very young children.

Strategy Use by Preschoolers

One important study establishing the strategic competence of preschoolers was conducted by De-Loache, Cassidy, and Brown (1985). They placed an object in a living room (e.g., under a pillow on the couch) as a child watched; the child was aware that he or she would have to retrieve the hidden object later. In this situation, even 2-year-olds are strategic. Although they will play in the living room during the retention interval (i.e., between when the object is hidden under the pillow and when they must retrieve it), preschoolers frequently look at the place where the object was placed, sometimes even pointing to the location and saying the name of the hidden object.

The research conducted by DeLoache and colleagues was sufficiently analytical to permit a strong conclusion that these "checking back" and simple rehearsal strategies were in fact memory strategies. One manipulation that was revealing on this point was the following: Sometimes the object was hidden in the room (e.g., under a pillow); other times it was placed in about the same position, but not hidden (e.g., on top of the same pillow). Only when the object was hidden from view did preschoolers look back at the spot or say the object's name during the retention interval. That is, the strategies occurred only when there was a memory demand. Even preschoolers are sometimes strategic, at least when simple strategies are considered or the children are tested in familiar surroundings or using methods that are sensitive to the strategies they use (Figure 2.1).

Prolonged Development of Strategic Competence as the Norm

The clear increases in rehearsal during the elementary years that have been documented in Western cultures are not paralleled by equally dramatic shifts in use of other strategies between 5 and 11 years of age. Consider, for example, how elementary school–age children tackle paired-associate learning. The most efficient strategies for learning paired associates involve **elaborations**, either a verbal elaboration in the form of a meaningful sentence containing both pair members (e.g., *turkeys* have *rocks* in their gizzards) or a meaningful interactive image

Figure 2.1 Even a young preschooler can be strategic when there is a need to remember something in a familiar setting such as the living room at home. This preschooler would be much less strategic if asked to perform a memory task in a laboratory at university. Context matters as a determinant of strategy application.

(e.g., a *turkey* scratching at *rocks* in the barnyard). The evidence is quite unambiguous that elementary-age children do not use such elaboration strategies on their own (e.g., Pressley & Levin, 1977a, 1977b); even many adults fail to do so (e.g., Bower, 1972; Kliegl, Smith, & Baltes, 1990; Rohwer, 1980a; Rohwer & Litrownik, 1983; Rohwer, Raines, Eoff, & Wagner, 1977).

More positively, by the end of the grade-school years, children elaborate somewhat with some materials and tasks, for example, when reading material that can be related to prior knowledge. For example, Chan, Burtis, Scardamalia, and Bereiter (1992) asked children to think aloud as they processed texts about dinosaurs and germs. With increasing age during the elementary years, students were less likely to rely on rote, surface-level processing and make irrelevant associations to text (e.g., associate to a single word in the text) and were more likely to relate ideas in the text to one another and to their own prior knowledge in ways that made the ideas more sensible. Even so, there was still room for much more integration and elaboration even among the oldest students, who were in grade 6.

Indeed, there is a recurring theme in the literature on higher education: University students often do not study effectively (e.g., Mathews, 1966, Chapter 7), with failure to use effective memory strategies usually cited prominently in this literature, alongside failures to use effective reading comprehension, writing, and problem-solving procedures. University students' lack of strategic sophistication is recognized by colleges and universities, with most campuses now having study skills courses available. A main focus of such courses is strategies. For example, Devine's (1987) text is one of the most sophisticated of the studies skills textbooks. A chapter in Devine's book is devoted exclusively to memory strategies, with instruction about imagery elaboration strategies and verbal elaboration procedures among others.

There are many strategies that adults do not use routinely. Those offering studies skills courses assume that strategies can be taught so that student academic performances increase. Some of the foundational literature supporting this assumption is taken up in the section on teaching of strategies.

Summary

Whether children use a memory strategy or not varies from strategy to strategy. Some simple strategies, such as looking at a spot where a to-be-remembered item has been hidden, are used routinely by preschool-age children. The familiar setting of their own living room, the familiar materials (e.g., a Bugs Bunny or Big Bird doll usually is the hidden object), and the familiar task (i.e., finding something in the living room) probably combine to permit greater strategic competence by preschoolers in this situation than in other situations (e.g., list learning in a laboratory). Many more complex strategies are not always common even among university students. Of course, there are strategies that fall in between in that they are not common with preschoolers nor during the early elementary grades but rather emerge during the later grade-school and high school years (e.g., associative elaboration of paired associates is one of these; Pressley, 1982). Even within Western culture, there is variety in the patterns of strategy development, diversity that cannot be captured by simple summaries.

Things get more complex when memory strategy data from other cultures are considered. Some cultures encourage use of some strategies more than do other cultures. What strategies a person uses is determined largely by his or her personal sociocultural history (Kurtz, 1990). Whether parents and educators encourage strategy use in children is an important determinant of whether or not children use strategies. In the next section, we expand on the theme that children often can learn strategies and how to use them.

TEACHING OF STRATEGIES

Early in the last section, it was established that young children often fail to use cumulative rehearsal strategies when they are asked to learn lists. Only brief instruction is required, however, to teach 6- and 7-year-olds how to rehearse lists so that they remember them later (e.g., Keeney, Cannizzo, & Flavell, 1967).

Children in kindergarten and grade 3 often fail to make use of organizational properties of lists that can aid memory. Thus, if given a list of items that could be sorted into different categories, which would facilitate memory, kindergarten to grade-3 children often fail to make use of the categories during learning. As was the case with rehearsal, however, it is fairly easy to teach children to sort list items into categories (Moely, Olson, Halwes, & Flavell, 1969).

Outcomes such as these motivated the hypothesis that when children fail to use efficient memory strategies, they can be taught to use them. This stimulated many attempts to teach memory strategies to children. By the middle 1970s, there was a massive literature demonstrating that children could be taught to use memory strategies that they did not evidence without instruction (see Pressley, Heisel, McCormick, & Nakamura, 1982, for an overview). Nonetheless, it was also clear that instruction in strategy use was not always sufficient to convert nonstrategic students into strategy users.

Age Differences in Susceptibility to Some Forms of Strategy Instruction

Not all strategies can be taught to all children. This point was established clearly in a number of studies concerned with pair-associate learning, learning of vocabulary-definition associations, and simple prose learning. In a number of studies, children were presented picture-paired associates (i.e., pairs of separate pictures with the task of remembering the pairings—a picture of a *turkey* and a *rock*). When preschoolers were asked to construct an interactive image for each pair, there was little facilitation of performance relative to a control condition in which children were given the paired pictures and simply asked to remember the pairings without instruction as to how to do so. This outcome was replicated a number of times by Levin and associates in the 1970s (e.g., Levin, McCabe, & Bender, 1975), with a great deal of evidence converging to suggest that the problem really was in the generation of an image rather than any other factor. Thus, if preschoolers are asked to generate a sentence linking paired items, they can do so easily and it facilitates memory (Levin et al., 1975), making obvious that the failure to benefit from imagery instructions is not due to inability to think of linking relationships.

A number of investigations also established that children up to 8 years of age experience difficulties when they are asked to generate images representing the content of prose (e.g., Guttmann, Levin, & Pressley, 1977; Shimron, 1975). More positively, slightly older children benefit from instructions to construct images of prose content (Gambrell & Bales, 1986; Pressley, 1976) as well as other material (e.g., vocabulary definitions; Pressley & Levin, 1978).

Some strategies that are helpful for older children and adults are not helpful at all for younger children. Generating images is one such strategy that has been explored in exceptional detail by researchers. Why susceptibility to imagery instructions increases with development will be taken up later in this chapter.

Continued Use of Strategies Following Instruction

Teaching students how to execute a strategy does not guarantee they will use the strategy on occasions when it would be appropriate to do so. Students sometimes fail to continue using strategies in situations almost identical to the instructional setting. That is, there are failures to **maintain** strategies. **Transfer** failures (sometimes referred to as **generalization** failures) occur when students do not apply strategies they have learned to new situations and tasks, where the strategies could be applied profitably.

Why are there maintenance and transfer failures? (1) Sometimes students simply do not recognize that a strategy they have learned could be used in a new situation, but they are able to apply the

strategy if given gentle hints to do so (Gick & Holyoak, 1980, 1983; Ross, 1984). (2) On other occasions, students recognize that a strategy they know is applicable, but their use of it in the particular situation is so jumbled that the strategy is neither recognizable nor effective (see Harris, 1988). (3) Sometimes students do not use a strategy because they do not enjoy carrying it out or do not think that the gains produced by the strategy are worth the effort (e.g., Rabinowitz, Freeman, & Cohen, 1992).

Although it is now recognized that there can be many reasons for maintenance and transfer failures, that was not always the case. A great deal of research was conducted in the last 20 years aimed at identifying the "cause" of maintenance and transfer failures. A popular hypothesis was that the failures represented a **metacognitive** problem and, in particular, were due to a failure of students to understand the utility of the strategies they were learning (e.g., Borkowski, 1985; Brown, Bransford, Ferrara, & Campione, 1983). This possibility will be explored in detail in the sections that follow. Suffice for now to make the point that simply instructing a student about how to carry out a strategy (i.e., without metacognitive information about why the strategy is useful or when it works) in no way assures maintenance or generalization of the strategy.

The failure of strategies to transfer beyond training situations is a specific instance of a phenomenon that will be encountered several times in this book. Learning tends to be tied to the context in which it occurs. This is something that has been recognized by researchers from many different perspectives, from Gestalt problem-solving theorists (e.g., Duncker, 1945) to behaviorists (e.g., Stokes & Baer, 1977) to modern cognitive developmentalists (e.g., Brown et al., 1983). One challenge for instruction is to produce learning that is not bound to specific contexts, with examples of how to do that scattered throughout this book.

Is Instruction Always Necessary? Are There Conditions That Might Facilitate Discovery of Strategies?

Best and Ornstein (Best, 1993; Best & Ornstein, 1986; also see Bjorklund, 1988) have studied whether children might continue to use categorization strategies during list learning, if they are induced to use such strategies by practicing list learning with lists that have saliently related items (i.e., items that are easily and obviously categorizable, such as "tiger, bus, carrot, giraffe, celery, van, beans, car, camel," which is obviously composed of zoo animals, vehicles, and vegetables). In fact, it seems that even children as young as third graders can do so, later using categorization strategies to learn lists containing not easily categorizable items. How is it certain that the learning of the highly related list caused the later strategy use? Because in other conditions of their studies, subjects first practiced learning with lists that did not have easily categorizable elements, with little evidence of use of categorization on subsequent lists. "Spontaneous" use of categorization on later lists was observed only when the third graders first studied lists containing highly relatable items.

Our view is that this is exceptionally important basic research, suggesting that students can discover strategies if they have experiences that support such discoveries. A real challenge is to explore in detail situations that might support the discovery of other strategies. Only through such investigations will it become clear whether it is realistic to expect that students can be encouraged to discover a number of different strategies through environmental manipulations that lead students to carry out the strategies because the materials so strongly suggest the strategic processing.

Summary

When given a memory task, students often fail to use a memory strategy that they could use if given a small amount of instruction about how to apply the strategy to the task in question. That such instruction is often successful was established in many experiments in which one group of children was taught to use a strategy and another group was left to their own devices as they attempted to learn some material. When learning in the instructed condition exceeded learning in the uninstructed condition, researchers concluded that the strategy could be learned and applied profitably to the task at hand by the types of students in the study. More negatively, not all strategies proved to be teachable to all students, with the example of mental imagery discussed explicitly here. Even when students can carry out strategic processes given instruction to do so, there is no guarantee that they will continue to use the strategies so learned. Indeed, there have been many demonstrations of failures to maintain and transfer strategies. Although these failures are prob-

ably caused by multiple factors, there was a great deal of research in the last decade examining whether such failures could be linked to metacognitive deficiencies—failures to understand when and where to apply strategies and failures to understand the gains produced by strategies when they are used. These possibilities are considered in detail in the next section.

METACOGNITION AND THE REGULATION OF STRATEGY USE

An important metacognitive hypothesis about strategy use was that simply teaching a student how to carry out a strategy in no way ensures that the student understands how the strategy benefits performance. Such understanding is critical for a student to continue to use a strategy following instruction. The theory is that such knowledge motivates use of the strategy being taught. This theoretical position stimulated a large number of experiments (e.g., Borkowski, Levers, & Gruenenfelder, 1976; Cavanaugh & Borkowski, 1979; Kennedy & Miller, 1976; Lawson & Fuelop, 1980; Rao & Moely, 1989; Ringel & Springer, 1980) of the following form: One group of students was taught a strategy for some task. A second group was taught the same strategy for the same task but also was provided information about the effects of using the strategy on the task (i.e., that use of the strategy would increase learning). The outcome in such experiments was always the same. Students who were informed about the utility of the strategy were more likely to maintain the strategy than students who were not provided the utility information (see Pressley, Borkowski, & O'Sullivan, 1984, 1985, for a review).

Although it was sensible that understanding utility might increase persistent use of a strategy in a situation extremely similar to the strategy instructional situation, it seemed likely that more would be needed to produce transfer of instructed strategies. For instance, O'Sullivan and Pressley (1984) hypothesized that embellishing strategy instruction with information about when and where the trained strategy might apply (sometimes referred to as **conditional knowledge** about a strategy; e.g., Paris, Lipson, & Wixson, 1983) would increase transfer of a strategy that was taught. It did. O'Sullivan and Pressley (1984) was an exceptionally clean test of the hypothesis that strategy-specific/task-specific meta memory affects transfer, a conclusion supported in subsequent research (e.g., Weed, Ryan, & Day, 1990).

An important hypothesis advanced in the late 1970s and early 1980s was that durable use of strategies might be especially likely if strategies were taught using what Brown et al. (1983) referred to as self-controlled training. Such instruction involves teaching a strategy, encouraging the student to evaluate the gains produced by the strategy (i.e., attend to information about the utility of the strategy), and instructing students to remind themselves to use the strategy using self-verbalizations.

Asarnow and Meichenbaum (1979) trained a cumulative rehearsal memory strategy using such an approach, with striking effects. Immediately following training, both self-control–trained students and conventionally instructed students outperformed control subjects who received no strategy instruction. The really interesting data came a week later on a test of strategy maintenance. Only the self-control–trained students used the cumulative rehearsal strategy on this delayed assessment.

This is the first of a number of outcomes that will be discussed in this book that suggest that long-term use of cognitive strategies requires instruction that involves a number of components: Effective instruction makes clear when and where to use cognitive strategies and makes obvious how useful cognitive strategies are for the learner. It is essential to do this because students often do not discover such utility information on their own, with this point made clear in the next section, which is concerned with whether and when students discover that cognitive procedures they are using are effective and how such knowledge regulates their use of strategies they know.

Monitoring Strategy Effectiveness: When Do Students Become Aware That a Strategy Is Affecting Their Performance Positively and What Difference Does Such Awareness Make?

Suppose that you are taught a new strategy for a familiar task and try it out. How can you know whether the strategy has worked for you, whether it has improved your performance relative to an old approach with the task? If you do recognize the value of the strategy, does it affect your decision to use the strategy in the future? These questions motivated a number of studies on **monitoring** of strategy effectiveness that were conducted in the 1980s, studies that yielded some surprising but consistent results.

In Pressley, Levin, and Ghatala (1984), adults and children in grades 5 and 6 were asked to learn some foreign vocabulary words. All participants were taught a powerful method of learning vocabulary involving construction of mental images and were required to use this method to learn half of the vocabulary items on a first list of words they were presented. For the remaining words on this first study list, the participants were required to rehearse the word and its meaning over and over, which is not effective in increasing memory of vocabulary-definition associations. As expected, items studied using the imagery method were learned better than those studied using rehearsal. More important, however, was that when the participants were asked to estimate how many vocabulary had been learned with imagery versus rehearsal immediately after the words were studied, *but before a memory test on the items,* neither the adults nor the children recognized that the imagery-studied items had been learned better. The students were not monitoring the effectiveness of the two strategies as they used them. Once given a test over the vocabulary items that had been studied with the two different procedures, there was clear perception by the adults that the items studied using the imagery method had been learned better than the ones studied using rehearsal. Following testing, children in the study also recognized there was a difference in learning favoring the imagery-studied items, although they were not as aware of how great an advantage the imagery method had produced.

That learners often fail to monitor how a strategy is affecting them as they use it has been demonstrated on a number of occasions. That learners can come to realize that a strategy is effective in promoting learning by being tested on what they learned with one strategy versus another also has been demonstrated on a number of occasions (Ghatala, 1986; Hunter-Blanks, Ghatala, Pressley, & Levin, 1988; Pressley & Ghatala, 1990).

What difference did awareness of differential strategy effectiveness have on decisions to use the more effective imagery strategy for future learning? After the test, when required to choose one of the two strategies to use to learn a new vocabulary list, both the adults and children overwhelmingly chose the imagery method, specifying that they were doing so because it was more effective than rehearsal. That is, knowledge of strategy utility determined subsequent use of the more effective strategy, consistent with the point made earlier in this chapter that knowing the utility of a strategy affects maintenance of it.

In Pressley, Levin, and Ghatala (1984), all of the participants had an opportunity to compare how they did with the imagery strategy versus rehearsal. Often when students are taught a new strategy, however, they are not given an explicit opportunity to compare it with other strategies. Rather, they are taught the strategy and asked to use it exclusively. Pressley, Levin, and Ghatala (1988) conducted a study to determine whether maintenance of the imagery-based vocabulary-learning strategy would be likely when students were taught the strategy and practiced it alone. The evidence was clear. Simply practicing the imagery method and taking a test on imagery-learned items without an opportunity to compare this performance with learning using other methods resulted in little maintenance of the imagery method 2 weeks later. When participants in the study were given a chance to compare how they did with the imagery method relative to more familiar methods, they recognized better the relative effectiveness of the imagery approach and were more likely to use it 2 weeks after their initial learning and practice of the strategy. This finding is important because instruction in new ways of doing things (i.e., new strategies) so often involves simply teaching the new procedure and having the student practice it. The Pressley, Levin, and Ghatala (1988) data suggest that maintenance of a newly taught strategy is unlikely given such instruction, and, indeed, failures of maintenance following such instruction are common (for a review, see Pressley, Borkowski, & O'Sullivan, 1984, 1985). "Try it" to see whether it works is not pedagogically sound advisement; "try it" and then "compare how you did with the new approach versus your old approach" is much sounder.

In concluding that strategy comparison opportunities can lead to better understanding of the utility of a strategy, which, in turn, leads to continued use of a newly learned, effective procedure, it is important to emphasize that this finding is robust with young adults. The effects of strategy comparison opportunities are not as certain with either children or older adults, as detailed in what follows.

Children In Pressley, Ross, Levin, and Ghatala (1984), 10- to 13-year-old students practiced learning vocabulary definitions with two strategies, one a powerful method similar to the imagery approach used in the previously discussed studies and the other a more familiar approach, although a technique that does not promote learning of vocabulary definitions well (see Pressley, Levin, & McDaniel, 1987, for a review)—composing sentences in which new vocabulary are used correctly. After studying lists of vocabulary using the two methods, all of the children took a test over the vocabulary that had been studied with the two procedures. As expected, the more effective method produced reliably better learning than the make-a-sentence method.

The critical data involved choice of a strategy when the children were asked to learn another list of vocabulary. After practicing the two strategies, taking a test and recalling better the vocabulary that were learned with the more effective method than with the sentence method, only 42 percent of the children selected the more effective approach for learning another list of definitions. This was despite the fact that three out of four of the students knew they had recalled on the test more items studied with the more effective approach.

Pressley, Ross, Levin, and Ghatala (1984) had anticipated this result based on other work they had done. They believed that in making a strategy choice, children would not make use of utility knowledge they possessed about the two strategies (knowledge derived from the previous practice list and test over words learned with the two strategies). If that was the case, the authors reasoned that cuing the students to make use of what they knew about the relative utility of the two strategies might make a difference in their strategy selections. Thus, Pressley, Ross, et al. (1984) included a condition in which subjects were told just before they made their strategy selection to consider how they had performed on the practice list and test as they made their strategy selection. When the children were so prompted before strategy selection, they selected the more effective strategy 89 percent of the time. What this study demonstrated was that children could possess metacognitive knowledge (i.e., in this case that the more effective imagery method worked better than the make-a-sentence method) but fail to use it in making a strategy selection. If children in the middle-elementary grades are to make use of their knowledge of strategy utility in making strategy selections, this study suggested it might be necessary to prompt them to make use of the utility knowledge they possess.

With younger children, it is clear given a series of studies that were supervised principally by Ghatala (Ghatala, Levin, Pressley, & Goodwin,1986; see Ghatala, 1986, for an overview) that even more is required. As in most of the other research described in this subsection, children in the early grade-school years practiced two strategies, one of which was much more effective than the other in mediating a learning task. Then the children were required to choose one or the other strategy on a maintenance test. Grade-2 children did not select the more effective strategy on a maintenance trial unless they were specifically instructed while they practiced the two procedures and took tests over the content learned with the two procedures to (1) assess how they were doing with the two strategies, (2) attribute performance differences as due to use of different strategies, and (3) use the knowledge they had gained about the utility of strategies in making their future strategy selections. When (but only when) the grade-2 children were instructed to assess, make attributions, and use strategy utility knowledge, they selected the more effective strategy 90 percent of the time. There was abundant evidence in this study that when grade-2 children simply practice two differentially effective strategies and take a test over practice

items, little usable metacognitive knowledge about strategies (i.e., understanding that one is more effective than the other) is produced. For children to come to understand that the more effective strategy is more effective and that its effects on performance should be taken into account in making future strategy selections, primary-grade children must be given explicit instruction to attend to their performance differences, interpret these differences as indicators of relative strategy effectiveness, and use this information in future decision making (Figure 2.2). For complementary data using different tasks that corroborates our conclusion that there is development during the grade school years in the coordination of performance awareness and decisions about academic processing, see Nelson-LeGall, Kratzer, Jones, and DeCooke (1990).

Older Adults Brigham and Pressley (1988) used a setup similar to all of the other experiments discussed in this subsection. As in Pressley, Levin, and Ghatala (1984), participants practiced learning vocabulary with two strategies, one a powerful method and the other a less powerful alternative, albeit one more familiar to the participants in the study because they used it frequently to learn things. The subjects in this study were younger (24 to 39 years of age) and older (60 to 88 years of age) adults.

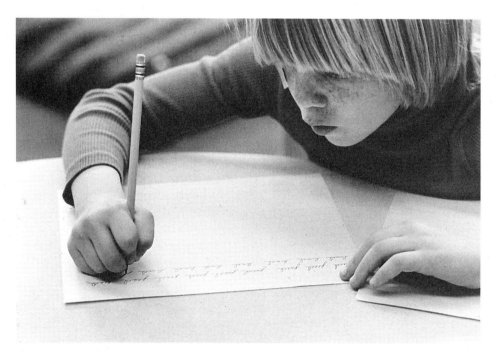

Figure 2.2 This 7-year-old is trying to learn spelling words by writing each one ten times. What might be done to help the child figure out whether the effort was worth it?

The younger adults behaved just as the younger adults in Pressley, Levin, and Ghatala (1984) had behaved: They recognized during the test that they had learned many more words using the more effective method than using the less effective method. When they were presented another list of vocabulary to learn, the younger adults selected the more effective method. They based their decision on the greater utility of the more effective method relative to the less effective method.

The older participants' behaviors were different. Although they recognized during testing that they had learned more using the more effective method than the less effective method, they were not as aware as the younger subjects just how great an edge the more effective method provided. More interesting, however, was that the greater utility of the more effective method was much less of a determinant of subsequent strategy selections for the older compared with the younger participants. Although 93 percent of the younger participants made their subsequent strategy choice based on relative utility of the two strategies, only 47 percent of the older adults did so. The older adults were much more likely than the younger adults to select the less effective strategy, basing their selection on factors other than effectiveness. Often they chose the less effective method because they perceived it to be easier to carry out than the more effective method or because it was more familiar. Selecting a strategy because it increases learning is much more an approach taken by younger than older adults, consistent with observations in other domains that older adults are much more likely to take a variety of factors into consideration when approaching a problem than are younger adults (Labouvie-Vief, 1985).

Summary

When trying a new strategy, people typically are not aware of the effect the strategy is having on their performance unless there is an opportunity to compare performance when the new strategy is used versus alternative procedures. Understanding the differential effectiveness of strategies also requires a test over content studied using the different strategies—people do not seem to monitor well how much they are learning while they are actually studying (a point taken up again later in this chapter). Compared with children and older adults, young adults more certainly use their perceptions of differential strategy utility in making decisions about subsequent strat-

egy use. When children monitor differences in test performance and understand that the differences are due to the differential effectiveness of strategies used during study, they seem not to understand that such information should be used in making subsequent strategy decisions. Other times they seem not to monitor the occurrence of differential performance effects or interpret such differences as reflecting differences in strategy effectiveness unless they are explicitly instructed to do so.

With older adults, their perceptions of differential strategy effectiveness may not be as accurate as those of young adults. There is more to their lower reliance on utility information in making strategy decisions, however. Although younger adults use knowledge of differential strategy utility to the exclusion of other considerations in making strategy selections, older adults are more likely to base their strategy selections on a variety of factors.

A good deal was learned about metacognitive regulation of strategies in the studies summarized in this section. A strong case could be constructed from this body of work that knowing when and where a strategy is useful can often be a determinant of strategy use. But it also must be emphasized that this is not a concrete rule. People sometimes know a strategy is useful and appropriate, and they still elect not to use it. That suggests that factors other than metacognition often determine how humans go about their learning, a theme advanced in most sections of this book.

We emphasize in closing this section that students who do not naturally discover strategies can come to use them—all of those university studies skills centers are not efforts in vain. Detailed evaluations of university-level studies skills courses complement well the themes covered in this chapter. Learning the strategies is not enough; improving achievement also depends on learning how to choose strategies and doing so (e.g., Nist, Simpson, Olejnik, & Mealey, 1991).

PRODUCTION SYSTEMS AND OTHER COGNITIVE-THEORETICAL CONSIDERATIONS RELATED TO THE USE AND INSTRUCTION OF STRATEGIES

A frequent claim that has been presented to us when we give talks about strategies and their metacognitive regulation is that strategies seem to be specific instances of **productions**, particularly as they are specified in a model of thinking known as **ACT* the-**

ory (e.g., Anderson, 1983). ACT* originated as artificial intelligence but Anderson and like-minded cognitive psychologists have used it to explain human thinking. There are important similarities between strategies already considered in this chapter and the productions of ACT*.

Discussion of productions at this point as conceived in ACT* theory permits introduction of some important theoretical distinctions regarding forms of knowledge and the relationship of knowledge to structures of the mind. Strategies are different from productions, however, and thus, this section concludes with an overview of some of the more striking differences between the two constructs.

At its most basic level, a production specifies some action a computer program can make and when the action should occur. Typically, productions are represented in "if-then" form in an artificial intelligence computer program, with the if portion establishing when the production will fire and the then portion establishing the action that will occur when the conditions specified by the if portion of the production are met.

One function of productions is to permit the ACT* artificial intelligence program to recognize and classify objects, such as the following:

If the animal has four legs,
and the animal has an elliptical head,
and the animal is longer than tall,
and the animal is less than a foot and a half high,
and the animal has claws,
Then classify the animal as a cat.

If equation has the form $y = ax^2 + bx + c$,
then classify equation as a quadratic.

These **pattern recognition** productions are important because a situation must be recognized before it is possible to determine whether the conditions are met for other actions. Thus, in the following example, cat and sofa must be recognized by the ACT* artificial intelligence system before it could be evaluated whether the conditions for the action "shoo the cat" are met:

If a cat is on the sofa,
then shoo the cat.

In the following, a quadratic must be recognized before there could be evaluation of whether the quadratic procedure applied:

If equation is quadratic,
and the goal is to know the value of x,
then apply formula of $x = (-b \pm \sqrt{(b^2 - 4ac)}/2a$.

What patterns must be recognized before the procedure "going to my ed psych course" could operated?:

If it is Monday,
and it is 2 P.M.,
then I go to my educational psychology course.

(Answer = Monday and 2 P.M.).

All of the if-information in these examples could be thought of as conditional knowledge, metacognitive information about when and where the action in question applies. In general, the if-information in action-sequence productions must be recognized via pattern-recognition productions before it can be determined that the conditions for the action sequence are met or not. With productions, whenever the if conditions are met, the "then" action associated with the if-information occurs. If this sounds mechanical, it should, for recall that production system models were developed and tested in artificial intelligence (i.e., computer) environments.

What is coded into the action portion of productions is **procedural** knowledge—knowledge of how to do things (e.g., strategic actions are procedures in this sense). Humans and computers, however, know much more than how to do things. They also possess a great deal of factual information, **declarative knowledge.** Procedural knowledge is knowing *how;* declarative knowledge is knowing *that,* a distinction that has been recognized for some time by philosophers (e.g., Ryle, 1949) and cognitive theorists (e.g., Kolers, 1975; Scheffler, 1965).

Returning now to human intelligence, the amount of declarative information possessed by any human is enormous. Here are some examples from author MP's own knowledge base:

I once lived outside Washington, D.C.
My son is Tim.
The New York Yankees dominated the American
    League in the 1950s.
A square has four sides and four right angles.
Dostoyevsky wrote *The Brothers Karamazov.*
Richard Nixon was the only U.S. president to resign
    from office.
The department secretary, Stacy, bought a lot of paper for this school year.

Of course, this declarative knowledge is not disconnected, but rather there are many interconnections to other knowledge. Thus, a Yankee fan's understanding that the Yankees dominated the American League in the 1950s is linked to knowledge of Mickey Mantle, Roger Maris, and Casey Stengel, all of whom were with the Yankees in the 1950s. It is also associated with knowledge that the Yankees' uniforms of that era had bold pinstripes on them. Moreover, some of the knowledge about the Yankees links to other knowledge about the American League. So, when baseball fans think of the 1950s Yankees, they think of DiMaggio, which leads to thoughts of Ted Williams, who played for Boston. Memories of the 1950s Yankees link the book, *The Year the Yankees Lost the Pennant,* which is associated with the play based on the book, *Damn Yankees,* which might prompt some "golden oldies" in the mind's ear, such as Buddy Holly songs or early Elvis Presley hits.

There are many distinctions between procedural and declarative knowledge (Tulving, 1983, pp. 8–9): For example, procedural knowledge can only be demonstrated by performing the procedure. Evidence of declarative knowledge can come in a variety of forms (e.g., verbal recall, recognition, application, association to other knowledge). Procedural knowledge is neither true nor false, whereas the truth value of much of declarative knowledge can be determined. Procedural knowledge is often acquired only after extensive practice. Much declarative knowledge is acquired with a single exposure.

Both procedural and declarative knowledge are stored in **long-term memory** stores. For all practical purposes, human long-term stores are unlimited, or at least there are no apparent limits. (Those who have run out of space on their computer hard drives know, however, that the same is not true of computers, although long-term storage on computers can be increased infinitely by adding "memory.")

When people or computers are using what they know—that is, when procedures are operating on declarative information, it happens in **working memory.** Working memory is often thought of as active consciousness or active memory. (Although there are some conceptual differences between working memory and **short-term memory,** these distinctions are more subtle than is required to understand the ideas used in this book, so working memory and short-term memory will be used somewhat interchangeably in this book and occasionally will be referred to as "attentional capacity.") The capacity of human short-term memory is extremely limited,

with Miller (1956) presenting data that humans can hold only seven plus or minus two pieces of information in active consciousness at any one time.

A short thought experiment will make apparent the capacity limitations of human short-term memory. Read the following list of digits one time, attempting to remember them, and then turn away from the page and try to recall them in order:

1, 8, 1, 2, 9, 8, 5, 8, 3

How did you do? A good bet is that you did not remember all nine digits despite the fact they had just been processed. You were certainly conscious of the numbers as you processed them (i.e., they were in short-term memory), but memory of each one faded quickly. That is what working memory is like—it is short-term, only lasting as long as there is active working on its content. All of human thinking has to deal with the short-term memory "bottleneck" (i.e., it is not big and it is fragile), and there will be several occasions in this book when specific recommendations will be made as to how to work around short-term memory limitations. (In this case, computers are not as limited as humans, with many machines having the capacity to hold many pieces of information in active memory as they make a large number of complex computations on them.)

For the time being, do not worry much about declarative knowledge, which is the focus of Chapter 3, or short-term memory, which will be encountered often in this book. We introduced declarative knowledge at this point (1) simply to stress that procedural and declarative knowledge work together in cognition, consistent with the claim introduced in Chapter 1 that strategies and nonstrategic knowledge work together, and (2) because in the next subsection the case will be made that procedural knowledge starts as declarative knowledge. What follows in the remainder of this subsection is mostly about procedural knowledge and mostly about when it is activated—that is, in working memory.

Many have espoused the view that development of procedural knowledge is an especially important mission of school. Tulving (1983, p. 52) provided an especially elegant statement of this point:

> . . . [P]rocedures learned in school—reading, writing, and arithmetic, and their higher-level equivalents— are better retained and more useful to people in life than is most [declarative] knowledge. A person who has learned how to learn and study in school, how to use sources of information, how to solve problems,

and other similar skills is much better equipped for what awaits him or her after school than is a hypothetical individual who has perfectly memorized everything in the curriculum.

Many of the chapters in this book specify educational programs that are intended to increase procedural knowledge. The steps of these procedures, which are often taught as strategies, can be put in production form. Consider this strategy for estimating the solution to a multicolumn addition problem (based on Reys, 1989):

If it is a problem with two multicolumn numbers
and a plus sign between them, then it is a multicolumn addition problem.
If it is a multicolumn addition problem and the goal
is to estimate, then use the front end digits in
the problem, rounding these based on the digits
in the second-to-front column (e.g., for
8294 + 3885, use 8 and 4).

Many writing strategies can be reduced to plan-translate-revise cycles (see Chapter 15). Here is a set of production-type statements specifying one cycle through these three phases:

If the goal is to write an essay on a content area,
search prior knowledge for information about
the content and search external sources for information about the content.
If information about the content has been identified,
organize that information in a fashion consistent with the message one wants to convey and
make an outline.
If an outline has been constructed, translate the outline into sentences and paragraphs until a first
draft is accomplished.
If a first draft is completed, reread the draft and revise.

In each case, the product produced by a previous procedure in the overall strategy serves as part of the condition specifying the firing of the subsequent procedure.

Acquisition of Procedural Knowledge

According to Anderson's ACT* theory (e.g., Neves & Anderson, 1981), all procedural knowledge starts out as declarative knowledge. That is, how to do something starts out as a verbal characterization of the procedure. When human learners (in contrast to artificial intelligence devices that learn) are first using a

procedure, they are conscious of each of the steps, perhaps even saying them aloud or at least verbalizing some of the steps. In addition, it is not at all unusual for there to be errors during this stage. With practice, errors become less frequent. There is less and less need to verbalize overtly. Execution of the entire sequence becomes smoother until the strategy is no longer a sequence of declarative directions but now one fluent procedure. The movement from declarative representation of a sequence of actions to a single procedure is known as **proceduralization.**

When a sequence of cognitive actions is represented declaratively, it is carried out slowly and with a high cost with respect to cognitive capacity (i.e., working or short-term memory). Most critically, more of this limited short-term capacity must be expended when executing a declarative sequence than an integrated procedure. For instance, when first learning an action sequence, the student will have to interpret each step as they do it. Such interpretation and step-by-step consideration requires cognitive capacity (i.e., short-term or working memory). With practice, the sequence can be executed automatically and without the need to interpret the steps in the sequence and with concomitant reductions in demands on capacity.

A nonstrategic example can illustrate proceduralization well. Last year, author MP's university acquired a new phone system with a phone mail system. The first time he used it, MP read each line of the direction from the card provided by the phone company and spent a lot of time making certain he understood each line. A few trials later, he was saying to himself, "Dial in 5-5-1-0-0 and wait until it answers, then punch in the extension." That did not work because MP forgot to hit the pound sign after keying in the extension number. One more trial later, he was still verbally directing himself step by step but hitting the pound signs appropriately. Gradually, there was less verbal self-cuing. In fact, MP can now do the entire key sequence without thinking about it, with his fingers moving automatically. The proof that not much short-term capacity is being used when he accesses the answering device is that he can easily do other things as his fingers run through the sequence (e.g., talk to a graduate student or think about what to put in one of the chapters of this book). For an example of how proceduralization of a skill frees up cognitive processing and thus permits a person to be able to be more strategic, see Wierda and Brookhuis's (1991) analysis of how skilled bicyclists can perform another task while bicycling much better than can unskilled bicyclists (Figure 2.3).

Short-Term Memory Capacity: A Critical Individual Differences Variable

One value of a well-worked-out, detailed theory such as the ACT* conception of how cognitive procedures are executed is that it illuminates many different factors that might affect procedural competence: Whether a procedure is executed in a situation in which it would benefit performance depends on a number of factors. One, of course, is whether the learner has the procedure in long-term memory (i.e., knows the strategy). The learner also requires conditional knowledge about procedures (the ifs) to use the procedures appropriately. Another determining factor is whether the learner possesses declarative knowledge that can be used in conjunction with the procedure. In addition to all of these components, all of which were considered earlier in the discussion of strategies, another determinant of whether and how well a strategy will be executed is that the learner has sufficient working memory capacity to execute the

Figure 2.3 Is what this person contemplating at this instant active in short-term (working) memory? In fact, he is thinking about what the interior of the family car is like, knowledge stored in long-term memory. Short-term and long-term memory interact routinely as part of good information processing.

strategy in question. Strategies, like all procedures, are always executed in short-term memory.

An hypothesis that follows from the fact that strategy execution is short-term memory capacity demanding is that those who have relatively larger short-term memory capacities will be more likely to be able to execute capacity-demanding strategies. Recall the earlier discussion about developmental differences in children's imagery-generation abilities. Pressley, Cariglia-Bull, Deane, and Schneider (1987) and Cariglia-Bull and Pressley (1990) investigated whether the ability to carry out imagery instructions is linked to differences in working-memory/short-term–memory capacity. The researchers anticipated a wide range of differences in the short-term capacities of the 6- to 12-year-olds who participated in their studies. Thus, tests were administered to participants to determine which students had relatively greater and which had relatively smaller short-term memory capacities. One of these tests involved learning lists of words varying from 3 items in length to 12 items in length. People with greater short-term capacity perform better on such tasks than people with lesser capacity, with those with greater capacity having less difficulty with the longer lists than those with less capacity. A second individual difference measure tapped in the study was general verbal competence of the participants (e.g., a measure of standardized reading achievement was used for this purpose in Cariglia-Bull & Pressley, 1990).

After the short-term memory and verbal competence individual differences measures were collected in both the Pressley et al. (1987) and Cariglia-Bull and Pressley (1990) studies, the grade-school students who served as subjects in the studies were presented 20 sentences to learn, such as, "The angry bird shouted at the white dog," "The toothless man sat on the orange couch," and "The fat boy ran with the grey balloon" (Cariglia-Bull & Pressley, 1990, p. 396). There were two conditions in both studies. In one condition, the children were instructed to attempt to visualize the meaning of each sentence in their head. Control subjects were left to their own devices to learn the sentences, instructed to try hard to learn them. After presentation of 10 sentences, the experimenter cued recall of each sentence by presenting the sentence subject (e.g., tell me about the boy sentence; tell me about the bird sentence).

The results were clear. As expected, general verbal competence did predict performance on this task.

More critically, however, in the imagery-instructional condition, short-term memory capacity predicted performance even after verbal competence and age of the learner were taken into account. Short-term capacity had no predictive value in the control condition. That is, when students were asked to use a capacity-demanding imagery strategy, the benefits of the instruction were greater for students with relatively great short-term capacity compared with students with less capacity. This was true even when general ability was taken into account. The ability to execute a short-term capacity–demanding strategy, such as imagery generation, depends on the amount of short-term capacity one has.

Capacity differences may affect use of strategies in other ways, however. Consider another digit-span task. Similar to the one presented earlier, you will be given a row of digits for each trial and should try to remember them in order. Once the list has been read once, turn away from the book and try to recall it. There are four lists that follow, so you will be reading four times and turning away to attempt recall four times. Here are the lists:

5, 4, 8, 5, 7, 3, 8, 5, 7, 0, 3, 5, 1, 7, 6, 7
4,8,7,3,5,6,7,3,4,5,2,9,3,5,9,8,6,8,5,6,8,5,0
9,2,4,7,5,9,2,3,8,7,4,2,9,8,4,1,3,0,9,4,8,4,1,3,8,4,5,7,1
4,6,4,3,8,7,9,4,5,7,8,5,4,3,3,5,6,7,8,6,8,9,3,2,6,5,7

Was it fun having heavy demand put on your capacity? Would you want to continue with more lists? If you are like many students we have taught, the answers are no and no: It is not fun doing a capacity-demanding task, and no thanks, most students pass on the opportunity to do more such lists. Guttentag (1984; also Guttentag, Ornstein, & Siemens, 1987) proposed that one of the reasons children may not use more strategies than they do is because many strategies are capacity demanding for them and thus somewhat unpleasant to carry out. Consistent with this hypothesis, as children's knowledge increases with development and is increasingly accessible (i.e., accessible with less effort), strategies that depend on knowledge for their operation (e.g., categorization during learning of categorizable lists; elaboration of paired associates) are easier to carry out and hence less capacity demanding. Moreover the less capacity demanding a strategy is with development, the more certain the strategy is to be used (e.g., Bjorklund & Harnishfeger, 1987; Kee, in press).

Low capacity has the potential to undermine strategic competence in several ways. Some strategies require more capacity than some students possess. For students who have sufficient capacity to carry out particular capacity-demanding strategies, the strain associated with doing so may be so great that they simply will not use the strategy when in a free-choice situation.

In summary, ACT* theory emphasizes the criticality of short-term capacity as a bottleneck in cognition, consistent with a long history of cognitive theory and research extending back to Miller (1956). Once ACT* theory was available, no discussion of procedural competence (e.g., strategic competence) has been considered complete without discussion of potential short-term capacity constraints. Thus, the discussion of ACT* theory led us to a brief reconsideration of strategy instruction and strategy use in light of short-term memory demands and limitations. At several points in the book, there will be explicit discussion about how educational psychologists deal with short-term capacity demands and constraints so as to design instruction that does not overwhelm the short-term capacities of students.

Summary: How Strategies and Productions Are Similar and Different

Strategies are like the productions of ACT* theory in that both strategies and productions specify cognitive actions, are stored in long-term memory, and are regulated by conditional knowledge. Both operate on external input and nonstrategic declarative knowledge, which is also stored in long-term memory, only transferred into a working, shorter-term store when needed as part of conscious thought involving procedures. According to ACT* theory, if the conditions associated with a procedure are met (i.e., if the ifs occur), the procedure is transferred from long-term memory to short-term memory and executed, with the nonstrategic knowledge required to carry out the procedure also activated into short-term memory because the procedure needs the knowledge to operate.

For strategies, things are not nearly so certain. Strategies often fail to be used even when all the ifs are met, even on occasions when efforts have been made to ensure that students know when and where a strategy applies. Whether a strategy is executed depends on other factors, not the least of which is student motivation. Motivation does not play a role in ACT* theory. In short, the theory of good thinking in this book is sensitive to more factors than is ACT* theory, although ACT* theory is a powerful theory as far as it goes. ACT* theory will come up again in the next chapter on knowledge and its representation.

CONCLUDING COMMENTS

The theory and data considered in this chapter suggest a number of conclusions that in fact will prove to be general, consistent with a great deal of theory and data presented in later chapters. Here are the most important of them:

- Even 2-year-olds evidence some simple strategies on some occasions.
- More negatively, young adults are not as competent as they could be.
- There is voluminous evidence that when people do not carry out a procedure when left unprompted, they often can carry it out if instructed to do so.
- Although transfer failures are common, much is being learned about how to encourage greater transfer of procedural knowledge learned through instruction.
- There are age-related increases in use of strategies during the schooling years, reflecting greater schooling (and other cultural) experiences for older compared with younger students.
- Conditional knowledge (i.e., metacognitive knowledge about where and when a procedure applies and the gains conveyed by a procedure)—and use of it during strategy decision making—is a critical determinant of whether maintenance and transfer of procedural knowledge occurs.
- Good human thinking does not always work as mechanically as the thinking specified by models such as ACT*. Human thinking involves more components, such as motivation.
- Acquisition of procedural knowledge often takes a while, at first, slow and supported by verbal representations of the sequence of actions composing the procedure. With experience, strategies are executed faster, with less explicit verbal mediation and with less demand on short-term capacity.
- Educational interventions must be designed so the procedures can be carried out given the short-term capacities of targeted students.

The basic research on strategies featured in this chapter is extremely important, for the insights produced in it have affected greatly the instruction of much more complex, academically important strategies—for reading, writing, and problem solving. A variety of strategies will be covered in this book with many associations documented between use of strategies matched to academic demands, developmental level, and academic achievement. Good students definitely know and use more strategies (as well as more effective strategies) to accomplish school tasks than do weaker students: Good students take notes, they plan essays, they prepare strategically for tests, and they schedule their time so that schoolwork and everything else in their lives can occur (e.g., Zimmerman, 1990a, 1990b; Zimmerman & Martinez-Pons, 1986, 1988). Although sophisticated task analyses of academic tasks contributed much to the development of academic strategies, so did the developmental and metacognitive basic research reviewed in this chapter.

Knowledge

Nonstrategic knowledge is extensive and diverse. Different theories have been proposed about how declarative and procedural knowledge are represented in the mind, with theoretical diversity necessitated in part because there are many types of representations that seem to function in thinking. The discussion of productions begun in Chapter 2 also continues in this chapter to illustrate how procedural, metacognitive, and declarative knowledge can operate in an artificial intelligence program designed to resemble human thinking. That thinking often depends on the situation in which it occurs is considered as well, making clear that the emphasis on mental representations in this chapter does not mean that only mental factors determine thinking.

This chapter is concerned with how knowledge can be represented and organized in long-term memory. Many alternative conceptions of knowledge that have been explored will be covered in this chapter.

Much of the research on knowledge and representation of knowledge involved evaluation of memory and hypotheses about factors affecting memory. Other research was concerned with comprehension and, in particular, identifying how particular forms of knowledge can affect the understanding of new information. Sometimes both memory and comprehension were implicated in the research—for example, the forms of knowledge mediating comprehension were sometimes inferred from qualitative characteristics of memory. Various types of problem-solving research also have played a role in research on knowledge and its representation, from studies about how people decide that two geometric objects are identical except for their angle of rotation to research on how students know which algebra algorithm to apply in a particular situation. Because this chapter is more about representation than memory, comprehension, or problem solving, however, no explicit attempt will be made to separate the contributions to representational theory that come from memory, comprehension, and problem-solving research. We begin by describing some simpler forms of representation.

NEURAL NETWORKS

A number of cognitive psychologists are interested in the most fundamental ways that knowledge can be represented. Although these scientists are ultimately interested in the brain, some of them also are interested in the implications of fundamental neural representations for education (Schneider & Graham,

1992). A good deal of the research on neural networks is done with computer simulations—that is, with programs that can encode information in artificial **neural networks.**

There are three basic components in the neural networks being studied on computers (Bechtel & Abrahamsen, 1991; Martindale, 1991): (1) Units or nodes are similar to neurons except they have only one property, whereas human neurons have many: That single property is that nodes can be activated at various levels. (2) There are connections between nodes. Two nodes are connected either by simultaneous excitation of the nodes (i.e., if one is excited, the other is) or inhibitions precluding joint excitement (i.e., if one node is excited, the other node cannot be). These connections between nodes are the stuff of long-term memory according to neural network theory. (3) Learning (i.e., development of long-term memories) is the creation of connections and changing the strength of connections. One of the most basic ways that connections are strengthened is by simultaneous activation of nodes in a fashion analogous to strengthening of connections between neurons (Hebb, 1949).

Consider a sample network dealing with some simple knowledge, the letters of the alphabet (Selfridge, 1959). The nodes in this case correspond to features that letters can possess, such as a horizontal bar, a vertical bar, an acute angle, a curve bulging to the right, and a diagonal bar. Suppose a letter is presented to the computer system, in this case a letter activating the vertical bar and rightward bulge features. Each of these features is strongly connected to the capital letters P, R, and Q if the machine has "seen" many Ps, Rs, and Qs before, with each exposure strengthening the connection between these two features and these capital letters. Thus, when a P is presented, the two activated features connect to the P, R, and Q, activating the nodes representing those letters. The computer decides that this is a P, however, because a clear signal that the letter is an R requires another feature be activated—a diagonal bar in the lower half of the letter. A clear signal that the letter is a Q requires activation of the lower-half diagonal bar feature as well as activation of a left-bulging curve feature. When the features add up to a P, inhibitory signals are sent out from the P node to the R and Q nodes as well as to all other letter nodes.

The child learning letters is building up connections between features and letters in much the same way according to **connectionist theories.** Thus, when a child is shown a P and is told it is a P, there is a strengthening of connections between the letter name P and the P features. With each subsequent encounter of a P and its name, the connections between the features of the letter P and the letter name strengthen. Eventually, whenever the feature complex defining P is encountered, there is automatic activation of the letter name.

The same type of strengthening of connections can be used to explain word recognition either in neural network computer programs or people according to connectionist theories (e.g., McClelland & Rumelhart, 1981). Consider what happens when the word EACH is presented. Connections are activated between the individual features defining each letter and between the letters. Connections between E and the first position in a word also are activated, as are connections between A and the second position, C and the third position, and H and the fourth position. That is, activating the E also partially activates connections with words beginning with E. Activating the A also partially activates connections with words having A in the second position. (This is why letters encountered in words are recognized faster than single letters.) For adults who have experienced the set of connections between first-E, second-A, third-C, and fourth-H many times before, there is activation of the word EACH and inhibition of other words (e.g., words sharing letters with EACH). For readers who want a state-of-the-science, detailed discussion of how connectionist models explain word learning, see Seidenberg and McClelland (1989).

Each set of nodes encodes particular information, and thus the human brain is like a large number of little machines according to connectionists, with each machine dedicated to learning a particular type of information. Of course, these little machines are interconnected and operate simultaneously, with the term **parallel distributed processing** (McClelland & Rumelhart, 1986; Rumelhart & McClelland, 1986) capturing this property. This parallel operation can be appreciated with respect to the letter and word examples just presented.

When presented the word EACH, there is not a linear analysis beginning with the first letter, proceeding to the second, and so on. Rather the connections between the letters and their positions are activated simultaneously. A number of constraints are considered all at once, and the decision that the word is EACH occurs after all of the relevant constraints have been considered. A lot is happening in parallel. Thus, there are features that define letters (Gibson,

1969). Activation of a particular subset of all features (and hence the connections between features) defines a letter. A particular set of letters activated in particular positions of a syllable (and the resultant pattern of connections) defines a particular syllable. A particular set of syllables activated and connected to particular positions in a multisyllable word permits recognition of a multisyllable word. All of this just to recognize one word!

According to connectionist models, for efficient performance, lower-order knowledge must be mastered before higher-order knowledge. Thus, knowledge of particular letters—that is, associations between patterns of feature activations and their corresponding letter names and sounds—must be well established before it is possible to learn to recognize words. Because knowledge begins with low-level features, which are progressively associated with one another to define higher-order units, this is decidedly a **bottom-up** approach to cognitive processing. This contrasts with **top-down** approaches to cognition, in which thinkers begin with hypotheses about higher-order units and then process lower-order units as part of evaluating the hypothesis (e.g., schema theory considereded later in this chapter).

We do not take a position on whether all human knowledge is reducible to neural networks, as connectionist theorists believe. We do believe, however, given the state of neural network theory and research at present, that other models of knowledge explain many patterns of human thinking data better than does connectionism. What follows is a sampler of highlights from this literature, featuring the models of knowledge having the greatest impact on education.

CONCEPTS

A person's **concept** of something is their understanding of it, which often corresponds to a larger societal conception (Klausmeier, 1990, whose historically rich coverage informed much of the discussion presented in this subsection). A concept is a decision rule for deciding whether an item is a member of a particular category. Thus, what a person thinks a dog is like is his or her concept of a dog; the labrador retriever next door, Lassie, and Big Red are members of the category "dog" (Bower & Clapper, 1989).

Many concepts are clear-cut so that independent observers readily agree on whether an item is an example of it or not. Thus, given a triangle, most North American adults recognize it as such. Other concepts are not as clear-cut and thus are referred to as "**fuzzy**" (Neisser, 1967; Oden, 1987). For example, it is not at all clear when a person stops being a juvenile and becomes a young adult or when a small business becomes a large business. There is a lot of conceptual fuzziness in the world.

Representation of Concepts

That people often can classify items into conceptual categories is more certain than exactly how they do it. Two approaches have received more research attention than others.

Classical Theory According to this theory, concepts can be defined with respect to the necessary and sufficient features for an item to qualify as a representative of the concept (e.g., Stillings et al., 1987, Chapter 3). Thus, a *triangle* is a closed, planar figure with three straight sides and three interior angles. Learning a concept is learning its defining features according to classical theory. An item is regarded as a member of a conceptual category to the extent that its features match the defining features for the concept.

Both **simple concepts** and **complex concepts** have been proposed. It has long been held that there are simple concepts that reflect innate sensory processes (e.g., James, 1983 edition of the text originally appearing in1890, Chapter 12). Thus, we have separate categories for red, orange, yellow, green, blue, indigo, and violet because of innate mechanisms for recognizing differences in color (e.g., Bornstein, Kessen, & Weiskopf, 1976). According to the classical view, complex concepts are learned and the result of combining properties of simple concepts. Thus, a triangle is defined by a conjunction of the simple concepts *closed, planar, figure, three-sided, straight-sided,* and *three-angled.* These features are sufficient and necessary to define the complex concept of a triangle.

This classical theory of concepts is easily comprehended in terms of neural networks. Thus, when the set of neural nodes associated with plane figures, closed figures, three-sided figures, and three-angled figures are simultaneously activated, the decision is made that the item in question is a triangle because of a long history of association between these coactivated features and the concept of a triangle.

Prototype Theory Classical theory is unsatisfactory for several reasons. First, it is often difficult to define many concepts in terms of simple concepts (i.e., perceptual features). Second, the evidence is fairly strong that many concepts are defined by their functional characteristics rather than their perceptual characteristics (e.g., Nelson, 1974). Thus, balls are coded as things that roll, bounce, and can be thrown, even by very young children. Third, fuzzy concepts (like juvenile and young adult) also pose a problem in that they are not obviously reducible to a set of particular features that uniquely define instances of the concept. Fourth, it should be possible, based on the number of features presumably defining a concept, to make predictions about how long it will take to process a concept relative to concepts with either fewer or more defining features. Such predictions, however, often do not transpire (Fodor, Fodor, & Garrett, 1975).

Rosch (1975, 1978) and colleagues (Rosch & Mervis, 1975) noted that people often classify based on resemblance rather than with respect to necessary and defining features. Thus, there are *typical* grandmothers, who are over 40 and gray-haired. *Atypical* grandmothers (e.g., a 35-year-old, whose child was born when she was 17 and who has, in turn, had a child at 17) are less readily classified as grandmothers. Because of its typicality, a robin is readily and quickly classified as a bird, whereas a penguin is less quickly classified as a bird. Rosch's theory is often referred to as **family resemblance theory.**

Family resemblance theory is a **prototype** theory because it is usually possible to construct a typical member of the category. Although a typical bird would be a concatenation of features that would never occur simultaneously in a real bird, the more an animal resembles this typical bird, the more certainly and quickly the animal would be classified as a bird (Figure 3.1). When given a robin and asked whether it is a bird, the response is faster than to the same question posed with respect to a chicken (Rips, Shoben, & Smith, 1973; Rosch, 1973; Rosch & Mervis, 1975). In addition, typical category members are first learned by children as being members of the category. Also, when people are given lists of category members and asked to recall them later, the more typical members are recalled before the atypical members. (See Smith & Medin, 1981, for a review of the relevant literature.)

How are such prototypes formed? They are a sort of mental average of the many instances of the concept that have been encountered in the world. Both adults (Posner & Keele, 1968, 1970; Reed, 1972) and children (e.g., Lasky, 1974) can construct such mental averages.

Figure 3.1 Which of these—the penguin, the robin, or the crane—is a prototypical bird? Which have the features of birds?

Features of stimuli are critical to classification in both classical and prototype theories. Prototype theories have been favored in recent years, however, although, to be sure, the debate between the classical and prototype theories rages on (e.g., see Ward, Vela, & Hass, 1990, favoring a feature-theory approach; also, a reply from Nelson, 1990, on the side of a prototype model of concept learning and categorization). How nondefinitive features contribute to classification (e.g., such as "over 40" for grandmothers) and how people classify instances of fuzzy concepts are more obvious with prototype theory.

Relations Between Concepts

Many complex connections between concepts are stored in long-term memory. Concepts are storied in hierarchies in memory, with each node in the hierarchy a whole that can be subdivided into parts. Thus, all living things can be subdivided into animals and plants. Animals can be further subdivided into reptiles, mammals, birds, insects, spiders, and so on, each with associated features (e.g., hair, vertebrate, warm-blooded for mammals). Mammals can be divided by *genus* (e.g., bears, elephants, giraffes, moles), each with associated features. Each *genus* is further divisible into species (e.g., bears can be polar,

black, brown, speckled). Each species has its associated features.

The most frequently cited evidence to support the existence of **hierarchical semantic networks** is that questions requiring consideration of information at different places in the hierarchy are answered more slowly than questions requiring consideration of information coded in nearby nodes (Collins & Quillian, 1969). Thus, the question, "Do birds have skin?" requires consideration of a feature (i.e., skin) coded with "animals" rather than directly with "birds." This question takes longer to answer than does, "Do robins have red breasts?" because "red breasts" is a feature stored directly with robins. Such an analysis is not above criticism, however, because it could be that "skin" is stored with robins but is a weak associate to robin, whereas "red breast" is a stronger associate (Conrad, 1972; Glass, Holyoak, & O'Dell, 1974).

Collins and Loftus (1975) proposed an updated model to attempt to account for this difficulty and other outcomes that could not be accounted for with the original model—for example, that people readily make acoustic associations to words (i.e., red breast and nest are acoustically linked) and that the decision speed for false facts (e.g., rocks can meow, dogs can meow) often cannot be predicted by the original model (Anderson, 1984). Collins and Loftus (1975) referred to their updated model as a **spreading activation** theory of semantic processing to emphasize that activation of any particular part of the network results in spread of activation with parts of the hierarchy that are "closer" and more highly associated with the activated concept. Only a little thought is required to make obvious that the interconnections in such a model are complex and the patterns of activation logically could be extensive.

The idea that concepts are linked associatively, with the links varying in strength is an old one (e.g., Deese, 1961, 1962, 1965; see Paivio & Begg, 1981, Chapter 5, for an overview). What is particularly striking about much of this work is how easy it is to demonstrate "clusters" of associations using various methods. Thus, "wings," "birds," and "fly" are strong associates. So are "yellow," "flower," "color," "sunshine," and "garden." One of the reasons that such association models are not studied as prominently today as they once were is that more powerful theories of knowledge representation have emerged that both capture the associations and specify more precisely the relations between associated elements (see the discussion of schemata later in this chapter). Even so, there are some tasks and some occasions when conceptual relations are perhaps best understood in terms of associations.

Consider the television game show *Family Feud.* Before each program, a panel of 100 people is given category labels (e.g., snack fruits) and is asked to generate associations (e.g., apple, banana, fig). Individual contestants on the show score points by "guessing" what the audience said. That individuals can do so reflects shared knowledge between members of the culture (for relevant analyses, see Garskof & Houston, 1963; Laffal, 1965). That individual contestants offer bizarre responses compared with the most frequent responses in the audience survey reflects that some knowledge is more personal.

An important consequence of spreading activation via hierarchical and associative networks is that activating some particular content can make it easier to understand related material. Thus, if the word "stone" is read by a person, followed by the word "rock," "rock" is recognized more quickly than if "stone" had not been presented (Meyer, Schvaneveldt, & Ruddy, 1975; Neely, 1976, 1977). The sentence, "The lawyer is in the bank," is understood more quickly if the sentence is preceded by a sentence containing words associated with *lawyer* and

bank (Anderson, 1984; McKoon & Ratcliff, 1979). That is, activation of a concept **primes** recognition of related concepts.

One caveat is that there is at least some evidence that the spread through semantic nets may not be as extensive as Collins and Loftus (1975) proposed. DeGroot (1983) developed word triads in which the first and second terms were strongly related, as were the second and third terms (e.g., *bull-cow-milk*). If spread is extensive, it might be expected that *bull* would serve as a prime for both *cow* and *milk*. It did not, only priming *cow*. It may well be that the spread of activation is only to near concepts and associations.

Development of Hierarchical Concepts in Children

Do children have hierarchical conceptual networks that resemble adult networks? Classic Piagetian theory included the claim that preschool (preoperational) children experience great difficulties doing tasks that involved classification. Particularly relevant here, preschoolers were assumed to be unable to accomplish **class inclusion** problems. Thus, according to Piagetian theory, if a preschooler is given a set of ten pictures of seven elephants and three bears, he or she should have difficulty with questions such as, "Are there more elephants or animals?" Piagetians assumed that preschooler difficulties with such tasks reflect a lack of understanding of the hierarchical relationship between animals and specific animals (Inhelder & Piaget, 1964).

Many researchers have generated data substantiating that the Piagetians underestimated the competence of young children (Brainerd, 1978a 1978b; see Chapter 7, this book), and so it has been the case with class inclusion. When children are carefully instructed about what is required in such tasks—that is, the instructions are simplified somewhat over those used in the original Piagetian studies—there is considerable evidence that children can do class inclusion problems and have hierarchical representations (Winer, 1980), at least for familiar classes (e.g., Markman & Siebert, 1976; Smith, 1979; Steinberg & Anderson, 1975).

Even so, children's categorization and processing of categories is anything but adultlike: (1) Children often fail class inclusion problems when unfamiliar concepts are presented. (2) Preschoolers also have difficulties when instructions do not make task requirements obvious. (3) Children's preferred way of representing categorizable content often is not along category lines but with respect to thematic relations they can detect between objects. Thus, when given a group of objects that can be sorted along categorizable lines (e.g., tiger, elephant, monkey, giraffe, banana, orange, grapes, apple), preschoolers often sort along thematic lines (e.g., monkeys eat bananas, elephants and giraffes live in the same house at the zoo, a tiger could eat an apple, mommy puts oranges and grapes in her fruit salad; Bruner, Olver, & Greenfield, 1966; Kagan, Moss, & Sigel, 1963). Such sortings suggest that schematic representations play a large role in children's early knowledge. (See the discussion of schemata later in this chapter.) (4) That children's categories do not always correspond to those of adults is also evident from their underextensions of concepts—using *duck* to refer only to one's pet duck—and their overextensions—using *duck* to refer to any bird larger than a robin (Bloom, 1973; Clark, 1973). (5) Children often sort into many more categories than adults do (Saltz, Soller, & Sigel, 1972). (6) Sophisticated studies of children's concepts have revealed striking qualitative differences between the concepts of preschoolers and those of older children and adults. For example, Carey (1985), in an investigation of children's biological knowledge, demonstrated that 10-year-olds' understanding of *animal* included relations between the processes of eating, breathing, growing, dying, and reproducing, whereas 4-year-olds did not understand the criticality of these functions in animals, although they could distinguish animals from nonanimals.

Although some of children's knowledge probably is in categorical hierarchies similar to those of adults, many concepts that children hold differ from those of adults. Moreover, children are less likely to rely on hierarchical categorical knowledge than are adults when they are performing tasks that could be mediated by hierarchical knowledge. How development of hierarchical categorical knowledge and its use occurs is not completely understood and is the target of current research (e.g., Markman, 1989). These developments probably are due in part to experience, however, with data from cross-cultural psychology informative on this point.

For instance, Sharp, Cole, and Lave (1979) established that rural Mexicans without formal schooling tended to classify objects based on functional properties (e.g., chicken and eggs would be seen as the two related objects in a triad composed of chicken, horse, and egg), whereas rural Mexicans with some formal schooling tended to use categories comparable to Western-educated adults (i.e., chicken and horse being selected as members of the same category—animals). Attendance in Western-style schools increases use of hierarchical categorical knowledge, just as it affects use of Western-style strategies (see Chapter 2, this book).

Summary

A mix of modern and classical thinking about concepts was represented in this section. We hope the simplicity of these models came through, however, for we want to emphasize that neither neural nor concept models capture well many relationships that exist between ideas stored in long-term memory (i.e., there are more than hierarchical and associative relations). Other types of representations do a better job of this, and these more complex approaches will be covered in sections that follow.

In admitting the limitations of neural network and concept models, that is not to denigrate them. Both connectionist and concept models account for some types of data well. The mind is complex enough for a variety of representational types, and, indeed, the many functions performed by the mind may require representational diversity.

SEMANTIC VERSUS EPISODIC MEMORY

Beginning with this section, we discuss ways of representing knowledge that can capture properties other than simple hierarchical categorizability and associative relatedness.

Tulving (1972) introduced the distinction between **semantic memory** and **episodic memory** as two ways to classify what is referred to in this book as declarative knowledge. Semantic memory is knowledge of the world that is now independent of specific experiences. Episodic memory is memory of personally experienced events. Thus, your semantic memory contains an image of a cat. You also have episodic memories of specific cats, perhaps including a pet or one that you have seen hanging around your neighborhood. Baseball fans have semantic knowledge of baseball games and episodic knowledge of specific games.

Tulving (1983, Chapter 3) provided a number of distinctions between semantic and episodic memory. A few are especially telling: (1) The point of reference for semantic knowledge is the world: Is this knowledge true about the world? The point of reference for episodic knowledge is the self: Did this event happen to me? Is this what really happened on that occasion? (2) Semantic memory is not coded with respect to *when* the information was acquired. Episodic information often is. (3) Semantic knowledge is less susceptible to context effects than episodic knowledge (e.g., Kintsch, 1980). That is, often episodic information is more likely to be remembered in situations in which it had originally been encoded than in other situations. Recall of semantic information is not nearly so context bound. (4) Semantic information is unlikely to be forgotten; episodic information is easily forgotten. (5) Semantic knowledge is *known;* episodic knowledge is *remembered.* (6) Education is more concerned with the development of high-quality semantic knowledge than development of episodic knowledge. Even so, there are often many episodic memories.

Both semantic and episodic knowledge function in cognition. Although people make a general association to *cat* when they read *dog,* they also sometimes think of particular cats and dogs they have known. Indeed, the argument is made later in this chapter that much of our most important knowledge is tied to the situation in which it was acquired—that much of thinking may be tied to the specific experiences giving rise to it—that abstract semantic knowledge may be much less prevalent in thinking than suggested by many cognitive models advanced in the past—that much of thinking is case based (i.e., episodic).

PROPOSITIONS AND MACROPROPOSITIONS

Propositions are descriptions specifying relationships between things and their properties (Clark & Clark, 1977; Kintsch, 1974). Every proposition specifies at least one such relationship. Each proposition contains a verb or preposition and specifies one or several semantic roles that are related by the verb or preposition. Thus, a proposition contains information about the agents performing actions specified by verbs, the objects of actions, goals accomplished by an action, the recipient of the action (referred to

as a patient in this system), time of the action, and so on. Propositions are equivalent to sentences in logic and are represented using a standard format that emphasizes the relationship specified by the verb or preposition. Thus, the proposition UNDER (DOG, HOUSE) specifies a relationship between a dog and a house, that the *dog is under a house.* Each of the propositional representations can be thought of as conveying one idea, one unit of meaning. What must be emphasized is that what is in the head is the abstract idea represented by the logical sentence, not the sentence itself, according to propositional theorists.

Substantially more complex ideas than category membership and associative relatedness can be expressed with propositions, especially multiple propositional units. Consider the sentence, "John carefully nailed down the loose shingles on the roof" (Kintsch, 1982). There are four units of meaning (**semantic units**) in this sentence: *Nailing is being done carefully, John nails shingles, shingles are on the roof,* and *shingles are loose* are the ideas that compose this sentence. These can be summarized in four propositions with NAIL as the main verb. JOHN is the agent performing the relation specified by this verb. The object of the relation is (LOOSE, SHINGLES). The location of the shingles is specified as (ON, SHINGLES, ROOF). The relation NAIL is modified by CAREFUL. Each of these four propositions is a **microproposition,** specifying a little bit of meaning in the text.

Many types of content can be specified propositionally (e.g., pictorial representations can be written as propositions, with how this can be done and the implications of this possibility taken up in the section on imagery later in this chapter). Even so, a great deal of research on propositional representations, and the most prominent work pertaining to propositions that is relevant to educational psychology, has been conducted with text, with the research and theoretical analyses provided by Kintsch and colleagues the most visible of these efforts.

In a nutshell, when a reader reads a text, Kintsch (e.g., 1983; van Dijk & Kintsch, 1983) believes the text is parsed implicitly by the reader into its micropropositions. These meaning units combine to capture the full meaning of the text. Of course, no one remembers everything about a text—no one can ever remember a text word for word unless they have gone to a great deal of difficulty to memorize the text verbatim. What people remember is the gist, which is the main idea of the text, which is encoded into **macropropositions,** which are not derived directly from the text—they are derived from the micropropositions. Thus, a macroproposition for the passage containing the sentence about John nailing shingles might be *John repaired the house.*

With respect to long discourse, such as a book, there are layers of macropropositions. Thus, at the top level, there is an overall summary of the book. Each chapter in the book can be captured by macropropositions, as can each paragraph in each chapter. The lower-level macropropositions collapse into one another to create the higher-level macropropositions (van Dijk & Kintsch, 1983, e.g., Chapter 2). In general, what ends up in our long-term memory are macropropositions, summaries of more detailed information we have experienced. Macropropositions preserve meaning of what has been processed (i.e., the gist), not the actual surface form of it.

Although it has been recognized for decades (at least since Bartlett, 1932) that gist is encoded during reading and that subsequent recall reflects memory for gist and reconstructions from world knowledge, Kintsch and associates have provided a sophisticated model of how macropropositional models of text are constructed. The differences between an original text and the meaning constructed by the reader are apparent in an example provided by Kintsch and van Dijk (1978, p. 384). Consider the following passage (attributed by Kintsch and van Dijk to an article by F. K. Heussenstam in a 1971 issue of *Transaction*):

> A series of violent, bloody encounters between police and Black Panther party members punctuated the early summer days of 1969. Soon after, a group of black students I teach at California State College, Los Angeles, who were members of the Panther party, began to complain of continuous harrassment by law enforcement officials. Among their many grievances, they complained about receiving so many traffic citations that some were in danger of losing their driving privileges. During one lengthy discussion, we realized that all of them drove automobiles with Panther Party signs glued to their bumpers. This is a report of a study that I undertook to assess the seriousness of their charges and to determine whether we were hearing the voice of paranoia or reality.

Here is a possible recall of that passage, one in which macropropositions are remembered. Some embellishment with bridging inferences is also apparent:

> In the sixties, there was a series of riots between police and the Black Panthers. The police did not like the Black Panthers. After that, students who enrolled at the California State College complained that the police were harrassing them. They were stopped and had to show their driver's license. The police gave them trouble because they had Black Panther signs on their bumpers. The police discriminated against these students and violated their civil rights. They did an experiment for this purpose.

There is actually an impressive array of evidence that propositions are important elements of meaning in much of cognition (see van Dijk & Kintsch, 1983, Chapter 2, for a review of the evidence). For instance, if you are asked to recall the information in a sentence that is presented for study, you are more likely to recall portions that are from the same idea unit than from other portions of the sentence (Lesgold, 1972; Wanner, 1975). For the sentence, *The mausoleum that enshrined the czar overlooked the square,* presentation of *overlooked* as a recall cue is more likely to elicit *mausoleum* than *czar,* even though czar was physically more proximus to *overlooked* in the sentence: Both *mausoleum* and *overlooked* are part of the idea unit OVERLOOK (MAUSOLEUM, SQUARE). In addition, there is evidence that when any part of a proposition is recalled, the whole of it tends to be recalled (Buschke & Schaier, 1979; Goetz, Anderson, & Schallert, 1981; Graesser, 1981; Kintsch, 1974). Another piece of evidence suggesting the psychological reality of propositional representations is that text containing more propositions requires more processing time, even if the number of words in the text is constant (e.g., Graesser, Hoffman, & Clark, 1980; Kintsch & Keenan, 1973; Kintsch, Kozminsky, Streby, McKoon, & Keenan, 1975).

An especially important property of propositions is that once a macrostructure is formed, subsequent exposure to some part of the macrostructure activates other parts of the macrostructure (see van Dijk & Kintsch, 1983, Chapter 6; also Kintsch, 1988). That is, there is **spreading activation,** much like that described with respect to semantic networks linking concepts. Spreading activation between propositions can also occur, for propositions are linked via **propositional networks.** Any two propositions that share common elements are directly linked in such networks (e.g., Hayes-Roth & Thorndyke, 1979). For example, the propositions representing, "Jane caught the ball," and "Jane bought a dress," are linked through *Jane.* Similar to other linkages, the strength of the connection between propositions can be increased by simultaneous activation of the propositions. Thus, when a person tells a story about Jane catching the ball that is the last out at a baseball game and then rushing off to buy a dress, the linkage between Jane catching the ball and her buying a dress increases.

General knowledge of the world, in contrast to memory of a specific text, also can be built up from text as Kintsch describes. Macropropositional representations of what has been read are integrated with prior knowledge to create new knowledge, some part of which is propositional in form. (Indeed, there are some propositional theorists who believe that all knowledge ultimately is represented in this form; e.g., Anderson & Bower, 1973). Thus, if you read a *Time* magazine article about overcoming infertility, you construct a macropropositional representation of that text. At a party tomorrow, you could rely on this macroproposition to guide partial retelling of the article to a friend who might be interested in infertility. In addition, and this is critical, your long-term knowledge of infertility in general might be changed by reading the article. Thus, 6 months from now, when someone makes a claim about infertility that conflicts with what was in the article, you can respond, "But I thought . . . ," going on to relate a general point from the article, perhaps no longer aware of where the information was acquired. What has been changed, to use Kintsch's term, is your **situation model** of infertility. Such a situation model is **schematic,** capturing and organizing a number of propositions about infertility. **Schemata** are more complex than any representations considered up until this point and are taken up in the next subsection.

FRAMES, SCRIPTS, AND SCHEMATA

Every adult knows what goes on at a birthday party. Description of that knowledge in terms of neural networks, concept models, or propositions, however, would be clumsy and long-winded at best. (Imagine the incredibly complex set of propositions required to represent everything that occurs at a birthday party.) Dissatisfaction with the inability of the theories of knowledge reviewed thus far to represent such common but complex events economically was part of the motivation for theories of knowledge considered in this section.

These new theories have been given different names by their creators, and each is particularly well matched to some situations better than others. Their common thread is that a number of concepts that commonly co-occur in particular situations are related to one another in orderly systems of procedures and expectations. Events and situations are presumed to have skeleton structures that are pretty much constant, although the particular ways the skeleton ends up taking on flesh varies from instance to instance.

Frame Theory

The first example of such a complex representation is Minsky's (1975) notion of a **frame:**

> A *frame* is a data structure for representing a stereotyped situation, like being in a certain living room, or going to a child's birthday party. Attached to each frame are several kinds of information. Some of this information is about how to use the frame. Some is about what one can expect to happen next. Some is about what to do if these expectations are not confirmed. We can think of a frame as a network of nodes and relations. The "top levels" of a frame are fixed, and represent things that are always true about the supposed situation. The lower levels have many *terminals*—"slots" that must be filled by specific instances or data. Each terminal can specify conditions its assignment must meet. . . . Simple conditions are specified by markers that might require a terminal assignment to be a person, an object of sufficient value. . . . More complex conditions can specify relations among the things assigned to several terminals. (p. 212)

A few examples will make more obvious what is implied here. Consider knowledge of birthday parties as Minsky (1975) did. There are certain objects that are always present and actions that always occur (Figure 3.2): (1) The attendees wear clothes. (2) They bring presents. (3) Games are played. (4) There are decorations. (5) There is a meal. (6) There is a cake. (7) There is ice cream. Items (1) through (7) specify the top level (i.e., the fixed level) of the birthday party frame. Associated with each of the parts of the fixed frame are constraints on how the frame can be filled out: (1) The clothes are usually Sunday best, although simply good clothes sometimes are acceptable. (2) The present must be something that the birthday child would like to receive. It is bought and wrapped in birthday gift wrap. (3) There are a set of acceptable games, such as hide-and-seek or pin-the-tail on the donkey. (4) The decorations often include balloons, streamers, and banners. Attendees are sometimes given party hats and noisemakers

Figure 3.2 What is going to happen next? What is it about representations in your long-term memory that permits you to predict with high confidence what is about to happen at this party? Would a 4-year-old know what is going to happen next?

(5) The "main dish" at the meal is kids' fare—hot dogs, hamburgers, or fried chicken. This is followed by cake and ice cream. (6) The cake is decorated and has candles, usually equal in number to the age of the birthday child. The cake is not cut until all party attendees have sung happy birthday, and the birthday child has blown out the candles. (7) Ice cream is chocolate, vanilla, or strawberry.

Script Theory

Schank and Abelson (1977) also sought to explain the common knowledge that people in a culture possess about recurring complex situations. They proposed that much of knowledge is represented in **scripts.** Although frames as just described can represent sequences of events, for a number of reasons that need not concern us here, scripts more completely capture sequences of events. Scriptlike representation of a sequence is an important human ability because there are many recurring sequences of events in life. For example, there is a *sequence* of events every time you go to a movie theatre, including traveling to the theater, buying the ticket, buying some food or beverage, giving the ticket to an usher, finding a seat, watching the film, leaving the seat and heading for the exit, dropping the food wrappers or paper cups

in the trash can near the exit, and leaving the building housing the theater.

That scripts are deeply engrained in all of us is apparent when a script is violated. Consider something that happened to us a few years ago. We were heading to dinner with a friend who wanted to show off his favorite fancy restaurant. After parking the car, we entered double glass doors that seemed to be part of a barber shop. We were confused to say the least. Our friend walked over to the barber's closet and pulled it open. We followed him into a restaurant in the motif of a speakeasy, with the barber shop front part of the camouflage. Until we were provided some explanation by our friend of this speakeasy motif, we were really lost about what was going on. The rest of the evening was a combination of familiar events, ones represented in the fancy restaurant and speakeasy scripts stored in our long-term memories. With both of these scripts activated, we were able to get through the evening without any more surprises.

Schema Theory

Although both frame and script theories have been important in cognitive psychology, their close relative, **schema theory** as developed by Richard Anderson and colleagues at the Illinois Center for the

Study of Reading (e.g., Anderson & Pearson, 1984), had much more impact in education. The similarity of a schema to frames and scripts will be apparent with the consideration of an example, one originally provided by Anderson and Pearson (1984, pp. 259–265). (The similarities between frame, script, and schema theories are such that from this point on, we will simply refer to any theory of this type as schema theory.)

The schema for a ship christening includes its purpose—to bless the ship. It includes information about where it is done (i.e., in dry dock), by whom (i.e., a celebrity), when it occurs (i.e., just before launching of a new ship). The christening action is also represented (i.e., breaking a bottle of champagne that is suspended from a rope). These parts of a schema are referred to as **nodes, variables,** or **slots.** At any particular christening, these slots are **instantiated** with particular instances (e.g., New Haven, with the President breaking a bottle of California-produced champagne on a particular new submarine). There are clear constraints on the instances that can occur in these slots. The celebrity would never be a person of ill repute (e.g., a smut publisher, a famous criminal). The champagne might be a bottle of Rothchild's, but a bottle of $7.00 champagne would be unlikely. Once instantiated, the schema can be represented as a series of propositions capturing that it was the President who christened the ship, the ship was in the New Haven yards, the champagne was produced in California, and so forth.

Once some small part of the ship christening schema is encountered, for example, by the first image in a news clip showing a bottle of champagne breaking on the bow of a ship, the entire schema is activated. Once activated, comprehension and processing of the ship christening event are different. (Schematic processing is decidedly **top-down** in that once activation of the higher-order idea occurs, it constrains thinking about the details of the situation.) The activated schema will permit reasonable inferences to be made about details of the event (e.g., as the bottle is seen breaking on the bow, the viewer might infer that there was a platform beside the ship with one or more persons on it, one of them a celebrity). The activated schema also affects allocation of attention (e.g., to the celebrity, to the name of the ship, and memory of the event).

Much of the research on schema theory was generated with respect to comprehension of texts. Schema activation can dramatically affect compre-

hension, inferences, attention allocation, and memory of what is read. (See Anderson & Pearson, 1984, for a review of the relevant data.) Sometimes readers activate a schema near the beginning of their processing of text, with the schema then affecting subsequent inferences that are made about the text.

Read the following text, which was used by Anderson, Reynolds, Schallert, and Goetz (1977):

> Every Saturday night, four good friends get together. When Jerry, Mike, and Pat arrived, Karen was sitting in her living room writing some notes. She quickly gathered the cards and stood up to greet her friends at the door. They followed her into the living room but as usual they couldn't agree on exactly what to play. Jerry eventually took a stand and set things up. Finally, they began to play. Karen's recorder filled the room with soft and pleasant music. Early in the evening, Mike noticed Pat's hand and the many diamonds. As the night progressed, the tempo of play increased. Finally, a lull in the activities occurred. Taking advantage of this, Jerry pondered the arrangement in front of him. Mike interrupted Jerry's reverie and said, "Let's hear the score." They listened carefully and commented on their performance. When the comments were all heard, exhausted but happy; Karen's friends went home. (p. 372)

Did you infer that the story was about cards or music? Either fits. If early in your reading you inferred that it was about cards, a number of inferences consistent with card playing were made as the rest of the passage was read. For instance, participants in Anderson et al. (1977) who thought the passage was about cards also mades inferences such as "She is playing with a deck of cards," and "Mike sees that Pat's hand has a lot of diamonds." Those who concluded the passage was about music made inferences such as "Mike brought out the stand and began to set things up," and, "As usual they couldn't decide on the piece of music to play." Once a schema is activated, it affects the inferences made about a situation, in this case, a text being read.

An activated schema also affects attention to information that would not be attended to if some other schema were activated. For instance, read the following passage (part of a passage used in Pichert & Anderson, 1977, and Goetz, Schallert, Reynolds, & Radin, 1983) as if you were a burglar making plans to rob the house described in the passage:

> The two boys ran until they came to the driveway. "See I told you today was good for skipping school," said Mark. "Mom is never home on Thursday," he

added. Tall hedges hid the house from the road so the pair strolled across the finely landscaped yard. "I never knew your place was so big," said Pete. "Yeah, but its nicer now than it used to be since Dad had the new stone siding put on and added the fireplace."

There were front and back doors and a side door that led to the garage, which was empty except for three parked 10-speed bikes. They went in the side door, Mark explaining that it was always open in case his younger sister got home earlier than their mother.

Pete wanted to see the house so Mark started with the living room. It, like the rest of the downstairs, was newly painted. Mark turned on the stereo, the noise of which worried Pete. "Don't worry, the nearest house is a quarter of a mile away," Mark shouted. Pete felt more comfortable observing that no houses could be seen in any direction beyond the huge yard.

Now reread the passage as if you were a potential homebuyer. What should be apparent during this second reading is that you attend to different parts of the passage when a burglar schema is activated versus when a homebuyer schema is activated. This was exactly the point of studies such as Goetz et al. (1983) and Pichert and Anderson (1977)—that schemata can guide attention.

The schemata that are activated when attempting to remember also can have a powerful impact on what is recalled. Thus, Anderson and Pichert (1978) had adults read the passage about boys playing hooky, again either reading from the perspective of a potential homebuyer or a burglar, followed by a memory test requiring recall of the passage. Then came the manipulation that is pertinent to the point being made here. Those participants who originally read and recalled from the perspective of a burglar were now asked to recall from the perspective of a homebuyer, and those who had read and recalled originally from the perspective of a homebuyer now attempted to recall from the perspective of a burglar. More information was recalled following this direction to switch perspectives, information consistent with the new perspective. An activated schema guides reconstruction of a previously encountered event (see also Kardash, Royer, & Greene, 1988). It can be used to guide retrieval, as it was in the case of this subject (cited by Anderson & Pearson, 1984) while attempting to recall the "hooky" passage from a burglar's perspective:

  I just thought of myself as a burglar walking through the house. So I had a different point of view, a different objective point of view for different details, you know. I noticed the door was open, and where would

I go here, go there, take this, take that, what rooms would I go to and what rooms wouldn't I go to. Like, you know, who cares about the outside and stuff? You can't steal a wall or nothing . . . I remember [the color TV] in the second one, but not in the first one. I was thinking about things to steal, things you could take and steal. In the den was the money. China, jewelry, other stuff in other places. [Q: Why do you think you remembered the color TV the second time and not the first time?] Because I was thinking of things to steal, I guess. (p. 283)

Children's Schemata The research produced by Anderson and colleagues substantiates that people have schematic knowledge and that it is used in processing new and recalling old information. Not surprisingly, this evidence has inspired a great deal of other work about the nature of human knowledge, with research conducted by Nelson, Hudson, Fivush, and their colleagues particularly important to educators. These investigators have asked whether children (e.g., preschoolers) store knowledge in schemata and, if they do, how such storage affects their processing of new material. In fact, children do use schematic representations much as adults do.

Not surprisingly, the schemata that children possess are determined by recurring events in their lives. Thus, children have schemata representing events such as dinner (at home and at McDonald's), bedtime, making cookies, birthday parties, and going to a museum (Hudson & Nelson, 1983; Hudson & Shapiro, 1991; Nelson, 1978; Nelson & Gruendel, 1981). For instance, if children are presented a brief story pertaining to one of their schemata, they can answer inferential questions about the story—that is, questions that require knowledge about the situation described in the text that is over and above the information specified in the text.

As an example, consider what happens when a child is questioned about the following short story:

  Johnny and his mom and dad were going to McDonald's. Johnny's father told him he could have dessert if he ate all his dinner. They waited in line. They ate their hamburgers. And they had ice cream. (Hudson & Slackman, 1990, p. 378)

When presented the question, "Why did they stand in line?," the 4- to 7-year-olds in the Hudson and Slackman study had no difficulty responding, despite the fact that there was no mention in the story of why they had stood in line. The McDonald's schema contains this information, a schema understood by many preschoolers in the United States.

That schemata can have a powerful effect on children's comprehension and memory is evident when they are presented stories that are not quite right in that they include information inconsistent with schemata stored by most children. Consider this less-than-perfect story that Hudson and Nelson (1983) presented to 4- to 7-year-olds:

> One day it was Sally's birthday and Sally had a birthday party.
> Sally's friends all came to her house.
> Sally opened her presents and found lots of new toys.
> Everybody played pin the tail on the donkey.
> Then Sally and her friends ate the cake.
> They had some chocolate and vanilla ice cream.
> Everybody had peppermint candy, too.
> Sally blew out all the candles on the cake.
> Sally's friends brought presents with them.
> Then it was time for Sally's friends to go home.

Most readers recognize that presents were opened before it was specified that the friends had brought the presents. In addition, the cake was eaten before the candles were blown out. These happenings are noted because they are inconsistent with the birthday party schema.

The use of the birthday party schema to comprehend and remember this story was apparent when the children in Hudson and Nelson (1983) attempted to recall the story. Sometimes the story was repaired during recall by failing to mention either one or both of the misordered elements. When the misordered acts were reported, they tended to be placed in schematically correct order rather than as specified in the story. Recall of the story was consistent with the schema for birthday party even though the original presentation of the story was not consistent with this schema.

In short, the evidence is quite compelling that adults and children have schemata for familiar events that determine how new information is processed, interpreted, and retrieved. What we emphasize in closing discussion of this point is just how early in development schematic-based knowledge occurs and affects thinking, with 1- to 2-year-olds definitely possessing schematic representations of common events in their lives (for a review, see Hudson, Fivush, & Kuebli, 1992).

Not surprisingly, students develop schemata for recurring intellectual tasks, with students' schematic understanding of academic tasks an arena of great interest to educational psychologists. Both students' knowledge of the schematic structure of texts and their understanding of the schematic structure of common mathematics problems have received attention from educational psychologists, with these two topics taken up in the next two subsections.

Text Structure Schemata   Texts have conventional structures that are familiar to readers (Kintsch & Greene, 1978). Both **narrative** text structures (i.e., the structures of fictional stories) and **expository** text structures (i.e., the structures of factual texts) have been studied. Although slightly different systems have been proposed by different researchers, there are great similarities in the various **story grammars** that have been proposed as capturing the structures of fiction and great similarities in the various schematic systems proposed as representing the structures of exposition. Thus, rather than worry about subtle differences between alternative story grammars and expository structures, we present well-known examples that convey the general sense of these schemata.

Mandler (e.g., 1978, 1987) has been particularly active in analyzing the structure of stories. According to Mandler's theory, a story consists of a setting and an event structure composed of episodes. Each episode has a beginning, which is an event initiating a complex reaction; a complex reaction, which is composed of an emotional or cognitive response and a state the protagonist wishes to achieve; a goal path, which involves a plan of action by the character and the consequences of setting the plan of action in motion; and an ending, which is a reaction.

There are at least four types of evidence that substantiate the existence and psychological importance of story grammar knowledge. (1) Stories that do not conform to the story grammar structure are difficult to remember (and are processed more slowly) compared with stories that do conform, with this finding holding for both children and adults (e.g., Kintsch, Mandel, & Kozminsky, 1977; Mandler, 1978; Mandler & Johnson, 1977; Stein & Nezworski, 1978). This conclusion holds not only for text that is heard, but also for stories presented on television (e.g., Collins, Wellman, Keniston, & Westby, 1978). (2) When story information is presented in an order other than one consistent with conventional story grammar, both children and adults tend to fix the story up at recall, remembering the elements of the story in an order consistent with the story grammar (Mandler, 1978; Mandler & DeForest, 1979; Stein & Glenn, 1979). (3) The probability that an element will be recalled from a story varies with the role it plays in the story as defined by story grammar. Thus, major setting, initiating event, and consequence elements are more likely to be recalled than attempts, which are more likely to be recalled than internal responses and reactions (Mandler, 1984; Mandler & DeForest, 1979; Mandler & Johnson, 1977; Stein & Glenn, 1979). (4) Reading times at the beginning of episodes are greater than for material in the middle of episodes. Content at the end of episodes is processed especially quickly (Haberlandt, 1980; Mandler & Goodman, 1982). There is a lot of reason to believe that people have schemata that specify the structure of fiction.

Anyone who has studied rhetoric knows that there is ample guidance in the classical rhetoric literature about how writers should process text. Kintsch (1982) argued that there are texts (and parts of expository texts) that simply identify things, specifying what they are. There also are definitional texts. Classification texts provide information about how to decide something is this or that. Some texts provide illustrations of general principles. There are compare-and-contrast texts and analysis texts, which break events down into their component parts, functions, or causes.

Whether people possess schemata for these various types of expositions has not been evaluated extensively, although the information that is available suggests that **expository text schemata** do function in adult learning and thinking. Kintsch and Yarbrough (1982) provided empirical validation of the psychological importance of expository text structures. University students read classification, illustration, compare-and-contrast, and procedural description texts in this study. The most critical manipulation in the study involved presentation of the text in either a good expository form or a poorly organized one. Thus, for the well-organized passage concerned with classification of primate locomotor patterns, the topic was introduced in the first paragraph. Then the classfications were presented in the next four paragraphs in their evolutionary order. In the poorly organized passage, the paragraphs were presented in a random order.

The results in the study were clear. Readers were much better able to state the main idea and recall ideas from well-organized compared with poorly organized passages. Even though the issue of whether adults possess schema for expository text is hardly resolved by a single study, it is heartening that the outcomes in Kintsch and Yarbrough (1982) were so clear-cut, for important reading comprehension interventions that are aimed at increasing reader knowledge of expository text forms are being proposed and disseminated. Some of these will be covered in subsequent chapters.

Mathematics Problem Schemata   Most of the mathematics problems presented in elementary and high school textbooks have typical structures. For instance, Mayer (1981) analyzed high school algebra texts and identified about 100 common problem types. Working through those problems has an effect on long-term knowledge of problems. Schematic representations of typical high school mathematics problem types reside in the long-term memories of people who have completed high school mathematics. For example, any algebra 1 textbook will contain a problem like this one: If a car travels 10 hours at 30 miles per hour, how far will it go? For many algebra 1 graduates, this problem activates their schemata for "distance = rate × time" problems.

Students who have taken algebra and science also have schemata for other types of problems (Mayer, Larkin, & Kadane, 1984, pp. 246–247), including the following: output = rate × time, total cost = unit cost × number of units, interest = interest rate × principal, profit = markup rate × cost, area = length × width, and current = voltage/resistance. For example, after completing algebra and science courses, students can classify problems into types (e.g., identifying problems as representing one of the example schemata presented in the last paragraph; e.g., Hinsley, Hayes, & Simon, 1977). In addition, students use their problem-solving schemata as they identify which information in problems is critical to process and which is not (e.g., Hayes, Waterman, & Robinson, 1977; Mayer, 1982; Robinson & Hayes, 1978). This may be one reason that students who possess greater knowledge of problem schemata—and hence are more proficient at problem classification—also are better able to solve problems (e.g., Silver, 1987). Expert problem solvers in an arena have well developed schemata (e.g., Riley, Greeno, & Heller, 1983).

Summary   People have schematic representations about familiar activities and recurring events. These schemata abstract the relationships between different parts of these activities and events. That these types of representations seem to be available as young as it is possible to measure their presence suggests that schematic representation is a fundamental human competency. That it is possible to specify many different types of schemata, from those that code scenes (e.g., frames; Minsky, 1975), sequences in an evening (i.e., scripts; Schank & Abelson, 1977), elements of text (e.g., story grammar; Stein & Glenn, 1979), and mathematical relationships (e.g., Hinsley et al., 1977), provides another angle on their power. Schematic representations are used by everyone and in many different situations.

CASES

Before there can be a schema, there must be individual cases that include information about concepts, procedures, and how the components of the case are related. Even after a schema is formed, representations of individual cases will remain. Thus, even though a person may have a schema for fancy restaurants in general, he or she will have memory of the specifics of a fancy restaurant in their neighborhood. Case knowledge is important, for decisions often are based on a single case encountered in the past.

Research examining the case versus schematic knowledge of young children has succeeded in documenting some important differences between memory for specific episodes and what is encoded in schemata. For example, Fivush, Hudson, and Nelson (1984) studied kindergarten children's memories for a specific trip to a particular museum, one distinguished because it was a museum of archeology, and their general memories of what happens on trips to museums. Memories of the specific museum trip were tapped immediately after the trip occurred, 6 weeks following the trip, and 1 year later. One striking result was that memory of the specific museum trip did not include intrusions from the more general "museum-trip" script, nor did events that occurred on the specific trip receive mention when the kindergarten students told about museum trips in general. We agree with Fivush et al.'s (1984) conclusion that the clear separation of the memory for the specific trip and the general event schema suggests that memory for specific cases and schematic memory are two different types of encodings of information. (This is consistent with the more general theory of memory advanced by Tulving, summarized earlier in this chapter, that there are episodic memories and more general, semantic memories.) The potential for case knowledge to have long-term impact on thinking is also supported by these data in that memory of the specific case (especially the ability to recognize specific parts of the museum in a picture recognition task) was still quite good 1 year after the trip to the museum. Indeed, some specifics of the museum trip were remembered even 6 years after the trip occurred (Hudson & Fivush, 1991a; see Wagenaar, 1986, for additional evidence that single events are remembered for at least 6 years). Hamond and Fivush (1991) also provided data that slightly younger children (i.e., 3- to 4-year-olds) remember important events in their lives (e.g., a visit to Disneyworld) at least a year and a half later. Rich preschool experiences create rich memories that endure.

Even though there are differences between memories for single events and generalized memories of events experienced repeatedly, an important direction in research on case-based reasoning is whether a generalizable approach to problem solving can be developed from experiencing a single example (see Chapter 13 for additional information on case-based reasoning during problem solving). The answer is "yes."

That generalizable problem-solving knowledge can be gained from an example was apparent in studies reported by Gick and Holyoak (1980, 1983), although these same studies made clear that people often do not use the procedural knowledge they acquire from an example, as have other more recent investigations (e.g., Reed, 1989). In the Gick and Holyoak studies, subjects—always at least in high school—read a sample problem and its solution, such as the following:

A small country was ruled from a strong fortress by a dictator. The fortress was situated in the middle of the country, surrounded by farms and villages. Many roads led to the fortress through the countryside. A rebel general vowed to capture the fortress. The general knew that an attack by his entire army would capture the fortress. He gathered his army at the head of one of the roads, ready to launch a full-scale direct attack. However, the general then learned that the dictator had planted mines on each of the roads. The mines were set so that small bodies of men could pass over them safely, since the dictator needed to move his troops and workers to and from the fortress. However, any large force would detonate the mines. Not only would this blow up the road, but it would also capture many neighboring villages. It therefore seemed impossible to capture the fortress.

However, the general devised a simple plan. He divided his army into small groups and dispatched each group to the head of a different road. When all was ready he gave the signal and each group marched down a different road. Each group continued down its road to the fortress so that the entire army arrived together at the fortress at the same time. In this way, the general captured the fortress and overthrew the dictator. (Gick & Holyoak, 1983, pp. 35–36)

Following presentation of this example, the participants were given another problem to solve. See if you can come up with a solution to this problem:

Suppose you are a doctor faced with a patient who has a malignant tumor in his stomach. It is impossible to operate on the patient, but unless the tumor is destroyed, the patient will die. There is a kind of ray that can destroy the tumor. If the rays reach the tumor all at once at a sufficiently high intensity, the tumor will be destroyed. Unfortunately, at this intensity the healthy tissue that the rays pass through on the way to the tumor will also be destroyed. At lower intensities the rays are harmless to healthy tissue, but they will not affect the tumor either. What type of procedure might be used to destroy the tumor with the rays, and at the same time avoid destroying the healthy tissue? (Gick & Holyoak, 1983, p. 3)

Gick and Holyoak's (1980, 1983) participants often did not generate reasonable answers to the "radiation" problem, even though it is a situation analogous to the situation in the "General" problem. The answer is to use a number of lower intensity rays coming in at different angles so that they meet at the point of the tumor—and thus, the intensity of the radiation at the tumor would be equal to the sum of the intensities of the individual rays, although no healthy tissue would be exposed to rays of such intensity.

Even though adults often fail to recognize the analogous relationship between the radiation and General problems and hence fail to generate a correct solution when first presented the radiation problem, Gick and Holyoak (1980, 1983) provided substantial evidence that much was learned from the sample problem. In particular, if, when the radiation problem was presented, adults were presented a vague hint to use the previous story to solve the new problem, the probability of solving the radiation problem was actually quite high. It was not that the subjects had not learned the dispersion solution presented with the General problem or could not apply it to a new problem with an analogous structure. The problem was that they did not recognize the relevance of the previous problem and its solution unless they were prompted to notice its relevance with the hint.

Quite a bit was learned from the single worked-out example—just not enough to assure recognition of new problems similar in structure to the sample problem. This, of course, is a metacognitive failure—not knowing when and where to apply a problem-solving procedure that one has learned.

Ahn (e.g., 1987) and colleagues (Ahn & Brewer, 1988; Ahn, Mooney, Brewer, & DeJong, 1987), in particular, have been exploring when general problem-solving approaches are derived from single examples. They present adults with anecdotes about how a particular problem was solved, such as the following:

Tom, Sue, Jane, and Joe were all friends and each wanted to make a large purchase as soon as possible. Tom wanted a VCR, Sue wanted a microwave, Joe wanted a car stereo, and Jane wanted a compact disk player. However, they each only had $50 left at the end of each month after paying their expenses. Tom, Sue, Jane, and Joe all got together to solve the problem. They made four slips of paper with the numbers 1, 2, 3, and 4 written on them. They put them in a hat and each drew out one slip. Jane got the slip with the four written on it, and said, "Oh darn, I have to wait to get my CD player." Joe got the slip with the 1 written on it and said, "Great, I can get my car stereo right away!" Sue got the number 2, and Tom got number 3. In January, they each contributed the $50 they had left. Joe took the whole $200 and bought a Pioneer car stereo. In February, they each contributed their $50 again. This time, Sue used the $200 to buy a Sharp 600 watt, 1.5 cubic foot microwave at Service Merchandise. In March, all four again contributed $50. Tom took the money and bought a Sanyo Beta VCR with wired remote at Service Merchandise. In April, Jane got the $200 and bought a Technics CD player at Service Merchandise. (Mooney, 1990, p. 502)

Depending on the experiment, subjects in Ahn's research either produced an abstract summary of the problem-solving rule illustrated by the story, wrote another anecdote illustrating the application of the approach to problem-solving illustrated in the story, or answered questions about the problem-solving tactic. In general, adults could perform these tasks after exposure to a single example—doing as well as subjects who had been presented a formal abstract summary of the problem-solving tactic. That is, they could induce a general principle based on a single example.

People often can and do reason about new situations based on analogies with previous situations (e.g., Hammond, 1990; Riesbeck & Schank, 1989)—

that is, people often engage in case-based reasoning. Some detail in today's problem often reminds a person of a situation encountered previously, with the dimension of similarity prompting creation of a solution for today's problem that has some similarity to the solution used to solve the previous problem. When some low-level superficial similarity cues transfer of a strategy from one situation to another, it is known as "low road" transfer (Salomon & Perkins, 1989). Low-road transfer is fairly common. For example, in Ross (1984), if a sample word problem illustrating a probability principle was based on the happenings in an IBM car pool, performance on a test item covering the principle was better if the test item story was about the happenings in an IBM car pool rather than the happenings among golfers or some other group of people. See Macario, Shipley, and Billman (1990) for evidence that children as young as 4 years of age can experience low-road, case-based learning of a generalizable rule.

The problem with low-road transfer, of course, is that often more than recognition of superficial similarity is required to solve a problem. Recognition of structural similarity between the current situation and a previously encountered situation is required. Salomon and Perkins (1989) refer to transfer based on recognition of structural similarity as "high-road" transfer. When taking the high road is required, people often act similar to Gick and Holyoak's (1980, 1983) subjects, failing to recognize analogies between new situations and situations they have dealt with in the past. Other times, people will ignore the deep structural cues and be reminded instead of something that is only superficially related to the present case, resulting in a poor solution being generated—as in the example of a person applying the solution used to solve a previous problem mentioning an IBM carpool when the current problem mentioning an IBM carpool required an altogether different approach (see Gentner, 1989, for an analysis).

Are there any general principles about the likelihood of solving new problems with solutions similar to ones used in analogous problems? Brewer (1989) proposed that there are two important ones, and we add two more: First, people often can make analogies between a new situation and an old one if they are given a prompt to do so (Gick & Holyoak, 1980, 1983) or something about the new situation reminds the learner about the old situation (e.g., Ross, 1984, 1987, 1989). Second, it will be easier to notice analogies between items in domains in which one has greater expertise—the learner is more likely spontaneously to detect an analogy for problems in a domain of expertise, and the learner is more likely to be able to determine how to apply old knowledge gained from examples to new problems when cued to do so. Prior knowledge is important, a theme that will be expanded on in the next chapter. Third, in general, low-road transfer is more certain than high-road transfer. Fourth, transfer of a problem solution to a new situation is more likely to the extent that people are taught when and where to apply a problem solution, why the solution works, and what outcomes the solution produces. For example, Chen and Daehler (1992) demonstrated that even children in the primary grades will transfer a problem solution from one situation to an analogous one if the initial presentation of the problem solution is metacognitively rich, specifying in particular the goals a problem solution facilitates and the outcomes it produces.

As we present this research on learning from one example, we feel some anxiety, for the conventional wisdom is that learning from examples is usually more certain when several examples are presented rather than one. Much of the work establishing the importance of multiple exemplars was generated in studies aimed at determining how people learn to identify new categories. Because much of this work was done with artificial materials, we do not want to emphasize it over some of the more ecologically valid research already presented in this section but think that the prominence of the work with artificial materials demands some mention of it.

For example, one paradigm establishing the role of multiple examples in acquiring categorical knowledge involved presentation to subjects of two five-dot patterns, each of which was presented as a prototype for a concept—A and B (for one such study, see Peterson, Meagher, Chait, & Gillie, 1973). Then a number of five-dot examples were presented to subjects, with their task to decide whether each example was representative of concept A or B, often with feedback provided as to the correctness of attempted classifications. A criterion in such studies is whether subjects can identify whether a dot pattern presented several days (weeks or months) later is representative of A or B.

Collapsing across studies of this genre (see Druckman & Bjork, 1991, for a brief review; also Smith & Medin, 1981), the following conclusions emerge: (1) Acquisition of concepts is more certain as the number of examples presented increases. (2) Training is more likely to permit identification of the full range of examples of the concept if the full range of examples is presented during training. (3) One hassle involved in presenting the full range of examples during training is that it increases errors during training. In short, there is substantial evidence in the concept acquisition literature that multiple and varied examples can have an extremely positive impact on acquisition of conceptual knowledge.

Is there really a dilemma here with respect to making practical recommendations? No. People sometimes generalize based on one case. Often, that is all they have to go on, and the situation is such that new cases cannot be created. (For example, an enormous amount of evidence in support of the claim that useful generalizations can emerge from single examples was generated by social learning researchers during the 1960s and 1970s; see Chapter 7.) In contrast, many of the concepts that must be discovered anew in school by each generation of students can be presented conveniently via multiple examples rather than just one. Although students may come to powerful understandings about the structure of a concept, procedure, or principle based on their first encounter with it or learn enough of its details to permit some low-road transfer, presentation of additional examples can permit practice working with the concept, procedure, or principle as well as exposure to various ways the concept, procedure, or principle can be packaged. A variety of examples seems like a good idea when it is possible, and it is often possible in school. Such variety fosters a schematic, generalized representation of the concept, procedure, or principle. When exposure to a variety of examples is not possible, the mind can store single cases that permit, at least some of the time, both low-road and high-road transfer.

VERBAL AND NONVERBAL REPRESENTATIONS: IMAGERY AND DUAL CODING

Paivio (e.g., 1971, 1986; especially Clark & Paivio, 1991, which provided the basis for much of what is presented in this subsection) posited that knowledge is composed of complex associative networks of verbal and imaginal representations (Figure 3.3). The verbal system contains wordlike codes for objects and events and abstract ideas, codes that are only arbitrarily related to what they represent (e.g., the

Figure 3.3 Allan Paivio's dual-coding theory and his research on the theory illuminated a psychological phenomenon known for over 2000 years—that people often construct images as part of their thinking. His brilliant experiments inspired a generation of researchers who have produced an enormous literature documenting when and how imagery functions in cognition. Although retired, Allan Paivio remains active as an emeritus professor at the University of Western Ontario.

word "book" has no physical resemblance to an actual book). The imagery system contains nonverbal representations that retain some resemblance to the perceptions giving rise to them (e.g., an image of a book shares features with the perception of an actual book). These include visual images (e.g., of a bell), auditory images (e.g., the sound of a bell), actions (e.g., ringing motion), skeletal sensations related to emotion (e.g., racing heart), and other nonlinguistic representations. Thus, the imagery representation for a book has visual and tactual qualities associated with books. Verbal representations tend to be sequential, whereas the imagery system can encode a number of features simultaneously. A single complex image (e.g., of a classroom) can encode a great deal about the classroom simultaneously, whereas a verbal representation of a classroom can only be made sequentially one bit of information at a time (e.g., the room has desks, aisles, and windows—until a sequence has been generated exhausting the details of the classroom). Images can be dynamically transformed, as when you mentally walk around an image of the classroom in which your educational psychology course meets.

Elements in the imagery representational system are linked to elements in the verbal representational system. Thus, there is a connection between most people's image of a book and their verbal representation of a book, with such **referential connections** permitting construction of mental images given words as stimuli and generation of names when objects are seen in pictures. (There is some evidence, in fact, that inefficiency in making such referential connections is implicated in learning disabilities, with that database interpreted as supportive of the hypothesis that dual coding is an important dimension of effective and efficient thinking; Swanson, 1989.)

The richness of verbal-imaginal referential connections can be understood by considering the nonverbal associations to a word such as "surgery." These can include vivid images of excruciating pain and memories of feelings of both "coming apart" and tightness along suture lines. When someone mentions "Canada," some people envision a map outline of the country and the first bar of "O Canada."

There are also **associative connections** within both the verbal and the nonverbal systems. In the verbal system, words are associated with other words, so that some students relate the word "school" with "hate," "boring," and "afraid." Categories and their instances are tied associatively within the verbal system, so that "tree" is associated with "maple," "oak," and "pine." Within the nonverbal system, there are associative connections between images within sensory or across sensory modalities. Thus, author CB's image of an elephant is associated with an image of big logs, since she has often seen elephants carrying big logs with their trunks. She also associates the visual image of elephants with her memory of the smell of elephants.

Paivio's dual-coding theory is supported by an enormous amount of evidence. For example, Paivio (1986) generated a list of 60 phenomena that can be explained by dual-coding theory. These include, among others, that concrete materials are more memorable than abstract materials, there are more synonym intrusions for concrete than abstract materials (consistent with greater spreading activation for the concrete materials), the amount of time taken to "generate" an image in response to an instruction to do so increases with the abstractness of the material, pictures are learned better than words, and words can be read faster than pictures can be named (suggesting the verbal code is accessed directly for words and only through the second, image code in reaction to pictures). A variety of evidence exists that activation of visual imagery interferes with visual perception and vice versa (Craver-Lemley & Reeves, 1992). There also is neuropsychological evidence supporting dual coding theory. For instance, left hemisphere lesions disrupt verbal processing more than nonverbal processing, whereas right hemisphere lesions have the opposite effect. See Farah (1988) and Tippett (1992) for compelling summaries of neurophysiological evidence supporting the conclusion that visual imagery and visual perception involve similar representations and are the products of the same regions of the brain.

The greatest challenge to Paivio's position came from his then colleague at Western Ontario, Pylyshen (1973), who argued that imagery effects could be explained in propositional terms (Anderson & Bower, 1973)—that, in fact, abstract propositional representations underpin images. It is true that any image can be defined by a propositional list—for instance, UNDER (DOG, TABLE); (RED, TABLE); (BROWN, DOG) is a list of propositions specifying an image of a brown dog under a red table. It takes little imagination, however, to recognize that even a moderately complex image can require many propositions to specify it. The real question, however, is whether the logical possibility of propositional encoding of images renders the idea of images as scientifically useless. That is, could it be that anything a propositional theory would predict and explain would be identical with what an imagery (dual code) theory would predict and explain, a possibility raised by some (e.g., Anderson, 1978)?

Kosslyn (1975) recognized that the two theories sometimes make unique predictions, however. Although the argument for the propositional position was complex, an important part of it was that imagery increased memory by activating the propositions defining the image. If that is so, and the image itself is simply an uninteresting byproduct of the propositional code, the size of the image "in the mind's eye" should not matter, or so reasoned Kosslyn (1975), for the relationships specified by propositions would be identical in big and little images.

Dual coding theory predicts that the relative size in the mind's eye does matter sometimes.

Thus, Kosslyn asked adults to imagine an animal, such as a rabbit, either next to a fly or next to an elephant. The subjects were then given the names of rabbit parts (e.g., eye, nose, ear) and were asked whether the part could be found on their image of the animal. The participants in fact "zoomed in" faster on features and made quicker decisions when the rabbit was next to a fly than when it was next to an elephant—that is, when the image of the rabbit was large compared with the image of the rabbit (Figure 3.4).

Kosslyn included a variety of controls to dismiss objections that might be raised by proponents of propositional theories. For instance, when subjects in Kosslyn (1976) were asked to verify in an animal image the existence of animal parts highly associated with the animal but perceptually small (e.g., whether an imagined cat had *claws*), their reaction times were slower than when they verified parts perceptually larger but less highly associated with the particular animal (e.g., whether an imagined cat had a *head*). When subjects did the same tasks without being instructed to consult an image (i.e., decide whether cats have *claws* and whether cats have *heads*), they reacted more quickly for parts highly associated with the animal compared with parts less highly associated with the animal. Findings such as this (see Finke [1989] for a stimulating summary of such evidence),

Figure 3.4 Can you spot the rabbit's claws faster in the small or large picture? Now, imagine a small rabbit. Zoom in on its claw. Imagine a big rabbit. Zoom in on its claw. What does the speed of "zooming in" on little and big images reveal about the nature of imagery? Do images and perceptions have similarities?

when combined with the vast amount of research evidence produced by Paivio and his co-workers at Western Ontario (see Paivio, 1971, 1986), make credible the claim that mental images can and often do function in human cognition—that part of our knowledge is composed of nonverbal images.

A number of educational interventions based on imagery have been proposed, studied, and disseminated, with some of these taken up in later chapters (e.g., Chapter 14). All of these interventions make the sensible assumption that people can create mental images that permit unique encodings relative to verbal encodings and that stimulate associations in a nonverbal representational system. For millennia, those interested in promoting learning have recognized the power of images to do so (Yates, 1966). The contemporary student of educational psychology must be cognizant of the potency of imagery in promoting thinking, understanding, and acquisition of new information.

PRODUCTIONS

In several important cognitive psychological theories, cognitive rules are represented as productions, which were introduced in Chapter 2 as procedural knowledge stored in "if-then" form—*if* these conditions hold, *then* execute this action. The argument was presented there that cognitive strategies resemble productions in many ways. How productions operate in thinking more generally can be illustrated by two models of thinking.

ACT*

ACT* was introduced in Chapter 2. ACT* is a knowledge system that includes procedural knowledge encoded into productions as well as declarative knowledge, the factual knowledge in the system. Although ACT* is an artificial intelligence system (i.e., a computer program), ACT* attempts to mirror human cognition and has been an influential model with educational psychologists. Consideration of the dynamics of ACT* can provide insights into how productions might function in human cognition. In particular, it is possible to see how procedural and declarative knowledge can interact during thinking. There are three types of declarative memory codes (Anderson, 1983, Chapter 2) in ACT*: (1) *Temporal strings* code the order of a set of items—which of a set of items occurs first, which second, third, and

so on. A whole event that is comprised of a sequence of steps can be captured by such a representation. (This is the ACT* version of a script, as discussed in the earlier section on schema theories.) (2) *Spatial images* code the spatial configuration of elements in an array (i.e., which items are above others, below others, to the left of others, and to the right of others). (This is the ACT* version of images.) (3) *Propositional representations* operate as they do in the Kintsch model discussed earlier—they encode meaningful relationships between elements.

In addition, declarative memory contains information about the category membership and attributes of the elements involved in each of these three types of representations. Consider two examples: (1) A square spatial array with a red triangle in the upper right corner, a blue circle in the upper left, a green rectangle in the lower right, and a black diamond in the lower right is encoded as a spatial image with four elements in the four corners of a square. The upper right element is categorized as a triangle, with its redness encoded as an attribute. The upper left element is categorized as a circle, with blueness being one of its features. (2) The sentence, "The tall lawyer believed the man came from Mars," is encoded BELIEVE (AGENT, OBJECT) with the object encoded as FROM (SUBJECT, MARS). The subject encodes that the category of the agent is lawyer, who has the attribute of being tall. The SUBJECT of the OBJECT is categorized as a man. The relation BELIEVE has the attribute of past tense.

Complex events can be represented in this system by combining the different types of declarative codes. Examples offered by Anderson (1983) included a baseball game encoded as a string of propositions, each proposition encoding some meaningful event in the game, with the events occurring earlier in the game coded earlier in the string (i.e., *strings* and *propositions* were coordinated). Anderson (1983) also provided an example of how ACT* would handle a restaurant script, such as the one studied by Schank and Abelson (1977). The central string (enter, order, eat, exit) has other strings branching from it. Thus, for an informal restaurant, the *enter* element on the main string branches to a string specifying how to enter an informal restaurant (walk in, look for table, decide, go to table, sit down). This hierarchy of strings has both propositional and imagery elements embedded in it. Thus, the *walk in* element in the informal restaurant string is the proposition WALKS

INTO (SUBJECT, RESTAURANT) with the subject categorized as a customer with two attributes—he or she is hungry and has money. The *go to table* proposition in the informal restaurant string includes an image of a table.

As just outlined, the declarative memory of the ACT* system includes many of the types of representations included in models of human representation that have been discussed in this chapter, from categories to images to propositional relations to schemas. This declarative knowledge is used in conjunction with procedural knowledge. For instance, during pattern recognition, some declarative knowledge will be activated, as when the pattern recognition productions identify an example of a category member. Thus, when encountering a four-legged animal with a longish elliptical head, sharp claws, and a meow, the pattern recognition productions identify a cat. This information is used to determine which action procedures to activate. If your goal is to make the animal happy, and if the animal is a cat (two conditionals), you give it some milk (an action).

A point of emphasis in Anderson (1983) is that procedural and declarative knowledge are stored in different parts of long-term memory. That is, procedural and declarative knowledge work together only when coactivated in short-term memory structures—there is no communication between them while they remain in long-term storage. When the set of conditionals for a production that is stored in long-term memory are met, the production is activated into short-term memory. It fires, sometimes activating declarative knowledge in the process, declarative knowledge required to carry out the proposition.

ACT* provides a possible model for the knowledge that underlies some educationally important cognitive competencies—most emphatically, the type of metacognitively guided strategy use coordinated with other knowledge that is discussed so prominently throughout this book. Young educational psychologists should be aware that some scientists interested in artificial intelligence are studying problems directly related to educational issues. For instance, ACT* can model how students approach geometry proofs and learn language (Anderson, 1983). Just and Carpenter (1987) have designed an artificial intelligence model of reading broadly conceived (CAPS)—attempting to simulate a variety of human reading performances from eye fixations to understanding of extended texts. The procedural

knowledge in their model includes productions for word encoding, accessing the meanings of words, syntactic analysis, semantic analysis, and text-schema processing. The declarative knowledge base includes representations of words, the concepts referred to by words, world knowledge, and text schemata (e.g., story grammar). It is impressive just how many different types of knowledge about reading and other complex academic competencies can be included in an artificial intelligence model. We do not go into more detail about ACT*, CAPS, or other artificial intelligence systems, however, because this book is about human abilities and performances rather than machine competencies.

One important characteristic of systems such as ACT* and CAPS is that many different types of representations are coordinated with one another—just as the many types of representations covered in this chapter are coordinated in human minds. The production system covered in the next subsection also displays this important property.

Mental Models

A number of researchers have been interested in **mental models** (Gentner & Stevens, 1983; Holland, Holyoak, Nisbett, and Thagard, 1986; Johnson-Laird, 1983). Their belief is that as people process the world, they construct a mental model (i.e., an internal representation) of what they are encountering. Holland et al. (1986) most explicitly spell out the role of productions in this process. Their theory is that as contact is made with the world, a number of productions are fired that contribute to a mental model of the situation.

Some of the productions that are activated by contact with the world permit categorization of elements in the world. Here are some examples (Holland et al., 1986, p. 42):

If an object is a dog, then it is an animal. [specifies superordinate categorization when dog is encountered]

If an object is a dog, then it can bark. [specifies feature defining category when dog is encountered]

In addition, there are productions that specify associations to elements encountered in the world. Consider the following productions that specify spreading activation from "dog":

If an object is a dog, then activate the "cat" concept.

If an object is a dog, then activate the "bone" concept.

In sum, the two types of productions considered thus far activate information in semantic nets—much as specified in the Collins and Loftus (1975) model.

Other productions that can be activated specify how change will take place—if particular conditions are met. Some of these are the basis for construction of expectations. Examples include the following:

If a person annoys a dog, then the dog will growl.
If a person whistles to the dog, then the dog will come to the person.

Others result in action on the environment, when particular conditions are met:

If a dog chases you, then run away.
If a dog approaches you with its tail wagging, then pet it.

Mental models also include productions that create new productions and modify old productions. What these creation and modification productions do is evaluate whether the productions that are being fired are working as anticipated. When they are not, new ones are created or the old ones are revised. In addition—and this is a critical function—these creation and modification productions generate associations between and clustering among productions to create larger knowledge structures, ones involving the articulation of various productions, each of which permits some progress toward a common goal.

There are important differences between mental models and the simpler ACT* production system. For one, more than one production can operate at a time in the creation of mental models, whereas productions fire in sequence, one at a time in ACT*. That is, there is **parallel processing** in mental models as productions in a mental model interact, sometimes cooperating. Successful productions in a mental model are strengthened and more likely to be used in the future. If progress is made when two productions are simultaneously active, the association between the productions is strengthened, and they are more likely to be used conjunctively in the future. Sometimes productions in a mental model compete, *bidding* to be the ones activated. The "winners" in this competition better match the current situation than the "losers," are stronger because they have

been more successful in the past in this situation than the losers, generate a better description of the situation than the losers, and are more compatible with other information activated in the system than the losers. Simultaneous activation of productions (as well as newly encountered information) is an important mechanism in the construction of higher-order knowledge. For example, simultaneous activation of the following productions eventually results in the construction of the category *zoo animal:*

If an object is an elephant, then it is a zoo animal.
If an object is a giraffe, then it is a zoo animal.
If an object is a monkey, then it is a zoo animal.
If an object is a zebra , then it is a zoo animal.

The mental modeling position is that representations of the world can be constructed using productions. Some of these productions have few and simple conditions and others have many and complex conditions for them to fire. Some specify simple actions if conditions are met; others specify complex reactions. All of the different types of productions in the system work together to generate inferences and expectations about the world and solutions to problems. In doing so, higher-order knowledge is constructed. Thus, coactivation of the following propositions on several occasions might lead to an integrated sequence that becomes a unified piece of knowledge:

If a person is saying an important telephone number, listen carefully.
If a person is saying an important telephone number, repeat it.
If a person is saying an important telephone number, write it down.

Success following simultaneous activation of this set of propositions should increase the likelihood of the listening-repeating-writing important number down sequence in the future.

If all of this seems vague at this point, keep reading in this subsection. What a mental model is—how it starts as prior knowledge that is transformed through encounters with new information and simultaneous activation with other prior knowledge and eventually represents something never encountered before—should become clearer with additional discussion and examples.

Example of Induction Holland et al. (1986, pp. 97–101) were particularly concerned with inductive processes during the creation of mental models. This was because they believe that prior knowledge could not possibly already hold all of the knowledge required to represent new situations—that is, as new circumstances are encountered in the world, new mental models must be constructed rapidly by processing of the new information in light of prior knowledge.

One of Holland et al.'s (1986) examples of induction during mental modeling involved a little girl who wanted to pet a cat: Jennifer sees a cat. Productions fire that activate the concept *cat* and its associated characteristics (e.g., animal; small, round head; longer than it is tall; four legs; sharp claws). Jennifer has a goal of getting closer to the cat to pet it. So far, nothing in her representation of cat includes information about how to approach a cat. Fortunately, as she searches for a solution to her problem, there is additional spreading activation. Productions fire activating associations to *cat,* such as *dog.* This provides useful information because *dog* has associated with it information about how to approach a dog: If person whistles, *dog* comes. Because both *cats* and *dogs* are *pets,* productions for creating new knowledge fire—in this case, productions for making analogies. The result is a new production: "If your goal is to summon X, and X is a certain kind of pet, then whistle." The result for Jennifer is a hypothesis, "The cat might come if I whistle." She does so, expecting the cat to come. The cat does not. This failure triggers the creation of new productions that compete with the active production. These might include, "If X is a pet and a cat, it will not come when you whistle," "If X is a cat, it won't come when you whistle," and "If X is a cat, then it ignores whistling children." The creation of these competing productions reduces the likelihood that Jennifer will whistle again upon encountering a cat. Perchance she does, the competing productions will strengthen when the cat does not come. If the competing productions are more powerful than the production governing "whistling," then Jennifer will cease attempting to summon the cat with a whistle. The new productions created during this episode are encoded into long-term memory and can affect future performance.

Nature of Factual Knowledge Mental models clearly make use of the conceptual and associative information in the semantic networks of long-term memory. They also include mechanisms for generat-

ing images, with images being one type of mental model (Johnson-Laird, 1983, especially Chapter 7; 1989). The particular strength of an image is that it contains information more directly corresponding to the structure of situations that it represents. Thus, Mani and Johnson-Laird (1982) presented subjects with sets of descriptions such as the following (Johnson-Laird, 1989, p. 472):

The spoon is to the left of the knife.
The plate is to the right of the knife.
The fork is in front of the spoon.
The cup is in front of the knife.

Their data generated in the study strongly supported the conclusion that such a set of relations was stored in a spatial array like the following:

spoon   knife   plate
fork   cup

That is, the verbal input stimulated the construction of a mental model in the form of an image. As Johnson-Laird (e.g., 1983, Chapter 7) might express it: The description of the place setting is initially represented in propositions capturing the meaning of the individual descriptive statements, with these linguistic expressions then translated into mental models via production rules, with the end product a mental image.

A development in mental model theory is the possibility that mental models are not entirely mental but rather often involve interactions between a partially complete internal representation and an environment that fills in the gaps in the mental model. For example, we use a word processing program (MacWrite), which requires users to access and select from menus specifying various word processing functions. If we were asked to recall the order of the menu cards or the actual items on the cards, we would have a tough time doing so. Our mental model contains information about the menu cards in general, their functions in general, and their location but does not include specifics. When we select functions with the program, some of the thinking goes on solely in our heads, and some depends on the presence of the screen—that is, thinking is distributed between the head and the computer screen (O'Malley & Draper, 1992). We will see in Chapter 8 that a number of scientists are beginning to think of thinking as more than an "in-the-head" thing and more of a "head-and-environment" thing, with cognition sometimes distributed across mind and the physical environment (as in the case of word processing) and sometimes distributed across minds (e.g., as with group problem solving) and sometimes distributed across minds and the physical environment (e.g., when two people work at a MacWrite screen and try to figure out how to accomplish a novel word processing task).

Holland et al. (1986, p. 12) and Johnson-Laird (1983) insist that mental models are not schemata. A schema is a chunk of information stored in long-term memory, specifying how a number of concepts relate to one another. In contrast, mental models are relationships that are constructed as input is encountered and processed. Mental models can involve schemata and use them in combination with new input and other knowledge. Thus, a restaurant schema might be activated from long-term memory when a person enters a restaurant. If a goat walks into the restaurant, however, there is nothing in most people's restaurant schema to deal with the goat. Another piece of knowledge—a production in long-term memory, such as "If a threatening or obnoxious creature intrudes, then eject it or escape from it"—can be combined with the restaurant script using the productions that permit construction of new knowledge (i.e., productions that generate inferences from old knowledge) to create a solution to this never-before-encountered problem. Mental models are about creating new knowledge and understandings from old knowledge and understandings.

In short, in constructing mental models, all of the forms of knowledge discussed in this chapter can come into play, a feature of many models of thinking that are being constructed around productions. Of course, what this really says is that production system–type mental models capture the procedural and declarative knowledge that interacts continuously as part of thinking and learning, a theme that will be reiterated in this book. One final point is that the exact form of a mental model will depend somewhat on the media in which information is presented to students. For example, mental models can be developed based on pictures alone or through consideration of both picture and verbal content. In addition, if the picture or the text content relates to prior knowledge possessed by the learner, the mental model will be different than if the picture or text is from an unfamiliar domain. Mental models are the result of complex interactions between new information, the way the new information is presented, and prior knowledge, with the mental model shifting as new information is encountered and the information already experienced is related to prior knowledge in various ways (Kozma, 1991).

Summary

The most comprehensive models of thinking developed to date include productions as part of their model of knowledge. Exactly how the productions function and the extent of their role in cognition varies within models. Models such as the one proposed by Holland et al. (1986) and others (e.g., SOAR; Newell, 1990) posit that most of cognition is productions. In part, this probably reflects that production systems run well on computers. Alternatively, this may reflect how critical it is to know how to do things—that much of thinking is knowing how (i.e., procedural knowledge) and using such knowledge appropriately (i.e., possessing conditional knowledge—metacognitive knowledge in humans—knowledge that relates to procedural knowledge).

SITUATED KNOWLEDGE

Brown, Collins, and Duguid (1989) believe that knowledge is not separable from the actions that give rise to it nor from the culture in which those actions occur, consistent with many ideas in Soviet psychological analyses of activity and thinking (e.g., Wertsch, 1985). (Note that this position is similar to the position introduced at the end of the mental models discussion—that thinking is not just an "in-the-head" thing.) What is critical to emphasize here is that *actions* undertaken in a *cultural milieu* largely determine the meaning of a concept rather than some abstract features.

Consider the "knowledge" of intelligence and its measurement possessed by a young psychologist who has never had an internship. It was developed in the culture of school through the actions required to pass examinations—and includes a lot of knowledge in the abstract, such as the types of items on IQ tests, and the professional party lines on appropriate environmental settings for giving such tests, and the professional standards for reporting and interpreting test data. We have yet to meet a graduate of such a class, however, who was ready to give an intelligence test on the first day of an internship or even understood how such tests are really used by mental health professionals. During many interactions with senior psychologists during the internship, however, the intern acquires many of the understandings held by senior psychologists about intelligence and testing for it.

Much of knowledge is implicit according to this framework, and it is obtained by acting in authentic situations—such as the intern giving an intelligence test to a real client in a real clinical setting. Much of the knowledge is built up through real problem solving and real dilemmas (e.g., how noncommunicative must a child be to decide to administer a nonverbal intelligence assessment). It is constructed rather than given—that is, the senior practitioner does not offer precise rules to the intern, but rather "brainstorms" with the intern about the options. There is reflection on the decision about what test to use, both during administration and after the session. The understanding of when to use nonverbal assessments is constructed through reflection on action.

The most intriguing part of Brown et al.'s (1989) proposal is that knowledge is intertwined with the activities and environments in which it develops, that knowledge is better thought of not as residing in the mind but spread across the mind and the environment. One proof of this is that there are some tasks that people can do only given environmental supports. For instance, a beekeeper's understanding of bees definitely involves an interaction between knowledge he can retrieve from his mind and information in the environment. This knowledge was built up largely by working with bees, with whatever "book learning" that occurred definitely expanded through interactions with beekeepers and bees. Any beekeeper's manual explains that swarming bees ordinarily will not sting while the swarm is being moved from a tree to a box hive (using a saw to cut off a branch). Real knowledge of the subtleties pertaining to this situation is gained only by removing a few swarms. Much of the knowledge gained is implicit (i.e., difficult to state). For instance, beekeepers often cannot convey in words how they know when some bees are about to attack out of a swarm, but they recognize the situation in an instant when holding in their hands a branch containing a swarm—knowledge about aggression by a swarm of bees is *distributed across mind and situation.* Because of cognitive psychologists' growing awareness about the situated nature of much of cognition, there is an effort in the 1990s to make education more authentic—for math problem solving and science teaching to involve more hands-on experiences and for reading—

ers to learn how to decode by processing authentic texts, with prominent examples of situation approaches to real-school learning featured in Chapters 12 through 15 of this book.

CONCLUDING COMMENTS

There is evidence that a variety of different types of representations function in thinking. Much of the research on mental representations has been concerned with identifying some knowledge structure that is more basic than others (e.g., research attempting to demonstrate that propositions underlie mental images). In the 1990s, research on connectionist models continues this tradition. Most researchers would concede that it is likely that there is some orderly neurological representational systems underlying higher-order representations such as images, schemas, and propositions. Whether connectionist research will be successful in explaining how representation occurs at the neurological-level and then be successful at explaining how neurological level representations translate into higher-order representations is an open question, however. We are skeptical that a neurologically based representational theory will emerge in the near future that has the power to explain the many outcomes that are accounted for by models of higher-order representations, such as dual-coding and schema theories. What should be noted is that attempts to explain the representations covered in this chapter in terms of more basic mechanisms have not been compelling. A striking example is the failure to generate evidence that imagery effects actually reflect the operation of propositional representations, despite substantial amounts of theoretical energy and research effort devoted to this problem.

At a phenomenological level, the analysis presented in this chapter is sensible. When we think about our own cognition, it is easy to generate examples of occasions when we depend on images and schemata. We also have a sense of thinking in terms of connected ideas. For example, we know that somewhere in our minds is stored the information that "dogs chase cats," and this is connected to the idea that "dogs chase postmen." There really is something to the idea of propositional representations that are connected in networks based on overlapping meanings. The idea of a semantic network is appealing for the same reason. We can easily think in categorical terms and know where many categories fit relative to other categories. We also have a vast network of associations between the concepts we know. Most people would concur that something like images, schemata, and abstract relationships between concepts (such as those represented by propositions) operate in their thinking, with the organization of these representations an important determinant of thinking.

The distinction between procedural and declarative knowledge also is a sensible one. Although we can state the steps involved in starting a car (i.e., generate a declarative representation of it), starting the car does not seem like a sequence of steps anymore but rather like one action—a compilation of steps that could be described declaratively because when first learned, it was represented declaratively. It is now represented in another form as well, one that cannot be talked about, a procedural representation that is evident only in its performance (i.e., in this case, in starting the car in one seamless motion).

By adulthood, adults have complex networks of procedural and declarative knowledge built up through experience. Again and again experience has been emphasized here. Procedures develop from declarative representations through repeated practice. Connections between procedures are strengthened when a sequence of procedures is executed with success. This process, which was taken up with respect to mental models here, is probably part of compilation, which is the integration of several procedures into a single procedure. Patterns of connections in neural networks are strengthened through repeated activation of the patterns, especially if activation of a pattern meets with some success in performing a task. Experience makes knowledge.

One question we are frequently asked by students is how the brain holds all that information. The brain not only holds information, but also is continuously constructing new information, as described briefly here with respect to mental models and inferences constructed when schemata are activated. With 100 billion neurons in the cortex, each of which has hundreds to thousands of synapses associated with them, with each synapse potentially making thousands of connections (e.g., Gardner, 1975), the capacity of the brain is great. There may be a quadrillion connections among neurons (Lerner, 1986). That capacity permits storage of a great deal of information and development of complex connections between different parts of the knowledge base. For example, it permits articulation between many pieces of procedural and declarative knowledge as part of carrying out a complex plan.

Even so, all of knowledge is not in the brain. Much of our knowing is situated, the result of mind and environment interaction at the moment. Moreover, new knowledge is constructed not simply in the mind but as the mind operates in the environment and as minds work together on problems. Increasingly, cognitive psychologists are realizing that thinking is not just an "in-the-head" thing and that the development of knowledge depends heavily on social interactions, themes that will be reiterated in later chapters (especially Chapter 8 and Chapters 12 through 15).

The Role of Knowledge in Cognition

High knowledge in a domain promotes performance in that domain. Expertise is considered in this chapter, with detailed consideration of the type of thinking enabled by high prior knowledge. Expert knowledge requires many years to develop and much experience. Because in the past, knowledge and strategies have been proposed as alternative explanations for increases in cognitive competence with development, the knowledge versus strategies debate is taken up here. What is concluded is that strategies and knowledge both operate in cognition and interact in complex ways. Research on expertise and knowledge has produced insights that are extremely important for educators to consider as they design curriculum and schooling as an institution. Some of the most important contemporary educational issues that relate to knowledge are taken up at the end of the chapter.

This chapter asks the questions: What difference does a large knowledge base make? What results from having extensive knowledge that is well organized? What can such a person do that cannot be done by a person lacking that knowledge base? The short answer to all of these questions is: Quite a bit.

KNOWLEDGE AS A DETERMINANT OF PERFORMANCE

Several of the studies in the next subsection are classics in educational psychology, ones cited frequently as powerful evidence in support of the hypothesis that prior knowledge and the extent of prior knowledge are powerful determinants of performance.

Demonstrations of the Potency of Knowledge as a Determinant of Performance

Suppose you know that 10-year-olds and adults are about to perform a memory task. The task involves memory for chess boards (i.e., chess pieces in particular, meaningful positions). Who would you bet on to perform better on this memory task? Make a prediction before reading on.

Now, consider this. The 10-year-olds are chess masters, and the adults are chess novices. Would you want to change your prediction? If you predicted that the 10-year-old chess experts would outperform the adult novices on this task, you made the right prediction (Chi, 1978).

Now, what if these two groups of subjects were given another memory task, perhaps a digit span task—a test in which a list of digits is presented one

at a time with subsequent recall of the list required. Who would do better? In this case, the adults outperform the children.

What is going on? The children are experts in a particular domain of knowledge—chess. When they are presented arrays of chess pieces, their knowledge of the game permits them to categorize the arrangement of pieces (e.g., this is a checkmate) so that they end up having only to remember a few chunks of information for each board. The adult novices see only chess pieces, with their relative positions meaningless, so they are learning the board on a piece-by-piece basis with little if any chunking. **Domain-specific knowledge** often permits those who possess it to process to-be-learned domain content differently than domain novices would process it. For a detailed analysis of what child chess experts know and how they think when operating in a chess-board environment, see Horgan and Morgan (1990).

Consider a second example. Suppose that university students are asked to learn some content pertaining to baseball and some content pertaining to music—in particular, lists of sentences such that given part of the sentence later on a test, they must recall the rest of the sentence. Suppose further that some of the students know a good deal about baseball and music already, some know only about baseball, some know only about music, and some have little familiarity with either baseball or music. Who remembers the most?

In Kuhara-Kojima and Hatano (1991), the students with prior knowledge in both areas outperformed students with prior knowledge in only one area. The students with prior knowledge in one of the two domains (either baseball or music) learned the content from their high-knowledge domain better than the content from their low-knowledge domain. Students lacking prior knowledge in either of the domains fared poorly in both domains.

Prior knowledge clearly mattered in this task. Consider what might have happened when a subject was presented the fact, "Kadota of the Hawks hit home runs in two consecutive at bats." For someone knowledgeable about Japanese professional baseball, this is a sensible statement—Kadota is a slugger who plays for the Hawks. Those who know a lot about Japanese baseball might know particular episodes that could be related to this fact. Later, when given the matching test, requiring matching of baseball players with their accomplishments, the baseball experts would have a rich network of associations linking Kadota and the hitting of multiple home runs, a network of associations stimulated as they studied the fact as originally presented. This network of associations would assist in making matches. (The series of studies conducted by Kuhara-Kojima and Hatano, 1991, included controls in which this matching test was administered without presentation of the facts for learning, with low performance in this case. High performance was possible only if there was an opportunity for learning.) Knowing about baseball was worthless in trying to learn the music facts. The knowledge of baseball experts who were music novices just could not be related to the music information. Baseball experts who were music novices performed poorly on the music task, much more poorly than music experts.

More than learning of single sentences is improved by prior knowledge. Classic work on learning of text as a function of prior knowledge was conducted by Voss and colleagues (Chiesi, Spilich, & Voss, 1979; Spilich, Vesonder, Chiesi, & Voss, 1979; Voss, Vesonder, & Spilich, 1980). The adults participating in this research varied from knowing a great deal about the game to knowing very little. During the study, the participants read texts about baseball games, although the texts also contained content not related to baseball. Those with high knowledge of baseball remembered more of the text content pertaining to the baseball game and had better organized memory of the game described in the text than did baseball novices (e.g., the experts remembered critical information rather than unimportant details). Recall of the nonbaseball content was equivalent for the baseball experts and novices, however. That is, the baseball experts did not have better memories across the board—only better memory for baseball content. The errors in recall were also telling. That the experts had substantial schematic knowledge of baseball, and the novices did not, was apparent in the patterns of errors. When baseball experts misrecalled, they misrecalled details. When novices misrecalled, they often reported illegal plays and impossible situations.

It has been known for some time that children also tend to learn more from text pertaining to their knowledge-rich domains (e.g., Pearson, Hansen, & Gordon, 1979). For example, Means and Voss (1985) analyzed the learning of *Star Wars* text by students in grades 2, 3, 5, 7, 9, and college. It was possible to identify both *Star Wars* experts and novices at each of these grade levels. Once again, learning was better for experts than novices at every grade level. An in-

teresting twist in this study was that expert performance increased with age, possibly owing to qualitative differences in the sophistication of *Star Wars* knowledge in older compared with younger students. Younger children saw *Star Wars* as being about good guys and bad guys, whereas older experts constructed layers of meaning, including themes of morality and the appropriateness of militarism.

Knowledge Versus Intelligence

The experts and novices were not randomly assigned to their statuses in the studies just summarized. A troubling possibility is that somehow only exceptionally intelligent people become experts at anything. Such speculation, especially when combined with the theoretical possibility that high intelligence might be reflected by high knowledge across a number of domains (e.g., Garcia, 1981; Sternberg & Wagner, 1985), motivated the investigation of the relative potency of domain-specific knowledge and general intellectual aptitude as predictors of various performances.

Schneider, Körkel, Weinert, and their colleagues (e.g., Schneider, Körkel, & Weinert, 1990) have provided some of the most impressive research to date on the power of domain-specific knowledge, especially relative to another intellectual factor often considered to be a potent determinant of performance—general intelligence (see Chapter 16).

Their initial studies (Körkel, 1987; Weinert, Knopf, Körkel, Schneider, Voegel, & Wetzel, 1984; Weinert, Schneider, & Knopf, 1988) involved 8-, 10-, and 12-year-old children who read passages about soccer, which is a popular sport in Germany, where the work was conducted. Even so, just as in the United States, sports are not for everyone, so it is easy to locate children who know a great deal about soccer and those who know little. An important characteristic of the text that the children in this study were asked to read was that it contained some contradictions. Moreover, there were several points at which inferences needed to be made to make sense of the content. Across the studies, there were measures of memory, construction of appropriate inferences, and detection of contradictions.

The outcomes, collapsing across studies, were generally as follows: Performances improved with age. More critically, soccer experts outperformed soccer novices. In addition, these data contained interactions reminiscent of Chi's (1978) outcomes. For example, in Körkel's (1987) study, the grade-3 experts recalled more than the grade-5 and grade-7 novices.

Schneider, Körkel, and Weinert (1989) and Schneider and Körkel (1989) measured both the soccer expertise and the general intelligence of their participants, in what were studies that otherwise resembled the earlier work. The data were absolutely striking. Again, performances (i.e., generation of appropriate inferences, detection of contradictions) improved with age from age 8 to 12. At every age level and on every measure, soccer expertise was associated with high performance compared with the performance of soccer novices (Figure 4.1). Most critically, general intellectual aptitude was not a strong determinant of performance (i.e., overall there was a slight tendency for high general aptitude subjects to do better than low aptitude subjects, although this was a small effect—especially compared with the huge effect of soccer expertise). For example, 8-year-olds high in soccer expertise detected about 10 times more contradictions than 8-year-olds low in knowledge of soccer. In contrast, there was minimal difference between the levels of contradiction detection for high-ability and low-ability domain experts. The corresponding difference for novices was also minimal.

The German results with children processing prose are complemented in the adult literature by Walker (1987), who demonstrated that low-general-aptitude baseball experts can learn more from a baseball passage than high-aptitude baseball novices. Recht and Leslie (1988) also reported that junior high students high in prior knowledge about baseball learned more from reading a passage about baseball than students low in prior knowledge of baseball. In their study, weaker readers with high prior knowledge learned more than otherwise stronger readers who were low in prior knowledge. Hall and Edmondson (1992) found that immediate comprehension and memory of a passage about basketball was affected by prior knowledge about basketball on both a posttest immediately following reading of the passage and a posttest delayed by several weeks. Comprehension was also predicted by general ability in the Hall and Edmondson (1992) study, however, suggesting that additional investigations are required before it will be possible to make strong claims about the generality of the prior knowledge effects that Schneider and associates obtained with German children. Even when general ability effects were greatest in Hall and Edmondson (1992)—which was at delayed testing, there was still a striking effect of prior knowledge on performance. We note as well that Schneider and colleagues never

Figure 4.1 Could you outperform these youngsters on a test of soccer knowledge? How about on a test of general world knowledge?

dismissed general aptitude as an important determinant of performance much of the time. For example, Schneider and Bjorklund (1992) reported that in list-learning situations, both general intelligence and prior knowledge have effects on recall: Soccer expertise predicted recall of lists composed of soccer terms but not recall of nonsoccer lists; intelligence predicted recall of both soccer and nonsoccer lists.

A memorable demonstration of the potency of domain-relevant knowledge in predicting performance compared to IQ was provided by Ceci and Liker (1986). They went to a racetrack and found patrons who knew a lot about horse racing and who had participated in betting on the sport for at least 8 years. Within this sample, however, were those who were extremely knowledgeable about how to handicap a horse race and those who were less knowledgeable. Thus, the 14 expert handicappers in Ceci and Liker's (1986) study were able, based on a large array of statistics pertaining to the horses and jockeys in races, to pick the horse most likely to be named "top horse" at race time for 9 out of 10 races. They were able to pick the top three horses for at least 5 of 10 races. In contrast, the 16 nonexperts picked the top horses much less often.

Ceci and Liker (1986) went to a good deal of trouble to make certain that the expert and nonexpert handicappers were otherwise comparable: The two groups had similar amounts of schooling (10 years on average), were similar in occupational prestige (full range, but with the mean in the craftsman range), and had comparable number of years of track experience (15 for the experts and 17 for the nonexperts). They also had comparable levels of general intelligence, with the mean IQ equal to approximately 100 for both samples (i.e., equal to the average intelligence for the general population) and the range from approximately 80 to 130 for both samples.

The task given to these experts and nonexperts was to handicap 50 two-horse races. Fifty horses that were unnamed but were described by extensive statistics (14 different statistics typically available to handicappers before a race) were pitted against a standard horse in each race. The standard horse was an average horse on a number of measures pertinent to handicapping, such as speed, lifetime earnings, and record of the jockey. The subjects were asked to compute the odds for each of the 50 races involving this standard and the 50 unnamed horses.

The handicapping of the experts reflected extremely complex reasoning about potential interactions between the variables described by the handicapping statistics, with the reasoning of experts approaching the complexity of the reasoning of a professional handicapper who was also included in the study. That IQ did not determine expertise was evident in that the complexity of reasoning for low IQ experts was greater than the complexity of reasoning for high IQ nonexperts. That experts were successful at picking winning horses validates the effectiveness of their thinking. It is also situated cognition (see Chapter 3). Ceci and Liker's (1986) experts did not manifest highly intelligent thinking across a variety of situations but only in selected domains. With a racing form in hand and talking about handicapping, their expert subjects were brilliant. When they were stripped of the racing form and asked to do another task, they performed slightly below the average level of the general population.

In short, the evidence is accumulating that knowledge relevant to the domain of a task is a much more important determinant of performance on many tasks than general intellect. When experts in a domain perform a task in their domain of competence, they invariably surpass novices, even those with high general intelligence. Cognitive psychologists have devoted considerable resources to locating (and sometimes developing) domain experts who are capable of fantastic cognitive feats. What has emerged from this work is a sophisticated understanding of how the knowledge of domain experts differs from that of domain novices. What will be apparent in the next section is that having extensive networks of concepts, schemata, and associations permits extremely sophisticated thinking—the type of good thinking that was introduced in Chapter 1 during the discussion of the *Hardy Boys*.

NATURE OF EXPERT THINKING

Expert performances in a number of domains have been studied, including research on chess, typewriting, memorizing restaurant orders, mental calculation, computer programming, judicial decision making, solving of poorly structured problems, and medical diagnosis (for examples, see Chi, Glaser, & Farr, 1988). The methods used in these studies have been diverse, although one of the most prevalent methods has been analysis of **verbal protocols** generated by subjects as they do tasks. That is, subjects are asked to tell what they are doing while they work on a problem or do a task, or, alternatively, they are asked to describe what they did on a task just completed. A number of generalities have emerged from research in this tradition, despite the fact that many domains of expertise have been studied.

Glaser and Chi (1988) provided an overview of the main findings from research on expert performance. Each of their main points captured an important characteristic of expert thinking:

- Experts excel mainly in their own domains.
- Experts perceive large meaningful patterns in their domains.
- Experts are fast. They are faster than novices at performing skills of their domain, and they quickly solve problems with little error.
- Experts have superior short-term memory for material in their domain of expertise.
- Experts see and represent problems in their domain at a deeper (more principled) level than novices; novices tend to represent problems at a superficial level.
- Experts spend proportionately more time analyzing problems qualitatively than do novices.
- Experts have strong self-monitoring skills.

The power of these conclusions about expert thinking is obvious when some examples of extremely expert behaviors in professions are considered (Figure 4.2.).

Expertise in Medical Diagnosis

Lesgold and colleagues (e.g., Lesgold et al., 1988) have been studying how expert and novice radiologists read x-ray films and thus provided an example of one of the most prevalent types of investigations in the study of knowledge: **expert-novice comparisons.** Lesgold et al. (1988) began their research by spending a lot of time watching expert radiologists work. They eventually devised a standardized situation involving reading of x-rays. This standard permitted them to do some analytical work that could not have been done by simply watching physicians at work. For instance, here were the procedures that were used in one of their more telling studies:

Subject examines [x-ray] film for as long as desired, thinking out loud.
Subject dictates formal diagnostic report as he would in his office.
Subject substantiates his diagnosis by drawing relevant anatomy and film features on the x-ray.
Subject draws all anatomy within a specified region of the film (previously known to be critical in diagnostic success). If it does not happen spontaneously, subject is asked to trace anatomical contours predetermined by the experimenters to be crucial.
Subject renders another diagnostic report. (p. 315)

The subjects in the study were highly experienced radiologists and residents in radiology. A number of interesting differences were noted between highly experienced and inexperienced radiologists as they performed this task.

The experts fairly quickly get a general idea of what might be going on in the x-ray. Which of the possible general schemata are activated depends on

Figure 4.2 In an emergency, which pilot is more likely to fly passengers out of danger? Keep in mind the reflexes of the younger pilot. Would the years of experience of the older pilot count for much in comparison to the quicker thinking of the youth?

the characteristics of the x-ray, with the expert selecting a general schema for additional consideration that is consistent with certain general features of the x-ray (schema invocation phase). Once a general schema is invoked, a series of additional tests are conducted to reach a diagnosis and confirm it (fine-tuning). The young radiologists were less likely to come to an appropriate general schema. Once they arrived at a general schema, they were less likely to apply additional tests that could confirm or refute the initial diagnosis. Often the details of these tests were less complete than the details of the tests of the experts. Experts were much more flexible in their thinking and took advantage of whatever clues could be found in the x-rays.

Here is how one expert responded to a film. He took a 2-second look and began searching for a general schema that might fit the situation: "We may be dealing with a chronic process here. . . . I'm trying to work out why the mediastinum and the heart is displaced into the right chest." The expert considered the possibility that the subject had not been facing the plate directly: "There is not enough rotation to account for this. I don't see displacement of fissures [lung lobe boundaries]." After doing some mental tests of this possibility, it was dismissed because there was little in the x-ray to confirm this possibility. Then the expert generated a "collapsed lung" schema and tested it: "There may be a collapse of the right lower lobe, but the diaphragm on the right side is well visualized and that's a feature against it. . . ." He continues to test this possibility, with it increasingly apparent that the collapsed lung schema would have to be fine-tuned quite a bit if it were to explain the pattern in the x-ray. In testing the collapsed lung schema, he noticed clues that there had been a previous surgery: "I come back to the right chest. The ribs are crowded together. . . . The crowding of the ribcage can, on some occasions, be due to previous surgery. In fact . . . the third and fourth ribs are narrow and irregular so he's probably had previous surgery. . . " The expert changes schemata and solves the problem: "He's probably had one of his lobes resected. It wouldn't be the middle lobe. It may be the upper lobe. It may not necessarily be a lobectomy. It could be a small segment of the lung with pleural thickening at the back." He keeps testing, however, especially the possibility that perhaps what is needed is an explanation involving both a collapsed lung and a lobectomy (i.e., he attempts to combine two schema to build a unique mental model of the situation): "I don't see the right hilium . . .

[this] may, in fact, be due to the postsurgery state I'm postulating. . . . Loss of visualization of the right hilium is . . . seen with collapse. . . " (Lesgold et al., 1988, pp. 319–320).

What was apparent was that the expert radiologist was building a mental model of the patient's anatomy while examining the x-ray, with the activation of schemata and attempts to fine-tune and test these schemata as part of the mental model construction process. An interesting difference between experts and novices was that the experts applied their knowledge of normal anatomy to the x-rays but did not try to force-fit pathological features into their normal schemata. Novices were much more likely to explain away pathological features as normal.

In building the mental model, the experts quickly generated a candidate schema that might explain the data in the x-rays. The experts seemed to know where to look on the film to obtain information that would permit a rough guess as to what was depicted in the x-ray. Once activated, the schema guided the processing of the experts, with experts much more likely to search information consistent with their candidate general schema than novices, who were more likely to be distracted by features of the x-ray irrelevant to the hypothesized explanatory schema. This difference showed up in the diagnostic reports, with the reports of experts concerned directly with the disorder depicted in the x-ray and the reports of novices more likely to be cluttered with mention of irrelevant x-ray features.

The fine-tuning of the experts was substantial compared with novices, who often were willing to accept a general schema as the correct diagnosis without attempts to check further. Thus, when an x-ray was presented that superficially suggested a lung tumor, the novices concluded lung tumor. Half the experts in the study, however, detected features in the film suggesting a less obvious—but, as it turns out, correct—diagnosis. One possibility suggested by Lesgold is that the novice radiologists may have had their short-term capacities full, using most of their capacity to discern just the gross features and come to an interpretation. If so, little capacity would be left over for consideration of nuances. Experts require less capacity to note gross features—years of experience make salient the telling features of the x-ray, with little investment of mental effort now required for experts to discern the informative parts of the picture.

Alternatively the novices might not yet know the possible follow-up tests that could be applied or may not be as sensitive to subtle features in the films. This latter possibility was suggested by the results of the tracing exercise in Lesgold et al.'s study, with the tracings of novices often failing to depict subtleties that were apparent in the tracings of the experts. There were multiple indicators that the experts understood better than novices the technical process of x-raying and the types of subtle features that can be in an x-ray, with these understandings combined in testing general schemata that are generated as potential explanations for the pattern in the x-ray.

The expert radiologists possessed substantial knowledge not possessed by residents. Their perceptual analyses skills were especially keen, there were strong linkages between particular perceptual patterns and explanatory schemata, and the schemata had associated with them knowledge about how to test to determine the fine-grained fit of the schemata to situations. A great deal of procedural and declarative knowledge was available, much of it schematically organized, although a schema would be revised in light of data. That is, there was construction of mental models here and not simply retrieval of a schema and interpretation of the situation in terms of the static schema.

Others studying medical diagnosis have provided additional evidence of flexible mental modeling. For example, Feltovich, Johnson, Moller, and Swanson (1984) studied decision making in pediatric cardiologists. A variety of input (e.g., patient histories, x-rays, electrocardiograms, other examination data) were given to specialists, residents, and students. The less experienced subjects focused in on one classic category of heart disease. The specialists were much more likely to work with several classic categories of disease to produce a diagnosis that uniquely combined characteristics from several types of disease. Pauker, Gorry, Kassirer, and Schwartz (1976) also observed that experienced doctors made an initial diagnosis and then adjusted it to take into account possible explanations of symptoms not consistent with the classic disease type. That extensive knowledge can be a powerful determinant of professional competence is considered additionally in the next subsection for the case of classroom teachers.

Expertise in Teaching

A number of programs of research on expertise in teaching have been carried out. We review briefly here some of the best of work in this tradition, research conducted by some of the leading figures in research on teaching.

Berliner's Research Berliner and associates (Berliner, 1986, 1988; Carter, Cushing, Sabers, Stein, & Berliner, 1988; Carter, Sabers, Cushing, Pinnegar, & Berliner, 1987) have studied teachers early in their careers (novices) and teachers nominated by their schools (and then screened by outside observers) as expert teachers. The perceptions of these teachers about classroom events were analyzed in several studies. Although the novices were broken down in these studies by their degree of experience, from none to advanced beginner, the distinctions within the less experienced group are not critical here, and thus we use the term *novice* to refer to any member of this less experienced group.

Sabers, Cushing, and Berliner (1991) had teachers watch a videotaped lesson. Using a complex setup involving three screens, the videotape depicted the simultaneous events occurring in all parts of the room (left, center, right). During part of the session, the participants were required to talk aloud about what was happening in the classroom. They were also asked questions about classroom events, including the routines in the lessons, the content covered, motivation in the classroom, students' attitudes, the teacher's expectations and roles, and the interactions between students and teacher. A number of findings emerged from the analyses of the data produced in this study. In general, the expert teachers had different understandings of the teaching they were watching than did the inexperienced teachers.

Sabers et al. (1991) concluded specifically that experts and novices differ in their abilities to monitor and interpret the complex set of events occurring in a classroom. Expert teachers made proportionately more interpretations and evaluations of what they saw and made more coherent interpretations and evaluations. The following sample of interpretations and evaluations from the experts make obvious that these teachers were able to make sense of what was going on in the videotaped classroom:

EXPERT 6: On the left monitor, the students' notetaking indicates that they have seen sheets like this and have had presentations like this before; it's fairly efficient at this point because they're used to the format they are using.

EXPERT 7: I don't understand why the students can't be finding out this information on their own rather than listening to someone tell them because if you watch the faces of most of them, they start out for about the first 2 or 3 minutes sort of paying attention to what's going on and then just drift off.

EXPERT 2: . . . I haven't heard a bell, but the students are already at their desks and seem to be doing purposeful activity, and this is about the time that I decide they must be an accelerated group because they came into the room and started something rather than just sitting down and socializing.

EXPERT 4: . . . I think there is an indication here of the type of structure of this classroom. It's pretty loose. The kids come in and go out without checking with the teacher. (Sabers et al., 1991, pp. 72–73)

In contrast, the less experienced teachers did not see as much and did not seem to perceive the overall structure of the classroom and the events taking place in it. A high proportion of the novice teachers' comments were simply descriptions of what was happening without interpretation or evaluations. When they attempted interpretations, they were less successful as evident in these comments:

NOVICE 1: . . . I can't tell what they're doing. They're getting ready for class but I can't tell what they're doing.

NOVICE 3: She's trying to communicate with them here about something, but I sure couldn't tell what it was.

ANOTHER NOVICE: It's a lot to watch.

The experts were more able to classify the type of instruction they were watching as activity oriented, Socratic, or process oriented. Such higher-order classifications did not occur in the reports of the novice teachers. The experts also took in more of the room, distributing their attention between the left, middle, and right portions of the room more evenly than the novice teachers did. An especially interesting difference was that the novices tended to be captured by the visual information, whereas the experts processed both the visual and the auditory input, using the language cues they picked up to aid in their interpretations of the classroom events. The result was that experts had a much better understanding of the managerial style of the classroom, the commitments of the teacher on the film, and the content being covered.

That the experts were attending to the verbalizations in the classroom was apparent in these rich descriptions:

EXPERT 3: In the middle . . . they're discussing notes that were taken on the reproductive system. On the right . . . she's asking specific individuals what the different parts of the digestive system are . . . she was very broad in just talking about the digestive system, rather than being specific and talking about parts or functions, and it seems like those are two separate objectives.

EXPERT 6: In the middle . . . she's talking about how the energy is released in the cell. Unless I missed it, she seemed to skip the lower digestive system, the two intestines, and how sugar and glucose get from the digestive system to the cells.

The novices did not understand as well the content being covered, with these comments about the verbalizations typical:

NOVICE 14: The teacher is talking a lot.

NOVICE 15: . . . she seems to be good at asking questions and getting the students to talk to her.

NOVICE 5: . . . it seems that the teacher is going over something; there doesn't seem to be much interest from the students . . . the teacher is still trying to get instructions across, and its hard to believe that everyone is comprehending what she's saying or even hearing what she's saying. (p. 78)

Novices noticed student misbehavior and were critical of it but did not make inferences about the underlying causes. The experts' perceptions of misbehavior were less evaluative and included explanations for the disruptions. For example, one expert explained inappropriate behavior at the end of a class period in the following way:

EXPERT 1: She [the teacher] seems like she's finished now, and she's not really going around to help students and to monitor how they're doing. There's time left in the class, and she's just kind of finished her work. She's not going around to check how students are doing. (p. 80)

Other experts had suggestions for improving the conduct in the class. In general, the experts were much more oriented to explaining the classroom behaviors than simply describing them or disapproving of the students.

Just as the expert radiologists were able to discern patterns in x-rays not apparent to novices, so it was with the expert teachers in Sabers et al. (1991). Just as the expert radiologists were able quickly to generate a possible general schema to explain the x-ray, expert teachers can size up a classroom quickly. Berliner (1988) described the differences between experts and novices in the descriptions of a classroom following a 1-second exposure to a slide of a classroom: The novices commented on superficial features of the class (p. 12): "A blond-haired boy at the table, looking at papers. Girl to his left reaching in front of him for something." ". . . a classroom. Student with back to camera working at a table." "A room full of students sitting at tables." In contrast, the experts perceived structure and organization and focused on instructionally important characteristics of the scene: "It's a hands-on activity of some type. Group work with a male and female of maybe late junior high school age." "It's a group of students maybe doing small group discussion on a project as the seats are not in rows." One second of viewing was all that was needed for experts to perceive structure, whether it was a blackboard activity, independent seatwork, or a laboratory exercise.

Peterson's Research   Berliner is not the only one to have considered the nature of expert teaching from the viewpoint of cognitive psychology. When others have looked at expert teaching (e.g., Swanson, O'-Connor, & Cooney, 1990), they too have produced data consistent with the expert literature in general. Peterson and Comeaux (1987) is one of the most cited studies illustrating this point.

Peterson and Comeaux (1987) studied how experienced and inexperienced high school teachers represented and remembered problem events that occur in classrooms. Their participants watched 4-minute videotapes of three such events, all involving misbehaviors common in classrooms. After watching each tape, the teachers were asked to describe what occurred in the incident, with the focus being exact recall of the behaviors and interactions depicted on the tape. Then the participants watched the same tape again, this time to identify places in the sequence where the teacher could have made a different decision than the one that was made. The participants were asked to generate alternative actions the taped teacher could have taken and to specify the action they themselves would have taken.

By a wide margin, the experienced teachers recalled more of the behaviors depicted on the tapes than did the novice teachers. A particular strength of the study was that another measure of memory was taken (i.e., digit span), with digit span not differentiating the two groups of subjects. This would suggest

that there is not an across-the-board difference in memory ability between experienced and inexperienced teachers, making more certain the conceptual significance of the greater recall of classroom events by the experienced high school teachers.

In addition, the alternative courses of action recommended by the two groups differed, with the more experienced teachers more likely to offer principled suggestions than the novices, such as the following:

> You can use the test as a learning experience rather than just to hand back.
> I think he could have done well to have thought of other ways of involving other students in what was going on.
> . . . [H]e . . . didn't really have classroom management.
> . . . [H]e can stimulate a little interest without always leaning on the test . . . it's just not motivational enough . . . isn't decisive enough . . . isn't well organized enough. (p. 324)

In contrast, the comments of the novices focused on particular alternative behaviors that could have been encouraged, rather than a conceptual analysis of the situation, as is evident in the following examples:

> He probably should have told them to get their notebooks out and take notes or ask for general attention before he started going into what he was going to talk about.
> I'd have handed out the test after they had cleared their desks of all other materials.
> [The teacher should have said] "If you have any questions . . . come up and see me" and then put himself in a position where he can scan the room. (p. 324)

Peterson and Comeaux (1987) concluded that the experienced teachers had more sophisticated schemata for encoding classroom events, with these schemata permitting more complete encoding and recall of the events and more principled interpretation of the classroom situation.

Borko's Research   How do differences in knowledge about teaching translate into differences in teaching? Although there has been little research done linking knowledge as we have been conceiving it here to teaching at a fine-grained level, the work that is available suggests that the extensive knowledge of expert teachers affects their teaching continuously and in many ways. An analysis that particularly highlighted the flexible use of schemata by expert compared with novice teachers was reported by Borko and Livingston (1989). They studied three experienced mathematics teachers and the student teachers who were assigned to these more experienced teachers. Teaching was observed, with an interview preceding each day of observation. This interview focused on planning for the lesson. The interviews following observed lessons tapped reflections on the teaching that had been watched.

The experienced teachers did much more planning for the long term than did the novices. Although both experienced and novice teachers made daily plans that were detailed, the novice teachers' planning was exclusively focused on the lesson for just that day, whereas the more experienced teachers continuously thought about coming sections in the text and the overall organization of the chapter. An even more striking difference was that much of the planning of the experienced teachers was done in the context of teaching. For example, experienced teachers did not concern themselves with which examples would be covered. They were always able to come up with apt examples, either ones they knew from experience or ones that they could locate quickly in the text. The novices agonized over which examples to present and how to present them.

The schism between planning and what actually occurred in the classroom was great for the novices compared with the more experienced teachers. In particular, the novices had difficulties with student questions and had difficulty adjusting to student misunderstandings. Student questions in particular often got the presentation off track, with the novice teachers having difficulty getting it back on track. In contrast, the experienced teachers were expert in using student errors and questions to guide and shape instruction in meaningful ways.

What accounted for the teaching differences between the experienced and the inexperienced teachers? Undoubtedly, one difference was content knowledge, which affected the quality of instruction. Part of the content knowledge of the experienced teachers resulted from interaction with students as they attempted problems. In particular, there was an increase in understanding which parts of the content pose difficulties for the students, with this increased understanding permitting preventive actions by the experienced teachers. Over the years, the experienced teachers accumulate cogent explanations and examples and developed understanding of when ex-

tensive explanations and demonstrations are in order and when more rapid coverage is possible.

In addition, there were multiple indicators in the study that the teaching schemata of novices were not as extensive as the teaching schemata of experts and that the schemata novices did possess were not as well connected nor as accessible as the schemata of experts: Planning took much more time for novices. The novices failed to see connections between questions asked by students and the lesson, connections that could have helped to keep lessons on track. In the postlesson reflections, the expert teachers selectively focused on classroom events that affected achievement, offering coherent and interpretive summaries of the day. In contrast, the postlesson reflections of the novices touched on many more aspects of the day, many of which were not relevant to student achievement.

Expert teachers have extensive and connected teaching schemata. These are not applied rigidly. Rather the teacher constructs a mental model (see Chapter 3) of a teaching situation and flexibly combines and adjusts prior knowledge to fit the current situation. A strength of Borko and Livingston's (1989) analysis was their emphasis on the ability of expert teachers to improvise. The ability to improvise—to adjust what one knows to new situations—is a mark of high competence.

Other Research   The nature of expert teaching and the knowledge base undergirding it have been the focus of intense study by a number of researchers besides the ones featured thus far. For instance, Leinhardt and colleagues (e.g., Leinhardt & Greeno, 1986) have established that expert teachers have definite routines that they use when teaching lessons, routines that are embedded in schemata about classrooms, teaching, and behavior/performance relationships in classrooms. Teachers have extensive hierarchical classification schemes for student abilities and characteristics (Calderhead, 1983). With experience, teachers increase in their understanding about how to be flexible in their thinking and how teaching behaviors interrelate—thinking about teaching is more complex in experienced compared with inexperienced teachers (e.g., Straham, 1989).

When the literature on teacher knowledge is read, it is clear that much of the knowledge of expert teachers is situated—they have built up coherent theories about and representations of good teaching through personal experiences. Experienced teachers claim they have "images" of good teaching that have developed as a result of their experiences in teaching. Here is how Elbaz (1983), summarizes the practical knowledge of teachers:

> The teacher's feeling, values, needs, and beliefs combine as she forms images of how teaching should be, and marshals experience, theoretical knowledge, and school folklore to give substance to these images. (p. 134)

Teachers' knowledge is often described in terms of metaphoric images, with a broad range of practices captured in this way, from the "classroom as home" (Clandenin, 1986; Connelly & Clandenin, 1985) to the curriculum as a "conduit" through which the teacher leads the students (Russell & Johnston, 1988). Morine-Dershimer (1979) suggested that teachers have images of what ideal lessons look like. Eraut (1985) described the images teachers possess of everyday situations in classrooms. Many teachers claim that such images guide their practice (e.g., Calderhead & Robson, 1991).

When all of the different types of evidence are combined, it is clear that experienced teachers have well-organized schemata for teaching, many of which are encoded as images. Experienced teachers are able to use what they know flexibly, so it is possible for them quickly to understand events in classrooms that are new to them.

Summary   Teachers, similar to other professionals, have vast knowledge that permits them to make rapid and powerful inferences about teaching and learning. Understanding this expertise is a relatively new direction for educational psychologists but one that deserves substantial attention in future research (see Shulman, 1986). All indications to date, however, are that good teachers have substantial procedural and declarative knowledge about classrooms and teaching. Such pedagogical knowledge will be considered often in this book as will teachers' knowledge of subject matter and the overall curricula (see Shulman [1986] for one conceptualization of the various types of knowledges teachers can possess; also Carter, 1990; for an entire volume on the topic of the knowledge required for teaching, see Reynolds, 1989). We are optimistic that studying teacher knowledge in greater detail will pay off.

One reason to be sanguine about additional research on the knowledge of expert teachers is that cognitive psychologists are getting good at devising ways of understanding high competence. The next section illustrates how great such competence can be when procedural and declarative knowledge are combined. The accomplishments presented in this next section also make the point emphatically that expertise is often extremely specific.

DEVELOPMENT OF HIGH COMPETENCE

What does it take to become an expert? What is required to acquire the many procedures involved in expert performance as well as detailed metacognitive understandings about those procedures (i.e., knowing when and where to use them)? How long does it take to acquire an expert vocabulary, with accompanying understanding of how the various categories in a domain interrelate? How long to be able to coordinate one's extensive procedural and declarative knowledge to solve new problems?

In many instances, the answer is that it requires many years of experience. Consider that expert chess players spend thousands of hours playing chess and studying the game; grandmasters invariably have played for 10 or more years (de Groot, 1965, 1966; Simon & Chase, 1973). Many of Lesgold et al.'s (1988) expert radiologists had read 200,000 x-rays in their careers. The expert teachers in Berliner's research had more than 5 years of teaching experience. In this section, we consider some analyses that have made cognitive psychologists aware that the brilliant performances of experts are the end product of years of training and practice (see especially Ericsson, Krampe, & Tesch-Römer, 1993).

Lives of Great Composers and Artists

Hayes (1985) analyzed the careers of the great musical composers and painters. He reasoned that if it takes a long time to become an expert, the early works of great composers and artists might not be as good as their later works. In the case of the composers, Hayes made the additional assumption that their better compositions would be recorded more often. As readers who are classical record buffs know, the publication *Schwann's Guide* provides listings of the recordings available for each composer.

By graphing the number of recordings for each piece against the year when the piece was composed, it is possible to summarize the relative popularity of compositions as a function of the composer's years of experience in composing.

Consider the case of Mozart. His productivity increased during the first decade of his career (from ages 4 to 14) from zero to about two compositions per year. For the remaining years of his career, he published between one and four pieces a year, with little consistency in total year-to-year productivity. That his early works were no great accomplishments, however, is reflected by the number of times these pieces have been recorded. Although 12 percent of Mozart's compositions were generated between 4 and 14 years of age, they represent only 5 percent of the total number of Mozart recordings (Figure 4.3). The early compositions were generally recorded for the sake of completeness, such as in anthologies. The first time that Mozart composed a piece that is preserved in as many as five recordings was when he was 16—12 years after he began to compose. All subsequent years resulted in pieces that are more popular than anything composed during Mozart's first decade.

Hayes analyzed an additional 75 composers. Their popularity curves were much like Mozart's. The number of pieces during the first decade was small compared with later periods in life. The pieces produced during the first 10 to 12 years are much less popular than pieces produced later in the career. There was a steep increase in the amount of work produced between years 12 and 24. In short, it took a while for a composer to get good and produce at a high, steady rate. More positively, once a composer achieved excellence, he maintained it for 30 years on average, with decline in distinguished works only apparent by the 50th year of a career on average. These data suggested that late blooming is the norm for great composers.

Hayes and colleagues did the same type of analysis for painters. The results were remarkably similar to those obtained for the composers. There was low productivity during the first 6 years for artists, with a steep increase in productivity between years 6 and 12 and steady productivity for many years after that.

Talented Young People

Bloom (1985) and his colleagues sought out top-flight concert pianists, sculptors, research mathematicians, research neurologists, Olympic swimmers, and tennis players. Most of the subjects were under age 35 at the time of the study. The purpose of the investigation was to determine the role of parents, teachers, and other factors in the development of extraordinary talent. The talented individuals were interviewed about how they became interested in their vocation and how they learned it. They were asked to pinpoint factors that contributed to their extraordinary attainments. Parents and influential teachers also were interviewed.

The 500+ page report is fascinating reading and strongly recommended for all who want detailed insights into development of great talent. Although there was some variability from talent area to talent area, there was also a great similarity across the talent areas. In every case, there were years of study and practice. These people had child-oriented parents who dedicated great resources to the development of their children. High achievement and striving for success was stressed in these homes. The work ethic was prominently in place: "To *excel*, to *do one's best*, to *work hard*, and to *spend one's time constructively* were emphasized over and over again" (p. 10). Good teaching in the area of expertise was available early in life. The kids liked the domain of expertise from first exposure. Initial success led to selection into even better educational environments—opportunities to be coached by more expert coaches, attend special classes, and so on. With success, students invested more effort into their talent, although more and more expert teachers played an ever greater role in the actual instruction and monitoring of practice. Student commitment grew ever stronger, with many hours per week devoted to the

Figure 4.3 Why are none of the young Mozart's compositions recorded much?

emerging vocation. Eventually the young talent was ready for the master teacher, with virtually all of the student's time then spent mastering the field. Most critical here, the typical time course for the complete education was 15 to 25 years.

A main message in Bloom's (1985) book is that great accomplishment is the product of years of high-quality education. There were no real child prodigies identified. Even at age 11 to 12, there was little suspicion by parents or teachers that the student would become one of the top 25 people in the world in their field of expertise, which was true for many of Bloom's subjects.

The view in Bloom contrasts with some stereotypes of genius, which portray geniuses as doing poorly in school. For instance, many know of Einstein's difficulties in the *gymnasium* in Munich. According to this stereotype, it is not long periods of immersion in a discipline that permits the expertise that is genius but some type of innate talent. Simonton (1988), as part of a book-length treatment of the psychology of creative genius, countered this point: Many geniuses earn doctorates fairly early in life, suggesting great focus and immersion early in life. Moreover, many of the best scientists went to the best schools. Finally, there are many scientific geniuses, including Marie Curie, Sigmund Freud, and Max Planck, who earned glowing marks throughout their educations, which extended over many years. Geniuses tend to do well in school, despite stereotypic impressions to the contrary. (See Chapter 18 for more on the development of gifted students.)

Summary

Great accomplishment does not just happen. It is the result of years of preparation. In many fields, it takes one to two decades to become an expert. It takes one to two decades to accumulate vast procedural, declarative, and metacognitive knowledge that can be used flexibly to great effect. Unfortunately, it is not possible to gauge how long it takes to become expert in the field most central to this book, which is teaching. Studies of expert teachers usually employ teachers with more than 5 years experience. Whether really high expertise in teaching can develop in 5 years should be studied. A good bet based on a growing body of evidence is that the answer is probably no. Retrospective interviews of superb teachers about their careers and the development of their expertise, something like the interviews conducted by Bloom

(1985), might be an efficient method to begin study of this problem.

Experts in an area possess a great deal of procedural and declarative knowledge relevant to an area. They often manifest strategies that novices would not evidence. They make many automatic associations, classifications, and analogies that could not be made by novices. Short of expertise, there are, of course, increases in knowledge with development and education, so that a grade-6 student is much more knowledgeable than a grade-1 student. A question that has been of great concern in the theoretical and basic research literature is whether improvements in performance associated with development and education are due to an increasing knowledge base or an increasing propensity to make use of the knowledge one possesses via strategies. Thus, the next section turns to extremely basic research conducted in typical laboratory situations rather than at racetracks or in x-ray departments. By turning to this work, we explicitly bring the reader back to the theoretical position introduced in Chapter 1, that good performance follows from components in interaction rather than the operation of single components—that capable performance could never be explained simply in terms of an expanding knowledge base that is applied automatically whether a person is attempting to apply the knowledge base to a task or not. Expertise reflects coordinated application of strategies and other knowledge, consistent with the perspective developed in the next section, which is devoted to basic research elucidating how knowledge and strategies determine intellectual competence.

PERFORMANCE INCREASES WITH DEVELOPMENT: INCREASES IN KNOWLEDGE OR STRATEGIES

Consider the following: Suppose children are given a list-learning task. Perhaps the list has 30 items on it. One-third of the list items are names of pieces of furniture (e.g., table, chair, piano), one-third the names of fruit (e.g., cherries, orange, melon), and one-third the names of zoo animals (e.g., lion, elephant, monkey). The items are presented in random order. If grade-1, grade-6, and grade-11 children are asked to learn such a list, memory performance increases. If asked simply to recall the items, with increasing age, students are increasingly likely to recall the pieces of furniture together, the fruit together, and the animals together—with increasing age, their recall is more **clustered** or **organized.**

One interpretation (e.g., Moely, 1977) of increasingly organized recall with development is that older students are more likely to use strategies intentionally, either to reorganize the input at study, and hence make to-be-learned content more memorable, or to use the category labels at testing to organize their recall. An alternative interpretation (Lange, 1973, 1978) is that the performance and organization increases represent nothing more than an expanding and ever more interconnected knowledge base. With increasing size and connectedness, the knowledge base is more accessible (see especially Rabinowitz & McAuley, 1990), so much so that presentation of a categorizable list results in automatic associations to category labels and interassociations between list items in the same category.

Bjorklund (e.g., 1985, 1987b), more than anyone else, has explored this problem, conducting many studies in which students at different developmental levels learn word lists. No complete discussion of the problem could exclude Bjorklund's research and the work of those who have emulated him. Even so, our view is that Bjorklund's research has not been (and could not be) definitive in determining whether increases in memory are due to increasing use of strategies or an expanding knowledge base: There is no pattern of outcomes that would definitely implicate either strategies or automatic use of knowledge-mediated associations and reorganizations, a point Bjorklund acknowledges (Bjorklund & Buchanen, 1989, p. 453).

There are some patterns, however, that Bjorklund believes are more telling than others. For instance, Bjorklund believes that if during recall, the latencies are short between same-category members (i.e., when people recall monkey, they also quickly recall elephant, zebra, or another zoo animal) and considerably longer between noncategory members (i.e., a much longer pause between recall of elephant and piano than between elephant and monkey), this is evidence that the categorical structure of the list is being used strategically.

Our interpretation of this situation, however, is that the same pattern of recall latencies would be produced by automatic reorganization at study stimulated by interassociations between the same-category items. We have never seen an outcome in-

volving recall of categorizable lists that could not be interpreted with respect to either strategies or knowledge base perspectives. When recall is low, it is always possible that the poor performance reflects failure to use strategies or lack of a knowledge base. When recall is high, it could be due to intentional use of categorization as a strategy, automatic mediation by the knowledge base, or a combination of strategy and knowledge-base mediation. This third possibility may be closest to the truth in the case of list learning: With increasing knowledge, it may be easier to apply a categorization strategy—the associations between list items and the category label would be stronger, and the associations between list members would be stronger and more diverse—and thus use of the categorization strategy might be more likely (Guttentag, 1984; Guttentag, Ornstein, & Siemens, 1987). People are often more likely to use procedures that are easier to apply rather than more difficult to use procedures. That is, the increasing knowledge base increases motivation to use categorization strategies by reducing the amount of effort required to apply them to lists.

Bjorklund's main conclusion is quite different, however. His reading of the data is that performance increases in categorizable list learning with development reflect expansion of an ever more accessible knowledge base. If strategic use of categorization occurs at all according to Bjorkland, it does not develop until adolescence, long after striking performance improvements in categorizable list learning have been observed during development.

Unfortunately the 15 years of research on knowledge and strategy tradeoffs has been less conclusive than research on other problems. To some extent, this is because of overreliance on the categorizable list-learning task by researchers interested in this problem. Moreover, researchers working in this paradigm have relied much less on sensitive research methods such as protocol analysis (thinking aloud; Ericsson & Simon, 1984) than other researchers interested in prior knowledge effects in cognition.

That is not to say that there has been no progress in understanding relationships between strategies and knowledge. In fact, it is possible to cite clear instances in which (1) possession of prior knowledge reduces dependencies on strategies, (2) possession of prior knowledge enables use of strategies that require prior knowledge for their execution, and (3) both strategies and automatic prior knowledge mediation have been demonstrated to make separable improvements in performance. (4) There have also been demonstrations that strategic use of errant prior knowledge can undermine effective performance. Examples of each of these possibilities provide windows on the complicated articulations between knowledge and strategies that occur as part of effective cognition.

Effects of Prior Knowledge on Learning and Performance

Knowledge-Base Mediation Can Replace Use of Strategies Sometimes children use strategies because they do not yet possess a knowledge base. For example, experienced readers have knowledge of thousands of words. Young readers, who do not, must rely much more on decoding strategies involving sounding out of words than do more experienced readers (see Chapter 14). Lesgold et al.'s (1988) experienced radiologists could recognize immediately many patterns in x-rays that less experienced radiologists could identify only by using inductive and deductive strategies.

The most complete analysis of tradeoffs between strategies and knowledge has been made with respect to development of children's knowledge of simple addition facts. Siegler and Shrager (1984) studied children's responding to simple addition problems such as 6 + 5 = 11, 3 + 4 = 7, and 2 + 5 = 7. Their younger participants (5- to 7-year-olds) could solve such problems, relying on strategies to do so: They used their fingers or other manipulatives to represent the problem and generate a solution (e.g., four fingers up and then three more put up for 4 + 3). Sometimes they used counting-up strategies (e.g., saying 4, 5, 6, 7 in response to 4 + 3). In contrast, older children (7- to 9-year-olds) rarely manifested these strategies. Rather they simply retrieved the answers to problems from long-term memory. A telling sign of such retrieval was rapid responding compared with the responding of younger children. Moreover, there was no evidence of fingers or anything else being manipulated by most 8-year-olds, nor was there overt counting up. Siegler and Shrager's interpretation of this pattern of data was that the younger children possessed some strategies for solving simple arithmetic problems but did not know their addition "facts" yet. Knowledge of arithmetic facts is built up during the first 3 years of school—school provides many trials on practice on

such problems. After a number of presentations of an addition problem followed by correct solution of the problem, an association is established between the problem and its correct answer. Eventually, presentation of the addition problem results in automatic activation of the answer. (Expanded discussion of Siegler and Shrager's work and related findings are presented in Chapter 13).

It is proving easy to demonstrate that people high in prior knowledge relevant to learning tasks and problems process differently than do people who lack relevant prior knowledge. **Think-alouds** are often helpful in demonstrating such differences, especially with adults. For example, Pritchard (1990) studied reading in grade-11 students, some of whom were students living on a South Pacific island (Palua) and others of whom were U.S. residents. These high school students read two types of texts, ones containing cultural schemata pertaining to the United States and others based on schemata related to Paluan culture. As these students read text, they thought aloud about what they were doing to understand the text. There were some key differences in reported strategies as a function of whether the text was matched to the background knowledge of the reader. Rereading and paraphrasing strategies were more common with culturally unfamiliar texts than with familiar ones. When reading culturally familiar texts, readers were more likely to relate what they were reading to previous text and previous experiences and more likely to extrapolate beyond the information presented in the text. In short, with culturally familiar text, processing largely involved relating to the knowledge base; with unfamiliar content, more general strategies such as rereading were common. Of course, this pattern is consistent with the pattern observed in all of the other studies addressed in this subsection.

Prior Knowledge Can Enable Use of Strategies Some strategies simply cannot be carried out profitably in the absence of particular forms of prior knowledge. An obvious example is prior knowledge activation (see Chapters 3 and 14). If a person is about to read a text on a particular content that is completely foreign to him or her, there would be little gain from asking the reader to think about related knowledge before reading the content or by instructing the reader to attempt to relate what he or she knows to the text.

Pressley and Brewster (1990) provided a telling demonstration that some strategies can only be executed if other knowledge has already been acquired. They asked Canadian middle-school students to learn some facts about Canadian provinces (e.g., Canada's first museum was in Ontario). The strategy that was studied in this investigation was an imagery strategy. Some students were instructed to construct an image depicting the fact occurring in a uniquely Ontario setting. Similarly, when presented facts about Nova Scotia, Saskatchewan, or British Columbia, students were instructed to construct images of the fact occurring in uniquely Nova Scotian, Saskatchewan, or British Columbian settings. The prior knowledge that was required, of course, was unique images for each province.

Pressley and Brewster (1990) determined in a pilot investigation, however, that many students lack unique images of the Canadian provinces in their long-term knowledge. Thus the study included a condition in which students acquired a vivid image for each province before attempting to learn the facts (e.g., the picture for Saskatchewan was of a wheat field, which is typical of the countryside in that province). These subjects were presented the 12 pictures corresponding to the 12 provinces until they could name perfectly the province shown in each picture. Those subjects who had acquired images of provincial settings in this fashion and who were instructed subsequently to remember each fact by imagining it occurring in the scene for the province in question learned the facts much better than students who were instructed to use imagery to learn the facts but who had not previously acquired an image corresponding to each province. Imagery participants who had learned the provincial scenes also outperformed control subjects. The imagery strategy of relating new facts about provinces to images of the provinces was potent—but only if the student already possessed an image corresponding to the province in question.

Knowledge-Base Mediation and Strategy Use Can Make Unique Contributions to Learning Even if students make some automatic associations to prior knowledge as they do a task, that does not mean that learning might not be improved additionally using strategies. For instance, there may be far more prior knowledge in long-term memory that could be related to a task than is related automatically by the learners. In some cases, the demands of the task are

such that more is required than simple associations to prior knowledge for the task to be accomplished.

Woloshyn, Pressley, and Schneider (1992) asked Canadian and German university students to learn some new facts about Canadian provinces and German states. Even in the absence of strategy instruction, learning of new facts pertaining to jurisdictions in one's own country was far superior to learning new facts about the other country. That is, prior knowledge was automatically applied to this learning task when it was available. Even so, the automatic use of prior knowledge did not maximize learning. When subjects were taught a strategy that prompted extensive search of fact-related prior knowledge (i.e., they were taught to attempt to learn each fact by figuring out why the fact made sense for the province in question), their learning improved over what was learned via automatic association to prior knowledge. That is, German students learning German facts in the absence of strategy instruction did not learn as many German facts as German students using the elaborative interrogation strategy. The same held for Canadian students learning Canadian facts. Strategies that increase attention to prior knowledge can produce greater learning than occurs through automatic association to what one already knows (see Martin & Pressley, 1991, for a telling analysis) because automatic activation of prior knowledge does not guarantee that all of the prior knowledge that is relevant will be used by a student.

Some tasks require more than the learning that is engendered by automatic activation of prior knowledge. For instance, a common writing strategy among young children is to rely heavily on prior knowledge, essentially to write down associations that occur given the topic of the writing assignment (Scardamalia & Bereiter, 1986). This automatic activation results in an incoherent and incomplete written product. As will be covered more extensively in Chapter 15, writing involves such activation embedded in a larger strategy comprised of planning activities, translation of plans into rough draft, and revisions of rough draft. Automatic prior knowledge association is not sufficient to accomplish this task completely because the task demands more— processes specified in plan-translate-revise writing strategies.

Knowledge-Base Activation Strategies Can Interfere with New Learning Not all prior knowledge possessed by students is accurate or consistent with new knowledge presented in school. Scientific misconceptions are a case in point. For example, students often believe that plants get food from soil and water. This misconception persists even after students learn about photosynthesis (e.g., Roth, 1990), which is a bad outcome. Even so, it can be worse. Activation of errant prior knowledge can substantially interfere with acquiring new information at all.

Alvermann, Smith, and Readence (1985) provided telling data on the impact of errant prior knowledge. Grade-6 children in their study either activated or did not activate knowledge relevant to a passage they were about to read. Those who activated prior knowledge were asked before they read the passage to write down everything they knew about "light and heat," the topic of the passage. There were plenty of misconceptions activated during this exercise. The passage that was read subsequently was on the topic of light and heat and contained information that clashed with these misconceptions. After reading the passage, memory of its content was tested in several ways. Participants wrote down what they could remember from the passage and then responded to multiple-choice items over the passage content, including ones that had wrong answers based on misconceptions about light and heat.

The results were striking. Free recall of the text was better when participants had not activated prior knowledge. Specifically, when prior knowledge had been activated, there was less recall of new information in the passage that was incompatible with students' prior knowledge about light and heat. In addition, multiple-choice items containing misconception foils were less likely to be responded to correctly in the prior knowledge activation condition. Activation of prior knowledge can undermine learning of content incompatible with it.

Williams (1993) produced data substantiating additionally the power of prior knowledge to disrupt learning of new content. She studied learning-disabled students who heard stories in a situation that encouraged them to make personal interpretations. What distinguished the interpretations offered by learning-disabled students compared with normally achieving readers was that their interpretations were bizarre. (For complementary data, see Purcell-Gates, 1991.) Moreover, these bizarre relationships persisted when the prose was recalled. Although encouraging students to activate prior knowledge related to the content of to-be-read mate-

rial has become common in reading instructional programs, data such as Williams (1993) and Alvermann et al. (1985) make clear that prior knowledge activation can be a double-edged sword, affecting learning of new content pejoratively in some cases.

Summary This section began with discussion of a program of research concerned with developmental changes in memory of categorizable lists. We argued that the paradigm in question made it difficult to separate out whether the development of accessible knowledge or the use of strategies accounted for developmental increases in memory of categorizable lists. Much of the other work in this section suggests that that may have been the wrong question.

The strategy versus knowledge base debate is strained as a legitimate question because part of any domain of knowledge is the strategies that can be used to learn new content in the domain. Students who are high with respect to declarative knowledge in a domain are also often high with respect to procedural knowledge for the domain, so a "strategic" younger student is not really the same as a "strategic" older student. Thus a grade-2 child who solves 3×13 using an addition strategy is strategic but not in as advanced a way as an older, more knowledgeable child who recognized $3 \times 13 = (3 \times 10) + (3 \times 3)$ and applied such an approach to the problem effortlessly because the multiplication facts $3 \times 10 = 30$, $3 \times 3 = 9$, and $30 + 9 = 39$ had been mastered long ago. The point of view adopted in this text is that with education and development, both strategic competence and other knowledge increases in completeness and complexity with ever better articulation between strategies and other knowledge. That is, performance increases with education or development are due to increases in strategies, increases in other knowledge, and increased efficiency in the articulation of strategies and other knowledge.

The effects of prior knowledge are diverse. For the most part, researchers have focused on how rich prior knowledge can empower learners, permitting them to complete some tasks more quickly and certainly than strategy use would, permitting them to carry out some strategies that can only be carried out when prior knowledge is high, and permitting additional learning over what is permitted by strategy use alone. Increases in prior knowledge enable diverse cognitive actions that have powerful positive effects on performance. Nonetheless, not all knowledge that students acquire is correct. Students often have great faith in and commitment to misconceptions. Such misconceptions can impede performance, with data reviewed in this section suggesting that such disruption may be especially likely if the misconceptions are activated. (In Chapter 12, there will be explicit discussion about how activation of misconceptions can be engineered so as to increase the likelihood that students will come to understand the inconsistency of new information with misconceptions and restructure their knowledge, so the new, more accurate concepts replace misconceptions.)

EDUCATIONAL IMPLICATIONS

The data in this chapter have important implications for educational policy decisions. The data reported in this chapter are extremely consistent and in ways that suggest that some instructional practices make more sense than others. We begin with some of the societal issues first and then take up some more precise recommendations for instruction.

Inequality of Educational Opportunity

High-quality performance in many arenas requires long-term, high-quality education. Sometimes the education that is required is available in the culture (e.g., in the case of baseball expertise) or in non-school settings (e.g., in the case of horse betting). For some of the most valued forms of expertise in our culture, however, years of formal schooling, including highly specialized training, is required (e.g., the talented youth in a variety of fields studied by Bloom and associates).

Analyses such as those reviewed in this chapter cast a special light on the many studies of inequality of educational opportunity in the United States. Because schools in the United States are financed largely with property taxes, students who live in high-income communities have more dollars spent on their education than students living in less economically advantaged communities. As this book was being written, Kozol's (1991) *Savage Inequalities* was attracting national attention. The book documents many such inequalities, both in cold terms (e.g., Chicago high schools spend about $5200 a year per pupil, whereas some Chicago suburban high schools spend $9300 per pupil) and in vivid, human

terms. The rich enjoy small classes in beautiful, well-furnished buildings, with lots of course diversity and enrichment. Their teachers are often exceptionally well qualified for their positions. In contrast, the poor reside in large classes in settings where even basic equipment is missing or broken. Although there are some exceptionally dedicated teachers, there are many ill-qualified teachers in these schools. We know of no analysis of inequality of schooling in the United States that does not conclude that the poor have much less access to knowledge and the instruction of knowledge than do the rich. For extremely scholarly analyses of the same points made by Kozol (1991), see Goodlad and Keating (1990). If knowledge is intellectual power, as suggested by the many analyses reviewed in this chapter, schooling in the United States is designed to be more empowering for the well-to-do than for the disadvantaged. Some have recognized that schooling is not producing certain increases in knowledge for many students and have offered potential solutions, with one of the most prominent of these in the early 1990s being the "cultural literacy" movement.

Cultural Knowledge

Hirsch (1987) and his supporters believe that to participate meaningfully in American society, it is necessary to have command of a certain core of knowledge that is essential to understand American life and thinking. Such a person is said to be in possession of **cultural literacy.** Important policy makers (e.g., Finn, 1991; Ravitch, 1989), who were close to the Bush administration, embraced this perspective. The most recent accomplishment of Hirsch has been the editing a series of books that specify what cultural literacy should be taught at each grade level. Thus, *What Your 2nd Grader Needs To Know* (Hirsch, 1991) covers the language arts, social studies, fine arts, mathematics, and natural sciences that grade 2 should cover.

What are the difficulties with this approach? Hirsch et al. (1988) presented what they regarded as important cultural knowledge in the form of a dictionary, with the result being pages and pages of fragmented information, thousands of short definitions of concepts. The scattered approach is not as extreme in the grade-school series of books, but the content is still fragmented. The lack of coherence in the grade-school series can be appreciated by considering what a second grader should know, for instance, in geography:

World Geography: The third-largest ocean, the Mediterranean and Aegean Seas, a review of the continents.
United States Geography: The U.S. map of states, including coverage of why some states have strange shapes; the first states.
Geography of Mexico, Central America, and South America: A smorgasbord of facts including that Spanish is the main language, a few explorers, Spanish ownership at one time except for Brazil, independence movements in Latin America.

In short, there are smatterings of information in the grade-2 curriculum (as well as the curricula specified for the other grade levels). The superficiality and lack of coherence so apparent in these volumes contrasts with everything that is now known about knowledge that permits powerful thinking: Knowledge that effectively mediates important performances is well organized and connected. Learning disconnected facts is a certain way to create what Whitehead (1929) referred to as inert knowledge, knowledge that can be remembered for a test but not applied elsewhere.

Although we do not want to imply that it is not important to build general knowledge in students, it is clear that general knowledge alone is not what is needed for high achievement in many fields. The contemporary world needs expertise in many domains, and analyses such as Bloom (1985) suggest that the development of many forms of expertise should begin in the grade-school years. Bloom's work, and other research on focused talent (see Chapters 6 and 18), suggests that specialized talent will not develop as a function of development of general cultural knowledge. We worry a great deal that an overemphasis on a common curriculum, which is what the cultural literacy approach advocates, would overshadow the importance of individualizing instruction to encourage the exceptional strengths and interests of students.

Even so, as this book is being written, we are aware of attempts to evaluate the impact of cultural literacy–inspired curricula in schools. Our view is that these evaluations should be studied carefully and with an open mind, for it may be that in the hands of experienced educators, the cultural literacy volumes will take on life not apparent from our reading of them.

One Way the Smart Get Smarter: Experts Become Their Own Teachers

All of the experts reviewed in this chapter exhibited **self-regulated** learning and problem solving. No one was leading them by the hand through the tasks they were doing or even providing hints. They kept themselves on task and guided their own thinking. That good thinkers invariably are self-regulated has provided great impetus for educational interventions that promote self-regulation, especially self-regulated use of complex sequences of procedures that are combined and coordinated with prior knowledge. What must be emphasized is that much of the self-regulation that goes on feeds back on the system, making the person an even more powerful thinker. Good thinkers can rapidly size up a situation in terms of their prior knowledge. To the extent that prior knowledge does not fit the current situation, the self-regulated expert makes adjustments and inferences, with the result being new knowledge that will be available in the future. Self-regulated thinking builds on itself, with the self-regulated thinker always becoming a better thinker.

CONCLUDING COMMENTS

Knowledge is intellectual power. A domain-knowledgeable 10-year-old often is more than equal to an adult lacking knowledge of the domain in question. For many tasks, the knowledgeable person with a 90 IQ has it all over the unknowledgeable person with a 130 IQ. The person high in knowledge about horses wins at the betting window; the soccer expert processes information about soccer more completely than a soccer novice, no matter how many IQ points the novice has.

Although expertise can be detected using a variety of measures, no method of investigation has been more helpful in understanding the nature of expertise than verbal protocol analysis—having experts and novices talk aloud as they do tasks. Regardless of area of expertise or task, many similarities in expert performance have emerged from such analyses and were highlighted in this chapter.

The knowledge of experts is rich in every way that knowledge can be rich. All of the forms of representation reviewed in Chapter 3 function in the mind of the expert. Highly organized, tightly connected, yet flexible knowledge empowers. Although experts have rich networks of concepts and associations, the schemata they possess have been singled out for scrutiny. Experts have many schematic images corresponding to situations common to the domain. Moreover, their images and other schemata are flexible, with experts modifying them as necessary to deal with new situations. Because experts are ever modifying their schemata, their education never stops.

That experts have a long education has been documented using a number of analyses. One to two decades of preparation is typical, with much of the second decade a period of immersion in the discipline. Chess masters have seen hundreds of thousands of chess boards, and expert radiologists have analyzed hundreds of thousands of x-rays.

One of the most important questions in the developmental literature during the 1970s and 1980s was whether performance increases with development reflected increases in use of strategies or increases in automatic mediation by the knowledge base (i.e., the ever-expanding and ever more accessible knowledge base permits more certain associations to prior knowledge when new content is processed). That proved to be the wrong question, with performance depending both on strategies and on other automatic knowledge-based mediation.

Chapters 3 and 4 provided an intellectual foundation for many of the interventions that will be presented in this book, and there will be frequent reference back to these chapters. Many of the interventions reviewed in this book can be thought of with respect to the representational systems reviewed in Chapter 3; the development of many academic competencies that will be covered here have been affected by the insights produced by analyses of expert performance—for example, many of the interventions reviewed in this book are long-term treatments, consistent with the perspective emerging from study of experts that skilled performance can only be developed in the long term. It is important that you connect what was presented in Chapters 3 and 4 with what follows, and we will provide cues at appropriate points along the way for readers to do so.

One way to remember some of the points covered in Chapters 3 and 4 is to think of the *Hardy Boys* again. The Hardy boys' knowledge of the criminal world was extremely well connected and could be applied in many different settings. They were capable of many complex sequences of behavior, sequences that seemed compiled (e.g., the entire sequence of events involved in lifting fingerprints and analyzing them might be thought of as a compilation). Many of their strategies (e.g., notetaking at the scene of a crime) were automatically carried out as part of an overall plan that was carefully controlled by each of the boys. They were constantly aware of what they wanted to accomplish and they kept themselves on task. For teenage boys to have achieved such expertise must have meant old Fenton Hardy had been at the boys since birth, for experts are educated over a long period of time and not born, although by the point in their development when they are introduced to readers of the *Hardy Boys* series, the boys are educating themselves, just by doing their trade. Practicing expertise is one way that the smart get smarter (Rohwer, 1980b).

Enhancing Student Motivation

In the last 15 years, there has been a revolution in understanding of academic motivation; much of that revolution is covered in this chapter. Particularly important, there have been many counterintuitive discoveries about how academic motivation is affected by schooling environments. The research covered in this chapter has profound implications about how to design education so it is maximally effective, so that students remain motivated throughout their academic careers.

This chapter is specifically devoted to insights about how to motivate students to learn and do well academically, although important principles of motivation are covered throughout the book. For example, in Chapter 2, the case was made that whether students use strategies they have learned depends on whether they understand their value. This is a specific instance of a general principle that will be presented more completely in this chapter and in Chapter 7, that the likelihood of a behavior that a person possesses occurring is a function of the expectancy of reward for performing the behavior and the value of the reward to the individual. A second example of motivation covered elsewhere in this book is the recurring theme that presentation of information just a bit beyond the current competence of the learner is motivating. The goal in this chapter is to present what are the most influential contemporary perspectives on the role of motivation in education. The most logical place to begin such a discussion is with evaluation of the need to understand student motivation.

THE NEED TO UNDERSTAND ACADEMIC MOTIVATION MORE FULLY: HOW MOTIVATION AND ACHIEVEMENT CAN BE UNDERMINED

In this section, we review three types of evidence that make clear that academic motivation can be undermined easily. Such evidence makes obvious that there is an urgent need to understand academic motivation better and to consider new ways of arranging schooling so that academic motivation is enhanced rather than destroyed by classroom experiences.

Expectations and Their Impact on Long-Term Motivations and Educational Outcomes

Most children entering elementary school have great expectations for success. Present them with a task—almost any academic task that could possibly be within their competence—and ask them how they will do. A high proportion of kindergarten, grade-1, and grade-2 children assume that they will do very well, something that has been confirmed in many investigations (e. g., Clifford, 1975, 1978; Entwisle & Hayduk, 1978; Flavell, Friedrichs, & Hoyt, 1970; Goss, 1968; Levin, Yussen, DeRose, & Pressley, 1977; Parsons & Ruble, 1977; Pressley & Ghatala, 1989; Stipek & Hoffman, 1980). Even more striking is the robustness of young children's optimism. Most children in the early grade-school years continue to believe they will do well even after they experience less than great success with a task (Clifford, 1975, 1978; Parsons & Ruble, 1977; Phillips, 1963; Pressley & Ghatala, 1989; Stipek & Hoffman, 1980).

Such optimism is generally not seen in older children (for a review, see Stipek & MacIver, 1989). (Many studies cited in the last paragraph provided striking data on this point.) Middle-grade and upper-grade elementary students are more aware of their academic failures than their academic successes (Kloosterman, 1988). Often, students perceive they are doing much worse than their teachers believe they are doing (Juvonen, 1988). The academic self-perceptions of lower-achieving students especially suffer (e.g., Renick & Harter, 1989). Not surprisingly, students' expectations about themselves as academic achievers decline during the elementary years. Once children decide that they cannot do well in school, their beliefs tend to persist, undermining future academic achievement (e.g., Fincham, Hokoda, & Sanders, 1989). The potential importance of this lack of optimism in older children compared with younger children is appreciated when it is remembered that motivation is largely a function of the expectation of reinforcement, with reinforcement in academic settings often boiling down to task success. As would be expected given declining expectations with advancing grades in school, there are clear declines with advancing grades in interest in school and what can be learned there (e.g., Harter, 1981; Wigfield, Eccles, MacIver, Reuman, & Midgley, 1991).

There is an interesting little twist, however. Boys' expectations about their academic performances tend to be higher than girls' expectations (e.g., Crandall, 1969; Entwisle & Hayduk, 1978; Frey & Ruble, 1987; Parsons & Ruble, 1977; Pressley & Ghatala, 1989; Pressley, Levin, Ghatala, & Ahmad, 1987; Stipek & Hoffman, 1980; Whitley, McHugh, & Frieze, 1986). The gender differences in expectations about academic achievement have been hypothesized to have enormous impact on girls' willingness to pursue some challenging academic arenas compared with boys' willingness to do so, an area of intense concern to Dweck and colleagues.

Dweck (e.g., 1986) and associates have been intrigued by the fact that during the early elementary years, girls exceed boys in mathematics achievement, with this pattern reversing at junior high and continuing reversed for the remainder of schooling. They have offered an explanation in terms of sex differences in expectations that translate into sex differences in motivation to tackle mathematics. This complex tale is among one of the more interesting in the contemporary literature on academic motivation.

Dweck (1986) reported a study in which otherwise high-achieving boys and girls reacted differently to a failure experience on a concept formation task. The high-ability girls tended to be devastated by the failure much more than the high-ability boys, with this affecting subsequent performances—the high-ability boys going on to outperform the high-ability girls on subsequent trials of the same task. High-ability girls seemed to be especially disadvantaged, with initial failures and difficulties disrupting their subsequent performances more than the performances of less able girls (Licht & Dweck, 1984). In

this same program of research, Dweck (1986) determined that girls are more likely than boys to prefer tasks they are good at. In contrast, boys prefer tasks that present some challenge for mastery. Girls are more likely than boys to attribute any difficulties they have to unchanging abilities (i.e., rather than to low effort, high task difficulty, or bad luck).

How girls think about task performances and task difficulties makes likely that they will reduce their motivation to continue a task when it proves difficult. That is, when they experience frustration, girls tend to believe it is because of low ability. Given a choice, they elect tasks that are not so frustrating, ones that are already familiar to them. Boys shrug off initial failures more certainly, attributing them to something other than their own ability. Because they prefer some challenge and novelty anyway, they are more likely to forge onward.

Believing that one is able can be extremely motivating even when it is not true. Believing one is not able can undermine motivation to try new and challenging tasks even when objective ability is high. That boys have more confidence in themselves in general relative to girls probably has a profound impact on their willingness to take on challenging academic domains such as mathematics (Dweck, 1986) (Figure 5.1).

Figure 5.1 Which of these students are most likely to be motivated to do mathematics and believe they can do it well? Why? Which of these students is least likely to be motivated to do mathematics and believe they can do it well?

Rewards and Their Impact on Intrinsic Motivations

The intuitively reasonable claim will be made in Chapter 7 that reinforcements (rewards) can increase the probabilities of behaviors that occurred just before the reward is administered (e.g., Skinner's perspective). Even so, rewards also have the potential for undermining performance, especially those behaviors that we might do in the absence of reward because they are intrinsically interesting to us. The researcher most frequently associated with this effect is Lepper, although as Lepper and Hodell (1989) made clear in their review of how intrinsic motivation can be undermined, this effect has been observed in diverse settings and with diverse tasks (e.g., Deci, 1971; Kruglanski, Friedman, & Zeevi, 1971; Lepper, Greene, & Nisbett, 1973).

A great deal of research has been devoted to determining when and why rewards undermine performance. They do so when initial interest in the rewarded activity is high and when the reward to perform the behavior is so salient that it could be construed as motivating the behavior (Lepper & Hodell, 1989). When subjects can justify their willingness to do something in terms of an extrinsic reward, it is harder in the long term to justify doing the same activity in the absence of reward—an outcome that Lepper et al. (1973) dubbed the **overjustification effect.** Rewards can be effective even when intrinsic motivation is high, however, if the situation is arranged so that the rewards come after the fact of performance—that is, as a bonus (Lepper, 1983; Lepper & Hodell, 1989).

Given this pattern of outcomes, why would anyone ever use rewards to motivate performance? When initial interest in a task is low (i.e., when a task is not intrinsically rewarding), rewards can increase the likelihood of academic engagement and performance of important academic tasks (Bandura & Schunk, 1981; Lepper & Hodell, 1989; Loveland & Olley, 1979; McLoyd, 1979), something that has been understood for many years by behavior modification theorists concerned with education (e.g., see Pitts, 1971).

Ego Involvement in Classrooms

Nicholls (e.g., 1989) has noted that most classroom reward (goal) structures foster ego involvement, with success in the classroom (especially relative to peers) implying high capacity (i.e., that one is smart) and failure implying low capacity. Such a system has high potential for undermining effort when success is not certain (e.g., with new task demands), for trying and failing leads to feelings of low ability. Attributing a failure to low ability does nothing to motivate additional effort: What good is it to try, since the student believes he or she lacks the ability to do the task.

Nicholls (1989) points to a variety of classroom practices that stimulate ego involvement and the conclusion for many students that they are not as able as their peers:

- Grading on the curve.
- Emphasis on student percentile ranks on standardized achievement tests.
- Making grades salient and public.
- Public teacher comments on the achievement of students, comments that tie achievement to worth. (pp. 153–154) (Author MP remembers vividly the first day in grade 7 when the principal introduced the 7-1 section as the students, "We really expect great things from." Section 7-6 was introduced as the students, "We know are going to have a lot of difficulty with grade-7 work.")

What is the result of this obsession with identifying publicly who is smart? Nicholls argues that such a practice probably undermines academic motivation for many children in the system. Students will often go to great lengths to avoid having to try something academic, rather than risk failure, public humiliation, and additional confirmation of low ability relative to other kids.

There is plenty of evidence to support Nicholls's beliefs, with substantial research on classroom structures that foster ego involvement (sometimes called by other names, such as competitive classrooms; e.g., Ames, 1984). In such classrooms, how a student does compared with others is an important determinant of whether he or she feels successful (e.g., Ames & Ames, 1981). Indeed, doing better than other kids in the class is far more important in determining whether one feels successful in competitive classrooms than is doing well in an absolute sense—that is, actually performing the educational task competently (Ames & Felker, 1979; Barnett & Andrews, 1977; Johnson & Johnson, 1974; Levine, 1983): Because most students will not end up doing "best" in the class, feelings of failure, self-criticism, and negative self-esteem often occur (Ames, 1984).

One likely reason that there is a clear decline in perceptions of academic self-efficacy from kindergarten to the middle grades is that comparative evaluations are less frequent and salient in the early primary years compared with the later primary and middle grades years (Harter, Whitesell, & Kowalski, 1992; Stipek & Daniels, 1988). With increasing age, children are more aware of the competitiveness in their classrooms (see Harter et al., 1992; also Schmidt, Ollendick, & Stanowicz, 1988) and of the implications of not succeeding. What is certain based on both the classroom research already cited and basic research (e.g., Wigfield, 1988) is that by the middle elementary years and continuing into the high school years, paying attention to how one does compared with others affects perceptions of one's own competency, with these perceptions having the potential to affect school performance. Thus, a student may have more positive perceptions about his or her own academic ability and better school performance (measured in some absolute way) if enrolled in a low-ability class rather than a high-ability class because what one thinks about one's own ability is determined with reference to class standing; such social comparisons with others can motivate additional effort (i.e., when one is at the top of a low-ability class) or undermine effort (i.e., when one is near the bottom of a high-ability class; e.g., Marsh, 1987).

More positively, there is another approach to schooling than the competitive classroom that is typical in the United States, one completely consistent with the reason society sends children to school—to improve themselves. Rather than rewarding students for being better than one another, it is possible to reward students for doing better than they did previously, to reward personal improvement on academic tasks. Nicholls refers to such classrooms as fostering task involvement, an apropos name in light of research findings by Nicholls and Thorkildsen (e.g., 1987): When these investigators rated and studied 30 grade-5 classrooms ranging in ego and task involvement, what they found was that work avoidance was much more commonly reported in ego-involved classrooms than in task-involved classrooms. That is, students in ego-involved classrooms were much more likely than students in task-involved classrooms to endorse claims such as the following: I don't have to do any homework, I don't have to work hard, all the work is easy, I don't have any tough tests, and the teacher doesn't ask hard questions. The students in the task-oriented class-

rooms believed that success in school depended on interest, effort, and attempting to learn, whereas the students in the ego-involved classrooms believed that success depended on being smarter than other kids and trying to beat out other students.

Nicholls (1989) summarized much additional evidence that task-oriented classrooms are much more likely to keep students interested in and committed to school than are ego-oriented classrooms. The problem is that many more classrooms are ego involved than task involved; many more classrooms are committed to motivational orientations that defeat student interest and effort than promote it; in far too many classrooms, the goal is to get better grades than the ones earned by peers rather than to learn (e.g., Ames, 1992; Blumenfeld, 1992).

A study by one of Nicholls's former students illuminates the relevance of work on classroom motivational orientation for the good information processing model. Nolen (1988) assessed whether grade-8 students were task or ego oriented. In addition, Nolen asked the students to indicate whether they would use particular strategies for reading and understanding textbook material, with their reported strategy use then compared with actual strategy use when the same students were observed while they studied some passages. What is important here is that although both task-oriented and ego-oriented students endorsed and used surface-level strategies for processing text (e.g., read the whole thing over and over), the task-oriented students were much more likely than the ego-oriented students to endorse and use strategies that involved deeper processing of text (e.g., try to see how this fits with what I've learned in class). What Nolen's (1988) study suggested is that task orientation and use of sophisticated strategies may be linked. A result like this makes it clear that good strategy instruction should include explicit efforts to encourage task orientation in students—to encourage students to recognize that the goal of education is to improve and that such improvement is possible in part through acquisition of powerful strategies.

Summary

There are three important messages in this section. The first is that conventional wisdom about motivation often is wrong (e.g., reinforcements effects are uniform; competition fosters achievement). The second message is that there is a lot wrong with student motivation in traditional classrooms. High expectations are transformed into low expectations as schooling continues. Many students view school as a place where inherent ability is more of a determinant of success than effort. Many students feel as if they are failing. Feelings of success are obtained by outperforming others, even if that does not require excellent performance in any absolute sense. In short, society is spending billions of dollars on an educational enterprise that more certainly undermines academic motivation than promotes it, with the result that far too many students are not academically motivated (Doyle, 1983; Harter, 1981; Lepper, 1983). The third message is much more positive. Researchers and theorists are more interested in student motivation now than at any previous point in history. There is increasing recognition that low student motivation often is the result of structural failures of schools rather than some inherent deficiency in students. We expect a great deal of research in the coming decade about how classroom goal structures affect motivation to learn (see especially Blumenfeld, 1992), about how school can be re-engineered to increase the interest, involvement, and achievement of most students, rather than just the top students.

WHAT CAN BE DONE TO MAKE SCHOOL MORE MOTIVATING AND TO CREATE MORE MOTIVATED STUDENTS?

This section comprises some theory, some data, and many hypotheses. To date, researchers have been better at figuring out the motivational properties of existing schools (e.g., Nicholls, 1989, analyses) than they have been at testing hypotheses that emerge from this work, hypotheses about how to increase interest in and engagement during schooling. We present some of the best hypotheses we have encountered related to increasing motivational properties of schools for three reasons: (1) It permits presentation of many ideas that motivational scholars have about specific mechanisms that influence student motivation. (2) This section provides a smorgasbord of ideas for readers who are future educational researchers. (3) We hope that those readers who are about to become teachers reflect carefully on the vast array of ways they could affect student motivation for the better.

We start this section with a discussion of one of the best validated approaches to increasing classroom motivation and learning. This work on cooperative learning should make clear that strong research on motivational interventions is possible, research that is readily translatable into real school interventions.

Cooperative Learning Rather than Competitive Learning

Cooperative learning interventions are now common in North American schools. Several prominent research groups have studied cooperative learning.

Johnson and Johnson's Approach to Cooperative Learning. Johnson and Johnson have been studying various ways of structuring classroom interactions since the 1970s (e.g., Johnson & Johnson, 1975, 1979). They argue that whether social interactions in classrooms are positive, negative, or neutral will have dramatic effects on long-term motivational achievement. Three types of social structures are considered in detail by the Johnsons (e.g., 1985):

> A *cooperative* social situation exists when the goals of the separate individuals are so linked together that there is a positive correlation among their goal attainments. An individual can obtain his or her goal only if the other participants can achieve their goals. Thus, a person seeks an outcome that is beneficial to all those with whom he or she is cooperatively linked. A *competitive* social situation exists when the goals of the separate individuals are so linked that there is a negative correlation among their goal attainments. An individual can obtain his or her goal only if the other participants cannot obtain their goals. Thus, the person seeks an outcome that is personally beneficial but is detrimental to the others with whom he or she is competitively linked. Finally, an *individualistic* social situation exists when there is no correlation among the goal attainments of the participants. Whether an individual accomplished his or her goal has no influence on whether other individuals achieve their goals. Thus, a person seeks an outcome that is personally beneficial, ignoring as irrelevant the goal achievement efforts of other participants in the situation. (Johnson & Johnson, 1985, p. 251)

Johnson and Johnson's analysis is that contemporary schooling is much too competitive and individualistic in orientation and too little cooperative, with the Johnsons estimating that cooperative learning occurs only 7 to 20 percent of the time in American education (Johnson & Johnson, 1985). How should learning occur according to the Johnsons? Four characteristics are essential (Johnson & Johnson, 1985, pp. 252–253):

1. Learning should be *interdependent.* Tasks should be large enough that more than one student is needed to get it all done. Rewards need to be structured so that everyone has incentive to pitch in and help.
2. There should be *face-to-face interactions among students within small learning groups.* The likelihood that all students will participate is greater with small groups than with large groups.
3. *Individual accountability* is essential. Students can assist one another effectively only if there is sufficient awareness among students about who knows what and who needs help.
4. Students need to be taught *interpersonal and small group skills.* Students who do not interact well in groups naturally can be provided the social skills that permit more productive interactions.

Great things happen when children learn in such small groups according to the Johnsons, with their conclusions supported by data from many different types of studies conducted at different sites. Getting students together in small groups to work on academic tasks has the following striking advantages:

It increases **intrinsic motivation.**
There are **high expectations** for success among cooperative learning participants.
The mutual benefits of cooperation increase **incentives** to learn.
There is high **epistemic motivation,** that is, high interest in the topic being studied, interest that extends beyond the small group. This is largely due to the motivational advantages provided by **cognitive conflict** in cooperative groups. (See the discussion of cognitive conflict later in this subsection.)
There is high task persistence.

It almost goes without saying that the Johnsons conclude that competitive and individualistic orientations do not have these advantages. They particularly point out, consistent with Nicholls's, Ames's, and Dweck's analyses presented earlier, that although the most able students may be motivated in competitive and individualistically oriented classrooms, these classrooms are likely to reduce the academic motivation of most students compared with what is possible in cooperative environments.

Does such cooperative learning improve academic achievement? Johnson, Maruyama, Johnson, Nelson, and Skon (1981) reviewed 122 studies that evaluated the effectiveness of cooperative learning, competitive learning, and individualistic learning. Cooperative environments produced better learning than the alternatives, with the overall effect sizes consistently in the "moderate" range (i.e., not small, but not large either).

Slavin's Research Program   Slavin and colleagues at Johns Hopkins University generally offer recommendations consistent with those made by the Johnsons, although they emphasize one aspect of cooperative learning more than others. Cooperative learning is most likely to be effective if there are both (1) group rewards and (2) individual accountability (e.g., Slavin, 1985a, 1985b). This works as follows: A cooperative group's score is calculated by summing over the scores of the individuals in the group on some individual assessment (i.e., perhaps at the end of a week or unit), with the group having the highest score receiving a reward. This effectively eliminates the freeloader problem, for capable students cannot sit by and allow teammates to learn nothing; if they did, the team score would suffer because one or more of the individual assessment scores would be low (i.e., those of the freeloaders).

An example of one of Slavin's programs, Team Assisted Instruction (TAI; e.g., Slavin, 1985b) for mathematics, illustrates the Hopkins approach to cooperative learning. A class is divided into four- to five-member teams, with each including both boys and girls, a racial mix, and a distribution of abilities. Students remain in their teams for 8 weeks or so at a time, changing teams at the end of this period.

Instructional sessions are divided into periods of individualized study and team study. During the individualized portion, each student works on self-instructional materials. Each such assignment includes an instruction sheet, detailing the skill to be mastered, including step-by-step instructions about how to do assigned problems. There are 20 problem work sheets followed by two practice tests and a final test.

During the team study period, students work with groupmates in pairs or in triads. The students do the work sheets, assisting one another with the instructions or with specific problems. Students work on problems and then check groupmates' answers against the answer key. If a student gets all four problems correct, he or she can go on to the next skill sheet. Otherwise, the student works another block of four problems from the same skill sheet, which is followed by checking. After working through all skill sheets, a student takes the first practice test which is then checked by a groupmate. If a student works 8 of the 10 practice test examples correctly, the student is certified by the team to proceed to the final examination. If the practice test score is less than 8, the adult teacher is called in to provide guidance, which usually means assigning the student to work on the skill sheets some more, leading up to a second practice test. Students monitor carefully whether groupmates make the required score of 8 on the practice test before they are permitted to proceed to the final test.

At the end of each week, a group score is calculated based on the total number of units completed per group member, with additional points given for exceptionally high performances on final tests. The teams that do exceptionally well receive certificates denoting their accomplishments. The teacher does not disappear completely in this process but rather provides tutorials to small groups of students daily, ones who are at about the same point in the various units, bringing students together to form tutoring groups of three to four students.

Slavin is a great respecter of data, and his endorsement of the TAI approach is based on a number of studies conducted by him and his associates with children in grades 3 through 6. In general, math achievement has proven superior in classrooms experiencing TAI compared with conventionally instructed classrooms. In addition, there is substantial evidence across the studies that students' attitudes toward mathematics improve following participation in TAI. See Slavin (1985b) for a review.

In recent years, Slavin has been especially interested in reading achievement, designing and studying the Cooperative Integrated Reading and Composition program (CIRC; Stevens, Madden, Slavin, & Farnish, 1987). The group arrangements are similar to TAI. Basal stories are read; reading and composition strategies are taught by the teacher to the class as a whole. Students read trade books at home.

Activities in small groups follow reading of a basal selection. These exercises include reading, analysis of narrative structures of stories, writing, word mastery and learning of definitions, story retelling, and spelling. All of this work is done with partners, who also monitor each other's progress as occurs in TAI in preparation for formal tests over stories and story-related activities.

In evaluations with grade-3 and grade-4 students to date, CIRC has fared well, improving standardized comprehension relative to control classes reading similar basal stories. Writing and oral reading effects have been positive as well.

Beyond What Works: Fantuzzo's Research Program
Johnson and Johnson are exemplary integrative scholars, complementing their research with fine overviews of the entire cooperative learning literature. Slavin is one of the most prolific educational psychologists in the United States. He has generated impressive programmatic research documenting the effectiveness of cooperative learning in improving what were already high-quality elementary arithmetic and reading programs. There is much to admire in both the research and the conceptions of the Johnsons and Slavin, although there has been a disturbing tendency by cooperative learning researchers to ask only whether cooperative learning works, rather than to focus on more analytical questions (e.g., Are some components more essential than others? Perhaps only the entire mix of components promotes performance, rather than a subset of them?)

In contrast, Fantuzzo and associates at the University of Pennsylvania are conducting exceptionally analytical research on cooperative learning, with their initial efforts yielding extremely interesting outcomes, especially given the challenging environments in which they have conducted their studies. Fantuzzo and colleagues (Fantuzzo, King, & Heller, 1992) went to one of Philadelphia's most economically disadvantaged schools. Their concern was the mathematics achievement of grade-4 and grade-5 students, individuals at great risk for school failure based on demographic predictors (e.g., Socioeconomic Status). The experiment included four conditions and permitted evaluation of the contributions of two cooperative learning components on achievement: the effects of group reward and paired learning. In the condition with both paired learning and group reward, two or more students worked together on math problems, alternating between teacher and student roles in a structured format: Students monitored each other's problem solving and prompted each other when one of the group experienced difficulties. They taught and encouraged one another. The rewards earned by the group were determined by combining the performances of all students so that there was incentive for pairmates (or for all group members, depending on the size of the particular group) to make certain that one's partner learned the material. In two other conditions of the study, students were taught to use the cooperative structure only, *or* they were administered group rewards so the effects of the individual components could be evaluated. In the control condition, students were teamed up to learn mathematics but were not required to use the student-teacher cooperative structure, nor were they provided group rewards.

The most critical variable in the study was a mathematics computation test that measured achievement in grade-4 and grade-5 mathematics, although the test covered the entire range of mathematics from grade-2 level to advanced grade-5 level. The test was timed, with the goal to complete as many of 48 problems in 20 minutes as possible. The results confirmed the importance of combining the cooperative learning components, with the performance of students in the cooperative pairing structure plus group reward condition clearly superior to performance in the other three conditions of the study. Neither providing the paired cooperative structure alone nor providing the group rewards alone produced performance better than in the control condition.

The Fantuzzo et al. (1992) outcome supports cooperative learning (Figure 5.2) : Gains did not follow from rewards alone or simply working together but from working together in the context of cooperative structures and incentives that promote the learning of all students in a group. Cooperative learning works because of the mix of components, rather than because of any one of the components constituting the intervention. In instructional research, there is a dialectical tension between designing and evaluating packages of components and evaluating the impact of individual components. The most informative way to resolve that tension is to conduct research permitting insights about both the packages as wholes and the individual components in the packages. That is what Fantuzzo et al. (1992) did.

Concluding Comments In closing this section on cooperative learning, we emphasize how flexible the approach is. Cooperative learning can be combined with other prosocial interventions (e.g., activities promoting social understanding, instruction highlighting social values through literature and content-area learning), and when it is for the long term, the effect can be a friendlier, more supportive, and

Figure 5.2 Is this game motivating the learning it is intended to motivate?

kinder classroom world than is typical in U.S. classrooms (Solomon, Watson, Delucchi, Schaps, & Battistich, 1988). Cooperative learning can be used with a variety of curricular contents, as exemplified by the reading and math examples presented in this subsection. Additional examples of cooperative learning appear in the chapters that follow—be on the lookout for them. We warn you, however, that sometimes the interventions will be more subtle than the examples discussed here. Thus, in Chapter 14, we will discuss reading groups that involve a lot of cooperation. In that case, the "group reward" is a more interesting story for all, produced by all students participating in the development of story interpretations. Great teachers often exploit natural rewards of group participation and cooperation, although there can be a positive side to conflict as well.

Stimulating Cognitive Conflict

We think about issues more deeply when challenged by others; we sometimes think about things in new ways and sometimes change our minds when interacting with folks who see the world differently than we do. When there is conflict between one's current knowledge or beliefs and new knowledge, the discrepancy motivates efforts to understand the new perspective, with it likely that knowledge will change as the new perspective is understood.

Piagetians (see Chapter 7) view such conflict as critically important to cognitive growth—much more important than other mechanisms. Kohlberg (e.g., 1969; see Chapter 9, this book) and Blatt (e.g., Blatt & Kohlberg, 1975; see Chapter 9, this book) were particularly instrumental in translating Piaget's ideas about cognitive conflict into educational methods. One of Kohlberg's greatest interests was in developing sophisticated moral reasoning in students. The principal pedagogical approach was to present groups of students with moral dilemmas—problems with alternative perspectives, problems that elicit spirited discussion and conflict. Cognitive growth was hypothesized to occur because ideas that come up that are different from one's own result in reflection on one's assumptions, the viewpoints of others, and the differences between one's own views and other perspectives.

There were many evaluations of the cognitive conflict hypothesis with respect to increases in the sophistication of moral judgment (see Enright, Lapsley, & Levy, 1983, for a definitive review). The evidence was orderly and generally positive, especially after the elementary years.

Although Piagetian thinking did much to inspire the cognitive conflict approach to learning, the idea that people are motivated to become more competent is an old one (see White, 1959). Being exposed to information that is discrepant with current knowledge or beliefs makes clear that one's knowledge may be off a bit, which motivates efforts to understand the new information. Cognitive conflict is bound to receive more attention in the coming years because discussions between students and between students and teachers that involve alternative interpretations is emerging as a favored approach to teaching and learning from a number of perspectives in science and mathematics education, with these analyses taken up in Chapters 12 and 13. Discussion of student dialogues is common in this book.

Encouraging Moderate Risk Taking

Many students are afraid to try for fear of failing. This is counterproductive, for learning inevitably involves some mistakes. Moreover, there is growing evidence that risk taking is motivating, with greater academic effort expended by risk takers than non–risk takers and greater achievement by risk takers compared with non–risk takers (Clifford, 1991). Perhaps it is not surprising that many of the curriculum interventions covered in Chapters 12 through 15 include encouraging students to take academic risks.

Praising Students

Brophy (1981) summarized the available literature on praise and offered a set of prescriptions about how praise should be delivered in classrooms to have maximally positive effects. Some of the most critical attributes of effective praise are the following:

- Effective praise is delivered contingent on desirable student behaviors (i.e., following desirable behaviors).
- In delivering the praise, the teacher makes clear what the student did that was praiseworthy.
- Effective praise is sincere.
- There is an implication that the student can be similarly successful in the future if they exert appropriate effort.
- There is a message that the student expended the effort that led to praise because the student enjoyed the task or wanted to develop the competencies that have been praised.

What a simple message, consistent with reinforcement theory (e.g., Bandura, 1986; Skinner, 1953; see Chapter 7, this book): Provide lots of positive reinforcement, with Brophy considering positive reinforcement as richly informative about what behaviors can lead to reinforcement and hence extremely motivating. (Contingent praise in particular should increase a student's perception that they are capable of performing an academic task—that is, increase their self-efficacy [e.g., Bandura, 1977a, 1986] regarding the task; see the discussion of self-efficacy later in this section.) What a simple message consistent with metacognitive theory (e.g., Borkowski, Carr, Rellinger, & Pressley, 1990): Provide lots of information about what it is that the student is doing right and why the student should engage in the desirable behaviors in the future. What a simple message designed to circumvent Lepper et al.'s (1973) overjustification effect: Efforts are made to convince the student they are carrying out the desirable behaviors because they want to do them, not simply to receive praise.

Effective praise as described by Brophy (1981) is difficult to do, however, and thus rarely occurs in classrooms. Rather, there is a lot of noncontingent praise in most classrooms, praise that does not make clear what the student did well and praise for behaviors that are not praiseworthy (e.g., praise for participation alone, rather than participation consistent with the processes being taught—"I'm so glad you are taking part"). When we review Brophy's (1981) discussion of praise, we always find ourselves wishing that some student would come along (maybe a reader of this book?) and run the study that needs to be done, comparing teachers who have learned how to praise effectively with those who have not. This is potentially a great program of research that would be informative about an inexpensive but too rarely exploited approach to classroom motivation.

Making Academic Tasks More Interesting

People pay more attention to content that is interesting (e.g., Hidi, 1990; Renninger, 1990; Renninger & Wozniak, 1985), prompting many materials developers to create academic materials that "grab" students. Of course, there is good reason to do this, for many students in school, especially ones at risk for school dropout, find what they are asked to learn to be boring (e.g., Farrell, Peguero, Lindsey, & White, 1988).

There is a terrible paradox in attempting to increase the interestingness of school learning, however. Sometimes motivational embellishments result in attention to and processing of something other than what the materials were intended to teach.

Learning From Text Anderson and colleagues at the University of Illinois Center for the Study of Reading (e.g., Anderson, Mason, & Shirey, 1984) largely reawakened interest in the study of interest as a mediator of learning from text. In the studies conducted at Illinois, children read sentences that had been rated either as interesting or uninteresting. Interesting sentences were much more certain to be remembered later than were uninteresting sentences, with the interestingness manipulation producing a large effect relative to the size of effects produced by other manipulations (e.g., readability of sentences).

Anderson's group (e.g., Anderson, Shirey, Wilson, & Fielding, 1987) also conducted some extremely analytical studies to determine the mechanisms underlying the interest effect, hypothesizing that more interesting materials were more likely to be attended. In fact, that seemed to be the case, with students spending more time reading interesting compared with less interesting texts; in addition, interesting texts were so absorbing that readers failed to respond to an external signal (e.g., pressing a button in response to a sound heard while one is reading) as quickly as they did when reading uninteresting texts. Even so, greater attention alone did not account for the greater learning of the interesting materials, for when differences in attention and effort are factored out of learning data (i.e., amount of time spent reading sentences was controlled statistically), there are still large differences owing to interest (e.g., Shirey & Reynolds, 1988). Thus, interest can affect directly both attention and learning, with only some of the increases in learning because of the effects of interest on attention to academic content.

Informed by the data collected at Illinois, Anderson, Shirey, Wilson, and Fielding (1987) offered some hypotheses about how to make texts more interesting:

- Include in them characters with whom readers can readily identify, such as characters similar in sex, age, race, religion, and occupation to readers, an hypothesis supported by subsequent research; e.g., Bleakley, Westerberg, & Hopkins, 1988).
- Ordinary occurrences bore; thus, place novel and extraordinary relations in text to the extent that it is possible to do so.
- Base the texts on life themes important to the readers.
- Construct texts that depict intense action and feeling rather than passive states. (pp. 293–295)

Anderson et al. (1987) acknowledged that the textbooks presented to children in school, especially social studies and science texts, are often dull. They also reviewed the ideas of others about how to make stories more interesting. These included Brewer and Liechtenstein's (1982) claim that good stories arouse emotions, Jose and Brewer's (1984) concern with suspense, and Bruce's (1983) analyses suggesting that complex stories with multiple interpretations are to be preferred over simpler, more literal stories.

Anderson et al. (1987) indicted the practice of adding interesting anecdotes to text as a motivational device, however. Texts filled with anecdotes often lack coherence (e.g., Anderson & Armbruster,

1984). In addition, although the anecdotes are often remembered, the point of the text is either missed or forgotten—personally stimulating information is recalled, but memory of the abstract and general points is unaffected (e.g., Hidi & Baird, 1988). Garner's work particularly is telling on this point.

Garner and colleagues (e.g., 1992; Garner, Gillingham, & White, 1989; Garner, Alexander, Gillingham, Kulikowich, & Brown, 1991) documented that readers often pay so much attention to interesting details and anecdotes in text—referred to as **seductive details** by Garner—they neglect the main ideas (see also Wade, Schraw, Buxton, & Hayes, 1993). For example, adults in Garner et al. (1989) read texts such as the following:

> Some insects live alone, and some live in large families. Wasps that live alone are called solitary wasps. A Mud Dauber Wasp is a solitary wasp. Click beetles live alone. *When a click beetle is on its back, it flips itself into the air and lands right up while it makes a clicking noise.* Ants live in large families. There are many kinds of ants. Some ants live in trees. Black ants live in the ground. (p. 46; seductive detail highlighted here but not in original text)

The most critical finding in the study was that recall of the main ideas was approximately half as likely when the text contained a seductive detail than when readers processed texts with the tantalizing details deleted. The effect has proven robust over texts and positioning of seductive details in text (Garner et al., 1991; for a complementary outcome, see Wade & Adams, 1990).

Since Dewey (1913), educational theorists have argued for increasing the interestingness of to-be-learned materials. Work like that of Garner makes clear that some thinking and research are required before Dewey's (1913) seemingly simple-minded recommendation can be carried out. Much work remains to be done to determine the most effective ways of simultaneously increasing the interestingness of expository text and its learnability.

Learning From Educational Software   Lepper and colleagues at Stanford (e.g., Lepper & Malone, 1987; Malone & Lepper, 1987) have taken the lead in analyzing the motivational properties of computer software. In general, they have had little difficulty demonstrating the motivational appeal of gamelike versions of computer programs compared with drill-and-practice programs that cover the same content (see also Rieber, 1991): Children are willing to spend

much more time with the games than the drills. Unfortunately, it is difficult to make the case that the gamelike programs produce greater academic achievement.

Lepper and Malone offered analyses of the motivational characteristics of these programs that would make them intrinsically appealing and motivating to students: They are appropriately *challenging*—not too easy but not so difficult that they cannot be played competently with some effort. They also *provoke curiosity:* How will the lights and sounds change *this?* They *provide a sense of control* to players, feelings that their actions determine what happens in the miniature world of the computer program, which is critical because controlling events is a powerful intrinsic motivator. The games involve *fantasy.* In addition, some of the games offer opportunities to cooperate with others, which can be interpersonally motivating; other games increase motivation by providing opportunities to compete. Some games provide explicit opportunity for recognition—for example, the program includes a "Hall of Fame" for players who have played exceptionally good games on the program (Figure 5.3).

Lepper and Malone also believe that computer games and software could be programmed so that they would be instructionally effective—that they could be programmed to enhance attention to to-be-learned content, provide appropriate feedback about learning and performance, increase the meaningful

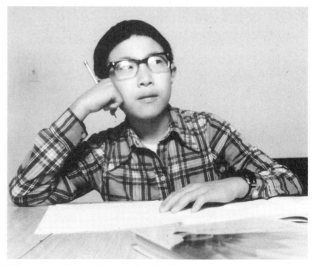

Figure 5.3 Does this student's distraction reflect a lack of motivation or volition? What might the student do to decrease the chances of future distractions?

processing of the content being taught by the program, and result in multiple representations of content (e.g., imagine all the ways that number concepts can be portrayed in computer environments—the numbers themselves, various sequential and simultaneous picture displays). The problem with the current generation of computer programs is that they were designed to be intrinsically motivating with less attention to whether the games would increase attention to and processing of the educationally relevant content. An anecdote provided by Lepper and Malone (1987) makes the point:

> . . . [We] have been watching young children learn to program in a Logo environment. Although most of the hard data are not yet in, it was difficult not to have the feeling that for every child lost in thought on some complex, planful, and potentially mind-expanding program, there was another in hot pursuit of what one might call a behavioristic "minimax" strategy—looking for the maximum payoff from a minimum investment of effort—leading to a plethora of programs exploring, for example, the results of sending the turtle forward 12,000 or 27,000 steps at a time and watching the screen successively fill with seemingly random lines. The path of least mental effort produced a big motivational "bang for the buck," but may have limited instructional value. (p. 281)

It is all too easy to have a lot of fun with many of the programs without learning much. In fact, during a visit to a school, we learned from a grade-5 student all the ways to trick a math program so as to extend one's turn and thus remain at the microcomputer (which was much preferred to working at one's seat). The "trick" was simply to make certain *not* to perform at mastery, for to do that meant the program would produce a fireworks display in celebration of the student's success, a display that ended the student's day at the computer.

Another motivational problem with computers and computer programs is that for some students, they are so motivating that these students would do nothing else except computing if given a free choice. From time to time in our careers, we have labored in university computer centers analyzing data. Thus, when we encountered this description by Weizenbaum (1976), we recognized immediately the type of student described:

> . . . [B]right young men of disheveled appearance, often with sunken glowing eyes, can be seen sitting at computer consoles, their arms tensed and waiting to fire their fingers, already poised to strike, at the buttons and keys on which their attention seems so riveted as a gambler's on the rolling dice. When not so transfixed, they often sit at tables strewn with computer printouts over which they pore like possessed students of a cabalistic text. They work until they nearly drop, 20, 30 hours at a time. Their food, if they arrange it, is brought to them: coffee, Cokes, sandwiches. If possible, they sleep on cots near the computer. But only for a few hours—than back to the console or the printouts. Their rumpled clothes, their unwashed and unshaven faces, and their uncombed hair all testify that they are oblivious to their bodies and to the world in which they move. They exist, at least when so engaged, only through and for computers. These are computer bums, compulsive programmers. (p. 116)

From the perspective of the development of expertise, perhaps these students should be viewed as a blessing: Many years of computer experience is required to be an expert in computing, and there is no shortage of need for such expertise now and in the future. From the perspective of educational well-roundedness, however, we do worry.

In short, producing motivating computer environments is not a problem. Assuring students learn well in these environments is an important issue; so is guaranteeing that some students who get hooked on computers also spend sufficient time in other pursuits. A great deal of research will be required to determine how to make the most of these extremely motivating tools.

Attributional Alternatives for School Successes and Failures

When a person succeeds or fails, they can explain their success or failure to themselves in various ways. Weiner (e.g., 1979) specified four types of explanatory attributions, with each of these having different motivational consequences. Students can explain outcomes by referring to their (1) efforts—success was due to hard work, and failure was due to lack of effort; (2) abilities—success was due to inherently high ability, and failure was due to low ability; (3) task factors—success occurred because the task was easy, and failure was caused by unreasonable demands of the task; or (4) luck—success reflects good luck, and failure reflects bad luck.

Only the first of these attributions, however, is likely to promote adaptive motivational tendencies. Believing that successes and failures are due to effort is believing that one's fate is personally controllable.

One can decide to try hard and be successful or to loaf and experience failure. The other explanatory possibilities—ability, task difficulty, and luck—are all out of one's control, due to genes, teacher task selection, or the whimsical nature of supernatural forces. Knowing that one's fate is under personal control has been referred to by motivational theorists as self-efficacy (e.g., Bandura, 1982; more about this later) or personal causation (e.g., deCharms, 1968), and self-agency (e.g., Martin & Martin, 1983). All theorists who have considered this type of knowledge recognize that those who believe they can control their destinies are likely to be more motivated to exert great effort in pursuit of goals than are those who believe their achievements are out of their control—for example, students with high mathematics self-efficacy have more positive attitudes about mathematics, which translates into higher mathematics achievement (Randhawa, Beamer, & Lundberg, 1993).

The role of attributions in motivating academic efforts has been studied especially with respect to the motivations of students who have experienced difficulties in school. For example, Jacobsen, Lowery, and DuCette (1986) interviewed learning-disabled and normally achieving students. Consistent with the results of other studies (e.g., Pearl, 1982), Jacobsen et al. (1986) determined that learning-disabled children were much more likely than their normally achieving classmates to believe that their achievements reflected low ability. Normally achieving children were more likely to believe that with effort they would be able to succeed in school. This belief in effort is telling even within low-achieving populations: Low achievers who believe they can control their academic progress through effort, in fact, do achieve at higher levels than low achievers who believe their low achievement reflects low ability (Kistner, Osborne, & LeVerrier, 1988).

That the attributions of many low-achieving children are dysfunctional (i.e., the students attribute their failures to uncontrollable ability factors and hence are not motivated to exert academic effort; e.g., Carr, Borkowski, & Maxwell, 1991) has inspired some to attempt to retrain attributional tendencies as part of larger educational programs aimed at children experiencing problems with school work, work that seems especially worthwhile given that academic progress in low-achieving children is related to the attributions they make: Borkowski and colleagues at Notre Dame (e.g., Borkowski, Weyhing, &

Carr, 1988; Reid & Borkowski, 1987) have provided the most compelling analyses and data about interventions aimed at shifting the attributions of low achievers to promote their academic performances.

Borkowski recognized that only getting students to attribute success to effort would probably do little for low-functioning students, consistent with the perspective offered since Chapter 1 of this book that sophisticated academic performances depend on a variety of factors. (Recall that Borkowski is one of the prime movers of the good information processor perspective; e.g., Pressley, Borkowski, & Schneider, 1987, 1989.) Thus, Borkowski's group has been training students to use strategies to accomplish intellectual tasks at the same time that they persuade students that their successes and failures on academic tasks are due to their efforts using appropriate strategies (Clifford, 1984; also, see the Chapter 2 discussion of the criticality of students understanding the value of academic strategies they are learning). That is, Borkowski and colleagues persuade students that as they learn strategies, they are acquiring tools that will permit them to improve their academic performances, which is a powerful motivation to use the strategies students are learning (Chapman, Skinner, & Baltes, 1990).

For example, in one study (Carr & Borkowski, 1989), underachieving elementary students were assigned to one of three conditions: (1) In the strategies plus attribution training condition, children were taught comprehension strategies. They were instructed to read paragraphs and to self-test whether they understood the content. The students were also taught summarization, topic sentence, and questioning strategies as means of understanding text (see Chapter 14). The attributional part of the training consisted of emphasizing to students that they could understand text by applying the comprehension strategies, that their comprehension of text was a function of how they approached text rather than any inherent comprehension abilities. (2) Strategies-only subjects were taught the strategies, without the benefit of attributional training. (3) Control subjects were provided neither strategies instruction nor attributional training.

Children in all conditions participated in 6 half-hour sessions. In the strategies plus attribution and strategies conditions, these sessions were devoted to receiving the instruction appropriate to the condition and to practicing the strategies with actual text. In the control condition, students practiced reading with the same tasks and passages processed by students in the instructional condition, although no information was provided about comprehension strategies.

What a difference in the strategies plus attributional training condition: When tested 3 weeks following the conclusion of the training sessions, the strategies plus attribution participants were more likely to be using the strategies than other participants in the study, with recall of text higher in this condition than in the other conditions of the study. In addition, the strategies plus attributions subjects seemed to be using the training strategies in the classroom much more than the students in the other conditions of the study.

Although much more work analyzing the effects of attributional retraining needs to be conducted to understand completely its potential for modifying views of oneself as a learner, many who work with learning-disabled students in particular are already including attributional retraining with their students. For example, a key ingredient in the University of Kansas strategies instructional model (e.g., Deshler & Schumaker, 1988) is promoting the understanding in students that they can do better if they master strategies well matched to the demands of school. As students are taught comprehension, writing, and memory strategies, there is consistent emphasis on the role of controllable factors, such as use of strategies, as a determinant of performance. That is, the Kansas group recognizes that the attributions made by learning-disabled students (e.g., I am stupid) are dysfunctional. Such attributions, if permitted to persist, have high potential for defeating other instruction, for believing that one is stupid is also believing that nothing can be done about it. Both applied efforts and basic research (e.g., Stipek & Kowalski, 1989) have documented that attribution retraining can make a substantial difference in the motivations of students who otherwise tend to attribute their poor performances to factors other than effort.

Incremental Development of Intelligence: Encouraging Students to Understand That Intelligence Is Not a Fixed Entity But an Incrementally Improving Function

Dweck and Leggett (1988; also Henderson & Dweck, 1990) have proposed that a critical determinant of achievement motivation is whether a person believes that intelligence is fixed biologically and hence not affected by environmental variables, or malleable. People who believe intelligence is fixed are said to possess an **entity theory** of intelligence—that is, that intelligence is a thing that one either has in great quantity or does not. Those who believe intelligence is modifiable subscribe to an **incremental theory** of intelligence.

The particular view of intelligence held by an individual has a powerful impact on his or her achievement behaviors. First, consider academic goals as a function of the theory held: Entity theorists are oriented to seek positive evaluations of their abilities and to avoid negative evaluations. Such a perspective can be damaging when negative feedback occurs, as it inevitably does in school. Such students are likely to interpret failures as indications of low intelligence and hence be discouraged by failures. In contrast, incremental theorists are much more oriented to increasing their abilities, believing that daily efforts lead to small gains, all of which can sum to substantially higher intelligence when effort is persistent and long term. Such students persist when obstacles occur because they see obstacles as a natural part of the learning process.

In short, entity theorists are more likely to experience negative emotion when confronted with failure, believing that failure signals low ability, with that belief undermining future attempts at the academic task in question. Indeed, the entity theorist may be motivated not to engage in the task in the future to avoid additional evidence of low ability. Incremental theorists experience much less negative affect in response to failure, interpreting the failure as part of the improvement process, which motivates high persistence. As long as there is success, there is little difference in the behaviors of entity and incremental theorists. When failure occurs, however, the differences in their outlooks become apparent, with the entity theorists much more at risk for believing they are helpless when they experience difficulties during challenging tasks, with low persistence and task avoidance the likely outcomes. Incremental theorists just keep plugging away following a failure.

Dweck and colleagues have produced quite a bit of evidence for this perspective (see Dweck & Leggett, 1988; Elliott & Dweck, 1988; Henderson & Dweck, 1990), as have others (e.g., Meece, Blumenfeld, & Hoyle, 1988; Wood & Bandura, 1989). Some of the most prominent research has been generated by

Ames and associates. For example, Ames and Archer (1988) studied students in grades 8 through 11, all of whom were attending a high school for academically gifted students. The students in this study answered a number of questions. Some of the questions were designed to determine whether students were incremental or entity theorists with respect to a particular class in which they were enrolled, with Ames and Archer (1988) believing that one's theory of achievement would vary depending on the reward structure in the class. Ames and Archer (1988) referred to incremental beliefs as **mastery-oriented** beliefs, reflecting that the incremental theorists are concerned with mastering material presented in class. They referred to entity beliefs as **performance-oriented** because such students are concerned with performing well. Items likely to be endorsed by students believing they are in a class promoting increments in ability (i.e., in mastery-oriented classrooms) included the following:

- The teacher makes sure I understand the work.
- The teacher pays attention to whether I am improving.
- Students are given a chance to correct mistakes.

Items likely to be endorsed by students believing they are in classrooms driven by an entity theory of intelligence (i.e., performance-oriented) included the following:

- Students want to know how others score on assignments.
- I really don't like to make mistakes.
- Only a few students can get top marks. (Ames & Archer, 1988, p. 262)

Other questions that were posed in the study were designed to determine the learning strategies used by students, their choice of academic tasks, their academic attitudes, and the causal attributions they make about school. Students who perceived themselves in classrooms that encouraged incremental improvements reported using more strategies and more effective strategies, seemed more open to challenging tasks, were more positive about their classes, and were more likely to believe that improvements follow effort. Those perceiving their classes to be driven by an entity model were more likely to have a negative view of their own ability and believe that classroom difficulties reflect low ability.

Ames (1990) believes that analyses such as Dweck's and her own have profound implications for education. She believes in particular that to the extent that classrooms foster performance goals rather than mastery goals—that is, are ego-oriented, to use Nicholls's (1989) term, or foster entity views of mind, to use Dweck's term—classroom goal structures discourage students from trying hard, using potentially effective learning procedures, or being optimistic in the face of academic difficulties. Our own reading of Ames, Nicholls, Dweck, and like-minded motivational theorists is that there is already substantial evidence in support of their perspective, which is one of the most important contemporary hypotheses motivating additional analyses of classroom processes that can foster student motivation and achievement. For now, we feel safe in concluding that students are better off in classrooms in which the mentally healthy messages associated with mastery-oriented classrooms are prominent: (1) Trying hard fosters achievement and intelligence. (2) Failure is a natural part of learning. (3) Being best is not what school is about; getting better is.

Possible Selves: Encouraging Students to Believe It Is Possible for Them to Learn and Do Well in School and in Life

Ask yourself the following question: What am I going to be in 10 years from now? What this question is tapping is your conception of "possible selves" that you might become, a concept developed most fully by Markus and colleagues (Cantor, Markus, Niedenthal, & Nurius, 1986; Markus & Nurius, 1986). We suspect that many readers of this book will provide answers to this question that reflect the expectation of upward mobility. Thus, undergraduates reading it may anticipate that they will be teachers or other professionals; teachers in master degree programs may envision that they will be principals, reading specialists, or curriculum developers; and graduate students in educational psychology may aspire to be professors, government officials, or product developers in business. What is critical to note here is that these possible selves are not frivolous fantasies but rather realistic goals, envisionments that provide a great deal of motivation to continue reading this book and completing the educational psychology course, to enroll in more courses next term, and to look for advancement opportunities (with the expectation of landing one), once school is through. As

Markus and Nurius (1986, p. 960) put it, a possible self can provide ". . . direction and impetus for action, change, and development." It can provide energy for behaviors that reduce the distance between the current true self and the possible self that one aspires to become.

Unfortunately, there is plenty of reason to suspect that many students do not have desirable or realistic possible selves. Last evening on the Washington, DC, news, we listened in horror to a conversation involving some 10-year-olds enrolled in schools in the District. One little boy related that he expected to become a drug dealer and maybe a pimp. A little girl reported that she suspected she would never have a job.

Almost as tragic are more positive but unrealistic possible selves because they can motivate enormous efforts during youth in directions that are unlikely to pay off for youth. A prime example is that many minority youth in the United States believe that they have a high probability of becoming a professional athlete, when in fact the odds against any particular youth attaining such a possible self are thousands to one (e.g., Edwards, 1973). Such unrealistic possible selves can motivate much effort directed toward athletic accomplishment, effort that could have been expended in pursuit of a self that is realistically possible. Gooden (1989), for example, presented analyses of how attainable "dreams"—to use Levinson et al.'s (1978) term for possible selves—could motivate young black males. For example, Gooden reported a dishwasher whose dream was to become a chef, a dream that motivated him to make it through cooking school. Gooden also presented cases of young black males with unrealistic horizons, such as becoming a famous scientist or physician. In these cases, however, the dream kept the young men on track academically, so that they did become professionals (teachers, for the group analyzed in Gooden, 1989). A young person's possible self (or dream) can be a powerful motivator.

Given the potential of possible selves for motivating interest in and commitment to academic attainment, and given that many students have dysfunctional possible selves, an obvious intervention possibility is to attempt to shift students' possible selves from unrealistic dreams to dreams that are more likely to keep the students on track. Day, Borkowski, Dietmeyer, Howsepian, and Saenz (in press) have begun to study such a possibility. They have particularly been concerned with improving the academic performances of Mexican-American students, enough so that these students will complete high school. Their studies to date have been with Mexican-American students in grades 3 through 7.

Most of the students come from neighborhoods with few, if any, professionals. Thus, there is little opportunity to see models of Mexican-Americans working in high status occupations, models that could inspire these children to believe they could become professionals. Even so, these children have ambitious possible selves: 92% expect to graduate from high school, 75% from college, and 17% from graduate or professional school. They highly value success in school (5.2 on a 6-point scale). They also fear that these dreams may not come true. Half of the children Day et al. (in press) have studied fear that they will end up in jobs that require less than a high school education.

Day et al. (in press) reasoned that even though Mexican-American children may have dreams, they may not know how to maintain those dreams through the many steps of the educational process, including frustrations that might be experienced along the way. The training package Day et al. developed is aimed at increasing awareness of the many types of jobs these students might attain in their lives and to make obvious that completion of middle school and high school is essential for obtaining multiple vocational opportunities. In addition, the training package focused on coping with negative feedback and failure, including unjustified reactions of others. Consistent with attribution theory, the training was designed to increase student understanding that their successes were under their control—that academic effort pays off.

The instruction involved a metaphorical piece of art, "The Possible-Me Tree." Two important leaves on the tree represent student hopes (e.g., a good job) and fears (e.g., dropping out of high school). These leaves are used in exercises designed to inspire students to work toward their goals and to avoid the feared outcomes. The give-and-take discussion, which is the intervention, emphasizes that there are various definitions of success, what people enjoy doing can become their life work, education is essential for obtaining desirable jobs, and obstacles are encountered in obtaining dreams.

The preliminary data regarding this intervention are promising, although not definitive at this point. Relative to control students not receiving the intervention, those participating in the Possible-Me Tree exercises have greater expectations of success in the future. Possible-Me-Tree students were more likely to believe they might attain especially high status occupations, such as judge or physician. There are modest improvements in grades (Estrada, 1990).

We believe that it is important to foster realistically ambitious possible selves and provide support to students so they maintain their motivation to pursue positive possible selves. Day and Borkowski's work is a first venture in this domain, an area that should be explored in great detail in future research.

Increasing Student Self-Efficacy

Social learning researchers (see Chapter 7) have increasingly offered perspectives that are consistent with views of good information processing that have been emphasized throughout this book. The concern of social learning theorists with motivation comes through in the definition of self-regulated learning provided by Zimmerman:

> [Self-regulated learners] approach educational tasks with confidence, diligence, and resourcefulness. Perhaps, most importantly, self-regulated learners are aware when they know a fact or possess a skill and when they do not. Unlike their passive classmates, self-regulated learners proactively seek out information when needed and take the necessary steps to master it. When they encounter obstacles such as poor study conditions, confusing teachers, or abstruse text books, they find a way to succeed. Self-regulated learners view acquisition as a systematic and controllable process, and they accept greater responsibility for their achievement outcomes. . . . [T]hese learners report high self-efficacy, self-attributions, and intrinsic task interest. . . . [T]hey are self-starters who display extraordinary effort and persistence during learning. . . . They seek out advice, information, and places where they are most likely to learn; they . . . self-reinforce during performance enactments. . . . (Zimmerman, 1989b, pp. 4–5)

A particularly critical part of this definition of self-regulated learning is the idea that self-regulated learners have high **perceived self-efficacy** (Bandura, 1977a, 1986; Schunk, 1990, 1991; Zimmerman, 1989a, 1989b, 1990a, 1990b)—that is, they believe they are capable of doing well on academic tasks. High self-efficacy in a domain is important because it motivates attempting tasks in the same domain in the future and thus is a causal factor in future academic achievement (e.g., Marsh, 1990a; Zimmerman, Bandura, & Martinez-Pons, 1992). For example, one motivation for a first-year university student to enroll in introductory calculus is previous success in mathematics. That is, the decision to pursue the goal of earning credit in first-year calculus is determined in part by previous success in prerequisite courses. Suppose that the calculus course goes well, with concepts learned easily and grades high on quizzes and tests. Self-efficacy with respect to mathematics is increased even more, which in turn can motivate future election of mathematics courses. What if things went badly in the calculus course? Self-efficacy with respect to mathematics should decline, with this reducing the likelihood of seeking mathematics credit in the future. Self-efficacy is determined in part by present attempts at learning and performance; it then affects future attempts at learning and performance.

What are the other determinants of self-efficacy besides previous success in the domain? For one, there are social models: When people who are similar to us can do something, we are more likely to believe that we could do it and should attempt to do so (Schunk, 1991). Other people also attempt to persuade us concerning our competencies. How many times did we hear from our gym teachers in junior and senior high school to try the parallel bars because they were sure we could do it! That motivated our attempts to learn how to perform on the parallel bars, as did watching classmates who did well on the parallel bars. Even so, we consistently received negative feedback for our efforts (i.e., we fell off the bar, executed maneuvers clumsily), with this feedback overriding the effects of modeling and teacher persuasion. Although modeling and the opinions of others have an impact on self-efficacy, feedback from one's own efforts has a greater impact (Schunk, 1990, 1991).

Self-efficacy is highly domain specific, so there are students who have high self-efficacy with respect to math and low self-efficacy with respect to composition—and this self-knowledge is generally accurate (i.e., people know their academic strengths and weaknesses: Marsh, 1990b, 1992a;—even middle-elementary-grades students: Marsh & Craven, 1991;—even children as young as 5 years of age: Marsh, Craven & Debus, 1991, although there certainly is greater differentiation with respect to academic self-concept with increasing age during the grade-school years, Stipek & MacIver, 1989). There are those with high self-efficacy with respect to most academic areas and low self-efficacy with respect to athletics. Within specific domains, there are differences in self-efficacy. As an illustration of the specificity, consider that as a senior in high school author MP had high self-efficacy with respect to tumbling and low self-efficacy with respect to the parallel bars. He had high self-efficacy with respect to the 440-yard dash and low self-efficacy with respect to the 220-yard race. He had high self-efficacy with respect to playing first base and low self-efficacy with respect to playing third base. All of us possess detailed knowledge about what we can do well (e.g., university students are aware of their proficiencies in reading and writing; Shell, Murphy, & Bruning, 1989), with the detailed perceptions of self-efficacy playing a large role in determining future efforts. For example, as a middle-aged adult who now only plays slow-pitch softball, author MP would never think of playing third base but would have no trepidation about playing first base.

The self-efficacy perspective makes clear why it is important to provide students with tasks that are just a bit beyond them. If subjects attempt an easy goal, they make progress rapidly, but the rub is that they do not acquire information about their abilities to tackle more ambitious tasks. If students attempt too difficult a task, there is little success in meeting the goal or making success toward meeting it, with the result diminished self-efficacy and motivation to continue with the task. Only tasks that are challenging for the learner, but not so challenging as to prevent progress, are capable of providing information to students that increases self-efficacy in ways that are likely to promote future attempts at challenging tasks.

Although self-efficacy theory can be related to a variety of theoretical perspectives pertaining to motivation (see Pintrich & deGroot, 1990; Schunk, 1991; Skinner, Wellborn, & Connell, 1990), one that seems particularly appropriate to consider is its relationship to **expectancy × value theory,** an important theory specifying when people will perform behaviors that they are capable of performing (see Chapter 7 for more extensive coverage of this theory). If self-efficacy is high in domain A, the expectancy of reinforcement contingent on performing in domain A is also high, and hence if the potential reinforcements for performing in domain A are also valued, the like-

lihood of domain A behaviors would also be high (i.e., high expectancy of reinforcement × high valuation of a reinforcement = high probability of performing the behavior, producing the reinforcement in question). If domain A behaviors occur and there is success, expectancy of reinforcement remains high contingent on domain A behaviors. In contrast, if domain A behaviors occur and there is failure, expectancy of reinforcement for domain A behaviors should decline, as should the likelihood of performing domain A behaviors in the future. Shifts in self-efficacy probably produce changes in expectations, which alter the likelihood of performing behaviors in a domain (Schunk, 1991).

A critical assumption of expectancy × value theories is that successful students both expect and value academic success. In a study analytical enough to determine whether there are strong relationships between expectations of academic success, valuation of success, and academic achievement, Berndt and Miller (1990) observed that the success of grade-7 students in English and math was linked strongly both to expectations of success in these domains and to valuation of potential rewards for success in math and English (i.e., successful students expected and valued academic success).

So far we have made it sound as if every attempt at doing something has great consequences for self-efficacy. In particular, this is not correct when a person already has a strong sense of self-efficacy built up over years. Consider the following: A major league batting star strikes out four times in one day. Is there an effect on the batting star's self-efficacy with respect to hitting? Probably not, or if it is, it is likely a specific shift, such as, "I have a lot of trouble against Lefty Smith (i.e., today's pitcher)." When attempting some new goal, the feedback on one occasion can have a dramatic impact on self-efficacy and long-term motivation; performing below par on one occasion in an arena in which one enjoys a long record of accomplishment has less impact on self-efficacy with respect to that goal (see Bandura, 1986, for other examples; also, Schunk, 1991).

In closing this discussion of self-efficacy, it is essential to emphasize that self-efficacy is only one determinant of motivation and selection of goals. One way to emphasize this is to reiterate that the probability of a behavior is a function of the expectation of reinforcement and the value of the expected reinforcement. If the expected reinforcement is of no value to the student, behavior is unlikely no matter how high the student's self-efficacy may be.

Encouraging Volition

Since the earliest formulation of the good information processing model (Pressley et al., 1987), there was recognition that good information processors "stick with" important tasks and are not easily distracted from them. The work of German psychologist Kuhl (e.g., 1985) influenced that early conception, with Kuhl claiming that people differ in the extent to which they can shield themselves from distractions, an individual difference that is an important determinant of performance on many tasks. Others (e.g., Corno, 1989) have also been impressed by Kuhl's analyses, with Corno arguing that Kuhl's work has special significance for understanding student **volition,** which contrasts with motivation in that motivation involves a decision to initiate action toward a goal, and volition involves continuing to pursue the goal once begun:

> Kuhl (1985) conceptualizes volition after Ach (1910) as a series of "action control processes," that is, "postdecisional, self-regulatory processes that energize the maintenance and enactment of intended actions" (p. 90). Although Kuhl's theory is general, the specific intended actions of concern here are concentrating and working toward the completion of academic tasks. That volitional processes are "postdecisional" is the distinguishing point between volition and motivation: Volitional processes come into play *after* the decision is made to learn or complete an academic task. Most motivational processes underlie or precede the decision to learn or complete a task—these include the weighing of success and outcome expectancies, the assessment of value, and so on. They *promote* the intent to learn. . . . A student brings in volition once there is a commitment to learn, and volition *protects* that commitment to learn and concentrate from competing action tendencies and other potential distractions. (Corno, 1989, p. 114)

Corno (1989) also analyzed what students would need to be taught to increase their volitional capabilities: They need to learn to control their attention to the task at hand, and especially to shield that attention from distractions in the environment, since schools are filled with distractions, from the antics of the class clown to the sounds of bell signals pertaining to other classrooms. How can this be accomplished?

One way is by teaching children to generate verbal self-instructions to attend to a task (e.g., Meichenbaum, 1977; see Chapter 7, this book, for extensive discussion of Meichenbaum's work and other self-instructional research). Students need to learn how to manage their study—for instance, knowing when to take much-needed breaks versus when to push on. Often, difficulty with an academic task is accompanied by emotional responses. Such responses need to be suppressed, for anxiety and distress can disrupt information processing. Often this also can be accomplished by teaching students to instruct themselves to remain calm and task focused (e.g., I can't worry about this, I can't get irrational; Corno, 1989, p. 120). Students need to learn how to motivate themselves if they begin to become discouraged. This can be accomplished by teaching them to review the dire consequences of failures and the rewards of successful task completion. Students can also be taught to self-verbalize encouragements (Corno, 1989), such as "I know this material, and I'll succeed next time," or to think of new strategies for reviewing the material on a next round (e.g., "This time I'm going to reread closely and take notes").

In addition to controlling themselves, good students learn to control their environments. Thus, if there are environmental distractions, one can move to a less distracting environment. If "bothered" by the poor lighting in a room, students can learn to take action to overcome the problem, such as fetching a lamp from another room or moving over to the window and taking advantage of sunlight. In short, students can learn strategies that will keep them focused on their ongoing work (see Corno & Kanfer, 1993, for an extensive discussion).

Much of the research on cognitive self-instruction during academic tasks is aimed specifically at volition, with a number of examples of self-instruction in chapters to follow. Classroom teachers' modeling of strategies for maintaining task persistence is an important starting point; for students who are especially distractible, explicit instruction to cue themselves in particular ways when they are at risk for distraction (e.g., in a noisy environment) can be extremely helpful. Much more work on the encouragement of volition is required, however. The research to date suggests there is great potential for increasing volition of students—the well-documented distractibility of many students (e.g., Messer, 1976) makes clear that there is also a need.

Informing Teachers About How to Motivate Students

This section has been about what can be done to enhance academic motivation in classrooms. One question that probably occurred to most readers is why teachers do not use these approaches already. An hypothesis offered by Brophy (1986, 1987) is that many teachers do not understand all that they could do and need to do to maximize motivation in their classrooms (for an example of a group of teachers who did not, see Newby, 1991). Thus, Brophy hypothesized that a profitable way to improve motivation in school would be to teach teachers the many tactics for increasing motivation that have been validated in various types of basic research. Brophy then proposed his own "greatest hits" list of motivational interventions, ones most defensible from classic conceptions of motivation. To motivate students, teachers should do the following according to Brophy:

- Model interest in learning: Teachers should let students know they like learning (e.g., reading, writing, problem solving) and find academic activities rewarding and generally satisfying.
- Communicate to students that there is plenty of reason to be enthusiastic about what is going on in school.
- Classrooms should be low-anxiety places.
- Send the message that what is occurring in school deserves intense attention.
- Induce curiosity and suspense.
- Make abstract material more personal, concrete, and familiar.
- Let students know the learning objectives—provide them with advance information about upcoming content.
- Provide informative feedback to students (e.g., feedback in the form of praise, as discussed in the last subsection).
- Adapt tasks to student interests as much as possible.
- Offer students choices between alternative tasks or alternative ways of learning content.

- Provide novel input as much as possible.
- Design instructional tasks to allow as much student autonomy as possible.
- Design tasks so there is opportunity for activity.
- Design learning tasks that produce a product (e.g., a class book).
- Include games as part of learning.

Brophy (1986, 1987) emphasized that simply attempting to add these components to instruction would do little good in the absence of other considerations, including some already encountered in this book:

- In general, classrooms should be orderly and well managed.
- Content should be at an appropriate level of content, not too easy, but not so difficult that most students will not be able to meet task demands with reasonable effort.
- What is being taught should be worth learning.
- A teacher's repertoire of motivational devices is extensive enough so that none must be used so frequently that it becomes "old hat."

In short, Brophy recognizes that effective instruction is not informed simply by one or even a few perspectives but by many traditions, including in this case motivational theories and research, research on classroom management, and understanding of age-appropriate and grade-appropriate curricula. Brophy's perspective is congruent with most of the thinking in this chapter, with his particular contribution an emphasis on the many things that can be done, whereas other theorists and researchers have usually been more narrow in their focus, either interested in or believing in one or a few motivational mechanisms more than others.

Brophy (1987) discussed a preliminary study in which grade-7 and grade-8 social studies teachers were provided brief training in the various ways for making instruction more motivating. The teachers in the study used the motivational tactics they learned with one of their classes and continued to teach another section in their customary fashion. Although the positive effects of the intervention were not great, and the effects were obscured somewhat by teachers carrying over what they had learned about motivation into their "control" classes, the outcomes were in the right direction. We did not find the outcome reported by Brophy (1987) to compel the conclusion that teachers could translate a few hours of training in how to motivate students into dramatic achievement gains for students. The possibility that teachers can be stimulated to develop more motivating classrooms by providing them much more information about motivation deserves much additional study.

Summary

When discussing motivation, it is tempting to parse up the discussion into environmental versus cognitive influences on motivation. The message encountered repeatedly in this section, however, is that such parsing misses an important point: Classroom environments can have powerful effects on cognitive processes affecting motivation. Thus, we summarize the main points in this section by offering a sample set of relationships between educational environments and cognitive-motivational processes:

- Providing positive reinforcement can decrease long-term motivation if the reinforcement is presented in such a way that students infer they are working for rewards per se. If students believe they are working for tangible rewards, their efforts are likely to diminish if they no longer receive the rewards.
- Classrooms filled with praise and other rewards can motivate students in the long term, if the reinforcement is presented so as to be informative (e.g., flagging what the child did that was praiseworthy). Some forms of praise, such as claims that, "You are so smart," have the potential for undermining effort, if the recipient begins to attribute their success or lack of it to ability rather than effort (e.g., Barker & Graham, 1987; Meyer et al., 1979).
- Task-oriented (or cooperative or mastery-oriented) classrooms produce high self-esteem for a much higher proportion of children than do ego-oriented (or competitive or performance-oriented) classrooms, which, in turn, accounts in part for the greater motivation in task-oriented classrooms. Such classroom environments increase student expectancies of success if appropriate effort is exerted. Such classrooms also sig-

nal that intelligence is incremental rather than an entity that is fixed.
- The ego (competitive, performance) orientation of many classrooms probably does much to undermine intrinsic motivation to learn and naturally high expectations that one can do well, hence the declines in academic motivation and expectations with additional years of schooling.
- Attempts to make tasks more interesting must be engineered so that attention and other cognitive processes are not diverted to the high interest part of the presentation at the expense of the intended content.
- Classroom environments that encourage the attribution that high performance follows from effort expended on appropriate academic strategies increase student awareness of the utility of the strategic knowledge acquired in school and hence student motivation to use what they have learned.
- Classroom instruction that highlights when and where new knowledge is useful has the potential to increase metacognitive awareness about knowledge (including knowledge of strategies) and hence increase motivation to use knowledge on occasions when it would be useful.
- Teachers can encourage students to believe that they can do well in school and in life and hence affect the possible selves the children imagine.
- When teachers consistently require students to work on tasks that are just beyond their competence, there is high potential for students to develop the understanding that effort pays off—to develop high self-efficacy with respect to academic tasks. Presentation of appropriately matched tasks increases cognitive conflict and engagement, with the resolution of such conflict following cognitive effort likely to increase self-efficacy and long-term academic efforts.
- Students who are especially distractible can be taught to self-instruct themselves to initiate academic efforts and to stay on task (see Chapter 7)—that is, instruction can be designed so that even the most difficult students can regulate their cognitive efforts, so that they can be motivated learners with high volition.

We could go on proposing additional relationships between educational environments, cognition, and motivation. The point is that educational environments are designed explicitly to develop mind, and there are some types of input to mind that can result in great long-term motivation to maximize one's mental resources and other inputs that can undermine long-term cognitive efforts. The trick is to design instruction to take advantage of as many motivational mechanisms as possible.

Theorists who are interested in good information processing (see Chapter 1) and instruction that encourages good information processing have been especially intrigued by the instructional implications of contemporary research on motivation. Borkowski and colleagues (e.g., Borkowski et al., 1990) have been at the forefront of these efforts, with their attention to the motivation literature apparent in Borkowski and Muthukrishna's (1992) list of essential elements in good information processing. The good information processor

- Knows a large number of learning strategies.
- Understands when, where, and why these strategies are important.
- Selects and monitors strategies wisely and is extremely reflective and planful.
- Adheres to an incremental view regarding the growth of mind.
- Believes in carefully deployed effort.
- Is intrinsically motivated, task-oriented, and has mastery goals.
- Does not fear failure and, in fact, realizes that failure is essential for success and hence is not anxious about tests but sees them as learning opportunities.
- Has concrete, multiple images of "possible selves"—hoped-for selves in the near and distant future.
- Knows a great deal about many topics and has rapid access to that knowledge.
- Has a history of being supported in all of these characteristics by parents, school, and society at large. (p. 483, adapted slightly)

Thus, this version of the model introduced in Chapter 1 maintains the importance of strategies, metacognition, knowledge, and motivation but highlights motivation. In doing so, it makes clear that without high academic motivation, many students will not develop extensive repertoires of strategies, the metacognition required to regulate the strategies they do have, or other knowledge.

The work on motivation is as important as anything covered in this book. If the new knowledge about motivating students is used well, there is high potential for increasing the achievement of U.S. schoolchildren. Not to use this knowledge would be deplorable, for there is nothing more tragic than a 10-year-old who has given up on himself or herself as a learner. Unfortunately, we have many personal memories of 10-year-olds who are academically discouraged and despondent. There seems to exist the potential to change this situation; we've got to try.

CONCLUDING COMMENTS

There is a new look to academic motivation research. Weiner (1990) made this point by reviewing the content of chapters on motivation in the editions of the *Encyclopedia of Educational Research* published since 1941. Physiological mechanisms underlying motivation dominated in the 1940s and 1950s, with a little bit of Freud (e.g., defense mechanisms) and behaviorism mixed in. Drives and grand theories (e.g., psychoanalytic) dominated the 1960s, with motivation in relation to the cognitive processes of learning, perception, and memory showing up in 1969. By 1982, about one-third of the chapters were concerned with issues covered in this chapter, with contributions on attribution theory, self-esteem, and reinforcement theory. The 1990 volume featured chapters on cognition, including causal attributions, self-efficacy, and learned helplessness. There were also chapters on environmental determinants of motivation, including cooperative and competitive structures, intrinsic and extrinsic rewards, and praise. Our reading of the 1990 volume makes us confident that what is presented here captures well much of the contemporary thinking on academic motivation.

We emphasize in closing that as we reflected on the data that informed this chapter, the case in favor of the perspective common to the writing of Dweck, Nicholls, Borkowski, and Ames is strong. There is a lot of evidence that one of the biggest problems with respect to reforming school so that it is more motivating is that Americans are caught up with rank ordering themselves and others. Whenever we talk with educators about restructuring their classrooms to enhance motivation, there is a terrible specter that always enters the conversation: report cards. The idea that everyone could make an "A" if every student was making progress just does not fit well with the evaluation system that is in place in American schools. Somehow it is seen as un-American or un-ethical or un-something not to rank order students. If Nicholls, Borkowski, Dweck, and Ames are right—and we think they are—we have a perspective on education (one that seems to pervade the nation) that is not only damaging to large numbers of individual children, but also to the United States as a whole. If it were possible to kill the obsession that classrooms always have a few "A" students, a few more "B" students, mostly "C" students, and a few who trail the pack, a lot of new life might be breathed into American students and schools. Powerful and revolutionary ideas are emerging from the careful scientific work conducted by the likes of Borkowski, Dweck, Nicholls, and Ames. We hope some readers of this book choose to join the revolution, either as researchers extending these ideas or as educators translating them into practice.

Biological Foundations

Methods in Biologically Oriented Research on Intellect
Psychophysiological Indicators of Intellectual Functioning
New Directions in Neurological Assessment

Neurological Foundations of Cognition, Learning, and Behavior
Neurological Development Following Birth
Physical Growth
Myelination
Development of Frontal Lobes
Concluding Comments

Biologically Determined Biases and Constraints in Cognition, Learning, and Behavior
Biological Preparedness for Particular Acquisitions
Biological Preparedness for Language
Biologically Determined Constraints in Cognitive Capacity
Biological Constraints on Intelligence and Academic Achievement
Concluding Comments About Biologically Determined Biases
and Constraints

How Contemporary Methods Are Increasing Understanding of the Biological Foundations of Academic Competence
Biological Studies of Reading
Biological Determination of Academic Dysfunctions

Biologically Determined Disruptions of Normal Development
Teratogens
Malnutrition
Neurological Injury and Trauma Early in Life

Just as there have been enormous increases in study of academic motivation during the last 15 years, there have also been enormous increases in understanding of thinking–human biology linkages. New methods have permitted measurement of mental processes not possible previously. In particular, these methods have allowed documentation of the dynamics of neurological development, especially during early childhood. The chapter includes summaries of many lines of research providing insights into important aspects of academic cognition, including reading. Nature-nurture is considered from the perspective of sophisticated behavior genetics models. The interactive roles of nature and nurture are explored specifically with respect to disruptions of development owing to environmental impacts on biological systems and the likelihood that gender differences in cognition are due to biological or environmental factors or both.

Although this chapter is concerned explicitly with biological factors that affect learning and cognition, what will become evident as it unfolds is that biology and environment are completely intertwined in determining learning. Biological potential can never be realized without relevant environmental input. The chapter begins with an overview of methods used by researchers to understand biology and its affects on learning and cognition. Then it moves on to sections detailing biological development and biological biases as determinants of intellectual functioning, followed by a section devoted to biological factors affecting specific academic competencies

(e.g., reading). The chapter concludes with three sections on extremely important problems in biological psychology related to education: the effects of disease on cognitive functioning, potential gender differences in intellect, and potential biologically determined modules of mind.

METHODS IN BIOLOGICALLY ORIENTED RESEARCH ON INTELLECT

Some biological methods have been used for a long time and are common in psychological studies. Others represent the cutting edge in the assessment of mind.

Psychophysiological Indicators of Intellectual Functioning

Typically, biologically oriented research psychologists rely on a variety of psychophysiological measurements that are revealing about basic neurological functioning. The first one to be described here is simple: Jensen and colleagues have been studying a simple form of **choice reaction time.** The subject sits in front of a panel with a 180-degree arc of lights (one, two, four, or eight lights, depending on the particular study). Below each light is a button. The subject's finger rests on a "home" button at the bottom and center of the arc. The task is to move as quickly as possible from the home button to the button next to a light on the arc as soon as the arc light comes on. Thus, the subject is touching the home button as one light of the arc comes on; the subject leaves the home button and quickly pushes the button adjacent to the lit arc light. Although a number of dependent variables can be extracted from such reactions, an important one is the subject's mean reaction time (i.e., time taken on average to depress the correct button once a light comes on). Jensen (see 1982, 1992) and colleagues have consistently obtained correlations between IQ (see Chapter 16) and mean choice reaction time (i.e., *r* often in the 0.3 to 0.4 range), documenting that more intelligent people react more quickly. One variation of the paradigm that is more complex involves three lights coming on, with two closer together than the third "odd-man-out" light. The subject's task is to hit the button adjacent to the odd-man-out light. This more complex variation produces correlations with intelligence measures in the 0.6 range (Frearson & Eysenck, 1986).

How could being quicker influence intelligence? Jensen's answer (see also Vernon, 1987) is **neural efficiency theory.** Recall that all conscious processing occurs in limited-capacity, short-term memory. Slow processes consume more capacity than do fast processes. Thus, those who process more quickly have greater functional capacity because they can perform more processes given the limited capacity they have. An important prediction from neural efficiency theory is that any capacity-demanding task should seem less demanding for intelligent compared with less intelligent people (e.g., note the position emission tomography [PET] scan correlations with intelligence that will be reported in a subsequent subsection of this chapter).

Other psychophysiological reaction time data support the conclusion that there are correlations between speed of information processing and psychometric intelligence and thus corroborate neural efficiency theory. For example, (1) Vernon (see 1991) is studying individual differences in **nerve conduction velocity,** with differences in conduction speed taken using electrodes attached to the arm. His initial studies are reporting correlations of 0.4 and better between this measure of the speed of information processing and psychometric intelligence. (2) In the Sternberg (1966, 1969) task, subjects are presented between one and seven digits to hold in short-term memory followed by a single digit, with the subject asked to decide whether the single digit is one of the numbers in short-term storage. More intelligent sub-

jects perform this **short-term memory scanning** task more rapidly than less intelligent subjects (e.g., Keating & Bobbitt, 1978; see Vernon, 1990a, 1990b for reviews). (3) In Posner's (1969) task, subjects are presented pairs of letters that are physically identical (AA, BB, aa, bb), semantically identical (Aa, bB), or different (AB, ab, Ab, aB). They must decide whether the letters presented are the same or different. Letters differing physically and semantically can be judged using recognition processes, whereas semantically identical letters require some retrieval of semantic information from long-term memory. The difference in reaction time for semantically identical pairs and semantically or physically different pairs is a measure of **speed of retrieval from long-term memory.** Again, more intelligent people retrieve information more quickly from long-term memory than less intelligent people. Some of the more complex variations on this paradigm can produce reaction time–intelligence correlations over 0.6 (Vernon [1990a] reviews this issue).

Some of the best-known work supporting neural efficiency theory involves one of the best-known psychophysical measures, the **electroencephalogram (EEG).** An EEG is an assessment of the electrical activity of the brain as detected by electrodes attached to the scalp (e.g., Marshall-Goodell, Tassinary, & Cacioppo, 1990) as a person performs various tasks. Correlations between such electrical activity and psychometric intelligence have been reported a number of times, although these tend not to be simple relationships (see Carlson & Widaman, 1987; Eysenck, 1987). For instance, relationships have been demonstrated between intelligence and what Jensen, Schafer, and Crinella (1981) referred to as "neural adaptability," which is producing greater electrical activity in reaction to an unexpected than to an expected stimulus, which represents efficient processing in that more processing should occur to comprehend a new compared with an old stimulus. Hendrickson and Hendrickson (e.g., 1980) have used EEG data to measure differences in ability to transmit error-free electrical impulses in reaction to stimuli, which they consider an indicator of the efficiency of the nervous system. They have reported correlations greater than 0.8 between their measures of brain efficiency and psychometric intelligence.

In short, there are multiple psychophysiological indicators (i.e., reaction time, nerve conduction rate,

EEG, pupil dilation) pointing to individual differences in the efficiency of basic information processing in humans, differences in processing that, in turn, are related to global intelligence. Studies assessing the heritability of speed of processing differences that are related to differences in intelligence (Baker, Vernon, & Ho, 1991; Ho, Baker, & Decker, 1988) have produced data consistent with the conclusion that speed of processing differences are highly heritable and that the association between speed of processing and intelligence is probably due to inherited common factors underlying both processing speed and intelligence. (A discussion about how psychologists study the heritability of intelligence and other characteristics is presented later in this chapter.)

We expect much more such work as psychologists continue to probe potential linkages between biological competence, developmental changes in biology, and intelligence. We also expect more research on the biological determinants of individual differences in memory, language, and other complex competencies, including propensity to monitor one's processing. For the moment, we remind readers that from the outset of this book, we have emphasized the need for a healthy nervous system if a person is to be a good information processor, including relatively large functional short-term capacity, which is largely determined by the efficiency of information processing. Work like that conducted by Jensen and colleagues supports these basic tenets of good information processing theory.

New Directions in Neurological Assessment

A variety of modern tools are being used in investigations of linkages between biology and thinking (Figure 6.1). **Computed tomography (CT** scanning) is a technology that involves x-ray beams projected

Figure 6.1 New methods of imaging are permitting much more analytical study of brain structures and functions than was possible in the past.

through the head from different angles, with the beams received by x-ray detectors on the opposite side of the head from where the x-ray is currently being projected. The x-ray detectors feed the input into computer programs, with the end result being x-ray images of sections of the brain (i.e., cross sections). These sections permit distinction between gray and white matter, with many structures within the brain distinguishable.

Positron emission tomography (PET scans) is an exceptionally important tool in studies of cognitive processing. As with CT scanning, x-rays are taken by rotating the camera around the head, producing images from a number of different angles. With PET scanning, however, the subject has either been injected with or has inhaled a substance that emits radiation. When neurons are active, they metabolize glucose. Some substances that emit radiation, such as radioactive fluorine, can bind with one of the products of metabolized glucose that accumulate in the active brain cells. The PET scan then detects the radiation being emitted from the active sites. The result is an image that literally glows. Because the PET scan is able to produce a number of cross sections of the head, it is possible to map out in some detail the location of conscious processing. That is, although CT scans can provide only information about brain **structures**, with PET scans, there is the possibility of generating information about brain **functions**.

As a research tool, PET scanning is being used to determine the parts of the brain that are active in reaction to particular types of sensory and psychological stimulation. For example, studies have been conducted determining that different regions of the brain are activated by simple compared with complex visual stimulation. Other studies have established the parts of the brain affected by listening to complex auditory input, such as a story, as well as the parts of the brain affected by various types of dementia (e.g., Phelps, Mazziotta, and Huang, 1982; Risberg, 1986; Vernon, 1991). In Haier et al. (1988), PET scans were made as subjects worked problems that appear on intelligence assessments. In Parks et al. (1988), PET scans were made as subjects performed verbal fluency items. There were clear correlations in these last two studies between brain activity as measured in the PET scans and performance on the intelligence test items. The interesting finding

was that less glucose was metabolized by the subjects who solved more problems and answered more verbal items. That is, more intelligent subjects exerted less intellectual effort to do the test items. As Vernon (1991) concluded: "Persons of higher intelligence can solve . . . more complex . . . problems . . . than can persons of lower intelligence, and expend less energy in the process" (p. 391).

Magnetic resonance imaging (MRI) is a further advance in CT, one permitting exploration of neurological structures with higher resolution than permitted by PET scans. This method involves placing the brain in strong magnetic fields (i.e., a person lies in the machine for about 15 minutes). Changes in the orientations of atomic nuclei in the molecules of the brain are induced and measured (Churchland & Sejnowski, 1992, Chapter 7). The precise measurement provided by MRI is permitting psychologists to resolve some old debates about intelligence. For example, MRI data are informing debates on the relationship of brain size to intelligence: Willerman, Schultz, Rutledge, and Bigler (1991) obtained a correlation of 0.41 between brain size as measured by MRI and psychometric intelligence, with other factors appropriately controlled in the calculation of this correlation.

Since the middle of the 19th century, there have been students of the brain who have postulated that particular functions are localized in particular parts of the brain–for example, Broca's 1864 claim after discovering left-hemisphere lesions during autopsies of the brains of people with verbal difficulties: *"Nous parlons avec l'hemisphere gauche"* (Kandel, 1991, p. 10; translation: "We speak with the left hemisphere"). Technology now exists to study in detail the anatomical regions involved in thinking by both healthy and injured brains, technology that can document the complex patterns of activation that undoubtedly underlie many functions. A great deal about the brain and how it functions is going to be learned as imaging research becomes more common. For example, although neural scientists have hypothesized for more than a century (e.g., J. Hughlings Jackson, who worked in the mid-19th century; Golden et al., 1992; Kosslyn & Koenig, 1992; McCarthy & Warrington, 1990) that complex cognitive functions involved interconnections between many parts of the brain, it is only as we approach the 21st Century that the technological (e.g., imaging techniques) and conceptual (e.g., connectionist theories;

see Chapter 3) machinery has existed to study how the brain does complex things. Some of the wonders that we have known about for some time will undoubtedly be understood better in the decades ahead.

NEUROLOGICAL FOUNDATIONS OF COGNITION, LEARNING, AND BEHAVIOR

There has been enormous progress in understanding connections between neurological development, thinking, and performance. We summarize in this section some of the most important relationships between neurology and learning. Command of this small amount of knowledge can go a long way in understanding neurological ideas relevant to education. For those readers, however, who desire more detailed coverage, we strongly recommend Brown, Hopkins, and Keynes (1991); Goldman-Rakic, Isseroff, Schwartz, and Bugbee (1983); Johnson (1993); Martinez and Kestner (1991); and Parmelee and Sigman (1983), all of which informed the discussion presented here.

Human neurology begins as a single layer of cells lining the neural tube (Goldman-Rakic et al., 1983) (Figure 6.2). These cells proliferate through normal cell division at an extremely rapid rate: At some points during development, approximately 48,000 new nerve cells are formed every second (Diamond, 1992). Through processes not completely understood, neural cells migrate to destinations corresponding to the beginnings of various parts of the nervous system. Most neurons are formed and have moved to their destinations by birth (Konner, 1991),

with many of them making the migration long before birth. Once this period of **neurogenesis** is concluded, there will be no new neurons. Any that are lost owing to disease, injury, or normal death will not be replaced.

Axons and dendrites appear once neurons have migrated to their designated locations. Each nerve cell normally has one **axon,** which conducts impulses away from the cell body. **Dendrites** are branchlike extensions of the cell body that transmit impulses toward the cell body from other cells. Eventually, **synaptic connections** between neurons are established. These connections involve an axon meeting a dendrite, a cell body, or another axon. Once the physical connections are formed, there can be development of physical and chemical characteristics that permit transmission of impulses (Gibson & Petersen, 1991). If that occurs, transmissions from a nerve cell to other cells can be sent via the synapses involving the axon for the cell (Gardner, 1975, Chapter 3).

Although the basic neuroanatomical structures that compose the human nervous system are in place by about 8 weeks following fertilization (Gardner, 1975, Chapter 9), human newborns are neurologically immature (Gibson, 1991a, 1991b), with substantial development of human neurological comp following birth.

Neurological Development Following Birth

Three-fourths of brain development occurs following birth, even though all of the neurons a person will ever have have been formed (Prechtl, 1986).

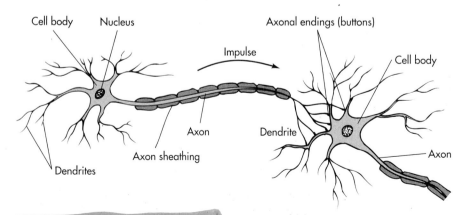

Figure 6.2 A nerve cell with its parts labeled.

Neurons take a long time to mature (Gibson & Petersen, 1991). With maturity, there are changes in the dendrites and the axons. Dendrites start out as short, tubular, and unbranched. With development, they become longer and have many branches. The longer and more numerous the branches, the more sources that potentially can stimulate the dendrites and thus result in transmissions to the nerve cell (e.g., Diamond, 1992). Neuronal cell functioning is increasingly more adaptive and flexible with increasing dendritic arborization.

As the dendrites are branching, the axons acquire a layer of axon sheathing. This permits more rapid firing of the axons and much greater specificity of firing. It then takes less stimulation for a myelinized axon to fire, and the recovery period between firings decreases.

Other structures that support the functioning of the nervous system are maturing at the same time (e.g., blood vessels). One type of cell that becomes more evident during this period, **glial cells,** is particularly interesting. Glial cells provide nourishment to neurons and thus are critical to the functioning of the central nervous system (Diamond, Scheibel, Murphy, & Harvey, 1985).

There are some forms of experience that the brain is genetically programmed to expect. Some areas of specialization in the brain correspond to perceptual systems (visual, haptic, gustatory, olfactory); others to affective systems, cognitive capacities, or linguistic competencies (Anastasiow, 1990; Fodor, 1983; Panksepp, 1986). One mechanism of genetic preparedness is the generation of **experience-expectant synapses** (Greenough & Juraska, 1986), with a proliferation of these 2 to 3 months following birth. Experience-expectant synapses for the visual system are sensitive to light; those corresponding to hearing are sensitive to auditory input. When relevant stimulation is encountered, neurons are activated and their functioning results in the establishment of permanent synaptic connections with other neurons. Experience-expectant synapses that do not stabilize die off—they are pruned (see Anastasiow, 1990, for a review of evidence pertaining to these conclusions; Black & Greenough, 1991; Crutcher, 1991). The existence of experience-expectant synapses makes clear that there can be simultaneous biological predetermination of learning and environmental determination of learning: Each member of a species is programmed to be sensitive to particular types of input,

but learning occurs only if that input is experienced. In general, experience-expectant synapses either stabilize or die off during **critical periods.** For the sensory systems, these critical periods tend to be early in life (Greenough, Black, & Wallace, 1987).

Other synapses, **experience-dependent synapses** (Greenough & Juraska, 1986), are not genetically predetermined. Instead, they stabilize in reaction to unique environmental stimulation that an individual encounters. The environment provides "unexpected" input to the organism that can be learned because of the possibility of stabilizing experience-dependent synapses. These types of synapses can be stabilized at any time during life (Anastasiow, 1990).

In addition to pruning of synapses (Gibson, 1991b; Gibson & Petersen, 1991), there also is substantial death of neurons during this early period of life. In fact, half of the neurons a person generates before birth have already died by the time birth occurs. Up to half of the remaining neurons in some sites of the brain die within a few years after birth (Crutcher, 1991; Diamond, 1992; Oppenheim, 1981; Shonkoff & Marshall, 1990). Such death is genetically preprogrammed for the most part, with the cells that are eliminated not critical to later functioning (e.g., Gardner, 1975, p. 183). In fact, it is likely that elimination of excess synapses and nerve cells is necessary for cognitive development to proceed to maturity (Goldman-Rakic, 1987).

The remainder of this section is concerned with three additional ways that the central nervous system matures (i.e., besides physical growth of neurons, formation of synapses, and pruning of excess synapses and neurons). Two of these additional mechanisms are global—physical growth and myelination; the third involves development of a particular region of the brain that is the contemporary focus of intensive investigations because of its probable contributions to self-regulation, with discussion of this region important in this book, for good information processing is self-regulated cognition if it is anything.

Physical Growth

There are striking changes in brain structure and function in the 2 years following birth (Konner, 1991). For instance, between birth and age 1, the brain doubles in volume. By age 1, it is a little more than half the size of an adult brain. The growth rate continues to be high during year 2.

The work of Marian Diamond (e.g., 1991) and colleagues with rats suggests that experience can play a large role in this physical development of the brain. They have conducted a number of experiments in which rats (from pups to "elderly" rats) have either received environmental enrichment (e.g., objects to explore, climb, and sniff) or they have not. In general, environmental enrichment has increased the size of the brain and in particular cortical thickness. Enrichment also increases dendritic branching and the number of the dendritic spines. It promotes proliferation of capillaries, increasing blood flow in the brain. The growth of glial-type cells also is stimulated by appropriate environmental stimulation (Diamond, 1992; Greenough, 1993).

Does enrichment as Diamond has defined it make a difference in learning? Diamond (1991, p. 117) concluded: "At every age at which they have been tested, enriched rats have run a maze better than the nonenriched animals." This, of course, parallels the finding that the physical size of the brain can be affected by experience across the rat's life span. In summary, M. Diamond and other researchers have amassed considerable evidence that the brain is plastic (at least in the case of rats), that its fundamental physical properties, including size and number of synaptic connections, varies with environmental stimulation.

Myelination

Myelin is a fatty sheath that insulates both peripheral and central nerve fibers in mammals (Konner, 1991). This sheath permits rapid conduction of impulses Myelination begins before birth in humans. Myelination continues for many years in humans, however, at least until adolescence and may do so until 30 years of age. In general, myelination occurs first in the inner areas of the cortex and later in the outer cortical areas.

The importance of myelination is obvious when it is lost owing either to disease or an intentional experimental manipulation (Konner, 1991): Impulse speed is slowed. It takes longer for a nerve cell to recover after firing (i.e., the latency between firings is greater). Conduction failures are more frequent. There is an increased likelihood of inadvertent electrical effects from neighboring axons. There is greater risk of dysfunction owing to mechanical and thermal factors as well as other stimulation. When myelin is reacquired, cell functioning returns to nor-

mal. In short, the evidence that myelination affects neural cell functioning is strong.

The evidence is also strongly suggestive (i.e., it cannot be definitive because other changes are correlated with myelination) that myelination makes a difference at grosser levels than the cell level (Konner, 1991). For example, just before birth, major neurons affecting vision are myelinated; there is rapid development of visual capability during this same period. Parts of the cerebral cortex concerned with hearing achieve myelination during the first 2 years of life, with myelination in these centers paralleling the development of language.

Development of Frontal Lobes

The frontal lobes are especially critical with respect to self-regulation and self-control, which are key as part of the development of good information processing. There are massive developments in these lobes during the first 2 years of life, including thickening, synaptic branching and connecting, and myelinization.

There also are corresponding changes in behavioral functioning, with the work of Adele Diamond (e.g., 1990a, 1990c, 1991) and colleagues especially illuminating with respect to relationships between frontal lobe development and cognitive functioning. The abilities of infants to relate information over space or time to solve simple problems (e.g., find a object just hidden from them) improves dramatically as the frontal lobes mature. In addition, there are increases in the ability to inhibit dominant responses when they are not appropriate (see Dempster [1992] for an expansive essay on the importance of inhibition in cognition across the life span; also Bjorklund & Harnishfeger, 1990). Both spatial-temporal integration and dominant response integration are key components in self-regulation and hence the development of self-regulative capabilities during the first 2 years of development. We expect that many intricate linkages between development of the frontal lobes and development of thinking and learning skills will be mapped out as researchers continue to study development of the frontal lobes in the early days and months of life.

Concluding Comments

With changes in neurological capacity, ones owing either to experience or normal development, there are changes in cognitive capabilities. All of the data discussed here suggest close linkages between neurological and psychological development during infancy. The importance of biology as a determinant of thinking, learning, and performance is apparent especially when something goes wrong, which is taken up later in this chapter.

One of the values of the type of research reviewed in this section is that it has helped in understanding some interventions that can prevent development from going terribly wrong. One famous example makes this point dramatically.

Some children are born with the inability to metabolize the amino acid phenylalanine. (Children with this deficiency have come to be known as PKU babies.) This is a problem because greater than normal amounts of phenylalanine can cause severe neurological damage. There is at least a partial cure, however. First, determine at birth whether a child lacks the capacity to break down phenylalanine, which can be done with a simple urine test. The diets of PKU children are then strictly controlled so that they ingest only a small amount of phenylalanine. If PKU is not detected until 3 years of age, intervention does little good, however, with profound retardation the outcome (see Zigler & Hodapp, 1986, Chapter 9, for a review). When dietary control commences shortly after birth, general intelligence seems to be impaired little, although there is evidence of subtle impairments in executive functioning (i.e., self-regulation of cognition; Welsh, Pennington, Ozonoff, Rouse, & McCabe, 1990), presumably because of subtle dysfunctions in the frontal lobes (see the discussion of the role of the frontal lobes in cognition presented earlier in this section). With increasing age, less strict dietary control is necessary (Scarr & Kidd, 1983); nonetheless, with increasing evidence that high levels of phenylalanine can produce damage even in later childhood, dietary controls are only relaxed and not eliminated (Stern, 1985).

Why so much damage if the disorder is not identified early in life and less need to control the diet later in life? The myelinated nervous system is much more resistant to the biological assault from high levels of phenylalanine than is the nervous system that is not yet myelinated. Moreover, the first several years of life are characterized by enormous growth in the central nervous system. During periods of growth, biological systems are much more vulnerable than at other times. Unfortunately, not all biolog-

ical risks are so easily handled as PKU, apparent from work reviewed later in this chapter.

BIOLOGICALLY DETERMINED BIASES AND CONSTRAINTS IN COGNITION, LEARNING, AND BEHAVIOR

There are many similarities in the knowledge that all people acquire and the things that people can do. The most likely explanation of human universals is that biology prepares humans to attend to some information more than other information and to be able to do some things and not others. Of course, this is an idea consistent with the earlier argument that there are experience-expectant synapses and with an argument that will be advanced later in this chapter, that there are modules of competencies sensitive to particular modes of input. Another possibility is that biological competencies constrain what can be learned. The credibility of both of these perspectives is taken up in this section.

Biological Preparedness for Particular Acquisitions

Seligman and Hager (1972) and others (e.g., Foree & Lolordo, 1973) advanced the theory that organisms are biologically prepared to emit some responses and learn some associations more easily than others. An example of biologically-mediated associative learning is that taste aversions to poisonous foods seem to be acquired easily by humans. This form of classical conditioning is the famous "sauce bernaise" effect (Seligman & Hager, 1972): Nausea shortly after eating a preferred food (e.g., sauce bernaise) can produce aversion to that food for a long time. Humans have evolved to avoid foods that make them sick because it often is dangerous to eat sickening food, and doing so reduces the likelihood that one will survive long enough to parent offspring who will carry one's genes into the future.

There is little doubt that from early in life (probably from birth), humans can learn some associations via classical conditioning readily (Lipsitt, 1990). Thus, if a puff of air to the eyelid, which elicits an unconditioned eyelid blinking response, is preceded consistently by a tone, which by itself has no capacity to elicit eye blinking, the tone alone eventually will come to elicit eye blinking. This ability to acquire conditioned blinking is inherited as part of the genetic blueprint for humanness; humans have evolved to be so readily conditioned to blink eyes because blinking before something hits the eye prevents injury of a critical sensory organ and thus increases the likelihood that the blinker will survive long enough to reproduce.

One possibility is that at least some biological preparedness may decrease with advancing age. This is because with advancing age, some forms of classical conditioning (e.g., eyelid conditioning) are much less certain than they were earlier in life (Woodruff-Pak, Logan, & Thompson, 1990) owing to neurological decline. From a biological perspective, this is an understandable development because what counts is preserving the young organism; once an organism is past the age of reproduction, there is less biological need for the organism's survival.

Biological Preparedness for Language

Biological preparedness is not limited to acquisition of simple associations or basic perceptual processing. Indeed, the evidence is strong that humans are unique in being biologically prepared to learn the exceptionally complex systems of representation that constitute language (e.g., Chomsky, 1965, 1980).

Theory linking biology and language comprehension and learning have been supported by a variety of data (Maratsos, 1989): For example, left-hemisphere damage results in language disabilities, with particular sites in the left hemisphere associated with particular language difficulties (McCarthy & Warrington, 1990). Children acquire languages in many different settings and in many different cultures. Despite such biological determinism, however, language learning is also diverse. Maratsos (1989) specified many ways that languages vary across cultures. For example, different parts of sentences receive focus in different languages. Also, the constituents of sentences (e.g., agents and patients [objects]) are typically ordered in one way in some languages such as English and are not marked for order in other languages. Some variation in what humans can acquire makes clear that humans have the capacity to learn a range of language rules, a capacity that is certainly biologically determined.

Biologically Determined Constraints in Cognitive Capacity

A final biologically determined constraint is due to short-term capacity limitations (see the discussions of short-term memory in all previous chapters). In particular, it has been known since Baldwin (Hollander, 1920) that how much children can attend at any one time increases with development. Baldwin assumed that the increases in **attention span** were somehow tied to maturation of the nervous system and that the attention span constrained a child's cognitive development. Variations on this theme have recurred in the developmental psychology literatures, with the most recent versions offered by Pascual-Leone (1970) and Case (1985).

Case's version of attention span is called **executive processing space** and refers to the number of pieces of information a child can have active at any one time while working toward some cognitive goal. Much of this executive processing space is **short-term storage space**, which is specifically dedicated to maintaining the activated information in consciousness rather than other executive activities (i.e., manipulations of the information aimed at accomplishing some cognitive goal). Much of Case's (1985) book is concerned with demonstrating that children can only do tasks that do not require more executive processing space than the children have. At several points in this book, there will be expansion of Case's views on the role of short-term memory in cognition. At this point, note that Case and Pascual-Leone before him viewed such short-term memory constraint as determined at least in part by human biology.

Biological Constraints on Intelligence and Academic Achievement

Beginning with Galton's 19th century insight that distinguished people tend to be closely related to one another, psychologists have entertained the hypothesis that talents of various sorts—including high psychometric intelligence—are inherited. Such hypotheses have not been accepted uncritically, however. When two bright people marry and have children, they would be expected to create a different environment for their offspring than would a husband and wife of average intelligence. That intellectually superior people and talented people provide environmental opportunities to their children not available to other children logically could be the critical factor in stimulating the intelligence or talents of the offspring rather than biological advantages.

A subfield of both psychology and genetics has emerged to address questions of nature or nurture through analyses of behavioral similarities as a function of biological relatedness. **Behavior geneticists** use several different approaches to unravel the relative contributions of heredity and environment to individual differences in human characteristics. We review the two most common methodological approaches used by behavior geneticists and the conclusions about biological determination of intelligence emanating from these studies.

Twin Studies Identical twins have the same genes because the two children were produced by a division of the same fertilized egg (Figure 6.3). When identical twins are reared together (i.e., in the same family), their environments are also similar, perhaps as similar as any two persons' environments could be. Thus, the high correlations in intelligence between identical twins (i.e., usually 0.80 to 0.90 or higher) reared together cannot alone be revealing

Figure 6.3 These identical twins share exactly the same biological endowment. Not only do they look the same, but also their IQs are similar. Behavior geneticists have observed similarity in the IQs of identical twins even when they are reared apart, and they believe such similarity is powerful evidence for biological determination of individual differences in intelligence.

about genetic versus environmental determinants of intelligence.

Sometimes, however, identical twins are reared apart. In that case, their genes are identical but their environments differ. If genes determine intelligence, the correlation in intelligence between identical twins reared apart should remain high; to the degree that environment determines differences in intelligence, the correlation in intelligence should be lower for identical twins reared apart than the correlation for identical twins reared together.

Another comparison possibility is to look at fraternal twins reared together. Fraternal twins share one-half of their genes (i.e., they are the product of two different fertilized eggs). When they are reared in the same family, they should have roughly comparable environments. If the correlations in their IQs are lower than the IQ correlations for identical twins reared together, the case would be bolstered for genetic determination of environment. If the IQs of fraternals raised together approximated the IQs of identical twins reared together, the environmental hypothesis would be supported.

Summarizing over 19 studies involving more than 5000 pairs of twins, Loehlin and Nichols (1976) concluded that the average IQ of identical twins is 0.86, which is higher than the 0.62 IQ correlation for fraternal twins. Bouchard and McGue (1981) reviewed the world twin literature, which includes data on more than 10,000 twin pairs, and concluded that the average IQ correlation for identical twins is 0.86 and for fraternal twins is 0.60. Bouchard and McGue (1981) identified three IQ correlations involving identical twins reared apart, with the average correlation being 0.72.

Behavior geneticists use such data to calculate the **heritability** of intelligence or the fraction of observed variation in intelligence that is due to genetic variability (Plomin et al., 1990, Chapter 9). In general, they have concluded that roughly half of the variability in intelligence is due to genes. That genes matter is obvious from the higher correlations for identical than for fraternal twins. That environment matters also is obvious: The IQs of identical twins reared together are more similar than the IQs of identical twins reared apart.

Family and Adoption Studies In family and adoption studies, family members are thought of as sharing either heredity only (i.e., parents and their biological children living in other families), family environment only (i.e., parents and adopted children), or both heredity and family environment (i.e., parents and biological children living in the same household). In general, if genes determine individual differences in intelligence, correlations should be higher when there is shared heredity. If family environment determines individual differences in intelligence, there should be higher correlations when correlated pairs live in the same family environment. If both genes and environment matter, the highest correlations in intelligence between family members should occur when there is both shared heredity and family environment. Thus, if intelligence is inherited, the IQs of adopted children should correlate with the IQs of their biological parents more than with the IQs of their adoptive parents. If environment matters more than genes, the IQs of adopted children should correlate more highly with the IQs of the adoptive than the biological parents. If intelligence is determined by genes, there should be a higher correlation for the intelligences of children who are biological siblings (i.e., because they have 50 percent of their genes in common) than for the intelligence of siblings by adoption (i.e., because they have no genetic relationship to one another).

Bouchard and McGue's (1981) review provided a comprehensive analysis of the available data up until 1981. In support of the role of heredity as a determinant of individual differences in IQ are comparisons such as the following: (1) The IQ correlation for parents and their offsprings when reared in the home of their biological parents is 0.42. This contrasts to a 0.19 correlation between adopting parents and adoptees. (2) The IQ correlation for biological siblings reared together is 0.47. This contrasts with the IQ correlation for biological half-siblings (who share one-quarter of their genes) reared together of 0.31 and the IQ correlation for nonbiological siblings of 0.32. (3) Parents share half their genes with their offspring; biological siblings share half their genes. It is striking that the biological parent-offspring correlation of 0.42 is close in magnitude to the biological sibling correlation of 0.47.

The role of the environment in the determination of differences in IQ is supported by the following comparisons in Bouchard and McGue (1981): (1) The IQ correlation for biological siblings reared together is 0.47 compared with an IQ correlation for biological

siblings reared apart of 0.24. (2) The IQ correlation between biological parents and their children when they live together is 0.42 versus 0.22 when they do not live together. (3) Half-siblings and cousins both share one-quarter of their genes; the IQ correlation for half-siblings is 0.31 compared with a 0.15 correlation for cousins. (4) That the IQ correlation of 0.47 for biological siblings raised in the same family is the highest correlation in the nontwin family data is consistent with the overall conclusion that emerges from considering the differences just summarized: Both genes and family environment are important in determining individual differences in IQ. Using some extremely sophisticated statistical methods, Chipeur, Rovine, and Plomin (1990) determined from the twin and family/adoption data that 45 percent of the variance in IQ scores is determined by heredity.

Three aspects of the adoption data provide especially striking support for the effects of environment in determining individual differences in intelligence. (1) The correlation in intelligence between adopted siblings increases as they live together longer, from 0.00 to 0.25 over the first 4 years of life in Plomin, DeFries, and Fulker's (1988) study; the correlation in intelligences of adopted children and their adopting parents increases from 0 to 4 years of age as well, from about 0.1 to 0.2 in the Plomin et al. (1988) study. The longer adoptive families are together, the greater the correlations in intelligence.

(2) As children grow up, the family accounts for less of their environment as friends become more important, and children make progressively greater inroads into the world. Perhaps not surprisingly, the intelligence level of the adopting family is progressively less of a determinant of individual differences in intelligence of adoptees as adoptees move through childhood into adolescence and adulthood (Loehlin, Horn, & Willerman, 1989).

(3) In a number of adoption studies, children have been raised in families in which the family level of intelligence was higher than the biological family intelligence of the adoptee. The intelligence of the adoptees tends to be higher on average than the average intelligence expected based on biological/socioeconomic group of the biological parents, often closer to the average of the biological/socioeconomic group means for the adopting family. This is one of the most frequently cited pieces of evidence favoring the hypothesis that environment makes a

profound difference with respect to level of intellectual functioning. These effects are especially likely when the adoption occurs at an early age for the child (e.g., Scarr & Weinberg, 1976, 1983; Weinberg, Scarr, & Waldman, 1992; see Storfer, 1990, Chapter 4, for a review of the adoption data supportive of strong environmental effects of rearing environment). Even those critical of adoption studies, and who tend to favor environmental interpretations over genetic explanations of intelligence differences, admit, based on the adoption data, that there is probably a 10- to 12-point IQ advantage associated with rearing in a more favorable environment (see Locurto's [1990] review of the adoption study data).

Academic Achievement   Academic success is substantially heritable (Plomin et al., 1990): The school grades of identical twins correlate more highly than do the school grades of fraternal twins (Husén, 1959). Correlations on standardized academic achievement tests are higher for identical than fraternal twins (Loehlin & Nichols, 1976). If one twin is reading disabled, an identical twinmate is more likely to be reading disabled than a fraternal twinmate (Bakwin, 1973; Decker & Vandenberg, 1985; DeFries, Fulker, & LaBuda, 1987). Analyses of adoption data also suggest that reading ability is largely, but not completely, inherited (Cardon, DiLalla, Plomin, DeFries, & Fulker, 1990), although the adoption data also substantiate that success in school is determined in part by the quality of the adopting environment (e.g., Duyme, 1988).

More Evidence of Both Biological and Environmental Determinism   There are three additional pieces of evidence that support the position that environment plays an important role in determining individual differences in intelligence: (1) The degree of heritability of a trait such as intelligence varies with environment. (2) One's genes (i.e., **genotype**) specify a potential range of outcomes (i.e., a **reaction range** of **phenotypes**); where one ends up in that range depends on environment. (3) Intelligence can be increased by environmental manipulations. These points are important to make because there are many misunderstandings about the roles and potential roles of biology and environment in shaping intelligence:

1. Heritability varies with environment: Even if the heritability of intelligence for white populations is about 0.50 based on studies to date, it is entirely possible that with a shift in environment, the heritability of intelligence would change dramatically:

> Heritability describes a situation involving a particular phenotype with a certain array of genetic and environmental factors at a given time. Heritability does not indicate an eternal truth concerning the phenotype, for it can vary from population to population and from time to time. (Plomin et al., 1990, p. 232)

In particular, if the range of environments experienced by different members of a population increase, heritability will decrease. Heritability is increased to the degree that there are few environmental options for a population. Most emphatically, heritability indices generated under one set of environmental conditions do not generalize to other environmental conditions (see Scarr & Kidd, 1983, for discussion of all of these points).

2. Genotypes specify a range of possible phenotypes: Any given set of genes specifies a variety of outcomes depending on the environment. For example, recall the case of PKU discussed earlier in this chapter. If a child with the genetically determined inability to metabolize phenylalanine experiences a nutritional environment rich in phenylalanine, the result is severe retardation. If the child experiences a nutritional environment in which phenylalanine has been eliminated, normal intelligence is the outcome. That is, genes and environment interact to determine outcomes: There is a **reaction range** of **phenotypes** associated with each **genotype** (Gottesman, 1963; Lewontin, 1974; Scarr & Kidd, 1983).

The concept of reaction range is an important one for interventionists. The goal of the interventionist should be to do all possible to insure students, patients, or clients end up on the favorable end of their reaction ranges. Thus, with respect to IQ, educators should be doing all possible to make certain that their students are as close as possible to the top of their reaction range for intelligence. There has been substantial progress in understanding how to accomplish this goal.

3. Psychometric intelligence is increased by exposure to high quality educational environments (Ceci, 1991; see Chapter 11, this book): High-quality environmental manipulations at home

and preschool produce increases in measured intelligence (for an especially complete review, see Storfer, 1990, Chapter 10; also Chapter 11, this book).

Concluding Comments About Biological Determination of Intelligence   Explanations of individual differences in intelligence in terms of either genetics or environment are off the mark: We conclude, as do others (e.g., Fletcher, 1991), that there is no reason to continue such debates, for they do not map on to the theories advanced either by sophisticated geneticists or sophisticated environmentalists. Genes provide potential; whether a person's intelligence is at the high or low end of that range of potential depends on the environments encountered during development. Rather than accept low levels of achievement, it makes good sense to provide educational environments that encourage students to function nearer the upper boundary of their reaction range than they would in conventional environments.

Based on current behavior genetics methods, given current environments, individual differences in intelligence and academic ability are determined in part by genetic factors, with estimates of heritability typically in the 50 percent range. Readers should bear in mind in interpreting this figure that there have been important methodological criticisms of both twin studies and adoption studies (e.g., see Lewontin, Rose, & Kamin, 1984; Locurto, 1990; Plomin et al., 1990). For example, two key assumptions in twin studies are that identical twins reared apart experience different environments, whereas fraternal twins reared together experience similar environments (Goldberger, 1977; Grayson, 1989; Wilson, 1982). The former assumption is strained by analyses of twin studies revealing that the adopting families of separated identical twins often are similar in socioeconomic status to the biological families; the latter assumption is strained by fraternal twins that all of us know who seem to lead extremely different lives—even during childhood. In adoption studies, there is an assumption that a reasonable estimate can be made of what IQ would have been for an adopted child if the child had been reared in the birth environment. Such estimations are often difficult to make, however, because of incomplete knowledge of the psychometric intelligence of biological parents. Despite the methodological limitations of particular studies, there are, nonetheless, enough replications

of twin studies and adoption studies with similar results—and the conclusions emerging from twin and adoption data converge—that confidence is growing in the conclusions emanating from behavior genetics analyses, including the major conclusion from such studies that both genetics and environment contribute to the determination of individual differences in intelligence.

Concluding Comments About Biologically Determined Biases and Constraints

Human biology biases humans to attend to certain types of information over others, makes some learning more likely than others learnings, determines that some learning (e.g., acquisition of language) will almost certainly occur given exposure to any part of the human family, and constrains other learning and performance demands to those not exceeding short-term capacity. Also, intelligence in general is partly determined by biology. Even more subtle relationships between academic performances and biology have been validated, with some of these taken up in the next section.

HOW CONTEMPORARY METHODS ARE INCREASING UNDERSTANDING OF THE BIOLOGICAL FOUNDATIONS OF ACADEMIC COMPETENCE

Biological studies offer a tremendous opportunity to expand understanding of important academic competencies. Without a doubt, the greatest progress in analyzing the biological foundations of academic achievement has been with respect to reading.

Biological Studies of Reading

Reading researchers are using psychophysiological and radiological imaging in combination with artificial intelligence analyses to provide windows on reading processes that cannot be understood using more conventional research tactics. Some of the most pertinent brain imaging studies of reading were conducted by Posner, Petersen, and their colleagues (e.g., Petersen, Fox, Posner, Mintun, & Raichle, 1988;

Petersen, Fox, Snyder, & Raichle, 1990; Posner, Petersen, Fox, & Raichle,1988). These investigators made brain images under a number of different conditions, such as when their subjects were looking at a dot, passively and silently reading a word (or pseudoword), reading a word aloud, repeating a word that was read, generating an associate to a word (e.g., given *hammer,* responding with *pound*), or determining whether a word referred to a member of a particular class (i.e., Is this a dangerous animal?). By "subtracting" the activations caused by tasks requiring less complete processing from the activations caused by slightly more complex tasks (e.g., subtracting activation associated with looking at a dot from activation owing to silent, passive reading), it is possible to determine the parts of the brain implicated in various types of word processing tasks.

Posner and colleagues have observed that passive reading of familiar words stimulates processing in the back part of the brain, more in the right hemisphere than the left, in an area of the brain known to be implicated in pattern recognition. This is a sensible result, because passive reading involves recognition of visual patterns. Passive reading of real words also activates the left frontal lobe (known to be implicated in associative memory), although reading of pseudowords does not. This is also sensible because there is a meaning to associate to a real word but not a pseudoword, with meaningful verbal processes conceptualized more as left-brain activities by neuroscientists than as right-brain activities. Consistent with this interpretation, the left frontal lobe activation is also prominent when subjects are generating associations to real words or attempting to determine whether a word refers to a dangerous animal. (See Kosslyn and Koenig, 1992, for a nontechnical summary of the subtractive method and its use in reading research as well as additional discussion of the results produced by Posner, Petersen, and their co-workers.)

The new neuroscience is permitting analyses of brain function that potentially may validate models such as connectionist approaches to word recognition (see Chapter 3) as well as identify their deficiencies as explanations of reading. For example, neuroscience analyses to date (such as those provided by Posner and Petersen) suggest that familiar word recognition involves parts of the brain specialized for pattern recognition, spatial relatedness, and association (Kosslyn & Koenig, 1992, p. 179). Suffice to conclude here that cognitive neuroscience and artificial intelligence will both play a role in evaluation of some new and some old theories of reading.

Biological Determination of Academic Dysfunctions

Some students experience extreme difficulties in acquiring particular academic competencies that others acquire given normal schooling. Sometimes these difficulties reflect biological differences between these students and other people.

Dyslexia **Dyslexia** is the failure to learn to read despite substantial instructional attempts to teach reading (e.g., Farnham-Diggory, 1992, Chapter 2). There has been progress in identifying different types of dyslexia (see Caplan, 1992, Chapter 5; also Rayner & Pollatsek, 1989, Chapter 11). One important distinction is between **acquired dyslexia** resulting from some type of brain injury and **developmental dyslexia,** which involves otherwise normal children experiencing difficulties in reading that cannot be explained easily (e.g., they are not due to obvious brain injury, such as the acquired dyslexias). Within the acquired and developmental categories, there are subcategorizations. For example, acquired phonological dyslexics cannot sound out nonsense words but can read actual words they learned before they suffered brain injury; in contrast, acquired surface dyslexics can sound out pseudowords but cannot read words they knew before their injury; and acquired deep dyslexics sometimes misread a word by producing semantically related items (e.g., saying *table* when presented the word *chair*).

Developmental dyslexia is much more important for most educators than is acquired dyslexia. There are a variety of potential symptoms of developmental dyslexia: eye-scan patterns that appear erratic or at least do not match the normal pattern of fixations and predominantly forward saccades, difficulties with spatial orientation including confusing left and right elements in arrays, and better reading of upside-down text than right-side-up reading. The particular symptoms manifested by particular developmental dyslexics differ from student to student, however. The most important one, however, is poor word recognition and decoding during childhood, persisting throughout life in most cases (Bruck, 1990).

Scarborough (1990) reported that as early as 2 years of age, dyslexic children are evidencing language difficulties not observed in children who will become normal readers. At 2 and 3 years of age, children who will become dyslexic produce relatively short utterances, ones not as syntactically complex as other children. Their pronunciations tend to be less accurate. Their receptive vocabularies are not as well developed, and they have more difficulties providing labels for common objects than do normal children. In short, Scarborough's data suggest that dyslexia is part of a more general language-processing deficiency, consistent with the best-supported theory of the cause of developmental dyslexia (Vellutino, 1979).

Many possibilities were considered before a research-defensible conception of the causes of dyslexia were uncovered. Some of the historically prominent explanations of developmental dyslexia that have been discounted (see Gaddes, 1985, Chapter 8; also Rayner & Pollatsek, 1989, Chapter 11, for reviews) include the following: Dysfunctional eye movements do not cause dyslexia (i.e., they are symptoms rather than causes); general perceptual deficiencies do not cause developmental dyslexia (Vellutino, 1979); the hypothesis that dyslexia reflects a "maturational lag" has failed; and the evidence favoring claims of an underdeveloped left hemisphere (claims beginning with Orton, 1925, 1926, 1937) are not well supported. Other studies using sophisticated methodological advances in neuropsychology (e.g., PET scans) as well as studies using old methods, such as autopsies, have provided evidence of physiological differences between developmental dyslexics and normal readers: Left-hemisphere activity (as reflected in brain imagery studies) is not as predictable in dyslexics as in normals. Abnormal tissue growth in the brain, especially in the left hemisphere, has been documented (see Galaburda, 1983). Taken as a whole, the best available evidence suggests that the probable cause of developmental dyslexia in many cases is a physiological difference or differences in the left hemisphere, ones translating into generalized verbal deficiencies (Scarborough, 1990; Vellutino, 1979). Among the various verbal abilities, the phonological processes implicated in decoding print to sound seem to be especially problematic for dyslexics (Rack, Snowling, & Olson, 1992). This conception of dyslexia is, in turn, stimulating research to identify the genetic underpinnings of such brain differences (e.g., claims that differences between dyslexics and normals on chromosome 15 might be responsible for the physiological differences; Smith, Kimberling, Pennington, & Lubs, 1983).

Disorders in Mathematics Competency Neuroscientists are increasingly interested in mathematical thinking skills. Some physiological psychologists have studied patients who have lost their capacity to calculate because of head injury or disease, who manifest **acquired dyscalculia.** McCloskey (1992) in particular has been attempting to validate a model of calculation consistent with the good information processor perspective favored in this book. McCloskey posits that calculation involves both knowledge of arithmetic facts and calculation procedures. To calculate, people must be able both to comprehend numbers and to produce them. Comprehension mechanisms translate numbers into internal representations, which can be operated on by mathematical procedures. The results of these procedures can be communicated to the outside world only if the person also has intact numerical production capabilities. The model specifies a number of complexities with respect both to comprehension and to production. Thus, one patient is described who can understand that a number such as 70 involves "tens" quantities but who cannot decide which of the tens quantities it is, with the result that the patient perceives sometimes that the number is 40, 50, 60, 80, and so forth. Some comprehension functions are intact; others are not.

In addition to studies of brain-damaged people, neuropsychologists also evaluate people who never acquire calculating competence, with the hypothesis that **developmental dyscalculia** (analogous to developmental dyslexia) is due to brain differences between those with dyscalculia and normal calculators. As with acquired dyscalculia, there are huge individual differences in the specifically impaired processes, including students whose problems are mainly verbal (e.g., they cannot name numbers, symbols, or mathematical relationships; they cannot read math; or they cannot write mathematical symbols) and others with problems that involve calculation and calculating subprocesses (Keller & Sutton, 1991).

When all of the physiological and psychological evidence on both acquired and developmental dyscalculia is considered, there is considerable regularity with respect to pinpointing specific brain sites implicated in mathematical disabilities (Keller &

Sutton, 1991): Difficulties in reading and understanding word problems as well as difficulties in understanding mathematical concepts and procedures involve the higher association areas of the individual's dominant hemisphere. Quick mental calculation ability is linked to the functioning of the frontal lobes, as is abstract conceptualizing and some problem-solving skills. Sequencing abilities depend on the left parietal lobe; visual processing of mathematical symbols involves the occipital lobes; and auditory perception of numbers requires intact temporal lobes. Progress is definitely being made in understanding the contributions of brain structures to mathematical cognition, and we expect it to continue. Such work has high potential for informing the good information processing perspective developed throughout this book.

BIOLOGICALLY DETERMINED DISRUPTIONS OF NORMAL DEVELOPMENT

Disease and injury are potential dangers from the moment of conception until old age. Tremendous progress has been made in understanding the effects of many neurological diseases and injuries, with important insights about the treatment and education of people following from this work.

Teratogens

A critical determinant of the effects of neurological disease or environmental insult to the nervous system is the timing of the sickness or trauma. A particularly bad period for adverse neurological events is during **neurogenesis,** when many new nerve cells are forming (i.e., during the first 2 to 3 months of life), and thus there is much greater concern about the impact of many **teratogens** (i.e., agents that can damage a developing brain and thus have effects on behavior) during the first trimester of a pregnancy than during the second and third trimesters. A large number of disease (e.g., cytomegalovirus, rubella, toxoplasmosis; Shonkoff & Marshall, 1990) and chemical (e.g., methylmercury, alcohol, lead; Vorhees & Mollnow, 1987) teratogens have been identified. In many cases, prenatal exposure to a disease or a chemical will do so much damage to the developing nervous system that normal learning and development can never occur. For example, rubella during pregnancy can produce extreme retardation as well

as a host of other symptoms, such as growth retardation and heart disease (Shonkoff & Marshall, 1990). Maternal alcoholism can produce the retardation associated with fetal alcohol syndrome. Prenatal exposure to PCBs (polychlorinated biphenyls) translates into visual information processing and short-term memory functioning deficits that are detectable during the preschool years (Jacobson, Jacobson, Padgett, Brumitt, & Billings, 1992).

Malnutrition

Prenatal and postnatal malnutrition also can reduce mental competency (Chase, 1973). The timing of malnutrition is an especially important determinant of outcomes (Morgan & Gibson, 1991). There is greater damage as a result of malnutrition when it occurs at periods corresponding to rapid development of the nervous system. Thus, from neurogenesis through the second year of life, when neural cell growth via arborization and proliferation of dendritic synapses is rapid, is an especially vulnerable period (Dobbing, 1974). Because substantial myelination occurs during the middle preschool years (3 to 4 years of age), this is also a period of great sensitivity to the effects of malnutrition. That the children who are most likely to suffer malnutrition are children from lower socioeconomic status homes does not improve the situation. Long-term malnutrition translates into lower cognitive development and reduced attentional capacity for many children (e.g., Sigman, Neumann, Jansen, & Bwibo, 1989).

Neurological Injury and Trauma Early in Life

Injury (e.g., during childbirth) can also reduce mental competency. Common forms of injury are asphyxiation during birthing and intracranial hemorrhage, with the latter especially probable among premature infants. Fortunately the incidence of these types of disorders is declining because of better fetal monitoring procedures and widespread dissemination of improved methods of delivery (Rosen, 1985). In many cases, however, children who are at biological risk at birth (e.g., low birth weight, birthing injury) manifest few if any long-term problems. For example, Sostek, Smith, Katz, and Grant (1987) found little difference at age 2 between children who had been preterms with intracranial hemorrhage and former preterms who experienced no hemorrhage.

Children who are at risk at birth are more certain to thrive if they experience diverse and stimulating environments during their first few years of life, environments with caregivers who are attentive and responsive to them (Anastasiow, 1990; Beckwith & Parmelee, 1986; Goldberg & DiVitto, 1983; Gottfried, 1984; Morgan & Gibson, 1991; Sameroff & Chandler, 1975; Sameroff & Fiese, 1990; Werner, 1990; Werner, Bierman, & French, 1971; Werner & Smith, 1982).

One of the most compelling demonstrations that a rich environment can do much to make up for initial biological disadvantage was provided by a true experiment conducted by The Infant Health and Development Project (1990; for complementary data, see Wasik, Ramey, Bryant, & Sparling, 1990). The target children were low-birth-weight infants, a group at substantial risk for later academic difficulties (Scott, 1987). The study was conducted at eight sites distributed across the United States, with this the largest multiple-site, randomized experiment of long-term early childhood intervention ever published. Approximately one-third of the children in the study were randomly assigned to the treatment condition and two-thirds to the control condition.

The treatment consisted of home visits during the child's first year of life. The visitor provided health and developmental information to the family as well as other forms of support as needed. Two curricula were introduced into the home during this first year. One was a cognitive, linguistic, and social development curriculum consisting of games and activities that encouraged parent-child interaction. The second curriculum provided child management information to parents, aimed specifically at problems parents often encounter with infants. At 1 year of age, and continuing until 3 years of age, the treated children attended a child development center 5 days a week. The learning curriculum initiated at home was continued and extended at the center, with adjustments made as the child developed to keep the curriculum consistent with the child's level and progress. There was an excellent adult-to-child ratio in these centers, with one adult for each three 1-year-olds and one adult for each four 2-year-olds. The parents of the children at the center met twice a month in groups to receive information about child rearing, safety, and health.

The effects produced by this treatment were dramatic. By age 3, the IQs of treated children were substantially higher than the IQs of controls. For those children who had weighed between 5 and 6 pounds at birth, there was a 13.5 IQ point advantage owing to the treatment (i.e., treated condition mean = 98.0; control mean = 84.8); the corresponding gain for infants who had weighed less than 5 pounds at birth was 6.6 points (i.e., treated condition mean = 91.0; control mean = 84.4), with the gains for both the heavier-birthweight and lighter-birth-weight infants statistically significant. The gain for the heavier children is especially striking in that all of these children were functioning almost at the mean of the normal distribution of intelligence. Their cognitive functioning could not possibly be construed as impaired.

What might explain the benefits provided to at-risk children by high quality early childhood environments? (Think back to the previous discussion of early education interventions in this chapter.) There is an overabundance of experience-expectant synapses during this interval. This abundance during the early preschool years permits greater plasticity than compared with later in development (Anastasiow, 1990). In addition, there seems to be a correlation between plasticity and myelination, which is sensible because myelination is an index of nervous tissue maturity. Once myelination occurs, the nervous system is less open to change than before myelination. Regardless of the specific mechanisms mediating the effects of interventions, it is clear that there are advantages to providing treatment to at-risk children early in life. Waiting until the grade-school years will often mean opportunity lost: Sensitive periods for stimulation will have passed.

We note in closing this subsection that although our concern here was with environmental effects on at-risk children, many of the same investigators doing such work are also providing striking demonstrations that intellectual outcomes for all children—not just those biologically at risk—are determined in large part by the quality of the home environment during the first 3 years of life. For dramatic evidence in support of this claim from six different sites in North America, see Bradley et al. (1989).

Children with Medical Conditions

Some children who attend school are seriously ill, and as a general rule of thumb, chronic physical illness is associated with increased risk for academic difficulties (e.g., Sexson & Madan-Swain, 1993). For some of these victims of disease and trauma, their illness is terminal; for others, there is complete recovery; some may live with lifelong handicaps caused by the childhood sickness. Some diseases and injuries cause mental impairment; some treatments produce side effects that affect participation and progress in school. We review in this subsection a few of the more prominent disease categories encountered in contemporary schooling, noting that other sicknesses also can cause disruption of education, including cystic fibrosis and hemophilia among others (Bartel & Thurman, 1992).

AIDS   Somewhere between 15,000 and 30,000 babies were born in 1992 with human immunodeficiency virus (HIV) infection (Stevens & Price, 1992). A critically important effect of acquired immunodeficiency syndrome (AIDS) early in life is that it causes central nervous system damage, including in many instances mental retardation. There is progressively greater brain damage as life proceeds from birth because the HIV virus produces powerful neurotoxins (Seidel, 1992). For children who contract the disease long after childbirth, the neurological assault is much less complete. Often the only obvious difference between such children and nondiseased children is the presence of the AIDS virus in their body. That is, the severe retardation that follows from AIDS during infancy does not occur with older children.

Although there are not a large number of studies assessing the impact of cognitive interventions on young children who are HIV infected, the available data support the use of cognitive stimulation programs for children with AIDS. For example, Seidel (1992) reported that a year of cognitive stimulation intervention resulted in cognitive and motor gains for a sample of preschool children with AIDS. More than 80 percent of the sample was at least holding steady. Given the neurological assault these children are experiencing, holding steady is a good sign. Another optimistic sign is that the use of drugs such as AZT to treat AIDS reduces brain infection and thus has a positive impact on cognitive performance (Armstrong, Seidel, & Swales, 1993).

Cancer   The most common childhood cancer is leukemia (Bartel & Thurman, 1992, for this point and what follows). Because of great advances in treatment, most childhood leukemia victims will survive, however, so there is reason for optimism about leukemic children. Brain tumors are the next most common form of childhood cancer, and although the survival probabilities are not as great as for leukemia, the chances of survival are increasing steadily with new understandings about effective treatments.

At a minimum, children treated for cancer are at risk for getting behind in school during their hospitalization. The illness and treatment dramatically disrupt normal school attendance and produce side effects, such as fatigue, that preclude normal academic engagement. The treatments also can affect long-term cognitive development negatively, with radiation because of a brain tumor especially likely to impair cognitive functioning in the long term (Brown & Madan-Swain, 1993). How much impairment depends on a number of factors, including the age of the child when the cancer occurs, whether there is postsurgical infection of the nervous system, and how much radiation therapy is administered. For example, brain tumors during the preschool years, when the brain is developing rapidly, seem to produce more impairment than brain tumors later in childhood. Even in the more favorable situation afforded by leukemia, many more post-leukemic students require special educational interventions to keep them at grade level than do children who are free of disease. More positively, with a reduction in the use of radiation therapy to the head to treat leukemia, there seems to be less impairment.

Medically Fragile Children   Some children have diseases or disabilities that require continuous life support, such as ventilation because of tracheotomy (Bartel & Thurman, 1992). The educational needs of these children are often increased because parental resources (e.g., financial and psychic) are completely expended in coping with the medical condition. Many of these children have limited energy; others experience chronic pain; it is often a struggle for these children to be in school at all, with little fight left to put into academic challenges. Many such children are absent from school frequently, sometimes because of prolonged hospital stays. In general, such children have less total academic engaged time than other children. At a minimum, there is a need for great flexibility in dealing with children with fragile medical conditions. Many more adjustments are required to meet these children's needs than those of other children.

Chemical Assaults   Perhaps the saddest cases of mental impairment are the ones due to chemical assaults on developing nervous systems, for in virtually all such cases, the assault did not have to happen: Parents who abuse chemical substances, especially mothers who drink or use drugs during pregnancy, create great risks for their children. Even if a child is in an environment filled with lead paint, that paint would do no harm with proper supervision of the child and management of the environment to prevent the child from ingesting paint chips.

More people are retarded because of prenatal exposure to *alcohol* than for any other reason (Burgess & Streissguth, 1992, for this point and the remainder of the commentary on alcohol effects). The child experiencing the full effects of **fetal alcohol syndrome** is born small and with low birth weight (itself a risk factor), has facial disfigurations, and experiences central nervous system damage that can translate into a small head and behavioral disorders ranging from retardation at the low end to learning disabilities and hyperactivity at the more favorable end of the spectrum of possibilities (e.g., the mean IQ is about 65 or 70, with a range of 30 to a little more than 100—that is, the distribution of IQ scores is significantly lower than the distribution of IQ scores in the normal population; see Chapters 16 and 18,). Often FAS children will be so impulsive and out of control that the school will refer the child for evaluation and treatment. Although not every mother who drinks heavily gives birth to such a disordered child, there is a 30 to 40 percent probability of fetal alcohol effects in heavy drinkers. Streissguth, Barr, Sampson, Darby, and Martin (1989) reported that on average, 4-year-olds whose mothers had consumed more than three drinks a day during pregnancy had an IQ 5 points lower than children of nondrinking mothers, with this effect obtained when many other potential factors that might have influenced IQ were controlled statistically. Even small and moderate alcohol consumption during pregnancy can result in detectable motor deficiencies in the preschool years (Barr, Streissguth, Darby, & Sampson, 1990).

A common problem for FAS children throughout their schooling years is inappropriate behavior, with lying, stealing, and acting out common. One interpretation of the lying is that it reflects limited communication abilities, so that the child is inadequately communicating what happened rather than intentionally telling mistruths. Of course, such poor communications skills also negatively impact social relations. If anything, the social problems worsen with advancing grade in school, with these dysfunctions producing an isolated and depressed adolescent in many cases.

At present, there is little hard knowledge about how to intervene with FAS children except there is general concensus that early intervention is better. In addition, there is a recognition of especially great need to improve the social and communications skills of FAS children.

Firm conclusions about the effects of other chemical addictions produced through prenatal exposure, including *cocaine* addiction, are difficult to put forward. One reason is that drug users rarely rely on one drug exclusively. Thus, the discussion now turns to "cocaine/polydrug-exposed" children (Griffith, 1992, for this point and the remainder of this subsection).

The effects of prenatal drug exposure are apparent early in life, effects due both to the neurotoxicity of the drugs directly and to indirect effects of drugs, such as retarded growth during the intrauterine period and abnormal, dysfunctional parent-infant interactions because of drug-induced characteristics of the infant (e.g., Lester et al., 1991; Lester & Dreher, 1989). A salient effect of prenatal exposure to drugs is poor self-regulation, with affected infants not displaying the "quiet alert" state that permits information from the environment to be processed. Much more swaddling, rocking, and pacification is required to induce quiet alertness in these children than in normal infants. Even so, these children can be overstimulated easily, with disorganized crying and extended sleeping ways of reacting to overstimulation. (That is, the flailing, crying infants commonly displayed on television as "crack" babies represent one type of reaction to overstimulation.) Great care must be taken to avoid overstimulation if drug-exposed infants are to be able to attend to their environments for prolonged periods of time, which is absolutely essential for cognitive growth.

At the time of this writing, little is known about the long-term effects of crack-cocaine exposure during the prenatal period on mental functioning. One possibility suggested by early studies is that at least for some children whose mothers opted into treatment during pregnancy and who experience postnatal environments that provide appropriate levels of stimulation, the long-term effects may be much less than suggested by the sensationalistic accounts in the mass media. Still, 3-year-olds who were drug-exposed prenatally have smaller heads on average than normal children, a symptom usually not associated with normal mental development. Also, a nontrivial proportion of those receiving the best treatments manifest communications and attentional problems at age 3. They are less likely to be able to control themselves and are easily overwhelmed by the environment, resulting in them withdrawing when challenged or going out of control. When working with such children, therapists attempt to determine variables that can overstimulate the youngster, setting him or her off, and adjust the environment as much as possible to eliminate potential overstimulation. We expect that there will be substantial research with such populations to determine if the approaches to increasing self-regulation that work with other populations (e.g., teaching children to self-instruct; see Chapter 7) can improve the adaptive functioning of drug-exposed children.

Unfortunately, chemical poisoning of a child can occur even if the parent is drug-free. For example, we live in a world of lead-based paint that chips, with many poor children especially at risk for unwittingly eating and breathing *lead*. The most visible American scientist studying the effects of lead on intelligence is Needleman (1992; Needleman & Bellinger, 1991). His main conclusion is that even low levels of lead exposure pose a long-term risk to neurological functioning. Needleman argues that 16 percent of American children have blood lead levels that are reason for concern, with poor children much more likely to be exposed to dangerous levels of lead in their environment. Lead exposure can reduce IQ, impair language, and decrease self-regulation and attention.

In one of Needleman's studies, teachers described students who had high blood lead levels as "... more distractible, less persistent, more dependent, less well-organized, less able to follow directions, and generally lower in overall functioning ..." (Needleman, 1992, p. 36) than students with low blood lead levels. Low levels of lead exposure in early childhood are associated with long-term risks as well, including reading disability and increased likelihood of failing to graduate from high school.

Concluding Comment

After seeing a crack baby, it is difficult even to contemplate supporting the legalization of now illicit drugs. After witnessing the effects of FAS, it becomes clear that funds for treatment of alcohol addiction in young women are well spent. When the costs of lead-induced retardation are factored into the costs of allowing American housing of the poor to continue to decay, there is additional impetus to support funding of new and repaired housing for those living in poverty.

The disorders covered in this section are in many ways the tip of the iceberg, with important programs of research now underway aimed at determining the effects of a number of disease and injury factors on school learning and achievement. Such research is paying off, even though only tentative conclusions can be advanced for many diseases because only a limited amount of research has been completed at this time. For example, although childhood *diabetes* is not associated with large deficits in cognitive functioning, there are subtle problems for diabetic children with respect to visuospatial and visuomotor processing (e.g., Rovet, Ehrlich, & Hoppe, 1988), verbal abilities (Kovacs, Goldston, & Ivengar, 1992), and memory and attention, which translate into increased risk for difficulties in academic achievement—that is, in reading, spelling, and arithmetic (Kovacs et al., 1992; Rovet, Ehrlich, Czuchta, & Akler, 1993). Particularly important given the themes emphasized in this book, diabetic children seem less likely to use strategies to mediate their learning than nondiabetic children (Hagen et al., 1990). Sickle cell anemia, an inherited disorder found in people of African descent, also produces some subtle cognitive impairments that affect school achievement negatively (Brown, Armstrong, & Eckman, 1993). Children who survive cardiac arrest perform at below-average levels on a number of intellectual measures (e.g., averaging almost a full standard deviation below the mean for overall intelligence; Morris, Krawiecki, Wright, & Walter, 1993). On the positive side, difficulties with school achievement seem less likely for children with asthma (Celano & Geller, 1993), a common childhood disorder and for children who receive kidney or liver transplants (Hobbs & Sexson, 1993). Just as medical advances are permitting many more children to survive and function well following serious illnesses, we expect that psychologists will come to understand the psychological effects of many illnesses well enough to be able to engineer interventions that will increase the educational achievements of children disadvantaged by medical conditions.

GENDER DIFFERENCES IN COGNITION

Are there any believable differences between males and females in their abilities to perform cognitive tasks? Are there differences in their fundamental cognitive processes? Are there biological differences in the central nervous systems of males and females that produce differences in their abilities to perform particular intellectual tasks? This section provides some answers to these questions, with what is presented here informed by the work of Halpern (e.g., 1992), who is now the most visible integrative scholar in the area of gender differences in thinking. For anyone seriously interested in gender differences in cognition, *Sex Differences in Cognitive Abilities* (2nd edition) by Halpern is a must read.

Although interpreting null effects can be dangerous, voluminous data exist supporting the conclusion of no overall difference in the intelligence of males and females as measured by psychometric tests of intelligence (i.e., the mean IQ scores for males and females are both about 100; intelligence is normally distributed for both males and females, with the standard deviation for IQs equal to 15 for both sexes; see Chapter 16). When processing and abilities are examined more closely, however, there are differences. Females are favored with respect to one extremely important ability: verbal ability. Males are superior to females for visual-spatial tasks, field independence (i.e., males are less influenced by context effects in perceptual tasks than are females), and quantitative skills.

One important characteristic of the differences favoring males is that males tend to be more variable than females for the characteristics in question (Feingold, 1992). A higher mean with much higher variability often implies that much of the mean difference is due to a relatively few outstanding performers and that, otherwise, there is great overlap in the distribution of scores. That conclusion does, in fact, hold for the few differences favoring males over females with respect to cognitive ability (Feingold, 1992).

There are several striking aspects to the entire list of differences. For one, it is so short. There are many aspects of performance that produce no gender differences, with the shortness of the list even more impressive when it is realized that most of the male differences can be accounted for by visual-spatial factors in measurements of field independence and mathematics abilities. We concur with Halpern's (1992, p. 97) conclusion, ". . . that cognitive similarities between the sexes are greater than the differences."

A question probably occurring to many of our readers is whether there are gender differences in use of cognitive strategies, metacognition about strategies, and other knowledge. The only gender difference in these areas consistently suggested in the literature is in computational versus problem-solving skills (strategies) at the elementary level favoring males. We note especially emphatically, however, that we know of no evidence that would suggest differences in the abilities of males and females to learn most problem-solving strategies (i.e., all except those involving visuospatial manipulation of mathematical representations).

Benbow and Lubinski have claimed (see Raymond, 1992; also Benbow, 1992) that motivations undermine the mathematics achievements of even the most highly mathematically talented of females. Benbow and Lubinski have been studying males and females who turn in the best performances on the math SAT to understand better why so few women choose careers in math and physics. They have found that even females who are strong in mathematics are less likely to aspire to scientific careers.

Are Gender Differences in Cognitive Abilities Due to Biological Differences Between Males and Females?

As with every other area of individual differences, there are two broad types of explanatory theories with respect to gender differences in cognition. Some theorists argue that gender differences can be explained via biological differences between males and females. Others argue that gender differences represent differences in the experiences of males and females. Halpern (1992) provides the most definitive review available of this evidence, with us relying on her review to formulate the conclusions that follow.

Some theories about how biology affects gender differences in cognition have received at least some support; others have failed to prove telling. The supportable ones include the following:

- Sex hormones may operate in various ways. Prenatal sex hormones are critical to the determination of sex, with testosterone particularly important (i.e., it stimulates the development of male external genitalia, with its absence resulting in female sex organs). Testosterone also affects development of gender differences in the brain, as do hormones secreted by the fetal ovaries. Studies of rats have manipulated the presence of such hormones at various points in development, producing changes in brain structures such as the corpus callosum, which is the bundle of fibers linking the two hemispheres of the brain. Although true experiments manipulating prenatal hormones are not possible with humans, there are medical conditions that result in abnormal levels of sex hormones during the fetal period. There is evidence that exceptionally high levels of androgen (a male hormone) increase spatial abilities in females. Some biological males do not respond to androgen and thus develop female characteristics, including a pattern of higher verbal than spatial ability. Women with Turner's syndrome have low levels of both male and female hormones, with strikingly reduced spatial skills relative to other females. In short, there are correlational differences 'favoring the hypothesis that prenatal hormones influence development of cognitive skills, but, of course, there are a host of other abnormal influences on individuals with abnormal sex hormone patterns and the differences associated with them. An especially prominent hormonal theory has been proposed by Geschwind and Galaburda (1987), who believe that high levels of prenatal testosterone slow development of the left hemisphere and reduce the size of the thymus gland, producing more left-handers in males, more immune disorders in males including allergies, and more pronounced superiority in males of right-hemisphere functions, such as spatial abilities. There is some support for this position, although much more research is needed.

- A related argument about gender differences being caused by differential brain lateralization in males and females is linked to the hypothesis that testosterone affects the development of the right and left hemispheres. Males have more clearly lateralized brains than do females, with verbal skills more a left-hemisphere function for males than females (e.g., Kee, Gottfried, Bathurst, & Brown, 1987). For females, verbal skills are carried out more by both hemispheres, with spatial abilities confined to the right hemisphere. The result is that there is less right-hemisphere capacity in females dedicated to spatial abilities than in males and more overall capacity in females dedicated to verbal skills. Thus, Levy (e.g., 1976) proposed that spatial skills get "squeezed out" of the right hemisphere in females to provide more verbal capacity. Support for this hypothesis comes in the form of sex by handedness interactions: Consistent with the theory, left-handed males perform more poorly on spatial tasks than right-handed males (i.e., in males, clearer differentiation of the hemispheric functioning is in right-handers, with the result better spatial performance for males who are not "squeezing" spatial abilities out of the right hemisphere). Also, consistent with the theory, left-handed females perform better than right-handed females (i.e., in females, clearer differentiation of hemispheric functioning is in left-handers, with the result better spatial performance for females who are not "squeezing" spatial abilities out of the right hemisphere; e.g., Harshman, Hampson, & Barenbaum, 1983).

- For females, cognitive abilities vary somewhat with **hormonal differences during the menstrual cycle.** The work of Hampson and Kimura at Western Ontario (e.g., Hampson, 1990a, 1990b; Hampson & Kimura, 1988) has been especially telling, with demonstrations of better performance by women at menstruation on tasks typically performed better by males, such as map problems, mazes, and visual-spatial problems. This was as predicted because female hormones are at the low ebb of the monthly cycle at this point in the cycle. When female hormones are at the peak of their cycle (i.e., at midcycle), females do better on tasks that are typically performed better by females than males, such as speech articulation, verbal fluency, and manual dexterity. It does seem that cognitive abilities in women vary with the point in their menstrual cycle.

- There are within-hemisphere differences in the organization of males and females. Kimura's (e.g., 1987) work on this problem has been conducted with patients having various types of brain injury. For example, although females' language areas in the left hemisphere are focused in some regions more than others, males processing tends to be more diffuse.

- Some portions of the *corpus callosum*—the bundle of fibers connecting the two hemisphere—are larger in females than in males, supporting the possibility that greater verbal facility in females is due in part to greater interhemispheric communication in females than in males.

In summary, there are three brain-based possibilities about gender differences in cognitive functioning: (1) They are due to gender differences in lateralization, (2) they are due to intrahemispheric differences in organization, and (3) differences in the size of the corpus callosum account for such differences. Of course, there is also the possibility that any two or all three of these brain differences are related in intricate ways to gender differences in cognition. Before there can be functional and structural differences, however, there are prenatal hormonal differences between males and females, differences that seem to affect development of the brain. In short, there is no simple biological explanation for the different patterns of male and female thinking but at best a developmentally complex explanation.

In finding favor with the biological perspective, we also note that some biological theories have *not* received support as potential explanations of gender differences. These include the following:

- Genetic theories that gender differences in cognition are **X-chromosome linked** have failed on examination. The argument is that females have two X chromosomes, whereas males have only one. Thus, if high spatial ability was a recessive trait carried on the X chromosome, females would require two recessives if they were to enjoy the advantages provided by such a gene, whereas any male with the gene on his single X chromosome would be advantaged.
- Differences in **pubertal hormones** and maturation rate at puberty have not produced reliable differences in the cognitive abilities that differentiate male and female thinking. The exception is that at least some testosterone at puberty seems necessary for normal spatial skills and that spatial abilities may vary with the level of the hormone estradiol.
- There are no differences in the size, weight, and complexity of male and female brains, although there has been frequent speculation of differences.

In concluding that there are probably biological foundations to gender differences in cognition, we recognize we are treading on an explosive topic, with many people opposed to such a conclusion (Halpern, 1992, Chapter 5). Such critics rightly point out that biologically oriented theorists and researchers usually have ignored environmental and social factors that might affect gender differences in cognition, some of which are taken up in the next subsection.

We close this subsection on biology noting the tendency of many to come to too strong conclusions about the inevitability of differences based on the findings reported here. Thus, the small verbal advantage for females is often exploded in the minds and rhetoric of some. That small advantage on average for females is swamped by the huge differences in verbal abilities within both sexes, so that there are many males who are more verbally facile than many females. Even the larger spatial abilities difference does not predict to individuals, with large numbers of females doing well on spatial tasks and in areas such as mathematics. Strong conclusions about how individuals will fare on cognitive tasks cannot be predicted from their sex.

Most emphatically, this work on gender differences is not evaluative with respect to whether the thinking patterns exhibited by one sex or the other are better or not. Halpern (1992) put it this way:

> To argue that female hormones are better than male hormones or that male brains are better than female brains is as silly as arguing which sex has the better genitals. It seems almost embarrassing and obvious to state that neither sex has the better biology for intellectual ability and that differences should not be confused with deficits. (pp. 169–170)

Psychosocial Theories of Gender Differences in Cognitive Abilities

Males and females are treated differently from the moment the delivery room nurse reaches for a blue blanket for a boy or a pink one for a girl. That differences in treatment exist is not the problem. The problem is that the behaviors encouraged in females are often less positively regarded and rewarded than the behaviors encouraged in males. Moreover, societal stereotypes often ascribe less valued roles for females compared to males (e.g., doctors are males and nurses are females; lawyers are males and paralegals are females; well-paid athletes are males and their admirers are females). The pervasiveness of such sexism can affect behavior if internalized, so that much of the reason girls might have less interest in math and careers requiring mathematics is that they internalized stereotypical beliefs, such as "Math is for boys," "Engineers and scientists are men," and "Science requires cold objectivity—a male stereotypic trait—rather than interpersonal warmth and human contact—female stereotypic traits." Parents, television, teachers, and community members all contribute to the stereotyping (see Halpern, 1992, for a review).

Halpern (1992, Chapter 7) considered some of the particular social-cognitive experiences that might contribute to the gender differences in cognition that have been observed, making the case that there is at least correlational evidence (and in some cases, experimental evidence) for each of the following possibilities: Gender differences in spatial abilities might be accounted for by greater male experience with games that require such skills (e.g., video games, billiards). Boys' toys and play activities in general may encourage development of spatial skills more than do girls' toys. Boys may be more curious about the environment than girls, a difference reinforced by adults who are more willing to allow boys to roam the world in search of new possibilities than they are willing to allow girls to do so (e.g., Lindow, Marrett, & Wilkinson, 1985). Greater exploration would be expected to foster visual-spatial skills. One dramatic piece of data consistent with the possibility that differences in experience cause gender-related differences in thinking abilities is that grade-school girls who are more interested in male activities than female activities become adolescent girls who have spatial abilities that exceed the spatial abilities of girls in general (Newcombe & Dubas, 1992).

With respect to gender differences in mathematics, the socialization differences are less subtle; there are many reports that boys are encouraged more in mathematics than are girls (Halpern, 1992, Chapter 7): Females take fewer mathematics courses, with much greater tolerance of high-ability girls dropping out of mathematics sequences than high-ability boys doing so. The majority of math teachers expect more from boys than girls and are more responsive to male achievements in mathematics than female achievements. Many adults who interact with children believe that math is harder for girls than boys, with such a bias expected to affect the messages sent to students about the possibility of mathematics achievement by girls. If we were attempting to design a world that would turn girls off to math and science, it seems unlikely we could be more successful than is the case now.

Concluding Comments

There are multiple forces that might affect gender differences in cognition. Contrary to many societal stereotypes, most differences in thinking that exist between men and women are small. Although some of the gender differences in cognition that do exist are probably due to biology, there are massive socialization differences between boys and girls that undoubtedly are important in determining how males and females construe the world and the academic content they encounter in it.

Differences in cognitive socialization become a problem to the extent that the knowledge and behaviors encouraged in one sex are more valued by the culture than the knowledge and behaviors encouraged in the other sex. Unfortunately, female-stereotypic behaviors do not have the payoff in our society that male-stereotypic behaviors do, nor do female ways of thinking pay off as well as male ways of thinking. Thinking about how to create more equitable experiences for males and females is in order. It is impossible to make a case on the basis of biology that males' ways of knowing, rationalizing, and problem solving are better than females' ways of dealing with the world.

GENETICALLY DETERMINED MODULES IN THE MIND AND MULTIPLE INTELLIGENCES

The idea that mind includes particular faculties that are specialized to deal with particular types of information has been around for a long time. It can be traced to Descartes's doctrine of innate ideas. Thinly disguised versions of the Descartes perspective appear periodically. These vary from the incredible (e.g., Gall's belief that the bumps on the head could provide insights about individual differences in capacities; Hollander, 1920) to credible, if not always well-supported, positions.

One piece of highly credible evidence supporting the hypothesis of separate mental faculties is that there are different sensitive periods for some acquisitions compared with others. Thus, the sensitive period for organization of visual processing in humans appears to be the first 4 or 5 years of life. The sensitive period for acquisition of language may be longer, perhaps the entire prepubertal period (Goodman, 1987). Many believe that the critical period for establishing a first intense attachment with another human being is in the first year of life (e.g., Bowlby, 1969).

Such observations fuel the argument that there are distinct human capacities that are inherited and that mind involves an interaction of faculties. The renaissance of faculty psychology was heralded in the first paragraph of Fodor's (1983) book *The Modularity of Mind*:

> Faculty psychology is getting to be respectable again after centuries of hanging around with phrenologists and other dubious types. By faculty psychology I mean, roughly, the view that many fundamentally different types of psychological mechanisms must be postulated in order to explain the facts of mental life. Faculty psychology takes seriously the apparent heterogeneity of the mental and is impressed by such prima facie differences as between, say, sensation and perception, volition and cognition, learning and remembering, or language and thought. Since, according to faculty psychologists, the mental causation of behavior typically involves the simultaneous activity of a variety of distinct psychological mechanisms, the best research strategy would seem to be to divide and conquer: first study the intrinsic characteristics of each of the presumed faculties, then study the ways in which they interact. Viewed from the faculty psychologist's perspective, overt, observable behavior is an interaction effect par excellent. (Fodor, 1983, p. 1)

Fodor goes on to argue throughout the book that humans inherit **cognitive modules;** these are "cognitive systems that are domain specific, innately specified, hardwired, autonomous . . . " (p. 37). An important point is that these modules are only independent, in Fodor's (p. 37) words, "to some interesting extent." That is, the modules interact, and there is some overlap in the architecture of the mind—there are many connections between the modules. (Minsky, 1986, pp. 314–317, provided a credible discussion of how there could be modules that interconnect.)

There are modules for each sensory/perceptual mode: hearing, sight, touch, taste, and smell. There are also modules for language (MIT-based Chomsky and Fodor are closely colleagual on this point). It must be emphasized that there are a number of specific modules within each mode:

> [These] . . . might include, in the case of vision, mechanisms for color perception, for the analysis of shape, and for the analysis of three-dimensional spatial rela-

tions. They might also include quite narrowly task-specific 'higher-level' systems concerned with the visual guidance of bodily motions or with the recognition of faces of conspecifics. Candidates in audition might include . . . systems that assign grammatical descriptions to token utterances; or ones that detect the melodic or rhythmic structure of acoustic arrays; or, for that matter, ones that mediate the recognition of *voices* of conspecifics. (p. 47)

How many modules there are could be debated at length, although Fodor suggests there are many, that we inherit diverse capacities that are at least partially separable and separated from one another. It must be stressed that Fodor's view is not really a particularly extreme one either, with many cognitive scientists voicing similar sentiments.

For example, Minsky (1986) offered *The Society of Mind*:

> I'll call 'Society of Mind' this scheme in which each mind is made of many smaller processes. These we'll call agents. Each mental agent by itself can only do some simple things that need no mind or thought at all. Yet when we join these agents in societies—in certain very special ways—this leads to true intelligence. (p. 17)

The specificity of the agents in Minsky's system is obvious from this analysis of the agents required to pick up a cup of tea:

Your GRASPING agents want to keep hold of the cup.
Your BALANCING agents want to keep the tea from spilling out.
Your THIRST agents want you to drink the tea.
Your MOVING agents want to get the cup to your lips. (p. 20)

> . . . If each [agent] does its little job, the really big job will get done by all of them together: drinking tea. (p. 20)

According to Minsky, learning is genetically predestined. What is inherited are agencies with particular structures that are sensitive to particular types of information and process such information in particular ways. The agencies and processes that are inherited by humans constrain what humans can learn, as does the physical world that humans inhabit (including our own bodies). Thus, how does

Minsky (1986) answer a question such as, "Is the child's conception of space acquired or inherited?" (p. 115):

> We acquire our conceptions of space by using agencies that learn in accord with processes determined by inheritance. These agencies proceed to learn from experience—but the outcomes of their learning processes are virtually predestined by the spatial geometry of our body parts. (p. 115)

Inherited capacities and processes operating in a real world with particular characteristics (including the constraints associated with human body structure) determine learning.

A conception that is related to that of modularity, and one that was informed directly by Fodor's views, is Gardner's (1983) **theory of multiple intelligences.** Gardner believes that people have a set of specific intelligences that are biologically determined—they are **biopsychological potentials** (Gardner, 1993). These include linguistic, musical, logic-mathematical, spatial, body-kinesthetic, interpersonal (i.e., ability to notice and make distinctions among other individuals), and intrapersonal (i.e., access to one's own feelings) intelligences. These seven abilities exist in the context of other abilities or knowledge that may be more general, such as common sense, originality, metaphorical abilities, and wisdom. One of the most critical features of Gardner's theory is that people vary in the strength of their particular faculties. From this perspective, it makes no sense to think of someone as smart or not-so-smart in general, as is implied in traditional psychometric theory (Chapter 16; see the discussion of the heritability of intelligence presented earlier in this chapter). Rather, people with musical intelligence would be expected to excel in music given appropriate stimulation; those who have superior capacity with respect to mathematics would be expected to do well given appropriate exposure to mathematics.

Gardner believes that a major problem with contemporary schooling is that linguistic, logical-mathematical, and intrapersonal intelligences are emphasized in school to the exclusion of others. There is little attempt to gauge the strengths and weaknesses of students with respect to the various intelligences.

Even if relative strengths and weaknesses were known, however, it would be difficult to know what to do. Should strengths be emphasized or weaknesses bolstered? What is known, based on the work of Bloom (1985), which was presented in Chapter 4, is that even when a person is favored biologically with respect to ability, enormous educational resources must be expended to produce someone who is expert with respect to the intelligence in question. Bloom's data make clear that if people inherit multiple intelligences, what they inherit are potentials, potentials that will be fully realized only given extremely favorable educational and environmental circumstances.

Of course, we hope it is obvious, in light of this lengthy discussion of biological determination of learning and cognition, that biological potential remains exactly that until it plays out in an environment that permits that potential to function. This is a fundamental understanding that is true no matter how fine or coarse the level of analysis: Environment-expectant synapses that organize visual competence do not stabilize unless there is appropriate visual stimulation; people high in body-kinesthetic intelligence do not become great athletes without years of coaching and practice.

As we close this subsection, we warn that Fodor, Minsky, and Gardner have yet to offer detailed research to support their positions, although there are lines of research that can support some of the assumptions of the theories they have proposed (e.g., Gardner, 1993). There are rich possibilities in these conceptions of mind for young educational researchers looking for good problems to study. For the budding educator, we are certain that Gardner's multiple intelligences theory is going to have an important impact on education, for it is often referred to in outlets designed for practitioners. The theory is viewed as strongly supportive of individualized instruction, and at least for some children, de-emphasizes language and mathematics instruction in favor of other faculties. It is a theory consistent with a long history of recognition of special abilities by psychologists. Gardner's and Fodor's new versions of faculty psychology, however, are substantially more refined and defensible than many of their predecessors and deserve more serious consideration than much of the faculty psychology of the past.

CONCLUDING COMMENTS

A great deal of research and theory generated during the last several decades supports the case that how learning occurs and what is learned is determined by biology. Humans are prepared better to learn some information than others. They are prepared to learn better some information at particular points in development compared with other points. Some humans are capable of learning contents that are much more difficult for others to acquire, possibly because of biologically based differences in faculty strengths.

Biology and Experience

In the past there have been many naive arguments about whether human intelligence is a product of heredity or environment. The answer, based on all of the biological perspectives reviewed here, is that human intelligence and competence depends both on biology and on environment. What biology provides is genetically determined potential. Whether that potential is realized depends critically on experiencing particular types of stimulation. The existence of critical periods with respect to neuronal plasticity makes obvious that it is often not possible to put off providing stimulation to a child until some later point in development. Throughout this book, we will present evidence that what is acquired during the early childhood years has great impact on later development. The critical period perspective reviewed here suggests that at least some of the reason that is true is tied to biological preparedness for learning from certain types of experiences during particular periods in life.

The data in this chapter also make clear that from the time of conception, there is reason to be concerned about the environment the child encounters. Maternal malnutrition, chemical dependency, or disease during a pregnancy can affect the biological development of an embryo or fetus. The result can range from mild mental handicap to severe retardation. There are good reasons to direct educational resources at children who have had adverse prenatal experiences, however, for the severity of disability at maturity can often be reduced or eliminated by responsive stimulation during infancy and the preschool years.

The hypothesis that individual differences in mental functioning might be based in part at least on biological differences between people has been entertained by psychologists throughout the 20th century, with a number of specific biological routes to individual differences proposed: Thus, prenatal exposure to testosterone may affect a person's pattern of cognitive strengths. Subtle individual differences

in neurological structure (e.g., number of dendrites) might make a difference in general intelligence achieved by adulthood. Differences in the extent of support tissues, such as capillaries and glial cells, could be implicated in the determination of individual differences in overall intellect. Perhaps the encapsulated modules inherited by different people differ in their relative strengths, a position consistent with Gardner's theory of multiple intelligences. In short, there is real progress in understanding the potential biological mechanisms that underlie human differences.

A Warning

In urging attention to biological evidence pertaining to and explanations about human commonalities and differences, we also urge some caution. All too often we have heard biologically oriented psychologists make exaggerated claims about the inevitability of function and inevitability of differences based on biology. Thus, a few years ago, we listened to a prominent physiological psychologist make the case that math and engineering were not subject areas for girls, with this claim made in light of some then current work on male-female differences in physiological mechanisms related to spatial representation. What this physiologist did not indicate (and perhaps did not understand) is that there are great overlaps in the distributions of males and females for most intellectual characteristics, including basic skills related to mathematics and science abilities (e.g., spatial thinking). Sweeping generalizations about ability based on gender, race, or health are not warranted.

In addition, some biologically oriented types have advanced extremely bad ideas, which have been translated into interventions that are disseminated. The Doman-Delacato "patterning" technique for the treatment of mental retardation and brain damage is an example (e.g., Doman, Spitz, Zucman, Delacato, & Doman, 1960). Consider the case of a brain-damaged child. The first step is to determine the developmental point at which the injury occurred. What follows is an attempt to "train" functioning from that point onward. The theory is that if the body can be exercised in particular ways that are associated with normal development, neurological organization will be achieved that will compensate for the neurological organization that cannot develop naturally because of the injury. The treatment

Part

2

Other Grand Theoretical Perspectives

7

Classical Theories of Learning and Development

This chapter summarizes important theories about education and development. Although all continue to have some implications for education, some are inspiring more educational research in the 1990s than are others. In particular, the social learning and cognitive-behavioral theories considered later in the chapter are stimulating more research than Gibson's approach to perceptual learning, Piagetian theory, or Skinnerian theory. All of these theories should be understood by contemporary educational psychologists and educators, for each is reflected in at least some important educational interventions.

In addition to information processing models of cognition, there are other theoretical perspectives that are important for educational psychologists to understand. These are covered in this second part of the book, with this chapter a summary of a diverse array of traditional theories that are of enduring importance. Chapter 8 is dedicated to the many social collaborative approaches to education proposed, covering both teacher-student interactions and student-student interactions that can contribute to long-term cognitive development. Chapter 9 continues the themes began in Chapter 8, focusing on the development of moral judgment and creation of thoughtful educational communities.

This chapter features traditional theories of learning and development, theories that would appear in most courses and texts in educational psychology. None of the theorists in this chapter offers a conception that can stand alone. Each of them, however, proposes mechanisms of knowledge acquisition that must be understood to have a complete understanding of the development of knowledge. Many of the mechanisms identified in this chapter probably play a role in knowledge acquisition. An important challenge is to understand how and when particular mechanisms are likely to be operative and to engineer educational opportunities so the various mechanisms in concert can have maximally positive effects.

The theories considered in this chapter are more psychological than the biologically oriented conceptions of knowledge acquisition considered in Chapter 6. Nonetheless, each theorist considered in this chapter has conceptions about how biology influences the development of knowledge and how biology interacts with experience. A recurrent theme in this chapter is that humans have evolved to be sensitive to particular forms of stimulation, stimulation that can be informative about the nature of the world. Thus, the case will be developed here that humans are hardwired to be sensitive to the types of sensory input that are in the world. We are also biologically prepared to process feedback offered by the world and to imitate behaviors we observe. What the theories in this chapter do well is to specify how particular biological proclivities translate into knowledge and behavior as a function of the natural environment.

PERCEPTUAL LEARNING

Perceptual learning theory highlights interactions between biologically determined potential and environment. A baby enters this world inherently active from this point of view. What is especially critical, according to Eleanor Gibson's (e.g., 1969) theory, is that the stimulation the baby encounters in the world is filled with information. For example, baby's rubber bathtub letters are composed of features that differentiate them (e.g., curves, straight lines, diagonals). Although a baby can tell when two letters are the same or different from an early age, he or she does not notice the features differentiating one letter from another until quite a bit later. By age 2½, baby probably can spot Mommy's letter (i.e., "M") and Daddy's letter (i.e., "D") reliably, not only when playing with the bathtub letters, but also whenever large block letters are encountered. At age 4, he or she might reliably spot all of the letters of the alphabet and name them, although there are occasional slipups, almost always involving letters that share features (e.g., "h" being mistaken for "n").

The features defining letters (and other things) are always out there in the world; with experience, people discover the critical features differentiating a set of items. Thus, for many preschoolers, every airplane is the same. After years of experience with aircraft, including many explicit attempts to figure out how particular aircraft and models differ from one another, experienced travelers can differentiate easily a 737 from a 747 and even a 737–100 from a 737–200, a 737–200 from a 737–300, and a 737–300 from a 737–400. With experience, frequent flyers develope knowledge of the **distinctive features** of different types of aircraft, sometimes as a function of incidental learning and sometimes by intentionally trying to distinguish the various aircraft at airports (Gibson, 1969, p. 83).

The distinctive features diffentiating members of a class are not isolated pieces of information but instead are in relation to one another. One manufacturer sells a customized car kit that is a small-scale front end of a Rolls Royce. This front end can be attached to the body of a Volkswagen. We have seen several such customized vehicles but have never once mistaken one of these cars for a Rolls Royce. A Rolls has more than a particularly shaped hood. There are many features in relation to one another that define a Rolls: The hood is proportional to the projected length of the car in particular ways. The ratio of the car body to the body in the driver's seat is much larger for the Rolls than for the kit car. The reflection off a Rolls is more striking because the paint is deeper in color and the surface smoother. Somehow the trim on a Rolls projects a sturdiness that is not projected by the trim on the kit car. So it is for any object, be it a letter of the alphabet, a person's face, or the leaves on trees. Thus, in the autumn, at one glance people fear red, three-leafed arrays that are near to the ground (i.e., poison ivy) but have no thoughts of danger when confronted with red leaves in general, other leaves near to the ground, or three-leaf clusters. Distinctive features are distinctive only in relation to one another.

Gibson's theory is that the processes underlying perceptual learning are the same in adults and children, although adults are sometimes quicker at any given perceptual learning task because their previous experiences have produced understanding of what to look for, what types of information define distinctive features. Thus, it takes most children several years to learn to differentiate the letters of the alphabet. In contrast, however, English-speaking adults who begin to study Russian acquire the distinctive features of the Cyrillic alphabet in a matter of days, largely because of a great deal of prior knowledge about the types of features that can differentiate letters of an alphabet.

What is required for perceptual learning to occur? Repeated exposure to a set of objects differing in particular ways is essential. In general, if the ways that the objects differ are essential to obtaining some goal, it is more likely the features will be noticed. With increasing practice, there is an **increase in specificity** of the objects that are classified in particular ways. At first, baby accepted any letter with verticals (e.g., H, M, N, P, R, D) as Mommy's letter. Then, two verticals were required (e.g., H, M, N). Then two verticals and at least one diagonal (e.g., M,

N) defined Mommy's letter. Finally, only "M"s were classified as Mommy's—although many variations on "M" would do, from *M* to *M* to **M** to ᴍ, and so on.

With increasing age and experience, children's attention to and processing of perceptual information becomes more efficient. Younger children's attention is often captured by salient environmental stimuli (see Turnure, 1970), whereas older children can more often ignore salient, distractible properties of stimulation that are not relevant to a task (e.g., Hagen & Hale, 1973). With increasing age, children are also much more likely to examine stimuli more systematically and completely. Thus, when Vurpillot (e.g., 1968) asked young children to examine visual patterns, preschoolers examined far fewer features and did so unsystematically compared with children 3 to 4 years older, who systematically and exhaustively scanned features that were potentially relevant in the task given to the children (i.e., to decide if two similar, complex patterns differed or were the same). In general, with development, children focus in on more information that is relevant to the task they are asked to perform; they are more flexible in attending to object features, sometimes systematically examining in one way and sometimes in another depending on the task; they learn to know what to expect and thus are better at knowing what to look for; and their attention becomes more economical in that task-relevant features come to dominate attention, with these increasingly perceived simultaneously or in quick succession. Thus, adult frequent flyers can quickly abstract many features of an airplane, whereas a preschooler covers features slowly one at a time. (e.g., Dad, it's got a door in the back, and there's two engines on the plane and one more on top, and this is a blue, red, and white plane—except up front, which is black on the nose!! And so it goes, slowly processing a feature at a time, ones a frequent-flyer Daddy picks up with a glance or two.)

Perceptual information is important because it often provides important information about how to use the objects in the world. James J. Gibson (e.g., 1979) proposed the concept of **affordances:**

> The *affordances* of the environment are what it *offers* the animal, what it *provides* or *furnishes,* either for good or ill. The verb *to afford* is found in the dictionary, but the noun *affordance* is not. I have made it up. I mean by it something that refers to both the environment and the animal in a way that no existing term does. It implies the complementarity of the animal

and the environment. The antecedents of the term and the history of the concept will be treated later; for the present, let us consider examples of an affordance.

If a terrestial surface is nearly horizontal (instead of slanted), nearly flat (instead of convex or concave), and sufficiently extended (relative to the size of the animal), and if its substance is rigid (relative to the weight of the animal), then the surface *affords support*. It is a surface of support, and we call it a substratum, ground, or floor. It is stand-on-able, permitting an upright posture for quadrupeds and bipeds. It is therefore walk-on-able and run-over-able. It is not sink-into-able like a surface or a swamp, that is, for heavy terrestial animals. Support for water bugs is different. (J. J. Gibson, 1979, p. 127)

Once again, human biology determines cognition. According to Gibson, there is something in our biology that makes us see a supporting structure when we perceive a terrestial, horizontal, flat, extended, and rigid surface. Once again, the environment determines cognition as well, for, "Affordances are not invented or read into events by the perceiver. They are there to be perceived" (E. J. Gibson, 1982, p. 57).

There are a few basic mechanisms of perceptual learning according to Eleanor Gibson. **Abstraction** is the finding of distinctive features or invariant relationships (i.e., relations that remain constant for a class of events). **Filtering** involves ignoring the irrelevant dimensions. A third mechanism is **peripheral attention:** processing of information that is out of central attention is critical to determining where next to focus attention. Peripheral visual mechanisms "look ahead" and guide the movement of the eyeball from fixation at one point A to a next point B (e.g., Just & Carpenter, 1987).

The Gibsons' view is that people are inherently motivated to learn from a world that is filled with what can be known. People are biologically prepared to abstract particular types of information from the environment. Learning is gradual and covaries with experience. Diverse perceptual experiences and many opportunities to interact with the world in meaningful ways is a Gibsonian prescription for high-quality perceptual learning. Humans have evolved to fit their environment (Gibson 1979)—human evolution has been shaped by the environment and in turn, each generation of humans comes to understand the environment in particular ways because of that evolutionary shaping. Our perception has evolved to guide our functioning in the world. We do not walk off cliffs because our perceptual apparati have evolved so that the perceptual array that defines the edge of a cliff affords falling to us (see Walk & Gibson, 1961).

PIAGETIAN THEORY OF COGNITIVE DEVELOPMENT: EQUILIBRATION AND COGNITIVE CONFLICT AS MECHANISMS FOR LEARNING AND DEVELOPMENT

No single individual has had as much impact on the study of children's mind and mental capacities as Jean Piaget (Figure 7.1). Although many of the specific descriptions and explanations of development offered by Piaget are no longer accepted, Piaget and his collaborators defined many of the problems that continue to occupy researchers interested in children's mind and the development of mental capacities. Moreover, his theory inspired a philosophy that continues to affect education, especially the education of young children.

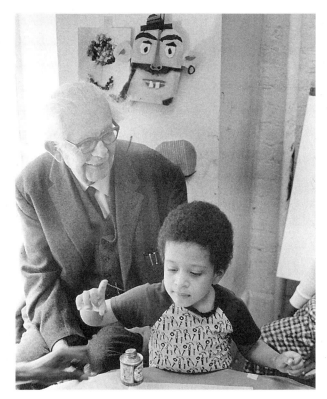

Figure 7.1 Although some of Jean Piaget's specific conclusions are debated, there is little doubt that he was the father of cognitive development psychology. His stage theory is much-knowledge for any educational psychologist.

Cognitive Development According to Piaget

Four Stages   According to Piaget (e.g., 1983), there are four stages of cognitive development that occur in an invariant sequence. Although Piaget frequently warned against applying age norms to the stages, the **sensorimotor stage** was generally considered as the first 2 years of life. Intelligence during this period of time is not yet in the mind but rather is in the actions of the child on the environment. Piagetians devoted substantial resources in the 1960s and 1970s to understanding the development of motor actions and the coordination of motor actions during infancy (schemes, in Piagetian terms). A particularly important acquisition during this period is the development of the **object concept,** the understanding that objects continue to exist independent of one's self. Before this acquisition, children act as if objects that are out of their sight no longer exist; once the object concept is acquired, the child understands that objects have an existence independent of their perception of the objects. By the end of the sensorimotor period, **symbolic functioning** has begun, especially the use of language. An organism that can use language and understands that there is a world independent of itself can no longer be considered to be functioning only on sensory and motor planes.

The **preoperational stage** roughly corresponds to the preschool years. There are significant advances in language and other competencies during this period. What is emphasized about the preoperational stage, however, are the child's incompetencies rather than competencies. The incompetency that has received the most attention from researchers is the preschool child's failure on **conservation tasks.** On a conservation problem, a substance is transformed in a way that does not alter its amount but changes its appearance (e.g., liquid is poured from a tall beaker to a stout beaker). The preschooler will claim that the amount changed despite the fact that nothing was added or subtracted. Thus, the preschooler might argue that there is more liquid after pouring because the water is wider or that there is less liquid because it is not as tall in the glass. The child is attending to and interpreting individual perceptual cues that are misleading with respect to the constancy of the amount of liquid.

Several years later, when the child can conserve, he or she gives explanations about how height and width offset one another and about how amount cannot change when nothing is added or subtracted.

That is not to say that there is no logic during the preschool years. Thus, if asked whether it is the same water when water is transferred from beaker A to beaker B, preschoolers understand that it is. Understanding that the **identity** of the water survives a perceptual transformation does not permit children to make logical claims about the relative amounts of water in the tall versus the wide beaker, however—the same child who will respond that it is the same water before and after pouring will also claim that there is now more or less water than there was before the pouring. Whatever logic is present is limited, however, with illogical responding produced easily by even small increases in difficulty of problems (e.g., asking whether it is the same amount of water versus the same water).

The preschool years are characterized, according to Piaget, by **egocentrism,** the inability to take the perspective of others. Thus, studies were offered by Piagetians in which preschoolers claimed that others, who viewed a set of objects from an angle different than their own angle of view, saw the set of objects from exactly the same perspective as they saw them. The Piagetians also contended that egocentric speech predominated in the language of preschoolers, so that a high proportion of utterances offered by preschoolers were not intelligible to others or social in the sense that they communicated information to other people well. In short, preschoolers generally were depicted as incompetent by Piagetians, despite a great deal of rhetoric by Piagetians about their focus on the competence of children.

The reason preschoolers' thought is so deficient according to Piaget is that they lack the logical **operations** that underlie mature thought. Basically, these are cognitive rules. One is the **identity** function already described. A second is **negation,** that an operation can be undone by returning to the point of departure (i.e., by reversing it, such as pouring the water back in the tall beaker—or doing so mentally). **Reciprocity** is recognition that change on one dimension can be compensated for by changes on another dimension (e.g., the same amount of water will be higher in a narrow than in a broad beaker).

Having such rules permits conservation according to Piagetians: The child with **operational intelligence** can reason that the amount of water in the wider beaker is the same as it was in the taller beaker because he or she can mentally undo the pouring (i.e., can reverse it). The child can also point out the reciprocal relationship between height and width of the liquid. The child who is in one of the two stages of operational intelligence is a much more powerful thinker than the preoperational preschooler.

During the **concrete operational stage**, which corresponds roughly to the elementary-grade years, the child can apply the cognitive operations, so long as the problem involves concrete objects (i.e., does not involve abstract manipulation or hypotheticals). Thus, if shown two rows of seven buttons lined up evenly, the child continues to believe the two rows contain the same number of buttons even when one of the rows is "stretched" so that there is greater space between individual buttons (i.e., the child can do number conservation problems). If two balls of clay are the same weight as evidenced by them exactly balancing a pan scale, the conserving child will predict that the scale will stay in balance even if one of the two balls is reshaped, perhaps flattened like a pancake or rolled into a snake (i.e., the child can do conservation of weight problems).

Concrete operations permit the performance of other tasks as well, such as **class inclusion** problems. These involve presenting children with sets of objects, some of which are subsets of each other. The child's task is to answer questions about the subset relationships. Thus, if given a set of five robins and four bluebirds, the conserving child understands there are more birds than robins, whereas the preoperational child is more likely to respond that there are more robins because there are more robins than bluebirds apparent in the perceptual array that the child is viewing. According to Piagetian theory, concrete operations also permit children to seriate items (i.e., ordering them on some dimension, such as shortest to tallest or lightest to heaviest).

Children who have acquired **formal operations** are capable of more still. First, they can handle problems that involve more factors. Thus, although the concrete operational child can seriate with respect to one dimension, the formal operational child can do so with respect to several dimensions simultaneously. Formal operational thinkers can also generate all combinations of possibilities for a given situation. Formal operational thinkers can infer "invisible forces" and thus can solve problems involving such forces (e.g., determining how hydraulic presses work given some weights and several presses).

In our classes, we frequently use one of the Piagetian tasks designed to tap formal operations to demonstrate the nature of formal operational thought to university students. For the pendulum

problem, we provide three lengths of string and three different weights that can be attached to the string. The question posed to students is to determine what factors determine the rate at which a pendulum swings. In most classes, the first student volunteer will propose the following: (1) Use one of the strings and try each weight in succession, and (2) use one of the weights and try each string in succession. What becomes apparent is that the speed of swinging varies with the length of the string, but not the weight. Good students will also vary systematically how much force they use to set the pendulum in motion, determining that this is not a critical factor in the speed of the pendulum swing. Some students act like fully rational scientists in this situation, varying one factor at a time while holding other factors constant. Such thinking is possible only with the onset of the formal operational stage according to Piagetian conceptions of intelligence.

Development according to the Piagetian perspective is biologically determined, following an inevitable sequence. Not surprisingly, the most important mechanisms underlying the movement through the stages are also biologically determined according to Piagetian theory.

Mechanisms of Cognitive Change Piaget (e.g., 1983) recognized that there were multiple determinants of developmental change. The first, **maturation**, is biological. Piaget's view was that as the organism matured physically, new possibilities for development were opened. Although biological development is necessary for cognitive growth, it is not sufficient for such growth to occur. **Experience** plays a role as well: New cognitive acquisitions are exercised (i.e., practiced). Experience with the physical world permits the abstractions of important regularities (e.g., that as the amount of something increases, its weight increases; color and weight do not always covary). There are also opportunities for what Piaget refers to as **logicomathematical experiences**, which involves learning about the effects of actions on objects:

> . . . For example, if a child, when he is counting pebbles, happens to put them in a row and . . . make[s] the astonishing discovery that when he counts them from right to the left he finds the same number as when he counts from the left to the right, and again the same when he puts them in a circle, etc., he has discovered experimentally that the sum is independent of order.

But this is a logicomathematical experiment and not a physical one, because neither the order nor even the sum was in the pebbles before he arranged them in a certain manner (i.e., ordered them) and joined them together as a whole. What he has discovered is a relation, new to him, between the action of putting in order and the action of joining together . . . and not . . . a property belonging to pebbles. (Piaget, 1983, p. 119)

The **social environment** also plays a role in development, with Piaget believing that the speed of movement through the stages could be affected by the quality of the child's social environment at home and school, with environments that permitted practice of new skills and logicomathematical experiences increasing the speed of movement from one stage to the next.

An especially critical mechanism affecting cognitive growth according to Piaget is **equilibration.** At any given point of development, children understand the world in terms of the cognitive operations they have developed (i.e., they **assimilate** new information). Thus, consider how a preoperational child, who does not have cognitive structures that permit understanding of compensation, responds to a conservation of weight problem. A ball of clay is presented. When rolled out into a sausage shape, the child indicates there is less clay now than when the clay was in a ball because the sausage is "thinner." The cognitive structures possessed by a preoperational child foster attention to only one dimension in making conservation judgments. If the experimenter continues to roll the sausage out, it gets longer and longer so that the length dimension becomes more salient and more difficult to overlook. Some of the time the child responds based on this increase in length, reporting that there is more clay when the clay is in the shape of a sausage than in the shape of a ball. The child eventually becomes aware of the oscillation between responding one way based on length and another way based on width, with the result being **cognitive conflict**—there is increasingly obvious difficulty in making a conservation judgment based on only one dimension. There is disequilibrium in that the cognitive structures that had been perceived by the child to work well on conservation tasks are no longer perceived to be adequate. This motivates reflection that results in the construction of new cognitive structures permitting compensation. This occurs through a process known as **accommodation:**

. . . [A]ccommodation [is] any modification of [an] assimilatory scheme or structure by the elements it assimilates. (Piaget, 1983, p. 107)

Once this accommodation occurs, there is a return to equilibrium: The structures that permit compensation produce solutions to conservation problems, responses that are perceived to be adequate.

We know from years of teaching these ideas that they are confusing, so here is another run through the notion of equilibration, this time with respect to conservation of liquid in Flavell's (1985) words:

. . . [T]he nonconserver usually focuses his attention only on the greater height of the liquid column in the taller, thinner glass, and therefore concludes that it has more liquid than the standard [in a shorter, wider glass]. His thinking about this problem is said to be in equilibrium, albeit at an immature, nonconservation level.

Suppose, however, that at some point he notices that the new column is thinner, a fact that by itself would incline him to conclude that the new glass contains less liquid than the standard. If he finds both of these opposing conclusions plausible at the same psychological moment, his cognitive system has moved from a state of equilibrium to one of disequilibrium or cognitive conflict with respect to this problem. According to Piaget, states of cognitive conflict and disequilibrium impel the child to make cognitive progress. In this case, the child achieves a new more intellectually advanced equilibrium state by conceptualizing both the height increase and the width decrease as predictable, mutually compensatory changes in a process of physical transformation that leaves liquid quantity unchanged. (Flavell, 1985, p. 289)

Natural development of conservation occurs when the child discovers the inadequacy of his or her belief in nonconservation (a belief long held without question and thus considered to be an **equilibrated** belief in Piagetian terms). A disconfirmation of such an expectation leads to destabilization of the belief that amount varies with appearance (such destabilization is **disequilibration**). Disequilibration motivates efforts to understand the principle that amount does not vary with appearance. Resolution of the cognitive conflict between a long-held belief and a new more adequate conception of a situation produces a new **equilibrium.**

Equilibration involves both assimilation and accommodation, with assimilation the tendency to interpret new situations in terms of existing cognitive structures and accommodation the tendency to adapt cognitive structures so that they produce expectations more in accord with what actually occurs in the world. This is the most important mechanism of cognitive change according to the Piagetians, with their assumption being that cognitive development is many cycles of equilibrium, disequilibrium, followed by equilibrium at a higher level of competence (see Piaget, 1983).

Although the Genevans resisted the idea that concepts such as conservation could be developed through instruction, they eventually conceded that instruction could affect conceptual development (e.g., Inhelder, Sinclair, & Bovet, 1974). Their concession was limited, however, and contrasts dramatically with alternative views of conceptual learning that will be presented later in this chapter.

Limits of Instruction According to Piagetian Theory One of the frustrations for educational psychologists who read Piaget is that he made few explicit recommendations for education. This was because of Piaget's conviction that cognitive development was largely a biological unfolding of cognitive stages. In 1974, the Genevans (Inhelder et al., 1974) produced a book on *Learning and the Development of Cognition*. The strong belief in biological inevitability came through clearly in this book. Piaget was an extreme "readiness" theorist. The view developed in Inhelder et al. (1974) was that instruction of a concept would be profitable only when children were on the verge of acquiring the concept naturally (i.e., acquisition of a concept might be speeded up but within the constraints of natural development— only for those concepts that are just a bit beyond where the child is already).

Piaget's distaste for research on educational acceleration is well-known, with Piaget and his Genevan colleagues derogating work on instruction as the "American question" (see Brainerd, 1978a). In conceding that a little acceleration was possible, Inhelder et al. (1974) made clear the Genevan view that the only educational mechanisms that could produce legitimate conceptual change were ones that mirror naturalistic development via equilibration (cognitive conflict).

Thus, a number of educators attempted to design environments encouraging discovery via equilibration, believing that such discovery would lead to deeper understanding than would other forms of learning, consistent with the general Piagetian theoretical position (see Brainerd, 1978a). The tasks given to children in such environments are ones that are developmentally appropriate, so it is essential to diagnose the child's current developmental stage and match instruction to it (Brainerd, 1978a; 1978b, Chapter 7). Instruction in such environments wa largely aimed at increasing children's awareness of conflicts between their approaches to problems and features of the problems (e.g., that in considering the width of a clay sausage, they are neglecting its length).

Kamii (1985, Chapter 8 written with DeClark) summarized Piagetian principles of education (adapted slightly here): (1) Adult power should be reduced as much as possible, with instruction encouraging the exchange of points of view between teachers and children and between children and children. (2) Children should be encouraged to think in their own ways rather than to produce the right answers in the right way as defined by a teacher. (3) Instruction should be intrinsically motivating. For example, much of arithmetic instruction can occur in the context of games. (4) Teachers should not correct wrong answers, but rather should provide hints and nudges about information the child might not be taking into account or may want to reconsider.

Kamii (1985), who was principally concerned with instruction of mathematics via Piagetian principles, urged teachers to tie instruction to problems of daily living (e.g., construct math lessons about potential outcomes in class votes; develop graphs and representations of attendance patterns in the class as well as demographics of the class). She encouraged teachers to provide students with challenging problems and to take the time necessary to solve the problems in ways that encourage deep student understandings of the problems and alternative solutions. Teaching of math should occur throughout the school day (e.g., graphing information generated during a class science experiment). Consistent with Piagetian principles, such teaching is concrete and tied to personal understandings that permit ready assimilation of much of the information. Piagetian views on education will be reiterated later, especially in the chapters on math and science instruction (see Chapters 12 and 13). In these two arenas, Piagetian-inspired thinking about education is enjoying a renaissance.

Evaluation of Piaget's Theory

From the mid-1960s to the mid-1970s, Piaget's theory was the preeminent theory of cognitive development. Much of the interest and enthusiasm followed publication of Flavell's (1963) book-length summary of the theory. Voluminous research on various aspects of Piaget's theory was generated during these two decades. Partially as a result of this work, however, much of the interest and enthusiasm for the theory died.

Many research outcomes were not consistent with Piaget's theory. Brainerd's (1978b) book was a culminating blow to the Piagetian perspective. Brainerd summarized evidence making obvious that some abilities were acquired earlier than Piaget had supposed (e.g., making simple inferences, some abstract logical processes). Other acquisitions came in later than specified by the theory (e.g., conservation of volume). Some behaviors reported by Piaget never were manifested anything like Piaget proposed (e.g., Piaget's depiction of preschooler speech as extremely egocentric was not consistent with the many communicative competencies possessed by preschoolers).

Some of the most important constructs and mechanisms specified in the theory proved challenging to study. For example, equilibration was almost impossible to operationalize. Measures of the various concrete and formal operations were difficult to devise. These difficulties resulted in great logical circularity in many tests of Piagetian ideas because there was no way to assess stage attainment independent of performing tasks presumably mediated by the cognitive structures characterizing a stage (Brainerd, 1978c). For example, arguments were made that if a child was concrete operational, the child should be able to do the concrete conservation tasks. How would one know if a given child possessed the concrete operations? He or she could do the concrete conservations.

While Piaget's theory was being challenged by disconfirming data, an alternative conception of thinking and the development of intellectual competence was faring well. Many information processing models and interventions based on information processing analyses of thinking and learning (i.e., models compatible with the models covered in Chapters 1 through 5) were being tested and validated. Moreover, information processing models could be applied more flexibly to analyses of many more school-valid tasks than could Piagetian perspectives. Thus, this book is filled with information processing analyses of writing, problem solving, reading, and science learning. The alternative was not only a better pre-

dictor of research outcomes, but also it was capable of producing predictions about and interventions relevant to more domains.

Two other limitations to the Piagetian approach became obvious as familiarity with the theory increased: (1) The theory is minimally informative about determinants of individual differences in mental functioning. Although information processing theories provided insights about intellectually disabled children as well as understandings about how to educate such populations (see Chapter 18), no such insights or guidance followed from Piagetian analyses. (2) Piaget's developmental theory accounts only for a fraction of life-span development. Once formal operations are obtained, Piaget's theory is, in general, silent about additional developments. Rarely did Piaget ever even discuss adult development. When he did (e.g., Piaget, 1972), development across the life span was seen as extending the operational competence developed during childhood and adolesence to new arenas and tasks. There have been only a few attempts to evaluate Piaget's thinking about adulthood, although studies to date in this tradition have generally confirmed Piagetian expectations. Thus, Kuhn, Kohlberg, Langer, and Haan (1977) demonstrated that formal operational competence does extend into new domains with increasing age and experience during adulthood. In contrast, the information processing frameworks have proven to be extremely helpful in understanding many more aspects of aging, from the mechanisms that underlie diseases of aging, such as Alzheimer's disease (see Poon, 1986), to explanations of exceptional competence during old age despite biological decline (e.g., Labouvie-Vief, 1985; Poon, 1985; see Chapter 18, this book). Information processing models have stimulated many more studies of intellectual development across the life span than have Piagetian conceptions.

Interest in Piaget's theory waned because of weaknesses in its predictive validity as well as limits in its scope (i.e., it was concerned mostly with development of normally functioning children). Piaget's thinking declined in prominence as well because of the success of other theories, such as the information processing conceptions of thinking and learning. Even so, Piagetian-inspired analyses continue to have powerful impacts in mathematics and science education today, and thus this is not the last mention of Piaget in this book. In addition, Piagetian thinking is inspiring new theoretical analyses of education that take into account information processing, with the most prominent of these approaches to development by Case and co-workers.

We close this coverage of Piaget's theory with brief discussion of Case's framework, a point of view that is not yet fully developed but is important because it is a thoughtful attempt to reconcile two important traditions in cognitive development, one in which stages of development are considered critical and the other in which processing mechanisms are the main concern. Case explains stages in terms of information processing mechanisms.

Case's Neo-Piagetian Theory of Development

Similar to Piaget, Case (e.g., 1991) argues for four distinct stages of cognitive development, which occur in an invariant sequence. The sequencing is invariant because each stage reflects differentiation, coordination, and consolidation of schemes present in the immediately previous stage. Case focuses on schemes rather than operations, however. According to Case, smaller schemes that were once separate combine to form larger, more powerful schemes. These larger schemes are increasingly coordinated with one another. More powerful schemes that are coordinated better permit more adequate performances.

Thus, a 4-year-old can draw a human figure that has many of the global features of humans. A slightly older child can draw a more differentiated figure and do so in relation to a larger scene. Case's explanation is that the drawings of the older child represent a differentiation not present in the younger children, with the parts of a drawing differentiated into figure (the human) and ground (the larger scene). The 6-year-old's systems for drawing figures and for drawing the larger scene also represent integrations of skills that are not integrated for 4-year-olds. The 6-year-old coordinates these two systems to produce the more complete pictures, a complex coordination relative to the coordinations possible for 4-year-olds.

How and why is there an improvement in drawing ability according to Case's theory? Part of the explanation is practice. Only schemes that are highly practiced can be differentiated into new schemes and then integrated with other schemes. Thus, a great deal of practice in drawing global figures is required before there is differentiation of drawing schemes. This practice must occur until the child can perform automatically the behaviors that once were done only with considerable effort and attention. Thus, although a young 4-year-old might have to expend all available mental energy to draw a stick figure, a slightly older child who has drawn many such stick figures can do so automatically, and thus less working memory is consumed during drawing of global human figures. This frees up some working memory for attention to other things, including acquisition of new understandings of how figure and ground can be separated. That is, with increasing automaticity in execution of skills, a child has more functional short-term capacity. The more functional short-term capacity, the better thinking in general.

Increasing functional short-term memory with development is the critical determinant of increases in cognitive competence according to Case's theory, with multiple factors accounting for developmental increases in working memory capacity: (1) As just explained, practicing a procedure increases its automatic functioning, with available capacity then used more efficiently, allowing more processes to be coordinated simultaneously and integrated in consciousness. (2) Children improve in their ability to shift their attention rapidly, getting better and better at moving between different sources of information and deploying attention (i.e., devoting capacity) to task-relevant information and ignoring task-irrelevant input (e.g., Bjorklund & Harnishfeger, 1990; Pearson & Lane, 1991; Tipper, Bourque, Anderson, & Brehaut, 1989). (3) In addition, as long-term memory develops and is better organized, information chunks are larger: The preschooler's "chunks" when attending to verbal material are single letters; the chunks held in memory by teenagers are whole words and phrases.

In addition to increases in functional capacity owing to increases in automaticity, ability to shift attention, and extent and organization of knowledge, the actual working memory available to a child probably increases as a function of neurological maturation according to Case. Because both functional increases and maturational increases in short-term capacity are indexed by age, it is difficult to determine how much of the increase in apparent short-term abilities with development is due to functional increases in capacity and how much is due to biological increases in capacity.

In short, with development, there are two sources of capacity-mediated increases in performance: There are both increases in functional capacity because of greater efficiency in executing skills and increases in actual capacity. Note that Case focuses on developmental increases in functional capacity, although classical neo-Piagetian theory based on Pascual-Leone's [1970] model focused much more on presumed actual increases in biological capacity. According to Case, the greater a child's functional short-term capacity, the more complex a task the child can undertake (i.e., the more schemes can be coordinated), so that a child whose entire attention once was required to draw a stick figure can eventually draw a much more sophisticated human figure in a much more complex scene—for as drawing skills are automatized, attention is more readily shifted between various component pieces in the scene, and larger, more complex parts of the scene can be juggled in the mind's eye (i.e., where once only a circle containing three dots and a smile, representative of a head, could be held in memory at one instance, an older child can hold a fully featured head in mind, for the older child's knowledge of head features is much more complete). Case and colleagues are testing their latest version of neo-Piagetian thinking (previous versions were provided by Pascual-Leone, 1970, and Case, 1985), with this work particularly important to educational psychologists because of Case's interest in developing instruction that is appropriate to the developmental level of the child.

In broad terms, Case (1991) argues for beginning instruction with a task the child can understand and perform. The child should be made aware of how they are performing tasks, with tasks practiced until the child can carry them out automatically. Gradually, task demands are increased, although care is taken to make certain that the working memory demands placed on the child by more demanding versions of a task do not exceed the child's capacity. Guidance is provided at first as the child attempts the task, with this guidance and support faded as the child is able to execute the new task independently. The amount of working memory required to execute this new task decreases with practice, as execution of it becomes more automatic. Case and colleagues have been investigating such an instructional approach with respect to a variety of tasks, including learning of mathematics and everyday quantitative skills, such as telling time and working with money (see Case, 1991).

That Case's analyses may be on target is suggested by the similarity of his approach to instruction of other theorists and researchers considered in this book. By the end of this book, readers will be familiar with the instructional prescription of starting with a task within the child's competence, gradually increasing the demands, with supports provided as needed. Concerns with the limits of short-term capacity also recur in this book. Case's approach is an important bridge between Piaget's historically important theory and contemporary theories of learning and instruction based on information processing analyses. Thus, Piaget's notion of stage development is translated into neo-Piagetian terms as reflective of development of capacity: Rather than explaining the superiority of the 8-year-old relative to the 4-year-old on conservation as a function of acquiring concrete operations—as Piagetians would—neo-Piagetians explain it as reflecting development of capacity, with the 8-year-old having the capacity to meet demands of conservation tasks (e.g., paying attention to several dimensions, such as the height and width of a column of liquid, and keeping track of their covariations) and the 4-year-old lacking the required capacity (e.g., Chapman & Lindenberger, 1989).

To understand contemporary approaches to instruction fully, more than Piaget and information processing is required, however. The behaviorists' long concern with problems of learning and instruction has produced an indelible mark on contemporary instruction, with the introduction to these approaches composing the remainder of this chapter.

THREE CLASSICAL MECHANISMS OF LEARNING: CLASSICAL CONDITIONING, REINFORCEMENT, AND PUNISHMENT

One of the best summaries of classical learning theory as it applies to education is an article in *Harvard Educational Review* by Michael and Meyerson (1962). Any discussion of behavioral approaches to education must touch on the categories covered in Michael and Meyerson (1962). Almost a quarter century later, Michael (1985) offered another summary of behavioral theory, this time as a master lecturer at a meeting of the American Psychological Association. Any contemporary discussion of the theoretical implications of B. F. Skinner's work must cover the categories in Michael (1985). We relied heavily on Michael's overviews of behavioral theory in constructing what follows.

The behaviorists had a different orientation than any of the other theorists and researchers considered in this book thus far. They focused on directly observable behavior rather than internal, unobservable explanatory variables. There are no schemata in behavioral theory, no cognitive strategies, and no metacognition. Thus, a behaviorist interested in reading would focus on observable reading behaviors, from orienting in the direction of and attending to a book to turning pages to completing whole books. If studying decoding, a behaviorist would be willing to accept attempted decodings of words (so long as such attempts were verbalized aloud and thus were observable) or eye movement data. A behaviorist would not make inferences about the representations of words or letter-sound associations that might account for decoding errors. A behaviorist would not make inferences about morphological knowledge that might account for eye movements while processing a word. Because of the emphasis on observable behaviors, many interested in education have considered behavioristic analyses to be superficial, believing that if education is anything, it is reshaping minds, which cannot be observed directly. Many educators accept that inferences about potential mental structures can be made from observable data and that to stop at the level of the observation is not to do justice to the complexity of human learning. For the most part, we agree.

Even so, the contributions of the Skinnerians to education cannot be questioned, and the importance of their perspective to students of educational psychology is undeniable. The teacher who understands behavioral principles will better understand behavior (Figure 7.2).

Basic Principles

The three most critical mechanisms in learning according to classical behaviorism are **classical conditioning** (sometimes known as respondent conditioning), **operant conditioning,** and **punishment.** **Classical conditioning** has been understood since the late 19th century, when the phenomenon was first explained by Ivan Pavlov (Bower & Hilgard, 1981). Pavlov observed that when meat powder is placed in a dog's mouth, the dog salivates. The food is an **unconditioned stimulus** that elicits an **unconditioned response,** salivation. As a boy, author MP knew that he could get the family's pet Irish Setter, Red, to salivate anytime, simply by approaching Red's dog house with a pan of food. The food pan was a **conditioned stimulus** that had acquired the power to elicit a **conditioned response,** salivation. That is, MP's approach with the food pan had rec-

Figure 7.2 Skinner believed deeply in the power of positive consequences. His insights are reflected in modern principles of classroom management. Although radical behaviorism is no longer fashionable, Skinner's work remains important, influencing modern conceptions such as cognitive behaviorism, which is taken up later in this chapter.

curred so many times that classical conditioning had occurred. A great deal of research (see Bower & Hilgard, 1981), beginning with Pavlov, has established which initially neutral stimuli that accompany (usually precede) unconditioned stimuli often become conditioned stimuli.

Although behaviorists such as Skinner and Michael acknowledge classical conditioning, behavioral theorists also emphasize that such conditioning is not a prominent part of human learning, especially human learning in school. Far more important than classical conditioning in human learning, however, is **operant conditioning.** Although the focus of learning with classical conditioning was with respect to the stimulus, the focus in operant learning is on an emitted response. Note that the operantly conditioned response is not elicited but emitted, reflecting that such responses are not reflexive behaviors but ones the organism can control. **The likelihood of an operant response being emitted in the future is increased when it is followed by a reinforcer.** This is the most fundamental principle in Skinner's psychology, a principle that is derived directly from Thorndike's **law of effect.**

Receiving a Coke after putting 75¢ in a Coke machine is an **unconditioned reinforcer** for depositing the money in that the Coke satisfies a biological deprivation. Other unconditioned reinforcers include food, sex, and exposure to aesthetically pleasing stimuli. Most reinforcers that people receive are not unconditioned reinforcers, however, but **conditioned reinforcers.** Thus, for coming to work daily, teaching class, supervising students, and doing research, the University gives your professor a check. No biological needs are satiated by the check directly. What the check permits is the purchase of goods and services that fulfill basic needs such as for food, beverage, and stimulation. As the label "conditioned reinforcer" implies, conditioned reinforcers have acquired their reinforcement properties by being paired with unconditional reinforcers (i.e., money was not always valuable to us but came to be so because its presence permitted acquisition of unconditioned reinforcers). For many schoolchildren, positive attention is an unconditioned reinforcer. Teachers also pass out conditioned reinforcers in the forms of grades and stickers, concrete rewards that often lead to unconditioned reinforcement, such as direct teacher praise and parental approval.

Reinforcement occurs only under particular conditions. If the conditions in the future are similar to the conditions that were in place when the reinforcement occurred, the response that was reinforced is more likely than if the conditions are different. This is known as **stimulus control of behavior.** The particular conditions that were in place when a response was reinforced come to be a **discriminant stimulus** for emitting the response, signaling that a reinforcement is likely if the response in question is emitted in this situation.

Reinforcements do not occur every time a person emits a response. Rather, they tend to occur intermittently. Such **intermittent reinforcement** has an interesting and important property. Learning that occurs via intermittent reinforcement is more resistant to extinction than learning that occurs under continuous reinforcement. Thus, perhaps one in three football games that football fans watch are exciting. They come back for more, however. Suppose a person's first exposure to football involved five exciting games in a row. If the sixth game were dull, that might tend to decrease the likelihood he or she would go to a seventh game than if only the first and fourth games seen previously had been exciting. Although Skinner did not use the term **expectation,** we do (and will develop the concept more fully later in

this chapter) because continuous reinforcement produces expectations about reinforcement every time a response is emitted, which increases vulnerability to extinction whenever a reinforcement fails to occur. In contrast, intermittent reinforcement creates an expectation that reinforcement is a sometimes occurrence and that if a person persists, reinforcement eventually occurs.

There are two ways that reinforcement can be intermittent. One is that it can follow a given number of responses (i.e., a **ratio reinforcement schedule**). Thus, a child who receives a sticker for completing 10 worksheets is on a ratio schedule of reinforcement. Alternatively, reinforcement can be delivered at particular time intervals. Some teachers reinforce a class on Fridays with extra afternoon recess if the class has been able to get weekly work in on time. This is an **interval reinforcement schedule.** The two types of schedules have dramatically different impacts on responding. The ratio schedule tends to produce high rates of responding that do not vary much except perhaps for a small reduction in responding immediately after payoff. The intermittent schedule tends to produce a rapid decline in performance immediately after payoff that only gradually increases until it reaches a maximum just before payoff. Thus, a teacher with a reinforcements-on-Friday schedule should expect fewer assignments coming in on Monday, Tuesday, and Wednesday, compared with Thursday and Friday.

Readers might be able to understand intermittent reinforcement by considering their own situation. The opportunities for reinforcement in university courses come at the examinations. Learning a great deal about educational psychology should result in reinforcement for studying. When does the most studying in this course occur, right before a test or after it? Is there an increase in studying as the time for an opportunity for reward (i.e., a test) draws nearer? Over the years, this example has convinced many students in our classes that their behaviors are often under the control of reinforcement contingencies.

There are two important classes of reinforcers, **positive reinforcers** and **negative reinforcers.** The occurrence of either of these types of reinforcers following a behavior increases the probability for future performance of the behavior preceding the reinforcement. Thus, many people are positively reinforced for turning on the radio and hearing classical music that they like. If many of these same people turn off a radio that is playing loud "heavy metal" music, negative reinforcement occurs. Positive reinforcement involves the presentation of a stimulus following a response; negative reinforcement involves the cessation of aversive stimulation following a response. Thus, if heavy metal music is aversive, any action leading to its cessation (e.g., turning off the radio) is negatively reinforcing. If listening to classical music is reinforcing, any action that results in classical music (e.g., tuning the radio to a classical station) is positively reinforced.

Negative reinforcement is often confused with punishment. **Punishment** involves presentation of aversive stimulation following a response. Thus, if a child sticks his finger in an electrical outlet, the jolt of electricity serves as a punisher. The response was sticking in the finger, which was followed by presentation of the aversive stimulation of electrical shock. The difference between negative reinforcement and punishment is that negative reinforcement involves the cessation of ongoing aversive stimulation as a result of an action taken by the responding organism, whereas punishment involves presentation of an aversive stimulus following a response, aversive stimulation that was not present before the response was emitted.

Students often experience great difficulty distinguishing these two terms, with the situation not helped much because many textbook authors mistakenly present negative reinforcement and punishment as synonymous. Check your understanding with these examples. Classify each of the following as an example of negative reinforcement or punishment:

- Jumping up after sitting on a tack. Jumping up is . . .
- Being spanked after swiping some money. Swiping money is . . .
- Receiving a ticket after speeding. Speeding is . . .
- Entering an air-conditioned building after near heat exhaustion outside. Entering the building is . . .
- Lifting one's hand from a hot stove. Lifting the hand is . . .

The answers were negatively reinforced, punished, punished, negatively reinforced, and negatively reinforced.

State of the Practice

In the 1960s, there was a great deal of thinking about how to use principles of operant psychology in

school. Although the first example discussed in this section, programmed instruction, is no longer being used widely as originally designed, it was the forerunner of much of the current generation of educational software and deserves mention for that reason alone. The second example, behavior modification and token economies in classrooms and other educational settings, is faring a little better, although it tends to be used in settings serving special populations more than in regular education classrooms. The third application, classroom management, is more than alive and kicking. Modern principles of classroom management are essential knowledge for any teacher.

Programmed Instruction and Teaching Machines

Conceptions of teaching machines appeared well before Skinner's views were well-known (e.g., Pressey, 1926), although Skinner's (e.g., 1961) writing would do more to spur the movement than previous contributions had done. The idea of programmed instruction was that if learning could be parsed up into small enough segments, with segments presented in sequence, exercises could be devised in which students would learn a little bit at a time with few misconceptions or misunderstandings. For each little bit of knowledge, students would be given an opportunity to respond. A correct response would be reinforced by showing the student that he or she was correct. Because learning was one little bit at a time, most responses would be correct and reinforced.

As an example, consider this sequence of frames from the Holland and Skinner (1961, pp. 52–56) program for teaching elementary behavioral principles (an example that fortuitously permits review of the difficult concept of negative reinforcement):

Reinforcement that consists of *presenting* stimuli (e.g., food) is called *positive* reinforcement. In contrast, reinforcement that consists of *terminating* stimuli (e.g., painful stimuli) is called _____ reinforcement. [Answer: negative]

Turning off a television commercial is reinforced by the *termination* of a(n) (1) _____ reinforcer; turning on a funny program is reinforced by the *presentation* of a(n) (2) _____ reinforcer. [Answers: (1) negative, (2) positive]

A stimulus is called a negative reinforcer if its _____-tion reinforces behavior. [Answers: termination or elimination]

Elimination of a television commercial may be a negative reinforcement. If so, the television

commercial is a(n) _____ reinforce-_____.
[Answers: negative, reinforcer]

Immediately after a student produces a response in reaction to a blank, there is an opportunity to check the response, in this case, by turning the page in the printed Holland and Skinner program (i.e., actual teaching machines had an answer window that could be opened). Determining that one's response matches the response provided by the program is reinforcing. Such reinforcement keeps motivation high, so the student stays the course and answers many such questions.

Pressey did much to start the programmed learning revolution, but he also did much to point out its limitations. As part of offering a number of criticisms of programmed instruction, Pressey (1963) elegantly summarized what was wrong with programmed mathematics:

> But did not Socrates so teach the slave boy? The boy could not read. What about the often-cited skilled tutor? He assumed that the student had done some reading. However, both Socrates and the tutor did further learning by asking questions. The writer would contend that neither simply presented an idea and then reinforced it. Brownell's (1928) early research regarding primary school children's learning of arithmetic here seems relevant. Simply telling them that $2 \times 3 = 6$ did *not* bring about real learning of that number combination. These sturdy little empiricists had not merely to be *told;* they had to be *shown,* as by putting out two sets each of three pennies and demonstrating that they did indeed count to six. They had similarly to verify, and to differentiate, that $2 + 3$ was 5 and $3 - 2$ was only 1. As Piaget (1954) and others have described, children gradually develop a number system, also cognitive schema as of space, causality; and they do this not by so crude a rote process as the accretion of bits of learning stuck on by reinforcements, but by progressive processes of cognitive integration and clarification. (p. 2)

The wisdom of Pressey's final comment in that quote will become obvious in Chapter 13, since this type of thinking is at the heart of contemporary conceptions of good mathematics instruction.

Although behaviorally oriented educators in the 1960s produced programmed materials for everything from beginning reading to mathematics to foreign language learning to science and religion (see de Grazia & Sohn, 1964, for a sampler of the range of possibilities), the movement died for the most part. Its appeal was theoretical—the prediction that high levels of learning could be produced by shaping through reinforcement of one small performance at a time was a straightforward extension of Skinner's theory. Programmed instruction was also taken seriously because it seemed to be a potentially economical way of teaching large bodies of knowledge. After all, programmed instruction was eliminating the need for teachers and tutors, with teachers and tutors often the greatest expense in any instructional system.

Although programmed instruction is rare today (albeit the Holland and Skinner [1961] program survives in some colleges in the United States), much of contemporary educational computing is constructed on similar principles. For example, many children today are becoming *Reader Rabbit* users. This popular program involves four different games (each with a number of variations) appropriate for children first learning to read words. Thus, there is a game involving an array of 12 "cards," each of which can be illuminated one at a time to reveal a word or a picture. The goal is to illuminate pairs of cards that go together, a word (e.g., bike) and its referent (e.g., a picture of a bike). Each time a match is made, there is positive reinforcement in that the two cards disappear and there is a bell sound. If the child makes all six matches in an efficient fashion, Reader Rabbit appears and does a little dance. Because there are different levels of each game (e.g., the easiest version of matching involves matching of pairs of pictures, so that matching two pictures of bicycles is reinforced; a somewhat harder version involves matching identical words, so that finding the two "bike" cards is reinforced), it is possible to find a level for most children that results in a high rate of correct responding and thus high reinforcement. Skinner and programmed instruction enthusiasts would feel good about *Reader Rabbit.*

Skinner never lost his intellectual commitment to programmed instruction (e.g., 1987, Chapter 8), largely because he so believed that students should not be required to advance at the same rate: "We could double the efficiency of education with one change alone—by letting each student move at his or her own pace" (Skinner, 1987, pp. 123–124). That idea comes up at a number of points in this book—recall the discussion of task-oriented classrooms in Chapter 5—although many educational theorists who are coming to the same conclusion often fail to realize that Skinner espoused such a position for most of his career and that student customizing of learning was one of the main motivations for programmed instruction.

Behavior Modification and Token Economies

One of the most salient interventions that evolved from behavioral conceptions of learning, behavior, and development was behavior modification. The main idea is to reinforce behaviors that are valued. If a person is not capable of those behaviors at present, reinforce behaviors they are capable of performing that are in the direction of the desired response, gradually increasing the criterion for reinforcement until the person can emit the desired response (i.e., shape the response). Thus, if a child does not do homework, find out what reinforcements matter to the child and provide those contingent on the completion of homework. If children in a class are not completing work carefully, provide reinforcements for carefully completed work. Sticker charts are used widely in American classrooms, with stickers earned for good grades on daily assignments. Such stickers are a form of **token reinforcement.** Other token reinforcements sometimes include chips that can be accumulated and eventually traded in for goodies or privileges.

Some behavior modification programs also include aversive components (i.e., punishment), although aversive stimulation was never an approach in favor with Skinner. The aversive stimulation that sometimes occurs as part of behavior modification has been the subject of much criticism and part of the reason for sensationalism with respect to such treatments. There are types of behavior modification that include, for example, use of cattle prods or other forms of electric shock on children. In the defense of these approaches, however, such aversive stimulation is provided in an attempt to eliminate more seriously injurious behavior. Children who self-stimulate by beating their heads against a wall are in grave danger of doing permanent and serious neurological damage. Even a mild electrical shock can sometimes disrupt such behaviors (e.g., Lovaas, Schaeffer, & Simmons, 1965; Merbaum, 1973; Tate, 1972). When aversive stimulation is used to eliminate behaviors as serious as self-mutilation, it is defensible.

Other punishments sometimes are acceptable as well. For example, if a teacher has set up a token economy in which children are rewarded for particular appropriate behaviors, it is reasonable for there to be a response cost in the form of forfeited tokens when the child engages in inappropriate behaviors. Another alternative acceptable in many settings is **time-out,** in which a child is physically removed from the other children or activities for a short period of time. Time-out can involve moving a child to an isolated corner of the classroom, to another room, or to a hallway. Sometimes it involves having a child sit on a chair while classmates are permitted to continue roaming freely in the setting.

Good behavior modification environments often have other features as well. Correct and preferred behaviors are consistently modeled by staff. Adult attention, which is a powerful reinforcement for many children, is provided for appropriate action rather than inappropriate action. Thus, if the teacher wishes to reduce aggression in a child, the child does not get attention when aggressive (which often occurs in many schools where aggression is met by teacher attention in the form of disapproval), but rather the teacher interacts with the child when the child is being good.

Behavioral contracting is another behavior modification option, in which the child makes an agreement with the educator to attempt to reach a particular goal. Usually the contract is negotiated, with the student involved in deciding what the goal will be, what reinforcement might be earned, and how much progress toward the goal is required before there is any reinforcement. Opportunities for rehearsal of new behaviors in nonthreatening, reinforcing environments often is provided. For example, children who may not know socially appropriate behaviors are taught them and provided opportunities to rehearse them with feedback. Often, classroom behavioral programs are complemented by parent training, in which parents are taught how they can use behavioral principles to provide reinforcement consistent with the school's program. Thus, if a teacher is reinforcing a child for bringing homework into school, the parent can be trained to reinforce the child at home for doing homework.

When reinforcement systems are used, almost invariably they are deployed on an intermittent basis, if for no other reason than it is hard for a classroom teacher to monitor and reinforce every appropriate response by all of the students in a classroom. An important goal of any token economy is to increase the ratio or interval between reinforcements, until the desired behaviors are occurring given only typical classroom reinforcements, such as praise. The gradual reduction in reinforcement is known as **fading.** Again, this is a principle that will come up at several points in this book, sometimes with a different label (e.g., in the next chapter as "scaffolding" of instruction).

Behavior modification and token economies of various sorts enjoy a long track record of success (e.g., see Hobbs & Lahey, 1983). Even if an educator does not wish to have a full-blown token economy or be completely committed to behavior modification, there are well-validated, theoretically sensible practices developed by behavioral psychologists that have great appeal to many teachers. A teacher who provides attention to students only when they are disruptive is simply asking for more disruptions. Thus, many skilled teachers ignore misconduct and pay great attention to positive behaviors. Unless the errant behavior causes harm to either the perpetrator or other children, ignoring the infraction is often a viable option. Contracting with students is commonplace in many school settings today. All teachers should be aware of their power as social models (also see next subsection) and behave accordingly. It can be damaging to a child to be exposed to a teacher who is a negative role model. For example, teachers who model sexism are shaping sexism. Teachers who smoke in front of their pupils are definitely encouraging smoking. The list goes on and on. One way a teacher can shape positive behaviors is by modeling positive behaviors. (As a preview, many of the principles that were developed as part of behavior modification show up in the next subsection on classroom management.)

Special educators and special education researchers, in particular, continue to have a great deal of interest in application of behavioral principles to education, with many specific applications to a variety of special populations being studied. For example, in the past few years, there have been studies of the effects of behavioral rehearsal and feedback on the generalization of question-asking behaviors from special education settings to regular classrooms (Knapczyk, 1989; Secan, Egel, & Tilley, 1989) as well as research on observational learning (see next subsection as well) of language by severely retarded children through modeling (Charlop & Milstein, 1989; Goldstein & Mousetis, 1989). For an excellent discussion of many ways that behavior modification is and can be used with mentally deficient students, see Kiernan (1985). The practicality of behavioral teaching for special populations is obvious, with studies about how to teach everything from clearly academic tasks, such as the basic arithmetic facts (e.g., Dunlap & Dunlap, 1989; Van Houten & Rolider, 1989), to life skills tasks, such as banking (McDonnell & Ferguson, 1989) and acting in socially appropriate

ways in employment settings (e.g., Park & Gaylord-Ross, 1989). That behavioral methods are more prominent in special education than regular education does not imply that there are not important applications and research in regular education. For instance, a number of fine programs aimed at focused, but important behaviors have been developed. For example, behaviorists have been active in developing effective procedures for teaching children how to fend off potential sexual abuse and abduction (Miltenberger & Thiesse-Duffy, 1988; Poche, Yoder, & Miltenberger, 1988).

Behavior modification is a success story for psychology. It is possible to redesign many aspects of an institutional or classroom environment to operate in ways consistent with behavioral principles, with substantial evidence that academic achievement can be improved (see Pitts, 1971; Thoreson, 1972; and Ulrich et al., 1970, for many examples of behavior modification in classrooms). Even so, classrooms that are set up completely along behavior modification lines are rare. Nonetheless, behavioral psychology is at the center of most contemporary approaches to classroom management.

Classroom Management Before it is possible to teach anything academic, it is essential that the teacher take control of the class. Modern principles of classroom management provide teachers with a great deal of guidance about how to maintain order in the classroom without creating an aversive environment. For excellent, brief reviews that informed what follows in this subsection, see Doyle (1986) and Evertson (1989).

Classroom management starts before the year begins. One essential is to arrange the physical classroom so that order can be maintained and students can be monitored easily. Thus, in many elementary classrooms, much of each morning is composed of small reading groups meeting with the teacher in one section of the room while the rest of the class does seatwork. It is essential that the furnishings of the classroom be positioned so the teacher can conduct the reading group and easily look up to scan the rest of the classroom. The teacher also needs to establish early the rules and procedures of the classroom. The beginning of the school day, including the opening activities and the morning's administrative activities (e.g., taking attendance, collecting lunch tickets) should be routinized so that they can be carried out automatically and quickly. Some teachers group students by rows and establish that movement is by rows. The point of these movement routines is not just quiet and order but also rapid transition. Time spent in transition is time lost, and student achievement in school depends on the amount of time students are engaged in instruction. More than anything, the expectations must be clear. Students must be made aware of what is permitted and what is prohibited.

Providing students positive reinforcement when they are consistent with classroom rules is a must. Teacher praise, such as, "Row 2 has really been working hard this morning—way to go!" is common in well-managed classrooms. Providing students feedback about their behavior as well as the adequacy of their academic performances is critical.

Good teachers signal their expectations. They signal when they are concerned about classroom misconduct well before the misconduct accelerates into a situation requiring sanctions. The good teacher constantly monitors the classroom and the activities of students. When sanctions are necessary, the good teacher deals with the situation quickly and as unobtrusively as possible. Good teachers are effective at dispensing mild punishers, such as telling eye contact and gentle touches to move students away from distractions. Persistent misconduct is dealt with more harshly but efficiently and with little, if any, disruption of the class. A skilled teacher informs a student of detention in less than a couple of seconds, with the student's behavior quickly improving in recognition of the teacher being in control of the situation. The student probably also expects that if he or she does not shape up, an even greater sanction will be administered, an expectation built up through consistent policies.

Good teachers are models of self-control and on-taskedness. They not only reinforce students for reading outside books and doing well in math, but also they make obvious their own enthusiasm for reading and mathematics. Good teachers model that they find their own academic competencies to be rewarding and that students can reap the same types of rewards by learning the lessons offered in school. Students in well-managed classrooms learn a great deal about how to achieve life's long-term rewards as well as how to achieve short-term reinforcements, such as positive teacher attention for carrying out assignments in ways consistent with classroom policies.

Implementing behavior management in schools continues to be researched. For example, Gottfred-son, Gottfredson, and Hybl (1993) studied how conduct in middle schools improved when school rules were made clearer, consequences for violating them were more certain, classrooms were organized and managed more efficiently, parents were kept informed about the good behavior and misbehaviors of their children, and reinforcement was increased for good conduct. If we have a complaint about this type of research, there still is little information available about how such management affects student and teacher perceptions about school—that is, it has been too behavioral and not enough cognitive. There is much to be learned about how students think about and make decisions in schools that are managed well versus those that are managed poorly. We urge such research because of our strong perception that students much prefer well-managed schooling environments. We doubt that students feel they are being "behavior managed" in such settings so much as they feel they are being better educated.

Punishment   For the most part, behaviorism is a positive approach to student learning and development. The emphasis is clearly on catching the students doing well and reinforcing them for it. If the students cannot do well given current competencies, reinforce them for whatever behaviors are in the right direction and gradually shape up more complete and adequate responses. This emphasis on the positive is directly due to Skinner's theory and philosophy. Chapter 12 in *Science and Human Behavior* (Skinner, 1953—Skinner's best-known and most definitive summary of his views on the relevance of behavioral principles to human behavior) was a complete indictment of punishment. He made the case there that reductions in the frequency of undesirable behaviors using punishment were short-lived. Skinner also argued that punishment led to undesirable byproducts, such as anxiety. Even so, punishment has come to be part of the behaviorist's repertoire of methods. Ever responsive to his environment, Skinner (1953, Chapter 12) in response to behaviorists commited to punishment argued that if punishment is to be used, there should be an alternative behavior available that can be reinforced. This became known as **differential reinforcement of other behavior (DRO)** (e.g., see Ross, 1981), an important principle of behavior change.

A number of other behaviorists have studied parameters that affect the potency of punishment. In general, many of these psychologists were more sanguine than Skinner was that punishment can have enduring effects on elimination of undesirable behaviors without enduring side effects (see Walters & Grusec, 1977, for a review). A number of investigators have studied ways of supplementing punishment, with researchers such as Cheyne and Walters (1969), Parke (1969, 1974), and LaVoie (1973, 1974) establishing that rationales for obeying a prohibition can make punishment more effective. In many cases, rationales alone are as effective or more effective than punishments, with a number of researchers believing that rationales help children internalize prohibitions (e.g., Hoffman, 1970; Kanfer & Zich, 1974). Although rationales presented to young children (e.g., preschoolers) need to be concrete (e.g., you might break this toy if you played with it because it is fragile), abstract rationales that focus on the rights and feelings of others (e.g., the owner of this toy will feel bad if you play with it) are increasingly effective with advancing age during childhood (LaVoie, 1974; Parke, 1974; for a review, see Walters & Grusec, 1977, Chapter 5), consistent with Piagetian theory that concrete thinking precedes abstract thinking developmentally. The literature on rationale effects provided a good deal of support for the general position that undesirable behaviors can often be suppressed without resorting to punishment.

Still punishment exists in schools. Mild sanctions as part of a larger program of classroom management are not troubling. What is troubling is that severe sanctions often are meted out in American schools, despite the fact that there is no compelling evidence that such actions lead to better behaved students (Edwards & Edwards, 1987). Corporal punishment is still legal in more than half of the U.S. states, and it is used frequently in many jurisdictions (Hyman, 1990; Hyman & Wise, 1977). Every day children in the United States are flogged by their teachers with paddles and straps. No one with an understanding of learning theory could endorse such actions.

In fact, Skinner (1977) delivered a scathing indictment of the practice, concluding with an easily defensible claim that corporal punishment teaches that might makes right: "The punishing teacher who punishes teaches students that punishment is a way of solving problems" (p. 336). Many other behaviorists have elaborated on that analysis, offering the compelling view that brutal punishment in school sends all the wrong messages to children (Edwards & Edwards, 1987): There is no teaching of appropriate behaviors by beating another human being. What is promoted is the lesson that retaliatory aggression is fine. There is also the possibility of reinforcing undesirable behaviors such as leaving school—we suspect many troubled high school students would rather abandon an institution than risk a severe paddling. A bad message to convey to a youngster who may already be troubled or aggressive is that aggression is sometimes okay to deploy, and that message comes through loud and clear during a spanking in the principal's office.

Skinner cared greatly about students and wanted to eliminate some of the worst practices in education in favor of more effective and humane techniques. His was one of the most powerful voices ever raised to promote the development of schools with strongly positive atmospheres where students are reinforced for getting better, consistent with the important motivational principle we favored in Chapter 5 of eliminating classroom competition in favor of improvement from baseline (to use terms with which Skinner would have been comfortable).

Closing Comment   The behaviorists offered many prescriptions about and much research relevant to classroom learning. Powerful methods for maintaining order and attention to academic tasks have emerged from behavioral analyses, with the fruits of these efforts apparent in everything from modern educational computer programs to the way Miss Jones keeps the rest of the class busy at seatwork while five students meet for reading group. No one studying learning in educational settings should neglect behavioral contributions to education. Still behaviorism does not go far enough.

Cognition and Behaviorism

Educational psychology has largely become a cognitive psychology of education (as we hope is apparent by this point in the book). This clashes with a powerful anticognitive stance that typified Skinner's thinking throughout his career, but especially during his later years, as his theory and worldview gave way to the cognitive revolution. That is, Skinner was not just indifferent to cognitive psychology and its constructs; he was hostile. His last public statement (Skinner, 1990), a speech given to the American Psychological Association 8 days before his death, was largely an indictment of cognitive psychology.

Skinner believed strongly that cognitive psychology did not pay enough attention to the role of the environment in determining the behaviors of individuals. He believed that his theory was consistent with evolutionary perspectives, that the species survive to reproduce largely because they are appropriately responsive to their environment. Skinner also believed that many cognitive explanations could be translated into behavioral terms, and he often did so.

For example, cognitive scientists maintain that what we perceive from an array of visual stimulation is affected by prior knowledge. Skinner's explanation of the same is in terms of reinforcement:

> Everyday perception is the product of a vast number of experiences in which fragmentary patterns of light, resembling those of the moment in many different ways, have been present when behavior has had many reinforcing consequences. (Skinner, 1987, p. 96)

No constructs are more sacred to cognitive psychology than cognitive representations and rules (see Chapter 3). Skinner reduces those rules to reinforcement histories in his theory:

> Cognitive scientists presumably appeal to the storage and retrieval of representations and rules because they can then explain behavior by pointing to conditions that are present at the time when behavior occurs. The rat was changed when pressing the lever was reinforced, but it presses now "because it knows that pressing brings food." That knowledge is a current surrogate of the history of reinforcement. (Skinner, 1987, p. 101)

Skinner's complete disdain for the cognitive approach comes through in the conclusion to the essay that provided the three quotes just presented:

> *I accuse* cognitive scientists of misusing the metaphor of storage. The brain is not an encyclopedia, library, or museum. People are changed by their experiences; they do not store copies of them as representations or rules.
>
> *I accuse* cognitive scientists of speculating about internal processes which they have no appropriate means of observing. Cognitive science is premature neurology.
>
> *I accuse* cognitive scientists of emasculating laboratory research by substituting descriptions of settings for the settings themselves and reports of intentions and expectations for action.
>
> *I accuse* cognitive scientists of reviving a theory in which feelings and states of mind observed through introspection are taken as the causes of behavior rather than as collateral effects of the causes.
>
> *I accuse* cognitive scientists, as I would accuse psychoanalysts, of claiming to explore the depths of hu-

man behavior, of inventing explanatory systems that are admired for a profundity more properly called inaccessibility.

> *I accuse* cognitive scientists of relaxing standards of definition and logical thinking and releasing a flood of speculation characteristic of metaphysics, literature, and daily intercourse, speculation perhaps suitable enough in such arenas but inimical to science. (Skinner, 1987, p. 111)

Fortunately, others found points of contact and ways that behavioral and cognitive psychologies can complement one another. Thus, many of the principles identified by Skinner occur in other theoretical traditions that are in greater favor with educators in the 1990s—for example, fading of reinforcement contingencies looks a lot like scaffolding of instruction, which will be taken up in Chapter 8. Many of the educator behaviors Skinner favored endure even if his explanation of their effectiveness does not.

COGNITIVE BEHAVIOR MODIFICATION

Many who were well educated with respect to Skinner's theory found greater favor with cognitive theory than Skinner did, largely because they recognized that many "behavioral" interventions had a strong cognitive component. One of the leading figures in the development of cognitive-behavioral interventions was Meichenbaum, who remains an important influence on educational research and theory (Figure 7.3).

Meichenbaum's Cognitive-Behavioral Analyses: Self-Instructional Approaches to Self-Regulation

Meichenbaum was aware of a large American and Soviet literature establishing that self-speech did and could be used to organize behavior. The prominent cognitive-developmental psychologist Kohlberg (Kohlberg, Yaeger, & Hjertholm, 1968) had reported self-verbalizations by preschoolers that served to organize complex behaviors. Meichenbaum (1977, p. 19) cited the following example of child speech that had a directive function during the construction of a tinker toy car:

> The wheels go here, the wheels go here. Oh, we need to start it all over again. We have to close it up. See it closes up. We're starting it all over again. Do you know why we wanted to do that? Because I needed it

selves not to pay any attention to the distractor. Wozniak (e.g., 1972) had provided thorough conceptual analysis of how speech for self could regulate preschoolers' motor behaviors. He especially analyzed how speech-for-self could be mobilized to inhibit impulsive responding.

In short, there was a body of research supporting the position that speech for self could organize behavior. Although there were indicators, such as Kohlberg et al. (1968), that young children often used such speech on their own, there was also a body of data (e.g., Patterson & Mischel, 1976; Wozniak, 1972) substantiating that young children often benefit from explicit instruction to self-verbalize, especially with respect to the inhibition of impulsive responses. The potential of speech-for-self to inhibit behaviors was important to Meichenbaum because he was particularly interested in increasing reflective behaviors in populations of children who are impulsive, who respond without thinking about their responses.

Meichenbaum and Goodman (1971), in what is now a classic study in cognitive-developmental psychology, demonstrated that the impulsive responding of hyperactive second-graders could be reduced through teaching children to instruct themselves to go slowly and reflect before responding. Using teacher modeling, guided practice, and the gradual fading of teacher cuing, the students were taught to make self-verbalizations consistent with this ideal model of self-instruction during a copying task:

> Okay, what is it I have to do? You want me to copy the picture with the different lines. I have to go slowly and carefully. Okay, draw the line down, down, good; then to the right, that's it; now down some more and to the left. Good, I'm doing fine so far. Remember, go slowly. Now back up again. No, I was supposed to go down. That's okay. Just erase the line carefully . . . Good. Even if I make an error I can go on slowly and carefully. I have to go down now. Finished. I did it! (Meichenbaum & Goodman, 1971, p. 117)

Of course, these students were being asked to do a lot, with the self-instruction focusing the students on the definition of the problem, providing guidance to the motor behaviors required in the task, reinforcing the drawing that occurs (e.g., "Good"), and cuing coping when there were difficulties (Meichenbaum, 1977, p. 32).

Using Meichenbaum's approach, the teacher first described and modeled self-verbalization. Then the teacher provided external support and guidance

Figure 7.3 Donald Meichenbaum recognized before others that cognitive and behavioral conceptions could be combined to produce powerful psychological interventions. His basic research was informed by careful readings of Soviet and American psychologies. Professor Meichenbaum remains an active researcher and theorist, working at the University of Waterloo in Canada.

to go a different way. Isn't it pretty clever, don't you think? But we have to cover up the motor just like a real car. (Kohlberg et al., 1968, p. 695)

Prominent Soviet psychologists such as Gal'perin (1969) and Vygotsky (e.g., 1962; see Chapter 8, this book) had argued that mature thinking was largely inner speech and dialogue representing the end product of a developmental process that began with external speech, including external dialogue with others, which evolved into external speech to self. External speech that directed behavior eventually internalized in the Soviet models, with inner speech playing a major role in thinking.

The power of speech-for-self in the regulation of children's behavior had been demonstrated in a number of studies in the 1970s. For example, Patterson and Mischel (1976) had taught preschoolers to resist a temptation by teaching them to tell them-as a student attempted to apply the approach to problems. The student was encouraged during this process to internalize the self-verbalizations, with the teacher eventually guiding the student to whisper rather than talk aloud and then eventually only to think about the problem definition, task focusing and guiding directions, and self-reinforcement as they performed the task. This is consistent with two general principles of instruction that will recur in subsequent chapters: (1) Instruction should be designed to encourage internalization of strategies. (2) Teachers can do so by prompting internalization and gradually fading their guidance of processing, intervening only on an as-needed basis.

The most striking data confirming that this type of instruction reduced impulsive responding were obtained on the Matching Familiar Figures Test (MFFT), an instrument that involves presentation of a picture that matches one of six similar pictures. The test taker's task is to identify which of the six pictures exactly matches the standard. Reflective and careful feature-by-feature comparisons of the standard to the six alternatives is the preferred strategy; rapid responding that does not include systematic comparisons (i.e., impulsive responding) undermines performance on the MFFT. In general, initially impulsive children in the Meichenbaum and Goodman (1971) study, who were trained to self-instruct, made fewer errors on the MFFT than control children, who were also impulsive, but who were not taught how to instruct themselves verbally to perform tasks requiring reflection.

Enthusiasm for self-instruction was fueled by a number of follow-up studies with various child populations who were impulsive. Data produced at a number of sites and with a number of tasks were consistent with the conclusion that self-instructional training could reduce impulsive responding (e.g., Bender, 1976; Bugenthal, Whalen, & Henker, 1977; Camp, Blom, Hebert, & van Doornink, 1977; Douglas, 1972; Douglas, Parry, Marton, & Garson, 1976; Finch, Wilkinson, Nelson, & Montgomery, 1975; Glenwick, 1976; Guralnick, 1976; Kagen, 1977). See Pressley (1979) for a review of these and related studies; Meichenbaum (1977) provided extensive commentary on the relevance of some of these investigations (as well as of other data) to his position that impulsive responding could be overcome with self-instructional training. More recently, Fjellstrom, Born, and Baer (1988) provided especially impressive evidence that children as young as preschoolers can learn to self-question while performing an intel-

lectual task, with the self-questioning dramatically affecting performance.

Manning's Extensions of Self-Instruction to Classrooms

Meichenbaum (1977) inspired many classroom researchers to develop and study interventions with self-instructional components. Manning (1991), based largely on her own previous research (e.g., Manning, 1988, 1990), has elaborated the self-instructional model so that it is applicable in elementary classrooms (see also, Hughes & Hall, 1989, however, for additional illustrations of self-instructional interventions in school). An important component in Manning's model is a teacher who consistently models self-control using self-instruction.

Anyone who has ever taught knows the frustration of trying to figure out what is wrong with the overhead projector. A self-instructing teacher might cope as follows: Consistent with Meichenbaum's research, the teacher would first define the problem verbally, followed by self-verbalizations to direct appropriate actions: "Why won't this overhead turn on? Let me see. I'll try all the switches again. This arrow points to the right. Did I turn left or right. Try again." When frustrated (which typically occurs when working with an overhead projector—especially the kind that are programmed once they have been switched off to remain shut off until they are cooled), the teacher models coping via self-instruction: "It's easy to get frustrated. Take a deep breath and relax. There must be a solution." Once a solution is found, the teacher self-reinforces: "Hey! I stuck with it and found the outlet is faulty. I'll try this other outlet. Yay! It works." If there is no success, the teacher models more coping and adapting: "I've tried all I know. I'll either show you this information by putting it on the board or call the media specialist to help fix the machine. Which would be fastest?" (Manning, 1991, p. 134). Of course, there are many opportunities for a teacher to model such self-control, with the teacher who does so projecting the clear message that such self-instruction and reasoning is a mature way to approach problems.

The self-instructing teacher also models for students how to cope with problems and temptations to behave impulsively or inappropriately. Thus, the teacher might model the following sequence for a student who is unprepared and caught attempting to cheat, again starting with a verbalization of the problem and proceeding to model self-direction and self-coping until a solution is achieved that can be self-reinforced: "I forgot to study for my test. Should I look at my friend's test? I can see her paper easily. But, is that right? Just do my best. I'll feel better about myself if I don't look. This is hard. I know my answers are wrong. That's okay. I've done the best I can. Next time I won't leave my book at school. I'm glad I didn't take answers that didn't belong to me. I feel good about that!" (p. 135)

Manning's (1991) book is filled with suggestions as to how to structure the classroom environment to foster self-instruction. She discusses how teachers and peers can model self-instruction and how self-instruction can be practiced in the context of games and school tasks. In short, Manning (1991) provides a compelling discussion of how to translate the self-instructional framework developed by basic researchers into classroom practice. Many of the cognitive strategies for reading, writing, and mathematics that will be covered in subsequent chapters could be self-instructed. Some self-instructional models have already been devised, including interventions to promote important academic competencies such as student writing (see Graham & Harris, 1989a, 1989b; Chapter 15, this book), arithmetic (e.g., Keller & Lloyd, 1989), and higher-order problem solving (e.g., King, 1991). Teacher modeling of self-instruction and self-control also will be evident in discussions of reading instruction in Chapter 14. The potency of self-instruction with academic content makes obvious the potential importance of Manning's model, which is the most complete conception of how to promote competence via self-instruction in the classroom. Anyone interested in conducting research on classroom self-instruction or in devising curriculam based on self-instruction should consult the Manning (1991) book as an essential resource detailing the state-of-the-art with respect to theory, research, and classroom practice.

Manning has conducted both true experiments (e.g., 1988) and intensive case studies (e.g., 1990). The experiments are essential to making the case that teaching self-instruction is a causal factor in improving classroom performance; the cases provide insights into the dynamics of this approach. In the 1988 experiment, the most behaviorally inappropriate grade-1 and grade-3 children in a school were assigned to either a self-instructional treatment group or a control condition that received additional instruction and attention except that the instruction did not include a self-instructional component. For example, when the experimental condition students

saw a teacher self-instruct to inhibit inappropriate behaviors, control students received additional explicit instruction in the school rules prohibiting the inappropriate behaviors. Both experimental and control subjects received 8 hours of instruction, with the classroom teachers blind as to the condition assignment of the children involved in the study. The data were striking both immediately following training and 3 months later. The students receiving self-instructional training were perceived as more self-controlled by their teachers, were assessed to be on task more during a series of formal assessments involving academic tasks, and believed themselves to be more in control of their behaviors. In the 1990 paper, Manning described how cognitive self-instruction was used to increase the on-task behavior of a grade-4 girl. At the beginning of the intervention, Jill (the student) was on task during school asssignments only 15 percent of the time. Following training in self-instruction, Jill was on task 80 percent of the time, with high on-task behavior still evident 3 months after the self-instructional training had occurred. Results such as these make clear that cognitive self-instruction is worthy of educational researcher and practitioner attention.

Summary

Instructions that include both behavioral (e.g., self-reinforcements) and cognitive (e.g., self-instructions) components are more powerful in many situations than ones that include simply behavioral components. As will be detailed in the next section and in subsequent chapters, it is necessary to know how to do something and to be motivated to do it. Learning "how" is more of a cognitive problem that can be addressed by interventions stimulating cognitive processes well matched to task demands; motivating use of such processes can be affected by behavioral interventions. Scientists like Meichenbaum and Manning clearly recognize the need for creating instruction that produces know-how and the desire to use that know-how. Both knowing how to learn and perform cognitive tasks and the motivation to perform cognitive tasks are necessary for people to perform at high levels of competence, a theme resounded throughout this book.

SOCIAL LEARNING THEORY

The main tenet of Bandura's **observational learning theory** (e.g., Bandura & Walters, 1963) is that much

Figure 7.4 Albert Bandura's social learning approach is a cognitive and a learning theory, one highlighting the important role of others in shaping mind. Professor Bandura continues to generate important insights about motivation, self-regulation, and self-control, working at Stanford University.

can be and is learned from observing others (i.e., behavioral models) (Figure 7.4). Because observation is a powerful method for acquiring many types of social behaviors (e.g., aggression, altruism, gender-appropriate behaviors) and because learning in this framework is by watching other people, the term social learning came to replace observational learning. Social learning theory has also evolved as a broader perspective than observational learning theory, encompassing some of the learning mechanisms identified in other theories of learning, most notably operant analyses of behavior.

Main Processes of Social Learning

How does learning proceed according to social learning theory?

1. When an action is followed by a positive consequence, the action often is more likely in the future. That is, the positive consequence is a reinforcer for the action it preceded. Skinner (e.g., 1953; see the discussion earlier in this chapter), in particular, provided substantial data that reinforcements can be used to shape behaviors. The mechanisms underlying reinforcement effects are not entirely understood, although some ways that reinforcements improve performance are by imparting information and motivating the behaviors that preceded them (Bandura, 1977, p. 17).

Thus, when a professor's class asks interesting questions following a well-prepared lecture, the professor is reinforced for preparing and delivering the lecture. The attention of the class is a reinforcement that informs the professor that he or she did a good job and motivates careful preparation of lectures in the future.

On days when professors are not prepared, they are often punished by students looking blankly at them and not taking notes. This is informative feedback that motivates not putting off lecture preparation in the future until it is too late. That is, such punishment should, if anything, reduce the likelihood of behaviors that preceded it.

If reinforcement or punishment were required for all learning to occur, learning would be much less efficient and certain than it is. For a reinforcement or punishment to occur, the behavior that is to be reinforced or punished must occur. When a person is incapable of that behavior, it is sometimes possible to reinforce a less demanding behavior that is part of or prerequisite to the desired behavior. Thus, when first learning to drive a car, the good driving instructor reinforces for behaviors that skilled drivers do not even think about. Thus, the student who checks carefully to see the brake is on, the car is in park, and the seat belt is fastened is reinforced for these behaviors, even though he or she may not really know what to do after turning the key. Once the student has mastered these preliminary steps, it takes more to get reinforced. So after several weeks of driving lessons, there may only be reinforcement if the day's drive was entirely smooth.

It is not possible to wait for some behaviors to occur in order to punish them because the behaviors are too dangerous. Thus, most people are never punished for driving over 100 miles an hour, and yet few people drive that fast. What is critical is that people know there are potential punishments for driving fast. They know because they have observed others be punished for such actions (e.g., they have seen wrecks by the roadway, listened to news reports of serious accidents involving high-speed driving, and know of others who have received citations and suspensions for fast and reckless driving). That brings the discussion to the most important mechanism for learning according to social learning analyses.

2. People learn by watching others. One child we know had never played basketball before he received an indoor hoop and ball for his third Christmas. The first thing he did was to pick up the ball

and throw it toward the hoop and scream, "Basket!" when it went in. He had learned a lot from watching older boys play basketball at the park.

3. People learn what to expect if they perform an action by observing others. Consider the following. How many different ways do you know for murdering a person? When we ask undergraduates this question, it is not unusual to receive over 100 responses, from the commonplace (e.g., shooting) to the creatively malicious (e.g., putting ground glass in food) to the extraordinarily inventive and specialized (e.g., using dissolving suture material in a heart surgery that requires the nondissolving variety). Most of the knowledge has been built up by observing murders on television, seeing them in movies, or reading about them in books. There have been many observational learning opportunities for learning about murder, and they have made a difference in people's long-term knowledge. (Like many other social scientists, we are extremely concerned about this type of observational learning from mass media.)

Even so, murders are statistically rare. Why? One reason is that people expect to be punished if they murder someone else. This **expectancy** has been established through years of observing that bad guys on television, in the movies, or in novels are caught and punished for their wicked deeds, or they self-punish themselves by torturous feelings of guilt. Whether or not a person performs a given behavior, one that he or she learned observationally, depends on expectations of rewards or punishments for performing the behavior and the value of the rewards and punishments. The **probability of performing a behavior X is a function of the expectancy of reward or punishment for X *and* the value of the reward or punishment;** this is sometimes expressed as $P_{behavior} = F(E_{reinforcement/punishment} \times V_{reinforcement/punishment})$. In the case of murder, expectancy of punishment is high: The negative values associated with the punishments of extreme guilt and potential imprisonment are also high. Thus, most people do not commit murder.

Consider another possibility. We have watched many people over the years adopt diet and exercise regimens and build up extensive knowledge bases about how to conduct such regimens based on their observations. People are both reinforced for dieting and exercising (i.e., by losing weight) and punished for it (i.e., suffering from perceived starvation and experiencing physical exhaustion). We engage in diet and exercise off and on, always expecting it will

reduce weight. What varies is the value of reinforcers and punishers. The heavier we get, the more valuable weight loss is. The heavier we get, the more likely the reinforcements from weight loss are greater in value than the punishments associated with going hungry and sweating. Our willingness to diet varies from day to day and situation to situation. The expectancy of a good time by going out to dinner with friends at a convention so outweighs the long-term reinforcements associated with weight loss that we often go out to dinner with friends when at conventions. We also expect the punishments associated with working up a sweat to be greater at a convention than at home—when we exercise in the morning of a convention day, legs often give out before the end of the day. Thus, whether diet or exercise occurs depends on the situation—what reinforcements and punishments we can expect in the situation and what those reinforcements and punishments mean to us. Today, author MP's weight is up a little; he expects that holding off on food and running at noon would bring his weight down some; he also expects that eating a meal at the student union would not be very reinforcing anyway. With those factors combined, he is not eating lunch today and jogging instead.

We discussed expectancy × value theory in Chapter 5 already. The important additional point in this context is that expectancies are often acquired through observational learning. Of course, that is adaptive in the case of terrible punishers. We are better off acquiring an expectation that touching a high tension wire will induce death or severe injury than acquiring such knowledge from direct experience. We are better off acquiring an expectation that driving at high speeds will result in a serious accident than being involved in a near-fatal collision.

We provided these home-spun examples illustrating expectancy-value theory because our years of teaching this concept has made clear to us that it is a difficult one for students to understand how performance varies as a function of both the expectancy of a reward or punishment and the perceived value of the reinforcer or punisher. (Even 4-year-olds understand the main idea of expectancy × value theory intuitively, however, and their willingness to exert effort is definitely a function of both expectancy of reinforcement or punishment and the value of the incentive; O'Sullivan, 1993)

4. In chapter 6, we described briefly how some emotional responses can be learned via **classical**

conditioning, such as aversions to foods that are eaten before experiencing illness! Thus, there is little debate that if a child approaches a dog and the dog counters aggressively, there is the possibility that the child will be fearful at the sight of the dog in the future, with the potential of the fearful responses generalizing to other dogs so that a phobia develops with respect to dogs (see Bandura, 1969, for an extensive analysis).

Fortunately, such emotional responses can sometimes be undone through observational learning opportunities. Thus, if children who are afraid of dogs have opportunities to see models approach and have contact with dogs with no adverse effects, negative emotional responding sometimes extinguishes, with the children able to approach and interact with dogs just as the models they had observed approached and interacted with dogs (e.g., Bandura & Menlove, 1968).

Social learning can occur via reinforcement, punishment, classical conditioning, or observation, with these mechanisms flexibly combining in many instances to affect learning. Thus, a child might acquire a classically conditioned aversion to collies, an aversion that is based in part on punishment for approaching a collie (i.e., after approaching a collie, the collie's negative reaction is a punisher that elicits negative emotion, which is subsequently elicited by the sight of a collie alone). Such a negative reaction can be modulated in the future by observation of other children having fun with collies and reinforcement from a parent for the child approaching and playing with a pet collie. Throughout this sequence, the child's expectancies about reinforcements and punishments change. Before approaching the offending collie, there is an expectancy of positive reinforcement that is valued (i.e., playing with a collie). After encountering the aggressive collie, the expectation changes so that punishment for approaching the collie is now expected. As the child observes other children having a good time with collies, expectancies about reinforcement increase. When the expectation of reinforcement exceeds the expectation of potential punishment, the child is likely once again to approach the collie, although there may be some conflict (i.e., this is known as an approach-avoidance situation, one in which both potential reinforcements and punishments can be anticipated, and thus there are both reasons to approach a stimulus and reasons to avoid it; e.g., Miller, 1944).

Although people sometimes experience reinforcements and punishments themselves, it is often the case that they learn through vicarious experiences: They see others experience reinforcements and punishments and thus form expectations about reinforcements or punishments that might accrue to them for performing particular behaviors through observational mechanisms. The social learning perspective is that much of human behavior is acquired via observation.

Example of Observational Learning of Behaviors and Expectancies: Classic Research Conducted by Bandura

No one has done as much to advance social learning theory as Bandura. His research on how and when people learn behaviors and expectancies through observation is now considered classic work in psychology. At least a 100-page chapter would be required to do justice to this research program. We do not have the luxury of such space here. Fortunately, a lot can be learned by reviewing some prototypical research conducted by Bandura and co-workers.

In Bandura (1965), young children viewed a film in which a child exhibited some novel physical and verbal aggressive behaviors toward a set of toys. At the completion of the film, the child model was either punished for the aggression (i.e., the child was spanked and verbally rebuked for the aggression), reinforced for it (i.e., given soft drinks, candy, and praise for the aggressive behaviors), or provided no consequences. After watching the film, the subjects were left alone in the room where the film was made with an opportunity to play with the toys seen in the film. When children watched the film involving reward or no consequences for the aggression, they were much more likely to exhibit the aggressive behaviors when interacting with the toys than if they viewed the film in which the model was spanked. Then, all children in the experiment were offered stickers and fruit juice if they would show the experimenter the aggressive behaviors that the film model had exhibited. The children had little difficulty in reproducing the behaviors.

What was going on in this situation? The children had clearly learned the aggressive behaviors in question because they could reproduce those behaviors when given an incentive to do so. They were less likely to perform the aggressive behaviors after viewing the punished model because they also learned to expect punishment from seeing the model punished. Performance of a behavior depends on knowing a response as well as expectation of reinforcements that are valued by the performer. When punishments are expected, performance often will not occur unless there are offsetting reinforcements. For many children in the Bandura (1965) study, the fun of playing with the toys aggressively was not worth the risk of getting a spanking.

During the late 1950s and 1960s, Bandura performed many experiments that shared features with his 1965 study. His work continued into the 1970s, in general, aimed at elaborating his view that observational learning is a powerful factor in the development of human behavior. The result is a highly cognitive account of social learning via observation, one that all students of educational psychology must understand.

Cognitive Mechanisms Mediating Social Learning Via Observation

Bandura's (1977b) *Social Learning Theory* was a book-length summary of the mechanisms underlying social learning and is still a well-regarded analysis. Bandura's (1986) *Social Foundations of Thought and Action* was a much longer analysis of social learning, relating it to many traditions in psychology. For students who need a short course in social learning theory that is more thorough than what is covered here, the 1977 book is recommended; for students who want to achieve professional-level understanding of social learning, the 1986 book is must reading.

At the heart of both of these books is a model of observational learning that includes **attentional, retentional, motor reproduction,** and **motivational processes.** Each of these four categories of processes are considered in detail by Bandura, with each category composed of multiple interrelated processes.

Attentional Processes What is attended to (i.e., observed) depends on characteristics of the model and characteristics of the observer. For example, not everyone has equal access to the same types of models. Children who are reared in environments with gentle people have more opportunities to view gentle behaviors than children who are raised in environments filled with aggressive people. Even so, all of us have some control as to the social models who are available to us and attended. Thus, when a person elects to go to college, he or she selects to be surrounded by students who model scholarly behaviors of various sorts. People who elect gang life rather than college select themselves into situations in which aggression is modeled.

In both the college and the gang situation, some of the people will command greater attention than others. Thus, the president of a fraternity is more likely to be observed and imitated than a pledge. The leader of a gang is much more likely to be watched and imitated than someone who is not as respected by gang members. The observer is more likely to attend to the behaviors of the fraternity president or the gang leader if they have been reinforced in the past for imitating such figures, which, of course, occurs often.

Advertisers have definitely figured out that high-status models are more likely to be imitated than low-status models. The power of stature to affect behavior is especially obvious when it is considered how much American presidents and their families can affect the behavior of Americans in general. How many rocking chairs were sold because Kennedy was often photographed in his rocker? More than a few of our more conservative friends had Nixon and Reagan haircuts. Older American women were much more comfortable in simple styles of dress when Barbara Bush lived in the White House.

When researchers have looked (e.g., Yussen, 1974), it has proven easy to demonstrate that what is attended is more likely to be learned than what is not attended. Such analyses have also made clear that sometimes learners benefit from instructions about what to watch. What is attended cannot be taken for granted by those wishing to teach via observational learning.

Retentional Processes Once a person attends to a behavior, it must be remembered if it is to affect future behaviors. Bandura's view is that imaginal and verbal coding of observed behaviors is critical to long-term memory of observations (see Chapter 3). Consistent with much of the thinking of the 1970s about memory (see Chapter 2), Bandura also considered rehearsal processes to be critical to improving memory of observed behaviors.

Bandura did not rely simply on the classical memory literature to make his case that imagery and rehearsal processes are mediators of observational learning. Rather, Bandura supervised a program of research documenting the potency of verbal, imaginal, and rehearsal processes in coding of observations (e.g., Bandura, Grusec, & Menlove, 1966; Bandura & Jeffery, 1973; Bandura, Jeffery, & Bachicha, 1974). Bandura's work was complemented by others who provided data demonstrating the criticality of encoding processes for observational learning (e.g., Coates & Hartup, 1969; Gerst, 1971). One important lesson from these studies was that instructions to construct imagery and verbal codes as well as instructions to rehearse often enhance learning of what was observed. As was the case with attention, it is often important to provide explicit information about how to retain what is observed if one wants to teach using observational learning opportunities.

Motor Reproduction Processes Not only must a person perceive and remember a behavioral sequence, but also they must be able to produce it themselves. In some cases, the sequence that is observed is readily reproducible. In other cases, the observer can carry out components but not the entire action. It is often necessary for individual components to be acquired before the entire sequence can be executed. For example, a skilled gymnast can sometimes watch another gymnast's routine (e.g., on the balance beam) and copy most or all of it immediately. Less skilled gymnasts often would have to break the routine into segments (e.g., practicing the mount over and over again, practicing a particular type of handstand over and over, practicing the dismount over and over) before attempting to integrate the segments. For some of us, it would never be possible to execute a routine on a balance beam.

Thus, reproduction following observation is often a demanding process, especially when it involves a skilled performance. Although the performance in question may be impossible for some, often it is attainable, although a great deal of practice may be required for that to occur. Moreover, additional observational learning opportunities may be necessary. We recall a Little League coach repeatedly demonstrating to an aspiring infielder how to position one's body to field a ground ball. Consistent with Bandura's theory, this young player was being provided both feedback about his performance and additional observational learning opportunities for a part of a larger sequence (i.e., fielding the ball and throwing it to first base):

> Skills are not perfected through observation alone, nor are they developed solely by trial-and-error fumbling. A golf instructor, for example, does not provide

beginners with golf balls and clubs and wait for them to discover the golf swing. In most everyday learning, people usually achieve a close approximation of the new behavior by modeling, and they refine it through self-corrective adjustments on the basis of informative feedback from performance and from focused demonstration of segments that have been only partially learned. (Bandura, 1977b, p. 28)

This quote from Bandura provides an opportunity to emphasize a point that will come up several times in this book. There are major debates between those who believe in discovery learning of various types and those who believe in learning through more direct instruction and explanation. There are also debates between those who believe that skills should be mastered first and those who believe that tasks should be tackled as wholes. Bandura clearly favors instruction via modeling over discovery. He also sides with the development of skills as a prerequisite to attempting the whole task.

Although we agree with Bandura in favoring instruction over discovery, the skills versus whole-task debate is somewhat overblown. That little boy who was drilled on how to position himself for a ground ball during infield practice spent the second half of practice playing in an actual game. There are many people who play entire rounds of golf after a bucket of balls at the driving range and 100 attempts on the practice putting green. Learning discrete skills and learning how to perform a whole task often can occur together; there are good reasons why they should. People are much more motivated to play whole baseball games and whole rounds of golf than to acquire component baseball or golf skills. In fact, the only motivation to learn the skills is to improve performance during a whole baseball game or round of golf, so that the "whole" task provides motivation for mastering subtasks. The way subtasks are combined in a baseball game or a round of golf is enormously complex. Learning how to combine skills flexibly as they are needed in the context of an actual game requires many years of practice. If the whole is ever to be accomplished, learners must have extensive experience participating at a level that requires coordination of all elements of the game. The reason there are Little Leagues and golf handicaps is so that people can participate in the whole activity while they are still mastering the skills that compose the activity.

Motivational Processes People can see an action, one that they are capable of doing, remember it, and still not perform it—such as the children who failed to perform the aggressive actions after seeing the aggressive model be punished. Performance depends on motivation, which, in turn, follows from an expectation of a valued reward if the behavior in question is performed. Sometimes this expectation follows from observing reinforcement of others who perform the behavior (i.e., vicarious reinforcement). Sometimes the expectation follows from a personal history of reinforcement for performing the behavior, as when a person continues to run in marathons simply to experience the runner's high and the congratulations from friends and strangers at the finish line. Sometimes the reward is expected because the person will reinforce themselves for performing the action. We know a writer who will only permit himself to relax in the evening by watching television once he has completed four pages of writing for the day.

Summary   All of us are constantly being exposed to behaviors, ones that we could learn and imitate. Of course, only some of the behaviors that are observed are learned, and few that are learned are performed. For a behavior to be observationally learned and performed requires attention to the behavior. Often, several exposures to the behavior are required, even to the point of breaking the behavior into parts that are modeled over and over as part of the learner attempting to master the complex sequence that is the total behavior in question. The performance of a previously observed behavior depends on retention of the behavior in memory. Imagery codes are especially emphasized by Bandura as critical in guiding performance of complex behaviors. Performance of a golf swing can be guided by an image of a previously modeled golf swing. In fact, one of the most interesting areas in sports research from the point of view of cognitive psychology is the study of how imagery can affect skilled motor performances. The evidence is growing that having an image of a to-be-performed action improves performance of the intended action (e.g., Hall, in press; Hall & Buckolz, 1983). Whether an observationally learned action occurs is a matter of intention, however. The motivation to carry out an action depends on the expectancies of the learner with respect to reinforcements for performing the action. The probability of any behavior, including those learned by observation, is a function of the expectancy of reinforcement and the value of the reinforcement to the performer.

The social in the phrase "social learning theory" is intended to emphasize that learning often occurs by observing others or through the reinforcement or punishment of others. What sometimes is obscured by the term "social learning" is that decidedly cognitive and academic behaviors can be acquired through observational mechanisms. In fact, from the perspective of this book, some of the most exciting work conducted within the social learning framework involves acquisition of conceptual and linguistic competencies.

Observational Learning of Conceptual and Linguistic Competencies

Awareness of the relevance of social learning theory to intellectual development was increased greatly with the 1978 publication of Rosenthal and Zimmerman's *Social Learning and Cognition* (Figure 7.5). During an era dominated by Chomsky's theory, which emphasized the innate determination of language acquisition, Rosenthal and Zimmerman (1978) specified how syntactical constructions could and often were acquired via social learning mechanisms. During an era dominated by Piaget's theory that much of

Figure 7.5 Barry Zimmerman is the most prominent social learning theorist who principally identifies with educational psychology. He has conducted many important experiments demonstrating that cognitive learning is affected by social imput. Professor Zimmerman works at the Graduate Center of the City University of New York.

conceptual learning was determined largely by biologically mediated stagelike progression, Rosenthal and Zimmerman (1978) specified how Piagetian concepts (e.g., conservation) could and often were acquired via social learning mechanisms. The worst part of it for those favoring Chomskian and Piagetian theories was that Rosenthal and Zimmerman (1978) were able to cite massive databases supporting their social learning analyses.

When Rosenthal and Zimmerman's book appeared in the fall of 1978, it was obvious that they had done much to advance social learning theory, especially with respect to education and educational psychology. The timing of the book was an important ingredient in its success. Bandura's (1977b) book, a cognitive account of social learning theory, was receiving a great deal of attention. Brainerd's (1978b) *Piaget's Theory of Intelligence* appeared at about the same time as the Rosenthal and Zimmerman book. Brainerd's book was the most complete critique of Piaget's theory ever published. Brainerd made the case that there was a massive database disconfirming Piaget's theoretical preferences. Brainerd also made clear that, in contrast, learning and social learning analyses of concept acquisition were well supported by existing data. A chapter by Brainerd published in the same year (Brainerd, 1978a) was a powerful and visible statement of how learning principles could better account for conceptual acquisitions such as conservation than did Piaget's theory. If that were not enough, Whitehurst and Zimmerman (1979) edited a book the following year that included a number of chapters specifying additionally the great support for social learning analyses of conceptual and language acquisition compared with more biologically oriented approaches, such as the theories of Chomsky, Piaget, and Kohlberg. In this section, we briefly describe the social learning perspective with respect to language and conceptual acquisition.

Language   Consistent with Chomsky, psycholinguists in the 1960s, 1970s, and 1980s often rejected imitation as a mechanism mediating language acquisition, with their view of imitation as mimicry (Whitehurst & Vasta, 1975). In contrast, sophisticated learning theorists viewed imitation as anything but mimicry. Imitation involves inducing rules from multiple exposures to examples of a phenomenon and using the rules that are constructed via induction to guide future behavior. Bandura's (1977b)

book is absolutely clear that this general formulation concerning rule induction through observation was intended to apply to language. He was on firm ground, for by that time a substantial body of evidence was accumulating that many grammatical rules can be learned via learning and social learning mechanisms (I. Brown, 1979; Rosenthal & Zimmerman, 1978, Chapter 2).

For example, I. Brown (1976) established that nursery school children could induce the grammatical rules governing the production of passive constructions if they were presented a sample of passive sentences accompanied by enactments of the actions specified by the sentences. After hearing 50 such sentences with enactments, the nursery school children were able to understand passive constructions involving different materials than had been used during the 50-sentence training. In fact, presentation of the sentences with enactments produced about 80 percent correct comprehension compared with 50 percent comprehension for controls who did not receive the 50-sentence training. What was most impressive were the large gains owing to exposure and enactment by children who had little understanding of passives at the beginning of the study. (Several other conditions were included in this study besides the exposure plus enactment and control conditions. These permitted elimination of alternative explanations of the findings, so that the conclusion that understanding of the passive construction was induced via observational learning was well supported.)

If there was doubt in the past about the teachability of language and the potential for learning mechanisms to mediate language acquisition, little doubt remains now (Speidel & Nelson, 1989): There is widespread agreement that the language structures acquired by a child are a function of the structures the child hears in the world. There is increasing understanding of how exposure to models with varying degrees of language competence can promote language development. There is also evidence that positively reinforcing children to use language, in fact, increases their competent use of it (e.g., Whitehurst & Valdez-Menchaca, 1988). Imitation as a mechanism mediating language learning is now a hot topic in psycholinguistics (see Speidel & Nelson, 1989).

Piagetian Concept Acquisition   No idea in Piagetian theory was researched more than the hypothesis that children in the preschool years do not conserve whereas older children do. That is, Piagetians believe that with development, there is increasing understanding from the preschool to the elementary-age years that the amount of a substance does not change because its appearance does—that amount changes only if something is taken away or added. Thus, a conserver knows that pouring water from one container to a different-shaped container does not change the amount of water; a conserver knows that seven beans in a 7-inch row (i.e., 1-inch spacing) is the same number of beans as seven beans in a 2-inch row (i.e., approximately a quarter-inch spacing); a conserver knows that a ball of clay does not change in weight or volume when it is reshaped as a pancake. In contrast, the classic Piagetian view was that preschoolers would claim that the amount of water would vary with the dimensions of its container, that the number of elements in a row would vary with the spacing in the row, and that the weight and volume of clay vary with shape of the clay.

Particularly critical here was the long-held Piagetian stance that conservation could not be taught and that attempts to do so would invariably disrupt natural development of the understanding of conservation. Americans studying the possibility that changes in conservation might be stimulated through instruction produced data that clashed with the Genevan assertion that cognitive restructuring could occur only through equilibration. Americans had little difficulty establishing conservation using conventional learning procedures (Rosenthal & Zimmerman, 1978, Chapter 4), such as simple correction, rule instruction (i.e., teach the child that the amount of something does not change unless something is added or subtracted), observational learning, and social interaction with children who conserve as they perform conservation problems (for reviews, see Brainerd, 1978a, 1978b). Particularly relevant here, two of the four procedures identified by American researchers involved clear imitative learning. The observational learning studies on Piagetian conceptual acquisitions were similar in structure and outcome to other observational learning studies: One group observed a person performing conservation and was more likely to exhibit conservation in the future than another group who had not observed conservation. In the studies of social interaction, nonconserving children were also exposed to a model doing conservation problems well—the more mature child in the dyad could and did perform the conservation tasks at a high level of competence in the presence of the nonconserving child. This database is certainly consistent with the general conclusion that imitation can play a powerful role in acquisition of cognitive concepts.

Summary A great deal of evidence has been generated that social learning mechanisms, and in particular observational learning, can produce changes in intellectual competence. The claims made by social learning theorists are at least as defensible, based on available evidence, as the claims made by others interested in problems of language and Piagetian conceptual development. That is not to dismiss the potential of mechanisms such as cognitive conflict to produce intellectual change. In fact, at several subsequent points in this book, cognitive conflict will be considered again as a mechanism promoting growth, with the perspective offered at those points that cognitive conflict can be an important factor in motivating and causing cognitive change.

Concluding Comments

People learn a great deal by observing others, an adaptive capacity since there are many things people need to learn that could never be learned by direct experience (e.g., one trial of learning via naturalistic punishment not to walk in front of speeding cars would certainly eliminate such behaviors, but the side effects would be intolerable—an organism requiring such direct consequation of behavior for any learning to occur would not survive long). Bandura and associates have done an admirable job in analyzing the cognitive underpinnings of observational learning. Their analyses leave little doubt that observational learning is a decidedly cognitive phenomenon.

CONCLUDING COMMENTS

As promised at the outset of this chapter, the theories offered here are filled with assumptions about biology: Gibson and Piaget emphasize the inherently active nature of humans and their inherent motivations to learn. Gibson's concern is especially with the types of stimulation that particularly catch the attention of humans, the types of information to which they are particularly sensitive because of genetic predisposition. Piaget proposed four stages that represent a biological unfolding; although Piaget always gives lip service to environment, stagelike progression is an inevitable consequence of biological maturation in his theory. Skinner believed that being susceptible to classical and operant conditioning provided biological advantages. That is, organisms that respond to feedback from the environment are more likely to survive than organisms that do not respond to environmental input. The Darwinian reasonableness of this claim is obvious. Bandura focuses on human's obvious ability to learn by watching and the inherited mechanisms that permit cognitive representation of what is observed. The cognitive-behaviorists accept all of the biological proclivities specified by the behaviorists (i.e., sensitivity to input from the environment) and cognitivists (i.e., biological mechanisms for representing information considered in previous chapters of this book).

Both the Gibsons and Piaget believed that most environments human children experience provide more than enough stimulation for their biological heritage to play out. In making that claim, however, we are aware that a particular child's perceptual learning depends on specific environmental inputs. Thus, many perceptual experiences with the letters of the Cyrillic alphabet permit abstraction of the distinctive features defining letters in that alphabet. Although Piaget always downplayed the differences in speed of acquisition associated with richer versus more impoverished environments, the associations between qualities of environment and Piagetian conceptual status are striking. The behavioral work on environmental determination of conservation ability did much to make these associations particularly clear: Children who are provided high-quality observational learning and cognitive conflict experiences with respect to concepts such as conservation are likely to acquire such concepts before children who do not receive such input.

Indeed, the qualities of environments and the quantities of environmental stimulation are critical determinants of learning and conceptual development according to behavioral theories. What a child learns depends on observational opportunities according to Bandura and the cognitive behaviorists. What a child does depends on which behaviors are reinforced and punished according to both the observational learning theorists and the operant theorists. The cognitive behaviorists especially contend that children's learning and performance depend

greatly on whether they are taught explicitly how to regulate their learning and behavior.

In general, when these theories are considered collectively, the case builds that high-quality environments sustained for long periods of time are absolutely essential if children's learning and conceptual development are to be optimized: Perceptual learning continues throughout life. Whenever there are new distinctions that are critical for thinking and performance, there is a need for long-term, high-quality perceptual learning opportunities. Think back to the radiologists who were discussed in Chapter 4. Tens of thousands of trials in reading x-rays seem to be required before a physician becomes expert in radiological diagnosis. In Chapters 12 and 13, the cases will be made that concrete conceptual experiences and opportunities to reflect on those experiences are essential for development of sophisticated scientific and mathematical understandings. It will be apparent during those discussions that it takes a long time to develop the conceptual understandings that constitute scientific and mathematical understanding.

An important conclusion that emerges from the theories and evidence considered in this chapter is that many different types of experiences and input are necessary during the development of mind. Our view is that development of mind and sophisticated behavioral repertoires involves all of the mechanisms reviewed in this chapter. Moreover, there is a great deal of commonality in the mechanisms proposed by the various theories. For instance, **discrimination** is required to abstract distinctive features in perceptual input. It is also required to learn that one occasion will lead to reinforcement for a behavior and another occasion will lead to punishment. Discrimination is also part of cognitive conflict in that cognitive conflict requires recognition that one's expectations are not consistent with the way the world actually works.

Consider a second common mechanism: **Feedback** is necessary for perceptual learning to occur, in that a child would never learn to discriminate a "b" from a "d" if there were no positive consequences for doing so. When one changes some Piagetian conceptual expectation, the feedback provided by the environment makes clear the greater adequacy of the new conception (e.g., an initially preoperational child receives more positive feedback from the world when he or she begins to predict that pouring a liquid makes no difference with respect to quantity than when the child predicted that the amount of liquid would change when pouring from one type of beaker to another). Whether something that is observationally learned is performed depends on expectations about future reinforcement based on the feedback received previously in the form of reinforcements or punishments for performing the behavior.

Finally, consider a third mechanism—**practice.** Gibsonians advocate practice as do Piagetians as do behaviorists. In short, all of these theories specify that practice making discriminations with feedback has important effects on learning and development.

There are important underlying commonalities across these theories.

Before closing this chapter, we want to emphasize that our commitment to information processing is a commitment to a theory of information processing that includes healthy respect for biological determination and the cultural specificity of learning and development. Information processing is enabled by biology; it is developed largely in a social context. Any successful theory of learning, development, and instruction will have to capture the mechanics of learning in terms of both biology and culture. Such a view will continue to emerge in the chapters that follow.

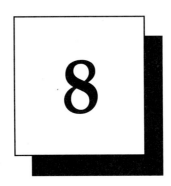

Social Interactional Theories of Learning and Development

An important hypothesis in the 1990s is that mental abilities develop largely through high-quality interactions with others. This perspective is inspired in part by renewed interest in Vygotsky's theories about the development of mind in society. Educational interventions informed by and theoretically related to Vygotskian theory are compared with other theories of instruction specifying particular types of teacher-student interactions. The most prominent of these approaches, one encountered often, is direct explanation, involving teacher modeling, explaining, and teacher-supported student practice of new competencies. Instructional conversations are also taken up in depth because new ways of conversing are at the heart of many modern recommendations in the curriculum and instruction literature, some of which are taken up in subsequent chapters.

People learn from other people, with some research documenting this claim reviewed in previous chapters (i.e., research on social learning and imitation). Some types of human interaction are more likely to foster learning and development than are other interactions, however, with a large number of researchers interested in determining qualities of interpersonal relationships that contribute to the development of sophisticated cognition. Without a doubt, one of the most influential theorists in this arena has been Lev Vygotsky, who lived in the first half of the 20th century in the former Soviet Union (Figure 8.1).

VYGOTSKY'S SOCIOCULTURAL APPROACHES TO MIND

There has been some awareness of Vygotsky and his perspective on the development of mind throughout the modern cognitive era, owing in part to the availability of a widely distributed English translation of *Thought and Language* (Vygotsky, 1962). Even so, until the late 1970s, as far as Western researchers and educators were concerned, Vygotsky was just one of those other theorists concerned with learning and development. Vygotsky certainly was not accorded the attention given to Piaget, Skinner, or Bandura. That changed in 1978 with the translation of Vygotsky's (1978) *Mind in Society: The Development of Higher Psychological Processes* and the promotion of Vygotsky's views by important developmental psychologists interested in education, in particular Brown (e.g., Brown & French, 1979) and Wertsch (e.g., 1985, 1991).

Figure 8.1 Lev Vygotsky's theories, formulated in the early 20th century in the then Soviet Union, have been resurrected in recent years by Western psychologists. Vygotsky's perspective is both developmental and sociocultural: Development depends on sociocultural factors, with cognitive maturity an internalization of skills mirroring earlier interactions with others.

The Developmental Relationship Between Thought and Speech

For many years, the only Vygotskian perspective well-known in the West was his view about relationships between thought and speech, which vary with developmental level.

Thought and Speech in Adults Vygotsky (1962) believed that for adults, inner speech was an important mechanism involved in thought. Inner speech is different from outer speech according to Vygotsky. In particular, inner speech is abbreviated and fragmentary, with the meaning of complex thoughts captured in few words. Vygotsky believed that thoughts often can only be completed via words, and words often play a role in shaping thought:

> The relationship of thought to word is not a thing but a process, a movement from thought to word and from word to thought. . . . Thought is not expressed but completed in the word. . . . Any thought has movement. It unfolds. It fulfills some function or resolves some task. This flow of thought is realized as an internal movement through several planes, as a transition from thought to word and word to thought. . . .

Speech does not merely serve as the expression of developed thought. Thought is restructured as it is transformed into speech. It is not expressed but completed in the word. (Vygotsky, 1987, pp. 250–251)

Although thought and speech are intertwined, they can be separated:

Thought does not consist of individual words like speech. I may want to express the thought that I saw a barefoot boy in a blue shirt running down the street today. I do not, however, see separately the boy, the shirt, the fact that the shirt was blue, the fact that the boy ran, and the fact that the boy was without shoes. I see all of this together in a unified act of thought. In speech, however, the thought is partitioned into separate words. Thought is always something whole, something with significantly greater extent and volume than the individual word. Over the course of several minutes, an orator frequently develops the same thought. The thought is contained in his mind as a whole. It does not arise step by step through separate units in the way that his speech develops. *What is contained simultaneously in thought unfolds sequentially in speech.* Thought can be compared to a hovering cloud which gushes a shower of words. (Vygotsky, 1987, p. 281)

When we read this passage by Vygotsky, we think about Paivio's dual coding theory, discussed in Chapter 3. Paivio (1971) argued that there is an imagery system (which is holistic) and a verbal system (which is sequential) that are constantly in communication, much as thought and word are constantly interacting according to Vygotsky. This distinction between holistic and sequential is an important distinction in understanding mind, whether thought of as a distinction between thought and word, as Vygotsky did, or as a distinction between imagery and verbal codes, which is Paivio's interpretation.

Some extremely important research in Soviet psychology has focused on when people subvocalize (i.e., use inner speech to mediate performance) and when they do not, with a summary of such work in English translation provided by Sokolov (1975), who was strongly influenced by Vygotsky. Sokolov summarizes studies, many of which were his own, in which subvocalization was measured using sophisticated psychophysical methods that involve measuring muscle tension in the vocal apparatus. Sokolov provides a substantial amount of evidence that whether subvocalization occurs or not depends on the difficulty of the problem facing a person, with more subvocalization when problems are taxing.

Though and Speech in Children Vygotsky's theory of the development of thought and speech specifies four stages. During the first 2 years of life, thought is nonverbal (largely sensorimotor as Piaget claimed), and speech is nonconceptual with no relationship between thought and speech. With the development of language (i.e., beginning at about age 2), thought and speech begin to merge, with the most obvious manifestations being a child who can label many objects by their "names" and who can communicate verbally with others. Self-speech is not used in any sense to direct thinking during this second stage, however, although the speech of others can and often is directive (see Luria, 1982). Although 2-year-olds are often reputed to be terrible, many times they really will "come," when you ask them to come. Such a reaction is less likely in younger children, unless there is a good deal of nonverbal cuing about the appropriateness of coming, such as an adult offering outstretched arms (see Service, Lock, & Chandler, 1989).

The role of self-speech in directing thought and behavior begins to emerge in the third stage, which is characterized by **egocentric speech.** When preschoolers do things, they often talk to themselves about what they are doing. Piaget argued that this represented a deficit in preschoolers, that they could not communicate meaning to others, a point of view that is contradicted by voluminous research that preschoolers more often than not do communicate successfully when they talk with others (see commentary in Chapter 7 on the inadequacies of Piaget's views concerning egocentric speech).

In contrast to Piaget, Vygotsky viewed the emergence of egocentric speech to be an advance, with such speech beginning to influence what the child thought and did. How many times did author MP hear his son say between 2 and 4 years of age, "I'm going to play with _____," before he went and played with _____; how many times did MP hear him say, "I'm going to _____," before Tim went and did _____. Often such utterances came when Tim was trying to figure out what to do, an observation completely consistent with Vygotsky. In fact, Vygotsky carried out studies with preschoolers in which the preschoolers were given tasks that were complicated by some obstacle (e.g., when a colored pencil, or paper, or paint that was needed was missing). When difficulties occur, the amount of egocentric speech is much greater than when preschoolers do the same tasks without obstacles. Consider this monologue produced by a preschooler faced with a task difficulty:

> Where is the pencil? I need a blue pencil now. Nothing. Instead of that I will color it red and put water on it— that will make it darker and more like blue. (Vygotsky, 1987, p. 70)

Speech produced by this child was clearly part of thinking.

During the fourth stage, the egocentric speech that was overt becomes covert and abbreviated, with the inner speech progressively reflecting predicates more than any other part of verbalizations, as in this example: "Where's the pencil? Need blue. Will use red, add water." The actions, specified by the predicates, are much more prominent in inner speech than in egocentric speech. Sokolov studied this fourth stage in the Vygotskian sequence.

For many years, this four-stage conception of the development of thought and speech was Vygotskian theory as far as Western readers were concerned. There were social contributions to this development, in that inner speech was considered to be internalized dialoguing. That is, the dialogue skills that began to develop in stage two affected the development of egocentric speech, which often involves a child conducting a monologue that can be heard by others, with this monologue eventually internalized.

Sophisticated Thought of Individuals Develops from Interactions Between Individuals

More complete understanding by Westerners of Vygotsky's conception of how others play a role in the development of a child's thinking abilities became possible with the publication of *Mind in Society*. Although other theorists in the early 20th century offered sociogenetic explanations of the development of mind that share features with Vygotsky's theory— most notably, the French psychologist Pierre Janet (Van der Meer & Valsiner, 1988)—their contributions are forgotten as scholars for the past decade and a half have pored over Vygotsky's writings.

Adults often assist children in thinking about problems they are confronting (e.g., how to solve a puzzle, trying to figure out how many "big sleeps" until Christmas). What goes on in these interactions is thinking, thinking that involves two heads. The child could not work through many problems with-

out assistance but with parental support makes fine progress. Years of participating in such interactions leads to internalization by the child of the types of actions once carried out between the child and the adult. That is, thought processes that were once interpersonal become intrapersonal. Probably the most frequently quoted statement by Vygotsky is his summary of this developmental progression:

> Any function in the child's cultural development appears twice, or on two planes. First, it appears on the social plane, and then on the psychological plane. First, it appears between people as an interpsychological category, and then within the child as an intrapsychological category. This is equally true with respect to voluntary attention, logical memory, the formation of concepts, and the development of volition. . . . Social relations or relations among people genetically underlie all higher functions and their relationships. . . . In their private sphere, human beings retain the functions of social interactions. (Vygotsky, 1981, pp. 163–164)

According to Vygotsky, cognitive development moves forward largely because the child is in a world that provides assistance when the child needs it and can benefit from it. The responsive social world lets the 2-year-old or 3-year-old solve for themselves those problems that they can handle. The child plays an important role in assuring some autonomous functioning: Any parent of a preschooler knows all too well the phrase, "I can do it myself!" There are other tasks that a 2-year-old or a 3-year-old could never perform, no matter how much assistance was provided. A responsive social environment does not even try to encourage children to do such tasks and, in fact, often discourages child attempts at behaviors far outside the range of preschooler competence (e.g., when a father physically lifts his son from the driver's seat of the car as the youngster urges the father to teach him to drive).

Critical developmental interactions occur with tasks in between these two extremes, tasks that the child could not do independently but can do with assistance. The responsive social world provides assistance on these tasks that are within the child's **zone of proximal development** according to Vygotskian theory. In fact, the "zone" is defined as behaviors beyond a child's level of autonomous functioning but within reach with assistance and, as such, reflect behaviors that are developing. Children learn how to perform tasks within their zone by interacting with more competent and responsive others who provide hints, prompts, and assistance to the child on an as-needed basis. These hints and prompts encourage the child to process the task appropriately, with such processing eventually internalized by the child—that is, the child ultimately performs the task without assistance, a development stimulated by the supportive interactions with others before autonomous functioning is possible.

What is critical is that more competent others scaffold (Wood et al., 1976) instruction about the task as they interact with the child. Scaffolding was introduced in Chapter 1, with this social-interactive model of teaching discussed at a number of points in the book. Recall that a scaffold is used when a building is being erected and is gradually removed as the building becomes self-supporting. So it is with the prompts and hints provided by an adult or older child to a younger child. It is important to provide enough support and assistance so the child does not fail (i.e., fall), with that support removed as the child is capable of performing autonomously. Scaffolding often takes place in the context of apprenticeships, an educational approach heavily favored by many of those now identifying with Vygotskian theory.

Apprenticeship

How did we become professors—how did we learn to do what professors do, to react as professors react? Yes, we went to school, took courses that included examinations and papers, and earned degrees. Although it is necessary to do that to become a professor, it is far from sufficient. We learned how to be professors by spending time around professors, as students and then as assistant professors. So it is with many professions and trades. People learn how to build houses by working with experienced builders as an apprentice. Airline captains learn how to fly from the left side of the plane by years of flying on the right side of the plane, as first officers working with captains. Medical residencies are apprenticeships, opportunities for young physicians to learn both the formal and informal knowledges possessed by senior physicians through direct contact with the senior physicians. (Of course, the Hardy boys apprenticed with Fenton Hardy, famous detective.)

Given how common apprenticeship experiences are in education, it is something of a wonder that educational researchers have only recently attempted to understand the nature of learning in such situations. Those who have begun to examine formally the nature of apprenticeship are concluding that it is a powerful approach to instruction, one that should be used not only to train young professionals and craftsmen, but also children in school as they tackle reading, writing, and problem solving.

An important idea here is that of situated cognition (e.g., Brown et al., 1989), which was introduced in Chapter 3. When students learn how to read, write, and problem solve in school, their understandings of reading, writing, and problem solving are largely tied to schooling environments. This is problematic because schooling environments are so different from the places where the reading, writing, and problem solving learned in school are to be put into practice. In contrast, trade and professional apprenticeships are highly situated, so that a young lad who learns the art and science of beekeeping by apprenticing with a beekeeper develops knowledge that is connected to the situations in which beekeepers must work. A person who acquires their understanding of beekeeping from taking a community college class on apiary science that involves three laboratory experiences with a beehive will not have the same situated knowledge. A real challenge is to make schooling sufficiently like the real world, so that reading, writing, and problem solving learned there are tied to important real-world situations. Many believe school should be reconstructed so that students serve as apprentices to people doing real reading of real books, real writing for real purposes, and solving of real problems (see Hamilton, 1990).

The best-known theoretical discussion of apprenticeship in school to date is Collins, Brown, and Newman (1989), although extensive discussions of apprenticeship in general are provided in Rogoff's (1990) and Hamilton's (1990) book-length treatments of the topic. We relied on these sources in constructing what follows.

What do apprentice learners do? (1) They observe. Thus, as graduate students, we observed senior professors in many settings, both informal and formal. For example, we learned how to submit a manuscript to a journal by watching a senior colleague do so, one who provided commentary about journal submissions over the course of a number of submissions and several years. In this relationship, we learned that it was all right to react negatively to a reviewer's comments in the privacy of one's office, but in the letter to the editor specifying how the reviewer's comments were handled, it is important to make the point that the reviewer comments were helpful and to make obvious to the editor that a good faith effort was made to accommodate the reviewer.

(2) Apprentices receive **coaching** from their mentors. Thus, when it came time to submit our first manuscripts to a journal, our graduate school mentor (the same individual for MP and CM) went over drafts of our papers, giving us pointers, helping us decide where to submit, and providing input and feedback about the form of the submissions. By the time a package left for the journal, we knew well that the editor who was receiving it insisted on a ribbon copy in addition to the three photocopies. We also knew that the editor receiving it had no patience for overly long abstracts or any departures from APA style, and our submission reflected this knowledge, which was passed from the mentor to us.

(3) Apprentices **practice** the tasks that are expected in the profession, although always being coached by the mentor. Thus, as graduate students, we did research and writing with our mentor coaching us along the way. A good mentor "scaffolds" (Wood et al., 1976) his or her input, providing assistance when it is needed but not so much that the student becomes dependent on it nor so little that the apprentice falters. Just as the scaffold of a building is removed as the building becomes free-standing, so it is with mentor scaffolding, with less and less of it provided as the apprentice is able to go it alone. There came a time when we were submitting papers on our own.

Apprenticeship for Elementary-Age Students   It is not hard to imagine an apprentice graduate student. But is it really sensible to think about teaching grade-school children within an apprentice relationship? Collins et al. (1989) think it is, and so do we. Studies of expert tutoring have provided important insights as to what high-quality tutoring can look like, and what it looks like is scaffolding.

One of our favorite examples was provided by Lepper and colleagues (Lepper, Aspinwall, Mumme, & Chabey, 1990). In this study, six expert tutors of elementary arithmetic were observed as they worked with individual students in grades 2 through 5. The tutors consistently let their students know that the task they were doing was a difficult one, but also that the students had great ability that could be applied to this task. There is a good reason for this. If the student fails, it is easy enough to blame the difficulty of the task, a type of attribution that should not dis-

courage the student (e.g., see Weiner, 1979). If they succeed, it is possible to highlight how bright the student is, an attribution that should encourage the student (Weiner, 1979). What is interesting from the perspective of scaffolding is that the tutor makes these attributions indirectly rather than directly—that is, the tutor provides support but not so much that the student will become dependent on it. Thus, after a student successfully completed a problem, a tutor might say, "I guess we'll have to try to find an even harder one for you," a subtle way of making the point that the last problem was hard and yet the student succeeded on it.

There are many more subtleties in the tutors' interactions with their students. There is little overt corrective feedback and little in the way of overt diagnoses about what the student is doing wrong. Indeed, 95% of the time errors are not labeled as such. There is little direct help, and rarely do the tutors give students the answers to the problems. When students made errors or were having difficulties, the tutors provided hints of three sorts:

- Questions or remarks implying that the previous move was an incorrect one.
- A suggestion about a potential direction the student might take with the problem, often in the form of a question.
- A hint about the part of the problem the student might want to think about, often in the form of a question.

What these tutors did when their students were in trouble was to ask them questions. (Readers with some knowledge of the history of education might be experiencing flashbacks about Socrates on one end of a log and one of the youth of Athens on the other end.) As an example, consider that when a student added 36 and 36 and came up with 126, the tutor commonly inquired, "Now how did you get that 6?" When this did not work, hints in the forms of questions became increasingly specific: "Which column do we start in? Where is the one column?

"Subtlety" is a word that comes to mind a lot when reviewing lessons taught by skilled math tutors. The tutor is not someone waiting to pounce on an error or full of directions. Rather the tutor is much more laid back, providing pretty good hints to students, hints that are full of information. Consider this dialogue from McArthur, Stasz, and Zmuidzinas (1990):

TEACHER: Okay, do you want to start on number 17? I don't know, have you done these before ever? [The equation is $x/3 = b/2 + c/6$]

STUDENT: I think we have. I don't remember.

T: Now usually the thing that bothers most students is fractions. They could do without them. So let's get rid of the fractions.

S: Okay.

T: Let us multiply every single term by what we refer to as the least common multiple, something all that can divide evenly into. What do you think that would be?

S: 6.

T: 6. So, I'm going to divide. And then it will turn into something you'll feel more comfortable with. Okay. Now, when I say, "Multiply each term by 6," I'm going to write in parentheses next to the object 6, okay? I'm multiplying each thing by 6. Three into 6 goes how many times? [T points to the 3 under x, then the parenthesized 6 above it.]

S: 2.

T: So what are you going to have left?

S: [No response]

T.: 2x. [S writes 2x below the x/3]

S: 2x.

T: 2 equals—2 goes into 6 how many times? [T points to the 2 under the b, then the parenthesized 6 above it.] (McArthur et al., 1990, pp. 210–211)

Now go back through this dialogue and look for some of the subtleties that Lepper et al. (1990) reported are part of scaffolded tutoring. Notice how the tutor provided prompts about potential directions the student might take. Were such hints in the forms of questions as Lepper et al. (1990) reported? Did the teacher give hints about the part of the problem the student might want to think about? Looking at this dialogue in this way makes obvious that there probably is a common core of behaviors that are part of expert math tutoring, behaviors that are what Wood et al. (1976) considered to be **scaffolding.** If we have a reservation about the Lepper et al. (1990) tutors, it is that they do not do much explaining, which is something that is often observed when a tutor works with a student.

Scaffolding is complicated, even in the context of one teacher with one student and fairly easy arithmetic. Good tutors know when and where to provide the hints, prompts, explanations, and modelings that they provide, and it is all contingent on the emerging needs of the student. Only people who are cognitively capable of attending vigilantly to several ongoing activities are likely to be good at scaffolding, and many people do not have such multiple-attention skills (Copeland, 1987). Scaffolding is going to be presented a number of times in this book, largely because there is a growing consensus that this is a good way of teaching and different from much of the teaching that is now going on.

This long aside about scaffolding, which is only one part of apprenticeship, was worthwhile because in every analysis of academic apprenticeship, such scaffolding is at the heart of the relationship. Increasingly, American educators believe that the apprenticeship model is the right one for elementary and secondary instruction.

Rogoff (1990) provided an exhaustive summary of the literature on apprenticeship, making the argument that such participation occurs in many cultures and may be a universal of human life. She reviews the literature documenting that apprenticeship adult-child relations are the principal means of passing on knowledge about the intellectual tools valuable in the culture, typically tools complex enough that years of apprenticeship are necessary. Thus, there are societies in which apprenticeships provide education in agriculture, hunting, fishing, weaving, and healing. Although there are cultural variations in the specific behaviors constituting apprenticeship relationships, Rogoff contends that there is great similarity across various types of apprenticeship:

- During an apprenticeship, the master provides bridges from what is known by the apprentice to the unknown. The master interprets the task into terms the apprentice can understand, and the master makes demands on the apprentice that the apprentice can meet, although the ante is always going up, with the apprentice required to learn more as subskills are mastered. That is, the master structures the task for the apprentice. Rogoff refers to this as a situation in which there is **guided participation** of the apprentice, with the guidance provided by the master.

- The master gradually transfers responsibility. Scaffolding is the key term here, with the master providing as much support as the apprentice needs to function but not more than enough, until support is entirely withdrawn because the student can do it alone.

In many cultures, apprenticeship is what Lave and Wenger (1991) refer to as **legitimate peripheral participation.** The apprentices are learning skills that are legitimately valued in the culture—skills that are directly valuable to the culture, in contrast to much of school learning, which is only indirectly valuable. For example, a high school student's learning of Latin in high school is not legitimate as Lave and Wenger use the term, although if there is a young monk somewhere learning Latin from a master so as to be able to participate fully in monastery life, that would be legitimate participation. Through the apprenticeship, the young monk would be able to participate somewhat in a community organized around Latin-based activities. Participation would not be as full as a master's participation and hence the appropriateness of the descriptor "peripheral" for the apprentice role. The master monk would scaffold Latin teaching for the younger monk because it is important to the monasterial culture that young monks learn Latin. A key attribute of situations in which apprenticeship is common is that there is a great cultural need for the apprenticed skills to be acquired.

More than skills are acquired. Legitimate peripheral participation "gobbles up" the apprentice and is all-consuming, and as a result, everything changes for the person. Lave and Wenger (1991) put it this way:

> An extended period of legitimate peripherality provides learners with opportunities to make the culture of practice theirs. From a broadly peripheral perspective, apprentices generally assemble a general idea of what constitutes the practice of the community. This uneven sketch of the enterprise (available if there is legitimate access) might include who is involved; what they do; what everyday life is like; how masters talk, walk, work, and generally conduct their lives; how people who are not part of the community of practice interact with it; what other learners are doing; and what learners need to learn to become full practitioners. It includes an increasing understanding of how, when, and about what old-timers collaborate, collude, and collide, and what they enjoy, dislike, respect, and admire. In particular, it offers exemplars (which are grounds and motivation for learning activity), including masters, finished products, and more advanced apprentices in the process of becoming full practitioners. (p. 95)

Legitimate peripheral participants have access to the experts in a culture that is not available to others, with the experts revealing much to the apprentices that they would never reveal to others. All of this is intended to reproduce new members of the culture that possess important skills for the culture, with the product someone who talks and thinks differently because they have changed.

We are beginning to get some idea about how students in school can be apprentice readers, apprentice writers, and apprentice mathematicians (as well as apprentice scientists, geographers, and so forth), with the models that are developing taken up at various points in this book. As a preview, however, consider that the apprenticeship model requires that teachers be real readers, writers, mathematicians, scientists, and social scientists, rather than people who talk about reading, writing, mathematics, science, and social science. Educational theorists such as Lave and Wenger believe that too much of school is talking about reading, writing, mathematics, science, and social science and not enough of talking within cultures of readers, writer, mathematicians, scientists, and social scientists. There is a challenging educational theory here, a whole new way of thinking about how learning in school might be accomplished.

Components of Apprenticeship The richness of apprenticeship can be appreciated by elaborative commentary on Collins et al.'s (1989) summary of its components, which expands on their three-part conceptualization of apprenticeship used to introduce this subsection on apprenticeship:

- *Modeling:* Experts show their apprentices how to do tasks that are important and explain the subtleties of such tasks to their charges. The expert tutor will make obvious to students his or her actions, often making overt actions that they normally would carry out automatically and covertly. The student sees the actions and hears a rationale as to why the actions were taken.
- *Coaching:* The master watches the student attempt a task and offers hints, feedback, and guidance. Sometimes the coach offers additional modeling or explanation. Coaching is pervasive during apprenticeship, so much so that if the apprenticeship process had to be described in a single word, the most appropriate single word would be coaching.
- *Scaffolding:* The master offers support, guidance, and reminders. The master does not offer too much support, however, pulling away as the ap-

prentice is able to function independently. Scaffolding requires great diagnostic skills on the part of the master, determining both when the apprentice is in need of help and offering appropriate redirection. The master must understand the many different types of errors that apprentices can make and how to deal with such errors. The flexibility of Lepper et al.'s (1990) math tutors is an enormous accomplishment, with such flexibility of input a hallmark of apprenticeship. Experts size up the needs of the apprentice in light of their expert knowledge of the demands of the task and make decisions about how to provide guidance so that the apprentice can proceed and learn how to cope with the task in question.

- *Articulation*: Articulation is a form of testing. Masters require their apprentices to explain what they are doing. Thus, an expert math teacher may require the tutee to explain how he or she went about solving a problem and why the particular solution method was used over alternative methods.

- *Reflection*: Apprentices are encouraged to compare their work with that of others, including the master and other apprentices. This aspect of the apprenticeship relationship has received an enormous amount of attention, largely because of Schön's (1983, 1987) influential writing about the role of reflection in the development of professional competence. Thus, young teachers often watch videotapes of themselves teaching and reflect on their teaching, perhaps discussing their teaching actions with more expert teachers or fellow apprentice teachers. Reflection by apprentice writers in grade-2 classrooms occurs when they have a conference with their teacher about a rough draft or have fellow students react to a draft during a peer conference. Thinking about how one is doing with the long-term goal of improving is an important component of apprenticeship.

- *Exploration*: Apprentices cannot be mere copies of their mentors. Thus, those who mentored our scholarship did not intend that we would simply spend our careers replicating their work but would instead strike out on our own. The apprenticeship relationship permits safe exploration. Thus, when we were graduate students, we tried out some crazy ideas in pilot studies. We still try out crazy ideas, but now we are more sophisticated in how to do such work. Part of

what we learned in graduate school was how to explore. Good mentors teach their apprentices how to explore and encourage them to do so.

That apprenticeship is a powerful perspective on education is apparent from the many references to it. Whether one is reading about the education of typical students (e.g., high school students in *Horace's Compromise* by Sizer, 1984) or the development of the most creative minds in science, humanities, and arts (see John-Steiner, 1985, especially Chapter 2), there are endorsements of coaching as a form of instruction and apprenticeship as a method of development. That apprenticeship is a powerful form of teaching is a hypothesis that has face validity to many with well-informed opinions about education at its best.

Research Validating Soviet Sociohistorical Positions

Vygotskian theory is inspirational, with many educators now couching their innovations in Vygotskian terms. Educators report that they are scaffolding instruction to students who are presented tasks that are within their zones of proximal development (i.e., just a little bit more difficult than what they are able to do on their own right now). Although we are enthusiastic about these theoretical directions, we share the concerns of many that the research support for many sociohistorical ideas is thin at best and nonexistent for some tenets of the theory.

Day and colleagues (1983; Day, Cordon, & Kerwin, 1989; Kerwin & Day, 1985), more than any others, have examined critically the research supporting sociohistorical instructional recommendations and found it wanting. Thus, do adults provide children with instruction for behaviors that are in their "zone of proximal development," that is, acquisitions that are now just forming and can be displayed by the child only with the assistance of an adult? Do adults assume the more demanding roles in such interactions to reduce the workload for the child, consistent with Vygotskian theory? Do adults eventually cede control of tasks to their students?

Day correctly points out how difficult it can be to generate research that is relevant to such questions:

> How are we to determine for instance that an adult provided just enough assistance and not too much assistance? How are we to know that the child is practicing nascent skills and not ones that have already been internalized? How can we show that the child ceded control quickly enough? (Day et al., 1989, p. 86)

Even so, researchers have tried to do so, with some success. Thus, researchers have demonstrated that adults regularly do provide instruction to children consistent with Vygotsky's thinking that adults should be supportive but not overly intrusive (e.g., Gardner & Rogoff, 1982; Heckhausen, 1987), and Day was able to identify instances where adults reduce the workload for children as a function of their developmental level and ability (e.g., Childs & Greenfield, 1980; Wertsch, 1979), consistent with the scaffolding perspective. For example, academic tutors provide more support to younger students (e.g., 7-year-olds) than older students (e.g., 11-year-olds) (Ludeke & Hartup, 1983). When expert weavers teach weaving, they intervene more with younger and less experienced learners (Greenfield, 1984). The best evidence that adults actively seek to adjust the workload demands come from the studies documenting that adults are more likely to intervene when children are experiencing difficulties with a task than at other times (e.g., Greenfield, 1984; McNamee, 1979).

One of the most analytical studies demonstrating parental scaffolding during problem solving appeared since Day's review: Freund (1990) observed mothers vary their support as a function of difficulties experienced by their children during problem solving. Using a true experimental design, Freund (1990) demonstrated that the parental scaffolding had an enduring effect on the children's problem solving, with the children who experienced scaffolding better able to perform a similar problem-solving task on their own than control children.

Unfortunately, however, instructional theorists who are attracted to Vygotskian theory have made stronger claims about the superiority of scaffolding compared to other forms of instruction than are justified based on the available data. In her own research, Day has obtained mixed evidence that children who receive scaffolded instruction from an adult learn faster or better than children who receive less competence-and-progress sensitive instruction (for positive evidence, see Day & Cordon, 1993; for more negative evidence, see Day et al., 1989). In experiments on scaffolded instruction, Day and her colleagues (personal communication, December 1991) have found that scaffolding had at best a small effect on learning. About the only consistent evidence of scaffolding effects on children has been reported by Rogoff and colleagues, who have observed that when an adult and child work together

on a task in a scaffolded fashion, the child is more likely to be planful when given other problems to solve (e.g., Gauvain & Rogoff, 1989; Radziszewska & Rogoff, 1988).

Just as Day has, Gelman, Massey, and McManus (1991) provided data suggesting overstatements by Vygotskian theorists. They designed a study aimed at elucidating the types of instruction that parents provide to their children during museum visits. Gelman et al. (1991) observed a number of different approaches to parent-child teaching besides scaffolding, not all of which could be considered good teaching. First, the types of interactions between parents and children varied with the type of exhibit. Thus, in an interactive grocery store exhibit, parents prompted, requested, and ordered their children to do things for much of the time. Certainly, in this setting, the adults provided support for their children, although there was little indication that the support was fine-grained—that is, adjusted to the level of the child's competence. Worse, in an exhibit intended to develop number skills, adults rarely helped their children despite the intention of the designers of the exhibit that it be approached as a parent-child interactive activity. Gelman et al. (1991) speculated that the adults may have felt more competent to assist their children in the more familiar grocery setting than in a math exhibit, since math is an area in which many adults do not have statable knowledge of many fundamental concepts. Gelman et al.'s (1991) pessimistic evaluation, that parents often do not scaffold instruction to their children when they could do so, was reinforced when she and her colleagues became involved in designing an exhibit intended to stimulate experimentation. Little scaffolded interaction was observed when children visited the exhibit with their parents. Other investigators as well have observed much less than universal scaffolding by parents to children in their charge (e.g., Pratt, Kerig, Cowan, & Cowan, 1988).

Summarizing across a great deal of research, we conclude that children receive a mix of different types of instruction (some scaffolded and some not). This is not particularly surprising, for scaffolding is extremely difficult to do (Day et al., 1989). It also is time-consuming and effortful. Based on existing data, it is also not clear that efforts to scaffold make that much difference relative to less scaffolded instruction.

Consistent with our conclusion, the National Research Council (1991, Chapter 4) reviewed the case for encouraging cognitive apprenticeship and concluded that this was an approach fraught with difficulties:

> . . . [C]ertain strategies of learning can be easily modeled . . . but the rationale for an expert's choice of strategies or solution routes may not be obvious, especially if a great deal of content knowledge is needed. Furthermore, monitoring a student's own understanding demands complex processing, and it is not clear that this is undertaken normally by tutors. Indeed, there is some evidence that teachers in a tutoring situation do not necessarily provide "intelligent" coaching and scaffolding, presumably because they have not monitored the student's understanding accurately. In fact, Putnam (1987) observed six teachers tutoring students in a one-on-one situation and found that they did not systematically diagnose students' misunderstanding and tailor feedback accordingly. Instead, they seemed to follow a structured and prescribed sequence of presenting subject-matter content to their students. (pp. 74–75) (See comments on Putnam's study earlier in this chapter.)

Think about this set of concerns with respect to what was presented in previous chapters. We make the case throughout this book that it is not enough to learn strategies. One must also learn when and where to use them. Thus, we find disturbing the conclusion by the National Research Council that it is difficult to discern why a model is executing a strategy. More positively, in some of the successful tutoring that will be reviewed later in this and subsequent chapters, experts make clear their reasons for doing what they do, perhaps because they are sensitive to the difficulties that students have in inferring such information.

This National Research Council point about monitoring another person's understanding makes contact with work discussed earlier as well. Recall in Chapter 2 that we established that monitoring is difficult, period. People often do not know how much they are learning when they are studying or even if they have figured out the main idea of a text. In light of these failures of people to monitor their own performances, is it surprising that teachers have difficulty monitoring how students are doing? Diagnosis of student difficulties (and the underlying problem causing the manifest difficulties) is hard even if an adult can work with a student in a one-on-one situation (see Flavell, 1972). Imagine the diagnostic challenges when there are 30 students in a classroom. Even so, we will present teachers in later chapters

who do seem to do a great deal of monitoring of student performance "on the run." Such teachers have built up long-term knowledge of their individual students' strengths and weaknesses as well as substantial craft and content knowledge (e.g., after years of teaching writing, one knows the errors that come up again and again and can spot them instantly). Thus, although the challenges of monitoring students and diagnosing their instructional needs must be acknowledged, we are convinced that such challenges are overcome at least by some skilled teachers.

A related difficulty with scaffolding is that children differ in their abilities to interpret teachers' appraisals and hints. In particular, children in the early grade-school years are less likely than older children to interpret accurately a teacher's comments about and actions in response to their academic behaviors (e.g., Lord, Umezaki, & Darley, 1990). What this means is that during the early grade-school years, scaffolding teachers must be especially sensitive about whether the messages they are sending to their students are getting through—the younger the child, the less reason there is to believe that the student understands subtle (and sometimes not so subtle) signals that her or his processing is off target.

Finally the closing comment in the National Research Council quote that teachers sometimes follow a predetermined sequence of instruction is critical. Scaffolded instruction is anything but tightly sequenced and predetermined, rather changing as the needs of the student change. Teachers are offered many sequences and scripts, especially by textbook publishers, sometimes with the message that the scripted lesson is more effective than anything a teacher would create, so teachers are intimidated into following the sequence specified by the script. Teaching at its best involves a teacher who is aware of her pupils and their needs, who knows the content area so well that many adaptations of content teaching are possible, and who is committed to expending the mental energy required to monitor student performance as students attempt tasks. Such teaching is never tightly sequenced or scripted.

While acknowledging the existence of many demonstrations of adult-child apprenticeships (see Rogoff, 1990, for a summary of the data), it is also necessary to acknowledge that parent-child and teacher-child scaffolding is anything but universal. Moreover, it is not clear that instruction that includes scaffolding is far superior to other forms of instruction, as supposed by many who find Vygotskian theory to be compelling. For example, there is always the possibility that children will attribute the help offered by the scaffolding adult as an indication that they are not very capable, and thus the adult assistance might undermine academic self-esteem and long-term academic achievement motivation (e.g., Graham & Barker, 1990). In a large classroom, the scaffolding teacher must depend on students to send signals that they need help. As it turns out, the students needing the help most may be the least likely to let the teacher know they need assistance (e.g., by asking questions; Newman & Goldin, 1990).

We are struck as well that scaffolding of instruction is just one of many important behaviors of excellent teachers. For example, Dillon (1989) describes an excellent secondary reading teacher who projects that he cares about his students' culture, has established a risk-free classroom and encourages active involvement in learning, assigns interesting materials, and plans and structures lessons carefully, but he also scaffolds a lot, individualizing instruction to children's difficulties and needs. Miller, Leinhardt, and Zigmond (1988) described a school that was extremely successful in keeping at-risk secondary students in school. Although teacher scaffolding occurred, there were many other forms of support provided as well, including policy accommodations (e.g., flexibility in attendance policy), careful selection of curricular items, and grading/testing policies that rewarded effort. Scaffolding is in high-quality instruction, but it is only one component in capable teaching.

We are struck, as Day was, that there have been so few analytical studies pertaining to Vygotskian theoretical conceptions of instruction. Moreover, little of what has been offered has been programmatic research. There has been some, however, with the work of Palincsar and Brown on reciprocal teaching the most obvious example of a research program that is often cited as pertinent to Vygotskian principles of instruction as they apply to an important type of elementary instruction, teaching of reading comprehension.

Reciprocal Teaching

Reciprocal teaching (e.g., Brown & Palincsar, 1989; Palincsar & Brown, 1984) involves instruction of comprehension strategies in the context of a reading group. Thus, students are taught to make predictions when reading, to question themselves about the text, to seek clarifications when confused, and to summarize content. The adult teacher initially explains and models these strategies for students, but the most unique part of reciprocal teaching is that quickly students are leading the group. That is, one student is assigned the role of group leader for a lesson, and this individual supervises the groups' generation of predictions, questions, and summaries as reading proceeds. The group leader also solicits points that need to be clarified and either provides clarifications or elicits them from other group members. The group interactions are cooperative. The adult teacher provides support on an as-needed basis—that is, he or she scaffolds. Brown and Palincsar summarized a typical discussion of text in a reciprocal teaching group:

> The dialogue leader begins the discussion by asking a question on the main content and ends by summarizing the gist. If there is disagreement, the group rereads and discusses potential candidates for question and summary statements until they reach consensus. Summarizing provides a means by which the group can monitor its progress, noting points of agreement and disagreement. Particularly valuable is the fact that summarizing at the end of a period of discussion helps students establish where they are for tackling a new segment of text. Attempts to clarify any comprehension problems that might arise are also an integral part of the discussion. And, finally, the leader asks for predictions about future content. Throughout, the adult teacher provides guidance and feedback tailored to the needs of the current discussion and his or her respondents. (p. 413)

Such instruction is full of good things from the perspective of the sociohistorical models, other social-interactive views, and even more purely cognitive views of learning and development (Brown & Palincsar, 1989). First, students are presented with multiple models of cognitive processing: The teacher models and explains. Every day the group comes together and executes a sequence of strategies well matched to the processes required to understand text, and thus peers in the group are continuously modeling reasoning about text. With respect to learning of content, students are led to make the types of elaborations and inferences that should facilitate learning of text (see Chapters 10 and 14)—that is, predictions, inferences required as part of question generation and elaboration, and summarization. The discussions permit various points of view to be aired and require students to justify and back up their claims (see the section on instructional conversations later in this chapter). These discussions permit review and commentary about the strategies being learned as well as the content being covered, so that reciprocal teaching offers opportunities to learn new content as it offers opportunities to learn how to process new content.

Perhaps most critical from the perspective of Vygotskian theory is the assumption that the teacher is progressively less involved as the students gain competence. The assumption is that by participating in the group, students will eventually internalize use of the four strategies encouraged as part of reciprocal teaching. That is, the processing that was once carried out between persons in the group will come to be carried out within the individual students, consistent with the Vygotskian perspective that individual cognitive development develops from participation in social groups.

The dialogue from a sample lesson, one involving low-achieving middle-school students, should help to make clear what occurs during a reciprocal teaching reading group. The dialogue that follows was generated by a group of students who had had 13 days of experience with the method and thus were accustomed to it. The students had just read the following brief text:

> *Text:* In the United States salt is produced by three basic methods: solar (sun) evaporation, mining, and artificial heat evaporation. For salt to be extracted by solar evaporation, the weather must be, hot and dry. Thus, solar salt is harvested in the tropic-like areas along our southern ocean coasts and at Great Salt Lake.

STUDENT LEADER (STUDENT C): Name three different basic methods how salt is produced.
STUDENT A: Evaporation, mining, evaporation . . . artificial heat evaporation.
STUDENT LEADER: Correct, very good. My summary on this paragraph is about ways that salt is produced.
TEACHER: Very good. Could you select the next teacher. (Student C does so, selecting Student L, with the reading continuing.)

> *Text:* The second oldest form of salt production is mining. Unlike early methods that made the work extremely dangerous and difficult, today's methods use special machinery, and salt mining is easier and safer.

The old expression "back to the salt mine" no longer applies.

STUDENT LEADER (STUDENT L): Name two words that often describe mining salt in the old days.
STUDENT K: Back to the salt mines?
STUDENT LEADER L: No. Angela?
STUDENT A: Dangerous and difficult.
STUDENT LEADER L: Correct. This paragraph is about comparing the old mining of salt and today's mining of salt.
TEACHER: Beautiful!
STUDENT LEADER L: I have a prediction to make.
TEACHER: Good.
STUDENT LEADER L: I think it might tell when salt was first discovered, well, it might tell what salt is made of and how it's made.
TEACHER: OK. Can we have another teacher?

> *Text:* Table salt is made by the third method—artificial evaporation. Pumping water into an underground salt bed dissolves the salt to make a brine that is brought to the surface. After purification at high temperatures, the salt is ready for our tables.

STUDENT LEADER K: After purification at high temperatures the salt is ready for what?
STUDENT C: Our tables.
STUDENT LEADER K: That's correct. To summarize: After its purification, the salt is put on our tables.
TEACHER: That was a fine job, Ken, and I appreciate all the work, but I think there might be something else to add to our summary. There is more important information that I think we need to include. This paragraph is mostly about what?
STUDENT A: The third method of evaporation.
STUDENT B: It mainly tells about pumping water from an underground salt bed that dissolves the salt to make a brine that is brought to the surface.
TEACHER: Angela hit it right on the money. The paragraph is mostly about the method of artificial evaporation and then everything else in the paragraph is telling us about the process. Okay. Next teacher.

> *Text:* For thousands of years people have known salt—tasting it, using it for their lives needs. Sometimes it has been treasured as gold; other times it has been superstitiously tossed over the shoulder to ward off bad luck. Somehow people and salt have always been together, but never is the tie more complete than when the best people are called "the salt of the earth."

STUDENT LEADER C: My question is, what are the best people called?

STUDENT L: The salt of the earth.

STUDENT LEADER C: Why?

STUDENT L: Because salt and the people have been together so long.

TEACHER: Do you have something to add to that? Okay. It really isn't because they have been together so long; it has to do with something else, Brian?

BRIAN: (reading) "People and salt have always been together but never has the tie been so complete."

TEACHER: All right, but when we use the expression, "That person is the salt of the earth," we know that means that person is a good person. How do we know that?

STUDENT B: Because we treasure salt, like gold. (pp. 421–422)

There are several interesting things about this lesson, not all of them reflecting positively on reciprocal teaching as a model. All students were participating, with a real structure to the participation. Even so, after 13 days of reciprocal teaching, there were no requests for clarification, despite the fact that some of the students were experiencing difficulties understanding the text. In addition, the questions generated in reaction to text by the student leaders required only low-level responses—they were all literal questions. Such questions do not stimulate people to think beyond the surface structure of the text. In addition, there seemed to be little scaffolding of the processing by the teacher here, with the teacher more someone who monitored whether the students were understanding the passage and providing clarification of the content as needed.

Our view of reciprocal teaching as operationalized by Palincsar and Brown (1984) is reserved. They have focused their efforts on low-ability readers and created a participation structure that invites these often passive students to take part in reading. We have watched many reciprocal teaching lessons in which there has been a preponderance of literal questions and little in the way of evidence that students are monitoring when they understand and when they do not understand, which is obvious from the striking lack of clarification questions in many reciprocal teaching lessons. Because reciprocal teaching so emphasizes that the teacher fade support, there are often long pauses in lessons with students fumbling because the teacher is uncertain whether to enter into the conversation and provide input.

That said, however, the evidence generated to date is more supportive of reciprocal teaching than not. An even-handed analysis provided by Rosenshine and Meister (1992) is particularly helpful here. They identified 19 experimental studies of reciprocal teaching (i.e., those that included both groups of students experiencing reciprocal teaching and groups experiencing some other form of instruction). Most of these interventions were brief, from 6 to 30 sessions—or a little more than a week of instruction to 6 weeks of instruction. Three investigations involved longer treatments, with two of these spanning 50 sessions and more than 100 sessions. Of course, the studies varied in other particulars, with some distinctions crucial in understanding the effects of the intervention: (1) Nine of the studies involved only reciprocal teaching (RT studies) in that the children were brought together and taught to dialogue as just described. The comprehension strategies were introduced as students first experienced dialoguing as a form of participation in reading instruction. In the 10 remaining studies, students received explicit teaching about how to execute the comprehension strategies before they began reciprocal teaching (ET/RT studies, for explicit teaching and reciprocal teaching). (2) Some investigations focused on students having decoding problems; others involved students who had no decoding difficulties but who experienced comprehension problems; still others involved students of all abilities. (3) Some studies included standardized tests; some used experimenter-generated tests, which typically tapped the processes encouraged by the four strategies; and some included both types of measures.

In general, the effects of reciprocal teaching were greater when explicit teaching of the comprehension strategies occurred before participation in reciprocal teaching (i.e., the size of the effect was greater in studies evaluating ET/RT than in studies evaluating RT). In general, when the main effects were considered, the effect of reciprocal teaching was about the same for all three ability types. When standardized tests were used, the effect of reciprocal teaching was modest, with the effects on standardized comprehension tests very modest with below-average readers, especially if they did not receive predialoguing instruction in execution of the four strategies (i.e., the effects were more modest in the RT than in the ET/RT studies for weaker readers when standardized measures were the criterion); with experimenter-constructed measures tapping the processes stimulated by the strategies, the effects of reciprocal teaching were quite striking, with the effect particularly striking in the ET/RT studies. The effects of reciprocal teaching did not seem to vary with the age or grade of the students: Most studies were conducted with students in the grade-school years, although several used the approach with adults. Ten of the investigations taught the 4 comprehension strategies favored by Palincsar and Brown (1984), with the other 11 studies involving between 1 and 10 strategies. There was no discernible effect of the number of strategies taught on the effects of reciprocal teaching.

This analysis of all available data on reciprocal teaching is important because it makes clear that even a small amount of reciprocal teaching of comprehension strategies (i.e., from a week of sessions to 6 weeks of sessions) can affect comprehension processing (i.e., students begin to use the comprehension strategies taught). It also makes clear that reciprocal teaching is not a panacea, however, for the effects on standardized comprehension were not consistently striking. This latter outcome is particularly important to emphasize because Brown and Palincsar (1989; also Brown & Campione, 1990) have made much of large standardized achievement gains (i.e., 2 years or more) by a few students who experience a month or so of reciprocal teaching. Although true enough (e.g., Brown & Palincsar, 1989, p. 424, Figure 13.1), almost as many control students experience such gains, suggesting that much of the largest gains are due to practice effects with the test. A realistic appraisal is that a week to a month and a half of reciprocal teaching has some discernible positive effects on the comprehension of elementary students, especially if measures directly tapping the comprehension strategies taught are the criteria (e.g., construct a summary of text, make predictions).

We emphasize in concluding this discussion of reciprocal teaching that there is nothing in the available data that permits great confidence that it is the Vygotskian aspects of reciprocal teaching that are potent. Even the most analytical of these studies (e.g., a study summarized in Brown & Palincsar, 1989, Figure 13.3) provided only a comparison between a condition in which the four comprehension strategies were taught using all of the reciprocal teaching components and another condition in which the four strategies were taught using conventional classroom explanation. That the reciprocally taught group outperformed the conventionally taught group could reflect the scaffolding of instruction by the teacher (which would probably be the Vygotskian interpretation) or the effects of the cooperative relations between peers in the reading groups (i.e., an interpretation that might be favored by cooperative learning theories; see Chapter 5) or a combination of scaffolding and cooperative learning.

Summary

The sociohistorical approach stimulated by Vygotsky's analysis is one of the most important theoretical directions in contemporary educational psychology. Conceptually attractive teaching constructs are associated with this approach, such as scaffolding and the zone of proximal development. Unfortunately the research generated by those interested in these theoretical ideas has not been analytical, limited to demonstrations that at least sometimes adults teach in a scaffolded fashion and that intervention packages that include scaffolding have some positive effects on performance.

In addition, questions about the conceptual uniqueness of some of the most important sociohistorical ideas (at least with respect to issues of instruction) are possible. For example, scaffolding seems a lot like what the behaviorists refer to as fading. Fading involves provision of reinforcement and modeling when it is needed, with both reinforcement and modeling withdrawn as the learner becomes more adept. With scaffolding, what is withdrawn is modeling and hints and prompts, some of which arguably serve as feedback that functions as reinforcement.

We have sympathy with our behaviorist friends, who believe that there is some conceptual plagiarism by the Vygotskians, especially when we consider how other theoretical persuasions have dealt with the zone of proximal development idea. According to the Vygotskians, instruction will go best if it is aimed at acquisitions that are in the "zone," acquisitions just a bit beyond where the learner now is. Concepts and behaviors in the zone are in their formation stage, and thus additional instructional input aimed at zone items will be more successful than instruction aimed at concepts and behaviors that are beyond the zone—that are not now in the process of acquisition. But is there any theory of learning that would not predict that concepts and behaviors already partially acquired would not be learned more easily than concepts and behaviors that have not been partially acquired? Indeed, a hallmark of many instructional theories, including Piaget's, is the principle of teaching just a bit beyond the current competency of the child (see Chapter 7 especially for discussion of this idea).

The point that there may be less unique in the sociohistorical theories than Vygotskian proponents might believe will be driven home more as this chapter proceeds. In the next section, we will present some interactional theories of teaching and learning that are viewed by some as different from Vygotskian perspectives. We will develop the case, however, that there really is quite a bit in common between these approaches and those inspired by Soviet theories of learning and development. Although extremists of various persuasions (e.g., dyed-in-the-wool Vygotskians and behaviorists) make much of the subtle differences between their own perspectives and other viewpoints that they do not favor, from the perspective of developing a psychology of instruction, it is heartening to find common recommendations flowing from a variety of theories. Indeed, there is what Mathison (1988) calls theoretical triangulation for instructional ideas like scaffolding and teaching in the zone of proximal development. That is, when different groups with different epistemological standards and methods come to similar conclusions about instruction, it increases confidence in those conclusions.

DIRECT INSTRUCTION AND EXPLANATION

If things are going well in a reciprocal teaching group, the adult teacher's presence hardly should be noticeable. The instructional theory is to reduce the teacher's input as much as possible, with student control of the interactions in the group an important part of eventual internalization by the students of the strategies being taught. In addition, there is a concern that the students construct content knowledge for themselves in the group, that the knowledge they construct via making predictions, generating questions, seeking clarifications when confused, and summarizing text will be more meaningful to them than if the teacher intervenes and provides information pertaining to the text. Those who identify with sociohistorical approaches to instruction are extremely concerned that the teacher cede control to the students as soon as possible.

Other perspectives on teacher-student interaction are not nearly so concerned with reducing the

teacher's role quickly, although we will argue after reviewing these perspectives that scaffolding occurs in the teaching captured by these models and that such instruction is usually offered in what the Vygotskians refer to as the zone of proximal development. Although many of the sociohistorical types consider the perspectives covered in this section to be antithetical to Vygotskian principles, our view is that there is much less distance between the instructional theories covered in this section and those reviewed in the previous section.

Direct Instruction

Although a number of researchers have contributed research on direct instruction, Rosenshine is associated with such teaching more than any other. Rosenshine (e.g., 1979; Rosenshine & Stevens, 1984) has provided the most complete and blunt appraisals of the variables that are associated with achievement gains in classrooms, especially gains related to reading and mathematics during the elementary years. There can be little doubt in reading Rosenshine that his emphasis is much more on behaviors of teachers and students (i.e., objective performances) than on internal changes in students. In this era when cognitive and sociocognitive theories are dominanting discussions of instruction, this emphasis on behavior is one reason many are turned off by Rosenshine's analyses of effective teaching. Even so, the scientific evidence pertaining to direct instruction is consistent with Rosenshine's conclusions.

What produces high levels of classroom learning according to Rosenshine? First, the more content covered, often measured in terms of time on academic tasks, the greater achievement. Rosenshine (1979) was particularly impressed with Bloom's (1976) conclusion, based on analysis of 15 studies, that the amount of time that students spent academically engaged was especially predictive of achievement (also Stallings & Kaskowitz, 1974): If there is one thing that is certain about direct instruction, most students are on task most of the time (e.g., Frick, 1990). Rosenshine (1979) concluded that learning was best accomplished in classrooms that were academically focused and teacher directed, ones in which academic content was presented in a sequenced and structured fashion. Direct instruction involves clear specification of goals to students. There is sufficient time for instruction, with continuous, extensive coverage of content. Student performance is monitored. Questions are asked that are at a level that students can handle them, so that lower-level and more literal questions are directed at weaker students, and more demanding questions are given to better students. Feedback is provided immediately and is academically oriented. Even with all of this academic work going on, Rosenshine's preferred classrooms are convivial and warm, democratic and cooperative. Although positive affect alone does not make a good classroom, positive affect when combined with an academic outlook does make for academic progress.

All of this should sound good, even to nonbehaviorists. So why the reservations about Rosenshine's proposal? One reason is that he made it sound so dreary. He found no problems with teaching in large groups, emphasized the teacher as decision maker rather than the student (e.g., in limiting the materials students can work with), embraced orderliness, endorsed asking questions that students can answer rather than questions that challenge them and require reflection, and recognized that drill and overlearning often have a place in school. For those many educators who are child centered or discovery oriented, Rosenshine's description was grim. In addition, it was unidimensional with respect to outcomes embraced, focusing on measurable student achievement (Peterson, 1979), ignoring that students have individual needs and talents that sometimes are not obvious on standardized assessments.

We are more enthusiastic about Rosenshine's approach than many commentators because it seems unlikely that things would go as well as they seem to go in direct instruction classrooms if the teachers were not highly responsive to the students. Indeed, there are plenty of provisions for such responsivity. For example, a key feature of direct instruction is to provide ample time. In many direct instruction classrooms, the teacher arranges schedules so that slower learners are permitted the time they need. In contrast, faster students are ushered into other academic content that goes beyond the minimum curriculum. To provide timely feedback, it is critical to be sensitive to students and their individual differences in needs and expression of needs and learning. In order for a teacher to ask questions that are likely to be answered correctly, he or she must be extremely aware of what students know already and be committed to taking their knowledge and perspectives into account in leading classroom discussions. Teachers who lack such sensitivity to student needs do not have classrooms that are convivial and warm. Thus,

our guess is that Rosenshine's preferred classrooms are more responsive than he describes. We are certain that he was relying on data sets that were not particularly sensitive to how teachers made decisions about students or provided feedback to them.

Even if direct instruction teachers are more student oriented than Rosenshine portrayed them, repackaging of the direct instruction approach was necessary if it was to be attractive to educators in the 1980s and 1990s. The cognitive revolution had in education forced a concern with developing strategies, knowledge, metacognition, and motivation in students. The direct explanation approach developed by Duffy, Roehler, and their colleagues at Michigan State went well beyond the direct instruction conceptualization of effective instruction, providing an attractive cognitively oriented theory of instruction that retained many of the best features of direct instruction.

Direct Explanation

There have been innumerable studies in which an adult has explained to a child how to do something and the child has been able to do it (see Pressley, Heisel, et al., 1982, for many examples involving memory strategies). As should be obvious by this point in the book, such explanations alone are not likely to result in the child continuing to use a strategy. If the teacher models the strategy for the student, it helps, as does having the student model the strategy for the teacher with feedback. Long-term maintenance and transfer are more likely if instruction includes information about when and where to use the strategy being taught as well as opportunities to practice the strategy and practice adapting it to new situations. All of these components are included in what Roehler and Duffy (e.g., 1984) have referred to as direct explanation.

Any strategy can be taught with direct explanation. It is an extremely fluid approach to teaching, usually beginning with teacher explanations and modeling and then proceeding to student practice. Practice is monitored with additional explanations and modeling provided as needed, with such feedback and instruction reduced as the student becomes more independent (i.e., direct explanations and feedback are provided in a scaffolded fashion). An important part of this instruction is what Duffy and Roehler refer to as **mental modeling** (e.g., Duffy & Roehler, 1989), which is simply showing the students how to apply the strategy by thinking aloud. (Mental *explaining things in appropriate for age*

modeling in this sense should not be confused with Johnson-Laird's mental models, which were covered in Chapter 3.) Another extremely important idea in this approach to instruction is **responsive elaboration:** That is, the information provided to students depends on the particular problems the students are encountering and the particular ways that their understandings are deficient. Reinstruction and reexplanations as well as follow-up mental modeling are responsive to student needs and usually are an elaboration of student understandings up until that point.

Duffy, Roehler, Sivan et al. (1987) produced an extremely well-designed study of the effects of direct explanation strategy instruction on grade-3 reading. They taught grade-3 teachers to explain directly the strategies and processes that are part of skilled grade-3 reading, for example, the prefix pronunciation strategy. The teachers were taught first to explain a strategy and then to mentally model use of the strategy for students. The mental modeling showed students how good readers apply the strategy when they read. Then came guided student practice with the students initially carrying out the processing overtly so that the teacher could monitor their use of the new strategy. At first, there was substantial assistance, which was reduced as students became more proficient. It must be emphasized, however, that reexplanations and remodeling and prescription of additional practice were on an as-needed basis. Thus, although there was scaffolding of instruction, the teacher was not at all reluctant to provide additional input when students needed it.

Teachers were also taught to encourage transfer of strategies by going over when and where the strategies being learned might be used. Teachers cued use of the new strategies when students encountered situations in which the strategies might be applied profitably, regardless of when these occasions arose during the school day. Cuing and prompting was continued until students autonomously applied the strategies they were taught.

A year of this type of instruction had an impact on grade-3 students. Students receiving direct explanations were more aware of lesson content and the strategic nature of reading at the end of the year than were control students receiving more conventional instruction. Even more important, however, was that the students in the direct explanation condition outperformed the control students on a number of measures of reading. In short, a full year of direct expla-nation of reading strategies made substantial difference in the reading achievement of grade-3 students.

Direct Explanation Compared With Direct Instruction How is this similar to Rosenshine's direct instruction? Direct explanation classrooms are certainly more teacher than student directed. Direct explanations are well structured and the goals of lessons are clear. Duffy, Roehler, and their colleagues are certainly concerned with using students' time well, with direct explanation and practice involving intensive academic engagement. Students are not rushed, however, with reexplanations and additional modeling occurring as needed. Thus, one of the most important roles for the direct explanation teacher is to monitor students—decisions to reexplain or remodel follow from teacher perceptions of student understandings and difficulties. The tasks (including questions) given to students are ones they can handle, at least with some support from the teacher. Direct explanations provide a great deal of feedback to students, and it is immediate academic feedback. Finally, direct explanation classrooms are friendly places. There can be little doubt that there is much in common between direct instruction and direct explanation.

There are also enormous differences, however, at least at a conceptual level. The direct explanation teacher's decisions are a function of the perceived needs of the students, needs that often are revealed by students' thinking aloud. The think-alouds are revealing about the students' cognitive processing. Direct explanation teachers care much more about process than products, whereas direct instruction, at least as it is described, is product oriented. (We emphasize, *as described*, for we sincerely believe that many direct instruction teachers monitor process as well—it is just that the direct instruction theorists and researchers never bother to pay attention to how the teachers are sensitive to student processing.) All of the mental modeling and explaining during direct explanations are aimed at making certain that the student understands what is being learned. Student understanding is not discussed much in direct instruction circles. (Again, however, many of the performances so valued by the direct instruction types would not be possible without understanding, so that direct instruction often must increase understanding, although such understanding is not the main concern of direct instruction theorists and researchers.) Duffy's direct explanation model is certainly a cognitive model, with the concern being deep understanding of strategies and when and how to use them. Although we believe that direct instruction often creates such understandings, its failing as a conceptual model of instruction is that it considers academic performances more than how those academic performances are achieved—and if there is anything that committed cognitively oriented educators (who are everywhere these days) care about, it is *how* academic performances are achieved.

Direct Explanation Compared With Reciprocal Teaching

We have argued since first reviewing reciprocal teaching and direct explanation that the two conceptions of instruction are similar (see Pressley, Snyder, & Cariglia-Bull, 1987). Both involve teaching of cognitive processes for coming to terms with text. Both involve modeling and explanation of strategies. During both, students have an opportunity to see multiple models of cognitive processing because during both types of groups, a number of students are going to be using the cognitive processes that are being instructed. The discussion of content that occurs during both reciprocal teaching and direct explanation, as students practice strategies, should increase incidental learning of the content covered in the readings used to practice the strategies being learned. Both involve teacher scaffolding of instruction—the teacher monitors what is going on and offers supportive instruction on an as-needed basis. The teacher's scaffolding of instruction necessarily results in a student-sensitive approach to instruction and a cooperative, supportive atmosphere in the reading group. The assumption in both approaches is that participating in the instructional group and receiving the scaffolded instruction will result in long-term internalization of the cognitive processes being fostered by the group, so that the teacher is progressively less involved as instruction proceeds. As striking as these similarities are, however, the differences between reciprocal teaching and direct explanation are also striking.

Reciprocal teaching was developed with respect to the teaching of four particular strategies—predicting, questioning, seeking clarification, and summarizing. Although it is possible to reciprocally teach with other strategies as the focus of instruction, most investigations of reciprocal teaching to date have involved the original four strategies used by Palincsar and Brown (1984). Direct explanation is more generic, in that it is easy to see how direct explanation could be applied with almost any strategy, including ones pertaining to reading, writing, or mathematical content. Indeed, our opening comment about direct explanation in this section was that there have been many studies in which adults have explained to children how to do something.

The most important difference between reciprocal teaching and direct explanation, however, is with respect to the saliency of the teacher. Those committed to reciprocal teaching are committed to reducing quickly the adult teacher's control. The belief is that if students are to internalize decision making with respect to cognitive processes, they need to be the ones controlling the cognitive processes. In contrast, the teacher is much more visibly in charge as part of direct explanations, although always with the goal of reducing teacher input—that is, direct explanation teaching really is scaffolded, with the teacher cutting back as soon as it is possible to do so.

There is an important consequence of this difference in saliency of the teacher in reciprocal teaching and direct explanation, one which, in our view, favors the direct explanation approach. In order for the teacher to be able to step back during reciprocal teaching, a fairly rigid sequence is set up. Go back to the sample reciprocal teaching lesson. Each time, after the text was read, the student leader of the moment posed a question for peers. The peers attempted to respond. Then the student leader proposed a summary. During reciprocal teaching, there are always questions and summaries from the student leaders, with other students encouraged to seek clarifications by posing questions. Predictions about upcoming text are offered. Those who favor reciprocal teaching point out correctly that a great deal of flexible discussion of text and issues in text can be covered with this framework. Moreover, they correctly argue that the particular processes are ones that are critical to comprehension of text (e.g., Baker & Brown, 1984). We contend, however, that the flexibility of discussion is greater during direct explanations and that the four processes favored during reciprocal teaching do not exhaust the strategies a good reader needs to deploy in order to understand text (see Chapter 14).

Impact of the Direct Explanation Model

We have been extremely impressed by how much impact Duffy and Roehler's (e.g., 1989) work on direct explanation is having on others who are attempting to devise cognitive process interventions for reading comprehension, a point that will be elaborated in Chapter 14. We personally believe that the most theoretically compelling instructional position developed in this chapter is Duffy and Roehler's direct explanation model, one that incorporates ideas like scaffolding and the zone of proximal development (i.e., the processes being directly explained are just a bit beyond what the students can do now) but keeps up front that student understanding of the processing is critical, understanding that permits autonomous functioning. Our belief is that the most important strengths of direct instruction and reciprocal teaching are represented in direct explanation, with direct explanation having some advantages that are not in the reciprocal teaching and direct instruction models.

Summary: Direct Explanation and Apprenticeship

We close in emphasizing that direct explanation at its best is cognitive apprenticeship. Someone who is definitely an expert in reading (or writing or mathematical problem solving) passes on expertise to the next generation. All of the elements of apprenticeship specified by Collins et al. (1989) are there: There is extensive modeling and scaffolding by a teacher who acts like a coach once students begin to practice the processes being explained. The students are required to be able to explain what they are doing (i.e., there is articulation of processing by students). Students have opportunities to compare how they are processing with how other students are approaching a task. Reflection on one's own processing is encouraged by the teacher/coach, as the teacher/coach provides feedback tailored to the difficulties the student may be having. Moreover, the teacher/coach strongly encourages the student to try out the newly learned processes in new situations and to use the processes being learned flexibly—that is, the students are encouraged to explore how the processes they are learning through direct explanations can be applied broadly. Our guess is that as the idea of cognitive apprenticeship in school is translated into practice, that practice is going to look a lot like direct explanation as Duffy and Roehler have conceived of it.

INSTRUCTIONAL CONVERSATIONS

Probably no form of human interaction is more common than conversation, and so it is in classrooms as well. Of course, the direct instruction, reciprocal teaching, and direct explanation approaches considered thus far in this chapter involve particular types of conversations, with the nature of these conversations taken up later in this section, after consideration of some of the most "classic" work on classroom discourse as well as emerging directions in research on conversations in classrooms.

Conversations as They Usually Occur in School: Initiate-Response-Evaluation Cycles

Conversations that are structured liked the following occur everyday in school:

TEACHER: Where is the Tomb of the Unknown Soldier? (Initiation)

STUDENT: In Arlington Cemetery? (Response)

T: That's right. (Evaluation) And what might you see at that tomb? (Initiation)

S: There's always a guard of honor there. (Response)

T: Yes. (Evaluation) Do you remember what is interesting about this guard? (Initiation)

S: Uh, uh, no. (Failed response)

T: Someone else? (Implied evaluation, initiation)

S2: He's a member of the Old Guard. Really hard to get into the Old Guard. (Response)

T: Correct. (Evaluation) What else is at Arlington Cemetery? (Initiation)

S: President Kennedy's grave. (Response)

T: Anything else? (Implied acceptance, initiation)

S: President Kennedy's brother's grave. It's over the hill a little bit down from the turning flame. (Response)

T: Eternal flame. (Implied evaluation) Yes, near President Kennedy's grave. (Evaluation)

The teacher initiates an interaction, often with a question; the student responds; and the teacher evaluates the response before making another initiation. We are certain all readers can recall many such interactions during their schooling. How pervasive initiate-response-evaluation (IRE) sequences are became clear with Mehan's (1979) classic analysis of classroom lessons. Teachers and students know how to interact with each other in this way. For example, teachers send clear nonverbal signals to students that such a sequence of questioning is about to begin and that student responses are expected, nonverbal signals that a teacher's students understand well (Figure 8.2) (see Cazden, 1988, Chapter 3).

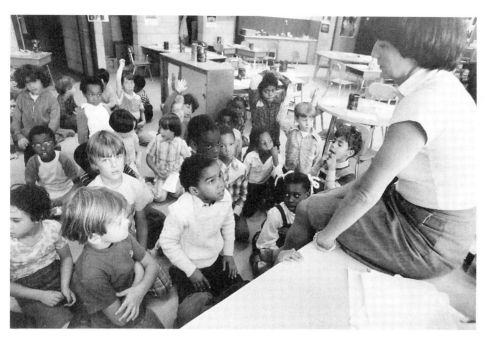

Figure 8.2 Teachers questioning students, students responding, and teachers then evaluating the responses (i.e., IRE cycles)—the most common type of teacher-student interaction in American schools. It is effective? As discussed in the text, the answer is complicated, but much theory suggests that classroom interactions that resemble naturalistic conversations may have benefits compared to IRE cycles.

Cazden sees such interactions as part of classroom management. To the extent that students do not have to think much about nonacademic aspects of their interactions (i.e., they know what is expected of them in IRE cycles because of participating in so many cycles during a school year), their attention can be to the content of the academic conversation. Moreover, it is possible for teachers to go through a lesson in an orderly fashion and make certain the points he or she considers important are "covered." The main motivation for many traditional classroom conversations is to cover a vast amount of content rather than to air alternative perspectives on the content being covered (e.g., Alvermann, O'Brien, & Dillon, 1990), is a tendency that is difficult for teachers to overcome even if they attempt to do so (Alvermann & Hayes, 1989).

Some of the negatives of such interactions are apparent, however. For example, questioning often tends to be lower level, filled with literal, factual questions. (Recall this was a criticism of direct instruction—and, of course, direct instruction is filled with IRE cycles.) Because only one student can be active at a time, this is a passive approach to learning for many students (for analysis, see Bowers & Flinders, 1990, Chapter 5). We suspect many readers remember such conversations as boring. Such criticisms resurface repeatedly in discussions of IREs (e.g., Cazden, 1988, Chapter 3).

For those who prefer students learning to control their thinking (and, of course, many if not most educators embrace such a goal), such recitation structures are particularly unattractive because IRE cycles are almost completely teacher controlled. This is one aspect of these interactions that some sociolinguists (i.e., scientists who study social factors in communications) consider to be particularly objectionable. Sociolinguists argue that how teachers interact with students and how dialogues are structured send powerful messages to students. In particular, the IRE structure provides teachers with many more options than students, rendering students powerless to do anything except bidding to answer and then answering questions that they had no part in formulating (Bowers & Flinders, 1990, Chapter 5). Students are being sent the message that education is receiving knowledge from an authority rather than working with knowledge to understand it in ways that are personally meaningful and in fashions that engender new knowledge. We believe, as do many others, that the message to send to students is that knowledge is something that is actively constructed by people just like them (and including them) rather than received from an external authority. Fortunately, there are other ways of dialoguing in school than IRE cycles. There is a great deal of contemporary interest in determining how to promote these alternatives to IRE cycles so as to empower teachers and students to participate in such discussions in ways that maximize educational benefits, including the construction of knowledge during academic discussions.

True Dialogues in School

In natural conversations, there are evolving meanings and real attempts to inform and persuade as participants try to understand what is going on. Consider the following snippet of conversation author MP had with his wife the other night over an upcoming schooling decision affecting their son:

MIKE: Did you call X School back? (Donna infers correctly that Mike is interested because this is a school he liked when he visited.)

DONNA: Yes, and we *are* going to go over for an interview; it's on the 23rd. I'll do that. (Mike inferred that Donna wanted to make certain she can size up the school without him present to highlight the features that excited him.)

MIKE: I feel badly because I'll be going to Chicago that day so I won't be able to take care of Tim at all. (Mike is trying to let her know that it is all right if she wants to go it alone for this interview.)

DONNA: What's in Chicago? (Change of topic, legitimately curious.)

MIKE: The basal publisher . . . (Mike consciously deciding to mention the business part of the trip as well as deciding to omit reference that he will be seeing some old friends on the trip and will probably be having a good time while Donna has a particularly hassled day.)

DONNA: I know you have to do these things. If you could keep the trip as short as possible I'd appreciate it, although I know it is often easier just to stay overnight after completing business. (Donna correctly inferring that Mike is going to have a good time, explicitly designing a comment to guilt trip him a bit but at the same time not make a big deal out of what she knows he will do no matter what she says.)

Quite a lot going on here. Two people who are very familiar with one another, including each other's habits and dispositions as well as biases and opinions, made powerful inferences based on prior knowledge, going well beyond the surface level of the conversation. There was strategy here motivated by particular goals (e.g., Mike was motivated to keep Donna from getting ticked off, as she might if he made it clear that he was going to be having a good time as she spent the day juggling the school interview, Tim, and her job). The particular choice of wording involved coordinating Mike's prior knowledge and Donna's prior knowledge with metacognition about which rhetorical tactics have worked in the past. Strategy, knowledge, metacognition, and motivation are all at work here—the same four elements emphasized since Chapter 1 of this book—with the outcome the type of outcome valued throughout this book: Both participants learned quite a bit from the conversation.

Nature of More Natural Classroom Dialogues

The analysis of the Mike-Donna conversation makes it easy to see why educators believe that conversations more natural than IRE cycles might go far in promoting learning in school. There are four important structural differences between "natural" classroom conversations and Mike's chat with Donna, however (see Cazden, 1988, Chapter 4, for some of these): (1) More people are typically involved. (2) Although students and teachers often know each other well, many of the relationships in the group will not even approximate the intimacy of knowledge shared by Mike and Donna. (3) One of the players in the classroom conversation is often someone who is much more knowledgeable and has the resources to exert control if he or she wishes—that is, of course, the teacher. (4) The topic of discussion shifts within narrower boundaries in instructional conversations. So, if the discussion of the day is about dinosaurs, it stays on dinosaurs rather than switching to how the local baseball team is doing. Natural conversations are much more far-ranging, as with Mike and Donna's conversation starting with comments about Tim's school and switching to a discussion of the Chicago trip.

Example of a Naturalistic Academic Conversation

Although study of more natural academic conversations is an emerging area of research, it is already clear that students and teachers in interaction can create conversations in which the teacher is much less in control, with the comments of students stimulating other students to participate in real interactions. Consider this example of conversation generated as kindergarten students and teacher discuss the story, "Tico and the Golden Wings," by Leo Lionni:

TEACHER: I don't think it's fair that Tico has to give up his golden wings.

LISA: It is fair. See, he was nicer when he didn't have any wings. They didn't like him when he had gold.

WALLY: He thinks he's better if he has golden wings.

EDDIE: He is better.

JILL: But he's not supposed to be better. The wishing bird was wrong to give him those wings.

DEANNA: She has to give him his wish. He's the one who shouldn't have asked for golden wings.

WALLY: He could put black wings on top of the golden wings and try to trick them.

DEANNA: They'd sneak up and see the gold. He should give every bird one golden feather and keep one for himself.

TEACHER: Why can't he decide for himself what kind of wings he wants?

WALLY: He has to decide to have black wings. (Cazden, 1988, p. 55, from a lesson taught in Vivian Paley's kindergarten class)

What a difference from IRE cycles! The students did not raise their hands to participate. The teacher did not evaluate their responses and decide who would next get a turn to answer a question. What happened instead is that these children applied their prior knowledge to this story and interpreted it. It is a good bet that the individual students reading alone would not have come up with many of the interpretations that emerged during the discussion and a certain bet that no one reader would have thought of all the counterarguments that were put on the table. There were so many **elaborations** of student knowledge and **inferences** in this few minutes of conversation. Many educational theorists are now thinking about the implications of encouraging such conversations in school.

Distributed Nature of Cognition in Naturalistic Classroom Conversations One of the most important analyses of naturalistic instructional conversations is that they are excellent examples of **distrib-**

uted cognition. The cognition—the thinking—that goes on here is not a product of one head but a product of *several heads in interaction* with one another (e.g., Bereiter, 1990; Hutchins, 1991). By heads coming together in such a fashion, it is likely that extremely powerful interpretations and understandings will emerge. First, the different heads have different prior knowledge. Moreover, the different heads have attended to different aspects of the information being considered. As the talk in the group proceeds, connections are made. Something Susie says connects with knowledge activated in Billy, who in turn responds. In doing so, Billy may combine some of what he knows in common with Susie and something Susie said that he did not know previously to produce a new inference. This inference might trigger something in Tommy, and so on.

What does the teacher do in all of this? He or she provides conversational starters and perhaps nudges the group one way or another with questions, as the kindergarten teacher did in the example. Those who study such groups (such as Hutchins, 1991) recognize that a powerful figure in a group can do much to shape the group opinion. One of the challenges for the teacher is to shape the group opinion to get some messages that are particularly important across to students but not to shape so much as to stifle creatively constructive and appropriate interpretations. This may be a difficult role for many teachers, especially those accustomed to IRE cycles during which they are in control of what happens in the group as well as the information that will receive positive evaluation. Electing to conduct real dialogues is electing to give up some of what has been a teacher's traditional power.

Let us now diverge for two paragraphs to point out how such research is making contact with one of the more abstract theoretical ideas developed earlier in Chapter 3. Hutchins's (1991) research has to do with applying connectionist models to the study of interaction in conversations. Thus, it is possible to construct simulations on computers in which all participants in a group have similar prior knowledge or all have different knowledge. That is, a computer program is constructed with group members, each of whom has a set of connections. Then a problem for discussion that connects with some parts of these knowledge bases is given to the "group members" for "discussion." It is possible to figure out much about the dynamics of the discussion and how an interpretation evolves from running such a program.

Figure 8.3 Where is the thinking going on as this group discusses a problem?

The outcome differs, for instance, if the programming was done by a group of equipotent peers versus a group that has one figure more powerful than others (e.g., such as a teacher). Some of Hutchins's simulations seem to capture what happens when humans interact and discuss, and thus we think there are important implications of connectionist models of knowledge for research on classroom communications (Figure 8.3).

Consider an example. What if everyone does come to the group with the same knowledge—the same connections, to use the term preferred by many neural network theorists. What a connectionist model predicts is that a group interpretation will emerge quickly once "discussion" begins and that interpretation will not change—and that is what happens when a program is run in which everybody thinks alike. When simulated people think differently, conclusions do not come nearly so rapidly, with many more novel inferences.

The idea that cognition can be distributed across members of a group, with novel interpretations reached when the groups members enter into **transactions** with one another, has been of great interest to organizational psychologists (e.g., Levine & Moreland, 1991; Schrage [1990] provided a nice popular summary; Wegner, 1987). No one in an organization can know everything about it. Parts of the organiza-

tion come together and combine their expertise to arrive at solutions for problems, solutions that could not be produced by anyone working alone.

Effects of Naturalistic Academic Conversations— the Exercise of Distributed Cognition—on the Learning and Thinking of Individual Students
Hatano and Inagaki (1991) provided important research substantiating the educational potential of interpretive discussion. Their starting premise was that a group of students interacting would understand a problem at a high level as a group. The issue for Hatano and Inagaki was whether the processing carried out by the group would transform the thinking of the individuals in the group. Specifically, Hatano and Inagaki explored an instructional procedure developed by another Japanese educator, Itakura (1967), a method referred to as hypothesis-experiment-instruction: The pupils are presented a question with several alternative answers. Each pupil chooses what they believe to be the correct answer, followed by a show of hands to determine how the various members of the group thought. The pupils then explain and discuss their choices, followed by another opportunity for individual students to select the correct answer. Pupils then have an opportunity to test their alternative by observing an experiment pertaining to the problem posed or

reading a passage concerning the problem. Here is how one teacher initiated such a sequence:

> Mr. Shoji started the lesson with a question: "Suppose that you have a clay ball on one end of a spring. You hold the other end of the spring and put half of the clay ball in water. Will the spring (a) become shorter, (b) become longer, or (c) retain its length. (Hatano & Inagaki, 1991, p. 337, based on an example from Inagaki, 1981)

Before the discussion, 12 children in the group selected (a), 8 selected (b), and 14 selected (c). The discussion clearly shifted individual student understanding, as evident by second attempts at the problem. This time 21 students selected the correct alternative, (a), with 5 and 8 selecting (b) and (c), respectively. The shifts to response (a) were almost certainly mediated by arguments presented during the discussion. Consider the following arguments in favor of alternative (a) made by supporters of response (a):

> [To a student who had selected (c)]: Your opinion is strange to me. You said, 'The weight of the clay will not change because it is only half immersed in water.' But you know, when a person's head is above the water, his weight is lighter in water.
>   I don't agree with the idea that the clay ball is as heavy in water as in air. I think that water has the power to make things float.
>   If the clay is a very small lump, I think the water can make it float. (Hatano & Inagaki, 1991, p. 338, based on an example from Inagaki, 1981)

Although shifts in perspective following such arguments are supportive of the position that opportunities to participate in group discussions can shift the thinking of individual students in the group, Hatano and Inagaki (1991) wanted more analytical information and, in particular, wanted to know if individual students' reasoning shifted as a function of participation in group discussions. That is, shifts in choices might reflect some change in understanding but not change sufficient to permit students to articulate why they changed their minds. Being able to explain why one has changed an opinion is a much more impressive accomplishment than simply changing an opinion. (The Inagaki [1981] result is reminiscent of when nonconserving children interact with conserving children on a conservation problem; they shift from claiming that the amount of a substance changes with a perceptual transformation to the position that the amount of something does not vary with perceptual transformations that do not involve adding or substracting something; see Chapter 7, this book.)

In Inagaki and Hatano (1989), fifth-graders read a passage about animal characteristics and lifestyles. Lions and moles were discussed as examples. Then the students were given a multiple-choice problem about the characteristics of a monkey, such as, "Do the thumbs of monkeys' forefeet oppose the other 'fingers' (like in human hands) or extend in parallel to other 'fingers' (like in human feet)? How about the thumbs of their hind feet?": (a) The thumbs are never opposing; (b) the thumbs are opposing only in the forefeet; or (c) the thumbs are opposing in both the fore and hind feet (pp. 341–342). (Alternative "c" was the correct response.) The students in a group discussion condition first made a choice individually, followed by group discussion, followed by a second opportunity to respond to the question. The students then read a passage that provided the correct answer but did not provide an explanation about why the answer might be correct. Students in the control condition made an initial choice of an answer and then read the passage containing the answer.

The most interesting outcome in this experiment was that the subjects in the group discussion condition provided more elaborate defenses of their answers, when prompted to do so, than did control students. Moreover, those subjects who had talked more during the discussion provided more elaborate answers than subjects who had talked less. In short, the data in this study converged to support the position that participating in the group discussions promoted learning by the individual participants in the group.

Confidence in Hatano and Inagaki's (1989, 1991) outcome is high because it complements a growing correlational and experimental literature documenting that when students in groups construct explanations about information they are learning, their acquisition and understanding of information are more certain. For example, Webb (see 1989, for a review) has conducted a number of studies in which students solved problems as group members. The students who did the explaining in the groups learned more (as determined by measures of individual achievement) than did students who were content to listen. Anderson, Wilkinson, and Mason (1991) observed that grade-3 students learned most during reading group when they were reading aloud and answering teacher's questions.

Although there are alternative explanations for the effects reported by Hatano, Inagaki, and Webb than that they reflect the positive effects of generating explanations (e.g., more able students might be expected to lead group discussions), such alternative explanations do not apply to experiments conducted by King (e.g., 1989) and colleagues. In King's studies, students have talked about to-be-learned content in groups. In some conditions of her experiments, subjects are taught how to generate thought-provoking questions by providing them with question frames with open slots. Thus, students are encouraged to generate questions over the content using frames such as the following: How would you use _____ to _____? What is a new example of _____? Explain why _____. How does _____ affect _____? Do you agree or disagree with this statement? Such question frames do stimulate discussions that involve considerable interaction and generation of new ideas, more so than if students are involved in unstructured discussion of content. In addition, learning of the to-be-learned content is improved when students are taught to use the question frames to structure discussion. See Pressley, Wood, Woloshyn, Martin, King, and Menke (1992) for a review of the relevant literature.

Group discussions can result in ideas related to content that would not have occurred to individual members of the group working alone. If learning is the goal, content seems to be better learned through group interaction, particularly if the situation is structured so there is substantial participation by each member, as in the studies reported by Hatano and Inagaki (1991) and those conducted by King. That the structure of discussion groups may be particularly critical for productive discussions that lead to new ideas and increase learning by the group has been a theme in theoretical analyses of interpretive discussions. Although the research literature pertaining to how group structure can affect thinking and learning is thin at present, there is a rich body of hypotheses emerging, ones that we believe will be evaluated extensively in the coming years.

Concluding Comments: Why Have More Naturalistic Instructional Conversations? Collaborative discussion is an exceptionally important form of instruction, one definitely acceptable (in fact, preferred) by students as a way to learn (e.g., Thorkild-

sen, 1989, 1991). From a Vygotskian perspective, the opportunities to participate in groups that dialogue about important content should have profound long-term effects on cognitive development. The Vygotskian theory is that opportunities to engage in interpersonal problem solving and thinking stimulate the development of personal problem-solving and thinking skills, in that many of the processes that the group carries out together eventually are internalized by individual members of the group. That is, there are long-term cognitive advantages from years of arguing with others about important ideas, reflecting as a group on strengths and weaknesses of proposals, elaborating as a group the good ideas of group members and rejecting the bad ones. Eventually the participant in such a group can construct arguments for himself or herself and has gotten in the habit of reflecting on ideas.

In addition, much of mature thinking is collaborative thinking (Resnick et al., 1991; Schrage, 1990). Flying an airplane requires several minds in collaboration to produce a safe flight. Controlling a large ship requires many more minds in interaction. Surgeons, anesthesiologists, and nurses think together to perform a complicated surgery. Innovative new products are not the inventions of individuals but the result of teamwork and groups of people reflecting and thinking together to create a better idea than any one of them could have produced on their own. Given the value of collaborative thinking in the modern world, it makes sense to foster such thinking in schools.

CONCLUDING COMMENTS

In presenting the argument in this chapter that much changed with the translation in 1978 of *Mind in Society*, we do not want to imply that Western researchers were completely oblivious to the potential impact of social interactional factors on cognitive development before that translation. In addition to the social learning theorists, who provided many experimental demonstrations in the early 1970s that children's thought could be affected by observations of and interactions with more competent others, there was substantial correlational data substantiating that growing up with parents who were responsive to their children's intellectual needs made a difference in intellectual outcome.

For example, Hess and Shipman (1965) found higher conceptual and linguistic functioning in children coming from homes in which parents encouraged their children to reflect before acting and to consider carefully before making choices. In homes producing more competent children, children were encouraged to size up a situation before acting rather than to apply a rigid rule. By the end of the 1960s, considerable evidence had amassed that some parents spent a great deal of time doing what is now thought of as scaffolding, providing children with intellectually engaging experiences, mediating these experiences so that children were not frustrated as they dealt with appropriately challenging intellectual content (e.g., Hess, Shipman, & Jackson, 1965; Katz, 1967; Jensen, 1968). That is, some parents read books to their children and help their children come to understand the content of those books; they reason with their children about why it is necessary sometimes to stop and think before acting; they play counting games with their children, help their offspring do the puzzles in children's magazines, and talk to their children about important categories of experience (e.g., which animals can be seen at the zoo and which ones live on farms). Unfortunately, it is only some children who received such input, with profound differences in cognitive development for those children who received such scaffolding compared with those who did not.

Work in this tradition continued in the 1970s and 1980s (e.g., Laosa 1978, 1980, 1982), with more demonstrations that some parents provide much more positive reinforcement and praise for their children than others, some ask more questions of their offspring, and some are more certain to assist their child in doing a task rather than simply doing the task for the child or leaving the task undone. Again, consistent correlations between such child-rearing behaviors, all of which are part of scaffolding, and intellectual outcomes were observed.

Other things equal, rank ordering of intellectual competence is going to favor children who have enjoyed sensitive intellectual input from parents and teachers. What Vygotsky suggests is that humans internalize cognitive processes first experienced in rich social situations—such as the favorable parent-child interactions just described—and that the ways of thinking in the surrounding social milieu become one's own ways of thinking. For that reason, it is important to do all possible to encourage parents, teachers, and peers to interact constructively with children.

In this chapter, we reviewed a number of different social interactional approaches to instruction. In some of these (e.g., IRE cycles, direct instruction), if there is scaffolding of learning, those concerned with developing and studying the form of instruction paid scant attention to the scaffolding that goes on. In contrast, scaffolding is at the center of apprenticeship, reciprocal teaching, and direct explanation models of teaching and learning.

Scaffolding is difficult to do well. Teachers must be tremendously motivated to do it. What is apparent to us is that some feminist scholars have hit on an important instructional ingredient not touched on in this book thus far, an ingredient that is essential if teachers are going to be willing to do the hard work that is scaffolded instruction. They have to care about their students (e.g., Noddings, 1984, especially Chapter 8). Noddings discusses how caring is at the center of a teacher-student apprenticeship situation and that this can be a wonderful and fulfilling situation for the teacher:

> . . . The teacher works with the student. He becomes her apprentice and gradually assumes greater responsibility in the tasks they undertake. This working together, which produces both joy in the relation and increasing competence in the cared-for . . . needs the cooperative guidance of a fully caring adult. . . . The . . . caring . . . teacher . . . has two major tasks: to stretch the student's world by presenting an effective selection of that world with which she is in contact, and to work cooperatively with the student in his struggle toward competence in that world. (pp. 177–178)

Throughout Noddings' discussion is the necessity of the teacher caring for the student, and she recognizes how difficult it is to do, so difficult that many believe it cannot be part of teaching:

> The sort of relatedness and caring I have been discussing is often dismissed as impossible [for the teacher] because of constraints of number, time, and purpose. Richard Hult, in his discussion of "pedagogical caring," notes that such requirements seem to require in turn close personal relationships. . . . He says, 'While these may sometimes occur and may be desirable, most pedagogical contexts make such relationships implausible if not undesirable.' He concludes that caring . . . 'cannot be the kind of caring demanded of teachers.' I insist that it is exactly the kind of caring ideally required of teachers. (p. 179)

What fascinated us in reading Noddings (1984, Chapter 8) is that so many of the themes discussed in this chapter are there. She urges teachers to give up some of their control and to foster trust between them and their students. She urges true dialogue and argues that it promotes deep contact with the ideas presented in the curriculum and stimulates the development of an active thinker. Noddings urges dialogical situations that permit and encourage students to take intellectual risks. Sensitive teaching that includes caring, however, does something else that has not been covered henceforth—it passes on an ethic of caring for others to the next generation.

We closed this chapter with Noddings to emphasize how frequently the main ideas in this chapter are encountered. Remember how we made the case earlier that many of the Vygotskian ideas overlap with behaviorist models of education as well as Piagetian thinking about the stimulation of cognitive development. That such ideas also resonate with feminist scholars should make apparent their broad appeal. Many educational theorists have come to the conclusion that these are powerful concepts that should be applied during instruction—there is theoretical triangulation here (Mathison, 1988), with Soviets in the early 20th century, American behaviorists in the mid-20th century, and feminists with an eye on the 21st century all professing faith in the advantages of matching instruction to student competence, providing just enough input so that educational progress occurs for every student.

In Chapter 9, we will conclude our sojourn through the grand theories of educational psychology. Just as was the case in this chapter, there will always be the message that there is something humanly universal about social forces as determinants of mind—that somehow we are hardwired to be susceptible to such forces, and thus, biological and social determinants of cognitive advance are inextricably intertwined. Minds have not evolved to function well alone.

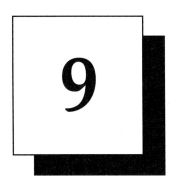

9

Preparing Students to Think Responsibly About Difficult Social Problems

There is a broad consensus that education for character and responsibility is important. More than anyone, Lawrence Kohlberg's work advanced understanding of how education can promote responsible thinking, with Kohlberg's theory and research an outgrowth of Piaget's theory of moral judgment. In the last decade, feminist scholars have simultaneously challenged and extended the theory proposed by Kohlberg, with their contributions also reviewed in this chapter. A variety of other perspectives that are also targeted at promoting education for character and responsibility have appeared, especially in recent years. These are taken up, with an emphasis throughout the chapter on common understandings about teaching and learning that emerge from this work. The most prominent similarity across perspectives is that interpersonal interactions stimulating cognitive conflict as part of considering moral and civic questions also stimulate growth of reflective and responsible thinking.

As a society, we want young people to emerge from school ready to make social and ethical decisions responsibly (e.g., Wentzel, 1991a, 1991b). A big bonus from the perspective of this book is that education for responsibility can contribute to cognitive development, with this a major theme in this chapter. Knowing how to read, write, and calculate can sometimes help with social decision making, but such knowledge is not sufficient to tackle the moral dilemmas that await each generation. Although development of academic competencies is not sufficient to ensure social responsibility, there are strong correlations (e.g., Hanson & Ginsburg, 1988; Wentzel, 1991a, 1991b) between academic competence and social responsibility, suggesting that there is nothing incompatible about academic education and developing reflective participants in democracy.

There is substantial theory and research on complex, socially responsible problem-solving. A great deal of the most credible theory-driven research on social problem solving was generated in reaction to Kohlberg's analyses of moral judgment, and that is where we begin our discussion of education for social responsibility.

THE DEVELOPMENT AND EDUCATION OF MORAL JUDGMENT ACCORDING TO KOHLBERG

Kohlberg advanced two important theories of moral judgment. One is a largely descriptive theory of the different stages of moral reasoning. The other is a

theory about how to advance moral reasoning through the stages, a theory of moral education. Before Kohlberg, however, there was another developmentalist with an enduring perspective on moral judgment—Piaget, whose position on moral judgment was Kohlberg's starting point.

Piaget's Theory of the Development of Moral Reasoning

Piaget's (1965) theory of the development of moral judgment was informed by his observations of children playing games, especially marbles. Naturally, there were some conflicts over rules as play proceeded. Piaget formulated hypotheses about children's moral understandings based on children playing by the rules, cheating, and changing rules. He then tested these hypotheses by asking children to reason for him about social dilemmas that he presented to them as short stories ending in a question. One of the more famous of these dilemmas involved children reasoning about whether a child who accidentally broke 15 cups was naughtier than one who intentionally broke one cup. Piaget eventually proposed a two-stage developmental description of two types of morality he had observed on the playgrounds and heard about in interviews, one reflecting the conceptions about rules held by preschoolers and children in the early primary years (stage of heteronomous morality) and the other reflecting the thinking of older children about rules (stage of autonomous morality).

Heteronomous and autonomous moralities differ from one another qualitatively. The heteronomously moral child focuses on the "objective" consequences of an action and thus concludes that the child breaking 15 cups is naughtier because more cups were destroyed by that child than by the one who intentionally broke one cup. In contrast, the autonomously moral child makes decisions based on the intentions of the actors, therefore concluding that breaking one cup intentionally is much worse than accidentally destroying many more cups. The heteronomously moral child respects and obeys those in control, those with the power. The autonomously moral child plays fairly (i.e., according to the rules) with other children, recognizing that the rules have been agreed on by the players, that obeying the rules of the game is a form of social contract. The heteronomous child views rules as sacred, as if they were written by the finger of God, never to be reconsidered. The autonomously moral child recognizes that rules are inventions of people and can be changed if people will it.

Similar to all Piagetian stages, there is an invariant order of development: The child must manifest heteronomous morality before autonomous morality. As is the case for all of cognitive development according to the Piagetian perspective (see Chapter 7), equilibration (cognitive conflict) is the main mechanism of cognitive change (i.e., movement from heteronomous to autonomous morality). Conflicts with peers that stimulate cognitive conflict are especially helpful (e.g., arguments about the rules of marbles). Such conflicts can be real mind stretchers, moving the child from viewing rules as given from above and inalterable to seeing them as agreements that the kids playing marbles can change by a show of hands or a chorus of protesting voices. Piaget's perspective that cognitive conflict was important in growth of moral thinking would be preserved in Kohlberg's theory, which elaborated and expanded the two stages of moral thinking favored by Piaget.

Kohlberg's Stage Theory

Kohlberg (e.g., 1969, 1981, 1984) posited progression through an invariant sequence of six stages (Figure 9.1). The first two of these are referred to as stages of **preconventional morality,** because they represent thinking that is certainly not what would be acceptable to most adults. Stages three and four are **conventional morality,** representing the type of moral thought most typically observed in adults. Stages five and six, the stages of **postconventional morality,** are reached by some but not all adults. Thus, the stages are invariant in that to get to stage four, one must go through stages one, two, and three. Achieving four, however, in no way guarantees achievement of five or six (nor does achieving two ensure further progress to three, or three to four).

In Kohlberg's original research establishing the stages, moral dilemmas in the form of stories were presented to adolescent boys, and thus Kohlberg's main research tactic was similar to one employed by Piaget. One of the most famous of Kohlberg's dilemmas involved a character named Heinz:

> In Europe, a woman was near death from a special kind of cancer. There was one drug that the doctors thought might save her. It was a form of radium that the druggist in the same town had recently discovered. The drug was expensive to make. He paid $400

Figure 9.1 Lawrence Kohlberg expanded Piaget's original two-stage model of moral judgment. His six-stage theory of moral judgment had impact far beyond psychology and education, from ethics and theology to law and political theory. The six-stage formulation was largely influenced by contemporary philosopher John Rawls' *theory of justice.*

> for the radium and charged $4000 for a small dose of the drug. The sick woman's husband, Heinz, went to everyone he knew to borrow the money and tried every legal means, but he could only get together about $2000, which is half of what it cost. He told the druggist that his wife was dying, and ask him to sell it cheaper or let him pay later. But the druggist said, "No, I discovered the drug and I'm going to make money from it." So having tried every legal means, Heinz gets desperate and considers breaking into the man's store to steal the drug for his wife. (Kohlberg, 1984, p. 640)

An interview tapping a subject's thinking about the dilemma then occurred that required the subject in the study to respond to the following questions:

1. Should Heinz steal the drug? 1a. Why or why not?
2. Is it right or wrong for him to steal the drug? 2a. Why is it right or wrong?
3. Does Heinz have a duty or obligation to steal the drug? 3a. Why or why not?
4. If Heinz doesn't love his wife, should he steal the drug for her? (If he favors not stealing the drug:) Does it make a difference in what Heinz should do whether or not he loves his wife? 4a. Why or why not?

5. Suppose the person dying is not his wife but a stranger. Should Heinz steal the drug for the stranger? 5a. Why or why not?
6. (If the subject favors stealing the drug for the stranger:) Suppose it's a pet animal that he loves. Should Heinz steal to save the pet animal? 6a. Why or why not?
7. Is it important for people to do everything they can to save another's life? 7a. Why or why not?
8. It is against the law for Heinz to steal. Does that make it morally wrong? 8a. Why or why not?
9. In general, should people do everything that they can to obey the law? 9a. Why or why not? 9b. How does this apply to what Heinz should do?
10. In thinking back over the dilemma, what would you say is the most responsible thing for Heinz to do? 10a. Why? (Kohlberg, 1984, pp. 640–641)

What mattered in the interview was not whether the subject thought Heinz should steal the drug but the reasons the subject gave for Heinz's actions, with the reasons varying from stage to stage.

In stage one, the reasons focused on obedience and avoiding punishment. Staying out of trouble is the concern that is more important than all others for the stage one thinker, exemplified by these rationales (all stage rationale quotes from Kohlberg, 1984, Tables 1.5 and 1.6, pp. 49–53, based on data reported originally by Rest, 1968): In favor of stealing the drug: "If you let your wife die, you will get in trouble. You'll be blamed for not spending the money to save her and there'll be an investigation of you and the druggist for your wife's death." Of course, a case also can be made that the best way to stay out of trouble is not to steal the drug: "You shouldn't steal the drug because you'll be caught and sent to jail if you do. If you do get away, your conscience would bother you thinking how the police would catch up with you at any minute." The stage one thinker is worried only about protecting his or her own hide—avoiding punishment.

The stage two thinker is only a slight advance, concerned only about his or her own pleasures. What is right is what brings pleasure to the self. Self-interest comes through clearly in this stage two justification for stealing the drug: "If you do happen to get caught, you could give the drug back and wouldn't get much of a sentence. It wouldn't bother you much to serve a little jail term, if you have your wife when you get out." Self-interest can be used to jus-

tify not stealing as well: "He may not get much of a jail term if he steals the drug, but his wife will probably die before he gets out, so it wouldn't do him much good. If his wife dies, he shouldn't blame himself; it isn't his fault she has cancer." By now it should be obvious why stage one and two thinking is considered preconventional. Any adult offering such justifications would be viewed with horror by most other adults, who long ago rejected such narrow self-interest as legitimate in decision making.

The stage three thinker is sometimes thought of as displaying "good boy–good girl" thinking, concerned with helping and pleasing others. This is conformist thinking in the sense of wanting to go along with the majority. Although saccharine, we suspect most readers know people who might offer stage three justifications. Consider this example in favor of stealing the drug: "No one will think you're bad if you steal the drug but your family will think you are an inhuman husband if you don't. If you let your wife die, you'll never be able to look anyone in the face again." The concern for the opinion of others comes through in this justification for not stealing the drug as well: "It isn't just the druggist who will think you're a criminal, everyone else will, too. After you steal it, you'll feel bad thinking how you've brought dishonor on your family and yourself; you won't be able to face anyone again." Something important to note is that this form of conventionality is decidedly not as advanced as stage four thinking according to Kohlberg's model. This is critical to remember because later we will take up an important dispute over Kohlberg's theory–whether Kohlberg's theory is sexist in part because stage three thinking, which some view as more consistent with women's way of thinking than men's approaches to morality, is considered less sophisticated than stage four thinking, which the critics claim is more consistent with men's conception of the world than with women's approach to it.

Although the stage three conventional thinker is concerned with the subjective perceptions of others, the stage four thinker is concerned with being in synchrony with the codified standards of his or her society—stage four thinkers have a deep respect for law and order. The stage four thinker is concerned with doing his or her duty to country, God, spouse, or whatever else commands allegiance by societal standards. This rationalization in favor of stealing the drug in reaction to the Heinz dilemma is based on the perception of duty to family members that is expected by society: "If you have any sense of honor, you won't let your wife die because you're afraid to do the only thing that will save her. You'll always feel guilty that you caused her death if you don't do your duty to her." Consistency with the laws of society comes through in this opposition to stealing the drug offered by another stage four thinker: "You're desparate and you may not know you're doing wrong when you steal the drug. But you'll know you did wrong after you're punished and sent to jail. You'll always feel guilty for your dishonesty and lawbreaking."

After some experience with conventional thinking, some come to reject it. The stage five postconventional thinker views rules and laws in terms of a contract, which is intended to protect the will and rights of others. One enters into this contract and obeys rules as part of a social understanding, rather than because of fear of retribution, respect for authority, or sense of duty. If the social purpose for the rules cannot be fulfilled by obeying them, it is all right to dispense with the rules according to stage five thinkers, as reflected in this opinion in favor of Heinz stealing the drug: "The law wasn't set up for these circumstances. Taking the drug in this situation isn't really right, but it's justified to do it." The social contract orientation also comes through in this stage five advisement against stealing the drug: "You can't have everyone stealing when they get desperate. The end may be good, but the ends don't justify the means."

Although there was certainly room for debate over the adequacy of the data supporting stages one through five (e.g. Kurtines & Grief, 1974), without a doubt, the greatest challenges were launched at Kohlberg's proposals about a stage six. The stage six thinker did not compromise in respecting the sanctity of life and human freedom. Kohlberg especially was influenced by Rawls's (1971) *Theory of Justice* in his portrayal of the stage six thinker, who is described as the ultimately just individual, one who could rationally make decisions without taking self-interest into account. That is, stage six thinkers decided dilemmas as if they knew they were one of the characters in the dilemma but did not know which one they were, with the result that these just individuals attempted to make decisions that would be viewed as fair as possible by all parties. That this stage was hypothetical became obvious when Kohlberg admitted in print that there was no con-

vincing evidence for it (see Kohlberg, Levine, & Hewer, 1983). This stage six conceptualization in terms of justice continues to be important, however, in that contemporary critics of Kohlberg point to his embrace of rationally determined justice as the highest of moral ideals to be narrow and, specifically, to reflect a masculine bias in his thinking.

Before concluding this discussion of moral reasoning stages, a few points need to be made. Classifying a person into a stage was never clear-cut, with many revisions of the Kohlberg scoring scheme. If you need evidence that the moral judgment interview approach produces ambiguous data, simply respond to the Heinz interview presented earlier. As you struggle attempting to classify the various responses you have to the dilemma, then consider that Heinz was one of nine dilemmas and interviews. Each interview resulted in a mass of data. It was not uncommon at all for subject protocols to reflect what became known as **stage mixture,** with the assignment of a subject to one particular stage based on the modal response category. Using the Kohlberg manuals, arriving at a diagnosis of someone's stage level took days and weeks of scoring in some cases.

Fortunately, others such as Rest (see 1979; also Rest et al., 1986) and Gibbs (Gibbs et al., 1984; Gibbs, Basinger, & Fuller, in press; Gibbs & Widaman, 1982; Gibbs, Widaman, & Colby, 1982) validated adaptations of the moral judgment interview that could be scored reliably and more easily than the original Kohlberg instrument. As with the Kohlberg measure, within-person variability in responding was the norm, however, so that a person might offer stage three, four, and five responses across dilemmas, with stage mixture even for the same dilemma not uncommon. Stage mixture should be remembered because later in the chapter, when we take up the debate regarding possible sexism in Kohlberg's thinking, new evidence of how people's moral judgments can include a mix of rationale types will be presented. Readers should recall at that point that diverse reasoning is more the rule than the exception in reaction to moral dilemmas.

Another important point to emphasize in closing this discussion of Kohlberg's (e.g., 1984) stage theory is that Kohlberg believed that in coming to the postconventional stages, people acquired an understanding of the universal applicability of particular values. These values include the sanctity of human life, personal property, and civil liberties. Kohlberg's stage six thinker would never be able to justify the taking of a life (e.g., Kohlberg was profoundly opposed to capital punishment; Kohlberg & Elfenbein, 1976) and requires great justification for the denial of civil liberties. Kohlberg's confidence that identification with such positions reflected moral sophistication was bolstered by his understanding of the lives of exceptionally moral individuals, from Christ, Socrates, and St. Thomas More to Gandhi and Martin Luther King (e.g., Kohlberg & Power, 1981). All of these ultimate moral thinkers lived lifes reflecting the universal values of life, liberty, and truthfulness, so much so that they were killed because of their commitments to such values.

Education and the Development of Moral Judgment

The scientific literature on moral education that accumulated in the 1960s until the early 1980s was competently summarized by Enright et al. (1983). They concluded that the approach to moral education favored by Kohlberg works well: Have students discuss and reason among themselves about moral dilemmas. This is sometimes referred to as the **plus-one approach** because it results in each student being exposed to information from a stage beyond him or her, which is considered an optimally motivating discrepancy in Kohlbergian theory between current level of functioning and level of input to the student. (That is, for each student in the discussion except the most advanced student, someone will be a bit beyond the student's current functioning; for the most advanced student, presumably the teacher would be beyond the level of moral sophistication of the student.) Kohlberg believed that a one-stage discrepancy would be likely to induce cognitive conflict, which motivates reflection on the new information, reflection that often results in coming to understand the adequacy of the slightly more advanced position relative to the position currently held by the student (see Chapter 5).

The first and most famous study in the plus-one tradition was Blatt and Kohlberg (1975) with junior and senior high school students. The teachers presented moral dilemmas to students, who debated the pros and cons of various resolutions to the dilemmas. Although the teachers sometimes clarified and summarized arguments and challenged low-level reasoning, the teachers definitely did not provide a

resolution to the dilemma. The moral discussions included a mixture of opinions, with some at a higher stage than others, so that everyone in the class was exposed to thinking at least a bit beyond them. (The teacher provided opinions in the discussion that were in advance of the most sophisticated student.) As was the case in a number of follow-up studies, students who participated in discussions of moral dilemmas reasoned at higher levels during moral judgment interviews than they did before experiencing the moral conflict discussions. Positive effects of plus-one moral reasoning discussions have been obtained both with short interventions—a single session—and long ones—full-semester courses (see Enright et al., 1983, for a summary).

Kohlberg was a man of great vision. One was to imagine large-scale environments—entire cultures—that would stimulate moral reflection. He believed that there was the potential for moral growth from community participation, in the sense of the traditional New England town meeting, participation that could be operationalized in schools and other institutions dedicated to improving their clients' thinking and morality. Thus, Kohlberg and his co-workers created "just communities" within the boundaries of institutional settings (see Power, Higgins, & Kohlberg, 1989, for a complete review of this approach).

For example, Kohlberg, Scharf, and Hickey (1972) took over part of a women's prison. The just community way of doing business was for decisions to be made in town meetings, including the development of rules for the prison community. Rather than discipline being a matter overseen by guards, juries took up offenses against the community, with these juries composed of both staff and inmates and reaching decisions based on discussion and reflection. Rather than letting the community slip into a lull of satisfaction with the rules as established by the community, there was continuous review of rules. Did living in such a community increase moral judgment skills as defined by the Kohlberg interview measures? Yes, a little.

Just communities were also set up in several schools, with both elementary and secondary just communities created. Town meetings and self-enforced discipline via reflective discussion was the order of business in these schools as well. Did attending a just-community school increase moral judgment skills as defined by the Kohlberg interview measures? Yes, a little (Power et al., 1989, Chapter 9).

This Kohlbergian approach to moral education is far from dead, with just communities implemented in schools (Higgins, 1987; Power & Power, 1992; Rulon, 1992), institutions serving emotionally disturbed adolescents (Blakeney & Blakenay, 1990), and prisons (Powell, Locke, & Sprinthall, 1991). In addition, there are many other settings providing students with experiences discussing difficult issues, consistent with the plus-one approach. The best-informed proponents of this type of instruction still are inspired by Piagetian and Kohlbergian thinking about the cognitive growth provided by cognitive conflict, although increasingly plus-one discussions occur in the context of educational environments designed to promote moral judgment and behavior using a variety of mechanisms (see Lickona, 1991, especially Chapters 12–15, and the discussion of Lickona's analysis presented later in this chapter).

Some new ways of operationalizing cognitive conflict discussions are being developed and used as part of contemporary plus-one interventions (Lickona, 1991, Chapters 12 and 13). For example, kids can be asked to deal with real moral issues, both ones in the news (e.g., should murderers receive capital punishment?) and ones pertaining to the school (e.g., how should students be punished for transgressions of school rules?). Important content dealing with civil liberties can be covered using such discussions. For example, we know of one Baltimore high school teacher who has a course on civil liberties. Rights and morality are debated by students and teacher as they consider court cases and decisions that have fleshed out the rights defined by the Bill of Rights and amendments to the Constitution. Evidence is accumulating that students can recognize situations that are controversial (e.g., whether the United States should spend more on health care and less on space exploration) from those that are not (e.g., whether astronauts should be warned about potential life-threatening flaws in the space shuttle) and understand the need for reflective consideration of multiple perspectives on controversial issues (e.g., Nicholls & Nelson, 1992).

One of the most ambitious models of school reform in the 1990s has as its most important feature that students participate in a living, breathing democracy. In many ways, the "microsociety" approach (e.g., Sommerfeld, 1992) to schooling is the ultimate just community. Microsociety is intended, in part, to provide hands-on experience with many aspects of economics but in doing so requires its members to engage in real community problem solving. Thus, when there is a crisis, such as when the school's legislature cannot pay its bills, the members of the society must wrestle with the problems that are created, including dealing with "civil servants" who are without paychecks and the potential consequences of deficit spending. Whether there is moral growth and increased understanding of ethical versus unethical conduct as a function of participating in microsociety schools is a question that is fertile for educational psychologists in the 1990s.

Challenge of Kohlbergian Educational Models

Kohlberg's educational theory is inspiring analyses of how difficult it is to carry out Kohlbergian-type programs of moral instruction. For example, Sharp (1987) made the case that the types of discussions required in just-communities of inquiry demand much of students. According to Sharp, just-community participants must be capable of all of the following: listen to others attentively, take another's ideas seriously, accept corrections by peers willingly, build on one another's ideas, develop one's own ideas without fear of rebuff or humiliation from peers, revise one's own view in light of reason from others, show concern for the rights of others to express their own views, detect underlying assumptions of ideas presented in discussion, show concern for consistency when arguing a point of view, ask relevant questions, verbalize relationships between ends and means, show respect for persons in the community, show sensitivity to context when discussing moral conduct, ask for reasons from one's peers, discuss issues with impartiality, and ask for criteria. Sharp's analysis of the complexity of plus-one exchanges makes clearer why moral discussions have not been successful with elementary students (Enright et al., 1983).

If plus-one is challenging for students, it is even tougher for many teachers. There is increasing evidence that many teachers do not feel comfortable serving as models of moral cognition, or they do not understand at all how to carry out Kohlberg's educational vision, identifying much more with the cultural transmission (i.e., teacher-as-teller of rules) approach to moral education (e.g., Bergem, 1990; Cox, 1988; Kutnick, 1988, 1990).

Concluding Comment

Our view is that there is a lot in Kohlberg's models for contemporary educational psychologists to consider and explore. This will become even more apparent when Kohlberg's perspective is contrasted with more recent analyses of moral reasoning, ways of thinking that reflect not only fairness and justice, but also concern for others, ways of thinking that reflect not only masculine, but also feminine perspectives.

The original Kohlbergian model was presented in terms of universals, reflecting the influence of Piaget on Kohlberg: Biology constrains stagelike progression according to Piaget and hence all of thinking, with humans prepared at different stages to manifest different reasoning abilities. Themes of universalism have given way over the years as it became increasingly obvious that stage six was a philosophical preference of Kohlberg's rather than an empirically documented reality and as the effects of social factors on moral judgment were taken more seriously, especially by feminists.

Lest readers think that the concerns in this chapter are totally divorced from good information processing, note that Stewart and Pascual-Leone (1992), consistent with neo-Piagetian theory (see Chapter 7, this book) believe that the critical determinant of moral reasoning ability is mental capacity (i.e., short-term capacity). In their one study of the problem, mental capacity as they measured it was an important determinant of the complexity and level of moral reasoning. Like Piagetians, neo-Piagetians view mental capacity as a developmentally expanding resource (see discussion of Case's theory in Chapter 7). Thus, they expect developmental improvement in moral reasoning because of functional increases in mental capacity.

SEX DIFFERENCES IN MORAL REASONING: THE DIFFERENT VOICE IDENTIFIED BY GILLIGAN

Up until this point, the discussion of Kohlberg's perspective has been positive. The possibility of sexism in the theory however, has fueled a reexamination of the moral judgments of males and females, one that is yielding new insights about the ways that both males and females reason about difficult issues. This work is making clear that educating people to be just in their thinking is not enough: Mature moral reasoning also reflects care about others and appreciation of connections that are more than the cold social contracts of Kohlberg's stage five thinker or the just outlooks emphasized by Kohlberg's stage six.

Gilligan (1982) forcefully summarized women's concerns about Kohlberg's theory in a scholarly book that received widespread attention, *In a Different Voice: Psychological Theory and Women's Development.* The perspectives developed by Gilligan (1982) were informed by a thorough understanding of Kohlberg's theory based on a long-term scholarly relationship with him. Gilligan's perspectives were also shaped by her own research and that of her colleagues at Harvard, including three studies that provided illustrations for many of the points made in the 1982 book. One was a study of the development of identity and moral thinking during the college years. The second tapped the moral thinking of young women as they contemplated having an abortion. The third was a study of thinking about rights and responsibilities, one conducted across the life span.

A main conclusion reached by Gilligan was that females were much more likely than males to consider issues of interpersonal caring and person-to-person connections as they reasoned about moral dilemmas, consistent with other feminist thinking that care is a much more important issue for women than for men (e.g., Brabeck, 1989; Noddings, 1984; see Chapter 8, this book). This conclusion was based on an examination of reasoning by males and females over many issues involving moral decisions.

The differences between reasoning that considers the interpersonal effects of decisions versus thinking that is concerned more with coming up with rational, just solutions can be illustrated by responses to the Heinz dilemma presented earlier. Female responses are much more likely than male responses to include arguments, such as "...I... think he [the druggist] had the moral obligation to show compassion in this case ... (p. 54)," "... if she [Heinz' wife] dies, it hurts a lot of people and it hurts her ... (p. 28)," "... you have to love someone else, because you are inseparable from them ... [t]hat other person is part of that giant collection of everybody (p. 57)," and "Who is going to be hurt more, the druggist who loses some money or the person who loses her life? (p. 95)" Compassion, connection, and concerns about minimizing hurt were issues raised by females in Gilligan's studies.

Gilligan, who was intimately familiar with Kohlberg's scoring scheme, recognized that, if anything, raising issues of care would reduce one's score in Kohlberg's traditional assessments. Her analysis was that the scoring scheme devised by Kohlberg was sensitive to a masculine strategy based on rationality and justice but insensitive to feminine thinking strategies, in which dilemmas are analyzed in terms of the human, interpersonal consequences of the various possible actions by the actors in a dilemma. Gilligan contended that, at a minimum, the traditional analyses of moral judgment missed the rich diversity of thinking about moral issues, something apparent in studies conducted in response to Gilligan's (1982) book.

For example, Johnson (1988) substantiated two different moralities (she referred to them as strategies) in the moral reasoning of adolescents. The subjects in her study were presented Aesop's fables and were questioned about them, with subjects first responding to the question, "What is the problem?" and then, "How would you solve it?" Follow-up questions were given to clarify responses, and countersolutions were presented for subject reactions. Consistent with Kohlberg's theory, themes of rights and justice were apparent in the reasoning about the fables. So were themes of response to others, of connection and caring, however. More than three-fourths of the time, the spontaneous solutions of males reflected the rights orientation. In contrast, rights predominated in the spontaneous solution of females about half the time. That is, there were sex differences in moral reasoning that were consistent with Gilligan's theory.

Lyons (1988) asked adults, "What does morality mean to you?" She also asked them to describe themselves in relation to others and to talk about their own real-life moral conflicts and issues. Consistent with Kohlberg's work, she found that her subjects talked about objective relations between people, duties and obligations, rules and standards—a morality of justice. She also found evidence of a morality of response and care, however, as predicted by Gilligan's theory. Consistent with Gilligan, the morality of justice predominated in men's responses, whereas response and care predominated in women's answers. In fact, about one-third of men made no references to response and care, and about one-third of women made no references to justice issues. Two-thirds of the subjects, however, represented both moralities in their responses, so that a scoring scheme based on justice alone would have misrepresented the moral reasoning of two-thirds of the men and all of the women.

Gilligan and Attannucci (1988) obtained evidence of a sex difference as well in a series of three studies involving upper-middle-class adolescents and adults. The participants were asked to identify an occasion when they were in a moral conflict and describe what they did, followed by reflection on whether their action was appropriate and why they thought their actions were justified or should have been different. The interview data were then analyzed for the types of moral considerations expressed by the subjects. Justice considerations predominated in the responses of two-thirds of the males, with all but one of the remaining third offering a mixture of justice and care considerations. In contrast, slightly more than one-third of females focused on issues of care, a little less than one-third focused on justice considerations, and the remaining third offered a mixture of care and justice considerations. If the data had been scored only for consideration of justice issues, the reasoning of one-third of the males and two-thirds of the females would have been misrepresented.

Gilligan and her associates believe that the identification of the two "voices" in their research on moral reasoning has far-reaching implications for education. Although their message of a sex difference is what has captured the most attention, the larger message seems to be that analyses of moral reasoning that only are rational, just, and attentive to rules and duties are narrow in their conceptualization of the world. There is another way to look at things, one emphasizing interconnections, caring, and responsibility for others.

Other Perspectives on "Different Voices" in Moral Reasoning

One reason there will be a great deal of additional research on sex differences in moral cognition is that Gilligan's conclusions are extremely controversial. Indeed, there is no more prominent issue in cognitive-moral and moral-education research of the 1990s than whether, in fact, there are gender differences in moral reasoning and, if there are, whether gender differences are the only differences in voice.

Why is this so? Most analyses of conventional moral judgment data—that is, data based on typical scoring of Kohlbergian or similar dilemmas—do not reveal striking sex differences (e.g., Gibbs, Arnold, & Burkhart, 1984; Rest, 1979; Rest et al., 1986; Walker, 1984, 1989). That is, as far as the conventional moral judgment data are concerned, it is fair to charge that Gilligan overattended to studies reporting sex differences.

Less conventional analyses also suggest less striking differences between males and females in their reasoning than Gilligan and her colleagues observed. In a test of Gilligan's hypothesis about sex differences in moral reasoning, Johnson, Brown, and Christopherson (1990) asked adolescents to talk about real-life moral dilemmas they face. Although both males and females described dilemmas in the context of human relationships, the males emphasized much more the effect of the conflict on themselves, whereas females emphasized the relationship aspect of conflicts much more. When Mellor (1989) administered instruments to males and females that were designed to determine how they identify themselves, females were slightly more likely to identify themselves by reference to connections to others than were males. Although the outcomes in these studies were consistent with Gilligan's conclusion that connectedness is a more important part of female than male thinking, the effects were not large.

Others using unconventional analyses have generated data even less consistent with analyses by Gilligan and her Harvard colleagues, however. For example, Galotti (1989) asked undergraduates, "When faced with a moral dilemma, what issues or concerns influence your decision?" Using analyses like the ones employed by Gilligan (1982), Galotti found little evidence of sex differences in response to this question, with both males and females including both masculine and feminine themes in their responses. (The only sex difference was that males were more likely to report that they reason systematically when working on a moral problem.) Galotti, Kozberg, and Farmer (1991) administered both conventional and unconventional moral judgment dilemmas to students in grades 8 and 11 as well as college sophomores. Again, male and female thinking was much more similar than different, although females tended to be more concerned with what others think about their judgments and the effects of their decisions on themselves, including personal guilt and social reactions. When Lawrence and Helm (1987) asked nurses to reason about ethical dilemmas they might face in their profession, the predominant theme in their reasoning was the concern for consistency with the law—that is, concern for rationality and justice rather than one of caring. Although

Bebeau and Brabeck (1987) observed more similarities than differences in the moral reasoning of dental students about ethical dilemmas in their profession; they did not observe differences between males and females with respect to their concern for care, as defined by Gilligan, with respect to the dental patients. Lonky, Roodin, and Rybash (1988) found that androgynous males reasoned in a more caring fashion than other males; they also observed that when people were urged to reason from their own perspectives, they were more likely to evidence stage three thinking—consistent with female perspectives—than if they reasoned from a more "objective" perspective. In short, whether one's reasoning reflects more masculine or feminine themes depends on sex-role orientation and how one approaches the task. It just is not as simple as Gilligan and her colleagues supposed. The conflicting data to date will inspire additional analyses (see Witherell, 1991, for a sampler of theoretical reactions to the inconsistencies in data regarding gender effects during the first decade since publication of Gilligan's [1982] book).

The feminists are not the only ones in the 1990s offering data challenging Kohlberg's thinking about universality, however. In particular, there now is an active cross-cultural psychology of moral cognition and education, with prominent studies from Asia and Israel placed in the literature (Gates, 1990; Iwasa, 1992; Luhmer, 1990; Maosen, 1990; Thomas, 1990; Tzuriel, 1992; Walker & Moran, 1991). In general, although the Kohlbergian pattern of development is observed, there are often differences in moral thinking that reflect the socialization pressures of the culture. For example, Chinese communists endorse practices such as capital punishment more readily than do many Westerners, emphasizing the benefits for the collective, rather than focusing on the individual rights of the victim (Walker & Moran, 1991). Also, Chinese are reluctant to claim that arguments made in response to a particular dilemma imply any general way of thinking (i.e., they seemed not to be case-based reasoners to the extent Western people are). Even relatively sophisticated Chinese thinkers believe more in analyzing the concrete specifics of situations in making moral judgments than do Western thinkers, at least according to Kohlbergian analyses. Of course, a fair criticism of Kohlberg's approach is that he ignored his subjects' attention to contextual factors affecting judgment, which, of course, was exactly Gilligan's main point. Just how similar Western and Asian thought are regarding moral issues may become more apparent as analyses such as Gilligan's are taken into account by cross-cultural researchers.

FROM DUALITY TO RELATIVISM TO COMMITMENT: THE MODELS OF PERRY AND ERIKSON

Mature people know who they are, defined largely by what they believe in. The firm beliefs of the 40-year-old, however, were not always held by him or her. How people develop from not even knowing about alternative beliefs to embracing particular beliefs was the focus of theories proposed by Perry and Erikson.

Perry's Theory of Intellectual Development

Perry set out to determine whether there were any fundamental changes during the college years in the ways that students think about issues. Although the study was conducted in the 1950s and 1960s, it remains an important examination of undergraduate thinking.

Perry's conclusions clashed with much of the 1960s thinking about thinking. Recall that Piaget had proposed that formal operations was the peak of intellect and was achieved during the adolescent years (see Chapter 7). Kohlberg, writing in the 1960s (e.g., 1969; see the discussion earlier in this chapter), claimed that postconventional thinking, the highest form of moral reasoning, was within reach of high school students. Thus, by claiming striking shifts in thinking between 18 and 22 years of age, Perry (1970) was anything but consistent with the intellectual opinions of the time. Perry was one of the first voices in what became a many-part chorus dedicated to proclaiming that much intellectual development remains for the 18-year-old (Figure 9.2).

Perry's study began with his observations in the counseling center at Harvard that students reacted differently to the **relativism** they encountered at the university—to the presentation of diverse points of view, including differing values systems, and arguments that right versus wrong relativism implies that the appropriateness of a perspective often depends on contextual variables. Difficulties in accepting multiplicity of opinion were striking to an academic counselor such as Perry because success at

Harvard requires relativistic thinking. For example, when freshman examination questions in government, history, English literature, and foreign literatures were analyzed for what they demanded of students, many required students to represent alternative perspectives respectfully. Making claims that one perspective was right and another wrong (i.e., **dualistic thinking,** to use a term favored by Perry) often did not earn points at Harvard.

Perry administered a questionnaire to a large sample of Harvard freshmen, one that determined where a student fell on a continuum from dualistic (i.e., engaging in "right-wrong" thinking) to relativistic (i.e., accepting a multiplicity of views and recognizing that the appropriateness of perspectives depends on the situation). Students falling at the extreme ends and the mean of the scale were selected to continue in the study. At the end of each of their four undergraduate years, these students were interviewed in an open-ended fashion about how they found meaning in their lives during the preceding academic year. Students provided information about their views of knowledge, how they studied, beliefs about social relationships, and their moral values.

There was evidence of dualism in the thinking of freshmen, which is not surprising because part of the sample had been recruited into the study because they were extreme in endorsing dualistic positions on the screening questionnaire. Only 3 or 4 of the 50 students who were interviewed in depth proved to be consistent with what Perry referred to as "position one," which was defined as right-wrong, yes-no, dualistic thinking: People agreeing with me are right; those disagreeing are wrong. The position one thinker views education as learning the right answers, with memory and hard work seen as the route to success in college. There are authorities out there with the answers, and there are absolute truths.

Dualistic thinkers are challenged, however, during bull sessions in the dorms and in class discussions. Immersion in a college world with many opinions reduces confidence in the righteousness of one's own beliefs. For example, one freshman on the screening questionnaire indicated that it was easy to disagree strongly with the following claim: "One thing is certain: even if there is an absolute truth, man will never know about it and therefore must learn to choose and venture in uncertainty" (Perry,

Figure 9.2 One of William Perry's great insights is that many a freshman arrives at college expecting to learn answers and leaves recognizing there are many different ways of viewing most problems.

1970, p. 69). By the spring interview of freshmen year, this same participant agreed with this item.

Students who conform to Perry's position two are in advance of position one in that they realize there is a multiplicity of views. Their view is that these alternatives are alien, and that those who hold them are wrong and confused. As a student, the game is to know the perspectives advanced by the professor, although the student may not identify with the professor's outlooks. Position 3 students still believe there are right answers but have doubts about whether authority figures (e. g., their teachers) have figured them out. Students perceive that they are evaluated simply for the form of their test answers, papers, and so on—not for the particular positions they advance because their teachers are too tentative about the various positions to feel confident in discriminating between students based on the positions they take.

Position four students embrace multiplicity in that it is believed that anyone has a right to their own opinion, although the multiple perspectives are seen as just that—personal opinions. They view authority as "wanting" them to think relativistically. Position four students do not yet recognize that the world really is inherently relativistic.

In contrast, students in position five believe that at least part of the world is relativistic—things are not true or false but true or false relative to a particular situation: That is, some students believe that some subdisciplines are relativistic (e.g., literature), whereas others are not (e.g., physical sciences); other position five students apply relativism more generally. Position five is clearly the swing stage in Perry's theory, the end of dualism and the beginning of relativism.

Students in position six accept relativism as the way of the world. A psychologically healthy position six outlook is to look forward to eventual commitments to particular positions with respect to religion, politics, friendships, social endeavors, and values. Thus, for example, a person comes to understand whether they prefer a wide range of friendships or a few. A less healthy outcome is retreating from commitment, perhaps through resentment of multiplicity of views or habitual negativism or rebellion against the perspectives of authority figures. Some position six students avoid commitment by taking an attitude of "anything goes." Position seven students are making initial commitments for themselves, recognizing the legitimacy of others' commitments. The process continues in position eight. By position nine, students are "in" one's life in the sense that they have made commitments to some perspectives. Thus, a position nine student may be committed to going to law school, practicing Catholicism, and staying single, while feeling perfectly comfortable and accepting of a friend who has decided on investment banking, converted to Judaism, and is marrying the girl back home, or another acquaintance who is going to teach grade school and continue to be an agnostic.

In short, what Perry observed was that there was a general movement during the undergraduate years from dualism to relativism—an increasing recognition of a variety of legitimate perspectives in the world. Some students begin to make commitments, tentatively in the beginning and advancing eventually to more complete commitments. Others become intent on avoiding commitments, recognizing the multiplicity of perspectives but unwilling to identify with any of them. In the original research, Perry (1970) reported that about three-fourths of the students he studied were making commitments by the end of their undergraduate years.

Although there has not been a tremendous amount of follow-up research on Perry's model per se, there is a substantial literature documenting that with increasing higher education, thinking is increasingly relativistic (see Pascarella & Terenzini, 1991, Chapter 4). For example, college seniors are much more likely than freshmen to understand and appreciate the validity of alternative perspectives on an issue like abortion (e.g., Winter, McClelland, & Stewart, 1981). As far as the development of commitments is concerned, however, the most prominent research has been conducted in reaction to Erikson's (1968) theory of identity development.

Erikson's Theory of Identity Development

Erikson (1968) proposed a life-span theory of development. People pass through eight stages according to Erikson (Figure 9.3). Each involves a central conflict, with either a positive or negative resolution of the conflict possible. These conflicts and roughly when they happen are as follows:

1. Trust versus mistrust: During infancy, the child either forms a trusting relationship with an adult or does not. Failing to interact with an adult who can be trusted to meet the infant's needs results in long-term mistrust.
2. Autonomy versus shame and doubt: During the early preschool years, children begin to do things on their own, and if they succeed in establishing some autonomy from others, that is a positive outcome. Part of autonomy is self-control, with much of the conflict involving self-control occurring during toilet training. If there are difficulties in establishing self-control and autonomy, there is the possibility of shame in not being more independent and doubt about whether one can be so.
3. Initiative versus guilt: As the preschool years proceed, there are many more initiations into the world and trying on of new roles. If the child is

Figure 9.3 Erikson proposed that identity develops across the life span, although adolescence is a period when identity issues are particularly intense.

overly punished for his or her burgeoning initiative, there is the potential for guilt.

4. Industry versus inferiority: With the schooling years, the child is expected to begin to master the skills of the culture. For example, in Western culture, children are expected to develop fundamental literacy and numeracy skills. Success in doing so leads to a sense of industry; failure to do so can lead to a sense of inferiority.

5. Identity versus identity confusion: During adolescence and early adulthood, the central crisis is the identity crisis. During this period, people struggle with determining who they are, what they believe in, and what they want to become. There are issues of sex-role identity and vocational identity to resolve. A positive outcome requires trying various possible identities and struggling with them. The successful outcome is emergence from the struggle with an understanding of one's sexual preferences, career aspirations, and intellectual commitments. Those who come to such conclusions without the struggle (e.g., they do as their parents expect) are at great risk for identity confusion later, confronting the fact that they are playing at roles that are not them; others simply continue to drift from role to role, with their identity confusion painfully obvious to those around them. From the perspective of Erikson's theory, it is a healthy pattern not to be committed early in adolescence but to come to commitments after experimenting with different roles and ideas.

6. Intimacy versus isolation: After youth, a person either achieves intimacy with others, usually a marital partner or the equivalent, or is at risk for feeling psychological isolation.

7. Generativity versus stagnation: Adulthood is either a period of contributing to society and to the development of the next generation, or there is a risk of stagnating.

8. Integrity versus despair: If a person resolves all of life's crises in a positive fashion, it is likely that he or she will be able to look back and feel a sense of integrity. Disgust and despair are possible if one fails to resolve positively one or more life crises.

Without a doubt, the most prominent crisis in Erikson's theory is the identity crisis, with it receiving more research attention than any of the other stages. According to Erikson's theory, during adolescence and youth, there are subcrises with respect to the identity issues that occur throughout life. These crises occur in part because of the quantum leap in intellectual sophistication that occurs with the onset of formal operations (see Piaget's theory, discussed in Chapter 7), permitting introspection and reflection on alternative possibilities, which is at the heart of the identity crisis. That is, there are identity-related conflicts during adolescence and youth with respect to development of trust versus mistrust, autonomy versus shame and doubt, initiative versus guilt, industry versus inferiority, intimacy versus isolation, generativity versus stagnation, and integrity versus despair. As part of these subcrises, adolescents and youth struggle to determine what they believe with respect to sexual orientation, intellectual interests, life philosophy, vocation, religion, and so on, with these struggles made possible by the intellectual power provided by formal operations—the power to think about hypothetical situations and to compare hypotheticals, a power that often increases doubt in what one has always believed (Boyes & Chandler, 1992).

One of the most prolific investigators in this area has been Marcia. Marcia generated substantial support for the conclusion that adolescents and youth make many choices and often come to commitments about important issues. In particular, he identified four different identity statuses (Marcia, 1966), reflecting the degree to which adolescents have experienced and resolved their identity crises. In our years of teaching undergraduates, we have had few students who have not been able to think of schoolmates who fit into each of the following four identity statuses:

- People in **diffusion** have not experienced crises in that they (1) have not tried out, nor are trying out, new roles and (2) have made no commitments. Youth and adolescents in diffusion often are perceived to be living lives without personal meaning. They are viewed as reluctant to make commitments to positions, avoiding close relationships, and unpredictable and changeable (Mallory, 1989).
- People in **foreclosure** have come to commitments without experiencing any crises. The stereotypical example is the young man or woman who follows the life plan devised by their parents (e.g., to go to a prestigious college followed by law school, accepting a place in the

family firm, while settling down in the same community and going to the same church as parents). They often have conservative values, are moralistic, conventional, sex-appropriate in their behaviors, and are satisfied with themselves (Mallory, 1989).

- People in **moratorium** are actively exploring. This is a healthy and appropriate status for adolescents and youth according to Erikson's theory. Young people who are in moratorium are viewed as introspective, anxious, philosophically concerned, and valuing independence (Mallory, 1989).
- People who are **identity achieved** have gone through crises and made choices. These people are perceived as productive, consistent, and independent.

The healthy progression according to Erikson's theory is into moratorium, with identity eventually achieved. Much less healthy is to come to an identity without conflict (i.e., moratorium) or to never experience conflict or identity (i.e., diffusion).

Our analysis of the four identity statuses in terms of Perry's theory is that diffusion and foreclosure reflect dualistic thinking; moratorium clearly involves relativism; and identity achieved is commitment as Perry conceived of it. If so, there should be more upperclassmen than freshmen in moratorium and identity-achieved stages, and, in fact, that seems to be the case.

Pascarella and Terenzini (1991, Chapter 5) reviewed the evidence pertaining to whether there was movement toward identity achievement during college—that is, increasing commitments with respect to vocation, lifestyle, and philosophy from freshmen to senior years. Their conclusion, based on a dozen studies inspired by Marcia's original work and another dozen testing Erikson's theory but not as follow-ups to Marcia's work, was that commitments develop during the college years. They speculated that college produced movement into moratorium followed by eventual identity achievement because the setting introduced students to diverse possibilities, a speculation supported by correlations between changes in identity status and exposure to diverse students (e.g., Henry & Renaud,1972; Komarovsky, 1985; Madison, 1969; Newman & Newman, 1978). Nonetheless, because few of the studies examined the identity status of comparably aged students not attending college, and when there were

such controls, there were other interpretive problems with the studies, it is impossible to conclude unequivocally that the college setting is what produces the development of identity as Erikson defines it—just as it is not possible based on Perry's work to conclude that college is the determining factor in the movement from dualism to relativism.

We close this subsection by emphasizing that identity achievement is anything but certain by the end of the college years. For example, Waterman and Goldman (1976) observed that only a little more than half of the college seniors they studied had achieved identity with respect to religious or political philosophies, a result consistent with other data reviewed by Pascarella and Terenzini (1991). Pascarella and Terenzini (1991) were especially conservative in concluding that all aspects of identity are worked out for many students by the end of the college years: ". . . if identity is defined as the *simultaneous* achievement of an identity in the occupational, religious, political, and sexual realms, then it [identity] remains a relatively infrequent occurrence during the traditional college years" (p. 183).

Concluding Comments

The college years are a time for sorting out values issues, including religious, philosophical, and political orientations, as well as other commitments, such as to vocation and family life. A consistent speculation is that college does so by forcing confrontation with alternatives not encountered before by students who have come from generally less diverse worlds. It is interesting that Kohlberg speculated (and Rest [1988], confirmed) that college affected movement from conventional to postconventional reasoning about moral issues in part because in college settings, students are exposed to moral arguments never encountered before by them. Such exposure produces cognitive conflicts not experienced previously, conflicts that stimulate hard thinking about moral choices and eventual reorganization of moral thought. The consistency of Kohlberg, Erikson, and Perry's thinking about the role of college in stimulating the development of thinking about values comes through in this quote from Kohlberg (1984, p. 203), who uses both Erikson's and Perry's terms as he explains moral growth in college: "One factor that appears to have precipitated the beginning of this [moral reasoning] shift was the college moratorium experience of responsibility and independence from authority together with exposure to openly conflicting and relativistic values and standards." There are other mechanisms stimulating social-cognitive growth, many of them taken up in the next section.

MANY MECHANISMS FOR STIMULATING SOCIALLY RESPONSIBLE THINKING AND BEHAVIOR: THE INTEGRATIVE APPROACH OF LICKONA

Lickona (1991), who has long been sympathetic to Kohlberg's perspective (Lickona, 1976), compiled what is without a doubt the most comprehensive sourcebook on techniques for moral education. The book is exceptionally well-informed by both research and classroom practice. Cognitive conflict and just community–type interventions are considered along with many other approaches by Lickona (1991), including the following:

- Teacher modeling of moral behavior and reasoning.
- Guest speakers.
- Storytelling and using literature. People can learn from symbolic models, either television characters or characters in books (Bandura, 1969, 1977b).
- Influencing television viewing. Social learning researchers established clearly in the last four decades that both antisocial and prosocial behaviors can be learned from television (see Comstock & Paik, 1991).
- Discussion of controversial, societal-scale issues. Students can learn that controversial issues are many-sided and complex by discussing them in class.
- Direct teaching. As we have reviewed throughout this book, direct explanations are often effective in changing student behavior. Teachers can make a substantial difference by communicating clearly that values matter.
- Mentoring and individual guidance.
- Asking students to be more ethical in their conduct; explaining why they should be. It has long been known that there are associations between prosocial behaviors and receiving explanations about why antisocial behavior is unacceptable compared with prosocial behavior (see Hoffman, 1970).

- Cooperative learning and fostering cooperation in general.
- Negative consequences for unethical conduct; positive consequences for the ethical, fair, and altruistic behavior.
- Using the curriculum to encourage moral growth. When opportunities arise to teach responsibility, do it. For example, the class pet (i.e., rabbit, hamster, ant farm) can be used in many ways for lessons in caring and responsibility. Make ethics an important theme in the school day.
- Idealism. Emphasize the moral responsibility to work and contribute cooperatively to society.
- High expectations. Send the message that there are high expectations about the moral, ethical, and civic development of students in the school, and then actually expect high moral, ethical, and civic responsibility.
- Reject ethics as simply matters of personal opinion. One movement in moral education, values clarification, encourages teachers not to make value judgments about student stances on ethical issues. Lickona, consistent with most in the Kohlbergian tradition, rejects this thinking, believing there are some clearly moral and immoral stances that are not controversial at all (more on this later in the chapter). The teacher should make clear to students when they voice ethical positions that are contrary to stances that are acceptable in society or when they engage in behavior that would be considered unethical by a moral person.

Lickona (1991) reviewed the different theoretical perspectives on moral education and the research related to them. He also visited and studied a number of moral education programs. The result is a book that is an impressive summary of many complementary approaches for increasing moral thinking. Lickona is not alone in coming to the recognition that single-mindedness, whether it is Kohlbergian in emphasizing cognitive conflict or behavioral in emphasizing modeling and reinforcement, is not defensible in moral education (e.g., see Marantz, 1988, analyses of preschool environments promoting prosocial behaviors and attitudes). Lickona's perspective is consistent with the point of view favored throughout this book that effective instruction is complex and multifaceted but understandable in terms of mechanisms highlighted in mainstream theories of development and instruction. Good moral education combines a variety of approaches.

THOUGHTFUL HIGH SCHOOL CLASSES AT THE END OF THE TWENTIETH CENTURY: THE WORKS OF NEWMANN, ONOSKO, BROWN, AND VOSS

All of the researchers considered in this chapter viewed adolescence and young adulthood as a period of great importance in the development of moral reasoning, reflection on values and beliefs, and the development of perspectives. Thus, it is not surprising that educational researchers would be interested in whether secondary schools are designed to promote thinking about alternative positions, ones that are important for students to understand in order for them to be able to make informed progress toward the development of identities, moral stances, or long-term commitments. Although there are many places in the curriculum that can contribute to the development of thoughtfulness in students, social understandings, and citizenship values, such human concerns have traditionally been viewed as a central mission of social studies instruction. Thus, Newmann of the University of Wisconsin at Madison and Onosko of the University of New Hampshire have been examining whether high school social studies classrooms in particular are thoughtful learning environments (Newmann, 1988, 1990a, 1990b, 1991a, 1991b, 1991d, in press; Newmann, Onosko, & Stevenson, 1990; Onosko, 1989, 1991, 1992; Onosko & Newmann, 1994; see also Chapter 11, this book).

First, Newmann and Onosko propose a model of cognitive components that contribute to in-depth understandings of social studies issues. This model includes all four of the main components of good information processing cited in this book : (1) At the heart of the social studies curriculum is content, and hence to think about social studies issues, one must have knowledge of content (e.g., historical facts; important sociological, economic, and political science concepts; and principles of various types of governments). (2) Excellent social studies instruction promotes the development of skills, some of which also might be thought of as strategies (see Nickerson, 1988), including identification of problems; formula-

tion of hypotheses and recognition of hypotheses when they are presented; and the detection of biases, logical consistencies, and inconsistencies. (3) Dispositions for thoughtfulness are necessary as well, with these tantamount to motivation to engage in hard thinking. Those with such a disposition consistently want arguments to be supported by reasons, enjoy reflecting on new information in light of what they already know, are curious, and habitually try to determine what type of thinking might be applied to present situations. (4) Although Newmann and Onosko do not list metacognition as a separate component, metacognition is included as part of their other components, including the disposition to monitor thinking, knowing when and where to use skills, and important beliefs about mind (e.g., knowledge is socially constructed, knowledge can be revised in light of new data, some things cannot be known, and hard thinking often leads to solutions of problems).

Newmann and Onosko developed a perspective on what a thoughtful social studies classroom might be like, one likely to increase knowledge, thinking skills and strategies, dispositions to think, and metacognition. This perspective was informed in part by observations of social studies classrooms in effective schools and by knowledge of the cognition and instruction literature, especially cognitive theoretical claims about effective instruction. The characteristics of effective classrooms identified by Newmann and Onosko included the following:

- There is sustained examination of a few topics.
- Lessons are substantive, are coherent, and build on previous knowledge.
- Students are permitted time to think, for example, time to formulate answers before responding to a question. (Compare this to the ideas about wait time presented in Chapter 11. Also, think about this characteristic of effective classrooms in comparison to other effective instruction considered in this book: The pace of effective instruction is always such that students respond only after they have reflected.)
- Teachers pose challenging questions to students and give themchallenging tasks.
- Teachers model thoughtfulness and flexibility in thinking. (Again and again in this text, there has been support for the social learning perspective that teachers should model effective thinking for their students, with such modeling including ex-

planations of the thinking processes demonstrated to students.)

- Students explain their thinking and provide reasons for their conclusions.

Newmann (1990b, 1991c, 1991d) studied 56 high school social studies classrooms across the United States, including observations of teaching and interviews of the teachers. Not surprisingly, he found variability with respect to the promotion of thoughtfulness in these classrooms. Schools that set the promotion of thinking skills as a priority, however, tended to have classrooms that were more thoughtful according to the Newmann criteria. Although there was more thoughtfulness in classrooms with generally higher-ability students, thoughtful instruction was offered to students at all ability levels in schools committed to stimulating the thinking abilities of their students.

Teachers presiding over thoughtful classrooms tended to be committed to promotion of thinking as an important goal of social studies instruction; they tended to be less committed than other teachers to having great breadth in their coverage. Schools with leaders (i.e., principals, department heads) committed to promoting thinking in the curriculum tended to have more thoughtful classrooms. (Compare this finding with the finding in the effective schools literature that good schools have a strong principal; see Chapter 11.) Perhaps most important, a variety of indicators suggested that thoughtful classrooms were more engaging for students (see especially Newmann, 1991b; see Chapter 11, this book)—that is, students really did spend more of their time thinking about the content in more thoughtful compared with less thoughtful classrooms; students viewed such classes as more challenging, engaging, worthwhile, and interesting.

With Newmann's summary rating of thoughtfulness calculated on a five-point scale, only one-fourth of the classrooms observed scored a four or higher. This was despite the fact that the study was intentionally biased in a number of ways to make it likely that a high proportion of the classrooms studied would be thoughtful. The obvious conclusion is that it is only a minority of American high school social studies classrooms that promote thoughtfulness in the ways Newmann surveyed. This is only one of many sets of data and analyses confirming that relatively few American classrooms stimulate students

to think deeply about issues (e.g., Brown, 1991; Cuban, 1984; Goodlad, 1984; Perrone, et al., 1985; Powell, Farrar, & Cohen, 1985; Sizer, 1984).

Others who have examined thoughtful classrooms have produced lists of characteristics comparable to the ones produced by Newmann and Onosko. For example, Brown (1991) offered the following list of characteristics (adapted from pp. xiv–xv):

1. Reference materials are available.
2. There is a lot to look at and touch in the schoolroom environment, including student work.
3. Students move around to gather information and work in groups.
4. There are few interruptions (e.g., by public address system).
5. Many students participate in discussions.
6. Students address one another in discussions.
7. The teacher permits enough time for students to respond toquestions.
8. The teacher seems to be a learner as well as the students.
9. Students and teachers ask questions that call for analysis, synthesis, interpretation, and evaluation.
10. Questions encourage deeper understanding of material.
11. The teacher encourages student questions.
12. The teacher encourages students to expand on their ideas.
13. The teacher represents concepts in several different ways (e.g., verbally and graphically) to ensure that many students understand them.
14. The teacher provides conceptual bridges from students' current understandings to new understandings; teachers try to lead students away from incorrect to correct understandings of content.
15. Students provide supporting evidence for their discussion comments and questions.
16. Teachers and students synthesize during discussions.
17. There is sufficient time for good discussion.
18. Teachers and students critique discussions.
19. Most students are alert and engaged.
20. Teachers and students listen carefully to one another and interact politely; they acknowledge and support each other's ideas.
21. There is humor and good will in the classroom.

22. Teachers praise student responses.
23. Teachers and students talk about thinking and the quality of it in their class.
24. Students can describe their thinking and strategies.
25. Students take notes and intend to use them later in a reflective fashion, revising or reorganizing them if necessary.
26. Multiple perspectives are accepted and encouraged.
27. Some uncertainty and ambiguity is accepted.
28. Students explore and brainstorm.
29. Students are encouraged to make mistakes—to take risks—and benefit from their mistakes.

What difference does it make that students do not encounter such engaging instruction? There are a variety of higher-order thinking skills that Newmann (1991a) believes may be affected by thoughtful teaching of the social studies, including the following:

- Students develop the ability to empathize with people in other circumstances and cultures.
- Transfer of abstractions—that is, understanding how abstract social studies concepts apply in life—may be promoted by thoughtful instruction.
- Students' abilities to make inferences and predictions from social data would be expected to improve.
- Students can engage better in critical discourse. They can dissent when they do not believe in a position taken by the government or a neighbor. They can debate another person who adopts a morally despicable position.

Our review of Newmann and Onosko's data as well as Brown's (1991) analyses is that they are not analytical enough to permit firm conclusions about whether thoughtful classrooms influence these student outcomes. There is important educational research waiting to be done here. To be sure, Newmann, Onosko, and Brown's hypotheses are in the tradition of Kohlberg, especially their positions that thoughtful interactions can lead to empathy with others (i.e., improved understanding of other people's perspectives and thinking) and better preparedness to participate in democracy. All of the cognitive benefits of thoughtful education are the same presumed benefits of active, progressive education in general.

Is schooling likely to change in the direction of greater thoughtfulness—even if a great deal of additional data accumulates documenting provable benefits of such teaching? Are we likely to see movement toward the development of many more thoughtful classrooms in thoughtful schools? Newmann and Onosko are realistic in recognizing that there are many challenges to the development of thoughtful classrooms. Others, notably Brown (1991, Chapter 8) and Voss (1991) also have concluded there are challenges in implementing such teaching. The barriers to thoughtful education perceived by Newmann, Onosko, Brown, and Voss include the following:

- Thoughtfulness is not appealing to many of those in charge of education because for it entails questioning conventional thinking and questioning fundamental societal assumptions. Brown (1991, p. 233) observed that schools that were thoughtful for students were also thoughtful environments for teachers and administrators, with open communication, inquiry, debate, problem solving, and collaboration. Too many schools are just the opposite, ones in which unquestioning deference to authority is the norm, and questioning that occurs goes on in secret. Perhaps as bad, many educators are isolated from other educators, with their days so full of demands in their classrooms that there is little opportunity to interact with their colleagues, to engage in reflection with intelligent others.
- There are few states or even school districts that have the development of thoughtfulness as a goal. (This is changing, with many states intrigued by programs such as "Dimensions of Thinking" [see Chapter 11], sometimes mandating such programs and often requiring achievement tests that are sensitive to critical thinking processes [see Chapter 17]).
- Critical discussion is hard work for students but also requires hard mental work by teachers. Often, it is easier for students to memorize and reproduce; often, it is easier for teachers to present material and oversee examinations that require only recall than ones that require reflective understanding and interpretation.
- Teachers often lack the in-depth knowledge required to be effective facilitators of classroom discussions of real-world problems.

- Teachers do not know how to conduct thoughtful education. They never saw it when they were in school. They were not taught it in teacher's college. There are no examples of such teaching in their own school. There are no in-services.
- The current generation of social studies textbooks is not matched to an in-depth discussion approach, rarely providing detailed information about even a single social problem. School libraries are often poor sources of information as well.
- In thoughtful classrooms, knowledge is constructed as part of active problem solving, discussion, and writing. Such construction takes time, with partial understandings and corrections along the way. One goal is to think critically about important social assumptions; another is to do more with knowledge than simply learn it (e.g., carry out projects, create integrative essays, publish books). Construction of knowledge and products based on knowledge involves taking intellectual risks and advancing ideas that sometimes conflict with conventional thinking. All of these activities may seem counterintuitive to students, parents, and teachers who have deeply held beliefs that: "(a) Most knowledge is certain, rather than problematic, (b) knowledge is created primarily by outside authorities, not within oneself, (c) knowledge is to be comprehended and expressed in small, fragmented chunks; (d) knowledge is to be learned as quickly as possible, rather than pondered; (e) knowledge may seem counterintuitive or mysterious with respect to one's experience, but it should be believed anyway; and (f) arguments and conflict about the nature of knowledge are personally risky because winners are favored over losers" (Newmann, 1991a, p. 393).
- There are many forces favoring breadth of coverage, and it is thus painful for many to contemplate cutting out some content to permit greater attention to fewer topics, which is essential for thoughtfulness. The knowledge transmission model is embraced by many as an ideal. Knowing facts is equated with knowing for many educators. (The enthusiasm by some for the "cultural literacy" [see Chapter 4], movement in education is one sign of this.)
- The reality of classroom life in American high schools is that 30 students of diverse abilities and interests come together for social studies classes. Teachers are responsible for four to six sections. The size of any one class makes reflective discussion challenging; overseeing ambitious projects or reflective writing exercises for so many students would challenge many teachers' personal resources. The study of many social problems requires more than knowledge from books and discussions; often contact with the real world would be helpful, with such contact typically difficult to arrange. The class is over when the 50-minute period ends, even though some reflective exercises and projects do not fit the 50-minute model well. Some projects (e.g., serving an internship in a community setting) might not be consistent with taking seven courses at a time. In short, school is an institution with a rigid structure, one not necessarily consistent with what is required for students and teachers to interact as they work on projects meaningful in scope.
- Many educators do not believe their students are intelligent enough to participate in a thoughtful classroom. (We do not believe this, however. We think about the hundreds of Chapter-1 primary students participating in thoughtful discussions of literature as part of the SAIL program [see Chapter 14] as we consider this objection to the creation of thoughtful classrooms. There is a great deal of data documenting that diverse populations react positively to intellectually rich and interesting environments, with data in support of this claim distributed throughout this book.) A corollary of this belief is that educators often have low expectations for their students, with some such as Voss (1991) believing that educator expectations that students will learn how to deal with social problems are even lower than their expectations that their students will learn science and mathematics.
- It is harder to grade thoughtfulness than performance on objective examinations. It is not impossible to do so, however, with new forms of assessment (see Chapter 17) being devised that are more sensitive to the processes that compose thoughtfulness.

So the answer to the question of whether widespread movement to thoughtful classrooms is likely is probably no. It is tragic that there are so few just communities, microsocieties, or even progressive schools, given almost a century of urging from Dewey, Kohlberg, Newmann, and like-minded progressives. We suspect that often progressive models of education seem incomprehensible to many teachers and potential teachers. One of our desires in writing this book was to ensure that a much higher proportion of the next generation of teachers and professional educators would understand the foundations of progressive education—or at least our cognitive instructional version of it—well enough that it seems doable and desirable.

Based on the barriers to transforming schools into communities that promote thoughtfulness, rational morality, and caring, it would be easy to give up in despair. We resist the temptation to do so, however, continuing to hope that the expanding knowledge about powerful educational reforms will eventually be too great to ignore (see Chapter 11). At the very least, research documenting the nature of thoughtful schools provides an envisionment of what schooling might become. Some of the schools that have developed exemplary thoughtful instruction serve challenging populations: This is not just a model that works in financially privileged environments that can afford extra staffing and resources of various types.

Brown (1991), for example, presented a series of case studies of thoughtful schools in what might seem unlikely places to many readers. Brown analyzed schooling in a traditional small town in the South, on an Indian reservation, in a major American urban district, and in a multicultural Canadian setting. More research documenting the benefits of thoughtful education as well as research establishing how teachers can learn how to carry out, thoughtful education can only help the greater educator community understand thoughtful classrooms. Even if it is a long shot that thoughtful education will become widespread, we believe it is one worth researching, for the potential gains for American students are great. We hope that some readers of this book will be educators making such gains happen and that other readers will dedicate their careers to studying such innovations.

CONCLUDING COMMENTS

Educators have long tried to create a more ethical, thoughtful, and caring citizenry through the design of school materials and schooling environments. It is no accident that the first mass-produced primes

were catechisms, beginning with Luther's *Little Catechism* in 17th century Sweden (Resnick, 1991). Understanding of liberty was promised by Elhanan's (1796) *Political Catechism, Intended for Use of Schools in the United States* (Resnick, 1991). Who could miss the moral education intentions in the instruction provided by sources such as the 1839 *New England Primer* (Chandler Press, 1988):

> *In Adam's Fall, We sinned all.*
> *Thy life to mend, God's book attend . . .*
> *A dog will bite, A Thief at Night. . . .*
> *The idle Fool Is Whipt at School . . .*
> *My Book and Heart, Shall Never Part.*
> *Job Feels the Rod, Yet Blesses God . . . (p. 11)*

Dewey's progressive school movement is well-known, but others also experimented with schools designed to encourage reflection (Tyler & Smith, 1942; see Cuban, 1991). Long before the current wave of efforts to increase thoughtfulness in school, governmental agencies sponsored programs to encourage the development of more thoughtful education (e.g., National Science Foundation, 1978; see Cuban, 1991). Even so, in the 1990s, we are faced with schools that are producing students whose abilities to think about social problems in realistic ways seem limited. Perhaps worse, the potential changes in schooling that might increase student thoughtfulness seem unworkable to many.

Many developmental theorists (e.g., Piaget, Erikson, Kohlberg) have offered the conclusion that reflective thinking is something that becomes possible with adolescence (i.e., the onset of formal operations). Thus, education to stimulate reflection, morality, caring, and thoughtfulness has been more targeted at adolescents than younger students, more a secondary school intervention than an elementary-level approach. Although some successes in improving high school education so that thoughtfulness is increased have been identified, they are not disseminated widely. One possibility is that the organizational characteristics of secondary schools may make them especially resistant to reform (Cuban, 1991), with content-driven curricula so completely accepted by so many secondary educators that process-oriented approaches simply do not have a chance. Another possibility is that despite the long history of schools attempting to influence values and social decision-making skills, there really is something too controversial about teaching students how to reason better about moral issues, consider issues of rationality versus care, and deliberate about the problems faced by their home communities and nation, perhaps even about working together.

Consistent with this possibility, Purpel (1989, Chapter 3), who has long identified with the movement to educate students to think about social issues (e.g., Purpel & Ryan, 1976), concludes that there are many pressures in society against educating the new generation to reflect on moral and social issues. For example, (1) individual thinking and accomplishment seems more valued now than ever, with the collective activities that are at the heart of the educational visions of Kohlberg, Newmann, and others discussed in this chapter at odds with the predominating individualistic, narcissistic focus (Lasch, 1979). The competition that is valued in our society and critical to conventional education is inconsistent with the cooperative educational options presented in this chapter.

(2) Many educators regard control of students as something that is essential to maintain; they really believe there are right ways of thinking, right answers, and right values. A great deal of control is given up with all of the educational options considered in this chapter. Communities in which patriotism is a high value might feel uncomfortable with schools that debated the ethics of government decision making. Schools located in religiously conservative areas of the United States might feel more comfortable transmitting particular views of morality than permitting the nature of morality to be a matter of debate. How many educators have we met who take pride in the peace and quiet in the hallways of their schools? There is much less peace and quiet when students are interacting with each other in thoughtful conversations, debates, and projects.

(3) Since the 1963 decision to ban prayer in U.S. public schools, any curriculum item suggesting that religion is being injected in schooling—and any curriculum in which universal values are considered is at risk for being viewed as somewhat religious—has produced discomfort in some school officials. Some educators hide behind the 1963 decision as a defense for not teaching values or even providing students with opportunities to think and talk about value-laden issues. Teachers are uncomfortable in making decisions about which values to teach (Boyd, 1988; Cox, 1988).

Even though the interventions considered in this chapter fly in the face of many social pressures af-

fecting American schools, Purpel (1989, Chapter 4) believes that many of the values and understandings promoted by such interventions are ones that are not debatable (although not all agree; e.g., Cox, 1988). Who would debate that it is a good thing to deepen understanding of democratic principles, which is a key outcome of interventions such as the just community approach? The United States is a country founded on and dedicated to principles of individual rights, justice, and political equality. The interventions considered in this chapter are concerned with deepening awareness of these principles and how they apply in life. On reflection, does it not make sense to do so? Many would argue that qualities such as forgiveness, mercy, and care are as American as apple pie. If they are, does it make sense for schools not to develop them? Perhaps most convincing of all, however, is Purpel's claim that our intellectual heritage is consistent with characteristics that are affected by thoughtful values and moral education:

> We value freedom of inquiry and expression, we revere creativity and originality, and we urge ourselves to be open and tolerant in the force of conflicting and differing ideas. We esteem a strong critical capacity. . . . We admire clarity as well as the provocative and the evocative. We recognize that the paths to truth are many, that they sometimes crisscross, and that we need to both challenge these paths as well as affirm them. Our culture values . . . the pursuit of knowledge. (Purpel, 1989, pp. 71–2)

Many of the interventions reviewed in this chapter were about that pursuit, learning how to reason about the complicated issues that will be reencountered throughout life.

We must point out, too, that there are those who believe the interventions reviewed in this chapter do not go nearly far enough with respect to educating different ways of thinking about society and personal management. For example, Martin (1992, Chapter 3) advances the perspective that boys' propensity for rationality needs to be curbed somewhat by education that promotes males' capacity to care. In contrast, females' too great propensity to care needs to be reeducated so that they are less likely to help others when the cost is great to themselves. Her proposal for implementing such education is part of what she calls the "schoolhome," which endeavors to provide much more teaching for living than is assumed by the current curriculum, teaching aimed at producing people who are more sensitive to the needs both of themselves and others. Based on Gilligan's analyses, she concludes this requires different education both for girls and for boys than they are currently receiving. That Gilligan's work fuels the enthusiasm of some dedicated to radical alternatives like the schoolhome concept may be one of the reasons that any movement toward thoughtful schools is scary to many conventional educators. Once thoughtfulness begins, it may become apparent that there is need for great change.

Our perspective is that if the schoolhome or any other alternatives designed to educate more thoughtful people are put into practice, educational psychologists should be there to assess the impact of these interventions. The goals of the educators devising these programs are noble; if they succeed, we must know and document the differences their interventions make on students' lives during the schooling years and afterwards.

A great accomplishment of cognitive research was reviewed in this chapter, which provided a window on sophisticated value-laden thinking, revealing its rational and caring sides and illuminating the reverence of the mature thinker for alternative positions as well as the ways good thinkers can come to commitments to some positions over others. Educational options were reviewed in the chapter as well, ones aimed at increasing the proportions of students who can systematically apply their understandings of justice, care, and diversity of ideas to the problems of tomorrow. We sincerely hope the future teachers reading this book use the instructional ideas in their classrooms; we also hope that at least a few burgeoning researchers are sufficiently stimulated by the hypotheses summarized here to expand on them as they develop and evaluate new approaches for increasing responsible and empathetic thinking in students.

There were assumptions in both Kohlberg's and Erikson's theories about how biology greatly biases people to think in particular ways and places some constraints on the potential sophistication of thinking at particular points in development (e.g., some forms of moral thought supposedly depend on formal operations). Kohlberg and Erikson and many others were aware, however, that how people think depends greatly on the social world in which they live. A main message emanating from the three chapters covering the grand theories in educational psychology is that biological and social forces are both powerful determinants of thought. Those who exclude either biology or social forces in their explanations of learning and cognition (there have been many instances in the history of educational psychology of theorists and researchers who did) fundamentally misunderstand much about the nature of mind and how it develops.

Even so, because educators have much more opportunity to manipulate environmental than biological variables, most of what follows in this book is concerned with environment without much consideration of biology. Also, as our knowledge about the limited biological determination of gender and race differences has increased, it has become apparent that some traditional biologically inspired hypotheses about learning, cognition, and instruction as a function of student diversity were, in fact, in error. There is no compelling reason to believe that there are biological differences between males and females or between the races that should affect what different people are taught or how they are taught. Thus, some work on biology makes it clear that the design of high-quality educational environments for all students is a sensible direction. We are going to follow that compass as we consider various interventions for improving learning and academic performance in the chapters that follow.

Part
3

Important Empirical Contributions in Educational Psychology

10

Basic Mechanisms Affecting Learning

Throughout its one-century history, educational psychology has been concerned with learning more than any other topic. This chapter covers some of the most important problems studied and conclusions generated about learning over the course of the 20th century. Some of the specific approaches to learning, such as mnemonics, are much older. Although work continues on many of the topics covered in this chapter, much of the work reviewed here has a more traditional look to it than other research considered in the book. From a positive standpoint, the main findings covered in this chapter are well supported by many replications. Thus, we know with certainty that meaningful processing of material (i.e., deep processing) can increase incidental learning (i.e., even when the purpose of the deep processing is not to promote learning), imagery mnemonics increase recall of associations, and spacing practice makes it more effective. Although such facts are well-known, educational psychologists continue to find ways to apply these understandings so to increase learning in school and other settings. The traditions reviewed in this chapter are as important at the dawn of the 21st century as they were throughout the first century of the scientific study of education.

Learning and cognition researchers have identified many mechanisms affecting learning and improving performance. In this chapter, some of the most important ones will be discussed. The chapter is organized into two sections: The first deals with ways of increasing memory and understanding. The second is concerned with the effects of practice on learning.

MECHANISMS AFFECTING MEMORY, COMPREHENSION, AND LEARNING

Historically, much of memory research in the 20th century focused on learning of discrete information in laboratory studies, such as the items on lists, vocabulary and their definitions, and countries and their capitals. Increased concerns in the last decade with generating information that is more certainly relatable to school learning and reflective of the demands of school have resulted in declining interest in such research in general. The late 1970s and early 1980s was a period of transition away from traditional investigations of learning and memory and toward more educationally valid studies. Thus, as this section proceeds, there is movement from learning of more discrete content (i.e., some would say more "artificial" materials) to acquisition of more connected and meaningful material.

Depth of Processing (Semantic Orientation)

One of the most important papers in the last 25 years in cognitive psychology was Craik and Lockhart (1972). They argued that what was remembered during a learning task depended on what the learner did during learning. Suppose, for example, that you are asked to process a list of words. Would you remember more of the words later if (1) you checked each word to determine whether it had an *e* or a *g* in it or (2) you rated the pleasantness of each word? As you probably guessed, you remember many more words following the pleasantness-rating task (Hyde & Jenkins, 1973). When do people remember more from a paragraph describing a person—When they read it to determine whether it desscribes them accurately or when they check for spelling errors (e.g., Reder, McCormick, & Esselman, 1987)? When they are concerned with the accuracy of the text's meaning?

One explanation of such differences in learning is that they reflect different depths of processing, with checking for spelling involving superficial processing of the meaning of material compared to instructions forcing orientation to meaning (e.g., pleasantness ratings or evaluating whether an article describes oneself). Craik and Tulving (1975) eventually came to the conclusion that **semantic orienting** directions are effective in promoting memory because they increase the number of elaborations to the material that is processed—the material is related more extensively to prior knowledge when a learner performs a semantic orienting task than when they focus on physical features of material they are processing.

That is not to say, however, that physical features cannot be processed deeply. Thus, Bower and Karlin (1974) provided a well-known demonstration of how memory for faces was affected by attending to meaning of faces rather than to physical features. When people rated whether faces were "honest," they remembered more of them than when they rated physical features of faces.

Although a great deal of important research on the effects of semantic orientation on memory have been conducted in the last 20 years, Craik and Lockhart (1972) *re*discovered semantic orientation rather than discovered it. Soviet psychologists were studying depth of processing effects decades ago. For example, Zinchenko (reported in English in 1981; also, see Smirnov, 1973, Chapter 2) presented adults with cards, each of which had a picture on it and a number. When the learners were given a task requiring categorization of the pictures, subsequent recall of the pictures was better than recall of the numbers. When subjects were asked to arrange the numbers in ascending order, subsequent recall of the numbers was greater than recall of the pictures. What is attended and processed meaningfully is what is learned.

Zinchenko's work is but one example of many research efforts in the Soviet Union aimed at establishing relationships between what people do and what they comprehend and remember—sometimes referred to as activity theory in the Soviet psychological literature. Readers who are interested in depth of processing should examine Smirnov's (1973) summary of the relevant Soviet literature for many examples of how orientation to information affects what is learned from it. Wertsch (1981) also provided translations of many fine essays by Soviet researchers interested in how meaningful activities affect learning and memory.

An appropriate way to sum up depth of processing is to recall the frequent teacher admonition to "pay attention." Such a command takes on meaning only when it is clear what should be attended. If students meaningfully process what is presented to them and attend to semantically rich aspects of the material, they are going to learn the meaning better than if they attend to physical features only. The head remembers what the head does (Jenkins, 1974).

Mnemonics

There have been many reports of magnificent feats of memory when people have used mnemonics (i.e., Memory tricks) to assist their learning. Indeed, at least since the 13th century, when Raimond Lullé dazzled France (Desrochers & Begg, 1987), some performers have made a living by using mnemonics to perform difficult memory tasks. Detailed, systematic accounts of how to improve memory using imagery mnemonics and other techniques have been in print since the early 19th century, when Fenaigle (1813) published his *New Art of Memory*. Yates (1966) provided a scholarly summary of the history of memory devices based on imagery, an overview making clear that imagery mnemonics and related procedures have been understood intuitively for about 2000 years.

What may be amazing, however, is that scientific analysis of imagery mnemonics has been under-

taken only in the last 30 years or so in the West. There were several reasons for this. First, for much of this century, thinking and mental phenomena were taboo in North America, with the study and measurement of overt behavior viewed as the only scientifically respectable pursuit for academic psychologists. (Recall Skinner's harsh words regarding cognitive psychology in Chapter 7.)

Second, for a phenomenon to be studied, there must first be a theory. There was no compelling theory about mnemonics until Miller, Galanter, and Pribram's (1960) *Plans and the Structure of Behavior*. Miller et al. (1960) discussed imagery effects in terms of information processing, then a new direction in psychology that seemed at the time especially promising and exceptionally scientific. Miller et al.'s (1960) main claim was that behavior is guided by cognitive plans, which are intentions to perform behaviors and a rough idea about how to carry out the plans. Such plans guide all of behavior. Imagery mnemonics are plans according to this framework. Miller et al.'s (1960) explanation of it to an academic guest for dinner is memorable:

> . . . "But what exactly is a Plan?" [the guest] asked. "How can you say that *memorizing* depends on Plans?"
>
> We'll show you," we replied. "Here is a Plan that you can use for memorizing. Remember first that:
>
> one is a bun,
> two is a shoe,
> three is a tree,
> four is a door,
> five is a hive,
> six are sticks,
> seven is heaven,
> eight is a gate,
> nine is a line, and
> ten is a hen."
>
> "You know, even though it is only ten-thirty here, my watch says one-thirty. I'm really tired, and I'm sure I'll ruin your experiment."
>
> "Don't worry, we have no real stake in it." We tightened our grip on his lapel. "Just relax and remember the rhyme. Now you have part of the Plan. The second part works like this: when we tell you a word, you must form a ludicrous or bizarre association with the first word in your list, and so with the ten words we recite to you."
>
> "Really, you know, it'll never work. I'm awfully tired," he replied.
>
> "Have no fear," we answered, "just remember the rhyme and then form the association. Here are the words:

1. ashtray
2. firewood
3. picture
4. cigarette
5. table
6. matchbook
7. glass
8. lamp
9. shoe
10. phonograph

The words were read one at a time, and after reading the word, we waited until he announced that he had the association. It took about five seconds on the average to form the association. After the seventh word he said that he was sure the first six were already forgotten. But we persevered. (pp. 134–136)

The dinner guest went on to recall the list, with him describing recall as "no sweat."

With a simple mnemonic plan, what had seemed like it would be a difficult task turned out to be a simple one. Anecdotes like this one have done more than their share to stimulate interest in imagery mnemonics in both the researcher and practitioner communities.

Imagery research did take off in the years following publication of the *Plans* volume. Important basic research on imagery was conducted by Paivio and his colleagues at Western Ontario as well as by Bower and his associates at Stanford, with this also fueling interest in applications of imagery, including mnemonics. Jensen and Rohwer at Berkeley would do research on the closely allied concept of **verbal elaboration,** especially in the context of associative learning, demonstrating huge effects on associative learning when learners place verbal pairs (e.g., *turkey-rock*) into meaningful verbal contexts (e.g., generating the sentence, "The *turkey* sat on the *rock*). Some of Jensen and Rohwer's students at Berkeley, such as Levin and Kee, became particularly interested in mnemonics, with their work also influenced strongly by the research conducted by Paivio during the 1960s. The conceptual overlap between verbal elaboration and constructing imagery mnemonics to link paired associates (e.g., making an image of a "turkey standing on a rock") was obvious—both involved taking arbitrarily paired items and creating a meaningful context that embedded the two elements in the pair, a context that could later be used in retrieving one of the two items given the other (i.e., presentation of *turkey* brings to mind the linking image, permitting recall of the *rock*).

Over the course of 30 years, Rohwer, Levin, Kee, and their students generated a large number of basic research studies concerned with verbal and imagery mnemonics, a body of data that proved to be coherent, sensible, and relevant to many important questions in memory development (Kee, in press; Schneider & Pressley, 1989). For example, one important question was whether young children could generate mnemonic images (i.e., imagery elaborations of paired associates), a specific instantiation of a general issue in memory development concerning the susceptibility of young children to strategy instruction. Whether imagery instructions for paired-associate learning promote learning depends in part on the age of the learner, something covered briefly in Chapter 2. Preschool children and children in the early elementary grades often experience difficulty in constructing images embedding paired associates—or, at least, if they construct imagery elaborations, the images do not mediate their learning.

For example, Pressley and Levin (1977b) presented 6- to 7-year-old children with paired associates, ones involving paired items not obviously related to one another (e.g., *turkey* and *rock* are not related to one another, whereas the pair *balloon-pin* involves an obvious semantic relation). When the pairs were presented at a relatively rapid rate (5 seconds per pair), instructions to generate linking images did not facilitate paired-associate learning relative to control instructions. Much more positively, however, the learning situation can be engineered so that images can be produced. Thus, in Pressley and Levin (1977b), when paired associates were presented at a much slower rate (i.e., 10 seconds per pair), the 6- to 7-year-olds benefited from the imagery instruction. Their analysis, based on both descriptive and experimental data, was that the 5-second presentation rate did not permit subjects enough time to determine and imagine a meaningful relationship between the paired items. Recalling that Miller et al.'s (1960) adult dinner guest required 5 seconds to construct linking images, isn't it sensible that 6- to 7-year-olds might need at least that much time to construct and imagine a linking relationship between two items not having any obvious relationship to one another?

Once beyond the early grade-school years, the evidence is actually quite strong that people often can generate imagery mnemonics when learning verbal associates (see Pressley, 1977). Even adults, however, do not generate mnemonic elaborations reliably in the absence of instruction, although there is an increase in the likelihood of students using verbal and imagery elaboration on their own with increasing age during adolescence (Beuhring & Kee 1987). That people can be taught to use mnemonics but do not use them autonomously in the absence of instruction has stimulated intensive study of how to teach people to generate mnemonics that might be useful in learning educational content, with one approach receiving more attention than any other.

Keyword Mnemonics   Atkinson's (1975) *American Psychologist* article was a turning point in the history of mnemonics. Atkinson summarized a series of studies conducted at Stanford (with Raugh) on the **keyword method.** The keyword method involves transforming some part of one of two to-be-associated pieces of information into what he called a "keyword," one familiar to the learner. For example, foreign vocabulary words and their definitions are frequent to-be-associated pieces of information for students in high school and college, with the foreign words the elements that are transformed into keywords because the foreign words are unfamiliar to the learners, and a keyword can transform an unfamiliar item into a familiar English concept. For example, to learn that *carlin* means *old woman,* first the learner identifies a word that sounds or looks like some part of *carlin:* Either *car* or *Carl* could serve as **keywords** for *carlin.* A concrete referent for the keyword would then be imagined in interaction with the definition referent. Thus, the learner might imagine an *old woman driving a car* or *Carl Yastremski, the Boston Red Sox Hall of Famer, giving his autograph to an old woman.* In general, Atkinson (1975) made the case that the keyword method facilitated the foreign language vocabulary acquisition of college students.

Pressley, Levin, and their colleagues went on to explore in detail whether keyword mnemonics might facilitate children's learning of new information. This seemed an important problem because children are often asked to learn the definitions of vocabulary, the associations between countries and their attributes, information about famous people, and so on. Indeed, if anything, children are asked to do more intentional associative learning than are adults. Pressley (1977) was the first study of whether grade-school children benefit from keyword method

instruction if they are provided mnemonic pictures. Thus, to learn that the Spanish vocabulary item *carta* means *letter,* Pressley provided elementary-level students with a picture of a letter in a shopping cart. The effects of these mnemonic pictures on learning were quite large for both grade-2 and grade-6 students: When given the foreign words on a test and the requirement to recall their definitions, the children seeing the keyword pictures were much more likely to remember the definitions than were the control subjects.

In a follow-up investigation, Pressley and Levin (1978) determined that providing pictorial support was much more critical with grade-2 than grade-6 students. At grade 2, keyword-method effectiveness varied with the amount of pictorial support provided: That is, complete mnemonic pictures produced better learning than provision of separate pictures of keyword and definition referents, which produced better learning than attempted keyword application given only the vocabulary word, its meaning, and the verbal keyword. (Readers might compare this finding with the Pressley & Levin [1977b] data discussed earlier in this subsection; both sets of data substantiate that imagery mnemonic instructions do not reliably facilitate the learning of 6- to 8-year-olds.) At the grade-6 level, however, students could easily generate their own linking images provided only the vocabulary word, its meaning, and a verbal keyword.

One of the most dramatic demonstrations of the potency of keyword-mediated learning was provided by Pressley, Samuel, Hershey, Bishop, and Dickinson (1981), who presented 10 Spanish words to 3-, 4-, and 5-year-olds, with each word presented one time. When left to their own devices to learn the words given one presentation of them (i.e., at 15 seconds per word), the children could recall about 2 of the 10 meanings on a posttest (i.e., given the Spanish word *pato,* there was only a 20 percent chance of remembering that the word meant *duck*). When same-age children were presented pictures depicting keyword referents (e.g., *pot* for *pato*) in interaction with definition referents (e.g., a *duck* with a *pot* on its head), about 70 percent of the vocabulary meanings could be recalled after one presentation. That is, learning was 3.5 times better when the keyword-interactive pictures were provided as an aid to learning than when the students attempted to learn the words on their own without the support of the transformational mnemonic pictures.

Levin (e.g., 1982, 1983, 1985, 1986) and his associates at Wisconsin as well as Mastropieri, Scruggs, and their colleagues at Purdue (e.g., Mastropieri & Scruggs, 1991), in particular, have produced many demonstrations of the utility of the keyword method for diverse students learning many types of factual content—contents requiring students to remember linkages between one type of information and other pieces of information. States and capitals can be remembered with the keyword method (e.g., for Madison, Wisconsin, imagine a *maid* [keyword for Madison] using a *whisk broom* [keyword for Wisconsin]). Artist and painting associations can be learned using the keyword method (e.g., imagine those huge Campbell Soup cans in a *war* to remember they were created by Andy Warhol; see Carney, Levin, & Morrison, 1988). Facts about American presidents can be encoded easily when the information is encoded in mnemonic pictures (e.g., many facts can be related to a mnemonic image of a *ray gun,* a keyword for Reagan, to remember information about the 40th president). The keyword mnemonic can be adapted so that hierarchies of scientific concepts are learned and interrelated (e.g., Levin & Levin, 1990).

Some especially striking keyword-method effects have been observed in prose-learning studies. McCormick and Levin (1987) presented short biographies to college students, with subsequent recall of name-biographical fact associations required (e.g., what did Charlene McKune do?). Subjects in the study attempted to learn biographies such as the following:

> Born and raised on a dairy *farm* where she helped take care of the cows, *Charlene McKune* has always been used to hard work. When she was a child, McKune enjoyed creating homes for her pets out of her toy *building blocks.* To earn extra money and because of her hatred for dirt of any kind, McKune began *washing cars* for her parents' friends . . . (p. 400).

Control students were left to their own devices to learn the passages. Mnemonic keyword subjects were instructed to use a keyword for Charlene McKune (*racoon*) and to construct an image linking the most important factual elements of the passage (e.g., an image of a pet *racoon* outside a *farmhouse* jumping over a row of *building blocks* with some kids *washing cars* nearby). Memory of the name-fact associations was much better in the mnemonic keyword condition than in the control condition, with this finding representative of many others in which keyword-

mnemonic intervention conditions have been contrasted with a variety of control procedures.

Despite the many demonstrations of improved learning via the keyword method, many educators are reluctant to try mnemonics. One of their concerns is that the method involves "artificial" learning, learning that is not deep because the method does not require the learners to think about the meaning of the association. One way that imagery enthusiasts have responded to this concern is with development of imagery-based procedures that do not involve keyword transformations, that more certainly represent the original meaning of the to-be-learned information.

Nonkeyword, Memonic Imagery   The imagery mnemonics described in the last subsection all involve some transformation of the to-be-learned material that introduces elements not meaningfully related to the original to-be-learned material (e.g., conversion of a foreign vocabulary word to a keyword, which only physically resembles part of the to-be-learned content). Powerful mnemonic images sometimes can be constructed that do not require keywords, however.

Woloshyn, Willoughby, Wood, and Pressley (1990) asked Canadian university students to construct representational images as they read paragraphs containing facts about particular Canadian universities, such as the following:

> The land on which McGill University stands was donated by a fur trader. The university's first faculty was a medical faculty. The university is also recognized for establishing the first medical faculty in Canada. The psychology department at the school is internationally acclaimed. The school has an extensive puppet collection. Many students consider the university's athletic facilities to be old and small. (p. 523)

The students in the imagery condition of the study were instructed to learn each fact about McGill by imagining the fact occurring in the school's geographical location. Thus, the mnemonic processing involved constructing relations consistent with the conceptual meaning expressed in the passage—that is, for McGill, students constructed images relating information about McGill to McGill's setting, which is Montreal. This imagery instruction studied by Woloshyn et al. (1990) dramatically increased recall of the facts for each school relative to performance in an uninstructed control condition.

Others have also been studying interventions that involve imagery transformations that relate to the meaning of the to-be-learned information, most notably Mastropieri and Scruggs. They have been devising mnemonics for teaching content, such as social studies. One type of imagery mnemonic they have devised requires the learner to engage in what they call *mimetic reconstruction* once the image is retrieved. Thus, a piece of factual information, such as "Early bridges often rotted and washed away," might be accompanied by a drawing of a rickety bridge with a woman in settler's clothing watching as the bridge beneath her feet is swept away by the rushing water of a stream. Later, by remembering the picture, the learner can reconstruct the more abstract fact—that bridges in the days of the settlers often did not hold up and were swept away by water. Another type of imagery Mastropieri and Scruggs have devised involves *symbolic reconstruction* at recall. Thus, an illustration accompanying text about American isolationism before World War I might involve Uncle Sam standing on a depiction of North America and looking towards fighting on a depiction of Europe. Uncle Sam could be saying, "Its not my fight" (Mastropieri & Scruggs, 1989, p. 97). Recalling this image later would permit reconstruction of the fact that the United States stayed out of the conflict in Europe for some time. To date, all indications are that embellishing texts with such mimetic and symbolic transformational mnemonic pictures increases learning of content.

In addition, mimetic and symbolic memory aids can be combined with pictures incorporating keyword mnemonics. Scruggs and Mastropieri are generating important studies establishing the effectiveness of embellishing traditional content with a variety of types of mnemonic pictures (e.g., Scruggs & Mastropieri [1989] provided several months of social studies instruction to learning-disabled students using various sorts of mnemonic pictures, producing large gains in performance).

In closing, we emphasize that experimental work has established that there are many ways of representing and transforming information into mnemonic pictures and images that can increase learning of new factual content. Moreover, the gains in learning often are striking, especially with populations that are otherwise difficult to teach, such as the learning-disabled. One of the most attractive features of imagery is how flexible it is. Thus, although young children sometimes have difficulties generat-ing their own images when asked to do so, it is, nonetheless, possible to devise mnemonic pictures that provide learning benefits (e.g., see the earlier discussion of Pressley, Samuel, et al.'s [1981] provision of keyword-mnemonic pictures to preschoolers learning foreign vocabulary). Young scholars reading this book should note that new research on old, established interventions often can do much to move the field beyond the traditional approach. What educational intervention could be more established than mnemonic imagery with its 2000+ year history (Yates, 1966). Providing new insights about traditional approaches often attracts positive attention. There is much educational benefit from imagery and related pictorial interventions and much study of imagery phenomena left to be done.

Enactment

When people are asked to remember actions, their memory is typically better if they carry out the actions rather than simply verbally rehearse their names. For example, if a list of actions, such as "Bounce the ball, drink from the cup, climb the tree...cut the paper," is presented to a person, he or she is more likely to recall the actions if each act is mimicked by the student as it is named than if the student only listens and tries to remember the list (Cohen, 1989). A likely explanation is that a form of dual coding (e.g., Paivio, 1971, 1986; Chapter 3, this book) is mediating the increase in memory owing to the actions. That is, hearing the list stimulates a verbal coding; hearing the list and acting it out stimulates verbal and motoric coding (Cohen, 1989).

Another possibility, however, is that acting out to-be-remembered items stimulates three codings—verbal, motoric, and imaginal, for motor processes have been hypothesized for a long time to increase the formation of images (e.g., Piaget & Inhelder, 1971; Zaporozhets, 1965). For example, recall from the last subsection that young elementary-school children often fail to learn more paired associations in reaction to imagery instructions than when left to their own devices to learn. Wolff and Joel Levin (Wolff & Levin, 1972; Wolff, Levin, & Longobardi, 1972) hypothesized that imagery instructions might be more effective in the early grade-school years if students were encouraged to act out the elaborative actions and they were attempting to imagine (e.g., act out with their hands a cow chasing a dog for the pair, *cow-dog*). In fact, imagery and motor instructions combined did increase associative learning at these developmental levels, with Wolff, Levin, and their colleagues concluding the motoric actions stimulated the development of imagery.

Baker-Ward, Hess, and Flannagan (1990) offered interesting new data suggesting that it may not be the motor activities per se. In that study, children's memories of activities were enhanced if they carried out the action rather than watched the action be carried out—unless the other person doing the action was familiar to them (i.e., a classmate). Recall was as high when grade-3 children watched a classmate perform actions as when they performed actions themselves and higher than when they watched an unfamiliar peer perform the action. Somehow, performing oneself and watching a friend perform creates deeper, richer encodings than watching a stranger. Regardless of the exact mechanism underlying enactment effects, however, it is clear that enactment often—although not always—is a powerful way to facilitate learning, with the benefits of enactment obtained across the life span, from preschool (e.g., Heindel & Kose, 1990) to old age (e.g., Knopf & Neidhardt, 1989).

Learning by Understanding: Relating New Information to Prior Knowledge

Learning can often be enhanced if learners understand the content they are being asked to learn. Educational psychologists have produced substantial evidence that understanding can affect memory of information dramatically. Although the effects on problem-solving have been studied less completely, there is a growing database substantiating that problem-solving also can be improved through manipulations that relate a current problem situation to prior knowledge.

Effects of Understanding on Learning and Memory

Try reading and learning the following passage so that you can look away from the book and recall it:

> The procedure is actually quite simple. First, you arrange the items into different groups. Of course, one pile may be sufficient depending on how much there is to do. If you have to go somewhere else due to lack of facilities that is the next step; otherwise, you are pretty well set. It is important not to overdo things. That is, it is better to do too few things at once than too many. In the short run this may not seem important, but complications can easily arise. A mistake can be expensive as well. At first, the whole procedure will seem complicated. Soon, however, it will become just another facet of life. It is difficult to foresee any end to the necessity for this task in the immediate future, but then, one can never tell. After the procedure is completed, one arranges the materials into different groups again. Then they can be put into their appropriate places. Eventually they will be used once more, and the whole cycle will have to be repeated. However, that is part of life. (Bransford & Johnson, 1972, pp. 722)

Most people experience a great deal of difficulty remembering the details of the procedure described in this passage. The points made seem so unconnected and arbitrary. If the title of the passage, "Washing Clothes," had been provided before you read the material, however, it would have permitted ready comprehension of the paragraph. The title would have activated all of the schemata (see Chapter 3) possessed by you about washing clothes, ones that would permit understanding of the paragraph content. These activated schemata would have permitted you to make sense of each part of the passage and the passage as a whole.

People often understand "new" material in terms of prior knowledge (e.g., Anderson & Pearson, 1984; Chapter 3, this book). The catch is that learners must activate their prior knowledge if it is to affect current comprehension and learning. Often the to-be-learned content includes cues associated with prior knowledge so strongly that relevant schemata are activated automatically. That is the case when college students are provided the title, "Washing Clothes." Once activated, the schemata affect interpretation of all that follows. Thus, the sentence, "That is, it is better to do too few things at once than too many," would have many meanings out of context. When encountered while reading a story entitled, "Washing Clothes," the interpretation is, "It is better to wash only a few pieces of clothing at once rather than overloading the washer." Knowing the title, the reader **infers** that the text is about washing a few pieces of clothing and the concern is with overloading the washer. The activated schemata also direct the **allocation of attention.** Thus, once the washing clothes schema is activated, the reader goes looking for elements of text related to washing clothes.

In short, once schemata are activated, they guide attention to text and permit inferences, with the result a mental representation of the text by the reader that is not identical to what was presented in text.

For the present example, the representation is likely to include text information central to the washing clothes schemata. More ambiguous information in the text will be translated into information about washing clothes (i.e., inferences will occur reconciling the ambiguous information with the rest of the text so that the entire representation is consistent with a clothes-washing framework). Part of the reason that recall of a text is not perfect is because activated prior knowledge supports the acquisition of some parts of to-be-learned content more than others and distorts other to-be-learned content to be consistent with activated schemata. That a learner's representation of a text is not an exact copy of the text has been understood for a long time (e.g., Bartlett, 1932).

But schemata affect more than encoding. They have an impact on retrieval as well. By thinking about washing clothes, the learner can think about each part of the washing clothes schema and recall whether that part of the schema was represented in the passage. If it was represented, the schema can aid recall additionally. Thus, as you thought about loading the washer, you might remember that the passage said it was better to do only a few things at a time and that complications arise if you do too many things at once. Those memories, in turn, might cue long-term knowledge of what can go wrong with a washer, stimulating memory of the hassles of overflows—which, in turn, might remind that the text said mistakes could be costly. Memory using this approach would not be perfect, although it would be better than without activation of the clothes-washing schemata at recall.

Some errors at retrieval will be errors of inference. So, if the washing clothes schema was used to guide recall of the washing clothes passage, some learners might infer that the passage mentioned detergent and "recall" that detergent was used. Such distortions are common, reflecting that recall involves **reconstruction** of to-be-learned information based on prior knowledge. Even so, all that is remembered are not reconstructions. Some of what is recalled is "in the memory trace."

The main point here, however, is that people's understanding of to-be-learned content in terms of prior knowledge affects both encoding and retrieval (see Anderson & Pearson, 1984, for extensive commentary). It makes a great deal of sense to do all possible to increase understanding of content by encouraging students to relate to-be-learned information to prior knowledge.

Even so, understanding material superficially often is not sufficient to ensure that new content will be learned. Bransford, who generated so much of the research supporting models of encoding and retrieval based on schemata, also provided data substantiating that superficial understanding is not enough to ensure high memory, at least in some situations.

Bransford and colleagues (e.g., Bransford et al., 1982; Stein & Bransford, 1979; Stein, Littlefield, Bransford, & Persampieri, 1984) reported a series of studies in which the subjects read sentences. Read the following and ask yourself as you are doing so whether each sentence can be understood:

The short man bought the broom.
The brave man gave money to the robber.
The fat man read the sign.
The tall man bought the crackers.
The thin man found the scissors.
The rich man picked up the chair.
The sad man looked at his new boat.
The kind man ate dinner.
The smart man went to work.
The bald man used the phone.
The artistic man put down the knife.
The frightened man ironed the sheet.
The sleepy man bought the mug.
The evil man wound up the clock.
The blind man hit the flea.
The bearded man threw out the coupon.
The crippled man flicked the switch.
The dying man used a feather.
The religious man used the saw.
The long-haired man looked for the pole.
The Irish man counted the leaves.
The weak man thanked the checkout girl.
The patriotic man memorized the words.
The dishonest man looked closely at the wrapper.
(Sentences used by Pressley, McDaniel, Turnure,
    Wood, & Ahmad, 1987, p. 300)

It was easy to understand each of the sentences in that list. Does understanding the sentences make it inevitable that they will be remembered? Here's a test. Without looking back, What did the sad man do? the sleepy man? the crippled man? the fat man? the Irish man? the evil man? Did understanding the sentences result in inevitable memory of them? As should be obvious by this point, for most readers, the answer is no. It is usually difficult for adults who read such sentences to remember which man did what. Even though each sentence can be understood as it is read, the relationship specified by the sentence is arbitrary. When so much arbitrary information is presented together, it is difficult to keep the arbitrary relationships sorted out. Understanding individual pieces of information does not insure memory of the pieces.

More positively, learners often possess a great deal of prior knowledge that they can relate to arbitrary pieces of information and, if they do so, render the material more meaningful and more memorable. In the case of the "man" sentences, learners can be asked to think about why the relationship specified in each sentence makes sense—they can be asked to think about "why" each man did what he did and especially why it is significant that a man with the specified characteristic performed the action indicated. When an instruction like that is provided to learners, the sentence, "The short man bought the broom," results in rationales such as, "Maybe it is a low room that needs to be swept," and "He could see how good the bristles were because he was so close to them." The sentence about a crippled man flicking a switch elicits rationales such as, "It's a switch on an electric wheelchair," and ". . . in a building with an elevator fully designed for the handicapped."

When university students are instructed to respond to such why-questions while reading such man-facts, their learning increases dramatically. For example, when university students read "man" sentences without being told in advance that there would be a memory test (i.e., in a study of **incidental learning;** Pressley, McDaniel, et al., 1987, Experiments 1 and 2), answering why-questions improved memory by more than 280%. When the students were aware they were reading the sentences in preparation for a memory test (i.e., in a study of **intentional learning;** Pressley, McDaniel, et al., 1987, Experiments 1 and 3), the improvement was less dramatic but still striking (i.e., more than 30 percent).

A series of experiments followed the initial Pressley, McDaniel, et al. (1987) finding. These studies established that why-questioning (referred to by Pressley and colleagues as **elaborative interrogation**) improves learning of facts, both when presented in lists and when presented in expository passages (e.g., Pressley, Symons, McDaniel, Snyder, & Turnure, 1988; Woloshyn, Pressley, & Schneider, 1992). The benefits of elaborative interrogation can be obtained with middle school–age students as

well, although the effects seem not to be as large as those obtained with adults (Wood, Pressley, & Winne, 1990).

The most important research in this series of studies, however, has pinpointed the cause of the elaborative interrogation effect. On the face of it, why-questioning might promote learning by encouraging greater effort by learners *or* increasing arousal *or* forcing more extensive, meaningful processing of to-be-learned content relative to what control subjects would be doing as they simply read facts. Pressley and his collaborators believed, however, that elaborative interrogation was effective because it prompted learners to activate prior knowledge related to the to-be-learned facts, prior knowledge that would not be activated by reading alone, for people often do not automatically access knowledge they possess that could be related to new information (e.g., Prawat, 1989).

Martin and Pressley (1991) produced evidence in favor of the prior knowledge activation hypothesis. In their study, Canadian students learned facts about Canadian provinces. In four conditions of the study, the subjects were asked why-questions, with the why questions varying from ones that directed attention to related prior knowledge to questions that directed attention away from relevant prior knowledge. If activation of prior knowledge is the active mechanism accounting for elaborative interrogation effects, performance in these four why-questioning conditions should have varied with the degree that questions oriented learners to relevant prior knowledge. Alternatively, all of the question types should have increased attention to the to-be-learned facts relative to reading alone; all question types should have increased arousal as well; and all question types should have increased meaningful processing. Thus, if increased attention, arousal, and meaningful processing account for elaborative interrogation effects, to-be-learned materials should have been learned better in all four questioning conditions relative to a reading control condition.

Martin and Pressley (1991) found that performance in the why-questioning conditions varied with the degree the why-questions forced attention to prior knowledge (e.g., "Why would the largest percentage of unionized workers be in British Columbia" orients toward prior knowledge supporting the claim that the largest percentage of unionized workers are in British Columbia; "Why is it surprising that the largest percentage of unionized workers are not in some other province" orients toward prior knowledge supporting the same fact much less so). In fact, for the questions that least directed attention to prior knowledge, there was little if any evidence of facilitation owing to elaborative interrogation. See Miller and Pressley (1989) for additional evidence that why-questions that direct attention away from critical content and toward not-so-critical information can undermine learning of essential information.

For additional evidence that prior knowledge plays a critical role in mediating the effectiveness of elaborative interrogation, see Woloshyn, Pressley, and Schneider (1992), who demonstrated that performance in why-questioning conditions depends greatly on the amount of prior knowledge possessed by learners pertaining to to-be-learned content. In their study, when Germans used elaborative interrogation to learn new information about Germany, they did better than when they attempted to learn new information about Canada using elaborative interrogation; when Canadians attempted to learn new information about Canada using elaborative interrogation, they did better than when they attempted to learn new information about Germany using elaborative interrogation.

When all of the data on elaborative interrogation are considered (for a review, see Pressley, Wood, Woloshyn, Martin, King, & Menke, 1992), it is apparent that learners often fail to relate what they already know to new material unless they are prompted to do so—such as when they are asked to answer why-questions pertaining to the material. As Langer (1989) puts it, people often process information "mindlessly." An important consequence of such mindlessness is that new content is understood less completely than it could be, and thus it is not as easily learned or remembered as it might be if the learner related prior knowledge to the task. Elaborative interrogation forces more extensive connection of new material to prior knowledge and hence greater understanding of the new to-be-learned content, with the consequence that learning is much better.

Effects of Understanding on Problem Solving

Understanding the significance of information affects not only memory, but also problem solving. One of the things that good learners do as they learn new ways to solve problems is that they construct explanations to themselves about the problem—that is, they relate a current problem to their prior knowledge. Chi, Bassok, Lewis, Reimann, and Glaser (1989; see also Chi & Bassok, 1989), for example, studied how physics students learn from worked-out example problems (see Chapter 3). The students were asked to think aloud as they went through the worked-out examples. There were large differences between students in the extent that they explained to themselves the significance of the sequence of steps in the worked-out problems. Moreover, there were clear correlations between the number and quality of self-explanations generated and success in solving subsequently presented problems that were analogous to the sample problems.

Of course, one reaction to Chi et al.'s (1989) finding is that more intelligent and better students would be more likely to generate explanations than would weaker students, so that there is no causal relationship between generation of the self-explanations and subsequent performance. That there might be ability differences between the good and poor problem solvers was suggested by clear differences in awareness of understanding by the good and poor problem solvers while processing the sample problems. The good problem solvers indicated much more often than the poor problem solvers when they were understanding the moves in the example and when they were not understanding the example moves. Thus, it could be that the more able students coming into Chi et al.'s (1989) study explained examples to themselves more, monitored their understanding of examples more, and solved problems better, without any necessary causal connections between self-explanations, monitoring, and subsequent performance.

There are, however, experimental data that permit stronger claims about cause-and-effect relationships between self-explanations that increase understanding and problem solving. For example, in Mayer and Cook (1981), adults listened to an expository passage about radar. For all subjects, there were pauses after every 4 to 7 seconds. Some participants in the study were required to say back the content they just heard; other subjects were instructed to try to understand the passage during these pauses by reflecting on the passage.

After listening to the passage, the subjects were asked to use the information in the passage in a new way. Subjects in the reflective condition did better on this test than did repetition subjects. During recall of the original passage, much more of the explanative material in the passage was recalled by reflection condition participants than by repetition condition subjects, although there was no difference between the two conditions for recall of other types of material in the passage. In general, it seemed as if the reflective group focused on the explanations more than did the repetition group, with this difference in attention between the two conditions the potential cause of the difference in problem-solving performance between the two conditions.

Consistent with research on elaborative interrogation, Mayer (e.g., 1980) has also demonstrated that asking readers to answer inferential questions about text they are reading (i.e., questions requiring them to compare content in one part of a text with content in another part of a text, to relate content in a text to a familiar situation) results in more certain application of knowledge gained from text. That is, readers who answer such questions are more likely to be able to solve problems requiring application of the text content in situations not specifically covered by the text. During learning of the original texts, subjects who answered inferential questions were more likely to focus on and remember the explanatory parts of the texts than were subjects who read the text as they normally would in preparation for a test (see Mayer, 1985). In general, Mayer's research is strongly supportive of the importance of encouraging learners to process parts of text that provide explanations that can increase understanding of the relationships covered in text. Answering integrative questions is one approach to doing so; simply asking learners to attempt to understand text can also improve learners' abilities to apply knowledge acquired from text.

Bielaczyc, Pirolli, and Brown (1991) provided an especially compelling experiment confirming that self-explanations can positively affect use of material read to solve subsequently presented problems. The university students in the study read lessons concerned with LISP programming. In previous research, Pirolli and Bielaczyc (1989) had determined that the best problem solvers following such lessons tended to (1) determine the main idea presented in lessons, (2) determine the meaning of the LISP code presented in examples, and (3) connect ideas in text with moves in the examples. Thus, in their study, subjects in the experimental condition were taught to look for the main ideas in text and to focus on the meaning of examples and how the examples related to the text. That is, the trained subjects were taught to generate self-explanations about relations between examples and text. Such instruction occurred in a socially interactive, scaffolded (see Chapters 1 and 8) fashion that began with the subjects watching a videotape in which the self-explanation strategies were applied aloud by a student. The instruction that was provided was sensitive to difficulties experienced by particular students and attempted to remediate difficulties. The self-explanation instruction also included teaching subjects to use a series of self-questions aimed at increasing learner awareness of whether they understood the lessons and increasing ability at finding particular pieces of information in text and understanding ideas. The self-questioning structures taught to the experimental participants were reminiscent of Meichenbaum's self-instructional approach (Chapter 7). Control subjects in the study spent the same amount of time in interaction with the experimenter, with the focus of their instruction being memory and recall of the content of the lessons.

As expected, the self-explanation instruction increased self-explanations dramatically, with much less pretest to posttest increase in self-elaborations in the control condition: The instructed students increased their identification of main ideas in lessons from the beginning to the end of the study; they were also more likely at the end of training to provide meaning-oriented elaborations explaining the significance of some aspect of an example, including elaborations connecting text and examples. The instructed subjects also monitored more, indicating more often when they understood text versus when they did not understand it.

Most important, self-explanation training improved students' abilities to apply the programming skills they had learned in the lessons to new problems. This experimental effect (i.e., difference between experimental and control conditions favoring the experimental condition) was complemented by within-condition differences. Within both the control and the experimental conditions, the subjects who were most self-explanative following training performed best on the programming exercises. All of the outcomes in this study were consistent with the general position that increasing the likelihood that students explain relations between text and problems—and hence try to understand how the coverage in the text maps onto the coverage in the problems—increases effective problem solving.

There is consistent evidence that trying to understand material—by searching prior knowledge for relationships between the new content and prior knowledge—can improve memory of the material (especially when there is salient between-item interference, as when many related facts are presented) and application of the content to new problems. Unfortunately, there is also substantial evidence that students often do not try to understand relationships presented in new material, failing to relate what they already know to new content or content covered in text through worked-out examples (Mayer, 1985; Woloshyn et al., 1992). Thus, substantial efforts are being made to determine how to increase student understanding of text (e.g., through self-questioning, including why-questioning), with the goal of eventually teaching such strategies so that students internalize them and subsequently use the strategies in a self-regulated fashion—thus, the scaffolded teaching in Bielczyc et al. (1991). One impetus for continuing such research are striking correlations between generation of explanations as part of learning and subsequent memory and problem solving (see Webb's [1989] review of studies in which being the explainer in small groups learned more than other members of the group). Another is consistent experimental outcomes in which learners taught to generate and respond to inferential questions requiring explanatory responses understand and remember text better than control subjects not taught to generate and answer such questions (e.g., King, 1989, 1990, 1992). Another way of encouraging students to relate new information to prior knowledge is taken up in the next subsection.

Processing Advance Organizers

Before reviewing the theory and research pertaining to advance organizers, we offer a warning. The term advance organizer has a checkered history (Corkill, l992). Although Ausubel (e.g., 1960) was the original theorist describing advance organizers and what he considered to be their potential effects on learning from text, the concept has undergone considerable reformulation since then. One reason is that research inspired by Ausubel's work, but not necessarily consistent with Ausubel's conception of advance organizer, failed to produce consistently positive results. That is, when people processed "advance organizers" that researchers claimed were consistent with Ausubel's formulation, there was often little if any improvement in comprehension and recall of text relative to when readers were not presented advance organizers before they read. A second reason for the reformulation of the concept of advance organizer is that cognitive theory in general shifted since

Ausubel's theory was proposed. Researchers such as Mayer and Derry reformed the concept of advance organizer to be consistent with one of the most prominent of these new directions.

Ausubel's Original Formulation and the Research It Inspired One difficulty with Ausubel's conception of an advance organizer was that it was vague. It was clear that advanced organizers should be processed by readers before they encounter to-be-learned content (and hence the "advance" part of the concept). Exactly what was to be presented in advance of reading was something of a mystery, except that it was supposed to be at a "...higher level of abstraction, generality, and inclusiveness" (Ausubel, 1968, p. 148) than the to-be-learned content. Ausubel believed that advance organizers could be used to mediate learning of both familiar and unfamiliar content, with familiar material defined as related to prior knowledge possessed by a learner.

In a series of experiments with college students, Ausubel claimed to have validated the advance organizer concept: In each study, Ausubel reported that students who read advance organizers before reading passages containing new content understood and remembered more of what they read than students who read passages not accompanied by advance organizers. One difficulty in interpreting the original Ausebelian results, however, is that the actual advance organizers used in the study were not provided in the reports (see Corkill, 1992). Such operational vagueness on Ausubel's part resulted in different readers of Ausubel's theory and studies conceiving of advance organizers differently. The result was a flurry of studies involving different prereading manipulations, all of which were identified as advance organizers by the researchers doing the work.

The concept of advance organizer was variously conceived as instruction to students to generate passage or paragraph headings, instructions to readers to predict the content of upcoming text, pictures summarizing the relations depicted in text, semantic maps of upcoming text, prequestions, outlines, and summaries presented at the beginning of a passage (Corkill, 1992). Enthusiasm for the concept of advance organizers waned because, more often than not, the operations passed off as advanced organizers failed to produce improved understanding or memory of text content, with the flood of negative evidence transparent to the entire profession with the publication of a review in the prestigious *Review of Educational Research* of 32 studies purporting to test the hypothesis that advance organizers improve learning of text, with only 12 deemed to have improved comprehension (Barnes & Clawson, 1975). Other prominent psychologists, most notably Mayer (1977), were more critical than Barnes and Clawson about how various researchers had defined the concept of advance organizer but nonetheless agreed that "[a]dvance organizers, as presently constructed, do not facilitate learning" (Barnes & Clawson, 1975, p. 651; quoted by Mayer & Bromage, 1980, p. 210).

Mayer and Derry's Revised Definition of Advance Organizer and Research Related to It   Shortly after the Barnes and Clawson (1975) review, schema theory would emerge as the leading model of text comprehension (e.g., Anderson, Spiro, & Anderson, 1978; see Chapter 3, this book). When it did, the notion of advance organizer would be rethought, with a number of new studies inspired by this reformulation. Mayer (1979) proposed that a good advance organizer would activate prior knowledge (i.e., schemata) that would increase the likelihood that the learner would be able to understand new information by relating the new content to prior knowledge (i.e., the learner would assimilate the new content to prior knowledge). Derry's (1984) addition to this definition was that learning the new content would result in an accommodation (i.e., "correction") of the original schemata.

Mayer and Bromage (1980) offered a test of the potency of advance organizers consistent with the new definition. Undergraduate students read a seven-page text explaining a simple computer language, with the text explaining command statements in the language and the operations defined by the command statements with respect to particular locations in the computer (i.e., input stack, memory, program, output) and objects operated on (i.e., number, pointer). For example, "FIND" could define an operation on the input stack involving a number: Find the number on the next data card waiting at the input stack. Alternatively, "FIND" operated on memory of a number: Find the number in the memory space indicated in the READ statement. "MOVE" could operate on a number in the input stack: Move the data card through the input stack to the finished pile. "MOVE" also could operate on a pointer with respect to the program: "Go on to the next statement."

The advance organizer that Mayer and Bromage (1980) created for this text was a diagram and text re-

lating the computer locations to objects familiar to the readers:

> The "input window" was likened to a ticket window, "memory scoreboard" was described as an erasable scoreboard with eight spaces, the "program list" and "pointer arrow" were described as a shopping list, and the "output pad" was described as a pad of message paper. (Mayer & Bromage, 1980, p. 217)

The manipulation in the study was whether subjects were presented this information before reading the text (i.e., in the advance organizer condition) or after they read it. Mayer and Bromage (1980) predicted different effects on learning as a function of this manipulation. In particular, they believed that if the organizer was presented before a text was read, the passage would activate prior knowledge in the readers that would aid their comprehension of the passage. Because prior knowledge would not be activated *before* the text was read when the information was presented after the reading, the expectation was that readers would not relate the content of the text to the prior knowledge reminded by the organizer in the after-passage condition.

In general, there was strong support for the hypothesis that presentation of the information in advance of reading affected understanding of the text. For example, when advance organizer subjects recalled information from the text, they were more likely to report integrations of ideas across the text. In contrast, the after-reading subjects kept the ideas in the text more clearly separated from one another during recall. Advance organizer students also were less likely to report inappropriate inferences in their recall (i.e., draw incorrect conclusions from the reading). This study would be one of the earliest in a substantial number of studies during the 1980s that would produce data consistent with a schema-based conception of advance organizers.

In Derry (1984), undergraduates read a text conveying the Greek mythological conception of creation. Here is part of the text that the undergraduates attempted to learn in the study:

> Before Prometheus could get there, he [Epimetheus] gave away all the best gifts: strength and swiftness and courage and shrewd cunning, fur and feathers and wings and shells and the like—until no good was left to work with, no protective covering and no outstanding qualities. Too late, as always, he was sorry for he thought the elders might be displeased. He couldn't think of what to do, so he asked his brother's help. Prometheus, then, took over the task and

thought out a way to make the next creations superior. He took ore and fashioned them in a noble form. And then he went to Nirvana where the sun was within reach, and there he lit a torch and brought down fire. (Derry, 1984, p. 100)

Students either read the passage accompanied by an advance organizer contrasting four themes in the myth with Biblical themes, which were presumably consistent with the students' prior knowledge, or they read the passage without the benefit of the advance organizer. Here is part of the advance organizer used in the study:

> Man created in God's image . . . the similarities between the Greek myth and Old Testament version of creation are striking. After beasts are made, Man is created by a kind, all-knowing heavenly father who strives to make humans superior to all animals. This is not an easy task in the Greek myth because of how beasts were created. But the father of Man does two things to insure Man's superiority. Like in the Old Testament, he fashions them from an earthly substance, in his own image. But the Greek myth also relates another account of how man was raised in status: the story of fire. (Derry, 1984, pp. 99–100)

The posttest required memory of the text, with some items requiring verbatim recall. Other items, however, involved selecting among potential answers, with some answers implied by the text only and some consistent with a modification of the text to accommodate the information in the advance organizer. One such question was the following:

> Prometheus took over the task of creation because
> a. Zeus asked him to because he was the wisest god.
> b. Epimetheus couldn't think of what to do.
> c. The gods had failed in their experiments with metals and called on Prometheus to help.
> d. Prometheus wanted to play a trick on Zeus.
> e. Prometheus wanted men to stand upright and be superior to beasts.

Selection of choice "e" would signal an advance organizer–modified representation of the text content; selection of "b" could be made based on the text alone. Derry's (1984) most striking result was that e-type answers were more common for students reading the advance organizers than for controls reading the same mythological text without exposure to the advance organizer.

Corkill (1992) reviewed all of the evidence pertaining to advance organizers effects, focusing on the studies conducted in the 1980s. She concluded that advance organizers can facilitate learning from text in some circumstances: When . . . "(a) subjects will not make appropriate connections between prior knowledge and the to-be-learned material without assistance, (b) attend to the advance organizer, (c) have adequate time to study the advance organizer and the to-be learned material, and (d) are tested for recall after at least a brief delay. In general, advance organizers that are written out in paragraph form seem to be more potent than briefer organizers. Many of the studies met these conditions, with advance organizers in the successful studies often provided to students in well-written paragraphs.

Reviewing Advance Organizers Before a Test

Corkill, Glover, Bruning, and King (1988) hypothesized that reviewing advance organizers just before taking a test over material covered in a text that included advance organizers would increase recall of the text on the test. Such facilitation was observed when the test occurred sometime after the text had been read (1 day to 2 weeks later). In the language of cognitive psychologists, advance organizers are terrific retrieval cues, and if a text includes them, reading them over just before a test is a smart study strategy.

Summary Although our reading of the literature is that advance organizer effects often are not large, there does seem to be consistent effects on learning of text that is accompanied by advance organizers that are 50 or more words in length. Corkill (1992) concluded that positive effects of advance organizers have been produced in diverse content areas, when subjects have read texts varying in length, under a range of testing conditions, and with delays of up to 2 to 3 weeks after reading of text.

One constraint that we would add, however, is that there has been relatively little study of advance organizer effects below the high school level. Given that other adjunct aids (e.g., questions posed before reading of a text, postquestions) have more limited effects on children's learning than adult learning (see Chapter 14), it may be that the gains for adults produced by advance organizers would not be obtained in the elementary years.

Notetaking

Notetaking is common, at least for college students (Hartley & Marshall, 1974; Nye, Crooks, Powley, & Tripp, 1984; Palmatier & Bennett, 1974), the primary means for creating an external, long-term record of

Figure 10.1 Notetaking is an almost universal experience among students in higher education. Scientific analyses of notetaking have confirmed that both taking notes and reviewing them later increases learning of lecture content.

what went on in class. No one doubts that taking notes aids college-level learning, for information contained in notes is much more likely than information not noted in lecture to be recalled later on tests (Figure 10.1) (Aiken, Thomas, & Shennum, 1975; Bretzing & Kulhavy, 1981; Einstein, Morris, & Smith, 1985; Kierwa & Fletcher, 1984).

Educational psychologists have been particularly interested in determining when learning occurs during notetaking, however. DiVesta and Gray (1972) suggested that both the act of taking notes (i.e., encoding) and subsequent review of notes increase learning. A number of studies have examined the effects of encoding notes without the opportunity of review, with the clear majority of studies favoring the conclusion that taking notes per se has a positive effect on learning; a number of studies have also examined the value of review of notes taken, with the majority of those studies favoring the conclusion that review of notes also increases learning, even if the notes were produced by someone else (Hartley, 1983; Kiewra, 1985, 1989a, 1989b; Kiewra, DuBois, Christian, & McShane, 1988; Ladas 1980).

Summary

Many of the various mechanisms described in this section that can affect learning, memory, and cogni-

tion can be thought of as processes that can be used strategically: Deciding to process deeply is strategic in that attention is directed to more meaningful rather than less meaningful aspects of to-be-learned content. The strategic value of imaginally elaborating arbitrary associations has been recognized for centuries. Acting out a sequence of events in order to fix the sequence in memory is also a strategy, as is attempting to relate new information to prior knowledge. A student can think hard about an advance organizer or pass over it in favor of getting on with the reading, with the former action certainly more strategic than the latter action. Notetaking is a strategy for creating a record that can be reviewed later.

The mechanisms reviewed in this section can also be thought about with respect to nonstrategic knowledge, another of the four most important components of good information processing. Thus, deep processing is enabled by a knowledge base that connects with the meaningful elements of new content. For example, deep processing of "beast" connects to images in long-term memory of many hideous creatures as well as to verbal associations from *Beauty and the Beast* to scripture references to the devil as a beast. Mnemonic elaborations require a great deal of prior knowledge. For example, to use the keyword method to learn foreign vocabulary, it is necessary to know first-language vocabulary that can be used as keywords. In addition, the interactive relationship between the keyword and definition referents cannot be arbitrary—if it is not meaningful, the interaction will not be retrievable later when the learner is tested. Acting out actions requires prior knowledge of the actions. All methods of relating new information to prior knowledge depend on rich prior knowledge. Advance organizers work only if they activate prior knowledge, which can, in turn, be related to the new content in the to-be-learned passage.

In short, the mechanisms reviewed in this section can be thought about with respect to strategy and knowledge components in interaction, completely consistent with the good information processor model. Because each mechanism affects only particular learning situations, students must have substantial metacognitive knowledge about where and when each mechanism can be applied. Because each mechanism requires effort to carry out, and in some cases substantial efforts, such as when elementary students construct mental images, autonomous use of the mechanisms covered in this section is unlikely without strong motivation, including motivational beliefs about the potency of the mechanisms covered here in general and confidence that intelligent use of the mechanisms covered here can improve learning and performance. The work covered in this section is all sensible from the perspective of the model featured in this book, that good thinking reflects interactions between strategic mechanisms (i.e., procedures), knowledge, metacognition, and motivation.

MANAGING OPPORTUNITIES TO LEARN: THE EFFECTS OF SIMPLE PRACTICE, DISTRIBUTED PRACTICE, AND TESTS

When new content is presented, there are many different possible ways to structure opportunities to learn. The case made in this section is that practice opportunities can greatly enhance learning of new ideas, especially if the presentations and practice are repeated on several different occasions. We close the section establishing that people often organize their opportunities to learn in light of their expectations about tests, and hence, it is important that students know the accountability demands they face.

Simple Practice

If practice does not make perfect, it certainly improves learning and performance. For example, writing a word over and over does help in learning to spell the word (e.g., Thomas & Dieter, 1987). Practice has other effects beyond long-term retention, especially with respect to learning of procedures.

Do you remember when you first learned to start a car? You intentionally buckled your seatbelt, checked to see if the parking brake was still on, put the car in park or set the stick into the first position, depressed the clutch (if driving a standard), turned the key, and so forth. Could you think about anything else when you were first learning how to start a car? The likely answer is no, or if you were able to think about other things, it was a "mental hassle" to do so. Compare how you started a car then with how you start it now. Do you intentionally go through each step, conscious of completing each one before proceeding to the next? Can you carry on a conversation easily as you start a car? The answers to these two questions are undoubtedly no and yes, respectively.

A sequence of procedures that once required conscious processing (**controlled** processing) can now be done automatically (Schneider, Dumais, &

Shiffrin, 1984; Schneider & Shiffrin, 1977; Shiffrin & Schneider, 1977). **Automaticity** is one of the byproducts of practice. As procedures become automatic, less attention (i.e., short-term capacity) is required to carry them out, so it is possible to do other things simultaneously or at least do them more comfortably.

Much about practice and its effects on learning has been understood for a long time (see Annett, 1989, for a review): (1) At first there are rather large gains in proficiency due to practice; even though the amount of improvement is less dramatic as practice continues, there is still improvement that is detectable after many trials and years (e.g., Crossman, 1959). (2) What is at first carried out as a sequence of distinct steps eventually becomes "chunked," (Newell & Rosenbloom, 1981) so originally separate steps become a whole.

Much of the changes that occur with practice have been summarized in a model of procedural learning proposed by Anderson (1983; Singley & Anderson, 1989) as part of ACT* theory (see Chapter 3). When new procedures are first learned, they are encoded as declarative knowledge—knowledge that can be stated. Thus, many students learn in driver's education classes how to talk about and describe various aspects of driving. Indeed, they learn many if-then statements about driving, for example, "If the safety belt is fastened and if the car is in park, then it is all right to turn the key." Such information can be used to mediate driving at first, with the student driver recalling each step in the sequence of steps required to get the car to go. Driving is difficult at this point, requiring a great deal of conscious attention to recall the steps and carry them out. There are also a lot of errors, in part because people often experience difficulty holding in short-term memory all that must be considered in order to recall declarative knowledge and apply it in a particular situation (Anderson, 1983, Chapter 6, this book). With practice, there is what Anderson (1983) refers to as **knowledge compilation** (first introduced in this book in Chapter 2): Productions are created from the declarative statements specifying a process. Productions can be acquired only by performing the actions specified by the productions. How can one know that compilation has taken place?: The actions occur more rapidly. There is less verbalization as the cognitive action proceeds. The process occurs more as a whole, rather than as one step at a time.

Knowledge compilation includes two subprocesses according to Anderson (1983). **Composition** involves taking a sequence of productions and collapsing them into a single production. Thus, for a child only beginning to learn how to dial telephone numbers, dialing might be conceived in terms of the following productions:

If the goal is to dial a telephone number,
 and if digit 4 is the first digit of the number,
 then dial digit 4.
If the goal is to dial a telephone number,
 and if 4 has just been dialed,
 and if 9 is after the 4 in the number,
 then dial 9.
(Continuing until all 7 digits have been dialed; based on an example in Anderson, 1983, p. 235)

Once compiled, the production operates much more like the following:

If the goal is to dial a telephone number,
 and if the number is 495-1212,
 then dial 4 first and then 9 and then 5, etc.
(Again, based on an example provided by Anderson, 1983, p. 235–236)

A **macroproduction** has been formed, one that collapses into one operation what was initially an ordered sequence of operations. Eventually, if the LV phone number is dialed frequently enough, the entire sequence fires off automatically once it is initiated. **Proceduralization** is said to have taken place. This can be represented as the following:

If the goal is to dial a telephone number,
 dial 4-9-5-1-2-1-2.

Once proceduralization occurs, there is no need to retrieve the number from long-term memory or hold it in working memory. The fingers dial it almost without the person thinking about it.

The sure signs of composition and proceduralization are speeded performance, reduced verbalization (reflecting less need for conscious processing), and increased execution of a task as a whole rather than as parts. An important benefit of knowledge compilation is that much less conscious capacity must be expended to carry out a compiled procedure relative to a sequence of productions. Once compiled, it is still possible to represent a procedure declaratively and to execute the steps consciously—the point is that it is no longer necessary to do so to accomplish the action captured by the compilation. The criticality of such **automaticity** to skilled performance often will be apparent in the chapters that follow (e.g., automatic decoding of words permits freeing up of capacity required to comprehend text; automatic retrieval of simple math facts, such as 3 + 2 = 5, allows the mathematical problem solver to focus on higher-order aspects of problems).

Practice is often costly in terms of time and effort, and thus there has been substantial research on whether the benefits of practice can be obtained in the absence of practice. A number of studies have been conducted in which actual practice has been compared with **mental practice.** Some of these studies have also evaluated the efficacy of combining actual and mental practice. The effects of practice for acquiring a number of different skills have been evaluated, from being able to speak quickly (e.g., Mackay, 1981, 1982) to tying knots (Annett, 1988) to completing peg boards (Hird, Landers, Thomas, & Horan, 1991). Feltz, Landers, and Becker (1988) provided a meta-analysis of the studies conducted up until that point in time. As previous reviews (e.g., Richardson, 1967; Singer, 1972; Weinberg, 1982) had concluded, Feltz et al. (1988) reported that mental practice produced better performance than no practice. Mental and physical practice combined was better still. Actual practice alone produced better performance than either physical and mental practice combined or mental practice alone (Figure 10.2). Although it is anything but clear what mechanisms mediate mental practice effects (Annett, 1989), that mental practice can improve linkages of a sequence of behaviors makes obvious that the effects of practice probably involve cognitive components—that the compilation that occurs when knot-tying im-

Figure 10.2 This student is cramming for a test. Why do three hours of study the night before an examination not pay off as much as an hour of study for each of three nights before an examination?

proves with practice is not a compilation of actions alone but a compilation of representations that mediate execution of the motor task.

Practice with Feedback

In general, if learners are provided feedback about when they are right and wrong, learning is more rapid than if they are not provided feedback (e.g., Lhyle & Kulhavy, 1987). Although feedback can be construed in behavioral terms as reinforcement, the more popular interpretation of feedback by cognitive psychologists is that feedback provides information about what has been learned and what remains to be learned. The more that feedback stimulates the learner to reflect on their errant responses in comparison to correct alternatives, the more likely it is to be effective. (Recall the discussion earlier in this chapter about reflection on errors.) Feedback involving explanations to the learner about the reasonableness of the correct approach compared with the learner's answer is more effective than other types of feedback, especially if the feedback results in the learner constructing a new, more adequate understanding of the material being learned (Bangert-Drowns, Kulik, Kulik, & Morgan, 1991). Simply telling a person when they are right or wrong is feedback but much less effective in improving performance.

Although the literature on the timing of feedback is somewhat confusing, immediate feedback seems to promote learning more than delayed feedback. The effects of immediate feedback in studies conducted in actual classrooms has been especially consistent, however, and thus, we have no hesitations in recommending that immediately after giving a test—preferably during the same class period—provide feedback about what constitutes a correct answer and what constitutes an error (Kulik & Kulik, 1988).

Total Time Spent Learning or On Task

Both basic (e.g., Bugelski, 1962) and applied (e.g., Brophy, 1988) researchers in educational psychology have observed that the total amount of time spent learning correlates with the amount and degree of learning. The proportion of classroom time engaged in academic activities predicts classroom achievement level. Even so, an important lesson reiterated throughout this book is that time spent learning and using effective strategies is going to be more productive than time spent learning and practicing ineffective procedures. It is not enough to consider just total time, but what one does with the total time.

Spaced Learning and Distributed Practice

Regardless of what one does with time and how much total time is available for learning, learning and practice opportunities can be scheduled in different ways. The temporal distribution of learning and practice opportunities is an important determinant of achievement. Suppose that you have a test on this chapter 1 week from today. Will you do better on that test if you study for 3.5 hours in one sitting or in seven sittings of a half hour? Or perhaps will you do equally well since the total amount of study time is the same in both cases? There is little doubt that you would do better after seven short sittings than after one long sitting. This is a specific instance of the principle of **spaced learning,** sometimes referred to as **distributed practice,** with the latter term especially appropriate if what is being learned is some procedure: If a given amount of study or practice time is distributed over several sessions, learning is greater than if the same amount of study or practice is massed into one session.

Distributed practice effects have been known for all of the 20th century, originally identified by Ebbinghaus (e.g., 1913) in his classic research on memory. The phenomenon has been demonstrated many times and across diverse materials and tasks, from basic verbal learning to acquisition of text content to motor learning (see Crowder, 1976; Dempster, 1988b; Lee & Genovese, 1988). It has been documented with children as young as preschoolers (Toppino, Kasserman, & Mracek, 1991).

The benefits of spaced practice endure. Bahrick and Phelps (1987) reported a study in which the critical data were collected 8 years after material was originally studied. The participants learned Spanish vocabulary words, distributed over 30 days or studied on 1 day. Eight years later, the 30-day distributed practice participants remembered twice as many Spanish words as the massed-practice subjects.

Why does distributed practice work? Researchers are not sure, but there are two probable mechanisms that underlie the effect (Hintzman, 1974; Madigan, 1969; Rundus, 1971): (1) When learning is massed, attention probably wanes over a long period of study. Thus, the total amount of attention and active attempts at learning may be greater with distributed presentation. This interpretation was especially supported in an analytical study of repeated text reading by Krug, Davis, and Glover (1990; also Glover & Corkill, 1987), who observed more waning of attention during massed than distributed repeated reading, but who also observed that attention during massed repeated reading was maintained when subjects read paraphrased versions of the same text rather than the exact same text twice. When subjects read the paraphrased versions of the same passage, memory was as high as when reading the same version of the passage was distributed; in contrast, massed reading of the same version of a passage resulted in less memory for the passage than distributed repeated reading of the same passage. The only explanation consistent with all of the effects observed in this study was that attention wanes when there is immediate reading of the same version of a passage, but is maintained if a paraphrased version is read or reading of the identical version is delayed (i.e., distributed). It is differences in attention that account for differences in memory associated with distributed and massed processing of a text.

(2) An alternative explanation of the distributed practice effect is that with multiple presentations, there is probably greater **encoding variability** than during a massed presentation. That is, each new presentation of something to be learned probably produces a slightly different approach to study and learning. Thus, one massed presentation likely results in continuous use of one or a few approaches, with attention during learning deployed in a particular way. This results in encoding of particular information. In contrast, several short presentations may produce attention to different aspects of the to-be-learned content and different ways of studying the content on each presentation, with the result being a richer representation of the to-be-learn content (Figure 10.3).

Practice Tests, Including Self-Tests

Practice tests improve learning of content (e.g., Foos & Fisher, 1988), even in the absence of opportunity for additional study following the practice tests. One possibility is that taking a practice test forces retrieval and review of material during the test, which strengthens memory of the material and connections between different parts of the material (e.g., Bahrick

& Hall, 1991; Glover, 1989). When there is an opportunity for restudy following a practice test, the practice test can heighten student's awareness of whether there is a need to restudy (Pressley, Snyder, Levin, Murray, & Ghatala, 1987; Walczyk & Hall, 1989).

Learners can create practice tests by self-testing themselves as they attempt a learning task. To the extent self-testing has been studied, it is clear that this is not an obvious strategy to children in the early elementary years. In some situations, it increases in likelihood with increasing age during the grade-school years (i.e., during list learning; e.g., Dufresne & Kobasigawa, 1989). That adults often have no idea whether they are ready to take a test over text that they have processed (e.g., Epstein, Glenberg & Bradley,1984; Glenberg, & Epstein, 1987; Glenberg, Wilkinson, & Epstein, 1982; Glenberg, Sanocki, Epstein, & Morris, 1987; Maki & Berry, 1984; Maki, Foley, Kajer, Thompson, & Willert, 1990; Maki & Serra, 1992; Pressley, Snyder et al.,1987; Walczyk & Hall, 1989), however, makes clear that people do much less self-testing than they could do. We believe that an important problem for educational psychologists is to determine if it is possible to teach students to self-test themselves consistently as a means of deciding whether additional study is necessary. The full effects of self-testing and how to develop self-testing are poorly understood.

Test Expectancy Effects

Do you study material differently as a function of the type of test you expect on it? The possibility that students do has been evaluated extensively by educational psychologists, with the conclusion offered that examination demands play a large role in determining how and what teachers teach and students study and learn in a course (e.g., Fredericksen, 1984). What Lundeberg and Fox (1991) found when they reviewed all of the available experimental studies is that this is one problem that was not served well by laboratory studies.

There were a number of laboratory studies in which students made preparations for either a recall or a recognition test and then received either a recall or a recognition test, with four possibilities: study for recall, recall test; study for recall, recognition test; study for recognition, recognition test; study for recognition, recall test. In fact, in laboratory studies, studying for a recall test when a recall test is given makes a big difference (i.e., studying for recognition—which is generally easier than recall—does not prepare a student for a recall test). Studying for a recognition test when a recognition test is given makes little difference (i.e., preparing for a harder recall test has a carryover effect such that a learner is also ready for the easier recognition test). In contrast, in real classrooms, studying for a recall test when a recall test is given makes a difference, as does studying for a recognition test (e.g., multiple-choice) when a recognition test is given. Test expectancy can affect performance on classroom tests, presumably by shaping how and how much one prepares for a test. Thus, the outcomes in the experimental literature suggest that it is important for students to know the type of test that will be given.

European researchers in particular have studied correlations between testing demands in courses and students' approaches to studying. Marton and Säljö (1976) proposed that students could either use **deep** or **surface** approaches to study. Deep processing entails looking for underlying meaning and linkages. (Note the use of the term "deep" to mean extensive meaningful processing, by both these European educational psychologists and North American depth-of-processing theorists, whose perspectives were reviewed earlier in this chapter.) Entwisle, a Scottish researcher, and his colleagues have been particularly successful in demonstrating that the more a course demands memory during evaluations, the more surface processing is apparent (e g., Entwisle & Ramsden, 1983). If a teacher wants students to think deeply about material, evaluations should reward students for coming up with insights that go beyond the information given, that require more than simple recall of the material. Many thoughtful educational researchers and theorists have concluded that the most potent way to affect student study strategies is through test demands, with students willing to learn how to process in ways that permit them to meet the demands of the tests they will face (e.g., Crooks, 1988; Elton & Laurillard, 1979)

Summary

More than teacher talk is required in effective educational presentations. Practice plays an important role in increasing acquisition and understanding of new knowledge; distributing presentation of content and practice opportunities across a number of occasions is supported by a broad base of evidence. An old hypothesis about time and learning was that total time (e.g., Bugelski, 1962) spent studying content—sometimes referred to as total time on task by classroom researchers (e.g., Doyle, 1983)—was a good predictor of learning. The distributed practice effect makes clear that that is not the case, however. Moreover, throughout this book, the case is made that what matters is not the amount of time spent doing something but what one does with the time. For example, a person applying an efficient strategy may learn much more in much less time than another person who applies a counterproductive strategy. An individual spacing practice learns more than someone who masses it.

CONCLUDING COMMENTS

There is more of an old-fashioned look to the work reported in this chapter compared with most of the material in this book. In fact, most of the ideas covered in this chapter were being studied before the cognitive revolution was fully underway in the mid-1970s. That makes the principles that emerge from this work no less valuable.

Whenever a person is confronted with a learning task (e.g., learning the ideas in a history chapter about the civil war in preparation for a test), there are a number of ways to react. The lesson in this chapter is that how the learner reacts will make a huge difference in memory. Thus, attempting to process text content deeply by relating it to prior knowledge should increase memory; inventing memory tricks to remember particular pieces of content improves learning of those details (e.g., one eighth-grade student told us about an image of how, "Lincoln *dug* a hole to bury his opponent in," as a way to remember that Douglas debated Lincoln); and taking notes is helpful in promoting learning, as is reviewing them later. If a student decides to spread studying out over an extended period of time (e.g., a little bit of studying each night for a week), learning is more certain than if the student attempts to cram for an examination. (Indeed, the best explanation to give to junior and senior high school students, who often have blind faith in cramming for examinations, is to explain the distributed practice effect.) That Ebbinghaus understood this principle more than a century ago—and it has endured more

Table 10.1 Practices That Promote Academic Performance

Deeply processing to-be-learned material (i.e., thinking about its meaning)

Mnemonics, often based on some form of imagery

Enactment of to-be-remembered content

Learning by understanding, including by relating new information to prior knowledge, responding to why-questions (i.e., elaborative interrogation), and constructing self-explanations

Processing advance organizers, including as a review before a test

Notetaking

Simple practice

Practice with feedback

Distributed learning

Practice tests, including self-tests

Forming accurate test expectancies that guide study (i.e., understanding accountability demands and responding to them; e.g., deep or surface processing required to meet course expectations)

than a century of scrutiny by researchers—suggests the conclusion that the principle of distributed practice is one of the most certainly correct pieces of advisement offered in this book.

As an *aide memoire,* Table 10.1 summarizes practices discussed in this chapter that facilitate learning.

11

Teaching Practices and the Development of Intellect

Although many educational psychologists interested in learning and thinking did concentrate on problems that could be tested in the laboratory, such as much of the work reviewed in Chapter 10, others raised their sights and definitely focused on learning, thinking, and achievement in school and because of school. This chapter summarizes findings that should be studied carefully by all who are concerned with schooling. We claim here that intelligence is definitely increased by attendance in school. We also review the strong evidence that some types of schools are much more effective in fulfilling their educational mission than are others. The effects of many specific schooling practices on achievement are also reviewed, permitting by the end of the chapter the presentation of a list of variables that certainly promote academic achievement and those that may be pretenders, in that they are claimed by some to be potent but do not enjoy empirical support. For example, one possible pretender is the boxed study skills programs published commercially and now used in many classrooms. More positively, higher education definitely seems to make a difference in cognitive competence. Even individual courses, such as this one, seem to have a long-term effect on knowledge.

By the end of this chapter, it will be clear that long-term schooling can make an important difference in thinking ability and that some schooling practices and policies can make a substantial difference in achievement at school. It will also be apparent, however, that some educational interventions specifically advertised as improving thinking do not do so. Attending college and taking a course like this one, however, are not included in the list of interventions that are falsely advertised, for the section that concludes this chapter presents substantial evidence that college makes a difference in the development of intellect and taking a course in cognitive psychology results in enduring understandings about the nature and education of mind.

EFFECTS OF SCHOOLING ON IQ

Going to school is so commonplace in Western life at the end of the 20th century that it is often overlooked as a cognitive intervention. In general, when researchers have evaluated the hypothesis that schooling profoundly affects mental abilities, there has been support for the conclusion that school affects the way that people think.

Ceci (1991), a Cornell University psychologist, more than anyone else has increased our awareness of the effects of schooling on the fundamental mental abilities tapped by intelligence tests. Ceci reviewed about 200 studies (many of which were conducted within the United States) that studied the relationship between schooling and IQ. He found a variety of evidence favoring the hypothesis that psychometric intelligence is increased by school attendance, including the following:

- There are high correlations (often 0.80 and greater) between the number of years of schooling completed and IQ.
- Summer vacation results in a drop in psychometric intelligence in children.
- Intermittent school attendance is associated with lower IQ than regular school attendance.
- For various reasons, the onset of schooling is sometimes delayed. Such delay is associated with reduced IQ.
- Leaving school before the completion of high school is associated with low IQ.
- The availability of schooling in various countries, and for various groups within countries, has fluctuated throughout the 20th century. In general, the more available schooling was during an era for particular populations, the greater the IQ scores for the group in question during that period.

Although any one of the results that Ceci (1991) examined might be explained away as artifactual (e.g., the reason students in some studies were not in school is because of low IQ), there were many attempts across the various investigations to consider alternative explanations, with many alternative explanations discounted. On the whole, the case that Ceci made is compelling: Schooling affects intelligence as measured by IQ tests (Figure 11.1).

Ceci also reviewed data supporting the conclusion that specific cognitive processes, such as fundamental perceptual abilities, conceptual capacities, and memory, are affected by school attendance. The type of evidence supporting this conclusion included the following:

- The abilities to use depth-perception cues, to disambiguate figures in a maze or in a larger scene, and to perform tasks with a high visual-spatial component all correlate with school attendance.
- Schooling is associated with the propensity to use conceptual dimensions, such as taxonomic class, rather than perceptual ones, such as color, to think about in both in terms of taxonomic and perceptual features.

Figure 11.1 Continuous participation in school has pronounced effects on the development, including development of intelligence as traditionally defined by IQ tests.

- Schooling influences memory performance on a variety of memory tasks, including all of the ones covered in chapters of this book.

Some of the most compelling evidence that schooling can affect intelligence has been produced in studies assessing the effects of early childhood interventions on the development of economically disadvantaged children. For example, consider the Carolina Abecedarian Project (e.g., Burchinal, Lee, & Ramey, 1989; Ramey & Campbell, 1987; Wasik et al., 1990). (*Note:* Abecedarian in this context means someone who is learning the alphabet, although the Carolina Project encompasses much more than alphabet acquisition. The Abecedarian Project and its precessor were the inspirations for the extremely successful Infant Health and Development Program described in Chapter 6.)

Experimental and control participants in the experimental evaluation of the Abecedarian Project began their participation shortly after birth. The experimental and control subjects were provided nutritional support, family-counseling contacts, and medical care. Most critically, however, the experimental children attended a high-quality preschool environment, attending for the entire day throughout the year. Parent meetings were held as part of this preschool program to increase parental awareness of how to stimulate child development and use community opportunities. A total 4.5 years of the Abecedarian Program produced moderate-sized gains in IQ (i.e., 8- to 12-point advantages at age 4.5 for experimentals over controls; Ramey, 1992).

More recently, however, the Abecedarian study has been extended so that it is possible to compare the effects of 8 years of Abecedarian intervention (i.e., through the first 3 years of schooling) with 5 years of Abecedarian treatment during the preschool years, 3 years of Abecedarian treatment during the elementary years, and no Abecedarian intervention. For children receiving Abecedarian treatment during the years of public schooling, efforts were made to maximize the likelihood of appropriate, stimulating educational experiences at school. Master teachers also visited with the students' parents and coached them about how they could stimulate their children's cognitive development. These master teachers were aware of the specific content being covered in school and provided ". . . literally thousands of specific activities and guides that parents could use in a gamelike manner to give their children extra practice and support in activities that

were directly related to classroom performance" (Ramey, 1992, p. 247).

The outcomes in this experiment were clear at age 8: eight years of Abecedarian treatment were superior to either 5 years of preschool Abecedarian intervention or 3 years of elementary-level Abecedarian treatment. In general, the more total Abecedarian treatment received, the lower the school failure rate and the higher the IQ at age 12 (Ramey, 1992). At-risk children's intelligence and academic achievement can be improved through intensive, long-term, academically oriented intervention. The Abecedarian studies are powerful evidence consistent with Ceci's general conclusion that schooling can affect intellectual development as defined by IQ measures.

SCHOOLS THAT ESPECIALLY PROMOTE INTELLECTUAL COMPETENCE

Do all Western schools have the same effects on intellectual competence? There have been many studies (see Firestone, 1991, for a review) in the past two decades documenting qualitative differences in schooling environments that produce differences in IQ and other achievement measures. One wing of this group is especially visible, known as the "effective schools movement" (e.g., Edmonds, 1979). Although a number of methods have been employed by those interested in effective schools, the effective schools movement has been especially interested in "outlier" schools, ones in which achievement is especially high relative to what might be expected in the school based on characteristics of its students, such as socioeconomic status (Firestone, 1991). Intensive case studies of such schools have been conducted.

One famous list of characteristics of effective schools was provided by Edmonds (1979). High achievement during the elementary years is obtained by inner-city youth, ones who are at risk of school failure because of socioeconomic disadvantage, when they attend schools having the following features:

- Strong administrative leadership.
- High expectations for all children.
- A safe, orderly but not rigid environment.
- Top priority given to student acquisition of basic school skills.
- Willingness to divert resources from other tasks to development of basic school skills.

- Frequent monitoring of pupil progress (based on Firestone, 1991, p. 15)

A similar list of characteristics emerges from analyses of effective secondary schools. Collapsing across analyses, the following are features of high schools that work:

- A shared sense of academic purpose by faculty, parents, and community.
- Recognition of student accomplishments.
- Recognition of good teaching.
- High involvement by parents and community in school affairs.
- A sense of caring and community (i.e., students care about school affairs, and educators are committed to student welfare).
- Academic emphasis (and coursework) for all students.
- Homework.
- High expectations that students can learn.
- Most class time is on-task (i.e., there is a great deal of instruction).
- School environment is orderly.
- Discipline is fair-minded.
- There is strong leadership that actively recognizes problems in the school and seeks to solve them.
- Teachers and administrators believe they are in control of the school and teaching.
- Staff collegiality. (Based on Newmann, 1991b, p. 58)

Although many criticisms can be levied against the studies of effective schools that have been done, it is difficult not to be impressed by two outcomes (Bliss, 1991; Firestone, 1991): (1) The consistency in results across studies is striking, with Edmonds's conclusions generally supported in many subsequent analyses (e.g., Bryk & Thum, 1989; Good & Brophy, 1986; Lezotte, 1986; Mortimore, 1991; Rutter, 1983; Stedman, 1988). (2) Many schools across the United States have paid attention to this research literature, with some estimates as high as 41% of U.S. schools influenced to some degree by the movement (General Accounting Office, 1989).

Others concerned with quality in education focused on what went on in particular classrooms. Rosenshine's (1979) analyses (see Chapter 8) were especially influential. Rosenshine identified classroom variables linked to high achievement: academic focus, teacher-directedness, orderly presentations of material, clear goals, sufficient time for instruction, high percentage of time devoted to academic content, monitoring of student performances, questioning with responding by students, immediate feedback, conviviality and warmth, democracy, and cooperation.

If Rosenshine's list is compared with the one generated by Edmonds (1979) and Newmann (1991b), it is clear that the conclusions are complementary. For example, all three analyses specified that achievement was greatest in environments with a high academic focus and clear academic leadership by educators (i.e., the principal at the school level and the teacher in the classroom).

Role of Academic Engagement in Fostering Academic Achievement

How can this literature be tied to Ceci's (1991) conclusion that the amount of schooling influences cognitive competency? Newmann (1991b) has provided a linking framework (see also Chapter 9): Newmann claims that effective schools are ones that permit and foster a high degree of pupil **engagement** in learning. Engaged students are invested in and committed to learning, understanding, and mastering what is presented in school. Engaged students concentrate on their work, are enthusiastic about it, and are deeply interested in academic content. They care about whether they are doing well in school.

Good schools present tasks that seem authentic to the students, lead them to inquire about important academic issues, require integration of knowledge, and produce outcomes that mean something besides the grade that results. Effective schools present their students with tasks that they "own" in part because they are involved in deciding what is done in school and how it is evaluated. There is flexibility in the pace and methods of teaching and learning, many opportunities for students to ask questions that are important to them, frequent occasions to pursue issues that students see as important, and many demands that students invent their own work—that is, create new understandings rather than simply parrot back what the teacher has said. Engagement is fostered by academic environments that encourage risk taking—there is no disrespect for trying and failing, but rather great respect for making an effort and support for making new attempts following a failure. Engagement is fostered by environments that respect student dignity and project a message that young people are important. Not least of all, engaging environments are fun.

Schooling as a Means of Overcoming Academic and Economic Disadvantages

A persistent hypothesis is that schooling can be used to elevate those who are now disadvantaged academically and economically. No one has done the experiment that needs to be done to evaluate this hypothesis. What is required is an experiment in which one group of at-risk students is provided high-quality educational input for their entire schooling career. The educational and economic outcomes for this group would be compared with outcomes obtained by students who are similar demographically and intellectually at the outset of the study but who receive instruction typically offered to the disadvantaged in the United States (i.e., instruction that is often poor by any standard).

Shorter-term interventions have been studied, however, with positive results. For example, the effects of Head Start and related preschool and extended-kindergarten interventions have been evaluated extensively. Intellectual gains (e.g., improvements in IQ) are obtained in the short term (e.g., Entwisle, Alexander, Cadigan, & Pallas, 1987). That environmental support beyond the preschool years is required, however, is evident in that Head Start kids are difficult to discriminate from non–Head Start students on purely intellectual measures (e.g., IQ) by grade 3. Nonetheless, there are clear, long-term, positive effects of early childhood interventions with disadvantaged populations. Disadvantaged children receiving high-quality preschool instruction subsequently are less likely to be referred into special education, fail a grade, or be charged with delinquency (Figure 11.2) (Consortium for Longitudinal Studies, 1983; Lazar, Darlington, et al., 1982). Although short-term interventions do not provide as striking long-term advantages as their developers anticipated (i.e., they had hoped the boost on measures such as IQ would be permanent), there are long-term academic and social advantages associated with experiencing high-quality preschool environments.

Longer-term educational interventions for at-risk students are being tested as this book is being written, with one of the best known of these developed by Slavin and colleagues at Johns Hopkins and dubbed, "Success for All" (e.g., Slavin, Madden, Karweit, Dolan, et al., 1991; Slavin, Madden, Karweit, Livermon, & Dolan, 1990). The goal of this program is to make certain that all at-risk students entering school arrive at grade-3 performing at grade level in basic skills, especially reading. Special enriched curricula are provided beginning in preschool and kindergarten. Those grade-1 students experiencing the greatest difficulties with reading receive one-on-one tutoring. Most students require no more than a semester of such tutoring to get them on track, although such tutoring could continue for years if necessary. Family support services are provided as well, especially ones targeted at solving problems that might interfere with academic progress. There is substantial assessment of students to make certain that problems are not overlooked and their treatment delayed. The data generated to date suggest positive effects of this approach, with substantial benefits especially apparent for extremely at-risk students who have received 3 years of Success for All (Madden, Slavin, Karweit, Dolan, & Wasik, 1993).

In short, to the extent that supplementary schooling has been attempted as an intervention, it works. A problem is that the enrichment typically ends after only a few years, with multiple indicators that longer-term support is necessary for lasting effects. Our view is that research on the effects of long-term enrichment should be a high priority.

SCHOOL AND AFTER-SCHOOL PRACTICES AFFECTING ACADEMIC GROWTH

Much of this book is about school interventions that can improve academic achievement. In a sense, this section is devoted to some practices that fall between the conceptual cracks in the commentary presented in other chapters, but practices that are nonetheless important to consider as part of school enrichment. Some occur daily in the classroom; others more affect the quality of intellectual life "after school."

Schooling Practices That Have Implications for Student Achievement

We proceed in this section from practices that individual teachers can control to ones that are controlled more at the level of the school or the district.

Teacher's Questioning of Students About Academic Content   At several points in this book, we discuss the effects of questioning on learning. For example, in Chapter 14, we consider whether adjunct questions in text improve learning—they do, although the effects are often not large. The elabora-

Figure 11.2 Although proponents of sex-segregated education often claim large advantages for single-sex classrooms and schools, the effects documented to date are modest, although consistently in favor of gender segregation, at least during high school.

tive interrogation strategy considered in Chapters 4 and 10 can be applied when learning a large number of facts.

One type of questioning not considered in detail at other points in this book, however, is teacher questioning. Many teachers feel compelled to ask questions all day. Who does not recall social studies, science, and literature classes that involved little more than one teacher question after another? (Recall from Chapter 8 that the most common discourse structure in school involves the teacher initiating a question, students attempting to respond, followed by a teacher evaluation—IRE cycles [Mehan, 1979].) Do the thousands of questions that students experience in school over their career make a difference in learning?

The answer is that they do. Two types of questions must be differentiated to appreciate fully the effects of classroom questioning on student learning. There are **higher-order questions**— ones requiring manipulation of information and reflection—and **lower-order questions**—ones requiring simple recall of information. One possibility supported in some data analyses (e.g., Brophy & Evertson, 1976) is that high proportions of higher-order questions are especially important in high-ability classes and that

predominantly lower-order questioning may lead to higher gains in achievement with weaker classes. Presumably, lower-order questions increase the likelihood that weaker classes will at least learn the facts; higher-order questions stimulate those students who acquire the facts with less effort to go beyond the information given—to think through it and relate the new content to prior knowledge, something that does not occur automatically (as demonstrated by the low level of control subject performances in the elaborative interrogation studies reviewed in Chapters 4 and 10). What about "typical" classrooms that have a mix of abilities? Redfield and Rousseau (1981) analyzed all available studies of higher-order and lower-order questioning effects in classrooms. In general, higher-order questioning was more potent in the studies reviewed by Redfield and Rousseau.

One variable that has been demonstrated to make a difference in questioning effects on achievement is whether teachers give students a chance to respond after they pose a question. When teachers wait for students to respond (i.e., provide **wait time**), they give the students a chance to think before responding, with such thinking time reliably associated with increases in achievement (e.g., in math and science classes; Tobin, 1987).

Encouraging Student Questions   Teachers can answer questions as well as ask them, and when they do, they often assist students to understand new material (e.g., Fishbein, Eckart, Lauver, Van Leeuwen, & Langmeyer, 1990; Ross & Balzer, 1975; Ross & Killey, 1977). The catch is that some of the students most in need of assistance often do not seek it out, wanting to be independent or believing that their efforts to seek help may be perceived as reflecting low ability (Newman, 1990; Newman & Goldin, 1990; van der Meij, 1988). For this reason, many educators encourage students to ask questions when they are not sure and send many messages in their classrooms that asking questions is not a sign of low ability but something a smart person does whenever they are in need of assistance.

A particularly important hypothesis is the possibility that teaching children how to ask questions about academic content can affect their processing of it. For example, Courage (1989) demonstrated that 4-, 5-, and 7-year-old students can be taught how to ask for categorical information about an object. Lyman (1992) is teaching elementary-level students to ask questions about text, tapping factual information, cause-and-effect relationships, temporal sequences, similarities and differences between ideas covered in the text, induction of generalizations from examples, and deduction of examples from generalizations. Just how such instruction affects academic processing remains to be documented, however. Evaluations of the effects of interventions that encourage student questions should be a high priority, given the popularity in the 1990s of all types of interventions that are aimed at increasing active student discussion (see Chapter 8 and Chapters 12 through 15).

Teacher Expectancies   If a teacher expects a child to do well in school, will that child excel academically? Will the teacher's prophecy be fulfilled—perhaps because the teacher acts differently toward the child than would occur in the absence of a belief in the child's ability? In one of the most famous studies in the educational psychology literature, Harvard psychologist Rosenthal and his colleague Jacobson (1968) reported data suggesting that teacher expectancies about student achievement were a powerful determinant of actual achievement.

Early in the school year, all children in one school were administered a standardized test that was represented as predictive of children who were about to blossom—that is, those who would be ex-

ceptionally likely to exhibit substantial intellectual growth in the next year. When the data from the test were reported to the teachers, 20 percent of the children in each classroom were identified as likely to make larger than typical gains during the current school year. This was a ruse, however, for these children had been selected at random, so that in reality there was no objective basis for believing these children would gain any more or less during the upcoming year than other children in the school. Nonetheless, when the children were tested at the end of the school year, the children who had been identified as likely to make differentially large gains in fact made larger gains during the year than the sample of students as a whole.

Similar to any visible piece of social science, Rosenthal and Jacobson (1968) inspired follow-up research. More often than not, other scientists did not obtain significant teacher-expectancy effects, and sometimes those expected to do poorly did well and those expected to do well did poorly (Goldenberg, 1992). Analyzing across studies, Rosenthal (1985) argued that Pygmalion effects were real, although they tended to be small. Our review of this literature led us to conclude that, at most, teacher beliefs alone have only a small effect on student achievement.

Readers will recall, however, that expectancies about performance were cited earlier in this chapter as potentially important in affecting academic success: Effective schools are characterized by faculty and administration who have high expectations about their students' abilities and potential for achievement. Although there are many doubts about whether expectancies alone can affect achievement, there are far fewer doubts (although again the evidence is not entirely unambiguous on this point; see Hall & Merkel, 1985, for a review) that teachers do behave differently as a function of their expectancies about students based on previous outcomes achieved by those students. That is, even if teachers do not react differently to children based on test reports about the children's abilities, they do react differently when they see evidence of high and low ability in their daily interactions with students.

Brophy and Good (1970) studied the teacher-student interactions in four grade-1 classrooms intensively. They observed that classroom life was different for higher-ability and lower-ability students. Based on their own work and other research on teacher-student interactions in classrooms, Brophy and Good (1974) compiled a list of ways that the classroom environments of low-ability and high-ability students differ, with this list elaborated by Brophy (1985):

- Teachers are less likely to wait for a low-ability child to respond to questions than for a high-ability child.
- When low-ability students hesitate to answer a question, teachers are more likely to give them an answer or call on another child to respond.
- Reinforcements are less likely to be contingent on correct responding for low-ability students compared with high-ability students.
- Low-ability students are criticized more often (e.g., in response to their failures).
- Low-ability students receive less praise than high-ability students.
- When low-ability students respond publicly, they are less likely to receive feedback than are high-ability students.
- Teachers generally pay less attention to low-ability students and interact with them less.
- Teachers call on low-ability students less often than on high-ability students.
- Teachers seat low-ability students further from the teacher than they seat high-ability students.
- Teachers interact with low-ability students more privately than publicly. They structure the activities of low-ability students more and control the behaviors of low-ability students more than they control the behavior of high-ability students.
- Teachers demand less from low-ability students.
- In matters of grading, low-ability students are less likely than high-ability students to receive the benefit of the doubt on close calls.
- Teachers are less friendly in their interactions with low-ability students.
- The questions of low-ability students receive briefer responses that are not as informative as the responses to questions of high-ability students.
- Low-ability students are less likely to receive effective but time-consuming instruction than are high-ability students. (List based on Brophy, 1985, pp. 309–310)

Brophy and Good (1970, 1974; Brophy, 1985) believe that such gross differential treatment affects student perceptions of themselves and their own abilities. The low-ability students come to perceive clearly that they are less likely to succeed than high-ability students—that is, they form a much more negative academic self-concept, which, in turn, reduces their motivation for school and learning and their levels of aspiration.

Even if teacher beliefs alone are not enough to create a Pygmalion from a weak student—and the evidence is mixed that such beliefs alone can even exert a weakly positive effect on student achievement—teacher beliefs and the behaviors fueled by those beliefs can go far in maintaining or even increasing achievement differences between students who are objectively strong and weak academically or objectively well-behaved and ill-behaved. Over the decades, social psychologists have established many times that people like to interact with and behave more favorably toward people that are like them. Capable, well-behaved students, with their commitments to things academic, are probably perceived more like comrades in intellect and behavior by teachers than are weaker students. Such cameraderie can serve strong, well-behaved students well, while undermining the education of weaker students. Given the perspective advanced throughout this book that all students are capable of learning how to learn and capable of learning a great deal when teachers construct a classroom environment that fosters learning, the behaviors of teachers toward weaker students—behaviors that certainly are not consistent with the models of good teaching featured in this book—are disturbing.

Volunteers in the Classroom There has been increasing emphasis on strengthening of school-community relationships. One way of doing so is to welcome community adults into schools as volunteers, with volunteer tutoring one of the most common contributions that citizens can make to schools. Such tutoring definitely increases the achievement of tutees (Michael, 1990, Chapter 4). College students often volunteer in schools, with their efforts clearly promoting the achievement of students they tutor (Reisner, Petry, & Armitage, 1989). Many teacher education reform efforts include requiring that potential teachers participate in tutoring programs throughout their 4 years of teacher training. In addition to providing hands-on experience in real schools to prospective teachers, such requirements provide an important resource to U.S. schools. The clear benefits of tutoring provided by volunteers should stimulate additional efforts to increase the use of volunteers in school, and we hope that educational psychologists will be there to study the volunteer tutoring process and experiment with ways to increase the efficacy of volunteer tutors.

Peer Tutoring   Not only can adult volunteers tutor, but also students can tutor other students. A consistent finding in the literature, going back to Allen's work in the 1970s (Allen, 1976), is that both the student tutor and tutee benefit from such interactions. If anything, long-term memory of course material is probably improved more by being a tutor than a tutee (Semb, Ellis, & Araujo, 1993), so peer tutoring is an even more positive educational opportunity for the tutor than the tutee. Although an intervention with a long history, there continue to be attempts to identify exceptionally powerful peer tutoring arrangements.

For example, Fantuzzo, Riggio, Connelly, and Dimeff (1989) generated the efficacy of a complex peer tutoring intervention relative to some simpler models. The complex approach was more potent than alternative approaches involving only some of the components of the complex approach. Fantuzzo et al. (1989) dubbed their best approach to peer tutoring as **reciprocal peer tutoring.** In their study, students in a university-level psychology course were paired with one another for most of the term. There were examinations in the course over each unit of material. Before each examination, each partner constructed 10 multiple-choice questions on the material in the unit. The partners then met and administered the examinations to one another, followed by a discussion in which the partner writing the examination question explained to the partner taking the examination the answer for each item answered incorrectly. It is easy to understand why this treatment was so effective. First, generating questions over academic content, such as was required by constructing the practice test for the partner, increases learning (Rosenshine & Trapman, 1992). So does taking practice tests (e.g., Glover, 1989; Chapter 10, this book), as does explaining academic content to another person (Webb, 1989).

Greenwood, Delquadri, and Hall (1989) offered an especially impressive analysis of peer tutoring, comparing a group of low–socioeconomic status students who had been in classrooms emphasizing peer tutoring all through grades 1 to 4 with an otherwise comparable group of children in more conventional classrooms. When assessed at the end of fourth grade, the children experiencing the peer tu-

toring–emphasis curriculum achieved at higher levels than the control children in reading, math, and language arts. The peer-tutored children were also better behaved in class and spent a higher proportion of class time engaged in academic activities. When the striking positive effects of this study and others are considered, it is clear that peer tutoring is an attractive form of instruction and one that is accepted and considered fair by students themselves (Thorkildsen, 1993). Because it is completely consistent with cooperative instruction models (see Chapter 5), we expect that peer tutoring will be common in American classrooms in the decade ahead.

Ability Grouping and Tracking by Ability Level
Ability tracking for instruction has been common in schools. It begins with three different groups for reading in grade 1 (good readers, average readers, weaker readers) and continues through the end of high school, with advanced placement courses for the best students and vocational education options for students who have not fared well academically in junior high school and the early years of high school. Special education has sometimes been offered as an extreme form of tracking, with "special" school, "special" classroom, and "resource room" placements given to students designated as learning-disabled or mildly retarded.

In the last two decades, the practice of ability grouping has come under attack. With respect to classified students, the law (in particular, **U.S. Public Law 94-142**) now requires that special education students be placed in minimally restrictive environments (i.e., environments as much as possible like normal schooling), which translates into a regular classroom placement whenever possible, with many efforts now underway to identify ways to maximize the learning of special education students in regular classrooms (for many examples, see Schloss, 1992).

Research bears out the wisdom of P.L. 94-142. Forming classrooms that are homogeneous with respect to student ability does not promote academic achievement (e.g., Oakes, 1987; Slavin, 1987a, 1990a). Putting a child in the middle or slower group guarantees different instruction relative to placement in the high group: He or she reads different materials; the pace is slower; and groupmates are less capable (Juel, 1990). In particular, segregation of students with special needs has exceptionally great potential for undermining their achievement: When special education students are isolated for instruction, the instruction often is not good. Even assignment to resource rooms for part of a day, which is a much less extreme form of special placement than assignment to a separate school or a special classroom for the entire day, has a bad impact on the quality of instruction offered to students.

Allington, McGill-Franzen, Meyers, and Gelzheiser, all of the State University of New York at Albany, in particular, have documented that when students receive resource room instruction, they actually receive less total instruction (e.g., time that might have been used for instruction is eaten up shuttling from the regular classroom to the resource room). In addition, the instruction offered to the students in the resource room is not well matched to the accountability demands that special education students face. Rather than addressing the content and skills required of these students during regular instruction, lower-level instruction is offered. The time spent in the resource room, in fact, reduces the amount of instruction these students receive with respect to the content and skills they are expected to be acquiring in the regular classroom. Indeed, rather than making these students' lives better, resource room instruction can make special education students' lives worse, fragmenting their day and their instruction and providing less opportunity for them to learn the material on which they are evaluated (graded) than they would have had in the absence of the resource room instruction.

Allington and McGill-Franzen's indictment of pulling children out of their regular classroom extends beyond special education placement: For example, they argue that special instruction offered to poor children through federally funded Chapter 1 services often has the same effect of fragmenting the day and reducing the amount of instruction matched to the accountability demands the students face (Allington, 1983, 1991a, 1991b; Allington & McGill-Franzen, 1989, 1991; McGill-Franzen, 1987; Meyers, Gelzheiser, Yelich, & Gallagher, 1990). O'Sullivan, Ysseldyke, Christenson, and Thurlow (1990) have generated independent evidence supportive of the main conclusions of the Albany group.

Oakes (1985) examined tracking in 25 high schools across the United States (schools originally studied by Goodlad, 1984), ones representing the full range of diversity in students and schools that was present in the United States in the late 1970s and early 1980s. All of these high schools included some form of tracking. Oakes studied these classrooms to determine if the opportunities to acquire knowledge differed as a function of how one was tracked and if the process of education was different for students in higher and lower tracks. (This research is especially interesting from the perspective of equity issues in that the poor and minorities more often end up in the lower tracks in high schools, including the ones studied by Oakes.)

There was considerable evidence that the students in the high tracks in Oakes' (1985) study were exposed to much more important content (i.e., rigorous academic content) than the students in the lower tracks (i.e., who received heavy doses of "life skills")—that schools offered the high-track students much greater opportunity to develop worthwhile knowledge.

Oakes (1985) also demonstrated that less of the total class time in lower-track classes is devoted to instruction than in higher-track classes: Students in low-track classes spend more time fooling around. They are assigned much less homework. In addition, there were multiple indications that the quality of school life was worse for low-ability compared with high-ability students: Teachers were less enthused about teaching them. Teacher communications were more likely to be understood by high-ability than lower-ability students. Grades were more clearly tied to effort and achievement for higher-ability students than lower-ability students. The high-track classes seemed better planned and organized than the lower-track classes. Teachers were more respectful of higher-track students; they were more punitive of lower-track students. Teachers were more open to questions from higher-track than lower-track students. Even peer relations were warmer and friendlier for higher-track students than lower-track students, who seemed to take their frustrations out on each other.

Although there has been progress with respect to integration of special education students into regular classroom settings—that is, in the 1990s, many special needs students are "mainstreamed"—progress in "untracking" students not classified as needing special education services (i.e., the types of lower-ability students studied by Oakes) has been slower. At the time of this writing, however, Wheelock's (1992) book, *Cross the Tracks: How "Untracking" Can Save America's Schools,* was receiving a great deal of attention, and we expect that there will be substantial efforts in the next decade to reduce ability grouping in schools.

Educational psychologists need to study carefully the impact of such efforts, for it is not entirely clear that untracking will, in fact, improve schooling for disadvantaged students. For example, mainstreaming of special education students might be used as an excuse for not providing special services for them. If so, special students' needs might be met even less well when they are mainstreamed than when they receive pullout instruction—even though pullout instruction has the disadvantages we reviewed earlier. Alternatively, mixing weaker and stronger students in high schools might result in a watering down of content for stronger students. Another possibility is that there will be additional frustration for weaker students, for example, if high school teachers were to teach to the top of mixed-ability classes. Moreover, when weaker students are placed in classes with stronger students, their weaknesses are ever more apparent to them, with the possibility that daily negative comparisons with students who are doing better in school will undermine achievement efforts (e.g., Renick & Harter, 1989; Reuman, 1989). There are no guarantees with untracking, with a clear need for objective assessment of the costs and benefits it affords.

Sex-Segregated Education   Although the evidence is mixed (Marsh, 1989a, 1989b), there is probably a small positive effect (i.e., 0.1 to 0.2 SD) of sex segregation on academic achievement at least at the secondary level (Figure 11.3) (Lee & Bryk, 1986, 1989).

Class Size   Virtually all reviewers of the literature on class size conclude that smaller classes boost achievement, particularly for weaker students (e.g., Cooper, 1989a; Educational Research Service, 1978; Glass & Smith, 1979; Hedges & Stock, 1983; Slavin, 1984). The debate is about how small classes must be before there are worthwhile gains in achievement, with some reviewers arguing that reducing classes to 15 pupils would make a difference (Glass & Smith, 1979) and others believing that gains are not large until class size is reduced to numbers more typical of small-group tutoring than classroom instruction (e.g., three students per teacher, Slavin, 1984; one-to-one tutoring, Slavin, 1989).

This is a problem now being attacked in true experimental studies, which allow clearer cause-and-effect conclusions than permitted by earlier research efforts on class size, which were nonmanipulative. For example, in 76 schools in Tennessee, Finn and Achilles (1990) assigned kindergarten students either to small classes (i.e., 13 to 17 students) or larger

Figure 11.3 Whether television increases or decreases academic achievement depends largely on what is viewed. Why might heavy doses of entertainment television impact bright children more negatively than other students?

classes (i.e., 22 to 25), with the presence or absence of an aid systematically manipulated in the larger classes. These class sizes and class assignments were held intact through grade 1. (Although some adjustments had to be made to deal with the realities of schools, the manipulation was reasonably clean, especially given the scope of the study.) The evidence in favor of the smaller classes was clear, with definitely greater achievement in mathematics and reading by the smaller classes at the end of grade 1. The advantages of the smaller class were especially striking for minority students. Although the presence of an aid helped, especially in grade 1, the smaller class students generally outperformed the students in larger classes taught by a teacher and aid. The definitiveness of outcome in this study when compared with the previous correlational efforts illustrates well the power of true experiments for illuminating important issues regarding schooling—Finn and Achilles (1990) demonstrated that large-scale experimentation is possible with respect to an important question pertaining to educational policy.

Retention   Should children be retained in a grade if their academic or social progress is not at the level of other children? The answer seems to be no, with retained children rarely measuring up academically to same-grade students several years after the retention experience (Holmes & Matthews, 1984), and when they do measure up, there is no advantage (i.e., retained and nonretained students perform comparably several years after the retention experience; e.g., Peterson, DeGracie, & Ayabe, 1987). More positively, perhaps, when all of the data are examined, stereotypical perceptions that retained children's self-esteem is reduced and their attitudes toward school negatively affected by the retention experience seem overblown, with only small negative effects of retention on self-esteem and attitudes toward school (Holmes & Matthews, 1984). In some cases, the motivations and attitudes of retained children seem to improve. For example, Plummer and Graziano (1987) studied more than 200 children (grades 2 and 5) retained in one Georgia county. They did not find across-the-board social rejection of such children. In fact, the self-esteem of retained children was higher than the self-esteem of nonretained children.

Even so, some analysts conclude that retained children do fine, and other observers catastrophize about the effects of retention on children. This is an area in which a great deal more research is required before it is reasonable to draw firm conclusions, especially because teachers endorse retention as an acceptable, helpful educational practice, especially during the primary years (e.g., Smith & Shepard, 1988; Tomchin & Impara, 1992). One problem that has received special attention has been kindergarten retention, with it not uncommon for one or two children in a kindergarten class to be retained, with younger children and boys more likely to be held back than other kindergarten students (e.g., Bryant, Clifford, & Peisner, 1991; Mantzicopoulos, Morrison, Hinshaw, & Carte, 1992). In general, kindergarten-retained children do worse in the early elementary years than do nonretained children (e.g., Mantzicopoulos & Morrison, 1992; Shepard, 1989), which on the face of it suggests the practice does not promote long-term academic success. The frustration in examining these studies is that it is never known how the retained children would be doing in the primary years if they had not been held back in kindergarten. We are not certain that well-controlled work on this problem is ethical (e.g., randomly deciding which kindergarten children should be retained from among the kindergarten children who are doing poorly in school), but better controlled studies might help to clear the air about what the actual effects of retention are: Is it helpful as teachers believe or harmful as suggested by the available correlational data?

Mastery Learning Mastery learning (Bloom, 1968) typically involves breaking course content up into manageable units, with students studying and taking quizzes on a unit until the test is passed at a high level of mastery (e.g., 80 to 100 percent). The course consists of the student proceeding through units, mastering each along the way. The assumption is that some students will need to study more than others, and some will require more instruction than will others. All students, however, can end up mastering the material and earning an "A," however, which is different from conventional instruction that involves all students receiving a fixed amount of instruction and a fixed number of quizzes, with some students learning more than others and thus, some making better grades than others. Mastery learning is consistent with the task-oriented, noncompetitive models of classroom motivation favored in Chapter 5.

Keller (1968), a distinguished behavioral psychologist interested in education, devised a version of mastery learning he dubbed **personalized systems of instruction (PSI)**. Keller favored reinforcement mechanisms more than Bloom, the other major mastery learning theorist, focusing on the consistent reinforcement for studying and learning afforded by quizzing with feedback until the student is successful.

Although mastery learning can and has been implemented in elementary and secondary schools, it is used much more frequently in higher education. When student achievement (e.g., on final examinations) in mastery courses is compared with learning and achievement in traditional courses, mastery learning boosts performance on teacher-constructed or experimenter-constructed tests (Kulik, Kulik, & Bangert-Drowns, 1990), a moderate-sized effect. Students in mastery courses also tend to like such courses better than traditional courses. One important factor that seems to increase the effect of mastery learning is to increase the passing criterion for the quizzes, with better final examination performance when students must perform perfectly on quizzes to proceed than when 70% on a unit quiz allows continuation to the next unit.

As we conclude that mastery learning seems to have positive effects, we are also aware of critics who cite failures of mastery learning to improve performance on more standardized measures than teacher-constructed tests (e.g., Slavin, 1990b). Still, in a school world of teacher-made tests tapping what the teacher expects students to learn, mastery learning effects on teacher-constructed instruments are important.

Summary   One reaction to much of what was presented in this subsection is that the conclusions are so commonsensical—that higher-order questions facilitate learning; teacher expectancies about achievement may affect teacher behaviors, which, in turn, affect student achievement; more teaching in the form of tutoring by volunteers improves achievement; and students in lower-ability tracks are provided less rich instruction, which undermines their achievement. Commonsensical or not, classroom questioning is often factual rather than higher order; negative teacher expectancies are all too common, especially with respect to disadvantaged students; many potential school volunteers remain at home; and there are many more tracked schools than untracked ones. Our understanding of factors that can improve the quality of schools is way ahead of school practice, a conclusion that we hope has been obvious at many points in this book.

Summer School

A persistent speculation is that there is some forgetting of what was learned during the school year over the summer. The Sustaining Effects Study (Heyns, 1987; Klibanoff & Haggart, 1981), a huge national effort mandated by Congress to assess the effects of schooling, generally concluded otherwise. By testing large samples of students in the spring and fall, it was possible to determine that there were actually summer gains in reading. As Heyns (1978, 1987) pointed out, however, the rate of growth in reading is less during the summer months than during the school year, however, with disadvantaged populations experiencing less growth during the summer in the absence of instruction than advantaged populations. There were slight losses over the summer in mathematics, especially at the high school levels.

The U.S. federal government, in particular, invests heavily in providing summer school programs to elementary and high school students, especially to disadvantaged students. Unfortunately the effects of these short-term programs, many of which are not well integrated with the curriculum experienced during the school year, tend to be small (Heyns, 1987).

It is heartening that there is not massive loss during the summer of academic skills gained during the year. Perhaps it should not be surprising that short-term summer programs would have little impact. What cannot be lost track of, however, is that the discontinuation of schooling does have a cost in that growth during the summer is slower than during the year. There is every reason to believe that if the United States were ever to opt for year-round schooling, there would be an increase in the achievement levels of American students. Based on Heyn's (1987) analyses, we conclude that for one-fourth of the year, American students' academic growth is at about one-third the rate it is for the remainder of the year. That is, a 20 percent increase in what is learned probably could be obtained by year-round schooling compared with the current 9-month school year.

After-School Educational Practices

What goes on after the school day ends can also affect achievement. All of the after-school factors are complex in that the decisions to engage in them are made by students, educators, and parents in interaction, sometimes explicitly (as when teachers assign homework) and sometimes implicitly (as when Japanese parents encourage their children to elect after-school tutoring).

Homework   For most American students, homework is a fact of life from the middle elementary grades through the remainder of their schooling. Not surprisingly, the effects of this pervasive educational "intervention" have been explored by educational researchers, who have asked whether, when, and how much homework improves academic achievement. Cooper (1989b) provided a definitive summary of the experimental and correlational research on homework. His conclusions included the following:

- The positive effects of homework are small in the upper elementary years and gradually increase in magnitude into the high school years.
- Although the evidence on whether homework makes a bigger difference for some school subjects compared with others is mixed, Cooper concluded that the effects of homework on math, reading, and English are probably greater than the effects of homework on social studies and science achievement. Cooper is more optimistic about the effects of homework on simple skills

that benefit from practice and repetition than more complex skills requiring integration and reflection.

- For junior high school students, 1 to 2 hours of homework per night seems optimal. High school students benefit from more homework, although it is not clear based on available data what a reasonable maximum might be.
- Just as distributed practice (spacing; see Chapter 10) works in other arenas, it works with homework. Homework that requires practicing material based on more than just today's lesson (or recent lessons) is more effective than massed practice of today's content.

After-School Tutoring   One way of providing remediation is to provide additional instructional time after school. For students who are slower to learn, this seems like a logical way of increasing the opportunities of such students to learn. Unfortunately, it is not elected often in the west (Rowan & Guthrie, 1989).

One culture where after-school instruction is common is Japan, with *juku* instruction commonly sought out by the brightest of Japanese students, who seek years of tutoring as preparation for the difficult university entrance examinations that will confront them eventually (e.g., White, 1987). There is a clear perception that such after-school and weekend tutoring makes a substantial difference in the ultimate achievement levels of Japanese students. Our view is that there has been much too little attention to the possibility of extending daily and weekly instructional time through outside tutoring. Educational psychologists should be interested in such tutoring because the dynamics of it will probably be different from the dynamics operating in school.

As an example of the extremely social and motivating nature of this type of instruction compared with normal schooling, consider this description of one *juku* tutor, Sagara:

> The students see him as on their side, as uncompromisingly working *with* them, and sometimes even as an ally against their parents. He constantly rewards them, and provides nurturance in the form of treats and surprises, such as getting them ice cream on a hot day or buying them books or special gifts. [One student] even received several comic books from Sagara when the young student was sick, and Sagara offered him a whole set of them if he'd promise to study hard for his high school entrance exam. Sagara's relation-

ship with his students is of the kidding, big-brother sort. Sagara once bet his students on the answer to a very hard problem and said that if he were wrong, he'd cut his hair very short. He was and he did. He is boyish and dresses casually, and the intensity of *juku* study is mitigated by Sagara's cheerful liveliness. . . . For the graduates, the *juku* experience seems to have been more meaningful than their time in regular schools, for they say "after I graduated from *juku*. . . " instead of "after I graduated from junior high. . . " They all say Sagara is one of the most important people in their lives. (White, 1987, pp. 148–149)

It is definitely an interesting question whether such people can make a difference in the academic achievement of their students, with the possibility that such relationships should be considered as one way to supplement schooling in the United States—or perhaps even as a means for restructuring school so that it is more personal and supportive. Although there are many reasons for Japanese superiority in mathematics achievement (see Chapter 13), one likely cause is that many university-bound Japanese students spend much of their out-of-school time with *juku* tutors. Tutoring—after-school and otherwise—is an intervention that works much of the time, one that needs to be explored further to understand how it works as well as how it might be incorporated more certainly in the lives of more students. (See the discussion of programs that involve one-to-one tutoring, such as Success for All earlier in this chapter, in Chapter 5, and Reading Recovery in Chapter 14.)

Extracurricular Activities   Does playing sports, cheerleading, participating in drama or debate, playing in the band, and a myriad of other activities affect student achievement? Using data collected in more than 1000 high schools by the federal government, Marsh (1992b) determined that there were small but consistently positive correlations between extracurricular participation and a variety of academic outcomes. Although it is impossible to determine from the Marsh (1992b) analysis whether such participation increases academic ability or more capable students elect to participate in extracurricular activities, there was nothing in the Marsh data to indict extracurricular involvement.

Holland and Andre (1987) offered an especially optimistic (and controversial; Brown, 1988; Holland & Andre, 1988; Taylor & Chiogioji, 1988) appraisal of extracurricular activities, claiming the literature supported correlations between such participation and higher self-esteem, better racial relations, more political and social involvement, feelings of greater control, lower delinquency, and higher grades and academic achievement and aspirations. One bonus finding was that students enrolled in smaller schools were more likely to partake of extracurricular activities and enjoy the benefits of such experiences.

After-School Employment   Extensive after-school employment work is associated with poorer school performance, more psychological distress, substance abuse, and delinquency (Steinberg & Dornbusch, 1991; Steinberg, Fegley, & Dornbusch, 1993). Unfortunately, students who are already having difficulty in school are most likely to elect outside work, which results in even lower in-school achievement (Steinberg et al., 1993).

Student Viewing of Popular Television and Interaction with Other Media   Although there is some disagreement about how negative the effects of television viewing are on academic achievement, all analysts who have worked through the relevant data sets conclude that there is a negative relationship between television viewing and academic achievement (Comstock & Paik, 1991, Chapter 3). The declines in achievement with increased television viewing are observed across virtually all academic subjects (e.g., California Assessment Program, 1988). The negative correlations between academic achievement/intelligence and overall television viewing cannot be interpreted as clear evidence of a causal relationship between television viewing and intellect. It is just as reasonable to argue that weaker students would choose to watch television as to argue that watching massive amounts of television reduces intellectual ability. Even so, when students watch large amounts of light-entertainment television (reruns of ."I Love Lucy" and contemporary counterparts) they are consuming time that could be devoted to activities that almost certainly improve intellect and academic achievement more—activities such as reading (e.g., Williams, 1986).

A balanced appraisal of television effects on mind requires consideration of the positive effects of television viewing on academic achievement. For example, there is no doubt that when preschoolers view "Sesame Street" for an extended period of time, they learn a great deal about basic literacy and numeracy concepts, such as the names of letters and the meaning of numbers (e.g., Ball & Bogatz, 1975). In Chapter 13, we will review evidence that PBS's

"Square One" television is increasing children's knowledge of mathematical concepts. The widespread availability of public television across North America has resulted in an intervention that is generally available to almost all children regardless of socioeconomic, racial, or ethnic status (Comstock, 1989; Comstock & Paik, 1991, Chapter 3)—which is not trivial given how scarce academic resources are for many of the least advantaged children: Indeed, for most children and many teenagers, television is their only source of news; television exposes children to occupational roles, ethnic groups, and information about settings that they would not experience otherwise—often with improvements in understanding and acceptance of diversity; television can be used to reverse stereotypes by presenting programming in which nontraditional roles (e.g., sex roles) are portrayed in a favorable light (Comstock & Paik, 1991, Chapter 4). In short, television definitely can improve children's knowledge of the world. The trick, of course, is to encourage viewing of programming that encourages ethically desirable, prosocial attitudes and the development of knowledge that is valuable both in and out of school, while discouraging heavy viewing of genetically altered reptiles, half-hour tales constructed to be amusing rather than informative, and mind-numbing music videos.

Summary   If the mind stops being engaged when the school bell rings at the end of the day, cognitive development is not as extensive as when the mind continues to be academically engaged through homework or tutoring. Many more waking hours are spent out of school than in school, and thus, there cannot be a complete understanding of education without an understanding of the educational experiences that occur before the pledge to the flag and after dismissal. Not everything that can occur between the morning and afternoon bells reliably promotes development of mind, however, with the next section devoted to curricular options that can be seductive entries into the school day but fail to deliver everything that they promise.

EXPLICIT TEACHING OF THINKING IN SCHOOLS: THINKING SKILLS PROGRAMS

There are many packaged programs aimed at increasing the thinking abilities of students. Many are sold by professional education associations and private publishers. The particular goals of programs vary, although all assume that many students do not develop the skills stimulated by the programs on their own. Of course, this is a fair assumption in light of the evidence that has been reviewed thus far in this book.

Consistent with the massive database supporting the teachability of many of these skills, including many of the studies already reviewed in this book, there is an assumption that effective thinking skills can be taught. Most of these programs are constructed by amalgamating a large number of individual instructional procedures, each of which has been validated in basic research, and thus, there are claims by program developers that their inventions are based on research. At best, however, these programs have been understudied, with many never evaluated as wholes in anything even resembling an experimental or quasiexperimental evaluation. This is an extremely unfortunate gap in the educational research literature, for many of these programs are implemented widely in schools. There are so many different programs that we can cover only some of the more famous ones.

CoRT Thinking Program

De Bono (e.g., 1985; also Nickerson et al., 1985, Chapter 7) of Great Britain has offered a number of thinking programs over the years, with the most extensive one, *CoRT* (which stands for "Cognitive Research Trust"), intended to be implemented over 3 years of instruction (i.e., with one lesson per week). The claim is made that CoRT can be used with children as young as 8 years of age and is appropriate for all subsequent age or grade levels. The program also is proposed as appropriate for slow and bright students and useful across cultures. It is based on de Bono's (1969) description of mind at its best, as a self-organizing, self-stabilizing, and active entity.

CoRT is a program intended to teach general thinking skills. Indeed, the claim is made that the program does not depend on the acquisition of prior knowledge. The CoRT skills can be applied across a wide range of situations and are particularly aimed at changing people's perceptions of situations. The program is designed to be simple and practical, emphasizing skills that are important in real life and transferable to a range of real-life situations.

There are six sets of 10 lessons, with each covering an important aspect of thinking:

1. **Breadth** of thinking. There is particular emphasis on examining ideas for their good, bad, and interesting points; there is also an emphasis on looking at a number of factors in a situation rather than focusing on a few, immediately salient features. Consequences of strategies are introduced, as is the idea of selecting and defining thinking objectives. Setting priorities is introduced. Generating alternatives rather than simply accepting a salient possibility is emphasized. Students are encouraged to consider all points of view in a situation.
2. **Organization** skills. These include labeling a situation based on key characteristics. Students are taught to divide up problems and situations to deal with them. They are taught about making comparisons and selecting among alternatives. Other skills include teaching how to start working on a problem, how to organize the steps of problem solving, and how to consolidate what one knows and generate conclusions.
3. **Interaction,** notably how to debate and discuss issues. These skills include examining both sides; evaluating types, value, and structure of evidence; determining how to structure evidence to increase agreements and reduce disagreements; and knowing the various ways of being right and wrong.
4. Increasing **creativity.**
5. Roles of **information** and **feeling** in thinking.
6. An **action** plan that teaches students how to use all of the skills taught in the previous lessons to produce powerful thinking. Students are taught to select a target for thinking and then to expand their thinking about the target followed by a narrowing of focus. Being clear about purpose is emphasized, as is identifying relevant inputs. Students are encouraged to generate alternative solutions to problems and to make choices among the alternatives.

CoRT lessons have a common structure (de Bono, 1983a, 1983b, 1985). Each has a focus, which is first explained by the teacher. Illustrations are provided that make clear the purpose of the lesson. There are practice items, which are accomplished in small groups. There is a great deal of feedback as part of instruction, emanating from teachers and students (i.e., to one another). There are discussions and projects involving application of the thinking skills (e.g., writing assignments requiring use of the CoRT skills). An important part of each lesson is a set of notes that are provided to students that summarize the points of the lesson. Although the focus of each lesson is on a particular type of thinking skill, review lessons integrate across lessons. de Bono is emphatic in arguing against attempting to combine the lessons with content instruction, believing that this would diminish attention to the thinking skills.

Unfortunately the evaluation of CoRT is thin at best (for a review, see Nickerson et al., 1985, Chapter 7). de Bono reports in his manuals and books that there have been experiments comparing CoRT students with students not receiving CoRT instruction. Not surprisingly, given the emphasis on production of ideas in CoRT, CoRT students produce more ideas regarding problems than non-CoRT students. There is also some evidence that the quality of ideas produced by CoRT students is better than the quality of ideas produced by non-CoRT students (e.g., CoRT students are more likely to examine several sides of an issue, rather than just one). Thus, following participation in the CoRT 1 lessons on breadth, more, slightly better ideas are generated in response to problems such as the following: "Should pupils have a say in making school rules?" and "A man is found to have stolen a huge pile of left shoes. What do you think he is up to?" Even so, there is no compelling evidence of sweeping improvements in thinking and academic achievement owing to CoRT participation.

Productive Thinking Program

Covington of the University of California at Berkeley and associates (Covington, Crutchfield, Davies, & Olton, 1974) devised a thinking skills intervention aimed at the later grade-school years (i.e., grades 5 and 6). There are 15 short booklets in the program, with these telling tales about a boy and a girl who are confronted with a series of mysteries that must be solved. The stories are conveyed using text and cartoons, with the books designed to be extremely attractive and interesting to elementary students. The characters in the story engage in a variety of problem-solving methods as they tackle these mysteries, continually sending the message that strategic effort is required to solve problems, ones that may prove challenging (i.e., there are failures of problem solving in the stories before there are successes). Students in the program are given many opportunities to generate solutions to problems. They are specifi-

cally taught a number of strategies for confronting the problems in the stories:

- Assemble the facts before attempting to problem solve.
- Formulate the problem carefully before attempting to problem solve.
- Generate many ideas.
- Try to think of unusual ideas.
- Realize there are many ways to solve a problem.
- Be planful, addressing problems systematically.
- Do not stay "stuck," but rather think of new approaches when having difficulty.
- Map out the various possibilities in a problematic situation.
- Think of general ideas and then variations on these general solutions. (Based on summary by Nickerson et al., 1985, p. 210)

To the extent that the program has been evaluated—and it has been evaluated more than most thinking skills programs (for reviews, see Covington, 1985; Mansfield, Busse, & Krepelka, 1978; Nickerson et al., 1985, Chapter 7)—the effects have been mixed. When presented problems similar to the ones presented in the program itself, Productive Thinking students produce more ideas and at least slightly better ideas than nontrained students. When confronted with problems that are somewhat different from problems encountered in the lessons, the effects are not as striking. In short, there is no evidence of broad transfer of thinking skills following participation in the Productive Thinking program.

Instrumental Enrichment

Feurstein (1979, 1980; for a review see Nickerson et al., 1985, Chapter 6) believes that poor cognitive performance involves failures of encoding and lack of elaboration of information that is presented and acquired (i.e., students do not relate what they know already to new information). When information is presented, the poor learner makes sweeping perceptions, rather than detailed, analytical ones; is unplanned and impulsive; fails to comprehend because of low verbal, spatial, and temporal abilities; does not conserve in the Piagetian sense (see Chapter 7); is not precise or accurate in measurement; and cannot deal with more than one source of information at a time. Elaboration is deficient in that the poor learner is not selective with respect to the information that is attended, fails to make important inferences and generate hypotheses, and thinks in terms of particulars of a situation rather than about how a situation is representative of a broader class of situations. Poor learners' responses tend to involve much trial-and-error responding, are often imprecise, and are impulsive.

Mediated learning experiences are crucial in overcoming these deficiencies according to Feurstein's view, with "mediated learning" virtually synonymous with "scaffolded" instruction (see Chapters 1 and 8). During mediated learning experiences, more knowledgeable adults assist children, modifying input that is provided to the child, so it can be comprehended by the child. The adult interprets the task for the child, and points out the relevant features of the situation that need to be considered to perform tasks given to the child. Sometimes, this means substantial reorganization and restructuring of a problem by the adult before the child is permitted to attempt it. The adult also assists at the response end, for example, making efforts to discourage impulsivity, so the child reflects before responding.

The instrumental enrichment program involves providing mediated learning experiences as students work on a series of paper-and-pencil exercises. The program is intended for low functioning adolescents and is delivered 3 to 5 hours a week for 2 to 3 years. While working on the exercises, the adult works closely with the student, helping the student understand the task, how he or she is approaching it, and how the task might be accomplished differently when the student uses more appropriate processes. After a student attempts the exercises independently, often there is a small-group discussion, which is aimed especially at producing insights about how to apply the processes practiced in the exercises to both school and out-of-school tasks. (These group discussions are reminiscent of the instructional conversations considered in Chapter 8 as part of socially mediated learning; the social-interactive aspects of this intervention are as striking in many ways as the specific curriculum materials that have been developed for the program.)

As in many other thinking skills programs, the thinking skills exercises are content-free and do not require any domain-specific knowledge. The exercises emphasize both perceptual and logical skills. For example, "organization of dots" involves organizing an array of dots by finding in them hidden figures that correspond to model figures shown to the learner. Feurstein's analysis of such tasks is that they require perceptual and search skills, with the task best accomplished if there is substantial planning by the learner. This task also requires inhibiting impulsivity. Because Feurstein believes that poor learners are "episodic" in their thinking, treating a current situation in an isolated fashion rather than as representative of a more general set of relations (i.e., students do not relate a current task to their prior knowledge; see Chapter 3 discussion of semantic versus episodic), a number of exercises are aimed at understanding how one situation relates to another. Thus, exercises are designed to develop the knowledge that how something looks depends on one's perspective on it. Exercises increase understanding that past and future exist as well as the present. There are many opportunities in the exercises to consider alternatives, and there is a consistent emphasis on learners explaining why and how they come to problem solutions. Exercises require learners to work with sets and subsets, with these requiring substantial logical skills as learners work with abstract elements.

Does this program work? At best, the evidence is mixed, and the most compelling support is difficult to interpret (see Nickerson et al., 1985, Chapter 6 for a review). Feurstein's own work (Feurstein, Rand, Hoffman, & Miller, 1979; Rand, Tannenbaum, & Feurstein, 1979) was with the children of African and Asian immigrants to Israel, groups that were decidedly out of the Israeli mainstream. As a group, these children were impoverished and low functioning relative to the general Israeli society. Progress following 2 years of instrumental enrichment was compared with progress made by comparable students who received the type of remedial instruction and enrichment typically offered to such immigrant children. After the intervention, there were clear differences between the instrumental enrichment and control students, although the effects of instrumental enrichment were not across the board but limited to particular competencies. Number, geometry, and addition skills were affected by instrumental enrichment as was performance on some spatial and figure grouping measures. Instrumental enrichment subjects displayed better interpersonal conduct in class than controls as well as greater self-sufficiency and adaptiveness to work demands. There were some academic and social-adjustment improvements attributed to instrumental enrichment in Feurstein's own studies, with the academic improvements generally on nonverbal measures, perhaps not surprising given that many of the exercises in the instrumental enrichment program are perceptual or logical and demand little in terms of verbal competency relative to what they demand with respect to perception and logic.

What do we make of Feurstein's outcomes, especially given they were produced with a population so atypical of students in Western schools? Our view is not to make much of them, consistent with the perspectives of other reviewers (e.g., Blagg, 1991, Chapter 2; Bradley, 1983), since evaluations of instrumental enrichment with Western populations (see Arbitman-Smith, Haywood, & Bransford, 1984) have produced statistically significant but generally modest effects (e.g., 5 to 10 IQ points gained over the course of the intervention). The methods in many of the existing studies have been severely criticized, especially because many of the design decisions, such as choice of dependent variables closely resembling training materials, were biased in favor of instrumental enrichment (e.g., Burden, 1987). When school achievement data are examined, there is little evidence of effect. For example, in a controlled study in South Carolina, O'Tuel and Darby (1993) evaluated the effects of receiving instrumental enrichment for the 3 years of grades 4, 5, and 6. There were no discernible effects on reading, math, or language as measured by standardized tests.

Philosophy for Children

Lipman (see 1985, 1991; also Nickerson et al., 1985, Chapter 10), who teaches at Montclair State in New Jersey, wrote a series of novels for students in the latter grade-school years (i.e., grades 5 and 6). In each of these, the main themes were thinking and reflecting on thinking. The core novel, *Harry Stottlemeir's Discovery* (Lipman, 1974; note the play on the name "Aristotle") is about Harry and his friends, who spend a lot of time talking about thinking and engaging in interactions that simulate thinking processes. There is coverage of how to conduct inquiries, discovery and invention, construction of inferences, causes and effects, and so on. Teachers who use the materials are provided information about

how to stimulate classroom discussions around the thinking themes in the texts. The readings and discussions are intended to encourage students to discover for themselves the thinking themes in the books, with those discoveries taking place in a classroom "community of inquiry" (see Lipman, 1991, especially Chapter 14). The types of classroom conversations that Lipman promotes are similar in design to the interpretive conversations considered in Chapter 8. How Philosophy for Children stimulates children's participation in authentic dialogues in the classroom has been a major focus of theoretical analyses of the intervention, with many claims that conversations about philosophical stories can foster the development of thinking abilities, moral understanding, and the existence of multiple perspectives (Lipman, Sharp, & Oscanyen, 1980; Sharp & Reed, 1992).

The evaluations that are available are positive (see Nickerson et al., 1985, Chapter 10, for a review). Improvements owing to reading and discussion of Philosophy have been reported in controlled studies. Philosophy students have outperformed controls on intelligence test items, reading comprehension, mathematics, and formal reasoning. Our own examination of *Harry Stotlemeir's Discovery* and the Philosophy texts that followed it are that they are interesting readings for elementary-school students, full of possibilities for interpretive discussions and collaborative problem solving. These texts would seem to fit well in the social-collaborative instructional settings that are evolving in the 1990s (see Chapter 8). That consistent benefits have been obtained is encouraging, even though the effects have not always been large.

Dimensions of Thinking

Marzano et al.'s (1988; Marzano, 1992) Dimensions of Thinking is a framework for encouraging critical and creative thinking in classrooms. According to this perspective, explicit instruction in how to form *concepts* should be provided to students, as should instruction in how to find *relationships* between concepts (i.e., principles). *Comprehension* processes should be taught, as should approaches to *problem solving* and *decision making.* Students should be taught methods of *scientific inquiry;* they should be taught how to *compose,* including written, musical, mechanical, or artistic products, depending in part on student interests and talents; and they should be provided opportunities to learn how to *talk* with other people. In addition, there are a set of thinking skills that need to be developed in every student, according to Dimensions. These overlap other thinking skills programs, including the CoRT program described earlier:

- *Focusing skills,* including defining problems and setting goals.
- *Information-gathering skills,* including systematic observation and formulation of questions.
- *Remembering skills*—both encoding and retrieval strategies.
- *Organizing skills,* such as comparing, classifying, ordering, and recoding from one form to another (referred to as "representing" in Dimensions).
- *Analyzing skills,* such as identifying attributes of things, relationships between elements, main ideas, and recognizing logical errors and other types of mistakes.
- *Generating skills,* including making of inferences, predictions, and elaboration of content.
- *Integrating skills,* such as summarizing and restructuring.
- *Evaluation skills,* such as establishing criteria and verifying whether criteria are met. (Based on Marzano et al., 1988, pp. 147–148)

In visits to schools, we often encounter the Dimensions of Thinking materials published by the Association for Supervision and Curriculum Development. We conclude from these observations that the Dimensions are on the mind of many educators, with many attempts across the United States to implement the instructional ideas supported by Dimensions. Our greatest concern with this direction is that we have not seen a single convincing evaluation of packages that are comprised of a large number of strategies aimed at diverse cognitive goals, including Dimensions, which is simply the most recent instantiation of multistrategy packages.

Most of the components in Dimensions have been validated, however. Two thick edited volumes (Jones & Idol, 1990; Idol & Jones, 1990) summarize basic research supporting various aspects of the Dimensions. That the components work tells us nothing about the efficacy of the package, however. At the time of this writing, how much effect Dimensions has on academic performance is indeterminate.

Summary

No one could read the literature on critical thinking packages and not wish for more data. There simply is not much research on these programs, which is especially disturbing because all of the programs discussed in this section are widely distributed. It is also disturbing that many of these programs are offered as "stand-alone" programs, rather than integrated with the curriculum. There is more teaching of strategies than anything else in these packages—with neglect of coordination of strategies with prior knowledge or application of strategies to other content in the curriculum. There is a lot of faith in transfer of the strategies taught, despite the fact that a great deal of research forces the conclusion that transfer occurs infrequently unless instruction is designed specifically to promote transfer. There is not nearly enough concern in some of these packages with the development of metacognitive understandings about the appropriate use of the strategies taught. Motivation to think well and use strategies is not a prominent concern in these packages either. We hope that teachers adopting these packages would be encouraging their students to find ways to apply the principles learned in the programs to content-area learning, explicitly attempt to develop metacognitive understandings in their students about when and where to use the strategies taught, and make efforts to motivate coordinated use of the strategies with other knowledge.

One striking consistency across these packages, however, is the encouragement of collaborative discussion about thinking and problem solving. In that way, they are consistent with many of the other interventions favored in this book. Even so, such discussions seem less rich than others considered in other chapters of this book because there is little concern with learning content as strategies are practiced in collaborative dialogues. The abstract problems favored in Instrumental Enrichment and CoRT contrast with discussion of material that can be related to children's prior knowledge—the type of material now covered routinely in many classrooms that have moved to cooperative models of learning. Although the novels in Philosophy for Children and the stories in the Productive Thinking program can be discussed as narratives, they are not the outstanding children's literature now prominently discussed daily in many classrooms. Although thinking skills programs favor discussion methods of learning, they seem to offer less to talk about than is offered in many classrooms now committed to collaborative discussion.

DOES HIGHER EDUCATION PROMOTE COGNITIVE COMPETENCE?

Most readers of this book will either have completed or be near the end of 4 years of college. A fair question to address as part of an educational psychology course is whether this 4-year intervention promotes cognitive development as advertised. Not surprisingly, substantial research has been directed at determining the effects of higher education on academic competence. Fortunately, for those of us who write books like this, Pascarella and Terenzini (1991; see also Astin, 1993) have compiled a 900-page summary of literature documenting how college affects students.

Thinking Skills Affected by College

Some of the positive effects of college documented by Pascarella and Terenzini (1991) include the following:

- Both general (math and verbal competence) and specific subject matter knowledge increase.
- College probably increases the likelihood that people will continue to engage in knowledge-enhancing activities following graduation. College graduates are more likely than high school graduates to read newspapers, magazines, and books; be informed about public affairs; and participate in continuing education (Hyman, Wright, & Reed, 1975). There is increased interest in classical music, reading and creative writing, theater, intellectual discussions, and the performing arts in general. Intrinsic interest in liberal education increases during the college years.
- Oral and written communication skills improve.

- Critical thinking improves, including the ability to deal with ill-structured problems and controversial issues.
- Flexibility in thinking improves (i.e., the ability to see several sides of an issue), as does the ability to deal with complex issues.
- Piagetian formal operational competence increases (e.g., Eisert & Tomlinson-Keasey, 1978; Mentkowski & Strait, 1983).
- Intellectual self-confidence (e.g., confidence in writing and math skills) increases, as does achievement motivation (e.g., Pascarella, Smart, Ethington, & Nettles, 1987).

Although the magnitudes of these effects are not always large, and alternative explanations of improvements (besides college attendance) are possible in most instances, it would be difficult given the many correlations between college attendance and subsequent cognitive change not to be convinced that cognitive competence increases during the college years. The case is similarly strong that commitment to long-term intellectual participation is fostered by what happens during the college years.

Effects of Particular Majors and Courses

An extremely interesting finding is that college major can affect undamental reasoning abilities. Lehman and Nisbett (1990) studied the reasoning abilities of University of Michigan students when they were first-semester freshmen and then again late in their senior year. A variety of reasoning tasks were administered. They found that majoring in a social science resulted in people who could use statistical reasoning to draw conclusions. Although there were improvements in statistical reasoning over the 4 years for students majoring in natural sciences and the humanities, the improvements were not as great as for the students in the social sciences. Natural sciences and humanities students improved in their conditional logical abilities (i.e., in their ability to solve problems requiring only logical reasoning rather than reasoning from evidence) more than social sciences students. In addition, the verbal reasoning abilities of natural sciences and humanities students improved slightly over the 4 years, compared with a slight loss in verbal reasoning skills for social sciences students. Given the differences in curricula for social sciences compared with natural sciences and humanities students, this was a sensible pattern of results. Drawing inferences from statistical evidence is at the heart of most social sciences; logical reasoning is demanded more often in the natural sciences and humanities. Four years of immersing a head in a particular type of reasoning affects the reasoning ability of that head.

Even particular courses have long-term impact on development of intellect. Bahrick of Ohio Wesleyan University is the most notable investigator who has studied the long-term effects of what is learned in high school and college courses. His 1984 study was concerned with how well people remember the Spanish they learned in school, with original learning occurring in some cases as long as 50 years ago. The answer is that people remember some of what they learn in courses well. Thus, for students who completed the equivalent of 5 semesters of college Spanish, there was about a 70 percent chance (collapsing across subtests) that they would be able to match the meanings of Spanish and English words—even 35 years later. More negatively, recall of the meanings of Spanish words or Spanish words given English meanings was much lower. Although there was decline across the 50 years in memory for diverse elements of Spanish, from grammar to idioms, memory was always greater than zero even after 50 years. That is, something was remembered. Bahrick (1984) observed substantial loss in knowledge of Spanish in the first 6 years, followed by a 30-year or so leveling off before there was additional noteworthy decline. At every retention interval, students receiving more training originally, in terms of the number of courses taken, had better long-term memory than students receiving less initial instruction. "A" students remembered more than "B" students. Bahrick's (1984) work makes obvious that there are long-term changes in knowledge as a function of foreign language instruction, although there is some forgetting as well.

What about this course? Will you remember much of what was presented in a course concerned principally with cognitive psychology and education? Of course, the only way to know if students will remember the content of courses such as this one is to study the long-term memories of students who have taken such a course. Conway, Cohen, and Stanhope (1991) approached that ideal study.

Conway et al. (1991) administered memory tests to former students in a cognitive psychology course (which was similar in content to much of what is covered in this book, although there was emphasis on more basic cognitive concepts rather than their applications in education). The "retention interval" (i.e., time since the course was taken) was as long as 10 years in some cases. Five different types of tests were administered:

1. Name and concept recognition: Lists of names and concepts were presented with the students required to recognize whether the names and concepts had been covered in the course. The concept list included the following: *chronometric cycle, eigen stimulus test, vector cells, quadratic activation effect, embedded figures test, texture cues,* and *preattentive processing.* (The last three are correct.)
2. Fact verification: True facts covered in the course were presented, as were false facts. The participants were required to distinguish the true and false facts. For example, one item was, "The behaviorists considered learning to be a passive process."
3. Concept grouping: Subjects were required to sort 24 concepts into six groups.
4. Cued recall of proper names and concepts: Items included, "E-- was an early German psychologist who studied the learning of nonsense syllables."
5. Research methods: Two-choice questions concerning methods were presented, including the following: "An experiment that uses different subjects in each experimental condition is known as (A) a between-subjects design, (B) a within-subjects design." "Data that can be ranked from best to worst is known as (A) ordinal data, (B) nominal data." (Conway et al., 1991, pp. 398–399)

With the exception of the research methods and fact verification data, there were clear declines in memory during the first 3 years following the course, with memory performances leveling off after 3 years. The research methods questions were answered at a level well above chance at all retention intervals with no apparent decline as a function of retention interval. There was little decline in recognition of general facts, both as indicated by correctness of responses to these items and confidence in responses; although correct recognition of specific facts did not decline with retention interval, confidence in these responses did.

In general, there was much in Conway et al.'s (1991) data to make those of us who labor as teachers of psychology to take heart. Much seemed to be remembered. More negatively, at least for some of the more demanding measures of memory (i.e., those involving recall and conceptual grouping), there was precipitous decline in the 3 years following the course. (A colleague observed that even this did not concern him because he had previously believed that many students learned it for the test and then forgot it immediately—only true for some types of information, according to Conway et al.'s [1991] or Bahrick's [1984] data.)

Stanhope, Cohen, and Conway (1993) studied former students' memory for a novel covered in a university course taken up to 39 months earlier. They reported outcomes generally consistent with those observed by Conway et al. (1991).

For a brief summary of the most important evidence to date on long-term retention of information learned in a university, see Conway, Cohen, and Stanhope (1993). The evidence as a whole suggests, however, that much of what is learned in college courses seems to be put in some type of "**perma-store,**" to use Bahrick's (1984) terminology. When combined with the data summarized by Pascarella and Terenzini (1991), there is reason to be confident that college experiences increase both competence in thinking and general knowledge.

CONCLUDING COMMENTS

Schooling can make a difference in cognitive development and competence. High-quality schooling can make more of a difference than does low-quality schooling.

Can student learning be maximized? Can the odds be increased that future generations of students will be good thinkers? The general message in this chapter and this book is yes, with it possible to improve education in various ways. Progress has been made at the elementary and secondary levels in identifying the characteristics of educational settings that predict long-term achievement; a great deal of research has been summarized in this book establishing ways of improving particular types of learning. Whether all of this research makes a difference depends on translation of research findings into actual curricula and widespread dissemination of instruction that is informed by theory and research—it is hoped with continuing study of the field-based interventions inspired by basic research.

Because this chapter presented a mixture of interventions that definitely work to improve student learning, thinking, and performance; others that have small or inconsistent effects at best; and still others that are untested for the most part, we summarize in Table 11.1 what was covered in this chapter with respect to documented efficacy with respect to stimulating student achievement.

Table 11.1 Interventions That Provide Certain Effects and Ones That Provide Either Small and Uncertain Effects or Have Not Been Tested Completely Enough

Certain Positive Effects

Attending school, especially "effective," orderly schools

Academically oriented, engaging classrooms

Head Start and early intervention programs

One-on-one tutoring, including as it occurs in programs such as Success for All and after school, as in the *Juku* system

Teacher questioning

Wait time during teacher questioning

Student questioning

Differential teacher reactions to students on basis of ability

Parental involvement in schooling

Volunteer tutors in classrooms

Peer tutoring

Smaller classes

Mastery learning

Homework, especially after the elementary-school years

Viewing educational television

Higher education

College major

Some college courses

Small, Uncertain, Negative, or Not Tested Satisfactorily

Teacher expectancies (mixed evidence)

Ability grouping and tracking (negative)

Sex-segregated classrooms (small)

Retention of students in a grade (negative)

Short-term summer school programs (small)

Extracurricular activities (uncertain)

After-school work (negative)

Viewing entertainment television (negative)

Thinking skills programs (not tested sufficiently)

Mentors in college (not tested sufficiently)

Part
4

Cognition and Instruction

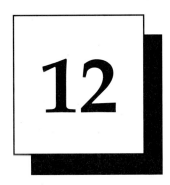

Science

Educational psychology is used by curriculum developers. Not surprisingly, many curriculum developers now are offering theories and conducting research that is decidedly psychological. Science educators are particularly concerned with prior knowledge that students possess, knowledge that is not consistent with scientific understandings students are expected to acquire in school. The problem is that such misconceptions seem to endure even following formal instruction presenting information inconsistent with the misconceptions. Piagetian theory and other cognitive analyses are now being used to devise instruction that might more certainly overcome such persistent errant prior knowledge. Beyond misconceptions, evidence is accumulating that development of scientific thinking is anything but certain, even if provided opportunities to engage in high-quality scientific educational activities. One paradox is that scientific learning is hypothesized by many science educators to be best if students largely construct their own understandings through active experimentation and discovery, and yet student discovery of scientific knowledge is often uncertain even in supportive environments. We make the case in this chapter and the next that one way to confront this paradox is through an approach to student construction of understandings that emphasizes scaffolded teaching, an instructional approach supported by a great deal of evidence summarized in this book. We also make the case, however, that many more effective learning mechanisms could be imported into science education than are now being used, with our view being that an educational psychology of science education is a possibility but one that is emerging rather than mature at this point. There is great opportunity for the next generation of educational psychologists and science educators to forge alliances to create much more complete understandings of science learning and teaching than now exist.

The scientific community believes that education in science can do more to produce good information processors than can other disciplines. Education in science can lead to habits of mind—strategies or higher-order thinking skills—that are less likely to be developed in other disciplines (e.g., Committee on High School Biology, 1990, Chapter 1; Murname & Raizen, 1988, Chapter 2, p. 19): These include (1) forming hypotheses in reaction to questions and problems; (2) seeking information that pertains to problems rather than simply attempting uninformed solutions; (3) using information to solve problems, although recognizing that the quality and generalizability of information are always constrained by limits on sampling; (4) mentally playing with information and thinking about it from alternative perspectives in order to solve problems; (5) offering arguments and counterarguments; and (6) building a consensus across individuals through collaboration and communication.

We are making substantial progress in understanding how to structure science education so it is more effective than it has been historically—so higher-order strategic thinking is fostered. Contemporary science education is informed by the nature and representation of knowledge (see Chapter 3), Vygotskian theories (see Chapter 8), and principles of motivation (see Chapter 5) as well as other psychological perspectives. Readers who have digested what has been presented up until this point in the book will find interventions described in this chapter that make good sense in light of a great deal of psychological theory and research.

MISCONCEPTIONS AND ALTERNATIVE FRAMEWORKS

One of Piaget's (e.g., 1929) most important insights was that people often have ideas about the world that clash with scientific viewpoints. For example, they often believe that inanimate objects are alive. Piaget believed that such **animism** was a symptom of preoperational intelligence and that with the development of concrete and formal operations, children's ideas about what is alive versus what is not alive would reflect conventional thinking about life. In a number of follow-up investigations, many of which were conducted in the 1930s and 1940s (for a brief review, see Brainerd, 1978b), it became apparent that although animism declined with development from the preoperational to the concrete and formal operational stages, it never extinguished. Animism persists throughout adulthood.

For years, the Piagetian-inspired discovery that nonscientific thinking was common in adults was largely forgotten. Then, in the late 1970s and in the 1980s, contemporary scientists and science educators noted that often people have important misconceptions about physical and biological relationships. "Intuitive physics" (e.g., McCloskey, 1983) is a set of different laws than the laws of actual physics: For example, if you were running with a football and dropped the ball, what would be the trajectory of the ball as it headed for the ground? Many people have the intuition that the ball will fall straight down, since only gravity would be acting on it. In reality, however, the ball continues to move forward all the time it is moving downward because no force has been exerted to change its forward velocity. When a discus thrower spins around in a 360-degree motion, what is the trajectory of the discus from the point of release? Intuitive physics puts a curve on the trajectory, although the actual trajectory is a straight line, consistent with Newton's first law that in the absence of a force being applied to it, an object in motion travels in a straight line. What forces operate on a baseball after it is hit into the air? Upward forces and gravity operate according to intuitive physics, when, in fact, gravity is the only force applied to the ball in flight (all of these examples based on Mc-Closkey, 1983). For many people, upward motion implies an upward force (see Clement, 1982).

Although scientific misconceptions in physics have been studied more than other misconceptions (Pfundt & Duit, 1991), people seem to have misconceptions about every scientific arena imaginable. Table 12.1 provides a listing of just a few of the common misconceptions that Woloshyn, Paivio, and Pressley (1992) uncovered in their review of the literature, a literature now comprised of more than 2000 studies (Duit, 1991). Scientific misconceptions can have a range of consequences, including ones that are tragic. Consider the pain that has been inflicted on victims of acquired immunodeficiency syndrome (AIDS) by people holding the following misconceptions (DiClemente, Pies, Stoller, Straits, Olivia,

---

Table 12.1 Common Scientific Misconceptions Identified by Woloshyn, Paivio, and Pressley (1992)

The Sun

The sun is a living organism—it is an animate object
The sun's surface is solid
The light of the sun is made up of only a few colors, mostly yellow and orange

Rattlesnakes

The rattlesnake is very dangerous and mean
The forked tongue of the rattlesnake is of little use to the snake
The rattlesnake smells objects with its nostrils

Water

One place where water does not exist is in the air
The distance between water molecules does not change when water is frozen
Good drinking water has an odor, some taste, and a slight color

Three States of Matter

Although molecules are small, they are still visible and can be seen with a
  microscope
Heat and light are matter and take up space
Molecules in solids are always still

Plants

All plants have roots, stems, leaves, and flowers
Plants eat soil and water
Plants use light energy from the sun to help them stay warm

Blood

All organisms have blood
Blood is made of only one component, red cells
The functions of the heart include cleaning, filtering, making, and storing blood

Animals

All animals have a backbone
People are not animals
Worker bees buzz to tell other bees where there is food

Genetics

Environmentally induced factors can be transmitted to offspring
A gene can be dominant in one offspring and recessive in another
Variations in an individual are caused by developmental deficits only

---

Haskin, Rutherford, 1989; DiClemente, Zorn, & Temoshok, 1986, 1987; Price, Desmond, & Kukulka, 1985): (1) A person can get AIDS by touching someone with the disease. (2) All gay men have AIDS. (3) AIDS can be spread by using someone's personal belongings like a comb or hairbrush. (4) A person can contact AIDS by being around someone with the disease. (5) All gay women have AIDS. (6) It is easy to detect a person with AIDS. (7) All persons exposed to the AIDS virus will get the disease. (8) A person can get AIDS by attending school with a student with AIDS. (9) It is unsafe for a person with AIDS to work near children.

Even after completing science courses covering scientific concepts and passing tests on them, misconceptions persist. (Indeed, even expert scientists will sometimes fail to recognize an exemplar of an elementary concept, such as acceleration [Reif & Allen, 1992].) Anderson's work at Michigan State has been especially revealing about the persistence of misconceptions following education.

For example, Anderson, Sheldon, and Dubay (1990) studied college students' conceptions of respiration and photosynthesis at the beginning and at the end of a year-long biology course. At the beginning of the course, students offered grossly deficient answers, even though most students had 1 or more years of biology previously. When asked on the pretest for a definition of respiration, few students mentioned energy, and fewer mentioned food, offering, in many cases, simplistic definitions such as the following: "Exhaling CO_2 for humans, exhaling O_2 for plants; breathing; has lungs to breath with; and air in, air out." The same held for pretest definitions of photosynthesis, another chemical process producing energy conversion. A minority of students mentioned food or energy in their definitions, which included the following: "Plants take in CO_2 and change it to O_2"; "I remember needing to know a formula for it in high school; keeps plants green; and green plants turn sun and CO_2 into chlorophyll." Students offered the following as explanations of "food for a bean plant": "Food for a bean plant is what is necessary for it to grow, water, soil, and minerals, sunlight"; "The chemicals it receives from the sunlight, soil, and fertilizer"; "Sunlight, water, soil"; and "The nutrients in the soil. The sun, the water, other animals that died and their body becomes part of the soil." In short, these students certainly did not understand that plants manufacture their own food.

What is much more disturbing than the pretest performances, however, is that at the end of the course, many students still had misconceptions: Almost 25 percent had little idea about the nature of respiration; about 20 percent did not understand that the essence of food is that it provides energy for metabolism and materials for growth; 40 percent did not completely understand that plants make their food; and more than 50 percent failed to understand that animals obtain energy from food, and plants obtain energy from sunlight. (Note that when stricter scoring was applied, the proportions of students having misconceptions at the end of the course were considerably higher.)

Bishop and Anderson (1990) reported a similar study tapping college students' understanding of some important ideas from genetics. Again, although most students had one or more years of biology before taking the course in biology, at pretesting it was apparent that the overwhelming majority did not understand fundamental ideas about how new traits arise via genetic mechanisms, about how variation in traits is related to reproductive success, and about how evolution is a change in the proportion of individuals with discrete traits. Again, and even worse, at posttesting more than one-third of the students could not answer applications questions based on these fundamental genetic principles, questions such as the following:

> While ducks were evolving webbed feet:
> (a) With each generation, most ducks had about the same amount of webbing on their feet as their parents.
> (b) With each generation, most ducks had a tiny bit more webbing on their feet than their parents. (*a* correct)
>
> If a population of ducks were forced to live in an environment where water for swimming were not available:
> (a) Many ducks would die because their feet were poorly adapted to the environment.
> (b) The ducks would gradually develop nonwebbed feet. (*a* correct)
>
> The populations of ducks evolved webbed feet because:
> (a) The more successful ducks adapted to their aquatic environment.
> (b) The less successful ducks died without offspring. (*b* correct)
> (Adapted from Bishop & Anderson, 1990, Figure 1, p. 418)

In contrast, many of these students could answer simple fact recall and recognition questions on this material. This suggests that they "knew the material" at some level. Whitehurst's notion of **inert knowledge,** introduced in Chapter 3, seems relevant here in that factual information learned in the course seems not to generalize to application questions. What is absolutely certain, however, is that misconceptions are not eliminated through courses, or at least by conventional science instruction. There is report after report in the science education literature about students having a misconception before taking a course or experiencing a lesson; learning an alternative, more scientifically defensible concept during the course or lesson; and then reverting to the logic of the misconception when given a subsequent problem that could be solved by applying the scientific concept. Those who argue that more traditional science coursework is what is required to reform science education need to ponder the implications of students just experiencing conventional instruction on chemical change and then failing to think about atoms and molecules when explaining chemical reactions, treating chemical changes like physical changes (e.g., thinking of rusting as only a form of decay rather than a chemical reaction), and failing to recognize that some reactions produce invisible products, such as gases.

We have been using the term misconception until this point because it is used frequently in the science education literature. What we have been discussing are misconceptions in the sense that they are not consistent with scientific ideas. Some researchers take exception to the term because they believe that what we have been discussing might better be regarded as **alternative frameworks** that provide people with guidance in many situations (e.g., Driver & Easley, 1978; see Duit, 1991). Another term that has been applied to the type of thinking considered here is **children's science;** still another is **children's conceptual frameworks.** All three of these terms suggest a dignity that is lacking from the term misconception. Nonetheless, because the term misconception is used more than any of the alternative terms, we use it here more often than the other terms, and we emphasize that misconceptions and alternative frameworks are operationally synonymous as far as we can tell (i.e., the subtleties differentiating the terms are ones that science educators may wish to debate, but most readers can ignore without loss of understanding).

The research on scientific misconceptions makes obvious that students do not arrive in the science classrooms as blank slates. Rather, they often possess prior knowledge that is inconsistent with the content they will be asked to learn in the science course.

Whether it is well-organized or fragmented prior knowledge is a matter of debate (e.g., DiSessa, 1982). Regardless of whether the errant prior knowledge forms a network of understandings, it often is so deeply entrenched that students will continue to apply alternative frameworks even after learning new science content that is inconsistent with the prior knowledge.

Why is errant prior knowledge so enduring? It has been built up over years of experience, and it is consistent with other knowledge possessed by the subject (Duit, 1991). Thus, how often have you talked about how something "burned up?" Such *language* suggests that what was burned was destroyed. It is counterintuitive for there actually to be more matter after burning than before. Nonetheless, weigh a piece of steel wool before and after it is burned, and it weighs more after. The chemical reaction during the fire created a product that weighs more than the original steel wool. Other times, *appearances are deceiving* (Eylon & Linn, 1988). The docility of a rattlesnake is not suggested by its appearance. The sun looks yellow and orange, and thus there is a perceptual basis for believing it produces mostly yellow and orange light. The *social environment* is filled with misinformation, such as the errant information about AIDS that has been spread by rumor and uninformed speculation. Finally, often *instruction provided to students is just plain wrong,* with students taught errant information. For example, we have encountered more than a few discussions of particle theories of light that make it seem as if light must be matter. Children live in a world that is filled with errant information, information that can seem sensible even if it is not correct.

Information that is learned well over time comes to mind more quickly than information that is not learned well, perhaps because it has been presented in an unconvincing fashion or simply has not been presented often. For new knowledge to replace old knowledge in the sense that the new knowledge would come to mind and be applied rather than the old knowledge, it is necessary for the learner to learn new information well. Contemporary science educators are convinced that most conventional science instruction does not permit learning that is extensive and meaningful enough (deep enough?—see Chapter 10) to permit the development of rich, strong connections to other knowledge.

Part of the problem is that learners' prior knowledge leads them to process new information in biased ways. In Piagetian terms, new information is assimilated to prior knowledge rather than prior knowledge being accommodated to new information. For example, Roth (e.g., 1991) has observed that when students read a text they frequently "remember" information that came not from the text but from their prior knowledge. Consider this example:

> Kevin, a seventh-grade student . . . had a rich prior knowledge about plants and food. He 'knew' that plants, like people, have multiple sources of food that they take in from the external environment. He wrote on a pretest:
>
>> Food (for plants) can be sun, rain, light, bugs, oxygen, soil, and even other dead plants. Also warmth or coldness. All plants need at least three or four of these foods. Plus minerals.
>
> When Kevin read a text that explained that minerals are not food for plants but that plants make their own food during photosynthesis, he ignored the statement that minerals are not considered food (even after a second reading of the key paragraph). This allowed him to incorporate inappropriately the concept of photosynthesis into his own schema of multiple foods for plants:
>
> INTERVIEWER: Could you summarize where does the plant get its food?
> KEVIN: Whew, from lots of places! From the soil for one, for the minerals and water, and from the air for oxygen. The sunlight for the sun, and it would change chemicals to sugars. It sort of makes it own food and gets food from the ground. And from air. (Roth, 1990, p. 145)

What is interesting is that Kevin's response actually includes a rough definition of photosynthesis. Even so, his belief in plants getting food from the ground persists. Roth (1990) viewed this as an example of **conceptual capture** (Posner, Strike, Hewson, & Gertzog, 1982) because some of the new conceptual information was captured and integrated into the student's knowledge, knowledge that is scientifically incorrect and actually contradictory to the scientific concept being studied. (Recall from Chapter 3 that new information is understood by relating it to prior knowledge.)

Similarly, Duit (1991) made the case that prior knowledge affects student observations, guiding them to information consistent with their own perspectives. Thus, classroom demonstrations intended to make one point can end up supporting an alternative perspective not consistent with scientific perspectives. As an example, Duit related how some students in a study conducted by Gunstone and White (1981) reacted to a demonstration involving a weight and a bucket of sand, which were in equilibrium on opposite sides of a pulley and extending downward an equal distance from the wheel of the pulley:

> A small spoonful of sand is added to the bucket. It is so small that no movement is caused. But the college students who have the idea that the bucket will sink "observe" this (well, it sinks just a little). Then so much sand is added that an accelerated movement of the bucket results. Students are asked to observe the speeds of the bucket at two positions. Students who believe that uniform speeds will occur, "observe" it. (Duit, 1991, pp. 71–72)

When presented science instruction, students often are looking to confirm what they "know" already, with the result both extremely selective attention and distortion of information provided during instruction.

Sometimes the prior knowledge is so strong that students will simply not believe what they see. Thus, when Gunstone and White pulled the bucket down, which raised the weight, students were asked to predict what would happen if the experimenter let go of the bucket. Many students predicted that the weight would drop and the bucket would return to its original position, something that, of course, did not happen (i.e., the equilibrium in such a system depends only on equal weight on each side of the pulley, not on the height of the two counterbalancing weights). Some of the students reacted to this outcome by trying to argue it away, claiming that somehow the pulley system in question was producing a nongeneralizable result (i.e., that there was something about the specific problem situation that resulted in a violation of the natural tendency of the bucket to return to its original height; Duit, 1991). That Gunstone and White's (1981) observation is not unusual is obvious from the many examples of working scientists who have refused to abandon deeply held scientific beliefs when confronted with evidence to the contrary (see Hull, 1988).

Another bias that reduces student comprehension of scientific content is a tendency to concentrate on big words, scientific facts, and details when reading science—to reduce learning of science to a rote exercise rather than as a task involving understanding. Here is how Roth (1991) described some middle school students in one of her studies processing information in scientific text:

... [R]eaders relied too heavily on details in the text, failing to attach any meaning to them. The details—most often specialized vocabulary words—were isolated fragments that students saw as having no relationship to one another or to their real world knowledge. ...

... [Other] students placed too much emphasis on facts, viewing science learning as a process of developing long lists of facts about natural phenomena. Their prior experiences in school had convinced them that memorizing unrelated facts constitutes satisfactory learning. They accumulated many facts from the text and described these facts accurately. But they treated all the facts as equally important, and they never attempted to relate facts to one another or to their real world knowledge about plants. (Roth, 1991, pp. 50–51)

The result was that the students "learned" what was in the text so they could report it back but they could not apply it:

... [t]he big words they picked up from the text were never used when they talked about real plants. Thus, school knowledge was something totally separate from the real world, and it was not expected to make sense or to relate to everyday phenomena.

[One student] ... remembered that the text described photosynthesis as the way plants make their food. However, when asked to explain how a plant sitting on the windowsill gets its food, she never mentioned photosynthesis or plants' ability to make food. (Roth, 1991, pp. 50–51)

Not only do students have alternative frameworks, but also these alternatives are persistent and can distort processing of more credible scientific concepts. Often, students process scientific content superficially, not attempting to understand it. Rather, they attempt to memorize it, a strategy that, unfortunately, often pays off, given the emphasis on rote memorization in many science courses.

There is reason for optimism, however, even when students are left on their own to process science content. Some students wrestle with science content, for example, attempting to understand the meaning and significance of science textbook presentations and actively seeking to accommodate (to use the Piagetian term) their beliefs about a phenomenon with the information in text. Roth (1991) reported how some of the middle school students in her studies reacted to text:

They recognized the conflicts between what the text said and their own personal theories and puzzled about these inconsistencies until they could resolve the conflict. Often, this meant changing their personal theories to accommodate scientific explanations ... the conceptual change readers:

1. Made efforts to link text ideas with their experiential knowledge.
2. Recognized and thought about central text statements that conflicted with personally held ideas.
3. Distinguished between main ideas and supporting details, often minimizing the importance of big words.
4. Experienced and recognized conceptual confusion while reading.
5. Worked to resolve this conceptual confusion.
6. Were aware that their own ideas about real world phenomena were changing.
7. Used concepts presented in the text to explain real world phenomena. (Roth, 1991, p. 52)

In short, some students activated prior knowledge related to text but recognized that their prior knowledge was not congruent entirely with meaning presented in text. These students worked at understanding the discrepancy so that their own thinking could be refined. The result is knowledge that can be applied, as exemplified by one student who used this **conceptual change strategy:**

INTERVIEWER: If I were to cover up all but one leaf of this plant, do you think the way it grows would change?
SUSAN: Yeah, it would, because there's only one leaf that can change the materials to food and regularly you have much more—and I don't think it could feed the whole plant. I just don't believe it.

The good news that some students do think hard about the meaning of scientific text and do attempt to correct misconceptions is complemented by more good news in the next section. A variety of instructional mechanisms have been proposed and are being investigated as means of increasing student understanding, memory, and use of scientific content, especially content that conflicts with everyday knowledge. At the heart of some of these interventions is the conceptual change strategy, with a number of science educators convinced that students can be taught to notice and resolve discrepancies between their own prior knowledge and science content, with deep understanding of science the result of such active processing.

TEACHING FOR CONCEPTUAL CHANGE

In this section, a number of interventions are described. A word of warning is that many of these interventions have not been evaluated as completely as we would like. The most prevalent designs used by science educators to evaluate interventions are qualitative case-study approaches and uncontrolled pretest-posttest designs. Of course, there are many alternative explanations besides the efficacy of a treatment when knowledge improves in a case study or from pretest to posttest, for example, testing effects (i.e., performance is better the second time a test is administered because of practice). More positively, there have been some true experiments and quasiexperiments, and some of these will be discussed. When the literature is considered as a whole, the positive results to date are sufficient to argue for much more intense study of interventions aimed at conceptual change, but there are not enough well-controlled evaluations reporting positive effects to justify strong conclusions about conceptual change teaching at this time. With that warning, we begin the discussion with one of the most famous of the conceptual change interventions.

Conceptual Conflict and Accommodation Model

Nussbaum and Novick (e.g., 1982) proposed that to overcome a misconception, a student first needs to be aware of their belief. Once aware, exposure to an event that cannot be explained by their belief or is inconsistent with it has the potential for producing cognitive conflict. Consistent with Piagetian thinking, such conflict motivates efforts toward conflict resolution and, in particular, motivates efforts to understand the scientific concept explaining the observed event. That is, conflict motivates efforts toward accommodation, setting up the possibility of modification of current cognitive structures (i.e., belief) and the creation of new ones.

In Nussbaum and Novick's (1982) study, primary-school children were given a lesson on the particle theory of gases and, in particular, a lesson establishing there is empty space between molecules of air. As part of the lesson, air was sucked from a flask with a hand pump. Students' awareness of their beliefs about air was induced by having them draw pictures of the flask and its contents before and after the air was removed. Some of the student drawings

and explanations were discussed by the instructor, as was the scientifically correct position that the flask contained particles of air with empty space between the particles before and only empty space after pumping. Of course, many of the students did not understand that the air molecules had empty space between them before the pumping began, for example, believing all of the space in the flask must have been occupied by air.

Then the instructor introduced a discrepant event. Students were shown syringes with equal volumes of air and water in them. The teacher attempted to compress the water, with no movement of the syringe plunger. Then, the teacher succeeded in compressing the air. If there was no space between air molecules, such compression should not have been possible. Discussion followed about how the student models of the flask situation might explain or be inconsistent with the compressibility of air but not water. The instructor's job was to help students see that the only model that could explain the evacuation of air from the flask and the compressibility of air in the syringe was the empty space theory. The success of this instruction was apparent to Nussbaum and Novick because many of the students accepted the empty space theory after such instruction, despite having no conception of empty space between air particles at the beginning of the lesson. They contended that conceptual conflict was created when errant beliefs were activated and confronted by an event inconsistent with the belief. This motivated cognitive accommodation, which operationalized as attention and openness to the scientifically correct conception.

Nussbaum and Novick's (1982) position can be criticized, however. For example, Posner, Strike, Henson, and Gertzog (1982) argued that more than just cognitive conflict is necessary for cognitive change to take place. They believe that effective instruction needs (1) to produce clear dissatisfaction with the errant belief and (2) to provide an intelligible and plausible alternative conception, and (3) the alternative must be fruitful in that it provides obvious intellectual power not permitted by the prior conception. In other words, students often need quite a bit of convincing before they give up a conception that is obviously correct to them in favor of a new one. The status of the prior conception often must be lowered (i.e., dissatisfaction induced), and the status of the new conception raised (i.e., proven useful), for the new conception to replace the old one (Hewson & Thorley, 1989).

Posner et al.'s (1982) elaboration of the conceptual conflict model is important: (1) There are many scientifically valid ideas that do not seem as plausible to students initially as their prior conceptions. For example, Clement, Brown, and Zeitsman (1989) noted that many students find implausible that static objects exert forces (e.g., a table exerting an upward force equal to the weight of the items on it). Osborne and Freyberg (1985) made the case that many ideas about force seem counterintuitive to young students: It is hard to accept that a ball thrown in an upward flight does not have an upward force operating on it while it is on the way up. It is hard to accept that a speeding bicycle that is no longer being pedaled does not have a forward force operating on it. (2) Often students find new conceptions to be unintelligible, with student exclamations such as, "I don't know what you're saying," or "I don't know what you mean" (Hewson & Thorley, 1989). (3) Students often prefer their prior conceptions to the new conceptions offered in school, believing that their own knowledge is consistent with the "real world" even if it is not consistent with what must be learned in school (Dreyfus, Jungwirth, & Eliovitch, 1990). If new knowledge is to prove fruitful, it often is going to have to prove more useful than everyday knowledge that the student trusts because it is grounded in experience.

Even though Posner et al.'s (1982) conditions for conceptual change learning are cited frequently and acknowledged as critical based on anecdotal and case-study information, there has been surprisingly little research on them, and the work that has been completed is not analytical (see Hewson & Thorley, 1989). Moreover, there has been little translation of the model into classroom practice. Part of the problem is that Posner et al.'s (1982) rationale for their position was presented in abstract, philosophical terms.

More positively, the relevant literature that is available largely has been summarized using sophisticated statistical techniques by Guzzetti, Snyder, Glass, and Gamas (1993). They concluded, based on all of the available studies, that conceptual conflict instruction was effective in promoting understanding of ideas in science not consistent with prior knowledge. Even more optimistic is that science educators are identifying additional strategies for imparting scientific concepts, ones that we believe often can be used in tandem with the conceptual change strategy as part of comprehensive science curricula.

Analogies

Making analogies involves finding similarities between a new concept and a familiar one to make the new concept more understandable. One reason it is good to teach students to think analogically is that scientists do things analogically (Glynn, 1991): Kepler explained planetary motion with analogies to clockwork; Priestley explained electrical force using analogies to gravitational force; and the physicist Campbell argued that particles of kinetic gases behave something like billiard balls (Figure 12.1). Powerful analogies can help teachers communicate to young minds as well and may be especially compelling when some scientific fact is difficult to comprehend to the point of being unbelievable. (See Chapter 3 for additional discussion of the power of analogies in thinking; e.g., Gick & Holyoak, 1980, 1983).

Recall a point made in the last subsection, that sometimes students find it difficult to accept that static objects exert force, so that it is somewhat unbelievable to many young students that the chair they are sitting on is exerting an upward force equal to their weight or that a table is exerting a force equal to the weight of the centerpiece, place settings, and food on top of it. Clement and colleagues (see Clement et al., 1989) had the insight that there were other physical situations analogous to static objects exerting force that are understood and accepted by many students and that these situations could be used as analogies to explain the more unbelievable idea, referring to the understandable situations as anchoring intuitions or bridging analogies. Clement et al.'s hypothesis was consistent with a report by an exceptionally talented physics teacher, Minstrell (1982), that student understanding of static objects producing forces could be increased by having students consider and discuss what happens when a weight is put on a table, a hand, or a spring balance.

In Clement et al.'s (1987) study, high school physics students received instruction about forces exerted by static objects, Newton's third law of collisions (i.e., if one object exerts a force on a second object, the second exerts an equal and opposite force on the first), and frictional forces. Students in the treatment classes were presented and discussed anchoring intuitions. For the example of a rigid table exerting force on a book lying on it (i.e., of a force exerted by a static object), students considered how a book might cause a piece of foam rubber to sag if placed

Figure 12.1 What properties of gases are captured by drawing an analogy between kinetic gases and billiard balls colliding? How does this analogy break down, as all anologies ultimately do?

on it or how a book might bend a "table" made of a flexible board (with the bending becoming less and less apparent as the board is thickened until the point when it is the thickness of a conventional table board). Students also reflected on how a spring would compress if a book were on it, and they experienced the force they exerted to hold a book in the palm of their hand. Although it took a number of discussions and bridging analogies to make the point, students in the classes receiving these analogies were better able to solve posttest problems involving forces exerted by static objects than were students receiving conventional instruction, with this advantage apparent even 2 months after instruction. Similar differences favoring analogical teaching were apparent for problems involving Newton's third law and frictional force.

Others have been able to replicate Clement et al.'s (1987) finding in true experimental comparisons (e.g., Brown, 1992; Stavy, 1991). One of the interesting features of Brown's study was the inclusion of an exceptionally difficult transfer problem requiring students to realize that when a 200-pound block is resting on a 40-pound block, the 40-pound block exerts 200 pounds of force—an idea totally foreign to those who do not understand Newtonian mechanics.

Brown also determined that bridging analogies establish a condition considered critical by Posner et al. (1982) in that they make Newtonian ideas more plausible to students. Given the success of bridging analogies in research studies, it is not surprising that instructional packages are now being developed that include bridging analogies. Although these packages are generally not evaluated in anything like true experiments, students do experience large gains in understanding from pretests to posttests as a function of experiencing these curricula (e.g., Summers, 1992).

Sometimes more than one analogy is available, and it can make a difference which analogy is applied in a situation. Thus, the flow of electricity can be understood either by analogy to flow of water (see Dupin & Joshua, 1989, for a review of evidence relevant to this point) or motion of a crowd of objects. The water flow analogy is as follows (Gentner & Gentner, 1983):

- Pipes correspond to wires, pumps to batteries, and narrow pipes to resistors.
- Water pressure is analogous to voltage, narrowness of pipes to resistance, and flow rate of water to electrical current.

- Connections in plumbing systems are like connections in electrical systems, involving pipes, pumps, and narrow pipes in the former case and wires, batteries, and resistors in the latter case. Just as flow rate increases with pressure, current increases with voltage. (Based on Gentner & Gentner, 1983, Table 6.1)

In contrast, the moving crowds analogy involves objects moving through passageways with all of the attendant characteristics of such crowds. For example, when the passageway narrows, there is a slowing down at the point where the narrowing occurs. Gentner and Gentner (1983) described it this way:

> Voltage corresponds to how powerfully they [moving objects] push. Like the water analogy, the moving-crowd model establishes a distinction between current and voltage. Further, the moving crowd model allows a superior treatment of resistors. In this model we can think of a resistor as analogous to a barrier containing a narrow gate. This "gate" conception of resistors is helpful in predicting how combinations of resistors will behave. . . . However, it is hard to find a useful realization of batteries in this model. (p. 111)

Gentner and Gentner (1983, Experiment 1) analyzed how high school and college students who used water flow and moving crowd models performed on circuit problems. The most pertinent result here is that performance depended on the model used by the subjects. Water flow subjects did better on problems involving serial and parallel combinations of two batteries than on ones involving serial and parallel combinations of two resistors. Exactly the opposite pattern was observed for moving crowd subjects.

In a second experiment, subjects were taught either the water flow or moving crowds analogy and were administered the same problems used in the first experiment. Subjects taught the moving crowd analogy performed much like the subjects who used the moving crowd analogy on their own in the first experiment (i.e., performing better than water flow subjects on the resistor problems). The water flow analogy did not produce superior performance on problems involving batteries, however. Qualitative follow-up data made clear what was going on and provided an important warning about analogies: The college students taught the water flow analogy did not understand how water behaves. *For an analogy to work, people must understand the analogue situa-*

tion. People who do not understand how water flows cannot productively use their deficient knowledge of water flow to solve problems about electrical flow—and, in fact, may make inferences about electricity that are not justified based on their errant understanding of water flow (see also Zook, 1991; Zook & DiVesta, 1991). In Gentner and Gentner (1983), misconceptions about water flow produced misconceptions about electrical flow when subjects were taught to think of electrical flow as analogous to water flow.

Additional support for the claim that the analogy used makes a difference in thinking about a target concept was produced by Dupin and Joshua (1989). They observed different ways of thinking about electricity when elementary and high school students were taught a mechanical train analogy versus a heat flow analogy. Also, Halpern, Hansen, and Riefer (1990) had adults read passages about the lymph system and about enzymes. When readers were alerted before reading the passage on the lymph system that the system could be thought about as operating like water through the pores of a sponge, there was greater comprehension of the passage than when the analogy was to blood through the veins. When readers read the passage on enzymes, an analogy to ministers and judges making and breaking matrimonial bonds was more effective than an analogy to heat as producing different effects.

Caution in the use of analogies in science instruction is justified for several reasons. First, as we have already seen, analogies work only if learners understand the analogy. Second, sometimes students have a difficult time mapping the relationship specified by the analogy to the material they are processing, as when Kloster and Winne's (1989) students had difficulty relating an analogical advance organizer about abuses involving office photocopiers to a passage about computer crime, even though the designers of the analogous advance organizer built in a one-to-one relationship between the elements of the photocopier example and the information about computer crime presented in the text. Third, analogies (and there are many analogies in science texts; Glynn, 1991) can produce misconceptions. For example, Walker and Wilson (1991) found the following analogy in a grade-4 science textbook, which induces the misconception that for raindrops to appear, a cloud must be squeezed, which is not consistent at all with the scientific explanation for why the molecules come closer together:

You might think of the air as a sponge. A sponge holds water until it is squeezed. Cooled air is like a sponge being squeezed. As air is cooled, its molecules lose energy and slow down. They come closer together. Some of the water molecules in the air are squeezed out. (Cooper, Blackwood, Bolschen, Giddings, & Carin, 1985, p. 169)

Fourth, even the best analogies break down at some point. Thus, even though water flow is a good analogy for electrical flow, when an electrical wire breaks, the electricity does not flow out of it as water flows out of a broken pipe (see Glynn, 1991).

One solution to the inadequacy of single analogies may be to present multiple analogies. Although each analogy breaks down in some way, in that it is incomplete, misleading, or fails to focus attention on important information (see Spiro, Feltovich, Coulson, & Anderson, 1989), several analogies can cover all of the important information pertaining to a to-be-acquired concept. Also, if a student does not understand one of the potential analogies or cannot map the analogous example to the to-be-learned relationship, they might understand a different analogy well enough to use it productively. This multiple-analogy approach currently is being explored for teaching of advanced concepts, such as biological information conveyed to medical students. We believe this approach should be explored in some detail for elementary science teaching as well, however. For example, recall in Clement et al. (1987) that it was possible to identify multiple analogies to explain basic physics concepts. Recall also that Clement et al. (1987) believed their intervention was successful because of the multiple analogies. Multiple analogies probably permit learner insights that single analogies cannot, highlighting different attributes of the concept (Glynn, 1991; Spiro et al., 1989). Multiple analogies also probably have persuasive force that single analogies do not.

On many occasions, however, the science teacher is only going to have a single analogy—for even a single analogy is sometimes hard to devise. Glynn's (1991) **teaching with analogies (TWA)** model has special promise in that situation. Glynn (1991) argued that to teach with an analogy, either as part of text or in a lecture, the target concept should be introduced, the retrieval of the analogue should be cued, the features shared by the target and analogue should be highlighted and the similarities mapped, the conclusions about the target intended by the analogy should be drawn, and where the analogy breaks down should be indicated. That is,

one way to handle analogy breakdown is simply to warn the learner. Indeed, by explaining where an analogy breaks down, it is possible to highlight the unique features of the concept being taught, as in this explanation of the breakdown of the water flow analogy for electrical flow cited by Glynn (1991):

The water analogy is quite useful for gaining a conceptual understanding of electric circuits, but it does have its limitations. An important one is that a break in a water pipe results in water spilling from the circuit, whereas a break in an electric circuit results in a complete stop in the flow of electricity. Another has to do with turning current off and on. When you *close* an electrical switch that connects the circuit, you allow current to flow in much the same way as you allow water to flow by *opening* a faucet. Opening a switch stops the flow of electricity. An electric current must be closed for electricity to flow. Opening a water faucet, on the other hand, starts the flow of water. Except for these and some other differences, thinking of electric current in terms of water current is a useful way to study electric circuits. (Hewitt, 1987, pp. 526–527)

Glynn and his colleagues are now conducting research aimed at identifying the strengths and weaknesses of the TWA model.

Analogies often can help students understand scientific concepts. Analogies have limits, however, in that the student must understand an analogue situation in order to use it to mediate learning of new content. In addition, no analogy completely captures a new concept, with analogical breakdowns having the potential for inducing misconceptions. Use of multiple analogies and presentation of explanations that warn of breakdowns may reduce the impact of this shortcoming of analogies, however. We expect considerable additional research on analogically mediated learning of science given the prominence of discussions of analogy in the science education literature. Such work has considerable promise for affecting educational practice, especially since even students as young as preschoolers can benefit from analogies at least in some cases (Alexander et al., 1989; Alexander, Willson, White, & Fuqua, 1987; Brown, 1989; Brown & Kane, 1988; Brown, Kane, & Echols, 1986; Brown, Kane, & Long, 1989; Goswami, 1991, 1992; Vosniadou & Schommer, 1988).

Refutation Text

One possible way to deal with misconceptions is simply to alert students to potential misconceptions and how the misconceptions differ from the scientific concept being taught. Consider the following example of text, which includes a refutation of potential misconceptions (highlighted here):

> A central point to be made is that the medieval impetus theory is incompatible with Newtonian mechanics in several fundamental ways. . . . To get a sense of some of the motion studies mentioned, imagine the following situation. A person is holding a stone at shoulder height while walking forward at a brisk pace. What kind of path will the stone follow as it falls? *Many people to whom this problem is presented answer that the stone will drop straight down, striking the ground directly under the point where it was dropped. A few people are even convinced that the falling stone will travel backward and land behind the point of its release. In reality,* the stone will move forward as it falls, landing a few feet ahead of the release point. Newtonian mechanics explains that when the stone is dropped, it continues to move forward at the same speed as the walking person, because (ignoring air resistance) no force is acting to change its horizontal velocity. (Hynd & Alverman, 1986, p. 444)

Adding refutational information to text has had variable effects on student learning in investigations to date. Adding refutations to text improved learning for low-achieving college students in Alvermann and Hague (1989) and Hynd and Alvermann (1986). Comparable effects with average-achieving college students have not been obtained in studies to date (Alvermann & Hynd, 1991). Perhaps less able students cling less tenaciously to their misconceptions because they are less certain of them, lacking confidence in their knowledge and abilities in general (Alvermann & Hynd, 1991).

An interesting possibility, however, is that refutation text will be more potent if efforts are made to assure that students do, in fact, experience cognitive conflict as they process the text. Thus, if students are warned that they are reading about a concept for which they may possess misconceptions and are urged to activate relevant prior knowledge that is not consistent with the to-be-acquired concept, refutation text may have more of an impact (Alvermann & Hynd, 1991). The effects of refutation text, including the possibility that it may need to be complemented by other instructional components that increase cognitive conflict, should be explored in greater detail, for, on the face of it, good refutations seem like a direct way to alert students to potential beliefs they may hold that are inconsistent with scientific conceptions.

Multiple and Alternative Representations

A recurring hypothesis in the science education literature is that students will learn science content better if they construct multiple and alternative representations of the content, stimulated in part by two types of reports: Distinguished scientists (Ben-Zvi, Eylon, & Silberstein, 1987; Miller, 1984) and good science students (e.g., Bowen, 1990) report constructing alternative representations as they think about scientific problems. The skilled chemist can represent a reaction with an equation, imagine the molecules interacting in his or her mind's eye, and imagine what the reaction looks like (e.g., memories of water drops on the sides of the many beakers used in classroom demonstrations of hydrogen and oxygen reacting). In contrast, many typical students do not construct multiple or alternative representations on their own (e.g., Ben-Zvi et al., 1987; Wandersee, 1988; Yarroch, 1985), for example, perhaps not thinking beyond the symbols in a chemical equation—so much so that the symbols are treated more as elements in a mathematical equation than as symbols for chemicals with physical characteristics. Consistent with expert theory (see Chapter 4), one possibility is that if students could only be taught and persuaded to construct multiple representations, their scientific learning and thinking would be improved. This hypothesis is particularly interesting because science educators have had it so long—generations of students have constructed ball and stick models in chemistry classes. Tens of millions of frogs have been dissected in hopes of increasing understanding of anatomy beyond insights produced by text and pictures. When dissection is not possible, such as in introductory courses in human anatomy, students have been presented many different depictions of the same anatomical features.

Some of the multiple/alternative representations hypotheses currently being explored in formal science education research mirror ones covered in earlier chapters: For example, to increase comprehension and recall of science, (1) read for main ideas and construct summaries capturing the important points in a piece of science text (e.g., Aulls, 1991); (2) create verbal and imaginal (pictorial) representations of the same concept, for concepts dually coded are more memorable than those coded verbally only or imaginally only (e.g., Vasu & Howe, 1989; Walker & Wilson, 1991); and (3) write about science in order to learn science (e.g., Santa & Havens, 1991).

Other multiple/alternative representation hypotheses are more unique to science education, such as the following: (1) Graphing data as it is collected increases understanding of the significance of data. For example, graphing the speed of an object as a function of time since it was thrown is a striking way of understanding acceleration, especially if it can be done quickly after the data pertaining to the physical event have been collected (e.g., Beichner, 1990; Brasell, 1987; Krajcik, 1991; Mokros & Tinker, 1987). Microcomputer technologies now exist that permit graphing of acceleration and velocity functions shortly after a movement occurs. A radar gun–type device directly feeds data into a microcomputer. Other types of physical relationships can be graphed quickly after data collection based on inputs from other probes, including thermometers as well as voltage, light, and pH meters. See Linn and Songer (1991) for an example of how such technology can be used to teach thermodynamics.

(2) Videodisc and microcomputer presentations of scientific events (e.g., chemical reactions) when combined with more conventional symbolic representational activities (e.g., writing and balancing equations) increase understanding of scientific concepts so represented (Krajcik, 1991; Smith & Jones, 1988). Videodisc visuals illustrating the particulate nature of matter are effective in combination with tutorial dialogue (Krajcik & Peters, 1989). Many such scientific **microworlds** (Pea & Kurland, 1984) are being created at present (Simmons, 1991), with it virtually certain that a great deal of research will be conducted in the near future to determine the effects of microworlds on student representation and understanding of scientific concepts. Microworlds afford the possibility of watching and rewatching scientific phenomena (e.g., chemical reactions) at various levels of analysis and from various perspectives (e.g., a time-lapse presentation of a plow rusting as well as a molecular-level animation of the molecules reacting).

(3) Scientific ideas can be rendered more understandable if students create **conceptual maps** focusing on the more important concepts and specifying relationships between more and less important terms and ideas. Because creation of conceptual maps is receiving a great deal of research attention at present, most of the remainder of this subsection is devoted to discussion of conceptual mapping research.

The hypothesis that conceptual mapping might be helpful is offered in the context of science instruction based on poorly organized textbooks and classroom instruction (Mason, 1992) that does not differentiate well between more central and less critical scientific information. Science educators such as Novak (e.g., Novak & Gowin, 1984) recommend conceptual graphing as a means of organizing scientific content that is presented initially in a poorly organized fashion. Once a decision has been made to map some content area, mapping proceeds as follows (Ault, 1985; Novak & Gowin, 1984; Okebukola, 1990):

- Key words and phrases are identified.
- Key concepts are ordered from the most general (i.e., most abstract and inclusive) to the most specific.
- The concepts are then clustered using two criteria. Concepts that interrelate are put together; concepts are classified with respect to their level of abstract (i.e., general concepts to specific ones). All of the concepts are then arranged loosely in a two-dimensional array with abstractness as one dimension and main ideas as the other.
- Related concepts are then linked with lines, with the lines labeled to specify the relationship between the concepts.

The concept maps produced by students will differ because a concept map represents an individual's construction of meaning from text. The idea is to get students to recognize not only hierarchical relationships between concepts, but also cross-linkages between various concepts. Concept maps need not capture just relations in a single text or in today's lecture. Good concept maps capture relationships across courses of studies. Concept maps can be extremely elaborate.

Two examples of concept maps generated in Okebukola's (1990) research are presented in Figures 12.2 and 12.3. Readers should study these maps carefully, noting the hierarchical relationships between concepts captured by going from the top to the bottom of the concept maps. Within each level of this hierarchy, concepts are roughly equal in abstraction and importance. Linkages between ideas within concepts and between concepts are specified in the maps. The flexibility of concept mapping and the intricacies of relationships that can be captured should be apparent with a few minutes' contemplation of the sample figures. It should also be apparent that construction of concept maps requires a great deal of active processing of content, including selective at-

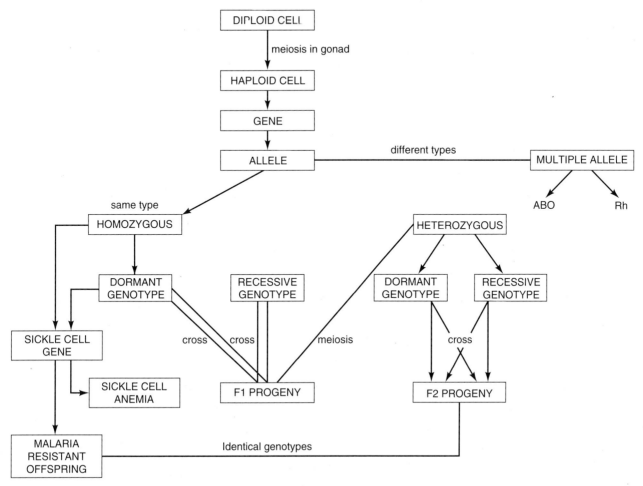

Figure 12.2 Concept map on simple Mendelian inheritance drawn by one of the subjects in Okebukola (1990). (Reprinted by permission of the author and the National Association for Research in Science Teaching.)

tention to and encoding of information, selective combination of information to make it interpretable, and selective comparisons of concepts to one another and to concepts known previously (Okebukola, 1990). Such selective encoding, combination, and comparisons would be expected to affect understanding and memory of scientific content.

Does concept mapping increase learning and understanding of science? The evidence is mixed (Willerman & MacHarg, 1991) at present. Some studies report significant, positive effects (e.g., Heinze-Fry & Novak, 1990; Okebukola, 1990), and others do not (e.g., Lehman, Carter, & Kahle, 1985). When we read a number of concept studies, we were struck that even when positive effects were produced, they were often small in magnitude. One possibility might be that inconsistencies in outcomes and small overall effects reflect differential impact of mapping,

with concept mapping helping some types of students but not others.

In fact, there is evidence supporting the differential-effect hypothesis: Only lower-ability students benefited from concept mapping in Stensvold and Wilson (1990). Sherris (1984) obtained concept mapping effects with students who had an external locus of control (i.e., students whose cognition and perception tends to be affected by external factors) but not with students with internal control. Students who mastered the techniques of concept mapping benefited more from construction of concept maps than students who had not mastered the techniques in Fraser and Edwards (1985).

One group, at Texas Christian University, has reported more success than others in improving learning through mapping (Lambiotte, Dansereau, Cross, & Reynolds, 1989). They have found that providing

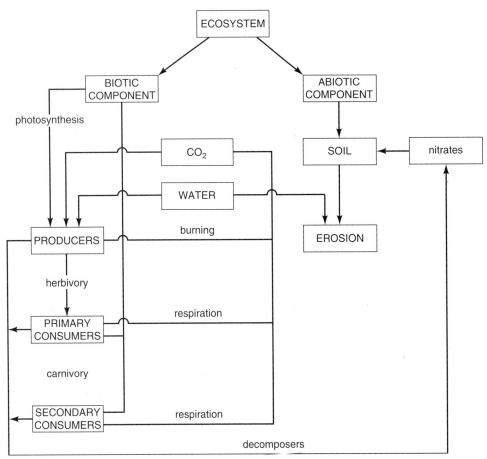

Figure 12.3 Concept map on ecology drawn by another student in Okebukola (1990). (Reprinted by permission of the author and the National Association for Research in Science Teaching.)

students with maps outlining a procedure or process (e.g., flow through the digestive system) are more effective in promoting learning than maps describing details related to other concepts (i.e., maps summarizing declarative knowledge), with such maps more effective in promoting learning than text describing the same process. Consistent with other investigators, they have observed greater mapping effects with lower-ability compared with higher-ability learners.

Our guess is that the great interest in concept mapping will continue. Our suspicion as well is that these procedures will seem more effective as investigators devise measurement procedures that are more sensitive to the strengths of conceptual mapping. For example, conceptual mapping does require interpretations by students resulting in selective attention to information and ultimately in differences in concept map representations. The richness of these interpretations has not been a focus of evaluations of concept mapping to date. If concept mapping does lead students to identify relationships they would otherwise miss and construct interpretations not obvious when mapping is not encouraged, these are important cognitive outcomes. More research and more creative research (especially with respect to dependent variables) should be conducted in this area.

In general, when all of the evidence on multiple and alternative representations is considered, there is modest support for encouraging students to construct alternative interpretations. Even though effects often are reported, they are not always large, however, so that there is nothing here to support the possibility that attempting to construct multiple representations alone leads to great expertise. When the interest in multiple representations in mathematics education (see Chapter 13) and science education are combined, however, it is clear that there is considerable intellectual momentum in the direction of expanding study of multiple representations. A number of research careers will be devoted to determine when and how instruction (and what types of instruction) in the construction of multiple representations produces important gains in science achievement.

Socially Supported, Collaborative Construction of Science Concepts

Many science educators would like students to engage in pure discovery learning, consistent, for instance, with Piagetian notions of learning (i.e., natural cognitive conflict, which is viewed as a powerful mechanism for cognitive change, often accompanies discovery). Such educators believe that discovery learning produces especially deep understanding of science and improves student attitudes toward science, hypotheses that have recurred throughout the 20th century from Dewey (e.g., 1933) to articles published in the 1990s (e.g., Ajewole, 1991). That there are so many science misconceptions among students who have acquired scientific knowledge on their own makes it obvious that pure discovery learning alone is not always a good idea, however, despite its enduring attraction to some science educators. Rather than abandon entirely the constructivist ideal of discovery, many other science educators are exploring a number of socially mediated types of instruction that permit guided discovery and scaffolded student exploration of science concepts. Thus, scaffolded instruction and various types of cooperative learning are being explored in science education, although these are always part of multicomponential instruction.

Consistent with this direction, social support is consistently observed in analyses of outstanding science teaching. Tobin of Florida State University has been especially active in studying outstanding science teaching, observing teachers nominated by teaching peers and other educators as outstanding at their craft. The findings from Tobin's studies are generally consistent with those of others studying exemplary science teaching (e.g., Garnett, 1987; Treagust, 1991).

For example, after studying 13 exemplary elementary and high school science teachers, Tobin and Fraser (1990) offered the following observations:

- Exemplary science teachers use management strategies that encourage *high student engagement*. They monitor their students and maintain control with quick, effective interventions. There is little need for teacher sanctioning, however, because there is little misbehavior. Instruction is well-organized with little time wasted moving from one activity to another. There are well-established routines in the class so that students know what to do when. There is a cooperative spirit in the classroom, with students consistently helping others.
- Teachers understand well the content they are teaching.
- Teachers are concerned with improving student *understanding* of content. Activities require student involvement and problem solving, with adequate materials and support for these activities. Concrete examples and analogies are used to explain abstract ideas. Most critically, teachers monitor student understanding and react when there is misunderstanding, posing questions to students that stimulate thinking in particular directions. Students elicit clarifications, and teachers react by prompting extensions of student thinking. Teachers do offer explanations on some occasions, however. That is, instruction is *scaffolded* in the sense of the term developed in Chapter 8. In particular, there are "safety nets" so that students can participate without risk of embarrassment or failure. For example, teachers treat all attempts at problem solving with respect and work with all misunderstandings, attempting to lead even students who have extreme misunderstandings to scientifically defensible perspectives.

Good science teachers are like other good teachers in having well-managed classrooms (see Chapter 7). They know what is happening in their class as a whole and with individual students, providing feedback and input that is tailored to student needs.

Theorists and educators such as Newman and colleagues (e.g., 1990; Newman, Griffin, & Cole, 1989) believe that socially interactive instruction permits students to experience distributed cognition (see Chapter 8)—to experience thinking in groups. Consistent with Vygotskian theory, they conceive of much of thinking happening outside the head of the student, with participation in thinking groups and in interaction with teachers who scaffold input as crucial to cognitive development and learning. Newman et al.'s (1989) commitment to Vygotskian ideas about instruction within the zone of proximal development (see Chapter 8), instruction that leads children to construct new knowledge in collaboration with others, is apparent from consideration of the title of their book—*The Construction Zone.*

One especially interesting point emphasized by Newman is that the meaning of a child's action is often determined by what follows the action, so teachers can respond either in ways that make a child's actions meaningful or in ways that do not link the student's actions to effective problem solving. An example of responding that enhances students' understanding of their own actions was provided by Newman et al. (1989) when they taught grade-4 students how to make all possible comparisons between pairs of objects.

An efficient way to generate all possible comparisons is first compare objects 1 and 2, then objects then 1 and 3, 1 and 4, until 1 and n is reached; then compare objects 2 and 3, 2 and 4, and so on, until 2 and *n* is reached; then compare 3 and 4 and so on, until 3 and n is reached; continue until n-1 and n are compared. This strategy usually is not observed in the absence of instruction until adolescence (e.g., Inhelder & Piaget, 1958). To teach this approach, first, Newman et al.'s (1989) tutor presented the student with a stack of picture cards of movie stars with the task of generating all possible pairs of movie stars. After the student generated a response, which invariably reflected generation of less than all possible pairings, the tutor reacted: "How do you know you have all pairs?" A typical response was, "I can't think of anymore," to which the tutor responded, "Could you check to see if you have all the pairs?" When the student fails to respond, the tutor says, "Well, I have a way to check. Do you have all the pairs with Mork?" (p. 191). Then the tutor went through a checking procedure asking about whether Mork had been paired with each of the other stars by the student, going through the deck on a star-by-star basis. Then the tutor did the same checking exercise with a second star, perhaps checking whether Mindy had been paired with every other star in the deck. Once the student understood this checking procedure, the tutor permitted the student to do it on his or her own.

When students were presented subsequent generate-all-pairs tasks, they were much more likely to be successful than they had been on the first trial in generating all possible pairings, despite the fact that they had never been taught directly to do so. What happened was that the tutor had taken the student's initial actions and rendered them more meaningful with the remarks about the checking strategy. These remarks made clear that the student's first pairings were incomplete. The comments also provided a powerful hint as to how more complete pairings might be generated. The student, however, generated the insight that the checking strategy could be used proactively. The tutor took what the youngster did and reacted to it so that the student would construct more powerful understandings of the inadequacy of the initial attempt and how the task might be done more effectively. Student cognitive growth occurred because of a particular reaction by the teacher in the context of supportive student-tutor interactions.

An important pedagogical principle emerges from Newman's analyses in particular. When students attempt an in-class experiment or work on problems, it is critical for there to be reflective discussion afterward. Thus, if small groups of students work on a chemistry laboratory exercise, bringing the group back together to discuss what happened makes a great deal of sense, in that alternative possibilities will be discussed with ensuing cognitive conflict. There is also the possibility for the teacher to react to what the students have done in order to stimulate them to think more about the problem. If the teacher is successful in providing hints and input that encourages students to understand the shortcomings of their problem solutions and, at the same time, encourages students to "figure out" more adequate solutions, he or she would be successful from Newman's perspective that teachers can encourage additional cognitive growth by encouraging reflection by students on their actions. If students provide such feedback to one another as well, the situation is even better. In that case, thinking would be fully distributed between teachers and students, with cognitive development of individual students stimulated by such thinking in social interaction consistent with Vygotskian ideals. Simultaneously the Piagetian ideal that knowledge is best developed through student constructions would be served. Reflective consideration of student attempts at problem solving has a lot going for it. (For another nice example of such socially interactive teaching in science, review discussion of Hatano and Inagaki [1991] in Chapter 8.)

An emerging consensus in science education is that social interaction around science problems is desirable, especially if a skilled teacher collaborates with students and scaffolds input to them. Consistent with direct explanation models, such teachers sometimes explain and sometimes model scientific thinking. There is also mounting evidence that such instruction produces great student involvement in learning, with students self-regulating their participation in group problem solving so that a high percentage of time is devoted to learning (e.g., see Pizzini & Shepardson's [1992] analysis of one socially interactive, problem-solving approach to science instruction; also, Amigues [1988] provided an important analysis of how interaction during physics problem solving heightened grade-10 students' self-monitoring and deliberate self-regulation).

Glynn, Yeany, and Britton (1991), in the introduction to their edited book on the psychology of science learning, provided a summary of socially interactive instruction that captures all of its most important features:

> Teachers should require students to reason scientifically. One way they can do this is by modeling scientific reasoning for their students. In effect, teachers and students should become collaborators in the process of scientific reasoning. Together, students and teachers should construct interesting questions about scientific phenomena; simply telling students the answers has little lasting value. Teachers and students should guess, or hypothesize, about the underlying causes of science phenomena. Teachers and students should collect data and design scientific tests of their hypotheses. And, finally, teachers and students should construct theories and models to explain the phenomena in question. Throughout all stages of this collaboration, teachers and students should be constantly "thinking out loud" (Glynn, Muth, & Britton, 1990). By means of the "thinking out loud" technique, teachers can help students to reflect on their own scientific reasoning processes (that is, to think metacognitively) and to refine these processes. (p. 4)

Teachers modeling and explaining processing to students as they attempt to work it out (i.e., construct their own understanding of the processing) in interaction with other students should be a familiar theme by now. This is how sophisticated cognitively based instruction is occurring across the curriculum. No teacher could possibly convey all of the tacit knowledge, the know-how, that is part of understanding any scientific concept (or any other concept for that matter). Students can acquire much tacit knowledge (e.g., Champagne & Bunce, 1991) by

working out problems with a little help from their classmates and their teachers.

We close this subsection with a warning, however. It is easy for socially interactive instruction and problem solving to go awry. For example, Gayford (1989) observed that in many cooperative science instruction groups, one person did most or all of the work. Not surprisingly, many members of such groups learn little (Gayford, 1992). Basili and Sanford (1991) found that there were good and poor cooperative group leaders, with conceptual change anything but certain in cooperative groups, especially ones with poor leaders. One difficulty in Basili and Sanford (1991) was that students often lacked critical prior knowledge that could not be remediated effectively by group cooperative discussion. Perlmutter, Behrend, Kuo, and Muller (1989) reported variable effects of cooperative pairing when children worked on problem solving together in a computer environment. Some children some of the time were helped by cooperation; some children some of the time were harmed by cooperation, with little basis for predicting when facilitation should be expected versus interference. Cooperative models that boil down simply to regrouping students for instruction often will fail to produce the types of high-quality social interactions considered in this section. Implementing cooperative learning alone guarantees nothing (e.g., Sherman, 1988; Tingle & Good, 1990). What is required is not social interaction per se but social interaction in which all students participate and learn without fear or intimidation; the presence of a science expert who can detect a variety of misunderstandings that students may possess and intervene to provide remediation may be necessary for instruction in advanced conceptual areas, such as most of science.

Closing Comments: Constructivist Nature of Conceptual Change Instruction

If there is any theme that pervades contemporary science education, it is that students must construct scientific understandings for themselves if they are to understand at a deep level. Consistent with Piaget (as well as other perspectives, such as schema theory; see Chapter 3), science educators recognize that the conceptual understandings a student brings to a situation play a large role in determining their understanding of the situation. If new information is inconsistent with the views already held by a child, there is the possibility for cognitive conflict, which motivates efforts by the child to comprehend the new input. Such conflict opens the possibility that the student will accommodate their current views to the new input, resulting in a new conceptualization of the situation by the student.

Analogies can aid in the process by connecting new information with understandings already possessed by the student but ones not activated by the student naturally (e.g., reminding the student of the clear effort exerted when books are held in the palm of the hand when the student is trying to comprehend that a table must exert a force equal to the weight of the objects on it). Other methods considered in this section also increase the likelihood that students will simultaneously activate newly presented science concepts and inconsistent prior knowledge, such as refutation text and socially interactive instruction. Although these interventions increase the likelihood that the student will exert cognitive effort to attempt to understand the scientific conception, science educators believe that analogies, texts, and social interaction advance scientific understanding by stimulating cognitive conflict, which results in reflection and, ultimately, in construction of new knowledge.

These interventions work because humans have an intrinsic motivation to be more competent than they currently are (e.g., White, 1959). Anything that makes obvious that current thinking is probably flawed, probably not competent, stimulates efforts toward greater competence. A new piece of information that is presented as more adequate than the student's current thinking is grist for the mill in this situation. Demonstrations and text accompanying this new information are especially likely to be processed at a deep level if the student is aware that the new information is not in synchrony with prior knowledge, and there is reason to believe that the "fault" is with the student's current understanding rather than the new information.

Although both instructors and students are making efforts with respect to all of the interventions considered in this section, the efforts of the students toward construction of meaning are much more critical than the efforts of the instructors. The instructional tactics taken here are important only because they make student construction of knowledge more likely.

DEVELOPMENT OF SCIENTIFIC THINKING SKILLS

As far as the great theorists in educational psychology are concerned (see Chapters 7 to 9), there is no doubt who is the greatest in the eyes of the science educator community. Long after most of the cognitive developmental and educational psychologists moved on to other ideas, the science educator community continues to find Piaget's theory helpful, which should have been obvious in the discussion of conceptual change. One of the greatest appeals of the theory is that the ultimate stage of development in Piaget's theory is formal operations, which is characterized by Piagetians as enabling the best of scientific thinking.

The classic reference on formal operations is *The Growth of Logical Thinking from Childhood to Adolescence* (Inhelder & Piaget, 1958). The formal operational adolescent's thinking is not confined to the world of concrete objects and facts as is the world of the elementary student. Adolescents are capable of reasoning about realities they have never experienced. They are capable of abstract thinking, fully hypothetico deductive reasoning. That is, the adolescent can make deductions given premises, which is critical as part of scientific reasoning.

Even more impressive, the adolescent can make inductions, reasoning from evidence to conclusions. The adolescent can form hypotheses, imagining what would happen if a particular theory held. Moreover, the adolescent can experiment, understanding how to vary single factors at a time while other factors are held constant (i.e., formal operational thinkers understand how to control variables). For example, think back to the pendulum problem described in Chapter 7. To determine the factors affecting the rate of pendulum swing, it is essential to vary the length of strings while holding the weight of the pendulum constant and to vary the weight of the pendulum while holding the string length constant.

A variety of other abilities are also hypothesized to follow from formal operations according to Piaget. One is the ability to generate all possible combinations when several factors can vary (e.g., given 4 binary characteristics [+ or −], the adolescent with formal operations can generate all 16 possibilities, from − − − − to + + + + and everything in between: +− − −, − +− −, − − +−, − − − +, + +− −, +−

+ −, + − − +, − + + −, − + − +, − − + +, + + + −, − + + +, + − + +, + + − +). Another is to be able to solve problems requiring comparison of several proportions. Adolescents also can understand probability, which is an extremely important competency for working scientists.

Piaget's claim was that formal operations permit all types of scientific feats that are beyond the concrete operational student (see Brainerd, 1978b, Chapter 6, for a more extensive review). The bad news is that many adolescents and young adults fail to achieve formal operations (e.g., Lawson, 1983; Piaget, 1972), and it may make a difference with respect to the development of their scientific thinking abilities.

A recurring hypothesis is that formal operational status will be associated with success in various types of science instruction. For example, Lawson and Renner (1975) produced a clear relationship between formal operational status and the ability to acquire scientific understandings that are not the result of direct experience (i.e., **hypothetical concepts**), such as knowing what a "gene" is or "DNA replication" or "natural selection." Such concepts were beyond all concrete operational thinkers; the more highly developed formal operational competencies were, the better the acquisition of such hypothetical concepts. More recent work by Lawson and associates (e.g., Lawson & Thompson, 1988) has produced additional support for the conclusion that many scientific concepts are acquired more certainly by students who have attained formal operations than by those who have not, with the relationship between formal operational status and concept acquisition obtained even when other factors such as verbal intelligence and age are controlled. Others (e.g., Gipson, Abraham, & Renner, 1989; Glasson, 1989), however, have produced evidence that Lawson may have overestimated the relationship between formal reasoning and acquisition of abstract scientific concepts, making obvious that debates about the role of formal operational competence in scientific reasoning continue.

Case's neo-Piagetian theory (see Chapter 7) is also receiving attention from the science educators, with the possibility that mental capacity as defined by Case (i.e., the neo-Piagetian version of working memory) is an important determinant of the ability to learn various types of science content. Although not all of the evidence is positive (e.g., Staver &

Jacks, 1988), researchers such as Niaz (e.g., 1988, 1989) are producing evidence that mental capacity can make a difference in learning scientific content such as chemistry. In particular, Niaz produced evidence that problems vary in difficulty to the extent that they demand students hold information in working memory. Many science educators continue to believe that cognitive demands of science can be understood in Piagetian and neo-Piagetian terms. Moreover, there is some evidence in support of the Piagetian and neo-Piagetian assumptions.

The most ambitious program of research on the development of scientific thinking skills has been conducted by Kuhn and colleagues, resulting in two book-length reports since 1988. Kuhn definitely begins with Piagetian thinking as a starting point, although there can be little doubt that her research significantly extends Piagetian analyses of scientific thinking and behavior. Thus, the remainder of this section on the development of scientific reasoning abilities is concerned almost exclusively with Kuhn's impressive contributions to our understanding of the development of scientific competence and the potential of her work for stimulating additional studies illuminating the development of scientific competence.

Evaluation of Scientific Evidence

Kuhn, Amsel, and O'Loughlin (1988) studied the scientific evaluation abilities of students from grade-3 through college, in some cases comparing their performances to the expert evaluations of five Ph.D. candidates in philosophy. (Well-trained philosophers have extensive knowledge about how to evaluate evidence and relate it to theory.) The method used in these studies was to present participants with a problem that some scientists wanted to solve. Although several different problems were used in these studies, the most frequently cited one was concerned with determining which of four factors affected the "servability" of balls in a paddle game that was under development:

> The subject was told that a sports company was conducting an investigation. A new game was being developed and different kinds of balls were being tried out to use in the game. All the rules of the game were not yet decided, but the game was to be played by two players, who hit a ball across a net to each other using a special kind of paddle. The interviewer also explained to the subject that the investigators at the

company had tried lots of different balls and found that some resulted in good serves and some in poor serves and that there really were not any balls in between.

A box 16 sample balls was then presented for the subject to examine. The four features of the balls, size (large or small), color (light or dark), texture (rough or smooth), and presence or absence of ridges, were then described . . . [and shown to subjects]. (Kuhn et al., 1988, p. 107)

Then, each subject was shown "good serve" and "bad serve" baskets, and the experimenter asked the participant which variables he or she thought determined whether balls would result in good or bad serves. The subjects were required to explain their opinions and eventually to rank order the variables with respect to the impact on serving. This permitted the experimenter to know the subject's theory of serving—that is, coming into the experiment, which variables the participant believed affected serving.

After their personal theories of variables affecting serving were assessed, subjects were presented a number of trials, each of which was "evidence" relevant to theories of servability. For example, in one of the simpler studies, on each trial, one ball was put in the good serve basket or in the bad serve basket. Then the subject was asked what the implication of the outcome was for the theoretical variable that the subject thought was most likely to be causal. Thus, a subject who believed that the ridging of a ball affected the quality of serves might be asked the implications of a large, light, rough, ridged ball producing a "good serve." If that same subject believed the color of the ball had the least effect on serving, they might be asked to evaluate the impact on this belief of the same ball producing a "poor serve."

More complex presentations were made in other studies, although the goal of the study was always the same, to evaluate the impact of the evidence on hand to the subject's theory. Thus, a subject holding the view that ridging was important might be presented a good serve basket containing the following balls:

- Large, dark, rough, ridged.
- Small, light, rough, ridged.
- Large, light, rough, ridged.
- Large, light, smooth, nonridged.
- Small, dark, rough, ridged.
- Small, dark, smooth, nonridged.

The same subject would be presented a poor serve basket containing the following balls:

- Large, light, rough, ridged.
- Small, dark, rough, ridged.
- Small, light, smooth, nonridged.
- Large, dark, smooth, nonridged.
- Large, light, smooth, nonridged.
- Small, dark, smooth, nonridged.

For this example, five-sixths of the evidence supports the view that ridging is a determinant of servability. Such an outcome is certainly consistent with the theory that ridging produces servability, although it does not prove it. (That is, correlation does not imply causation.) An outcome that would not be consistent with the theory that ridging affected servability would be half the balls in the good basket were ridged and half were not ridged.

By getting judgments from grade-3 through college students and philosophers on such problems, it was possible to come to a number of conclusions about how students evaluate scientific data, both the strengths and the weaknesses of such evaluation efforts (Figure 12.4). Some of the more important conclusions from this series of studies were the following:

- There is improvement in evidence evaluation skills from childhood to adolescence to adulthood, although even adult college students do not evaluate evidence as skillfully as philosopher experts.
- People often ignore evidence that is not consistent with their preferred theories. They sometimes distort evidence to make it consistent with their own theories (e.g., explaining away discrepant evidence by appealing to some third variable that must be operating to distort the situation).
- People often make the mistake that correlation implies causation. For example, that five of the six balls in the good basket are ridged and five of the six balls in the bad basket are not ridged does not prove that ridging causes servability. An alternative possibility is that ridging covaries with some other variable—perhaps the ridged balls are made of a different material than the nonridged balls.
- Many people do not understand the concept of covariation, for example, believing that some in-

children have more difficulty than adults in coordinating theories and evidence potentially relevant to theories (Kuhn, 1989), there was still great variability in the abilities of adults to interpret evidence. Philosophers rarely made logical errors; college students did not do as well as philosophers but were much better at evaluation of evidence than adults not enrolled in college. Kuhn et al. (1988) complemented this research on evaluation with research on whether people can generate evidence consistent with particular theories, with that work generating additional evidence of difficulty in separating theory and evidence.

Generation of Evidence

A critical scientific skill is knowing what types of outcomes would support a theory and what would not support it. For example, a scientist cannot begin to plan a test of a theory without knowing in advance the nature of evidence that would provide compelling support for the theory as well as the nature of evidence that would be inconsistent with the theory. For example, to evaluate the development of competence to generate scientific evidence, Kuhn et al. (1988) asked subjects to generate evidence supporting their preferred explanation of servability (e.g., that size of the ball affects servability) and evidence that would be contrary to a particular theory.

In general, the outcomes were consistent with the evaluation study outcomes:

- In general, there were developmental improvements from grade 3 to college, with college students better at generation of evidence than noncollege adults.
- Participants were better able to produce evidence of covariation than evidence of noncovariation.
- The most prevalent difficulty in generating covariation evidence was a failure to control other variables. For example, subjects were willing to make claims of a clear covariation between ridging and servability with presentation of a confounded comparison, perhaps of a large, light, rough, ridged ball producing a good serve and a small, dark, smooth, nonridged ball producing a poor serve. Ridging is confounded (covaries) with all three other variables in this example. A

Figure 12.4 How likely is it that these college students are good at scientific thinking according to Kuhn's work? Is it likely they could design a well-controlled experiment?

ference about covariation could be made given only one ball in one of the baskets.
- People have difficulties comparing two theories at once, paying attention only to a subset of the information available.
- People do not recognize that when variables do not covary, causality is not possible. (Correlation does not imply causation, but causation implies correlation.)
- People have difficulty making sense of mixed evidence.

Kuhn et al. (1988) produced evidence that people often failed to see relationships that existed in data. Other times, their subjects claimed the existence of relationships that could not be inferred rationally from the evidence on hand. Although there were developmental improvements in the evaluation of evidence, consistent with the conclusion that two-ball example providing clearer support of covariation between ridging and servability would be a large, light, rough, ridged ball producing a good serve and a large, light, rough, nonridged ball not doing so.

- It was easier to generate evidence compatible with one's own theory than evidence incompatible with one's own beliefs.

Consistent with the evaluation data, there were substantial difficulties in the generation of evidence, and, in particular, there were more difficulties in working with noncovariation than with covariation. Although there was evidence in both the evaluation and the generation data that younger students in particular experience difficulties isolating and manipulating single variables (or understanding manipulations of single variables).

In contrast to Piaget's (e.g., Inhelder & Piaget, 1958) theory, however, Kuhn et al. (1988) do not ascribe the difficulties they observed to lack of formal operations. Rather, they raised the possibility that young students lack "experimentation strategies." A person with an experimenting strategy knows to focus on one variable at a time—varying that variable while holding other factors constant. Thus, information about roughness is provided when a small, dark, rough, ridged ball is compared to a small, dark, smooth, ridged ball but not if a large, dark, rough, ridged ball is compared to a small, dark, smooth, ridged ball (i.e., size and roughness-darkness are confounded in the latter comparison). The importance of having such an experimenting strategy will be considered further later in this section.

Scaffolded Practice Performing Experiments

In a number of studies, Kuhn and colleagues have evaluated the possibility that students may learn scientific procedures through practice doing tasks requiring the procedures for success. In the two studies discussed here, subjects were provided multiple trials working on scientific problems designed to illuminate particular scientific procedures. The first was concerned with children learning how to evaluate and generate evidence. The second focused on children learning how to make unconfounded comparisons, learning how to control variables (i.e., how

to make the tests Piagetians consider indicative of formal operational competence, as discussed earlier in this section). The adult experimenter provided scaffolded support in these studies, nudging the child gently to "discover" a strategy or way of thinking about data. There were substantial improvements in many children's scientific thinking skills observed in these studies.

Kuhn et al. (1988, Study 5) investigated the acquisition of evidence evaluation and generation skills in the context of the "balls" problem considered earlier in this section. Over the course of nine sessions, grade-5 and grade-6 students were asked to generate evidence to show a theory to be correct, generate evidence of theory incorrectness, evaluate insufficient evidence, evaluate theory-consistent and theory-inconsistent covariation evidence, evaluate mixed evidence, and evaluate unequal evidence for two competing theories. As subjects attempted problems, the experimenter provided prompts directing attention to important evidence that the subject ignored. For example, if the subject only used evidence from one of the two baskets to generate an evaluation, the experimenter pointed out the evidence in the basket that was ignored. Sometimes the experimenter would elicit information about potential strategies that might be used by asking the subject to reflect and respond to how someone else performed a task (e.g., Another person thought that size was what caused them to come out different. What do you think of that person's idea?).

Many of Kuhn et al.'s (1988, Study 5) students (but not all) made progress in learning how to evaluate and generate evidence. A particular strength of Kuhn et al. (1988, Study 5) was the inclusion of a control condition that did not receive practice on the balls task but did receive experimenter attention by working on another problem-solving task during the time corresponding to when the "balls" subjects worked on balls problems. Although the balls subjects and the control subjects performed identically and poorly on a pretest involving evaluation and generation of evidence on balls problems, the balls subjects were much better able to evaluate and generate evidence on the posttest.

In Kuhn and Phelps (1982), grade-4 and grade-5 subjects who did not have an isolation-of-variables strategy were presented problems involving mixtures of chemicals producing reactions. Thus, they observed an experimenter pour three chemicals in a beaker containing a fourth chemical with a resulting reaction (liquid turns red). The experimenter then poured three other chemicals in a container with the same fourth chemical and produced a different reaction (liquid turns cloudy). The subjects were then asked to plan and carry out experiments to determine what caused the reaction producing red and the other reaction that produced cloudiness. (In both cases, combining one of the three chemicals with the fourth chemical was sufficient to cause the reaction observed.) As the child attempted a solution to this problem, the experimenter encouraged the child to analyze what they were doing and to interpret their results. There were 11 to 13 sessions of such problem solving, with problems becoming more complicated as sessions continued (i.e., combinations of several liquids produced reactions instead of combinations of two chemicals). An optimal response in this situation included generating a genuine *hypothesis* (e.g., "It could be either B or C that is making it red," or "I want to see if D has anything to do with it"), a genuine *experiment involving manipulation* of a variable or variables of interest while holding other variables constant, and a legitimate *inference* based on the manipulation (e.g., "It's B because it turned cloudy when we tried it by itself," or "It's not C because C alone didn't do anything"). Such an optimal approach reflects understanding and use of the isolation-of-variables strategy.

At first, none of the subjects engaged in valid, efficient experimentation. By the end of the 11 to 13 trials, many subjects were performing experiments and making valid inferences. This outcome led Kuhn and Phelps (1982) to conclude that strategic experimenting behaviors (i.e., isolation-of-variables, to use the Piagetian term) can become more sophisticated when students work in a problem arena, albeit with prompts and hints and indirect feedback about how to proceed. What was also apparent in the study, however, was that figuring out how to experiment was a long-term affair with uneven progress. It was not unusual for a student to perform a true experimental manipulation during one session and then revert to less systematic testing at the beginning of the next session. Kuhn and Phelps concluded that their subjects not only were learning the new isolation-of-variables strategy, but also had to extinguish inefficient strategies (i.e., simply to proceed unsys-

tematically, messing around) and that inefficient strategies were slow to go. (Recall from Chapter 2 the discussion of how elementary students can benefit from applying a new strategy relative to a more familiar approach and yet not use the new strategy in the future. Experiencing success with a new strategy one time is not enough to ensure that a new strategy will be adopted and used in the future.)

It was also not unusual for students to believe they understood the factors affecting the chemical reaction before they actually did so (i.e., they failed to monitor their understanding, consistent with other reports of failure to monitor discussed previously; see Chapter 2). In short, the scaffolded discovery learning that was observed here (i.e., students tried out strategies while receiving feedback from an adult) required a number of trials for students who were successful in acquiring the isolation-of-variables strategy, with these successful students manifesting a number of processing deficiencies (e.g., failing to monitor their understanding, failing to stick with a successful strategy). In addition, almost half of the students were not successful in consistently applying the isolation-of-variables strategy.

There is evidence of increases in knowledge of scientific procedures (e.g., control-of-variables strategy, rules for evaluating evidence) through scaffolded experience in attempting to evaluate and generate evidence or conduct miniexperiments. The type of teaching considered in this subsection is completely constructivist, involving adults structuring the situation so students are likely to discover how to be scientific. These studies seem important to us because they are addressing the effects of a type of learning that science educators value, students learning from personal experimentation and grappling with evidence. Moreover, this is a type of learning that has been valued at least since Dewey (see Robertson, 1992). What the research reviewed in this chapter reveals, however, is that children are not nearly as facile at drawing conclusions from trial-and-error experiences as Dewey believed, and thus this work is not rewarmed Dewey but rather a whole new vision of the challenges a child faces in constructing an understanding of the world through experimentation.

More work of this type is needed, and we are optimistic it will get done. One reason is that scientific microworlds are becoming more common, and as they do, they permit a perfect opportunity for experiments in which student experiences in such worlds are structured in various ways (e.g., White, 1984). For example, it should be possible to determine if science procedures might be learned more certainly and efficiently with slightly more direct explanations and modeling. This seems likely since other researchers have succeeded in teaching students to control variables using explicit instructions and feedback, at least with respect to some traditional tasks used to tap formal operational competence. For example, Case (1974) taught 7- to 8-year-olds how to control other variables to determine factors affecting the flexibility of rods. Lawson and Wollman (1976) taught grade-5 and grade-7 students to control variables on the same task with some transfer to other Piagetian tasks observed (e.g., pendulum). In research to date (see Ross, 1988, for a review), training students to control variables has been more effective with more intense instruction of individual students than during classroom instruction and when training has occurred across contexts (e.g., school and nonschool).

As working scientists, we know that there are no more important scientific skills than understanding how to make controlled comparisons and knowing how to evaluate and generate scientific evidence. As university-level teachers of scientific methods, we are also aware, however, that there is little time in the curriculum to teach these skills. One traditional solution for experimental psychologists has been to teach methods and content simultaneously (e.g., Underwood, 1966), with scientists designing and carrying out studies related to some important content in experimental psychology (e.g., designing studies of distributed practice effects as such effects are discussed as content in a course on learning). We believe that such combined methods and content teaching ought to be possible in developing high-quality methods instruction for elementary and high school students. We are heartened by demonstrations of exciting attempts to do so, such as Linn, Clement, Pulos, and Sullivan's (1989) teaching of the control-of-variables strategy as content about blood pressure was taught to high school students. Carey, Evans, Honda, Jay, and Unger (1989) taught grade-7 students about the nature and purpose of science, hypothesis testing, experimentation, and evaluation of data as part of lessons on yeast. Lawson and Snitgen (1982) taught college students about how to make controlled tests as biology content was covered.

MORE THOUGHTS ON DISCOVERY LEARNING

Many science educators seem to remain committed to discovery learning experiences as part of science education, despite the fact that induction is inefficient at best and uncertain in outcome. There is no research on the horizon that is likely to identify ways of overcoming these limitations. Schauble (1990) provided an example of how even guided discovery (i.e., participation scaffolded by an adult who nudges the student in the direction of potentially important information) is associated with slow progress in coming to understand a scientific problem and a substantial percentage of students who do not solve a problem after a reasonable period of time.

Grade-5 and grade-6 students in Schauble (1990) interacted with a microworld involving racing cars (i.e., a racing game run on a microcomputer). Children planned, carried out, and evaluated experiments aimed at determining the variables affecting the speed of the racing cars. The game permitted the construction of 48 different racing cars by selecting one value for each of five features: (1) engine: large or small? (2) fin: on or off? (3) wheels: large, medium, or small? (4) color: red or blue? (5) muffler: on or off? Other things equal, large-engined cars were faster (i.e., went farther given the time permitted for the race) than small-engined cars. Medium-wheeled cars were faster than small-wheeled or large-wheeled cars. Not having a fin increased the speed of large-engined cars but had no effect on the speed of small-engined cars. Neither color nor the muffler variables affected speed. The computer program permitted the racing of up to three cars at a time as well as the storage of results from experiments for review.

Over the course of the 8 weeks, there were improvements in understanding the variables affecting the speed of the cars. In particular, 2 of the 22 participants figured out that the presence of the tail fin interacted with engine size; the number who believed the muffler was not a causal factor more than doubled from 8 students at pretest to 17 students at the end of 8 weeks; and 21 participants believed by the end of the study that medium wheels were fastest, compared with 5 who held this belief at the pretest.

Increases in knowledge about the variables affecting speed permitted much better predictions at the end of the 8 weeks than at the beginning of the study.

In short, consistent with the Kuhn studies, Schauble observed that students could induce understandings by personally experimenting with variables, at least given the cuing provided by the experimenter, which included some powerful hints about what might be gained from controlled comparisons. Nonetheless, the students were not efficient in generating information, sometimes figuring out a causal relation in one session and then forgetting about it in the next session (see Hancock, Kaput, & Goldsmith, 1992, for another example of students failing to coordinate across days progress made during scientific exploration). Schauble's students were not adept at monitoring their progress in understanding the causal variables in the microworld. Some children, however, consistently made confounded comparisons (e.g., trying to interpret a comparison between a large-engined, finless, medium-tired, *red*, *mufflerless* car with a large-engined, finless, medium-tired, *blue*, *mufflered* car). Invalid inferences (i.e., from invalid comparisons) included both attributions of covariation (e.g., that a noncausal variable was causal) when covariation could not be inferred logically and failures to recognize noncovariation. Many invalid judgments reflected distortions (neglect) of evidence in ways that served to preserve the children's initial theories, with such distortions more common for children who had not acquired the control-of-variables strategy during the study.

Lest readers think that inefficiencies during discovery learning are restricted to children, reports of adult difficulties during discovery learning are published regularly. For example, Hardiman, Pollatsek, and Weil (1986) presented college students with Piaget's balance beam problems, which requires subjects to determine the rule for placing weights on a beam so that the beam balances on a fulcrum at the midpoint of the beam. The college students required a mean of 49 problems before they figured out the principle for balancing the beam, with the most efficient student needing only 30 trials. Even after inducing the rule, the students sometimes reverted to solving subsequent balance beam problems with an incorrect procedure.

Given these difficulties with induction, is there any reason to continue with at least some discovery learning opportunities? Logically the answer is yes.

If real science is anything, it is an inductive enterprise. The scientist's job largely is to discover the solutions to problems. There have been many examples in this book of the principle that part of learning to do complex tasks (e.g., read for comprehension, write coherent essays) is to practice doing them. It makes good sense from this perspective to give students discovery learning experiences if we want them to be able to discover in the future.

McDaniel and Schlager (1990, Experiment 2) provided evidence that experience in discovering problem solutions increases the ability to discover solutions for subsequent problems. College students were first given experiences with water jar problems:

> In a typical water-jar problem, the subject is asked to imagine a number of empty jars (usually three) on a counter, near a sink. Each jar can hold a specified volume of water but has no graduated markings with which to hold fractional amounts. The subject is given the capacities of the three jars and an amount of water to be obtained. The object is to figure out a sequence of filling and emptying operations that will result in the goal amount residing in one of the jars. For example, the subject is told that Jar A can hold 7 units, Jar B can hold 24 units, and Jar C can hold 98 units. The goal is to obtain 60 units of water in Jar C. (McDaniel & Schlager, 1990, p. 142) [Solution to problem: Fill Jar C with 98 units of water, take out 7 units of water two times using Jar A and remove 24 units of water one time with Jar B, resulting in 60 units in Jar C.]

All subjects in the study were given 16 practice problems, in sets of four. Each of the problems in a 4-problem set could be solved using a particular "formula": (1) Fill one jar, twice remove the contents of another jar, and then add the contents of the third jar; (2) fill one jar and twice remove the quantity in one of the other jars and three times remove the quantity in the remaining jar; (3) fill one jar and remove once the quantity for one jar and twice the quantity for the other jar; and (4) fill one jar, twice remove the quantity for the other jar, and four times add the quantity of the third jar. In one condition, before attempting a set of four problems, the experimenter provided the solution rule; in the other condition of the study, subjects had to infer the rule themselves.

There were two types of transfer tasks, water jar problems involving applications of the exact rules that applied to the practice problems and water jar problems requiring discovery of novel rules. All participants were required to solve these transfer problems on their own (i.e., the experimenter did not provide the rules for solving any of the transfer problems). In general, there were small advantages for the "discovery" subjects in the speed of solving the transfer problems that involved application of previously practiced rules. More importantly, there were quite large advantages on problems requiring the discovery of new rules. The previous practice in inducing the solutions to problems seemed to increase the efficiency with which these college students grappled with problems in pursuit of a solution.

The McDaniel and Schlager (1990) data make obvious that we dare not abandon providing discovery learning experiences as part of science education. The inefficiencies of discovery learning make clear as well, however, that if the purpose of an exercise is to ensure that all participants understand a scientific principle, more than an opportunity to discover the solution may be required. In addition, when time is a factor, and it is given the extent of the contemporary science curriculum, there are more efficient methods of conveying information than discovery learning. There is little evidence that not providing discovery experiences will limit the extent to which students can apply a procedure taught through direct explanation to situations requiring exactly that principle. (McDaniel & Schlager's [1990] subjects, given direct explanation of the strategies that solved the practice problems, applied those strategies quite well relative to control participants not taught the principles or provided practice with problems that could be solved with the procedures that were explained.)

Research on the appropriate balance of direct explanation and discovery experiences is needed. The either-or quality of this debate in the past is missing the possibility that these two approaches can both be used to accomplish different objectives in a science curriculum that contains a number of goals, including making certain that students know certain classic approaches to solving particular types of problems (which often can be accomplished using direct explanation) and guaranteeing that students are able to induce new solutions when presented new types of problems (which requires skills at discovery).

CONCLUDING COMMENTS

A theme that appears repeatedly in the science education literature is that the amount of material covered in science should be reduced, in favor of a strategy of covering especially important concepts in depth. We recognize fully that the instructional strategies favored in this chapter require more than the typical lecture or textbook presentations usually found in conventional science education and thus agree with the general sentiment that if important concepts are to be taught thoroughly, there will probably need to be some reduction in the overall coverage. One of the reasons that science education is challenging is because to participate in scientific discourse, it is necessary to be armed with a large technical vocabulary, so it is not realistic to believe that there can be wholesale elimination of much of the factual learning that has traditionally been associated with science instruction.

A realistic psychology of science learning must be multifaceted, dealing both with deeply held misconceptions and factual information that is completely new or almost so. There are many techniques already covered in this book that are equal to the second task. In fairness to the science education community, some of their members are already studying some of the conventional mechanisms that can improve comprehension and learning of science and other things. For example, there are demonstrations of the positive effects on learning of science from advance organizers (e.g., Healy, 1989; Willerman & MacHerg, 1991), adjunct questions (e.g., Holliday & Benson, 1991; Holliday & McGuire, 1992; Pearson, 1991), elaborative interrogation (see Chapters 4 and 10, this book; e.g., Woloshyn, Paivio, & Pressley, 1994; Wood, Pressley, & Winne, 1990), alternative types of discourse (e.g., Dhindsa & Anderson, 1992), and dual coding through instructive illustrations and animation. Studies of the effects of dynamic pictures on learning are particularly timely because they may stimulate the construction of mental models (Mayer, 1989a; see Chapter 3, this book). Illustrations and animations may facilitate the construction of both verbal and imaginal representations of dynamic processes (e.g., how a pump works as in Mayer & Anderson [1991, 1992], Mayer & Gallini [1990], Rieber [1990]; how a brake works, Mayer [1989b]). Illustrations can also increase the memorability of important details (e.g., Waddill, McDaniel, & Einstein, 1988). Dee-Lucas and Larkin (1991) have demonstrated that students often can understand scientific proofs better if they are explained using ordinary language rather than mathematical equations. In addition, there have been studies of new technologies, such as interactive videodiscs (e.g., Hofmeister, Engelmann, & Carnine, 1989; Leonard,

1989, 1992) and microworlds (e.g., Faryniarz & Lockwood, 1992), technologies that permit much more "experimentation" as part of simulations compared with the experimentation permitted when materials must be gathered as part of a "wet" or hands-on laboratory.

Our view is that many of these approaches that are now on the periphery of the science education discipline, which has been and is obsessed with conceptual change, should probably be moved more toward center stage. There needs to be some hard thinking about how various methods of teaching can be combined to achieve a variety of science education goals, including conceptual change, construction of multiple representations of concepts entirely new to students, and development of scientific habits (e.g., commitment to isolation-of-variables strategies because of many demonstrations in microworlds that such a strategy permits generation of interpretable data).

As we conclude this chapter, we are especially disturbed about Kuhn's findings. Many students, including college students, cannot reason scientifically. There are no skills more valuable to a scientist than knowledge of the methods that permit creation of new knowledge and evaluation of scientific evidence. Kuhn's data make clear that much attention needs to be given to increasing a few fundamental thinking skills in U.S. students, including abilities to understand and generate experiments and correlational data.

We are encouraged that Kuhn and associates view important scientific competencies such as control-of-variables as strategies that can be learned by students, rather than competencies determined by factors generally considered to be out of instructional control (e.g., Piagetian stages). Not surprisingly, given the lack of concern with procedural knowledge, however, there is little about metacognition in the science education literature. More positively, a great deal of thought about other types of knowledge has occurred, although there has been emphasis on misconceptions and conceptual change to the exclusion of other problems of knowledge. Thinking about motivation is rudimentary. Yes, there is a strong belief that conceptual conflict motivates conceptual change. Even so, motivation is treated superficially in the science education literature compared with other educational arenas. It will be a while before it will be possible to construct an empirically defensible description of science learning consistent with the strategies-metacognition-knowledge-motivation framework that pervades this book.

Mathematical Problem Solving

We begin this chapter with a review of a famous set of recommendations about problem solving offered by the mathematician Polya. Our review of effective problem-solving instruction is that it stimulates the general processes that Polya cited as important in problem-solving—understanding the problem, devising a solution plan, trying it, and checking to see whether it worked—although it does much more, specifically developing important, more specific problem-solving strategies. One of the most important contemporary approaches to problem-solving instruction, offered by Schoenfeld, is completely consistent with the good information processor model featured in this book. The natural development of mathematical competence also is reviewed and is understandable from the good information processing perspective. Many specific interventions for increasing mathematical competence are discussed in this chapter, as are several specific topics that have been of particular interest to psychologists interested in mathematics achievement. These include cross-cultural differences in mathematics achievement as well as gender, racial, and socioeconomic differences in mathematics competence within Western cultures.

Research presented in this chapter is simultaneously representative of contemporary research on mathematical problem solving and directly pertinent to mathematics education. Because much of the most educationally relevant research in mathematical cognition has been conducted in elementary mathematics, there is a great deal of work pertaining to arithmetic.

INSTRUCTION OF GENERAL PROBLEM-SOLVING STRATEGIES

When I [MP] was a sophomore in high school, a classmate once asked his grade-10 algebra-2 teacher, "Is there anything we could read that would tell us how to solve word problems?" The teacher responded, "There is . . . a book called *How to Solve It* by a mathematician named George Polya." Unfortunately, none of the students in the class tracked down the book.

If they had, what they would have found was a set of general strategies designed to be used whenever attempting to solve a problem (adapted from Polya, 1957):

Understand the problem. Example approaches for doing so:
Ask yourself, "What am I looking for?"
Ask yourself, "What information is given in the problem?"
Try drawing a diagram to illustrate what is given in the problem and what needs to be solved.

Then, devise a plan for solving the problem. Example approaches for doing so:
Ask yourself, "Do I know a similar problem?"
Ask yourself, "Do I know an easier problem that might be related to this one or be one of the components of this one?
Ask yourself, "Can I restate the problem?"

Try solving a related problem.

Try to solve part of the problem.

Carry out the plan.

Look back. Example approaches for doing so:

Check the calculations and result.

Try to get the same result using a different method.

Ask yourself whether this solution plan might work for another problem (e.g., in your present homework set).

Readers should recognize some of the strengths of Polya's approach: (1) Formulating a plan and carrying it out is consistent with the perspective that tasks should be approached strategically. (2) Looking back is mostly monitoring. (3) The recommendation to attempt to apply the solution plan to another problem was aimed at developing case-based knowledge of solution strategies.

One obvious quagmire in the Polya four-step scheme is coming up with a plan (i.e., step 2). Isn't that the crux of the problem?: The potential problem solver does not know which processes to use to solve the problem at hand. Aware that people often do not know specific strategies that could be applied to problems they face, some psychologists devised general plans for solving problems (Newell & Simon, 1972). The most popular of these approaches became known as **means-end analysis.**

The person using the means-end plan is constantly aware of the end state they wish to achieve (e.g., knowledge of how many hours is required to drive 650 miles). They are also aware of what they know now (e.g., that the speed limit for 300 of the miles is 55, the speed limit for 325 miles is 65, and the speed limit for 25 miles is 45). The idea is to make progress from the initial state to the desired end state, deciding on steps that permit progress. A first step that might be elected would be to figure out how long it takes to go through each speed zone by dividing the total distance for the zone by the speed limit: 5.45 hours for the 55-speed zone, 5.00 hours for the 65-speed zone, and 0.55 hour for the 45-speed zone. Has progress been made toward the goal? Absolutely, for at least now, we have total times spent on various parts of the trip, which is progress because the final solution must be expressed in terms of total time on the road. What next? We could add the time spent on each segment: 5.45 hours + 5.00 hours + 0.55 hour = 11.00 hours. Have we come to the end? Yes, we know how long it would take to drive the 650 miles in question. The means-end problem solver is always asking how to reduce the difference in present state and desired end state and carries out operations that makes progress until the end state is reached.

The teaching of general planning strategies fell out of favor in the 1970s and 1980s, however, largely because of the recognition that the most powerful problem solving in any domain is done by individuals with a great deal of domain knowledge (e.g., Owen & Sweller, 1989). Domain knowledge often includes knowledge of extremely efficient strategies for accomplishing common problems in the domain, so that working from a starting state to an ending state would be less efficient than just applying well-known approaches that are almost "rules-of-thumb."

Another difficulty with means-end analysis also became apparent in the early 1980s. People have a difficult time abstracting specific problem-solving schemes when they use means-end analysis to solve problems (e.g., Sweller & Levine, 1982; Sweller, Mawer, & Ward, 1983). That is, they do not emerge from means-end–mediated problem-solving experience with generalizable knowledge of the specific strategies that can be applied to the types of problems they have been solving. For example, after solving a group of distance = rate × time problems through means-ends analysis, students might not know to look for the distance, rate, or time in the given information of the problem and solve for the missing value, which is the strategy that practice with such problems is intended to instill. Because the goal of problem-solving instruction is to produce students who can recognize problem types immediately and solve them using efficient procedures, encouraging students to rely on means-end as a way to "discover" specific problem-solving strategies seems unwise.

Sweller (1988, 1989) and Owen and Sweller (1989) proposed several reasons why solving problems using means-end analyses might not result in abstraction of strategies useful when encountering problems of the same type in the future: (1) Means-end focuses attention on reducing the discrepancy between what is known now and what needs to be known; it does not encourage stepping back at the end of problem solving and getting the whole picture, which is absolutely necessary if there is to be understanding of the approach used to solve a problem. (That is, when using means-end analysis, people do not seem to follow through with Polya's fourth step, which is to check their answer, including figuring out if the solution plan they devised for this problem might apply to other problems.) (2) Means-end analysis also consumes a great deal of short-term capacity (Owen & Sweller, 1985), for the present state must be held in memory and compared with the end state as the problem solver tries to figure how to reduce the difference between the present and end states. With so much mental juggling going on, there may be little capacity left over for remembering the sequence of steps that produced a problem solution.

Despite these problems with general problem-solving plans such as means-end analysis, we are not convinced that general problem solving strategies should be abandoned entirely. Indeed, a great deal of evidence favors Polya's four-step approach. That general problem-solving plans, such as Newell and Simon's means-end approach, are ineffective tells us nothing about the efficacy of the much more encompassing Polya approach. An analysis by Burkell, Schneider, and Pressley (1990) was informative on this point.

Burkell et al. (1990) analyzed studies in which elementary-age students had been taught successfully how to solve problems. They found in every one of the successful studies that Polya's four steps were taught, although the researchers did not always use Polya's terms. In every one of the studies, students were encouraged first to make certain they understood the problem before they attempted to solve it (Polya's first step). The specific recommendations for doing so differed from study to study: Students can attempt to understand a problem by (1) reading the problem aloud (presumably, slowly and deliberately, thinking hard about it), (2) identifying the problem being asked, (3) identifying important information specified in the problem statement, (4) defining terms, (5) paraphrasing the problem, (6) making a list or table summarizing the important elements in the problem, (7) creating a representation of the problem using objects, and (8) drawing a diagram representing the problem.

Students in the problem-solving studies identified by Burkell et al. (1990) were also encouraged to devise and carry out strategies for solving problems (i.e., follow Polya's steps 2 and 3). To this end, they were encouraged to (1) relate the present problem to easier examples they might have encountered, (2) identify a familiar pattern in the problem, or (3) con-

struct hypotheses and potential operations for solving the problem (and, of course, then carrying out the operations). Of course, some of the operations used to understand the problem also led to generation of problem solution plans, with plans often discovered by representing the problem using concrete objects or by using a diagram or even from listing the critical information in the problem.

All of the successful problem-solving regimens also encouraged students to review and reflect on their work (Polya's fourth step). Specifically, students were encouraged to (1) check their answer, (2) compare the answer they obtained through problem solving with an estimated answer, (3) solve the problem another way, (4) summarize what they did to solve the problem, and (5) construct a problem that would be similar to the present one and require the same solution strategy.

It is important to emphasize that more than Polya's four general strategies were taught in the studies in which problem solving improved. Rather the general Polya-type problem-solving instruction was integrated with other mathematics instruction. Review of one of the best-designed and most convincing of the studies analyzed by Burkell et al. (1990) makes clear that development of skilled problem solving involves long-term teaching of general and specific problem-solving approaches.

Charles and Lester (1984) conducted their experiment in grade-5 and grade-7 classrooms. At each grade level, teachers were assigned to an experimental or a control condition. Control teachers carried on business as usual in their mathematics classes. So did the experimental teachers except that they supplemented their mathematics instruction with teaching of a Polya-like approach to problem solving.

To understand problems, experimental students in Charles and Lester (1984) were encouraged to (1) read and reread problems carefully, (2) write down what is known, (3) look for key phrases, (4) find the important information in each problem, (5) paraphrase the problem, and (6) make certain of what must be found out. For generation and execution of a strategic plan, students were taught to (1) look for a pattern resembling one they had seen in other problems, (2) draw a picture representing the problem, (3) make a list or table summarizing what is known and needs to be known, (4) use objects to depict the problem, (5) simplify the problem, (6) guess and check, and (7) write an equation. After generating an answer, students were encouraged to (1) determine whether all of the important information stated in the problem was used, (2) decide whether the answer made sense, and generally (3) check the answer.

Instruction to use these general problem-solving strategies took place over 23 weeks, with students taught to apply the strategies to the problems normally covered in their courses. Pretest and posttest assessments were made, with a great deal of evidence that the strategy instruction made a substantial difference. There were indications at posttest that the strategy-trained students were more likely than control participants to develop a plan when attempting to solve new problems, although using the general problem-solving strategies did not always translate into finding a problem solution. That is, although there was a problem-solution advantage for trained over control students, it was not huge. The trained students, however, seemed to have better understanding than control students about how and when to use the mathematical skills they were acquiring.

The recommendation to teach general problem-solving strategies, including the four steps outlined by Polya and means-end analysis, has something of a checkered history. On the one hand, such strategies are not substitutes for instruction of more specific problem-solving approaches, and solving problems using general strategies in no way guarantees discovery and acquisition of more specific skills. On the other hand, teaching of general strategies as part of mathematics instruction makes some sense, with teaching of Polya's four steps prominent in interventions that improve problem solving.

If readers return to the discussion of experts in Chapter 4, it is easy to see general problem-solving strategies in expert performances, especially when experts are confronted with difficult problems. For example, radiologists attempting to make a difficult diagnosis first make certain they understand the problem, then they evaluate alternative ways of analyzing the x-ray film before advancing a tentative diagnosis, and finally they check their diagnosis (Lesgold et al., 1988). The general understanding-planning-solving-checking sequence is informed at all times by extensive domain-specific knowledge, however, and proceeds largely because of this domain-specific knowledge. Effective problem solving for experts is an articulation of general strategies and domain-specific strategies and declarative knowledge.

Can the problem-solving of poor problem solvers be understood in terms of Polya's general model? Montague and Bos (1990) administered questionnaires, reasoning tests, and mathematics achievement tests to high-achieving, average-achieving, low-achieving, and mathematics learning-disabled grade-8 students (i.e., students whose only problem in school was with math). All students in the study were filmed as they solved five problems, so they could watch the videotape later with a researcher and explain what they were doing. The interview used to elicit student descriptions of their problem solving covered all parts of Polya's four-step problem-solving process as well as some more specific problem-solving strategies.

There were several aspects of the Montague and Bos (1990) data that are relevant to the present discussion: First, the higher the mathematical achievement level of the student, the more of the Polya problem-solving steps evidenced during problem solving. Second, the higher the mathematics achievement, the more knowledgeable the student about strategies as reflected by responses to the interview items. Third, better students were more likely to indicate that they actually used the problem-solving strategies routinely than were weaker students. Montague and Bos (1990) confirmed that knowledge and use of the Polya strategies varied from extensive by good problem solvers to unlikely by weaker problem solvers. Such correlational data make clear that the interventions reviewed by Burkell et al. (1990) reflect the problem solving of good students, consistent with Polya's analysis 40 years ago.

Without a doubt, however, the most extensive analysis of the general processes in skilled problem-solving was a statistical analysis of 487 studies conducted between 1920 and the present (Hembree, 1992). Collapsing across studies (both experimental investigations manipulating problem-solving components such as strategies and correlational studies of problem-solving), there were clear associations between each of the Polya strategies and problem-solving performance. For example, the correlation between comprehending a problem and performance was 0.54, between selecting the correct problem-solving operations and performance was 0.72, and between checking work and performance was 0.25. There were positive effects of performance for using a variety of specific strategies as part of problem-solving plans (e.g., $r = 0.31$ for drawing a diagram). There also were large effects for teaching a variety of specific strategies.

The most interesting relationship identified by Hembree (1992), however, involved the effects of teaching the Polya heuristics. The teaching of the Polya strategies had a greater impact with advancing age, with the overall correlation between teaching of Polya strategies and performance only 0.17 for children in grades 4 to 5, increasing to 0.26 at grades 6 to 8, increasing much more to 0.72 at grades 9 to 12, and decreasing to 0.40 when postsecondary students were instructed in use of the strategies.

A reading of Polya's books (e.g., 1954, 1957, 1981) makes clear that the effective problem solvers he considered were rich in knowledge of mathematics, and the effective problem solving he wrote about was articulation of general and domain-specific approaches. Polya's idea that students benefit from instruction to organize their application of domain-specific knowledge and strategies using general strategies is doing well in the 1990s (see Lawson, 1990), a theme that will recur in this chapter. Indeed, Hembree's (1992) review suggests that at the secondary level at least, the case in favor of teaching Polya's heuristics is already strong; both Hembree and Burkell et al. (1990) offered analyses supporting the teaching of the Polya strategies to even younger children.

The best bet based on the extant data is that effective problem-solving education will include teaching of the general strategies favored by Polya as well as instruction of domain-specific concepts and strategies. It includes a great deal of practice solving problems requiring articulation of Polya's general strategies and specific mathematical concepts and problem-solving procedures.

INSTRUCTION THAT PROMOTES MATHEMATICAL UNDERSTANDING

Contemporary mathematics educators believe that too much of traditional mathematics instruction has been conveying information from teacher or textbook to student. That is, the teacher or textbook attempts to give knowledge to the student rather than encourage the student to construct knowledge for himself or herself. Students are taught methods of doing problems without being taught why the methods work. There is too much memorization of math facts and procedures. Math is taught as a 20- to 60-minute segment in the school day, rather than as a

useful part of life, with few attempts to map mathematical concepts and procedures to real-world relationships. The result of such conventional pedagogy is less-than-complete understanding of the mathematics taught.

If you were to ask many contemporary mathematics educators what good mathematics instruction does—that is, how it contrasts with conventional instruction—they would tell you that it promotes understanding of mathematical concepts and procedures, understanding that is essential if mathematics is to be used broadly and flexibly (e.g., Baroody, 1987; Fennema, Carpenter, & Peterson, 1989; Hiebert & Carpenter, 1992; National Council of Teachers of Mathematics, 1989, 1991; Scheid, 1993, Chapter 4; Schoenfeld, 1987; Schroeder & Lester, 1989; Silver, 1985, 1987; Skemp, 1989). Such understanding entails all of the following:

- Recognizing that mathematics is a way of thinking about and organizing real experiences.
- Recognizing why the mathematical concepts and procedures being learned are important.
- Recognizing how the particular mathematical concepts and procedures being learned are related to one another and are related to information already understood by the student.
- Knowing when, why, and where to apply mathematical concepts and procedures and being able to do so when confronted with situations that call for particular mathematical knowledge and use of mathematical procedures.
- Being able to explain why particular mathematical concepts and procedures are used to solve particular problems.

These views of mathematical understanding lead to certain assumptions about the teaching of mathematics:

- Learning of mathematics is best when it results from children's own mathematical activities—that is, when they generate their own understandings of problem solving and mathematics concepts rather than when problem solving and mathematics concepts are taught by a teacher or textbook. When children construct their own mathematical understandings, the knowledge is intimately related to what the children know already. As they discover new knowledge, children also gain experience self-regulating themselves as they do mathematics, which is important, since self-regulated application of mathematical concepts and procedures is an important goal of mathematics education.

- Students should learn to approach problems in the fashion prescribed by Polya, involving reflection on the problem situation, planning, and monitoring the effectiveness of solution attempts. Strategies such as representing problems with diagrams (which really is effective; e.g., Lewis, 1989) and checking and reflecting on one's work stimulate deep understanding of problems and should be encouraged. (Nonetheless, sometimes reflection on more than one problem of a given type is required—and sometimes, even then, a general solution strategy is not abstracted [e.g., Reed, 1989], so that there is a lot to be said for instruction that provides explicit information about how to solve particular problem types, a theme reiterated throughout this chapter, even though such instruction might seem hypocritical to the most devoted of radical constructivist mathematics educators, who unquestioningly embrace discovery approaches to learning.)

- Problem solving is a means for learning about new ways of solving problems, not just an activity that the student does after being taught methods of problem solving. That is, just as Polya prescribed, students should be encouraged to reflect on their problem solving in order to abstract general problem-solving principles and procedures from working particular problems.

- Often mathematical concepts can be grasped by children through manipulatives before they can be grasped symbolically, a conclusion supported by voluminous research (see Sowell, 1989). Understanding how mathematical symbols relate to the world can be fostered by encouraging children to connect operations performed with manipulatives to symbols (e.g., after observing a row of 8 buttons being extended by 3 buttons, resulting in an 11-button row, the symbolic equivalent of $8 + 3 = 11$ can be related to the physical representation of buttons) relating an equation to such a concrete representation is considered to be an especially effective way of increasing young children's understanding of concepts such as "addition" and "equation." In general, concrete, incomplete, and unsystematic (e.g., informal) learning of mathematics precedes abstract (i.e., symbolic), complete, systematic, and formal learning. Formal learning is at its best when it is connected and related to students' informal understanding (e.g., Putnam, Lampert, & Peterson, 1990).

- Students should be encouraged to use technology such as calculators as part of problem solving because these devices eliminate much of the lower-order computational demands of problem solving, permitting more attention to the higher-order, executive decisions.

- Instruction should emphasize how mathematical symbols are related to events and relationships in the world, especially events and relationships already understood by the child (e.g., relating the mathematical operation of division to sharing, such as when three children share six cookies with each child receiving two cookies).

- Word problems should be used from the beginning of mathematics instruction. Word problems require students to map the relationships expressed in the problems verbally to mathematical concepts, symbols, and procedures.

- Instruction should permit students to observe how the mathematical concepts and procedures they are learning apply in a variety of situations, with such experiences necessary for students to acquire understandings about when and where to use mathematics, understandings that are essential if mathematical knowledge is to be used generally and flexibly.

- Students should experience many examples illustrating concepts and procedures they are learning.

- Much of problem solving should occur in everyday situations.

- Instruction should foster beliefs that support student behaviors likely to motivate appropriate efforts and persistence in learning mathematics. Thus, students should be encouraged to believe that it makes sense to ask questions when a concept or procedure is not understood, errors are to be expected when doing mathematics and do not reflect low ability, and the mathematics learned in school relates to everyday life.

- Teachers should question students about how they are solving problems and listen to student answers because such answers can be revealing about what students understand and do not yet grasp. This is part of ongoing assessment of student progress in understanding the mathematical ideas they are being taught.

- Problem solving in small groups is often effective, especially in getting students to explain their reasons for problem solving in particular ways, but also in exposing students to alternative solution methods, exposure that should foster understanding that problem solving is a flexible enterprise. Small-group problem solving also permits students to experience the understanding-solving-checking cycle recommended by Polya. For example, Artzt and Armour-Thomas (1992) observed groups of grade-7 students while they solved problems: The students recursively read problems, attempted to understand them, explored, analyzed, planned, carried out plans, and checked. That students can experience such high-quality problem-solving experiences in small groups is one reason that leading mathematics educators, such as Schoenfeld (e.g., 1992), are emphatic that real mathematics is a social and collaborative enterprise, that it involves talking and explaining and making false starts with other people.
- Teachers should model problem solving, making obvious as they do so that problem solving is not always straightforward but often involves false starts and consideration of many factors.

These pedagogical perspectives on teaching for understanding are summarized in two volumes published by the National Council of Teachers of Mathematics (NCTM), known for short as the *Standards* (i.e., *Curriculum and Evaluation Standards for School Mathematics* and *Professional Standards for Teaching Mathematics*). These *Standards* are having a great deal of impact on mathematics education reform across the United States.

Many different psychological theories influenced the NCTM as they developed their positions on teaching, including the following: (1) *Piaget:* Some of the instructional recommendations in the *Standards* are based on progressive, constructivist philosophy. It is hard to miss the Piagetian influence on recommendations to teach mathematics to young children using concrete materials. The Piagetian themes of exploration and discovery pervade the NCTM recommendations. The Piagetian emphasis that instruction should be matched to the child's level of functioning (Inhelder et al., 1974) comes

through as well, with teachers urged to diagnose continually the level of functioning of the child and provide instruction just beyond the current levels of their students.

(2) *Traditional learning theory and direct explanation models:* Although the mathematics educators often are reticent to admit it, elements of traditional learning theory and direct explanation are prominent in their recommendations as well. Teachers are urged to model problem solving for children and to make certain that instruction includes explanations for mathematical relationships. Indeed, our reading of the NCTM *Professional Standards for Teaching Mathematics* is that the teaching recommended there resembles in many ways the best of direct explanation approaches (see Chapters 1 and 8): Teacher explanations and modeling are provided on an as-needed basis and flexibly; the emphasis is on thorough understanding rather than on moving through the curriculum at a rapid pace.

(3) *Representational theories of mind:* Contemporary mathematics educators also recognize that information is represented in various ways in the human mind (see Chapter 3), with the recommendation to present alternative representations of concepts and procedures stimulated in part by the understanding that mind includes both concrete, imaginal conceptions (e.g., a vision of a row of 8 buttons joined by a row of 3 buttons to form 11 buttons) as well as more abstract codes that are closer to formal mathematical symbolism (e.g., $8 + 3 = 11$).

(4) *Network theories of representation:* Cognitive theorists and researchers recognize that people can connect related representations but often fail to do so on their own. The recognition that connections are anything but automatic, based on knowledge of cognitive theory and years of experiences with students who did not recognize mappings between equations (e.g., $x^2 + y^2 = 4$) and their concrete representations (i.e., a circle with radius of 2), resulted in the NCTM recommendation for mathematics teachers to encourage connections between alternative representations of mathematical ideas.

The mathematics educators have done a good job of reading the cognition and instruction literatures and culling from them instructional recommendations. Most cognitive psychologists find much that pleases them in the NCTM *Standards*. What is even more pleasing to the psychological researcher community, however, is that some members of the mathematics education profession are conducting impressive experimental evaluations of their ideas, evaluations that are providing high-quality information about the effects of some of the instructional practices favored in the *Standards*.

Examples of Instructional Experiments Validating the Importance of Teaching Mathematics So as to Enhance Student Understanding of Mathematical Content

The experiments conducted by mathematics educators range from ones that are short term and focused to those that evaluate entire curricula implemented over an extended period of time. We consider three such studies here, to illustrate better what is meant by teaching for mathematical understanding as well as the research tactics being employed by some of the more analytical researchers in the mathematics education community.

Evaluation of a Kindergarten Part-Part-Whole Curriculum

A powerful mathematical understanding is that any number can be decomposed into parts (e.g., Resnick, 1983; Riley, Greeno, & Heller, 1983). Thus, 14 can be decomposed into a 10 and a 4. The number 7 can be decomposed into a 4 and a 3 or alternatively into two 2s and a 3. Complete understanding of addition and arithmetic is not possible without part-part-whole understanding, with the evidence mounting that instruction of part-part-whole can increase children's understanding of basic arithmetic operations.

For example, Fischer (1990) evaluated the consequences of teaching kindergarten children the first seven whole numbers using a part-part-whole approach compared to conventional mathematics instruction. Two kindergarten classes received 25 days (20 minutes a day) of part-part-whole instruction. The children receiving the part-part-whole curriculum also counted sets of objects, but in doing so they were required to create subsets (e.g., if counting five objects, to create two subsets). The exercises emphasized counting various combinations of subsets in order to establish that whole numbers can be decomposed into components and that however decomposed, the parts sum to the whole.

Two control condition classes experienced a curriculum based on counting, saying, and writing the first 7 whole numbers. Control students practiced counting items in sets, including verbalization of the numbers involved in counting, and writing the number of items in a just-counted set. The control curriculum was rich compared with much of conventional kindergarten instruction because it was supplemented with manipulatives, and there were more total counting exercises than in many conventional textbooks (i.e., this was not a "straw-man" control). There was equivalent instruction about the whole numbers from 1 to 7 in the experimental and control classrooms. There were also the same number of opportunities to count sets of 7 items and comparable worksheet opportunities.

The part-part-whole curriculum made a slight difference on a number concept posttest (i.e., part-part-whole students answered questions requiring counting and knowledge of the first 7 whole numbers slightly better than control students). When asked to do some simple problems requiring dividing numbers such as 12, 14, and 15 into two sets, the part-part-whole students did slightly better than controls. A striking advantage for part-part-whole students was observed, however, in solving simple word problems, even though neither group of students had experienced instruction in solving word problems. This is an important finding, for solution of word problems requires understanding the relationships specified in the word problems and performing the arithmetic operations. Such problems often pose difficulties for older children (e.g., Morales, Shute, & Pellegrino, 1985) and sometimes even for university-level students (e.g., Lewis & Mayer, 1987).

Students receiving part-part-whole instruction were better able to understand and solve problems such as the following (Carpenter, 1985):

Sam had 2 books. Mom gave him 4 more. Now how many books does Sam have?
The cat has 9 kittens. Six are brown and the rest are white. How many white kittens are there?

It takes only a little thought to recognize that awareness of how parts combine to produce wholes could facilitate representation and solution of such problems. Fischer's (1990) demonstration of increased competence in mathematics when important mathematical understandings are developed is one of a growing number of such demonstrations.

Evaluation of a Grade-1 Curriculum for Increasing Understanding of Place Value Hiebert and Wearne (1992) evaluated a grade-1 curriculum covering place values, with extensive coverage of the tens-place and ones-place value and an introduction of the hundreds-place value. Understanding of place value was developed in the experimental curriculum by relating concrete representations of numbers (e.g., 56 represented as 5 bars of 10 units and 6 unit bars) and symbolic representations (i.e., the number 56 with a 5 in the tens place and a 6 in the units place). Hiebert and Wearne (1992) described the experimental curriculum as follows:

> The . . . lessons began by posing problems of finding how many objects there were in large sets, most sets between 50 and 100. Class discussions and suggested strategies began with counting by ones and shifted to counting more efficiently by regrouping and counting by twos, fives, and, eventually, tens. One kind of object investigated was Unifix cubes. These were eventually grouped into quasipermanent bars of 10. Two-digit numerals were introduced as efficient ways of recording the size of sets. Discussion frequently included the two ways of interpreting the written number—as ones and as tens and ones. For example, 57 was interpreted as 57 individual objects and as 5 groups of 10 objects with 7 leftover objects. Base-10 blocks were introduced as tools, like Unifix cubes but already hooked together. Most tasks at this point were story situations that involved dealing with large sets by, for example, packaging them for sale in groups of 10. Students used base-1 blocks or pictures of the blocks or written numbers to help them solve the problems and then described the strategies they used (Hiebert & Wearne, 1992, p. 101).

Such instruction continued through coverage of two-digit addition and subtraction without regrouping (i.e., for readers from another generation, problems not requiring "borrowing" or "carrying"). Physical and symbolic representations were related to one another throughout instruction on addition and subtraction. Students shared with one another their strategies for solving problems. The teacher encouraged student reflection on the various strategies and solutions as well as emphasizing the relationships between physical and symbolic representations.

The experimental curriculum differed from the control curriculum, which was conventional grade-1 instruction, with respect to the interactions between students and the reflection encouraged by the teacher. The textbook presentation in the control condition involved showing bundles of 10 sticks to represent 10-place elements and single sticks to represent units. It continued with exercises involving different types of objects so grouped. Control students also had some opportunity to work with one actual physical representation (i.e., 10 beans glued to a stick to represent one 10 in the tens place). For two-digit addition and subtraction without regrouping, most of the instruction involved workbook pages of problems. These were introduced with "beanstick" representations of addition and subtraction and some instruction about checking addition and subtraction using estimation. Although the controls received high-quality conventional instruction, what they did not experience were the discussions intended to increase understanding of place-value concepts. These discussions covered various strategies for representing numbers and for adding and subtracting two-digit numbers, strategies requiring knowledge and use of place-value knowledge. The control students were able to practice many more problems than did the experimental students, for the in-depth discussion in the experimental classrooms consumed a great deal of time. Although the control students actually covered more topics in each lesson, the experimental students generated more numerous representations for each of the problems they practiced.

Did the instruction designed to inculcate understanding make a difference? Did making certain that the students understood relationships between the physical and symbolic worlds affect their ability to do problems involving place value? It did. The students in the experimental classes did better on posttest problems similar to the ones covered in class (e.g., two-digit addition and subtraction problems not requiring regrouping). More impressive, however, was that experimental students were much better able than control students to do addition and subtraction problems that required regrouping (i.e., problems requiring "carrying"), despite the fact that no instruction on regrouping had been given to them. The deep understanding of place value developed in the experimental classrooms increased transfer of addition skills especially (i.e., addition with regrouping was accomplished better by experimental students than subtraction with regrouping).

Evaluation of a Problem-Centered Grade-2 Mathematics Curriculum   Cobb and colleagues at Purdue University (Cobb, Wood, Yackel, Nicholls, Wheatley, Trigatti, and Perlwitz, 1991) compared performance in 10 grade-2 classrooms receiving arithmetic instruction consistent with NCTM recommendations (see description earlier in this section) and 8 classrooms receiving conventional instruction. Children in the NCTM classrooms solved challenging problems continuously, with students engaged in constructing solutions to the problems presented to them. The students were encouraged to reflect on their problem-solving activities and to construct knowledge about how to solve problems. The problem solving generally took place in interactive, cooperative classroom groups, groups in which the role of the teacher was to provide support and gentle guidance in the direction of productive problem solving, rather than to provide solutions or explicit instruction about how to solve problems. The grade-2 experimental curriculum focused on addition and subtraction and with the development of strategies for solving such problems. Students were encouraged to believe that success in mathematics was possible through individual and collective efforts. The experimental students were encouraged to feel successful when they solved challenging problems. In short, the NCTM curriculum combined Vygotskian notions (see Chapter 8) that sophisticated thinking can be developed in social interactions and contemporary motivational perspectives (see Chapter 5) that long-term motivation is most likely when students attribute success to effort and reinforce themselves for taking on and persisting with challenging tasks. Consistent with Cobb et al.'s identification with radical constructivist theories of the development of mind, which posit that socially mediated discovery and construction of knowledge is to be preferred over any form of explicit instruction, the Cobb et al. curriculum downplayed elements of direct explanation compared with other interventions consistent with the NCTM perspective (e.g., 1991).

Did the NCTM-type instruction make a difference? It did on state-administered assessments of mathematics achievement as well as on an experimenter-produced test of mathematics achievement. Differences favoring the experimental students were especially notable on items requiring application of the concepts covered in the curriculum. The students in the experimental classes reported that they valued collaboration more than did control students; the experimental students did not identify with academic competition as much as control students.

Commentary: Teaching for Understanding

The formalization of the NCTM *Standards* (1989, 1991) is stimulating substantial instructional research on mathematics education, with the constructivist-theoretical underpinnings of the NCTM perspective now being examined in ambitious instructional experiments. Although it is possible to find flaws in individual studies, the strengths are more striking. There is a growing database supportive of the proposition that mathematics instruction stimulating deep understanding of mathematical concepts and procedures promotes mathematics achievement.

SCHOENFELD'S MODEL OF MATHEMATICAL COGNITION

Some outstanding mathematics educators, including Schoenfeld of the University of California at Berkeley, have offered models of competent mathematical cognition that are consistent with the good information processor model featured in this book. For the past decade, Schoenfeld has explored mathematical thinking and the development of mathematical abilities via instruction. What has emerged from his work is a model of thinking that includes four information processing components (Schoenfeld, 1992): (1) The knowledge base, (2) problem-solving strategies, (3) monitoring and control, and (4) beliefs and affects. A fifth component in the model are instructional practices that foster effective mathematical cognition. The information processing hardware (especially short-term memory) also figures in Schoenfeld's formulation.

The components Schoenfeld describes overlap considerably with the components considered throughout this book.

Knowledge

Schoenfeld's (1985, 1992) conception of mathematical thinking begins with mathematical knowledge, including both the declarative and procedural knowledge (see Chapter 2) required to do mathematics: Algorithms are procedures that the thinker can execute flawlessly and does so whenever they can be applied appropriately. Other procedures (i.e., routine procedures) are also likely to be used correctly and to be executed without great difficulties, but there is less of a guarantee than with algorithms. The good thinker articulates declarative knowledge of mathematical concepts and procedural knowledge when solving problems.

For example, the student who begins with two intersecting lines, with a point P on one of them, and constructs a circle tangent to both lines and to point B using a straightedge and a compass, uses both declarative and procedural knowledge to do so (Schoenfeld, 1985, Chapter 2; 1992, pp. 349–350). The declarative knowledge includes knowing that a tangent to a circle is perpendicular to a radius drawn to the point of tangency and that any two constructible loci are sufficient to determine the location of a point. The procedural knowledge includes understanding how to bisect an angle and drop a perpendicular to a line from a point. With a moment's thought about any mathematical problem, it is easy to identify both mathematical facts that contribute to solving the problem and mathematical procedures that do so.

Knowledge Effects on Functional Short-Term Capacity

Schoenfeld recognizes that problem solving depends on short-term capacity, which is limited. That the long-term knowledge of mathematics is well-organized and "chunkable" for the expert does much to reduce demands on capacity and is one source of expertise in mathematics: Good problem solvers are able to juggle more in their limited capacity than weaker problem solvers in part because their chunks are bigger and better organized. There have been multiple confirmations that good problem solvers have more extensive working memory capacities than weaker problem solvers, at least with respect to mathematical symbols and operations (e.g., Cooney & Swanson, 1990; Dark & Benbow, 1990). For any particular student, one reliable way to make problems more difficult is to set them up so that a great deal of working memory capacity is required to construct a solution. For example, problems that require three pieces of information to be held in memory in order to solve them are more difficult than those re-

quiring two pieces of information to be held in memory; those requiring computations not yet automatized are more demanding than those requiring only calculations that are automatized (e.g., Fayol, Abdi, & Gombert, 1987). When students can rapidly recall math facts as they work word problems, short-term memory demands are reduced—that is, having to reflect on 3 + 2 = 5 consumes short-term capacity: In a study examining various factors that could contribute to word problem–solving ability, Zentall (1990) observed that only speed of math fact retrieval predicted performance on word problems, consistent with the hypothesis that problem solving is less certain when short-term memory is strained. In short, there is diverse evidence substantiating that short-term or working memory figures largely in skilled problem solving, consistent with Schoenfeld's theory.

Problem-Solving Strategies

At the center of Schoenfeld's conception of problem-solving strategies are Polya's strategies. Schoenfeld recognizes that these work only if the thinker is armed with a great deal of other knowledge, including strategies specialized for particular types of problems.

Schoenfeld's best-known study (Schoenfeld, 1979) involved an evaluation of the teaching of Polya-like strategies to university students in a mathematics course. The strategies included analyzing the problem (e.g., draw a diagram, try to simplify the problem), exploring it with the goal of coming up with a solution plan (e.g., relate the current problem to equivalent, slightly modified, or similar problems), and verifying the solution (e.g., checking whether the solution uses all the relevant data, is reasonable, can be obtained using another procedure). Such strategies can only be applied to specific problems by someone who knows a great deal about the specific mathematics concepts and procedures relevant to a problem being attempted. What is interesting given the current emphasis by mathematics educators on understanding, especially understanding through reflective discussion of problem solving, is that such discussion was important in the Schoenfeld intervention. Students practiced problems and then reflectively discussed how the problem-solving strategies taught in the course were applied to the practice items.

Did Schoenfeld's university-level students benefit from learning and using the general problem-solving strategies? Comparisons of problem solving before and after the strategies instruction as well as comparisons to students enrolled in another mathematics-oriented course revealed that the course had substantial impact (Schoenfeld, 1985, Chapters 6–9). There was no doubt that strategies-instructed students benefited from the problem-solving instruction they received. There were clear differences favoring trained students both in problems similar to ones covered in the course and in problems quite different from those practiced and discussed as part of the class requirements. The difficult problems included some that Schoenfeld put on the final test simply because they had stumped him for some time. The students taught to analyze problems using the problem-solving strategies were less distracted by surface details of the new problems on the test than were control students. The strategies-instructed students focused more on the aspects of the problems that provided the information needed to solve the problem (Schoenfeld & Herrmann, 1982). Think-aloud protocols confirmed extensive use of the general strategies to organize application of specific mathematical concepts and procedures by the students who took the course.

Although Schoenfeld's training clearly involved some student discovery and guided discovery via teacher coaching, there is no doubt that Schoenfeld's instruction was more explicit than the instruction prescribed by many radical constructivists (e.g., see Schoenfeld, 1989b). Our interpretation of Schoenfeld's work is that it is direct explanation in the best sense of the term (see Chapter 8), in that the teacher provides the students with a good start on the processes that compose effective problem solving, but students and teachers then work together to develop a much fuller understanding of the problem-solving strategies. Schoenfeld's students worked hard to figure out how to adapt and elaborate the strategic scheme Schoenfeld provided to them, with the result an internalization of a flexible approach to problem solving, an approach to problem solving that students constructed for themselves. Although Schoenfeld typically refers back to his training studies as evidence favoring articulation of general strategies and more specific knowledge, including specific mathematics procedures that could be thought of as task-specific strategies, there were other sets of data generated in the 1980s that also

supported models of mathematical cognition that include strategies. Some of these will be touched on as the discussion of other components in Schoenfeld's model proceeds.

Monitoring and Control (Self-Regulation)

Monitoring is an aspect of metacognition that Schoenfeld highlights. Schoenfeld focuses on how monitoring contributes to self-regulated use of knowledge, including procedural knowledge. Schoenfeld recognizes that an expert electing a strategy to make a first attempt at solving a problem uses metacognitive understandings to do so as part of planning a candidate problem solution. For instance, Schoenfeld (1992) reports how professional mathematicians spend a great deal of time analyzing problems before making a first move to problem solve compared with novices, many of whom spend almost no time in planning. Once a strategy is activated, the expert monitors whether progress is being made in solving the problem, with shifts in strategies when the expert senses that progress is not occurring or that there may be a better approach. Such shifts are much less common when novices attempt problems, with much less on-line monitoring of progress during problem solving by novices compared with skilled problem solvers.

Schoenfeld believes that the good math instructor can do much to foster understanding of where and when particular mathematics strategies work as well as foster a general tendency in students to monitor their progress during problem solving—to ask questions when problem solving seems not to be proceeding well or important information seems to be missing (e.g., Graesser & McMahen, 1993). This can be accomplished using scaffolded instruction as groups of students attempt to solve problems. Good mathematics teachers coach their students during their problem-solving attempts, posing questions such as the following:

What (exactly) are you doing? Can you describe it precisely?
Why are you doing it? How does it fit into your solution?
How does it help you? What will you do with the outcome when you obtain it? (Schoenfeld, 1992, p. 356)

Such questions, when posed consistently as part of mathematics instruction, sensitize students to monitor their problem solving and to become aware of the effects of the strategies they are using as well as where and when positive effects can be obtained.

Schoenfeld believes (informed in part by research by Lester; see the earlier discussion of Charles & Lester, 1984) that teachers can improve student understanding of mathematics and self-regulated problem solving by modeling for students the monitored use of mathematical concepts and strategies and coaching students to monitor and self-regulate. He recognizes that the development of self-regulated problem solving requires long-term input, however, and that our understanding of how to structure classrooms and coaching interactions so as to foster best self-regulated problem solving is far from complete.

Schoenfeld is aware that students often have misconceptions and misunderstandings about when and where to use the mathematical procedures they know (see also Confrey, 1990, and Putnam et al., 1990); sometimes their execution of strategies is systematically flawed as well, as in the case of the many subtraction bugs (i.e., consistent errors made during subtraction; van Lehn, 1990). If students are to become aware of errant metacognitive and procedural knowledge and correct it, it is essential that they monitor whether the strategies they are using are effective. From Schoenfeld's perspective, it is not surprising that there are clear correlations between problem-solving and monitoring competencies (e.g., Slife, Weiss, & Bell, 1985; Van Haneghan, 1990; Van Haneghan & Baker, 1989). Consistent with this relationship, problem solving instruction that includes monitoring is more effective than otherwise comparable instruction that does not encourage students to monitor their progress toward solutions (Delclos & Harrington, 1991). Also, students with extensive metacognition are better problem solvers than students who are not (Swanson, 1990).

Beliefs and Affect

Students construct beliefs about mathematics, often ones based on the experiences they have as part of mathematics instruction. These beliefs are sometimes errant in ways that undermine the development of sophisticated mathematical behaviors (Schoenfeld, 1989a and 1992, provided all of the beliefs described here; see also Ball, 1988; Lampert,

1990; Schommer, Crouse, & Rhodes, 1992; Stodolsky, 1985). For example, the common beliefs that, "Mathematics problems have only one right answer," and "There is only one correct way to solve any mathematics problem—usually the rule the teacher has most recently demonstrated to the class," have high potential for discouraging reflective problem solving, including the generation of alternative ways of tackling particular problems. So does a belief such as, "When the teacher asks a question in math class, the students who understand only need a few seconds to answer correctly." Perhaps it should not be surprising in light of such beliefs that some students conclude that math learned in schools is "Mostly facts and procedures that have to be memorized." Many students come to believe more in memorizing as a process underlying achievement in mathematics than in reflection, endorsing perspectives such as, "The best way to do well in math is to memorize all the formulas," and "You have to memorize the way to do constructions (from students in a geometry class)." Moreover, by high school, students are making attributions that clearly undermine exerting effort when having difficulty with mathematics (see Chapter 5), often attributing achievement in mathematics to uncontrollable factors such as ability: "Some people are good at math and some aren't."

The experiences that shape these beliefs include many nights of homework that has only one final answer as well as years of taking tests that require quick responding. By emphasizing speed of responding, teachers often discourage reflection and encourage the belief that if a student cannot do a problem in a few minutes, it is probably beyond the student (Schoenfeld, 1985, 1992). Of course, such teaching is the result of teacher beliefs that their job is to prepare students to work the "problem" typically covered in elementary-level arithmetic, algebra, geometry, or calculus and to work it quickly, for that is what is required on the SAT and other instruments in the accountability system.

Beliefs affect motivations and hence determine behavior. Traditional mathematics instruction is rigged to encourage the beliefs that memorizing is problem solving, problems that require reflection are problems that cannot be solved, and if math does not come easily, the ability to do mathematics is not there. Such beliefs motivate memorizing and rapid responding and giving up when a problem solution is not immediately obvious. Such beliefs must be turned around if students are to become reflective problem solvers who persist in the face of difficulties during problem solving.

Practices

Just as conventional mathematics instruction undermines reflective problem solving, there are instructional practices that promote it, ones consonant with effective instructional practices we have encountered before. Students and teachers can engage in reflective dialogue, with the teacher providing challenging problems, ones that are, nonetheless, within reach of the students. Effective teachers also provide support on an as-needed basis. In such classes, there are collaborative attempts to make sense of problems and discussions of potential alternative solutions. There are thoughtful arguments. Teachers do not tell answers or how to get them. Students and teachers cooperatively interact to construct and evaluate potential solutions.

Schoenfeld is aware of mathematics educators who manage to teach mathematics as a collaborative enterprise. He also recognizes that such instruction is too rare and that we know too little about it. There is much research to be done here. Such work has high potential for informing the larger educator community: As we have reviewed in previous chapters, teacher-student collaborative problem solving and meaning-making are at the heart of contemporary models of learning to read and write as well as considered essential in contemporary science instruction. (More about cooperative models in mathematics education later in this chapter.)

Schoenfeld's Model and the National Council of Teachers of Mathematics Standards

The NCTM *Standards* (1989, 1991) address all of the factors Schoenfeld believes are important in mathematical thinking and problem solving. Problem solving is at the heart of mathematics consistent with the *Standards* calling for students to be taught the general Polya-type strategies as well as many specific procedures for particular types of problems. These specific strategies are viewed as procedures to be used flexibly and in combination with other mathematical knowledge as part of problem solving. Monitoring of performance is one of the general strategies, with students consistently encouraged to reflect on their problem solving. Such reflection is in-

tended, in part, to encourage the development of sophisticated metacognition about specific problem-solving strategies and the applicability of particular mathematics concepts. Consistent with Schoenfeld, the NCTM *Standards* particularly encourage instruction that promotes beliefs that will motivate persistence and effort during problem solving as well as long-term commitment to mathematics as a way of thinking about the world that is accessible to most students.

Summary

Schoenfeld's perspectives on mathematical cognition are consistent with what we call good information processing, which includes knowledge, strategies, metacognition, and motivational beliefs in interaction. An important mechanism in the development of good information processing is teacher-student collaborative instruction that begins with teacher modeling and explanations but that expands as teachers and students work together in applying new strategies to diverse tasks.

Author MP first summarized the nature of good information processing in mathematical cognition in an article published 1 year after Schoenfeld's (1985) classic, *Mathematical Problem Solving* (Pressley, 1986). The article was written in 1984 before I encountered the Schoenfeld book. As the years have passed, both Schoenfeld's perspectives and the points of view in Pressley (1986) have endured, with virtually every claim in both sources now more supportable than it was at the time of publication. Both have had impact on development of new models of problem-solving instruction.

For example, Derry (e.g., Derry, Hawkes, & Tsai, 1987; Derry & Kellis, 1986) cited both the Schoenfeld model and the good information processing perspective as important in her thinking as she developed her TAPS (Training Arithmetic Problem-Solving Skills) model of problem-solving instruction. She taught middle-school, high school, and young adult populations strategies for solving simple word problems, instruction that emphasized when the strategies taught could be applied. Derry's students were taught to react to a problem by first attempting to understand it. Then, they came up with a plan based on matching strategies they had learned to the demands and constraints of the problem and monitor their problem solving. TAPS proved effective in promoting the arithmetic word problem-solving skills in several studies and provided additional validation for both Schoenfeld's model and the good information processing perspective.

NATURAL DEVELOPMENT OF MATHEMATICAL UNDERSTANDINGS

Mathematics education researchers such as Carpenter, Romberg, and Moser of the University of Wisconsin; Fuson of Northwestern; and Baroody of the University of Illinois have studied extensively the natural development of young children's arithmetic competence. They contend that conventional mathematics instruction does not build on what the child knows already about numbers and mathematical operations. This is unfortunate from their perspective because they believe that children are most likely to understand completely the mathematics they are taught if it is related to prior knowledge, again a prescription encountered repeatedly in this book as part of effective instruction. Much of the research on the development of mathematical cognition has focused on preschool and primary-grade children's acquisition of addition and subtraction.

Mathematical Understandings Developed During the Preschool Years

There is substantial development of mathematical understandings during the preschool years (e.g., Baroody, 1987; Fuson, 1988, 1992; Romberg & Carpenter, 1986). We summarize in this section some of the most important discoveries of Baroody, Fusen, Carpenter, Romberg, and their like-minded colleagues. (We make no attempt in this subsection to attribute the documentation of specific competencies to specific researchers, pointing out that what follows in this subsection is an abstraction across the writings of Baroody, Fusen, Carpenter, and Romberg.)

Many 2-year-olds can report to their parent when there are two toys. Three- to 4-year-olds also can point out three cookies or four people. Recognition of such small sets seems to be based more on perceptual differences between one, two, three, and four items, rather than on a deep conceptual understanding of the concepts of number or the amounts represented by the numbers 1 through 4, with the term **subitizing** often used to refer to young children's abilities to identify the number for small sets

of objects. Identification of larger sets of objects by number is infrequent for 2- to 4-year-olds.

With small numbers, addition and subtraction operations are sometimes performed by preschoolers, in the sense that they can "get some more" and "lose some." Preschoolers also can conserve in the Piagetian sense when small numbers of objects are involved (Piaget, 1965): Suppose a row of three objects is shown to a child. Then the row is covered with the middle object surreptitiously removed. When the cover is lifted, the child will definitely notice that the number of objects in the row has changed, not fooled for an instant by the fact that the row of two objects spans the same distance as the row of three objects did (Gelman & Gallistel, 1978). In contrast, with larger numbers of objects, preschoolers perceive that a 10-inch row of n objects has the same number of objects as a 10-inch row of n + 2 or n + 3 objects; also, two rows with n objects are perceived as having different numbers of objects if one row is 10 inches long and the other 13 inches long. That is, preschoolers do not conserve larger numbers—perceptual qualities other than the number of objects are used to decide equivalency and nonequivalencies of amount. With one-, two-, and three-object quantities, however, the number of objects in a set is used to determine equivalency of sets, rather than any other physical property of the sets, such as length of the row in which the set members are displayed.

Many preschoolers learn the whole-number sequence from 1 to 10, and often preschoolers acquire the sequence from 1 to 20. It is common for a child to arrive at kindergarten able to write the whole numbers to 20. Some kindergarten children learn to count by single units to 100 as well as by tens to 100. On their way to learning these sequences, consistent errors are common, with a frequent error being that some numbers are skipped in number sequences (e.g., 13, 14, 16, 18 . . .). Much of the learning of sequences is more memory work than conceptual: Children do not recognize that 1, 2, 3, and so forth are related to 11, 12, 13, and so forth or to 10, 20, 30 and so forth perhaps because it is not obvious how 2 is related to 12 or 20 given that the word two is not perceptually salient to the preschooler in the pronunciation of twelve and twenty.

Preschoolers begin to learn how to count objects, recognizing that they need to arrange items so that each item is counted once and only once using the whole-number sequences they have learned. Even so, preschoolers sometimes do not arrange relatively large numbers of objects, and they sometimes point to an object and fail to count it or point to an object and say two numbers. By 5 years of age, it is not unusual for children to be able to count up to 20 or more objects, although it takes a lot of effort on behalf of the child. If the child attempts effort-reducing shortcuts during counting, such as simply looking at each object rather than pointing at or touching them, errors are common and likely: Number sequences and the operations of counting are anything but automatic for the 5-year-old, with the result that high effort is required and errors are common. For the 5-year-old, counting is a short-term memory capacity–demanding activity.

An important acquisition is the development of understanding that the last number uttered in a count is the number of objects in the set counted (i.e., the **cardinal number**). The development of understanding of cardinality as it relates to counting is known as the **count-to-cardinal** transition. Many 5-year-olds recognize that if the count of two sets of objects ends in the same number the two sets have the same number of objects (e.g., 1,2,3,4,5,6 apples in this row is equal to 1,2,3,4,5,6 apples in that row). This is an important understanding because a cognitive prerequisite for learning simple addition and subtraction is the ability to note equivalence of two sets. Beyond having this prerequisite knowledge, kindergarten and grade-1 entry-level students often know much more, including how to add and subtract, at least in some situations.

Naturally Developed Addition and Subtraction Skills of Primary-Grade Children

As we just reviewed, children entering kindergarten or grade 1 have many fundamental mathematical understandings. In fact, they arrive at kindergarten and grade 1 already able to do much of what they are supposed to learn in primary mathematics: Even before receiving instruction in addition and subtraction, children often can do a variety of elementary addition and subtraction if they are provided concrete objects to manipulate (Figure 13.1).

Addition   In a prominent 3-year longitudinal study of children's addition and subtraction, Carpenter and Moser (e.g., 1982) and their colleagues (e.g., Car-

Figure 13.1 What mathematical concepts do preschoolers possess? What can their fingers reveal about their abilities to carry out mathematical procedures?

penter, Hiebert, & Moser, 1981) evaluated how school-entry children solved two types of addition problems:

Joining problems involve putting together two quantities, as in "Connie had 5 marbles. Jim gave her 8 more marbles. How many marbles did Connie have altogether?" Joining problems involve a dynamic, changing relationship.

Part-part-whole problems require analyzing an existing quantity and decomposing it into its components, such as in "There are 6 boys and 8 girls on the soccer team. How many children are on the team altogether?" Part-part-whole problems involve a static, descriptive relationship.

Carpenter, Moser, and their colleagues were able to discern several different strategies used by children beginning school. Some used their fingers or other concrete objects to solve the problems. Others used counting sequences; sometimes, children relied on number facts they had learned (i.e., if a child "knew" 8 + 5 = 13 based on prior experience, there was no need to use fingers or counting to solve the problem). In general, Carpenter and associates noted that these strategies were used for both joining and part-part-whole problems, with no consistent differences in the way that the preschoolers tackled the two types of problems.

Often, strategies were combined, with **counting all with models** a strategy combination discussed frequently in the literature. This combination involves establishing two sets as the addends and then counting all of the elements, beginning the count with the whole number 1. Some of the best-known counting strategies in children's addition, ones documented since the late 1960s and early 1970s (e.g., Groen & Parkman, 1972; Suppes & Groen, 1967) also were observed. One was **counting all without models,** which is the same as counting all with models except that no concrete objects are used to represent the addends and sum. Another counting strategy observed was **counting on from first** (i.e., start from the addend mentioned first and count up by the number represented by the second addend) and **counting on from larger** (which involves starting with the larger addend and counting up the number specified by the smaller addend). Counting on from larger is often referred to as the **MIN** strategy (Groen & Parkman, 1972) because it minimizes the number of counts required to solve an addition problem when using a counting strategy.

Consistent with young children being more facile in their perception, representation, and use of small compared with large numbers, problems involving small numbers were especially likely to be solved in the studies conducted by Carpenter and associates. In general, early in grade 1, counting all with models was the predominant strategy. By the end of grade 1 and, thus, following some instruction in addition, counting on was observed more than other strategies. The most important point, however, is that even at entry to grade 1, children were strategic problem solvers, able to do something that had not yet been covered in school formally.

Subtraction Just as children entering primary school can do several types of addition problems, they can also solve different types of subtraction problems. For example, consider Romberg and Carpenter's (e.g., 1986, Table 29.2, for all examples provided in this paragraph) analysis of subtraction word problems: Some problems require **separation** of one set of objects from another, such as the following:

> Tom has 13 marbles. He gave 5 marbles to his sister Connie. How many marbles does Tom have left?

Others are **join/missing addend** problems, similar in structure to this one:

> Tom had 5 marbles. His sister Connie gave him some more marbles. Now Tom has 13 marbles. How many marbles did Connie give him?

A **compare** problem involving Tom and Connie might be the following:

> Tom has 5 marbles. His sister Connie has 13 marbles. How many more marbles does Connie have than Tom?

A **combine** problem involves specification of a total, with one of the numbers contributing to the total given and the other missing, as in this problem:

> There are 13 marbles in the bag. Five of them are red and the rest are blue. How many blue marbles are in the bag?

Several strategies were observed as grade-1 students attempted these problems. One, the **separating from given** strategy, involves constructing a set of concrete objects representing the larger number in the problem and then separating out (i.e., by counting) the number to be subtracted from the larger number. The **counting down from given** strategy is like the separating from strategy except no concrete objects are used. Counting down from involves starting with the larger number in the problem and counting down from that number, one count at a time, equal to the total number of counts in the smaller number in the problem. The **adding on** strategy begins with setting up the number of objects equal to the smaller number cited in the problem. Objects are then added on one at a time until the larger number cited in the problem is reached. The number of objects added on is then counted to provide the solution. A pure counting version of adding on (i.e., involving no concrete objects) is called **counting up from given.** A third strategy involving manipulation of concrete objects was termed **matching.** Two sets of concrete objects corresponding to the numbers in the problem are established. Then, objects from the two sets are paired in a one-to-one fashion. When one set still has remaining items, those are counted, with that count being the correct answer to the problem.

Importance of Word Problems and Children's Use of Natural Strategies to Solve Them All of the problems discussed in the last two subsections were word problems, consistent with the NCTM recommendation to present word problems to young children. Analysis of such word problems to produce solutions using concrete representations requires real mathematical understandings, more so than the mechanical addition and subtraction exercises that typify much conventional primary addition and subtraction problems (e.g., ones in which number sentences are set up and the student need only solve the setup problem, such as $13 - 5 =$ ____, $8 + 5 =$ ____, or $13 -$ ____ $= 5$, exercises that are intended to develop long-term memory of the basic addition and subtraction "facts" and facility in using the facts).

Conventional thinking is that children are not ready for word problems until they have mastered the relevant addition and subtraction facts. That children can solve word problems before relevant addition and subtraction facts have been memorized and automatized is clear evidence that the conventional wisdom is wrong, at least with respect to the prerequisites for word problems. Carpenter and Moser's (1983) position is that the conventional wisdom is essentially backwards: Solution of word problems should be used to stimulate the development of knowledge of mathematical facts (i.e., knowledge of facts such as $13 - 5 = 8$, $8 + 5 = 13$, or $13 - 8 = 5$ will increase as an incidental byproduct of solving problems involving the facts); memorization of facts should not be used to set the stage for presentation of word problems. Carpenter and Moser's position is consistent with the recurring contemporary emphases on student construction of mathematical knowledge as a means of developing mathematical understandings.

Even so, we believe there is reason for caution in coming to general prescriptions about the use of word problems as children's introduction to arithmetic problems. A study by Levine, Jordan, and Huttenlocher (1992) is telling with respect to this point. They presented simple addition and subtraction problems to children ages 4 to 6. When the children were given word problems like the ones used in Carpenter et al. (1981), the 6-year-olds solved the problems about two-thirds of the time. The 4-year-olds and young 5-year-olds, however, rarely solved these word problems. In contrast, when 4-year-olds and 5-year-olds were presented problems comparably difficult but with concrete referents (black buttonlike disks) that could be added or subtracted, they solved many more problems, with the difference in solution

rates for 4- and 5-year-olds versus 6-year-olds small when problems were presented with discs but much larger when the children attempted word problems. There may be a lower developmental limit on the usefulness of word problems in beginning arithmetic instruction, with word problems more appropriate for grade-1 and older children than for preschoolers.

Readers who experienced conventional grade-1 mathematics instruction will recognize how radically different the developmental point of view is compared with conventional outlooks about the teaching of addition and subtraction. For example, we both can remember that our grade-1 teachers did everything possible to dissuade students from solving addition and subtraction problems on their fingers. In contrast, the contemporary outlook is that the fingers are a natural set of concrete objects and that using them to solve problems involving addition and subtraction is developmentally appropriate.

Readers might also note that the use of mathematical strategies by preschoolers is consistent with previous discussions in this book about preschoolers' strategic competence (see Chapter 2). Implicit throughout this book is that use of strategies is important in the construction of declarative knowledge. The effects of children's problem-solving efforts on the development of mathematical knowledge during the preschool and primary-grade years has been of special interest to Siegler of Carnegie-Mellon University.

Development of Knowledge of Math Facts: Distribution of Associations Model

Siegler's work (covered briefly in Chapter 4) emphasizes that most children eventually abandon the counting and concrete manipulation strategies identified by Carpenter and colleagues. They come to rely on knowledge of math facts when presented simple problems (e.g., given "$2 + 5 =$", they retrieve the answer "7" from long-term memory). Siegler's (e.g., 1987, 1988, 1989; Siegler & Shrager, 1984) theory is that as children use strategies to work addition and subtraction problems, they develop associations between the problem statements (e.g., $2 + 5$) and the answers they generate for problems (i.e., the association between "$2 + 5$" and "7" is strengthened when a child solves $2 + 5$ using fingers or through counting). Of course, children do not always produce the correct answer to problems, and thus they also form associations between problem statements and incorrect answers (e.g., the association between "2 + 5" and "6" is strengthened when a child errantly generates 6 as an answer to the problem 2 + 5). Because the most frequently experienced answer is the correct one (i.e., when children are shown complete number facts, such as on flash cards, they experience correct associations; adults or other children often correct errant answers by providing the correct answer; and the most frequent answer produced by most children in reaction to a problem is the correct answer), the strongest association between a math fact problem (e.g., 2 + 5) and an individual number is with the number corresponding to the correct answer (e.g., 7).

When the associative strength between the problem and the correct answer is sufficiently stronger than any other math fact-number association, the math fact comes to elicit the correct answer reliably. The student no longer needs to solve the problem using concrete aids or counting—they can simply "look it up" in long-term memory (e.g., Ashcraft & Battaglia, 1978; Ashcraft & Stazyk, 1981), although some students will continue to count or use other strategies in order to "just make certain" he or she is reporting the correct answer (Siegler, 1988). What Siegler is describing is a shift from reliance on problem-solving strategies to reliance on the knowledge base (see Chapter 4).

In general, Siegler's most important results have been replicated by others as part of analyses supporting the model developed by Siegler, in particular that development of associations between simple problems and their answers permits retrieval of correct answers to become a preferred approach when solving simple problems (e.g., Geary & Burlingham-Dubree, 1989; LeFevre, Kulak, & Bisanz, 1991). Even so, it must be remembered that Siegler's studies were of children answering "number-fact" problems devoid of external referents. This is an important limitation, for children do not seem to use the strategies Siegler studied (e.g., use of fingers) as certainly when they are confronted with problems depicted concretely (e. g., addition and subtraction problems presented with black buttons) or when presented word problems based on number facts (Levine et al., 1992). Nonetheless, given the many occasions when children are presented math fact problems without concrete supports, there is no doubt that Siegler has provided an important window on a salient part of many children's mathematical experiences. The importance of this developmental model is obvious from the amount of follow-up research it has inspired.

Additional Understandings of Basic Mathematical Skills Produced in Research Evaluating Developmental Shifts from Reliance on Computing Strategies to Reliance on Fact Retrieval

The orderly outcomes produced by the Wisconsin and Carnegie-Mellon groups have stimulated much follow-up research, with this work providing increasingly detailed understanding of basic addition and subtraction. A brief review of some of the more interesting of these studies makes obvious that this is an exceptionally active area of research. This work also makes obvious that basic addition and subtraction competencies are enormous intellectual accomplishments. Consider the following examples:

- Children's facility in using counting as a problem-solving procedure improves considerably during the preschool years, with counting applied to an increasing range of problems from 3.5 years of age onward (Sophian, 1987).
- Among the computational strategies based on counting that preschoolers use, some are more efficient than others. There have been suggestions in the literature since Groen and Parkman (1972) that with practice doing addition problems, children eventually discover and use the more efficient MIN strategy rather than less efficient procedures. Siegler and colleagues (e.g., Siegler & Crowley, 1991; Siegler & Jenkins, 1989) reexamined this issue by observing children solve many problems and interviewing them after they solved them. They believed that the preschoolers they watched discovered the MIN strategy. In short, work continues on preschoolers' use and discovery of strategies, with the aim of providing more detailed understanding of the origins and nature of preschoolers' strategic competencies. There is no doubt that preschoolers discover many strategies as they practice solving addition problems (e.g., Christensen & Cooper, 1991).
- Widaman, Little, Geary, and Cormier (1992) studied the addition competencies of students in

grades 2, 4, and 6 and college. In two experiments, students were provided simple math facts, with each fact accompanied either by a correct or an incorrect answer (e.g., $2 + 5 = 7$ or $2 + 5 = 8$). The second experiment also included more complex problems, one involving addition of two-digit numbers with two-digit numbers (e.g., $41 + 25$), again accompanied either by a correct or an incorrect answer. The students' task was to decide as quickly as possible when presented a problem and answer whether the answer was correct. The reaction time data were analyzed to make inferences about strategies used by the students and shifts in use of strategies. One important conclusion was that at each developmental level, there were students using strategies to solve problems and others relying on retrieval of math facts. (See Geary & Brown, 1991, for an analysis of differences in solution strategies among grade-3 and grade-4 students; see Geary, 1990; Geary, Brown, & Samaranayake, 1991; and Geary, Bow-Thomas, & Yao, 1992, for evidence that some students are much more likely to develop a repertoire of addition strategies than are other children, and some children are more likely to come to rely on retrieval of math facts than are other students.) Although this was not surprising at the grade-2 level in Widaman et al. (1992), it was striking that nontrivial proportions of grade-6 (30 percent) and college (20 percent) students use computational strategies: Is it possible that even some college students do not know their basic addition facts, or were they computing the answer just to be sure they were right? Widaman et al. (1992) believe the answer is that fact retrieval from long-term memory is anything but certain for some adults. Complementary analyses document that for most adults, even simple addition problems require some cognitive effort to solve (Kaye, deWinstanley, Chen, & Bonnefil, 1989).

- That simple addition is problematic for some middle-grade children was illuminated by the work of Goldman and colleagues at Vanderbilt. Goldman, Mertz, and Pellegrino (1989; also Goldman, Pellegrino, & Mertz, 1988) studied students in grades 3 and 4 who had not reached the point of being able to retrieve their math facts automatically, continuing to rely extensively on MIN and other counting strategies. Using a microcomputer program, the students

were given extensive practice (i.e., sessions provided over 3 months) in generating the answers to basic single-digit addition problems. In general, student responding quickened over the period of practice, although even at the end of 3 months, virtually all participants seemed to use counting strategies (particularly MIN) at least some of the time, consistent with other data that mathematically disabled students overrely on counting strategies (Geary et al., 1992; Geary & Brown, 1991; Geary et al., 1991).

- Just as many children come to "know" addition facts and rely on retrieval of facts rather than computation when presented simple addition problems, they also come to know other math facts, with fact retrieval eventually supplanting counting strategies when presented elementary multiplication problems (Cooney, Swanson, & Ladd, 1988; Geary, Widaman, & Little, 1986; Koshmider & Ashcraft, 1991). For example, Campbell and Graham (1985) studied the development of associations between the single-digit math problems up to 9×9 and the answers to these problems. In general, Siegler's distribution-of-associations model fits the data, with the strength of association between a problem and its answer eventually stronger than any competing associations. By grade 5, children's use of multiplication-fact retrieval resembled multiplication-fact retrieval by adults.

- Widaman et al. (1992) also validated three different component skills involved in multidigit addition (Widaman, Geary, Cormier, & Little, 1989) that are performed slowly at first and eventually can become automatized. The three skills are (1) initial coding of the digits in a problem, (2) computing or retrieving the correct sum for each column from long-term memory, and (3) carrying to the next column. Others (e.g., Wolters, Beishuizen, Broers, & Knoppert, 1990), who have been studying mental addition of multidigit numbers, have also identified ways in which long-term knowledge of addition facts is essential as part of the problem-solving process, which often depends heavily on reformulating addends into parts and adding the parts, for example, thinking of $29 + 64$ as $(30 - 1) + (60 + 4)$, which can be calculated quickly as $30 + 60 + 4 - 1 = 93$. Siegler and Shrager's (1984) insights about the use of long-term–remembered math facts to solve simple addition problems is helping to explain how people solve even more complex problems than the ones Siegler studied.

Children acquire simple problem-solving strategies before they come to school. A consequence of practicing these strategies and generating answers to problems is the development of associations between problems (e.g., 4 + 3, 2 + 7) and the answers generated in response to problems. Because the correct answer to a problem (e.g., 7 and 9 for the example problems) is associated with the problem more often than any other answer, this association becomes stronger than competing problem-number associations, so eventually the correct answer is elicited reliably and automatically whenever the problem is presented. By the middle elementary grades, many children are relying on retrieval of answers from long-term memory over any other strategy in generating answers to single-digit addition problems. With practice performing other operations, such as subtraction and multiplication, there is strengthening of associations between subtraction and multiplication problems and their correct answers, so that by the middle-to-late elementary grades, many children rely on retrieval from long-term memory to respond to basic subtraction and multiplication problems as well as addition problems. It is important to recognize that there are individual differences, however, with respect to whether students come to use the retrieval strategy. For example, a nontrivial proportion of adults continues to rely on counting strategies to solve single-digit arithmetic problems.

Another Developmental Model of Procedural and Knowledge Contributions to Early Arithmetic Competence

Byrnes of the University of Maryland (e.g., 1992; also Byrnes & Wasik, 1991) believes that mathematical concepts and procedures are stored in separate memory systems, consistent with the ACT* model reviewed in Chapters 2 and 3 and with the specification throughout this book of procedural and declarative knowledge as distinguishable components in good information processing. Byrnes also believes, however, that mathematical procedures index pieces of conceptual knowledge that must be understood for the procedure to be carried out. For example, the procedure of "adding fractions" is indexed to the concept of "least common denominator," since a

least common denominator must be found as part of the fraction addition operation. Concepts are also linked to one another in long-term memory according to Byrnes' viewpoint (e.g., "fractions" is indexed as connected to "least common denominator").

Despite these interconnections when procedures and concepts are understood well, Byrnes believes it makes sense to separate them for several reasons: One is that people can know concepts but not be able to carry out the procedures that call for them (e.g., understanding the idea of lowest common denominator without understanding how to add fractions); moreover, sometimes people can execute procedures without fully understanding the concepts relating to the procedures (e.g., adding fractions using an algorithm). Another support for separation of conceptual and procedural knowledge is psychophysiological evidence (e.g., Squire, 1987) substantiating that mathematical-conceptual and procedural knowledge involve different regions of the brain. Even so, most mathematical operations involve dynamic interaction and simultaneous use of procedural and mathematical conceptual knowledge.

Byrnes (1992) offered impressive evidence in favor of this perspective. He studied grade-7 students who had just received their first instruction about the concept of integers. They had been taught about the negative and positive parts of the number line, but they had not yet been taught about how to do computations involving integers (i.e., how to add and subtract positive and negative numbers). Byrnes first measured how much conceptual knowledge each of 25 students had acquired from instruction they had received thus far about integers: The conceptual knowledge measure required students to place four positive and four negative integers on a number line; the students also placed the same numbers on an analogous "staircase," which had a landing corresponding to zero and steps descending from it to the left to represent negative numbers and ascending from the right to represent positive numbers, with the numbers –4 and +2 already placed on the correct steps of the staircase. The conceptual measurement also required students to decide which of two integers presented to them was larger. Byrnes assessed how much procedural knowledge the students possessed with respect to addition and subtraction of integers. This measurement required students to show, using a number line, the results of adding or subtracting particular integers from a particular starting point on the number line. Students also attempted a number of computational problems involving signed numbers.

After these assessments of conceptual and procedural knowledge were taken, instruction in computation (addition, subtraction, multiplication, division) of integers was provided to students. Computational skill was measured again. The most interesting relationship between pretest assessments and postinstructional computational performance was that pretest conceptual understanding of order was correlated with final computational facility. That is, children's conceptual understanding of integers was related to their ability to acquire procedural skills involving integers, consistent with Byrnes' belief that although mathematical conceptual and procedural knowledge can be separated, they interrelate to determine mathematical competence.

In a second experimental study, Brynes (1992) manipulated adults' conceptual understanding of "prime number," teaching either a correct or incorrect definition of it. All subjects were then taught a set of mathematical operations requiring knowledge of prime numbers. There was a striking effect of conceptual knowledge on the acquisition of these novel procedures in this study: Students who had learned the errant definition of prime numbers performed the new mathematical procedures more poorly than students taught the correct definition of primes. Once again, acquisition of a mathematical procedure depended on understanding a mathematical concept. We expect more experiments from Byrnes and others specifying in greater detail how conceptual and procedural knowledge interact to affect the development of and developmental differences in mathematical competence.

Instructional Implications

There are some important instructional messages in these data. Carpenter, Romberg, and Moser's work made obvious that word problems are not beyond the capabilities of primary students, and, indeed, their perspective is that working such problems is much more mathematically meaningful for primary students than drilling on the basic math facts. Knowing the math facts by heart is not necessary for grade-1 students to be able to solve many word problems. Even so, retrieval of the single-digit math facts is essential for performing more complex functions (e.g., single-digit addition facts are used to solve multiple-digit addition problems), so that it is disturbing that many students in the later elementary grades and even a number of adults do not au-

tomatically retrieve the answers to single-digit problems. Practice doing such problems helps, but there is no quick fix here. Even after 3 months, many of Goldman et al.'s (1989) grade-3 and -4 students were still relying on counting strategies some of the time. A great deal of work remains to be done to determine how to ensure that most students will leave the primary grades "knowing" their math facts—with it likely based on the work of Carpenter and other mathematics educators that much of the instruction intended to produce such knowledge should involve much more than drill and practice: The goal must be students who reliably retrieve facts such as 2 + 7 = 9, understand how such facts relate to the world, and connect the mathematical facts they know to other mathematical knowledge. Both knowing math fact associations *and* understanding addition, subtraction, multiplication, and division are essential if a student is to be competent in elementary mathematics and beyond.

Although many mathematics educators seem uncomfortable with the idea of direct teaching of problem-solving skills, believing that mathematics is better learned by students constructing their own understandings, there is substantial evidence of positive effects of explicit mathematics instruction. For example, kindergarten and grade-1 students can solve some types of simple addition and subtraction problems much more reliably if they are given instruction. Problems involving comparison of one set size with another set size can be difficult for primary students who have not been taught a strategy for constructing comparisons (Riley & Greeno, 1988). One reason is that kindergarten and grade-1 students misinterpret statements such as Mary has 5 more marbles than John" to mean "Mary has 5 marbles" (Cummins, 1991). Bebout (1990), however, demonstrated that with instruction, primary students can learn to solve such problems. The children in her study were taught how to use concrete aids to represent the problems and then how to translate the concrete representations into symbolic representations. For example, given a comparison problem such as "Bill found 9 pennies. Rosemary found 6 pennies. How many more pennies did Bill find than Rosemary?", Bebout taught students to represent the problem with concrete manipulatives. Then, students were shown corresponding number sentences capturing the important elements in the problem (e.g., 9 − 6 = ___), with teacher-student interactions until the students could see how the concrete situation was represented with the number sentence. Instruction continued with students inventing word problems given number sentences (e.g., developing their own word problem that could be represented with 6 + ___ = 14). In short, there was a great deal of direct instruction of how to construct number sentences. Fourteen lessons produced a great deal of improvement in the students' construction of correct number sentences for a variety of problem types.

Finally, we emphasize that the notion of strategy teaching, which is featured in this book, makes sense in the context of primary arithmetic. For example, many children do not naturally develop some effective elementary problem-solving strategies (e.g., counting up from the subtracted number to the larger number to determine a difference—such as counting up from 8 to establish that 6 digits intervene between 14 and 8 and thus represent the answer to 14 – 8). Fuson and colleagues (e.g., Fuson & Fuson, 1991; Fuson & Willis, 1988) have demonstrated that the counting-up strategy can be taught profitably to primary students, with Fuson's group relying on direct explanation that emphasizes subtraction conceptualized as "adding on." Fuson's work and studies such as Bebout (1990) make clear that direct explanation of elementary problem solving can emphasize understanding. Such instruction can result in students who are more adept at representing the world with mathematical expressions and better able to solve math problems that are presented to them. Our view is that study of conceptually rich instruction of mathematics strategies should be a high priority in the next decade and that the models of information processing theorists such as Siegler and Byrnes do much to inspire testable hypotheses that are advancing understanding of how children do problems and can learn to do them better. Such theoretically rich research, however, is occurring simultaneous with research that is more obviously applied in focus.

APPLIED RESEARCH INCREASING UNDERSTANDING OF EFFECTIVE MATHEMATICS INSTRUCTION

Mathematics educators are as much as any educator group "on the cutting edge" of new instructional approaches. This section covers some salient instructional and technological innovations currently being evaluated by mathematics educators and researchers interested in mathematical problem solving. Some of these interventions depend on direct explanations of content and procedures that are intended as a start-

ing point for additional student construction of knowledge; other interventions are more consistent with radically constructivist perspectives on mathematics teaching and learning, in that they leave more for the student to discover. Readers should reflect on the direct explanatory and radical constructivist aspects of the various interventions covered in this section.

Cooperative Learning

Cooperative learning (introduced in Chapter 5) is used for many content areas but is especially appropriate for mathematics education, given the importance that contemporary mathematics educators place on social collaboration in problem solving. Davidson of the University of Maryland and his colleagues (e.g., Bassarear & Davidson, 1992; Davidson & Kroll, 1991) have been at the vanguard in developing cooperative methods for mathematics instruction. They believe that cooperatively interacting to solve problems can be a transformative experience for many students, with the following advantages:

- Students come to value the process of problem solving rather than production of a correct answer.
- Davidson and colleagues have observed that mathematics anxiety is reduced when students work in cooperative groups.
- Cooperative instruction permits more challenging and less conventional problems to be presented to students.
- Cooperation fosters student explanations and reexplanations to one another, which is important since explaining difficult ideas to others is an effective method of forcing people to understand the ideas fully (e.g., Webb, 1989, 1991). The discussions bring to light misconceptions, which can sometimes be resolved via discussion. Students make connections to other knowledge as they discuss, with different students offering to the group differing insights about how the mathematics being learned connects to the world.
- Multiple representations of problem situations are offered in discussions, which is important, for mathematical people realize that any situation can be represented in a variety of ways.

Although not all studies comparing cooperative learning of mathematics with more conventional instruction have produced significant effects favoring cooperation, many studies have done so (Davidson, 1985). The evidence is simply overwhelming that usually at least small positive effects of cooperation are obtained with respect to objective mathematics performances (e.g., students can solve problems on standardized assessments better as a function of participating in cooperative learning experiences).

A healthy turn in cooperative learning research as part of mathematical problem solving is the analysis of the dynamics and structures of groups. Webb (1989, 1992) has established (both in her own research and through systematic review of studies conducted by Peterson and colleagues; e.g., Peterson & Janicki, 1979; Peterson, Janicki, & Swing, 1981; Peterson & Swing, 1985) both the positive effects of generating explanations in cooperative groups and the negative effects on achievement of only being told correct answers when seeking assistance.

Webb has observed that cooperative groups have the potential of allowing only some members to benefit, however, so that some caution in constituting groups is in order: Because the higher-ability students in a group are more likely to dominate interactions (also see Dembo & McAuliffe, 1987) and provide explanations, the higher-ability students in a cooperating group of students benefit more from participation in the group. With groups composed of a wide range of abilities, one interesting dynamic is that the high-ability students often form teacher-learner relationships with the low-ability students, with the unfortunate result that medium-ability students are less involved in group interactions than other students. Medium-ability students are much more active and learn more in homogeneous groups and in groups in which the range of abilities is more narrow (i.e., in groups composed of high-ability and medium-ability students or of medium-ability and low-ability students). Homogeneously high-ability groups tend to be less engaging for high-ability students than mixed-ability groupings, perhaps because the high-ability students assume that other high-ability students do not need their assistance; homogeneously low-ability groups are filled with incorrect explanations, with the result that low-ability students benefit less from homogeneous grouping than from mixed-ability grouping. When all factors are considered, mixed-ability grouping representing less than the full range of abilities seems to be the best combination (i.e., "highs" and "mediums" together, "mediums" and "lows" together).

Webb (1984) has also studied the effects of gender balance in cooperative groups. She reported that girls were more likely to be interactive in cooperative groups that were gender balanced (i.e., equal numbers of boys and girls), with majority-boy groups resulting in girls being ignored and majority-girl groups resulting in disproportionate interactions directed at the boys in the group. Achievement was greater for girls when they participated in gender-balanced groups.

We expect much more study of cooperative-learning group dynamics, especially with the development of analyses that are sensitive both to the cognitive strategies being used in the groups and to the metacognitive information conveyed by group members to one another (e.g., Artzt & Armour-Thomas, 1992). Such research is important, for it is becoming apparent that group problem-solving sometimes goes awry.

Stacey (1992), for instance, collected verbal protocols of students in grades 7 to 9 while they attempted challenging problems in small groups. What was disturbing was that the group members were often willing to go along with a simple and wrong method of problem solution that was put on the floor by one member of the group. Sometimes good solutions were rejected. Cooperative grouping is no guarantee of successful problem solving (see also Tudge, 1992). Much more research is needed to map in detail when groups work and what can be done so that they work better.

Parental Help with Homework

To the extent it has been studied (i.e., in six studies with students in grades 4 to 6), parental assistance with homework is associated with improved student problem solving (Hembree, 1992). This association is striking because *assignment* of homework has only a small effect on elementary student achievement in problem solving (Hembree, 1992). Just getting assignments does not stimulate understanding; getting help with assignments from a parent does.

Learning from Examples

Although social interactions can increase mathematical understandings, there are also nonsocial ways of increasing knowledge of mathematical problem-solving procedures. We both took calculus in university. We remember almost never bothering with the textbook in math courses. Rather, we purchased and studied supplementary texts filled with worked problems, believing that the way to do well in calculus was to understand the worked problems and be able to do ones like them. Research outcomes are consistent with our undergraduate intuitions about the importance of worked examples in learning how to solve problems.

One of the most important studies evaluating the role of examples in acquisition of problem solving was reported by Sweller and Cooper (1985). In their studies, grade-8 and grade-9 algebra students were either provided worked examples of problem types or practiced solving such problems on their own. The first finding was that it took subjects less time to process the worked problems than to work through the practice problems on their own.

After presentation of practice problems, the participants in the study were presented identically structured test problems. The students who had been given the worked examples during practice solved these new problems more rapidly than did the students who had worked the practice problems on their own. Moreover, the students who had received worked examples made fewer errors on the test problems than did the practice control participants (see also Cooper & Sweller, 1987). These advantages with identically structured problems did not transfer to problems that were not identical in structure, however, even though they involved the same problem-solving operations as the practiced problems. That is, the procedural competence acquired from studying the worked examples did not generalize to new problem types in Sweller and Cooper (1985), something that has been noted in other investigations of short-term instruction as well (e.g., Eylon & Helfman, 1982; Reed, Dempster, & Ettinger, 1985).

When longer-term instruction involving presentation of worked-out examples has been studied, there has been evidence of long-term retention of skills learned through worked-out examples as well as acquisition of understandings about when the skills learned should be applied. Zhu and Simon's (1987) outcome was exemplary in this regard. As part of their work in high school mathematics instruction, they studied instruction of factoring of quadratic expressions (i.e., expressions of the form $x^2 + ax + b$), multiplication involving exponents (i. e., operations of the form $a^m \times a^n = a^{m+n}$, $(a^m)^n = a^{m \times n}$, and $(ab)^m = a^m \times b^n$), geometry proofs, ratios, proportions, and fractions. In general, across their experiments, problem-solving procedures were acquired more quickly with greater final competence when students were provided worked example problems. Perhaps the most impressive achievement is that a 3-year mathematics curriculum (2 years of algebra and 1 year of geometry) has been developed based on

worked-out examples. This is now being implemented in some Chinese high schools, with all indications that problem-solving achievement is higher, and learning occurs more rapidly in this program of instruction than in traditional programs. This is impressive because greater overall performance in mathematics requires that students not only learn the procedures taught, but also how, when, and where to apply the procedural competence they have acquired.

Although learning from examples is a preferred mode of learning for students (e.g., Anderson, Greeno, Kline, & Neves, 1981; LeFevre & Dixon, 1986; Pirolli & Anderson, 1985), much less effortful than attempting to derive principles by working out practice problems (Paas, 1992), and simply placing examples in texts seems to make texts more effective in conveying understanding of problem-solving procedures (e.g., Reder, Charney, & Morgan, 1986), there are many subtle factors that can make a worked example more or less effective.

Sweller (1989) warned that worked examples are effective only if the to-be-learned relationships are apparent without a lot of mental juggling—without a lot of integration that consumes short-term capacity, for learning the solution is a capacity-demanding process. Conventional worked examples, such as the following, were not effective in teaching students how to do problems in a study conducted by Ward and Sweller (1990; also see Tarmizi & Sweller, 1988):

> A car is accelerated in a straight line from rest for 10 seconds and in this time travels 100 meters. What is the final velocity of the car?
>
> Solution:　$s = vt$
> 　　　　　$v = s/t$
> 　　　　　　$= 10$ meters/second
> 　　　　　$V = 2v$
> 　　　　　　$= 2 (10)$
> 　　　　　　$= 20$ meters/second
> 　　　　　　　　(Sweller, 1989, p. 464)

A much better approach was to integrate the solution information into the problem so that students could easily map the solution components to the problem components, as in this revised version of the same worked problem:

> A car is accelerated in a straight line from rest for 10 seconds and in this time travels 100 meters [$s = vt$; $v = s/t = 100/10 = 10$ meters/second]. What is the final velocity of the car? [$V = 2v = 2(10) = 20$ meters/second]

Although there is a great deal of work to be done to determine exactly how to design worked examples so that they maximize understanding of solution processes, it is work well worth doing and is being pursued (e.g., Paas, 1992). A trip to any college bookshop to survey the stacks of worked example books for every area of mathematics, physics, chemistry, statistics, and engineering makes obvious that worked examples are important instructional resources for many students.

Computer Programming Experiences

A recurring hypothesis in the mathematics education literature is that experiencing computer programming should enhance mathematical problem-solving abilities. Because many programs include experience with particular mathematical contents, some also hypothesize that programming experiences have positive effects on mathematical content knowledge.

One of the most popular computer programs for elementary students is LOGO. Children can construct patterned images by commanding the cursor (referred to as a "turtle" because of its triangular turtlelike shape) to move in particular directions (specified in terms of left and right and by degrees) and to go particular distances.

One mathematical content-enhancement hypothesis is that LOGO programming should increase knowledge of geometric concepts. It does (e.g., Clements & Battista, 1989, 1990; Edwards, 1991; Lehrer, Guckenberg, & Lee, 1988; Lehrer, Randle, & Sancilio, 1989; Olive, 1991). For example, compared with grade-3 students not receiving LOGO instruction, grade-3 students who received 26 weeks of it (three times a week) learned a great deal of geometry. For example, they were more likely to be able to draw an angle when asked to do so, draw a larger angle than a given angle, and recognize right angles. LOGO students were more likely to know the number of angles in a triangle and a rectangle. They were better able to sort quadrilaterals into piles corresponding to classic categorizations of quadrilaterals (i.e., squares, rectangles, parallelograms, trapezoids). They could explain better the concept of "shape."

Unfortunately the evidence that LOGO programming experiences produce general improvements in problem-solving competencies is less compelling (see Lehrer, 1989, for a review; also Palumbo, 1990; Pea & Kurland, 1984). When generalization of problem-solving has been observed, either the effects have been subtle (e.g., Clements, 1990; Lehrer et al., 1988), or the transfer problem included salient elements shared by LOGO and the problem context (e.g., Lehrer, 1989, describes a chore task that is solved better by LOGO students that involves helping a "turtle" pick up its toys given some constraints regarding the order of the chores). Such shared elements are powerful clues to apply the skills learned as part of LOGO programming.

Perhaps it should not be surprising that LOGO experience per se does not produce large general increases in problem-solving skills. Recall the discussion in Chapter 5 about how educational computing programs often do not produce intended effects because they do not motivate or require the processes that are intended. Noss and Hoyles (1992) analyzed LOGO and concluded that many versions of the program do not stimulate the type of reflection that is required to build understanding of the processes performed when the turtle follows commands to move in particular ways. Moreover, children often prefer to construct figures by approximation and guessing rather than by working out a plan mathematically, and the program works regardless of which tactic the child takes. More positively, Noss and Hoyles (1992) concluded, as have others such as Lehrer (1989; e.g., Lehrer & Littlefield, 1991), that hints and prompts from live teachers (i.e., teacher scaffolding) can do much to increase student reflection on LOGO problem-solving activities. Such hinting can increase student understanding of the relationships between the symbols manipulated in the program and the movements observed on the screen. Studying the effects of LOGO programming when students receive scaffolded instruction should be a high priority, especially since mathematicians have analyzed LOGO in great detail to determine many different types of mathematical understandings that might be promoted by it (see Hoyles and Noss, 1992). Another possibility, suggested by the results of a study by Clements and Nastasi (1988) is that if children practice LOGO programming in small groups, reflection may be more likely and that LOGO programming may be a good stimulus for interactions that promote cognitive development (e.g., experiencing social-cognitive conflict as part of trying to identify a way to program some particular movements of the turtle). In short, there are converging data suggesting that programming experiences may be a good deal more enriching if experienced with other people—but more than that, that the problem-solving required by programming may encourage interpersonal interactions that stimulate the cognitive development of participants.

The evidence of generally improved problem solving following instruction in other programming languages is not much more compelling than it is for LOGO. For example, Blume and Schoen (1988) provided one of the more positive reports we have encountered, with the outcomes mixed in favor of programming effects on more general problem solving. Grade-8 participants in Blume and Schoen (1988) either learned how to program in the language BASIC or they were provided no such instruction. The criterion problem-solving test required facility in solving word problems and logic exercises. In support of the case that programming produced positive effects on problem solving, the programmers were more systematic in their problem-solving attempts and seemed to check their work more carefully. Nonetheless, the programmers did not seem to plan more and were no more successful in solving problems than were the nonprogrammers. In short, some problem-solving processes were stimulated by the programming experience, but the overall effectiveness of problem solving was not improved by learning to program in BASIC, consistent with all other available data on the effects of programming on problem-solving abilities.

Calculators

Cognitive psychologists believe that the tools one uses to think can affect the way one thinks. Thus, children who use an abacus to calculate come to perform mental calculations differently than do children who use nonabacus methods, with substantial evidence that long-term use of an abacus results in an internal abacus (i.e., an image of an abacus that is used to make mental calculations; e.g., Hatano, Miyake, & Binks, 1977; Hatano, Amaiwa, & Shimuzu, 1987; Hatta, Hirose, Ikeda, & Fukuhara, 1989; Hishitani, 1990; Stigler, 1984).

With respect to more up-to-date technology, use of electronic calculators can increase mathematical conceptual understandings, problem-solving abilities, and attitudes toward mathematics (Hembree & Dessart, 1986). For example, recall from Chapter 1 that Russow and Pressley (1993) explored the effects when college-level students used graphing calculators in a basic mathematics course covering mathematical functions. Compared with control students

who hand-graphed functions, the graphing calculator students came to understand the concept of function much more completely than controls, with graphing calculator students solving more problems on final examinations that required understanding of the relationship between mathematical functions and their graphs than did control students. These results were consistent with the observations of mathematics educators who have observed student use of calculators in classroom applications without conducting formal experiments of the effects of calculator assistance (see Demana & Leitzel, 1988).

Interactive Videodiscs

Interactive videodisc technology offers opportunities to present richly contexted problems to students. Students can be presented a complex set of relationships in such a movielike presentation, with realistic depiction of the many features that define the complex contexts in which realistic problems can occur. It is a format that permits easy review of a section of the presentation. Thus, viewers can interact with it, reexamining the images and screenplay to gather information needed to make a decision.

The Cognition and Technology Group at Vanderbilt University (e.g., 1992; Van Haneghan, Barron, Young, Williams, Vye, & Bransford, 1992) is pioneering research in applications of videodisc technology to teaching and learning of mathematical problem solving. Much of their early work involved creating problem sets to be solved in light of information in commercially made movies (e.g., *Raiders of the Lost Ark*), information that could be viewed and reviewed as part of attempting to solve a problem. More recently, they have produced their own series of shows, dubbed the *Jasper* series, about the adventures of a character named Jasper Woodbury. The first tape in the series was a 17-minute adventure ending in a problem.

The plot of *The Journey to Cedar Creek* was as follows:

> . . . [A] person named Jasper Woodbury takes a river trip to see an old cabin cruiser he is considering purchasing. Jasper and the cruiser's owner, a woman named Sal, test-run the cruiser, after which Jasper decides to purchase the boat. As the boat's running lights are inoperative, Jasper must determine if he can get the boat to his home dock before sunset. Two major questions that form the basis of Jasper's decision are presented at the end of the disc: Does Jasper have enough time to return home before sunset, and is

there enough fuel in the boat's gas tank for the return trip? The story indicates that Jasper decides he can get home before sunset. (Van Hanaghan et al., 1992, p. 22)

The students must attempt to solve the problems Jasper had to solve in reaching his conclusion, discussing and reviewing information in the videotape in order to solve the problems. Just as real-life problems are often complex and the essential facts buried in many irrelevant details, so are the facts in the *Jasper* stories. Just as there are alternative ways of figuring out the solution to the complex problems that fill the real world, so there are alternative routes to solution in the *Jasper* problems.

The complexity of the situations presented to students is apparent from consideration of the plot outline of another Jasper adventure, *Rescue at Boone Meadow:*

> . . . [W]e see Jasper Woodbury's friend, Larry Peterson, flying his ultralight into Cumberland City, their hometown. We soon learn that Larry is not only a very good pilot, he also gives flying lessons. One of his pupils is Emily Johnson. During Emily's lessons, she (and the viewers) learns much about the ultralight, including information on landing, payload, fuel capacity, fuel consumption, speed, and how the shape of the wing produces lift.
>
> After several weeks of lessons Emily has a successful first flight, and she, Larry, and their friend Jasper celebrate at a local restaurant. During dinner, Jasper reveals that he will soon be taking his annual fishing trip. He plans to drive to Hilda's (where she has a house and her gas station), park his car, and hike about 18 miles into his favorite fishing spot, Boone's Meadow. We also learn that Larry recently flew his ultralight to see Hilda and landed the plane at the field next to Hilda's house. As they leave the restaurant, Emily and Larry stop and weigh themselves.
>
> Next, we see Jasper fishing and eating his catch. As he is eating he hears a gunshot and he investigates. He finds a wounded bald eagle and uses his CB radio to call for help. Hilda answers Jasper's call and relays the information to Emily. Emily consults the local veternarian, Doc Ramirez, and they discuss additional information on eagles, distances, and so forth. The map on his wall reveals there are no roads from Cumberland City (where Emily and Doc Ramirez are located) to Boone's Meadow (where Jasper and the eagle are located). Nor are there roads from Hilda's to Boone's Meadow. Doc Ramirez leaves to attend an-

> other patient but emphasizes that time is essential if they are to save the eagle.
>
> The adventure ends with Emily posing the challenge to herself: What is the fastest way to rescue the eagle, and how long will it take? The challenge is presented to the students, and they are told that all the facts that they need to solve the problem are presented in the video. (Cognition and Technology Group at Vanderbilt, 1992, pp. 297–298)

The solution of this problem involves generating alternative rescue plans and making calculations about them. Three characters potentially can be involved in the rescue, and there are at least two vehicles available. Information about many possible routes is presented in the film. If the ultralight is chosen, there are constraints with respect to payload, including constraints on the amount of gasoline that can be put on the plane, which varies depending on the weight of the pilot. The possible complications go on and on. Students working together usually require several hours of problem solving to generate the optimal solution, including a great deal of exploration of the tape for important clues. The exploration of the tape requires students to attend to both visual and auditory information and to separate out problem-relevant and problem-irrelevant information as they build a mental model (see Chapter 3) of the problem situation. Teachers provide guidance and support on an as-needed basis (i.e., problem solving is scaffolded). After students attempt to solve the problems, they view the resolutions presented on the disc. Once the problems posed in the tape are solved, teachers present additional problems to the students, which can be solved using material in the tape.

Does experience with the Jasper problems affect problem-solving abilities? Van Haneghan et al. (1992) summarized the results of a controlled study in which the grade-5 experimental participants experienced the Cedar Creek tape and problems. Rather than working the problems related to Jasper, control students received instruction and practice on problems using conventional textbook materials, with problems relevant to competencies and topics covered during the time corresponding to the Jasper problem-solving experiences for participants in the experimental condition. The controls also received some instruction about Polya's general four-step model of problem solving and were urged to apply the Polya model while they attempted their practice problems.

There were no important differences in the problem-solving performances of experimental and control participants at the start of the study. Following problem-solving experiences with *Jasper,* however, experimental subjects performed better on a transfer task involving watching a short video and solving a problem. The think-aloud protocols of *Jasper* students reflected more sophisticated problem-solving. The overall solution rate of *Jasper* students was twice that of control participants. The *Jasper* students also performed better on written word problems, despite the fact that the controls had practiced solving word problems and the *Jasper* students had not. In short, this first test of *Jasper* provided support for its efficacy in promoting problem-solving performances.

The Cognition and Technology Group (1992) reported the results of a much more ambitious evaluation of Jasper, conducted in the middle grades in 11 school districts. Five of the districts included both experimental and control condition classes, permitting an interpretable comparison of the effects of *Jasper.* The *Jasper*-site students experienced at least three *Jasper* adventures. Some sites experienced four of the adventures. Controls received practice doing word problems. Pretest measures revealed no problem-solving differences between experimental and control students at the outset of the study.

As in the Van Haneghan et al. (1992) study, however, there were striking differences on posttests favoring students who had experienced *Jasper.* Performance on word problems was better for *Jasper* students. Because *Jasper* emphasizes planning skills, problems requiring planning were given at pretest and posttest. Although such problems were difficult for all students at pretesting, at posttesting *Jasper* students planned much more effectively than did control participants—they constructed a mental model of the problem situation and generated alternative solutions before deciding on one approach over others. A variety of attitude measures were collected as well. After experiencing *Jasper,* students were less likely to believe that math was scary, more likely to believe that mathematics has many uses, more interested in math, and more likely to enjoy the challenge of solving complex problems than were control students. In addition, the teachers liked *Jasper* and believed it facilitated students' learning of mathematics and problem solving.

Interactive videodisc presentations can be prepared that provide challenging and interesting problem-solving opportunities for students. Although *Jasper* is still in the evaluation stages, the positive outcomes to date should stimulate additional development of this technology. As interactive videodisc technology becomes more common, the commercial viability of this approach to problem-solving instruction should increase as well. The Vanderbilt-based group is continuing their creative evaluations of video presentations, extending their work upward, examining the effects of video learning opportunities for college students as they learn about complex theories and their application to real-world problems (e.g., Michael, Klee, Bransford, & Warren, 1993).

Educational Television Programming

Children's Television Workshop (CTW) has a long history of success in producing programming that positively affects children's cognitive growth, with *Sesame Street* and *Electric Company* their best-known products. Both of these shows increase children's understanding of important literacy and numeracy concepts (Comstock & Paik, 1991, Chapter 3). CTW's *Square One,* was designed specifically to stimulate positive attitudes and enthusiasm for mathematics in 8- to 12-year-olds, encourage development of problem-solving processes, and present important mathematical content. This programming has appeared 5 days a week on public television. Math is presented via enjoyable detective stories. The show is a mathematized version of *Dragnet* in many ways, with the detectives encountering many problems that can be solved using math.

Well-designed evaluations of *Square One* television are beginning to appear. Thus, in Hall, Esty, and Fisch (1990), grade-5 children were pretested with respect to their mathematical problem-solving abilities. Some of the children then watched 30 episodes of *Square One,* with controls not exposed to the program. Careful matching based on pretest scores ensured that the *Square One* viewers and controls were equal in problem-solving competence at the outset of the study. At posttesting, the students who watched the series episodes outperformed the control students on a number of measures of problem solving. The children who had watched the program manifested a greater variety of problem-solving behaviors in reaction to posttest problems, offering solutions that were both more complete and sophisticated than the solutions proposed by control participants. *Square One* is entertaining programming that stimulates development of problem-solving competence.

Summary and Commentary

A variety of methods for enriching mathematics instruction have been proposed and studied. These are not competitors but rather complementary approaches. For example, interventions such as problem solving in reaction to interactive videodisc presentations would seem naturally to fit into cooperative-group arrangements because group sifting through and selection of information from videodisc adventures is a natural part of coming up with a solution plan. Although individuals can use calculators, they are also instruments that can be employed as groups of students explore mathematics, with the calculator a device so portable that it can go anywhere that students might engage in problem solving.

In applauding the technological advances reviewed in this section, we are haunted by the reality that such advances are not distributed equitably to American schoolchildren (see Scott et al., 1992). The more expensive the technology or intervention, the more likely that its implementation will widen the gap between the education offered to the rich and poor, for expensive educational supplements are deployed only in districts that can afford them. The American track record on educating disadvantaged children with respect to high techonolgy is terrible compared with the record in educating more advantaged children (e.g., Sutton, 1991). In addition, even within a school, the intellectually rich may get richer and the poor get poorer in high-technology environments, which often impose new intellectual demands on students that are easier for high-ability students to handle than low-ability students (e.g., all the commands one must learn to use a computer; Hativa, 1988). Given that technological competence will be a requirement for more jobs in the coming economy, it is imperative that the United States devise plans to ensure that all children are given high-quality educational experiences involving computers, interactive videos, calculators, and whatever other electronic wizardry emerges as an important problem-solving tool in the soon-to-be 21st century.

This may be easier with each passing year, both because the prices of high-technology equipment come down and because such environments are always being made more user friendly, with the former factor important for economic equality of opportunity and the latter factor important for equality of opportunity for students varying in ability.

What about the question posed at the beginning of this section concerning direct explanation and radical constructivism? As it turns out, there is direct explanation with respect to every one of the interventions covered in this section, but there is also a great deal of knowledge construction. All of these interventions require students to solve real problems, which is always going to require taking what one knows and constructing innovative solution plans. The new media products and technologies do not just give information; rather, they encourage students to use ideas that are new to them in ways that require flexibility in application and reflection before and during problem solving. This technology at its best permits alternative ways of examining mathematics and encourages active interaction with important mathematical concepts and procedures.

Although we do not expect any school to include all of the approaches covered in this section, combining powerful elements of mathematics instruction has a good track record (e.g., cooperative learning and interactive, scaffolded instruction; Hawkins, Doueck, & Lishner, 1988). We expect much mixing of the components in the years to come.

MATHEMATICS ACHIEVEMENT IN ASIAN SCHOOLS

American students do not do as well in international comparisons of mathematics achievement as do students in many other countries, notably Japan and China (National Center for Education Statistics, 1992). Stevenson at the University of Michigan and colleagues have studied intensively the differences between American and Asian educational systems in an attempt to understand the academic achievement differences between these cultures (e.g., Stevenson, 1990, 1992; Stevenson et al., 1990a, 1990b; Stevenson, Lee, & Stigler, 1986; Stevenson, Lummis, Lee, & Stigler, 1990; Stigler, Lee, Lucker, & Stevenson, 1982; Stigler, Lee, & Stevenson, 1987, 1990; see also d'Ailly, 1992).

Stevenson's studies included both formal quantitative comparisons and more qualitative assessments to elucidate potential factors that might account for at least some of the achievement differences between Asians and Americans. After considering many potential explanations, many of which proved not to be credible (e.g., differences in innate ability), the Michigan group has produced a list of likely contributors to the Asian-American achievement gap, including the following factors:

- American students and parents are satisfied with lower levels of mathematics achievement than are Asians (Crystal & Stevenson, 1991).
- The Asian curricula are more difficult in that more advanced concepts tend to be introduced earlier.
- Asians attribute successes and failures to effort, a factor under the control of students; Americans are much more likely to attribute successes and failures to ability (Hess, Chih-Mei, & McDevitt, 1987; Holloway, 1988), which does not motivate effort because ability is out of the learner's control (see Chapter 5).
- Many more hours are spent on mathematics in Asian classrooms compared with American classrooms.
- Asian students are on task for a greater proportion of classroom time than are Americans, with Stevenson believing that this may be due to differences in scheduling of the school days in Asia so that children have more breaks for play during an overall longer school day. It is easier to be attentive during class time when there are periods of relaxation during the school day.
- Asian teachers are more energetic in class because they teach fewer hours per day than American teachers and have much greater opportunity for preparation.
- Achievement in school is much more valued in Asia than it is in the United States.
- Asian children spend more time on homework than do Americans (Chen & Stevenson, 1989).
- There are demanding, national mathematics curricula in Asian countries, in contrast to local decision making in the United States and hence greater variability in curricular expectations in the United States.
- Mathematics instruction in Asian schools involves high-level interactions and teachers monitoring students to determine whether and how well they understand. That is, Asian instruction already resembles the NCTM ideal, whereas much of American mathematics instruction still resembles the conventional instruction stereotype. The extensive seatwork given in the United States compared with Asian schools does not promote teacher-student interactions.
- Consistent with NCTM ideals is the use of many more manipulatives in Asian classrooms than in American classrooms.
- Word problems, another favored curriculum item by the NCTM, are more common in the Asian elementary experience than in the American experience.
- Feedback to students is much more common in Asian classrooms.
- Asian teachers do more to relate mathematics to the lives of their students than do American teachers.
- Asian teachers question their students more about mathematical concepts and about mathematics strategies that might be used to solve problems (Perry, VanderStoep, & Yu, 1993). Such questioning probably stimulates deeper thinking about mathematics in Asian classrooms, beginning in the primary grades at which Perry et al. (1993) made their observations of questioning during mathematics instruction in Asian and American classrooms. (Recall the discussion of elaborative interrogation in Chapters 4 and 10—questioning often stimulates students to relate new content more completely to what they know already than students do in the absence of questioning.)

In short, it is impossible to single out a single factor as *the* cause of superior mathematics achievement in Asian schools. The most likely explanation is that there are many ways that Asian instruction differs, with the Asian curriculum filled with components that, if anything, should promote mathematics achievement. Interestingly, when Song and Ginsburg (1987) compared the mathematics achievement of Korean elementary students with American students, they observed increasing Korean superiority with each additional year of schooling and concluded, as Stevenson and his colleagues have, that a variety of teaching practices, parental attitudes and expectations, and cultural values combined to promote achievement in mathematics (see also Holloway, 1988).

GENDER, RACE, AND SOCIOECONOMIC DIFFERENCES IN MATHEMATICS ACHIEVEMENT

U.S. females historically have not achieved at the same level in mathematics as U.S. males, especially when the benchmark was achievement on standardized mathematics assessments. American minorities perform more poorly in mathamatics than do members of the majority culture. Poor children do not perform as well in mathematics as children from middle-class and upper-class families. The result is that females, racial minorities, and people with lower-class origins are underrepresented in the pool of mathematics majors and in professions that require mathematics competency (Maple & Stage, 1991).

On the positive side, male-female differences in U.S. mathematics achievement are not large and have declined in recent years (Figure 13.3) (Friedman, 1989; Hyde et al., 1990). As far as classroom grades are concerned, females do better than males, with male advantages confined to math achievement as defined by standardized tests (Kimball, 1989). There also have been detailed analyses of factors that promote and undermine female students' motivation with respect to mathematics for example, females who are good at math are much less likely to continue taking math than their male counterparts. With these analyses informing the mathematics reform movement (see Chapter 5, this book). In addition, international comparisons are making obvious that there is no inherent biological reason for female underachievement on standardized tests and lack of interest in mathematics, for there are cultures in which males and females perform comparably on mathematics assessments and participate at equally high levels (e.g., Walberg, Harnisch, & Tsai, 1986). There also has been some closing of the white-minority achievement gap in recent years (Dorsey, Mullis, Lindquist, & Chambers, 1988; Jones, 1984). Still, there is much gap that remains to be closed, and we expect a great deal of research in the next decade aimed at identifying mathematics instruction that works with minority students, studies that would complement and inform efforts to involve more females, minorities, and lower-class students in mathematics and science (see Chapter 12).

There is reason to be hopeful that it might be possible to produce large achievement gains for some groups. For example, Cardelle-Elawar (1990) taught Hispanic grade-6 students who were experiencing difficulties in mathematics to apply a variation of Polya's model to the solution of problems: The students were taught first to understand a problem, translating it into questions that could be answered. Essential knowledge and algorithms needed to solve the problem were then identified and a solution plan devised. Students were taught to monitor their execution of the problem-solving plan. Control students in Cardelle-Elawar (1990) received more conventional instruction, emphasizing feedback about the correctness of answers to problems. There was a huge effect of this intervention on problem-solving performance on a mathematics achievement posttest (i.e., more than 3 SD difference), with both boys and girls benefiting from the intervention. Recall as well the demonstration by Fantuzzo et al. (1992) of the effectiveness of a math tutoring program in an inner-city elementary school, discussed in Chapter 8. Effective instruction can and is being devised, instruction that works well in schools that predominantly serve minority students (Figure 13.4).

Although Cardelle-Elawar's (1990) outcome is encouraging, what must be emphasized is that wait-

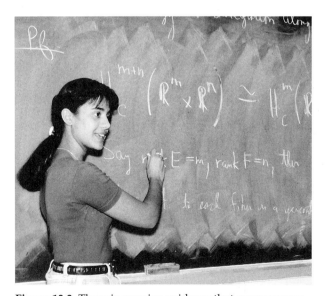

Figure 13.3 There is massive evidence that many young women can excel at advanced mathematics. In fact, if there are any differences in female-male mathematical conpetencies, they are very small.

Figure 13.4 The evidence is growing that children enjoy mathematics when mathematical understanding is the focus of instruction.

ing until grade 6 may be waiting too long. Mathematical competency group differences favoring majority-group students can be detected at the onset of schooling (e.g., Entwisle & Alexander, 1990). At special risk are minority students whose parents dropped out of school themselves or who do not value academic achievement (Entwisle & Alexander, 1990). The differences in the primary grades are most striking when children are given demanding mathematics tasks for their age, such as word problems (e.g., Jordan, Huttenlocher, & Levine, 1992). Can the differences detectable in mathematics competence in kindergarten and grade 1 be eradicated through instruction? We do not know at this time. As a society, we need to know what difference it makes if children receive high-quality mathematics instruction throughout their schooling, with the possibility that some who have done poorly in conventional mathematics programs might do much better if provided other instruction.

There is a lot of reason to conduct studies in which the mathematics achievement of girls, minorities, and economically underprivileged students is targeted. One is that different factors may determine mathematics achievement and participation for girls, minorities, and the disadvantaged than for white, middle-class boys. For example, Ethington (1992) analyzed some of the data from the Second International Mathematics Study (Crosswhite, 1986) and concluded that for boys, mathematics achievement could be predicted from their previous achievements in mathematics and their expectations of success or failure in math. For girls, previous achievement and expectations of achievement, predicted achievement but so did three other factors: (1) Ethington found that girls who were less likely to receive help in mathematics from their families suffered for it more than did boys. (2) The achievement of girls who view math as a male dominion is lower than the achievement of other girls. (3) If girls view math as difficult, it has a negative impact on their math achievement. As far as intentions to take mathematics in the future, Ethington (1991) reported that grade-8 boys' expectations of success in math and their valuation of math powerfully affected their plans to take math in the future; for girls, expectations of success had little impact on their plans, with valuation of mathematics a much more important determinant of whether they intended to take additional mathematics. In short, there are different determinants of math achievement and motivation to take mathematics for boys and girls.

In arguing for greater attention to the math achievement of underrepresented groups, we do not want to send the message that there is no real concern with the achievement of whites and males. The fact is that too few Americans are becoming highly proficient in mathematics, with this claim true for whites and males as well as other groups (Maple & Stage, 1991). Much more research on how to increase all students' mathematics achievement and interest in mathematics is needed. The intervention research covered in this chapter is only a start.

CONCLUDING COMMENTS

Mathematical cognition and teaching of mathematics is being studied from a variety of perspectives in the 1990s. One reason is that it is so easy to document poor problem solving even in university-level students (Perkins & Simmons, 1988), including use of trial-and-error rather than planful analysis, persevering with approaches that are leading nowhere or quitting once a difficulty is encountered, guessing, and equation cranking (a mindless form of working backwards from a solution, looking only for equations that yield the solution rather than for equations that correspond to elements in the problematic situation). We close by reviewing the most important perspectives driving research in mathematics education and by touching on some emerging approaches to the study of mathematical thinking and the teaching of mathematics.

Understanding Mathematical Concepts

The emphasis on understanding that is so prominent in the thinking of contemporary mathematics educators is different than previous conceptions of learning mathematics. Davis (1992, pp. 226–228), summarized the differences between the old and new views:

- Whereas the old view was that "... mathematics is about symbols written on paper," the new perspective is that, "... 'mathematics' is a way of thinking that involves mental representations of problem situations and of relevant knowledge, that involves dealing with these representations, and that involves heuristics. It may make use of written symbols ... but the real essence is something that takes place within the student's mind."
- The old view was that, "... knowledge of mathematics is constructed from words and sentences".... The new view is that knowledge of mathematics is built up from "previous experience." "This often means concrete experience...." Although "[w]ords may be used ... to guide the construction of mental representations, ... the mental representations themselves are *not* built out of words."
- The conventional perspective was that teaching meant, "... getting students to write the right thing in the right place on the paper".... The current conception is that, "... '[t]eaching mathematics' is a matter of guiding and coaching the student's own development of his/her repertoire of basic building blocks (from which mental representations can be constructed), and helping students to develop skill in building and using mental representations."
- It once was thought that, "The point of learning mathematics ... [was] to learn a few facts..., a few standard algorithms..., and a few definitions" and that "... [A]dvanced mathematics ... [involved] ... memoriz[ing] a few proofs." In contrast, the reason for studying mathematics

today, "... is to learn to think in a very powerful way...."
- It was once thought that, "... students would not be able to invent algorithms themselves." Now, it is acknowledged that, "... students often invent their own algorithms, even though they may conceal them from view of adults who would probably diapprove." (See Rohwer, 1980b, for commentary on children's invention of powerful algorithms that they carry out in secret.)

Regardless of the problems with conventional mathematics, many of the claims about the constructivist approach are not as well grounded in research as we would like. Indeed, we often think that the mathematics educators have done a better job of specifying the problems with mathematics education than they have in producing an alternative that can be recommended to the United States with confidence. If we were charged with writing a chapter summarizing credible research consistent with the radical constructivist instructional agenda, it would be a short chapter. In fact, the vague terms of reference used by many constructivist theorists, such as Davis's "way of thinking," his allusions to mathematical representations by specifying what they are not (*not* words) rather than what they are, and Davis's advancement of extremely general goals (e.g., "thinking in a very powerful way"), does much to undermine research in mathematics education. We find much attractive about talking in more concrete terms, such as those offered by other perspectives, some of which will be considered in the remainder of this section. At the same time, the commitment of the likes of Carpenter, Cobb, and Hiebert to models of mathematics education emphasizing understanding, ensures much more research in this tradition. We look forward to it, for the work to date is advancing the understanding of the nation about how theoretically inspired mathematics education can make a difference in what students learn about fundamental mathematical ideas and their application in the world.

Situated Knowing About Mathematics

There also is progress in understanding the social-environmental contributions to mathematical thinking, with a growing number of scholars conceptualizing mathematical cognition as situated knowing

(Greeno, 1991, 1992). A heuristic study for this perspective was conducted by Carraher, Carraher, and Schliemann (1985). They identified young Brazilians who make a living as entrepreneurs in city streets. As part of their business operations, these children perform complex calculations efficiently. When given problems in a formal testing situation, however, ones requiring exactly the same computations as the problems worked in the street, these children falter. Their mathematical competence is situated, tied to the world in which the mathematical operations typically are carried out. People develop nonstandard ways of doing the math that the world requires of them (see also Saxe, 1988).

Given the general interest of cognitive psychologists in situated learning (see Chapter 3) and the compelling demonstrations to date of context effects in academic cognition, we expect much more of such work. We believe that analyses of situational factors will only enrich understanding of the instruction and processing models favored throughout this chapter and book.

Good Information Processing and Its Development Via Instruction

Although research on mathematical cognition and instruction is being framed with respect to a number of exceptionally modern theoretical frameworks, including contemporary neuropsychological, situational, and constructivist theories, both the instructional and the cognitive-theoretical models featured in this book fare well when considered in light of the research conducted by math educators and psychologists interested in mathematics.

Direct Explanation Theories   Recall the analysis of effective problem-solving studies conducted by Schneider et al. (1990): Effective problem-solving instruction includes teaching specific problem-solving competencies in the context of explanations and efforts to insure that students first attempt to understand problems, then formulate and carry out problem-solving plans, and conclude by monitoring the adequacy of their solutions (although, of course, these are recursive processes so that linear progress from understanding to planning to calculating to checking is approximate at best). Good mathematics instruction is multicomponent, similar to all of the effective instruction featured in this book. We emphasize this point because some reform-minded mathematics educators, in the name of constructivism, sometimes argue for instruction that is not explicit in directing students and not filled with the components observed in studies of effective problem-solving. We agree wholeheartedly with the reformers' goal that students should understand the mathematics they are learning; we disagree that understanding is most likely when students receive largely nondirective and discovery-oriented instruction.

The direct explanations we favor are just a starting point for students—enough information that they can at least make some progress on routine problems. Additional instruction is provided in the form of hints and clues and elaborations (scaffolding) as the effective direct explanation teacher pushes her students on to more challenging problems. That is, the teacher explanations are only a beginning for students who construct much more elaborate conceptions of the instructed ideas and procedures as they work on mathematics problems. Explanations about mathematical concepts and procedures were provided to students in many of the more successful instructional studies reviewed in this chapter. We emphasize as well that the best of direct explanation research is as situationally contexted as instruction favored by constructivist educators—that excellent mathematics strategy instructors present problems from the real world to students. Although many math educators, and even some educational psychologists (e.g., Derry, 1992), view strategy instructional models as different from constructivist, situated teaching, we know of enough examples of strategy construction in authentic situations following introduction of a strategy through instruction to be confident that at least some strategy instruction is constructivist and situated.

In contrast, less directive instruction has been less studied, and when it has been examined, nondirective approaches often have been compared to instruction known to be ineffective. (Recall our discussion of the instructional studies designed to make the case that increasing students' conceptual understanding of mathematics would improve mathematics achievement.) The empirical case in favor of nondirective, radical constructivist instruction is not extensive nor strong compared with the empirical case favoring teacher presentation of high-quality explanations followed by scaffolded opportunities to apply the mathematical knowledge to meaningful problems. For example, there are the many explanations that occur when students scaffold each other by cooperating to solve problems. Explaining to other students how to do mathematics is an approach that increases the understanding of the explainer as well. Despite constructivist attacks on explanation models of instruction, there is plenty of evidence justifying resistance to those attacks—evidence that instruction followed by scaffolded problem-solving is effective

Good Information Processing   Just as the instructional perspectives featured in this book are consistent with much of the evidence in the mathematics education literature, so is the model of thinking that we favor consistent with models embraced by many mathematics educators. Earlier in the chapter, we made the case that Schoenfeld's perspective was consistent with good information processing. We close by returning to the theorist whose ideas opened the chapter, Polya (1954a, 1954b, 1957, 1981), whose description of how highly effective mathematicians think is wholly consistent with the good information processing model.

Strategies are everywhere in Polya. These range from particular strategies—such as focusing attention on the unknowns, data, and conditions of a problem to drawing figures to enhance problem comprehension to looking for analogies with other problems to decomposing a problem into subproblems—to the higher-order, problem-solving strategy for which Polya is best-known (i.e., attempting to understand, solve, and check a problem, with understanding, solving, and checking processes applied recursively). Polya recognized that use of these problem-solving strategies improves with practice: "Problem solving is a practical skill like, let us say, swimming. We acquire any practical skill by . . . practice" (Polya, 1957, p. 4).

Polya understood the importance of metacognition, such as the criticality of knowledge about where and when to use particular strategies, as illustrated by this quote:

> Look out for such features of the problem at hand as may be useful in solving problems to come—try to disclose the general pattern that lies behind the present concrete situation. (Polya, 1981, p. 116)

There are many instances in Polya's writings when he instructs students to determine whether a present problem might be analogous to a previous problem that the student already knows how to solve (e.g.,

Polya, 1957, pp. 110–112; Polya, 1981, pp. 81–82). In short, Polya emphasizes that students should always be attempting to increase their understanding of when and where particular problem solutions can be applied, and they should always be sizing up new problems to determine if they might already know how to solve the problem at hand.

Another aspect of metacognition that is important in good information processing is monitoring. Polya recognized well that such awareness of cognitive actions and how they affect problem solving is salient in the thinking of good problem solvers. Here is how Polya on one occasion described what is referred to in this book as monitoring:

> You keenly feel the pace of your progress. . . . Whatever comes to your mind is quickly sized up: "It looks good," "It could help," or "No good," "No help" . . . such judgments are important to you personally, they guide your effort. (Polya, 1954b, pp. 145–146)

What contemporary educational psychologists think of as metacognition pervades Polya's descriptions of effective problem solving.

Polya also understood how declarative knowledge can be critical to problem solving and how such knowledge must be used in conjunction with procedural competence in order to solve problems. For example, Polya (1981, p. 37) explained how it would be impossible to solve a problem about iron spheres floating in mercury without a great deal of knowledge about both iron and mercury.

Motivation is in Polya, too. He believed that good problem solvers really "get into" problem solving, to use a contemporary expression. He believed that motivated intensity such as the following was typical during effective problem solving:

> [As you solve a problem,] . . . [y]our mind becomes more selective; it becomes more accessible to anything that appears to be connected to the problem, and less accessible to anything that seems unconnected. You eagerly seize upon any recollection, remark, suggestion, or fact that could help you to solve your problem, and you shut the door upon other things. When the door is so tightly shut that even the most urgent appeals of the external world fail to reach you, people say that you are absorbed. (Polya, 1954b, p. 145)

All of the elements of good information processing have been in Polya's writings for more than 40 years. Polya's perspectives are even more relevant today than they were in the 1950s, however, for there now exists a more substantial database to support his theories about instruction and mathematical thinking. The good information processing perspective gets a big boost of support from Polya's theories, just as it does from Schoenfeld's more contemporary approach and the expanding database in mathematical cognition documenting that strategies, metacognition, nonstrategic knowledge, and motivation are key determinants of success in mathematical problem solving. We expect that as work on mathematical thinking inspired by traditions such as neuropsychology, situationism, and constructivism proceeds, new understandings about the physical and social determinants of strategies, metacognition, nonstrategic knowledge, and motivation to do mathematics will be identified. We expect the new theoretical lenses being applied to mathematical thinking and mathematics education to provide complementary explanations of thinking and learning rather than competing ones.

Literacy I: Reading

Both psychologists and reading educators have conducted important research on the psychology of reading. In the 1990s, we know a great deal about what to do during the preschool and primary grades years to increase the likelihood that children will develop into good readers. Much of that evidence is reviewed in this chapter. Beyond learning how to decode, a problem traditionally studied by psychologists, much psychological research was carried out in the past 15 years to determine how to improve reading comprehension. That basic research is now being used to devise educational interventions that are also the focus of psychological investigations. Unfortunately, the intensive research at the preschool and elementary levels has not been matched by equally intensive efforts at the secondary and adult levels. The result is that much remains unknown about how to teach older students and adults to be better readers, although the need is great with these populations. Although psychologists have typically thought in terms of interventions that improve the students' processing abilities, an alternative approach to increasing comprehension is by modifying materials so they more certainly stimulate effective comprehension processes. Thus, this chapter closes with an overview of what psychologists have learned about changing text so that meaning making is more certain and the meanings intended by text authors are more likely to be constructed by readers.

In recent years, American political leaders and the citizenry have concluded that there is a literacy crisis. The shock wave began with the 1975 publication of *The Adult Performance Level Study* (Northcutt, 1975). The shock magnified with *A Nation at Risk* (U.S. Department of Education, Commission on Excellence in Education, 1983). The literacy deficiencies of the United States have also been apparent in the "nation's report card," the National Assessment of Educational Progress (NAEP; e.g., Kirsch & Jungeblut, 1986): Many Americans lack fundamental literacy skills. More positively, by age 17, virtually 100 percent of current American students can perform the most simple of literacy tasks: They can write a simple description of a job they would like; they can locate a single piece of information in a newspaper article of moderate length; they can select words, phrases, or sentences to describe a simple picture (Kirsch & Jungeblut, 1986). The problem, of course, is that much more is demanded in our complex society, and only a small proportion of students seem to be able to carry out literacy tasks equal to these demands (Mikulecky, 1987). For example, fewer than 5 percent of 17-year-olds can extend and work with ideas in specialized, complex text. That is, most stu-

dents have a tough time with demanding scientific materials, critical essays, historical source documents, and technical materials such as those experienced in the workplace. They have trouble linking ideas in more complex essays and are not facile at making generalizations based on such texts.

The shock wave produced by the many analyses suggesting that Americans are much less literate than they need to be contributed in part to the great interest in the last two decades in reading. The information processing theory emphasized in this book also had an impact, with information processing analyses of many aspects of literacy produced in the last 20 years. Other theories of literacy and how to promote it flourished as well in the 1970s and 1980s. For example, "whole-language" theorists considered the acquisition of literacy in terms of natural language development in the context of a linguistically rich environment. Social constructivist views of cognitive development (e.g., Vygotsky) contributed to new conceptualizations of preschoolers as emergent literates.

In general, this chapter is about reading (Chapter 15 is devoted to writing), organized developmentally, with discussion of reading in the preschool years followed by discussion of elementary-level reading and reading by adolescents. Some thoughts on the challenges in promoting adult literacy then follow. Before setting out on this developmental description, however, we begin with a description of what good reading looks like.

NATURE OF GOOD READING

Good reading is similar to other types of good information processing and can be described using many of the same terms (e.g., strategies, metacognition, nonstrategic knowledge, motivation). Consider some of the attributes of good readers confirmed by information processing research and summarized by Oakhill and Garnham (1988):

- Their eyes take in text in an efficient fashion. There are **fixations** and **saccades** (i.e., pauses of about a quarter of a second a piece and jumps accomplished in a twentieth of a second). The movements are planned: The next saccade is determined during this fixation, with some perception of the next 15 or so letters to the right of the point of the current fixation. Most of the time, the next jump is forward, but some of the time, there are regressive saccades.

- Letters and words are recognized automatically because the good reader has knowledge of many words in a **mental lexicon,** containing the many words the reader has learned in his or her lifetime.
- The good reader's knowledge of syntax is so complete and used so automatically that even the most difficult syntactic constructions can be rendered sensible.
- The good reader has sufficient working memory to be able to hold "in mind" some of what was read previously as new information now fixated is taken in, permitting integration of what has been read and what is being read (e.g., Dixon, LeFevre, & Twilley, 1988; Just & Carpenter, 1992).
- The good reader has extensive background knowledge that permits inferences (Dixon et al., 1988), ones that elaborate on the stated meanings in the text and others that permit linkages between ideas in the text and between this text and other texts the reader has encountered in the past (Hartman, 1992).
- Their knowledge includes knowledge of text structures (i.e., the typical elements in narratives and expositions), which permits good readers to abstract main points and important details from text.

Given the emphasis on strategies and metacognition in this book, it should not surprise readers that strategies and monitoring play prominent roles in skilled reading and work in concert (e.g., Baker, 1989; Walczyk, 1990). Moreover, the best bet is that strategic and monitoring competence continue to grow well into adulthood (Baker, 1989).

One study was especially revealing about how exceptionally skilled readers read. Wyatt, Pressley, El-Dinary, Stein, Evans, and Brown (1992) asked 15 accomplished social science professors to select a journal article that would be interesting to them and in an area of great expertise for them. These professors were required to think aloud as they read their article, with their think-alouds audiotaped for later analyses. Their behaviors as they read were recorded as were any markings on the articles. Despite the fact that these professors came from different areas of competence and were reading different articles, there were great similarities in the way they read. At least 12 of the 15 professors used each of the following comprehension strategies:

- Anticipated or predicted information in text.
- Looked for information relevant to personal goals, such as their own research, writing, or teaching.
- Went backwards or forwards in text looking for particular pieces of information.
- Reread information when uncertain about meaning.
- Attended closely to tables and figures.
- Varied their reading style according to the relevance of the text to their reading goals.
- Paraphrased or explained what was in the text and gave examples illustrating text content.
- Summarized.

Other strategies were observed as well, although these were not as frequent (i.e., used by at least 5 of the 15 participants but by less than 12 of the professors):

- Decided early in the reading that they were looking for specific information.
- Noted parts of the text to be read later or particular citations in the text to be looked up later.
- Related content in one part of text to content in another part.
- Watched for particular information throughout the reading.
- Read the article's reference list to activate prior knowledge.
- Decided to read parts of the text in a particular order.
- Noted relations among parts of an argument in the text.
- Underlined or made other markings.
- Read aloud.

Monitoring, which is critical to regulation of strategies (see Chapter 2), was observed as well. At least 12 of the 15 professors monitored their reading and comprehension in the following ways:

- Noted how difficult or easy the text was to read.
- Noted when text content was already known or not known.
- Evaluated the relevance of text information to reading goals.

Other types of monitoring occurred, although less frequently (i.e., used by between 5 and 11 of the 15 professors):

- Indicated awareness of personal biases about text content.
- Noted when something was worth or not worth knowing.
- Noted when content was taken from another source.
- Adjusted attention depending on relevance to reading goals.
- Noted when the text contradicted a belief held by them.

Finally the professors experienced great affect as they read—consistent with the perspective that the entire range of human affective responses can be produced in response to text (e.g., Goetz, Sadoski, Olivarez, Calero-Breckheimer, Garner, & Fatemi, 1992). In particular, the professors produced affectively charged evaluation as they read. Eighty percent of the professors did the following:

- Reacted to information in the text based on their prior knowledge, often their own theories, writing, or personal contacts with the author of the text being read.
- Evaluated the quality of the text (e.g., the quality of the literature review, theoretical perspectives, methods, analyses, results, conclusions, discussion, writing or editing style, or biases of the author).
- Expressed negative affective reactions, including anger, weariness, or boredom.
- Expressed interest in the text.

Less frequent evaluative reactions included the following:

- Expressed surprise by what was in the text.
- Responded evaluatively using nonverbal expression (laughed, looked puzzled, made gestures, gave the raspberry, scratched the chin, slapped the forehead).
- Swore.
- Expressed positive affect about the text content.

Wyatt et al. (1992) demonstrated that good readers are active readers. Good readers use diverse strategies, they monitor their understanding in many different ways, and they react to what they are reading. Good readers separate the wheat from the chaff as they read, expending more effort to process parts of text that are important than parts of text covering information not well matched to the reader's needs (e.g., Reynolds, 1992; Reynolds, Shephard, Lapan, Kreek, & Goetz, 1990). They evaluate the sensibility of text in light of what they already know (see Baker & Brown, 1984). One of the most interesting aspects of the Wyatt et al. (1992) data was the great correlation between use of monitoring strategies and evaluations ($r = 0.77$). The correlation between use of comprehension strategies in general and evaluations was much smaller ($r = 0.45$, and $r = 0.31$ when the relationship between use of comprehension strategies and monitoring was taken into account): Good readers assess the worth and credibility of what they read as they process text in their area of expertise.

Documenting the many comprehension strategies and monitoring tactics used by good readers has been pursued vigorously by educational psychologists (e.g., Afflerbach, 1990; Lundeberg, 1987; Pritchard, 1990; Wade, Trathen & Schraw, 1990). Documenting that readers with extensive prior knowledge make interpretive evaluations of what they read is a related scholarly activity carried out by rhetoricians (i.e., those interested in how scholarly arguments are constructed), with a number of rhetorical analyses of experts reacting to text in their domain (e.g., Bazerman, 1985; Charney, in press; Geisler, 1991; Haas & Flower, 1988, Schwegler & Shamoon, 1991; Wineberg, 1991a, 1991b). The strength of Wyatt et al. (1993) is that it captured the strategies and monitoring favored in psychological analyses as well as the interpretive processes that have been the concern of rhetoricians.

Good Reading Compared with Expert Problem Solving

Skilled reading by domain experts shares many similarities with problem solving by domain experts (Chapter 4), and perhaps it should, as abstracting meaning from complicated text is a form of problem solving:

- Domain experts use their prior knowledge extensively during problem solving, recognizing large patterns and strong connections with previous experience.
- Experts are opportunistic during problem solving, using clues they encounter while solving a problem to assist in deciding next moves. So are good readers, as when they move forward and backward in text to find particular pieces of information they think might be important.

- Experts exhibit flexibility as they solve problems. So it is with good readers, who use diverse tactics to come to terms with text.
- Experts monitor their performances (Baker, 1989). Analogously, good readers monitor understanding, difficulty of text, and pertinence of a text to the reader's goals.
- Experts process "deeply" as they solve problems, using prior knowledge in conjunction with strategies, continually monitoring progress in understanding the problems. So it is with extremely sophisticated readers.

It is a long developmental trip to expert reading, however.

EMERGENT READING DURING THE PRESCHOOL YEARS

Not so long ago, a common question asked by parents and educators was: "Is my child ready to read?" Typically, this question was posed when the child had reached 5 or 6 years of age. Whatever happened before that was viewed simply as "getting the child ready to read." That is not how many contemporary educators think, however. Rather, there is a recognition that a great deal of literacy development occurs during the preschool years, that this is a period of **emergent literacy,** a term coined first by Clay (1966, 1967), a prominent New Zealand reading educator. Sulzby's (1988) definition is a good one: Emergent literacy is reflected in the reading and writing behaviors during the preschool years that precede and develop into conventional literacy.

Literacy begins in infancy according to this perspective; it is a home and school thing, something that develops anywhere young children are. Children are seen as active in the development of their own literacy, seeking out and initiating many behaviors that are literate and literacy fostering. The social environment can support and facilitate such literacy activities. Unfortunately, however, not all children live in worlds that are as supportive as they could be: Environments that support emergent literacy include (1) rich interpersonal experiences with parents, brothers and sisters, and others; (2) physical environments that include literacy materials, from plastic refrigerator letters to storybooks to writing materials; and (3) high positive regard by parents and others for literacy and its development in children (Leichter, 1984; Morrow, 1989).

Insights about the factors supporting emergent literacy can be gained by considering the characteristics of homes in which children learn to read before they start school (Briggs & Elkind, 1973; Clark, 1976; Durkin, 1966; King & Friesen, 1972; Morrow, 1983; Plessas & Oakes, 1964; Teale, 1978):

- The children were interested in and experienced paper-and-pencil activities, letters, and words at an early age.
- Parents read to the children, helping them with their "reading" and "writing." Parents frequently read themselves, valuing reading as a source of pleasure.
- There were books everywhere around the home.
- Parents took their children to libraries and bookstores.
- Early readers tended to come from smaller families.
- The literacy richness of the environment was more important than parental education or economic status (Hansen, 1969).
- Television viewing was limited.

In short, for these children, literacy often began before the first birthday, perhaps through experiences with plastic "bathtub" books filled with colorful pictures or from mothers and fathers who read nursery rhymes to their children as they rocked them to sleep. These early beginnings expand into a rich array of literacy experiences, from scribbling letters to grandma to experiencing stories on grandma's lap. Such experiences are so important that entire programs of research have been devoted to them, as exemplified by research on storybook reading.

Storybook Reading

Scientific interest in storybook reading predates the concept of emergent literacy. See Sulzby and Teale (1991) for a review of the literature establishing correlations between amount of storybook reading during the preschool years and vocabulary and language development, children's interest in reading, and success in early reading. Research on storybook reading has been substantially more analytical (Sulzby & Teale, 1991).

What do we now know about storybook interactions? Whether storybook reading occurs at home or at school, there are rich discussions and animated conversations between the reader and the child. The adult and child work out the meaning of the text, and they have a lot of fun doing it (Morrow, 1989). There is questioning, both by the adult and the child; there is modeling of dialogue by adults, with children sometimes participating; the adult praises the child's efforts to get meaning from the pictures and print; adults offer information to children and respond to children's reactions to text; and both adults and children relate what is happening in the text to their lives and the world around them (Applebee & Langer, 1983; Cochran-Smith, 1984; Flood, 1977; Pellegrini, Perlmutter, Galda, & Brody, 1990; Roser & Martinez, 1985; Taylor & Strickland, 1986).

Consistent with the Vygotskian ideas about scaffolding described in Chapter 8, parents seem to encourage children to participate as much as possible in storybook interactions, providing support as children need it, providing input that children can understand (e.g., DeLoache & DeMendoza, 1987). With increasing age during the preschool years, parents do more of the reading—the children are attentive to longer sections of text (Heath, 1982; Sulzby & Teale, 1987). With increasing experience reading storybooks, adults and children have more complex discussions about text (Sulzby & Teale, 1991). Children who experience a lot of storybook reading are accustomed to interacting with an adult about story content; they are appropriately attentive during storybook reading, much more so than same-age children who have not experienced storybook reading (Bus & Van Ijzendoorn, 1988).

There has been some attention to differences in style of storybook reading and the effects of such variation on cognitive development. There is better vocabulary development for children who interact with adults who are skillful at eliciting verbal interactions from their children during reading (e.g., Ninio, 1980). Heath (e.g., 1982) established a correlation between the degree to which parents prompted and provided elaborations of book content and the eventual literacy attainment of their children: Children who experienced rich elaborations of text meaning did better on higher-order comprehension tasks than other children.

This correlational evidence favoring the hypothesis that quality of storybook reading affects long-term literacy development is bolstered by evidence from an impressive experiment conducted by Whitehurst et al. (1988). In that study, the parents of 14 children between $1\frac{3}{4}$ and 3 years of age participated in a 1-month intervention designed to improve interactions between parents and children during story-

book reading. Parents were taught to asked more open-ended questions and more questions about the functions and attributes of objects in stories as they read stories with their preschoolers. The parents were also given instruction in how to respond appropriately to their children's comments during story reading and how to expand on what the children had to say. The parents in this treatment group were also taught to reduce the amount of straight reading that they did as well as to eliminate questions that the child could answer simply by pointing to something in an illustration. Fifteen other children and their parents served as control participants in the study, with these families encouraged to continue reading storybooks as they normally did with their children.

First, the intervention parents were able to implement the treatment. That is, they could learn to interact differently with their children during storybook reading and in ways that increased the qualities of interactions between the children and their parents. Although there had been no differences between intervention and control children at the beginning of the study with respect to language variables, there were clear differnces at the end of the month of treatment, ones favoring the intervention participants: At the end of the study, the intervention participants outscored the control subjects on a standardized measure of psycholinguistic ability and on two vocabulary tests. What was most striking in this study was that when the same measures were repeated 9 months later, the intervention subjects still had an advantage over the control participants, although the differences were not as large on the 9-month follow-up as at immediate posttesting. In general, however, everything in Whitehurst et al. (1988) was consistent with the hypothesis that high-quality storybook reading can have a positive impact on long-term language development, which is a critical emergent literacy ability. Notably, Valdez-Menchaca and Whitehurst (1992) replicated and extended the Whitehurst et al. (1988) finding with Mexican children.

As Sulzby and Teale (1991) concluded, most of the storybook reading data have been interpreted with respect to Vygotsky's theories of scaffolding and gradual internalization of cognitive skills: Within the context of the adult-child dyad, the child learns how to attend to text and how to participate in discussions of complex issues about stories, such as cause-and-effect in story sequences. Much is learned in these interactions—including both procedural knowledge, such as how to identify the main ideas in stories (Lehr, 1988), and declarative knowledge, such as cultural information incidentally conveyed in high-quality literature (e.g., Cornell, Sénéchal, & Broda, 1988). Much is learned largely because parents help the child as needed and "up the ante" when the child is ready for it (i.e., reads longer sequences to the child, urges the child to sit still for more). Such storybook reading does not occur in isolation, however, with many preschoolers in the last and present generations experiencing high-quality entertainment that is explicitly designed to stimulate literacy.

Sesame Street

Since fall 1969, American preschoolers have had *Sesame Street* in their living rooms, with a typical audience of about 10 million homes (e.g., Palmer, 1984). All systematic evaluators of *Sesame Street* (e.g., Anderson & Collins, 1988; Ball & Bogatz, 1970; Bogatz & Ball, 1971) have concluded that children learn a great deal about the alphabet and language from watching the program, much more so than from entertainment television, with *Sesame Street* making contributions to the development of literacy over and above family interactions and other sources of stimulation (e.g., Rice, Huston, Truglio, & Wright, 1990). *Sesame Street* is designed to grab children's attention through use of elements such as animated films, second-person address, and lively music (Campbell, Wright, & Huston, 1987), with the result substantial learning of the material featured on the show.

Concluding Comment

The more parents interact verbally with their children, the more verbally competent the children are (e.g., Huttenlocher, Haight, Bryk, Seltzer, & Lyons, 1991); watching Ernie, Bert, Big Bird, and Cookie Monster can stimulate some fundamental literacy understandings as well. Preschoolers especially seem to learn a great deal about literacy when adults read to them (e.g., they come to understand what words are and how they function from such interactions with elders and books; Roberts, 1992). Not surprisingly, 5-year-olds who are more emergent literate—reflected by greater competence in reenacting stories, writing individual words, "writing" stories, and "reading"—tend to outperform less emergent

literate 5-year-olds in reading during the primary grades, which can be interpreted as a validation of sorts for emergent literacy experiences (Barnhart, 1991): That is, emergent literacy competence at age 5 predicts later more conventional reading competence. We believe, as did Feitelson (1988), who studied early reading instruction around the world, that ". . . informed opinion as well as the results of experimental studies seem to indicate that a particularly good way to use the years *before* children enter school may be to emulate what middle-class parents seem to have been doing intuitively all along, namely reading intensively to their children" (p. 153).

A great deal is being learned about how to structure children's worlds to increase their emergent literacy experiences. For example, more emergent literacy experiences are observed when children's play areas include props that encourage literacy. Thus, labeling of objects in the child's world can stimulate interaction with print and words. The world of play can include paper, pencils, and pens; "stores" and "offices" in play settings can include "order forms" and letters, appointment books, and message pads; and children's attempts at drawing and writing can be displayed. The presence of magazines and books as well as cozy corners in which to read them also stimulate emergent reading and writing activities (e.g., Morrow, 1990; Morrow & Weinstein, 1986; Neuman & Roskos, 1992).

READING DURING THE ELEMENTARY YEARS

Elementary reading, especially beginning reading, has fueled enormous controversies. Twenty-five years ago, the whole-word versus phonics debate was detailed by Chall (1967) in *The Great Debate*, although data then and now (e.g., Byrne, Freebody, & Gates, 1992; Freebody & Byrne, 1988) support the phonics approach much more than whole-word reading. The winds of war between beginning reading camps stir again in the 1990s with extremely rancorous debates about the relative merits of whole language, which emphasizes comprehension and does not include explicit decoding instruction (e.g., Goodman & Goodman, 1979) and instruction that includes explicit teaching of decoding skills.

The evidence is simply overwhelming that explicit decoding instruction benefits most children and might be essential for many if they are to make rapid progress in becoming readers during the elementary years (e.g., Adams, 1990). Given the scientific stance taken in this book, we have no choice but to emphasize the decoding literature in the discussion that follows. In arguing for explicit phonics instruction, however, we caution that we do not dismiss the many potential advantages of whole language. In fact, we believe that excellent beginning reading instruction includes many of the elements favored by whole-language enthusiasts. Before elaborating on that conclusion, however, we cover some of the best science that is informing the teaching community about the importance of phonemic awareness and explicit decoding instruction in beginning reading.

Research on Phonemic Awareness

Emergent literacy experiences, such as child-adult book reading, do not produce all of the competencies that are essential for success at reading during the elementary years. One such critical competency is **phonemic awareness,** which is awareness that words are composed of separable sounds (i.e., phonemes) and that phonemes are combined to say words. Phonemic awareness is one of the best predictors of success in early reading in school (e.g., Adams, 1990; Bond & Dykstra, 1967; Scarborough, 1989). Children who fail to learn to read during the first several years of schooling often lack phonemic awareness (e.g., Pennington, Groisser, & Welsh, 1993; Stanovich, 1986, 1988). Children who lack phonemic awareness have a difficult time learning to spell and to develop understanding of letter-sound relationships (Griffith, 1991; Juel, Griffith, & Gough, 1986). Poor phonemic awareness at 4 to 6 years of age is predictive of reading difficulties throughout the elementary years (Juel, 1988; Stuart & Masterson, 1992). Poor readers at all age levels often are less phonemically aware than same-age good readers (e.g., Pratt & Brady, 1988), with low phonemic awareness, which persists despite instruction, almost certain in dyslexic readers (e.g., Bruck, 1992; Bruck & Treiman, 1990; Pennington, Van Orden, Smith, Green, & Haith, 1990).

In normal readers, for phonemic awareness to develop, formal instruction in reading seems essential (i.e., only a small proportion of children develop phonemic awareness in the absence of such instruction; e.g., Lundberg, 1991). Notably the one emergent literacy experience that predicts phonemic awareness is parental teaching of letters and their sounds (Crain-Thoreson & Dale, 1992). Many parents, however, do not engage in such teaching, so that education that impacts phonemic awareness typically occurs in school.

Without a doubt, the best-known experimental study of the effects of instruction aimed at increasing phonemic awareness was conducted in England by Bradley and Bryant (e.g., 1983), although it was not the first (see Williams, 1980). They hypothesized, based on analyses of correlations between children's rhyming and alliteration skills (which require understanding that words are composed of sounds; i.e., phonemic awareness) and later reading achievement (e.g., Calfee, Chapman, & Venezsky, 1972; Calfee, Lindamood, & Lindamood, 1973), that providing instruction to children about how to categorize words based on their sounds would increase phonemic awareness and hence long-term reading achievement.

An important principle emphasized in the Bradley and Bryant (1983) training was that the same word can be categorized in different ways based on sound when it is in different sets of words. Thus, if *hen* is in a group of words that include *hat, hill, hair,* and *hand,* it would make sense to categorize all of these words together as starting with *h,* especially in contrast to other words starting with another letter (e.g., *b* words such as *bag, band, bat*). If *hen* were on a list with *men* and *sun,* however, these three words could be categorized as ones ending in *n.* If *hen* were on a list of words that included *bed* and *leg,* it would be possible to categorize the words as ones with *short e* in the middle.

The training involved 40 10-minute sessions spread out over 2 years, although a more recent version of the instruction was implemented over a period of 4 months (Bradley, 1988). During the first 20 sessions, 5- and 6-year-olds who initially lacked phonemic awareness were taught to categorize words based on common sounds using pictures of the objects (i.e., pictures of a *hen, men,* and a *leg*). For example, in one lesson, a set of pictures representing the letter *b* was shown to the child, who named the objects. The child repeated the names with the teacher urging the child to listen to the sounds. The child then was asked if he or she could hear a sound common to each word. This continued until the child could identify the common sound, with the adult providing help and hints if the child experienced difficulty doing this.

The sound identification task was repeated many times during training, and there were variations (e.g., presentation of *bus* with the child required to pick out a picture starting with the same sound from an array of pictures; presentation of *bus* with the direction to pick out pictures starting with a different sound than the one at the beginning of *bus*). Children were given sets of pictures and asked to group them together based on common sounds, with them also required to justify their classifications. Odd-one-out was played, with the child required to eliminate a word starting (or ending or containing) a sound different than the other pictures in a set. Many such exercises were given for each sound (e.g., *b*), with the teacher moving on to a new sound only when the child seemed to be proficient with the sound previously introduced. Of course, as new sounds accumulated, the difficulty of tasks increased (e.g., there can be depictions of items starting with many different sounds rather than just one or two, as is the case at the beginning of training).

The 20 sessions with pictures were followed by 20 sessions with words, with children required to determine whether words rhymed or began with the same sound (alliteration). After the child was proficient at this task, there were lessons on end sounds (e.g., odd-word-out exercise requiring elimination of the word ending in a sound different than the others). After the child could manage categorizing based on final sounds, there was instruction of categorization based on middle sounds in words.

Pictures yielded to purely aural presentations in this training. Various discrimination exercises eventually gave way to production exercises, so that children had to recall words containing particular sounds in particular positions. In the latter half of the curriculum, children were required to spell words using plastic letters, with the teacher providing help as needed, up to and including spelling the word for the child if that was what was needed to move the lesson along. Spelling exercises included sets of words sharing common features. Thus, for a set involving *hat, cat,* and *rat,* an efficient strategy was simply to change the first plastic letter as each new word was requested. The saliency of many different sound patterns was illustrated with such spelling lists.

This training produced substantial gains in standardized reading performance (i.e., about a year advantage) relative to a control condition in which children were trained to categorize pictures and words conceptually (e.g., *cat, bat,* and *rat* are all animals).

The sound categorization-trained students were even further ahead of control participants who had received no supplementary categorization training. Even more striking, however, were the results of a 5-year follow-up. Even though many of the control subjects had received substantial remediation during the 5-year interval following participation in the study, there were still striking reading advantages for students who had experienced the sound categorization training when they were in the primary grades. See Bradley (1989) and Bradley and Bryant (1991) for discussion of these data.

Since the appearance of the Bradley and Bryant (1983, 1985) study, there have been a number of other experimental confirmations that phonemic awareness training promotes reading achievement (e.g., Ball & Blachman, 1988, 1991; Blachman, 1991; Cunningham, 1990; Lie, 1991; Lundberg, Frost, & Peterson, 1988; Tangel & Blachman,1992). Goswami and Bryant (1992) elegantly summarized the findings:

> There can be little doubt that phonological awareness plays an important role in reading. The results of a large number of studies amply demonstrate a strong (and consistent) relationship between children's ability to disentangle and to assemble the sounds in words and their progress in learning to read. . . . There is also evidence that successful training in phonological awareness helps children learn to read. . . . Put together, these two sets of data are convincing evidence that phonological awareness is a powerful causal determinant of the speed and efficiency of learning to read. . . . The enterprise of establishing the importance of phonological awareness . . . has immediate educational implications, and it will also undoubtedly play a great part in theories about learning to read. However, it is only a first step. (p. 49)

We concur and follow up on Goswami and Bryant's (1992) opinion that there is more to early reading than phonemic awareness: In the next section, various mechanisms that have been implicated in early reading are reviewed. Learning to read is an elegant intercoordination of a number of processes.

Other Processes in Learning to Read Words

This section is arranged with respect to the complexity of the mechanisms that permit decoding of individual words, with the less complex mechanisms presented first. One possibility is that the simpler mechanisms would be operative before the more complex ones, so that moving from the beginning to the end of this list would be a rough developmental progression. We resist that conclusion, for some mechanisms that appear complex seem to be used by quite young children under at least some circumstances (e.g., analogy; Baron, 1977; Goswami & Bryant, 1992). Although perhaps it goes without saying at the beginning of a section on other processes, we emphasize from the outset that there is more than one way to read a word (see Ehri, 1991, which informed much of what follows, for elaborate discussion of this point). We also emphasize that how beginning and skilled readers read words is an extremely active area of research, and there is much debate. That such decoding is extremely complicated is not debated. Thus, what is presented in this subsection is an overview of some of the more important ideas, with no attempt to present exhaustive coverage of the mechanisms defining either beginning or skilled decoding.

Logographic Reading Logographic reading (sometimes referred to as **visual cue reading;** e.g., Ehri, 1991) involves using only salient visual characteristics of a word rather than relying on letter-sound correspondences. There is an association for these children between the visual cue and the word. This generation of children often can read the word "apple" on a computer or the same word on television when it is accompanied by the company's multi-colored apple with a bite out of it; the word *Jello* has a memorable shape; *STOP* is read correctly by some children so long as it is in the middle of a red hexagon; many 5-year-olds can read the words SCHOOL BUS on the back of a large, yellow vehicle; and virtually no 4- to 5-year-old has trouble decoding Disney's signature, even though it is written in script.

Gough (reported in Gough, Juel, & Griffith, 1992) presented 4- to 5-year-olds with four words to read, one on each of four flashcards. One of the flashcards had a blue thumbprint on it. The participants went through the deck of cards until they could say each word given its card. Then came the interesting part. Could the children say the word that had been presented with the blue thumbprint if they were shown the word on a clean card devoid of the thumbprint? No. Could they say the word if they were shown just the blue thumbprint? Yes. In days of old, when verbal learning was popular, this would have been explained as a case of the blue thumbprint being a functional stimulus for saying the word. Gough et al. (1992) refer to this as **selective association,** which is another name for logographic reading

or visual cue reading. Regardless of what it is called, it is the same process.

Alphabetic Reading Traditional decoding instruction emphasizes sounding out words using letter-sound relations. This mechanism is operative in both reading and writing well before the time when children know *all* of the letter sound correspondences (e.g., Ehri & Wilce, 1985; Huba, 1984; Scott & Ehri, in press). For example, preschoolers who know some letter-sound correspondences use what they know to attempt invented spellings of familiar words. When readers know some letter-sound relationships, they are capable of doing what Ehri (1991) refers to as **phonetic cue reading.** Ehri (1991) contrasted such reading with logographic reading using the following example:

> . . . [L]ogographic readers might remember how to read *yellow* by the "two sticks" in the middle (Seymour & Elder, 1986). In contrast, phonetic cue readers might see the two l's in *yellow,* hear their name in the pronunciation, and use this information to connect the spelling to the word in memory. (p. 391)

To be certain, however, such reading has its hazards. If the same letter cues are used for several words or a cue used to decode some word is experienced in a new word, there may be mix-ups. For example, it is not uncommon for a child to misread a sight word, referring to it as another word that is known to the child that is similar in length and shares common letters (e.g., *yellow* read for *pillow;* Ehri's [1991] interpretation of Seymour & Elder's [1986] data; Ehri & Wilce, 1987a, 1987b). Of course, phonetic cue readers have a difficult time if asked to learn a set of words that share letters (e.g., *pots, post, spot, stop;* e.g., Gilbert, Spring, & Sassenrath, 1977).

Eventually, young readers learn all of the letter-sound relationships. They acquire what Gough and colleagues (e.g., Gough et al., 1992) refer to as **the cipher,** which is a code mapping the sounds of a language (i.e., **phonemes**) onto its alphabet. The complexity of the cipher is clear from this brief description of it:

> The orthographic cipher of English (in short, the cipher) is very complex. Simple cipher would map each letter onto a single phoneme and each phoneme onto a single letter. But English has only 26 letters to map into more than three dozen phonemes, so it could not be simple; either a letter must represent more than one phoneme, or some phonemes must be represented by more than one letter. . . .

Consider only the mappings of the initial letters onto initial phonemes. For only a minority of the letters (*b, d, f, l, n, r, v, z*) it is possible to identify the phoneme it represents. For the other 19, at least one additional letter must be identified before the identity of the word's first phoneme can be determined; in some cases, at least four more letters are required (compare *chord* and *chore*). The vast majority of the letter-sound correspondences of the English cipher are context dependent. (Gough et al., 1992, p. 39)

Acquiring the cipher and using it increases speed and accuracy in reading of unfamiliar words.

Before students acquire the cipher, they must understand the **alphabetic principle**—"that all 26 of those strange little symbols that comprise the alphabet are worth learning and discriminating one from the other because [they stand] for . . . the sounds that occur in spokewords" (Adams, 1990, p. 245). Once these realizations occur, there are a number of specific decoding "rules" that must be acquired as part of cipher learning. Some are easy because they require only one piece of information: The letter *b* is pronounced the same regardless of context; the same is true for *d, f, l, n, r, v, z*, the easy initial letters cited in the previous Gough et al. (1992) quote. Other letters sound differently, depending on other letters in the word, with the most common example being that vowels are long if there is a final -*e* in a syllable and short if there is not. Another example is that *c* is pronounced differently if followed by an *e* or an *i* than if followed by an *a, o,* or *u* (e.g., compare the pronunciation of the *c* sounds in *celestial, city, cat, cot,* and *cut*). In general, conditional rules (i.e., involving consideration of more than one letter to determine the sound of a particular letter) are acquired later than rules involving one letter-sound association (e.g., Venezky & Johnson, 1973).

An important point to emphasize here is that knowing about letters, their names, and sounds may not be sufficient if the student does not possess phonemic awareness (i.e., thorough understanding that words are composed of sequences of sounds). Thus, Tunmer, Herriman, and Nesdale (1988) observed that grade-1 children were especially likely to make good progress in decoding instruction if they possessed both phonemic awareness and high levels of letter-name knowledge. Even more relevant was the work of Byrne and Fielding-Barnsley (1990, 1991), who observed that preschoolers with phonemic awareness who also knew the sounds associated with letters were particularly adept at decoding unfamiliar words. Alphabetic reading may depend on phonemic awareness—a proposition that seems reasonable when it is understood that alphabetic reading involves mapping sounds onto letter sequences that must be decomposed. Such decomposition would seem to depend on understanding first that there is a sequence of sounds in each word that can be separated.

Explicit Phonics-Rule Application   Much of this early reading is probably rule-based decoding, if for no other reason than that much of early reading instruction involves teaching of phonics rules. Every morning in grade-1 classrooms, children experience letter-sound association drills. There are then opportunities to experience the letter-sound associations in the contexts of real words, with stories in phonics-based reading programs filled with regularly spelled words, preferably ones containing the letter-sound relations already presented to the children.

Students in phonics-based programs are taught other rules as well ("When two vowels go walking . . . "; "When there is an -*e* at the end of a syllable . . . "). There are a manageable number of such rules (e.g., Clymer [1963] produced a list of 45 of them). Although termed rules, phonics generalizations never hold 100 percent of the time. For example, "Two vowels go walking . . . " works about 66 percent of the time according to Clymer. Thus, it almost always works when *oa* is the vowel combination as in *boat*; it rarely works for *ui* (i.e., it works for *suit* but not for most other *ui* words like *build, quill*). The final -*e* rule really is a host of rules of varying utility: "When there is one *e* in a word that ends in a consonant, the *e* usually has a short sound" works about 76 percent of the time (e.g., for *leg* but not *blew*). "In many two-syllable and three-syllable words, the final *e* lengthens the vowel in the last syllable" works 46 percent of the time (e.g., for *invite* but not *gasoline*).

Although whole-language enthusiasts and theorists disagree, the consensus opinion based on an analysis of the scientific data is that such instruction is extremely profitable for many children, assisting them in learning to read (Adams, 1990; Anderson, Hiebert, Scott, & Wilkinson, 1985; Ehri, 1991). "Sounding out" of words is more likely among children receiving explicit phonics instruction than among children receiving no such instruction (e.g., Barr, 1974–75). The value of phonics instruction is in giving students a good start. Although the phonics rules do not always work, they seem good enough.

Sight Word Reading   We doubt that anyone reading this book has had to sound out a single word in this chapter except perhaps for unfamiliar proper names such as Ehri. Every word in it is in readers' sight vocabularies. There probably was a time when each and every word in this chapter was sounded out. Many trials of successfully sounding out a word, however, increase the connections between the letter pattern defining the word and the word in memory (Adams, 1990, Chapter 9; Ehri, 1980, 1984, 1987, 1992; see the discussion of connectionism in Chapter 3 of this book). Thus, on initial exposure to a word like *frog,* the word is sounded out. Such sounding out begins a process in which the connections between each letter and adjacent letters are strengthened (e.g., between *fr* and *og*) and connections defining the entire sequence of letters and letter combinations in the word (strengthening of the connection between *fr* and *og*). Eventually the spelling is represented in memory as a unit consisting of *frog.* By repeated reading, there is also a strengthening of the connections between this visual stimulus and the conceptual understanding in long-term memory that defines a frog so that eventually even the briefest exposure to the word *frog* elicits thoughts of a green, jumpy thing.

Orthographic Reading   This can occur only after a child has experience with alphabetic reading. Eventually, meaningful letter strings are perceived as wholes (i.e., repeated co-occurrence of *i, n,* and *g* in that order results eventually in *-ing* being perceived as a unit; e.g., Stanovich & West, 1989). Prefixes and suffixes are obvious examples, but there are other recurring combinations, many of which are root words (e.g., *-take, mal-, ben-, rog-, do-*). When familiar orthographic patterns are encountered, it is not necessary to decode alphabetically. Rather, there is a direct connection with the sound sequence in memory and probably direct connections with meaning as well. For example, when author CBM encountered the word *maleic acid,* she really had no idea what the substance was but was certain at first glance—based on the "mal-" part—that there was something bad about it.

There are tremendous advantages when words can be read by sight and orthographic chunks can be processed as wholes, with these advantages addressed in what LaBerge and Samuels (1974; also Samuels, Schermer, & Reinking, 1992) dubbed as **automaticity theory.** Two tasks are required to get the meaning out of a word: (1) It must be decoded. (2) What is decoded must be comprehended. Both require use of short-term memory, that extremely limited resource that can be thought of as one's attentional capacity. Decoding operations and comprehension processes can be thought of as competing for such capacity.

Alphabetic decoding or phonics rule application requires a great deal of attention on the part of the reader. Walk into any grade-1 classroom on any morning and there will be children who will have all of their mental energy and attention devoted to the task of sounding out the words when they read. If all of the attentional capacity is consumed by decoding, there is nothing left over for comprehension, with the result that the word may be pronounced but not understood. One solution for the slow alphabetic decoder might be to decode first and then comprehend. The cost of this is enormous: It is slow. Because decoding and comprehending are done in sequence, the phonological representation of the word must be held in short-term memory, which involves reduction of capacity that is needed for comprehension. No matter how the alphabetic reader approaches the task, there is strain on short-term capacity.

Automatic sight word reading and automatic recognition of orthographic chunks, in contrast, require little effort or attention, and thus there is substantial mental capacity left over for comprehension when decoding is automatic. Indeed, for many sight words and orthographic chunks, there are probably automatic connections between the sight words and the chunks, the phonological representations of the word and the chunks, and the meanings of the words and the chunks (e.g., Baron, 1977). The result is faster, more accurate, and less effortful reading with experience and development (e.g., Horn & Manis, 1987). That is right. A paradox of slow, high-effort, alphabetic reading is that it is less certain to result in accurate decoding than fast, low-effort automatic decoding via sight words and orthographic chunks, with the reader who recognizes orthographic regularities automatically especially advantaged when words are encountered in isolation (e.g., Barker, Torgesen, & Wagner, 1992; i.e., there are no external context clues about the word or its meaning).

Reading by Analogy   Words that sound the same often have the same spelling patterns. Thus, a child who knows how to pronounce *beak* could make a good guess at *peak* the first time it is encountered simply by decoding by analogy (i.e., this is like *beak* only it starts with a *p*). That same *beak*-word knower would have a fighting chance with *bean, bead,* and *beat* as well using the analogy strategy. Adams (1990, pp. 210–211) provided the example that good readers quickly pronounce the word *kail* to rhyme with *ail, bail, tail, Gail,* and *hail.* Adams (1990, Chapter 9) in particular favors the connectionist theories (see Chapter 3, this book) to explain such decoding by analogy. Each time a word with *-ail* in it is encountered and pronounced with the long *-a* sound, there is a strengthening of the association between *-ail* and the long *-a* sound. Thus, when *kail* is encountered by someone who has had many exposures to the *-ail* and long *-a* association, there is automatic activation of *kail,* and the word is pronounced correctly almost without thinking.

For the most part, analogy has been considered an advanced strategy used only by children who had been reading a while or by adults, with Marsh and colleagues especially strong advocates of this position (e.g., Marsh, Desberg, & Cooper, 1977; Marsh, Friedman, Desberg, & Saterdahl, 1981; Marsh, Friedman, Welch, & Desberg, 1981). Although there are procedural aspects of these studies that reduce confidence in Marsh's conclusions about the advanced nature of analogy (see Goswami & Bryant, 1992), we concentrate here on the positive evidence produced by others that analogy is a tactic available even to beginning readers, focusing, in particular, on evidence produced by Goswami and Bryant (see 1992, for a review) because it is particularly convincing.

In one study (Goswami, 1986), 5- to 8-year-olds were asked to read words that were either analogous or not analogous to "clue" words such as *beak,* which was shown and pronounced for the child. Although children were not instructed how to use the clue words, they were better able to read words that were analogues to the clue words than words that were not analogues. Even nonreaders were able to do this in some cases (i.e., with respect to words sharing simple endings such as *-at*). Later, Goswami (1988) replicated this finding.

One especially interesting aspect of Goswami's results is that analogies based on word endings are especially likely to be made by young children (i.e., words that rhyme are decoded as such). We like this finding because it connects to historically important work on what children remember about words they encounter, with children frequently confusing words that they have heard in a learning task with words that rhyme (e.g., Bach & Underwood, 1970). The historical learning research established that children are attentive to rhyme; Goswami's research establishes that they are inclined to use rhyme to figure out new words. Goswami and Bryant (1990, 1992) are developing a theory that children's rhyming categories (which are established early in life, including in the context of learning nursery rhymes and playing word games) are the basis of orthographic categories that permit decoding by analogy.

In closing this subsection, we must point out again that Goswami's results are controversial. For example, Ehri and Robbins (1992) found that only children who already had some phonological decoding skills were able to decode words by analogy, a finding inconsistent with Goswami's conclusion that nonreaders can decode by analogy; Peterson and Haines (1992) produced results complementary to the Ehri and Robbins outcome. In addition, Bruck and Treiman (1992) demonstrated that even when young children can use analogies, they rely greatly on decoding of individual phonemes and orthographs in decoding new words they encounter. Given the commitment of Goswami, Ehri, Bruck, Treiman, and their associates, we suspect there will be substantial additional research addressing the issue of whether decoding by analogy depends on being able to decode using letter-sound associations.

Using Semantic Context Clues When Words Are Presented in Meaningful Text   A popular hypothesis with whole-language theorists and enthusiasts (e.g., Goodman, 1967; Smith, 1971) is that when words are read in context, decoding is really a "psycholinguistic guessing game." That is, reading of isolated words (which is frequently how decoding was studied in the investigations summarized in this section) is nothing like reading of words in real text because real text offers many cues about the meaning of words that facilitate decoding. The classic study supporting this position was by Goodman (1965), who demonstrated that children's reading accuracy for words improved 60 to 80 percent when the words were in text compared with when the same words were presented on lists.

A number of follow-up investigations have produced generally consistent results. When there have been positive effects of context on reading of words, the effects have generally been smaller than the effects obtained by Goodman (1965). Nicholson's work, in particular, has been informative with respect to this issue. Nicholson found (Nicholson, 1991; Nicholson, Bailey, & McArthur, 1991; Nicholson, Lillas, & Rzoska, 1988) that younger children in the primary years are more likely to benefit from context than older primary-level readers; poor readers benefit more than better readers. Goldsmith-Phillips (1989) and Schwantes (1991) also reported that reliance on context was a strategy used by younger grade-school readers much more than by more mature readers. Nicholson (1991) and Goldsmith-Phillips interpreted these results in terms of compensation (Stanovich, 1980): Poor readers rely on context in an attempt to compensate for poor decoding skills. See Stanovich (1986) for a review of other evidence—which is massive—supportive of this conclusion. Although Corley (1988) was not willing to rush to the conclusion that relying on semantic cues undermines the development of sound-analysis and syntax-analysis skills, she also observed weaker readers who relied too much on meaning cues as they processed sentences and not enough on phonological and syntax-analysis skills.

Summary Except for the youngest of readers, who might know only some logographs, readers do not use only one approach to decoding of words, although there is no doubt that with increasing experience, students use a greater variety of word-level strategies and do so more flexibly (e.g., Rayner, 1988). One popular theory of flexibility in decoding that emerges from much of the research (Baron, 1977; Barron, 1981, 1986; Bryant & Bradley, 1980; Coltheart, Davelaar, Jonasson, & Besner, 1977; Frith, 1979; Treiman & Baron, 1983) is **dual route theory.** Ehri (1992) summarized this perspective as involving knowledge of some words based on their visual representation versus derivation of a word's pronunciation when the word is not visually familiar and then matching this pronunciation to an item in the mental lexicon. The visual route, of course, is faster than the phonological route, not requiring linear processing of the letter and sound relationships. An interesting new development is that Ehri (1992) believes that the faster visual route probably still involves some phonological decoding. She makes a case in her 1992 chapter that there is a need to study carefully exactly what happens when reading seems direct and is fast.

Still, for the present, the more extreme version of the dual route theory is a good way to organize the processes covered in this section. When readers engage in logographic decoding, sight word reading, or orthographic reading, their processing is more on the side of faster, more direct, visual accessing of the lexicon (although there may still be some phonological coding as part of this process); when readers engage in alphabetic reading or phonics rule application, their processing is more of the slower, less direct, extensively phonological sort. Reading by analogy could be either.

When good readers read text that is easy for them, much of it is sight word reading. On other occasions, skilled reading involves other mechanisms. Thus, when an adult sees a Russian can of Pepsi, there is logographic reading of Pepsi. When teachers read the roll the first day, much of the reading of unfamiliar last names involves alphabetic reading and sometimes reading by analogy (e.g., guessing the pronunciation of *Baser* given its resemblance to *laser*). The full repertoire of decoding strategies taken up in this section is available to good readers. That is not the case with young readers. It takes the young reader a while to build up a sight vocabulary. It takes a while to build up sufficient knowledge of orthography to use analogy strategies to the full extent. That there is so much to learn in order to decode reliably and so much practice required in order to decode most words reasonably automatically has been respected in school for years: Most of the first 3 years of formal reading instruction is dedicated more to decoding instruction than anything else; decoding instruction continues through grade school and in many cases into middle school. Some specific mechanisms that have been proposed as means of making decoding instruction more efficient are taken up in the next section.

Before leaving this subsection, however, we think it important to point out two of the important discoveries of the last 15 years: One is that when good readers read, they process the words in a text thoroughly. Studies of eye movement during skilled reading have established that not only are good readers reading every single word when they are trying to learn what is in text (e.g., McConkie, Zola, Blanchard, & Wolverton, 1982; for a discussion, see Carver, 1990, Chapter 5), but also they are processing every single letter (e.g., Rayner, Inhoff, Morrison, Slowiaczek, & Bertera, 1981 (for commentary and reviews, see Adams, 1990, Chapter 6; Stanovich, 1986). A good college-level reader has no difficulty reading at a rate of 200 to 300 words per minute, at least when reading easy text (Carver, 1990). Such a reader is processing an enormous amount of information quickly—30 or so letters a second. Years of reading are required before such an information processing feat is possible. When the reader first starts to read, often all attentional capacity is fixated on single letters, with several seconds sometimes spent on a letter (Samuels, Miller, & Eisenberg, 1979). Think about it, from several seconds to process a single letter (and then sound it out correctly only some of the time) to 30 milliseconds or less with 100 percent accuracy (Carver, 1990).

The second important finding we emphasize in closing is that one of the best ways to increase competence with respect to many aspects of reading is to read more. The evidence is simply overwhelming that better readers do, in fact, read more (see Allen, Cipielewski, & Stanovich, 1992; Allington, 1977; Cipielewski & Stanovich, 1992; Cunningham & Stanovich, 1990, 1991; Juel, 1988; Samuels et al., 1992; Stanovich, 1986). By doing so, they make themselves even better readers (Taylor, Frye, & Maruyama, 1990) and more knowledgeable people in general (Stanovich & Cunningham, 1993). To appreciate the literacy advantages that a good reader creates for himself or herself, consider the following numbers generated by Nagy and Anderson (1984): A middle-school student who is not motivated to read may read 100,000 words a year. An average-achieving, average-motivated middle school reader might read 1 million words a year. In contrast, the best, most voracious readers will read between 10 million and 50 million words a year.

Of course, Stanovich and everyone else who has studied the effects of amount of reading on reading achievement believe that such practice affects a number of reading competencies, not just adequacy of decoding. Thus, this is a good jumping-off place with respect to coverage of decoding.

Comprehension Strategies Instruction

The long-term goal of reading instruction is not the training of readers so they can "say" words but the development of readers who can construct meaning—who can comprehend. Just as there have been

exciting research findings in the last two decades about how decoding occurs, there have been exciting research findings with respect to comprehension, with much of the research aimed at increasing comprehension instruction during the elementary years.

One of the most important research studies about reading comprehension instruction was conducted by Durkin (1978–79). She observed that elementary reading instruction included little teaching aimed at fostering comprehension. Instead of teaching comprehension, teachers seemed to be testing it all of the time, asking lots of questions about what had been read in the text, with Durkin noting many IRE cycles (see Chapter 8) but little information provided to students about how they might prepare themselves to answer questions about text they were reading.

That study did much to motivate research on how to increase reading comprehension. An important assumption was that comprehension could be increased if students were encouraged to create coherent representations of text. Recall from Chapter 3 the various ways that scientists have thought about representations in memory. Such theories inspired a number of instructional interventions.

Much of the research on comprehension strategies instruction was of the following form: A researcher believed that if students constructed a particular type of representation (e.g., mental images representing the story told in a narrative, summaries) or reacted to texts in a particular way (e.g., relating it to prior knowledge, explicitly seeking clarifications when unsure of meaning), comprehension and hence long-term memories of text would be improved. The experimenters testing these strategies usually had reasons to believe that students were not already engaging in such processing when reading, or they were doing so less systematically and completely than they could.

In these studies, the reading comprehension of students receiving instruction typically was measured by some type of objective test of understanding (e.g., multiple-choice items over literal and potentially inferred messages in text). The performances of instructed subjects on such tests were compared with the performances of students not receiving strategy instruction (e.g., control subjects permitted to read as they normally would in preparation for an objective test). If the strategy-trained students outperformed the control students on the test, there was support for the conclusions that the students (1) probably were not using the trained strategy on their own or were not using it systematically, but, more positively, (2) they can be taught to do so. In addition, (3) there was some additional validation of the theory of representation of knowledge that gave rise to the intervention (e.g., when imagery instructions improved learning, it bolstered confidence that people really can represent material with images).

There were many such experiments in the 1970s and 1980s, producing evidence that students could benefit from instructions to use a number of individual strategies aimed at improving learning from text (see Haller, Child, & Walberg, 1988; Pearson & Dole, 1987; Pressley, Johnson, Symons, McGoldrick, & Kurita, 1989). We illustrate these interventions and the research on them with brief discussion of summarization, mental imagery, and story grammar training.

Summarization   Kintsch and van Dijk's (e.g., 1978; van Dijk & Kintsch, 1983) theory was that good readers store the main ideas presented in text, the macropropositions. In contrast, children are much less likely to store the main ideas of what they read (e.g., Brown & Day, 1983; Brown, Day, & Jones, 1983). A number of reading researchers reasoned that if children were taught to extract the main ideas and summarize text, their comprehension and memory of text should improve.

Summarization strategies were devised and tested and proved their worth in controlled studies. For example, Brown and Day (1983) devised an intervention based on the summarization principles that mature readers use, as specified in the van Dijk and Kintsch (1983) framework (see Chapter 3). Brown and Day's summarization rules were to (1) delete trivial information, (2) delete redundant information, (3) substitute superordinate terms, (4) integrate a series of events with a superordinate action term, (5) select a topic sentence, and (6) invent a topic sentence if there is none. Bean and Steenwyk (1984) successfully instructed grade-6 students in the use of these rules. After the students were taught to apply such rules to paragraph-length texts, their performances on standardized reading comprehension tests, which generally involves reading short texts, improved.

A number of other summarization interventions have also improved the comprehension and memory of grade-school students:

- Taylor and associates (Taylor, 1982; Taylor & Beach, 1984) taught students to outline text using text headings and subheadings. Main idea statements were generated for every paragraph and embedded in this outline.
- Rinehart, Stahl, and Erickson (1986) taught children to produce summaries that included main ideas and important supporting details. Their instruction involved Brown and Day's (1983) summarization rules and instruction to relate the various parts of text in a hierarchical outline form, as in Taylor's instruction.
- Berkowitz (1986) taught students to construct maps of passages. They wrote the title of the passage in the middle of a page and then identified six or so main ideas in the passage. These were placed in boxes surrounding the title. Each of these boxes was then filled with supporting details for the main idea placed in it.
- Armbruster, Anderson, and Ostertag (1987) taught students the problem/solution structure, which is characteristic of many social studies texts: Students were taught to summarize the problem covered by a passage and the actions taken to resolve the problem.

That memory and comprehension were consistently improved by summarization instruction has done much to stimulate the teaching of summarization in elementary classrooms. Sometimes, summarization is taught alone, but a more defensible approach is to teach it as one of several strategies that is used in combination with others. Theoretically, this makes sense because, in any particular text, there are both specific pieces of information and relations between different facts, with discrete information and relational information acquired in different ways (McDaniel & Einstein, 1989). For example, discrete pieces of information in a text can be encoded via imagery. In contrast, attending to story grammar elements definitely focuses attention on key elements in stories and how they relate to one another.

Mental Imagery   At least after the age of 8, memory and understanding of text improves when children are instructed to create images depicting what they have read (e.g., Gambrell & Bales, 1986; Pressley, 1976), possibly because of dual coding of what is read (i.e., construction of both verbal and imagery codes; see Chapter 3, this book; Paivio, 1971). Often the gains in learning owing to imagery instructions are not large, but they are consistent (see Pressley, 1977, for a review; also Pressley, Borkowski, & Johnson, 1987). The exception to this generalization is when the learner is required to learn material that includes many relationships that might seem arbitrary. If there are a lot of them, such situations have high potential for interference. The construction of an image for each confusing fact seems to reduce interference and thus greatly increases the likelihood that learners will keep the various facts straight. Pressley, Symons, McDaniel, Snyder, and Turnure (1988) provided an example of such facilitation.

In their Experiment 1, Pressley, Symons et al. (1988) asked university students to learn sentences about things that various types of men had done—the same sentences presented earlier in Chapter 10 as part of the Pressley, McDaniel et al. (1987) study. Thus, when presented the sentence, "The bald man used the phone," they were to imagine a bald man using a phone. When presented, "The crippled man flicked the switch," they were to imagine that. The effect of imagery on learning was huge. Subjects who constructed images remembered a mean of 18.45 of the 24 sentences compared with controls, who remembered 9.15 of 24 sentences on average—more than a 100 percent improvement in learning as a result of the use of imagery. Thus, when learning confusing content, construction of images that represent as exactly as possible the meaning of the text has the potential to produce large learning gains.

The most compelling reason for encouraging students to construct images comes not from cognitive psychology but from literary (reader) response theories (e.g., Rosenblatt, 1978). One of the principal ways that good readers respond to text is that they construct images of the meanings conveyed by the text. These images are interpretive and personal. Images are important forms of aesthetic response to text. Indeed, many texts are written explicitly to elicit vivid images in readers. Unfortunately, however, not all readers respond as intended by authors, with the potential consequence that readers will miss the point of many tales they read.

Much of Sadoski's work (e.g., 1983, 1985) has been directed at the consequences of readers constructing images in reaction to text, images that are essential for deriving important understandings from text. In his research, students in the middle-elementary grades read stories, ones that have a climax.

For example, the grade-5 students in Sadoski (1983) read "Freddie Miller, Scientist":

> The story concerns the plight of a boy scientist whose frequent home experiments go awry and get him into trouble. In the end, the boy becomes the family hero when he aids his sister, who has become locked in a closet, by constructing a home-made flashlight and lowering it to her through the transom vent above the closet door. The story contains three illustrations. Two depict experiments at the beginning and middle of the story, and the third is a diagram of the home-made flashlight. The illustration shows only the flashlight and does not illustrate the climactic event in which the flashlight was used. (pp. 111–112)

One important finding in this research is that about half of the children reported images at the point of climax in this story (a finding replicated with grade-3 and grade-4 children in Sadoski, 1985). Moreover, understanding of the story varied in an interesting way with whether subjects reported climax imagery or not. The subjects who reported climax imagery were much more likely than subjects who did not to be able to provide the theme of the story during their recall of it (again, a finding replicated in Sadoski, 1985). This is powerful evidence in favor of reader response claims that imagery reactions are a part of acquiring a deep understanding of what is read.

Sadoski and Quast (1990; also Sadoski, Goetz, & Fritz, 1993a, 1993b) extended the previous work. In Sadoski and Quast (1990), college students read feature articles from popular magazines (e.g., *Time, Newsweek*). They found that college students still remembered quite a bit from such articles when they were tested 16 days after reading them. What was interesting was the parts of the texts that were recalled: The sections of the text that were most easy to imagine were more likely to be remembered than other sections of the text. This contrasted with no significant relationship between the importance of the information and memory. In Sadoski et al. (1993a, 1993b), adults read biographical texts: How easy it was to generate an image of the text predicted recall of the text much better than did the rated interestingness of the material or even its familiarity to readers. Sadoski's work supports the conclusion that texts evoking powerful images are more memorable than texts that do not invoke such images.

Although psychologists have emphasized memory in their research on imagery, some of the most exciting thinking about imagery pertains to its role in understanding of text. Literary response theorists such as Iser (e.g., 1978) believe that the "image" of a story unfolds as readers proceed through text—and that images are highly personal, reflecting prior knowledge and personal interests (see Sadoski, Goetz, & Kangiser, 1988, for data confirming this view of reader imagery). Such images are the heart of aesthetic understanding, with thinking that parallels Iser's prominent in theoretical analyses of comprehension.

For example, Langer (1986, 1990) believes that how a reader's **envisionments** of text content change can be extremely revealing about how the reader is relating prior knowledge to text or constructing and understanding the underlying morals of tales. At their best, these envisionments are extremely dynamic and rich, including deep understanding of character motivations and suppositions about why the plot is unfolding as it is. (See Wittrock and Alesandrini, 1990, for additional evidence that summarization-integration and imagery processes are related.) How imagery as conceptualized by more information processing–oriented researchers, such as Sadoski and Paivio, relates to conceptions of text understanding emerging from literary response theory is an important area of research. Complete understanding of representational imagery and its effects on understanding both particular parts of texts and the emerging messages in text will require investigations that are sensitive to both dual coding and literary response theories.

Story Grammar Training Some children do not possess knowledge of story grammar (see Chapter 3). Short and Ryan (1984) reasoned that teaching such children the elements of a story and to use these elements to understand text would improve comprehension and memory of stories. They taught grade-4 poor readers to ask themselves five questions in order, questions corresponding to the elements of story grammar, as they read stories:

1. Who is the main character?
2. Where and when did the story take place?
3. What did the main characters do?
4. How did the story end?
5. How did the main character feel?

Students who received this training were able to recall more of stories they read than students who did not receive training. The facilitation was large, great enough to improve the reading of the poor grade-4 readers to the level of skilled grade-4 readers.

Other research has been conducted since Short and Ryan's (1984) path-breaking study. Idol (1987; Idol & Croll, 1987) taught 9- to 12-year-old poor readers to construct a story map as they read stories, a map containing the elements of story grammar: setting, problem, goal, action, and outcome. Memory of stories improved following this training. Nolte and Singer (1985) taught students to ask themselves questions as they read, questions focusing attention on the story grammar elements of stories. The students were taught to ask themselves about the setting, the main characters, the goals of the characters, and the obstacles encountered on the way to the goal. This instruction had a large effect on students' ability to answer short-answer questions over text.

Other Strategies Many other strategies have been evaluated as well, including (1) **mnemonic imagery,** construction of images that transform text meaning in some way to make it more memorable (e.g., when reading a biography of Charles Dickens, imagining each of the events occurring to a "Mr. McGoo" Scrooge to remember these were events in Dickens' life, rather than events from some other biography; see Chapter 10); (2) **question generation,** thinking of questions about the meaning of text as reading proceeds (e.g., Rosenshine & Chapman, 1992); and (3) **prior knowledge activation,** relating what one already knows to information encountered or expected in text. If this activation occurs before reading, it often involves prediction of text content (e.g., as in reciprocal teaching; Palincsar & Brown, 1984, which was introduced in Chapter 8).

From these studies, a collection of strategies resulted that could be applied before (e.g., making predictions based on prior knowledge), during (e.g., imagery generation), and after (e.g., summarization) reading (Levin & Pressley, 1981). Even so, this research was not aimed at coordinated use of strategies before, during, and after reading but rather was aimed at the validation of particular individual strategies. More complicated studies of strategies instruction were required, for many sophisticated models of thinking specified that multiple strategies could help students make sense of the world, including worlds created in texts (e.g., Baron, 1985; Brown et al., 1983; Levin & Pressley, 1981; Nickerson et al.,

1985). A few prominent investigations of this type were conducted in the 1980s.

Multiple-Strategies Instruction   Scott Paris and his University of Michigan associates (e.g., Paris & Oka, 1986) developed a set of strategies lessons that could be used across a year of elementary reading instruction. The curriculum included instruction of many of the individual strategies validated in research as well as some attention to metacognitive and motivational components in strategy use. Although approximately 20 weekly lessons resulted in improved performance on some of the specific tasks covered in the curriculum, more general changes, such as improvements on standardized reading comprehension tests, did not occur.

The best-known multiple-strategies intervention developed during the 1980s was reciprocal teaching of comprehension strategies, perhaps because it was the first report of a classroom-deployed, multiple-strategies intervention that seemed to promote reading comprehension (Palincsar & Brown, 1984). As discussed in Chapter 8, this intervention—which involves teaching students to predict, self-question, clarify when confused, and summarize—produced consistent increases in lower-ability students' use of the processes taught (i.e., prediction, seeking clarification, question generation during reading, and summarization); often, this type of instruction also produced at least modest gains on more general measures (e.g., standardized reading comprehension; Rosenshine & Meister, 1992).

Others also reported improvements in student reading as a function of teaching multiple strategies, however: Yuill and Oakhill (1988) improved the comprehension of weaker 7- to 8-year-old readers by teaching them to generate questions about text, make predictions about text content, and analysis of individual words in text as a clue to overall text meaning. In Duffy et al. (1987), grade-3 teachers recast the skills taught during grade-3 reading as strategies, with the teachers providing many direct explanations about how to attack text and comprehend it (see Chapter 8). Collins (1991) improved comprehension in grade-5 and grade-6 students by providing a semester (3 days a week) of lessons on reasoning skills. The students were taught to seek clarification when uncertain, look for patterns and principles, analyze decision making that occurs during text processing, problem solve (including the use

of backward reasoning and visualization), summarize, predict, adapt ideas in text (including rearranging parts of ideas in text), and negotiate interpretations of texts in groups. Although the trained students did not differ from controls before the intervention with respect to standardized comprehension performance, there was a large difference between treated and control conditions on the posttest. Bereiter and Bird (1985) demonstrated that students in grades 7 and 8 benefited from instructions to use a few comprehension strategies used by older, more sophisticated readers (i.e., restate difficult text, backtrack as necessary, watch for pertinent information in text, and resolve apparently anomalous information in text). Their findings could be combined with Duffy et al.'s (1987) and Collins's (1991) data to produce optimism that instruction of multiple strategies is an intervention that is potentially effective during most of the elementary-school years.

Notably, Duffy et al. (1987), Collins (1991), and Bereiter and Bird (1985) all involved extensive direct explanations of strategies by teachers to students, with these direct explanations conveying both information about how to carry out strategies and metacognitive information about the role strategies play in thinking and when they can make a difference in comprehension (see Meloth, 1990). In all three studies, the teachers made visible otherwise invisible mental processes by thinking aloud (i.e., mental modeling; Duffy, Roehler, & Herrmann, 1988). In all three cases, students had extensive practice opportunities, with teacher assistance provided during practice as required by students. In all three cases, there was opportunity for gradual acquisition of the repertoire of strategies and long-term instruction about the coordination of the strategic competencies acquired.

Summary   By the end of the 1980s, there had been substantial success in demonstrating that instruction of some individual cognitive processes improves comprehension of text. In addition, a few investigators succeeded in teaching multiple strategies in ways that improved reading comprehension. The multiple-strategies approach is especially appealing theoretically because learning from text involves remembering specific items mentioned in text as well as how the various pieces of information in text relate—such generative processes at multiple levels are more likely when readers apply both strategies that increase memory and understanding of particular parts of text and ones that promote integration across various parts of the reading (McDaniel & Einstein, 1989; Wittrock, 1990).

Missing in this research, however, was information about how real educators might translate strategies instruction into effective educational practice. Indeed, the true experiments just discussed were not at all revealing about the instructional dynamics of lessons—the interweaving of teacher and student behaviors that is instruction. They did not answer some extremely important questions, such as "What do complete strategies instruction lessons look like?" and "What do years of such lessons look like?" Getting answers to such questions was important because widespread dissemination and acceptance of effective strategies instruction would be unlikely in the absence of high-quality knowledge about how strategies can and should be taught. Fortunately, analyses of important reading programs, including strategies-based ones, are now available, with some of these reviewed in the next subsection.

Before moving on, however, we point out that an emerging direction in reading comprehension research is to find ways to increase comprehension by manipulations that decrease the demands on short-term memory. For example, when text is presented more rapidly than readers normally read, more of the text can be held in short-term memory than is normally held, with increases in comprehension (e.g., Breznitz, 1987; Breznitz & Share, 1992). Thus, a new twist on reading strategies is probably going to be to teach young readers how to make the most of their short-term capacity, which will probably include teaching children to read more quickly than they are inclined to do so naturally. Part of this effort will involve familiarizing students with many more vocabulary so that the words can be rapidly accessed when encountered in text, consistent with the observation that functional short-term memory is greater for familiar words than for unfamiliar ones (Engle, Nations, & Cantor, 1990).

Reading Programs

The three reading programs reviewed here are covered in "developmental order," with whole language being implemented from the onset of schooling, reading recovery applied when decoding problems are evident (i.e., at end of grade 1), and transactional

strategies instruction appropriate for children who can decode, with its focus on comprehension.

Whole Language   Whole language is difficult to define (e.g., see Watson, 1989, for an entire article on the challenges of defining it). Whole-language educators are determined that the integrity of language be preserved in literacy education, that children deal with "whole" language rather than be presented language skills instruction. There is reading of "whole" texts and writing of "whole" texts. Language instruction is done within the context of the "whole" life of the child. If it is not clear what is whole about whole-language instruction, try rereading from the beginning of this paragraph and substituting "authentic" for every appearance of "whole" (Weaver, 1990, p. 6). If whole language is difficult to define, it is not difficult to identify its chief advocate—Goodman of the University of Arizona, who has written extensively on how whole-language philosophy is consistent with a broad range of scientific and philosophical traditions, from psycholinguistic analyses of language development to Dewey's methods of education through real-world problem solving to integrated curricular perspectives on language arts (i.e., language arts across the school day).

Some of the tenets of whole-language instruction include the following (adapted from Weaver, 1990, p. 6):

- Children learn to read and write as they learned to talk, which means as a gradual and natural process, one in which instruction is downplayed. The teaching role is that of someone who assists rather than instructs the child.
- Children are encouraged as they work with language. For example, creative inventive spellings that reflect the sounds of the language are praised.
- Children read real stories, poems, and books every day.
- Children write something for a real audience every day (e.g., they write a story that will be read to classmates).
- Reading and writing occur across the school day as part of art, social studies, science, and so on.

Our view is that whole language is an important approach to literacy instruction that should be evaluated in a serious fashion by the research community, if for no other reason than its prevalence in

American and Canadian education. No movement has had a greater impact on the education of children in recent years than has whole language.

Although supporters of whole language (e.g., Goodman, 1989; Weaver, 1990, Chapter 6) make the case that there already exists a scientific database supporting whole-language philosophy and practice, it is not large. Only a handful of studies compare whole language approaches directly with other approaches to literacy instruction (e.g., basal reader programs, which have predominated in early literacy education for the last 50 years). Moreover, the comparisons that have been made do not favor whole language over other instruction (Stahl & Miller, 1989). Particularly disturbing, however, is that there are at least hints in the literature that whole language may make little difference for average-ability or high-ability readers and actually negatively affect the reading progress of weaker students (Stahl & Miller, 1989).

That whole language has the potential for doing harm is the greatest concern with the approach. In particular, there is substantial evidence that explicit teaching of phonics and explicit attempts to increase phonemic awareness benefit students who are at risk for difficulties in learning to read because the home environments did not support and encourage emergent literacy during the preschool years (Adams, 1990). The problem is that such explicit teaching of decoding is seen as skills instruction by whole-language advocates and considered inconsistent with the development of reading via authentic approaches. Our view is that the scientific database favoring explicit instruction in decoding for at-risk primary students far outweighs the database favoring whole-language instruction with such students. Indeed, the assumption that reading and writing should or could be acquired naturally, without instruction, by most students seems flawed. It is based on an analogy to the acquisition of a first language. Although the natural learning of a first language is well established, there is no credible scientific evidence that humans have evolved so that learning to read and write is an inevitable consequence of experience with print and other authentic language and literature experiences (Bertelson & De Gelder, 1989; Liberman & Liberman, 1990).

Even so, there is still much that is attractive about the whole-language approach. Who could argue that reading fine literature is not a good thing for

children to do? Who could argue with daily writing? Our guess is that such experiences have profound effects on children, ones that may not be captured readily by standardized tests such as those used in evaluations to date. The challenge for whole-language researchers is to design evaluations that are convincing to the scientific and educational policy making communities, evaluations that include measures sensitive to the advantages whole language might confer on young readers.

For example, tests sensitive to the development of prior knowledge about contemporary children's authors should reveal advantages for whole-language students over participants in basal programs because of the whole-language emphasis on exposing students to texts by the best of children's writers. In short, our view is that the scientific analyses of whole language have barely begun, but that thorough analyses are needed because of the widespread dissemination of the approach based on claims made by advocates such as Goodman. Although some in the whole-language movement believe such research is not possible, not necessary, and perhaps even destructive (e.g., Edelsky, 1990), we think that legitimate and fair inquiry is possible and essential.

Reading Recovery   Many grade-1 students make little progress in learning how to read. Such students are at long-term risk for academic difficulties. An important program aimed at such children was developed by Clay (e.g., 1985). It involves daily one-teacher, one-child sessions for 10 to 20 weeks, with each session lasting approximately 30 to 40 minutes. The goal is to help the student catch up with peers. The starting assumption is that students may be learning too narrow a range of strategies for dealing with print and may not be flexible in their use of the strategies they have acquired. For example, students may attempt to sound out every word, when, in fact, a variety of strategies (see the earlier discussion in this section) can be applied during the identification of words in texts.

Much of reading recovery is teaching students strategies, which are defined by Clay (1985; Pinnell, 1989) as the processes required to read, including the following:

- Reading left to right on a page.
- Using a return sweep from the right-hand side of the page rather than a slow return to the left side.

- Monitoring whether what is being read makes sense.
- Using cross checks on meaning-making processes, such as illustrated by the following:

  A reader might use one kind of information to predict a word but will check that prediction by using another source of information. For example, glancing at a picture of the Billy Goats Gruff going across a bridge, a young reader might predict the word "water" in the text. Checking the print, however, the reader might notice that the word "stream" is not visually consistent with that prediction. This cross checking may lead to a self-correction or other indication from the child of an awareness of a discrepancy. (Pinnell, 1989, p. 166)

- Searching for cues to meaning from pictures, language structures, and visual cues in print.
- Rereading when meaning is unclear.
- Self-correction rather than waiting for teacher correction of errors.

The emphasis on strategies in Reading Recovery comes through in quotes such as the following:

> . . . [A]ttention of teacher and child must be on strategies or operations—mental activities initiated by the child to get messages from a text. If the teacher becomes involved in teaching items rather than strategies—particular letter-sound correspondences or sight vocabulary words, for example, rather than the strategy of checking a word that would make sense in the context against the information in the print—the prospect of accelerated learning is seriously threatened. Letter-sound correspondences and spelling patterns are learned, but in the course of reading and, especially, writing meaningful text, [Reading Recovery] teachers praise children for generative strategies, not for items learned. (Clay & Cazden, 1990, p. 208)

There is a common structure to each Reading Recovery lesson: (1) First the child rereads two or more short, familiar books. (2) Then the child reads a book introduced the day before, with the teacher keeping track of errors that are made. (This provides baseline information, with the goal of the child eventually reading the book with 90 percent accuracy on subsequent days as part of step "1." (3) There is a letter identification exercise involving plastic letters that attach to a metal board. (Once children know letters, this step is deleted or other decoding or vocabulary teaching is substituted.) (4) The child composes and writes out a story. (5) The child reassembles the story after the teacher cuts it up into pieces. (6) A new book is introduced and read by the child.

The interaction that goes on around composing and reading of the new books is definitely scaffolded, with the student receiving hints and support as needed (Clay & Cazden, 1990). For example, during writing, the teacher calls attention to the sounds of words and spelling patterns by urging the student to listen carefully to words that will be written, prompting the child to write out a new word several times so that it will be memorable, praising progress, and so on. Consistent with Clay's (1991) perspective that reading instruction should develop inner control (i.e., internalized use of strategies taught to children), such support is faded as the child is able to function independently, with additional support provided as more challenging texts and tasks are presented following success with easier texts and tasks.

Does Reading Recovery work? Evaluations have been conducted in both New Zealand and in Ohio (see Pinnell, 1989). In both settings, most (at least two-thirds is the lowest estimate we have seen) of the Reading Recovery students catch up with their classmates. More impressively, 2 or 3 years later, Reading Recovery students still have some advantage relative to controls not receiving the intervention. Many educators are excited about Reading Recovery as an intervention, as they are about other one-to-one tutoring programs that seem to be effective (see Wasik & Slavin, 1993; also, the discussion of "Success for All," in Chapter 11, this book).

Critics, however, point to the cost of one-to-one tutoring for half a year. Our reaction is that it is a small price to pay relative to the long-term costs when students do poorly in school, and it is a good bet that a fair proportion of students who go through Reading Recovery would have done much worse in school without the intervention. Wasik and Slavin (1993) offered a brief but reflective discussion of the cost-effectiveness of one-to-one tutoring that complements our perspective.

Conceptually, we find Clay's (1991) analysis of reading as the development of inner control to be appealing, with it similar to other ideas about internalization of cognitive processes such as those offered by Vygotsky (1978; see Chapter 8, this book). We also find the Reading Recovery results reported thus far to be compelling evidence of the program's efficacy. Even so, we are also struck that some are finding ways to improve on it—such as Iversen and Tumner (1993), who produced quicker improvement when reading recovery was complemented with more explicit instruction about phonology and decoding. We are also struck that some much less expensive approaches to one-to-one tutoring, such as parental tutoring, have the potential to encourage inner-controlled reading by primary students who had previously experienced difficulty with grade-1 reading (e.g., Mudre & McCormick, 1989).

Transactional Instruction of Comprehension Strategies Pressley knew of a number of sites where comprehension strategies instruction was documented to be done well. At the end of the 1980s, I began visiting these sites. I visited Michigan State to deepen my understanding of Palincsar's work and Duffy and Roehler's direct explanation model. I had frank conversations with Bereiter about the Bereiter and Bird research. My trips included a visit with Deshler and Schumaker's (e.g., 1988) group at the University of Kansas, who were responsible for a learning strategies curriculum that was disseminated nationwide and that was researched extensively as it was developed. Mastropieri and Scruggs (e.g., 1991) welcomed me to Purdue for detailed explanations of their work on teaching learning-disabled students to use elaboration strategies to remember academic content. In addition, there were trips to many individual teachers who were doing what they could to implement strategies instruction based on what they could glean from the existing literature.

After the visits came a series of qualitative investigations in two settings. One was Benchmark School near Philadelphia, which serves bright elementary-school children who experienced great difficulty learning to read in regular schools. At the heart of the Benchmark curriculum is the teaching of cognitive strategies, so that study of the school's approach to teaching and learning was ideally informative about how strategies instruction might be implemented, especially because of the school's long track record of success with children who had failed elsewhere. A large-scale interview study was conducted at Benchmark (Pressley, Gaskins, Cunicelli et al., 1991), as was an intensive case study of a semester in one Benchmark classroom (Pressley, Gaskins, Wile, Cunicelli, & Sheridan, 1991) and an analysis of the classroom discourse at Benchmark (Gaskins et al., 1993; see Chapter 8, this book). The second set of studies

was conducted in a public school strategies instruction program (i.e., *Students Achieving Independent Learning* [SAIL]), which was targeted at Chapter 1 students and seemed to produce impressive outcomes (based on quasiexperimental achievement evaluations conducted by the United States) relative to other Chapter 1 interventions. As at Benchmark, the SAIL teachers participated in interviews, observations, and case studies (e.g., El-Dinary, Pressley, & Schuder, 1992; Pressley, El-Dinary, Gaskins et al., 1992; Pressley, Schuder, SAIL Faculty and Administration, Bergman, & El-Dinary, 1992).

When the visits and the qualitative analyses were combined, it was clear that there was great commonality of philosophy and method across the Benchmark and SAIL settings. The developers of these programs operate on the following assumptions about skilled reading: Good readers make decisions about reading rate and focus; which basic processing strategies to use (e.g., word-for-word reading, skimming); and how to coordinate strategies for monitoring, problem solving, and evaluation. Good readers anticipate what might happen subsequently in a text, evaluate their expectations as reading proceeds, generate questions about the text content, visualize the meanings conveyed in the text, seek clarifications when confused, identify main ideas, and selectively attend to important and interesting parts of the material. Good readers are generally active as they read, making associations between their prior knowledge and content encountered in text. Good readers evaluate the text (e.g., whether they like it, whether it is serving its intended purpose). Good readers possess extensive metacognition about the strategies they use (e.g., Flavell, 1985, Chapter 4; Chapter 2, this book), especially recognizing where and when those strategies can be applied profitably (see Pressley, Borkowski, & O'Sullivan, 1984, 1985). Such metacognition is crucial to the regulation and appropriate use of the strategies learned in the curriculum. (Comparing the list of reading behaviors summarized here with those reported by the expert social science readers, discussed earlier in this chapter, reveals great consistency between the educators' understandings of skilled reading and the skilled reading observed in analytical investigations of good reading, such as Wyatt et al., 1993.)

The strategies instruction programs that Pressley and colleagues evaluated used direct explanation and mental modeling to teach students the processes that constitute capable reading. Thus, students in these programs are taught a manageable number of comprehension strategies. For example, students in the SAIL program are taught to predict, visualize, and summarize as they read. Generally active processing of text is stimulated by having SAIL students think aloud during reading instruction, with associations to background knowledge encouraged as part of think-alouds. Such thinking aloud is expected to reduce impulsive responses and encourage planning before and during reading. This use of language to support cognitive actions is consistent with theoretical positions developed by Vygotsky (1978, 1987) as well as Meichenbaum (1977), ones reviewed in Chapters 7 and 8. That is, thinking aloud about cognitive processes can promote self-regulation of those processes: Thinking aloud during application of reading strategies should promote student control of attention, the contents of thoughts, and the use of strategies. In addition, thinking aloud gives the teacher and other members of the reading group access to a student's thought processes, so that members of the reading group are continually modeling active thinking about text for their peers. This is critical because such mental modeling by peers can influence those exposed to it (e.g., Bandura, 1986; Duffy, Roehler, & Herrmann, 1988).

Because SAIL students always receive reading instruction in texts at or above grade level, they are taught problem-solving strategies for dealing with difficult words when reading for gist. For instance, when encountering a new word in text, students are taught that it could be sounded out, skipped, guessed, or context clues could be used to infer its meaning, rereading if necessary for additional clues.

Pressley and colleagues observed in their studies at Benchmark and in the SAIL program teachers modeling and explaining comprehension strategies as part of regular reading group lessons. The teachers used outstanding children's literature from trade books, magazines, or basal reader anthologies as they did so. A lesson might begin with the teacher reading first, thinking aloud about how the text ought to serve his or her purposes and how its content and structure might relate to prior knowledge. The teacher might make predictions, report images stimulated by the text, or note consistencies and inconsistencies between text content, text structure, and reader expectations. Then the teacher might invite students to try using the strategic procedures with the text. Members of the reading group would

take turns reading aloud. Throughout the process, student interpretations of text are encouraged, and thus reading group participants are exposed to a variety of interpretations of text and the processes for constructing and evaluating those interpretations.

Pressley, El-Dinary, Gaskins, et al. (1992) refer to this type of instruction as **transactional strategies instruction,** so dubbed because what happens during reading group is codetermined by a teacher and student in interaction with a text (Bell, 1968; Bjorklund, 1989, pp. 228–231; Sameroff, 1975), and; in particular, the interpretations of text are codetermined by teacher-student-text transactions (e.g., Rosenblatt, 1978). Years of transactions involving predictions, questioning, clarifications, visualizations, associations, and summaries are intended to produce independent, successful readers who engage in such processes on their own. For example, the average Benchmark student stays at the school for 4 years, with some attending for up to 7 years; SAIL is implemented in grades 1 through 5. Internalizing the cognitive processes taught as comprehension strategies and learning how to use such processes in a flexible fashion with diverse types of texts is an impressive intellectual accomplishment that cannot be accomplished in a few lessons or a few months. As this book went to press, Rachel Brown, Pressley, and colleagues submitted a year-long quasiexperimental study for publication consideration. They reported striking benefits for grade-2 children who experienced a SAIL program.

For detailed commentary about the nature of transactional strategies instruction lessons, see Pressley, El-Dinary, Brown, et al. (1994, in press). We note in closing this section that an important part of transactional strategies instruction is the motivational component. Students are taught about strategies and encouraged to use them in contexts that do much to maximize academic motivation, with the teachers in these settings aware of and using many of the motivational recommendations presented in Chapter 5. Some consideration of these motivational features will highlight again a theme running throughout this book, that there is no one component that defines effective instruction. Rather, effective instruction promotes strategies well matched to task requirements (e.g., such as prediction, self-questioning, seeking clarifications, summarization), development of nonstrategic knowledge (e.g., the type of information that might be acquired from the fine literature read in the transactional strategies instruction classrooms), enhancement of metacognition about strategies learned (e.g., knowledge of when and where to use strategies that follows from practice using them in many contexts, the practice that can occur over multiple years of instruction), and motivation to use what one knows to accomplish academic tasks.

Pressley, El-Dinary, Marks, Brown, and Stein (1992) identified some of the motivational features of good strategies instruction classrooms:

- Task involvement and task orientation are encouraged rather than ego orientation (Nicholls, 1989). Each student's improvement is emphasized rather than how students are doing relative to one another. (See Chapter 5.)
- Success is ensured when strategies are taught and practiced, largely through scaffolding. (See Chapter 8.)
- Teachers reinforce thinking that reflects strategic engagement. It is not the correctness of answers that is reinforced but how students generate responses.
- The utility of strategies—how they help students—and when they help is emphasized (see Chapter 2). Teachers do all possible to identify many occasions when strategies being taught might be helpful to students (e.g., prediction is helpful in math and science as well as in the context of reading group).
- Students practice strategies with authentic, appropriately challenging (i.e., not too difficult but not too easy), and interesting tasks. The tasks are made more interesting because the strategies are applied as part of the process of personally interpreting the task. (See Chapter 5.)
- There is little criticism in these classrooms. The overall environment is positive.
- An exceptionally important characteristic of this instruction is that student choice is emphasized. Transactional strategies instruction teachers do not tell students to do this strategy or that one but rather remind students of the comprehension strategies they know and urge them to choose a strategy that is appropriate for a current comprehension demand. When a reader encounters a problematic word, the teacher might remind the student of the various problem-solving strategies in the student's repertoire of strategies but would not prescribe one over another. The message is that the student is in con-

trol and that self-regulation of cognition is being developed. Students are not learning to take orders from teachers; they are learning to make the types of choices good readers make, similar to the choices their teachers, who are good readers, model for them.

Our view is that it may be absolutely necessary for strategies instructional environments to promote student motivation. Strategies instruction benefits may be more likely when (1) there are clear messages to students that improvement is the goal of schooling rather than student performance relative to other students, (2) there are efforts to match various aspects of strategies instruction and other teaching to particular student interests and abilities, and (3) instruction occurs in a generally cooperative atmosphere, one in which students help one another in the application of strategies and in the development of understandings (e.g., interpretations of texts).

Effective comprehension instruction is multicomponent. Students are taught a small repertoire of powerful comprehension strategies. Teaching takes place over a number of years via explanations, modeling, and practice opportunities. As the strategies are practiced by students, metacognition that permits their informed use develops (i.e., students discover when the strategies help them and when they do not). Motivation develops as students come to understand the utility of strategies in an instructional environment that sends the message that students can become better learners, especially if they learn the procedures and other knowledge taught in school.

Concluding Comment   In the 1990s, there has been substantial study of important reading interventions that are based on psychological analyses of reading. Even so, much more about the effects of various types of reading instruction could be known. Reading instructional programs are dynamic, evolving entities that have been affected by research in the past and will be affected by research in the future.

Before leaving elementary reading, it is hard not to be struck by how much instructional good is coming from understandings produced in basic research. There is now a firm scientific database supporting explicit decoding instruction, especially for students who enter school without phonemic awareness. Teaching students to apply flexibly a few powerful comprehension strategies (e.g., prediction, self-questioning, seeking clarification, summarization), all of which were evaluated in basic research studies, stimulates much active reading and increases the likelihood students will get the big ideas from text. Teaching text analyses strategies (e.g., to analyze stories into story grammar components, expositions into their logical structures such as cause-and-effect), again strategies validated in basic studies, can aid reading comprehension and permit a reading-writing connection (i.e., using the same analyses strategies to plan and generate stories and expositions).

Those who might question whether basic research can provide knowledge that is translated into important educational practices and policies should study how elementary reading has changed: Groan-and-grunt phonics instruction has been replaced by well-validated methods of decoding. The vacuum in comprehension instruction identified by Durkin (1978–79) has been filled by instruction stimulating the comprehension processes used by exceptionally sophisticated readers. Educational scientists studying elementary reading have definitely made an impact on elementary reading education.

READING DURING ADOLESCENCE AND EARLY ADULTHOOD

In contrast to the admirable research efforts at the elementary-school level, there has been much too little study of literacy and literacy instruction during middle school, high school, and college. This is regrettable because it is clear that there is still a great need for reading and writing instruction after elementary school: Far too many students receive high school diplomas even though their literacy skills are weak compared with what they should or could be; far too many students arrive at universities ill-prepared for the demanding reading and writing expected of college students, with deficiencies in such skills predictive of difficulties in college (e.g., Royer, Marchant, Sinatra, & Lovejoy, 1990).

Why the neglect of research on reading and writing during the middle-school, high school, and college years? Perhaps the main reason is that the principle educational goal at these levels of schooling is not the development of basic competencies but instruction of specific contents—literature, social studies, history, and sciences. More positively, there have been some distinguished analyses of literacy and literacy instruction after childhood. Those are featured in this section.

Alvermann and Moore (1991) provided an exceptionally complete summary of secondary school reading. When their conclusions are combined with ones that can be abstracted from Weinstein and Mayer's (1986) review of learning strategies research, it is possible with some confidence to generate a list of strategies that can promote comprehension and memory of text by postelementary students. These are mentioned briefly here, as they have been described in previous chapters and sections of this chapter:

- **Using/analyzing text structure** to abstract main ideas.
- **Summarizing, outlining, and mapping** of text, if substantial instruction is provided about how to do it.
- **Notetaking.**
- **Self-questioning,** with the benefits seemingly greater for lower-ability students. This can include self-questions designed to prompt students to look for main ideas and elaborate on them.
- **Elaborations of text** of various sorts, including representational imagery, relating to prior knowledge, and thinking about why the relationships specified in text hold (see Pressley, Wood et al., 1992).
- **Creating mnemonic images** (e.g., an image capturing many of the features of the Whiskey rebellion, which also incorporates a big bottle of whiskey as a distinctive encoding cue) are proving especially effective with special education populations (e.g., Masteropieri & Scruggs, 1991), although there is no reason to limit their use to such populations.

One especially interesting point is that some strategies recommended widely in the studies skills literature simply do not seem to be effective:

- **Rehearsal** of complex materials seems effective only if the greater amount of time required to rehearse (e.g., copy a passage) is ignored. Also, rehearsal may depress more conceptual analyses of text. Tobias (1987) offered an interesting twist on this theme, demonstrating that students do not benefit much if left on their own to choose what to reread. If they are in a computerized instructional environment that mandates rereading of the parts of text that are important or that they are not understanding (i.e., as evidenced by performance on adjunct questions accompanying the reading), rehearsal is effective. In general, however, because high school students are not effectively selective in what they reread, there is usually little, if any, gain produced by rereading.

- **Underlining** of text produces small, inconsistent improvements in learning at best.
- **SQ3R** (*Survey, Question, Read, Recite, Review*), although recommended in many studies skills courses, does not have a track record of exceptional effectiveness (Forrest-Pressley & Gilles, 1983).

What might be noted about all three of these less effective techniques is that they involve largely simple rehearsal (attention) to material rather than extensive recoding and relating of new content to other knowledge. In contrast, all of the unambiguously effective procedures require more of the learner with respect to the meaning of the text. The learner works with the text content, analyzing relationships between elements of the text as given or considering the text that is given in light of other knowledge already possessed by the learner.

Important insights about comprehension strategies instruction are still emerging. For example, one of the real challenges for high school–level and college-level students is to read expository texts in their content area courses, especially science. Cook and Mayer (1988) studied one approach for improving comprehension of scientific texts. They taught students the types of ideas that can appear in a scientific text and how these ideas are structured in scientific texts, including (1) generalizations, (2) enumerations, (3) sequences, (4) classification, and (5) comparison-and-contrast structures. Junior college students who were given instruction about these types of text structure, along with some practice in identifying such structures as part of trying to understand text, in fact, were better able to comprehend scientific texts than were uninstructed control students. The basic research significance of such a finding is high—as any student of the rhetoric knows, the expository structures taught by Cook and Mayer are basic argument structures. Teaching students to look for such structures and use them to understand text is a strategy that should be of great general utility. Whether it is or not is a question that remains to be studied, perhaps one that some readers of this text will tackle. For another example of a sequence of

processes that can be taught profitably to college students for improving comprehension of content area text, see Simpson, Hayes, Stahl, Connor, and Weaver's (1988) analysis of PORPE, which teaches students to *p*redict, *o*rganize, *r*ehearse, *p*ractice, and *e*valuate.

One of the intriguing aspects of the postelementary comprehension data is that a good deal of effort has been made to establish which procedures facilitate comprehension and memory of text, but that relatively little effort has been put into determining *how* to teach comprehension strategies. There are no theoretical or empirical analyses that correspond to the analyses of reciprocal teaching, direct explanation, and transactional strategies instruction in the elementary literature. The most frequent method of instruction used in the secondary and college years is to teach a large number of strategies in a relatively short period of time, such as in the context of a studies skills course. There are few evaluations of such courses. The ones that do exist suggest small to inconsistent effects. Unfortunately, most of the attempted validations of such courses contain methodological problems serious enough to undermine confidence in the conclusions emanating from the studies. Such warnings are especially telling when it is realized that careful, longer-term, scaffolded instruction is often required to ensure that students can carry out particular strategies in the curriculum (e.g., the summarizing, outlining, and mapping strategies cited earlier in this subsection).

We have talked with many studies skills counselors who firmly believe that building up repertoires of strategies is essential for many high school and college students. They also recognize that traditional studies skills courses provide too much, too fast. Our view is that it makes a great deal of sense to take what we have learned about individual strategies that work and do some hard thinking about how high school and college students could receive systematic instruction in ways that would complement rather than threaten the content-driven curricula that is secondary and postsecondary education. At present, we are probably failing large numbers of students who could be better learners if they were taught powerful comprehension tools in ways that made sense to them (e.g., slowly enough that the strategies can be understood, in the context of realistic assignments)—something brought home by strong correlations between reading ability and achievement in college-level courses (e.g., Royer, Abranovic, & Sinatra, 1987). That college-level achievement in general might be increased by thorough teaching of comprehension strategies in high school and early in a college career is a hypothesis that could keep more than one newcomer to the field of educational psychology busy.

MODIFYING TEXTBOOKS SO THEY ARE EASIER TO READ AND UNDERSTAND

A great deal of effort has been expended by information processing researchers attempting to devise ways to modify texts so that the information in them is easier to comprehend and remember (Glynn, Andre, & Britton, 1986). Four approaches to text modification have been studied in more detail than others: signaling, adding elaborations and connections, adjunct questions, and illustrations.

Four Approaches to Text Modification

Signals Meyer (e.g., 1975) has provided some of the most explicit arguments in favor of putting **signals** in text. Types of signals include the following:

- Use of text conventions that flag the structure of the text. For example, when a cause-and-effect relationship is specified in the text, signaling the cause with the introductory clause, "The cause of X is. . . ."
- Advance organizers summarizing a main point can be provided, with these sometimes in the form of a summary statement early in the passage (see Chapter 10).
- Summary statements can be put at the end of sections of text.
- A variety of words specifying the information considered important by the author can be placed in text, such as "Of less consequence. . . ," and "More to the point. . . ."

In general, signaling seems to provide at least slight comprehension advantages to readers (e.g., Lorch, 1989; Meyer, Brandt, & Bluth, 1980). Even more explicit signals are being studied by some investigators, such as providing a graphical outline of the text summarizing the main points in the text and how the points relate to one another (e.g., Arm-

bruster, Anderson, & Meyer, 1991; Guri-Rozenblit, 1989). One important conclusion supported by some studies is that signaling is especially helpful in making difficult conceptual information comprehensible and useful—for example, permitting readers to solve problems related to the topic of a passage (e.g., Loman & Mayer, 1983). More negatively, although signals promote learning of the content and its organization, rarely is there any carryover benefits to other parts of text (Lorch, 1989; Lorch, Lorch, & Inman, 1993). One way to overcome that limitation, however, is to organize the entire text well: Texts with clear hierarchies, topical structures, sequences, and causal chains are understood better than texts lacking salient organization (Calfee & Chambliss, 1987; Chambliss & Calfee, 1989).

Elaborations and Connections In a series of investigations, Beck and associates at the University of Pittsburgh (Beck, McKeown, Sinatra, & Loxterman, 1991; McKeown, Beck, Sinatra, & Loxterman, 1992) have claimed that textbooks used by elementary-level students often fail to provide enough information so that students can detect and understand the interconnections between ideas. Often the students lack prior knowledge assumed by the texts; in addition, many textbook passages are poorly written if not downright incoherent.

The Pittsburgh group (as do others—Britton, Van Dusen, & Gülgöz, 1991; Britton, Van Dusen, Gügöz, & Glynn, 1989; Duffy et al., 1989; Graves & Slater, 1991) believes that the solution is to modify textbooks so that essential background information is contained in readings, and linkages between ideas in text are made more explicitly (i.e., to **add elaborations and connections** to text). Thus, consider a text for use in grades 4/5 American history:

The French and Indian War

In 1763, Britain and the colonies ended a 7-year war with the French and Indians. As a result of this war, France was driven out of North America. Britain would now rule Canada and other lands that had belonged to France. This brought peace to the American colonies. The colonists no longer had to fear attacks from Canada. The Americans were happy to be a part of Britain in 1763. Yet a dozen years later, these same people would be fighting the British for independence, or freedom from Great Britain's rule. This war was called the War for Independence, or the American Revolution. A revolution changes one type of government or way of thinking and replaces it with another. (Beck et al., 1991, p. 275)

Now, consider this elaborated version, which fills in some gaps in information and increases the connectedness of the text in general:

The French and Indian War

About 250 years ago, Britain and France both claimed to own some of the same land, here, in North America. This land was just west of where the 13 colonies were. In 1756, Britain and France went to war to see who would get control of this land. Because the 13 American colonies belonged to Britain, the colonists fought on the same side as Britain. Many Indians fought on the same side as France. Because we were fighting against the French and Indians, the war has come to be known as the French and Indian War.

The war ended in 1763. Britain won the war. Now Britain had control of North America, including Canada. The French had to leave North America.

The colonists were very glad that Britain had won. They now felt safer in their homes. Before the war, Indians had often attacked colonists who lived near the borders. Now Britain owned these lands where the Indians lived. The colonists were sure that Britain would protect them.

The colonists were happy to be part of Britain, but that was about to change. They began to decide that they would rather have their own country, independent from Britain. So a dozen years later, the colonists would be fighting the British for freedom from Great Britain's rule. This later war would be called the War for Independence, or the American Revolution. (Beck et al., 1991, p. 275–276)

Beck and associates have reported modest increases in learning as a result of revisions. More positively, the benefits of revision at the high school and college levels have been greater (Britton et al., 1989, 1991; Duffy et al., 1989; Graves & Slater, 1991). The idea of writing more complete texts that explain important ideas more completely is appealing from a number of perspectives.

Adjunct Questions   Another classic way to increase learning of text content is to place **adjunct questions** in the text (e.g., Rothkopf, 1966, either before the text [prequestions] or after the text [postquestions]). The outcomes produced in studies of adjunct questioning were orderly (Anderson & Biddle, 1975). Both prequestions and postquestions enhance memory for material covered by questions. Prequestions either do nothing to enhance learning of other information in the text, or they actually reduce memory of nonquestioned information. A prequestion directs attention to questioned information and thus reduces attention to other information in the passage. In contrast, postquestions improve learning of both questioned and nonquestioned material. Postquestions seem to increase review and reflection of more than just the information that answers the postquestion, although the types of information tapped by postquestions over present content can increase differential attention to the same type of information in subsequent sections of text (e.g., Mayer, 1975; McConkie, Rayner, & Wilson, 1973; McGaw & Grotelueschen, 1972; Sagerman & Mayer, 1987). In general, however, it should be noted that adjunct questioning effects typically are not dramatically large, consistent with the general tendency of most text modifications to produce small effects. In general as well, adjunct question effects tend to be smaller with children than with adults (see Pressley & Forrest-Pressley, 1985). Still, textbooks that include a variety of signals or adjunct questions should promote learning at least slightly, making it easier for readers to comprehend and remember the messages in the text.

Illustrations   The fourth approach is to provide illustrations as accompaniments to text. Memory of text is improved to the extent that illustrations overlap the meaning conveyed by the text (Levin, 1982, 1983; Levin & Lesgold, 1978; Pressley, 1977), consistent with Paivio's (e.g., 1971) dual-coding theory (see Chapter 3). Pictures also sometimes stimulate inferences that would not occur if the text alone were read (e.g., Holmes, 1987). The only consistently negative effect of pictures on learning that has been reported is with beginning readers. Pictures can reduce decoding demands for these readers and thus reduce their attention to the words they are reading. If children read words accompanied by their illustrations, their acquisition of the words as sight vocabulary is less likely than if they read them without accompanying illustrations (Samuels, 1970)—that is, a great deal more attention to and analysis of the words, "A boy rides the bike," occur when the sentence is read alone than when it is read in the context of a picture depicting a boy riding a bicycle.

Summary

A good deal is now known about how to modify texts so as to increase the comprehensibility and learnability of them, although the types and amounts of gain vary depending on the modifications made. Interestingly, texts that are modified in ways to increase their learnability are obviously clearer: When asked to evaluate a variety of textbooks (Britton, Van Dusen, Gülgöz, Glynn, & Sharp, 1991), 95 percent of college students were able to discriminate texts that were constructed to be highly learnable from texts that were not carefully constructed with respect to comprehensibility and learnability.

CONCLUDING COMMENTS

There is a long history of claims that reading can be improved. Many are scandalous, including assertions that phonics and decoding can be learned only by listening to audio tapes and that people can learn to read thousands of words per minute by enrolling in a course that meets for a few hours a night for 10 to 20 weeks (e.g., 600 word per minute is probably the maximum a person can read given physiological constraints; Carver, 1990, Chapter 19). In contrast to such incredible claims, the benefits owing to the instruction summarized in this chapter are credible. Notably, there were no quick fixes in this chapter. Years of high-quality, theoretically reasonable instruction is a potential solution to many of the literacy problems of the United States.

Broad-based conclusions about reading that emerge from the well-conducted, systematic study of important reading problems and processes include the following:

1. There are concerns about inadequate reading skills at every age level. Some children go through their preschool years without exposure to emergent literacy experiences. Many children arrive at grade 1 lacking phonemic awareness. National tests document lower than desired levels of literacy throughout the elementary and secondary years.

2. There are psychologically sound (or at least promising) interventions for every age level. Understanding how good readers read has done much to increase understanding about how to devise interventions that promote the literacy of lower-achieving readers. Despite increases in knowledge about how to foster literacy, we suspect the minority of children receive literacy instruction even approximating the best practices described in this chapter. More positively, there are greater commitments to high-quality emergent literacy experiences and reading comprehension instruction than there were a decade ago, largely because of the understandings produced by research reviewed in this chapter.

3. We have come to understand that good reading is a specific instance of good problem solving: Both involve strategies, metacognition, knowledge, motivation, capacity, and constructive social interactions. Teaching of general problem-solving strategies would not produce good readers, however, for effective readers have developed strategies that are exceptionally well matched to the particular demands of reading.

4. Effective reading instruction is definitely long term, with instructional packages conceptualized in terms of months and years more than often than days or weeks. In the best possible world, a newborn would experience high-quality literacy experiences matched to needs, interests, and abilities for every day of her or his life.

5. Meaning construction is the emphasis in contemporary reading instruction. How to teach decoding and comprehension strategies to foster efficient abstraction of meaning from text is the overarching issue. Skills and drills are not the orders of the day. Rather the concern is with students coming to understand the cognitive processes that compose skilled reading so that those processes can be used to derive meaning from texts and create new meanings in new texts.

6. Direct explanation, including modeling, of effective reading processes, which is then followed by scaffolded student attempts to use the processes, emerges as a sound method of teaching reading. Rich teacher-student interactions aimed at encouraging students to become interpreters of text, to construct their own understandings of text, are gaining in prominence. As will be considered in detail at the conclusion of Chapter 15, student construction of knowledge about reading is key. Students can be assisted to learn how to read, but they are the ones who figure out how to do it. Good direct explanations with follow-up scaffolding encourage construction of knowledge, with students made aware that the processes modeled by the teacher are flexibly adaptive.

We recognize that a large amount of information was covered in this chapter. One way that our students found it helpful to organize the various topics covered is with respect to whether the research on them is revealing about decoding or comprehension or both. Although such a separation is an artificial one—for example, when a word is decoded by a skilled reader, comprehension processes are operating as well—it does seem to help make a large and potentially difficult-to-organize literature more comprehensible. Thus, we conclude the chapter with Table 14.1 as a summary.

Table 14.1 Organization of Reading Research with Respect to Whether Decoding or Comprehension Was the Main Focus

---

Decoding

Research on phonemic awareness and its development through instruction

Research on logographic reading, alphabetic reading, phonics rules, sight words, orthographic reading, reading by analogy, and use of semantic context cues to infer words

Research on various forms of experience (e.g., repeated readings, just reading more) that promote decoding competence

Study of fixations and saccades and other word-level processes

Comprehension

Cognitive processes apparent in think-aloud analyses of good reading

Comprehension strategies instruction (e.g., imagery, summarization), including instruction of coordinated use of multiple comprehension strategies (e.g., transactional strategies instruction)

Whole language

Secondary and college-level reading

Textbook modification

Both Decoding and Comprehension

Emergent literacy experiences (e.g., decoding: plastic letters, alphabet song; comprehension: reenactments, joint meaning construction during storybook reading)

One-on-one tutoring such as Reading Recovery and Success for All

---

15

Literacy II: Writing

For generations, educators have lamented student writing abilities. One of the great success stories in the analyses of academic information processing is writing. In the past two decades, composition researchers and cognitive psychologists have offered analyses of writing that focus on the planning, drafting, and revising processes that are composition. These analyses stimulated the development of new forms of writing instruction that definitely improve composing abilities. The writing of both children and adults, normal learners and learning-disabled populations, is improved through teaching of coordinated planning, drafting, and revising processes. The chapter closes with a discussion of the constructivist nature of literacy strategies instruction. We emphasize the general point that all of the strategy instruction favored in this book stimulates student construction of understandings about important cognitive procedures, such as reading and writing strategies.

In the past 15 years, there have been intense analyses of the nature of good writing. In part, this was due to growing awareness that most students left U.S. schools unable to communicate their ideas clearly in writing (e.g., Beach, 1976; Emig, 1971; Shaughnessy, 1977). We begin this chapter with an overview of the nature of good writing. This will be followed by discussion of writing instructional research and commentary about reading and writing connections.

NATURE OF GOOD WRITING

Although there are some disagreements about details, there is little disagreement among investigators in this field about the essentials of excellent writing. Rohman's (1965) early model of writing, involving three stages, proved to be nearly on the mark: Rohman conceived of writing as involving (1) prewriting (planning), (2) writing (composing a draft), and (3) rewriting (editing and revising). The only problem with this perspective was its linearity. People do not plan, write, and revise. Rather, they plan a little, write a little, plan some more, and write some more. Perhaps as they revise some of what they have already written, the need for more planning and writing becomes obvious, and so on. Flower and Hayes (1980) noted this recursive property of good writing: Planning occurs before and during writing, revision can occur from the moment something is first penned, and a final draft may require many trips through planning-writing-revision cycles before a composition is ready.

According to the Flower and Hayes' (1980) model, writing can be understood by considering the author's long-term memory, the environment the writer inhabits, and the composition being developed. How long-term memory, the environment, and the composition interact will become clearer by considering the writing subprocesses of **planning, translating,** and **revising** in more detail.

Good writers spend a lot more time planning than do weak writers, with their planning activities focusing on the higher-order meanings that the composition is intended to convey (Bereiter & Scardamalia, 1987). There are three subprocesses to such planning, with these occurring recursively. First, it is necessary to **generate the information** that might go in the composition. This can be done by retrieving information from long-term memory or from seeking information in the environment, such as when a reporter interviews witnesses to an accident or a student searches a library for material for a paper. Second, planning involves **setting writing goals.** Occasionally a goal is provided, such as when a teacher assigns an essay topic: "What I Did on My Summer Vacation." More often, however, it is up to the writer to decide on the topic of the composition and what effect the writer wishes to have on readers. For example, an essay on a condemned killer could be written to elicit sympathy from readers, acceptance of capital punishment as necessary, or political action from readers in the form of protest to the governor. Often, what the goals should be becomes clear only as planning proceeds (e.g., deciding to write an essay on how behaviorism is not incompatible with doctrines of free will can occur only after the writer discovers that the behaviorism–free will controversy exists and determines that this seems like a fairly interesting topic compared with the other information about behaviorism that was covered in trips to the library). Third, planning involves **organizing the information** retrieved, a large part of which is selecting information that is relevant to the writing goals that have emerged during the planning phase.

The translating phase of composing is transforming the sketch of a paper that emerges from planning into standard English sentences, ones that go together reasonably well to form paragraphs and represent the arguments intended by the writing plan. Sometimes deficiencies in the plan will become evident during the translating phase, in which case, more planning occurs. Although good writers plan before they write, they also do a lot of planning once writing has begun (Humes, 1983), fixing up and elaborating the plan in light of what they discover as they write, including change of their writing goal (Flower & Hayes, 1980). Often, additional planning is required because a gap in knowledge becomes evident as the writer tries to craft a coherent essay.

Revision is usually considered to begin once a draft is completed, although, of course, it can begin earlier with the decision to scrap a paragraph, word, or sentence that one has just written during the translating phase. There are essentially two subprocesses to revision: One is reading what has been written, and the second is editing. Editing involves looking for technical errors, such as noun-verb disagreements and punctuation errors. If a reading of the draft creates the sense that the message is not getting across, the point of editing is not technical accuracy but getting the meaning more in line with the intentions of the writer. The writing goals are always in mind during revision. If the draft falls far short of meeting the goals, substantial additional planning and rewriting may be required.

Challenges of Planning, Translating, and Revising

When we teach educational psychology courses, students easily remember that skilled writing involves planning, translating, and revising. They often fail to appreciate what a revolutionary perspective the Flower and Hayes' (1980) model is—somehow forgetting years of schooling that emphasized good spelling and correct punctuation as the heart of good writing—or how complex planning, translating, and revising are. Brief review of some subprocesses of planning, translating, and revising that have been studied as problems in their own right will make clear how challenging composition is. We particularly highlight here subprocesses research that has been conceptualized in psychological terms.

Planning   One subprocess of planning is searching for information that might be placed in an essay, with clear individual differences between students in how they search for information. For example, Nelson and Hayes (1988) studied how college students search for material for term papers. Some students went to the library shortly before the due date for the paper, completed their search in one afternoon and evening, with their selection of books anything but exhaustively systematic. Other students

headed to the library much more in advance of the deadline and were extremely systematic and selective in their choice of references.

Suppose for the moment that the student is far enough along with the project to have a fairly clear goal and has photocopies of some articles identified by the computerized abstracts as relevant. Will the student find the information he or she is seeking—even if the article has been retrieved, photocopied, and read? Guthrie and colleagues (e.g., Guthrie, 1988; Dreher & Guthrie, 1990; Guthrie, Bennett, & Weber, 1991) have determined that search of documents is extremely complex, involving the following steps:

- **Goal formation,** in which an objective is specified. For example, to discover information supporting the thesis that behaviorism and free will are compatible.
- **Category selection,** in which relevant parts of the document being read are identified. Thus, if an article contained only some sections containing information about free will, it is important to find those sections.
- **Extraction of information,** involving the identification of the critical information within relevant sections of a text.
- **Integration** of the new information found with prior knowledge and other relevant information in the document.

Of course, this is not a linear process but one that is also recursive. Thus, it may become obvious when reading one section of an article that has been categorized as potentially relevant that it is not relevant at all. This might stimulate reconsideration of the other sections of the text that have been singled out for more detailed search. In addition, some information found in the third or fourth section of the text searched might make clear that something read earlier was more relevant than the writer thought it was, stimulating a search for the material that was dismissed when covered previously (Figure 15.1).

Finding information in a text is difficult even for bright high school and university students. Often, they fail to identify the information they are seeking in a text even though it is there (e.g., Guthrie & Dreher, 1990). Often, people will read the relevant information and not recognize that that is what they are looking for (Symons & Pressley, 1993) or understand it (Grabe, 1989). The document search problems of students have been well documented in the

Figure 15.1 Part of the planning process is searching for information from sources. This is a difficult process even for college students.

National Asssessment of Educational Progress, which includes data on Americans up to 21 to 25 years of age. Only about one-third of young adults can find a piece of information in a newspaper article that involved consideration of three features. Perhaps most readers would not be surprised to learn that the college students who went to the library near the paper deadline in Nelson and Hayes (1988), which was discussed earlier in this section, were also ineffective when it came to searching in the texts they located. They tended to do a lot of copying of quotes from sources without reflecting much on the appropriateness of the quotes. In short, document search is challenging but an essential part of planning when writers must retrieve information from archival sources in order to have sufficient information to write an essay.

Researchers in writing have documented a number of other difficulties during planning (see Harris & Graham, 1992, for commentary): A common one is that some student writers do not plan but rather simply write, doing what Bereiter and Scardamalia (e.g., 1987, Chapter 1) refer to as **knowledge telling,** illustrated by this description of writing by one 12-year-old:

> I have a whole bunch of ideas and write down until my supply of ideas is exhausted. Then I might try to think of more ideas up to the point when you can't get

any more ideas that are worth putting down on paper and then I would end it. (Bereiter & Scardamalia, 1987, p. 9)

Some writers have a great deal of difficulty generating ideas for compositions and cannot zero in on an appropriate topic (Morocco & Neuman, 1986). Some have a lot of information in their heads about their writing topic but seem not to be able to access it or do so inefficiently (see Englert & Raphael, 1988; Graham & Harris, 1989a).

Translating   Any trip to a bookstore will confirm that there are no end to writing style manuals, most of which are filled with technical rules, detailing everything from when to use a semicolon to how to cite a reference. Readers of this book who continue their study of psychology will undoubtedly be exposed to the *Publication Manual of the American Psychological Association.* There are plenty of rules of writing in that source. It would be easy to get the impression from sources such as the APA *Manual* that good writing required only knowledge and application of such rules, a perspective reinforced for years by educators who emphasized such rules. Knowledge of such rules does not produce good writers or even people who can translate a writing plan into good prose. In fact, overconcern with such rules might actually interfere with the construction of text that conveys what the author wants to say (e.g., Bereiter & Scardamalia, 1987, Chapter 4). There has been ample documentation that students often receive negative feedback about technical problems in their writing, with such negative feedback discouraging rather than encouraging additional student efforts to write (Daiker, 1983, 1989; Dragga, 1986; McCarthy, 1987; Rose, 1985, 1989). Think back to the issues of self-efficacy discussed in Chapter 5, and the motivational implications of persistent negative feedback should be obvious. Recall the limits of short-term memory, and it is easy to imagine that if much of short-term capacity is consumed with attending to technical matters, there may be little short-term capacity left over to attend to developing the meaning of the text—so much effort is put into punctuating and capitalizing correctly by some writers that they forget what they want to say (see Bereiter & Scardamalia, 1987, Chapter 4).

The real challenge in writing is developing text that expresses the intended meaning: That is what good writers can do and poor writers cannot do. Thus, there has been increasing emphasis in developing writers who can write what they mean. (Some of the most important of this work will be taken up later in the chapter.)

One important difficulty in creating texts that convey meaning is that writers must respect what Nystrand (1986) refers to as the **reciprocity principle.** In constructing a text that makes sense, the writer must be aware of what the potential reader knows already. Thus, when one of us writes the introduction to a technical article in educational psychology, we do not spell out the meanings of all of the terms we use—as we have been doing while we write this text for you. It is safe for us to assume that readers of our technical articles would be familiar with most of the terminology in our introductions. In fact, to define terms in such an article might be seen as an insult to the readership. If we were not to define our terms in the chapters in this book, few of you would be reading this book because few of your instructors would have deemed it appropriate for their students. Good writers keep their audience in mind as they construct text. Because the reader is not there to ask questions of the writer as the composition is created, the writer must anticipate the questions that readers might have and answer those questions (see McCutchan & Perfetti, 1983; Scardamalia & Bereiter, 1986) as part of constructing the text. Psychologists think of this as a problem of **social cognition:** Good writers are aware of the state of the readers' minds and adjust their writing so that readers can understand the meaning intended by the writer.

Revising   Revision has proven to be an extremely intriguing problem for psychologists. Again, getting the meaning of the text right is critical in revision. Worrying about the mechanics alone does not result in effective revisions (e.g., Graham, Schwartz, & MacArthur, 1991; MacArthur & Graham, 1987; MacArthur, Graham, & Schwartz, 1991).

Suppose that a writer is confronted with a text in need of revision because it does not convey the intended meaning or does so poorly. Why might the writer fail to revise?: The writer may not detect that there is a problem with the text. More positively, if someone else points out that there is a difficulty, writers are often capable of fixing up problems they initially fail to detect (e.g., Beal, 1987; see Beal, 1989, for additional discussion), although there are developmental differences such that the ability to correct initially undetected problems (i.e., once they are

pointed out) increases during the grade-school years (Beal, 1990). Also, students can be taught to monitor whether there are inconsistencies in a piece of writing. For example, Beal, Garrod, and Bonitatibus (1990) taught grade-3 and grade-5/6 children to self-question themselves about drafts of narratives using a set of questions that any complete, consistent narrative should be able to answer: Who are the people in the story and what are they like? What is happening in the story? Why are they doing what they did? Where does the story take place? When does the story take place? Such instruction increased detection of errors and construction of revisions. Even more effective detection and revision was obtained with grade-3 students when the instruction they were given about revision included exposure to example stories containing parts that should be revised. Beal et al. (1990) provided compelling evidence that detection of problems in stories can be taught so that young children can identify when to make revisions—although the main point here is that in the absence of instruction, children often fail to detect difficulties with text.

Writers may fail to identify problems because they lack adequate criteria about what makes a piece of writing appropriately communicative (e.g., McCormick, Busching, & Potter, 1992). For example, based on much of the feedback about writing given in school, students sometimes accept text as adequate if the mechanics of the writing (i.e., spelling, punctuation, capitalization) are fine and the writing is neat. Alternatively, they may be seduced by interesting details (see Chapter 5). For example, they may believe a text is communicative because they like the examples used in the text (e.g., anecdotes about pets), failing to recognize that the anecdotes are not good illustrations of the phenomena being explained in the text.

Even when writers detect problems, sometimes they do not know how to revise to express the meaning they intend. Some students do not know how to make additions, deletions, substitutions and text rearrangements as revisions (e.g., Fitzgerald & Markham, 1987).

Fortunately, some people do learn how to revise well. A number of studies have been conducted in which think-aloud data have been collected as writers revise. Fitzgerald (1992) summarized how good revisers approach the task. First, they keep the overall meaning of the text in mind and what the reader needs to get out of the text (Berkenkotter & Murray,

1983; Hayes, Flower, Schriver, Stratman, & Carey, 1987). If there is a particular writing style that they want reflected in the writing, that is considered prominently as revision proceeds (e.g., Graves, Slater, Roen, Redd-Boyd, Duin, Furniss, & Hazeltine, 1988). They do not worry about problems at the sentence and word level as much as they worry about problems at a higher level of organization—for example, concentrating more on the overall organization of the text than the construction of individual sentences (Hayes et al., 1987). Although attention to higher-order meaning takes precedence, expert revisers also evaluate grammar and spelling and some writing maxims, such as to use parallel constructions and to avoid wordiness (Hayes et al., 1987; Hull, 1987).

In short, expert revisers have a repertoire of strategies that they apply while they are revising, from ones that are directed at the main messages of the text to others that are directed at details of grammar, spelling, and punctuation. Throughout Fitzgerald's (1992) review of revision, she keeps returning to Nystrand's (e.g., 1986) reciprocity principle, that good revisers are aware of the needs of the reader. For that reason among others, a popular instruction option is for students to revise in small groups, with peers reading one another's work and reacting with constructive criticism. Consistent with Vygotskian theory (Chapter 8), many who favor revision groups believe that participating in such discussions will lead to long-term internalization of the revision processing carried out in the group (e.g., DiPardo & Freedman, 1988).

Good Writing Compared with Expert Problem Solving

Just as good reading is an example of expert problem solving (see Chapter 14), so is good writing:

- Domain experts use their prior knowledge extensively during problem solving. So it is with skilled writers who have a great deal of knowledge about the specific topics they are writing and ways of expressing their ideas.
- Experts are opportunistic during problem solving, using clues they encounter while solving a problem to assist in deciding next moves. So it is with skilled writing, with writing plans changing as writers encounter gaps in the texts they are creating.

- Experts exhibit flexibility as they solve problems. So it is with skilled writing, with the good writer juggling the plan until it seems right, experimenting with different ways of expressing a thought and revising by applying multiple criteria simultaneously.
- Experts monitor their performances. So it is with good writers, who size up when they need to plan more as they experience difficulties with writing and who explicitly approach revision as an exercise involving error detection and correction (see Beal's [1989] analysis).
- Experts process "deeply" as they solve problems; that is, expertise in problem solving produces a complex thinker who does not simply apply readily available prior knowledge to a problem but rather uses prior knowledge in conjunction with strategies, continually monitoring progress in understanding the problems. So it is with writing, with the skilled writer thinking extensively about the essay and how it can be crafted best to express intended meaning.
- Finally, expertise in problem solving takes a long time to develop. So it is with writing. Good writers write a lot (Applebee, 1984; Applebee, Langer, & Mullis, 1986).

Good writing is so much a problem-solving process that Flower has produced a college-level introductory writing textbook entitled, *Problem-Solving Strategies for Writing* (1989). We strongly recommend this book as a tutorial for those who wish a full-blown exposition on how writing can be approached as problem solving.

Closing Comment on Good Writing

The analyses of skilled writing presented here were intended to make obvious that writing can be understood in terms of information processing but that being able to explain it in such terms does not diminish the enormity of the task. Good writing involves the integration of a number of skills that require a great deal of time and experience to develop. What is shocking is that American education traditionally has required little writing of students, a point forcefully made by Applebee (1984). Consider the following claims from the conclusions section of that study of high school writing in the United States:

> The majority of school assignments provide little room for writing of even paragraph length.

When more extended writing is required, it still tends to be rather limited in scope. The typical assignment is a first-and-final draft, completed in class, and requiring a page or less of writing. Topics for these assignments are usually constructed to test previous learning of information or skills; hence the students' task is to get the answer "right," rather than to convince, inform, or entertain a naive audience. (pp. 183–184)

How could we expect to develop excellent writers in such a schooling environment? Fortunately, since Applebee's (1984) study, and in part because of it, there has been renewed interest in increasing the amount of writing done in school, with some of the most important discoveries about the effects of such writing instruction considered in the pages that follow. As a preview of what is to come, we simply say that writing opportunities and writing instruction is a concern at all levels of contemporary schooling, and the development of competent writers is of great interest to both educators and researchers.

EMERGENT WRITING DURING THE PRESCHOOL YEARS

If a child can hold a crayon, it is likely that he or she will engage in writing at some level according to the emergent literacy perspective. There is a clear developmental progression during the preschool years for children who live in an environment supportive of writing (Sulzby, 1985): Drawing and then scribbling are significant precursors to conventional writing. Eventually, scribbling is not random, with letter like features observed both in drawings and scribbling. The child will learn to draw some letters, such as the ones in his or her name, although often the letters are far from perfect or in the correct order. With time and experience, the child can write many more, often inventing spellings based on the sounds of the word (e.g., GNYS for GENIUS; Bissex, 1980). Invented spellings gradually approximate conventional spellings, until there comes a time that spelling is completely conventional.

When invented spelling is allowed, the child is free to write much more than if adults are hung up about conventional spelling. Preschools and kindergartens are now filled with writers. It is not unusual, in fact, to see all types of writing in any given kindergarten, from drawings and scribbling to short sentences and phrases written with conventional

spelling (Allen et al., 1989; Sulzby & Teale 1991). Variations on writing such as invented spelling will persist into the early elementary years. An assumption of many language arts educators who are committed to positions such as "whole language" is that letting the kids write as they will and can is essential if children are to be motivated to be writers. Recall the point made earlier in this chapter about how overconcern with mechanics can interfere with writing and reduce the motivation to write. IMURJENT RITing iS A WUNDuRFULL IDiR!

WRITING DURING THE ELEMENTARY YEARS

Walk into an American elementary classroom on any given morning. What are the three most likely events to occur? One is the pledge to the flag, an American institution (or singing of *O Canada!* north of the border). The second is reading group, a staple of elementary education for more than a century. The third is **Writers' Workshop,** which is less than a decade old (Atwell, 1987; Calkins, 1986) but is becoming as commonplace as the pledge and reading group. Children are learning that to write every day is natural.

Writers' Workshop is designed to be motivating: For example, students often are permitted to choose their own topics for writing rather than writing to some teacher-prescribed topic. Students control other aspects of their writing as well, such as how long their essays will be and how they will revise. Just as good readers experiencing transactional strategies instruction are taught that they must make choices for themselves, so it is with Writers' Workshop participants, something hypothesized to increase the likelihood of eventual self-regulated writing. As part of the writing process, students in Writers' Workshop receive feedback from their peers, with a great deal of sharing of writing between students. We have many memories of children listening to peers and then explaining what it is they like about a peer's essay, what they do not understand, and what might be a good way to extend the piece. Students do much to teach each other how to communicate effectively as part of the Writers' Workshop experience. That students provide feedback to one another does not deny the role of the teacher in instruction, however. One prominent instructional role for the teacher is to listen to student essays just as the peers do and provide the same type of feedback, about strong points and aspects that might be elaborated or clarified.

When students reach the end of this process, many Writers' Workshops provide another lesson in writing—a lesson about another important reason that writers write. The completed essay is "published," perhaps in a class book or for display on a bulletin board.

In describing these salient features of Writers' Workshop, many of which are explicitly aimed at increasing both knowledge of writing and motivation to write, we have downplayed one of its most important components. In many Writers' Workshops, teachers provide a great deal of direct explanation and modeling about the writing process, with the Flower and Hayes' (1980) model considered earlier in this chapter (and variations of it) guiding much of contemporary writing instruction. As it turns out, there is great need for such instruction.

Deficiencies in the Writing of Elementary Students

There are five potential problems that students can have with writing (Harris & Graham, 1992; Langer, 1986; Scardamalia & Bereiter, 1986). They can fail to do the following:

1. Establish a writing goal: They do not establish whether the task is to be persuasive or to tell a tale; they fail to identify their audience. More positively, there are age-related increases in student awareness of the communication possibilities that writing permits, although these understandings of communication possibilities are much less developed in the elementary years compared with the high school years (Langer, 1986, Chapter 3).
2. Generate enough content: They may fail to search their memories or environments completely for information that could be put in an essay.
3. Organize what they write: They do not plan enough, often only doing what Scardamalia and Bereiter (1986) refer to as "knowledge telling," which is simply writing without planning or re-organizing.
4. Do the mechanics of writing efficiently: Their writing, spelling, or sentence construction is weak, or they get so hung up on the mechanics that they pay little attention to the meaning and organization of what is being written. That children often are overly concerned about mechanics probably reflects that many schooling environments overemphasize mechanics such as spelling and sentence construction skills (Langer, 1986, Chapter 3).
5. Revise, including shifting goals if that seems appropriate based on what was discovered during planning, drafting, and previous revisions (see Fitzgerald, 1987).

In short, elementary student writing is often deficient with respect to the processes associated with good writing. More positively, elementary writing instruction is an area in which there have been many successes. Students can learn to write well.

Writing Instruction

Although Scardamalia and Bereiter (e.g., 1986) generated the first large-scale systematic program of investigations of writing instruction during the elementary grades, there is a growing fraternity of process-oriented writing researchers. Graham and Harris are particularly prominent members of this group, having identified a number of ways that the writing performance of elementary-age learning-disabled students can be improved. Based on their own research on writing, especially with learning-disabled students, and the research of others concerned with writing by elementary students, Harris and Graham (1992; but also Graham & Harris, 1988, 1992; Graham, Harris, MacArthur, & Schwartz, 1991; Sawyer, Graham, & Harris, 1992) provided a particularly thorough review of their perspectives on writing instruction.

According to Harris and Graham, writing should proceed as follows:

> First, students could be urged to concentrate on topic choice, planning, and content generation [planning stage in the Hayes and Flower frame work]. Once a first draft is generated [writing stage], students could then concentrate on revising their paper with an eye focused on content and organization [revision stage]. When students feel comfortable that their paper is complete, then editing for mechanical errors could take place. A routine of this nature focuses students' efforts on content and meaning. . . . Hence, they will

not be needlessly distracted by errors of mechanics and usage. . . . However, students do not forget that the paper will eventually need to be edited. . . . As students master such a routine, they should further be encouraged to see the various processes recursively.

It is not only critical that students become comfortable with the various stages involved in writing, they also need to develop effective strategies for executing these processes. Within the Writers' Workshop, one way teachers can help students develop these strategies is to model the pertinent strategies and the thought processes involved in executing them. For instance, a teacher may demonstrate how to gather raw material, mentally rehearse ideas and images to write about, talk to others to gain information, or use brainstorming and webbing activities to generate content for a topic. Modeling will not be enough. . . . Current research . . . suggests that . . . contextualized and explicit instruction is highly effective in promoting the development of cognitive and self-regulation skills central to academic success (Duffy & Roehler, 1986). (Harris & Graham, 1992, pp. 314–315)

There it is: Plan, write, and revise, with direct explanation and modeling of strategies for each of these stages. The strategies that can be applied during planning, writing, and revision include the following:

- *Strategies predominantly addressing the planning stage.* Because students sometimes do not search their memories thoroughly for everything they might know about a topic (see Scardamalia & Bereiter, 1986, for an analysis) either before or while they write, strategies that promote more thorough search of memory for ideas can increase the quantity of material written on a topic. For example, Humes (1983) recommended providing sets of question prompts that would stimulate systematic search of memory for relevant content. (Such prompts are a specific instance of **procedural facilitators** [Scardamalia & Bereiter, 1986], in that they make more likely execution of procedures that will result in a more complete and well-organized piece of writing.) Thus, if the student were writing about a sequence of events, the questions included the following: What happened first? What happened next? Next? What happened last? When did it happen? Where did it happen? To whom did it happen? Similarly, Harris and Graham (1985) taught students a rou-

tine for searching their memories to find action verbs, adjectives, and adverbs that would be sensible in their essays, with this search routine increasing the amount written and the quality of the text. Bereiter and Scardamalia (1982) provided students with sentence openers such as, "One reason . . . ," "Even though . . . ," "For example,. . . ," and "I think. . . ." Perhaps the most intuitively obvious approach, however, is simply to ask the child who writes a short essay to write some more (Graham, 1990; Scardamalia & Bereiter, 1986), a command that children can internalize and make to themselves if they are taught to do so (Graham & Harris, 1987).
- *Strategies predominantly addressing the writing stage.* Students can learn to instruct themselves to respond to a series of probes that are matched to the information contained in essays in the genre. Thus, to write a short persuasive essay, students can be taught to respond to the following four prompts in order: (1) Generate a topic sentence. (2) Note reasons. (3) Examine the reasons and ask if readers will buy each reason. (4) Provide an ending (Graham & Harris, 1988). A second example is a set of questions for generating a narrative with conventional story grammar (Harris & Graham, 1992): Who is the main character? Who else is in the story? When does the story take place? Where does the story take place? What does the main character do or want to do? What do other characters do? What happens when the main character does or tries to do it? What happens with other characters? How does the story end? How does the main character feel? How do the other characters feel?
- *Strategies predominantly addressing the revision stage.* After teaching students the elements of a good essay, Graham and MacArthur (1988) taught learning-disabled students to revise by cycling through six steps: (1) Read the essay. (2) Find a specific sentence that tells what the student believes and wants to say. (3) Add two reasons to the essay for the belief. (4) Scan each sentence of the essay. (5) Make changes on the computer (or paper, if handwritten). (6) Reread and make final changes. Fitzgerald and Markham (1987) taught grade-6 students to approach revision as a problem-solving task, a problem that could be solved by making additions, deletions, substitutions, and rearrange-

ments. Graham and MacArthur (1988) taught students to revise by adding details, examining the clarity and cohesiveness of the paper, and fixing mechanical errors. Peers can be asked to give feedback on the content and the structure of the paper (e.g., MacArthur, Schwartz, & Graham, 1991). (Recall as well the description earlier in this chapter of the self-questioning strategy taught to elementary students by Beal et al., 1990.)

We assume by this point that it is obvious to readers that there is much to be learned for a student to plan, write, and revise an essay. Not surprisingly, writing instruction is long term, although it is often possible to observe some benefits after a few weeks or months of some specific type of strategy instruction. For example, Harris and Graham's (1992) review of their own writing research included information about how long it took to teach the writing strategies covered in each of their studies (some of which have been mentioned already). The length of instruction varied greatly, typically involving 6 or more hours of teaching distributed over several weeks of lessons. This time was well spent, with Harris and Graham consistently observing maintenance of training (i.e., continued application of the strategies taught when doing the same writing task), sometimes measured as long as 16 weeks after the instruction was completed. In addition, Harris and Graham (1992) have observed some transfer of the strategies they have taught, for example, to different settings (teachers) and writing genres.

Harris and Graham (1992) not only spend a good deal of time instructing students (which is essential for students to learn writing strategies, especially the learning-disabled students who are their particular concern), but also they teach according to a model of instruction that is consistent with many other types of effective strategies instruction (including a number already reviewed in this chapter):

1. There is an initial conference with students to explain the goals of the strategy instruction and why such instruction is important (i.e., benefits of instruction are explained).
2. Prerequisite skills are taught to students who may be deficient. For example, if knowing con-

ventional story grammar is critical to execution of the strategy, students who may not understand the conventional structure of stories can be taught what they need to know.
3. There is initial discussion of the strategy, during which the instructor explains each step and its significance to the overall process.
4. The teacher models use of the strategy being taught. As part of this, the teacher talks aloud about his or her problem that might be solved with the writing strategy. The teacher self-evaluates as his or her writing proceeds, correcting errors and providing self-reinforcement (e.g., hey, this is really coming along) as the essay develops.
5. The student memorizes the steps of the strategy.
6. The student receives scaffolded instruction from the teacher while practicing the strategy.
7. Eventually the student can execute the strategy independently, with talk-aloud data reflecting use of all of the steps of the strategy.
8. The student and teacher discuss how to apply the strategy in other settings and with other tasks and, then the student attempts to use the strategy during the regular school day.

We assume readers have no difficulty discerning the by now familiar pattern of explicit explanation and modeling followed by scaffolded practice until the student is ready for independent performance. This is a winning formula, although one that can take years to complete, as illustrated by one of the most important instructional studies of student writing reported to date, which is taken up in the next subsection.

Englert, Raphael, Anderson, Anthony, and Stevens (1991)

Englert and colleagues at Michigan State set out to teach grade-4 and grade-5 students (both regularly achieving students and special education students) how to construct particular types of expositions: explanations and compare-contrast essays. The study took place over the course of an entire academic year. They dubbed their approach **Cognitive Strategy Instruction in Writing (CSIW).**

CSIW has much in common with other Writers' Workshop approaches:

1. There is direct explanation of writing strategies and modeling of their use.
2. There is daily writing, usually on topics selected by the students.
3. Procedural facilitators are provided to increase the likelihood that children will execute completely the processes they have been taught.
4. Peers evaluate each other's papers and provide revision comments.
5. Teachers and students have frequent writing conferences.
6. There is "publication" of student papers.

First, the text structures that students were learning were introduced using examples (see Chapter 3), ranging from extremely well-structured ones to completely disorganized passages. As part of this introduction via examples, students were provided information about the types of questions the text structure in question addresses and the types of text signals that authors can build into such text to make the text work as intended. There was discussion of appropriate ways to begin such an essay, how to construct opening sentences that catch the attention of readers. As the teacher went over the good and bad examples, he or she thought aloud for students in ways that were revealing about strengths and weaknesses of the text (e.g., "I wonder how the author got into this situation?") or structural elements the student should note (e.g., "Did the author address what is being explained?", "Who is involved?"; "What materials are needed?"; "Did (s)he explain where it was taking place?"; and "What are the steps?"). As examples continued, students played an ever-increasing role in these analyses activities, doing so at the invitation of the teacher who scaffolded their participation in the analysis process.

Second, teachers modeled the writing of texts conforming to the structure being instructed. They talked aloud as they did so, telling students what they were doing and how they were doing it. While thinking aloud, teachers provided information about when to use the text structure under instruction and the text-construction strategies being modeled. For example, a teacher modeling the construction of an explanation-type text would first think aloud about planning: "Who am I writing for?" "Why am I writing this?" "What do I know about this?" "How can I organize all of this?"

Third, the teacher introduced a "planning think sheet," a type of procedural facilitator, something intended to assist planning of the essay. Thus, the planning think sheet for explanation essays included the types of questions, the teacher previously modeled as part of his or her planning:

WHO: Who am I writing for?
WHY: Why am I writing this?
WHAT: What do I know? (Brainstorm)
HOW: How can I group my ideas?
How will I organize my ideas?: _____ comparison/
    contrast, _____ problem/solution
    _____ explanation _____ other

Students then wrote class papers in dialogue with the teacher, with the teachers and students using the planning sheets collaboratively to construct essays. As this writing proceeded, the students took more responsibility. That is, instruction was scaffolded, with the teacher providing no more help than needed. After the group construction efforts came attempts by students to construct their own essays, again with scaffolded instruction from teachers. The students worked collaboratively with one another as they worked on essays. Essay writing continued in this fashion until the student was ready to prepare an essay that could be published in the class book. Throughout the process, however, whenever students needed additional explanations or modeling, they received it.

CSIW was evaluated in a quasiexperiment in which comparable control students and teachers carried on their instructional business as usual. The control students were receiving high-quality language arts instruction, including some instruction in process writing (i.e., the controls were learning to plan, draft, and revise as part of writing). That the instruction in the control classrooms was good teaching bolsters confidence in the claims of effectiveness made by Englert et al. (1991)—Englert et al. had a challenging control condition rather than a "straw man" control.

On the posttest, participants in the study were asked to explain in writing how to do something they were familiar with (e.g., how to play a game or make some object), keeping in mind that the reader would know little about the topic before reading the essay. They also wrote a compare-and-contrast paper, comparing two different people, places, or things. A third writing assignment required the students to write about something that they knew a great deal about, which was a transfer task because CSIW students had never been taught a text structure strategy for such writing.

In general, the posttest essays of CSIW students were superior to those of controls, both when judged holistically (i.e., readers rated the overall quality of the essay) and with respect to important characteristics of explanatory (i.e., introduction of topic; a sequence of steps; key words such as first, second, third; and closure, approximately in that order) and compare-and-contrast (i.e., identification of two things compared; similarities; differences; keywords such as alike, different, but; and conclusion, roughly in that order) essays. Three other outcomes were important as well, however: (1) The texts of CSIW students were more sensitive to the needs of readers as reflected by more interesting introductions, explicit statements of purpose, anticipating and answering potential reader questions, and an explicit author voice indicating that personal opinions were being expressed, with the writer's personality injected in the essay in various ways. (2) The CSIW students wrote better "expert" papers as well, even though they were not taught text structure strategies for such texts. Englert et al. (1991) intepreted this as evidence of transfer of writing strategies to a novel writing task. (3) At posttest, students in CSIW had much more metacognitive knowledge about the writing process than control students: For example, they could talk about writing as a process involving planning, writing, and revising. They understood the importance of essay organization and that revising was to establish coherence (i.e., rather than to correct grammar, spelling, and so forth) and knew more ways of producing coherence (e. g., putting closely related ideas in the same paragraph).

In general, there was a great deal of evidence in Englert et al. (1991) supporting the general conclusion that a year of expository writing instruction benefited students. CSIW students produced better organized and more interesting essays at the end of the year of instruction than did control students experiencing otherwise high-quality language arts instruction. The effects were pronounced both for normally achieving students and for learning-disabled students.

The plan-write-revise framework can be taught to grade-school students of varying abilities, including those who are experiencing special education interventions because of previous difficulties in language arts. A number of specific approaches have been developed to address each of the three recursive phases of writing. Good instruction provides students with a repertoire of specific procedures for facilitating planning, writing, and revising and permits a great deal of scaffolded practice of expository writing. Procedural facilitators in the form of lists of elements that should be in an essay are used frequently as part of writing instruction. (See Zellermayer, Salomon, Globerson, & Givon, 1991, for an evaluation of computerized scaffolding and provision of procedural facilitators to high school students, one in which 20 hours of interaction with the computerized "writing partner" improved the quality of students' essays.) Even short-term writing instruction aimed at improving some specific writing competency occurs over hours and days; impressive writing gains, such as the transfer documented by Englert et al. (1991), occur after weeks and months of instruction. Fortunately, long-term writing instruction is part of many educators' conceptions of high-quality language arts instruction, instruction that is decidedly multifaceted.

Summary

The work reviewed in this section has been produced by cognitive scientists and psychologists, specialists in curriculum and instruction, rhetoricians, and special educators. Various specialists have combined basic ideas from cognitive psychology with their knowledge of the literacy needs and capabilities of students to design interventions that improve children's writing. What is gratifying to cognitively oriented educational psychologists is that it is now possible to walk into classrooms and see theoretically motivated practice that is effective and received enthusiastically by students and teachers alike.

If there is a "secret" here, it is that a lot can be had from simple but powerful ideas: When students learn to plan, write, and revise compositions—and specific ways to accomplish each of these stages of composition—they have learned important literacy lessons: Good text does not just happen but rather is a human construction, one usually accomplished only with hard work and many reworkings.

WRITING DURING ADOLESCENCE AND EARLY ADULTHOOD

Without a doubt, the two most prominent researchers studying high school writing and writing instruction are Applebee and Langer (e.g., Applebee, 1984; Langer & Applebee, 1987). Their work and that of their colleagues at the federally sponsored National Center for the Study of Writing has involved a number of methods, from detailed case studies of student writing and the teaching of writing to analyses of the writing samples of hundreds of students and the collection of questionnaire data from teachers across the United States. A coherent set of important conclusions emerged from their analyses.

Nature of Student Writing

Much of the writing done by students is to convince the teacher that they have learned content that has been taught. Often, this writing is in response to a short-answer question on a test. Such writing is undemanding, with teachers rarely worried about whether answers are communicative so long as the student touches on the points that he or she was to learn for the examination.

More positively, there are clear developments in writing skills moving from the elementary years through secondary schooling, largely in response to new demands made by schooling. Thus, during the elementary years, children in Applebee's and Langer's (e.g., Langer, 1986) studies could write simple reports and simple stories, narratives containing story grammar elements and other features common in stories (e.g., starting with, "Once upon a time. . . " and ending with, "They lived happily ever after. . . "). (Given the increased prominence of writing instruction in the elementary years since Applebee's and Langer's investigations, much more might be expected from grade-school students if the study were to be repeated now.) By the end of the grade-school years and in the middle-school years, students are writing book reports. These are typically not more than a page or two in length, requiring description of the text and some evaluative commentary. Although most students learn to cope with these styles and offer acceptable stories and book reports, individual differences in qualities of text are evident even with respect to these simple forms of writing. For example, some students will provide interpretations of books they have read, whereas others will simply offer evaluative commentary (Durst, 1984).

In contrast, high school requires more analytical forms of writing. Thus, English and social studies courses include assignments in which students must present a thesis and defend it. Science courses include laboratory reports. Although students experience difficulties in learning how to produce such essays, they eventually succeed (Durst, 1984). What is somewhat disturbing, however, is that they seem to learn a formula for generating the writing required for specific classes. Once that formula is understood and mastered, it is followed (Applebee, 1984; Marshall, 1984b).

For example, students learn that thesis essays open with a paragraph stating the thesis, followed by several paragraphs (often three) supporting the thesis. Each of the supporting points is explicitly tied to the main idea of the thesis. There is a concluding paragraph that ties up the essay, offering a conclusion or perhaps a generalization. Students' understandings of this frame are so specified that many seem to have the goal of writing paragraphs that are precisely three sentences long, a minimum prescribed length for paragraphs in some middle-school and high school textbooks presenting information to students about how to write effective thesis-type essays. Similarly, students learn that science laboratory reports include (in order) the following: statement of purpose, hypothesis, materials, procedures, results, and conclusions. Once the basic form is mastered, students generate essays consistent with the form (Durst, 1984; Marshall, 1984b).

The positive of all of this is that students can produce essays of different types. In addition, many students do understand the necessity of revising, especially with respect to longer essays that are developed over a period of time, with good high school writers often first revising to produce a clear meaning, worrying about revisions involving mechanics only near the due date for the essay (Butler-Nalin, 1984). Even so, many students do not revise or do not do so effectively; many high school students have learned skills rather than strategies, formulas that are applied rigidly rather than heuristics that are creatively adapted, expanded on, and applied in new ways in new settings and with new tasks (Applebee, 1984; Durst, 1984; Marshall, 1984a, 1984b). Applebee believes that the rigid use of writing formulas largely reflects ineffective writing instruction in high school.

Writing Instruction

Applebee and Langer clearly subscribe to the plan-write-revise model presented earlier. Moreover, they are convinced that effective writing instruction must be scaffolded. Consistent with the Vygotskian principles discussed in Chapter 8, their view of writing instruction is that it should possess the following characteristics (Langer & Applebee, 1987, Chapter 9):

- Students should recognize that they are not simply to obey the instructions presented to them. They need to understand why they are learning a writing process and how it can help them. Instruction must send a message that writing is for students to say what they mean. Writing instruction should permit students to codify their own ideas, with the result that students have a sense of **ownership** about the essays they write.
- The writing tasks should be at an **appropriate level of challenge,** not so easy that no effort is required but not so difficult that they are beyond students even if the students are given teacher support.
- Teacher support should be aimed at making the structure of the writing task clear. Teachers need to convey that the strategies being taught can be used to produce a variety of texts and that the purpose of the instruction is to prepare students to produce texts in the future. Students need to be impressed that the **purpose** of writing instruction is for them to learn how to convey meaning rather than for them to acquire low-level skills (e.g., punctuation, grammar, knowledge of a writing formula that can be applied mechanically).
- Good writing instruction is **collaborative,** with teachers **scaffolding instruction:** They provide the support and assistance needed by a student but no more.
- The goal is **internalization** of the writing strategies taught. What this requires is for the teacher to let go of the student when the student can proceed autonomously. Teachers must understand that they are successful to the degree that they exert less and less control over students.

Unfortunately, the writing instruction that Applebee, Langer, and their associates found in schools was far from this ideal. First, most writing was brief and intended to let the teacher know that particular content was learned. Such a situation does little to inspire a sense of ownership. This situation was caused in part by textbooks filled with assignments requiring knowledge of content. A second cause was teachers' concerns with accountability—If writing contains the "right" information, it is easier to defend a grade than if writing is more creative, interpretive, or evaluative. Third, teachers provided little instruction in writing as the creation of meaning, with much attention instead devoted to the mechanics of writing. Fourth, even teachers who taught according to some form of the plan-write-revise model were only partially consistent with the model: Their concern with evaluation led such teachers to emphasize the correctness of information in essays over the creation of a novel writing product (Marshall, 1984a): That is, the correctness of the final product (e.g., a science laboratory report) was more important than the writing process that produced it.

Why is writing instruction like this? Langer and Applebee (1987, Chapter 9) offered analyses consistent with the realities of contemporary schooling:

1. Plan-write-revise strategies promote in-depth learning (see next subsection). In contrast, the schooling accountability system emphasizes breadth of learning and, in particular, at the high school level, emphasizes knowledge of content. The science teacher recognizes that his or her students must know a lot of science facts at the end of the year; whether they can write inventive, reflective laboratory reports or essays about science is not captured by the conventional evaluation system.
2. The easiest way to grade a student essay is to check off the points made that are consistent with points that should have been made in an essay on a particular topic. This approach to grading is consistent with the ongoing accountability system but stifles student ownership of writing.
3. The textbooks on writing are woefully inadequate and not consistent with the modern approaches to writing instruction considered in this chapter.

4. High school teachers are overloaded with work; reading student essays puts a heavy demand on already hectic programs.

5. Many teachers are not good writers themselves with respect to the genres of their discipline.

In short, there are many aspects of contemporary schooling and school life that make it difficult for classrooms to be communities of writing scholars rather than acquirers of information that is to be remembered and will be tested. Langer and Applebee's (1984) clear opinion is that if writing instruction is to improve, "The role of the teacher must shift, from an evaluator of what has already been learned to a collaborator who can help the student accomplish more complicated or sophisticated purposes" (p. 179). The teacher who scaffolds student writers who are trying to create their own meanings does this; the teacher who corrects grammar, punctuation, and correctness of content does not.

Reading-Writing Connections

That reading and writing instruction now occur together with increasing frequency in school would be more than enough reason to study potential reading and writing connections. Such analyses make sense theoretically as well, however, for example, with respect to consideration of common information processes in reading and writing. Information processing theorists, who believe that individual differences in fundamental processing are responsible for individual differences in many areas of functioning, could produce a great deal of support for their positions if they could identify meaningful relationships between reading and writing that reflect the operation of fundamental processes (e.g., monitoring, active use of strategies). Without a doubt, the most complete review and commentary on potential reading-writing connections was provided by Shanahan and Tierney (1990), both prominent literacy researchers. They have identified three approaches to the study of reading and writing connections.

1. *Reading and writing require common knowledge and share common processes.* According to this perspective, there should be correlations between writing and reading competence because of common components in the two tasks: They both require knowledge of vocabulary, syntax, and understanding of text organization alternatives. Competent reading and writing both require monitoring, predicting and idea generation, revising of thinking, and so on. Consistent with this hypothesis, there are, in fact, correlations in reading and writing ability, although these tend to be small-to-moderate in size (i.e., 0.30 to 0.40 with a maximum of 0.60). Because such a correlation could be due to the relationship of reading and writing to a third factor, such as general intelligence, the significance of these correlations is not entirely clear. Other evidence of common processes affecting reading and writing simultaneously has been produced in studies in which learning to read better has improved writing, *or* learning to write better has promoted reading. Unfortunately, however, Shanahan and Tierney (1990) estimate that such conjoint improvement has been obtained only in 30 percent of the studies in which researchers have looked for simultaneous improvement. Although armchair task analyses of reading and writing suggest that there are connections between reading and writing, such connections have not been easy to demonstrate, and promoting reading through writing instruction and promoting writing through reading instruction is much less certain than proponents of this position would like.

2. *Reading and writing both involve communications skills.* "Writers anticipate the needs of potential readers, and . . . readers use their thinking about authors to enhance their reading comprehension" (Shanahan & Tierney, 1990, pp. 18–19). Some of the most persuasive evidence that communication skills are an important reading-writing connection is that interventions designed to increase writers' awareness of audience needs do seem to improve the quality of writing (Black, 1989; Cohen & Riel, 1989; Greenlee, Hiebert, Bridge, & Winograd, 1986; Schriver, 1986). Another type of evidence supportive of links between literacy and communications comes from think-aloud data generated during reading. When readers experience difficulty understanding a text, they often report attempting to think about the author's intentions, perspectives, and meanings (e.g., Flower, 1987; Tierney, LaZansky,

Raphael, & Cohen, 1987). The communications hypothesis would be especially compelling if there were data establishing that learning to think about readers during writing improves reading or learning to think about authors during reading affects writing. No such data exist at this point.

3. *Reading and writing are used jointly to accomplish some tasks.* If students are asked to take notes, write answers to questions, or construct essays in response to reading, they sometimes learn more (e.g., Marshall, 1987; Newell, 1984; Newell, Suzynski, & Weingart, 1989), although the exact mechanisms mediating the learning gains are not well understood and may reflect only greater total reading time when written responses to text are required (Shanahan & Tierney, 1990). Such activity does not always lead to greater learning and may, in fact, reduce learning (e.g., if summary essay writing is required and memory for details in text is later tested). It seems that whether writing during reading aids learning probably depends on what the student must recall or do later—if memory of detail is critical, writing answers to detail questions or notetaking may help a little; if recall of the big ideas of the text is important or using the big ideas of a text to frame an argument is the task the student must do later, more integrative writing in reaction to text that is read helps more (see the earlier discussion of Langer & Applebee, 1987).

Some of the most interesting research on reading and writing together has been conducted at Carnegie-Mellon University, although work on coordination of reading and writing is also being conducted at other laboratories as well (e.g., McGinley, 1992; Nash, Schumacher, & Carlson, 1993). In this paradigm, students are given several texts about a topic to read with the assignment of constructing an integrative essay of some sort. Flower and colleagues (Flower et al.,1990) provided book-length coverage of their work on this problem with university freshmen. Although all of the students attempted to get the big ideas of the passages that were read, university students nonetheless differed in their reading strategies: (1) Some students did what Flower et al. (1990) referred to as gist and list. They simply listed out the big ideas in the text in

preparation for writing. (2) Others were more selective and evaluative, deciding whether the information being processed was true, important, or something they agreed with (i.e., they used the "True, Important, I Agree" strategy—TIA for short). This strategy has a lot of power, providing the reader-writer with ideas that are appealing and worth putting in an essay from the perspective of the reader-writer. The problem, of course, is that the student reader-writer's perspective can predominate rather than the messages that the writers of the text intended or emphasized. (3) The third strategy, the dialogue strategy, involved the student reader-writer comparing the texts being read (i.e., creating a dialogue between the authors of the texts), generating counterexamples to information in text (i.e., debating the ideas in the text), imagining occasions when the point made in the text might hold, and a fourth and extremely complicated form of dialogue: statements synthesizing ". . . two claims by qualifying both or at least putting them into relation with one another." These qualifications were sometimes insights and sometimes counterexamples.

Once the reading was done in Flower et al. (1990), it was time to write the essay. Students differed in how they planned their essays: (1) Some hardly planned at all, simply writing an essay that reflected the ideas they had come up with as they gisted and listed, TIAed, or dialogued during reading. (2) Others relied almost exclusively on the ideas generated during reading but were more planful in the sense of carefully classifying and organizing the content. The difficulty with both approaches (1) and (2), however, is that they really are simply what Scardamalia and Bereiter (e.g., 1986; Bereiter & Scardamalia, 1987, Chapter 1; see the discussion of knowledge telling by children presented earlier in this chapter) refer to as "knowledge telling" strategies. This is the strategy of an elementary-age student. When more is expected, as it is of university student writers, knowledge telling is not a good strategy. Unfortunately, it was the strategy of choice for the majority of the freshmen in Flower et al.'s (1990) study.

(3) A better approach, used by about 40 percent of the Flower et al. (1990) sample is to do **constructive planning.** Constructive planners ". . . spent time thinking about not only the content, as did everyone, but about the goals for the paper, about criteria for judging it, about problems in designing it, and/or al-

ternative ways to handle the task. They became reflective, strategic thinkers, looking at their writing as a rhetorical problem and a constructive act. . . . Constructive planning . . . often came as a response to a problem" (p. 240). Yes, the constructive planner uses the knowledge gained from the texts that were read, but the constructive planner tries to go beyond those texts, creating elaborations that permit a more creative essay. One of Flower et al.'s (1990) subjects provided the following protocol, which is representative of constructive planning:

> Unless I just restate a lot of this stuff, talk about the fact that, you know, it is important . . . but that's not what they want. They want me to assimilate this, come up with some conclusions, they [should] be related to something. . . .
>
> [He rereads his assignment and appears to conceive a new goal.]
>
> I guess I'm gonna have to deal with how, how to attack the problem of time management. It sounds good, write this down and attack problem. Yeah! Great! Things I can think of off hand, you got to put in there about. . . . [At this point he begins to review notes, to search the text and to rethink his response. . . . A few minutes later he returns to his plan.]
>
> I guess I can do a little bit more than restate what they have in the text. I can relate to my situation as a college student. It would be easier to relate to a college student! Well, wonderful. (p. 241)

Spivey and King (1989), in another study conducted at Carnegie-Mellon, examined how sixth-grade, eighth-grade, and tenth-grade students write from sources. The students were given three encyclopedia articles on the topic of "rodeo," with the assignment to write a report about rodeos. The most important finding in this study was that although there were some improvements in organization of writing and the resulting texts with increasing grade level, there was a much more striking effect for reading ability, with more able readers planning more and spending more total time writing, with the result better organized and more compelling texts. Writing from multiple sources—a typical student writing activity—is greatly affected by reading ability.

Summary The search for reading-writing process connections, including ones based on communication functions, is an active area of interest for researchers, including both applied researchers and

those interested in the most fundamental properties of mind (e.g., its monitoring capacities, strategic tendencies). In many ways, however, the most interesting and challenging reading-writing connection work may be the studies in which the articulation of reading and writing are studied. So many important tasks depend on both understanding and interpreting text and then conveying our reactions to texts to others.

That even Carnegie-Mellon students (i.e., freshmen at a highly selective university) are sometimes prone to uncreative reading-writing strategies, such as gist and list, and the majority engage in knowledge telling is depressing. Rose's (1989, Chapter 7) commentaries on his work at the tutorial center at UCLA illustrate that, if anything, however, the situation is worse at other major universities. Most of the students he worked with at UCLA had done well in beleaguered urban high schools:

> They were the kids who held class offices and saw their names on the honor role; they went out for sports and were involved in drama and music and a variety of civic and religious clubs. If they had trouble with mathematics or English or science, they could depend on the fairness of the system that rewarded effort and involvement: They participated in class discussions, got their work in on time, helped the teacher out, did extra-credit projects. In short, they were good academic citizens, and in some high schools—especially beleaguered ones—that was enough to assure them a B. (p. 172)

Despite success in their high schools, at UCLA, these students ended up in remedial courses or received poor grades in their freshman work. Their self-esteem suffers—they begin to think that they are stupid. They feel isolated in the university and alienated from it. What is offered currently to these students does little—the remedial skills programs consist of "dumping a bunch of strategies" on them, without scaffolded instruction (or sensitive instruction of any kind) about how to use the strategies. The inabilities of these students (e.g., not being able to identify the theme of a piece of unfamiliar poetry) are striking in the context of UCLA, where students are supposed to be able to identify the main themes in sophisticated writing produced by the likes of Bronowski and Szasz.

In short, much additional research is needed on how to increase the reading and writing competence of bright university students who come from backgrounds that do not prepare them for the literacy demands of university study. One reason to conduct such research is that many of these students are within reach—several years of high-quality enrichment might do much to make up for previous educational disadvantages. We conclude this section with commentary on a program of research and development that makes clear that it is possible to devise and disseminate on a large scale cognitive instruction for adolescents and youth that makes conceptual sense and can be validated.

Kansas Strategies Instruction Model

Deshler, Schumaker, and their colleagues at the University of Kansas (Deshler & Schumaker, 1988; Schumaker & Deshler, 1992) have devised reading (e.g., paraphrasing) and writing (e.g., paragraph writing) strategy interventions aimed at improving important academic competencies in high school students, with learning-disabled students the target population for their interventions. We cover the Kansas work here because it provides a model of how to devise, validate, and distribute cognitively based instruction that can promote the literacy of large numbers of secondary students, including their abilities to acquire, store, and communicate important information.

There are five phases in the Kansas curriculum development model, with these occurring roughly in the following order:

1. *Identification phase.* This involved determination of the demands placed on students in school. As part of this effort, the Kansas group spent time in high school settings determining what high school students are asked to do. This information was combined with knowledge of deficiencies of weaker students, such as their memorizing, organizing, reading, and writing problems as documented in the research literature and evident in schools studied by the Kansas group.
2. *Design phase.* Once a performance goal is targeted (e.g., to increase learning-disabled students' abilities to write paragraphs), the literature is searched for information about strategies that may have already been identified in meeting the need. Often, there have been. Once a strategy has been identified as profitable to teach, step-by-step instruction is devised, as are methods of measuring whether students are

learning the strategy. For example, when the goal was to teach students how to write paragraphs (see Schumaker & Lyerla, 1991), a strategy involving the writing of paragraphs that integrated topic sentences, detail sentences, and clincher sentences was devised. Explicit descriptions of the strategy were created, as were methods of modeling the strategy. Various types of scaffolded practice were designed into the instructional package (i.e., Kansas uses a direct explanation model of strategy instruction). There was clear understanding at the outset about the type of paragraph writing that was expected at the end of the instructional unit and specification about how students could be taught to generalize the paragraph strategy across their school day once they had learned to construct such paragraphs as part of controlled instruction.
3. *Pilot-test phase.* The intervention is tried out with a small number of students, with the researchers attempting to determine whether the instruction is sound, the measures reliable, and the strategy practical for students.
4. *Research phase.* One or several formal research studies are carried out. Typically the research is school-based with actual teachers teaching the strategy package. The strategy may be revised (or abandoned) in light of the data generated in the formal studies. See Schumaker and Deshler (1992) for a review of the research studies supporting their model.
5. *Refinement phase.* The goal is to make the intervention as useful as possible for a number of different settings. Feedback from teachers who have used the intervention is helpful during this phase. Once this phase is completed, the package is ready for widespread dissemination.

There are some exceptionally important features to the research approach used by the Kansas team: (1) The goals of the instruction are socially valid ones (i.e., the strategies meet demands students actually face). (2) Conventionally accepted research designs are used, often the multiple-baseline procedures developed as part of research on behavior modification (see Chapter 7). (3) The research and development are conducted in actual school settings. (4) Every effort is made to design instruction that teachers will accept and be enthused about, for without teacher acceptance, there will be no dissemination. (5) The criterion measures are ones tapping valuable outcomes; they are the indicators of school success and failure that are routinely collected in school. For example, the goal is not to produce statistically significant effects but effects that are significant in the lives of the students. Thus, improving grades a little bit can be statistically significant with enough subjects in the research study. That would not be enough. Going from *F*s to *B*s on school assignments (e.g., ones involving writing of paragraphs) is the type of shift that the Kansas researchers attempt to produce (and often do produce).

Kansas instruction is not a quick fix, with a new strategy learned over a period of several months. Years of participation is required for students to acquire a repertoire of strategies providing diverse means of acquiring, retaining, and writing about academic content. The instruction is developed by teachers who have received intensive instruction about how to use direct explanations, modeling, and guided practice during the initial acquisition of strategies and as part of teaching for generalization. Teacher training is offered by a national network of trainers, with teachers often participating in such instruction for several years. Because of the concern with learning-disabled secondary students, most of the instruction has been provided by special education teachers. What is exceptionally exciting, however, are successful efforts to teach strategies to junior college and university students as well as minority students (Bulgren, McKnight, Deshler, & Schumaker, 1989; Denton, Seybert, & Franklin, 1988; Moccia, McKnight, Deshler, & Schumaker, 1990; see Schumaker & Deshler, 1992, for a review). Basketball fans might want to note that Deshler and Schumaker do their bit for the Kansas basketball program, which is a perennial contender for national ranking. They teach members of the team how to apply learning strategies in their university courses, providing a valuable source of assistance to student athletes who are often at academic risk but who always need to get the most out of the study time that is available to them during the season (Hock, Deshler, & Schumaker, 1991).

Despite the effort required by teachers to learn the Kansas model and the amount of time required by students to acquire a repertoire of strategies, such instruction is extremely well received by teachers, administrators, parents, and students, with the learning and performance gains that result from the program worth the investment in instructional re-

sources and student efforts. Although reservations about some of the particular validation studies are sometimes expressed, no one could examine the entire body of evidence generated by Deshler, Schumaker, and their colleagues and not conclude that they have devised important instructional programming that is effective. The completeness of their approach is unprecedented in the history of the design, validation, and implementation of curricula based on scientific analyses. The list of strengths is longer than the list of strengths for any other intervention discussed in this book. Their work is distinguished by (1) careful assessment of students' needs; (2) well-informed design of strategies based on extensive knowledge of the cognitive, behavioral, special education, and educational psychology literatures; (3) validations in actual school settings; (4) attention to acceptability issues; (5) design of instructional methods that work to ensure acquisition and increase the likelihood of transfer; (6) design of effective teacher education; and (7) distribution and administration of teacher training across the United States and Canada. As far as the research-based curriculum development community is concerned, the Kansas group is the best of us. The rest of us can learn much from them. Students contemplating careers as curriculum designers should study the Kansas work carefully for guidance about how to devise instruction that works and will be used by the educator community.

For the most part, the need for better reading and writing instruction for adolescents and young adults is great. What the Kansas group teaches us is that it is possible to do research and development that is scientifically credible and has an impact on instruction in the United States. It is particularly important that Deshler, Schumaker, and their colleagues are now working with young adults, for no one has done for young adults what the Kansas researchers have done for adolescents: No one has conducted complete analyses of adult literacy needs, which stimulate development of instruction that transforms the lives of low literate and illiterate adults.

CONSTRUCTIVIST NATURE OF LITERACY STRATEGIES INSTRUCTION

A criticism of strategy instruction that has been made by some (e.g., Poplin, 1988a, 1988b) is that it is reductionist, stimulating students to copy the processing of others rather than constructing their own approaches to important cognitive tasks, such as reading and writing. We do not concur with these evaluations because the evidence is overwhelming that strategy instruction done well is student sensitive, stimulating students to experiment with strategies and to construct their own personalized versions of efficient information processing, with adaptation of strategies continually occurring as they are used flexibly in coordination with diverse knowledge to accomplish diverse goals in diverse situations (Harris & Pressley, 1991; Pressley, Harris, & Marks, 1992; for other versions of the perspective that what is taught by the teacher is a beginning point for student construction of knowledge, see Elbers, 1991; Iran-Nejad, 1990; Wittrock, 1992).

None of the strategy instructors considered in Chapters 14 and 15 expect students to carry out mechanically the strategies that are explained and modeled by the teacher. One of the reasons that teaching and practice extends over a long period of time is so that students can explore how the strategies can be flexibly adapted to different tasks, so they can observe how their execution of the strategies is both similar to and different from the strategic efforts of classmates. Moreover, teacher modeling of strategies is certainly not algorithmic. In fact, often it happens on the run, when an academic task calls for it. Such opportunities to model rarely afford "canned" responses but rather require creative application, modification, and combination of strategies.

If the explanations of strategies do not make clear the personalized nature of such processing, the reexplanations offered in light of student difficulties certainly should. Reexplanations and additional modeling invariably require the teacher to model "gerry-rigging" of strategies. These reexplanations are dialogic, with the student and teacher working together to figure out how to apply strategies to a situation that poses difficulty for the student. The teacher is not content until he or she believes the student understands what they are doing; that is, the reexplanations are aimed at helping students "figure out" the situation rather than simply directing them about how to make correct responses.

Strategies are not forced on students. Rather the students are taught procedures that permit them greater success with less effort. Students come to value the strategies because they recognize that strategies are intellectually empowering. Good strategy instruction sends the message that students can control how they do academically, with much gained by creatively applying the cognitive strategies that are taught to them. Good strategy instruction encourages student reflection, permitting powerful tools for reflective meaning-getting from texts, creation of reflective stances via writing, and reflective decision making about whether and how to use strategies they know to tackle new situations.

A variety of characteristics of and constraints on human communication abilities make it inevitable that students will construct their understanding of strategies from strategy instruction:

- Teachers' understandings of strategies differ, so their explanations will differ. In addition, any one teacher's approach to a particular strategy will vary from situation to situation.
- In making a good faith attempt to explain a strategy, even experienced, exceptionally competent strategy teachers do not cover a strategy completely or provide exhaustive information about where or when to use the strategy or completely cover all of the benefits of deploying the strategy. Thus, there is always plenty left for the student to figure out. If the teacher's presentation is so deficient that students cannot even begin to understand and apply the strategy, the teacher will be cued by students to provide more input (e.g., reactions such as "huh?" or looks of puzzlement).
- When students ask questions of teachers about the strategies they are attempting to learn, there are always a variety of responses. The teacher who is scaffolding instruction provides enough of a response that students can then begin to make progress on their own in applying and understanding strategies.

Pressley, Harris, and Marks (1992) summarized the inevitability of student construction of knowledge during strategies instruction as follows:

> Teacher-student interactions during strategy instruction are not tightly scripted in advance, but rather worked out as instruction proceeds. The good strategy teacher tries to provide instruction about strategies that is clear and can be grasped by students. No matter how well the teacher expresses her or his knowledge of a strategy, the student's understanding of the procedure will differ somewhat from the teacher's conception. The teacher and student will have exchanges throughout the instructional process,

with the nature and content of these exchanges determined largely by the student's progress in coming to understand the strategy and how to execute it, as well as the teacher's perceptions of the student's progress. Exactly what is taught and learned during strategy-instructional sequences is a function of many reactions and adjustments during teacher-student exchanges, adjustments that often represent best guesses by the teacher and student about what the other one means or understands. . . . what a student experiences during good strategy instruction and what he or she takes away from the experience varies enormously from student to student and from class to class. Strategies are not rigidly formulated, exacting cognitive rules; rather, they entail personal interpretation. . . . (pp. 15–16)

What we emphasize most here, however, is that when the teaching procedures of those who profess to be constructivist teachers (e.g., Ferreiro, 1985; Petitto, 1985; Pontecorvo & Zuccchermaglio, 1990) are analyzed and compared with good strategy instruction, there are remarkable similarities:

- Students interact with teachers attempting to construct understandings for the student, with both agreements and disagreements during these interactions, with the interactions going smoothly sometimes and not so smoothly on other occasions.
- There is group instruction, with peers providing input and feedback to one another.
- Teachers continuously monitor the student's understanding of what is being taught, with additional instruction provided on a personalized, as-needed basis. The better the student's progress, the fewer reexplanations and less remodeling of strategies.
- Dialogues between students and teachers are not scripted.
- Teachers continuously encourage students to apply what they are learning to new situations.
- Individual differences in students' rates of progress are permitted.
- It is clear that teacher explanations and modeling of strategies are intended to be transformed by students; students know that they are not just to mimic the teacher's actions but rather use the teacher's actions as a starting point for the construction of personalized actions.
- There is great emphasis on learning through understanding. Understanding is the most valued educational outcome.

There is, of course, a difference between instruction provided by professed constructivists and good strategy instructors. Good strategy instructors are much more explicit in their explanations. Even though they expect that students will interpret and adapt the procedures that are explained and demonstrated, the good strategy teachers do offer explicit explanations and demonstrations. Our view is that how learning begins is not what is critical. What counts is that students come to understand the procedures they are learning, coming to know the procedures in ways that permit them to use the procedures flexibly to accomplish goals that are important to students. Our view, consistent with many perspectives on mind (e.g., Piaget, 1970; White, 1959) is that humans inevitably construct understandings from input that is presented to them, that they are highly motivated to do so. The extent to which they are successful in coming to sophisticated understandings depends on the input with which they work, however, with exceptional understanding more likely with high-quality instruction that stimulates student construction.

As Resnick (1987) concluded, good instruction provides ". . . the 'material' upon which constructive mental processes work" (p. 47). Good strategy instructors provide the best explanations they can and then encourage their students to take it from there, providing additional assistance as they can as students work it out. Our view, along with others (e.g., Graham & Perry, 1993), is that it is exceptionally important to understand more about students' knowledge when they are first beginning to learn something—how the beginnings of understanding motivate students to work on constructing additional understanding. (See Moshman, 1982, for an exceptionally lucid discussion of the range of instruction that is constructivist, from discovery approaches to explicit instruction models that lead students to construct their own understandings.)

We provide this input about the constructivist nature of strategy instruction at this point in the book because we believe that enough information about strategy instruction has been presented by now to permit understanding of our perspective on the constructivist nature of strategy instruction. From this point on, additional allusions will be made to the constructivist perspective. One of the most irritating characteristics of constructivist educators is that the constructivist nature of the instruction they provide is emphasized repeatedly, overshadowing many other properties of effective instruction. Although we are constructivists, our recognition that many other factors play an important role in intellectual advancement compels us not to provide obsessive discussions of the constructivist nature of the instruction considered in this book. Still, much of it is constructivist, and readers should keep that in mind as they consider what follows and reconsider material covered earlier.

CONCLUDING COMMENTS

Meaning construction is the emphasis in contemporary writing instruction. How to teach writing so that writers can communicate ideas that are important to them is the overarching question in writing instructional research. Understanding how good writers write has done much to stimulate the development of such instruction. Just as good reading is an instance of good problem solving, good writing is good problem solving. Just as with reading, writing can be understood in terms of strategies, metacognition, knowledge, motivation, capacity, and constructive social interactions. Just as with effective reading instruction, effective writing instruction is long term, lasting years. Just as direct explanation followed by scaffolding was a sound approach to reading instruction, it is also a sound approach to writing instruction.

The historical tendency to treat reading and writing separately is yielding to the study of reading and writing connections and instruction designed to foster reading and writing connections. Just as literacy is both reading and writing, we expect that much of the future research on literacy will capture reading and writing simultaneously.

In closing, we emphasize that the high-quality literacy instruction featured in this chapter and Chapter 14 are aimed at teaching strategies well matched to the demands of literacy tasks: for example, comprehension strategies that enhance understanding and memory of text; also, writing strategies that increase the likelihood that compositions will be comprehensible. The high-quality strategy instruction featured in these chapters is intensive and long term, permitting many opportunities for students to learn when and where to use the strategies they are learning and permitting many opportunities for students to practice adapting strategies to new situations. High-quality literacy instruction is designed to make reading and writing enjoyable experiences for students, experiences that make sense to students. The goal is not to get the "right" interpretation from text but to process and build one's own meaning; the goal is not to produce an essay that is just "good English" but rather an essay that says something important, with mechanics considered after the meaning is established. High-quality literacy instruction undoubtedly builds other knowledge as well. Students are reading excellent texts with important messages, messages that are more likely to be understood and reflected on because of the strategy instruction. When students write, they are often writing about important content; information used to create new texts is going to be thought about in a "deep" fashion, increasing the likelihood that the student writer will make connections to prior knowledge. Good literacy instruction enhances the good information processing that is the focus of this book, increasing knowledge of strategies, metacognitive understandings, other knowledge, and important motivational beliefs about what counts in school and in literacy. Such instruction deserves the research attention of the next generation of educational researchers, such as some of the readers of this book, for this already rich instruction has much potential for extension as it continues to be translated into educational practice.

Part

5

Assessment and Individual Differences

16

Traditional Assessments and Conceptualizations of Intelligence and Academic Competence

Testing has always been an important part of educational psychology. For example, some of the earliest volumes of the Journal of Educational Psychology published in the first two decades of the 20th century included articles that detailed analyses of early IQ tests, a form of assessment destined to change the way both psychologists and laypeople think about mental ability. This chapter reviews several important standardized tests and the technical requirements such tests must meet. We then develop understandings of mind and mental ability that have been permitted by IQ testing, including dynamics of development revealed through analyses of psychometric intelligence data. Even so, there is a dark side to standardized testing: the possibility of test bias. How psychologists think about test bias and attempt to eliminate it are covered in more detail than in most educational psychology texts because standardized testing is so common in our society, and thus issues of bias must be understood if educators are to make intelligent decisions based on testing data.

Much of this book is about individual differences and how differences affect competency: People perform differently on memory and comprehension tasks depending on the strategies they know and use; differences in metacognition predict differences in strategy use; knowledge differences between experts and novices influence problem solving; and differences in motivational beliefs affect the willingness to attempt academic tasks. Our view is that future study of individual differences will be attuned to the types of differences highlighted in this book. Traditionally, however, the term "individual differences" in psychology has been used most often to refer to differences in competencies tapped by psychometric instruments, such as traditional intelligence tests.

Issues of assessment and individual differences are often seen as dull and far removed from education by many students in educational psychology courses. One of the best ways to dispel these impressions is to cover an educational assessment students know well because they have experienced it, one that has made a difference in their lives. The two tests covered in the next section are important assessments faced (or in the case of the Graduate Record Examination, will be faced) by readers of this book.

HIGHER EDUCATION ADMISSIONS TESTS

Admissions to college or graduate school invariably involves standardized testing. Students, however, often do not understand well the entrance examinations they are asked to take. (Perhaps even more distressing is that many people involved in the admissions decision process do not either.) Most students new to educational psychology find the information that follows to be enlightening.

Scholastic Aptitude Test

Many readers of this book will have taken the Scholastic Aptitude Test (SAT). (Others will have taken the American College Test [ACT], which in many ways in similar in design to the SAT.) The SAT is usually taken in the junior year of high school or early in the senior year. There are typically five sections on the test, divided between math and verbal sections. The math section includes traditional high school mathematics problems. The verbal section taps knowledge of vocabulary (e.g., identifying a response opposite in meaning to a given vocabulary item; verbal analogies) and comprehension (i.e., reading passages and answering questions about the meaning of texts). Both the verbal and math scores can range from 200 to 800. An excellent review of the SAT, its history, and the controversies surrounding it was provided by Hanford (1991), a former President of the College Entrance Examination Board, which administers the SAT. Much of what follows about the SAT is covered in Hanford's autobiography, which we recommend for students who wish an insider's understanding of academic admissions tests.

In the late 19th century, only some colleges had admissions tests. Each college created its own test. The problem this created for secondary schools was enormous as they attempted to prepare their students for admissions to many different colleges with different expectations and admissions criteria. In 1900, a group of U.S. East coast colleges attempted to solve the problem by establishing the College Entrance Examination Board at Columbia University. At first, the College Board administered essay examinations, tapping a prescribed high school curriculum. Thus, two benefits of the early tests were that students could apply to more than one school without taking multiple admissions tests and what would be tested became more predictable.

The test evolved throughout the 20th century. During World War I, the U.S. Army conducted research on an intelligence test (the Army Alpha Test), which involved multiple-choice questions. Brigham of Princeton University applied this new multiple-choice approach to the SAT. At about the same time, there was a movement away from a curriculum-based assessment to testing of general verbal and math abilities that might be expected to develop given a variety of high school curricula. Multiple-choice SAT testing of general math and verbal abilities was in place by the mid-1920s—that is, the SAT began to resemble the test administered today.

In those days, the administrators of the test could have reverted back to essay examinations if the multiple-choice format had proven unsatisfactory, for only a select group of students attempted to enter college. As the century progressed, more students would aspire to college, so that more than 2 million students take the SAT annually. Hanford estimated that if essay examinations were administered today, the SAT would have to rent out Madison Square Garden to seat all the readers employed to correct it. A computer-scored, objective test is the only option when so many students are tested at once. Thus, a third advantage of the SAT is that it can be administered economically to many students, with quick reporting results (usually 1 to 2 months after the testing date).

A fourth advantage is that until 1994, a current SAT score meant the same as a SAT score from the 1950s, 1960s, 1970s, and 1980s. The meaning of a SAT score remained constant from 1941 to 1994. First, the higher a score is on the 200 to 800 scale, the better the score was. Second, a score of 500 meant the student was exactly in the middle of the range of 1941 performances. A 600 placed the student at about the 84th percentile of the 1941 distribution of performances. A 700 score meant that 98 percent of the 1941 sample performed more poorly than the 1990s student in question. That is, SAT scores were figured for the past 50 years with respect to how a student performed relative to the 1941 sample. Because of declines in overall performance on the SAT, however, a 500 score in the 1990s was well above the average for students taking the test in the 1990s. We emphasize this latter point because of many high school counselors we have encountered who believed that 500 was the mean score on the SAT and thus sent a signal to 500-scoring students that they had average SAT scores. In 1991, the mean verbal SAT score was 422 and the mean math score was 474 (*Chronicle of Higher Education*, 26 August 1991, p. 9). A 500 score on either the verbal or math scale was above average relative to the scores of the 1941 students.

All of this changed in 1994 with the test rescaled so that 500 is now the mean for scores produced when the test is administered. In addition, new types of items were added to the test in 1994 and some new formats (e.g., calculators can now be used). The SAT is changing.

A fifth advantage of the SAT is that the test has excellent psychometric properties. First, the test is **reliable.** What that means is that if a student takes one form of the test today and a second form of it tomorrow, there is a good chance that the scores for the two sittings will be within 30 points of one another (actually about a two in three chance). Indeed, SAT scores are often thought of and expressed as ranges, so that a score of 470 means that there is a good chance (two in three) that the student's **true score** is in the 440 to 500 range.

In addition, the SAT is a **valid** predictor of academic performance in college. In fact, it predicts about as well as high school grades. When high school grades and SAT scores are used together in statistical formulas for predicting grades, prediction is better than when either is used alone—that is, even when high school grades are already taken into account, the SAT improves the prediction of college grades. Many colleges have conducted studies of how well high school grades and SAT scores predict success at their institutions, with the consensual conclusion that the SAT is useful in deciding who might do well at a given college and who is likely to do poorly. To be certain, such predictions are not perfect. For example, collapsing across 685 colleges, the combined verbal and math SAT score correlates 0.42 with freshmen grades, which is roughly comparable to the 0.48 correlation between high school grades and freshman grades. When SATs and high school grades are combined, they predict freshman grades with a correlation of 0.55 (Anastasi, 1988, Chapter 11). Although not perfect, admissions tests and high school grades are the best predictors available.

One exceptionally interesting strength of the test is how well it predicts exceptionally talented people. If the test is given to grade-7 and grade-8 students, those scoring in the top one-fourth of 1 percent of the population taking the math test (i.e., the absolute top scorers on the test) do much better in high school, college, and graduate school than those who are in the top 1 percent of test takers but not in the top one-fourth of 1 percent of the distribution (Benbow, 1992).

With so many advantages, what is the down side of the SAT? First, there has been an overall decline in performance, with some believing the decline reflects the increasing irrelevancy of the SAT. There are more than 80 possible alternative explanations for the decline, however, with two of the most likely of these being the following: The College Board believes much of the decline is due to a broadening of the range of people taking the test, a conclusion based on careful study of the populations of students taking the test between 1963 and 1977 (Donlon, 1984; Turnbull, 1985; Wirtz, 1977). The decline also may reflect a shift in the courses students take in high school. That is why new types of items are now being devised for the SAT—for example, being able to use a calculator is an essential 1990s competency, so the test now permits calculator use.

A second negative for the SAT is that some groups do better on the test than do other groups. Whites do better than minorities; men do better than women. For example, whites enjoyed at least a 50-point advantage on both verbal and math SATs in 1991 over American Indians, blacks, Mexican-Americans, Puerto Ricans, and Hispanics (*Chronicle of Higher Education,* 26 August 1992, p. 9). One possibility is that this reflects bias in the test. The College Board points out in its defense that the SAT is a good predictor of college success for all groups, however (see Reynolds & Kaiser, 1990a, 1990b, for a brief review of the relevant issues and literature). That is, when only blacks are considered, those blacks who score better on the SAT are more likely to do well in college than blacks who score poorly. That is, the test is a valid predictor of college success for blacks just as it is a valid predictor of college success for whites. The College Board also discourages the use of its test data in ways that are blatantly discriminatory—for example, it opposed a New York State Regents plan that provided scholarships based on SAT scores because such a policy would discriminate against women and minorities.

A third negative perceived by some is that the test does not provide enough of a boost in predictability over high school test scores to justify its expense. Countering this claim are arguments that standardized tests are great equalizers. Every college "knows" certain high schools better than others because of proximity or a long history of alumni from the high school proceeding to the college. It is easy to prove biases toward particular high schools and toward particular groups of people by some colleges. The SAT is the one hurdle faced by all applicants, giving the student from a backwoods or distant high school a chance to distinguish himself or herself (see Jensen, 1981, Chapter 1). In addition, the SAT is used by some national scholarship agencies to identify talented youth. Many such youth would be overlooked in other types of talent searches.

Even though the SAT is a psychometrically sophisticated instrument (i.e., it is reliable and valid), it is subject to many of the same criticisms as other tests, most notably bias against particular groups of people. That it is predictive of college outcomes for all groups is what saves it. One interesting direction in higher-education research is to determine whether the strategy-use perspective detailed in this book is more predictive of college success than tests such as the SAT. For example, Britton and Tesser (1991) examined whether reported use of study time management strategies (i.e., responses to a questionnaire tapping whether students plan their study time, make good use of available study time, and make long-range plans to complete papers and prepare for examinations) predicted overall success in college as reflected by grade-point averages. Consistent with the perspective in this book that strategies are an important determinant of academic success, strategic study time management accounted for four times as much variance in predicting college success as did the SAT. Although the SAT is a benchmark, it is a benchmark that may be surpassed in predictive validity as more sophisticated measures of strategic engagement in college are developed.

We cannot leave our discussion of the SAT without commenting on a frequent question posed to us: whether it is possible to improve SAT scores through specific educational experiences, such as taking widely advertised test-preparation courses. Short-term courses produce only small effects (Becker, 1990). Courses that involve long-term participation have greater effects, with the best preparation for SAT tests being a demanding curriculum throughout the high school years (Messick & Jungeblut, 1981).

Graduate Record Examination

The General section of the Graduate Record Examination (GRE) includes math and verbal sections (see Anastasi, 1988, Chapter 11). Although more advanced than the corresponding SAT sections, there is a great similarity between the GRE and SAT, including with respect to scoring. In addition to the General sections, there are Subject Tests for many areas of university study (e.g., psychology, history, mathematics, education).

The GRE is scored with reference to a 1952 sample of seniors at 11 colleges. Thus, a score of 500 means that the test taker would have been in the middle of the 1952 sample. The test is reliable with

0.90 correlations between scores obtained at different administrations of the test. In general, GRE scores are slightly better predictors of graduate school performance than is undergraduate grade point average, although best prediction of graduate school performance is obtained by statistically combining GRE scores and undergraduate grades. Those readers of this book enrolled in graduate study in psychology might be interested that the correlation between the GRE Psychology Subject Test and the likelihood of completing a Ph.D. in psychology is 0.34. That is, there is a modest but positive relationship between the Subject Test score and making it through graduate school (Anastasi, 1988). What is amazing about the SAT and GRE tests is that 3-hour assessments predict future educational achievement almost as well as the years of grades summarized on high school and undergraduate transcripts.

Do not fear if all of the ideas covered in this section are not yet clear. The most important concepts introduced here will be expanded on in the next section, with the SAT and GRE examples referred to in the next section to provide readers with somewhat familiar examples.

PSYCHOMETRIC QUALITIES OF TESTS

A first requirement of a test is that it be **reliable;** without reliability, it cannot possibly be **valid.** Reliability and validity are concepts that must be understood by all students of educational psychology. Only tests that are reliable and valid for the purpose of the tester should be administered. The SAT has survived so long and is used so widely largely because it is extremely reliable, and it validly measures what admissions committees are interested in determining—the likelihood of academic success in college (i.e., it is valid). What follows is a distillation of the most important ideas regarding reliability and validity found in most leading psychometric textbooks (e.g., Anastasi, 1988; Cronbach, 1990; Jensen, 1980; Nunnally, 1978; Sattler, 1992). For those students desiring more information, an outstanding low-cost publication that provide definitive professional-level information about test construction is the *Standards for Educational and Psychological Testing* (American Psychological Association, 1985). An interesting historical perspective on test validity is provided by Geisenger (1992b).

Reliability

To understand reliability, it is essential to understand that any **observed score** on a test can be decomposed into two scores, the **true score** and **error.** The following equation summarizes this relationship: **observed score = true score + error**

Error represents the part of the score that is due to irrelevant and chance factors. If the same test could be administered to a person many times with each testing independent of the other (i.e., under the impossible constraint that taking a test on one occasion would not affect test performance on a second occasion), the errors would cancel each other out over the many test administrations so that the mean score over all testings would reflect the subject's true score for the test. The error for any single administration would be the difference between the score on the single administration and the overall mean score collapsing across administrations.

A reliable test has relatively low error, so that from one administration of the test to another, a person will score about the same. One method of determining a test's reliability is simply to administer the same test twice, with the correlation in the scores between the two testings defined as reliability using this **test-retest** method. Another type of reliability, **alternate-forms reliability,** can be assessed when there are multiple forms of a test, such as with the SAT and GRE examinations. People are assessed with two forms of the measurement. The correlation between performances on one form of the test and the other form is the reliability for the test. Estimates of the reliability of a test are even possible if only one form of a test is available, a form that is administered only once. An historically prominent approach was to calculate the **split-half reliability.** test was literally split in half using this method, for example, constructing scores based on the odd items and the even items on the test. The correlation between the half-test scores was the estimate of reliability. The problem with this approach is that the estimate of reliability will vary depending on how the items are split, so that in most cases the correlation between odd-even halves would differ from a correlation based on halves produced by randomly assigning items to half-test scores. Cronbach (1951) proposed a solution to this dilemma: **coefficient alpha,** which is the mean of all possible split-half reliabilities. A variation of the procedure, the **Kuder-Richardson 20 formula** (Kuder & Richardson, 1937), can be used if all items on the test can be scored as either right or wrong. Although the formulas for these methods are presented in all psychometrics texts, in practice, most people generate them using computer programs, with these reliability indices available on most commercially produced advanced statistics packages.

Although exact guidance on acceptable reliabilities is difficult to provide, in general, reliabilities above 0.70 are viewed as adequate for many purposes. How can such reliability be attained?

- The more items on a test, the greater its reliability. Hence, if an initial version of a test is unreliable, increase the number of items.
- Avoid ceiling and floor effects. If the test is so easy that many people get everything right or so hard that few people get anything right, the reliability of the test will be low. In general, a good test produces a range of performance, with few people (if any) scoring zero (i.e., on the floor of the scale) or achieving a perfect score (i.e., at the ceiling of the scale).
- The more objective the scoring of the test items, the greater the reliability.
- The wider the range of abilities taking the test, the greater the reliability.
- If the test is taken by people with similar backgrounds (other things being equal), reliability will be higher than if the test is given to people with diverse backgrounds.
- Straightforward, clearly worded questions increase the reliability of a test.
- Good directions increase the reliability of a test.
- Reliability is increased if the people taking the test are well rested, calm, well, and are taking the test seriously.

Validity

The reliability of a measurement is not enough, however. The measurement must also be valid for its purpose. Thus, although we can measure the circumferences of children's heads with high reliability, head circumference is not a valid measure of intelligence (see Gould, 1981), with even proponents of such measurement able to produce only low correlations between head girth and intelligence (e.g., Rushton, 1992).

Does this assessment measure what it is supposed to measure? That is the main validity question. More exacting validity questions are posed,

however, depending somewhat on the nature of the characteristic being assessed. The various ways that validity can be construed are considered briefly in the three subsections that follow. For readers who wish an expansive discussion of contemporary perspectives on test validity, see Shephard (1993).

Content Validity   Does this test cover the content it is supposed to cover? Suppose I want to devise a test of high school mathematics achievement. What should my test include? A content valid assessment would include items from general mathematics, algebra, geometry, trigonometry, and calculus. Depending on the test's purpose, the proportions of such items might vary. Thus, if the desire was to do a good job of discriminating whether students had obtained the most basic numerical competencies required of citizens, the test might consist entirely of general math items. If the test is to decide who should be selected as a finalist for scholarship consideration in mathematics, there would be a much greater proportion of calculus and trigonometry items than general math items; challenging algebra and geometry problems might also be included on such a test.

When devising an educational achievement test, content validity is often a paramount concern. Thus, when test developers are devising a subject area test to assess knowledge in some undergraduate major area (e.g., GRE in psychology), they first plan carefully about what should be covered and in what proportions. Thus, the test developers might lay out all of the subfields of psychology that they wish to cover, such as experimental, social, clinical, physiological, statistics, educational, and so on. Then, they decide the proportions of items for each subfield, using some conception about which areas deserve emphasis relative to others (e.g., areas that would be covered by all psychology majors would receive more emphasis than completely elective areas). Within a subfield (e.g., educational psychology), additional decisions are made about what topics to cover (e.g., theories about learning, assessment and individual differences, motivation), with the proportions of items for each of these topics decided based on the centrality of the topic to the subdiscipline (e.g., for educational psychology, many more items about cognitive theories than motivation).

If a test developer is planful, there is no excuse for not achieving content validity. All that is required is laying out what topics should be covered by a test and in what proportions.

Criterion Validity Does this test make the discriminations it is supposed to make? For example, does the SAT discriminate between students who will be successful in college and those who will not be successful? It does (as discussed earlier in this chapter): There is a positive correlation between SAT performance and grades in college. When the criterion is prediction into the future, as it is when the SAT is used to predict college grades, the criterion-related validity is referred to as **predictive validity.** When both a measure and its criterion can be collected close in time, criterion-related validity is sometimes referred to as **concurrent validity.**

Construct Validity Does this test measure the construct it is intended to measure? To understand this question, it is first necessary to define a construct. Many psychological variables are abstract rather than concrete (Nunnally, 1978). "Ability" cannot be observed directly, nor can "intelligence." **Constructs** must be inferred from behavioral observations. Thus, "mathematical ability" is inferred from consistent, exceptional mathematics performance. "Anxious personality" is inferred from many instances of anxiety in situations that do not provoke anxiety in others. Intelligence is inferred from performances on intelligence test items.

If a test developer is attempting to create a new test for a construct measured by existing instruments—for example, attempting to create a short intelligence test that can be given in groups and thus one that can be administered much less expensively than psychometrist-administered, individual tests of intelligence—construct validation requires demonstrating that the new test correlates with the accepted tests assessing the construct. Again, because the maximum values for such correlations are constrained by the reliabilities of the measurements correlated, it is essential that the new measure be reliable (presumably, the old, accepted measure is reliable, or it would not have attained the status of a standard).

In addition to creating new tests to measure familiar constructs, psychologists are forever attempting to validate new constructs. Campbell and Fiske (1959), in a classic paper, provided exceptionally clear guidance as to how to do this. First, establishing the reliability of the measures of the new construct is essential. Second, it is necessary to demonstrate that the new construct is not identical to another construct. That is, that it does *not* correlate with other familiar constructs. (If there is a high correlation, it is hard to make the case that a unique new construct is being tapped by the new measure.)

For example, one set of test developers wanted to make the case that they were measuring "psycholinguistic ability." The claim has not been widely accepted because their measure correlates highly with psychometric intelligence, suggesting that their test is really tapping IQ rather than some unique psycholinguistic ability (see Sattler, 1992, pp. 345–347). Because many intellectual tests do correlate with IQ, demonstrating a low correlation with IQ is a standard for some in establishing the **discriminant validity** of a measurement claiming to tap a new cognitive construct (e.g., Mischel, 1968).

Rigid insistence on such a standard would not be reasonable, however, in many cases, such as when the unique construct might be expected to affect intelligence test performance. Thus, reading disability is likely to affect performance on IQ tests that are filled with verbal competence items so that years of reading disability should depress IQ. Another possibility is that the unique competence depends on intelligence so that creativity may only be possible given at least moderate intelligence (see Haensley & Torrance, 1990).

In the best of all possible psychometric worlds, Campbell and Fiske also specify a third criterion that is met for establishing the validity of a construct: More than one measure of the construct is created, with the two measures correlating highly (and, of course, neither of the two measures correlates with other, familiar constructs). When two or more measures of a construct correlate highly with one another, there is said to be **convergent validity** for the construct. Thus, a construct such as attention deficit/hyperactivity is convergently validated because various measures of attention deficit and hyperactivity correlate with one another (i.e., performances on maze, attention, and frustration measures correlate with classroom observational scales indicative of poor attention and hyperactivity). At the same time, there is no pattern of performance on standardized IQ tests that is a sure tipoff of hyperactivity, providing some discriminant validation for the hyperactivity/attention deficit construct (see Sattler, 1992, Chapter 20).

Summary and Concluding Comments Good tests are well-validated ones, although there is flexibility in making claims of validity, something implied in this section emphasizing the various ways validity is construed. Familiar tests that have survived the test of time almost always have been validated in many different ways. Unfortunately, there are many other tests on the market with questionable validations at best. Before adopting a test for a particular purpose, educators have an obligation to their students to obtain validation information about an instrument. This information is often supplied by publishers of reputable tests. If it is not, an invaluable source of information is the *Buros Mental Measurements Yearbook* which publishes reviews specifying the psychometric characteristics of many tests.

INTELLIGENCE ASSESSMENT

Psychometricians are exceptionally aware of their history, how contemporary psychometric theory and practice have been influenced by well over a century of theoretical and test-development work. The history is a rich one, although charged with controversy from its beginning. An exceptionally interesting history of the *mismeasurement* of intelligence was provided by anthropologist Stephen Jay Gould (1981). Block and Dworkin (1976) provided a documentary history of the checkered history of mental tests and their interpretation. Excellent shorter histories are provided by Brody (1992, Chapter 1); Kaufman (1990, Chapter 1); Plomin, DeFries, and McClearn (1990); and Sattler (1992, Chapter 3 and frontleaf), all of which informed the short history that follows.

The origins of psychometric intelligence theory often are traced back to Galton's (1869) *Hereditary Genius: An Inquiry into Its Laws and Consequences*. He made the important observation that bright people often had bright offspring. Using rudimentary ideas about the normal curve, Galton argued that blood relationships between geniuses were much closer than would be expected by chance. To support his case, he analyzed the lives of eminent individuals of the day from a variety of walks of life, discovering for example that the 1000 most eminent men he could identify came from only 300 families. This statistic is striking given the 1 in 4000 chance of attaining eminence in Galton's analyses. Within these families, Galton was also able to show that eminence was more likely in close relatives than in distant relatives. For example, eminent men often had eminent fathers, with about a one in four probability. They were less likely (1 in 12 probability) to have eminent grandfathers. Galton

concluded from these probabilities that genius was inherited.

Although Galton's strong claims about the heritability of genius did not hold up, Galton's contributions to the scientific analysis of intelligence were enormous. For example, he devised a rudimentary individual differences test based on reaction time, strength, eyesight, and motor abilities. He also devised rudimentary correlation coefficients as well as medians and percentiles to analyze the data he collected. Galton performed the first twin studies in an attempt to separate the contributions of heredity and environment in determination of individual differences. Although Galton did not develop an instrument resembling contemporary intelligence tests, others provided more refined approaches to statistical analyses, and Galton's twin studies were merely precursors of what studies of twins would be, Galton's thinking was a source of stimulation for both European and American workers who were interested in individual differences in intellectual abilities.

European interest in individual differences in intelligence grew in the late 19th century (e.g., Binet & Henri, 1896), concomitant with the birth of what is now recognized as the discipline of psychology, signified by the opening of a psychology laboratory at Leipzig by Wundt in 1879. In the United States, Cattell (1890; Cattell & Farand, 1890) established a mental testing laboratory at the University of Pennsylvania, collaborating with Wissler (1901) at Columbia University, using correlation to identify mental measurements that were related to one another.

An extremely important advance was Spearman's (1904) paper, which conceptualized intelligence as consisting of multiple factors, one general factor (g) and the others more specific (s): Every item on an intelligence assessment was assumed somehow to be related to general intelligence, with the degree of correlation to g varying among measures. Every measure of intelligence also tapped specific functions s independent of g. Spearman definitely understood that intelligence was a construct, something that had to be inferred. He also understood that powerful inferences could be made based on intercorrelations of measurements and developed the statistical methods that permitted analyses of large numbers of correlations so that factors giving rise to patterns of correlation could be identified. The pattern of correlation giving rise to g was that every mental test correlated somewhat with every other mental test: The fundamental importance of this discovery is obvious in that no one has ever devised a mental test that does not correlate positively with other mental tests (see Jensen, 1992).

Spearman was a theoretical giant, with his conception of intelligence fueling theoretical debates about the nature of intelligence for much of the first half of the 20th century. Thomson, for example, argued that the single factor *g* was a statistical artifact and deflected attention from the true nature of intelligence, which was a large set of independent bonds in the mind. Thurstone emphatically made the point that a "factor" could emerge in a correlation matrix because of similarities in test items that had nothing to do with any abstract factor (e.g., verbal test items are similar in many ways besides their relevance to verbal intelligence; spatial test items share similarities besides tapping spatial abilities). Thurstone's position was that there are several important factors underlying intelligence, not just *g* and a collection of myriad characteristics specific to each of the many items on intelligence assessments. Based on a large battery of tests administered to hundreds of subjects, Thurstone (1938) concluded that the **primary mental abilities** were spatial, perceptual, numerical, verbal, memory, word fluency, inductive, arithmetical reasoning, and deduction factors.

The early years of the 20th century witnessed the proliferation of intelligence tests, including Binet and Simon's (1905a, 1905b, 1905c) intelligence scale for children; Terman's revision of the Binet-Simon scale, which was carefully normed on American children (i.e., the Stanford-Binet scale; Terman & Childs, 1912); and the Army Alpha and Beta tests, which were a group-administered adaptation of the Binet test (Yoakum & Yerkes, 1920). It is impressive that there remains a great deal of resemblance between these early tests and contemporary intelligence assessments, although it must be emphasized that these tests were the survivors, for a number of other tests of intelligence were proposed and dismissed or discontinued after a short period of use. That Terman's test and the Army tests were derived from Binet's scales makes clear that the testing giant in the early 20th century was Binet. Theoretical thinking was driven by Spearman; testing applications were stimulated by Binet.

Why were intelligence tests developed? Binet was charged by the Minister of Public Instruction in Paris to find a way to discriminate between normal and retarded children. Terman shared Binet's vision that useful discriminations could be made between normal and low intelligence children but also thought the tests could be useful in identifying feebleminded adults. The Army tests were designed to discriminate the mentally unfit from those who attempted to fake stupidity to avoid World War I. These tests proved able to make discriminations in ability, with some validations exceptionally convincing. For example, performances on the Army tests generally were better for higher ranking than lower ranking troops (Yoakum & Yerkes, 1920).

In the 1930s, Wechsler began work on the test that would become the standard for the assessment of adult intelligence, the *Wechsler Adult Intelligence Scale–Revised (WAIS-R)*. He borrowed liberally from previously validated tests, although his instrument was unique in its balance of nonverbal and verbal items (i.e., verbal items had predominated in most previous assessments). Because this is the most frequently used assessment of adult intelligence, educational psychologists must be familiar with it. An overview of the *WAIS-R* illustrates many of the conceptual ideas already developed in this chapter.

Wechlser Adult Intelligence Scale–Revised

Wechsler's first intelligence test was the *Wechsler-Bellevue Intelligence Scale* (Wechsler, 1939), revised in 1955 as the *Wechsler Adult Intelligence Scale (WAIS)*, and revised again in 1981 as the *Wechsler Adult Intelligence Scale–Revised*. Although there was substantial overlap in items from version to version, there was also some updating to modernize the test with respect to cultural considerations (e.g., the *WAIS-R* includes new items that mention prominent black Americans). In addition, *WAIS* items that produced floor or ceiling effects were eliminated from the *WAIS-R*. Although there are many sources of information about the *WAIS-R*, we recommend (and used in the writing of this chapter), the *WAIS-R Manual* (Wechsler, 1981), Kaufman (1990), and Sattler (1992).

The test can be administered to adults between 16 and 75 years of age. It is administered to one person at a time by a psychometrist or psychologist . The test is composed of six Verbal Scales and five Performance Scales. The Verbal Scales include the following:

1. Information: 29 questions tapping general knowledge from literature, history, and geography.

2. Digit span: lists of digits (up to 9 for forward digit span and 8 for backward digit span) that must be recalled either in order of presentation (forward span) or reverse order of presentation (backward span).
3. Vocabulary: 35 words that the examinee is asked to define.
4. Arithmetic: 14 problems that the examinee is asked to solve.
5. Comprehension: 16 questions dealing with organization of the government, the nature of law, health standards, social relations, and proverbs.
6. Similarities: 14 pairs of words, with the examinee asked to explain the similarity between the words in each pair.

The Performance Scales are the following:

1. Picture completion: 20 drawings of well-known objects are presented, each of which is missing some essential component, with the examinee asked to indicate the missing part (timed).
2. Picture arrangement: examinee is asked to sequence series of pictures logically, with 10 problems of this type (timed).
3. Block design: examinees are shown red-and-white pictures of designs and must construct a matching design with red-and-white plastic blocks (timed).
4. Object assembly: examinee solves four jigsaw puzzles to produce pictures of well-known objects (timed).
5. Digit symbol: examinee must copy symbols presented as paired with numbers—that is, after presentation of the digit-symbol pairings, 93 digits alone are presented with the subject required to copy the appropriate symbol for each one (timed).

The *WAIS-R* manual specifies in detail how to derive an IQ score from performance on these 11 subtests. Mean performance on the test is set at 100 with a standard deviation of 15 (normed with a national sample of 1900 respondents representative of the racial, gender, and regional mix of people in the United States). If the distribution in IQ were normally distributed (as described in many textbooks), less than 2 percent of the population would have an IQ less than 70, approximately 14 percent would have an IQ between 70 and 85, 68 percent would have IQs between 85 and 115, 14 percent would score

between 115 and 130, and 2 percent would have scores greater than 130. The reason for the *if* is that the distribution of intelligence is not entirely normal, with a slightly greater proportion of people in the tails of the distribution (i.e., less than IQ of 70 and greater than IQ of 130) than occurs in a normal distribution (see Brody & Brody, 1978). One reason for this is that people do not marry by chance, with smart people more likely to marry other smart people and feebleminded people more likely to marry other feebleminded people than would occur by chance (Gilger, 1991; Neale & McArdle, 1990). Even so, thinking about IQ as normally distributed is close enough for most purposes, with the following intelligence classifications attached to various IQ ranges for the *WAIS-R* (and other Wechsler scales):

- 130 and above: Very superior
- 120–129:   Superior
- 110–119:   High average
- 90–109:   Average
- 80–89:   Low average
- 70–79:   Borderline
- 69 and below: Mentally retarded for the *WAIS-R*; mentally deficient for the *WISC-R* and *WPPSI* (described later)

One the of strengths of the *WAIS-R* is that it has extremely high reliability (0.97). That the reliabilities of each of the 11 subtests is lower than the overall reliability is due in part to the fact that scores based on more items (i.e., full-scale IQ is based on all items from all subscales) are more reliable than scores based on fewer items. (Remember the point made earlier in the chapter that longer tests are more reliable than shorter tests.) There is about a two in three chance that the IQ score obtained for a person with the *WAIS-R* is within 5 points of the score the person would obtain on a retesting (i.e., the confidence band for the test is 10 points, IQ score ± 5 points).

The concurrent validity (and to some extent the construct validity as well) of the *WAIS-R* was determined by correlating *WAIS-R* IQ scores with IQ scores obtained with other tests, including the 1955 *Wechsler Scale* and the *Stanford-Binet* (Thorndike, Hagen, & Sattler, 1986) scale. In general, these correlations were high (e.g., 0.94 with the *WAIS* and 0.85 with the *Stanford-Binet*). Factor analyses were used to determine that all of the subtests load on the *g* factor.

The *WAIS-R* is a good test with excellent psychometric properties. It is an adult scale, however, and thus not appropriate to administer to children, who are the concerns of many educators. A downward extension of the test, the *Wechsler Intelligence Scale for Children Revised (WISC-R)* is appropriate for school-age children.

Wechsler Intelligence Scale for Children–Revised

The *Wechsler Intelligence Scale for Children (WISC)* was published in 1949 (Wechsler, 1949), with the revision, the *WISC-R*, published in 1974. The tests were based on the *WAIS* and *WAIS-R*, and, thus, there is a great deal of similarity between the *WAIS-R* and the *WISC-R*. What follows is based based on the *WISC-R Manual* and Sattler's (1992) article on the *WISC-R*.

The *WISC-R* is appropriate for children 6.5 to 16.5 years of age. Similar to the *WAIS-R*, there are Verbal and Performance Scales. Child-relevant versions of the 11 subtests of the *WAIS-R* are included on the *WISC-R*, with one additional Performance test: A mazes subtest requires subjects to complete a series of mazes. The full-scale IQ for the *WISC-R* is based on only 10 of the subtests, however, with the digit span and mazes data eliminated from the computation. Similar to the *WAIS-R*, the mean for the *WISC-R* is 100, and the standard deviation is 15. There is a two in three chance that an IQ score is within 6.5 points as determined by a *WISC-R* retest (i.e., 13-point confidence band, IQ ± 6.5 points). Often educators think about intelligence data in terms of **mental age,** which can be calculated with the *WISC-R*.

The reliability is high (i.e., 0.96 for test-retest). As with the *WAIS-R*, none of the subscales have as great reliability as the full-scale IQ. Concurrent validity is also high, with the test correlating with other standardized measures of intelligence (e.g., correlation with the *Stanford-Binet* was 0.80), including traditionally well-regarded measures of children's intelligence. For example, the *WISC-R* correlates with the *McCarthy Scales of Children's Abilities* (0.72), the *Kaufman Assessment Battery for Children* (0.70), and the *Peabody Picture Vocabulary Test* (0.68). Performances on five subtests of the *WISC-R* are strongly associated with *g* (i.e., Vocabulary, Information, Similarities, Block Design, Comprehension); four are moderately associated with *g* (i.e., Arithmetic, Object Assembly, Picture Completion, Picture Arrangement); and three are correlated weakly with *g* (i.e., Digit Span, Mazes, Digit-Symbol). (Notably, two of the three subtests that load weakly on *g* are not included in the calculation of the full-scale score.)

The *WISC-R* has desirable psychometric properties. Its limitation is that it is not appropriate until the grade-school years. Because many decisions must be made about children during the preschool years, Wechsler (1967) developed a test for younger children.

Wechsler Preschool and Primary Scale of Intelligence (WPPSI)

The *WPPSI* (see Sattler, 1992; Wechsler, 1967) is appropriate for children 4 to 6.5 years of age. It has eight subtests that are similar to the *WISC-R* (Information, Vocabulary, Arithmetic, Similarities, Comprehension, Picture Completion, Mazes, Block Design) and three subtests unique to it:

- Sentence: examinee repeats sentence read by tester.
- Animal house: examinee places colored cylinders in a board with holes, with matching of cylinders and holes based on matching of four different animals.
- Geometric design: examinee copies geometric designs from printed cards.

Similar to the other Wechsler tests, the mean IQ on the *WPPSI* is set at 100 with standard deviation of 15. The test was normed on a sample of 1200 children (200 at each of six age levels), balanced to reflect the racial, gender, and regional mix of the United States. Mental ages can be calculated from the test data.

The reliability for full-scale IQ is 0.96. At all age levels, there is a two in three chance that the reported full-scale IQ is within 6 points of an IQ score obtained on a retest. The test also has good concurrent validity, correlating highly with other intelligence scales used with children. Yule, Gold, and Busch (1982) also demonstrated the predictive validity of the *WPPSI*, with *WPPSI* scores predicting *WISC-R* scores obtained 11 years after the *WPPSI* was administered (i.e., $r = 0.86$ between the intelligence rank orderings at 5.5 and 16.5 years of age). See Sattler (1992, Chapter 9) for review of several other studies that also reported long-term prediction of intelligence differences from *WPPSI* scores. These predictive studies provide especially impressive support for use of the *WPPSI* as a meaningful measure of intellectual ability. All of the *WPPSI* subtests are strongly related to *g*.

Despite the fact that the *WPPSI* is administered to an age range that has often been considered difficult to assess reliably, the *WPPSI* does well as a measure. The predictive validity data on the *WPPSI* as well as the substantial overlap for subtests on the *WPSSI, WISC-R,* and the *WAIS-R* suggest that if for some reason it is desirable to have longitudinal intelligence data on children (and often it is for both clinical and research purposes), a reasonable strategy would be to administer the *WPPSI* during the preschool years, the *WISC-R* during elementary and the early to mid high school years, and the *WAIS-R* during the late high school and adult years. Wechsler made an enormous contribution to the assessment of individual differences in intelligence.

Other Intelligence Tests

There are many intelligence tests (sometimes going by other names) that have been published. First, there are tests that are sensitive to the needs of diverse groups of children, including minority, handicapped, and the very young. Some are as well designed and validated as the Wechsler (e.g., *McCarthy Scales of Children's Abilities, Stanford-Binet Intelligence Scale*), and these scales are the ones used much of the time by competent examiners, such as professional psychometrists and psychologists. If we had the space to provide information about these tests, the writeup would share many points with the writeup of the Wechsler scales: good reliability, concurrent validity, perhaps even predictive validity, and high loadings on *g*.

Unfortunately, there are many other published instruments purporting to measure intelligence that have not been prepared or studied with the same care as the Stanford-Binet and the Wechsler scales. If there is a need for intelligence test data on a child, it is best to go to a well-qualified professional who will identify an appropriate instrument and know how to administer it. At the same time, we emphasize that there are some group tests of mental ability (i.e., they can be administered to groups of children by guidance counselors or other education professionals) that have been carefully validated and are reliable. Tests such as the Otis-Lennon School Ability Test (OLSAT), the Cognitive Abilities Test (CogAT), the Detroit Tests of Learning Aptitude (DTLA), and School and College Ability Tests (SCAT) provide a great deal of help-

ful data to teachers and school personnel at low cost (see Sattler, 1992, for reviews of these tests). Readers should emerge from this section on intelligence testing aware that an extensive, sophisticated testing technology exists, with this technology influenced deeply by a rich heritage of intellectual assessment (e.g., many *WAIS-R* items are updated versions of items on the earliest intellectual assessments).

WHY TEST INTELLIGENCE? WHAT DOES PSYCHOMETRIC INTELLIGENCE REVEAL ABOUT THE DEVELOPMENT OF MIND?

Psychometric intelligence is useful both to practitioners and to researchers. In general, the careful work involved in developing these tests has paid off in that orderly, replicable relationships between intelligence and other variables are common: The high reliability of intelligence assessments makes it possible for respectably high correlations with other variables.

Educational Success

There is voluminous evidence that IQ correlates with current and future successes in school, with Brody (1992) estimating that overall the correlation between IQ and school performance and achievement is about 0.50. It is impressive that success in reading at grade 6 correlates 0.45 or higher with intelligence as measured in kindergarten (Butler, Marsh, Sheppard, & Sheppard, 1985; Feshbach, Adelman, & Fuller, 1977). The *WISC-R* validation data includes report of a 0.39 correlation between performance on the *WISC-R* and school grades (Sattler, 1992); there are a number of reports of *WPPSI* performance in the preschool, kindergarten, and grade-1 years predicting performance on academic achievement tests several years later (Sattler, 1992); and the *WAIS-R* correlates (typically, 0.6 or higher) with academic achievement as measured by psychometric assessments (Sattler, 1992).

The amount of schooling completed also varies with IQ. For example, consider the following data for the *WAIS-R* reported by Reynolds, Chastain, Kaufman, and McLean (1987):

College graduates	Mean IQ = 115, IQ range = 87–148 95 percent have IQ of 96 or higher

Some college	Mean IQ = 107, IQ range = 76–139 95 percent have IQ of 89 or higher
High school graduate	Mean IQ = 100, IQ range = 63–141 95 percent have IQ of 81 or higher
Some high school	Mean IQ = 96, IQ range = 59–146 95 percent have IQ of 72 or higher
Elementary graduate	Mean IQ = 91, IQ Range = 65–125 95 percent have IQ of 76 or higher
Some elementary school	Mean IQ = 82, IQ range = 53–139 95 percent have IQ of 59 or higher

Bookkeeper	Mean IQ = 120.0, IQ range = 70–157
Salesperson	Mean IQ = 115.1, IQ range = 60–153
Machinist	Mean IQ = 110.1, IQ range = 38–153
Mechanic	Mean IQ = 106.3, IQ range = 60–155
Bartender	Mean IQ = 102.2, IQ range = 56–137
Chauffeur	Mean IQ = 100.8, IQ range = 46–143
Truck driver	Mean IQ = 96.2, IQ range = 16–149

Although there are high-ability individuals in every one of the categories of educational completion, low-ability individuals are rare at the college completion level. These data (and other data on the relationship of intelligence to completion of schooling; see Kaufman, 1990, Chapter 6) suggest that there is a minimum amount of intelligence required to complete each level of education, with the minimum increasing with more advanced educational level. Overall, Kaufman (1990) estimated about a 0.60 correlation between IQ and level of education completed.

IQ predicts the occupational status that one will achieve as well. Harrell and Harrell (1945; summary data reproduced in Brody & Brody, 1978) measured the intelligence level of a number of professions. There was a clear relationship between IQ and mean educational status, although there was also clear evidence in the data that high intelligence did not guarantee a high status occupation. Consider the following examples:

| Lawyer | Mean IQ = 127.6, IQ range = 96–157 |
| Chemist | Mean IQ = 124.8, IQ range = 102–153 |

What is especially striking in these data is that as the status of a job and the years of education required to perform a job decline, the lower the intelligence of the least intelligent people performing the job and the lower overall intelligence of all the people in the occupation. Even so, there are people with high intelligence performing every one of the jobs just listed—and, in fact, every one of the jobs in Harrell and Harrell's (1945) study. Brody and Brody's (1978) interpretation seems correct to us: "... individuals who score low on intelligence tests have limited opportunity to enter more prestigeful occupations" (p. 95). The psychometrically smart in our society have more opportunities and more freedom of choice than the less intelligent.

A traditional conclusion (see Brody & Brody, 1978) based on some work by Ghiselli (1966, 1973) was that even though intelligence predicted occupational level, it did not correlate with success within an occupation. Hunter and Hunter (1984) reanalyzed the studies and data considered by Ghiselli and reached different conclusions based on more modern and sensitive statistical methods. Their conclusion was that occupational success, based on measures such as supervisor ratings, correlated 0.53 with intelligence, a substantial relationship. The smarter one is in a psychometric sense, the more likely one is to do well at one's job.

IQ is a proven predictor of important life outcomes, including success at school, level of educational and occupational attainment, and success within an occupation. When decisions are being made about the allocation of scarce and valuable resources—for example, "high-tech" training opportunities in the military—using IQ as one indication of who should receive the resources is fully justified. When employers are attempting to determine who to hire, many factors weigh in. That there is a moderate relationship between IQ and occupational success makes clear that taking the intelligence of a potential employee into account as part of the hiring decision is justified. There is simply no other measure that does as well as IQ in predicting school and life success.

Intellectual Competencies Across the Life Span

Studies of human intelligence have played a prominent role in producing contemporary views of intellectual functioning across the life span. Analysis of intelligence functions is one of the most salient areas of research in the area of life-span cognitive development.

Early Childhood to Adulthood   Although it has been known for some time that IQ scores at age 7 will correlate at least 0.6 or 0.7 with IQ scores at age 18 (see Brody & Brody, 1978), the general conclusion has been that test data generated during the first years of life have no predictive value and that the correlations between preschool measures and intelligence at age 18 fall far short of the 0.6 to 0.7 level. There is an important exception, however, based on new measures emanating from research in the last 15 years.

Fagan (e.g., 1991; Fagan & McGrath,1981; Thompson, Fagan, & Fulker, 1991) has determined that infant susceptibility to a process known as **habituation** predicts psychometric intelligence in childhood. Habituation is measured using a preference paradigm. In one variation of the preference paradigm, an infant is shown two identical visual stimuli, such as two copies of the same face. Then, two more pictures of faces are shown, one identical to the original faces and one a new face. The measure of habituation is the degree of preference for the new face, with individual differences in habituation obtained during the first year of life correlating with individual differences in intelligence at ages 5 to 7 (see Goodman, 1990, for a review). To habituate, a child must efficiently form an internal representation of a currently perceived stimulus and note the discrepancy between what was just seen and a new source of stimulation—processes that more intelligent infants might be expected to carry out more certainly than less intelligent infants. Sometimes the correlations between infant habituation and later intelli-

gence have been as high as 0.60 (see Fagan, 1985). Fagan has developed an apparatus that is being sold to hospitals and other infant assessment professionals that simulates the testing conditions in his original studies and provides information about individual differences in infant habituation. Given both the predictive validity of Fagan's measurements and the predominance of information processing as a perspective for understanding mental processing in the 1990s, it seems likely that Fagan's approach to measurement of individual differences in intellectual abilities of infants will become much more popular than it is now. See Rose (1989) for discussions of extensions of Fagan's work and an illuminating perspective on the psychometric challenges of devising infant intelligence measures (e.g., low Cronbach alphas when habituation is measured with several different types of visual stimuli). See Ruff, Lawson, Parrinello, and Weissberg (1990) for research using other attention paradigms confirming long-term stability of individual differences in attention from infancy to the preschool years.

Across the Adult Life Span   One stimulus to the study of intelligence across the adult life span was an exceptionally unbelievable conclusion that was believed by many people. For many years, a classic introductory psychology–textbook conclusion was that intelligence as measured by psychometric tests decreases with increasing age during adulthood. After age 20, it was all downhill. We are certain that many readers—especially those who are no longer in their 20s—immediately question the credibility of this conclusion. Consider, however, the following mean IQ scores as a function of adult age for the *Wechsler-Bellevue (WB)*, the *WAIS*, and the *WAIS-R* (from Kaufman, 1990, Table 7.1, p. 185):

20–24 years of age	WB = 103.1, WAIS = 99.8, WAIS-R = 97.2
25–34 years of age	WB = 100.2, WAIS = 99.9, WAIS-R = 98.2
35–44 years of age	WB = 95.4, WAIS = 97.5, WAIS-R = 93.5
45–54 years of age	WB = 90.6, WAIS = 93.4, WAIS-R = 91.8
55-64 years of age:	WB = 87.6, WAIS = 89.6, WAIS-R = 87.6
65–69 years of age	WB = —, WAIS = 85.5, WAIS-R = 84.4
70–74 years of age	WB = —, WAIS = 78.5, WAIS-R = 81.7

75+ years of age $WB =$ —, $WAIS = 72.9$, $WAIS\text{-}R =$ —

It is easy to understand why researchers might conclude from data such as these that intelligence declines with increasing age during adulthood.

Some German developmental psychologists understood, however, that there was an important confounding in such data (e.g., Baltes, 1968; Baltes, Reese, & Nesselroade, 1977, Chapter 13; Schaie & Labouvie-Vief, 1974; Schaie, 1980): The data were generated in cross-sectional studies. That is, different people provided the intelligence data at each age level, and, thus, there was a confounding of age level and cohort of people providing the data. Thus, it could be that the 55- to 64-year-olds have not declined to high-80s intelligence. Rather, 55- to 64-year-olds might never have been able to obtain a score in the high 90s or at a mean of 100 if tested against the people currently taking the test. A little more explanation will clear up what must seem terribly confusing.

With every generation, there are increased educational and cultural opportunities. Thus, many of today's 25-year-olds have had richer and broader educational experiences than today's 50- to 70-year-olds. For example, a 15-year-old of today is more than twice as likely as a contemporary 55-year-old person to have completed college (Kaufman, 1990, Table 7.3, p. 187). If somehow it were possible to obtain data on the same test when today's 50 to 70-year-olds were 25, it seems likely that the performance of today's 25-year-olds might be higher than the hypothetical performance of 25-year-olds of yesteryear. If that were true, it would be expected that if intelligence data were collected longitudinally—thus, eliminating the confounding between age level and the particular cohort of people tested—the decline in IQ might be less dramatic than it seems when cross-sectional data are examined.

There now have been a number of such longitudinal investigations (see Schaie, 1990, for a review), and the consensus is that a simple conclusion of across-the-board decline in psychometric intelligence is unjustified. A little review of the composition of intelligence tests and a little theory will help move this discussion along.

Recall that the Wechsler tests have two scales, Verbal and Performance. The verbal scales tap knowledge that an individual has; the performance scales require quickness and flexibility in mental functioning. Many intelligence tests have items that can be thought of as tapping either knowledge or ability to process quickly and adeptly.

Cattell (e.g., 1987; also, Horn, 1985) has argued that g should be thought of as two separate factors, which he labeled **fluid** and **crystallized ability.** Fluid intelligence is the biological ability to acquire knowledge and adapt to new situations and is presumably tapped by tests such as those on the Performance Scale of the Wechsler tests. Any task tapping visualization, ability to discern figural relations between elements, ability to make inferences, short-term memory, or sensory discrimination would be expected to "load" on the fluid factor. Although all of these abilities depend heavily on a fully functioning nervous system, proposed revisions of Cattell's original approach have downplayed the biological claims, claiming that fluid intelligence is simply a summary label for nonverbal reasoning and reflects learning as well as biological endowment (e.g., Horn, 1985).

Crystallized ability is influenced more by acculturation according to the classic Cattellian formulation, with revisionists such as Horn (1985) relaxing the emphasis on the environmental determination of crystallized intelligence in favor of both biological and environmental influences. Vocabulary knowledge is the premier crystallized intelligence task, with the vocabulary a person possesses determined largely by their environmental experiences according to Cattell's reasoning.

With respect to development during the childhood and adolescent years, Cattell claimed that both fluid and crystallized abilities increase. In fact, that is the case. For example, both the proportions of Verbal and Performance Scale items on the Wechsler scales that are answered correctly increase during childhood and adolescence (Sattler, 1992). During adulthood, however, there are important differences in the course of fluid and crystallized intelligence.

There is one certain fact about the human nervous system: It declines with advancing age during adulthood, losing something like 50,000 neurons a day. Thus, it would make sense that intellectual functions that strongly depend on biological integrity would decline with advancing age. Consistent with this supposition, a variety of longitudinal and cross-sectional evidence supports the conclusion that fluid intelligence declines with advancing age during adulthood (see Brody, 1992, Chapter 8; Kaufman, 1990, Chapter 7). This translates into dramatic reductions in the ability to reason about new problems and to be able to execute quickly the many operations that often must be executed quickly to solve demanding problems (see Salthouse, 1982, 1985, 1988, 1992).

For crystallized intelligence, it is a different story. One of the most dramatic findings in Schaie and Labouvie-Vief's (1974) report of 14 years of longitudinal intelligence data was that some indicators of crystallized intelligence actually improved with advancing age into the seventh decade of life.

Some impressive evidence in favor of the view that crystallized intelligence increases was produced by Hertzog (1989), who statistically adjusted crystallized performance measures to eliminate individual differences in processing speed with advancing age (i.e., to control statistically for declines in fluid abilities). With speed of processing controlled, there was evidence for increases in crystallized abilities until age 70.

Kaufman and associates (Kaufman, Reynolds, & McLean, 1989; see also Kaufman, 1990, Chapter 7) also addressed whether differences in education between cohorts could account for the appearance of decline in IQ across adulthood. What they discovered was that once age was controlled statistically, there was still substantial decline with advancing age in cross-sectional fluid intelligence measures; with education controlled statistically, there was little decline with advancing age in crystallized abilities. Kaufman (1990, p. 191) summarized the result this way:

> Regardless of chronological age (and, hence, *when* people were educated), adults with the same amount of formal education earned about the same mean sum of scaled scores on the Verbal Scale. . . . This relation maintained whether the adult was 25, 50, or 65, and whether he or she was educated in the 1910s, 1930s, or 1950s. . . . Unlike Verbal sums, Performance sums *decreased steadily* [with increasing chronological age] within each educational category. . . .

When the developmental functions for the various Verbal subtests are examined in Kaufman's analyses, which controlled for different levels of education at the various age levels, there is strong support for the supposition that knowledge continues to grow through most of the adult life span. For example, the peak age for performance on the Information subtest was 62; for Vocabulary, 72; and for Comprehension, 62.

Even if older people cannot respond as quickly and perform cognitive processes as adeptly, they "know" more information. This is despite the fact that intelligence test items, if anything, are biased toward younger generations with respect to the particular information tapped on information, vocabulary, and comprehension subtests, reflecting the type of information prevalent in contemporary schools. Because standardized testing is more prevalent now than it was earlier in the century, contemporary students may benefit from better general test-taking skills as well. Because there are these reasons for believing that crystallized measures are loaded in favor of the young, it is especially impressive that people do better with advancing age on items tapping crystallized intelligence. If anything, the analyses documenting life-span increases in crystallized knowledge probably underestimate such increases.

That the thinking of older adults prevails in the larger culture, despite clear declines in fluid abilities—for example, how many political leaders in the world are old—may reflect that knowledge really is intellectual power. Knowledge often boils down to "knowing" the solutions to problems based on previous experience rather than having to reason about a problem situation because the problem (or one like it) has not been encountered before. Case-based reasoning (see Chapter 3) rather than reasoning using only logical abilities becomes much more possible as knowledge of cases increases through experience in the world. A pessimistic way of looking at the life-span intelligence data is that it is difficult to teach old dogs new tricks. More optimistically, old dogs already know so many tricks that they have no need of easily learning new ones to stay ahead of a pack of puppies that have intact nervous systems but little experience tackling the challenges of the kennel.

A case can be made that most creative work in many fields (athletics to mathematics and physical sciences to biological and social sciences) is produced by young people (e.g., Mattarazzo, 1972; Simonton, 1990). Kaufman (1990, p. 229) believes that this may reflect the relatively intact fluid abilities of younger people, arguing that creative flexibility is determined by fluid factors.

We believe that an important direction in intelligence theory in the near future will be to determine more completely the role of general reasoning and other fluid abilities versus knowledge and crystallized abilities at different points in the life span. Such work has already permitted great insights, such as debunking the myth that it is all downhill intellectually after the 20s: Even though thinking will be slower as a person ages, people tend to know more with advancing age. Given the importance of knowledge built up over many years in many forms of expertise, it seems likely that future analyses may be emphasizing the strengths of such thinking (e.g., the nature of wisdom, Simonton, 1990) rather than the weaknesses of it.

The model of thinking that emerges from Schaie, Cattell, and Horn's work is more compatible with the perspective that has dominated this book than is *g* theory: Intelligent functioning is due to a number of factors in interaction, with much of intellectual development and functioning explained by development of knowledge through environmental input, although this knowledge always depends on biological resources. As knowledge increases with advancing age, however, it is less necessary to rely on biological resources to reason through situations, which is fortunate because biological capacities decline with increasing age.

Analyses of Individual Differences Leading to Conceptions of Intelligence That Dovetail with Information Processing Analyses

Much of cognitive research involves comparisons of mean performances—how people do on average under one set of conditions (e.g., instructions) versus another set of conditions. Within any condition, however, there are always individual differences in performance. When the concern is with comparing means, these individual differences are treated as error. In contrast, for researchers interested in individual differences, it is this within-cell variability that is interesting. Individual differences theorists believe that much about human mind can be learned by explaining differences in performance between people. Intelligence testing forces attention to individual differences, and as theorists and researchers have attempted to understand the nature of intelligence as measured by intelligence tests, they have stimulated much thinking about the many processes involved in thinking. Two of the more prominent traditions in the cognitive analysis of intelligence data are taken up in this subsection.

Factor Analytic Approaches Implicating Cognitive Processes Thurstone (e.g., 1938, 1947) conducted some especially thorough factor analyses of intelligence tests, concluding in the first half of the 20th century that intelligence test data reflected the operation of at least nine **primary mental abilities:** inductive reasoning, deductive reasoning, practical problem reasoning, verbal comprehension, associative short-term memory, spatial abilities, perceptual speed, numerical competence, and word fluency (see Horn & Hofer, 1992, for a concise, informative history of this work and research stimulated by it). Subsequent analyses by others hypothesized many more factors, with Guilford (e.g., 1967), who worked from this model, eventually proposing that there might be 120 primary mental abilities defined by 5 types of operations × 6 types of products × 4 types of products matrix.

Cattell and Horn (e.g., Horn & Cattell, 1967; Horn, 1968; Cattell & Horn, 1978) and their colleagues (e.g., Hakstian & Cattell, 1978; Horn & Stankov, 1982) also conducted research within this framework, producing the theory of fluid and crystallized intelligence presented earlier in this section. As it turns out, however, those are only two of nine factors these investigators believe to be implicated in intelligence. Horn and Hofer (1992) summarized the nine factors as follows:

1. Fluid reasoning (G_f) measured in tasks requiring inductive, deductive, conjunctive, and disjunctive reasoning to arrive at understanding relations among stimuli, comprehend implications, and draw inferences.
2. Acculturation knowledge (G_c) measured in tasks indicating breadth and depth of the knowledge of the dominant culture.
3. Quantitative knowledge (G_q) measured in tasks requiring under-standing and application of the concepts and skills of mathematics.
4. Short-term apprehension-retrieval (G_{sm}), also called short-term memory, measured in a variety of tasks that mainly require one to maintain awareness of, and be able to recall, elements of immediate stimulation—that is, events of the last minute or so.
5. Fluency of retrieval from long-term storage (G_{lr}), also called long-term memory, measured in tasks that indicate consolidation for storage and mainly require retrieval, through association of

information stored minutes, hours, weeks, and years before.

6. Visual processing (G$_v$), measured in tasks involving visual closure and constancy, and fluency in "image-ing" the way objects appear in space as they are rotated and flip-flopped in various ways.

7. Auditory processing (G$_a$), measured in tasks that involve perception of sound patterns under distraction or distortion, maintaining awareness of order and rhythm among sounds, and comprehending elements of groups of sounds, such as chords and the relations among such groups.

8. Processing speed (G$_s$), although involved in almost all intellectual tasks (Hertzog, 1989), measured most purely in rapid scanning and responding in intellectually simple tasks (in which almost all people would get the right answer if the task were not highly speeded).

9. Correct decision speed (CDS), measured in quickness in providing answers in tasks that require one to think (Horn & Hofer, 1992, pp. 56–57).

What is important at this point is that such an analysis points out that the cognitive products that are counted up as part of calculating an IQ are the results of processes, each of which is performed better by some people than others. Presumably, if we knew how well a person could perform each of the individual processes specified by the nine factors considered critical by Horn and his colleagues, we would be in a good position to estimate how well they would do on an IQ test. The estimate would not be perfect because intelligence is the result of the coordinated use of the nine processes, not simply the sum of the nine processes.

More process-oriented factor analyses of individual differences in psychometric intelligence (and explanations of intelligence factors in terms of processes) stimulated a great deal of theory and research aimed at elucidating individual differences in cognitive processes, with many workers in this arena believing that if individual differences in information processing components are understood, individual differences in intelligence will be understood (Das, 1992; Hunt, Frost, Lunneborg, 1973): For example, psychometric intelligence is related to differences in speed of information processing (see Chapter 6), with speed differences related to *g* (and hence, highly heritable; e.g., Baker, Vernon, & Ho, 1991; Jensen, 1982; Vernon, 1983, 1985; for comprehensive

reviews, see Vernon, 1987). There are also strong relationships between working memory capacity/functioning (perhaps best thought of as attentional capacity/functioning; e.g., Tomporowski & Simpson, 1990) and IQ (e.g., Necka, 1992).

Triarchic Theory of Intelligence   Sternberg, a cognitive psychologist at Yale, has proposed a **triarchic theory** of intelligence. At the heart of Sternberg's theory (e.g., 1985) are **components,** which are elementary information processes that operate on internal representations of objects or symbols (Sternberg, 1977; 1980; 1985, pp. 97–98). Components can ". . . translate a sensory input into a conceptual representation, transform one conceptual representation into another, or translate a conceptual representation into a motor output" (Sternberg, 1985, p. 98). The theory is referred to as triarchic because there are three main types of components involved in intelligent functioning:

1. "**Metacomponents** are higher-order executive processes used in planning, monitoring, and decision making in task performance" (Sternberg, 1985, p. 99). These include the following (Sternberg, 1985, pp. 99–105):

   a. Deciding what the problem is that requires solution.
   b. Selecting a set of lower-order components to solve the problem.
   c. Selecting one or more organizations or representations of information for other components to work on.
   d. Selecting a strategy for combining lower-order components.
   e. Deciding how to allocate short-term memory (i.e., limited-capacity attentional resources).
   f. Monitoring solution of the problem as processing proceeds.
   g. Attending to and processing feedback.

2. "**Performance components** are processes used in the execution of a task" (Sternberg, 1985, p. 99). These include the following (Sternberg, 1985, pp. 105–106):

   a. Encoding components that are involved with initial perception and memory of new information.
   b. Combination and comparison components that are involved in integrating and comparing pieces of information.
   c. Response components involved in outputting solutions once they are determined.

3. "**Knowledge-acquisition components** are processes used in gaining new knowledge" (Sternberg, 1985, p. 107). These include the following:

   a. Selectively encoding by sifting relevant from irrelevant information.
   b. Selectively combining selectively encoded information into a coherent whole.
   c. Selectively comparing new information with information acquired in the past.

The components of intelligence can also be classified in another important way, with respect to their level of generality. **General components** are required to perform all tasks. **Class components** can be used for a number of similar tasks but do not apply to all tasks. **Specific components** apply to individual tasks.

Sternberg believes that the factors identified in factor analyses by intelligence theorists can be explained in terms of components. For example, individual differences in general components lump to produce a *g* factor: Many metacomponents are general components because planning and monitoring are required for many if not all tasks. Some knowledge acquisition and performance components apply across most tasks as well (e.g., most problems require encoding and responding). A second example is Sternberg's explanation of crystallized and fluid intelligence in terms of component: Crystallized intelligence is the product of knowledge-acquisition components. That is, those who are better at acquiring knowledge will have more of it as reflected by vocabulary and general information subtests on IQ scales. Fluid ability depends more on the performance components. Because both crystallized and fluid intelligence depend on the operation of metacomponents, crystallized and fluid intelligence should be correlated somewhat, which they are.

Is there any reason to be cautious about enthusiasm for this conceptually appealing approach to individual differences in intelligence? One good reason for caution is that correlations between information processing components and psychometric tests generally have proved small (see Sternberg, 1983, 1991a). Cognitive components work has not succeeded in explaining IQ differences among people.

Summary and Concluding Comments Intelligence data have inspired information processing analyses to explain them. Work such as Thurstone's provided powerful insights about the complexities

of thinking that a theory of information processing would have to explain. Although the information processors now talk as if psychometric intelligence theory and research is passé, we are impressed that psychometric intelligence theory seems healthy. Our suspicion is that both psychometric intelligence approaches to mind and information processing approaches will continue to cross-fertilize one another—indeed, there will be substantial discussion in Chapter 17 about how information processing theory is stimulating the development of new types of psychometric instruments. One reason psychometric and information processing conceptions both will continue to exist is that it has not yet proved possible to "explain" intelligence in terms of the information processing components favored by Sternberg or others (i.e., with high correlations between information processing and intelligence differences a necessary starting point for such explanations).

We cannot close this short section on the relationship of psychometric intelligence theory to information processing theory without discussing the good information processing model featured in this book. Strategies, metacognition and monitoring, knowledge, and short-term memory show up in all information processing analyses as they do in the good information processing model. An important difference, however, between other information processing frameworks and good information processing is that motivation is highlighted in good information processing. Another important difference between other information processing perspectives and good information processing is that good information processing research has been aimed at tasks considerably more complex than the tasks on intelligence tests—tasks considerably more educationally valid (see Sternberg, 1991a, for discussion of the limitations of information processing approaches to intelligence that focus on explaining performance differences on tasks traditionally appearing on IQ tests).

Our confidence in traditional psychometrics research and information processing analyses of psychometric intelligence is undermined by the lack of measurement of educationally realistic reading comprehension, writing, and problem solving. One of the reasons that the alternative assessments considered in Chapter 17 are stimulating so much interest is that testing is finally taking on tasks that are educationally valid, such as reading comprehension, actual writing, and mathematical and scientific problem solving like that expected in school. One challenge is to devise tests measuring educationally valid processes that have psychometric properties rivaling the scales developed by traditional intelligence testers such as Wechsler. This is an enormous challenge and one that will require a marriage of psychometric specialists who know the technical aspects of measurement and cognitive instructional psychologists who know what to measure and can provide some insights to the psychometrists about how to do it. If these new assessments prove to be predictive of school achievement, they might also correlate with psychometric intelligence because psychometric intelligence correlates with school achievement. If that happens, great progress will have been made in identifying the long-sought theoretical linkages between information processing and intelligence.

Concluding Comments About the Value of Intelligence Tests

Intelligence tests permit insights about individual students, providing excellent data predicting the probability of academic success. Such tests must not be seen as providing an inevitable prediction, however. Correlations between IQ and academic success are never perfect, for there are other determinants of individual differences. Indeed, much of this book has been about environmental interventions that can increase academic success.

The evidence in this section has been consistent with a main theme in this book, that intellectual performance is multiply determined, with both biology and environment critical in the formation and development of competence. Many of the process-oriented investigators conducting the research covered in other chapters of this book have shunned psychometric intelligence analyses. Our view is that there is more than enough room for both perspectives and that these two perspectives will do more than coexist: Psychometric theorists and information processing theorists will goad each other on to make testing more informative to the issues favored by information processors and to make information processing analyses more informative about what sophisticated tests may be testing. In fact, psychometric research also has stimulated the development of information processing theories of mind. Indeed, as will become even clearer in Chapter 17 on alternative assessments, testing and information processing research traditions are interacting in the 1990s.

There is another reason besides theoretical advance that psychometric conceptions of intelligence are more out of favor today than they once were. For many, there is a dark side to testing. They believe testing is biased against some groups of people. The depressed performances of some groups compared with others on IQ tests has enormous potential for stimulating discrimination, something that is apparent to many critics of testing and all too often ignored by advocates of testing.

BIAS IN MENTAL TESTING

In 1969, Jensen, a Berkeley psychologist who had devoted most of his previous scholarly efforts to studies of laboratory learning, published an article in the prestigious *Harvard Educational Review* (Jensen, 1969), "How much can we boost IQ and scholastic achievement?", touching off an explosion. What was so disturbing about the Jensen article?

Although most academics concerned with intelligence testing had known for a long time that blacks traditionally score much lower than whites on IQ tests (i.e., usually about a standard deviation, or 15 points for most IQ measures), this article (more correctly, second-hand reports of it in the media) made many more Americans aware that the measured IQs of blacks were on average quite a bit lower than the IQs of whites. If Jensen's article had only increased awareness of the 15-point difference in the average IQs of whites and blacks, that would have been bad enough. It went much further, however, making the case that the 15 point difference reflected an essential biological difference between blacks and whites, one favoring whites with respect to intelligence.

By 1969, there was substantial study of the heritability of IQ, including the work of Burt (e.g., Burt, 1966), a strong advocate of the position that intellectual differences reflect genetic differences. Most of the work had been conducted with white populations, with the conclusion that within these populations, differences in intelligence were largely inherited. Jensen (1969) extrapolated from the within-white-population claims of heritability to explain between-population differences in mean intelligence: He concluded that the 15-point disadvantage for blacks compared with whites on IQ tests was not due to socioeconomic disadvantage or culturally biased tests (alternative hypotheses that might explain at least part of the 15-point difference) but due to genetic differences between blacks and whites. That conclusion enraged many.

Our view is that that rage was justified. It had been understood for a long time that within-population estimates of heritability cannot be generalized to estimate between-population differences (e.g., see Plomin et al., 1990, Chapter 14). We explain this to classes using our version of a well-known example among behavior geneticists: Suppose we take the seeds from a watermelon. Make two piles. Plant both piles of watermelon seeds in side-by-side plots with equally good soil, excellent fertilizer, appropriate amounts of water, and weekly weeding of both plots. Is it likely that better watermelons are going to be produced in one plot or the other? No, the two piles of seeds are biologically equivalent, and the environments are equivalent.

Now, what if we had started with the same two piles of seeds. Instead of putting them in identical plots with identical care, suppose one pile is treated as described previously. Suppose the other is put in a plot with inferior soil and denied fertilizer. Suppose as well that the inferior plot is put under a translucent tent that cuts out most of the sunlight and precludes rain from falling directly on the plot. Which plot will yield the better melons? All students recognize that there will be different yields when the plot environments differ. Then, we ask, "Why the difference?" Everyone claims it is environment. No one ever claims it is innate difference in the seeds. That is the point, of course: There can be massive differences between two groups who have essentially the same genetic endowment, differences that must be due entirely to environment.

That environment may make a difference in IQ is suggested by the consistent correlation observed between IQ and socioeconomic status, a correlation observed within both white and black groups (e.g., Jensen, 1973, Chapter 6; Sattler, 1992, Chapter 4). One possibility is that the inferior environment has caused depression in intelligence, a position attractive to the detractors of IQ testing and biological explanations of between-population differences in IQ (e.g., Mensh & Mensh, 1991). Alternatively, of course, it may be that less intelligent people simply do not do as well in this world, and, thus, they end up worse off than others, an explanation of socioeconomic differences acceptable to supporters of IQ

testing and biological explanations of between-population differences in IQ. One attack on the intellectual problem of determining whether racial differences in intelligence might be wiped out if socioeconomic differences between blacks and whites could be eliminated is to control statistically for socioeconomic status in analyses of intelligence data. When that is done, some of the difference is wiped out (perhaps a third; see Jensen, 1973), but there is still an 8- to 10-point discrepancy. Another possibility is to look at the types of items that high and low socioeconomic status populations answer correctly and determine if the overall pattern of black-white performance differences on the various subtests of IQ scales are similar to the pattern of differences between high and low socioeconomic status populations: They are not (see Jensen, 1992).

The most obvious case to make against the part of the black-white discrepancy that cannot be explained as due to socioeconomic-mediated differences is to argue that the test is unfair: IQ tests are biased against various groups, including blacks and other minorities. This possibility of bias has been raised repeatedly, including in many courtrooms (e.g., see Jensen, 1980, Chapter 1; Reynolds & Kaiser, 1990a, 1990b). For many, the fact of racial or ethnic differences in IQ scores is proof enough that test bias exists (see Reynolds & Kaiser, 1990a, 1990b, for a review of such arguments). There is much more to proving bias than that, however.

Potential Sources of Test Bias

Bias can be introduced in a number of ways, with those reviewed by Reynolds and Kaiser (1990a, 1990b) overviewed here. First, and most obvious to many, is that the content of items can tap concepts and experiences more familiar to some racial and ethnic groups than others. There are many possible variations on this theme, such as differing answers to the same item in different cultures and failure to use vocabulary in testing a concept that is equally familiar to all people taking the test. Although a great deal of effort is expended by many test constructors to eliminate bias, it is definitely not clear how to ensure that tests are content unbiased. One of the greatest difficulties is that even experts in a culture cannot identify reliably items that will pose difficulty for children in their culture—with judges disagreeing between themselves and judges' rating of item difficulties for their culture correlating poorly with actual item difficulties (Jensen, 1976; Sandoval & Mille, 1980). Test constructors have generated a great deal of evidence that weighs against the claim that there is gross cultural bias in well-constructed intelligence tests: For example, across a number of well-designed tests, there are remarkably high correlations (i.e., mostly 0.94 and above) in the difficulty level of items across populations (see Reynolds & Kaiser, 1990b). If there were many cultural boners in the items sets, such high correlations would seem unlikely.

A second possible bias is with respect to the constructs measured by the test: The test might measure one thing for one population and something different for another population (e.g., intelligence for the majority population and language proficiency for minorities). If that is the case, one might expect different factor analyses outcomes for different racial and cultural groups: Attempts at identifying differences in the factors underlying the IQ performances of different groups have generally produced comparable factors for the groups studied (Reynolds & Kaiser, 1990a, 1990b).

A third possible bias is with respect to predictive validity, with tests predicting educational or other types of successes better for some groups than others. Again, that has been investigated for a variety of good tests, including IQ and SAT tests, with the general conclusion that these tests predict equally well across racial and cultural groups. Even when test means differ between populations and even when the correlations between the predictor (i.e., test score) and predicted outcomes (e.g., educational attainment) differ between groups, it is possible statistically to construct equations that minimize the number of errors in decision making for all groups in question (e.g., Cleary, Humphreys, Kendrick, & Wesman, 1975)—and that is what is required for a test to be unbiased in a predictive validity sense: For example, if the test is asked, "Will this person do well in this college?", it is unbiased if the answer it generates is "right" the same proportion of times for all groups. For a test to be right with equal probability for various groups can require a different prediction equation for each group in question, but such equations can be constructed if the test is reliable and representative, and sizable norming samples have been generated for each of the populations in question.

A fourth potential source of bias is with respect to the standardization samples. Examination of a volume such as Sattler (1992), which provides extensive norming information, makes clear, however, that more recent, generally well-constructed tests are aware of the need for representative, national norming samples, and they generate such samples. Examination of a volume such as Sattler (1992) also makes clear, however, that there are many tests on the market that have not been normed with representative samples.

A fifth potential source of bias is mismatch between the race or culture of the examiner and the test taker. This hypothesis has been studied extensively with respect to race, however, with little evidence that the race of an examiner makes a difference in the test score earned by a person being examined (Graziano, Varca, & Levy, 1982). An examiner variable that does seem to matter is familiarity between examiner and person being tested, with personal familiarity between tester and examinee slightly boosting the performance of the examinee. What is especially important in this context is that the familiarity effect seems to be especially large for lower socioeconomic status populations (Fuchs & Fuchs, 1986).

Test constructors are extremely sensitive to many ways that tests can be biased and are attempting to devise unbiased tests. Testing at its best involves instruments without blatant cultural bias in content, tests normed with representative samples and demonstrated to be measuring the same constructs in various cultures. These tests are administered by examiners who do all possible to make certain that blatant cultural differences do not interfere with a fair assessment (e.g., language differences between the tester and the student). At the other extreme, however, are tests that are biased with respect to content (e.g., dated tests often have content bias) and that have not been normed with data generated by populations being tested with the instrument. Sadly, there are examiners who simply are insensitive to problems that minorities may face in taking a test and do not hesitate to report low test scores as valid despite many indications during testing of language barriers or failures of the student in question to cooperate with the tester or to understand the consequences of the assessment. Of course, the closer an assessment is to the first description, the more weight should be given to the test data; it is essential that the education community do everything possible to eliminate assessments made with instruments of uncertain reliability and validity or conducted by examiners who ignore examinee characteristics that might preclude a valid assessment. If such tests cannot be eliminated, they should, at least, be ignored in decision-making processes.

CONCLUDING COMMENTS

It is difficult to grow up in the United States without experiencing standardized achievement tests. For example, many readers will have taken the *Iowa Test of Basic Skills* during their elementary years. Those who aspire to higher education invariably take either the *SAT* or the *ACT American College Testing Progam).* Postgraduate work requires *GREs* or the *LSAT (Law School Aptitude Test)* or the *GMAT (Graduate Management Aptitude Test)* or a similar examination. All of these examinations have characteristics similar to the *SAT* and *GRE:* They have been normed on large, nationally representative samples. They are reliable and valid in predicting future academic achievement. Indeed, school grades and standardized test performance together provide greater predictive power than any other predictor.

For many years, intelligence assessment was almost as prevalent as other forms of standardized testing, with many school jurisdictions routinely administering group tests of intelligence to their students. Such tests are not as widespread as they once were: It has become recognized that abuse of such data was common, especially since many teachers who had access to such numbers were not trained in the proper interpretation of psychometric assessments. Also, that minorities often perform at lower levels than members of the majority population on such assessments has reduced their attractiveness to many educators who have been under substantial pressure in the last two decades to be sensitive to minority concerns.

Nonetheless, IQ testing is still extremely common as part of the assessment of children referred for assessment and treatment. Whenever there is a need to do a complete assessment of a person (e.g., attempting to determine the cause of a student's difficulty in learning to read), IQ testing is likely to oc-

cur. Indeed, many mental health classifications require psychometric assessment of intelligence. For instance, classification of learning disabilities is in terms of academic performance relative to what would be expected based on intelligence, with academic performance lower than expected based on intelligence the telltale sign of learning disabilities.

It is essential for students of educational psychology to understand standardized tests, for such tests are used to make many important decisions, such as whether a student should be placed in special education or enrolled in a gifted program. This chapter summarized the essential points about reliability and validity that all educational psychology professionals should understand. The student who understands the various types of reliability and validity covered in this chapter would be able to understand much of the commentary in technical writeups accompanying many tests or articles in sources such as the *Buros Mental Measurements Yearbook* or Sattler (1992).

Scholars interested in standardized assessments are immersed in historically prominent issues, including the relative roles of nature and nurture in development, the appropriateness of using intelligence assessment with nonmainstream populations, and continuities and discontinuities in the nature of mind across the life span. A variety of extremely sophisticated tools are employed to answer such questions, including the twin and adoption methods of behavior genetics (see Chapter 6) and the longitudinal experimental designs of interventionists interested in the long-term effects of high quality educational experiences. Such work affects both the development of new educational theory and practice.

Although measurement professionals are aware of the intellectual foundations of their work, foundations that permit a strong case for standardized testing and traditional intelligence assessment, these same workers are always looking for new ways to assess competence. A variety of new methods have been inspired by theory and new technology as well as new societal demands. Some of the most intriguing of the new approaches to assessment of individual differences will be taken up in the next chapter.

17

Alternative Assessments

Chapter 16 was about types of testing that have been around for a long time. This chapter is about more modern forms of assessment. Both federal and state governments are concerned with achievement in schools, resulting in the development of standardized tests that result in "report cards" on the schools. Some of these assessments are important from the good information processing perspective because they are designed explicitly to assess whether students are learning the competencies emphasized in this book. Such performance assessments are not understood as well as they need to be understood at this point to be generally useful as assessments, but this is an important direction in testing that is theoretically defensible from the point of view favored in this book. Other modern forms of assessment, all of which can be related to instructional practices defensible based on analyses offered in this book, are also taken up. These include portfolio assessments, dynamic assessments—which have a scaffolded teaching component, curriculum-based assessments—which operationalize the task-oriented possibilities considered in the chapter on motivation, and new neuropsychological tests. Testing is an exciting area of educational psychology in the 1990s.

As the 20th century nears its end, there is much rethinking about how to measure competence. Many new measurements are providing important ways of thinking about learning, thinking, and intelligence. Explored in this chapter are many of the most prominent of these "new" assessments, with *new* defined as having been developed in the last quarter century or so.

NATIONAL AND STATE ASSESSMENTS

American students are tested extensively, with the National Commission on Testing and Public Policy (1989) estimating that American students take on average three standardized tests a year. Many are conventional standardized achievement tests that have been normed in a rigorous fashion, such as the SAT, described in Chapter 16. Their purpose is to provide information about the progress of individual students, although many jurisdictions use them to make decisions about whether or not their schools are doing well. Thus, many U.S. states and Canadian provinces conduct statewide/province-wide assessments of student competence. So does the U.S. federal government, with the *National Assessment of Ed-*

ucational Progress (NAEP) the best-known of the national testing efforts.

This section includes an overview of the *NAEP* because it is such a prominent test, with statistics from it presented almost continuously in the media. This section will also cover some of the newer, more innovative assessments being developed for use at the federal and state levels. Testing is being transformed from conventional multiple-choice into radical visions that attempt to measure academic abilities more directly than the traditional assessments. By beginning with the *NAEP*, this section will proceed from more conventional to less conventional tests, although the *NAEP* also has many innovative aspects to it.

Before proceeding, there is one important point. Most national and many state assessments are aimed at evaluating the performance of educational institutions through assessments of their students. That is, the focus in many national and state assessments is not on the achievement of the individual student, as it was for the assessments covered in Chapter 16 and later in this chapter. Rather the focus is on group differences: How do minorities fare compared with white students? How do students living in various types of urban environments fare compared with students living in rural areas? How do the performances of public and private school students compare? How do students in "Our County" fare compared with students in "Their County"?

National Assessment of Educational Progress

The *NAEP* is billed as "The Nation's Report Card" by Educational Testing Service (ETS), its most visible analyst.

Development and Administration The Congress mandated the *NAEP* with legislation in the late 1960s. The original assessment was devised by the National Commission of the States to provide information to policymakers about the state of education in the United States. This was done under the direction of Tyler, one of the great curriculum and measurement figures of the 20th century. There are periodic assessments of 9-, 13-, and 17-year-olds in school, with data collected biannually; there are also assessments of young adults, up to 35 years of age. Exactly which subject areas are tested varies from assessment to assessment. Over the years, reading, writing, mathematics, science, social studies, literature, art, music, citizenship, computer skills, and career development have been evaluated. ETS goes to great lengths to ensure content validity of the examination, using a broad base of experts to generate and evaluate items before the test is used. Every effort is made to make certain that the test covers content that students should know (or processes they should be able to carry out) without them having to use some particular textbook or experience some particular curriculum. Items are reviewed carefully to make certain they are not offensive to some subcultural groups. Measurement specialists review items in detail to ensure that they are constructed properly.

Once the test is constructed, great efforts are made to identify and test a nationally representative sample. For example, the 1988 civics assessment (Anderson et al., 1990), which will be used in this subsection to represent the type of outcomes generated by the *NAEP*, was administered to 11,000 students in more than 1000 public and private schools distributed across the United States. The sampling was sufficient to permit meaningful comparisons across demographic, school, and home characteristics.

Sample Test Items From the 1988 Civics *NAEP*
Most of the items on the civics *NAEP* were multiple choice in format. Among the easiest items on the test (passing rate = 71 percent at grade 4, 94 percent at grade 8, and 99 percent at grade 12) were the following:

> Who would become President of the United States if the President dies?
> A. The Secretary of State
> B. The Speaker of the House
> C. The Chief Justice of the Supreme Court
> D. The Vice-President
>
> Suppose a person has just been arrested because the police have evidence that he or she has stolen some money. Does the accused have the right to know what he or she is accused of?
> A. Yes
> B. No
> C. I don't know (Anderson et al., 1990, p. 31)

The following items are slightly more difficult (passing rate = 10 percent at grade 4, 61 percent at grade 8, 89 percent at grade 12):

> In the United States, an individual citizen has the right to:
> A. Impeach the President
> B. Vote for government officials
> C. Make new laws
> D. Collect taxes
>
> Under the law, United States citizens may work to change government policy by doing all of the following *except:*
> A. Making public speeches
> B. Writing letters of protest
> C. Persuading legislators to change laws
> D. Refusing to pay taxes (Anderson et al., 1990, pp. 34–35)

These are even more challenging (passing rate less than 1 percent at grade 4, 13 percent at grade 8, 49 percent at grade 12):

> How is the Chief Justice of the United States Supreme Court selected?
> A. By a national election with approval by a majority of state governors
> B. Through a majority vote by the existing Supreme Court justices
> C. By constitutional amendment and presidential signature
> D. Through appointment by the President with the consent of the Senate (Anderson et al., 1990, p. 36)

These were among the most difficult items on the test (passing rate less than 1 percent at grades 4 and 8, 6 percent at grade 12):

> Bicameralism is best defined as a
> A. Government composed of two principal branches
> B. Multilevel judicial system containing a higher court of appeals
> C. System of checks and balances between two branches of government
> D. Legislative system composed of two houses or chambers
>
> In the execution of its responsibilities, which of the following is *least* likely to be influenced by lobbying?
> A. The Supreme Court
> B. The House of Representatives
> C. The Senate
> D. A state governor (Anderson et al., 1990, p. 39)

In addition to the multiple-choice questions, students at grades 8 and 12 responded to an essay question requiring them to name the President and to write during a 15-minute period a description of his responsibilities.

Outcomes for the 1988 Civics *NAEP* *NAEP* data are analyzed so as to provide indications of how students across the United States are doing, with a variety of comparisons possible. For example, the civics test confirmed a steady increase in civics knowledge from grades 4 to 12. There were small, inconsistent gender differences. Whites outperformed blacks and Hispanics. Students residing in urban advantaged environments outperformed rural students, who did better than students from urban disadvantaged backgrounds. Children with parents who were more highly educated outperformed children from homes with less educated parents. Having both parents at home was associated with better performance than living with one parent; children living with one parent outperformed those living with people other than their parents. There were only small differences associated with maternal employment. Grade-12 students enrolled in academic programs (i.e., rather than vocationally oriented programs) and those planning to attend postsecondary education outperformed other students. The only consistent regional difference was that students in the Southeast performed slightly worse than students in other regions of the United States. (Although this evaluation of the 1988 *NAEP* did not break down outcomes on a state-by-state basis, analyses for *NAEPs* collected from 1990 on do so, with such data first released in 1991.)

One aspect of the essay data provided one of those shocking tidbits of information that the media often pick up and report: Eleven percent of grade-8 and 6 percent of grade-12 students did not know that Ronald Reagan was president of the United States (at the time the test was taken). Close analyses of the civics *NAEP* revealed that many students do not know much of the vocabulary pertaining to civics, lack knowledge of many important political processes, and are deficient in their understandings of many aspects of government history and tradition.

NAEP Outcomes in General and What They Mean
There are several important general conclusions that emanate from *NAEP* data, with these frequently reported in the media. We make the case in this section that there is reason to be cautious in making too-general claims based on this test.

Poor Performance of Contemporary Students. A consistent trend over the years has been for Amer-

ican students to perform at lower levels on *NAEP* assessments than is desirable (e.g., review the discussion of *NAEP* performance levels in reading that were covered in Chapter 14)—at least in the eyes of some prominent policy makers who publish analyses of *NAEP* data along with stinging criticisms of American students and the schools that are educating them (e.g., Bennett, 1984; Cheney, 1987, Ravitch & Finn, 1987). A theme in such commentaries, and those of like-minded politically conservative thinkers (e.g., Bloom, 1987; Hirsch, 1987), is that schools are not preparing students as well as they used to be prepared. Careful analyses of tests from previous eras and of opinions of previous generations of students do not support the supposition of the conservatives that there was once an educational golden era (e.g., Maxwell, 1979, p. 279; Whittington, 1991; Wyatt, 1992).

Narrowing of the Gap Between Black and White Achievement. *NAEP* data have been analyzed for racial differences in performance since this testing program started. Whites always outperform blacks. Even so, the gap in black-white performance differences has been narrowing, with the most prominent analyses for reading and mathematics (Jaynes & Williams, 1989, Chapter 7; Mullis, Owen, & Phillips, 1990). Although there has also been a narrowing of black-white differences in performance on tests such as the *SAT* during this same period, the *NAEP* data are seen as more telling because these data are more representative of the entire population, since the *SAT* is a test elected only by those interested in postsecondary education.

Not all who examine this closing of the gap are sanguine about it (Darling-Hammond & Snyder, 1992; Secada, 1992). First, at least for some of the *NAEP* assessments, the narrowing represents both a decline in white achievement and a gain in black achievement, so that focusing on the black-white difference misses the point that there have not been especially striking improvements in black performance. In addition, when there is close analysis of the pattern of performances within tests, much of the black performance improvement (e.g., in mathematics) is with respect to lower-level competencies rather than the more advanced competencies tapped by the test (Jaynes & Williams, 1989, Chapter 7;

Kirsch & Jungeblut, 1986). The critics of these tests argue that the closer one looks at *NAEP* data, the more clear it is that there is a long way to go if minorities are to perform at the higher level of competencies tapped by these tests, levels of competency that reflect the ever-increasing literacy and numeracy demands of modern life. Those who focus simply on the narrowing of the black-white gap are missing the point that education is still failing to be effective with many more minority than white majority children.

Other Potential Failings of the **NAEP**, *Analyses, and Interpretations of It.*

Besides the danger of projecting an overly pessimistic outlook on the current generation compared with past generations, there are a number of other failings of the *NAEP*, at least in the eyes of its critics. These include the following:

- The *NAEP* tests basic skills much more than higher-order skills (Squire, 1991). Many of the content items require only superficial acquaintance with the material (e.g., knowing who wrote what) rather than the deep understanding that comes from critical reading, reflecting, discussing, and acting on important content (Rosenblatt, 1991).
- The *NAEP* data are used by policy makers to leverage for reforms consistent with their agendas (e.g., Darling-Hammond & Snyder, 1992; Early, 1991; Farr & Beck, 1991; Ruth, 1991), which are not always consonant with educator agendas. One of the most debatable of these is the push by conservative groups for a common curriculum, one based on what they perceive to be the great Western ideas (e.g., Finn, 1991; Hirsch, 1987) but not one considered broad enough by many nor necessarily representative of the best of all thought and ideas.
- There are some important sampling problems with the *NAEP*. In particular, only children who are enrolled in school are measured. Because minorities and members of economically disadvantaged groups tend to drop out in larger proportions from school, they may be underrepresented in the high school data especially (Secada, 1992).
- Some claims made in light of the test data may be flagrant overstatements (e.g., the conclusion

that American students lack higher-order thinking skills). One possibility is that the higher-order thinking skills that students possess will not be evident in all situations, with a standardized testing situation being one in which reflective, higher-order thinking may not occur as readily as it would in other situations (Newkirk, 1991).

Summary   Although the *NAEP* is an impressive assessment achievement yielding voluminous, but generally orderly, data for the last 25 years here are doubts. As was the case with the standardized assessments covered in Chapter 16, there are doubts about how well minority populations are measured by the *NAEP*, although some of the specific concerns differ from the ones raised about IQ testing. In addition, just as many believe that IQ testing is a tool of the political right, the *NAEP* raises suspicion that it is a political lever of the reactionary United States: The political right publicly embrace *NAEP* data more uncritically than others and seem to use it to push their own agenda toward a curriculum emphasizing American and Western knowledge and values.

Without a doubt, however, there has been more discussion about *NAEP* conclusions regarding higher-order thinking than about almost any other topic. Too few students are scoring near the top of the *NAEP* scales; too few are getting the most difficult items on the tests correct. One possibility is that most U.S. students are not developing higher-order academic skills such as being able to coordinate strategies to find information in texts; plan, write, and revise texts; and understand, plan, and carry out complex solutions in an attempt to solve problems. Alternatively, perhaps the tests simply are very good at assessing these competencies. This possibility is one impetus for the development of new assessments that tap higher-order skills more directly.

Performance Assessments

There are substantial data documenting that if students are tested on particular content, teachers will teach to that content (e.g., Darling-Hammond & Snyder, 1992; F. Smith, 1986, Chapter 6; M. L. Smith, 1991a, 1991b). What is also interesting, however, is that they will teach some processes that they believe will be useful on the test: They teach students how to take the test, most prominently test-taking skills and strategies, from those with implications only for test taking, such as eliminating obviously incorrect multiple-choice answers before making a guess if not sure, to those that have some educational value beyond the test, such as converting story problems into equations that can be solved (Smith, 1991a).

One of the rationales behind performance assessments is that this powerful tendency of teachers to prepare their students for national, state, and other standardized assessments can be exploited for some good (Popham, 1987)—if the tests require processing abilities that are valuable in and of themselves: Performance assessments are being designed explicitly to force change in what students are learning in school, with performance assessment one of the most active areas in measurement research and development. Policy makers who have been influenced by educational researcher findings have decided that it is a good thing for students to learn (1) how to plan, write, and revise essays, with the result that performance assessments are being devised that require students to demonstrate how they write; (2) to perform scientific experiments, from hypothesis formation to hypothesis testing, with the outgrowth the development of assessments that require students to conduct experiments from hypothesis formation to actual experimentation to writeup of the outcomes of the experiment; and (3) the skills necessary to work mathematics problems and explain them at a conceptual level, stimulating the creation of math assessments in which students must explain their answers and how the answer was generated (O'Neil, 1992).

Some examples of performance assessments will make more obvious how different these assessments are from the standardized tests considered in Chapter 16 and in this chapter thus far. For readers who wish more examples and extensive descriptions of performance assessments, Mitchell's (1992) *Testing for Learning: How New Approaches to Evaluation Can Improve American Schools* is an excellent, accessible sourcebook. This book also provides substantial input about the many different groups that are working on development of performance assessments; it is an excellent history of this short-lived movement that is expanding its intellectual scope as the 1990s proceeds, with many more jurisdictions coming on board as political support for new assessments increases.

Maryland Reading-Writing Assessment (Maryland State Performance Assessment Project) Many leading literacy theorists believe that reading and writing should be taught together and are naturally related activities (see Chapter 15). One way to encourage teachers to teach that way is to use assessments that require simultaneous, coordinated reading and writing, which is one of the approaches used in the Maryland State Performance Assessment Project (MSPAP).

Consider an assessment used at grade 8 (Mitchell, 1992, pp. 47–49; also see *Educational Leadership,* May 1992, p. 17): Each student is given some texts (Jack London's classic story, "To Build a Fire," and a short piece from a book by Robert Pozos and David O'Born, *Hypothermia: Causes, Effects, and Prevention*). Each student also receives a map of North America, including Alaska and Canada's Yukon Territory.

The students are asked first to think about when they have been cold. They are given 10 minutes to write about their experiences being cold in a response journal. This is followed by reading of the London story, with students then responding to a series of comprehension questions. Some questions can be answered by constructing drawings; most require written responses. One question asks them to compare their own experiences with the cold with those of the dying man in "To Build a Fire." The students also assess how difficult the reading was for them; they are asked to write about the reading strategies they employed while reading the story by responding to a question about what they did when they came to a word or reference that they did not understand. That is day 1.

The test continues on day 2. First, students write a 5-minute letter to the dying man in "Fire," advising him about what to do to save his life. What follows is a class discussion of this topic, with the teacher recording on the board student ideas, especially in response to some of the words in the story (succumb, insidious). Students then read the piece from the book on hyperthermia and respond in writing to a series of comprehension questions, some of which can be answered by constructing pictures and diagrams. That is day 2.

Day 3 is concerned with integrating the information in the two pieces that were read. Students are required to write one of three types of responses:

- An essay informing friends what they need to do to be safe on a weekend trip.
- A poem, story, or play capturing the feelings associated with extreme states of heat, cold, hunger, or fatigue.

- A speech attempting to persuade people not to travel to the Yukon.

The teachers of students, however, do not know which of these types of writing will be required, although they have been informed in advance that students will be required to construct one of these three types of responses. The idea, of course, is to encourage teachers to teach students how to compose essays, poems, stories, plays, and persuasive speeches. The idea is to force the curriculum to cover particular types of writing processes in reaction to material that is read.

As they construct their day 3 writing, students are required to show their process. They must list words they have brainstormed in planning the essay or record in their journal a semantic web of ideas used in planning the essay. Then, they write a rough draft and revise it. The examination concludes with the participants using a proofreading guidesheet to check their final copy.

All of this material is graded on two criteria. One is for comprehension of what was read. That is, there is scoring of whether the student seemed to understand what was read. In addition, there is scoring of the quality of writing and how the writing task was done.

Mathematics and Science Performance Assessments   Such assessments are different from conventional assessments because there is observation of the decision making process, either decision-making in groups of students or by individual stuents (Figure 17.1) (Berk, 1986; Webb, 1992). For example, if attempting to assess students' measurement skills, performance assessment at its best involves observation of students as they use rulers, tape measures, different types of scales, and so on. That is, they are not shown a drawing of a ruler next to an object and asked to read off the length from the depiction. Rather, the assessor sizes up the procedures used and the attitudes and confidence of students as they proceed with problem solving using an actual ruler.

Mathematics educators are also working on performance assessments that are paper-and-pencil assessments, although ones with a difference: These assessments require students to reveal their understanding of process. Consider the following example, which involves presentation of this problem and the solution attempted by another student:

Figure 17.1 Science performance assessments measure the processes students carry out as they work on solving science problems. Teams of students work together, with the goal of the assessment the evaluation of the educational program rather than the individual students.

A bowl contains 10 pieces of fruit (apples and oranges). Apples cost 5 cents each, and oranges cost 10 cents each. Altogether the fruit is worth 70 cents. We want to find out how many apples are in the bowl. Kelly tried to solve the problem this way:

$10 \times 5 = 50$	$8 \times 5 = 40$
$2 \times 10 = 20$	$3 \times 10 = 30$
70	$4 \times 10 = 40$
	$6 \times 5 = 30$

There was 30 apples in the bowl. (Szetala & Nicol, 1992, p. 44)

The student taking the assessment is then asked to evaluate the performance of the student whose answer is shown, by responding to the following questions:

1. Is Kelly's way of solving the problem a good one? Tell why you think it is or is not a good way.
2. Did Kelly get the right answer? Explain why she did or did not. (Szetala & Nicol, 1992, p. 44)

Most readers will have figured out that Kelly's solution contained serious errors (e.g., 30 apples as a response makes no sense when there are only 10 pieces of fruit total in the bowl; the correct solution is 6 apples, with Kelly's error that she copied the wrong piece of information from her computations and failed to check her answer against the reality of the situation). To evaluate Kelly's solution, a student must be able to represent the problem and compare his or her representation with Kelly's. The questions posed about Kelly's solution require that students reveal their thinking about the problem.

Closing Comments on Testlike Performance Assessments   A diverse range of competencies can be tested via performance assessment. A major question, however, is how good these tests are: Are they reliable and valid? Shavelson and associates (e.g., Shavelson, Baxter, & Pines, 1992) have been evaluating science performance assessments for grade-5 and grade-6 science. For example, in one, students were asked to test three different types of paper towels to determine which soaked up the most and least water. In addition to the towels, the students were provided water, beakers, a scale, a timer, and other utensils. In a second assessment, students were "given" mystery boxes containing circuit components in a MacIntosh computer microworld simulation. Using wires, batteries, and bulbs, they were to determine what was in these boxes. The students were appraised that each box had (a) two batteries linked into the circuit, (b) a wire in the circuit, (c) a light alone, (d) a battery and light, or (e) nothing. In a third assessment, students experimented with sow bugs to determine the bugs' environmental preferences, with the bugs and manipulations carried out in a MacIntosh simulation. They were to determine whether the bugs liked damp or dry environments and light or dark environments. In all three assessments, students were required to keep records of what they did and report their conclusions.

Could student performances be assessed reliably with these tests? Yes and no. On the positive side of the ledger, it was easy to get agreement between raters with respect to the scoring of individual assessments. It was more difficult to produce consistent results across tasks, however, with some students performing better on one assessment than another. What this latter result means is that to obtain reliable performance assessment data, a number of tasks will have to be included in such assessments. This is a formidable demand given that the expenses in developing, administering, and scoring single performance assessments are high. More positively, it did seem in Shavelson's studies that reliable scoring of student writeups of their assessments was possible; in addition, presentation of the problems on a microcomputer with subsequent experimentation in the simulation environment (and recorded by the program) also seemed satisfactory. Thus, there do appear to be cost-saving "short-cuts" to actual hands-on student performances observed and scored by raters.

With respect to validity, Shavelson et al. (1992) expected that students who had been enrolled in "hands-on" science courses that taught process would outperform students in traditional textbook-oriented courses. That proved to be the case. In addition to testing subjects with the performance assessments, Shavelson's group also tested other students with paper-and-pencil tests designed to assess the experimental competencies measured in the performance assessments. The most interesting finding with respect to these tests was that they did not differentiate students with hands-on science instruction from those receiving traditional instruction, although the performance assessments had done so, which, of course, provides some validation for the performance assessments.

One major concern with performance assessments is their expense relative to traditional assessments. As professionals who have been close to groups developing such tests, it is striking how much time and effort—many committees and many pilot assessments—go into the development of performance assessment items. Then, there are the administration costs, with these tests extending over days of school rather than over hours of school. Finally, there is scoring, which requires many person-hours of effort compared with the rapid machine scoring permitted by multiple choice. Mitchell (1992) estimated that these tests may be 10 times more costly than conventional assessments. Although research such as Shavelson et al. (1992) suggest some cost-saving possibilities, such as reliance on journals and written products rather than actual observations of students, there are also indicators that more resources may have to be put into future assessments than present ones: Recall that Shavelson et al. (1991) observed that a large number of items would be required for reliable performance assessments, which involves the costs of designing the items and then administering them. If Shavelson et al. (1991) are right, the 3-day tests that are performance assessments in the early 1990s may seem like "quickies" compared with future performance assessments.

Consideration of whether what is gained by performance assessment is worth the cost of it is needed.

In addition, the problems students have been presented on performance assessments to date often are simple or contrived compared with the types of problems we would like students to be able to solve; the essays that emanate from the writing assessments are short and without feeling compared with the essays educators want to stimulate their students to write. In short, our perception of testlike performance assessments is that they are not authentic enough. That is one reason another form of performance assessment, portfolios, covered in the next subsection, is much more appealing to us. Portfolios include authentic student products, student's best efforts, efforts most likely to reveal their competence. Even so, we will conclude the section on portfolios with a continuation of this discussion of reservations about new forms of assessment.

Portfolios: A Form of Long-Term Performance Assessment

Educational portfolios are intended to provide information so that inferences can be made about student knowledge, ability, and their attitudes toward their work. It is a file of a student's best work in writing, math, science, or any area of competence that is the target of education (Collins, 1992; Goodman, 1991; O'Neil, 1992). Educators are thinking hard about how student portfolios can and should be used, what should be included in portfolios for various educational tasks and contents (e.g., science, writing, mathematics), and how complete such files should be. Ultimately the portfolio is a collection of objects, often a file of completed projects. Some portfolios might be more specific than others, such as Collins's (1992) suggestion that physics students could be asked to develop portfolios of evidence over some set period of time to verify their understanding of some physics concept (e.g., a file of examples of how physics impacts everyday life). In short, portfolios are **collections of objects assembled for a purpose** (Bird, 1990; Collins, 1992). The purpose must be clear before setting out to develop a portfolio.

Portfolio Examples From the Classroom As part of Hansen's Literacy Portfolios Project in Manchester, New Hampshire, fourth-grade students prepare portfolios to document their literacy. Hansen (e.g.,

1992) believes such folders provide students much opportunity to know themselves and how rich their literacy lives are as they provide opportunity for educators to get to know and understand students and their literacy better.

Literacy portfolios in New Hampshire often contain evidence of reading and writing outside of school as well as inside school because children often engage in significant literacy that is not school reading and writing. Hansen and her colleagues recognize the importance of documenting such activity if an assessment is to be a comprehensive representation of a child's literacy. The purpose of the portfolios is not only to document reading-writing growth of the child, but also to be an expression of who the child is, both as a literate person and more broadly: Thus, one grade-1 student's portfolio includes a book about a character who has trouble speaking, a book important to the child because he has a speech problem, too. One junior high student's portfolio includes a book about a juvenile who had stolen a car, went to prison, and reformed. This book meant something to the young reader because he had been expelled from a previous school for misconduct and found the story inspirational as he attempted to make good in a new school.

Hansen (1992) and her colleagues believe it important that portfolios capture children's perspectives on their literacy, at least some of the reasons why reading and writing are important to them, and why some books they read and some things they write are more important to them than others. One reason is that such a literacy portfolio provides a great deal of information to new teachers the student will encounter, information that can be used to aid in planning a literacy curriculum that is sensitive to student needs, concerns, and interests.

Collins (1992) provides a description of potential grade-4 science portfolios. There are four classes of objects in such a portfolio: (1) *artifacts,* such as written reports of experiments and tests; (2) *reproductions,* such as a photo of a bulletin board display created by the student; (3) *attestations,* which are appraisals of the student by someone other than the student and his teacher who reviews the portfolio, with examples being letters of gratitude for something a student did (e.g., organized an environmental clean-up day) or a note from other members of the students' cooperative learning group praising a particular contribution made by the student; and (4) *productions,* objects prepared especially for inclusion in the portfolio, including goal statements from the teacher about the purpose of the portfolio, reflective statements by the student indicating the importance and relationship of the various documents in the portfolio, and captions attached to each document in the portfolio to describe what the object is and why it is significant.

One fourth-grade teacher's goal was for students to document that they had acquired balanced science knowledge during the year. Thus, students were required to include documentation about their learning in the content area they liked best during the year of science instruction, two thinking skills they had mastered, and evidence that they had learned about some topic of public concern. (These three categories mapped the particular instructional objectives the teacher had for the class during the year, to develop in-depth knowledge about a range of topics, to increase thinking skills, and to stimulate awareness of the social relevance of science.) To do so, the portfolios could include worksheets from problem-solving activities, diagrams or pictures that had been graded, and products from group work. The number of pieces of evidence was limited, and students were required to develop captions for each exhibit and a reflective statement summarizing how the various exhibits related to one another. The individual students consulted with their teacher about what ought to be included in their portfolio, with the construction of the portfolio a dynamic experience, permitting review of the year's work and increased self-understanding by the students:

> Knowing the purposes of the portfolio and its structure, students have saved their work throughout the year. . . . Now, as the year ends, they sit in teams with all their evidence spread before them discussing which topic was their favorite and why, or which assignment from that topic best illustrates their mastery; they have all their problem-solving sheets and can see how their skills have changed; they recognize that each has different strengths—the future artist, future mechanic, and future author. As the students write their reflective statements, they integrate their experiences in science class with their experiences from other classes. (Collins, 1992, p. 462)

Such a science portfolio provided a great deal of information about what had been accomplished by the student for that year and was especially rich documentation for parents about their own child's progress. The grade-4 teacher was able to make evaluations of individual students and assign grades for the year, with the portfolios extremely helpful in this process. The portfolios as a collection provided the next year's teachers with a rich fund of evidence about the science coverage experienced in grade 4. For this grade-4 science teacher, the portfolios provided assessment information, a rich educational experience for the students, and a window on the students' knowledge for subsequent educators.

Knight (1992) is a middle-school mathematics teacher in California. She had her students keep exhaustive files of their work for the year, including some long-term projects, notes they had taken, tests, problems of the week, homework, and journal remarks about especially difficult examination problems. At the end of the year, she had them go through their folders and select five items that would represent their knowledge of math and the efforts they had expended during the year. The students attached a personal statement to each of these exhibits. Here is an example of one set of comments:

> I chose three papers for my portfolio because they show my best work and my worst work. They portray both sides of my academic performance in math this last semester.
>
> The 45 percent math test is in my portfolio because it shows that I have some problems in math. It shows my bad work. It shows that sometimes I have a bad day. It shows also that I forgot to study (ha, ha, ha).
>
> I can sum up three papers in this paragraph. Those are the Personal Budget, the James project, and the $2000 lottery project. On all of these papers, I did really well. That shows I do much better on those projects, especially the creative ones. I have a bit more fun doing them rather than doing just normal take-home math assignments. These papers definitely show me at my best. (Knight, 1992, p. 72)

One of the most immediately obvious effects of this new form of assessment for Knight was that it did what performance assessment is intended to do: It changed her teaching:

> As a result of trying to implement portfolio assessment, my classroom has definitely changed. It became apparent early on that if I wanted variety in my children's portfolios, I had to provide variety in assignments. I have changed my curriculum to include more problem-solving opportunities with written explanations. I have also had my students do two long-term situational problems. In the past, although I knew my algebra classes found such problems entertaining, I

had questioned their lasting value. Now I see that these problems are the ones the kids remember the most. (Knight, 1992, p. 72).

The portfolios were used as part of assessing students in the course, providing about 20 percent of the total grade. Knight believed that the portfolio provided her with increased understanding of student maturity, self-esteem, and writing. She also believed that student self-assessment was an important gain from construction of the portfolios, with the portfolio construction project forcing them to review their strengths and weaknesses and what had been accomplished in the class.

In closing this subsection on examples of evaluations with portfolios, we emphasize that these reports are typical of many we have been encountering, in published accounts of teacher use of portfolios and as we interact with teachers in the field. The three essential steps to construction of a portfolio are the following: Students (1) collect their work over a reasonable period of time; (2) review it at some point, selecting some "best" work or most representative work for inclusion in a portfolio; and (3) assemble the portfolio, including reflective, integrative commentary about the pieces selected and their significance. Typically, teachers provide criteria to students to help them select and reflect on their work.

Many teachers believe portfolio construction increases student review and reflection on their work. As an assessment device, it informs them as teachers about strengths and weaknesses of their curriculum and is informative to parents and future teachers about the curricular accomplishments of individuals as well as groups of students.

NAEP and Portfolio Assessment: The 1990 Writing Portfolio Pilot Study Although the *NAEP* has been criticized for relying too much on multiple-choice tests, it also has a distinguished track record for integrating new and innovative methods into large-scale assessments (e.g., the presidential responsibilities essay on the civics test). *NAEP* is now studying the possibility of national portfolio assessment of writing, with Gentile (1992) reporting the results of a 1990 pilot study related to that effort.

NAEP has been conducting writing assessments for some time. The typical format for these assessments is for students to be provided a writing assignment that can be completed in 15 minutes. A great failing of this type of assessment is that much of writing requires more than 15 minutes. Indeed, most of the process writing instruction that is favored by writing researchers and theorists—and is being translated into instruction in many schools—involves multiple sessions of planning (perhaps including library or other research) and revisions after the completion of a first draft. These revisions often involve student conferencing with teachers, peers, or parents. Given the growing commitment of many educators to plan-write-revise models, the *NAEP* is questioning the validity of its 15-minute, first-and-final draft writing assessment. Consistent with their commitment to research-based conclusions, however, *NAEP* has decided to study the situation as part of piloting portfolio assessment of writing rather than simply concluding that the 15-minute format is inadequate. We applaud such a commitment to research rather than armchair analyses of assessment.

The portfolio project involved grade-4 and grade-8 students who had participated in the regular *NAEP* writing assessment. The teachers of these students were contacted and asked to assist the students in selecting one piece of their *best* writing from the grade-4 or grade-8 school year. More than 1000 students were tapped at each age level. (One reason this was a pilot is that the sample ended up not being as carefully constructed with respect to national representation issues as other *NAEP* samples, although none could read the description of the sampling without thinking that the study was adequate to permit at least tentative conclusions about the writing of American grade-4 and grade-8 students.)

Once the essays arrived at *NAEP,* a great deal of effort was devoted initially to determining how to analyze them. One of the first analyses was to examine exactly what type of writing was submitted. There were some surprises. First, more than half of the writing samples (51 percent at grade 4, 59 percent at grade 8) were informative essays. The second most common type of writing was narratives (36 percent at grade 4, 30 percent at grade 8). An especially striking finding was that there was little persuasive essay writing, striking to the *NAEP* because their assessments so often ask students to write persuasive essays. (Thus a first major finding was that a type of essay frequently tapped on more traditional *NAEP* writing assessments probably is not practiced much in school writing.) There was also little poetry, few letters, and almost no research reports. One disturbing finding was that 7 percent of the grade-4 and 5 percent of the grade-8 submissions were skill sheets, with teachers indicating that they had not started writing instruction by the spring. (Thus, another important finding is that despite the claim in Chapter 15 that writing instruction is common in American elementary schools, there are some schools where it does not happen or does not happen until late in the year.)

The papers were assessed for several other features early in this analysis process, with substantial important information emerging from these analyses. First, almost all of the papers were written to an unspecified audience, despite the fact that many believe skilled writers write to specific audiences and shape essays according to audience background knowledge and need. Second, fewer than half of the papers showed evidence of using the plan-write-revise approach. The most common process that was evident was minor revision. Although the *NAEP* had requested that drafts accompany the submissions, they recognized the possibility that many teachers sent best drafts and that their assessment of process on this pilot might underestimate the amount of process students use. They gathered more extensive information about process in their 1992 portfolio assessment, which was being analyzed when this book went to press. Third, the most frequently used resource for papers were students' own ideas rather than material from sources. Fourth, only 2 percent of the papers were written on computers, suggesting a low level of computer use for word processing in schools. Fifth, the majority of papers were written in response to general prompts from the teacher, such as, "write about Thanksgiving," or "write about bicycles." A great deal about student writing in the United States was discerned from even these preliminary assessments.

After reviewing the papers systematically, the *NAEP* came up with ways of scoring the various types of writing to reflect the characteristics of good versus poor writing. Thus, the worst narratives described only a single event, often minimally with a list of sentences. Then came undeveloped stories, followed by stories that contained all of the main story grammar elements (i.e., a series of events carried out by characters confronting problems; see Chapters 3 and 14). It was also possible to discern better-developed stories, with these classified as extended stories, developed stories, and elaborated stories (with elaborated best of these three, which included all of the story grammar elements with elaborated problems and resolutions to problems).

Similar scoring schemes were developed for informational essays and persuasive writing, with the weakest examples of each genre scored as 1's (e.g., single events in the narrative category) and the best examples scored as 6's (i.e., elaborated stories for narratives). A critical part of this analysis work was establishing the reliability of these scoring schemes: Two different raters agreed on the exact rating for an essay more than three-quarters of the time; two different raters were within one category (e.g., one gave it a 3, the other a 4) a minimum of 96 percent of the time, ranging up to 100 percent of the time (i.e., for grade-4 narratives and informative essays). The scoring was reliable.

The outcome was not entirely different from other *NAEP* assessments, however, including the writing assessments used to generate the *Writing Report Cards* for the United States to date. First, most students performed on the low end of the scale. Collapsing across all types of writing, 88 percent of grade-4 students and 70 percent of grade-8 students received a 1, 2, or 3. Virtually none of the students received 6's. Only 1 percent of the grade-4 narratives received a 5; only 2 percent of the grade-4 informative essays did so; there were no grade-4 persuasive essays earning a 5. Only 8 percent of the grade-8 narratives earned a 5; only 8 percent of the grade-8 informative essays did so; no grade-8 persuasive essays earned a 5.

A critical question for the *NAEP* was whether students would score differently on this portfolio assessment compared with the more traditional *NAEP* writing assessment. At the grade-4 level, if they did poorly or well on the portfolio assessment, they did the same on the *NAEP Writing Report Card* assessment 77 percent of the time. The corresponding figure at the grade-8 level was only 55 percent, however. That is, the grading of students on the two assessments was more similar at the grade-4 than at the grade-8 level. When there was a discrepancy in student performance at either grade level, students were more likely to score well on the portfolio assessment than on the 15-minute, first-and-last-draft assessment. Our reading of these data is that the portfolio was providing unique information at both grade levels and, if anything, information that is more telling to the United States about the type of writing that many educators wish to foster.

Although there were glitches in the 1990 *NAEP* portfolio pilot, such as the need for more extensive information about the processes students used to produce their portfolio essay, the assessment process seemed to have proceeded smoothly with this new format, producing data directly relevant to contemporary writing instruction and models of excellent writing instruction. That *NAEP* conducted the 1992 assessment with refinements over the 1990 pilot is indicative of their commitment to this new type of assessment tool, one that promises to deliver a more interesting and probably more valid writing report card to the United States in the future.

Concluding Comments Portfolio assessment is stimulating a great deal of interest among teachers and those responsible for national assessments. One of its great appeals is that the assessment and the educational product are the same; the items placed in the portfolio are ones that should be produced in a high-quality educational environment. Of course, in some cases, the portfolio assessment stimulates teachers to require their students to do the type of high-quality work required for a successful portfolio.

The effects portfolios have on students and teachers need to be studied closely, however: If portfolios have the positive effects on self-esteem suggested by some of the educators discussed in this subsection, that is an important benefit. If they stimulate student understanding of their work and how it fits together, that is an important benefit. If they lead to more effective review of material covered in a course, that is also a benefit that needs to be documented. The research opportunities are great here, both for those interested in testing and those more concerned with instruction.

Our general enthusiasm for portfolios is held in check, however, by many concerns about performance assessment in general. One way to think about the concerns, however, is as challenges to overcome. If the benefits of portfolios can be documented better, there is every reason to believe that educators and educational researchers will devise ways to overcome obstacles. Our guess is that for portfolios, the obvious external validity of this form of assessment is going to have tremendous appeal to many constituencies, and, thus, thinking about how to overcome concerns is more appropriate than trying to make the case that defensible portfolio assessment is impossible.

One critical concern is that portfolios, similar to other performance assessments, are capturing only a small part of academic achievement. There are many sources of information that teachers have available to them that provide information about whether their students are making progress. For example, for primary teachers who are charged with the development of literacy in their students, they observe (1) changes in how students respond to stories, (2) whether students engage in independent reading, and (3) the development of oral reading fluency. Teachers obtain data about student reading achievement throughout the school day (e.g., Chittenden, 1991). When these many sources of information about children's literacy are considered, it is clear that even the richest portfolios are going to miss a lot. Thus, one reaction we have to portfolios is to applaud that they are more comprehensive than traditional assessments and more authentic to boot; another reaction is that they could be even more comprehensive and tap a broader range of authentic classroom experiences.

Are the New Assessments Improved Enough to Justify Eliminating the Old in Favor of the New?

No one could read the new assessment literature without discerning contempt by some of the new assessors about old assessment practices (e.g., Wolf et al., 1991). Our own view is that the new assessments represent an evolutionary development that has benefited enormously from the psychometrics work that preceded it. For example, the evaluations of new assessments in terms of reliability and validity are informed by years of work in standardizing traditional instruments. We fear that some extremely useful, more traditional tests may be dismissed too readily, however, if the aggressive antistandardized testing rhetoric of the new assessors becomes the politically correct position, which is pretty clearly a goal of many of the new breed of testers. (There is no quicker way to elicit turned-up noses from many testing reformers than to mention IQ!)

One of the old assessment practices that comes under attack is measuring individual students at all. The result is that many performance assessment products are team products, such as a group of students conducting experiments together, with their collaborative efforts and products examined. This reform raises some important questions: Are children well served by never measuring how they perform as individuals, given that individualized accounting systems await them outside of school? Isn't it important to know if some students are more in need of help than others?

Given the limited remedial resources available, it is often necessary to make a strong case based on objective measurement that students who are receiving special assistance need it more than others in a school. We worry that individual students might be forgotten more easily in schools that orient exclusively to the testing of group performances rather than individual children. The dynamics of individual children's learning and intelligence still seem important to us, with the work of some like-minded testing reformers considered in the next section.

DYNAMIC ASSESSMENT (LEARNING POTENTIAL ASSESSMENT)

Those who identify with the dynamic assessment movement are concerned that traditional IQ measures underestimate the competencies of many children. They view an IQ test like an achievement test—that is, a measure of skills and knowledge already acquired. The assumption of those constructing IQ tests is that smarter people will have acquired more than same-age people of lesser intelligence because the smarter people learn more quickly. This assumption is filled with additional assumptions about equal opportunity, however, assumptions that clearly do not hold for many segments of society: For example, children living in poverty do not have the same opportunities for exposure to the type of information tapped on IQ tests as do majority children (Budoff, 1987b).

For more than 30 years, intelligence researchers such as Budoff (e.g., Budoff & Friedman, 1964) have argued that a fairer test of intelligence would measure speed of learning more directly, that high intelligence would come to be defined as being able to benefit from experience reality, and low intelligence would be reflected by inability to benefit from environmental experiences. The general approach taken by Budoff was to design assessments that involved a teaching component. Students are tested, then taught, followed by retesting. For example, a student might be given a problem to solve and, after failing to solve it, be provided problem-solving instruction, with subsequent retesting on the problem. If the child benefits from a short period of training, the inference is made that the child profits from experience. (Readers should note that this is a different approach to linking assessment to teaching than performance assessment, with learning potential assessment directly assessing whether the child can benefit from instruction.)

In much of Budoff's work, a block design task (Kohs, 1923) was used in the assessment. In this task, the subject is provided a picture of block design involving red, white, blue, yellow, blue/yellow, and red/white sides. The task is to duplicate the depicted design with blocks that are provided. A subject is presented 15 of these problems, increasing in difficulty as testing during the first session proceeds. Then, there is coaching, which includes the following:

1. Maximizing success by the possibility of working down to the simplest elements in the design.
2. Freely offering praise and encouragement.
3. The strategy of motorically checking the construction, block by block, against the design card to encourage an active, planned, and systematic work approach and to allow the subject to see concretely the success he or she is achieving.
4. Emphasis on the concept of two-color blocks as the elements composing the design (e.g., by teaching the process of building a stripe and the concept of orientation of the blocks in a design by constructing a diamond). (Budoff, 1987a)

One day and 1 month after the coaching session, student performance on the designs is tested again.

Budoff and Friedman (1964) were able to demonstrate in a true experiment that retarded children benefited from the training they provided. More importantly, regardless of IQ, some subjects benefited more from training than did other subjects. In addition, there were indicators in subsequent work that those who gained the most from training achieved at a higher level in school than did low gainers (Babad & Budoff, 1974; Budoff, Gimon, & Corman, 1974). One of the most impressive demonstrations of the predictability of learning potential classification was conducted at the middle-school level. Gainers acquired more from a science unit on electricity than did nongainers (with IQ controlled statistically). In short, Budoff and colleagues provided substantial data to support the hypothesis that susceptibility to instruction, which is what learning potential is, predicts academic achievement. Budoff's work has done much to fuel enthusiasm for dynamic assessment in North America.

The approach favored by Budoff has been "discovered" by other intelligence theorists working in other cultures, which is, perhaps, a testimony to its appeal. Thus, Feurstein (e.g., 1979) developed dynamic assessment approaches to measure Israeli juveniles who had been living outside mainstream Israel, including many post–World War II immigrants. Feurstein's (1979) test includes many items that resemble traditional IQ test items, although ones that presumably require high-order thinking to accomplish. For example, consider the "organization of dots" task. A subject is given a card with dots on it, with the dot patterns varying from item to item on the test. The subject is also shown geometric figures. The task is to find the same figures in the dot patterns and connect the dots. Feurstein (e.g., 1979) contends that this task involves a number of higher-order processes, including discriminations of form and size, restraint of impulsivity, planning, and systematic search and comparison among others.

As with Budoff's test, subjects are tested first and then provided some training in the strategies and principles required to perform the test task. This instruction is individualized to deal with particular problems that subjects may encounter. Thus, teaching is not rigidly standardized but flexible. The teaching phase is followed by retesting. The focus is on the processing strengths of the person being assessed (i.e., the peaks in their performances).

The main finding from Feurstein's work (e.g., Rand & Kaniel, 1987) is that performance on test items does improve with training: Posttraining performance of socioculturally deprived children often approaches the level of performance of mainstream children. Feurstein (1979) believes that this pattern of results confirms one of his most important claims—that static measures of IQ (e.g., simulated with the learning potential pretests, which are always lower for deprived children compared with mainstream populations) underestimate the competencies of socioculturally deprived populations. Moreover, Feurstein and colleagues (e.g., Tzuriel & Feurstein, 1992) contend that their studies confirm that children who initially test poorly can improve dramatically if given high-intensity, responsive teaching at a high level of abstraction, teaching that emphasizes strategies and principles. (See the discussion of instrumental enrichment in Chapter 11.)

Soviet psychologists developed testing procedures consistent with dynamic assessment as well (e.g., Luria, 1961). One important Soviet idea that has been linked to dynamic assessment, by Feurstein (e.g., 1979) originally but more recently by Campione and Brown (1987), is the zone of proximal development: Vygotsky (e.g., 1978; see Chapter 8,

this book) argued that much of learning is mediated by interactions with others, who provide support for the young child attempting to acquire new concepts and procedures. There are some things that a child can do unaided. There are others that the child can accomplish if provided some assistance from an adult. There are still other skills and competencies that are beyond the child at present. Those competencies that can be carried out by the child with assistance define the child's zone of proximal development. ("Proximal development" refers to the assumption that those skills that the child can perform with assistance are partially developed already— the child's development is in the proximity of these capacities, although not yet achieving them.) An important measure of individual differences is the "width" of this zone, with more capable children able to perform many more tasks with assistance than less capable children (i.e., more capable children have wider zones of proximal development than do less capable children). A critical assumption is that the width of the zone can change for a child, for example, after high-quality instruction has begun following years of neglect, so that today's appraisal of the width of the zone may be invalid in a few weeks or months depending on what happens in the child's environment (see Campione & Brown, 1987).

Campione and Brown's (1987) approach to dynamic assessment is similar in many ways to Budoff's and Feurstein's, although there are also unique elements. Their studies involve variants of traditional psychometric tasks (e.g., matrix problems). Subjects are pretested; then they receive instruction about ways to solve the problems; then they are tested again, with maintenance problems (i.e., identical in format to pretest items) and transfer problems (i.e., items related in format to pretest items but requiring slightly different operations). Thus, if subjects are trained to solve matrix problems that require using one of three rules, maintenance problems would require using one of three rules, but transfer problems might require using two rules simultaneously.

Some of the research from Campione and Brown's group was conducted with preschool children (e.g., Bryant, 1982; Bryant, Brown, & Campione, 1983). The preschoolers were given simple matrices tasks. Consistent with Campione and Brown's findings in general in this area (as well as others such as Budoff), static measures of ability (i.e., IQ) did predict learning and transfer to some degree. In particular, Campione and Brown's group found that higher-ability children required fewer hints to learn during training than did the lower-ability participants. Moreover, higher-ability subjects as defined by IQ required fewer hints to do the transfer tasks than did low-ability subjects. Importantly, however, even when IQ was controlled, there were still relationships between the pretest-to-posttest gain scores (i.e., the index of learning potential) and the number of hints required at transfer. What Campione and Brown's (1987) data suggest is that both the static and the dynamic measures are useful in predicting transfer. People with high psychometric intelligence transfer more readily (i.e., with fewer hints) than people with lower psychometric intelligence; after intelligence is accounted for, however, there are differences in how quickly people learn. Those who learn more quickly transfer more readily (i.e., require fewer hints to apply skills learned on one task to another related task).

The Campione and Brown emphasis on predictive validity as reflected by transfer data is important. Good thinkers can use what they know broadly—they can transfer. That there is a relationship between the susceptibility to instruction and transfer makes clear that by measuring differences in learning when given instruction, the assessor is tapping into competencies at least related to the broad use of what has been learned.

We view the predictive validity issue as especially critical with respect to dynamic assessment. After all, one of the reasons traditional intelligence tests have endured is that they are predictively valid: They predict well who will succeed in school. A reasonable expectation is that alternative measures that might be proposed as replacements for traditional assessments would have greater predictive validity than IQ. Besides the Budoff studies and the work of Campione, Brown, and their associates, there are other data consistent with the perspective that dynamic measures provide better predictions of academic achievement (at least in some situations) than do other measurements. For example, Luther and Wyatt (1989) reported that dynamic assessments predicted the school success of English-second-language students better than did traditional IQ. Dynamic assessments predicted better than conventional intelligence test data which preschool handicapped students would do well enough in school so that 2 years later they would be in regular classrooms rather than in special education placements

(Samuels, Killip, MacKenzie, & Fagan, 1992). Shochet (1992) reported that for disadvantaged students entering college, traditional static measures did a reasonable job of predicting the success of students who proved less modifiable in dynamic assessments; the success of students proving more modifiable in dynamic assessments was not predictable from static assessments. Gullke and Wingenfeld (1992) reported that among disadvantaged children in particular, dynamic assessments did a better job of predicting academic achievement longitudinally than did static tests.

Even so, we believe a great deal of work needs to be done before firm claims can be made about the value of dynamic assessment. First, there are issues of reliability, with little attention to this critical psychometric consideration in the dynamic assessment literature to date (Laughon, 1990; Samuels, Tzuriel, & Malloy-Miller, 1989). Second, much more work needs to be done on the predictive validity of dynamic assessment relative to conventional assessment. The small amount of data that is available, however, is supportive of the conclusion that dynamic measures are better predictors of achievement than static measures. A second problem is that there are only a few studies examining prediction of real-school academic performance, which, of course, is the predictive validity of greatest concern.

Dynamic assessment is extremely attractive to many who are concerned about disadvantaged students, believing that such students are discriminated against by conventional assessments. For example, some of those fighting the legal battles to prevent standardized assessment from being used to assign minority children to special education view dynamic assessment as potentially fairer to minority children, permitting more certain identification of students who would benefit from particular types of educational interventions (Elliott, 1992; Utley, Haywood, & Masters, 1992). That is, one possibility with dynamic assessment is for the assessor to try a variety of teaching methods during the teaching phase of the test-teach-retest cycle, until the assessor zeroes in on methods that work with this particular student. If dynamic assessors can succeed in reliably identifying treatments that work for particular students but not others, this would be a tremendous accomplishment (e.g., Utley et al., 1992). What an exciting approach to assessment this would be compared with more conventional approaches, which are aimed largely at gauging who will make it and who will not in conventional school. Consistent with this general direction, the next section describes some approaches for deciding whether particular forms of instruction are working for particular students as they face real-school academic demands.

CURRICULUM-BASED ASSESSMENT/MEASUREMENT

Most of the measurements detailed in Chapter 16 and this chapter have involved tasks and materials removed from actual classroom tasks and materials, with the most conspicuous exception being portfolio assessment. Not surprisingly, the recommendations that emerge from such assessments often are not helpful in instructional decision making. Classroom-based assessment/measurement contrasts with most other approaches to assessment with respect to the classroom authenticity of the materials used in the evaluations and generation of recommendations that are explicitly relevant to the curriculum the student is experiencing.

Shinn, Rosenfeld, and Knutson (1989), based in part on Deno (1987), defined classroom-based assessment as, "... *any* set of measurement procedures that use direct observation and recording of a student's performance in the local curriculum as a basis for gathering information to make instructional decisions" (p. 300). They go on to describe some variations on this approach, concluding that there are four different models of assessment that qualify:

(1) *Curriculum-based assessment for curriculum design* was proposed by Gickling and colleagues (e.g., Gickling, Shane, & Croskery, 1989). Consistent with the motivational principle of optimal levels of challenge (see Chapter 5), Gickling believes that students are best served if they are being ask to learn material that is just a bit beyond them, material that presents some challenge but is not overwhelming. The key is to test students to find out where they are in the curriculum, to determine which tasks they can do with little challenge, which can be done only with hesitation or with assistance, and which are completely beyond them. Thus, a student is in the appropriate reading level according to this model if the student can perform the skill and drill exercises for the level with 70 to 85 percent correct responses and recognizes 93 to 97 percent of the words in the reading. Note that such levels of correctness permit the student to do well much of the time, although there is still some learning for the student to master the level.

Gickling and Armstrong (1978) studied the academic achievement and behaviors of students who were matched well to curricular level versus those provided tasks beyond their current competence and those presented tasks that were too easy. Students given assignments that were too difficult did not do as much work as well-matched students, with more off-task behaviors by the overchallenged mismatched students. Off-task behavior was common when tasks were too easy as well. Academic engagement was greatest with appropriate matching to difficulty level.

The assessments conducted by a teacher to determine level of placement are constructed from course materials. Once the initial placement is made, based on determining which part of the curriculum offers optimum challenge, there is ongoing assessment to determine whether the student is making progress. If the student masters the current level, he or she moves on in the curriculum. If not, there may be reason to consider alternative instruction from what is being provided. In short, such assessment is for instructional planning. Many readers will certainly have noted that it is "dynamic" (see Haywood, Tzuriel, & Vaught, 1992, who make an explicit case that curriculum-based assessment is dynamic). Shinn et al. (1989) acknowledged its potential for determining who should be referred for special educational services versus students who can make progress in the regular education environment: That is, if students do not make progress given current instruction that is aimed at a level matched with their current level of functioning, that is a sign that other instructional measures are appropriate. Because such an assessment is grounded in the curriculum for which the student is accountable, and because the focus is on whether and how the student can learn, it is an admirable form of dynamic assessment.

(2) *Curriculum-based measurement.* This approach, favored by Deno (e.g., 1986; also Fuchs & Fuchs, 1990) involves assessing students continuously with respect to a long-term goal. Perhaps the goal is for a student to be able to read at a second-grade, second-semester level 1 year from now. Beginning now and throughout intervention, there will be measurement of the student's reading of second-grade, second-semester materials, perhaps including responses to comprehension questions, ability to retell what has been read, or oral fluency. The teacher often will graph the student's progress so that the student can

have visual evidence of improvement when it occurs. If improvement is not occurring, it is a signal to the teacher to make some changes in the instruction that is occurring, and such monitoring does seem to increase the number of curricular adjustments that teachers make (Fuchs, Fuchs, Hamlett, & Stecker, 1991). This type of measurement is entirely forward looking, with students expected to do poorly at first because they are responding to material far beyond them. The goal is to be able to perform capably in the long term the tasks that are frustrating today.

(3) *Criterion-referenced models (also known as mastery learning approach).* Students are tested on content they are currently learning, with large chunks of content often broken down into smaller units (Fuchs & Fuchs, 1990; see the discussion of mastery learning in Chapter 11 of this book). If the students meet some predetermined criterion for a unit test (e.g., 80 percent of the comprehension questions correct)—one devised by the teacher over unit content—they are deemed to have learned the material for the unit and can move on in the curriculum to the next unit. If the students fall below the criterion on the mastery test, there is additional teaching and subsequent retesting.

(4) *Curriculum-based evaluation.* Howell and Morehead (1987) argued that good teachers should, ". . . test what you teach and teach what you test," contending that alignment of instruction and assessment was one way to increase learning. Those favoring this approach emphasize breaking tasks down into their subskills. During the initial assessment, students are asked to perform the task of interest to the assessor (e.g., subtraction of multidigit numbers). The student errors are analyzed by the assessor to generate hypotheses about what the student might be doing wrong while working problems (e.g., the student cannot regroup during subtraction). Assessments are then designed that tap the presumed problems the student is experiencing (e.g., a number of subtraction problems requiring regrouping are constructed, with student performance explicitly compared on otherwise similar problems that do not require regrouping). Decisions are made from these follow-up tests about the deficiencies of the student so that appropriate instruction can be planned to remediate the shortcomings.

Curriculum-based assessment/measurement is actually a family of procedures that have similarities. First, the assessments are based on the curriculum and viewed as informing instruction. The assessments tend to be brief and inexpensive, or, at least no more expensive than any other teacher-made tests. All of these approaches are sensitive to student improvement, and when students fail to improve, signal that there is a need for change in instruction or, at least, additional instruction. In general, the evidence is growing that use of curriculum-based assessment has a positive effect on the students measured in that their progress is more certain if they experience curriculum-based assessment as an integral part of instruction than if they do not (e.g., Deno & Fuchs, 1987; Fuchs, Fuchs, & Maxwell, 1988; Marston & Magnusson, 1985).

As with dynamic assessment, there is an assumption that most students can learn and improve and that one role for the assessment process is to stimulate the identification and development of instruction that works with particular children. In contrast to standardized assessments conducted by professionals from outside the classroom using measurements not reflecting classroom tasks, curriculum-based assessment is teacher controlled and administered and tied to actual curricula. There is high content validity here.

Unfortunately, other reliability and validity issues have been neglected in the development of curriculum-based measurements. In addition, much of the concern is with short-term gains, with notable exceptions such as Deno's curriculum-based measurement, which entails monitoring progress toward long-term goals. The most promising, most up-to-date approaches to curriculum-based assessment, however, combine approaches identified by Shinn et al. (1989): These combined approaches include monitoring of progress toward long-term goals, assessing short-term gains, and diagnosing weaknesses in current abilities (e.g., Fuchs, Fuchs, Hamlett, & Stecker, 1990; Shapiro, 1990). That the four approaches identified by Shinn et al. (1989) can be combined makes clear that the four approaches tap different, complementary information.

Great efforts are now being made to train young teachers in curriculumbased assessment (e.g., Howell & Morehead, 1987; Salvia & Hughes, 1990), with these textbooks providing examples and stimulating the practice of curriculum-based assessment/measurement across the entire curriculum. Although some teachers perceive that curriculum-based measurement is costly in terms of time (King-Sears, Richardson, & Ray, 1992), once teachers learn how to do it, their perceptions improve (King-Sears et al., 1992). Moreover, there are some short-cuts, such as students monitoring one another (e.g., Bentz, Shinn, & Gleason, 1990).

In closing this section, we must emphasize how enthused we are about this approach to assessment. Recall from Chapter 5 the motivational benefits from focusing on student improvement. Curriculum-based assessment/measurement makes improvement salient. Teachers who do it can defend grading practices based on improvement because there are objective records. Curriculum-based assessment may be an important development in the eradication of the competitive classroom, a classroom structure that undermines academic motivation. In making this conjecture, we note that, at present, curriculum-based assessment is used much more in special education than regular education. There is nothing, however, about this combined assessment and intervention that limits its use to special education populations. We hope that regular educators begin to use this approach to monitor sensitively the progress of students as well as to identify their students' instructional needs.

NEUROPSYCHOLOGICAL ASSESSMENTS

Before proceeding with a discussion of neuropsychological assessments, the difference between **structure** and **function** must be appreciated (see Chapter 6). In a complete diagnosis of a brain disorder or injury, information would be produced about the parts of the brain involved (i.e., brain structure) and the processing (i.e., functioning) that is disrupted. An extremely important point is that there is not a one-to-one relationship between brain structures and functions. Often, functions normally accomplished by one region of the brain sometimes can be taken up by another region of the brain, with the ability of the brain to compensate in this way inversely related to age (i.e., younger children are more likely to exhibit compensation than older children or adults; see Chapter 6).

For example, the two largest structures in the brain are the right and left cerebral hemispheres. Different regions in these structures are normally associated with different functions, for example, the frontal lobes with planning and carrying out higher-order functions (see Chapter 6). A particularly important functional distinction is that the right hemisphere often is involved more with nonverbal

abilities than is the left hemisphere, which specializes in verbal functions. Often, if the right hemispheric structure is damaged, there is functional loss of depth perception, spatial reasoning, and recognition of faces. Left hemisphere injuries are more likely to result in loss of speech, reading, or writing abilities. The extreme plasticity of the brain with respect to function—at least when brain injury occurs early in life—is illustrated by outcomes in some cases of left hemisphere removal, usually because of a tumor. When adults lose their left hemisphere, there is massive loss of language functioning. When young children lose the left hemisphere, however, they occasionally (e.g., Dennis & Whitaker, 1977; Woods, 1980) develop into adults with nearly normal language and intellect (e.g., McCarthy & Warrington, 1990, Chapter 1; McFie, 1961; Smith & Sugar, 1975). That is, the right hemisphere performs some of the functions normally performed by the left hemisphere. A complete neuropsychological assessment of such a patient documents will identify exactly the structures that have been damaged or removed as well as the neuropsychological functions that are normal versus those that are disrupted. Historically, medical diagnoses have provided structural information (see medical approaches to such assessments discussed in Chapter 6), and neuropsychological diagnoses have provided functional information.

Less extreme examples make the point how important complete and complementary medical and psychological diagnoses are. It is not at all unusual for even young people to experience small strokes, with some damage to small areas of brain tissue. The presenting symptom that lands the victim in the emergency room in many cases is something like loss of speech or sudden onset of blindness. Such symptoms stimulate physicians to perform diagnostic procedures that produce images of the brain (see Chapter 6), which often provide definitive information about the location of the problem in the brain. Additional medical tests usually are done to attempt to determine the underlying cause for the stroke (e.g., atherosclerosis, hypertension; Brust, 1991). Neuropsychological diagnoses are routinely done as the patient is recovering to assess functional losses. What is important to emphasize is that often there is spontaneous recovery of function, so that the individual appearing at the emergency room unable to talk will be talking normally a month later. The brain has found another way for the function that was disrupted by the small stroke to be performed, a not uncommon occurrence. Extensive neuropsychological diagnoses can often determine the completeness of such functional recovery, with this information critical in determining whether there is a need for long-term rehabilitative interventions. The focus in this section is on such assessments.

Neuropsychological test batteries are more recent developments than traditional intelligence tests or the SAT (although notably the Wechsler scales can be used for neuropsychological assessment; Golden, Zillmer, & Spiers, 1992; Sattler, 1992, Chapter 22), but they are not that new. For example, the Halstead-Reitan Neuropsychological Test Battery was developed in the 1940s (Halstead, 1947). The Luria-Nebraska Neuropsychological Battery was developed in the 1970s by Golden and colleagues, although it was based on tests developed by Luria, the great Soviet neuropsychologist who developed his assessments many years earlier (see Luria, 1966, 1973). Both of these important adult scales have been adapted for use with children (see Sattler, 1992, Chapter 22). The Halstead-Reitan Battery consists of a series of cognitive (e.g., concept formation, expressive and receptive language, memory) and perceptual-motor (e.g., finger-tapping, marching, rhythm, tactile form recognition) tests. The Luria-Nebraska also includes basic cognitive and perceptual-motor tasks, but also tasks that are recognizably academic tests, such as reading, writing, and arithmetic scales. In addition to these batteries, large numbers of neuropsychological tests are designed to tap specific functions (see Spreen & Strauss, 1991).

What these tests do well when administered by well-qualified neuropsychologists is to discriminate between people who are brain-injured or suffering from some serious brain disorders (e.g., aphasias of various sorts, which are receptive and productive language disorders; epilepsy; dyslexia; short-term memory loss) from those who have normally functioning brains (Golden, Zilmer, & Spiers, 1992). In making this generalization, however, it must also be pointed out that great skill is often required for the diagnostician to differentiate various types of brain dysfunctions and brain dysfunctions in general from other disorders, for example, hearing loss, delayed speech, autism, or various forms of psychoses, such as schizophrenia (Golden et al., 1992; Sattler, 1992). The skilled diagnostician compares patterns of performance across tests and within tests to make an assessment decision. There is a great deal of flexibility in the assessment procedure, with the assessor often

deciding in the middle of the assessment to test some function that emerged as suspect in subtests already administered.

There are many children who require neuropsychological assessments, with possible brain damage suffered by some children prenatally (see Chapter 6) and by others who contract disease, experience physical trauma, or are exposed to hazardous environmental agents, including some illicit drugs. In most cases, the neuropsychological assessment is part of a much larger assessment that includes extensive medical evaluation. By examining the patterns of performances on the various subtests in light of medical outcomes, the neuropsychologist often can make credible predictions about brain damage and functioning. Because a great deal of knowledge has accumulated about how specific brain injuries and disorders are related to important academic competencies, such as reading, writing, calculation, and problem solving (see McCarthy & Warrington, 1990), neuropsychologists believe such knowledge is invaluable in educational planning. It should increase awareness of the potential limitations of brain-injured students but, more importantly, also increase awareness of functions that are unimpaired, functions that might be exploited to compensate for other dysfunctions (e.g., knowing that the ability to read sight words is intact for a child even if his or her ability to decode using letter-sound rules is missing might be extremely helpful in planning reading instruction for the student).

In closing this subsection on neuropsychological tests, we emphasize that these tests are largely still in development. A serious problem is the reliability of neuropsychological assessments: The reliabilities of the full neuropsychological batteries are not as great as the reliabilities of tests such as the Wechsler. With the test battery customized for each patient, as it is when testers pick and choose subtests as they test hypotheses about patients, it is impossible to gauge the reliability of the assessment provided to any particular person.

It seems virtually certain that how these tests are used is going to change in the coming years as a function of development of other assessments, such as neural imagery (see Chapter 6). Nonetheless, many of the "high-tech" measures are far from ready for widespread deployment, and many have serious drawbacks. For example, many of the new "high-tech" measurements are limited in what they reveal, excellent at providing only particular information. A second problem is that some of the "high-tech" measures lost thousands of dollars for a single measurement. We believe that the neurological test batteries, which generate many different types of information at relatively low cost, will continue to be developed and play a role in diagnosis when brain damage or difference is suspected.

CONCLUDING COMMENTS

A number of measurement approaches were considered in this chapter and Chapter 16. Individual differences are assessed in different ways for different purposes. Thus, some tests provide information about the promise of individual students based on what they have learned so far. These include conventional IQ assessments and SATs. Others provide information about differences in student susceptibility to instruction and different types of instruction. Both dynamic assessments and curriculum-based assessments are suited to this purpose. Some assessments are designed to determine how well schools are doing, with aggregate statistics summarizing individual student performances a window on school impact. The *NAEP* and the state assessments do this, with these measurements increasingly attempting to capture whether students have acquired important procedural knowledge—important strategies for reading, writing, and scientific and mathematical problem solving. Some of the most "high-tech" of assessments are designed to illuminate the biological foundations of human competence.

In classifying tests with respect to purpose, as we did in the last paragraph, that is not to deny flexibility in purpose. For example, we suspect that biologically based assessments of individual differences in intelligence are possible. Moreover, portfolio assessments, which are being used at the state and national level to characterize achievement at the school level, can be modified and used by individual teachers to assess individual students, with examples of portfolios used in this way included in this chapter. In addition, results from tests such as the SAT are often aggregated over populations or regions to provide composite information. That is, good tests can do a lot of good: For example, the SAT has proved useful to students as they plan for college and to colleges as they select their classes. It also is an indicator of national patterns of academic achievement and as much as any test has provided a wake-up call of

sorts to educators and the policy community about the possibility of declining achievement in American schools. Because tests provide so much helpful information, we generally are enthused about their use and development.

Standardized testing has also been associated with harm to some groups. For example, minority groups have often made the case that tests are biased against them. In the sense that some minority groups consistently score lower on such assessments than do members of the majority culture, there is bias. Some extreme proponents of testing argue that such differences are real and reflect fundamental, and perhaps biological, differences between members of the majority and minority communities. We not only do not identify with that sentiment, but also find compelling that tests are better matched to the majority culture than they are to many minority cultures, and this mismatch might account for much of the differences in performance observed between majority and minority cultures.

Dana (1993) summarizes the case that many minorities have different world views that can affect their responses in testing situations. For example, the Anglo-American perspective of personal control and responsibility is not shared by Native Americans, which can undermine propensity to problem solve. Native Americans may be disadvantaged on assessments calling for active problem solving because of this difference in style. In addition, many minorities do not have a strong commitment to assimilation, resulting in acquisition and display of behaviors appropriate in their setting but not captured or valued by assessments matched to the culture they are resisting. Finally, it is difficult to escape that even if tests were culture free (which they are not), there would still be some racism in some individual assessors. For example, it is racist when a psychologist tries hard to determine if a white student's poor showing on an assessment might be accounted for by motivational or ameliorating factors (e.g., illness) but on the same day is willing to accept low scores from a black student at face value. Readers should be assured that good training programs do all possible to educate psychologists about the inappropriateness of such differential assessment; even so, many of the racist tendencies in the larger society will be reflected in any professional activity, including psychologist assessment. Competent psychologists, however, recognize the ambiguities in the measurement of minorities and take those ambiguities into account when they generate competency reports and make recommendations with respect to treatment.

In closing this chapter on alternative assessments, we urge readers never to lose track of the basics with respect to assessments: (1) It is necessary always to be asking whether a test is valid for the purpose it is being used for. One strength of newer assessments is that their purpose is more immediately obvious from the operations of the test. Thus, math portfolios are obviously related to math achievement and more certainly so than performance on a standardized math test. (2)The other basic is reliability, which is often ignored by psychologists as they use measurements (Rushton, Brainerd, & Pressley, 1983). Psychologists have erred many times by relying on low reliable tests, and those failures should be remembered whenever there are questions about reliability of tests, as there are for many of the newer assessments.

Psychological measurements are used to come to conclusions about individuals and groups. At the individual level, academic evaluations frequently are made to determine whether students are retarded or normal, learning-disabled or retarded, learning-disabled or normal, or gifted. Because of the importance of classifications of students in terms of intellectual abilities, Chapter 18 on individual differences takes up retardation, learning disabilities, and giftedness.

Various Types of Learners

The good information processor perspective provides a powerful way of analyzing individual differences. Mental retardation, learning disabilities, and giftedness have been studied in information processing terms. Changes in cognition across the life span also can be rendered sensible in terms of good information processing. Much work on individual differences remains, however, with increasing awareness of the need for research on the learning of non-native-speaking students in majority-population schools. The understandings developed in this book about mind and factors affecting it are a powerful starting point for study of diverse learners in terms that are likely to emphasize the information processing strengths of such populations.

By this point, it should be clear that assessment is about measurement of differences between people. One byproduct of this assessment enterprise has been the creation of entire new fields of inquiry aimed at understanding particular types of learners. The purpose of this chapter is to provide an overview of some of the types of learners and learner differences that have captured the attention of educational psychologists. Throughout the chapter, there will be attention to the ways that various groups differ and the similarities in information processing across groups.

The first part of the chapter reviews three classifications commonly used with learners with special needs: mental retardation, learning disabilities, and giftedness. Following is an overview of important psychological issues when dealing with non–English-speaking students. The chapter concludes with discussion of an individual differences dimension that affects all of us: cognitive changes during the adult years.

MENTAL RETARDATION

All psychological classifications are inexact, with mental retardation no exception (Clarke, Clarke & Beng, 1985). The American Association on Mental Deficiency reflected extensively on the various factors involved in retardation in attempting to construct a definition of the disorder (Grossman, 1983). Three points must hold for a person to be considered retarded by their criteria:

- There is significantly subaverage general intellect, which is usually operationalized as IQ of 70 or lower.

- There are deficits in adaptive behaviors. That is, personal and social behaviors are atypical.
- Retardation is manifested during childhood.

An important distinction within the retarded population is between those who are retarded because of known organic causes and those who are socially/culturally retarded (Burack, 1990). There are a number of causes of organic retardation, including the following:

1. Chromosomal anomalies, including Down syndrome, which usually is due to three copies of chromosome 21 (rather than two, which is normal; i.e., trisomy 21).
2. Prenatal factors, including disease and infection (e.g., Berg, 1985; Stern, 1985).
3. Injury at birth, including oxygen deprivation and mechanical injury (e.g., Berg, 1985).
4. Premature birth, with factors such as greater susceptibility to injury (e.g., hemorrhage in the brain) playing a role (e.g., Berg, 1985).
5. Neonatal hazards, including disease (e.g., meningitis), head injury, chemical assault, and disorders induced by malnutrition (e.g., Berg, 1985; Stern, 1985).
6. Inborn errors in metabolism (i.e., genetically determined enzyme deficiency), with these often resulting in structural damage to the nervous system caused by profound biochemical abnormalities (e.g., Stern, 1985).
7. Childhood psychosis, including autism, schizophrenia, and neuroses (Clarke, 1985).

Sociocultural retardation tends to run in families, although it is extremely difficult to draw firm conclusions as to why this is so. One obvious possibility is heredity, with parents of below-average intelligence more likely to give birth to children of lower intelligence than are parents of average intelligence (i.e., parents at the lower end of the normal distribution of intelligence provide a genetic endowment to their children that puts them at the lower end of the normal distribution). There is always the possibility, however, that sociocultural retardation is not just the lower end of the normal distribution but is due to some inherited but undetected organic disorder. The difficulty with drawing any conclusion based on biological endowment, however, is that parents of lower intelligence often provide less stimulating environments for their children than do parents of higher intelligence. In short, there probably are multiple determinants of familial retardation. That is, when an unfortunate genetic endowment encounters the nonstimulating environment provided by parents who are of low intelligence themselves, the result is that the child ends up at the bottom of his or her reaction range of intelligence, which from the moment of conception was a lower range compared with many other children born of parents with more fortunate genetic characteristics.

Determining the prevalence of retardation is extremely difficult, dependent on factors such as the exact definition used and the age level considered. Even so, Richardson and Koller (1985) were able to construct an estimate of the prevalence of severe retardation based on a survey of the world literature on retardation, concluding the overall rate was 4 in every 1000 children (see also Zigler & Hodapp, 1986, Chapter 5). The prevalence rates for mild retardation are much more variable from setting to setting, ranging from 3 or so per 1000 children in some urban areas to 70 or 80 per 1000 in some poor and rural areas. About 75 percent of all retardations are of the nonorganic type, with the more common nonorganic retardation presenting much less severe impairment than organic retardation. One good ballpark number to remember is that at most 1 in 100 people are severely retarded, with most of these organically caused. Another 2 to 3 per 100 are mildly retarded, with more of these representing sociocultural retardation than organic retardation. In the most unfortunate of populations, the rate of retardation runs as high as 8 in 100 people, with sociocultural retardation predominating in these groups.

Information Processing in the Retarded

There has been extensive study of many aspects of retarded children's information processing. This research provided windows not only on the processing of retarded people, but also on the information processing determinants of intelligent behavior in general.

Strategies and Metacognition   In the absence of instruction, retarded individuals are less likely to develop a variety of strategies than are normally intelligent individuals (see Ellis, 1979). Even so, there have been many demonstrations of retarded individuals being able to carry out basic memory strategies

following instruction in the processes composing the strategies. Retarded children can be taught to rehearse during list learning, use categories to cluster categorizable lists that are to be memorized, and construct elaborations that mediate paired-associate learning (e.g., Blackman & Lin, 1984; Brown, 1978; Taylor & Turnure, 1979). Such training demonstrations suggest much greater competence than is apparent from the naturally mediated performances of retarded individuals (i.e., how they remember on their own in the absence of instruction).

An important hypothesis advanced by Brown and colleagues (e.g., Brown, 1974; Brown & Campione, 1978) was that retarded children could carry out strategies but often do not do so on occasions when it would be appropriate—even when it is assured through training that they know relevant strategies. Brown argued that retarded children have an executive deficiency: They do not regulate their use of strategies they know.

Belmont, Butterfield, and Ferretti (1982) offered an analysis supporting this executive deficiency hypothesis, but also making clear that with more elaborate instruction, retarded children can improve the regulation of their use of strategies. Belmont et al. examined more than 100 strategies training studies conducted with mentally handicapped students, identifying seven investigations that included some evidence of transfer. In six of these seven studies, not only had a strategy or strategies been trained, but also students had been taught how to self-regulate their use of the strategy using a variant of the self-instructional approach originally devised by Meichenbaum (1977; see Chapter 7, this book). That is, when presented with a memory task, these students were taught to do the following:

- Decide on a goal.
- Make a plan to attain the goal.
- Try the plan.
- Ask themselves after their attempt, "Did the plan work?"
- If yes, no more is required; if no, ask, "Did I actually follow the plan?" If no, try the plan. If yes, ask, "What was wrong with the plan?" Devise a new plan and try it. (Adapted from Figure 2, Belmont et al., 1982)

That teaching students to self-regulate their use of strategies increases transfer of rehearsal, elaboration, and problem-solving procedures provides important support for Meichenbaum's (1977) perspective that explicitly teaching disadvantaged students how to self-regulate can increase their use of know-how they acquired through instruction (see Chapter 7, this book). There is a great deal of know-how (i.e., strategies) that retarded children can acquire, but for them to use such know-how broadly, they often have to be taught much more than simply how to carry out the operations that define the strategic process.

Why might self-instruction work? One possibility is that use of strategies in such a self-controlled fashion increases metacognition about the strategies (e.g., Borkowski & Kurtz, 1987). Because retarded students are often impulsive in their responding, they do not naturally plan as extensively as normals. By forcing such planning, as self-instruction does, the learner must reflect on his or her actions and the characteristics of the situation. When students check their performance outcomes following use of a strategy, they are attending to utility information, which is important in promoting maintenance of strategies being learned (see Chapter 2). Attempting to devise a new plan when an old plan fails also forces attention to information about when and where the strategies being learned are helpful. Thus, the research on higher-order, self-regulated strategies instruction is also consistent with the perspective that improved metacognition about strategies increases transfer of newly learned procedures (see Chapter 2).

When students transfer procedural knowledge they have acquired, it is an excellent sign that they are self-regulating, which is an important marker of competence. Indeed, a mainstream theory of mental retardation is that retardation is a self-regulatory disorder (e.g., Whitman, 1990), with language critical to self-regulation: Language can be used in the formulation of cognitive plans (e.g., asking oneself, "Have I seen a problem like this one before?"), to cue oneself to do something (e.g., "First I should do this and this and then this"), and as part of organizing one's thoughts (e.g., "These are *farm* animals and those are *zoo* animals, so they're different types of animals"). Whitman believes that one reason retarded people do not self-regulate as normals do is because of their language deficiencies, although he also recognizes that relative to normals, retarded children are strategy deficient, less metacognitively developed, and less likely to have an extensive knowledge base, with all of these factors probably contributing to self-regulation failures in the retarded.

In pointing out these deficiencies, we also emphasize that the potential is great because retarded people can learn a great deal and do so, especially when provided long-term exposure to material that is functionally important to them. For example, many retarded individuals learn important life scripts (e.g., washing hands, how to prepare and eat meals appropriately, getting off to school in the morning; Soodak, 1990). In addition, although there is variability in reading achievement in retarded populations, it is not unusual for middle school–age retarded children to be decoding near grade level with some evidence of comprehension (Rynders & Horrobin, 1990). Although more explicit prompting and more support may be required than with normal children, the retarded can learn many behaviors via scaffolding and reinforcement of correct responding (e.g., Butterfield & Nelson, 1991; Day & Hall, 1988; Demchak, 1990). Other behavioral learning mechanisms work with retarded children as well, such as punishment (see Mulick, 1990), classic conditioning (e.g., Ross & Ross, 1976), and observation and imitation (e.g., Kreitler & Kreitler, 1990)—that is, the four mechanisms that permit social learning by normally intelligent people (see Chapter 7) affect the learning of the retarded. Although there have been attempts to discredit studies demonstrating cognitive gains in retarded children and children at risk for retardation when these children are exposed to environments providing stimulation and enriched opportunities for learning (e.g., Spitz, 1986a, 1986b), such gains are not easily explained away (see Garber, Hodge, Rynders, Dever, & Velu, 1991; also Storfer, 1990). There are multiple indications in the literature that retarded children can learn to do quite a bit when placed in environments carefully engineered to foster learning. Such careful engineering is more critical with retarded children than with normally intelligent students, however, for left on their own, the retarded often undermine their own learning, for example, by making attributions that reduce effort, as taken up in the next subsection.

Motivation Retarded children's attributions about their own academic performances are likely to discourage future intellectual efforts (see Chapter 5, this book; Merighi, Edison, & Zigler, 1990; Zigler & Hodapp, 1986, Chapter 6). When retarded children fail at tasks, they tend to blame themselves more than do normally intelligent children (e.g., MacMillan &

Knopf, 1971). Retarded children's failures lead them to doubt whether they could possibly solve problems presented to them and increase their dependency on others to provide solutions to them (e.g., Achenbach & Zigler, 1968; Zigler & Balla, 1982), although they also tend to be more wary of potentially helpful adults than are other children (Merighi et al., 1990). Retarded people often have little confidence in themselves as learners or problem solvers.

More positively, some motivational interventions work extremely well with the retarded (e.g., Kiernan, 1985). Behavior modification, which involves the provision of reinforcements (see Chapter 7) for appropriate behaviors, has been used with great success with retarded populations. Retarded individuals can be taught self-help skills (e.g., self-feeding) and self-regulation (e.g., neat eating rather than sloppy eating) with behavior modification; there have been a number of behavior modification successes in improving communication skills, increasing attention span, decreasing hyperactivity, and increasing social interaction. Punishments (e.g., time-out) and reinforcements can be used to eliminate undesirable behaviors (e.g., aggression), with **differential reinforcement of other behavior** (i.e., reinforcing a desired behavior while punishing a nondesired behavior) working well with retarded populations. What the behavior modification literature demonstrates is that the retarded population is susceptible to motivation interventions, with a variety of reinforcers (e.g., from opportunities to interact with others to money) proving to be powerful motivators for behavior change in the retarded.

One important direction that needs to be explored is how retarded individuals' feelings about themselves as learners—that is, their feelings of competence—change as a function of improved behavior owing to behavior modification. On the one hand, provision of reinforcement has the potential for damaging belief in one's own abilities—people can come to believe they are performing well only because they are being rewarded (e.g., Weiner, 1979). On the other hand, knowing that you can can do well at all might give a big boost to self-esteem if that success follows a long history of failure in other settings (with retarded individuals, that is usually the case).

Whitman (1990) recognized how critical motivation is if retarded individuals are to learn how to self-regulate. He argued that any instruction that would succeed in increasing self-regulation would need to

produce high success in retarded students. Influenced by his Notre Dame colleague, Borkowski, Whitman also recognized the need for retarded individuals to come to understand that they can control their academic outcomes to some degree by exerting effort in the execution of effective strategies—and that failure often reflects lack of effort and failure to use task-appropriate strategies. That is, retarded learners need to acquire beliefs that are likely to motivate cognitive effort and strategy use rather than persist with beliefs that support passivity (e.g., "I am dumb," and, thus, there is little reason to try).

Processing Efficiency: Interactions Between Working Memory, Speed of Processing, and Knowledge

Tasks that are presumed to require substantial working memory to be performed well—typically requiring recall of information presented rapidly without the opportunity for reflective study (e.g., digit span)—are performed much more poorly by retarded than by normally achieving people (for a review of data, see Torgesen, Kistner, & Morgan, 1987). There is substantial evidence that working memory capacity probably is more limited in retarded people than in normally achieving individuals (Hulme & Mackenzie, 1992), although it is difficult to know for certain whether there is really less neurological capacity, or it only seems so because the capacity is used inefficiently: There is inefficiency because the information processing of retarded individuals is slower than the processing of nonretarded individuals (Brewer, 1987; Detterman, 1979; Nettelbeck & Brewer, 1981; Torgesen et al., 1987). Although the retarded can learn to do many tasks faster with practice, they remain far slower than normally intelligent individuals given equivalent practice (Brewer, 1987). The efficient use of working memory capacity is further undermined in the retarded because they are often less fully attentive to task-relevant information than are normals (e.g., Ross & Ross, 1984; Zeamon & House, 1979). Retarded individuals do not possess nearly as much knowledge of the world and academic content areas as normally intelligent people, so that information that can be "chunked" into larger units by normally intelligent people—and thus be easier to hold in short-term memory—cannot be chunked by the retarded. A variety of factors combine to reduce the efficiency of processing by retarded individuals compared with normal individuals, with the evidence clear that other things being equal, retarded individuals do not process as much in any given instant of time as do normally intelligent individuals. If the actual working memory capacity of retarded people is not less than normals, their functional short-term capacity certainly is.

Summary   When the thinking of the retarded is conceived in terms of strategies, metacognition, knowledge, and motivation, it is obvious why enormous efforts are required to improve the functioning of the retarded. It will not be enough to teach strategies alone or only embellish strategy instruction with metacognition or only increase content knowledge or only shift motivational beliefs. All of these factors must be attended to and much more intensively than with normally intelligent children who are underperforming.

In addition, other possibilities besides cognitive training alone should be pursued, including the design of environments that maximally stimulate retarded individuals and provide great cuing to them about appropriate cognitive actions (Baer, 1990). Reinforcement can be used to increase the independent functioning of the retarded (e.g., Baer, 1990; Kendall, 1990). One of the heartening aspects of much of contemporary special education intervention research is that cognitive, environmental, and behavioral interventions are being combined (e.g., Kendall & Braswell, 1985).

We close this section on information processing by emphasizing that we favor much more work on the development and evaluation of treatments that combine all of the best thinking about how to improve mental functioning by the mentally retarded. This includes creating rich environments filled with reinforcement for appropriate behaviors and cognitive stimulation to maximize the acquisition of strategies, metacognition, and other knowledge. As Pressley (1990) put it:

> What would happen: If retarded children were immersed in environments where important social and academic procedures were taught using detailed explanations and modeling? If extensive feedback and corrective, constructive, and elaborative commentary were provided—even if such scaffolding were imperfect because of poor cues from retarded children or limited patience by teachers? If important metacognitive information about when and where to use academic strategies was emphasized as well? If educators consistently presented important world knowledge in

> digestible quantities? If retarded students were taught that appropriately directed effort (i.e., use of strategies and application of knowledge that they already have or could acquire) determines performance more than does ability or other uncontrollable factors . . . ? Some work evaluating such a large-scale intervention might provide important guidance to the educational community about how to promote self-regulation in the very next cohort of retarded children. (Pressley, 1990, p. 370)

Even as we are sanguine, however, we remain open to the possibility that even the most favorable of instruction and environments might not be able to overcome some of the biological limitations (e.g., speed of processing) that seem to be inherent in retardation.

LEARNING DISABILITIES

The term "learning disabilities" evolved in the late 1960s and early 1970s (Wiederholt, 1974). Since its inception, definitional debates over learning disabilities have raged and continue (see Kavale & Forness, 1992; Stanovich, 1991; Torgesen, 1991), although a majority view has emerged:

> Learning disabilities is a general term that refers to a heterogeneous group of disorders manifested by significant difficulties in the acquisition and use of listening, speaking, reading, writing, reasoning, or mathematical abilities. The disorders are intrinsic to the individual, presumed to be due to central nervous system dysfunction, and may occur across the life span.
>
> Problems in self-regulatory behaviors, social perception, and social interaction may exist with learning disabilities but do not by themselves constitute a learning disability.
>
> Although learning disabilities may occur concomitantly with other handicapping conditions (for example, sensory impairment, mental retardation, serious emotional disturbance) or with extrinsic influences (such as cultural differences, insufficient or inappropriate instruction), they are not the result of those conditions or influences. (National Joint Commission on Learning Disabilities, Memorandum, 1988; reported in Torgesen, 1991, p. 21)

What does this definition imply? About the only thing obviously wrong with the learning-disabled student is that he or she is having trouble in some academic area. If academic difficulties can be explained as symptoms of other handicapping conditions or environmental deprivations, the problems do not reflect learning disabilities. The use of the conjunctive *or* in the list of problem areas is important. Learning disabilities are specific to one or two competencies or to a cluster of closely related competencies (e.g., reading and writing). Although terms such as general learning disabilities have been used to classify children who are having difficulties in most academic areas, many would argue such use of the term learning disabilities is a euphemism for below-average intelligence, mild retardation, or behavioral/emotional disturbance (e.g., Gajar, 1980).

What should be obvious from the conjunction *or* is that learning disabilities is a family of disorders, something that makes research on learning disorders per se extremely difficult or impossible. Indeed, one of the most critical sections in any learning disabilities journal article is the subjects subsection of the methods. Although it is important in any scientific article to specify who was studied, the need is especially urgent with respect to learning disabilities. In general, to make the case that a sample of children is learning-disabled, it is necessary to establish that they are performing below expected levels in some academic arena, but that other functioning is within expected levels of achievement for age/grade. In many articles, mean intelligence scores will be reported with the claim made of normal intelligence despite low performance in the deficit area.

The assumption of central nervous system dysfunction is often exactly that, supported at best by "soft signs" of neurological impairment, including the following:

- Speech/language delay.
- Motor clumsiness.
- Perceptual deficits.
- Poor right-left orientation.
- Meaningless and hyperactive motor behavior.
- Awareness that only one hand is being touched when both are being manipulated.
  (All of the above are especially applicable after age 8)
- Inability to copy simple geometric forms.
- Sloppy writing and copying.
- Faulty hand-eye coordination. (Based on Gaddes, 1985, pp. 12–13)

These signs are tapped by neuropsychological assessments and can be combined with other measures (e.g., patterns of differences on subscales of intelligence measures and standardized neuropsychological assessments, such as the Halstead-Reitan and the Luria-Nebraska; see Chapters 16 and 17) to make a case for learning disabilities.

Although more direct measures are possible—such as neurological surgery or neuroimaging (see Chapters 6 and 17), these are rarely used to diagnose learning disabilities. Readers may recall from Chapters 6 and 17, however, that progress in research has been made in identifying neurological abnormalities (especially for reading disabilities) using such procedures. For example, using a variety of techniques—from studies of cerebral blood flow to autopsies—abnormal structures and dysfunctions of the left hemisphere have been detected in the reading disabled (e.g., Flowers, Wood, & Naylor, 1991; Galaburda, Sherman, Rosen, Aboitiz, & Geschwind, 1985; Gross-Glenn, Duara, Yoshii, Barker, Chen, Apicella, Boothe, & Lubs, 1988; Hier, LeMay, Rosenberger, & Perlo, 1978; Johnson & Myklebust, 1967). Although it was a controversial study (see Lyon, Newby, Recht, & Caldwell, 1991), Duffy, Denckla, Bartell, and Sandini (1980; see also Duffy & McAnulty, 1990) used an electroencephalogram (EEG) procedure to provide preliminary evidence of different patterns of left-hemisphere electrical activity in dyslexics and normal readers. Abnormal electrical activity in reaction to visual information (e.g., Conners, 1971; Harter, 1991) has been recorded with reading-disabled students. There are patterns in EEGs when normal readers read silently and aloud that are less pronounced when dyslexic readers read silently and aloud (Galin, 1989). One interesting finding produced using magnetic resonance imaging (MRI) technology is that regions of the brain implicated in language processing tend to be smaller in reading-disabled students than in normal learners (Hynd & Semrund-Clikman, 1989); MRI studies have also detected abnormal brain structures at the back of the left hemisphere of dyslexics (Jernigan, Hesselink, Sowell, & Tallal, 1991; Larsen, Hoien, Lundberg, & Ødegaard, 1990). In addition, there also are abnormalities of blood flow in the frontal lobes of attention deficit children (Lou, Henriksen, & Bruhn, 1984), which is sensible in light of the criticality of the frontal lobes in self-control and self-regulation (see Chapter 6).

One point about biology and learning disabilities especially deserves commentary. For many years, learning-disabled students were referred to as "minimally brain damaged," reflecting the assumption that some unknown brain trauma had occurred at some point in life. One form of support for this supposition was that known brain damage does sometimes produce the same intellectual impairments experienced by learning-disabled students. Nonetheless, what the best physiological data are now suggesting is that these children are brain different—usually in the left hemisphere (i.e., at least for language/reading deficiencies, which have been studied most extensively using advanced physiological techniques)—not brain damaged.

That learning disabilities involve biological differences is also supported by behavior genetics research. For example, Smith and Pennington and their colleagues (e.g., Smith, Pennington, Kimberling, & Ing, 1990) have experienced some success in determining the chromosomal locations of genes affecting reading ability and disability. Some of the most theoretically interesting data have been produced in twin studies, however, with reasonable heritability estimates for individual differences in phonological processing, including the ability to sound out novel words (see Stevenson, 1992, for a review). In contrast, there is little heritability for individual differences in the ability to read sight words (Stevenson, 1992). Readers should recall the discussion in Chapter 14 about the importance of phonemic awareness and decoding ability. The evidence is mounting that there is an inherited biological basis for differences between children in their ability to analyze words and sound them out. What is also apparent is that such heritabilities are in the 0.40 to 0.75 range, meaning that there is a substantial environmental component and, thus, every reason to expect that environmental interventions can be developed that improve phonological processing—even for those children who may have a biological endowment that supports phonological processing less than does the biological endowment of other students.

In concluding that there are biological factors in the determination of learning disabilities, that is not to say that environment plays no role. In fact, there is growing evidence that some parental behaviors probably are dysfunctional in that they lead to maladaptive outcomes for children who may be at risk for various forms of learning disabilities. For example, Jacobvitz and Sroufe (1987) studied children who manifested attention deficit disorder in school at 6 years of age. These children were part of a larger longitudinal study that involved taking many measures on the children and their interactions with their parents. When these children were observed during the preschool years in problem-solving situations with their parents (e.g., solving an Etch-a-sketch maze-tracing problem), the interactions were different than were the interactions between other parents and children. The parents of children who eventually would be diagnosed as attention deficit tended to overstimulate their children as they solved problems, either physically touching them or interacting with the child in ways that more provoked or teased than helped. In general, during daily interactions, these same parents were more likely than parents of other children to interfere with the child's ongoing activity without taking into account the child's state, mood, or interest. Buhrmester, Camparo, Christensen, Gonzalez, and Hinshaw (1992) also observed that parents of hyperactive children have more provocative and interfering interactions with their children than do parents of normal children. Such observations suggest that the parents may have played a role in shaping the child's attention deficit, which is a source of difficulty in performing the academic demands of schooling.

Generating reliable incidence figures for learning disabilities is impossible, precluded largely by the debates over definition and the uncertainty in many cases about whether a child is learning-disabled or simply manifesting symptoms consistent with learning disabilities, symptoms caused by some as yet undiagnosed alternative causal factor. When more than 100 experts in learning disabilities were polled in 1983, all offered estimates between 0 and 5 percent of the school-age population (*Journal of Learning Disabilities,* January 1983, Volume 15). Even so, there was little agreement within that range as to what the incidence might be. Figures can be provided for the percentage of students classified as learning-disabled in schools, with this figure often between 4 and 5 percent of the population of children in school (see Kavale & Forness, 1992).

As Kavale and Forness (1992) point out, there are a myriad of reasons for students being classified as learning-disabled, with some, such as government funding formulas (i.e., formulas determining what percentage of the school population is eligible for special education funds), prompting suspicion that too many students are currently being classified as learning-disabled. For example, teachers taking our graduate classes have frequently told us that the only way to obtain needed services for some students is to have them classified as learning-disabled, although there is no reason to believe that these students have learning disabilities (e.g., the evidence more suggests that the students are far behind in school because their parents did not provide academic stimulation during the preschool years). In recent years, with increasing pressure from the federal government to identify no more than 2 percent of the total school-age population as learning-disabled, there has been a trend to reduce the number of students so classified.

A final consideration is that many readers may have the impression that one type of learning disability—dyslexia, which is the inability to decode words well despite intensive educational efforts—is "learning disabilities." Dyslexia accounts for only a small proportion of all learning-disabled. Again, incidence figures are difficult to gauge, but a fair guess is that no more than half of 1 percent of all people suffer from dyslexia. What that means is that if a school district is classifying 4 percent of its students as learning-disabled, about one in eight of these children might be dyslexic. Learning disabilities is more than dyslexia, including difficulties in comprehending once decoding is accomplished, difficulties in remembering what has been read as well as nonverbal disabilities such as extreme difficulties in calculating (i.e., dyscalculia).

Problems of definition and diagnosis abound in the area of learning disabilities. Even so, the more that is learned about biological and behavioral differences between learning-disabled and normal students, the more defensible is the category of learning disabilities.

Information Processing by Learning-Disabled Students

There has been a great deal of description of the deficiencies of students with various types of learning disabilities (e.g., how the mathematical computations by people with dyscalculia differ from the mathematical computations of people who are normally achieving in arithmetic). There has also been progress in understanding the processing differences between the learning-disabled and normal achievers. Indeed, learning-disabled students have been studied intensely as part of attempts to build models of effective and ineffective cognition (e.g., Larson & Gerber, 1992). In part, these efforts were stimulated by persistent hypotheses offered by learning disabilities theorists about the probable

causes of learning disabilities, with a number of single factors proposed as determinants of learning dysfunctions over the years (Willis, Hooper, & Stone, 1992).

One prominent proposal was that visual-perceptual problems were the cause of learning disabilities. Such a position was supported by correlations between perceptual disorders and learning disabilities (see Kavale, 1982), such as erratic eye movements during reading in learning-disabled readers compared with normal readers (e.g., Pirozzolo, 1979). A variety of data combined to undermine the hypothesis that the perceptual dysfunctions caused the learning dysfunctions. For example, interventions designed to improve reading by modifying eye movements fail to do so (Daneman, 1991).

An alternative to the perceptual deficiency hypothesis is that learning disabilities are due to underlying problems in processing of language, with Vellutino (1979) offering a book-length summary of the evidence supporting the claim that verbal information processing deficiencies underlie dyslexia. Of the single-factor theories offered, this one certainly has the greatest support, continuing to mount with advances in neuropsychology: When neuropsychological correlates of reading and learning disabilities have been detected, more often than not they have been in the left hemisphere and often in areas of the brain known to be implicated in processing of language.

Even if differences in parts of the brain underlying language competence prove to be the most fundamental cause of many learning disorders, it is important to understand learning disabilities at a psychological level, for information processing models have proven important in designing treatments that dramatically affect the learning and performance of learning-disabled students. Again, thinking about learning disabilities in terms of the elements of good information processing makes them more comprehensible.

Strategies and Metacognition   Some of the earliest analytical research on learning disabilities focused on the use of strategies by learning-disabled students as they attempted the types of basic memory tasks that had been studied extensively in normal children (see Chapter 2). Learning-disabled students proved less likely than normally achieving students to use strategies such as rehearsal and category reorganization during list learning (e.g., Bauer, 1977a,

1977b; Dallago & Moely, 1980; Kastner & Rickards, 1974; Tarver, Hallahan, Cohen, & Kauffman, 1977; Tarver, Hallahan, Kauffman, & Ball, 1976; Torgesen, 1977; Torgesen & Goldman, 1977). More positively, learning-disabled students are able to carry out these strategies and others when instructed to do so (e.g., Bauer, 1977b; Tarver et al., 1976, Experiment 2; Torgesen, 1977), making clear that their deficiencies did not prevent them from carrying out processes such as rehearsal and categorical reorganization of material.

One of the leaders of this basic research thrust, however, Torgesen (1979, 1980; Torgesen & Houck, 1980), led the way in urging the study of processing with tasks better matched to the ones learning-disabled students actually faced in school. In the 1980s, studies of strategy use and strategy instruction in basic task situations gave way to studies of strategy use and strategy instruction in exactly the types of situations confronted by learning-disabled students in school. The concern of learning disabilities researchers for improving the processing of problem learners in school has done much to move the entire field of cognition and instruction, with learning disabilities researchers generating some of the best, most ecologically valid research on strategies instruction.

The strength of that research already might be apparent to readers in that it has been featured in previous chapters. Thus, reciprocal teaching of prediction, questioning, clarification, and summarization strategies was designed to teach middle-school students with reading problems how to increase their comprehension (Chapters 8 and 14). The most convincing data to date on the effectiveness of transactional instruction of comprehension strategies has been generated with weak readers (Chapter 14). Some of the best writing intervention studies, including research by Englert, Raphael, Harris, and Graham, were produced with learning-disabled students, with the case strong that students experiencing specific learning deficiencies can learn complex strategies. For example, students who have difficulties in language arts can learn to use plan-write-revise approaches to composition (Chapter 15). Deshler, Schumaker, and their associates at Kansas (Chapters 14 and 15), in particular, have validated and disseminated a number of comprehension, writing, memory, and problem-solving strategies designed explicitly for use with the learning-disabled.

When these strategy instructional packages are examined, there is always extensive attention to metacognition, emphatic efforts to increase student awareness of when and where the strategies being learned can be used, and many prompts encouraging students to monitor their performance. The reason for this is that there have been many demonstrations in the literature that weaker students, and learning-disabled students in particular, often are not as aware as normally achieving students of their cognition. As Larson and Gerber (1992) summarized it:

> ... [P]oor readers are found to be less aware of the purpose of reading as meaning-getting, less knowledgeable about strategies for decoding, comprehending, and reading for a specific purpose, less sensitive to important parts of text, and less aware of text inconsistencies. ... In the area of spelling, learning-disabled students have difficulty with ... error monitoring. ... In the area of math, learning-disabled students have been described as having significant difficulties selecting correct algorithms ... using strategies correctly ... and monitoring procedures. (pp. 128–129).

Of course, as emphasized throughout this book, if learners are to make the most of the strategies they are learning and know, they must know when and where the procedures apply, which is often reflected by effective selection of strategies; they must also monitor whether the tactic they are taking at present is paying off or whether some other approach might work better. Certainly, learning-disabled students are not unique in their lack of awareness of the appropriateness of various strategies or their awareness of the status of their cognition, for a variety of evidence has been presented in this book of how increasing metacognition in normal learners can increase the use and generalization of new strategies. Moreover, a variety of evidence has been presented about how normal learners vary in metacognitive status and use of metacognition (e.g., elementary children may use what they know about the relative effectiveness of strategies only when prompted to do so; people tend to monitor how they do during testing much more than they monitor their performances during learning; see Chapter 2).

Just as Torgesen led the way in urging more ecologically valid study of strategies, he provided some of the earliest thinking on the possible role of metacognition in mediating learning disabilities. Torgesen (1975, 1977, 1979), in noting the passivity of learning-disabled students relative to other students, proposed that these students were not as aware as other students about the value of planning and monitoring or of the situational value of strategies they might know and be able to use. Differences in such metacognitive understandings overlap with differences in the motivational beliefs held by learning-disabled students, with their motivational beliefs actually another form of metacognition (i.e., knowledge of the value of cognitive activities), which is often deficient in ways that undermine active attempts to tackle academic tasks.

Motivation   Learning-disabled children often are caught in a terrible cycle. Because they have done poorly in school, they begin to think of themselves as academic failures—they begin to believe they are stupid. Such a belief does nothing to motivate academic effort, which results in additional failure, which, if anything, strengthens the perception of low ability (e.g., Borkowski et al., 1990; Licht, 1983, 1992; Torgesen, 1977; see Chapter 5, this book). The evidence is overwhelming that compared with normally achieving children, learning-disabled students lack academic self-esteem (e.g., Licht, 1992; Rogers & Saklofske, 1985; Winne, Woodlands, & Wong, 1982). They expect to do poorly in school (e.g., Butkowski & Willows, 1980; Rogers & Saklofske, 1985). The instruction they are receiving does not make sense to them, and they know it has not been effective in the past (e.g., Kos, 1991). In general, conventional remedial instruction does not reduce the gap in academic self-esteem between normally achieving students and those with learning disabilities (e.g., Chapman, 1988).

Rather, conventional schooling does much to reinforce the negative academic self-esteem of children with learning disabilities. American classrooms are filled with reminders to students who are doing poorly that they are experiencing difficulties: Their papers are not displayed with the "A" papers, their names are not part of the "Geographer of the Week" display, they are not honored by placement on the classroom's "Tip-Top Speller" list, and they are not members of the reading group that includes all the smartest children in the class. The more the classroom publicly honors its high achievers, the worse the social comparison for the low achievers (Ames & Archer, 1988; Stipek & Daniels, 1988). If anything, the situation is worse for girls because boys more readily explain away their failures as caused by factors other than their low ability (e.g., the teacher doesn't like me, the tests aren't fair; e.g., Licht, Kistner,

Ozkaragoz, Shapiro, & Clausen, 1985; see Chapter 5, this book). Hyperactive children seem to be especially likely to believe that academic matters are out of their control (e.g., Hartsfield, Licht, Swenson, & Thiele, 1989).

This situation is not hopeless, however, with growing evidence that as students are taught ways of tackling academic tasks that improve their task-related performances, they can also be taught to attribute their task-performances to use of the strategies they are learning (for reviews, see Borkowski et al., 1990; Licht, 1992; also Chapter 5, this book). Borkowski and colleagues have experienced substantial success in increasing the long-term commitment of learning-disabled students to use of new strategies they are learning by making certain their students understood as part of instruction that their performances were improving because of their use of strategies (see Chapter 5).

There are also other instructional procedures that increase sense of competence and control (Licht, 1992). Bandura and Schunk (1981) reported that focusing students' attention on successful attainment of concrete and immediate goals (e.g., getting today's problems correct) increases student **self-efficacy,** which is their term for learners believing that their performances are under their own control. Focusing on progress toward long-term goals (e.g., thinking about today's performance with respect to how many days it will take to cover the entire unit of material) has much less of an impact on self-efficacy. When students perform strategies in ways that make it salient that they are doing something to attempt to perform a task (e.g., they self-verbalize the strategy), self-efficacy seems to be enhanced as well (Schunk & Cox, 1986). When children see another person like themselves coping with a task but finally accomplishing it, their self-efficacy is likely to improve (Schunk, Hanson, & Cox, 1987). In addition, children seem to have greater self-efficacy, more positive feelings of competence, and better performance in classrooms emphasizing improvement rather than performance relative to peers (e.g., Nicholls, 1989).

What is heartening is that review of the academic interventions with learning-disabled and low-achieving students featured in previous chapters (e.g., Deshler and Schumaker's work on a variety of learning strategies, Graham and Harris's writing interventions, transactional reading comprehension instruction) makes clear that such interventions are rich with instruction to shift motivational beliefs that might undermine academic effort. Students are taught that their performances can improve through use of strategies that are under their control. They receive substantial here-and-now feedback about improvement. Their improvements are emphasized rather than their absolute level of performance or their standing relative to classmates. Students see models coping and struggling to apply the strategies being taught. At least initially, they perform strategies using self-verbalization, which makes obvious *how* they are coping with the academic task. That successful instructional packages do include these motivational components provides some validation of the theoretical stance that it is essential to alter the dysfunctional motivational beliefs of learning-disabled students if great progress is to be made in advancing the academic achievements of learning-disabled students.

It must be emphasized in closing, however, that altering motivation is not enough. Programs that are effective with learning-disabled students teach strategies, teach metacognition about those strategies, and have students apply their newly learned information processing tools to content worth learning, content that can stimulate increases in a student's declarative knowledge base. The consistent message throughout this book is that academic success is a mixture of factors, most notably strategies, metacognition, conceptual knowledge, and motivation.

Processing Efficiency: Interactions Between Working Memory, Speed of Processing, and Knowledge

Memory span tasks—typically requiring recall of information presented rapidly without the opportunity for reflective study (e.g., digit span)—often are performed much more poorly by learning-disabled than by normally achieving students (e.g., Torgesen & Houck, 1980). Why? (1) The verbal processing difficulties experienced by many learning-disabled children are a factor in memory span, with the phonetic coding demands of such tasks interfering with performance (e.g., simply saying "four, seven, nine, one, three, five, and two" may require substantial effort for a child with language/learning difficulties). (2) Although the pervasive slowness of processing observed in the retarded is not evident in the learning-disabled, learning-disabled students are slower for some processes than are normally achieving students (e.g., initial processing of sequentially presented information, such as saying the to-be-remem-

bered items to oneself). (3) The efficient use of working memory capacity also is undermined in some learning-disabled students because of attention problems (e.g., Shaywitz & Shaywitz, 1992). (4) To the extent that academic prior knowledge has been reduced by the learning disability (i.e., learning-disabled children learn less content in school because of their learning disability), there also is reduced ability to recode information into larger meaningful chunks efficiently—to do so requires prior knowledge that makes clear which particular pieces of new information relate to one another.

One of the more interesting observations about working memory and learning-disabled children is that reading-disabled children may have a more generalized impairment in working memory than other learning-disabled children. Siegel and Ryan (1989) observed that reading-disabled children had difficulty with a memory span task involving processing of sentences and another working memory task requiring counting. In contrast, arithmetic-disabled children had difficulty only with the working memory–counting task. The possibility of working memory difficulties varying with type of learning disability (see also Siegel & Ryan, 1988) deserves further study.

Although processing inefficiencies in children with learning disabilities are not as pronounced as in the retarded, there is less efficient use of limited capacity working memory by learning-disabled students compared with normally achieving students, at least some of the time. Most analyses are consistent with the conclusion that, if anything, learning-disabled students and many students experiencing academic problems (e.g., weaker readers) have less working memory or short-term capacity than do normal achievers (e.g., Hulme & Mackenzie, 1992; Swanson, 1992; Swanson & Cooney, 1991). As is always the case in analyses of working/short-term memory, however, it is impossible to be absolutely certain that there is less capacity for the learning-disabled. It may only seem that way because of processing inefficiencies: For example, so much effort can be expended phonetically coding the to-be-remembered digits that there is little capacity left over for the memory part of the task. So much attention can be diverted from the task by irrelevancies in the environment that little of the total capacity is available for the memory demand. Lacking prior knowledge possessed by many others prohibits the learning-disabled from forming meaningful "chunks," such as recoding the sequence 7-4-7 as "747 jet," 4-1-1 as "directory assistance," or 2-8-2-7 as the "score of a football game in which both teams scored four touchdowns and one missed one extra point."

Summary and Commentary   If information processing analyses of learning disabilities are correct—that learning disabilities can be understood largely in terms of strategies, metacognition, knowledge, and motivation—educational environments developed in light of information processing analyses might be especially effective. Formal study of such environments has only just begun, but the data generated to date inspire additional confidence in information processing approaches to instruction with these children.

Benchmark School, outside of Philadelphia, is dedicated to the education of otherwise high-ability children who have already experienced great difficulties in school (Figure 18.1). The Benchmark student is an otherwise intelligent child who cannot learn to read in regular schooling.

During the first year or two at Benchmark (see Gaskins & Elliot, 1991, for a book-length description of the school, its programs, and students), students

are taught to decode, using an approach to decoding developed at the school. Right from the start, however, Benchmark students learn that reading is not just sounding out words but meaning getting. As decoding skills develop, students read increasingly challenging literature; they are taught to tackle such challenging reading by using the comprehension strategies that work for all elementary children (see Chapter 14). In addition, there is daily instruction in writing, again involving instruction of higher-order strategies, such as the planning-translation-revising strategies featured in Chapter 15. Content-area instruction is not neglected, but rather the strategies that the students learn to read, write, and problem solve are applied to social studies and science texts (Pressley, Gaskins, Wile, Cunicelli, & Sheridan, 1991).

The Benchmark model of instruction is consistent with the model of instruction favored throughout this book (Pressley, Gaskins, Cunicelli et al., 1991)—long-term instruction of strategies well matched to important academic tasks; development of metacognition about strategies through direct explanation, modeling, and scaffolded practice; reinforcement for improvement rather than for outper-

Figure 18.1 A Benchmark School classroom looks much like any elementary classroom in a still photo, but the instruction is anything but commonplace. Students receive high-quality instruction in decoding, strategies, and problem solving. Much of the research featured in this book has inspired curricular innovations used daily in the school. Benchmark is recognized as a model school for students who experience difficulties in learning to read in regular schools.

forming other students in a class, with every effort made to encourage healthy motivational beliefs (e.g., I can do well if I apply the right strategies, the ones being learned in school); and expansion of content knowledge.

Does it work? An 8-year-old who cannot read, which is the status of most entry-level Benchmark students, is at great risk for long-term academic failure. In contrast, most Benchmark students leave the school in an average of 4 years (some stay as long as 7 years) to return to normal schooling. When they do so, typically they are at least average students or better. Virtually all Benchmark alumni graduate from high school; many go on to college. The success of Benchmark illustrates that high-ability learning-disabled students can achieve in school when they are offered high-quality instruction that stimulates the development of good information processing.

GIFTEDNESS

Who is gifted? What defines a gifted student? There is great debate over these questions (Hoge, 1988). One criterion is IQ, although many different IQ cutoff points have been used as the starting point for giftedness. Often scores of 130 to 140 are considered the lower boundary of the gifted range. Of course, high IQ alone is not sufficient to define giftedness. For example, some students are much stronger on some subscales of intelligence tests than on other subscales, so an overall IQ score does not represent adequately their giftedness.

Not surprisingly, there have been diverse pressures to expand the definition of giftedness beyond being a label for the upper end of the IQ distribution (e.g., Richert, 1991). Recall, for example, the discussion of Gardner's **multiple intelligences** (Chapter 6). A person can have much greater intelligence in music or math or for physical activities than for other competencies. Even if their specialized competence is not so great as to be considered prodigious, there is often little doubt that these people have better ability in one area than in others.

What does it mean to be prodigious? We favor a definition offered by Radford (1990, Chapter 11, p. 200): "Statistically, a prodigy comes at the extreme end of a distribution of achievement in a particular activity . . .": Thus, in recent National Hockey League all-star games, Wayne Gretsky has clearly been the best of the best, a hockey prodigy, with his talent apparent since he first showed up at the neighborhood rinks in Brantford, Ontario. Liona Boyd received a guitar for Christmas when she was 12 and as a young adult established herself as the first lady of classical guitar. Stevie Wonder was a successful songwriter and singer at age 12 and continues at the top of the profession today. Prodigies have generated a great deal of attention in the last decade, with several book-length treatments of their accomplishments.

Prodigies

A main question posed by many studying prodigious genius is how to foster the giftedness of such individuals: What environmental variables have an impact on whether a person with a great talent becomes a leading figure in a field of specialization? If the talent is there, how can we increase the odds of producing a great mathematician, scientist, or artist? Although each reviewer of the lives of prodigies comes up with a slightly different list, and although each reviewer has a factor or two they view as particularly critical, the following are mentioned often as important to the development of prodigious genius (e.g., Bloom, 1985; Feldhusen, 1986; Feldman, 1988; Radford, 1990; Renzulli, 1986; Tannenbaum, 1986):

- High general intellect.
- A distinctive aptitude or aptitudes (although some authors dispute whether such aptitudes are innate, emphatically arguing that many aptitudes can be rendered "special" by high-quality instruction and experience, pointing to data supporting their claim; see Howe, 1990, pp. 31–34).
- Instruction related to exceptional abilities, with this often extensive to the point of mentoring.
- A series of teachers of increasing sophistication who coach the student in the area of giftedness.
- Nurturant and supportive parents, who are particularly supportive of the development of the particular talent.
- Long-term motivation to develop the ability—often to the point of being uncontrollably "turned on" by the activity or obsessively devoted to the field.
- Great rewards to the prodigy for engaging in the activity.
- A great deal of practice of the special ability or abilities.
- Confidence in their special ability.

- Meshing of the ability with a field in which recognized accomplishment is possible.

A moment's thought about this list makes it clear that prodigious talent is the happy coincidence of many factors, something borne out not only in the rich bibliographic studies that inspired the list we just presented, but also in harshly quantitative analyses of high achievement based on data sets in which the prodigious are anonymously represented to the researchers (e.g., Benbow & Arjmand, 1990; Reynolds & Walberg, 1991; Tomlinson-Keasey & Little, 1990). The right genes are born into a supportive family (or at least the family fosters a talent that can be developed by the child); the child is excited by the special competency and dedicated to developing it; and the talent is one that is needed by society, one matched to the state and needs of the world at the time. Prodigy is not just intellect or special talent. There are factors that are at least partially nonintellectual, such as motivation; there are factors external to the individual, such as family support and historical circumstance. For example, would Steven Jobs of MacIntosh computer fame have been a prodigy if he had been born in the late 19th century? Perhaps his ability to work inventively with complex relationships would have translated into genius resulting in turn-of-the-century inventions complementing the work of Edison, and then again, maybe his innate abilities would not have been as powerfully matched to the level of development and the needs of that era of invention as they were to the level of development and the needs of the modern computing age. A lot of prodigy is probably lucky coincidence of genes and resources and the state of the world—consistent with a general perspective that intelligence is a product of both an individual's competencies and the opportunities afforded by society (Kornhaber, Krechevsky, & Gardner, 1990).

People Who Are Generally Highly Intelligent

In contrast to individuals with high specialized talents, there are people who are generally smart but not exceptionally talented in any one domain. Suppose that we accept IQ = 130 as the cutoff for high general ability. With that figure representing roughly only 2.5 percent of the population, it is obvious that general intelligence is a scarce resource but not so rare that most educators are not going to be dealing with it on a regular basis. If a person is teaching 125

students a day at a high school with an absolutely average group of students, 3 or 4 of that teacher's students would have IQs exceeding 130. Teachers who teach in socioeconomically advantaged communities could have a much higher percentage of such pupils because socioeconomically advantaged communities tend to have a larger proportion of residents of above-average intelligence. Thus, all educators should have a working understanding of such people.

Any discussion of high general intelligence must include coverage of one of the most distinguished longitudinal studies ever conducted, begun in the 1920s by Terman (i.e., the Stanford professor who developed the Stanford-Binet IQ test; see Chapter 16), which continues to generate new analyses and perspectives today (e.g., Schuster, 1990; Shurkin, 1992; Tomlinson-Keasey & Little, 1990).

Terman's Kids   Genius fascinated Lewis Terman. During the years when he was developing the Stanford-Binet test, Terman encountered a number of children who scored in the 140 range or higher; he was fascinated by the tales the parents of these children told of their sons and daughters reading and writing early. Terman knew of the stereotypes—that geniuses were quirky, eccentric, and even unhealthy. Terman also recognized as he became acquainted with geniuses firsthand that he was meeting a well-adjusted and happy group of people, whose sole peculiarity was that they were extremely smart. Word spread throughout the Stanford community of Terman's interest in child brilliance, and the faculty made it a point of bringing around new examples. The more of these people he met, the more convinced Terman was that brilliance and good mental health were complementary (Shurkin, 1992, Chapter 2, for this and other points in this subsection; Terman, 1925; Terman & Oden, 1947; Terman & Oden, 1959).

In the early 1920s, he sought and received funding to begin a longitudinal study of bright children. To do so, he administered intelligence tests and other assessments to a large number of children throughout California, many of whom had been nominated by their teachers as exceptionally bright. Others were nominated in a haphazard fashion by those acquainted with the study; some were brothers and sisters of nominated children. In the end, a sample of 643 children was identified as gifted in the sense of having IQ scores of 135 or higher. Other children from outside the geographical areas searched were added to the sample, as was a group of children with special talents, so that the final sample was composed of more than 1500 children.

Terman's kids were studied extensively, including evaluations of their health and physiques, with them proving both healthy and physically normal. They were more healthy and slightly superior physically to the population as a whole, contrary to stereotypes of the day. Terman's subjects were excelling in school, often moved ahead in the curriculum. Half of the sample were able to read before they began school. They read more than other children, they read "better" books than other children, and their reading interests were more diverse than the interests of the typical child. Their zeal for the written word remained high into high school and college and adult life, with more than three-quarters of the sample reporting as adults that they read "literature." They tended to graduate from high school early and enter college at a young age, with most "Termites" going to college or wanting to go (90 percent went relatively early in life; 70 percent graduated relatively early in life). The Terman kids excelled in college, outperforming their classmates. This was true even for the students who attended the highly selective Stanford—the Terman kids did better than other students admitted to one of the West Coast's best colleges. A high proportion of Terman's subjects made Phi Beta Kappa. Despite their academic successes, these gifted people were socially adept and accepted; they were well-behaved and had normal sexual urgings. The exceptions—the nerds—were among the brightest in the sample, however.

Terman's adults were more likely to earn doctorates and professional degrees than members of the general population, with the majority of the sample eventually earning graduate degrees. Their incomes were well above population averages. They published many more books than any random sample of 1500 adults (200+ books). They averaged more than one published article per person (i.e., 2500+ articles). They produced 350 patents. Quite a few earned fame in their fields, even if very few earned widespread recognition. Alcoholism was low for the group; so was criminality. Their mental abilities during adulthood, as measured by conventional psychometric instruments, continued to be impressive relative to the general population.

The majority were satisfied with their life and life's work. Family was important to them, as was joy of life. In general, personal satisfaction was more important than occupational satisfaction. Terman's subjects married other bright people and gave birth to children with IQs that were well above average. An intriguing outcome, from the perspective of the sexually liberated 1990s, is that the majority of Terman's women became nonincome-producing homemakers. Even so, in the later years of their lives, the Terman men and women who remain alive seem happy as a group.

One of the more interesting differences involved comparison of successful Terman kids with less successful Termites. The successes were more likely to have parents who pushed them to achieve in school and to go to college. Thus, as with prodigies, parents seemed to play a guiding, shaping role in the lives of successful people with high intelligence. Ability alone does not produce great success; ability is fostered by supportive family and friends.

The Terman study is admirable if for no other reason than so many people were studied for so long, with Shurkin (1992) expecting data collection on Terman's kids to continue until the last one of them dies. We expect secondary analyses to continue for some time after that. Although this study provided many measures of the participants' competence, it was not as analytical as studies directed at specific aspects of information processing, with more focused studies providing essential data about the good information processing of gifted individuals compared with the population at large.

Information Processing Cognitive theorists (e.g., Borkowski & Peck, 1986; Jackson & Butterfield, 1986; Sternberg, 1986, 1991b) concerned with giftedness cite the factors highlighted in this book as critical to gifted performances:

- Strategies: repeated observations of great facility by the gifted in combining information and working with knowledge to produce new ideas and products (e.g., Feldman, 1982; MacKinnon, 1978); use of more advanced strategies than average-intelligence age-mates on a variety of academic tasks (e.g., Jackson & Butterfield, 1986; Robinson & Kingsley, 1977; Zimmerman & Martinez-Pons, 1990); enhanced ability to translate problems into mathematical expressions (e.g., Dark & Benbow, 1990).

- Metacognition: superior in regulating and coordinating cognitive processes and knowledge (Sternberg, 1981; Zimmerman & Martinez-Pons,1990); gifted children are more likely to transfer new strategies they have learned from one task to another task that can be mediated by strategies (Borkowski & Peck, 1986; Jackson & Butterfield, 1986); when asked questions tapping knowledge of cognition in general, gifted children outperform children of average intelligence (Borkowski & Peck, 1986).
- Knowledge: early mastery of the knowledge required for the field in which the person is gifted (Feldhusen, 1986); deeper and broader knowledge than people of normal intelligence (e.g., Gagné & Dick, 1983; Rabinowitz & Glaser, 1985; Sternberg, 1981; Tannenbaum, 1983).
- Motivation: high commitment to excellent performance in one or more fields (Feldhusen, 1986; Feldman, 1979; Terman & Oden, 1959); high self-concept (e.g., Feldhusen, 1986; Feldhusen & Kolloff, 1981; Ketcham & Snyder, 1977; Ringness, 1961), although a minority of gifted children greatly underestimate their abilities, perhaps reflecting parental underestimation of their children's talents (e.g., Phillips, 1987).

One important point relating to good information processing is that gifted people process information more efficiently than do more typical peple, for example, being able to scan a set of items being held in memory more rapidly than people of average intelligence (i.e., they can decide more quickly than normals whether a particular letter is included in a set of letters being held in memory; Keating & Bobbitt, 1978; McCauley, Kellas, Dugas, & DeVillis, 1976). The gifted tend to have superior short-term memory for material pertaining to their area of great competence—for example, highly gifted mathematics students have better short-term memory for digits than do people gifted in other arenas (Dark & Benbow, 1990, 1991). Gifted individuals also can retrieve information more rapidly than can people of average intelligence (i.e., the speed difference in deciding that two physically identical letters are the same [e.g., AA] and deciding that two physically different letters have the same name [e.g., Aa] is small relative to average-ability people; e.g., Borkowski & Peck, 1986; Hunt, Lunneborg, & Lewis, 1975; Jackson & Myers, 1982; Keating & Bobbitt, 1978). Another index of retrieval efficiency is the speed of deciding

whether two objects are members of the same category; gifted people perform such categorizations more rapidly (e.g., Goldberg, Schwartz, & Stewart, 1977) and certainly (Rabinowitz & Glaser, 1985) than others: Gifted students process information more efficiently than do less talented people, with their superior efficiency freeing up more of their short-term capacity for consideration and manipulation of strategies and other knowledge.

In short, relative to comparably aged individuals, gifted people have more and better strategies, metacognition, other knowledge, and motivation (at least with respect to fields in which their giftedness is expressed). In addition, their information processing is faster and more efficient. Gifted people transfer what they know how to do more readily to new situations than less talented people. Their extensive knowledge permits insights that elude others, ways of seeing relationships that are novel (Sternberg & Davidson, 1983).

One important information processing characteristic of the gifted is extremely important. Gifted people do not just solve problems, they discover new ones (e.g., Perkins, 1981)—sometimes they invent entire new arenas of inquiry. For example, Piaget was a great psychologist because he made the world aware of the developing mind. Flavell is a great developmental psychologist because he pioneered the study of strategies and metacognition in development. An entire new area of inquiry was opened up after Miller wrote about the 7 ± 2 chunks of memory. Think about the impact of Edison with his light bulb, Marx and his views of economics, or Jefferson and his ideas about democracy. The gifted often invent concepts that change the world—they identify new technologies and ideas that become the passions and concerns of many others. Giftedness is intellectual leadership.

Comparison of the Information Processing Characteristics of Retarded, Learning-Disabled, Normally Achieving, and Gifted Students

The processing of all types of children has been studied with respect to the information processing components featured in this book. Although it is something of an oversimplification, in general, evidence of strategy use increases going from retarded to learning-disabled to normally achieving to gifted students, as does evidence of metacognition, extensive world knowledge, and motivation supporting academic behaviors. In addition, there is increasingly efficient information processing in terms of speed moving from retarded to gifted students. Although it is not possible to know if the amount of neurological capacity allocated for short-term processing differs between these classifications, functional short-term capacity certainly does, with performance on short-term memory tasks improving steadily going from retarded to learning-disabled to normally achieving to gifted classifications.

We emphasize, however, it is not just that better learners have "more" of each of the components of skilled processing. The coordinated use of information processing components is also more certain for gifted achievers than normally achieving students, who articulate their cognitive components more effectively than do learning-disabled or retarded students. Also, it should be noted that although the retarded versus normally achieving comparison is a main effect in that normally achieving students are generally better off than retarded students, both learning disabilities and giftedness often reflect particular deviations from typical abilities and performances. That is, an otherwise normally achieving student who does poorly in math is math disabled; an otherwise normally achieving person who is superior in mathematics is mathematically gifted. Thus, in the cases of learning disabilities and giftedness, it might be expected to see vast differences in information processing from normally achieving students for the particular disability or gift but otherwise observe strategies, metacognition, knowledge, and motivations typically observed in the general population. The information processing model featured so prominently in this book is a powerful way of thinking about learner differences, with this becoming more evident as other dimensions of learner differences are considered.

What is disappointing is that despite much scientific progress in understanding such individual differences, schools generally do not use cutting-edge knowledge in classifying students, with great variability in how decisions are made from district to district (e.g., Singer, Palfrey, Butler, & Walker, 1989). The reasons for this neglect range from ignorance to exploitation: As one school administrator admitted to author MP a few years ago, "If there is state funding for 2 percent of the total school population to be educated as learning-disabled, we find 2 percent of the kids to be learning-disabled. If we can economi-

cally support gifted and talented instruction for 10 percent of students, 10 percent of students are designated as gifted and talented." The distance between science and practice in many diagnostic decisions is staggering. We hope the situation will change as the research just covered is disseminated and better understood.

CHILDREN WHOSE NATIVE LANGUAGE IS NOT THE MAJORITY LANGUAGE

This section focuses on one of the most salient groups of at-risk students in American education, non–English-speaking North Americans. For the most part, the literature relevant to the populations is not as extensive as the literature pertaining to the mainstream culture. Moreover, when there has been substantial study, it usually has not been informative with respect to the factors we consider critical to efficient thinking—strategies, metacognition, other knowledge, and motivation.

It is not unusual in major urban environments in the United States and Canada to have 20 to 40 different first languages in a school population. All of the points made with respect to multiculturals and people in poverty hold for many of the children with a first language different than English. In addition, these children are faced with the challenge of learning English as a second language (or French in some parts of Canada). A few important conclusions have emerged from sophisticated cognitive analyses of second-language learning and second-language learners.

Challenge of Second-Language Learning for Children

A well-known hypothesis (Lenneberg, 1967) is that learning a second language is much easier for children than adults. Despite the popularity of this idea, there is no evidence to support it. In fact, the evidence is consistent with the opposite conclusion, that second-language learning is more challenging for young children than for adults (Hakuta, 1986, Chapter 6; McLaughlin, 1984, Chapter 3). Even so, on average those who learn a second language during childhood are more likely to sound like natives once the second language is acquired, and they will have better grammar (Hakuta, 1986, Chapter 6). Although true, on average, it must be emphasized that there are many adults who acquire a second language, with little, if any, detectable accent.

Attitudes About and Motivation to Learn the Second Language

Some of the most important research on second-language learning in school contexts has been conducted in Canada. Lambert of McGill University and Gardner of the University of Western Ontario (e.g., Gardner & Lambert, 1972) have provided the premier analyses of the relationship between attitudes about a target second language (i.e., French in the Gardner and Lambert investigations) by first-language-English students and learning of the second language. Using several clever measures of attitude (e.g., personality ratings of French and English speakers), Lambert and Gardner documented clear individual differences among English-speaking Canadian students in their attitudes toward the French language. (Anyone who has spent time in Canada immediately recognizes the validity of this claim. There are intense feelings about language in Canada, an officially bilingual country, which, nonetheless, has many more monolingual enclaves than regions that are truly bilingual.) Important in this context, the differences in attitudes about French by English-speaking Canadians are associated with differences in success in learning French (Gardner, 1980). By measuring the language attitudes of members of the students' families, Gardner and Lambert have been able to make the case that the causal direction is from attitude to achievement: Better attitudes about French cause higher achievement in French, with students who have a negative attitude about French coming from families who foster negative feelings toward French language and culture (Gardner, 1983). These Canadian findings provide plenty of reason for pause when it is recognized that relations between American bilingual minorities and English-speaking Americans are often hostile. The contemporary political climate favoring multiculturalism rather than assimilation may, in fact, do much to undermine the motivations of individual non–English-speaking students to learn and use English.

Intelligence, School Achievement, and Bilingualism

The literature contains the contradictory hypotheses (and contradictory data) that bilingualism reduces

intelligence and that bilingualism increases intelligence (e.g., Hakuta, 1986, Chapter 2). Such a mix of positions and results does not inspire confidence for either position, however, and conclusions about the relationship of cognitive competence to bilingual status should be avoided. In fact, the data are contradictory even within individual investigations, with Hakuta (1987) reporting that bilingualism improved cognitive functioning in the grade-school years, with corresponding effects not detectable during the middle-school years. Any real or enduring effects of bilingualism on intellectual processing are probably small at best and possibly fleeting.

One of the most important tasks facing a second-language child is learning to read in the second language. Verhoeven (1990) studied this process as Turkish immigrant children learned Dutch in the Netherlands and concluded that learning to read in Dutch was facilitated by learning to speak Dutch. For primary-grades children, both word recognition and comprehension in Dutch were related to oral proficiency in Dutch. This study highlights the importance of encouraging spoken language skills in the majority language as a determinant of success in learning to read in the majority language.

Immersion Programs

Immersion programs were developed in Canada and have been adapted by Americans. In the primary years of immersion, most of the school day is spent in the second language. Beginning at about grade 3, the day is more evenly split between instruction in the second language and instruction in the first language. By high school, the majority of instruction is in the first language, although a large proportion of the day (e.g., 40 percent) is spent in classes conducted in the second language. The immersion model is intended to stimulate the development of both the first-language and second-language skills. Although the outcomes are complex, acquisition of both first and second languages is generally satisfactory. Academic achievement seems not to be reduced when it is provided in the second language (Genesee, 1985).

Canadian-type immersion programs are unique in that there is a substantial database available for them (including U.S. data). A number of other types of second-language programs are now being explored in the United States (see Ovander & Collier, 1985). The relative benefits of these are difficult to assess at the time of this writing, with a clear need for extensive evaluation of the various alternatives. To the extent that program alternatives have been evaluated in the United States, the evaluations have been weak methodologically (Lam, 1992).

There are many pressures for increased bilingual instruction, including legal ones. For example, in *Lau v. Nichols* (1974), the U.S. Supreme Court ruled that non–English-speaking children had to be provided instruction that permitted their participation in school, including the possibility of instruction in English or instruction in the native language. In addition, the Bilingual Education Act, originally passed in 1968, has been amended considerably since then, each time increasing the pressures on educators to provide bilingual education.

Particularly heartening from the perspective of this book, second-language educators are exploring how students can be taught strategies for learning second language as well as the metacognition to regulate use of strategies, with substantial evidence that many of the strategies useful for mainstream students are also useful for second-language students (e.g., Langer, Bartolome, Vasquez, & Lucas, 1990; O'Malley & Chamot, 1990). Consistent with the good information processing model, however, such strategies are often more evident with materials related to the reader's background (i.e., their cultural schemata; e.g., Malik, 1990). Second-language education is an area of research in which it is especially likely there will be great progress in research in the near future, and we suspect that many of the processes reviewed in this book will prove important in reshaping education of bilinguals so that it is increasingly effective.

Testing and Educational Placement of Non–English-Speaking Students

The Hispanic population of the United States has increased dramatically in size in the last 15 years and is projected to continue increasing in size, one factor motivating critical examination of the appropriateness of standardized testing with Spanish-speaking Americans. Until recently, there were laws in some parts of the United States—ones now struck down by courts, litigation, and changing professional standards—requiring that all children be tested in English, with decisions about school placement into special education or giftedness classes based on such tests (e.g., Donlon, 1992; Rodriguez, 1992). It is easy to understand why disproportionately higher numbers of Spanish-speaking children ended up in special education and disproportionately low numbers of Spanish children experienced accelerated offerings when placement was based on a test administered in English (Donlon, 1992; Pennock-Román, 1992; Schmeiser, 1992).

Positively speaking, progress has been made in eliminating the abuses of tests with non–English-speaking minorities, with the *Standards for Educational and Psychological Tests* (American Psychological Association, 1985) making clear that the scores of many standardized tests may be distorted because of language problems if the tests are administered to non–English-speaking minorities. For example, ability tests administered in English to Spanish-speaking students sometimes correlate 0.00 with ability tests administered in Spanish (Pennock-Román, 1992). That is, the distortions are sometimes massive to the point of transforming a test that is highly valid and interpretable with English-speaking students to one that is of no value for assessing minority students.

Because of litigation, there have been increases in protection of non–English-speaking students (Donlon, 1992; Rodriguez, 1992; Schmeiser, 1992): The ruling in *Diana vs. California State Board of Education* (1970) was that students must be tested in their native language (Geisenger, 1992a). In this case, an English-administered IQ test had been used to place Spanish-speaking students in special education. The Court determined that all Spanish-speaking and Chinese-speaking children in the state who were in classes intended for retarded children had to be retested using procedures that did not discriminate based on language. The Court also ruled that the retesting had to eliminate test items tapping vocabulary and general information that might not be encountered in the minority cultures. The retesting determined that seven of the nine students who had brought the case were much more intelligent than originally assessed (i.e., more than 15 points better, a full standard deviation; Constantino, 1992). The students were taken out of the classes for retarded students after the new, fairer assessment data were collected. The California legislature subsequently passed new laws to prevent the abuses that had produced the *Diana* case (Geisenger, 1992a), and there has been additional court action in California to prevent overrepresentation of minorities in special education classes (Constantino, 1992).

Another important case was *Larry P. vs. Riles* (1979), in which a federal judge ruled that California's mandate that IQ tests be used to decide special education placements for blacks and minorities was inappropriate. Tests that have been normed without sufficient samples of minorities are being rejected as a reasonable basis for making decisions about minorities (e.g., *Rivera vs. City of Wichita Falls,* 1982). Courts are recognizing when tests are being used with the intent to segregate students and are rejecting the use of tests in this way (e.g., *Morales vs. Shannon,* 1975).

Concluding Comments

The families of non–English-speaking students are often supportive of schooling and more committed to their children doing well in school than are majority parents (e.g., Delgado-Gaitan, 1992). They are more likely to be supportive of homework, comparative achievement testing, and longer school days. These family values translate into students who try hard to do well in school, although their efforts are often not sufficient to overcome institutional barriers to achievement by non–English-speaking students (Duran & Weffer, 1992).

There is no compelling evidence that non–English-speaking students are any less intelligent than majority students. We are especially hopeful that the next decade will produce work in educational psychology that permits more analytical conclusions about non–English-speaking populations, including investigations about how the development of strategic competence, metacognition, other knowledge, and supportive motivational beliefs can be developed to ensure that high proportions of such students develop their information processing capabilities in school.

DIFFERENCES IN THINKING ABILITIES ACROSS THE LIFE SPAN

Now more than ever, education occurs across the life span. It is not unusual for university-level and graduate students to be in their 30s, 40s, and 50s. Many universities now have programs for people in their 60s and older. Many of these people are returning to school, perhaps fulfilling an educational dream that was suspended some years before in favor of marriage or children or because of the economic infeasibility of pursuing higher education during youth. In addition to college-level returnees, many seek to complete high school equivalency work. Others are remediating basic skills deficiencies, with national efforts now underway to reduce adult illiteracy. In parts of the United States, 10 to 20 percent of the population are illiterate in the sense that they cannot read at a grade-4 level with comprehension. There is a real need for 21st century educational psychologists to understand adult thinking and learning abilities.

Strategies

A number of studies have been conducted in which elderly were presented some basic memory task, such as paired-associate or list learning. Subjects in one condition were taught a strategy well matched to the task (e.g., making interactive images for paired associates, organizing list materials by categories); control subjects were left to their own devices to process the material. Consistently in these studies, the elderly who were given the strategy instruction outperformed control subjects (for a review, see Meyer, Young, & Bartlett, 1989, Chapter 2; also, Roberts, 1983). What is clear is that, typically, if left to their own devices, the elderly are not as strategic as they could be. Nonetheless, they are quite capable of carrying out a number of strategies if provided brief instruction about how to do so.

When these studies have included younger adults as well, a common finding is that younger control participants outperform elderly controls, and that younger strategy-trained subjects outperform elderly strategy-trained subjects. That is, although it is not uncommon for strategy-trained elderly to outperform young adult controls, strategy-trained elderly do not perform anywhere near the level of strategy-trained young adults. Cognitive strategy training can improve the functioning of the elderly, but it usually does not permit the levels of performance that are possible during youth and younger adulthood.

For example, in Kliegl, Smith, and Baltes (1990), when younger and older adults performed a serial learning task under control instructions, the older subjects remembered about 12 percent of the list items, and the young adults recalled about 25 percent. Following a type of imagery mnemonic instruction (i.e., a one-is-a-bun pegword strategy; see Chapter 10), the recall of the elderly increased to the 40 percent level; the recall of the younger participants, however, soared to 75 percent. Under control instructions, there was substantial overlap in the scores of older and younger subjects (i.e., some older subjects outperformed some younger participants). Under the imagery instruction, few of the elderly outperformed any of the younger adults. After a lot of practice with the imagery mnemonic strategy, the elderly were able to boost their learning to about 50 percent; the younger adults went over the 80 percent level with practice.

There was another striking finding in the Kliegl et al. (1990) study. Large gains as a result of strategy training occurred for the elderly only when lists were presented slowly (i.e., 10 seconds per item or more). In contrast, younger subjects experienced great gains even at a faster rate (i.e., 5 seconds per item) and some gains at a much faster rate (i.e., 1 to 3 seconds per item). When all of the Kliegl et al. (1990) data are combined (see also Kliegl, Smith, & Baltes, 1989, as well as Baltes & Kliegl, 1992), what is apparent is that although the imagery strategy is helpful for the elderly, it is more helpful for younger adults and can be used by younger adults in more situations. Perhaps it should not be surprising that the elderly are less likely than younger adults to want to continue using imagery strategies they are taught (Brigham & Pressley, 1988; see Chapter 2, this book), for strategies produce greater benefits for younger adults than for the elderly.

A fair criticism of the adult literature on strategies is that there has been far too little evaluation of strategy use with ecologically valid materials. More positively, some such work is appearing. An example is Meyer et al.'s (1989) development and evaluation of a complex text learning strategy.

Meyer et al. (1989) were aware of a number of analyses of adult deficiencies in expository text processing; they were also aware of a number of successful attempts to teach young adults to analyze the structure of expository texts (i.e., determine whether the text is descriptive, a sequence of events, a cause-and-effect sequence, a problem-solution structure, a comparison, or a listing of related elements) and to use the structural cues to guide reading and learning from text (see Meyer et al., 1989, Chapter 2). They were interested in whether older adults could be taught to identify the structures in expository text and use this information to increase their learning from text. Meyer et al. (1989) evaluated the value of their training in a true experiment involving both younger (mean age = 24) and older (mean age = 68) subjects.

Participants in the strategy-training condition were taught the "Plan Strategy." This involved iden-

tifying the writing plan of the author of an expository piece. For each type of expository structure, participants were taught the structures and words in a text that could signal the use of the structure. For example, they were taught that descriptive text is signaled by phrases such as the following: for example, which was one, this particular, for instance, specifically, such as, attributes of, that is, namely, properties of, characteristics are, qualities are, marks of, in describing.

Knowledge of such signals is a form of metacognition, tipping off the reader about the type of text the author composed. Other metacognition about strategies was developed as well, with instruction provided about when the Plan Strategy works: It works when readers want to be able to recall the most important information in a text. It is not a useful strategy when the goal is simply to find some particular piece of information in a text. Thus, the training of the Plan Strategy was rich in information about when and where to use the plan as a whole and where and when to use particular expository structures to analyze text.

During training, participants applied the Plan Strategy to a variety of materials. Instruction occurred over five sessions.

There were two conditions in the study besides the Plan Strategy–training condition (henceforth, the strategy-training condition). A practice control condition (henceforth, the practice condition) practiced reading and remembering texts during the time corresponding to training in the Plan Strategy condition. There was also a no intervention/no practice control condition (henceforth, the control condition).

The findings were orderly and striking. Whether subjects used one of the expository structures to organize their recall of text was examined. The only pretest-to-posttest increases in the use of such structures occurred in the strategy-training condition for both younger and older participants. In general, there was slightly more pronounced evidence of pretest-to-posttest shifting in the younger than in the older sample, although the increases were quite striking for both younger and older participants. There were also posttest measures of the ability to identify types of passage structure, with strategy-trained subjects outperforming practice and control subjects. Again the tendency was for younger subjects to be at least slightly more proficient in making such identifications. In addition, the strategy report questionnaire data confirmed predominant use of the Plan Strategy in the strategy-trained condition, although there was slightly more reported use of it among younger than older subjects.

Strategy training increased recall of passage ideas in the elderly (from 21 percent at pretest to 32 percent at posttest) and in the young (from 20 percent at pretest to 35 percent at posttest). Much of this gain may have been due simply to the practice component, however, for there was an 18 to 25 percent increase in recall in the elderly practice condition and a corresponding 23 to 30 percent increase in the young adult group. More importantly, however, the strategy-trained subjects were more likely to recall higher-order information than were the subjects in the practice and control conditions. Also, when asked to identify the main ideas in passages, the trained subjects were slightly better at it than the practice or control participants.

The Meyer et al. (1989) results suggest to us that there is good reason to believe that the investment in long-term comprehension strategy instruction with adults might pay off, for the positive effects of training were consistent even if they were not large. Meyer et al. (1989) was an exceptional study of strategy instruction with young and elderly adults that deserves a great deal of follow-up. Many adults are faced with the need of getting information from expository materials. Unfortunately, in the absence of instruction, many adults are not armed with the strategies to extract such information efficiently.

There is substantial evidence of plasticity in human cognition across the adult life span (Lerner, 1990)—that thinking and performance can vary depending on conditions, with one important condition that can improve thinking being instruction. Life-span researchers have made this point through studies of strategy instruction. Strategies can be taught across the life span. Strategy instruction is not a magic bullet, however, eradicating age differences completely. Younger people using a strategy often outperform older people using the same strategy. What is particularly optimistic is that adults can learn complex strategies that have real world value, such as Meyer et al.'s (1989) Plan Strategy.

Metacognition

Because decline in memory with increasing age has been a particular concern of life-span developmental psychologists, metamemory has been assessed more often than other types of metacognition in life-span studies. One of the most important ways that metacognition has been examined in adulthood has been with metacognitive questionnaires. For example, here are some items that appear on one questionnaire:

1. How would you rate your memory in terms of the kinds of problems you have?
2. How often do you need to rely on your memory without the use of remembering techniques, such as making lists, when you are engaged in . . . (a) social activities?
3. How is your memory compared to the way it was . . . (b) one year ago?
4. How often do these present a problem to you . . . (a) names?
5. As you are reading a novel, how often do you have trouble remembering what you have read . . . (a) in the opening chapters once you have finished the book?
6. How well do you remember things that occurred . . . (a) last month?
7. When you actually forget in these situations, how serious a problem do you consider the memory failure to be . . . (a) names?
8. How much effort do you usually have to make to remember in these situations? . . . (a) names. (Adapted from Gilewski & Zelinski, 1986, Table 11.7, and Kausler, 1991, Table 9.3).

A variety of metamemory questionnaires are now available, with them tapping adults' knowledge of strategies, task variables affecting memory, and understanding of capacity and capacity limits. There are also questions about how people perceive their memory abilities changing with development, how much having a good memory means to them, whether they are anxious about memory, and whether they believe that they can exert control over their intellectual performances (Kausler, 1991, Chapter 9).

The most striking finding in this literature is that older adults are extremely pessimistic about their memory capabilities (e.g., Devolder & Pressley, 1991) and attribute difficulties they are experiencing to mental decline—to use a term from the motivational literature that has been adopted by metacognitive theorists and researchers interested in memory across the life span, there is a decline in **memory self-efficacy** (e.g., Berry, West, & Dennehey, 1989; Hertzog, Hultsch, & Dixon, 1989). One possibility is that reduced memory self-efficacy undermines motivation to remember and hence memory itself. That is, believing that you have a poor memory due to aging, which is out of your control, would not motivate efforts to remember, efforts that if made would improve memory (e.g., Bandura, 1989). It is not clear, however, that these beliefs, in fact, undermine motivation to attempt to remember new information, with mixed evidence of relationships between pessimism about memory and objective memory performances (Kausler, 1991, Chapter 9). We note, however, that leading contributors to the instructional literature with the elderly are now calling for studies in which strategies are taught as measures are taken to increase older adults' expectations about their intellectual abilities (e.g., Best, Hamlett, & Davis, 1992).

Another metacognitive possibility raised in the literature on aging is that older adults do not monitor their memories as well as do younger adults, with this often measured by examining the difference in how people believe they will perform a task and how well they actually perform the task. The literature is extremely mixed on this possibility as well, however, with some studies reporting declines in accuracy and others reporting equally accurate monitoring in younger and older adults (see Devolder, Brigham, & Pressley, 1990, for a review of the various studies).

Metacognition and monitoring are important to the extent that they are determinants of performance and efforts to affect performance. Thus, if a learner monitors that they have not yet mastered a task and reacts to that perception by working on the task some more, monitoring has played an important role in cognitive control. One possibility is that objective performances, and perceptions of objective performances, are not as critical in determining the behaviors of older learners compared with younger learners (again, see the discussion of Brigham & Pressley, 1988, in Chapter 2, this book).

Strong conclusions about monitoring in the elderly and its role in the cognition of the elderly are not possible based on the extant data. We are struck, however, by how salient efforts to increase metacognitive understandings are in successful training studies with the elderly (e.g., Meyer et al., 1989), consistent with successful intervention packages reviewed throughout this book.

Knowledge

One well-known measure of knowledge, the crystallized intelligence factor, was discussed in Chapter

16. Crystallized intelligence increases across the adult life span, an unsurprising finding on reflection. What is more interesting, however, are potential qualitative differences in the knowledge possessed by younger and older people, with developmental psychologists searching for such differences. The conclusion based on a large body of work at this point, however, is that the commonalities in the qualities of knowledge possessed by younger and older adults are greater than the differences.

One problem of great interest to life-span psychologists is whether there are differences in the scripts (see Chapter 3) possessed by younger versus older adults. When younger and older adults are asked about common activities, both groups provide descriptions that are recognizable as the activity. That is, their scripts are similar. Nonetheless, the scripts of older adults are more idiosyncratic in content than the scripts of younger adults (e.g., Hess, 1992; Light, 1992; Ross & Berg, 1992). The scripts provided by older adults reflect peculiar experiences and perspectives more clearly than do the scripts of younger adults. Consider how one elderly woman responded to the question, "What happens when you go on an airplane trip starting with the decision to take the trip and ending when you are called to enter the plane?":

> Son sends the ticket. Get ticket. Become paralyzed with fear. Cut off appointments for 2 weeks. Tell people when I'll be gone. Look through my clothes to find the nicest. Put clothes on the davenport. Look at clothes. Pack by process of elimination. Take out what looks too shabby. Take out what looks too small. Take out suitcase. Take out the list of what I brought before.
>
> Judge by the list what I will need now. Put the list with the ticket. Wait for the day I go. Ask friend to take me. He takes me there 1 hour early. Get there. They assign a seat. They put me in a wheelchair because the distance is long. They ask me which seat I prefer. Get an aisle seat. They write the number of my seat. Sit. Read. They open the door to the plane. (p. 39)

The significance of such quirky knowledge is that it can affect other learning. Thus, when Ross and Berg (1992) presented younger and older adults with script-type information to learn, they found that adults at both age levels had an easier time learning script-type information consistent with the idiosyncracies of their scripts. Even so, it seemed likely that the younger adults were making use of their personalized scripts to encode new material more than did the older adults, for the difference in recall between information consistent with idiosyncratic versus nonidiosyncratic scripts was greater for younger subjects than for older subjects.

Another possible difference in the knowledge of younger and older adults is with respect to semantic network organization, which would be reflected by different associations to vocabulary items. Thus, if given "table," different semantic organizations in long-term memory would be assumed if one person responded "chair" and another responded "legislation." One hypothesis, supported in some studies, but not in ones in which level of education and vocabulary knowledge are carefully controlled (see Kausler, 1991, Chapter 9, for a review; also, Light, 1992), is that the semantic networks of older adults are more idiosyncratic than the semantic networks of younger adults. If so, more younger adults would offer a first response of "chair" given "table," than would older adults, who would offer a variety of first responses to "table." The problem is that in some studies they do, and in some studies, they do not. That they do not in the more carefully controlled studies encourages the conclusion that the organization of concepts in memory may not differ dramatically during adulthood as a function of age. Other methods (besides word association) that potentially might reveal differences in semantic organization also have failed to produce evidence of age-related differences in conceptual relations, however.

Regardless of whether semantic memory is organized differently as a function of age during adulthood, there is little doubt that older adults make less use of their semantic memory to organize study and recall than do younger adults. For example, when studying lists of words that could be grouped into categories, the recall of older compared with younger adults is less likely to be organized with respect to the categories (see Kausler, 1991, Chapter 7). In addition, there is some evidence that the ability to retrieve information from long-term memory may decline with advancing age. One type of information supportive of this conclusion is that recognition memory shows less decline with advancing age than does recall, which implicates retrieval as a possible causal factor in the decline of recall because greater retrieval is required for recall than recognition. Similar differential declines with advancing age have been noted in other tasks that differ in the role of retrieval, with greater retrieval requirements associ-

ated with greater decline over the adult life span (see Salthouse, 1992, for a review of the relevant data).

When all of the data are reviewed, most of it suggests qualitative similarity in the structure of knowledge in younger and older adults, with the organization of concepts and the structure and content of scripts and schemata studied more completely than other types of knowledge. The more striking difference between young adults and the elderly is that knowledge is more certainly accessed and used to assist the accomplishment of new tasks by the young compared with the elderly. One possibility is that if new material is saliently consistent with schemata possessed by the elderly person, the information is processed relative to the schemata and memory is fine—for example, if to-be-learned information is presented in an organized picture that is easily related to a schema possessed by the older adult (e.g., recognition of a kitchen setting given an organized picture of a kitchen and the objects in it). If some effort is required to identify schemata that might be used to organize the information presented (e.g., to-be-learned kitchen items are presented in a disorganized picture), older adults are less likely to expend the effort required to identify and use schemata that might facilitate the learning of the material (Hess & Slaughter, 1990).

Motivation

A variety of motivational hypotheses have been advanced to explain, at least in part, the lower performances of older compared with younger adults. Only some of these have received support (Kausler, 1990, 1991; Willis, 1985). The following ideas about motivation in the elderly enjoy some support:

- Older adults have slightly less need for cognitive stimulation than do younger adults, resulting in at least slightly less engagement in cognitive activities by the elderly (Salthouse, Kausler, & Saults, 1988).
- Older adults have difficulties inhibiting task-irrelevant behaviors and thoughts relative to younger adults (e.g., Hasher, Stotzfus, Zacks, & Rypma, 1991). That is, the problem is not an age-related difference in motivation to do something; it is an age-related difference in staying on task (i.e., a volitional difference; e.g., Corno, 1989; see Chapter 5, this book).

- Older adults are more likely than younger adults to believe their performances are out of their control (i.e., older adults are more likely to attribute their cognitive difficulties to impaired ability, whereas younger adults attribute performance differences to controllable factors, such as effort and use of inappropriate strategies; e.g., Devolder & Pressley, 1992), with correlations between believing that cognitive performances are under personal control and objective performance levels (e.g., Devolder & Pressley, 1992).

Other potential motivational explanations of age differences have not been supported:

- Potential age differences in performance-disruptive anxiety (i.e., older people are more anxious and hence more likely to experience anxiety-related disruption of performance) have not been observed reliably.
- The need to achieve does not reliably decline with increasing age during adulthood as hypothesized by some. Enjoying learning for the sake of learning does not seem to vary with age during adulthood either.
- Older adults do not seem to be underaroused by cognitive tasks relative to younger adults, as proposed by some theorists interested in aging; nor do they seem to be overaroused reliably relative to younger adults, an hypothesis offered by some other workers in aging.

Some of the obvious ways that motivation could differ between older and younger adults have not proved telling. The more promising age-related motivational differences are understudied at this point, however. If older adults do not enjoy thinking as much as younger adults, if they are less likely to stay on task, and if they are less likely to believe that they can control their performances, these are serious deficiencies that adult educators should be aware of. Based on attribution-retraining successes with other populations (e.g., learning disabled; see Chapter 5), we would be optimistic that dysfunctional attributions might be reduced through instruction; given the success of self-instructions in keeping other populations on task (e.g., see Chapter 7), we think it possible that inhibition can be developed in the elderly if inhibition is indeed a serious problem for older adults. We expect educational psychologists to be active in studying academic motivation across the life span, including investigation of ways to modify instruction so that older adults are more likely to try hard to undertake a task and stay with it.

Processing Efficiency: Developmental Changes During Adulthood in Speed of Processing and Working Memory

One of the best substantiated findings in the literature on aging is that with advancing age, processing of information slows (e.g., Salthouse, 1982). In addition, although the data are not completely conclusive, slowing with increasing age during adulthood probably translates into decline in functional short-term capacity with advancing age (e.g., Hertzog, 1989; Salthouse & Babcock, 1991). Regardless of whether speed underlies declines in short-term or working memory, however, the evidence is mounting that short-term or working memory capacity decreases with advancing age (e.g., Kausler, 1991, Chapter 8). For example, recency effects in list learning (i.e., recall of the last few items from a list that has been studied), which are determined mostly by short-term memory factors, vary with age, with older adults less likely to recall the last items in a list than are younger adults (for a review of the relevant studies, see Kausler, 1991, Chapter 8). Campbell and Charness (1990) studied how young, middle-aged, and older adults perform mathematical computations in their head. With advancing age, there are many more errant substitutions, deletions, and omissions in performing calculations, errors that are due to short-term processing difficulties rather than long-term knowledge of mathematics facts and procedures. When older people retell stories, they are more likely than younger adults to make references to characters or events in ways that it is unclear which particular characters or events are intended, a failure of working memory: The frequency of such errors correlates with working memory differences in the elderly (Pratt, Boyes, Robins, & Manchester, 1989).

In addition to behavioral slowing, other factors contribute to decline of functional capacity as well. For instance, older adults are less likely to use their prior knowledge to chunk information into fewer, more meaningful pieces—that is, older adults are less likely than younger adults to use their knowledge to render demanding cognitive tasks easier (e.g., Taub, 1974; see also the earlier comments in the knowledge subsection). In short, several factors combine to undermine the efficiency of thinking by older adults compared with younger adults.

Concluding Comment

Something that is striking is that the differences in the thinking of younger and older adults are not great (Figure 18.2). A number of subtle differences, nonetheless, combine to reduce the overall performance of older adults compared with younger adults: The older adults are not as quick in their thinking; they are less likely to adopt newly offered strategies; they do not apply prior knowledge to tasks as certainly; their motivation for many tasks is less than that of younger adults; and their recall tends to be filled both with quirky irrelevancies and broad generalizations, whereas younger adults focus more on the objective and particular in their recall.

CONCLUDING COMMENTS

Within each individual differences classification considered here (i.e., retarded, learning-disabled, or gifted; non–English-speaking students; younger adults and older adults), there are distributions of abilities. Little is known about a person by knowing any of the classifications considered in this chapter relative to what must be known to make informed judgments about that person, their thinking quali-

ties, or that might be effective with them. Thus, our view is that knowledge of individual differences as covered in this chapter is useful with respect to understanding how psychology has illuminated ways that people can differ from one another. What is presented in this chapter is useless, however, in making decisions about individuals.

Decisions about individuals require extensive information about how that person performs various tasks and what the person's needs are. Often, classroom teachers can gather that information using informal assessments, teacher-made tests, and so on. In cases in which a child or adult has exceptional difficulties, more formal assessments can be helpful, sometimes including the intelligence or neuropsychological assessments detailed in Chapters 16 and 17 or other standardized measures of academic achievement. When information from these tests is considered by a professional psychologist working with educators who know the person well, there is good reason to believe that testing can provide some important data that can supplement other information (e.g., classroom performance and behavior) in making educational decisions about the person in question. The value of such standardized assessments is apparent when an important insight emerges that was not apparent to family members or teachers previously (e.g., that a person may be suffering from a sensory impairment, such as hearing loss, that accounts for poor achievement; when a

Figure 18.2 The good information processor model can be used to describe the thinking of all three of these males. All three of these people can learn strategies, regulate their use of strategies using metacognition, and possess a great deal of knowledge about the world that can be used in their thinking. How might the strategies, metacognition, knowledge, and motivation to do things academic and effortful differ between these three people, however?

child does well on an IQ test when evaluated by a psychologist who overcomes a child's shyness to reveal the active mind living behind a reticent veneer).

In concluding this chapter on individual differences, we feel frustrated. Although there has been much progress in understanding many groups of children for whom school is a challenge, there are other groups that are virtually ignored, groups that represent nontrivial proportions of the school-age population. We do not yet have an educational psychology that assists teachers in dealing with students who exhibit recalcitrant behavior problems, including, in the 1990s, those who bring guns to school and use drugs. We do not know much about how to reduce the likelihood of students dropping out of school or how to design educational alternatives that might be appealing enough to keep them in school. Although the challenges of studying such marginal students are great, it seems timely to do so. About all that we know now is that schools with rigid schedules, demands, and offerings do not work well for these students, if they work at all (Sinclair & Ghory, 1987).

One of the next missions for educational researchers interested in learner differences should be to attempt to understand "rebel" students as well as we understand more conventional students. The rebels of the 1990s are as much understudied by educational psychologists as multiculturals and middle aged adults returning to school. It is time for researchers to get to know many more types of learners than they have known in the past, for the 21st century demands that we educate better people of color, those challenged by poor health, and adults attempting to learn new skills required by technological advances as well as kids in leather jackets experimenting with drugs and exhibiting unacceptable behaviors. We will all benefit if school works for everyone, and it is more likely to do so if there is more extensive study of how all of us can succeed in school. We hope some readers found inspiration in this book to join us and other educational psychologists in the research and application challenges that are ahead.

References

Ach, N. (1910). *Uber deb willensaks und das temperament.* Leipzig Germany: Quelle & Meyer. (Cited in Corno, 1989.)

Achenbach, T., & Zigler, E. (1968). Cue-learning and problem-learning strategies in normal and retarded children. *Child Development, 3,* 827–848.

Adair, J. G., Sharpe, D., & Huynh, C-L. (1989). Hawthorne control procedures in educational experiments: A reconsideration of their use and effectiveness. *Review of Educational Research, 59,* 215–228.

Adams, M. J. (1990). *Beginning to read.* Cambridge, MA: Harvard University Press.

Afflerbach, P. P. (1990). The influence of prior knowledge on expert readers' main idea construction strategies. *Reading Research Quarterly, 25,* 31–46.

Ahn, W. (1987). *Schema acquisition from a single example.* Unpublished master's thesis. Urbana, IL: University of Illinois, Department of Psychology.

Ahn, W., & Brewer, W. F. (1988). Similarity-based and explanation-based learning of explanatory and nonexplanatory information. *Proceedings of the Tenth Annual Conference of the Cognitive Science Society* (pp. 524–530). Hillsdale, NJ: Erlbaum & Associates.

Ahn, W., Mooney, R. J., Brewer, W. F., & DeJong, G. F. (1987). Schema acquisition from one example: Psychological evidence for explanation-based learning. *Proceedings of the Ninth Annual Conference of the Cognitive Science Society* (pp. 50–57). Hillsdale, NJ: Erlbaum & Associates.

Aiken, E. G., Thomas, G. S., & Shennum, W. A. (1975). Memory for a lecture: Effects of notes, lecture rate, and information density. *Journal of Educational Psychology, 67,* 439–444.

Ajewole, G. A. (1991). Effects of discovery and expository instructional methods on the attitude of students in biology. *Journal of Research in Science Teaching, 28,* 401–409.

Aks, D. J., & Coren, S. (1990). Is susceptibility to distraction related to mental ability? *Journal of Educational Psychology, 82,* 388–390.

Alexander, P. A., & Judy, J. E. (1988). The interaction of domain-specific and strategic knowledge in academic performance. *Review of Educational Research, 58,* 375–404.

Alexander, P. A., Willson, V. L., White, C. S., & Fuqua, J. D. (1987). Analogical reasoning in young children. *Journal of Educational Psychology, 79,* 401–408.

Alexander, P. A., Willson, V. L., White, C. S., Fuqua, J. D., Clark, G. D., Wilson, A. F., & Kulikowich, J. M. (1989). Development of analogical reasoning in 40 5-year-old children. *Cognitive Development, 4,* 65–88.

Allen, J. B., Clark, W., Cook, M., Crane, P., Fallon, I., Hoffman, L., Jennings, K. S., & Sours, M. A. (1989). Reading and writing development in whole language kindergartens. In J. Mason (Ed.), *Reading and writing connections* (pp. 121–146). Needham Heights, MA: Allyn & Bacon.

Allen, L., Cipielewski, J., & Stanovich, K. E. (1992). Multiple indicators of children's reading habits and attitudes: Construct validity and cognitive correlates. *Journal of Educational Psychology, 84,* 489–503.

Allen, V. L. (Ed.) (1976). *Children as teachers: Theory and research on tutoring.* New York: Academic Press.

Allington, R. (1977). If they don't read much, how they ever gonna get good? *Journal of Reading, 21,* 57–61.

Allington, R. L. (1983). The reading instruction provided readers of differing ability levels. *Elementary School Journal, 83,* 548–559.

Allington, R. L. (1991a). Effective literacy instruction for at-risk children. In M. S. Knapp & P. M. Shields (Eds.), *Better schooling for the children of poverty: Alternatives to conventional wisdom* (pp. 9–30). Berkeley, CA: McCutchan Publishing Co.

Allington, R. L. (1991b). The legacy of "slow it down and make it more concrete." In J. Zutell & S. McCormick (Eds.), *Learner factors/teacher factors: Issues in literacy research and instruction: Fortieth Yearbook of the National Reading Conference* (pp. 19–29). Chicago: National Reading Conference.

Allington, R. L., & McGill-Franzen, A. (1989). School response to reading failure: Chapter 1 and special education students in grades 2, 4, & 8. *Elementary School Journal, 89,* 529–542.

Allington, R. L., & McGill-Franzen, A. (1991). *Unintended effects of educational reform in New York state.* Unpublished paper. Albany: State University of New York, School of Education.

Alvermann, D. E., & Hague, S. A. (1989). Comprehension of counter-intuitive science text: Effects of prior knowledge and text structure. *Journal of Educational Research, 82,* 197–202.

Alvermann, D. E., & Hayes, D. A. (1989). Classroom discussions of content area reading assignments: An intervention study. *Reading Research Quarterly, 24,* 305–335.

Alvermann, D. E., & Hynd, C. R. (1991). The effects of varying prior knowledge activation modes and text structure on nonscience majors' comprehension of physics text. *Journal of Educational Research.*

Alvermann, D. E., & Moore, D. W. (1991). Secondary school reading. In R. Barr, M. L. Kamil, P. B. Mosenthal, & P. D. Pearson (Eds.), *Handbook of reading research,* Vol. II (pp. 951–983). New York: Longman.

Alvermann, D. E., O'Brien, D. G., & Dillon, D. R. (1990). What teachers do when they say they're having discussions of content area reading assignments: A qualitative analysis. *Reading Research Quarterly, 25,* 296–322.

Alvermann, D. E., Smith, L. C., & Readence, J. E. (1985). Prior knowledge activation and the comprehension of compatible and incompatible texts. *Reading Research Quarterly, 20,* 420–436.

American Psychological Association (1985). *Standards for educational and psychological testing.* Washington, DC: American Psychological Association.

Ames, C. (1984). Competitive, cooperative, and individualistic goal structures: A motivational analysis. In R. Ames & C. Ames (Eds.), *Research on motivation in education,* Vol. 1 (pp. 117–207). New York: Academic Press.

Ames, C. (1990). Motivation: What teachers need to know. *Teachers College Record, 91,* 409–421.

Ames, C. (1992). Classrooms: Goals, structures, and student motivation. *Journal of Educational Psychology, 84,* 261–271.

Ames, C., & Ames, R. (1981). Competitive versus individualistic goal structures: The salience of past performance information for causal attributions and affect. *Journal of Educational Psychology, 73,* 411–418.

Ames, C., & Archer, J. (1988). Achievement goals in the classroom: Students' learning strategies and motivation processes. *Journal of Educational Psychology, 80,* 260–270.

Ames, C., & Felker, D. W. (1979). Effects of self-concept on children's causal attributions and self-reinforcement. *Journal of Educational Psychology, 71,* 613–619.

Amigues, R. (1988). Peer interaction in solving physics problems: Sociocognitive confrontation and metacognitive aspects. *Journal of Experimental Child Psychology, 45,* 141–158.

Anastasi, A. (1988). *Psychological testing* (sixth edition). New York: MacMillan.

Anastasiow, N. J. (1990). Implications of the neurobiological model for early intervention. In S. J. Meisels & J. P. Shonkoff (Eds.), *Handbook of early childhood interventions* (pp. 196–216). Cambridge, UK: Cambridge University Press.

Anbar, A. (1986). Reading acquisition of preschool children without systematic instruction. *Early Childhoo Research Quarterly, 1,* 69–83.

Anderson, C. W., Sheldon, T. H., & Dubay, J. (1990). The effects of instruction on college nonmajors' conceptions of respiration and photosynthesis. *Journal of Research in Science Teaching, 27,* 761–776.

Anderson, D. R., & Collins, P. A. (1988). *The impact on children's education: Television's influence on cognitive development.* (Office of Research Working Paper No. 2). Washington, DC: U.S. Department of Education, Office of Educational Research and Improvement.

Anderson, J. R. (1978). Arguments concerning representations for mental imagery. *Psychological Review, 85,* 249–277.

Anderson, J. R. (1983). *The architecture of cognition.* Cambridge, MA: Harvard University Press.

Anderson, J. R. (1984). Spreading activation. In J. R. Anderson & S. M. Kosslyn (Eds.), *Tutorials in learning and memory: Essays in honor of Gordon Bower* (pp. 61–90). San Francisco: W. H. Freeman & Co.

Anderson, J. R., & Bower, G. H. (1973). *Human associative memory.* New York: Wiley.

Anderson, J. R., Greeno, J. G., Kline, P. J., & Neves, D. M. (1981). Acquisition of problem-solving skill. In J. R. Anderson (Ed.), *Cognitive skills and their acquisition* (pp. 191–230). Hillsdale, NJ: Erlbaum & Associates.

Anderson, L., Jenkins, L. B., Leming, J., MacDonald, W. B., Mullis, I. V. S., Turner, M. J., & Wooster, J. S. (1990). *The civics report card.* Washington, DC: U.S. Department of Education, Office of Educational Research and Improvement.

Anderson, R. C., & Biddle, W. B. (1975). On asking people questions about what they are reading. In G. Bower (Ed.), *The psychology of learning and motivation,* Vol. 9. New York: Academic Press.

Anderson, R. C., Hiebert, E. H., Scott, J. A., & Wilkinson, I. A. G. (1985). *Becoming a nation of readers.* Washington, DC: National Institute of Education.

Anderson, R. C., Mason, J. M., & Shirey, L. (1984). The reading group: An experimental investigation of a labyrinth. *Reading Research Quarterly, 20,* 6–38.

Anderson, R. C., & Ortony, A. (1975). On putting apples into bottles: A problem of polysemy. *Cognitive Psychology, 7,* 167–180.

Anderson, R. C., & Pearson, P. D. (1984). A schema-theoretic view of basic processes in reading. In P. D. Pearson (Ed.), *Handbook of reading research.* New York: Longman.

Anderson, R. C., & Pichert, J. W. (1978). Recall of previously unrecallable information following a shift in perspective. *Journal of Verbal Learning and Verbal Behavior, 17,* 1–12.

Anderson, R. C., Reynolds, R. E., Schallert, D. L., & Goetz, E. T. (1977). Frameworks for comprehending discourse. *American Educational Research Journal, 14,* 367–382.

Anderson, R. C., Shirey, L. L., Wilson, P. T., & Fielding, L. G. (1987). Interestingness of children's reading material. In R. E. Snow & M. J. Farr (Eds.), *Aptitude, learning, and instruction, Volume 3: Conative and Affective Process Analyses* (pp. 287–299). Hillsdale, NJ: Erlbaum & Associates.

Anderson, R. C., Spiro, R. J., & Anderson, M. C. (1978). Schemata as scaffolding for the representation of information in connected discourse. *American Educational Research Journal, 15,* 433–439.

Anderson, R. C., Wilkinson, I. A. G., & Mason, J. M. (1991). A microanalysis of the small-group, guided reading lesson: Effect of emphasis on global story meaning. *Reading Research Quarterly, 26,* 417–441.

Anderson, T. H., & Armbruster, B. B. (1984). Content area textbooks. In R. C. Anderson, J. Osborn, & R. J. Tierney (Eds.), *Learning to read in American schools* (pp. 193–226). Hillsdale, NJ: Erlbaum & Associates.

Annett, J. (1988). Motor learning and retention. In M. Gruneberg, P. Morris, & R. Sykes (Eds.), *Practical aspects of memory 2.* Chichester, UK: John Wiley & Sons.

Annett, J. (1989). Training skilled performance. In A. M. Colley & J. R. Beech (Eds.), *Acquisition and performance of cognitive skills* (pp. 61–84). Chichester, UK: John Wiley & Sons.

Applebee, A. N. (1984). *Contexts for learning to write.* Norwood, NJ: Ablex.

Applebee, A. N., & Langer, J. A. (1983). Instructional scaffolding: Reading and writing as natural language activities. *Language Arts, 60,* 168–175.

Applebee, A. N., Langer, J., & Mullis, I. (1986). *The writing report card: Writing achievement in American schools.* Princeton, NJ: Educational Testing Service.

Arbitman-Smith, R., Haywood, W. C., & Bransford, J. D. (1984). Assessing cognitive change. In P. Brooks, R. Sperber, & C. M. McCauley (Eds.), *Learning and cognition in the mentally retarded.* Hillsdale, NJ: Erlbaum & Associates.

Armbruster, B. B., Anderson, T. H., & Meyer, J. L. (1991). Improving content-area reading using instructional graphics. *Reading Research Quarterly, 26,* 393–416.

Armbruster, B. B., Anderson, T. H., & Ostertag, J. (1987). Does text structure/summarization instruction facilitate learning from expository text? *Reading Research Quarterly, 22,* 331–346.

Armstrong, F. D., Seidel, J. F., & Swales, T. P. (1993). Pediatric HIV infection: A neuropsychological and educational challenge. *Journal of Learning Disabilities, 26,* 92–103.

Artman, L., & Cahan, S. (1993). Schooling and the development of transitive inference. *Developmental Psychology, 29,* 753–759.

Artzt, A. F., & Armour-Thomas, E. (1992). Development of a cognitive-metacognitive framework for protocol analysis of mathematical problem solving in small groups. *Cognition and Instruction, 9,* 137–175.

Asarnow, J. R., & Meichenbaum, D. (1979). Verbal rehearsal and serial recall. *Child Development, 50,* 1173–1177.

Ashcraft, M. H., & Battaglia, J. (1978). Cognitive arithmetic: Evidence for retrieval and decision processes in mental arithmetic. *Journal of Experimental Psychology: Human Learning and Memory, 4,* 527–538.

Ashcraft, M. H., & Stazyk, E. H. (1981). Mental addition: A test of three verification models. *Memory & Cognition, 9,* 185–196.

Astin, A. W. (1993). *What matters in college? Four critical years revisited.* San Francisco: Jossey-Bass.

Atkinson, R. C. (1975). Mnemotechnics in second-language learning. *American Psychologist, 30,* 821–828.

Atwell, N. (1987). *In the middle: Reading, writing, and learning from adolescents.* Portsmouth, NH: Heinemann.

Aulls, M. W. (1991). Main ideas: keys to learning science. In C. M. Santa & D. E. Alvermann (eds.), *Science learning: process and applications* (pp. 96–103). Newark, DE: Int'l. Reading Assn.

Ault, C. S. (1985). Concept mapping as a study strategy with earth science. *Journal of College Science Teaching, 15,* 38–44.

Ausubel, D. P. (1960). The use of advance organizers in the learning and retention of meaningful verbal learning. *Journal of Educational Psychology, 51,* 267–272.

Ausubel, D. P. (1961). Learning by discovery: Rationale and mystique. *Bulletin of the National Association of Secondary School Principles, 45,* 18–58.

Ausubel, D. P. (1968). *Educational psychology: A cognitive view.* New York: Holt, Rinehart, & Winston.

Babad, E. Y., & Budoff, M. (1974). Sensitivity and validity of learning potential measurements in three levels of ability. *Journal of Educational Psychology, 66,* 439–447.

Bach, M. J., & Underwood, B. J. (1970). Developmental changes in memory attributes. *Journal of Educational Psychology, 61,* 292–296.

Baddeley, A. (1986). *Working memory.* New York: Oxford University Press.

Baer, D. M. (1990). Why choose self-regulation as the focal analysis of retardation? *American Journal of Mental Deficiency, 94,* 363–364.

Bahrick, H. P. (1984). Semantic memory content in permastore: Fifty years of memory for Spanish learned in school. *Journal of Experimental Psychology: General, 113,* 1–29.

Bahrick, H. P., & Hall, L. K. (1991). Preventive and corrective maintenance of access to knowledge. *Applied Cognitive Psychology, 5,* 1–18.

Bahrick, H. P., & Phelps, E. (1987). Retention of Spanish vocabulary over 8 years. *Journal of Experimental Psychology: Learning, Memory, and Cognition, 13,* 344–349.

Baker, L. (1989). Metacognition, comprehension monitoring, and the adult reader. *Educational Psychology Review, 1,* 3–38.

Baker, L., & Brown, A. L. (1984). Metacognitive skills and reading. In P. D. Pearson, R. Barr, M. Kamil, & P. Mosenthal (Eds.), *Handbook of reading research* (pp. 353–394). New York: Longmans.

Baker, L. A., Vernon, P. A., & Ho, H-Z. (1991). The genetic correlation between intelligence and speed of information processing. *Behavior Genetics, 21,* 351–367.

Baker-Ward, L., Hess, T. M., & Flannagan, D. A. (1990). The effects of involvement on children's memory for events. *Cognitive Development, 5,* 55–69.

Bakhtin, M. M. (1981). *The dialogic imagination: Four essays by M. M. Bakhtin* (Edited by Michael Holquist; Translated by Caryl Emerson & Michael Holquist). Austin: University of Texas Press.

Bakwin, H. (1973). Reading disability in twins. *Developmental Medicine and Child Neurology, 15,* 184–7.

Ball, D. L. (1988). *Knowledge and reasoning in mathematical pedagogy: Examining what prospective teachers bring to teacher education.* Unpublished doctoral dissertation. Michigan State University.

Ball, E. W., & Blachman, B. A. (1988). Phoneme-segmentation training: Effect on reading readiness. *Annals of Dyslexia, 38,* 203–225.

Ball, E. W., & Blachman, B. A. (1991). Does phoneme segmentation training in kindergarten make a difference in early word recognition and developmental spelling? *Reading Research Quarterly, 26,* 49–66.

Ball, S., & Bogatz, G. A. (1970). *The first year of "Sesame Street": An evaluation.* Princeton, NJ: Educational Testing Service.

Ball, S., & Bogatz, G. A. (1975). Some thoughts on this secondary evaluation. In T. D. Cook, H. Appleton, R. F. Conner, A. Shaffer, G. Tamkin, & S. J. Weber, *"Sesame Street" revisited.* New York: Russell Sage Foundation.

Baltes, P. B. (1968). Longitudinal and cross-sectional sequences in the study of age and generation effects. *Human Development, 11,* 145–171.

Baltes, P. B., & Kliegl, R. (1992). Further testing of limits of cognitive plasticity: Negative age differences in a mnemonic skill are robust. *Developmental Psychology, 28,* 121–125.

Baltes, P. B., Reese, H. W., & Nesselroade, J. R. (1977). *Life-span developmental psychology: Introduction to research methods.* Monterey, CA: Brooks/Cole.

Bandura, A. (1965). Vicarious processes: A case of no-trial learning. In L. Berkowitz (Ed.), *Advances in experimental social psychology,* Vol. 2 (pp. 1–55). New York: Academic Press.

Bandura, A. (1969). *Principles of behavior modification.* New York: Holt.

Bandura, A. (1977a). Self-efficacy: Toward a unifying theory of behavioral change. *Psychological Review, 84,* 191–215.

Bandura, A. (1977b). *Social learning theory.* Englewood Cliffs, NJ: Prentice-Hall.

Bandura, A. (1982). Self-efficacy mechanism in human agency. *American Psychologist, 37,* 122–147.

Bandura, A. (1986). *Social foundations of thought and action: A social cognitive theory.* Englewood Cliffs, NJ: Prentice-Hall.

Bandura, A. (1989). Regulation of cognitive processes through perceived self-efficacy. *Developmental Psychology, 25,* 729–735.

Bandura, A., Grusec, J. E., & Menlove, F. L. (1966). Observational learning as a function of symbolization and incentive set. *Child Development, 37,* 499–506.

Bandura, A., & Jeffrey, R. W. (1973). Role of symbolic coding and rehearsal processes in observational learning. *Journal of Personality and Social Psychology, 26,* 122–130.

Bandura, A., Jeffrey, R. W., & Bachicha, D. L. (1974). Analysis of memory codes and cumulative rehearsal in observational learning. *Journal of Research in Personality, 7,* 295–305.

Bandura, A., & Menlove, F. L. (1968). Factors determining vicarious extinction of avoidance behavior through symbolic modeling. *Journal of Personality and Social Psychology, 8,* 99–108.

Bandura, A., & Schunk, D. H. (1981). Cultivating competence, self-efficacy, and intrinsic interest through proximal self-instruction. *Journal of Personality and Social Psychology, 41,* 586–598.

Bandura, A., & Walters, R. H. (1963). *Social learning and personality development.* New York: Holt, Rinehart, & Winston.

Bangert-Drowns, R. L., Kulik, C-I. C., Kulik, J. A., & Morgan M. (1991). The instructional effect of feedback in test-like events. *Review of Educational Research, 61,* 213–238.

Barclay, C. R. (1979). The executive control of mnemonic activity. *Journal of Experimental Child Psychology, 27,* 262–276.

Barker, G., & Graham, S. (1987). Developmental study of praise and blame as attributional cues. *Journal of Educational Psychology, 79,* 62–66.

Barker, T. A., Torgesen, J. K., & Wagner, R. K. (1992). The role of orthographic processing skills on five different reading tasks. *Reading Research Quarterly, 27,* 334–345.

Barnes, B. R., & Clawson, E. U. (1975). Do advance organizers facilitate learning? Recommendations for further research based on analysis of 32 studies. *Review of Educational Research, 45,* 637–659.

Barnett, M., & Andrews, J. (1977). Sex differences in children's reward allocation under competitive and cooperative instructional sets. *Developmental Psychology, 13,* 85–86.

Barnhart, J. E. (1991). Criterion-related validity of interpretations of children's performance on emergent literacy tasks. *Journal of Reading Behavior, 23,* 425–444.

Baron, J. (1977). Mechanisms for pronouncing printed words: Use and acquisition. In D. LaBerge & S. J. Samuels (Eds.), *Basic processes in reading: Perception and comprehension* (pp. 175–216). Hillsdale, NJ: Erlbaum & Associates.

Baron, J. (1985). *Rationality and intelligence.* Cambridge, UK: Cambridge University Press.

Baron, J. (1988). *Thinking and deciding.* New York: Cambridge University Press.

Baron, J. (1990a). Reflectiveness and rational thinking: Response to Duemler and Mayer (1988). *Journal of Educational Psychology, 82,* 391–392.

Baroody, A. (1987). *Children's mathematical thinking.* New York: Teachers College Press.

Barr, H. M., Streissguth, A. P., Darby, B. L., & Sampson, P. D. (1990). Prenatal exposure to alcohol, caffeine, tobacco, and aspirin: Effects on fine and gross motor performance in 4-year-old children. *Developmental Psychology, 26,* 339–348.

Barr, R. C. (1974–75). The effect of instruction on pupil reading strategies. *Reading Research Quarterly, 10,* 555–582.

Barron, R. W. (1981). Development of visual word recognition: A review. In G. E. MacKinnon & T. G. Waller (Eds.), *Reading research: Advances in theory and practice,* Vol. 3 (pp. 119–158). San Diego: Academic Press.

Barron, R. W. (1986). Word recognition in early reading: A review of the direct and indirect access hypotheses. *Cognition, 24,* 93–119.

Bartel, N. R., & Thurman, S. K. (1992). Medical treatment and educational problems in children. *Phi Delta Kappan, 74,* 57–61.

Bartlett, F. C. (1932). *Remembering.* Cambridge, UK: Cambridge University Press.

Basili, P. A., & Sanford, J. P. (1991). Conceptual change strategies and cooperative group work in chemistry. *Journal of Research in Science Teaching, 28,* 293–304.

Bassarear, T., & Davidson, N. (1992). The use of small group learning situations in mathematics instruction as a tool to develop thinking. In

N. Davidson & T. Worsham (Eds.), *Enhancing thinking through cooperative learning* (pp. 235–250). New York: Teachers College Press.

Bauer, R. H. (1977a). Memory processes in children with learning disabilities. *Journal of Experimental Child Psychology, 24,* 415–430.

Bauer, R. H. (1977b). Short-term memory in learning disabled and nondisabled children. *Bulletin of the Psychonomic Society, 10,* 128–130.

Bazerman, C. (1985). Physicists reading physics: Schema-laden purposes and purpose-laden schema. *Written Communication, 2,* 3–23.

Beach, R. (1976). Self-evaluation strategies of extensive revisers and nonrevisers. *College Composition and Communication, 27,* 160–164.

Beal, C. R. (1987). Repairing the message: Children's monitoring and revision skills. *Child Development, 58,* 401–408.

Beal, C. R. (1989). Children's communication skills: Implications for the development of writing strategies. In C. B. McCormick, G. Miller, & M. Pressley (Eds.), *Cognitive strategy research: From basic research to educational applications* (pp. 191–214). New York: Springer-Verlag.

Beal, C. R. (1990). The development of text evaluation and revision skills. *Child Development, 61,* 247–258.

Beal, C. R., Garrod, A. C., & Bonitatibus, G. J. (1990). Fostering children's revision skills through training in comprehension monitoring. *Journal of Educational Psychology, 82,* 275–280.

Bean, T. W., & Steenwyk, F. L. (1984). The effect of three forms of summarization instruction on sixth graders' summary writing and comprehension. *Journal of Reading Behavior, 16,* 297–306.

Bebeau, M. J., & Brabeck, M. M. (1987). Integrating care and justice issues in professional moral education: A gender perspective. *Journal of Moral Education, 16,* 189–203.

Bebout, H. C. (1990). Children's symbolic representation of addition and subtraction word problems. *Journal for Research in Mathematics Education, 21,* 123–131.

Bechtel, W., & Abrahamsen, A. (1991). *Connectionism and the mind.* Cambridge, MA: Basil Blackwell.

Beck, I. L., McKeown, M. G., Sinatra, G. M., & Loxterman, J. A. (1991). Revising social studies text from a text-processing perspective: Evidence of improved comprehensibility. *Reading Research Quarterly, 26,* 251–276.

Becker, B. J. (1990). Coaching for the Scholastic Aptitude Test: Further synthesis and appraisal. *Review of Educational Research, 60,* 373–417.

Beckwith, L., & Parmelee, A. H., Jr. (1986). EEG patterns of preterm infants: Home environments and later IQ. *Child Development, 57,* 777–789.

Beichner, R. J. (1990). The effect of simultaneous motion presentation and graph generation in a kinematics lab. *Journal of Research in Science Teaching, 27,* 803–815.

Bell, R. Q. (1968). A reinterpretation of the direction of effects in studies of socialization. *Psychological Review, 75,* 81–95.

Belmont, J. M., Butterfield, E. C., & Ferretti, R. P. (1982). To secure transfer of training: Instruct self-management skills. In D. K. Detterman & R. J. Sternberg (Eds.), *How and how much can intelligence be increased* (pp. 147–154). Norwood, NJ: Ablex.

Benbow, C. P. (1992). Academic achievement in mathematics and science of students between ages 13 and 23: Are there differences among students in the top one percent of mathematical ability? *Journal of Educational Psychology, 84,* 51–61.

Benbow, C. P., & Arjmand, O. (1990). Predictors of high academic achievement in mathematics and science by mathematically talented students: A longitudinal study. *Journal of Educational Psychology, 82,* 430–441.

Bennett, W. L. (1984). *To reclaim a legacy: A report on humanities in higher education.* Washington, DC: National Endowment for the Humanities.

Bentz, J., Shinn, M. R., & Gleason, M. M. (1990). Training general education pupils to monitor reading using curriculum-based measurement procedures. *School Psychology Review, 19,* 23–32.

Ben-Zvi, R., Eylon, B., & Silberstein, J. (1987, July). Students' visualization of a chemical reaction. *Education in Chemistry,* 117–120.

Bereiter, C. (1990). Aspects of an educational learning theory. *Review of Educational Research, 60,* 603–624.

Bereiter, C., & Bird, M. (1985). Use of thinking aloud in identification and teaching of reading comprehension strategies. *Cognition and Instruction, 2,* 131–156.

Bereiter, C., & Scardamalia, M. (1982). From conversation to composition: The role of instruction in a developmental process. In R. Glaser (Ed.), *Advances in instructional psychology,* Vol. 2 (pp. 1–64). Hillsdale, NJ: Erlbaum & Associates.

Bereiter, C., & Scardamalia, M. (1987). *The psychology of written communication.* Hillsdale, NJ: Erlbaum & Associates.

Berg, J. M. (1985). Physical determinants of environmental origin. In A. M. Clarke, A. D. B. Clarke, & J. M. Berg (Eds.), *Mental deficiency: The changing outlook* (4th edition) (pp. 99–134). New York: Free Press.

Bergem, T. (1990). The teacher as moral agent. *Journal of Moral Education, 19,* 88–100.

Berk, R. A. (1986). *Performance assessment: Methods and application.* Baltimore: Johns Hopkins University Press.

Berkenkotter, C., & Murray, D. (1983). Decisions and revisions: The planning strategies of a publishing writer and responses of a laboratory rat—or being protocoled. *College Composition and Communication, 34,* 156–172.

Berkowitz, S. J. (1986). Effects of instruction in text organization on sixth-grade students' memory for expository reading. *Reading Research Quarterly, 21,* 161–178.

Berliner, D. (1986). In pursuit of the expert pedagogue. *Educational Researcher, 15 (7),* 5–13.

Berliner, D. C. (1988). *The development of expertise in pedagogy.* Washington, DC: American Association of College for Teacher Education.

Berndt, T. J., & Miller, K. E. (1990). Expectancies, values, and achievement in junior high school. *Journal of Educational Psychology, 82,* 319–326.

Berry, J. M., West, R. L., & Dennehey, D. M. (1989). Reliability and validity of the memory self-efficacy questionnaire. *Developmental Psychology, 25,* 701–713.

Bertelson, P., & De Gelder, B. (1989). Learning about reading from illiterates. In A. M. Galaburda (Ed.), *From reading to neurons* (pp. 1–23). Cambridge, MA: MIT Press.

Best, D. L. (1993). Inducing children to generate mnemonic organizational strategies: An examination of long-term retention and materials. *Developmental Psychology, 29,* 324–336.

Best, D. L., Hamlett, K. W., & Davis, S. W. (1992). Memory complaint and memory performance in the elderly: The effects of memory-skills training and expectancy change. *Applied Cognitive Psychology, 6,* 405–416.

Best, D. L., & Ornstein, P. A. (1986). Children's generation and communication of mnemonic organizational strategies. *Developmental Psychology, 22,* 845–853.

Beuhring, T., & Kee, D. W. (1987). Developmental relationships among metamemory, elaborative strategy use, and associative memory. *Journal of Experimental Child Psychology, 44,* 377–400.

Bielaczyc, K., Pirolli, P., & Brown, A. L. (1991, March). *The effects of training in explanation strategies on the acquisition of programming skills.* Presented at the annual meeting of the American Educational Research Association, Chicago.

Binet, A., & Henri, V. (1896). La psychologie individuelle. *L'Annee Psychologique, 2,* 411–465.

Binet, A., & Simon, T. (1905a). Sur la necessite d/etablit un diagnostic scientifique des etats inferieurs de l'intelligence. *L'Annee Psychologique, 11,* 163–190.

Binet, A., & Simon, T. (1905b). Methodes nouvelles pour le disagnostic du niveau intellectual des anormaux. *L'Annee Psychologique, 11,* 191–244.

Binet, A., & Simon, T. (1905c). Application des methodes nouvelles au diagnostic du niveau intellectual chez des enfants normaux et anormaux d'hospice et d'ecole primaire. *L'Annee Psychologique, 11,* 245–336.

Bird, T. (1990). The schoolteacher's portfolio: An essay on possibilities. In J. Millman & L. Darling-Hammond (Eds.), *Handbook of teacher evaluation: Elementary and secondary personnel, second edition* (pp. 241–256). Newbury Park, CA: Sage.

Bishop, B. A., & Anderson, C. W. (1990). Student conceptions of natural selection and its role in evolution. *Journal of Research in Science Teaching, 27,* 415–427.

Bissex, G. (1980). *GNYS at work: A child learns to write and read.* Cambridge MA: Harvard University Press.

Bjorklund, D. F. (1985). The role of conceptual knowledge in the development of organization in children's memory. In C. J. Brainerd &

M. Pressley (Eds.), *Basic processes in memory development: Progress in cognitive development research* (pp. 103–142). New York: Springer-Verlag.

Bjorklund, D. F. (1987b). How age changes in knowledge base contribute to the development of children's memory: An interpretive review. *Developmental Review, 7,* 93–130.

Bjorklund, D. F. (1988). Acquiring a mnemonic: Age and category knowledge effects. *Journal of Experimental Child Psychology, 45,* 71–87.

Bjorklund, D. F. (1989). *Cognitive development.* Monterey, CA: Brooks/Cole.

Bjorklund, D. F., & Buchanen, J. J. (1989). Developmental and knowledge base differences in the acquisition and extension of a memory strategy. *Journal of Experimental Child Psychology, 48,* 451–471.

Bjorklund, D. F., & Harnishfeger, K. K. (1987). Developmental differences in the mental effort requirements for the use of an organizational strategy in free recall. *Journal of Experimental Child Psychology, 44,* 109–125.

Bjorklund, D. F., & Harnishfeger, K. K. (1990). The resources construct in cognitive development: Diverse resources of evidence and a theory of inefficient inhibition. *Developmental Review, 10,* 48–71.

Blachman, B. A. (1991). Phonological awareness: Implications for prereading and early reading instruction. In S. A. Brady & D. P. Shankweiler (Eds.), *Phonological processes in literacy: A tribute to Isabelle Y. Liberman* (pp. 29–36). Hillsdale, NJ: Erlbaum & Associates.

Black, J. E., & Greenough, W. T. (1991). Developmental approaches to the memory process. In J. L. Martinez Jr., & R. P. Kesner (Eds.), *Learning and memory: A biological view,* 2nd ed. (pp. 61–91). San Diego: Academic Press.

Black, K. (1989). Audience analysis and persuasive writing at the college level. *Research in the Teaching of English, 23,* 231–253.

Blackman, L. S., & Lin, A. (1984). Generalization training in the educable mentally retarded: Intelligence and its educability revisited. In P. H. Brooks, R. Sperber, & C. McCauley (Eds.), *Learning and cognition in the mentally retarded* (pp. 237–263). Hillsdale, NJ: Erlbaum & Associates.

Blagg, N. (1991). *Can we teach intelligence?: A comprehensive evaluation of Feurstein's instrumental enrichment program.* Hillsdale, NJ: Erlbaum & Associates.

Blakenay, R., & Blakenay, C. (1990). Reforming moral misbehaviour. *Journal of Moral Education, 19,* 101–113.

Blatt, M., & Kohlberg, L. (1975). The effects of classroom moral discussion upon children's level of moral judgment. *Journal of Moral Education, 4,* 129–161.

Bleakley, M. E., Westerberg, V., & Hopkins, K. D. (1988). The effect of character sex on story interest and comprehension in children. *American Educational Research Journal, 25,* 145–155.

Bliss, J. R. (1991). Strategic and holistic images of effective schools. In J. R. Bliss, W. A. Firestone, & C. E. Richards (Eds.), *Rethinking effective schools research and practice* (pp. 43–57).

Englewood Cliffs, NJ: Prentice-Hall.

Block, N. J., & Dworkin, G. (Eds.) (1976). *The IQ controversy.* New York: Pantheon.

Bloom, B. S. (1968, May). Mastery learning. In *Evaluation comment* (Vol. 1, No. 2). Los Angeles: UCLA, Center for Evaluation of Instructional Programs.

Bloom, B. S. (1976). *Human characteristics and school learning.* New York: McGraw Hill.

Bloom, B. S. (1985). *Developing talent in young people.* New York: Ballantine Books.

Bloom, B. S. (1987). A response to Slavin's Mastery Learning reconsidered. *Review of Educational Research, 57,* 507–508.

Bloom, L. (1973). *One word at a time.* The Hague, Netherlands: Mouton.

Blume, G. W., & Schoen, H. L. (1988). Mathematical problem-solving performance of eighth-grade programmers and nonprogrammers. *Journal for Research in Mathematics Education, 19,* 142–156.

Blumenfeld, P. C. (1992). Classroom learning and motivation: Clarifying and expanding goal theory. *Journal of Educational Psychology, 84,* 272–281.

Bogatz, G. A., & Ball, S. (1971). *The second year of "Sesame Street": A continuing evaluation.* Princeton, NJ: Educational Testing Service.

Bogen, J. E. (1975). The other side of the brain. VII: Some educational aspects of hemispheric specialization. *UCLA Educator, 17,* 24–32.

Bond, G. L., & Dykstra, R. (1967). The cooperative research program in first-grade reading instruction. *Reading Research Quarterly, 2,* 5–142.

Borko, H., & Livingston, C. (1989). Cognition and improvisation: Differences in mathematics instruction by expert and novice teachers. *American Educational Research Journal, 26,* 473–498.

Borkowski, J. G. (1985). Signs of intelligence: Strategy, generalization, and metacognition. In S. R. Yussen (Ed.), *The growth of reflection in children* (pp. 105–144). Orlando, FL: Academic Press.

Borkowski, J. G., Carr, M., Rellinger, E. A., & Pressley, M. (1990). Self-regulated strategy use: Interdependence of metacognition, attributions, and self-esteem. In B. F. Jones (Ed.), *Dimensions of thinking: Review of research* (pp. 53–92). Hillsdale, NJ: Erlbaum & Associates.

Borkowski, J. G., & Kurtz, B. E. (1987). Metacognition and executive control. In J. G. Borkowski & J. D. Day (Eds.), *Cognition in special children: Comparative approaches to retardation, learning disabilities, and giftedness* (pp. 123–152). Norwood, NJ: Ablex.

Borkowski, J. G., Levers, S., & Gruenenfelder, T. M. (1976). Transfer of mediational strategies in children: The role of activity and awareness during strategy acquisition. *Child Development, 47,* 779–786.

Borkowski, J. G., & Muthukrishna, N. (1992). Moving metacognition into the classroom: "Working models" and effective strategy teaching. In M. Pressley, K. R. Harris, & J. T. Guthrie (Eds.), *Promoting academic competence and literacy in schools* (pp. 477–501). San Diego:

Academic Press.

Borkowski, J. G., & Peck, V. A. (1986). Causes and consequences of metamemory in gifted children. In R. J. Sternberg & J. E. Davidson (Eds.), *Conceptions of giftedness* (pp. 182–200). Cambridge, UK: Cambridge University Press.

Borkowski, J. G., Weyhing, R. S., & Carr, M. (1988). Effects of attributional retraining on strategy-based reading comprehension in learning-disabled students. *Journal of Educational Psychology, 80,* 46–53.

Bornstein, M. H., Kessen, W., & Weiskopf, S. (1976). Color vision and hue categorization in young infants. *Journal of Experimental Psychology: Human Perception and Performance, 2,* 115–129.

Bouchard, T. J., Jr., & McGue, M. (1981). Familial studies of intelligence: A review. *Science, 212,* 1055–1059.

Bowen, C. W. (1990). Representational systems used by graduate students while problem solving in organic synthesis. *Journal of Research in Science Teaching, 27,* 351–370.

Bower, G. H. (1972). Mental imagery and associative learning. In L. Gregg (Ed.), *Cognition in learning and memory* (pp. 51–87). New York: Wiley.

Bower, G. H., & Clapper, J. P. (1989). Experimental methods in cognitive science. In M. I. Posner (Ed.), *Foundations of cognitive science.* Cambridge, MA: MIT Press.

Bower, G. H., & Hilgard, E. R. (1981). *Theories of learning,* 5th ed. Englewood Cliffs, NJ: Prentice-Hall.

Bower, G. H., & Karlin, M. B. (1974). Depth of processing pictures of faces and recognition memory. *Journal of Experimental Psychology, 103,* 751–757.

Bowers, C. A., & Flinders, D. J. (1990). *Responsive teaching: An ecological approach to classroom patterns of language, culture, and thought.* New York: Teachers College Press.

Bowlby, J. (1969). *Attachment and loss,* Vol 1. *Attachment.* New York: Basic Books.

Boyd, D. R. (1988). Perspectives on moral education within the Canadian multicultural mosaic. *Journal of Moral Education, 17,* 148–160.

Boyes, M. C., & Chandler, M. (1992). Cognitive development, epistemic doubt, and identity formation in adolescence. *Journal of Youth and Adolescence, 21,* 277–304.

Brabeck, M. M. (Ed.) (1989). *Who cares? Theory, research, and educational implications of the ethic of care.* New York: Praeger.

Bracht, G. H., & Glass, G. V. (1968). The external validity of experiments. *American Educational Research Journal, 5,* 437–474.

Bradley, L. (1988). Making connections in learning to read and to spell. *Applied Cognitive Psychology, 2,* 3–18.

Bradley, L. (1989). Predicting learning disabilities. In J. Dumont & H. Nakken (Eds.), *Learning disabilities,* Vol. 2, *Cognitive, social, and remedial aspects* (pp. 1–18). Amsterdam: Swets Publishing.

Bradley, L., & Bryant, P. E. (1983). Categorizing

sounds and learning to read—a causal connection. *Nature, 301,* 419–421.

Bradley, L., & Bryant, P. (1985). *Rhyme and reason in reading and spelling.* International Academy for Research in Learning Disabilities Series. Ann Arbor, MI: University of Michigan Press.

Bradley, L., & Bryant, P. (1991). Phonological skills before and after learning to read. In S. A. Brady & D. P. Shankweiler (Eds.), *Phonological processes in literacy: A tribute to Isabelle Y. Liberman* (pp. 37–45). Hillsdale, NJ: Erlbaum & Associates.

Bradley, R. H., Caldwell, B. M., Rock, S. L., Ramey, C., Barnard, K. E., Hammond, M. A., Mitchell, S., Gottfried, A. W., Siegel, L., & Johnson, D. L. (1989). Home environment and cognitive development in the first 3 years of life: A collaborative study involving six sites and three ethnic groups in North America. *Developmental Psychology, 25,* 217–235.

Bradley, T. B. (1983). Remediation of cognitive deficits: A critical appraisal of the Feuerstein model. *Journal of Mental Deficiency Research, 27,* 79–92.

Brainerd, C. J. (1978a). Learning research and Piagetian theory. In L. S. Siegel & C. J. Brainerd (Eds.), *Alternatives to Piaget: Critical essays on the theory* (pp. 69–109). New York: Academic Press.

Brainerd, C. J. (1978b). *Piaget's theory of intelligence.* Englewood Cliffs, NJ: Prentice-Hall.

Brainerd, C. J. (1978c). The stage question in cognitive developmental theory. *Behavioral and Brain Sciences, 1,* 173–213.

Bransford, J. D., & Johnson, M. K. (1972). Contextual prerequisites for understanding: Some investigations of comprehension and recall. *Journal of Verbal Learning and Verbal Behavior, 11,* 717–726.

Bransford, J. D., Stein, B. S., Vye, N. J., Franks, J. J., Auble, P. M., Mezynski, K. J., & Perfetto, J. A. (1982). Differences in approaches to learning: An overview. *Journal of Experimental Psychology: General, 111,* 390–398.

Brasell, H. (1987). The effect of real-time laboratory graphing on learning graphic representations of distance and velocity. *Journal of Research in Science Teaching, 24,* 385–395.

Bretzing, B. H., & Kulhavy, R. W. (1981). Note-taking and passage styles. *Journal of Educational Psychology, 73,* 242–250.

Brewer, N. (1987). Processing speed, efficiency, and intelligence. In J. G. Borkowski & J. D. Day (Eds.), *Cognition in special children: Comparative approaches to retardation, learning disabilities, and giftedness* (pp. 15–48). Norwood, NJ: Ablex.

Brewer, W. F. (1989). The activation and acquisition of knowledge. In S. Vosniadou & A. Ortony (Eds.), *Similarity and analogical reasoning* (pp. 532–545). Cambridge, UK: Cambridge University Press.

Brewer, W. F., & Liechtenstein, D. H. (1982). Stories are to entertain: A structural affect theory of stories. *Journal of Pragmatics, 6,* 473–486.

Breznitz, Z. (1987). Increasing first graders' reading accuracy and comprehension by accelerating their reading rates. *Journal of Educational Psychology, 79,* 236–242.

Breznitz, Z., & Share, D. L. (1992). Effects of accelerated reading rate on memory for text. *Journal of Educational Psychology, 84,* 193–199.

Briggs, C., & Elkind, D. (1973). Cognitive development in early readers. *Developmental Psychology, 9,* 279–280.

Brigham, M. C., & Pressley, M. (1988). Cognitive monitoring and strategy choice in younger and older adults. *Psychology and Aging, 3,* 249–257.

Britton, B. K., & Tesser, A. (1991). Effects of time-management practices on college grades. *Journal of Educational Psychology, 83,* 405–410.

Britton, B. K., Van Dusen, L., & Gülgöz, S. (1991). Reply to "A response to 'instructional texts rewritten by five expert teams.'" *Journal of Educational Psychology, 83,* 149–152.

Britton, B. K., Van Dusen, L., Gülgöz, S., & Glynn, S. (1989). Instructional texts rewritten by five expert teams: Revisions and retention improvements. *Journal of Educational Psychology, 81,* 226–239.

Britton, B. K., Van Dusen, L., Gülgöz, S., Glynn, S. M., & Sharp, L. (1991). Accuracy of learnability judgments for instructional texts. *Journal of Educational Psychology, 83,* 43–47.

Brody, E. B., & Brody, N. (1978). *Intelligence: Nature, determinants, and consequences.* New York: Academic Press.

Brody, N. (1992). *Intelligence.* San Diego: Academic Press.

Brophy, J. (1981). Teacher praise: A functional analysis. *Review of Educational Research, 51,* 5–32.

Brophy, J. (1985). Teacher-student interaction. In J. B. Dusek (Ed.), *Teacher expectancies* (pp. 303–328). Hillsdale, NJ: Erlbaum & Associates.

Brophy, J. (1986, October). *On motivating students.* Occasional Paper No. 101. East Lansing: Michigan State University, Institute for Research on Teaching.

Brophy, J. (1987). Socializing students' motivation to learning. In M. L. Maehr & D. A. Kleiber (Eds.), *Advances in motivation and achievement: Enhancing motivation,* Vol. 5 (pp. 181–210). Greenwich, CT: JAI Press.

Brophy, J. (1988). Research linking teacher behavior to student achievement: Potential implications for instruction of Chapter 1 students. *Educational Psychologist, 23,* 235–286.

Brophy, J., & Evertson, C. (1976). *Learning from teaching: A developmental perspective.* Boston: Allyn & Bacon.

Brophy, J., & Good, T. (1970). Teachers' communication of differential expectations for children's classroom performance: Some behavioral data. *Journal of Educational Psychology, 61,* 365–374.

Brophy, J., & Good, T. (1974). *Teacher-student relationships: Causes and consequences.* New York: Holt, Rinehart, & Winston.

Brown, A. L. (1974). The role of strategic behavior in retardate memory. In N. R. Ellis (Ed.), *International review of research in mental retardation,* Vol. 7. New York: Academic Press.

Brown, A. L. (1978). Knowing when, where, and how to remember: A problem of metacognition. In R. Glaser (Ed.), *Advances in instructional psychology,* Vol. 1. Hillsdale, NJ: Erlbaum & Associates.

Brown, A. L. (1989). Analogical learning and transfer: What develops? In S. Vosniadou & A. Ortony (Eds.), *Similarity and analogical reasoning* (pp. 367–412). Cambridge, UK: Cambridge University Press.

Brown, A. L., Bransford, J. D., Ferrara, R. A., & Campione, J. C. (1983). Learning, remembering, and understanding. In J. H. Flavell & E. M. Markman (Eds.), *Handbook of child psychology,* Vol. III, *Cognitive development* (pp. 77–166). New York: Wiley.

Brown, A. L., & Campione, J. C. (1978). Permissible inferences from cognitive training studies in developmental research. In W. S. Hall & M. Cole (Eds.), *Quarterly Newsletter of the Institute for Comparative Human Behavior, 2 (3),* 46–53.

Brown, A. L., & Campione, J. C. (1990). Interactive learning environments and the teaching of science and mathematics. In M. Gardner, J. G. Greeno, F. Reif, A. H. Schoenfeld, A. DiSessa, & E. Stage (Eds.), *Toward a scientific practice of science education* (pp. 111–139). Hillsdale, NJ: Erlbaum & Associates.

Brown, A. L., & Day, J. D. (1983). Macrorules for summarizing texts: The development of expertise. *Journal of Verbal Learning and Verbal Behavior, 22,* 1–14.

Brown, A. L., Day, J. D., & Jones, R. S. (1983). The development of plans for summarizing texts. *Child Development, 54,* 968–979.

Brown, A. L., & French, L. (1979). The zone of proximal development: Implications for intelligence testing in the year 2000. *Intelligence, 3,* 253–271.

Brown, A. L., & Kane, K. J. (1988). Preschool children can learn to transfer: Learning to learn and learning from example. *Cognitive Psychology, 20,* 493–523.

Brown, A. L., Kane, M. J., & Echols, K. (1986). Young children's mental models determine analogical transfer across problems with a common goal structure. *Cognitive Development, 1,* 103–122.

Brown, A. L., Kane, M. J., & Long, C. (1989). Analogical transfer in young children: Analogies as tools for communication and exposition. *Applied Cognitive Psychology, 3,* 275–294.

Brown, A. L., & Palincsar, A. S. (1989). Guided, cooperative learning and individual knowledge acquisition. In L. B. Resnick (Ed.), *Knowing, learning, and instruction: Essays in honor of Robert Glaser* (pp. 393–451). Hillsdale, NJ: Erlbaum & Associates.

Brown, B. B. (1988). The vital agenda for research and extracurricular influences: A reply to Holland and Andre. *Review of Educational Research, 58,* 107–111.

Brown, D. E. (1992). Using example and analogies to remediate misconceptions in physics: Factors influencing conceptual change. *Journal of Research in Science Teaching, 29,* 17–34.

Brown, I. (1976). Role of referent concreteness in the acquisition of passive sentence comprehension through abstract modeling. *Journal of Experimental Child Psychology, 22,* 185–189.

Brown, I. (1979). Language acquisition: Linguistic structure and rule-governed behavior. In G. J. Whitehurst & B. J. Zimmerman (Eds.), The functions of language and cognition (pp. 141–173). New York: Academic Press.

Brown, J. S., Collins, A., & Duguid, P. (1989). Situated cognition and the culture of learning. *Educational Researcher, 18 (1),* 32–42.

Brown, M. C., Hopkins, W. G., & Keynes, R. J. (1991). *Essentials of neural development.* Cambridge, UK: Cambridge University Press.

Brown, R. (1973). A first language: The early stages. Cambridge, MA: Harvard University Press.

Brown, R. G. (1991). *Schools of thought.* San Francisco: Jossey-Bass.

Brown, R. T., Armstrong, F. D., & Eckman, J. R. (1993). Neurocognitive aspects of pediatric sickle cell disease. *Journal of Learning Disabilities, 26,* 33–45.

Brown, R. T., & Madan-Swain, A. (1993). Cognitive, neuropsychological, and academic sequelae in children with leukemia. *Journal of Learning Disabilities, 26,* 74–91.

Brownell, W. A. (1928). The development of children's number ideas in the primary grades. *Supplement to Education Monographs,* No. 35.

Bruce, B. (1983). A new point of view on children's stories. In R. C. Anderson, J. Osborn, & R. J. Tierney (Eds.), *Learning to read in American schools* (pp. 153–174). Hillsdale, NJ: Erlbaum & Associates.

Bruck, M. (1990). Word-recognition skills of adults with childhood diagnoses of dyslexia. *Developmental Psychology, 26,* 439–454.

Bruck, M. (1992). Persistence of dyslexics' phonological awareness deficits. *Developmental Psychology, 28,* 874–886.

Bruck, M., & Treiman, R. (1990). Phonological awareness and spelling in normal children and dyslexics: The case of initial consonant clusters. *Journal of Experimental Child Psychology, 50,* 156–178.

Bruck, M., & Treiman, R. (1992). Learning to pronounce words: The limits of analogies. *Reading Research Quarterly, 27,* 374–398.

Bruner, J. S., Olver, R. R., & Greenfield, P. M. (1966). *Studies in cognitive growth.* New York: Wiley.

Brust, J. C. M. (1991). Cerebral circulation: Stroke. In E. R. Kandel, J. H. Schwartz, & T. M. Jessel (Eds.), *Principles of neural science* (pp. 1041–1049). New York: Elsevier.

Bryant, D. M., Clifford, R. M., & Peisner, E. S. (1991). Best practices for beginners: Developmental appropriateness in kindergarten. *American Educational Research Journal, 28,* 783–803.

Bryant, N. R. (1982). *Preschool children's learning and transfer of matrices problems: A study of proximal distance.* Unpublished master's thesis, University of Illinois, Urbana. (Reported in Campione & Brown, 1987.)

Bryant, N. R., Brown, A. L., & Campione, J. C. (1983, April). *Preschool children's learning and transfer of matrices problems.* Paper presented at the Society for Research in Child Development meetings, Detroit.

Bryant, P. E., & Bradley, L. (1980). Why children sometimes write words which they do not read. In U. Frith (Ed.), *Cognitive processes in spelling* (pp. 355–370). San Diego: Academic Press.

Bryk, A. S., & Thum, Y. M. (1989). The effects of high school organization on dropping out: An exploratory investigation. *American Educational Research Journal, 26,* 353–383.

Budoff, M. (1987a). Measures for assessing learning potential. In C. S. Lidz (Ed.), *Dynamic assessment: An interactional approach to evaluating learning potential* (173–195). New York: Guilford Press.

Budoff, M. (1987b). The validity of learning potential assessment. In C. S. Lidz (Ed.), *Dynamic assessment: An interactional approach to evaluating learning potential* (pp. 52–81). New York: Guilford Press.

Budoff, M., & Friedman, M. (1964). Learning potential as an assessment approach to the adolescent mentally retarded. *Journal of Consulting Psychology, 28,* 434–439.

Budoff, M., Gimon, A., & Corman, L. (1974). Learning potential measurement with Spanish-speaking youth as an alternative to IQ tests: A first report. *Intraamerican Journal of Psychology, 8,* 233–246.

Bugelski, B. R. (1962). Presentation time, total time, and mediation in paired-associate learning. *Journal of Experimental Psychology, 79,* 383–384.

Bugenthal, D. B., Whalen, C. K., & Henker, B. (1977). Causal attributions of hyperactive children and motivational assumptions of two behavior-change approaches: Evidence for an interactionist position. *Child Development, 48,* 874–884.

Buhrmester, D., Camparo, L., Christensen, A., Gonzalez, L. S., & Hinshaw, S. P. (1992). Mothers and fathers interacting in dyads and triads with normal and hyperactive sons. *Developmental Psychology, 28,* 500–509.

Bulgren, J. A., McKnight, P., Deshler, D. D., & Schumaker, J. B. (1989). *The 1989 INROADS program report.* Lawrence, KS: University of Kansas, Institute for Research in Learning Disabilities.

Burack, J. A. (1990). Differentiating mental retardation: The two-group approach and beyond. In R. M. Hodapp, J. A. Burdack, & E. Zigler (Eds.), *Issues in the developmental approach to mental retardation* (pp. 27–48). Cambridge, UK: Cambridge University Press.

Burchinal, M., Lee, M., & Ramey, C. (1989). Type of day-care and preschool intellectual development in disadvantaged children. *Child Development, 60,* 128–137.

Burden, R. L. (1987). Feurstein's Instrumental Enrichment program: Important issues in research and evaluation. *European Journal of Psychology of Education, 2,* 3–16.

Burgess, D. M., & Streissguth, A. P. (1992). Fetal alcohol syndrome and fetal alcohol efects: Principles for educators. *Phi Delta Kappan, 74,* 24–30.

Burkell, J., Schneider, B., & Pressley, M. (1990). Mathematics. In M. Pressley & Associates, *Cognitive strategy instruction that really improves children's academic performance* (pp. 147–177). Cambridge, MA: Brookline Books.

Burt, C. (1966). The genetic discrimination of differences in intelligence: A study of monozygotic twins reared together and apart. *British Journal of Psychology, 57,* 137–53.

Buschke, H., & Schaier, A. H. (1979). Memory units, ideas, and propositions in semantic remembering. *Journal of Verbal Learning and Verbal Behavior, 18,* 549–564.

Butkowski, I. S., & Willows, D. M. (1980). Cognitive-motivational characteristics of children varying in reading ability: Evidence for learned helplessness in poor readers. *Journal of Educational Psychology, 72,* 408–422.

Butler, S. R., Marsh, H. W., Sheppard, M. J., & Sheppard, J. L. (1985). Seven-year longitudinal study of the early prediction of reading achievement. *Journal of Educational Psychology, 77,* 349–361.

Butler-Nalin, K. (1984). Revising patterns in students' writing. In A. N. Applebee (Ed.), *Contexts for learning to write: Studies of secondary school instruction* (pp. 121–133). Norwood, NJ: Ablex.

Butterfield, E. C., & Belmont, J. M. (1977). Assessing and improving the executive cognitive functions of mentally retarded people. In I. Bialar & M. Sternlicht (Eds.), *Psychological issues in mental retardation* (pp. 277–318). New York: Psychological Dimensions.

Butterfield, E. C., & Nelson, G. D. (1991). Promoting positive transfer of different types. *Cognition and Instruction, 8,* 69–102.

Byrne, B., & Fielding-Barnsley, R. (1990). Acquiring the alphabetic principle: A case for teaching recognition of phoneme identity. *Journal of Educational Psychology, 82,* 805–812.

Byrne, B., & Fielding-Barnsley, R. (1991). Evaluation of a program to teach phonemic awareness to young children. *Journal of Educational Psychology, 83,* 451–455.

Byrne, B., Freebody, P., & Gates, A. (1992). Longitudinal data on the relations of word-reading strategies to comprehension, reading time, and phonemic awareness. *Reading Research Quarterly, 27,* 140–151.

Byrnes, J. P. (1992). The conceptual basis of procedural learning. *Cognitive Development, 7,* 235–257.

Byrnes, J. P., & Wasik, B. A. (1991). Role of conceptual knowledge in mathematical procedural learning. *Developmental Psychology, 27,* 777–786.

Calderhead, J. (1983, April). *Research into teachers' and student teachers' cognitions: Exploring the nature of classroom practice.* Paper presented at the annual meeting of the American Educational Research Association, Montreal.

Calderhead, J., & Robson, M. (1991). Images of teaching: Student teachers' early conceptions of classroom practice. *Teaching & Teacher Education, 7,* 1–8.

Calfee, R. C., & Chambliss, M. J. (1987). The structural design features of large texts.

Calfee, R. C., Chapman, R., & Venezsky, R. (1972). How a child needs to think to learn to read. In L. W. Gregg (Ed.), *Cognition in learning and memory.* New York: Wiley.

Calfee, R. C., Lindamood, P., & Lindamood, C. (1973). Acoustic-phonetic skills and reading—kindergarten through twelfth grade. *Journal of Educational Psychology, 64,* 293–298.

California Assessment Program (1988). *Annual report: 1985–86.* Sacramento: California State Department of Education.

Calkins, L. M. (1986). *The art of teaching writing.* Portsmouth, NH: Heinemann.

Camp, B. W., Blom, G. E., Hebert, F., & van Doorninck, W. J. (1977). "Think aloud": A program for developing self-control in young aggressive boys. *Journal of Abnormal Child Psychology, 5,* 157–169.

Campbell, D. T., & Fiske, D. W. (1959). Convergent and discriminant validation by the multitrait-multimethod matrix. *Psychological Bulletin, 56,* 81–105.

Campbell, D. T., & Stanley, J. C. (1966). *Experimental and quasi-experimental designs for research.* Chicago: Rand-McNally.

Campbell, J. I. D., & Charness, N. (1990). Age-related declines in working-memory skills: Evidence from a complex calculation task. *Developmental Psychology, 26,* 879–888.

Campbell, J. I. D., & Graham, D. J. (1985). Mental multiplication skill: Structure, process, and acquisition. *Canadian Journal of Psychology, 39,* 338–366.

Campbell, T. A., Wright, J. C., & Huston, A. C. (1987). Form cues and content difficulty as determinants of children's cognitive processing of televised educational messages. *Journal of Experimental Child Psychology, 43,* 311–327.

Campione, J. C., & Brown, A. L. (1987). Linking dynamic assessment and school achievement. In C. S. Lidz (Ed.), *Dynamic assessment: An interactional approach to evaluating learning potential* (pp. 82–115). New York: Guilford Press.

Cantor, N., Markus, H., Niedenthal, P., & Nurius, P. (1986). On motivation and self-concept. In R. M. Sorrentino & E. T. Higgins (Eds.), *Motivation and cognition: Foundations of social behavior* (pp. 99–127). New York: Guilford.

Caplan, D. (1992). *Language: Structure, processing, and disorders.* Cambridge, MA: MIT Press.

Cardelle-Elawar, M. (1990). Effects of feedback tailored to bilingual students' mathematics needs on verbal problem solving. *Elementary School Journal, 91,* 165–175.

Cardon, L. R., DiLalla, L. F., Plomin, R., DeFries, J. C., & Fulker, D. W. (1990). Genetic correlations between reading performance and IQ in the Colorado adoption project. *Intelligence, 14,* 245–257.

Carey, S. (1985). *Conceptual change in childhood.* Cambridge, MA: MIT Press.

Carey, S., Evans, R., Honda, M., Jay, E., & Unger, C. (1989). "An experiment is when you try it and see if it works": a study of grade 7 students' understanding of the construction of

scientific knowledge. *International Journal of Science Education, 11,* 514–529.

Cariglia-Bull, T., & Pressley, M. (1990). Short-term memory differences between children predict imagery effects when sentences are read. *Journal of Experimental Child Psychology, 49,* 384–398.

Carlson, J. S., & Widaman, K. F. (1987). Elementary cognitive correlates of g: Progress and prospects. In P. A. Vernon (Ed.), *Speed of information-processing and intelligence* (pp. 69–99). Hillsdale, NJ: Erlbaum & Associates.

Carney, R. N., Levin, J. R., & Morrison, C. R. (1988). Mnemonic learning of artists and their paintings. *American Educational Research Journal, 25,* 107–125.

Carpenter, T. P. (1985). Learning to add and subtract: An exercise in problem solving. In E. A. Silver (Ed.), *Teaching and learning mathematical problem solving: Multiple research perspectives* (pp. 17–40). Hillsdale, NJ: Erlbaum & Associates.

Carpenter, T. P., Hiebert, J., & Moser, J. M. (1981). Problem structure and first-grade children's initial solution processes for simple addition and subtraction problems. *Journal for Research in Mathematics Education, 12,* 27–39.

Carpenter, T. P., & Moser, J. M. (1982). The development of addition and subtraction problem-solving skills. In T. P. Carpenter, J. M. Moser, & T. A. Romberg (Eds.), *Addition and subtraction: A cognitive perspective* (pp. 9–24). Hillsdale, NJ: Erlbaum & Associates.

Carpenter, T. P., & Moser, J. M. (1983). The acquisition of addition and subtraction concepts. In R. Lesh & M. Landau (Eds.), *The acquisition of mathematics concepts and processes* (pp. 7–44). New York: Academic Press.

Carr, M., & Borkowski, J. G. (1989). Attributional training and the generalization of reading strategies with underachieving children. *Learning and Individual Differences, 1,* 327–341.

Carr, M., Borkowski, J. G., & Maxwell, S. E. (1991). Motivational components of underachievement. *Developmental Psychology, 27,* 108–118.

Carraher, T. N., Carraher, D. W., & Schliemann, A. D. (1985). Mathematics in the street and in schools. *British Journal of Developmental Psychology, 3,* 21–29.

Carter, K. (1990). Teachers' knowledge and learning to teach. In W. R. Houston (Ed.), *Handbook of research on teacher education* (pp. 291–310). New York: MacMillan.

Carter, K., Cushing, K., Sabers, D., Stein, P., & Berliner, D. (1988). Expert-novice differences in perceiving and processing visual classroom information. *Journal of Teacher Education, 39,* 25–31.

Carter, K., Sabers, D., Cushing, K., Pinnegar, S., & Berliner, D. C. (1987). Processing and using information about students: A study of expert, novice, and postulant teachers. *Teaching & Teacher Education, 3,* 147–157.

Carver, R. P. (1990). *Reading rate: A review of research and theory.* San Diego: Academic Press.

Case, R. (1974). Structures and strictures: Some

functional limitations on the course of cognitive growth. *Cognitive Psychology, 6,* 544–573.

Case, R. (1985). *Intellectual development: Birth to adulthood.* Orlando, FL: Academic Press.

Case, R. (1991). A developmental approach to the design of remedial instruction. In A. McKeough & J. L. Lupart (Eds.), *Toward the practice of theory-based instruction* (pp. 117–147). Hillsdale, NJ: Erlbaum & Associates.

Cattell, J. M. (1890). Mental tests and measurement. *Mind, 15,* 373–380.

Cattell, J. M., & Farand, L. (1890). Physical and mental measurements of the students of Columbia University. *Psychological Review, 3,* 618–648.

Cattell, R. B. (1987). *Intelligence: Its structure, growth, and action.* Amsterdam: North-Holland.

Cattell, R. B., & Horn, J. L. (1978). A check on the theory of fluid and crystallized intelligence with description of new subtest designs. *Journal of Educational Measurement, 15,* 139–164.

Cavanaugh, J. C., & Borkowski, J. G. (1979). The metamemory-memory "connection": Effects of strategy training and maintenance. *Journal of General Psychology, 101,* 161–174.

Cazden, C. B. (1988). *Classroom discourse: The language of teaching and learning.* Portsmouth, NH: Heinemann.

Ceci, S. J. (1991). How much does schooling influence general intelligence and its cognitive components? A reassessment of the evidence. *Developmental Psychology, 27,* 703–722.

Ceci, S. J., & Liker, J. K. (1986). A day at the races: A study of IQ, expertise, and cognitive complexity. *Journal of Experimental Psychology: General, 115,* 255–266.

Celano, M. P., & Geller, R. J. (1993). Learning, school performance, and children with asthma: How much at risk? *Journal of Learning Disabilities, 26,* 23–32.

Chall, J. S. (1967). *Learning to read: The great debate.* New York: McGraw-Hill.

Chambliss, M. J., & Calfee, R. C. (1989). Designing science textbooks to enhance student understanding. *Educational Psychology, 24,* 307–322.

Champagne, A. B., & Bunce, D. M. (1991). Learning-theory-based science teaching. In S. M. Glynn, R. H. Yeany, & B. K. Britton (Eds.), *The psychology of learning science* (pp. 21–41). Hillsdale, NJ: Erlbaum & Associates.

Chan, C. K. K., Burtis, P. J., Scardamalia, M., & Bereiter, C. (1992). Constructive activity in learning from text. *American Educational Research Journal, 29,* 97–118.

Chandler Press (1988). *Early American school books.* Maynard, MA: Chandler Press.

Chapman, J. W. (1988). Cognitive-motivational characteristics and academic achievement of learning disabled children: A longitudinal analysis. *Journal of Educational Psychology, 80,* 357–365.

Chapman, M., & Lindenberger, U. (1989). Concrete operations and attentional capacity. *Journal of Experimental Child Psychology, 47,* 236–258.

Chapman, M., Skinner, E. A., & Baltes, P. B.

(1990). Interpreting correlations between children's perceived control and cognitive performance: Control, agency, or means–ends beliefs? *Developmental Psychology, 26,* 246–253.

Charles, R. I., & Lester, F. K., Jr. (1984). An evaluation of a process-oriented instructional program in mathematical problem solving in grades 5 and 7. *Journal for Research in Mathematics Education, 15,* 15–34.

Charlop, M. H., & Milstein, J. P. (1989). Teaching autistic children conversational speech using video modeling. *Journal of Applied Behavior Analysis, 22,* 275–285.

Charney, D. (1993). A study in rhetorical reading: How evolutionists read "The Spandrels of San Marco." In J. Selzer (Ed.), *Understanding scientific prose.* Madison, WI: University of Wisconsin Press.

Chase, H. (1973). The effects of intrauterine and postnatal undernutrition on normal brain development. *Annals of the New York Academy of Sciences, 205,* 231–244.

Chen, C., & Stevenson, H. W. (1989). Homework: A cross-cultural examination. *Child Development, 60,* 551–561.

Chen, Z., & Daehler, M. W. (1992). Intention and outcome: Key components of causal structure facilitating mapping in children's analogical transfer. *Journal of Experimental Child Psychology, 53,* 237–257.

Cheney, L. V. (1987). *American memory: A report of the humanities in the Nation's public schools.* Washington, DC: National Endowment for the Humanities.

Cheyne, J. A., & Walters, R. H. (1969). Intensity of punishment, timing of punishment, and cognitive structure as determinants of response inhibition. *Journal of Experimental Child Psychology, 7,* 231–244.

Chi, M. T. H. (1978). Knowledge structure and memory development. In R. S. Siegler (Ed.), *Children's thinking: What develops?* (pp. 73–96). Hillsdale, NJ: Erlbaum & Associates.

Chi, M. T. H., & Bassok, M. (1989). Learning from examples via self-explanations. In L. B. Resnick (Ed.), *Knowing, learning, and instruction: Essays in honor of Robert Glaser* (pp. 251–282). Hillsdale, NJ: Erlbaum & Associates.

Chi, M. T. H., Bassok, M., Lewis, M., Reimann, M., & Glaser, R. (1989). Self-explanations: How students study and use examples in learning to solve problems. *Cognitive Science, 13,* 145–182.

Chi, M. T. H., Glaser, R., & Farr, M. J. (1988). *The nature of expertise.* Hillsdale, NJ: Erlbaum & Associates.

Chiesi, L., Spilich, G. J., & Voss, J. F. (1979). Acquisition of domain-related information in relation to high and low domain knowledge. *Journal of Verbal Learning and Verbal Behavior, 18,* 257–273.

Childs, C. P., & Greenfield, P. M. (1980). Informal modes of learning and teaching: the case of Zinecanteco weaving. In N. Warren (Ed.), *Studies in cross-cultural psychology,* Vol. 2 (pp. 269–316). London: Academic.

Chipeur, H. M., Rovine, M. J., & Plomin, R. (1990). LISREL modeling: Genetic and environmental influences on IQ revisited. *Intelligence, 14,* 11–29.

Chittenden, E. (1991). Authentic assessment, evaluation, and documentation of student performance. In V. Perrone (Ed.). *Expanding student assesment* (pp. 22–31). Alexandria, VA: Association for Supervision and Curriculum Development.

Chomsky, N. (1965). *Aspects of the theory of syntax.* Cambridge, MA: MIT Press.

Chomsky, N. (1980a). Initial states and steady states. In M. Paittelli-Palmarini (Ed.), *Language and learning: The debate between Jean Piaget and Noam Chomsky* (pp. 97–130). Cambridge, MA: Harvard University Press.

Chomsky, N. (1980b). Rules and representations. *Behavioral and Brain Sciences, 3,* 1–61.

Christensen, C. A., & Cooper, T. J. (1991). The effectiveness of instruction in cognitive strategies in developing proficiency in single-digit addition. *Cognition and Instruction, 8,* 363–371.

Churchland, P. S., & Sejnowski, T. J. (1992). *The computational brain.* Cambridge, MA: MIT Press.

Cipielewski, J., & Stanovich, K. E. (1992). Predicting growth in reading ability from children's exposure to print. *Journal of Experimental Child Psychology, 54,* 74–89.

Clandenin, D. J. (1986). *Classroom practice: Teacher images in action.* London: Falmer Press.

Clark, E. V. (1973). What's in a word? On the child's acquisition of semantics in his first language. In T. E. Moore (Ed.), *Cognitive development and the acquisition of language* (pp. 65–110). New York: Academic Press.

Clark, H. H., & Clark, E. V. (1977). *Psychology and language.* New York: Harcourt, Brace, Jovanovich.

Clark, J. M., & Paivio, A. (1991). Dual coding theory and education. *Educational Psychology Review, 3,* 149–210.

Clark, M. M. (1976). *Young fluent readers: What can they teach us?* London: Heinemann.

Clarke, A. M. (1985). Polygenic and environmental interactions. In A. M. Clarke, A. D. B. Clarke, & J. M. Berg (Eds.), *Mental deficiency: The changing outlook* (4th ed.) (pp. 267–290). New York: Free Press.

Clarke, A. M., Clarke, A. D. B., & Berg, J. M. (1985). *Mental deficiency: The changing outlook* (4th ed.). New York: Free Press.

Clay, M. M. (1985). *The early detection of reading difficulties: A diagnostic survey with recovery procedure.* Portsmouth, NH: Heinemann.

Clay, M. M. (1991). *Becoming literate: The construction of inner control.* Portsmouth, NH: Heinemann.

Clay, M. M., & Cazden, C. B. (1990). A Vygotskian interpretation of Reading Recovery. In L. C. Moll (Ed.), *Vygotsky and education: Instructional implications and applications of sociohistorical psychology* (pp. 206–222). Cambridge, UK: Cambridge University Press.

Cleary, T. A., Humphreys, L. G., Kendrick, S. A., & Wesman, A. G. (1975). Educational uses of tests with disadvantaged students. *America Psychologist, 30,* 15–41.

Clement, J. (1982). Students' preconceptions in introductory mechanics. *American Journal of Physics, 50,* 66–71.

Clement, J., with the assistance of Brown, D., Camp, C., Kudukey, J., Minstrell, J., Palmer, D., Schultz, K., Shimabukuro, J., Steinberg, M., & Veneman, V. (1987). Overcoming students' misconceptions in physics: The role of anchoring intuitions and analogical validity. In J. Novak (Ed.), *Proceedings of the second international seminar: misconceptions and educational strategies in science and mathematics,* Vol. III (pp. 84–97). Ithaca, NY: Cornell University Press.

Clement, J., Brown, D. E., & Zeitsman, A. (1989). Not all preconceptions are misconceptions: finding 'anchoring conceptions' for grounding instruction on students' intuition. *International Journal of Science Education, 11,* 554–565.

Clements, D. H. (1990). Metacomponential development in a Logo programming environment. *Journal of Educational Psychology, 82,* 141–149.

Clements, D. H., & Battista, M. T. (1989). Learning of geometric concepts in a LOGO environment. *Journal for Research in Mathematics Education, 20,* 450–467.

Clements, D. H., & Battista, M. T. (1990). The effects of LOGO on children's conceptualizations of angle and polygons. *Journal for Research in Mathematics Education, 21,* 356–371.

Clements, D. H., & Nastasi, B. K. (1988). Social and cognitive interactions in educational computer environments. *American Educational Research Journal, 25,* 87–106.

Clifford, M. M. (1975). Validity of expectation: A developmental function. *Alberta Journal of Educational Research, 21,* 11–17.

Clifford, M. M. (1978). The effects of quantitative feedback on children's expectations of success. *Journal of Educational Psychology, 48,* 220–226.

Clifford, M. M. (1984). Thoughts on a theory of constructive failure. *Educational Psychologist, 19,* 108–120.

Clifford, M. M. (1991). Risk taking: Theoretical, empirical, and educational considerations. *Educational Psychologist, 26,* 263–297.

Clymer, T. (1963). The utility of phonic generalizations in the primary grades. *Reading Teacher, 16,* 252–258.

Coates, B., & Hartup, W. W. (1969). Age and verbalization in observational learning. *Developmental Psychology, 1,* 556–562.

Cobb, P., Wood, T., Yackel, E., Nicholls, J., Wheatley, G., Trigatti, B., & Perlwitz, M. (1991). Assessment of a problem centered second-grade mathematics project. *Journal for Research in Mathematics Education, 22,* 3–29.

Cochran-Smith, M. (1984). *The making of a reader.* Norwood, NJ: Ablex.

Cognition and Technology Group at Vanderbilt (1992). The Jasper series as an example of anchored instruction: Theory, program description, and assessment data. *Educational Psychologist, 27,* 291–315.

Cohen, M., & Riel, M. (1989). The effect of distant audiences on students' writing. *American Educational Research Journal, 26,* 143–159.

Collins, A. (1992). Portfolios for science education: Issues in purpose, structure, and authenticity. *Science Education, 76,* 451–463.

Collins, A., Brown, J. S., & Newman, S. E. (1989). Cognitive apprenticeship: Teaching the crafts of reading, writing, and mathematics. In L. B. Resnick (Ed.), *Knowing, learning, and instruction: Essays in honor of Robert Glaser* (pp. 453–494). Hillsdale, NJ: Erlbaum & Associates.

Collins, A. M., & Loftus, E. F. (1975). A spreading-activation theory of semantic processing. *Psychological Review, 82,* 407–428.

Collins, A. M., & Quillian, M. R. (1969). Retrieval time from semantic memory. *Journal of Verbal Learning and Verbal Behavior, 8,* 240–247.

Collins, A., & Stevens, A. L. (1982). Goals and strategies of inquiry teachers. In R. Glaser (Ed.), *Advances in instructional psychology,* Vol. 2 (pp. 65–119). Hillsdale, NJ: Erlbaum & Associates.

Collins, C. (1991). Reading instruction that increases thinking abilities. *Journal of Reading, 34,* 510–516.

Collins, W. A., Wellman, H., Keniston, A. H., & Westby, S. D. (1978). Age-related aspects of comprehension and inference from a televised dramatic narrative. *Child Development, 49,* 389–399.

Coltheart, M., Davelaar, E., Jonasson, J. T., & Besner, D. (1977). Access to the internal lexicon. In S. Dornic (Ed.), *Attention and performance VI* (pp. 535–555). Hillsdale, NJ: Erlbaum & Associates.

Committee on High School Biology (1990). *Fulfilling the promise: Biology education in the nation's schools.* Washington, DC: National Academy Press.

Comstock, G. (1989). *The evaluation of American television.* Newbury Park, CA: Sage.

Comstock, G., & Paik, H. (1991). *Television and the American child.* San Diego: Academic Press.

Confrey, J. (1990). A review of the research on student conceptions in mathematics, science, and programming. In C. B. Cazden (Ed.), *Review of Research in Education,* Vol. 16 (pp. 3–56). Washington, DC: American Educational Research Association.

Connelly, F. M., & Clandenin, D. J. (1985). Personal practical knowledge and the modes of knowing: Relevance for teaching and learning. In E. Eisner (Ed.), *Learning and teaching the ways of knowing (84th yearbook of the National Society for the Study of Education,* Part II) (pp. 174–198). Chicago: University of Chicago Press.

Conners, C. K. (1971). Cortical visual evoked response in children with learning disorders. *Psychophysiology, 7,* 418–428.

Conrad, C. (1972). Cognitive economy in semantic memory. *Journal of Experimental Psychology, 92,* 149–154.

Consortium for Longitudinal Studies (1983). *As the twig is bent.* Hillsdale, NJ: Erlbaum & Associates.

Constantino, G. (1992). Overcoming bias in the educational assessment of Hispanic students. In K. F. Geisinger (Ed.), *Psychological testing of Hispanics* (pp. 89–98). Washington, DC: American Psychological Association.

Conway, M. A., Cohen, G., & Stanhope, N. (1991). On the very long-term retention of knowledge acquired through formal education: twelve years of cognitive psychology. *Journal of Experimental Psychology: General, 120,* 395–409.

Cook, L. K., & Mayer, R. E. (1988). Teaching readers about the structure of scientific text. *Journal of Educational Psychology, 80,* 448–456.

Cooney, J. B., & Swanson, H. L. (1990). Individual differences in memory for mathematical story problems: Memory span and problem perception. *Journal of Educational Psychology, 82,* 570–577.

Cooney, J. B., Swanson, H. L., & Ladd, S. F. (1988). Acquisition of mental multiplication skill: Evidence for the transition between counting and retrieval strategies. *Cognition and Instruction, 5,* 323–345.

Cooper, E., Blackwood, P., Bolschen, J., Giddings, M., & Carin, A. (1985). *Science,* level 4. Orlando, FL: Harcourt, Brace, Jovanovich.

Cooper, G., & Sweller, J. (1987). Effects of schema acquisition and rule automation on mathematical problem-solving transfer. *Journal of Educational Psychology, 79,* 347–362.

Cooper, H. M. (1989a). Does reducing student-to-instructor ratios affect achievement? *Educational Psychologist, 24,* 79–98.

Cooper, H. (1989b). *Homework.* New York: Longman.

Copeland, W. D. (1987). Classroom management and student teachers' cognitive abilities: A relationship. *American Educational Research Journal, 24,* 219–236.

Corkill, A. J. (1992). Advance organizers: Facilitators of recall. *Educational Psychology Review, 4,* 33–67.

Corkill, A. J., Glover, J. A., Bruning, R. H., & King, D. (1988). Advance organizers: Retrieval context hypotheses. *Journal of Educational Psychology, 80,* 304–311.

Corley, P. J. (1988). A developmental analysis of sentence comprehension abilities in good and poor readers. *Educational Psychologist, 23,* 57–75.

Cornell, E. H., Sénéchal, M., & Broda, L. S. (1988). Recall of picture books by 3-year-old children: Testing and repetition effects in joint reading activities. *Journal of Educational Psychology, 80,* 537–542.

Corno, L. (1989). Self-regulated learning: A volitional analysis. In B. J. Zimmerman & D. H. Schunk (Eds.), *Self-regulated learning and academic achievement: Theory, research, and practice* (pp. 111–141). New York: Springer-Verlag.

Corno, L., & Kanfer, R. (1993). The role of volition in learning and performance. In L. Darling–Hammond (Ed.), *Review of research in education,* Vol. 19 (pp. 301–341). Washington, DC: American Educational Research Association.

Courage, M. (1989). Children's inquiry strategies in referential communication and in the game of twenty questions. *Child Development, 60,* 877–886.

Covington, M. V. (1985). Strategic thinking and fear of failure. In J. W. Segal, S. F. Chipman, & R. Glaser (Eds.), *Thinking and learning skills,*

Vol. 1, *Relating instruction to research* (pp. 389–416). Hillsdale, NJ: Erlbaum & Associates.

Covington, M. V., Crutchfield, R. S., Davies, L. B., & Olton, R. M. (1974). *The productive thinking program: A course in learning to think.* Columbus, OH: Merrill.

Cox, E. (1988). Explicit and implicit moral education. *Journal of Moral Education, 17,* 92–97.

Craik, F. I. M., & Lockhart, R. S. (1972). Levels of processing: A framework for memory research. *Journal of Verbal Learning and Verbal Behavior, 11,* 671–684.

Craik, F. I. M., & Tulving, E. (1975). Depth of processing and the retention of words in episodic memory. *Journal of Experimental Psychology: General, 104,* 268–294.

Crain-Thoreson, C., & Dale, P. S. (1992). Do early talkers become early readers? Linguistic precocity, preschool language, and emergent literacy. *Developmental Psychology, 28,* 421–429.

Crandall, V. C. (1969). Sex differences in expectancy of intellectual and academic reinforcement. In C. P. Smith (Ed.), *Achievement-related behaviors in children.* New York: Russell Sage Foundation.

Craver-Lemley, C., & Reeves, A. (1992). How visual imagery interferes with vision. *Psychological Review, 99,* 633–649.

Cronbach, L. J. (1951). Coefficient alpha and the internal structure of tests. *Psychometrica, 16,* 297–334.

Cronbach, L. J. (1957). The two disciplines of scientific psychology. *American Psychologist, 12,* 671–684.

Cronbach, L. J. (1990). *Essentials of psychological testing,* 5th ed. New York: Harper & Row.

Cronbach, L. J., & Snow, R. E. (1977). *Aptitudes and instructional methods: A handbook for research on interactions.* New York: Irvington.

Crooks, T. J. (1988). The impact of classroom evaluation practices of students. *Review of Educational Research, 58,* 438–481.

Crossman, E. R. F. W. (1959). A theory of the acquisition of speed skill. *Ergonomics, 2,* 153–156.

Crowder, R. G. (1976). *Principles of learning and memory.* Hillsdale, NJ: Erlbaum & Associates.

Crutcher, K. A. (1991). Anatomical correlates of neuronal plasticity. In J. L. Martinez, Jr., & R. P. Kesner (Eds.), *Learning and memory: A biological view,* 2nd ed. (pp. 93–146). San Diego: Academic Press.

Crystal, D. S., & Stevenson, H. W. (1991). Mothers' perceptions of children's problems with mathematics: A cross-national comparison. *Journal of Educational Psychology, 83,* 372–376.

Cuban, L. (1984). Policy and research dilemmas in the teaching of reasoning: Unplanned designs. *Review of Educational Research, 54,* 655–681.

Cummins, D. D. (1991). Children's interpretations of arithmetic word problems. *Cognition and Instruction, 8,* 261–289.

Cunningham, A. E. (1990). Explicit versus implicit instruction in phonemic awareness. *Journal of Experimental Child Psychology, 50,* 429–444.

Cunningham, A. E., & Stanovich, K. E. (1990). Assessing print exposure and orthographic processing skill in children: A quick measure of reading experience. *Journal of Educational Psychology, 82,* 733–740.

Cunningham, A. E., & Stanovich, K. E. (1991). Tracking the unique effects of print exposure in children: Associations with vocabulary, general knowledge, and spelling. *Journal of Educational Psychology, 83,* 264–274.

Daiker, D. (1983). *The teacher's options in responding to student writing.* Paper presented at the Conference on College Composition and Communication, Washington, DC.

Daiker, D. (1989). Learning to praise. In C. M. Anson (Ed.), *Writing and response: Theory, practice, and research* (pp. 103–113). Urbana, IL: National Council of Teachers of English.

d'Ailly, H. H. (1992). Asian mathematics superiority: A search for explanations. *Educational Psychologist, 27,* 243–261.

Dallago, M. L. L., & Moely, B. E. (1980). Free recall in boys of normal and poor reading levels as a function of task manipulations. *Journal of Experimental Child Psychology, 30,* 62–78.

Dana, R. (1993). *Multicultural assessment perspectives for professional psychology.* Needham Heights, MA: Allyn & Bacon.

Daneman, M. (1991). Individual differences in reading skills. In R. Barr, M. L. Kamil, P. B. Mosenthal, & P. D. Pearson (Eds.), *Handbook of reading research,* Vol. II (pp. 512–538). New York: Longman.

Dark, V. J., & Benbow, C. P. (1990). Enhanced problem translation and short-term memory: Components of mathematical talent. *Journal of Educational Psychology, 82,* 420–429.

Dark, V. J., & Benbow, C. P. (1991). Differential enhancement of working memory with mathematical versus verbal precocity. *Journal of Educational Psychology, 83,* 48–60.

Darling-Hammond, L., & Snyder, J. (1992). Curriculum studies and the traditions of inquiry: The scientific tradition. In P. W. Jackson (Ed.), *Handbook of research on curriculum* (pp. 41–78). New York: MacMillan.

Das, J. P. (1992). Beyond a unidimensional scale of merit. *Intelligence, 16,* 137–149.

Davidson, N. (1985). Small-group learning and teaching in mathematics: A selective review of the research. In R. Slavin, S. Shara, S. Kagan, R. Hertz-Lazarowitz, C. Webb, & R. Schmuck (Eds.), *Learning to cooperate, cooperating to learn* (pp. 211–230). New York: Plenum.

Davidson, N., & Kroll, D. L. (1991). An overview of research on cooperative learning related to mathematics. *Journal for Research in Mathematics Education, 22,* 362–365.

Davis, R. B. (1992). Understanding "understanding." *Journal for Research in Mathematics Education, 11,* 225–241.

Day, J. D. (1983). The zone of proximal development. In M. Pressley & J. R. Levin (Eds.), *Cognitive strategy research,* Vol. 1, *Psychological foundations* (pp. 155–175). New York: Springer-Verlag.

Day, J. D., Borkowski, J. G., Dietmeyer, D. L., Howsepian, B. A., & Saenz, D. S. (1994). Possible selves and academic achievement. In L.

Winegar & J. Valsiner (Eds.), *Children's development within social contexts.* Hillsdale, NJ: Erlbaum & Associates.

Day, J. D., & Cordon, L. A. (1993). Static and dynamic measures of ability: An experimental comparison. *Journal of Educational Psychology, 85,* 75–82.

Day, J. D., Cordon, L. B., & Kerwin, M. L. (1989). Informal instruction and development of cognitive skills: A review and critique of research. In C. B. McCormick, G. Miller, & M. Pressley (Eds.), *Cognitive strategy research: From basic research to educational applications* (pp. 83–103). New York: Springer-Verlag.

Day, J. D., & Hall, L. K. (1988). Intelligence–related differences in learning and transfer and enhancement of transfer among mentally retarded persons. *American Journal of Mental Deficiency, 93,* 125–137.

de Bono, E. (1969). *The mechanism of mind.* New York: Simon & Schuster.

de Bono, E. (1983a). *CoRT thinking: CoRT I, II, III, IV, V: Teacher's notes.* Oxford: Pergamon Press.

de Bono, E. (1983b). *CoRT thinking: Notes.* Oxford: Pergamon Press.

de Bono, E. (1985). The CoRT thinking program. In J. W. Segal, S. F. Chipman, & R. Glaser (Eds.). *Thinking and learning skills,* Vol. 1, *Relating instruction to research* (pp. 363–388). Hillsdale, NJ: Erlbaum & Associates.

deCharms, R. (1968). *Personal causation.* New York: Academic Press.

Deci, E. L. (1971). Effects of externally mediated rewards on instrinsic motivation. *Journal of Personality and Social Psychology, 18,* 105–115.

Decker, S. N., & Vandenberg, S. G. (1985). Colorado twin study of reading disability. In D. B. Gray & J. Kavanaugh (Eds.), *Biobehavioral measures of dyslexia* (pp. 123–135). Baltimore: York.

Dee-Lucas, D., & Larkin, J. H. (1991). Equations in scientific proofs: Effects on comprehension. *American Educational Research Journal, 28,* 661–682.

Deese, J. (1961). From the isolated verbal unit to connected discourse. In C. N. Cofer (Ed.), *Verbal learning and verbal behavior.* New York: McGraw-Hill.

Deese, J. (1962). On the structure of associative meaning. *Psychological Review, 69,* 161–175.

Deese, J. (1965). *The structure of associations in language and thought.* Baltimore: Johns Hopkins Press.

DeFries, J. C., Fulker, D. W., & LaBuda, M. C. (1987). Evidence for a genetic aetiology in reading disability of twins. *Nature, 329,* 537–539.

de Grazia, A., & Sohn, D. A. (Eds.) (1964). *Programs, teachers, and machines.* New York: Bantam Books.

de Groot, A. D. (1965). *Thought and choice in chess.* The Hague: Mouton.

de Groot, A. (1966). Perception and memory versus thought: Some old ideas and recent findings. In B. Kleinmuntz (Ed.), *Problem solving* (pp. 19–50). New York: Wiley.

de Groot, A. M. B. (1983). The range of automatic spreading activation in word priming.

Journal of Verbal Learning and Verbal Behavior, 22, 417–436.

Delclos, V. R., & Harrington, C. (1991). Effects of strategy monitoring and proactive instruction on children's problem-solving performance. *Journal of Educational Psychology, 83,* 35–42.

Delgado-Gaitan, C. (1992). School matters in the Mexican-American home: Socializing children to education. *American Educational Research Journal, 29,* 495–513.

DeLoache, J. S., Cassidy, D. J., & Brown, A. L. (1985). Precursors of mnemonic strategies in very young children's memory. *Child Development, 56,* 125–137.

DeLoache, J. S., & DeMendoza, O. A. P. (1987). Joint picturebook interactions of mothers and 1-year-old children. *British Journal of Developmental Psychology, 5,* 111–123.

Demana, F., & Leitzel, J. (1988). Establishing fundamental concepts through numerical problem solving. In A. F. Coxford & A. P. Shulte (Eds.), *The ideas of algebra K-12: 1988 yearbook of the National Council of Teachers of Mathematics.* Reston, VA: National Council of Teachers of Mathematics.

Dembo, M. H., & McAuliffe, T. J. (1987). Effects of perceived ability and grade status on social interaction and influence on cooperative groups. *Journal of Educational Psychology, 79,* 415–423.

Demchak, M. (1990). Response prompting and fading methods: A review. *American Journal of Mental Deficiency, 94,* 603–615.

Dempster, F. N. (1985). Short-term memory development in childhood and adolescence. In C. J. Brainerd & M. Pressley (Eds.), *Basic processes in memory development: Progress in cognitive development research* (pp. 209–248). New York: Springer-Verlag.

Dempster, F. N. (1988b). The spacing effect: A case study in the failure to apply the results of psychological research. *American Psychologist, 43,* 627–634.

Dempster, F. N. (1992). The rise and fall of the inhibitory mechanism: Toward a unified theory of cognitive development and aging. *Developmental Review, 12,* 45–75.

Dennis, M., & Whitaker, H. A. (1977). Hemisphere equipotentiality and language acquisition. In S. J. Segalowitz & F. A. Gruber (Eds.), *Language development and neurological theory.* New York: Academic Press.

Deno, S. L. (1987). Curriculum-based measurement. *Teaching Exceptional Children, 20,* 41.

Deno, S. L., & Fuchs, L. S. (1987). Developing curriculum-based measurement for special education problem solving. *Focus on Exceptional Children, 19* (8), 1–16.

Denton, P. H., Seybert, J. A., & Franklin, E. L. (1988). Ideas in practice: A content-based learning strategies program. *Journal of Developmental, 11,* 20–24.

Derry, S. J. (1984). Effects of an organizer on memory for prose. *Journal of Educational Psychology, 76,* 98–107.

Derry, S. J. (1992). Beyond symbolic processing: Expanding horizons for educational psychology. *Journal of Educational Psychology, 84,* 413–418.

Derry, S. J., Hawkes, L. W., & Tsai, C. (1987). A theory for remediating problem-solving skills of older children and adults. *Educational Psychologist, 22,* 55–87.

Derry, S. J., & Kellis, A. (1986). A prescriptive analysis of low-ability problem-solving behavior. *Instructional Science, 15,* 49–65.

Deshler, D. D., & Schumaker, J. B. (1988). An instructional model for teaching students how to learn. In J. L. Graden, J. E. Zins, & M. J. Curtis (Eds.), *Alternative educational delivery systems: Enhancing instructional options for all students* (pp. 391–411). Washington, DC: National Association of School Psychologists.

Desrochers, A., & Begg, I. (1987). A theoretical account of encoding and retrieval processes in the use of imagery-based mnemonic techniques: The special case of the keyword method. In M. A. McDaniel & M. Pressley (Eds.), *Imagery and related mnemonic techniques: Theories, individual differences, and applications* (pp. 56–77). New York: Springer-Verlag.

Detterman, D. K. (1979). Memory in the mentally retarded. In N. R. Ellis (Eds.), *Handbook of mental deficiency: Psychological theory and research* (pp. 727–760). Hillsdale, NJ: Erlbaum & Associates.

Devine, T. G. (1987). *Teaching study skills: A guide for teachers.* New York: Allyn & Bacon.

Devolder, P. A., Brigham, M. C., & Pressley, M. (1990). Memory performance awareness in younger and older adults. *Psychology and Aging, 5,* 291–303.

Devolder, P. A., & Pressley, M. (1991). Memory complaints in younger and older adults. *Applied Cognitive Psychology, 5,* 443–454.

Devolder, P. A., & Pressley, M. (1992). Causal attributions and strategy use in relation to memory performance differences in younger and older adults. *Applied Cognitive Psychology, 6,* 629–642.

Dewey, J. (1913). *Interest and effort in education.* Boston: Riverside.

Dewey, J. (1933). *How we think: A restatement of the relation of reflective thinking to the education process.* Boston: Heath.

Dhindsa, H. S., & Anderson, O. R. (1992). A model of the effects of rate of teacher communication on student acquisition of information. *Science Education, 76,* 353–371.

Diamond, A. (1990a). Developmental time course in human infants and infant monkeys, and the neural bases, of inhibitory control in reaching. In A. Diamond (Ed.), *The development and neural bases of higher cognitive functions* (pp. 637–676). New York: New York Academy of Science.

Diamond, A. (1990c). The development and neural bases of memory functions as indexed by the A[not]B and delayed response tasks in human infants and infant monkeys. In A. Diamond (Ed.), *The development and neural bases of higher cognitive functions* (pp. 267–317). New York: New York Academy of Science.

Diamond, A. (1991). Frontal lobe involvement in cognitive changes during the first year of life. In K. R. Gibson & A. C. Petersen (Eds.), *Brain maturation and cognitive development: Comparative and cross-cultural perspectives* (pp. 127–180). New York: Aldine de Gruyter.

Diamond, M. C. (1991). Environmental influences on the young brain. In K. R. Gibson & A. C. Petersen (Eds.), *Brain maturation and cognitive development: Comparative and cross-cultural perspectives* (pp. 107–124). New York: Aldine de Gruyter.

Diamond, M. C. (1992, October). Plasticity of the brain: enrichment versus impoverishment. In C. Clark & K. King (Eds.), *Television and the preparation of the mind for learning.* Washington, DC: U.S. Department of Health and Human Services.

Diamond, M., Scheibel, A., Murphy, G., & Harvey, T. (1985). On the brain of a scientist: Albert Einstein. *Experimental Neurology, 88,* 198 204.

Diana v. State Board of Education, C-70-37 RFP (N. D. Cal. June 18, 1973) (stipulated settlement).

DiClemente, R. J., Pies, C. A., Stoller, E. J., Straits, C., Olivia, G. E., Haskin, J., & Rutherford, G. W. (1989). Evaluation of school-based AIDS education curricula in San Francisco. *The Journal of Sex Research, 26,* 188–198.

DiClemente, R. J., Zorn, J., & Temoshok, L. (1986). Adolescents and AIDS: A survey of knowledge, attitudes, and beliefs about AIDS in San Francisco. *American Journal of Public Health, 76,* 1443–1445.

DiClemente, R. J., Zorn, J., & Temoshok, L. (1987). The association of gender, ethnicity, and length of residence in the bay area to adolescents' knowledge and attitudes about acquired immune deficiency syndrome. *Journal of Applied Social Psychology, 17,* 216–230.

DiPardo, A., & Freedman, S. W. (1988). Peer response groups in the writing classroom: Theoretic foundations and new directions. *Review of Educational Research, 58,* 119–149.

DiSessa, A. (1982). Understanding Aristotelian physics: A study of knowledge based learning. *Cognitive Science, 6,* 37–75.

DiVesta, F. J., & Gray, G. S. (1972). Listening and notetaking. *Journal of Educational Psychology, 63,* 8–14.

Dixon, F. W. (1972). *The Hardy Boys detective handbook.* New York: Grosset & Dunlop.

Dixon, P., LeFevre, J–A., & Twilley, L. C. (1988). Word knowledge and working memory as predictors of reading skill. *Journal of Educational Psychology, 80,* 465–472.

Dobbing. J. (1974). The later growth of the brain and its vulnerability. *Pediatrics, 53,* 2–6.

Doman, R. J., Spitz, E. B., Zucman, E., Delacato, C. H., & Doman, G. (1960). Children with severe brain injuries. *Journal of the American Medical Association, 174,* 219–223.

Donlon, T. F. (Ed.) (1984). *The College Board technical handbook for the Scholastic Aptitude Test and achievement tests.* New York: College Entrance Examination Board.

Donlon, T. F. (1992). Legal issues in the educational testing of Hispanics. In K. F. Geisinger (Ed.), *Psychological testing of Hispanics* (pp.

55–78). Washington, DC: American Psychological Association.

Dorsey, J. A., Mullis, I. V. S., Lindquist, M. M., & Chambers, D. L. (1988). *The 1986 mathematics report card.* Princeton, NJ: Educational Testing Service, National Assessment of Educational Progress.

Douglas, V. (1972). Stop, look, and listen: The problem of sustained attention and impulsive control in hyperactive and normal children. *Journal of Behavioral Science, 4,* 259–276.

Douglas, V. L., Parry, P., Marton, P., & Garson, C. (1976). Assessment of a cognitive training program for hyperactive children. *Journal of Abnormal Child Psychology, 4,* 389–410.

Doyle, W. (1983). Academic work. *Review of Educational Research, 53,* 159–199.

Doyle, W. (1986). Classroom organization and management. In M. C. Wittrock (Ed.), *Handbook of research on teaching,* 3rd ed. (pp. 392–431). New York: MacMillan.

Dragga, S. (1986). *Praiseworthy grading: A teacher's alternative to editing error.* Paper presented at the Conference on College Composition and Communication, New Orleans.

Dreher, M. J., & Guthrie, J. (1990). Cognitive processes in textbook search processes. *Reading Research Quarterly, 25,* 323–339.

Dreyfus, A., Jungwirth, E., & Eliovitch, R. (1990). Applying the "cognitive conflict" strategy for conceptual change—some implications, difficulties, and problems. *Science Education, 74,* 555–569.

Driver, R., & Easley, J. (1978). Pupils and paradigms: A review of literature related to concept development in adolescent science students. *Studies in Science Education, 5,* 61–84.

Druckman, D., & Bjork, R. A. (Eds.) (1991). *In the mind's eye: Enhancing human performance.* Washington, DC: National Academy Press.

Duemler, D., & Mayer, R. E. (1988). Hidden costs of reflectiveness: Aspects of successful scientific reasoning. *Journal of Educational Psychology, 80,* 419–423.

Duffy, F. H., Denckla, M. B., Bartels, P. H., & Sandini, G. (1980). Dyslexia: Regional differences in brain electrical activity by topographic mapping. *Annals of Neurology, 7,* 412–420.

Duffy, F. H., & McAnulty, G. (1990). Neuropsychological heterogeneity and the definition of dyslexia: Preliminary evidence for plasticity. *Neuropsychologica, 28,* 96–103.

Duffy, G. G., & Roehler, L. R. (1986). *Improving classroom reading instruction: A decision-making approach.* New York: Random House.

Duffy, G. G., & Roehler, L. R. (1989). Why strategy instruction is so difficult and what we need to do about it. In C. B. McCormick, G. Miller, & M. Pressley (Eds.), *Cognitive strategy research: From basic research to educational applications* (pp. 133–154). New York: Springer-Verlag.

Duffy, G., Roehler, L., & Herrmann, G. (1988). Modeling mental processes helps poor readers become strategic readers. *Reading Teacher, 41,* 762–767.

Duffy, G. G., Roehler, L. R., Sivan, E., Rackliffe,

G., Book, C., Meloth, M., Vavrus, L., Wessel-man, R., Putnam, J., & Bassiri, D. (1987). Effects of explaining the reasoning associated with using reading strategies. *Reading Research Quarterly, 22,* 347–368.

Dufresne, A., & Kobasigawa, A. (1989). Children's spontaneous allocation of study time: Differential and sufficient aspects. *Journal of Experimental Child Psychology, 17,* 274–296.

Duit, R. (1991). Students' conceptual frameworks: Consequences for learning science. In S. M. Glynn, R. H. Yeany, & B. K. Britton (Eds.), *The psychology of learning science* (pp. 65–85). Hillsdale, NJ: Erlbaum & Associates.

Duncker, K. (1945). On problem solving (L. S. Lee, Trans.). *Psychological Monographs, 58,* 407–416.

Dunlap, L. K., & Dunlap, G. (1989). A self-monitoring package for teaching subtraction with regrouping to students with learning disabilities. *Journal of Applied Behavior Analysis, 22,* 309–314.

Dupin, J. J., & Joshua, S. (1989). Analogies and "modeling analogies" in teaching: Some examples in basic electricity. *Science Education, 73,* 207–224.

Duran, B. J., & Weffer, R. E. (1992). Immigrants' aspirations, high school process, and academic outcomes. *American Educational Research Journal, 29,* 163–181.

Durkin, D. (1966). *Children who read early.* New York: Teachers College Press.

Durkin, D. (1978–79). What classroom observations reveal about reading comprehension instruction. *Reading Research Quarterly, 14,* 481–533.

Durst, R. K. (1984). The development of analytic writing. In A. N. Applebee (Ed.), *Contexts for learning to write: Studies of secondary school instruction* (pp. 79–102). Norwood, NJ: Ablex.

Duyme, M. (1988). School success and social class: An adoption study. *Developmental Psychology, 24,* 203–209.

Dweck, C. S. (1986). Motivational processes affecting learning. *American Psychologist, 41,* 1040–1048.

Dweck, C. S., & Leggett, E. L. (1988). A social-cognitive approach to motivation and personality. *Psychological Review, 95,* 256–273.

Early, M. M. (1991). Major research programs. In J. Flood, J. M. Jensen, D. Lapp, & J. R. Squire (Eds.), *Handbook of research on teaching the English language arts* (pp. 3–17). New York: MacMillan.

Ebbinghaus, H. (1913). *Memory.* New York: Teachers College.

Edelsky, C. (1990). Whose research agenda is this anyway? A response to McKenna, Robinson, and Miller. *Educational Researcher, 19,* 8–11.

Edmonds, R. R. (1979). Effective schools for the urban poor. *Educational Leadership, 37 (1),* 15–24.

Educational Research Service (1978). *Class size: A summary of research.* Arlington, VA: Educational Research Service.

Edwards, H. (1973). *Sociology of sport.* Homewood, IL: Dorsey Press.

Edwards, L. D. (1991). Children's learning in a computer microworld for transformation geometry. *Journal for Research in Mathematics Education, 22,* 122–137.

Edwards, R., & Edwards, J. (1987). Corporal punishment. In A. Thomas & J. Grimes (Eds.), *Children's needs: Psychological perspectives* (pp 127–131). Washington, DC: National Association of School Psychologists.

Ehri, L. C. (1980). The development of orthographic images. In U. Frith (Ed.), *Cognitive processes in spelling* (pp. 311–338). London: Academic Press.

Ehri, L. C. (1984). How orthography alters spoken language competencies in children learning to read and spell. In J. Downing & R. Valtin (Eds.), *Language awareness and learning to read* (pp. 119–147). New York: Springer-Verlag.

Ehri, L. C. (1987). Learning to read and spell words. *Journal of Reading Behavior, 19,* 5–31.

Ehri, L. C. (1991). Development of the ability to read words. In R. Barr, M. L. Kamil, P. B. Mosenthal, & P. D. Pearson (Eds.), *Handbook of reading research,* Vol. 2 (pp. 383–417). New York: Longman.

Ehri, L. C. (1992). Reconceptualizing the development of sight word reading and its relationship to recoding. In P. B. Gough, L. C. Ehri, & R. Treiman (Eds.), *Reading acquisition* (pp. 107–143). Hillsdale, NJ: Erlbaum & Associates.

Ehri, L. C., & Robbins, C. (1992). Beginners need some decoding skill to read words by analogy. *Reading Research Quarterly, 27,* 12–27.

Ehri, L. C., & Wilce, L. S. (1985). Movement into reading: Is the first stage of printed word learning visual or phonetic? *Reading Research Quarterly, 20,* 163–179.

Ehri, L. C., & Wilce, L. S. (1987a). Does learning to spell help beginners learn to read words? *Reading Research Quarterly, 18,* 47–65.

Ehri, L. C., & Wilce, L. S. (1987b). Cipher versus cue reading: An experiment in decoding acquisition. *Journal of Educational Psychology, 79,* 3–13.

Einstein, G. O., Morris, J., & Smith, S. (1985). Note-taking, individual differences, and memory for lecture information. *Journal of Educational Psychology, 77,* 522–532.

Eisert, D., & Tomlinson-Keasey, C. (1978). Cognitive and interpersonal growth during the college freshman year: A structural analysis. *Perceptual and Motor Skills, 46,* 995–1005.

Elbaz, F. (1983). *Teacher thinking: A study of practical knowledge.* New York: Nichols Publishing.

Elbers, E. (1991). The development of competence and its social context. *Educational Psychology Review, 3,* 73–94.

El-Dinary, P. B., Pressley, M., & Schuder, T. (1992). Becoming a strategies teacher: An observational and interview study of three teachers learning transactional strategies instruction. In C. Kinzer & D. Leu (Eds.), *Forty-first Yearbook of the National Reading Conference.* Chicago IL: National Reading Conference.

Elliott, E. S., & Dweck, C. S. (1988). Goals: An approach to motivation and achievement. *Journal of Personality and Social Psychology, 54,* 5–12.

Elliott, R. (1992). Larry P., PASE, and social science in the courtroom: The science and politics of identifying and educating very slow learners. In H. C. Haywood & D. Tzuriel (Eds.), *Interactive assessment* (pp. 470–503). New York: Springer-Verlag.

Ellis, N. R. (Ed.) (1979). *Handbook of mental deficiency: Psychological theory and research.* Hillsdale, NJ: Erlbaum & Associates.

Elton, L. R. B., & Laurilland, D. M. (1979). Trends in research on student learning. *Studies in Higher Education, 4,* 87–102.

Emig, J. (1971). *The composition process of twelfth graders.* Urbana, IL: National Council of Teachers of English.

Engle, R. W., Nations, J. K., & Cantor, J. (1990). Is "working memory capacity" just another name for word knowledge? *Journal of Educational Psychology, 82,* 799–804.

Englert, C., & Raphael, T. (1988). Constructing well-formed prose: Process, structure, and metacognitive knowledge. *Exceptional Children, 54,* 513–520.

Englert, C. S., Raphael, T. E., Anderson, L. M., Anthony, H. M., & Stevens, D. D. (1991). Making strategies and self-talk visible: Writing instruction in regular and special education classrooms. *American Educational Research Journal, 28,* 337–372.

Enright, R. D., Lapsley, D. K., & Levy, V. M. (1983). Moral education strategies. In M. Pressley & J. R. Levin (Eds.), *Cognitive strategy research: Educational applications* (pp. 43–83). New York: Springer-Verlag.

Entwisle, D. R., & Alexander, K. L. (1990). Beginning school math competence: Minority and majority comparisons. *Child Development, 61,* 454–471.

Entwisle, D. R., Alexander, K. L., Cadigan, D., & Pallas, A. M. (1987). Kindergarten experience: Cognitive effects or socialization. *American Educational Research Journal, 24,* 337–364.

Entwisle, D., & Hayduk, L. (1978). *Too great expectations: The academic outlook of young children.* Baltimore: Johns Hopkins Press.

Entwisle, N. J., & Ramsden, P. (1983). *Understanding student learning.* London: Croom Helm.

Epstein, W., Glenberg, A. M., & Bradley, M. M. (1984). Coactivation and comprehension: Contribution of text variables to the illusion of knowing. *Memory and Cognition, 12,* 355–360.

Eraut, M. (1985). Knowledge creation and knowledge use in professional scientists. *Studies in Higher Education, 10,* 117–133.

Ericsson, K. A., Krampe, R. Th., & Tesch-Römer, C. (1993). The role of deliberate practice in the acquisition of expert performance. *Psychological Review, 100,* 363–406.

Ericsson, K. A., & Simon, H. A. (1984). *Protocol analysis.* Cambridge, MA: MIT/Bradford.

Erikson, E. H. (1968). *Identity, youth, and crisis.* New York: W.W. Norton.

Estrada, M. T. (1990). *Improving academic performance through enhancing possible selves.* Unpublished master's thesis. University of Notre Dame, Notre Dame, IN.

Ethington, C. A. (1991). A test of a model of achievement behaviors. *American Educational Research Journal, 28,* 155–172.

Ethington, C. A. (1992). Gender differnces in a psychological model of mathematics achievement. *Journal for Research in Mathematics Education, 23,* 166–181.

Evertson, C. M. (1989). Classroom organization and management. In M. C. Reynolds (Ed.), *Knowledge base for the beginning teacher* (pp. 59–70). New York: Pergamon Press.

Eylon, B., & Helfman, J. (1982, February). *Analogical and deductive problem-solving in physics.* Paper presented at the annual meeting of the American Educational Research Association, New York.

Eylon, B., & Linn, M. (1988). Learning and instruction: An examination of four research perspectives in science education. *Review of Educational Research, 58,* 251–301.

Eysenck, H. J. (1987). Speed of information processing, reaction time, and the theory of intelligence. In P. A. Vernon (Ed.), *Speed of information processing and intelligence* (pp. 21–67). Norwood, NJ: Ablex.

Fagan, J. F. (1985). A new look at infant intelligence. In D. K. Detterman (Ed.), *Current topics in human intelligence,* Vol. 1, *Research methodology in human intelligence* (pp. 223–246). Norwood, NJ: Ablex.

Fagan, J. F. (1991). The paired-comparison paradigm and infant intelligence. In A. Diamond (Ed.), *The development and neural bases of higher cognitive functions.* New York: New York Academy of Sciences.

Fagan, J. F., & McGrath, S. (1981). Infant recognition memory and later intelligence. *Intelligence, 5,* 121–130.

Fantuzzo, J., King, J., & Heller, L. R. (1992). Effects of reciprocal peer tutoring on mathematics and school adjustment: A component analysis. *Journal of Educational Psychology, 84,* 331–339.

Fantuzzo, J. W., Riggio, R. E., Connelly, S., & Dimeff, L. A. (1989). Effects of reciprocal peer tutoring on academic achievement and psychological adjustment: A component analysis. *Journal of Educational Psychology, 81,* 173–177.

Farah, M. J. (1988). Is visual imagery really visual? Overlooked evidence from neuropsychology. *Psychological Review, 95,* 307–317.

Farnham-Diggory, S. (1992). *The learning-disabled child.* Cambridge, MA: Harvard University Press.

Farr, R., & Beck, M. D. (1991). Formal methods of evaluation. In J. Flood, J. M. Jensen, D. Lapp, & J. R. Squire (Eds.), *Handbook of research on teaching the English language arts* (pp. 489–501). New York: MacMillan.

Farrell, E., Peguero, G., Lindsey, R., & White, R. (1988). Giving voice to high school students: Pressure and boredom, ya know what I'm sayin'? *American Educational Research Association, 25,* 489–502.

Faryniarz, J. V., & Lockwood, L. G. (1992). Effectiveness of microcomputer simulations in stimulating environmental problem solving by community college students. *Journal of Research in Science Teaching, 29,* 454–470.

Fayol, M., Abdi, H., & Gombert, J-E. (1987). Arithmetic problems formulation and working memory load. *Cognition and Instruction, 4,* 187–202.

Feingold, A. (1992). Sex differences in variability in intellectual abilities: A new look at an old controversy. *Review of Educational Research, 62,* 61–84.

Feitelson, D. (1988). *Facts and fads in beginning reading.* Norwood, NJ: Ablex.

Feldhusen, J. F. (1986). A conception of giftedness. In R. J. Sternberg & J. E. Davidson (Eds.), *Conceptions of giftedness* (pp. 112–127). Cambridge, UK: Cambridge University Press.

Feldhusen, J. F., & Kolloff, M. B. (1981). Me: A self-concept scale for gifted students. *Perceptual and Motor Skills, 53,* 319–323.

Feldman, D. H. (1979). The mysterious case of extreme giftedness. In A. H. Passow (Ed.), *The gifted and the talented: Their education and development.* The Seventy-Eighth Yearbook of the National Society for the Study of Education. Chicago: University of Chicago Press.

Feldman, D. H. (1982). *Developmental approaches to giftedness and creativity.* San Francisco: Jossey-Bass.

Feldman, D. H. (1988). *Nature's gambit: Child prodigies and the development of human potential.* New York: Basic Books.

Feltovich, P. J., Johnson, P. E., Moller, J. H., & Swanson, D. B. (1984). LCS: The role and development of medical knowledge in diagnostic expertise. In W. J. Clancey & E. H. Shortliffe (Eds.), *Readings in medical artificial intelligence: The first decade.* Reading, MA: Addison-Wesley.

Feltz, D. L., Landers, D. M., & Becker, B. J. (1988). A revised meta-analysis of the mental practice literature on motor skill performance. In D. Druckman & J. A. Swets (Eds.), *Enhancing human performance: Issues, theories and techniques: Background papers* (pp. 1–65). Washington, DC: National Research Council.

Fenaigle, G. von (1813). *The new art of memory.* London: Sherwood, Neely, & Jones.

Fennema, E., Carpenter, T. P., & Peterson, P. L. (1989). Teachers' decision making and cognitively guided instruction: A new paradigm for curriculum development. In K. Clements & N. F. Ellerton (Eds.), *Facilitating change in mathematics education.* Geelong, Victoria, Australia: Deakin University Press.

Ferreiro, E. (1985). Literacy development: A psychogenetic approach. In D. R. Olsen, N. Torrance, & A. Hildyard (Eds.), *Literacy, language, and learning: The nature and consequences of reading and writing.* Cambridge, UK: Cambridge University Press.

Feshbach, S., Adelman, H., & Fuller, W. (1977). Prediction of reading and related academic problems. *Journal of Educational Psychology, 69,* 299–308.

Feuerstein, R. (1979). *The dynamic assessment of retarded performers: The Learning Potential Assessment Device, theory, instrument, and techniques.* Baltimore: University Park Press.

Feuerstein, R. (1980). *Instrumental enrichment: An intervention program for cognitive modifiability.* Baltimore: University Park Press.

Feuerstein, R., Rand, Y., Hoffman, M., & Miller, R. (1979). Cognitive modifiability in retarded adolescents: Effects of instrumental enrichment. *American Journal of Mental Deficiency, 83,* 539–550.

Field, T. (1991). Quality infant day-care and grade school behavior and performance. *Child Development, 62,* 863–870.

Finch, A., Wilkinson, M., Nelson, W., & Montgomery, L. (1975). Modification of an impulsive cognitive tempo in emotionally disturbed boys. *Journal of Abnormal Child Psychology, 3,* 45–52.

Fincham, F. D., Hokoda, A., & Sanders, R., Jr. (1989). Learned helplessness, text anxiety, and academic achievement: A longitudinal analysis. *Child Development, 60,* 138–145.

Finke, R. A. (1989). *Principles of mental imagery.* Cambridge, MA: MIT Press.

Finn, C. E., Jr. (1991). *We must take charge: Our schools and our future.* New York: Free Press.

Finn, J. D., & Achilles, C. M. (1990). Answers and questions about class size: A statewide experiment. *American Educational Research Journal, 27,* 557–577.

Firestone, W. A. (1991). Educators, researchers, and the effective schools movement. In J. R. Bliss, W. A. Firestone, & C. E. Richards (Eds.), *Rethinking effective schools research and practice* (pp. 12–27). Englewood Cliffs, NJ: Prentice-Hall.

Fischer, F. E. (1990). A part-part-whole curriculum for teaching number in the kindergarten. *Journal for Research in Mathematics Education, 21,* 207–215.

Fishbein, H. D., Eckart, T., Lauver, E., Van Leeuwen, R., & Langmeyer, D. (1990). Learners' questions and comprehension in a tutoring setting. *Journal of Educational Psychology, 82,* 163–170.

Fitzgerald, J. (1992). Variant views about good thinking during composing: Focus on revision. In M. Pressley, K. R. Harris, J. T. Guthrie (Eds.), *Promoting academic competence and literacy in school* (pp. 337–358). San Diego: Academic Press.

Fitzgerald, J., & Markham, L. (1987). Teaching children about revision in writing. *Cognition and Instruction, 4,* 3–24.

Fivush, R., Hudson, J., & Nelson, K. (1984). Children's long-term memory for a novel event: An exploratory study. *Merrill-Palmer Quarterly, 30,* 303–316.

Fjellstrom, G. G., Born, D., & Baer, D. M. (1988). Some effects of telling preschool children to self-question in a matching task. *Journal of Experimental Child Psychology, 46,* 419–437.

Flavell, J. H. (1963). *The developmental psychology of Jean Piaget.* Princeton, NJ: van Nostrand.

Flavell, J. H. (1972). An analysis of cognitive-developmental sequences. *Genetic Psychology Monographs, 86,* 279–350.

Flavell, J. H. (1985). *Cognitive development.* Englewood Cliffs, NJ: Prentice-Hall.

Flavell, J. H., Beach, D. H., & Chinsky, J. M. (1966). Spontaneous verbal rehearsal in a memory task as a function of age. *Child Development, 37,* 283–299.

Flavell, J. H., Friedrichs, A. G., & Hoyt, J. D. (1970). Developmental changes in memorization processes. *Cognitive Psychology, 1,* 324–340.

Fletcher, R. (1991). Intelligence, equality, character, and education. *Intelligence, 15,* 139–149.

Flood, J. (1977). Parental styles in reading episodes with young children. *Reading Teacher, 30,* 864–867.

Flower, L. (1987). *Interpretive acts: Cognition and construction of discourse* (Occasional Paper No. 1). Berkeley: University of California, Center for the Study of Writing.

Flower, L. (1989). *Problem-solving strategies for writing,* 3rd ed. San Diego: Harcourt, Brace, Jovanovich.

Flower, L., & Hayes, J. (1980). The dynamics of composing: Making plans and juggling constraints. In L. Gregg and E. Steinberg (Eds.), *Cognitive processes in writing* (pp. 31–50). Hillsdale, NJ: Erlbaum & Associates.

Flower, L., Stein, V., Ackerman, J., Kantz, M. J., McCormick, K., & Peck, W. C. (1990). *Reading to write: Exploring a cognitive and social process.* New York: Oxford University Press.

Flowers, D. L., Wood, F. B., & Naylor, C. E. (1991). Regional cerebral bloodflow correlates of language processes in reading disability. *Archives of Neurology, 48,* 637–643.

Fodor, J. A. (1983). *The modularity of mind.* Cambridge, MA: MIT Press.

Fodor, J. D., Fodor, J. A., & Garrett, M. (1975). The psychological unreality of semantic representation. *Linguistic Inquiry, 6,* 515–531.

Foos, P. W., & Fisher, R. P. (1988). Using tests as learning opportunities. *Journal of Educational Psychology, 80,* 179–183.

Ford, D. H. (1987). *Humans as self-constructing living systems: A developmental perspective on behavior and personality.* Hillsdale, NJ: Erlbaum & Associates.

Foree, D. D., & LoLordo, V. M. (1973). Attention in the pigeon: Differential effects of food-getting versus shock-avoidance procedures. *Journal of Comparative and Physiological Psychology, 85,* 551–558.

Forrest-Pressley, D. L., & Gilles, L. A. (1983). Children's flexible use of strategies during reading. In M. Pressley & J. R. Levin (Eds.), *Cognitive strategy research: Educational applications.* New York: Springer-Verlag.

Forrest-Pressley, D. L., & Waller, T. G. (1984). *Cognition, metacognition, and reading.* New York: Springer-Verlag.

Fraser, K., & Edwards, J. (1985). The effects of training in concept mapping on student achievement in traditional tests. *Research in Science Teaching, 15,* 158–165.

Frearson, W. M., & Eysenck, H. J. (1986). Intelligence, reaction time (RT), and a new "odd-man-out" RT paradigm. *Personality and Individual Differences, 7,* 807–817.

Fredericksen, N. (1984). The real test bias: Influences of testing on teaching and learning. *American Psychologist, 39,* 193–202.

Freebody, P., & Byrne, B. (1988). Word-reading strategies in elementary school children: Relations to comprehension, reading time, and phonemic awareness. *Reading Research Quarterly, 23,* 441–453.

Freund, L. S. (1990). Maternal regulation of children's problem-solving behavior and its impact on children's performance. *Child Development, 61,* 113–126.

Frey, K. S., & Ruble, D. N. (1987). What children say about classroom performance: Sex and grade differences in perceived competence. *Child Development, 58,* 1066–1078.

Frick, T. W. (1990). Analysis of patterns in time: A method of recording and quantifying temporal relations in education. *American Educational Research Journal, 27,* 180–204.

Friedman, L. (1989). Mathematics and the gender gap: A meta-analysis of recent studies on sex differences in mathematical tasks. *Review of Educational Research, 59,* 185–213.

Frith, U. (1979). Reading by eye and writing by ear. In P. A. Kolers, M. Wrolstad, & H. Bouma (Eds.), *Processing of visible language,* Vol. 1 (pp. 379–390). New York: Plenum Press.

Fuchs, D., & Fuchs, L. S. (1986). Test procedure bias: A meta-analysis of examiner familiarity effects. *Review of Educational Research, 56,* 243–262.

Fuchs, L. S., & Fuchs, D. (1990). Curriculum-based assessment. In C. R. Reynolds & R. W. Kamphaus (Eds.), *Handbook of psychological and educational assessment of children: Intelligence and achievement* (pp. 435–455). New York: Guilford.

Fuchs, L. S., Fuchs, D., Hamlett, C. L., & Stecker, P. M. (1990). The role of skills analysis in curriculum-based measurement in math. *School Psychology Review, 19,* 6–22.

Fuchs, L. S., Fuchs, D., Hamlett, C. L., & Stecker, P. M. (1991). Effects of curriculum-based measurement and consultation on teacher planning and student achievement in mathematics operations. *American Educational Research Journal, 28,* 617–641.

Fuchs, L. S., Fuchs, D., & Maxwell, L. (1988). The validity of informal measures of reading comprehension. *Remedial and Special Education, 9* (2), 20–29.

Fuson, K. (1988). *Children's counting and concept of numbers.* New York: Springer-Verlag.

Fuson, K. C. (1992). Research on learning and teaching addition and subtraction of whole numbers. In G. Leinhardt, R. Putnam, & R. A. Hattrup (Eds.), *Analysis of arithmetic for mathematics teaching* (pp. 53–187). Hillsdale, NJ: Erlbaum & Associates.

Fuson, K. C., & Fuson, A. M. (1991). Instruction supporting children's counting on for addition and counting up for subtraction. *Journal for Research in Mathematics Education, 22,* 72–78.

Fuson, K., & Willis, G. (1988). Subtraction by counting up: More evidence. *Journal for Research in Mathematics Education, 19,* 402–420.

Gaddes, W. H. (1985). *Learning disabilities and brain function,* 2nd ed. New York: Springer-Verlag.

Gagné, R. M. (1965). *The conditions of learning.* New York: Holt.

Gagné, R. M., & Brown, L. T. (1961). Some factors in the programming of conceptual learning. *Journal of Experimental Psychology, 62,* 313–321.

Gagné, R. M., & Dick, W. (1983). Instructional psychology. *Annual Review of Psychology, 34,* 261–295.

Galaburda, A. (1983). Developmental dyslexia: Current anatomical research. *Annals of Dyslexia, 33,* 41–53.

Galaburda, A. M., Sherman, G. F., Rosen, G. D., Aboitz, F., & Geschwind, N. (1985). Developmental dyslexia: Four consecutive patients with cortical anomalies. *Archives of Neurology, 35,* 812–817.

Galin, D. (1989). EEG studies in dyslexia. In D. J. Bakker & H. van der Vlugt (Eds.), *Learning disabilities,* Vol. 1, *Neuropsychological correlates and treatment.* Amsterdam: Swets Publishing.

Galotti, K. M. (1989). Gender differences in self-reported moral reasoning: A review and new evidence. *Journal of Youth and Adolescence, 18,* 475–488.

Galotti, K. M., Kozberg, S. F., & Farmer, M. C. (1991). Gender and developmental differences in adolescents' conceptions of moral reasoning. *Journal of Youth and Adolescence, 20,* 13–30.

Gal'perin, P. (1969). Stages in the development of mental acts. In M. Cole & I. Maltzman (Eds.), *A handbook of contemporary Soviet psychology* (pp. 249–273). New York: Basic Books.

Galton, F. (1869). *Hereditary genius: An inquiry into its laws and consequences.* London: MacMillan.

Gambrell, L. B., & Bales, R. J. (1986). Mental imagery and the comprehension-monitoring performance of fourth- and fifth-grade poor readers. *Reading Research Quarterly, 21,* 454–464.

Garber, H. L., Hodge, J. D., Rynders, J., Dever, R., & Velu, R. (1991). The Milwaukee Project: Setting the record straight. *American Journal of Mental Deficiency, 95,* 493–525.

Garcia, J. (1981). The logic and limits of mental ability testing. *American Psychologist, 36,* 1172–1180.

Gardner, E. (1975). *Fundamentals of neurology,* 6th ed. Philadelphia: W.B. Saunders Co.

Gardner, H. (1983). *Frame of mind: The theory of multiple intelligences.* New York: Basic Books.

Gardner, H. (1993) Multiple intelligences: *The theory in practice: A reader.* New York: Basic Books.

Gardner, R. C. (1980). On the validity of affective variables in second language acquisition: Conceptual, contextual, and statistical considerations. *Language Learning, 30,* 255–270.

Gardner, R. C. (1983). Learning another language: A true social psychological experiment. *Journal of Language and Social Psychology, 2,* 219–239.

Gardner, R., & Lambert, W. (1972). *Attitudes and motivation in second language learning.* Rowley, MA: Newbury House.

Gardner, W., & Rogoff, B. (1982). The role of instruction in memory development: Some methodological choices. *Quarterly Newsletter of the Laboratory of Comparative Human Cognition, 4,* 6–12.

Garner, R. (1992). Learning from school texts. *Educational Psychologist, 27,* 53–63.

Garner, R., Alexander, P. A., Gillingham, M. G., Kulikowich, J. M., & Brown, R. (1991). Interest and learning from text. *American Educational Research Journal, 28,* 643–660.

Garner, R., Gillingham, M. G., & White, C. S. (1989). Effects of "seductive details" on macroprocessing and microprocessing in adult and children. *Cognition and Instruction, 6,* 41–57.

Garnett, P. J. (1987). Exemplary practice in secondary chemistry education. In K. Tobin & B. J. Fraser (Eds.), *Exemplary practice in science and mathematics education.* Perth, Western Australia: Western Australian Institute of Technology. (Cited in Garnett, P. J., & Tobin, K. [1988]. Teaching for understanding: Exemplary practice in high school chemistry. *Journal of Research in Science Teaching, 26,* 1–14.)

Garskof, B. E., & Houston, J. P. (1963). Measurement of verbal relatedness: An idiographic approach. *Psychological Review, 70,* 277–288.

Gaskins, I. W., Anderson, R. C., Pressley, M., Cunicelli, E. A., & Satlow, E. (1992). The moves strategy instruction teachers make. *Elementary School Journal, 93,* 277–304.

Gaskins, I. W., & Elliot, T. T. (1991). *Implementing cognitive strategy instruction across the school: The Benchmark manual for teachers.* Cambridge, MA: Brookline Books.

Gates, B. (Guest Ed.) (1990). Special Issue: Perspectives on morality and moral education east and west. *Journal of Moral Education, 19* (3).

Gauvain, M., & Rogoff, B. (1989). Collaborative problem solving and children's planning skills. *Developmental Psychology, 25,* 139–151.

Gayford, C. (1989). A contribution to a methodology for teaching and assessment of group problem-solving in biology among 15 year old pupils. *Journal of Biological Education, 23,* 193–198.

Gayford, C. (1992). Patterns of group behavior in open–ended problem solving in science classes of 15-year-old students in England. *International Journal of Science Education, 14,* 41–49.

Geary, D. C. (1990). A componential analysis of an early learning deficit in mathematics. *Journal of Experimental Child Psychology, 49,* 363–383.

Geary, D. C., Bow-Thomas, C., & Yao, Y. (1992). Counting knowledge and skill in cognitive addition: A comparison of normal and mathematically disabled children. *Journal of Experimental Child Psychology, 54,* 372–391.

Geary, D. C., & Brown, S. C. (1991). Cognitive addition: Strategy choice and speed-of-processing differences in gifted, normal, and mathematically disabled children. *Developmental Psychology, 27,* 398–406.

Geary, D. C., Brown, S. C., & Samaranayake, V. A. (1991). Cognitive addition: A short longitudinal study of strategy choice and speed-of-processing differences in normal and mathematically disabled children. *Developmental Psychology, 27,* 787–797.

Geary, D. C., & Burlingham-Dubree, M. (1989). External validation of the strategy choice for addition. *Journal of Experimental Child Psychology, 47,* 175–192.

Geary, D. C., Widaman, K. F., & Little, T. D. (1986). Cognitive addition and multiplication: Evidence for a single memory network. *Memory and Cognition, 14,* 478–487.

Geisenger, K. F. (1992a). Fairness and selected psychometric issues in the psychological testing of Hispanics. In K. F. Geisinger (Ed.), *Psychological testing of Hispanics* (pp. 17–42). Washington, DC: American Psychological Association.

Geisenger, K. F. (1992b). The metamorphosis of test validation. *Educational Psychologist, 27,* 197–222.

Geisler, C. (1991). Toward a sociocognitive model of literacy: Constructing mental models in a philosophical conversation. In C. Bazerman & J. Paradis (Eds.), *Textual dynamics of the professions: Historical and contemporary studies of writing in professional communities* (pp. 171–190). Madison: University of Wisconsin Press.

Gelman, R., & Gallistel, C. R. (1978). *The child's understanding of number.* Cambridge, MA: Harvard University Press.

Gelman, R., Massey, C. M., & McManus, M. (1991). Characterizing supporting environments for cognitive development: Lessons from children in a museum. In L. Resnick, J. M. Levine, & S. D. Teasley (Eds.), *Perspectives on socially shared cognition* (pp. 226–256). Washington, DC: American Psychological Association.

General Accounting Office (1989). *Effective schools programs: Their extent and characteristics.* Washington, DC: General Accounting Office.

Genesee, F. (1985). Second language learning through immersion: A review of U.S. programs. *Review of Educational Research, 55,* 541–562.

Gentile, C. (1992). *Exploring new methods for collecting students' school-based writing.* Washington, DC: U.S. Department of Education.

Gentner, D. (1989). The mechanisms of analogical learning. In S. Vosniadou & A. Ortony (Eds.), *Similarity and analogical reasoning* (pp. 199–241). Cambridge, UK: Cambridge University Press.

Gentner, D., & Gentner, D. (1983). Flowing waters or teeming crowds: Mental models of electricity. In D. Gentner & A. Stevens (Eds.), *Mental models* (pp. 101–129). Hillsdale, NJ: Erlbaum & Associates.

Gentner, D., & Stevens, A. (Eds.) (1983). *Mental models.* Hillsdale, NJ: Erlbaum & Associates.

Gerst, M. S. (1971). Symbolic coding processes in observational learning. *Journal of Personality and Social Psychology, 19,* 7–17.

Geschwind, N., & Galaburda, A. M. (1987). *Cerebral lateralization: Biological mechanisms, associations, and psychology.* Cambridge, MA: MIT Press.

Ghatala, E. S. (1986). Strategy-monitoring training enables young learners to select effective strategies. *Educational Psychologist, 21,* 43–54.

Ghatala, E. S., Levin, J. R., Pressley, M., & Goodwin, D. (1986). A componential analysis of the effects of derived and supplied strategy-utility information on children's strategy selections. *Journal of Experimental Child Psychology, 41,* 76–92.

Ghiselli, E. E. (1966). *The validity of occupational aptitude tests.* New York: Wiley.

Ghiselli, E. E. (1973). The validity of aptitude tests in personnel selection. *Personnel Psychology, 26,* 461–477.

Gibbs, J. C., Arnold, K. D., & Burkart, J. E. (1984). Sex differences in the expression of moral judgment. *Child Development, 55,* 1040–1043.

Gibbs, J. C., Basinger, K. S., & Fuller, D. (1992). *Moral maturity: Measuring the development of sociomoral reflection.* Hillsdale, NJ: Erlbaum & Associates.

Gibbs, J. C., & Widaman, K. F. (1982). *Social intelligence: Measuring the development of sociomoral reflection.* Englewood Cliffs, NJ: Prentice-Hall.

Gibbs, J. C., Widaman, K. F., & Colby, A. (1982). Construction and validation of a simplified, group-administrable equivalent to the Moral Judgment Interview. *Child Development, 53,* 895–910.

Gibson, E. J. (1969). *Principles of perceptual learning and development.* New York: Appleton-Century-Crofts.

Gibson, E. J. (1982). The concept of affordances in development: The renascence of functionalism. In W. A. Collins (Ed.), *The concept of development: The Minnesota symposium on child psychology,* Vol. 15 (pp. 55–81). Hillsdale, NJ: Erlbaum.

Gibson, J. J. (1979). *The ecological approach to visual perception.* Boston: Houghton-Mifflin.

Gibson, K. R. (1991a). Basic neuroanatomy for the nonspecialist. In K. R. Gibson & A. C. Petersen (Eds.), *Brain maturation and cognitive development: Comparative and cross-cultural perspectives* (pp. 13–25). New York: Aldine de Gruyter.

Gibson, K. R. (1991b). Myelination and behavioral development: A comparative perspective on questions of neoteny, altriciality and intelligence. In K. R. Gibson & A. C. Petersen (Eds.), *Brain maturation and cognitive development: Comparative and cross-cultural perspectives* (pp. 29–63). New York: Aldine de Gruyter.

Gibson, K. R., & Petersen, A. C. (1991). Introduction. In K. R. Gibson & A. C. Petersen (Eds.), *Brain maturation and cognitive development: Comparative and cross-cultural perspectives* (pp. 3–12). New York: Aldine de Gruyter.

Gick, M. L., & Holyoak, K. J. (1980). Analogical problem solving. *Cognitive Psychology, 12,* 306–355.

Gick, M. L., & Holyoak, K. J. (1983). Schema induction and analogical transfer. *Cognitive Psychology, 15,* 1–38.

Gickling, E. E., & Armstrong, D. L. (1978). Levels of instructional difficulty as related to on-task behavior, task completion, and comprehension. *Journal of Learning Disabilities, 11,* 559–566.

Gickling, E. E., Shane, R. L., & Croskery, K. M. (1989). Developing mathematical skills in low-achieving high school students through curriculum-based assessment. *School Psychology Review, 18,* 344–355.

Gilbert, N., Spring, C., & Sassenrath, J. (1977). Effects of overlearning and similarity on transfer in word recognition. *Perceptual and Motor Skills, 44,* 591–598.

Gilewski, M. J., & Zelinski, E. M. (1986). Questionnaire assessment of memory complaints. In L. W. Poon (Ed.), *Handbook for clinical memory assessment of older adults* (pp. 93–107). Washington, DC: American Psychological Association.

Gilger, J. W. (1991). Differential assortative mating found for academic and demographic variables as a function of time and assessment. *Behavior Genetics, 21,* 131–150.

Gilligan, C. (1982). *In a different voice: Psychological theory and women's development.* Cambridge, MA: Harvard University Press.

Gilligan, C., & Attanucci, J. (1988). Two moral orientations. In C. Gilligan, J. V. Ward, & J. M. Taylor with B. Bardige (Eds.), *Mapping the moral domain: A contribution of women's thinking to psychological theory and education* (pp. 73–86). Cambridge, MA: Harvard University Press.

Gipson, M. H., Abraham, M. R., & Renner, J. W. (1989). Relationships between formal-operational thought and conceptual difficulties in genetics problem solving. *Journal of Research in Science Teaching, 26,* 811–821.

Glaser, R., & Chi, M. T. H. (1988). Introduction: What is it to be an expert? In M. T. H. Chi, R. Glaser, & M. J. Farr (Eds.), *The nature of expertise* (pp. xv–xxiix). Hillsdale, NJ: Erlbaum & Associates.

Glaser, B., & Strauss, A. (1967). *The discovery of grounded theory.* Chicago: Aldine.

Glass, A. L., Holyoak, K. J., & O'Dell, C. (1974). Production frequency and the verification of quantified statements. *Journal of Verbal Learning and Verbal Behavior, 13,* 237–254.

Glass, G. V., & Smith, M. L. (1979). Meta-analysis of the research on class size and achievement. *Educational Evaluation and Policy Analysis, 1,* 2–16.

Glasson, G. E. (1989). The effects of hands-on and teacher demonstration laboratory methods on science achievement in relation to reasoning ability and prior knowledge. *Journal of Research in Science Teaching, 26,* 121–131.

Gleitman, L. R. (1986). Biological preprogramming for language learning. In S. L. Friedman, K. A. Klivington, & R. W. Peterson (Eds.), *The brain, cognition, and education* (pp. 120–151). Orlando, FL: Academic Press.

Glenberg, A. M., & Epstein, W. (1987). Inexpert calibration of comprehension. *Memory and Cognition, 15,* 84–93.

Glenberg, A. M., Sanocki, T., Epstein, W., & Morris, C. (1987). Enhancing calibration of comprehension. *Journal of Experimental Psychology: General, 116,* 119–136.

Glenberg, A. M., Wilkinson, A. C., & Epstein, W. (1982). The illusion of knowing: Failure in the self-assessment of comprehension. *Memory and Cognition, 10,* 597–602.

Glenwick, D. S. (1976). Training impulsive children in verbal self-regulation by use of natural change agents (Doctoral dissertation, University of Rochester, 1976). *Dissertation Abstracts International 459-B.* (University Microfilms No. 76–14, 758.)

Glover, J. A. (1989). The "testing" phenomenon: Not gone but nearly forgotten. *Journal of Educational Psychology, 81,* 392–399.

Glover, J. A., & Corkill, A. J. (1987). Influence of paraphrased repetitions on the spacing effect. *Journal of Educational Psychology, 87,* 198–199.

Glynn, S. M. (1991). Explaining science concepts: A teaching-with-analogies model. In S. M. Glynn, R. H. Yeany, & B. K. Britton (Eds.), *The psychology of learning science* (pp. 219–240). Hillsdale, NJ: Erlbaum & Associates.

Glynn, S. M., Andre, T., & Britton, B. K. (1986). *Design of instructional text. Educational Psychologist* (Special issue), *21 (4).*

Glynn, S. M., Muth, K. D., & Britton, B. K. (1990). Thinking aloud about concepts in science text: How instructional objectives work. In H. Mandl, E. De Corte, S. N. Bennett, & H. F. Friedrich (Eds.), *Learning and instruction: European research in an international context,* Vol. 2 (pp. 215–223). Oxford, UK: Pergamon Press.

Glynn, S. M., Yeany, R. H., & Britton, B. K. (1991). A constructive view of learning science. In S. M. Glynn, R. H. Yeany, & B. K. Britton (Eds.), *The psychology of learning science* (pp. 3–19). Hillsdale, NJ: Erlbaum & Associates.

Goetz, E. T., Anderson, R. C., & Schallert, D. L. (1981). The representation of sentences in memory. *Journal of Verbal Learning and Verbal Behavior, 20,* 369–385.

Goetz, E. T., Sadoski, M., Olivarez, A., Jr., Calero-Breckheimer, A., Garner, P., & Fatemi, Z. (1992). The structure of emotional response in reading a literary text: Quantitative and qualitative analyses. *Reading Research Quarterly, 27,* 360–372.

Goetz, E. T., Schallert, D. L., Reynolds, R. E., & Radin, D. I. (1983). Reading in perspective: What real cops and pretend burglars look for in a story. *Journal of Educational Psychology, 75,* 500–510.

Goldberg, R. A., Schwartz, S., & Stewart, M. (1977). Individual differences in cognitive processes. *Journal of Educational Psychology, 69,* 9–14.

Goldberg, S., & DeVitto, B. A. (1983). *Born too soon: Preterm birth and early development.* San Francisco: W.H. Freeman & Co.

Goldberger, A. S. (1977). Twin methods: A skeptical view. In P. Taubman (Ed.), *Kinometrics: Determinants of socioeconomic success between and within families.* North-Holland: Amsterdam.

Golden, C. J., Zillmer, E., & Spiers, M. (1992). *Neuropsychological assessment and intervention.* Springfield, IL: Charles C. Thomas.

Goldenberg, C. (1992). The limits of expectations: A case for case knowledge about teacher expectancy effects. *American Educational Research Journal, 29,* 517–544.

Goldman, S. R., Mertz, D. L., & Pellegrino, J. W. (1989). Individual differences in extended practice functions and solution strategies for basic addition facts. *Journal of Educational Psychology, 81,* 481–496.

Goldman, S. R., Pellegrino, J. W., & Mertz, D. L. (1988). Extended practice of basic addition facts: Strategy changes in learning-disabled students. *Cognition and Instruction, 5,* 223–265.

Goldman-Rakic, P. S. (1987). Development of cortical circuitry and cognitive function. *Child Development, 58,* 601–622.

Goldman-Rakic, P. S., Isseroff, A., Schwartz, M. L., & Bugbee, N. M. (1983). The neurobiology of cognitive development. In M. M. Haith & J. J. Campos (Vol Eds.) and P. H. Mussen (General Ed.), *Handbook of child psychology,* Vol. II, *Infancy and developmental psychobiology* (pp. 281–344). New York: John Wiley & Sons.

Goldsmith-Phillips, J. (1989). Word and context in reading development: A test of the interactive-compensatory hypothesis. *Journal of Educational Psychology, 81,* 299–305.

Goldstein, H., & Mousetis, L. (1989). Generalized language learning by children with severe mental retardation: Effects of peers' expressive modeling. *Journal of Applied Behavioral Analysis, 22,* 245–259.

Good, T. L., & Brophy, J. E. (1986). School effects. In *Handbook of research on teaching,* 3rd ed. (pp. 570–602). New York: MacMillan.

Gooden, W. E. (1989). Development of black men in early adulthood. In R. L. Jones (Ed.), *Black adult development and aging* (pp. 63–89). Berkeley, CA: Cobb & Henry.

Goodlad, J. I. (1984). *A place called school: Prospects for the future.* New York: McGraw-Hill.

Goodlad, J. I. (1990). *Access to knowledge: An agenda for our nation's schools.* New York: College Entrance Examination Board.

Goodman, J. F. (1990). Infant intelligence: Do we, can we, should we assess it? In C. R. Reynolds & R. W. Kamphaus (Eds.), *Handbook of psychological and educational assessment of children: Intelligence and achievement* (pp. 183–208). New York: Guilford Press.

Goodman, K. S. (1965). A linguistic study of cues and miscues in reading. *Elementary English, 42,* 639–642.

Goodman, K. S. (1967). Reading: A psycholinguistic guessing game. *Journal of the Reading Specialist, 6,* 126–135.

Goodman, K. S. (1989). Whole-language research: Foundations and development. *Elementary School Journal, 90,* 207–221.

Goodman, K. S., & Goodman, Y. M. (1979). Learning to read is natural. In L. B. Resnick & P. A. Weaver, *Theory and practice of early reading,* Vol. 1 (pp. 137–154). Hillsdale, NJ: Erlbaum & Associates.

Goodman, R. (1987). The developmental neurobiology of language. In W. Yule & M. Rutter (Eds.), *Language development and disorders* (pp. 129–145). Oxford, UK: Blackwell.

Goodman, Y. M. (1991). Informal methods of evaluation. In J. Flood, J. M. Jensen, D. Lapp, & J. R. Squire (Eds.), *Handbook of research on teaching the English language arts* (pp. 502–509). New York: MacMillan.

Goss, A. M. (1968). Estimated versus actual physical strength in three ethnic groups. *Child Development, 39,* 283–290.

Goswami, U. (1986). Children's use of analogy in learning to read: A developmental study. *Journal of Experimental Child Psychology, 42,* 73–83.

Goswami, U. (1988). Orthographic analogies and reading development. *Quarterly Journal of Experimental Psychology, 40,* 239–268.

Goswami, U. (1991). Analogical reasoning: What develops? A review of research and theory. *Child Development, 62,* 1–22.

Goswami, U. (1992). *Analogical reasoning in children.* Hillsdale, NJ: Erlbaum & Associates.

Goswami, U., & Bryant, P. E. (1990). *Phonological skills and learning to read.* Hillsdale, NJ: Erlbaum & Associates.

Goswami, U., & Bryant, P. (1992). Rhyme, analogy, and children's reading. In P. B. Gough, L. C. Ehri, & R. Treiman (Eds.), *Reading acquisition* (pp. 49–63). Hillsdale, NJ: Erlbaum & Associates.

Gottesman, I. I. (1963). Genetic aspects of intelligent behavior. In N. Ellis (Ed.), *Handbook of mental deficiency.* New York: McGraw-Hill.

Gottfredson, D. C., Gottfredson, G. D., & Hybl, L. G. (1993). Managing adolescent behavior: A multiyear, multischool study. *American Educational Research Journal, 30,* 179–215.

Gottfried, A. W. (1984). Home environment and early cognitive development: Integration, meta-analyses, and conclusions. In A. W. Gottfried (Ed.), *Home environment and early cognitive development: Longitudinal research* (pp. 329–342). Orlando, FL: Academic Press.

Gough, P. B., Juel, C., & Griffith, P. L. (1992). Reading, spelling, and the orthographic cipher. In P. B. Gough, L. C. Ehri, & R. Treiman (Eds.), *Reading acquisition* (pp. 35–48). Hillsdale, NJ: Erlbaum & Associates.

Gould, S. J. (1981). *The mismeasure of man.* New York: W.W. Norton Co.

Grabe, M. (1989). Evaluation of purposeful reading skills in elementary-age students. *Journal of Educational Psychology, 81,* 628–630.

Graesser, A. C. (1981). *Prose comprehension beyond the word.* New York: Springer-Verlag.

Graesser, A. C., Hoffman, N. L., & Clark, L. F. (1980). Structural components of reading time. *Journal of Verbal Learning and Verbal Behavior, 19,* 135–151.

Graesser, A. C., & McMahen, C. L. (1993). Anomalous information triggers questions when adults solve quantitative problems and comprehend stories. *Journal of Educational Psychology, 85,* 136–151.

Graham, S. (1990). The role of production factors in learning disabled students' compositions. *Journal of Educational Psychology, 82,* 781–791.

Graham, S., & Barker, G. P. (1990). The down side of help: An attributional-developmental analysis of helping behaviors as a low-ability cue. *Journal of Educational Psychology, 82,* 7–14.

Graham, S., & Harris, K. R. (1987). Improving composition skills of inefficient learners with self-instructional strategy training. *Topics in Language Disorders, 7,* 66–77.

Graham, S., & Harris, K. R. (1988). Instructional recommendations for teaching writing to exceptional children. *Exceptional Children, 54,* 506–512.

Graham, S., & Harris, K. R. (1989a). A components analysis of cognitive strategy instruction: Effects on learning disabled students' composition and self-efficacy. *Journal of Educational Psychology, 81,* 353–361.

Graham, S., & Harris, K. R. (1992). Self-regulated strategy development: Programmatic research in writing. In B. Y. L. Wong (Ed.), *Contemporary intervention research in learning disabilities: An international perspective* (pp. 47–64). New York: Springer-Verlag.

Graham, S., Harris, K. R., MacArthur, C., & Schwartz, S. (1991). Writing instruction. In B. Wong (Ed.), *Learning about learning disabilities* (pp. 309–343). New York: Academic Press.

Graham, S., & MacArthur, C. (1988). Improving learning disabled students' skill at revising essays produced on a word processor: Self-instructional strategy training. *Journal of Special Education, 22,* 133–152.

Graham, S., Schwartz, S., & MacArthur, C. (1991). *Learning disabled and normally achieving students' knowledge of the writing process: Attitudes toward writing and self-efficacy.* College Park, MD: University of Maryland, Department of Special Education.

Graham, T., & Perry, M. (1993). Indexing transitional knowledge. *Developmental Psychology, 29,* 779–788.

Graves, M. F., & Slater, W. H. (1991). A response to "Instructional texts rewritten by five expert teams." *Journal of Educational Psychology, 83,* 147–148.

Graves, M., Slater, W. H., Roen, D., Redd-Boyd, T., Duin, A. H., Furniss, D. W., and Hazelton, P. (1988). Some characteristics of memorable expository writing: Effects of revisions by writers with different backgrounds. *Research in the Teaching of English, 22,* 242–265.

Grayson, D. A. (1989). Twins reared together: Minimizing shared environmental effects. *Behavior Genetics, 19,* 593–603.

Graziano, W. G., Varca, P. E., & Levy, J. C. (1982). Race of examiner effects and the validity of intelligence tests. *Review of Educational Research, 52,* 469–498.

Greenfield, P. M. (1984). A theory of the teacher in the learning activities of everyday life. In B. Rogoff & J. Lave (Eds.), *Everyday cognition: Its development in social context* (pp. 117–138). Cambridge, MA: Harvard University Press.

Greenlee, M. E., Hiebert, E. H., Bridge, C. A., & Winograd, P. N. (1986). The effects of different audiences on young writers' letter writing. In J. Niles & R. Lalik (Eds.) *Solving problems in literacy: Learners, teachers, and researchers* (pp. 281–289). Rochester, NY: National Reading Conference.

Greeno, J. G. (1991). Number sense as situated knowing in a conceptual domain. *Journal for Research in Mathematics Education, 22,* 170–218.

Greeno, J. G. (1992). Mathematical and scientific thinking in classrooms and other situations. In D. F. Halpern (Ed.), *Enhancing thinking skills in the sciences and mathematics* (pp. 39–62). Hillsdale, NJ: Erlbaum & Associates.

Greenough, W. T. (1993). Experience and brain development. *Child Development, 58,* 539–559.

Greenough, W. T., Black, J. E., & Wallace, C. S. (1987). Experience and brain development. *Child Development, 58,* 539–559.

Greenough, W. T., & Juraska, J. M. (1986). *Developmental neuropsychobiology.* Orlando, FL: Academic Press.

Greenwood, C. R., Delquadri, J. C., & Hall, R. V. (1989). Longitudinal effects of classwide peer tutoring. *Journal of Educational Psychology, 81,* 371–383.

Griffith, D. R. (1992). Prenatal exposure to cocaine and other drugs: Developmental and educational prognoses. *Phi Delta Kappan, 74,* 30–34.

Griffith, P. L. (1991). Phonemic awareness helps first graders invent spellings and third graders remember correct spellings. *Journal of Reading Behavior, 23,* 215–233.

Groen, G. J., & Parkman, J. M. (1972). A chronometric analysis of simple addition. *Psychological Review, 79,* 329–343.

Groen, G., & Resnick, L. (1977). Can preschool children invent addition algorithms? *Journal of Educational Psychology, 69,* 645–652.

Gross-Glenn, K., Duara, R., Yoshii, F., Barker, W. W., Chen, J. Y., Apicella, A., Boothe, T., & Lubs, H. A. (1988). PET-scan reading studies of familial dyslexics [Abstract]. *Journal of Clinical and Experimental Neuropsychology, 10,* 34–35.

Grossman, H. J. (Ed.) (1983). *Manual on terminology and classification in mental retardation* (3rd revision). Washington, DC: American Association on Mental Deficiency.

Guba, E. G. (Ed.) (1990). *Paradigm dialog.* Newbury, CA: Sage.

Guilford, J. P. (1967). *The nature of human intelligence.* New York: McGraw-Hill.

Gunstone, R. F., & White, R. T. (1981). Understanding of gravity. *Science Education, 65,* 291–299.

Guralnick, M. J. (1976). Solving complex perceptual discrimination problems: Techniques for the development of problem-solving strategies. *American Journal of Mental Deficiency, 81,* 18–25.

Guri-Rozenblit, S. (1989). Effects of a tree diagram on students' comprehension of main ideas in an expository text with multiple themes. *Reading Research Quarterly, 24,* 236–247.

Guthke, J., & Wingenfeld, S. (1992). The learning test concept: Origins, state of the art, and trends. In H. C. Haywood & D. Tzuriel (Eds.), *Interactive assessment* (pp. 64–93). New York: Springer-Verlag.

Guthrie, J. T. (1988). Locating information in documents: Examination of a cognitive model. *Reading Research Quarterly, 23,* 178–199.

Guthrie, J. T., Bennett, S., & Weber, S. (1991). Processing procedural documents: A cognitive model for following written directions. *Educational Psychology Review, 3,* 249–265.

Guttentag, R. E. (1984). The mental effort requirement of cumulative rehearsal: A developmental study. *Journal of Experimental Child Psychology, 37,* 92–106.

Guttentag, R. E., Ornstein, P. A., & Siemens, L. (1987). Children's spontaneous rehearsal: Transitions in strategy acquisition. *Cognitive Development, 2,* 307–326.

Guttmann, J., Levin, J. R., & Pressley, M. (1977). Pictures, partial pictures, and young children's oral prose learning. *Journal of Educational Psychology, 69,* 473–480.

Guzzetti, B. J., Snyder, T. E., Glass, G. V., & Gamas, W. S. (1993). Promoting conceptual change in science: A comparative meta-analysis of instructional interventions from reading education and science education. *Reading Research Quarterly, 28,* 117–159.

Haas, C., & Flower, L. (1988). Rhetorical reading strategies and the the construction of meaning. *College Composition and Communication, 39,* 167–183.

Haberlandt, K. (1980). Story grammar and reading time of story constituents. *Poetics, 9,* 99–116.

Haensly, P. A., & Torrance, E. P. (1990). Assessment of creativity in children and adolescents. In C. R. Reynolds & R. W. Kamphaus (Eds.), *Handbook of psychological and educational assessment of children: Intelligence and achievement* (pp. 697–722). New York: Guilford Press.

Hagen, J. W., Barclay, C. R., Anderson, B. J., Feeman, D. J., Segal, S. S., Bacon, G., & Goldstein, G. W. (1990). Intellective functioning and strategy use in children with insulin-dependent diabetes mellitus. *Child Development, 61,* 1714–1727.

Hagen, J. W., & Hale, G. A. (1973). The development of attention in children. In A.D. Pick (Ed.), *Minnesota symposium on child psychology.* Minneapolis: University of Minnesota Press.

Haier, R. J., Siegel, B. V., Nuechterlein, K. H., Hazlett, E., Wu, J. C., Paek, J., Browning, H. L., & Buchsbaum, M. S. (1988). Cortical glucose metabolic rate correlates of abstract reasoning and attention studied with positron emission tomography. *Intelligence, 12,* 199–217.

Hakstian, A. R., & Cattell, R. B. (1978). Higher stratum ability structure on a basis of twenty primary abilities. *Journal of Educational Psychology, 70,* 657–659.

Hakuta, K. (1986). *Mirror of language: The debate on bilingualism.* New York: Basic Books.

Hakuta, K. (1987). Degree of bilingualism and cognitive ability in mainland Puerto Rican children. *Child Development, 58,* 1372–1388.

Hall, E. R., Esty, E. T., & Fisch, S. M. (1990). Television and children's problem-solving behavior: A synopsis of an evaluation of the effects of *Square One* TV. *Journal of Mathematical Behavior, 9,* 161–174.

Hall, V. C., & Edmondson, B. (1992). Relative importance of aptitude and prior domain knowledge on immediate and delayed posttests. *Journal of Educational Psychology, 84,* 219–223.

Hall, V. C., & Merkel, S. P. (1985). Teacher expectancy effects and educational psychology. In J. B. Dusek (Ed.), *Teacher expectancies* (pp. 67–92). Hillsdale, NJ: Erlbaum & Associates.

Haller, E. P., Child, D. A., & Walberg, H. J. (1988). Can comprehension be taught? A quantitative synthesis of "metacognitive" studies. *Educational Researcher, 17 (9),* 5–8.

Halpern, D. F. (1992). *Sex differences in cognitive abilities,* 2nd ed. Hillsdale, NJ: Erlbaum & Associates.

Halpern, D. F., Hansen, C., & Riefer, D. (1990). Analogies as an aid to understanding and memory. *Journal of Educational Psychology, 82,* 298–305.

Halstead, W. C. (1947). *Brain and intelligence.* Chicago: University of Chicago Press.

Hamilton, S. F. (1990). *Apprenticeship for adulthood: Preparing youth for the future.* New York: Free Press.

Hammond, K. J. (1990). Case-based planning: A framework for planning from experience. *Cognitive Science, 14,* 385–443.

Hamond, N. R., & Fivush, R. (1991). Memories of Mickey Mouse: Young children recount their trip to Disneyworld. *Cognitive Development, 6,* 433–448.

Hampson, E. (1990a). Estrogen-related variations in human spatial and articulatory-motor skills. *Psychoendocrinology.*

Hampson, E. (1990b). Variations in sex-related cognitive abilities across the menstrual cycle. *Brain and Cognition.*

Hampson, E., & Kimura, D. (1988). Reciprocal effects of hormonal fluctuations on human motor and perceptual-spatial skills. *Behavioral Neuroscience, 102,* 456–495.

Hancock, C., Kaput, J. J., & Goldsmith, L. T. (1992). Authentic inquiry with data: Critical barriers to classroom implementation. *Educational Psychologist, 27,* 337–364.

Hanford, G. H. (1991). *Life with the SAT: Assessing our young people and our times.* New York: College Entrance Examination Board.

Hansen, J. S. (1969). The impact of the home literacy environment on reading attitude. *Elementary English (46)* 17–24.

Hansen, J. (1992). Literacy portfolios: Helping students know themselves. *Educational Leadership, 49 (8),* 66–68.

Hansen, J., & Pearson, P. D. (1983). An instructional study: Improving the referential comprehension of good and poor fourth grade readers. *Journal of Educational Psychology, 75,* 821–829.

Hardiman, P. T., Pollatsek, A., & Weil, A. D. (1986). Learning to understand the balance beam. *Cognition and Instruction, 3,* 1–30.

Harrell, R., Capp, R., Davis, D., Peerless, J., & Ravitz, L. (1981). Can nutritional supplements help mentally retarded children? *Proceedings of the National Academy of Science, 78,* 574–578.

Harrell, T. W., & Harrell, M. S. (1945). Army General Classification Test scores for civilian occupations. *Educational and Psychological Measurement, 5,* 229–239.

Harris, K. R. (1988, April). *What's wrong with strategy intervention research: Intervention integrity.* Presented at the annual meeting of the American Educational Research Association, New Orleans.

Harris, K. R., & Graham, S. (1992). Self-regulated strategy development: A part of the writing process. In M. Pressley, K. R. Harris, & J. T. Guthrie (Eds.), *Promoting academic competence and literacy in school* (pp. 277–309). San Diego: Academic Press.

Harris, K. R., & Pressley, M. (1991). The nature of cognitive strategy instruction: Interactive strategy construction. *Exceptional Children, 57,* 392–404.

Harris, L. J. (1988). Right-brain training: Some reflections on the application of research on cerebral hemispheric specialization to education. In D. L. Molfese & S. J. Segalowitz (Eds.), *Brain lateralization in children* (pp. 207–236). New York: Guilford Press.

Harshman, R. A., Hampson, E., & Barenboim, S. A. (1983). Individual differences in cognitive abilities and brain organization: Part I: Sex and handedness differences in ability. *Canadian Journal of Psychology, 37,* 144–192.

Harter, M. R. (1991). Event-related potential indices: Learning disabilities and visual processing. In J. E. Obrzut & G. W. Hynd (Eds.), *Neuropsychological foundations of learning disabilities: A handbook of issues, methods, and practice* (pp. 437–473). San Diego: Academic Press.

Harter, S. (1981). A new self-report scale of intrinsic versus extrinsic orientation in the classroom: Motivational and informational components. *Developmental Psychology, 17,* 300–312.

Harter, S., Whitesell, N. R., & Kowalski, P. (1992). Individual differences in the effects of educational transitions on young adolescent's perceptions of competence and motivational orientation. *American Educational Research Journal, 29,* 777–807.

Hartley, J. (1983). Notetaking research: Resetting the scoreboard. *Bulletin of the British Psychological Society, 36,* 13–14.

Hartley, J., & Marshall, S. (1974). On notes and notetaking. *University Quarterly, 28,* 225–235.

Hartman, D. K. (1992). Eight readers reading: The intertextual links of able readers using multiple passages. *Reading Research Quarterly, 27,* 122–123.

Hartsfield, F., Licht, B., Swenson, C., & Thiele, C. (1989, August). *Control beliefs and behavior problems of elementary school children.* Paper presented at the meeting of the American Psychological Association, New Orleans.

Hasher, L., Stoltzfus, E. R., Zacks, R. T., & Rypma, B. (1991). Age and inhibition. *Journal of Experimental Psychology: Learning, Memory, and Cognition, 17,* 163–169.

Hatano, G., Amaiwa, S., & Shimuzu, K. (1987). Formation of a mental abacus for computation and its use as a memory device for digits: A developmental study. *Developmental Psychology, 23,* 832–838.

Hatano, G., & Inagaki, K. (1991). Sharing cognition through collective comprehension activity. In L. Resnick, J. M. Levine, & S. D. Teasley (Eds.), *Perspectives on socially shared cognition* (pp. 331–348). Washinton, DC: American Psychological Association.

Hatano, G., Miyake, Y., & Binks, M. G. (1977). Performance of expert abacus operators. *Cognition, 5,* 47–55.

Hativa, N. (1988). Computer-based drill and practice in arithmetic: Widening the gap between high- and low-achieving students. *American Educational Research Journal, 25,* 366–397.

Hatta, T., Hirose, T., Ikeda, K., & Fukuhara, H. (1989). Digit memory of Soroban experts: Evidence of utilization of mental imagery. *Applied Cognitive Psychology, 3,* 23–33.

Hawkins, J. D., Doueck, H. J., & Lishner, D. M. (1988). Changing teaching practices in mainstream classrooms to improve bonding and behavior of low achievers. *American Educational Research Journal, 25,* 31–50.

Hayes, J. R. (1985). Three problems in teaching general skills. In S. F. Chipman, J. W. Segal, & R. Glaser (Eds.), *Thinking and learning skills,* Vol. 2, *Research and open questions* (pp. 391–405). Hillsdale, NJ: Erlbaum & Associates.

Hayes, J. R., Flower, L., Schriver, K., Stratman, J., & Carey, L. (1987). Cognitive processes in revision. In S. Rosenberg (Ed.), *Advances in applied psycholinguistics: Reading, writing, and language processing.* Cambridge, UK: Cambridge University Press.

Hayes, J. R., Waterman, D. A., & Robinson, C. S. (1977). Identifying relevant aspects of a problem text. *Cognitive Science, 1,* 297–313.

Hayes-Roth, B., & Thorndyke, P. W. (1979). Integration of knowledge from text. *Journal of Verbal Learning and Verbal Behavior, 18,* 91–108.

Haywood, H. C., Tzuriel, D., & Vaught, S. (1992). Psychoeducational assessment from a transactional perspective. In H. C. Haywood & D. Tzuriel (Eds.), *Interactive assessment* (pp. 38–63). New York: Springer-Verlag.

Healy, V. C. (1989). The effects of advance organizer and prerequisite knowledge passages on the learning and retention of science concepts. *Journal of Research in Science Teaching, 26,* 627–642.

Heath, S. B. (1982). What no bedtime story means: Narrative skills at home and school. *Language in Society, 11,* 49–76.

Hebb, D. O. (1949). *The organization of behavior.* New York: Wiley.

Heckhausen, J. (1987). Balancing for weaknesses and challenging developmental potential: A longitudinal study of mother-infant dyads in apprenticeship interactions. *Developmental Psychology, 23,* 762–770.

Hedges, L. V., & Stock, W. (1983). The effect of class size: An examination of rival hypotheses. *American Educational Research Journal, 20,* 63–85.

Heindel, P., & Kose, G. (1990). The effects of motoric action and organization on children's memory. *Journal of Experimental Child Psychology, 50,* 416–428.

Heinze-Fry, J. A., & Novak, J. D. (1990). Concept mapping brings long-term movement toward meaningful learning. *Science Education, 74,* 461–472.

Hembree, R. (1988). Correlates, causes, effects, and treatment of test anxiety. *Review of Educational Research, 58,* 47–77.

Hembree, R. (1992). Experiments and relational studies in problem solving: A meta-analysis. *Journal for Research in Mathematics Education, 23,* 242–273.

Hembree, R., & Dessart, D. (1986). Effects of hand-held calculators in precollege mathematics education: A meta-analysis. *Journal for Research in Mathematics Education, 17,* 83–99.

Henderson, V. L., & Dweck, C. S. (1990). Motivation and achievement. In S. S. Feldman & G. R. Elliott (Eds.), *At the threshold: The developing adolescent* (pp. 308–329). Cambridge, MA: Harvard University Press.

Hendrickson, D. E., & Hendrickson, A. E. (1980). The biological basis of individual differences in intelligence. *Personality and Individual Differences, 1,* 3–33.

Henry, M., & Renaud, H. (1972). Examined and unexamined lives. *The Research Reporter, 7,* 5–8.

Hertzog, C. (1989). Influences of cognitive slowing on age differences in intelligence. *Developmental Psychology, 25,* 636–651.

Hertzog, C., Hultsch, D. F., & Dixon, R. A. (1989). Evidence for convergent validity of two self-report metamemory questionnaires. *Developmental Psychology, 25,* 687–700.

Hess, R. D., Chih-Mei, C., & McDevitt, T. M. (1987). Cultural variations in family beliefs about children's performance in mathematics: Comparisons among People's Republic of China, Chinese-American ,and Caucasian-American families. *Journal of Educational Psychology, 79,* 179–188.

Hess, R. D., & Shipman, V. C. (1965). Early experience and the specialization of cognitive modes in children. *Child Development, 36,* 869–886.

Hess, R. D., Shipman, V., & Jackson, D. (1965). Early experience and the socialization cognitive models in children. *Child Development, 36,* 869–886.

Hess, T. M. (1992). Adult age differences in script content and structure. In R. L. West & J. D. Sinnott (Eds.), *Everyday memory and aging: Current research and methodology* (pp. 87–100). New York: Springer-Verlag.

Hess, T. M., & Slaughter, S. J. (1990). Schematic influences on scene memory. *Developmental Psychology, 26,* 855–865.

Hewitt, P. G. (1987). *Conceptual physics.* Menlo Park, CA: Addison-Wesley.

Hewson, P. W., & Thorley, R. (1989). The conditions of conceptual change in the classroom. *International Journal of Science Education, 11,* 541–553.

Heyns, B. (1978). *Summer learning and the effects of schooling.* New York: Academic Press.

Heyns, B. (1987). Schooling and cognitive development: Is there a season for learning? *Child Development, 58,* 1151–1160.

Hidi, S. (1990). Interest and its contribution as a mental resource for learning. *Review of Educational Research, 60,* 549–571.

Hidi, S., & Baird, W. (1988). Strategies for increasing text-based interest and students' recall of expository text. *Reading Research Quarterly, 23,* 465–483.

Hiebert, J., & Carpenter, T. P. (1992). Learning and teaching with understanding. In D. A. Grouws (Ed.), *Handbook of research on mathematics teaching and learning* (pp. 65–97). New York: MacMillan.

Hiebert, J., & Wearne, D. (1992). Links between teaching and learning place value with understanding in first grade. *Journal for Research in Mathematics Education, 23,* 98–122.

Hier, D. B., LeMay, M., Rosenberger, P. B., & Perlo, V. P. (1978). Developmental dyslexia: Evidence for a subgroup with a reversal of cerebral asymmetry. *Archives of Neurology, 35,* 90–92.

Higgins, A. (1987). A feminist perspective on moral education. *Journal of Moral Education, 16,* 240–247.

Hinsley, D., Hayes, J. R., & Simon, H. A. (1977). From words to equations. In P. Carpenter & M. Just (Eds.), *Cognitive processes in comprehension.* Hillsdale, NJ: Erlbaum & Associates.

Hintzman, D. L. (1974). Theoretical implications of the spacing effect. In R. L. Solso (Ed.), *Theories in cognitive psychology: The Loyola symposium.* Hillsdale, NJ: Erlbaum & Associates.

Hird, J. S., Landers, D. M., Thomas, J. R., & Horan, J. J. (1991). Physical practice is superior to mental practice in enhancing cognitive and motor performance. *Journal of Sports & Exercise Psychology, 13,* 281–293.

Hirsch, E. D., Jr. (1987). *Cultural literacy: What every American needs to know.* Boston: Houghton Mifflin Co.

Hirsch, E. D., Jr. (1991). *What your second grader needs to know: Fundamentals of a good second-grade education.* New York: Doubleday.

Hirsch, E. D., Kett, J. F., & Trefil, J. (1988). *The dictionary of cultural literacy.* Boston: Houghton Mifflin.

Hishitani, S. (1990). Imagery experts: How do expert abacus operators process imagery? *Applied Cognitive Psychology, 4,* 33–46.

Ho, H-Z., Baker, L. A., & Decker, S. N. (1988). Covariation between intelligence and speed of cognitive processing: Genetic and environmental influences. *Behavior Genetics, 18,* 247–261.

Hobbs, S. A., & Lahey, B. B. (1983). Behavioral treatment. In T. H. Ollendick & M. Hersen (Eds.), *Handbook of child psychopathology* (pp. 427–460). New York: Plenum.

Hobbs, S. A., & Sexson, S. B. (1993). Cognitive development and learning in the pediatric organ transplant recipient. *Journal of Learning Disabilities, 26,* 104–114.

Hock, M., Deshler, D. D., & Schumaker, J. B. (1991). *Annual report on the GOALS program.* Lawrence, KS: University of Kansas, Institute for Research in Learning Disabilities.

Hoffman, M. L. (1970). Moral development. In P. H. Mussen (Ed.), *Carmichael's manual of child psychology*, 3rd ed., Vol. 2 (pp. 261–360). New York: John Wiley & Sons.

Hofmeister, A. M., Engelmann, S., & Carnine, D. (1989). Developing and validating science education videodiscs. *Journal of Research in Science Teaching, 26*, 665–677.

Hoge, R. D. (1988). Issues in the definition and measurement of the giftedness construct. *Educational Researcher, 17* (7), 12–16.

Holland, A., & Andre, T. (1987). Participation in extracurricular activities in secondary school: What is known, what needs to be known? *Review of Educational Research, 57*, 437–466.

Holland, A., & Andre, T. (1988). Beauty is in the eye of the reviewer. *Review of Educational Research, 58*, 113–118.

Holland, J. G., & Skinner, B. F. (1961). *The analysis of behavior.* New York: McGraw-Hill.

Holland, J. H. Holyoak, K. J., Nisbett, R. E., & Thagard, P. R. (1986). *Induction: Processes of inference, learning, and discovery.* Cambridge, MA: MIT Press.

Hollander, B. (1920). *In search of the soul.* New York: E. P. Dutton.

Holliday, W. G., & Benson, G. (1991). Enhancing learning using questions adjunct to science charts. *Journal of Research in Science Teaching, 28*, 97–108.

Holliday, W. G., & McGuire, B. (1992). How can comprehension adjunct questions focus students' attention and enhance concept learning of a computer-animated science lesson? *Journal of Research in Science Teaching, 29*, 3–15.

Holloway, S. D. (1988). Concepts of ability and effort in Japan and the United States. *Review of Educational Research, 58*, 327–345.

Holmes, B. C. (1987). Children's inferences with print and pictures. *Journal of Educational Psychology, 79*, 14–18.

Holmes, C. T., & Matthews, K. M. (1984). The effects of nonpromotion on elementary and junior high school pupils: A meta-analysis. *Review of Educational Research, 54*, 225–236.

Horgan, D. D., & Morgan, D. (1990). Chess expertise in children. *Applied Cognitive Psychology, 4*, 109–128.

Horn, C. C., & Manis, F. R. (1987). Development of automatic and speeded reading of printed words. *Journal of Experimental Child Psychology, 44*, 92–108.

Horn, J. L. (1968). Organization of abilities and the development of intelligence. *Psychological Review, 75*, 242–259.

Horn, J. L. (1985). Remodeling old models of intelligence. In B. Wolman (Ed.), *Handbook of intelligence* (pp. 267–300). New York: Wiley.

Horn, J. L., & Cattell, R. B. (1967). Age differences in fluid and crystallized intelligence. *Acta Psychologica, 26*, 107–129.

Horn, J. L., & Hofer, S. M. (1992). Major abilities and development in the adult period. In R. J. Sternberg & C. A. Berg (Eds.), *Intellectual development* (pp. 44–99). Cambridge, UK: Cambridge University Press.

Horn, J. L., & Stankov, L. (1982). Auditory and visual factors of intelligence. *Intelligence, 6*, 165–185.

Howe, K. R. (1988). Against the quantitative-qualitative incompatibility thesis. *Educational Researcher, 17* (8), 10–16.

Howe, M. J. A. (1990). *The origins of exceptional abilities.* Oxford, UK: Basil Blackwell.

Howell, K. W., & Morehead, M. K. (1987). *Curriculum-based evaluation for special and remedial education: A handbook for deciding what to teach.* Columbus, OH: Merrill Publishing Co.

Hoyles, C., & Noss, R. (Eds.) (1992). *Learning mathematics and LOGO.* Cambridge, MA: MIT Press.

Huba, M. E. (1984). The relationship between linguistic awareness in prereaders and two types of experimental instruction. *Reading World, 23*, 347–363.

Huberman, M. (1987). How well does educational research really travel? *Educational Researcher, 16* (1), 5–13.

Hudson Institute (1987). *Workforce 2000.* Indianapolis, IN: Hudson Institute.

Hudson, J. A., & Fivush, R. (1991a). As time goes by: Sixth graders remember a kindergarten experience. *Applied Cognitive Psychology, 5*, 347–360.

Hudson, J. A., Fivush, R., & Kuebli, J. (1992). Scripts and episodes: The development of event memory. *Applied Cognitive Psychology, 6*, 483–505.

Hudson, J., & Nelson, K. (1983). Effects of script structure on children's story recall. *Developmental Psychology, 19*, 625–635.

Hudson, J. A., & Shapiro, L. R. (1991). From knowing to telling: The development of children's scripts, stories, and personal narratives. In A. McCabe & C. Peterson (Eds.), *Developing narrative structure* (pp. 89–136). Hillsdale, NJ: Erlbaum & Associates.

Hughes, J. N., & Hall, R. J. (Eds.) (1889). *Cognitive behavioral psychology in school.* New York: Guilford Press.

Hull, D. L. (1988). *Science as a process.* Chicago: University of Chicago Press.

Hull, G. A. (1987). The editing process in writing: A performance study of more skilled and less skilled writers. *Research in the Teaching of English, 21*, 8–29.

Hulme, C., & MacKenzie, S. (1992). *Working memory and severe learning difficulties.* Hillsdale, NJ: Erlbaum & Associates.

Humes, A. (1983). Putting writing research into practice. *Elementary School Journal, 81*, 3–17.

Hunt, E., Frost, N., & Lunneborg, C. (1973). Individual differences in cognition. In G. Bower (Ed.), *The psychology of learning and motivation: Advances in research and theory*, Vol. 7 (pp. 127–139). New York: Academic Press.

Hunt, E., Lunneborg, C., & Lewis, J. (1975). What does it mean to be high verbal? *Cognitive Psychology, 7*, 194–227.

Hunter, J. E., & Hunter, R. F. (1984). Validity and utility of alternative predictors of a job performance. *Psychological Bulletin, 96*, 72–98.

Hunter-Blanks, P., Ghatala, E. S., Pressley, M., & Levin, J. R. (1988). Comparison of monitoring during study and during testing on a sentence-learning task. *Journal of Educational Psychology, 80*, 279–283.

Husén, T. (1959). *Psychological twin research.* Stockholm: Almqvist & Wiksell.

Hutchins, E. (1991). The social organization of distributed cognition. In L. Resnick, J. M. Levine, & S. D. Teasley (Eds.), *Perspectives on socially shared cognition* (pp. 283–307). Washinton, DC: American Psychological Association.

Huttenlocher, J., Haight, W., Bryk, A., Seltzer, M., & Lyons, T. (1991). Early vocabulary growth: Relation to language input and gender. *Developmental Psychology, 27*, 236–248.

Hyde, J. S., Fennema, E., & Lamon, S. J. (1990). Gender differences in mathematics performance: A meta-analysis. *Psychological Bulletin, 107*, 139–155.

Hyde, J. S., & Jenkins, J. J. (1973). Recall for words as a function of semantic, graphic, and syntactic orienting tasks. *Journal of Verbal Learning and Verbal Behavior, 12*, 471–480.

Hyman, H., Wright, C., & Reed, J. (1975). *The enduring effects of education.* Chicago: University of Chicago Press.

Hyman, I. A. (1990). *Reading, writing, and the hickory stick: The appalling story of physical and psychological abuse in American schools.* San Diego: Lexington Books.

Hyman, I. A., & Wise, J. H. (Eds.) (1977). *Corporal punishment in American education.* Philadelphia: Temple University Press.

Hynd, C. R., & Alvermann, D. E. (1986). The role of refutation text in overcoming difficulty with science concepts. *Journal of Reading, 29*, 440–446.

Hynd, G. W., & Semrud-Clikeman, M. (1989). Dyslexia and brain morphology. *Psychological Bulletin, 106*, 447–482.

Idol, L. (1987). Group story mapping: A comprehension strategy for both skilled and unskilled readers. *Journal of Learning Disabilities, 20*, 196–205.

Idol, L., & Croll, V. J. (1987). Story-mapping training as a means of improving reading comprehension. *Learning Disability Quarterly, 10*, 214–229.

Idol, L., & Jones, B. F. (Eds.) (1990). *Educational values and cognitive reform: Implications for reform.* Hillsdale, NJ: Erlbaum & Associates.

Inagaki, K. (1981). Facilitation of knowledge integration through classroom discussion. *The Quarterly Newsletter of the Laboratory of Comparative Human Cognition, 3*, 26–28.

Inagaki, K., & Hatano, G. (1989). *Learning histories of vocal and silent participants in group discussion.* Paper presented at the annual meeting of the Japanese Psychological Association, Tsukuba Japan.

Infant Health and Development Program (1990). Enhancing the outcomes of low-birth-weight premature infants. *Journal of the American Medical Association, 263*, 3035–3042.

Inhelder, B., & Piaget, J. (1958). *The growth of logical thinking from childhood to adolescence.* New York: Basic Books.

Inhelder, B., & Piaget, J. (1964). *The early growth*

of logic in the child. New York: W.W. Norton Co.

Inhelder, B., Sinclair, H., & Bovet, M. (1974). *Learning and the development of cognition.* Cambridge, MA: Harvard University Press.

Iran-Nejad, A. (1990). Active and dynamic self-regulation of learning processes. *Review of Educational Research, 60,* 573–602.

Iser, W. (1978). *The act of reading: A theory of aesthetic response.* Baltimore: Johns Hopkins University Press.

Itakura, K. (1967). Instruction and learning of concept "force" in static based on Hypothesis-Experiment-Instruction: A new method of science teaching. *Bulletin of the National Institute for Educational Research, 52,* 1–121.

Itard, J. (1801). The wild boy of Aveyron. In L. Malson (Ed.) (E. Fawcett & J. White, translators), *Wolf children.* London: New Left Books.

Iversen, S., & Tumner, W. E. (1993). Phonological processing skills and the reading recovery program. *Journal of Educational Psychology, 85,* 112–120.

Iwasa, N. (1992). Postconventional reasoning and moral education in Japan. *Journal of Moral Education, 21,* 3–16.

Jackson, N. E., & Butterfield, E. C. (1986). A conception of giftedness designed to promote research. In R. J. Sternberg & J. E. Davidson (Eds.), *Conceptions of giftedness* (pp. 151–181). Cambridge, UK: Cambridge University Press.

Jackson, N. E., & Myers, M. G. (1982). Letter naming time, digit span, and precocious reading achievement. *Intelligence, 6,* 311–329.

Jacobsen, B., Lowery, B., & DuCette, J. (1986). Attributions of learning disabled children. *Journal of Educational Psychology, 78,* 59–64.

Jacobson, J. L., Jacobson, S. W., Padgett, R.J., Brumitt, G. A., & Billings, R. L. (1992). Effects of prenatal PCB exposure on cognitive processing efficiency and sustained attention. *Developmental Psychology, 28,* 297–306.

Jacobvitz, D., & Sroufe, L. A. (1987). The early caregiver-child relationship and attention-deficit disorder with hyperactivity in kindergarten: A prospective study. *Child Development, 58,* 1488–1495.

James, W. (1983). *The principles of psychology.* Cambridge, MA: Harvard University Press.

Jaynes, G. D., & Williams, R. M. Jr. (1989). *A common destiny: Blacks and American society.* Washinton, DC: National Academy Press.

Jenkins, J. J. (1974). Remember that old theory of memory? Well, forget it! *American Psychologists, 29,* 785–795.

Jensen, A. R. (1968). Patterns of mental ability and socioeconomic status. *Proceedings of the National Academy of Science, 60,* 1330–1337.

Jensen, A. R. (1969). How much can we boost IQ and scholastic achievement? *Harvard Educational Review, 39,* 1–123.

Jensen, A. R. (1973). *Educability and group differences.* New York: Harper & Row.

Jensen, A. R. (1976). Test bias and construct validity. *Phi Delta Kappan,* December, 340–346.

Jensen, A. R. (1980). *Bias in mental testing.* New York: Free Press.

Jensen, A. R. (1981). *Straight talk about mental tests.* New York: Free Press.

Jensen, A. R. (1982). Reaction time and psychometric g. In H. J. Eysenck (Ed.), *A model for intelligence.* Berlin: Springer-Verlag.

Jensen, A. R. (1992). Understanding g in terms of information processing. *Educational Psychology Review, 4,* 271–308.

Jensen, A. R., Schafer, E. W. P., & Crinella, F. M. (1981). Reaction time, evoked brain potentials, and psychometric g in the severely retarded. *Intelligence, 5,* 179–197.

Jernigan, T. L., Hesselink, J. R., Sowell, E., & Tallal, P. A. (1991). Cerebral structure on magnetic resonance imaging in language- and learning-impaired children. *Archives of Neurology, 48,* 539–545.

John-Steiner, V. (1985). *Notebooks of the mind: Explorations of thinking.* Albuquerque: University of New Mexico Press.

Johnson, D. K. (1988). Adolescents' solutions to dilemmas in fables: Two moral orientations—two problem-solving strategies. In C. Gilligan, J. V. Ward, & J. M. Taylor with B. Bardige (Eds.), *Mapping the moral domain: A contribution of women's thinking to psychological theory and education* (pp. 49–72). Cambridge, MA: Harvard University Press.

Johnson, D., & Johnson, R. (1974). Instructional goal structure: Cooperative versus competitive or individualistic. *Review of Educational Research, 44,* 213–240.

Johnson, D. W., & Johnson, R. (1975). *Learning together and alone: Cooperation, competition, and individualization.* Englewood Cliffs, NJ: Prentice-Hall.

Johnson, D. W., & Johnson, R. (1979). Conflict in the classroom: Controversy and learning. *Review of Educational Research, 49,* 51–70.

Johnson, D. W., & Johnson, R. (1985). Classroom conflict: Controversy over debate in learning groups. *American Educational Research Journal, 22,* 237–256.

Johnson, D., Maruyama, G., Johnson, R., Nelson, D., & Skon, L. (1981). Effects of cooperative, competitive, and individualistic goal structures on achievement: A meta-analysis. *Psychological Bulletin, 89,* 47–62.

Johnson, D., & Myklebust, H. R. (1967). *Learning disabilities: Educational principles and practice.* New York: Grune & Stratton.

Johnson, M. H. (Ed.) (1993). *Brain development and cognition.* Cambridge, MA: Blackwell.

Johnson-Laird, P. N. (1983). *Mental models.* Cambridge, MA: Harvard University Press.

Johnson-Laird, P. N. (1989). Mental models. In M. I. Posner (Ed.), *Foundations of Cognitive Science* (pp. 469–499). Cambridge, MA: MIT Press.

Jones, B. F., & Idol, L. (Ed.) (1990). *Dimensions of thinking: Review of research.* Hillsdale, NJ: Erlbaum & Associates.

Jones, L. V. (1984). White–black achievement differences: The narrowing gap. *American Psychologist, 39,* 1207–1213.

Jordan, N. C., Huttenlocher, J., & Levine, S. C. (1992). Differential calculation abilities in young children from middle- and low-income

families. *Developmental Psychology, 28,* 644–653.

Jose, P., & Brewer, W. F. (1984). The development of story liking: Character identification, suspense, and outcome resolution. *Developmental Psychology, 20,* 911–924.

Juel, C. (1988). Learning to read and write: A longitudinal study of 54 children from first through fourth grades. *Journal of Educational Psychology, 80,* 417–447.

Juel, C. (1990). Effects of reading group assignment on reading development in first and second grade. *Journal of Reading Behavior, 22,* 233–254.

Juel, C., Griffith, P. L., & Gough, P. B. (1986). Acquisition of literacy: A longitudinal study of children in first and second grade. *Journal of Educational Psychology, 78,* 243–255.

Just, M. A., & Carpenter, P. A. (1987). *The psychology of reading and language comprehension.* Needham Heights, MA: Allyn and Bacon.

Just, M. A., & Carpenter, P. A. (1992). A capacity theory of comprehension: Individual differences in working memory. *Psychological Review, 99,* 122–149.

Juvonen, J. (1988). Outcome and attributional disagreements between students and their teachers. *Journal of Educational Psychology, 80,* 330–336.

Kagen, R. M. (1977). Generalization of verbal self-instructional training in cognitively impulsive children. Doctoral dissertation, University of Texas at Austin, 1976. *Dissertation Abstracts International, 37,* 4148B.

Kamii, C. K. (1985). *Young children reinvent arithmetic.* New York: Teachers College, Columbia University.

Kandel, E. R. (1991). Brain and behavior. In E. R. Kandel, J. H. Schwartz, & T. M. Jessel (Eds.), *Principles of neural science* (pp. 5–17). New York: Elsevier.

Kanfer, F., & Zich, J. (1974). Self-control training: The effect of external control on children's resistance to temptation. *Developmental Psychology, 10,* 108–115.

Kardash, C. A. M., Royer, J. M., & Greene, B. A. (1988). Effects of schemata on both encoding and retrieval of information from prose. *Journal of Educational Psychology, 80,* 324–329.

Kasik, M. M., Sabatino, D. A., & Spoentgen, P. (1987). In S. J. Ceci (Ed.), *Handbook of cognitive, social, and neuropsychological aspects of learning disabilities,* Vol. 2 (pp. 251–272). Hillsdale, NJ: Erlbaum & Associates.

Kastner, S. B., & Rickards, C. (1974). Mediated memory with novel and familiar stimuli in good and poor readers. *Journal of Genetic Psychology, 124,* 105–113.

Katz, I. (1967). Some motivational determinants of racial differences in intellectual achievement. *International Journal of Psychology, 2,* 1–12.

Kaufman, A. S. (1990). *Assessing adolescent and adult intelligence.* Boston: Allyn & Bacon.

Kaufman, A. S., Reynolds, C. R., & McLean, J. E. (1989). Age and WAIS-R intelligence in a national sample of adults in the 20- to 74-year-old age range: A cross-sectional analysis with education level controlled. *Intelligence, 13,* 235–253.

Kausler, D. H. (1990). *Motivation, human aging, and cognitive performance* (pp. 172–182). San Diego: Academic Press.

Kausler, D. H. (1991). *Experimental psychology, cognition, and human aging.* New York: Springer-Verlag.

Kavale, K. A. (1982). Meta-analysis of the relationship between visual perceptual skills and reading achievement. *Journal of Learning Disabilities, 15,* 42–51.

Kavale, K. A., & Forness, S. R. (1992). History, definition, and diagnosis. In N. N. Singh & I. L. Beale (Eds.), *Learning disabilities: Nature, theory, and treatment* (pp. 3–43). New York: Springer-Verlag.

Kaye, D. B., deWinstanley, P., Chen, Q., & Bonnefil, V. (1989). Development of efficient arithmetic computation. *Journal of Educational Psychology, 81,* 467–480.

Keating, D. P., & Bobbitt, B. (1978). Individual and developmental differences in cognitive processing components of mental ability. *Child Development, 49,* 155–169.

Kee, D. W. (in press). Developmental differences in associative memory: Strategy use, mental effort and knowledge-access interactions. In H. W. Reese (Ed.), *Advances in child development and behavior,* Vol. 25. New York: Academic Press.

Kee, D. W., Gottfried, A. W., Bathurst, K., & Brown, K. (1987). Left-hemisphere language specialization. Consistency in hand preference and sex differences. *Child Development, 58,* 718–724.

Keeney, F. J., Cannizzo, S. R., & Flavell, J. H. (1967). Spontaneous and induced verbal rehearsal in a recall task. *Child Development, 38,* 953–966.

Keller, C. E., & Lloyd, J. W. (1989). Cognitive training: Implications for written language. In J. N. Hughes & R. J. Hall (Eds.), *Cognitive-behavioral psychology in the schools* (pp. 280–304). New York: Guilford Press.

Keller, C. E., & Sutton, J. P. (1991). Specific mathematics disorders. In J. E. Obrzut & G. W. Hynd (Eds.), *Neuropsychological foundations of learning disabilities* (pp. 549–571). San Diego: Academic Press.

Keller, F. S. (1968). "Good-bye teacher . . . " *Journal of Applied Behavior Analysis, 1,* 79–89.

Kendall, P. C. (1990). Challenges for cognitive strategy training. *American Journal of Mental Deficiency, 94,* 365–367.

Kendall, P. C., & Braswell, L. (1985). *Cognitive-behavioral therapy for impulsive children.* New York: Guilford.

Kennedy, B. A., & Miller, D. J. (1976). Persistent use of verbal rehearsal as a function of information about its value. *Child Development, 47,* 566–569.

Kersh, B. Y. (1958). The adequacy of "meaning" as an explanation of superiority of learning by independent discovery. *Journal of Educational Psychology, 49,* 282–292.

Kerwin, M. L. E., & Day, J. D. (1985). Peer influ-

ences on cognitive development. In J. B. Pryor & J. D. Day (Eds.), *The development of social cognition* (pp. 211–228). New York: Springer-Verlag.

Ketcham, R., & Snyder, R. T. (1977). Self-attitudes of the intellectually and socially advantaged student: Normative study of the Piers-Harris' children's self-concept scale. *Psychological Reports, 40,* 111–116.

Kiernan, C. (1985). Behaviour modification. In A. M. Clarke, A. D. B. Clarke, & J. M. Berg (Eds.), *Mental deficiency: The changing outlook* (pp. 465–511). New York: Free Press.

Kiewra, K. A. (1985). Investigating notetaking and review: A depth of processing alternative. *Educational Psychologist, 20,* 23–32.

Kiewra, K. A. (1989a). A review of note-taking: The encoding-storage paradigm and beyond. *Educational Psychology Review, 1,* 147–172.

Kiewra, K. A. (1989b). Cognitive aspects of autonomous note taking: Control processes, learning strategies, and prior knowledge. *Educational Psychologist, 23,* 39–56.

Kiewra, K. A., DuBois, N. F., Christian, D., & McShane, A. (1988). Providing study notes: Comparison of three types of notes for review. *Journal of Educational Psychology, 80,* 595–597.

Kiewra, K. A., & Fletcher, H. J. (1984). The relationship between notetaking variables and achievement measures. *Human Learning, 3,* 273–280.

Kimball, M. M. (1989). A new perspective on women's math achievement. *Psychological Bulletin, 105,* 198–214.

Kimura, D. (1987). Are men's and women's brains really different? *Canadian Psychology, 28,* 133–147.

King, A. (1989). Effects of self-questioning training on college students' comprehension of lectures. *Contemporary Educational Psychology, 14,* 366–381.

King, A. (1990). Enhancing peer interaction and learning in the classroom through reciprocal questioning. *American Educational Research Journal, 27,* 664–687.

King, A. (1991). Effects of training in strategic questioning on children's problem-solving performance. *Journal of Educational Psychology, 83,* 307–317.

King, A. (1992). Comparison of self-questioning, summarizing, and notetaking-review as strategies for learning from lectures. *American Educational Research Journal, 29,* 303–323.

King, E. M., & Friesen, D. T. (1972). Children who read in kindergarten. *Alberta Journal of Educational Research, 18,* 147–161.

King-Sears, M. E., Richardson, M., & Ray, R. M. (1992). Generalizing curriculum-based measurement from university coursework to school-based practice: Train and hope? *LD Forum, 17* (3), 25–28.

Kintsch, W. (1974). *The representation of meaning in memory.* Hillsdale, NJ: Erlbaum & Associates.

Kintsch, W. (1980). Semantic memory: A tutorial. In R. S. Nickerson (Ed.), *Attention and performance 8.* Hillsdale, NJ: Erlbaum & Associates.

Kintsch, W. (1982). Text representations. In W. Otto & S. White (Eds.), *Reading expository material* (pp. 87–102). New York: Academic Press.

Kintsch, W. (1983). Memory for text. In A. Flammer & W. Kintsch (Eds.), *Discourse processing* (pp. 186–204). Amsterdam: North-Holland.

Kintsch, W. (1988). The role of knowledge in discourse comprehension: A construction-integration model. *Psychological Review, 95,* 163–182.

Kintsch, W., & Greene, E. (1978). The role of culture-specific schemata in the comprehension and recall of stories. *Discourse Processes, 1,* 1–13.

Kintsch, W., & Keenan, J. M. (1973). Reading rate and retention as a function of the number of propositions in the base structure of sentences. *Cognitive Psychology, 5,* 257–279.

Kintsch, W., Kozminsky, E., Streby, W. J., McKoon, G., & Keenan, J. M. (1975). Comprehension and recall as a function of content variables. *Journal of Verbal Learning and Verbal Behavior, 14,* 196–214.

Kintsch, W., Mandel, T. S., & Kozminsky, E. (1977). Summarizing scrambled stories. *Memory and Cognition, 5,* 547–552.

Kintsch, W., & van Dijk, T. A. (1978). Toward a model of discourse comprehension and production. *Psychological Review, 85,* 363–394.

Kintsch, W., & Yarbrough, C. J. (1982). Role of rhetorical structure in text comprehension. *Journal of Educational Psychology, 74,* 828–834.

Kirsch, I. S., & Jungeblut, A. (1986). *Literacy: Profile of America's young adults.* Princeton, NJ: Educational Testing Service.

Kistner, J. A., Osborne, M., & LeVerrier, L. (1988). Causal attributions of learning-disabled children: Developmental patterns and relation to academic progress. *Journal of Educational Psychology, 80,* 82–89.

Klausmeier, H. J. (1990). Conceptualizing. In B. F. Jones & L. Idol (Eds.), *Dimensions of thinking and cognitive instruction* (pp. 93–138). Hillsdale, NJ: Lawrence Erlbaum Associates.

Klibanoff, L. S., & Haggart, S. A. (1981). *Report No. 8: Summer growth and the effectiveness of summer school.* Technical Report prepared for the Office of Program Evaluation, U.S. Department of Education, Mountain View, CA: RMC Research Corporation.

Kliegl, R., Smith, J., & Baltes, P. B. (1989). Testing-the-limits and the study of adult age differences in cognitive plasticity of a mnemonic skill. *Developmental Psychology, 25,* 247–256.

Kliegl, R., Smith, J., & Baltes, P. B. (1990). On the locus and process of magnification of age differences during mnemonic training. *Developmental Psychology, 26,* 894–904.

Kloosterman, P. (1988). Self-confidence and motivation in mathematics. *Journal of Educational Psychology, 80,* 345–351.

Kloster, A. M., & Winne, P. H. (1989). The effects of different types of organizers on students' learning from text. *Journal of Educational Psychology, 81,* 9–15.

Knapczyk, D. R. (1989). Generalization of student question asking from special class to regular class settings. *Journal of Applied Behavior Analysis, 22,* 77–83.

Knight, P. (1992). How I use portfolios in mathematics. *Educational Leadership, 49* (8), 71–72.

Knopf, M., & Neidhardt, E. (1989). Aging and memory for action events: The role of familiarity. *Developmental Psychology, 25,* 780–786.

Kohlberg, L. (1969). Stage and sequence: The cognitive-developmental approach to socialization. In D. Goslin (Ed.), *Handbook of socialization theory and research.* New York: Rand McNally.

Kohlberg, L. (1981). *The philosophy of moral development: Moral stages and the idea of justice: Essays on moral development, 1.* San Francisco: Harper & Row.

Kohlberg, L. (1984). *The psychology of moral development: Essays on moral development, 2.* San Francisco: Harper & Row.

Kohlberg, L., Levine, C., & Hewer, A. (1983). Moral stages: A current formulation and a response to critics. *Contributions to Human Development, 10.* Basel: S. Karger.

Kolhberg, L., Scharf, P., & Hickey, J. (1972). The justice structure of the prison: A theory and intervention. *Prison Journal, 51,* 3–14.

Kohlberg, L., Yaeger, J., & Hjertholm, E. (1968). Private speech: Four studies and a review of theories. *Child Development, 39,* 691–736.

Kohs, S. C. (1923). *Intelligence measurement.* New York: MacMillan.

Kolers, P. A. (1975). Specificity of operations in sentence recognition. *Cognitive Psychology, 7,* 289–306.

Komarovsky, M. (1985). *Women in college: Shaping new feminine identities.* New York: Basic Books.

Konner, M. (1991). Universals of behavioral development in relation to brain myelination. In K. R. Gibson & A. C. Petersen (Eds.), *Brain maturation and cognitive development: Comparative and cross-cultural perspectives* (pp. 181–223). New York: Aldine de Gruyter.

Körkel, J. (1987). *Die Entwicklung von Gedächtnis und Metagedächtnisleistung in Abhängigkeit von bereichsspezifischen Vorkenntnissen.* Frankfurt/Main: Lang.

Kornhaber, M., Krechevsky, M., & Gardner, H. (1990). Engaging intelligence. *Educational Psychologist, 25,* 177–199.

Kos, R. (1991). Persistence of reading disabilities: The voices of four middle school students. *American Educational Research Journal, 28,* 875–895.

Koshmider, J. W., & Ashcraft, M. H. (1991). The development of children's mental multiplication skills. *Journal of Experimental Child Psychology, 51,* 53–89.

Kosslyn, S. M. (1975). Information representation in visual images. *Cognitive Psychology, 7,* 341–370.

Kosslyn, S. M. (1976). Can imagery be distinguished from other forms of internal representation? Evidence from studies of information retrieval times. *Memory and Cognition, 4,* 291–297.

Kosslyn, S. M., & Koenig, O. (1992). *Wet mind: The new cognitive neuroscience.* New York: Free Press.

Kovacs, M., Goldston, D., & Ivengar, S. (1992). Intellectual development and academic performance of children with insulin-dependent diabetes mellitus: A longitudinal study. *Developmental Psychology, 28,* 676–684.

Kozma, R. B. (1991). Learning with media. *Review of Educational Research, 61,* 179–212.

Kozol, J. (1991). *Savage inequalities: Children in America's schools.* New York: Crown.

Krajcik, J. S. (1991). Developing students' understanding of chemical concepts. In S. M. Glynn, R. H. Yeany, & B. K. Britton (Eds.), *The psychology of learning science* (pp. 117–147). Hillsdale, NJ: Erlbaum & Associates.

Krajcik, J. S., & Peters, H. (1989). *Molecular velocities* [microcomputer program]. Oakdale, IA: Conduit, University of Iowa.

Kreitler, S., & Kreitler, H. (1990). Cognitive antecedents of imitativeness and persistence in children with mental retardation. *American Journal of Mental Deficiency, 94,* 342–343.

Krug, D., Davis, T. B., & Glover, J. A. (1990). Massed versus distributed repeated reading: A case of forgetting helping recall? *Journal of Educational Psychology, 82,* 366–371.

Kruglanski, A. W., Friedman, I., & Zeevi, G. (1971). The effects of extrinsic incentives on some qualitative aspects of task performance. *Journal of Personality, 39,* 606–617.

Kuder, G. F., & Richardson, M. W. (1937). The theory of estimation of test reliability. *Psychometrica, 2,* 151–160.

Kuhara-Kojima, K., & Hatano, G. (1991). Contribution of content knowledge and learning ability to the learning of facts. *Journal of Educational Psychology, 83,* 253–263.

Kuhl, J. (1985). Volitional mediators of cognition-behavior consistency: Self-regulatory processes and action versus state orientation. In J. Kuhl & J. Beckmann (Eds.), *Action control: From cognition to behavior.* West Berlin: Springer-Verlag.

Kuhn, D. (1989). Children and adults as intuitive scientists. *Psychological Review, 96,* 674–689.

Kuhn, D., Amsel, E., & O'Loughlin, M. (1988). *The development of scientific thinking skills.* San Diego: Academic Press.

Kuhn, D., Kohlberg, L., Langer, J., & Haan, N. (1977). The development of formal operations in logical and moral judgment. *Genetic Psychology Monographs, 95,* 97–188.

Kuhn, D., & Phelps, E. (1982). The development of problem-solving strategies. In H. Reese (Ed.), *Advances in child development and behavior,* Vol. 17 (pp. 1–44). New York: Academic Press.

Kulik, C-L. C., Kulik, J. A., & Bangert-Drowns, R. L. (1990). Effectiveness of mastery learning programs: A meta-analysis. *Review of Educational Research, 60,* 265–299.

Kulik, J. A., & Kulik, C-L. C. (1988). Timing of feedback and verbal learning. *Review of Educational Research, 58,* 79–97.

Kurtines, W., & Grief, E. B. (1974). The development of moral thought: Review and evaluation of Kohlberg's approach. *Psychological Bulletin, 81,* 453–470.

Kurtz, B. E. (1990). Cultural influences on children's cognitive and metacognitive development. In W. Schneider & F. E. Weinert (Eds.), *Interactions among aptitudes, strategies, and knowledge in cognitive performance* (pp. 177–199). New York: Springer-Verlag.

Kutnick, P. (1988). "I'll teach you!" Primary school teachers' attitudes to and use of moral education in the curriculum. *Journal of Moral Education, 17,* 40–51.

Kutnick, P. (1990). A survey of primary school teachers' understanding and implementation of moral education in Trinidad and Tobago. *Journal of Moral Education, 19,* 48–57.

LaBerge, D., & Samuels, S. J. (1974). Toward a theory of automatic information processing in reading. *Cognitive Psychology, 6,* 293–323.

Labouvie-Vief, G. (1985). Intelligence and cognition. In J. E. Birren & K. W. Schaie (Eds.). *Handbook of the psychology of aging,* 2nd ed. (pp. 500–530). New York: Van Nostrand Reinhold.

Ladas, H. S. (1980). Note taking on lectures: An information-processing approach. *Educational Psychologist, 15,* 44–53.

Laffal, J. (1965). *Pathological and normal language.* New York: Atherton Press.

Lam, T. C. M. (1992). Review of practices and problems in the evaluation of bilingual education. *Review of Educational Research, 62,* 181–204.

Lambiotte, J. G., Dansereau, D. F., Cross, D. R., & Reynolds, S. B. (1989). Multirelational semantic maps. *Educational Psychology Review, 1,* 331–367.

Lampert, M. (1990). When the problem is not the question and the solution is not the answer: Mathematical knowing and teaching. *American Educational Research Journal, 27,* 29–64.

Lange, G. (1973). The development of conceptual and rote recall skills among school age children. *Journal of Experimental Child Psychology, 15,* 394–406.

Lange, G. (1978). Organization-related processes in children's recall. In P. A. Ornstein (Ed.), *Memory development in children* (pp. 101–128). Hillsdale, NJ: Erlbaum & Associates.

Langer, E. J. (1989). *Mindfulness.* Reading, MA: Addison-Wesley.

Langer, J. A. (1986). *Children reading and writing: Structures and strategies.* Norwood, NJ: Ablex.

Langer, J. A. (1990). The process of understanding: Reasons for literary and instructional purposes. *Research in Teaching of English, 24,* 229–258.

Langer, J. A., & Applebee, A. N. (1984). Language, learning, and interaction: A framework for improving the teaching of writing. In A. N. Applebee (Ed.), *Contexts for learning to write: Studies of secondary school instruction* (pp. 169–181). Norwood, NJ: Ablex.

Langer, J. A., & Applebee, A. (1987). *How writing shapes thinking: A study of teaching and learning.* Champaign, IL: National Council of Teachers of English.

Langer, J. A., Bartolome, L., Vasquez, O., & Lucas, T. (1990). Meaning construction in school literacy tasks: A study of bilingual students. *American Educational Research Journal, 27,* 427–471.

Laosa, L. M. (1978). Maternal teaching strategies in Chicano families of varied educational and socioeconomic levels. *Child Development, 49,* 1129–1135.

Laosa, L. M. (1980). Maternal teaching strategies in Chicano and Angle-American families: The influence of culture and education on maternal behavior. *Child Development, 51,* 759–765.

Laosa, L. M. (1982). School, occupation, culture, and family: The impact of parental schooling on the parent-child relationship. *Journal of Educational Psychology, 74,* 791–827.

Larry P. v. Riles 343 F. Supp. 1306 (N. D. Cal. 1979), aff'd 502 F. 2d (9th Cir. 1974); 495 F. Supp. 926 (N. D. Cal. 1979), aff'd. in part and rev'd in part, 793 F. 2d 969 (9th Cir. 1984).

Larsen, J. P., Hoien, T., Lundberg, I., & Ødegaard, S. (1990). MRI evaluation of the size and symmetry of the planum temporale in adolescents with developmental dyslexia. *Brain and Language, 39,* 289–301.

Larson, K. A., & Gerber, M. M. (1992). Metacognition. In N. N. Singh & I. L. Beale (Eds.), *Learning disabilities: Nature, theory, and treatment* (pp. 126–169). New York: Springer-Verlag.

Lasch, C. (1979). *The culture of narcissism: American life in an age of diminishing expectations.* New York: Norton.

Lasky, R. E. (1974). The ability of six-year-olds, eight-year-olds, and adults to abstract visual patterns. *Child Development, 45,* 626–632.

Lau v. Nichols (1974). 414 U. S. 563.

Laughon, P. (1990). The dynamic assessment of intelligence: A review of three approaches. *School Psychology Review, 19,* 459–470.

Lave, J., & Wenger, E. (1991). *Situated learning: Legitimate peripheral participation.* Cambridge: Cambridge University Press.

LaVoie, J. C. (1973). Punishment and adolescent self-control. *Developmental Psychology, 8,* 16–24.

LaVoie, J. C. (1974). Cognitive determinants of resistance to deviation in seven-, nine-, and eleven-year-old children of low and high maturity of moral judgment. *Developmental Psychology, 10,* 393–403.

Lawrence, J. A., & Helm, A. (1987). Consistencies and inconsistencies in nurses' ethical reasoning. *Journal of Moral Education, 16,* 167–176.

Lawson, A. E. (1983). Predicting science achievement: The role of developmental level, disembedding ability, mental capacity, prior knowledge, and beliefs. *Journal of Research in Science Teaching, 20,* 117–129.

Lawson, A. E., & Renner, J. W. (1975). Piagetian theory and biology teaching. *American Biology Teacher, 37,* 336–343.

Lawson, A. E., & Snitgen, D. A. (1982). Teaching formal reasoning in a college biology course for preservice teachers. *Journal of Research in Science Teaching, 19,* 233–248.

Lawson, A. E., & Thompson, L. D. (1988). Formal reasoning ability and misconceptions concerning genetics and natural selection. *Journal of Research in Science Teaching, 25,* 733–746.

Lawson, A. E., & Wollman, W. T. (1976). Encouraging the transition from concrete to formal cognitive functioning: An experiment. *Journal of Research in Science Teaching, 13,* 413–430.

Lawson, M. J. (1990). The case for instruction in the use of general problem-solving strategies in mathematics teaching: A comment on Owen and Sweller. *Journal for Research in Mathematics Education, 21,* 403–415.

Lawson, M. J., & Fuelop, S. (1980). Understanding the purpose of strategy training. *British Journal of Educational Psychology, 50,* 175–180.

Lazar, I., Darlington, R., Murray, H., Royce, J., & Sipper, A. (1982). Lasting effects of early childhood education: A report from the consortium for longitudinal studies. *Monographs of the Society for Research in Child Development, 47* (2–3, Whole No. 195).

Leal, L. (1987). Investigation of the relation between metamemory and university students' examination performance. *Journal of Educational Psychology, 79,* 35–40.

Lee, T. D., & Genovese, E. D. (1988). Distribution of practice in motor skill acquisition: Learning and performance effects reconsidered. *Research Quarterly for Exercise and Sport, 59,* 277–287.

Lee, V. E., & Bryk, A. S. (1986). Effects of single-sex secondary schools on student achievement and attitudes. *Journal of Educational Psychology, 78,* 381–395.

Lee, V. E., & Bryk, A. S. (1989). Effects of single-sex schools: Response to Marsh. *Journal of Educational Psychology, 81,* 647–650.

LeFevre, J., & Dixon, P. (1986). Do written instructions need examples? *Cognition and Instruction, 3,* 1–30.

LeFevre, J-A., Kulak, A. G., & Bisanz, J. (1991). Individual differences and developmental change in the associative relations among numbers. *Journal of Experimental Child Psychology, 52,* 256–274.

Lehman, D. R., & Nisbett, R. E. (1990). A longitudinal study of the effects of undergraduate training on reasoning. *Developmental Psychology, 26,* 952–960.

Lehman, J. D., Carter, C., & Kahle, J. B. (1985). Concept mapping, Vee mapping and achievement: Results of a field study with black high school students. *Journal of Research in Science Teaching, 27,* 663–674.

Lehr, S. (1988). The child's developing sense of theme as a response to literature. *Reading Research Quarterly, 23,* 337–357.

Lehrer, R. (1989). Computer-assisted strategic instruction. In C. B. McCormick, G. Miller, & M. Pressley (Eds.), *Cognitive strategy research: From basic research to educational applications* (pp. 303–320). New York: Springer-Verlag.

Lehrer, R., Guckenberg, T., & Lee, O. (1988). Comparative study of the cognitive consequences of inquiry-based Logo instruction. *Journal of Educational Psychology, 80,* 543–553.

Lehrer, R., & Littlefield, J. (1991). Misconceptions and errors in LOGO: The role of instruction. *Journal of Educational Psychology, 83,* 124–133.

Lehrer, R., Randle, L., & Sancilio, L. (1989). Learning preproof geometry with LOGO. *Cognition and Instruction, 6,* 159–184.

Leichter, H. P. (1984). Families as environments for literacy. In H. Goelman, A. Oberg, & F. Smith (Eds.), *Awakening to literacy.* Exeter, NH: Heinemann.

Leinhardt, G., & Greeno, J. G. (1986). The cognitive skill of teaching. *Journal of Educational Psychology, 78,* 75–95.

Leonard, L. H. (1989). A comparison of student reactions to biology instruction by interactive videodisc or conventional laboratory. *Journal of Research in Science Teaching, 26,* 95–104.

Leonard, W. H. (1992). A comparison of student performance following instruction by interactive videodisc versus conventional laboratory. *Journal of Research in Science Teaching, 29,* 93–102.

Lepper, M. R. (1983). Extrinsic reward and intrinsic motivation: Implications for the classroom. In J. M. Levine & M. C. Wang (Eds.), *Teacher and student perceptions: Implications for learning.* Hillsdale, NJ: Erlbaum & Associates.

Lepper, M. R., Aspinwall, L. G., Mumme, D. L., & Chabey, R. W. (1990). Self-perception and social-perception processes in tutoring: Subtle social control strategies of expert tutors. In J. M. Olson & M. P. Zanna (Eds.), *Self-inference processes: The Ontario symposium* (pp. 217–237). Hillsdale, NJ: Erlbaum & Associates.

Lepper, M. R., Greene, D., & Nisbett, R. E. (1973). Undermining children's intrinsic interest with extrinsic rewards: A test of the "overjustification" hypothesis. *Journal of Personality and Social Psychology, 28,* 129–137.

Lepper, M. R., & Hodell, M. (1989). Intrinsic motivation in the classroom. In C. Ames & R. Ames (Eds.), *Research on motivation in education,* Vol. 3, *Goals and cognitions* (pp. 73–105). San Diego: Academic Press.

Lepper, M. R., & Malone, T. W. (1987). Intrinsic motivation and instructional effectiveness in computer-based education. In R. E. Snow & M. J. Farr (Eds.), *Aptitude, learning, and instruction,* Vol. 3, *Conative and affective process analyses* (pp. 255–286). Hillsdale, NJ: Erlbaum & Associates.

Lerner, R. M. (1986). *The nature of human plasticity.* New York: Cambridge University Press.

Lerner, R. M. (1990). Plasticity, person-context relations, and cognitive training in the aged years: A developmental contextual perspective. *Developmental Psychology, 26,* 911–915.

Lerner, R. M., & Busch-Rossnagel, N. (Eds.) (1981). *Individuals as producers of their own development: A life-span perspective.* New York: Academic Press.

Lesgold, A. M. (1972). Pronominalizations: A device for unifying sentences in memory. *Journal of Verbal Learning and Verbal Behavior, 11,* 316–323.

Lesgold, A., Glaser, R., Rubinson, H., Klopfer, D., Feltovich, P., & Wang, Y. (1988). Expertise in a complex skill: Diagnosing x-ray pictures. In M. T. H. Chi, R. Glaser, & M. J. Farr (Eds.),

The nature of expertise (pp. 311–342). Hillsdale, NJ: Erlbaum & Associates.

Lester, B. M., Corwin, M. J., Sepkoski, C., Seifer, R., Peucker, M., McLaughlin, S., & Golub, H. L. (1991). Neurobehavioral syndromes in cocaine-exposed newborn infants. *Child Development, 62,* 694–705.

Lester, B. M., & Dreher, M. (1989). Effects of marijuana use during pregnancy on newborn cry. *Child Development, 60,* 765–771.

Levin, J. R. (1982). Pictures as prose-learning devices. In A. Flammer & W. Kintsch (Eds.), *Discourse processing* (pp. 412–444). Amsterdam: North-Holland.

Levin, J. R. (1983). Pictorial strategies for school learning: Practical illustrations. In M. Pressley & J. R. Levin (Eds.), *Cognitive strategy research: Educational applications* (pp. 213–237). New York: Springer-Verlag.

Levin, J. R. (1985). Educational applications of mnemonic pictures: Possibilities beyond your wildest imagination. In A. A. Sheikh (Ed.), *Imagery in education: Imagery in the educational process* (pp. 63–87). Farmingdale, NY: Baywood.

Levin, J. R. (1986). Four cognitive principles of learning strategy research. *Educational Psychologist, 21,* 3–17.

Levin, J. R., & Lesgold, A. M. (1978). On pictures in prose. *Educational Communication and Technology, 26,* 233–243.

Levin, J. R., McCabe, A. E., & Bender, B. G. (1975). A note on imagery-inducing motor activity in young children. *Child Development, 46,* 263–266.

Levin, J. R., & Pressley, M. (1981). Improving children's prose comprehension: Selected strategies that seem to succeed. In C. M. Santa & B. L. Hayes (Eds.), *Children's prose comprehension* (pp. 44–71). Newark, DE: International Reading Association.

Levin, J. R., Yussen, S. R., DeRose, T. M., & Pressley, M. (1977). Developmental changes in assessing recall and recognition memory. *Developmental Psychology, 13,* 608–615.

Levin, M. E., & Levin, J. R. (1990). Scientific mnemonies: Methods for maximizing more than memory. *American Educational Research Journal, 27,* 301–321.

Levine, J. M. (1983). Social comparison and education. In J. M. Levine & M. C. Wang (Eds.), *Teacher and student perceptions: Implications for learning* (pp. 29–55). Hillsdale, NJ: Erlbaum & Associates.

Levine, J. M., & Moreland, R. L. (1991). Culture and socialization in work groups. In L. Resnick, J. M. Levine, & S. D. Teasley (Eds.), *Perspectives on socially shared cognition* (pp. 257–279). Washington, DC: American Psychological Association.

Levine, S. C., Jordan, N. C., & Huttenlocher, J. (1992). Development of calculation abilities in young children. *Journal of Experimental Child Psychology, 53,* 72–103.

Levinson, D. F., Darrow, C. N., Klien, E. B., Levinson, M. H., & McKee, B. (1978). *The seasons of a man's life.* New York: Ballantine Books.

Levy, J. (1976). Cerebral lateralization and spatial ability. *Behavior Genetics, 6,* 171–188.

Lewis, A. B. (1989). Training students to represent arithmetic word problems. *Journal of Educational Psychology, 81,* 521–531.

Lewis, A. B., & Mayer, R. E. (1987). Students' miscomprehension of relational statements in arithmetic word problems. *Journal of Educational Psychology, 79,* 363–371.

Lewontin, R. C., Rose, S., & Kamin, L. J. (1984). *Not in our genes: Biology, ideology, and human nature.* New York: Pantheon Books.

Lezotte, L. (1986). *Reflections and future directions.* Paper presented at the Annual Meeting of the American Educational Research Association, San Francisco.

Lhyle, K. G., & Kulhavy, R. W. (1987). Feedback processing and error correction. *Journal of Educational Psychology, 79,* 320–322.

Liberman, I. Y., & Liberman, A. M. (1990). Whole language versus code emphasis: Underlying assumptions and their implications for reading instruction. *Annals of Dyslexia, 40,* 51–76.

Licht, B. (1983). Cognitive-motivational factors that contribute to the achievement of learning-disabled children. *Journal of Learning Disabilities, 16,* 483–490.

Licht, B. (1992). Achievement-related beliefs in children with learning disabilities. In L. J. Meltzer (Ed.), *Strategy assessment and instruction for students with learning disabilities: From theory to practice* (pp. 195–220). Austin, TX: PRO-ED.

Licht, B. G., & Dweck, C. S. (1984). Determinants of academic achievement: The interaction of children's achievement orientation with skill area. *Developmental Psychology, 20,* 628–636.

Licht, B. G., Kistner, J. A., Ozkaragoz, T., Shapiro, S., & Clausen, L. (1985). Causal attributions of learning disabled children: Individual differences and their implications for persistence. *Journal of Educational Psychology, 77,* 208–216.

Lickona, T. (Ed.) (1976). *Moral development and behavior.* New York: Holt, Rinehart, & Winston.

Lickona, T. (1991). *Educating for character: How our schools can teach respect and responsibility.* New York: Bantam Books.

Lie, A. (1991). Effects of a training program for stimulating skills in word analysis in first-grade children. *Reading Research Quarterly, 26,* 234–250.

Light, L. L. (1992). The organization of memory in old age. In F. I. M. Craik & T. A. Salthouse (Eds.), *The handbook of aging and cognition* (pp. 111–165). Hillsdale, NJ: Erlbaum & Associates.

Lincoln, Y. S., & Guba, E. G. (1985). *Naturalistic inquiry.* Newbury Park, CA: Sage.

Lindow, J., Marrett, C. B., & Wilkinson, L. C. (1985). Overview. In L. C. Wilkinson & C. B. Marrett (Eds.), *Gender influences on classroom interaction* (pp. 1–15). Orlando, FL: Academic Press.

Linn, M. C., Clement, C., Pulos, S., & Sullivan, P. (1989). Scientific reasoning during adolescence: The influence of instruction in science

knowledge and reasoning strategies. *Journal of Research in Science Teaching, 26,* 171–187.

Linn, M. C., & Songer, N. B. (1991). Teaching thermodynamics to middle school students: What are appropriate cognitive demands? *Journal of Research in Science Teaching, 28,* 885–918.

Lipman, M. (1974). *Harry Stottlemeier's Discovery.* Upper Montclair, NJ: International Association of Philosophy for Children.

Lipman, M. (1985). Thinking skills fostered by philosophy for children. In J. W. Segal, S. F. Chipman, & R. Glaser (Eds.), *Thinking and learning skills,* Vol. 1, *Relating instruction to research* (pp. 83–108). Hillsdale, NJ: Erlbaum & Associates.

Lipman, M. (1991). *Thinking in education.* Cambridge, UK: Cambridge University Press.

Lipman, M., Sharp, A. M., & Oscanyan, F. S. (1980). *Philosophy in the classroom.* Philadelphia: Temple University Press.

Lipsitt, L. P. (1990). Learning processes in the human newborn: Sensitization, habituation, and classical condition. In A. Diamond (Ed.), *The development and neural bases of higher cognitive functions* (pp. 113–127). New York: New York Academy of Sciences.

Locurto, C. (1990). The malleability of IQ as judged from adoption studies. *Intelligence, 14,* 275–292.

Loehlin, J. C., Horn, J. M., & Willerman, L. (1989). Modeling IQ change: Evidence from the Texas adoption project. *Child Development, 60,* 993–1004.

Loehlin, J. C., & Nichols, R. C. (1976). *Heredity, environment, and personality.* Austin: University of Texas Press.

Loman, N. L., & Mayer, R. E. (1983). Signaling techniques that increase the understandability of expository prose. *Journal of Educational Psychology, 75,* 402–412.

Lonky, E., Roodin, P. A., & Rybash, J. M. (1988). Moral judgment and sex role orientation as a function of self and other presentation mode. *Journal of Youth and Adolescence, 17,* 189–195.

Lorch, R. F. Jr. (1989). Text-signaling devices and their effects on reading and memory processes. *Educational Psychology Review, 1,* 209–234.

Lorch, R. F. Jr., Lorch, E. P., & Inman, W. E. (1993). Effects of signaling topic structure on text recall. *Journal of Educational Psychology, 85,* 281–290.

Lord, C. G., Umezaki, K., & Darley, J. M. (1990). Developmental differences in decoding the meanings of the appraisal actions of teachers. *Child Development, 61,* 191–200.

Lou, H. C., Henriksen, L., & Bruhn, P. (1984). Focal cerebral hypoperfusion in children with dysphasia and/or attention deficit disorder. *Archives of Neurology, 41,* 825–829.

Lovaas, O. I., Schaeffer, B., & Simmons, J. Q. (1965). Building social behavior in autistic children by use of electric shock. *Journal of Experimental Research in Personality, 1,* 99–109.

Loveland, K. K., & Olley, J. G. (1979). The effect of external reward on interest and quality of task performance in children of high and low intrinsic motivation. *Child Development, 50,* 1207–1210.

Ludeke, R. J., & Hartup, W. W. (1983). Teaching behaviors of 9- and 11-year-old girls in mixed-age and same-age dyads. *Journal of Educational Psychology, 75,* 909–914.

Luhmer, K. (1990). Moral education in Japan. *Journal of Moral Education, 19,* 172–181.

Lundberg, I. (1991). Phonemic awareness can be developed without reading instruction. In S. A. Brady & D. P. Shankweiler (Eds.), *Phonological processes in literacy: A tribute to Isabelle Y. Liberman* (pp. 47–53). Hillsdale, NJ: Erlbaum & Associates.

Lundberg, I., Frost, J., & Peterson, O. (1988). Effects of an extensive program for stimulating phonological awareness in preschool children. *Reading Research Quarterly, 23,* 263–284.

Lundeberg, M. A. (1987). Metacognitive aspects of reading comprehension: Studying understanding in legal case analysis. *Reading Research Quarterly, 22,* 407–432.

Lundeberg, M. A., & Fox, P. W. (1991). Do laboratory findings on test expectancy generalize to classroom outcomes? *Review of Educational Research, 61,* 94–106.

Luria, A. R. (1961). An objective approach to the study of the abnormal child. *American Journal of Orthopsychiatry, 31,* 1–14.

Luria, A. R. (1966). *Higher cortical functions in man.* New York: Basic.

Luria, A. R. (1973). *The working brain.* New York: Basic.

Luria, A. R. (1982). *Language and cognition.* New York: Wiley.

Luther, M., & Wyatt, F. (1989). A comparison of Feuerstein's method of LPAD assessment with conventional IQ testing on disadvantaged North African high school students. *International Journal of Dynamic Assessment and Instruction, 1,* 49–64.

Lyman, F. Jr. (1992). Think-pair-share, thinktrix, thinklinks, and weird facts: An interactive system for cooperative learning. In N. Davidson & T. Worsham, *Enhancing thinking through cooperative learning* (pp. 169–181). New York: Teachers College Press, Columbia University.

Lyon, G. R., Newby, R. E, Recht, D., & Caldwell, J. (1991). Neuropsychology and learning disabilities. In B. Y. L. Wong (Ed.), *Learning about learning disabilities* (pp. 376–406). San Diego: Academic Press.

Lyons, N. P. (1988). Two perspectives: On self, relationships, and morality. In C. Gilligan, J. V. Ward, & J. M. Taylor with B. Bardige (Eds.), *Mapping the moral domain: A contribution of women's thinking to psychological theory and education* (pp. 21–48). Cambridge, MA: Harvard University Press.

Macario, J. F., Shipley, E. F., & Billman, D. O. (1990). Induction from a single instance: Formation of a novel category. *Journal of Experimental Child Psychology, 50,* 179–199.

MacArthur, C., & Graham, S. (1987). Learning disabled students' composing with three methods: Handwriting, dictation, and word processing. *Journal of Special Education, 21,* 22–42.

MacArthur, C., Graham, S., & Schwartz, S. (1991). Knowledge of revision and rising behavior among learning disabled students. *Learning Disability Quarterly, 14,* 61–73.

MacArthur, C. Schwartz, S., & Graham, S. (1991). Effects of a reciprocal peer revision strategy in special education classrooms. *Learning Disabilities Research and Practice, 6,* 201–210.

MacKay, D. G. (1981). The problem of rehearsal or mental practice. *Journal of Motor Behavior, 13,* 274–285.

MacKay, D. G. (1982). The problem of flexibility, fluency, and speed-accuracy trade-off in skilled behavior. *Psychological Review, 89,* 483–506.

MacKinnon, D. W. (1978). *In search of human effectiveness.* Buffalo: Creative Education Foundation.

MacMillan, D. L., & Knopf, E. D. (1971). Effects of instructional set on perceptions of event outcomes by EMR and nonretarded children. *American Journal of Mental Deficiency, 76,* 185–189.

Madden, N. A., Slavin, R. E., Karweit, N. L., Dolan, L. J., & Wasik, B. A. (1993). Success for all: Longitudinal effects of a restructuring program for inner-city elementary schools. *American Educational Research Journal, 30,* 123–148.

Madigan, S. A. (1969). Intraserial repetition and coding processes in free recall. *Journal of Verbal Learning and Verbal Behavior, 8,* 828–835.

Madison, P. (1969). *Personality development in college.* Reading, MA: Addison-Wesley.

Maki, R. H., & Berry, S. L. (1984). Metacomprehension and text material. *Journal of Experimental Psychology: Learning, Memory, and Cognition, 10,* 663–679.

Maki, R. H., Foley, J. M., Kajer, W. K., Thompson, R. C., & Willert, M. G. (1990). Increased processing enhances calibration of comprehension. *Journal of Experimental Psychology: Learning, Memory, and Cognition, 16,* 609–616.

Maki, R. H., & Serra, M. (1992). The basis of test predictions for text material. *Journal of Experimental Psychology: Learning, Memory, and Cognition, 18,* 116–126.

Malik, A. A. (1990). A psycholinguistic analysis of the reading behavior of EFL-proficient readers using culturally familiar and culturally nonfamiliar expository texts. *American Educational Research Journal, 27,* 205–223.

Mallory, M. E. (1989). Q-sort definition of ego identity status. *Journal of Youth and Adolescence, 18,* 399–412.

Malone, T. W., & Lepper, M. R. (1987). Making learning fun: A taxonomy of intrinsic motivation for learning. In R. E. Snow & M. J. Farr (Eds.), *Aptitude, learning, and instruction,* Vol. 3, *Conative and affective process analyses* (pp. 223–253). Hillsdale, NJ: Erlbaum & Associates.

Mandler, J. M. (1978). A code in the node: The use of a story schema in retrieval. *Discourse Processes, 1,* 14–35.

Mandler, J. M. (1984). *Stories, scripts, and scenes: Aspects of schema theory.* Hillsdale, NJ: Erlbaum & Associates.

Mandler, J. M. (1987). On the psychological reality of story structure. *Discourse Processes, 10,* 1–29.

Mandler, J. M., & DeForest, M. (1979). Is there more than one way to recall a story? *Child Development, 50,* 886–889.

Mandler, J. M., & Goodman, M. S. (1982). On the psychological validity of story structure. *Journal of Verbal Learning and Verbal Behavior, 21,* 507–523.

Mandler, J. M., & Johnson, N. S. (1977). Remembrance of things parsed: Story structure and recall. *Cognitive Psychology, 9,* 111–151.

Mani, K., & Johnson-Laird, P. N. (1982). The mental representation of spatial descriptions. *Memory and Cognition, 10,* 181–187.

Manning, B. H. (1988). Application of cognitive behavior modification: First and third graders self-management of classroom behaviors. *American Educational Research Journal, 25,* 193–212.

Manning, B. H. (1990). Cognitive self-instruction for an off-task fourth grader during independent academic tasks: A case study. *Contemporary Educational Psychology, 15,* 36–46.

Manning, B. H. (1991). *Cognitive self-instruction for classroom processes.* Albany: State University of New York Press.

Mansfield, R. S., Busse, T. V., & Krepelka, E. J. (1978). The effectiveness of creativity training. *Review of Educational Research, 48,* 517–536.

Mantzicopoulos, P., & Morrison, D. (1992). Kindergarten retention: Academic and behavioral outcomes through the end of second grade. *American Educational Research Journal, 29,* 182–198.

Mantzicopoulos, P., Morrison, D. C., Hinshaw, S. P., & Carte, E. T. (1992). Nonpromotion in kindergarten: The role of cognitive, perceptual, visual-motor, behavioral, achievement, socioeconomic, and demographic characteristics. *American Educational Research Journal, 26,* 107–121.

Maosen, Li (1990). Moral education in the People's Republic of China. *Journal of Moral Education, 19,* 159–171.

Maple, S. A., & Stage, F. K. (1991). Influence on the choice of math/science major by gender and ethnicity. *American Educational Research Journal, 28,* 37–60.

Marantz, M. (1988). Fostering prosocial behaviour in the early childhood classroom: Review of the research. *Journal of Moral Education, 17,* 27–39.

Maratsos, M. P. (1989). Innateness and plasticity in language acquisition. In M. L. Rice & R. L. Schiefelbusch (Eds.), *The teachability of language* (pp. 105–125). Baltimore: Paul H. Brookes.

Marcia, J. E. (1966). Development and validation of ego-identity status. *Journal of Personality and Social Psychology, 3,* 551–558.

Markman, E. M. (1989). *Categorization and naming in children.* Cambridge, MA: MIT Press.

Markman, E. M., & Siebert, J. (1976). Classes and collections: Internal organization and resulting holistic properties. *Cognitive Psychology, 8,* 561–577.

Markus, H., & Nurius, P. (1986). Possible selves. *American Psychologist, 41,* 954-969.

Marsh, G., Desberg, P., & Cooper, J. (1977). Developmental strategies in reading. *Journal of Reading Behavior, 9,* 391–394.

Marsh, G., Friedman, M., Desberg, P., & Saterdahl, K. (1981). Comparison of reading and spelling strategies in normal and reading-disabled children. In M. P. Friedman, J. P. Das, & N. O'Connor (Eds.), *Intelligence and learning* (pp. 363–367). New York: Plenum.

Marsh, G., Friedman, M., Welch, V., & Desberg, P. (1981). A cognitive-developmental theory of reading acquisition. In G. E. MacKinnon & T. G. Waller (Eds.), *Reading research: Advances in theory and practice* Vol. 3 (pp. 199–221). New York: Academic Press.

Marsh, H. W. (1987). The big-fish-little-pond effect on academic self-concept. *Journal of Educational Psychology, 79,* 280–295.

Marsh, H. W. (1989a). Effects of attending single-sex and coeducational high schools on achievement, attitudes, behaviors, and sex differences. *Journal of Educational Psychology, 81,* 70–85.

Marsh, H. W. (1989b). Effects of single-sex and coeducational schools: A response to Lee and Bryk. *Journal of Educational Psychology, 81,* 652–653.

Marsh, H. W. (1990a). Causal ordering of academic self-concept and academic achievement: A multiwave, longitudinal panel analysis. *Journal of Educational Psychology, 82,* 646–656.

Marsh, H. W. (1990b). The structure of academic self-concept: The Marsh/Shavelson model. *Journal of Educational Psychology, 82,* 623–636.

Marsh, H. W. (1992a). Content specificity of relations between academic achievement and academic self-concept. *Journal of Educational Psychology, 84,* 35–42.

Marsh, H. W. (1992b). Extracurricular activities: Beneficial extension of the traditional curriculum or subversion of academic goals? *Journal of Educational Psychology, 84,* 553–562.

Marsh, H. W., & Craven, R. G. (1991). Self-other agreement on multiple dimensions of preadolescent self-concept: Inferences by teachers, mothers, and fathers. *Journal of Educational Psychology, 83,* 393–404.

Marsh, H. W., Craven, R. G., & Debus, R. (1991). Self-concepts of young children 5 to 8 years of age: Measurement and multidimensional structure. *Journal of Educational Psychology, 83,* 377–392.

Marshall, J. D. (1984a). Process and product: Case studies of writing in two content areas. In A. N. Applebee (Ed.), *Contexts for learning to write: Studies of secondary school instruction* (pp. 149–168). Norwood, NJ: Ablex.

Marshall, J. D. (1984b). Schooling and the composing process. In A. N. Applebee (Ed.), *Contexts for learning to write: Studies of secondary school instruction* (pp. 103–119). Norwood, NJ: Ablex.

Marshall, J. (1987). The effects of writing on students' understanding of literary text. *Research in the Teaching of English, 21,* 31–63.

Marshall-Goodell, B. S., Tassinary, L. G., & Cacioppo, J. T. (1990). Principles of bioelectrical measurement. In J. T. Cacioppo & L. G. Tassinary (Eds.), *Principles of psychophysiology* (pp. 113–148). Cambridge, UK: Cambridge University Press.

Marston, D., & Magnusson, D. (1985). Implementing curriculum-based measurement in special and regular education settings. *Exceptional Children, 52,* 266–276.

Martin, J., & Martin, W. (1983). *Personal development: Self-instruction for personal agency.* Calgary, Alberta, Canada: Detselig Enterprises.

Martin, J. R. (1992). *The schoolhome: Rethinking schools for changing families.* Cambridge, MA: Harvard University Press.

Martin, V. L., & Pressley, M. (1991). Elaborative-interrogation effects depend on the nature of the question. *Journal of Educational Psychology, 83,* 113–119.

Martindale, C. (1991). *Cognitive psychology: A neural-network approach.* Pacific Grove, CA: Brooks/Cole.

Martinez, J. L. Jr., & Kesner, R. P. (1991). *Learning and memory: A biological view,* 2nd ed. San Diego: Academic Press.

Marton, F., & Säljö, R. (1976). On qualitative differences in learning: I: Outcome and process. *British Journal of Educational Psychology, 46,* 4–11.

Marzano, R. J. (1992). *A different kind of classroom: Teaching with dimensions of learning.* Alexandria, VA: Association for Supervision and Curriculum Development.

Marzano, R. J., Brandt, R. S., Highes, C. S., Jones, B. F., Presseisen, B. Z., Rankin, S. C., & Suhor, C. (1988). *Dimensions of thinking: A framework for curriculum and instruction.* Alexandria, VA: Association for Curriculum and Supervision.

Mason, C. L. (1992). Concept mapping: A tool to develop reflective science instruction. *Science Education, 76,* 51–63.

Mastropieri, M. A., & Scruggs, T. E. (1989). Constructing more meaningful relationships: Mnemonic instruction for special populations. *Educational Psychology Review, 1,* 83–111.

Mastropieri, M. A., & Scruggs, T. E. (1991). *Teaching students ways to remember: Strategies for learning mnemonicall.* Cambridge, MA: Brookline Books.

Mathews, M. M. (1966). *Teaching to read: Historically considered.* Chicago: University of Chicago Press.

Mathison, S. (1988). Why triangulate? *Educational Researcher, 17 (2),* 13–17.

Mattarazzo, J. D. (1972). *Wechsler's measurement and appraisal of adult intelligence,* 5th ed. Baltimore: Williams & Wilkins.

Maxwell, M. (1979). *Improving student learning skills.* San Francisco: Jossey-Bass.

Mayer, R. E. (1975). Forward transfer of different reading strategies evoked by testlike events in mathematics text. *Journal of Educational Psychology, 67,* 165–169.

Mayer, R. E. (1977). The sequencing of instruction and the concept of assimilation-to-schema. *Instructional Science, 6,* 369–388.

Mayer, R. E. (1979). Can advance organizers influence meaningful learning. *Review of Educational Research, 49,* 371–383.

Mayer, R. E. (1980). Elaboration techniques that increase the meaningfulness of technical text: An experimental test of the learning strategy hypothesis. *Journal of Educational Psychology, 72,* 770–784.

Mayer, R. E. (1981). Frequency norms and structural analysis of algebra story problems into families, categories, and templates. *Instructional Science, 10,* 135–175.

Mayer, R. E. (1982). Memory for algebra story problems. *Journal of Educational Psychology, 74,* 199–216.

Mayer, R. E. (1985). Structural analysis of science prose: Can we increase problem-solving performance? In B. K. Britton & J. B. Black (Eds.), *Understanding expository prose: A theoretical and practical handbook for analyzing explanatory text* (pp. 65–87). Hillsdale, NJ: Erlbaum & Associates.

Mayer, R. E. (1989a). Models for understanding. *Review of Educational Research, 59,* 43–64.

Mayer, R. E. (1989b). Systematic thinking fostered by illustrations in scientific text. *Journal of Educational Psychology, 81,* 240–246.

Mayer, R. E., & Anderson, R. B. (1991). Animations need narrations: An experimental test of a dual-coding hypothesis. *Journal of Educational Psychology, 83,* 484–490.

Mayer, R. E., & Anderson, R. B. (1992). The instructive animation: Helping students build connections between words and pictures in multimedia learning. *Journal of Educational Psychology, 84,* 444–452.

Mayer, R. E., & Bromage, B. K. (1980). Different recall protocols for technical texts due to advance organizers. *Journal of Educational Psychology, 72,* 209–225.

Mayer, R. E., & Cook, L. K. (1981). Effects of shadowing on prose comprehension and problem solving. *Memory and Cognition, 9,* 101–109.

Mayer, R. E., & Gallini, J. K. (1990). When is an illustration worth ten thousand words? *Journal of Educational Psychology, 82,* 715–726.

Mayer, R. E., Larkin, J. H., & Kadane, J. (1984). A cognitive analysis of mathematical problem solving ability. In R. Sternberg (Ed.), *Advances in the psychology of human intelligence* (pp. 231–273). Hillsdale, NJ: Erlbaum & Associates.

McArthur, D., Stasz, C., & Zmuidzinas, M. (1990). Tutoring techniques in algebra. *Cognition and Instruction, 7,* 197–244.

McCarthy, L. P. (1987). A stranger in strange lands: A college student writing across the curriculum. *Research in the Teaching of English, 21,* 233–265.

McCarthy, R. A., & Warrington, E. K. (1990). *Cognitive neuropsychology: A clinical introduction.* San Diego: Academic Press.

McCauley, C., Kellas, G., Dugas, J., & DeVillis, R. F. (1976). Effects of serial rehearsal training of memory search. *Journal of Educational Psychology, 68,* 474–481.

McClelland, J. L., & Rumelhart, D. E. (1981). An interactive activation model of context effects in letter perception: Part 1. An account of basic findings. *Psychological Review, 88,* 375–407.

McClelland, J. L., & Rumelhart, D. E. (1986). *Parallel distributed processing,* Vol. 2. Cambridge, MA: MIT Press.

McCloskey, M. (1983). Naive theories of motion. In D. Gentner & A. Stevens (Eds.), *Mental models* (pp. 299–324). Hillsdale, NJ: Erlbaum & Associates.

McCloskey, M. (1992). Cognitive mechanisms in numerical processing: Evidence from acquired dyscalculia. *Cognition, 44,* 107–157.

McConkie, G. W., Rayner, K., & Wilson, S. J. (1973). Experimental manipulation of reading strategies. *Journal of Educational Psychology, 65,* 1–8.

McConkie, G. W., Zola, D., Blanchard, H. E., & Wolverton, G. S. (1982). Perceiving words during reading: Lack of facilitation from prior peripheral exposure. *Perception and Psychophysics, 32,* 271–281.

McCormick, C. B., Busching, B. A., & Potter, E. F. (1992). Children's knowledge about writing: The development and use of evaluative criteria. In M. Pressley, K. R. Harris, & J. T. Guthrie (Eds.), *Promoting academic competence and literacy in school* (pp. 311–336). San Diego: Academic Press.

McCormick, C. B., & Levin, J. R. (1987). Mnemonic prose-learning strategies. In M. A. McDaniel & M. Pressley (Eds.), *Imagery and related mnemonic processes: Theories, individual differences, and applications* (pp. 407–427). New York: Springer-Verlag.

McCutchen, D., & Perfetti, C. A. (1983). Local coherence: Helping young writers manage a complex task. *Elementary School Journal, 84,* 71–75.

McDaniel, M. A., & Einstein, G. O. (1989). Material-appropriate processing: A contextualist approach to reading and studying strategies. *Educational Psychology Review, 1,* 113–145.

McDaniel, M. A., & Schlager, M. S. (1990). Discovery learning and transfer of problem-solving skills. *Cognition and Instruction, 7,* 129–159.

McDonnell, J., & Ferguson, B. (1989). A comparison of time delay and decreasing prompt hierarchy strategies in teaching banking skills to students with moderate handicaps. *Journal of Applied Behavior Analysis, 22,* 85–91.

McFie, J. (1961). The effects of hemispherectomy on intellectual functioning in cases of infantile hemiplegia. *Journal of Neurology, Neurosurgery Psychiatry, 24,* 20.

McGaw, B., & Grotelueshen, A. (1972). Direction of the effect of questions in prose material. *Journal of Educational Psychology, 63,* 580–588.

McGill-Franzen, A. M. (1987). Failure to learn to read: Formulating a policy problem. *Reading Research Quarterly, 22,* 475–490.

McGinley, W. (1992). The role of reading and writing while composing from sources. *Reading Research Quarterly, 27,* 226–248.

McKeown, M. G., Beck, I. L., Sinatra, G. M., & Loxterman, J. A. (1992). The contribution of prior knowledge and coherent text to comprehension. *Reading Research Quarterly, 27,* 78–93.

McKoon, G., & Ratcliff, R. (1979). Priming in episodic and semantic memory. *Journal of Verbal Learning and Verbal Behavior, 18,* 463–480.

McLaughlin, B. (1984). *Second-language acquisition in childhood.* Hillsdale, NJ: Erlbaum & Associates.

McLoyd, V. C. (1979). The effects of extrinsic rewards of differential value on high and low intrinsic interest. *Child Development, 50,* 1010–1019.

McNamee, G. D. (1979). The social interaction origins of narrative skills. *Quarterly Newsletter of the Laboratory of Comparative Human Cognition, 1,* 63–68.

Means, M., & Voss, J. (1985). Star Wars: A developmental study of expert and novice knowledge structures. *Journal of Memory and Language, 24,* 746–757.

Meece, J. L., Blumenfeld, P. C., & Hoyle, R. H. (1988). Students' goal orientations and cognitive engagement in classroom activities. *Journal of Educational Psychology, 80,* 514–523.

Mehan, H. (1979). *Social organization in the classroom.* Cambridge, MA: Harvard University Press.

Meichenbaum, D. (1977) *Cognitive behavior modification.* New York: Plenum.

Meichenbaum, D., & Goodman, J. (1971). Training impulsive children to talk to themselves: A means of developing self-control. *Journal of Abnormal Child Psychology, 77,* 115–126.

Mellor, S. (1989). Gender differences in identity formation as a function of self-other relationships. *Journal of Youth and Adolescence, 18,* 361–375.

Meloth, M. S. (1990) Changes in poor readers' knowledge of cognition and the association of knowledge of cognition with regulation of cognition and reading comprehension. *Journal of Educational Psychology, 82,* 792–798

Mensh, E., & Mensh, H. (1991). *The IQ mythology.* Carbondale, IL: Southern Illinois University Press.

Mentkowski, M., & Strait, M. (1983). *A longitudinal study of student change in cognitive development, learning styles, and generic abilities in an outcome-centered liberal arts curriculum* (Final Report to the National Institute of Education, Research Report No. 6). Milwaukee, WI: Alverno College, Office of Research and Evaluation.

Merbaum, M. (1973). The modification of self-destructive behavior by mother-therapist using aversive stimulation. *Behavior Therapy, 4,* 442–447.

Merighi, J., Edison, M., & Zigler, E. (1990). The role of motivational factors in the functioning of mentally retarded individuals. In R. M. Hodapp, J. A. Burack, & E. Zigler (Eds.), *Issues in the developmental approach to retardation* (pp. 114–134). Cambridge, England: Cambridge University Press.

Messer, S. B. (1976). Reflection-impulsivity: A review. *Psychological Bulletin, 83,* 1026–1052.

Messick, S., & Jungeblut, A. (1981). Time and method in coaching for the SAT. *Psychological Bulletin, 89,* 191–216.

Meyer, B. J. F. (1975). *The organization of prose and its effects on memory.* Amsterdam: North Holland.

Meyer, B. J. F., Brandt, D. H., & Bluth, G. J. (1980). Use of top-level structure in text: Key for reading comprehension of ninth-grade students. *Reading Research Quarterly, 16,* 72–103.

Meyer, B. J. F., Young, C. J., & Bartlett, B. J. (1989). *Memory improved: Reading and memory enhancement across the life span through strategic text structures.* Hillsdale, NJ: Erlbaum & Associates.

Meyer, D., Schvaneveldt, R. W., & Ruddy, M. G. (1975). Loci of contextual effects on word recognition. In P. M. A. Rabbitt & S. Dornic (Eds.), *Attention and performance V* (pp. 98–118). London: Academic Press.

Meyer, W., Bachmann, M., Biermann, U., Hempelmann, M., Ploger, F., & Spiller, H. (1979). The informational value of evaluative behavior: Influence of praise and blame on perceptions of ability. *Journal of Educational Psychology, 71,* 259–268.

Meyers, J., Gelzheiser, L., Yelich, G., & Gallagher, M. (1990). Classroom, remedial, and resource teachers' views of pullout programs. *Elementary School Journal, 90,* 533–545.

Michael, A. L., Klee, T., Bransford, J. D., & Warren, S. F. (1993). The transition from theory to therapy: Test of two instructional methods. *Applied Cognitive Psychology, 7,* 139–153.

Michael, B. (Ed.) (1990). *Volunteers in public schools.* Washington, DC: National Academy Press.

Michael, J. L. (1985). Behavioral analysis: A radical perspective. In B. L. Hammonds (Ed.), *Psychology and learning: Master lectures.* Washington, DC: American Psychological Association.

Michael, J., & Meyerson, L. (1962). A behavioral approach to human control. *Harvard Educational Review, 32,* 382–402.

Mikulecky, L. (1987). The status of literacy in our society. *Research in literacy: Thirty-seventh yearbook of the National Reading Conference* (pp. 24–34). Chicago: National Reading Conference.

Miller, A. I. (1984). *Imagery in scientific thought: Creating 20th-century physics.* Boston: Birkhaüser.

Miller, G. A. (1956). The magical number seven, plus-or-minus two: Some limits on our capacity for processing information. *Psychological Review, 63,* 81–97.

Miller, G. A., Gallanter, E., & Pribram, K. H. (1960). *Plans and the structure of behavior.* New York: Holt, Rinehart, & Winston.

Miller, G. E., & Pressley, M. (1989). Pictures versus question elaboration on young children's learning of sentences containing high- and low-probability content. *Journal of Experimental Child Psychology, 48,* 431–450.

Miller, N. E. (1944). Experimental studies in conflict. In. J. McVicker Hunt (Ed.) *Personality and the behavior disorders* (pp. 431–465). New York: Ronald Press.

Miller, S. E., Leinhardt, G., & Zigmond, N.

(1988). Influencing engagement through accommodation: An ethnographic study of at-risk students. *American Educational Research Journal, 25,* 465–487.

Miltenberger, R. G., & Thiesse-Duffy, E. (1988). Evaluation of home-based programs for teaching personal safety skills to children. *Journal of Applied Behavior Analysis, 21,* 81–87.

Minsky, M. (1975). A framework for representing knowledge. In P. H. Winston (Ed.), *The psychology of computer vision* (pp. 211–277). New York: McGraw-Hill.

Minsky, M. (1986). *The society of mind.* New York: Simon & Schuster.

Minstrell, J. (1982, January). Explaining the "at rest" condition of an object. *The Physics Teacher, 20,* 10–14.

Mischel, W. (1968). *Personality and assessment.* New York: Wiley.

Mitchell, J. V., Jr. (Ed.) (1985). *The ninth mental measurements yearbook* (Vol. 1–2). Lincoln: The Buros Institute of Mental Measurements of the University of Nebraska–Lincoln.

Mitchell, R. (1992). *Testing for learning: How new approaches to evaluation can improve American schools.* New York: Free Press.

Moccia, R. E., McKnight, P., Deshler, D. D., & Schumaker, J. B. (1990). *The 1990 INROADS Program Report.* Lawrence, KS: University of Kansas, Institute for Research on Learning Disabilities.

Moely, B. E. (1977). Organizational factors in the development of memory. In R. V. Kail & J. W. Hagen (Eds.), *Perspectives on the development of memory and cognition* (pp. 203–236). Hillsdale, NJ: Erlbaum & Associates.

Moely, B. E., Olson, F. A., Halwes, T. G., & Flavell, J. H. (1969). Production deficiency in young children's clustered recall. *Developmental Psychology, 1,* 26–34.

Mokros, J. R., & Tinker, R. F. (1987). The impact of microcomputer-based labs on children's abilities to interpret graphs. *Journal of Research in Science Teaching, 24,* 369–383.

Montague, M., & Bos, C. S. (1990). Cognitive and metacognitive characteristics of eighth grade students' mathematical problem solving. *Learning and Individual Differences, 2,* 371–388.

Mooney, R. J. (1990). Learning plan schemata from observation: Explanation-based learning for plan recognition. *Cognitive Science, 14,* 483–509.

Morales v. Shannon, 516 F. 2d 411 (1975).

Morales, R. V., Shute, V. J., & Pellegrino, J. W. (1985). Developmental differences in understanding and solving simple word problems. *Cognition and Instruction, 2,* 41–57.

Morgan, B., & Gibson, K. R. (1991). Nutritional and environmental interactions in brain development. In K. R. Gibson & A. C. Petersen (Eds.), *Brain maturation and cognitive development: Comparative and cross-cultural perspectives* (pp. 91–106). New York: Aldine de Gruyter.

Morine-Dershimer, G. (1979). *Teacher plan and classroom reality: The S. Bay study, part 4.* Research Monograph, Institute for Research on Teaching, University of Michigan.

Morocco, C., & Neuman, S. (1986). Word processors and the acquisition of writing strategies. *Journal of Learning Disabilities, 19,* 243–247.

Morris, R. D., Krawiecki, N. S., Wright, J. A., & Walter, L. W. (1993). Neuropsychological, academic, and adaptive functioning in children who survive in-hospital cardiac arrest and resuscitation. *Journal of Learning Disabilities, 26,* 46–51.

Morrow, L. M. (1983). Home and school correlates of early interest in literature. *Journal of Educational Research, 76,* 221–230.

Morrow, L. M. (1989). *Literacy development in the early years: Helping children read and write.* Boston: Allyn & Bacon.

Morrow, L. M. (1990). Preparing the classroom environment to promote literacy during play. *Early Childhood Research Quarterly, 5,* 537–554.

Morrow, L. M., & Weinstein, C. S. (1986). Encouraging voluntary reading: The impact of a literacy program on children's use of library corners. *Reading Research Quarterly, 21,* 330–346.

Morson, G. S., & Emerson, C. (1990). *Mikhail Bakhtin: Creation of a prosaics.* Stanford, CA: Stanford University Press.

Mortimore, P. (1991). Effective schools from a British perspective: Research and practice. In J. R. Bliss, W. A. Firestone, & C. E. Richards (Eds.), *Rethinking effective schools research and practice* (pp. 76–90). Englewood Cliffs, NJ: Prentice-Hall.

Moshman, D. (1982). Exogenous, endogenous, and dialectical constructivism. *Developmental Review, 2,* 371–384.

Mudre, L. H., & McCormick, S. (1989). Effects of meaning-focused cues on underachieving readers' context use, self-corrections, and literal comprehension. *Reading Research Quarterly, 24,* 89–113.

Mulick, J. A. (1990). The ideology and science of punishment in mental retardation. *American Journal of Mental Deficiency, 94,* 142–156.

Mullis, J. V. S., Owen, E. H., & Phillips, G. W. (1990). *Accelerating academic achievement.* Princeton, NJ: National Assessment of Educational Progress, Educational Testing Service.

Murnane, R. J., & Raizen, S. A. (1988). *Improving indicators of the quality of science and mathematics education in grades K–12.* Washington, DC: National Academy Press.

Mussen, P. H. (ed.) (1983). *Handbook of child psychology.* 4th ed. New York: John Wiley & Sons.

Muth, K D., Glynn, S. M., Britton, B. K., & Graves, M. F. (1988). Thinking out loud while studying text: Rehearsing key ideas. *Journal of Educational Psychology, 80,* 315–318.

Nagy, W., & Anderson, R. (1984). How many words are there in printed school English? *Reading Research Quarterly, 19,* 304–330.

Nash, J. G., Schumacher, G. M., & Carlson, B. W. (1993). Writing from sources: A structure-mapping model. *Journal of Educational Psychology, 85,* 159–170.

National Center for Education Statistics (1992). *Digest of education statistics.* Washington, DC: U.S. Department of Education.

National Commission on Testing and Public Policy (1989). *From gatekeeper to gateway: Transforming testing in America.* Chestnut Hill, MA: National Commission on Testing and Public Policy, Boston College.

National Council of Teachers of Mathematics (1989). *Curriculum and evaluation standards for school mathematics.* Reston, VA: National Council of Teachers of Mathematics.

National Council of Teachers of Mathematics (1991). *Professional standards for teaching mathematics.* Reston, VA: National Council of Teachers of Mathematics.

National Science Foundation (1978). *Report of the 1977 national survey of science.* Washington, DC: Natural Science Foundation.

Neale, M. C., & McArdle, J. J. (1990). The analysis of assortative mating: A LISREL model. *Behavior Genetics, 20,* 287–297.

Necka, E. (1992). Cognitive analysis of intelligence: The significance of working memory processes. *Personality and Individual Differences, 13,* 1031–1046.

Needleman, H. L. (1992). Childhood exposure to lead: A common cause of school failure. *Phi Delta Kappan, 74,* 35–37.

Needleman, H. L., & Bellinger, D. (1991). The health effects of low level exposure to lead. *Annual Review of Public Health, 12,* 111-140.

Neely, J. H. (1977). Semantic priming and retrieval from lexical memory: Roles of inhibitionless spreading activation and limited capacity attention. *Journal of Experimental Psychology, 106,* 226–254.

Neisser, U. (1967). *Cognitive psychology.* New York: Appleton-Century-Crofts.

Nelson, D. G. K. (1990). When experimental findings conflict with everyday observations: Reflections on children's category learning. *Child Development, 61,* 606–610.

Nelson, J., & Hayes, J. R. (1988). *How the writing context shapes college students' strategies for writing from sources.* (Technical Report No. 16.) Berkeley: University of California and Carnegie-Mellon University, Center for Study of Writing at University of California and Carnegie-Mellon.

Nelson, K. (1974). Concept, word, and sentence: Interrelations in acquisition and development. *Psychological Review, 81,* 267–285.

Nelson, K. (1978). How children represent their world in and out of language. In R. S. Siegler (Ed.), *Children's thinking: What develops?* (pp. 255–273). Hillsdale, NJ: Erlbaum & Associates.

Nelson, K., & Gruendel, J. (1981). Generalized event representations: Basic building blocks of cognitive development. In A. Brown & M. Lamb (Eds.), *Advances in developmental psychology,* Vol. 1 (pp. 231–247). Hillsdale, NJ: Erlbaum & Associates.

Nelson-Le Gall, S., Kratzer, L., Jones, E., & De-Cooke, P. (1990). Children's self-assessment of performance and task-related help seeking. *Journal of Experimental Child Psychology, 49,* 245–263.

Nettelbeck, T., & Brewer, N. (1981). Studies of mild mental retardation and timed performance. In N. R. Ellis (Ed.), *International review* of research in mental retardation, Vol. 10 (pp. 61–106). New York: Academic Press.

Neuman, S. B., & Roskos, K. (1992). Literacy objects as cultural tools: Effects on children's literacy behaviors in play. *Reading Research Quarterly, 27,* 202–225.

Neves, D. M., & Anderson, J. R. (1981). Knowledge compilation: Mechanisms for the automatization of cognitive skills. In J. R. Anderson (Ed.), *Cognitive skills and their acquisition* (pp. 251–272). Hillsdale, NJ: Erlbaum & Associates.

Newby, T. J. (1991). Classroom motivation: Strategies of first-year teachers. *Journal of Educational Psychology, 83,* 195–200.

Newcombe, N., & Dubas, J. S. (1992). A longitudinal study of predictors of spatial ability in adolescent females. *Child Development, 63,* 37–46.

Newell, A., & Rosenbloom, P. S. (1981). Mechanisms of skill acquisition and the law of practice. In J. R. Anderson (Ed.), *Cognitive skills and their acquisition* Hillsdale, NJ: Erlbaum.

Newell, A., & Simon, H. A. (1972). *Human problem solving.* Englewood Cliffs, NJ: Prentice-Hall.

Newell, G. (1984). Learning from writing in two content areas: A case study/protocol analysis. *Research in the Teaching of English, 18,* 205–287.

Newell, G., Suszynski, K., & Weingart, R. (1989). The effects of writing in a reader-based and text-based mode on students' understanding of two short stories. *Journal of Reading Behavior, 21,* 37–58.

Newkirk, T. (1991). The high school years. In J. Flood, J. M. Jensen, D. Lapp, & J. R. Squire (Eds.), *Handbook of research on teaching the English language arts* (pp. 3–17). New York: MacMillan.

Newman, D., Griffin, P., & Cole, M. (1989). *The construction zone: Working for cognitive change in school.* Cambridge, UK: Cambridge University Press.

Newman, L. S. (1990). Intentional and unintentional memory in young children: Remembering versus playing. *Journal of Experimental Child Psychology, 50,* 243–258.

Newman, P., & Newman, B. (1978). Identity formation and the college experience. *Adolescence, 13,* 311–326.

Newman, R. S., & Goldin, L. (1990). Children's reluctance to seek help with schoolwork. *Journal of Educational Psychology, 82,* 92–100.

Newman, F. (1988). Can depth replace coverage in the high school curriculum? *Phi Delta Kappan, 68 (5),* 345–348.

Newmann, F. (1990a). Higher–order thinking in social studies: A rationale for the assessment of classroom thoughtfulness. *Journal of Curriculum Studies, 22,* 41–56.

Newmann, F. (1990b). Qualities of thoughtful social studies classes: An empirical profile. *Journal of Curriculum Studies, 22,* 253–275.

Newmann, F. (1991a). Higher-order thinking in the teaching of social studies: Connections between theory and practice. In J. F. Voss, D. N. Perkins, & J. W. Segal (Eds.), *Informal reasoning and education* (pp. 381–400). Hillsdale, NJ: Erlbaum & Associates.

Newmann, F. M. (1991b). Promoting higher order thinking in social studies: Overview of a study of 16 high school departments. *Theory and Research in Social Education, 19,* 324–340.

Newmann, F. M. (1991c). Student engagement in academic work: Expanding the perspective on secondary school effectiveness. In J. R. Bliss, W. A. Firestone, & C. E. Richards (Eds.), *Rethinking effective schools research and practice* (pp. 58–75). Englewood Cliffs, NJ: Prentice-Hall.

Newmann, F. (1991d). The prospects for classroom thoughtfulness in high school social studies. In C. Collins (Ed.), *Building the quality of thinking in and out of our schools in the twenty-first century.* Hillsdale, NJ: Erlbaum & Associates.

Newmann, F., Onosko, J., & Stevenson, R. (1990). Staff development for higher-order thinking: A synthesis of practical wisdom. *Journal of Staff Development, 11 (3),* 48–55.

Niaz, M. (1988). Manipulation of M demand of chemistry problems and its effect on student performance: A neo-Piagetian study. *Journal of Research in Science Teaching, 25,* 643–657.

Niaz, M. (1989). Relation between Pascual-Leone's structural and functional M-space and its effect on problem solving in chemistry. *International Journal of Science Education, 11,* 93–99.

Nicholls, J. G. (1989). *The competitive ethos and democratic education.* Cambridge, MA: Harvard University Press.

Nicholls, J. G., & Nelson, J. R. (1992). Students' conceptions of controversial knowledge. *Journal of Educational Psychology, 84,* 224–230.

Nicholls, J. G., & Thorkildsen, T. A. (1987, October). *Achievement goals and beliefs: Individual and classroom differences.* Presented at the meeting of the Society for Experimental Social Psychology, Charlottesville, VA.

Nicholson, T. (1991). Do children read words better in context or in lists? A classic study revisited. *Journal of Educational Psychology, 83,* 444–450.

Nicholson, T., Bailey, J., & McArthur, J. (1991). Context cues in reading: The gap between research and popular opinion. *Journal of Reading: Writing and Learning Disabilities, 7,* 33–41.

Nicholson, T., Lillas, C., & Rzoska, A. (1988). Have we been misled by miscues? *The Reading Teacher, 42,* 6–10.

Nickerson, R. S. (1988). On improving thinking through instruction. In E. Z. Rothkopf (Ed.), *Review of Research in Education,* Vol. 15 (pp. 3–57). Washington, DC: American Educational Research Association.

Nickerson, R. S., Perkins, D. N., & Smith, E. E. (1985). *The teaching of thinking.* Hillsdale, NJ: Erlbaum & Associates.

Ninio, A. (1980). Picture-book reading in mother-infant dyads belonging to two subgroups in Israel. *Child Development, 51,* 587–590.

Nist, S. L., Simpson, M. L., Olejnik, S., & Mealey, D. L. (1991). The relation between self-selected study processes and test performance. *American Educational Research Journal, 28,* 849–874.

Noddings, N. (1984). *Caring: A femine approach to ethics and moral education.* Berkeley: University of California Press.

Nolen, S. B. (1988). Reasons for studying: Motivational orientations and study strategies. *Cognition and Instruction, 5,* 269–287.

Nolte, R. Y., & Singer, H. (1985). Active comprehension: Teaching a process of reading comprehension and its effects on reading achievement. *Reading Teacher, 39,* 24–31.

Northcutt, N. (1975). *Adult functional competency: A summary.* Austin, TX: Adult Performance Level Project.

Noss, R., & Hoyles, C. (1992). In C. Hoyles & R. Noss (Eds.), *Learning mathematics and LOGO* (pp. 431–468). Cambridge, MA: MIT Press.

Novak, J. D., & Gowin, D. B. (1984). *Learning how to learn.* New York: Cambridge University Press.

Nunnally, J. C. (1978). *Psychometric theory,* 2nd ed. New York: McGraw-Hill.

Nussbaum, J., & Novick, S. (1982). Alternative frameworks, conceptual conflict and accomodation: Toward a principled teaching strategy. *Instructional Science, 11,* 183–200.

Nye, P. A., Crooks, T. J., Powley, M., & Tripp, G. (1984). Student note-taking related to university examination performance. *Higher Education, 13,* 85–97.

Nystrand, M. (1986). *The structure of written communication: Studies in reciprocity between writers and readers.* New York: Academic Press.

Oakes, J. (1985). *Keeping track: How schools structure inequality.* New Haven, CT: Yale University Press.

Oakes, J. (1987). Tracking in secondary schools: A contextual perspective. *Educational Psychologist, 22,* 129–154.

Oakhill, J., & Garnham, A. (1988). *Becoming a skilled reader.* London: Basil Blackwell.

Oden, G. C. (1987). Concept, knowledge, and thought. *Annual Review of Psychology, 38,* 203–227.

Okebukola, P. A. (1990). Attaining meaningful learning of concepts in genetics and ecology: An examination of the potency of the concept-mapping technique. *Journal of Research in Science Teaching, 27,* 493–504.

Olive, J. (1991). LOGO programming and geometric understanding: An in-depth study. *Journal for Research in Mathematics Education, 22,* 90–111.

O'Malley, C., & Draper, S. (1992). Representation and interaction: Are mental models all in the mind? In Y. Rogers, A. Rutherford, & P. A. Bibby (Eds.), *Models in the mind: Theory, perspective, and application* (pp. 73–99). London: Academic Press.

O'Malley, M., & Chamot, A. U. (1990). *Learning strategies in second language acquisition.* Cambridge, UK: Cambridge University Press.

O'Neil, J. (1992). Putting performance assessment to the test. *Educational Leadership, 49 (8),* 14–19.

Onosko, J. (1989). Comparing teachers' thinking about promoting students' thinking. *Theory and Research in Social Education, 17,* 174–195.

Onosko, J. (1991). Barriers to the promotion of higher-order thinking in social studies. *Theory and Research in Social Education, 19,* 340–365.

Onosko, J. (1992). Exploring the thinking of thoughtful teachers. *Educational Leadership, 49 (7),* 40–43.

Onosko, J. J., & Newmann, F. M. (1994). Creating more thoughtful learning environments. In J. Mangieri & C. C. Block (Eds.), *Advanced educational psychology: Enhancing mindfulness.* Fort Worth, TX: Harcourt, Brace, Jovanovich.

Oppenheim, R. W. (1981). Neuronal cell death and some related phenomena during neurogenesis: A selective historical review and progress report. In W. M. Cowman (Ed.), *Studies in developmental neurobiology* (pp. 74–133). Oxford University Press: New York.

Ornstein, P. A., Naus, M. J., & Liberty, C. (1975). Rehearsal and organizational processes in children's memory. *Child Development, 46,* 818–830.

Ornstein, R. (1977). *The psychology of consciousness.* New York: Harcourt, Brace, Jovanovich.

Ornstein, R. (1978). The split and whole brain. *Human Nature, 1,* 76–83.

Orton, S. T. (1925). "Word-blindness" in school children. *Archives of Neurology and Psychiatry, 14,* 581–615.

Orton, S. T. (1926). Reading disability. *Genetic Psychology Monographs, 14,* 335–453.

Orton, S. T. (1937). *Reading, writing, and speech problems in children.* New York: W.W. Norton.

Osborne, R., & Freyberg, P. (1985). *Learning in science: The implications of children's science.* London: Heinemann.

O'Sullivan, J. T. (1993). Preschoolers' beliefs about effort, incentive, and recall. *Journal of Experimental Child Psychology, 55,* 396–414.

O'Sullivan, J. T., & Pressley, M. (1984). Completeness of instruction and strategy transfer. *Journal of Experimental Child Psychology, 38,* 275–288.

O'Sullivan, P. J., Ysseldyke, J. E., Christenson, S. L., & Thurlow, M. L. (1990). Mildly handicapped elementary students' opportunity to learn during reading instruction in mainstream and special education settings. *Reading Research Quarterly, 25,* 131–146.

O'Tuel, F. S., & Darby, D. (1993, April). Instrumental enrichment for 4–6 grades: Can it raise achievement scores? Is three years too few? Presented at the annual meeting of the American Educational Research Association, Atlanta.

Ovander, C. J., & Collier, V. P. (1985). *Bilingual and ESL classrooms.* New York: McGraw-Hill.

Owen, E., & Sweller, J. (1985). What do students learn while solving mathematics problems? *Journal of Educational Psychology, 77,* 272–284.

Owen, E., & Sweller, J. (1989). Should problem solving be used as a learning device in mathematics? *Journal for Research in Mathematics Education, 20,* 322–328.

Paas, F. G. W. C. (1992). Training strategies for attaining transfer of problem-solving skill in statistics: A cognitive-load approach. *Journal of Educational Psychology, 84,* 429–434.

Paivio, A. (1971). *Imagery and verbal processes.* New York: Holt, Rinehart, & Winston.

Paivio, A. (1986). *Mental representations: A dual-coding approach.* New York: Oxford University Press.

Paivio, A., & Begg, I. (1981). *Psychology of language.* Englewood Cliffs, NJ: Prentice-Hall.

Palincsar, A. S., & Brown, A. L. (1984). Reciprocal teaching of comprehension-fostering and monitoring activities. *Cognition and Instruction, 1,* 117–175.

Palmatier, R. A., & Bennett, J. M. (1974). Note-taking habits of college students. *Journal of Reading, 18,* 215–218.

Palmer, E. L. (1984). Providing quality television for America's children. In J. P. Murray & G. Salomon (Eds.), *The future of children's television* (pp. 103–124). Boys Town, NE: Boys Town Center.

Palumbo, D. B. (1990). Programming language/problem-solving research: A review of relevant issues. *Review of Educational Research, 60,* 65–89.

Panksepp, J. (1986). The neurochemistry of behavior. *Annual Review of Psychology, 7,* 77–108.

Paris, S. G., Lipson, M. Y., & Wixson, K. K. (1983). Becoming a strategic reader. *Contemporary Educational Psychology, 8,* 293–316.

Paris, S. G., & Oka, E. R. (1986). Children's reading strategies, metacognition, and motivation. *Developmental Review, 6,* 25–56.

Park, H-S., & Gaylord-Ross, R. (1989). A problem-solving approach to social skills training in employment settings with mentally retarded youth. *Journal of Applied Behavior Analysis, 22,* 373–380.

Parke, R. D. (1969). Effectiveness of punishment as an interaction of intensity, timing, agent nurturance and cognitive structuring. *Child Development, 40,* 213–236.

Parke, R. D. (1974). Rules, roles, and resistance to deviation in children: Explorations in punishment, discipline and self-control. In A. D. Pick (Ed.), *Minnesota symposium on child psychology,* Vol. 8. (pp. 111–144). Minneapolis: University of Minnesota Press.

Parks, R. W., Loewenstein, D. A., Dodrill, K. L., Barker, W. W., Yoshii, F., Chang, J. Y., Emran, A., Apicella, A., Sheramata, W. A., & Duara, R. (1988). Cerebral metabolic effects of a verbal fluency test: A PET scan study. *Journal of Clinical and Experimental Neuropsychology, 10,* 565–575.

Parmelee, A. H., Jr., & Sigman, M. D. (1983). Perinatal brain development and behavior. In M. M. Haith & J. J. Campos (Volume Ed.) and P. H. Mussen (General Ed.), *Handbook of child psychology,* Vol. II, *Infancy and developmental psychobiology* (pp. 95–155). New York: John Wiley & Sons.

Parsons, J., & Ruble, D. (1977). The development of achievement-related expectancies. *Child Development, 48,* 1075–1079.

Pascarella, E. T., Smart, J. C., Ethington, C. A., & Nettles, M. T. (1987). The influence of college on self-concept: A consideration of race and gender differences. *American Educational Research Journal, 24,* 49–77.

Pascarella. E. T., & Terenzini, P. T. (1991). *How college affects students.* San Francisco: Jossey-Bass.

Pascual-Leone, J. (1970). A mathematical model for the transition rule in Piaget's developmental stages. *Acta Psychologica, 32,* 301–345.

Patterson, C. J., & Mischel, W. (1976). Effects of temptation-inhibiting and task-facilitating plans on self-control. *Journal of Personality and Social Psychology, 33,* 209–217.

Pauker, S. G., Gorry, G. A., Kassirer, J. P., & Schwartz, W. B. (1976). Towards the simulation of clinical cognition: Taking the present illness by computer. *The American Journal of Medicine, 60,* 981–996.

Pea, R. D., & Kurland, D. M. (1984). On the cognitive effects of learning computer programming. *New Ideas in Psychology, 2,* 137–168.

Pearl, R. (1982). LD children's attributions for success and failure: A replication with a labeled LD sample. *Learning Disability Quarterly, 5,* 173–176.

Pearson, D. A., & Lane, D. M. (1991). Auditory attention switching: A developmental study. *Journal of Experimental Child Psychology, 51,* 320–334.

Pearson, P. D., & Dole, J. A. (1987). Explicit comprehension instruction: A review of research and a new conceptualization of instruction. *Elementary School Journal, 88,* 151–165.

Pearson, P. D., Hansen, J., & Gordon, C. (1979). The effect of background knowledge on young children's comprehension of explicit and implicit information. *Journal of Reading Behavior, 11,* 201–209.

Pellegrini, A. D., Perlmutter, J. C., Galda, L., & Brody, G. H. (1990). Joint reading between black head start children and their mothers. *Child Development, 61,* 443–453.

Pennington, B. F., Groisser, D., & Welsh, M. C. (1993). Contrasting cognitive deficits in attention deficit hyperactivity disorder versus reading disability. *Developmental Psychology, 29,* 511–523.

Pennington, B. F., Van Orden, G. C., Smith, S. D., Green, P. A., & Haith, M. M. (1990). Phological processing skills and deficits in adult dyslexics. *Child Development, 61,* 1753–1778.

Pennock-Román, M. (1992). Interpreting test performance in selective admissions for Hispanic students. In K. F. Geisinger (Ed.), *Psychological testing of Hispanics* (pp. 99–136). Washington, DC: American Psychological Association.

Perkins, D. F. (1981). *The mind's best work.* Cambridge, MA: Harvard University Press.

Perkins, D. F., & Simmons, R. (1988). Patterns of misunderstanding: An integrative model for science, math, and programming. *Review of Educational Research, 58,* 303–326.

Perlmutter, B. F. (1987). Personality variables and peer relations of children and adolescents with learning disabilities. In S. J. Ceci (Ed.), *Handbook of cognitive, social, and neuropsychological aspects of learning disabilities,* Vol. 1. (pp. 339–359). Hillsdale, NJ: Erlbaum & Associates.

Perlmutter, M., Behrend, S. D., Kuo, F., & Muller, A. (1989). Social influences on children's problem solving. *Developmental Psychology, 25*, 744–754.

Perrone, V., et al. (1985). *Portraits of high schools: A supplement to high school: A report on secondary education in America.* Princeton, NJ: Carnegie Foundation for the Advancement of Teaching.

Perry, M., VanderStoep, S. W., & Yu, S. L. (1993). Asking questions in first-grade mathematics classes: Potential influences on mathematical thought. *Journal of Educational Psychology, 85*, 31–40.

Perry, W. (1970). *Forms of ethical and intellectual development in the college years.* New York: Holt.

Petersen, S. E., Fox, P. T., Posner, M. I., Mintum, M., & Raichle, M. E. (1988). Positron emission tomographic studies of the cortical anatomy of single-word processing. *Nature, 331*, 585–589.

Petersen, S. E., Fox, P. T., Snyder, A. Z., & Raichle, M. E. (1990). Activation of extrastriate and frontal cortical areas by visual words and word-like stimuli. *Science, 249*, 1041–1044.

Peterson, M. E., & Haines, L. P. (1992). Orthographic analogy training with kindergarten children: Effects of analogy use, phonemic segmentation, and letter-sound knowledge. *Journal of Reading Behavior, 24*, 109–127.

Peterson, M. J., Meagher, R. B., Jr., Chait, H., & Gillie, S. (1973). The abstraction and generalization of dot patterns. *Cognitive Psychology, 4*, 378–398.

Peterson, P. L. (1979). Direct instruction reconsidered. In P. L. Peterson & H. J. Walberg (Eds.), *Research on teaching: Concepts, findings, and implications* (pp. 57–69). Berkeley, CA: McCutchan.

Peterson, P. L., & Comeaux, M. A. (1987). Teachers' schemata for classroom events: The mental scaffolding of teachers' thinking during classroom instruction. *Teaching & Teacher Education, 3*, 319–331.

Peterson, P., & Janicki, T. (1979). Individual characteristics and children's learning in large-group and small-group approaches. *Journal of Educational Psychology, 71*, 677–687.

Peterson, P., Janicki, T., & Swing, S. (1981). Ability X treatment interaction effects on children's learning in large-group and small-group approaches. *American Educational Research Journal, 18*, 452–474.

Peterson, P., & Swing, S. R. (1985). Students' cognition as mediators in effectiveness of small-group learning. *Journal of Educational Psychology, 77*, 299–312.

Peterson, S. E., DeGracie, J. S., & Ayabe, C. R. (1987). A longitudinal study of the effects of retention/promotion on academic achievement. *American Educational Research Journal, 24*, 107–118.

Petitto, A. L. (1985). Division of labor: Procedural learning in teacher-led small groups. *Cognition and Instruction, 2*, 233–270.

Pfundt, H., & Duit, R. (1991). *Bibliography: Students' alternative frameworks and science education*, 3rd ed. Kiel, Germany: IPN.

Phelps, M. E., Mazziotta, J. C., & Huang, S-C.
(1982). Study of cerebral function with positron computed tomography. *Journal of Cerebral Blood Flow Metabolism, 2*, 113–162.

Phillips, B. N. (1963). Age changes in accuracy of self-perceptions. *Child Development, 34*, 1041–1046.

Phillips, D. A. (1987). Socialization of perceived academic competence among highly competent children. *Child Development, 58*, 1308–1320.

Piaget, J. (1929). *The child's conception of the world.* London: Routledge & Kegan Paul.

Piaget, J. (1965). *The moral judgment of the child.* New York: Free Press.

Piaget, J. (1970). Piaget's theory. In P. H. Mussen (Ed.), *Carmichael's manual of child psychology*, 3rd ed., Vol. 1 (pp. 703–732). New York: John Wiley & Sons.

Piaget, J. (1972). Intellectual evolution from adolescence to adulthood. *Human Development, 15*, 1–12.

Piaget, J. (1983). Piaget's theory. In W. Kesson (Ed.) & P. H. Mussen (General Ed.), *History, theory, and methods*, Vol. 1, *Handbook of child psychology* (pp. 103–128). New York: John Wiley & Sons.

Piaget, J., & Inhelder, B. (1971). *Mental imagery in the child.* New York: Basic Books.

Pichert, J. W., & Anderson, R. C. (1977). Taking different perspectives on a story. *Journal of Educational Psychology, 69*, 309–315.

Pinnell, G. S. (1989). Reading recovery: Helping at-risk children learn to read. *Elementary School Journal, 90*, 161–183.

Pintrich, P. R., & deGroot, E. V. (1990). Motivational and self-regulated learning components of classroom academic performance. *Journal of Educational Psychology, 82*, 33–40.

Pirolli, P. L., & Anderson, J. R. (1985). The role of learning from examples in the acquisition of recursive programming skills. *Canadian Journal of Psychology, 39*, 240–272.

Pirolli, P., & Bielaczyc, K. (1989). Empirical analyses of self-explanation and transfer in learning to program. *Proceedings of the Ninth Annual Conference of the Cognitive Science Society* (pp. 450–457). Hillsdale, NJ: Erlbaum & Associates.

Pirozzolo, F. J. (1979). *The neuropsychology of developmental reading disorders.* New York: Praeger.

Pitts, C. E. (Ed.) (1971). *Operant conditioning in the classroom.* New York: Crowell.

Pizzini, E. L., & Shepardson, D. P. (1992). A comparison of the classroom dynamics of a problem-solving and traditional laboratory model of instruction using path analysis. *Journal of Research in Science Teaching, 29*, 243–258.

Plessas, G. P., & Oakes, C. R. (1964). Prereading experiences of selected early readers. *Reading Teacher, 17*, 241–245.

Plomin, R., DeFries, J. C., & Fulker, D. W. (1988). *Nature and nurture during infancy and early childhood.* New York: Cambridge University Press.

Plomin, R., DeFries, J. C., & McClearn, G. E. (1990). *Behavioral genetics: A primer,* 2nd ed. New York: W.H. Freeman & Co.
Plummer, D. L., & Graziano, W. G. (1987). Impact of grade retention on the social development of elementary school children. *Developmental Psychology, 23*, 267–275.

Poche, C., Yoder, P., & Miltenberger, R. (1988). Teaching self-protection to children using television techniques. *Journal of Applied Behavior Analysis, 21*, 253–261.

Polya, G. (1954a). *Mathematics and plausible reasoning: (a) Induction and analogy in mathematics.* Princeton, NJ: Princeton University Press.

Polya, G., (1954b). *Patterns of plausible inference.* Princeton, NJ: Princeton University Press.

Polya, G. (1957). *How to solve it.* New York: Doubleday.

Polya, G. (1981). *Mathematical discovery* (combined paperback edition). New York: Wiley.

Pontecorvo, C., & Zucchermaglio, C. (1990). A passage to literacy: Learning in social context. In Y. M. Goodman (Ed.), *How children construct literacy: Piagetian perspectives* (pp. 59–98). Newark, DE: International Reading Association.

Poon, L. W. (1985). Differences in human memory with aging: Nature, causes, and clinical implications. In J. E. Birren & K. W. Schaie (Eds.), *Handbook of the psychology of aging* (pp. 427–462). New York: van Nostrand.

Poon, L. W. (1986). *Handbook for clinical memory assessment of older adults.* Washington, DC: American Psychological Association.

Popham, W. J. (1987). The merits of measurement-driven instruction. *Phi Delta Kappan, 68*, 679–682.

Poplin, M. S. (1988a). Holistic/constructivist principles of the teaching/learning process: Implications for the field of learning disabilities. *Journal of Learning Disabilities, 21*, 401–416.

Poplin, M. S. (1988b). The reductionistic fallacy in learning disabilities: Replicating the past by reducing the present. *Journal of Learning Disabilities, 21*, 389–400.

Posner, M. L. (1969). Abstraction and the process of recognition. In G. H. Bower & J. T. Spence (Eds.), *The psychology of learning and motivation*, Vol. 3 (pp. 43–100). New York: Academic Press.

Posner, G. J., Strike, K. A., Hewson, P. W., & Gertzog, W. A. (1982). Accommodation of a scientific conception: Toward a theory of conceptual change. *Science Education, 66*, 211–227.

Posner, M. I., & Keele, S. W. (1968). On the genesis of abstract ideas. *Journal of Experimental Psychology, 77*, 353–363.

Posner, M. I., & Keele, S. W. (1970). Retention of abstract ideas. *Journal of Experimental Psychology, 83*, 304–308.

Posner, M. I., Petersen, S. E., Fox, P. T., & Raichle, M. E. (1988). Localization of cognitive operations in the human brain. *Science, 240*, 1627–1631.

Powell, A. G., Farrar, E., & Cohen, D. K. (1985). *The shopping mall high school.* Boston: Houghton Mifflin.

Powell, R. E., Locke, D. C., & Spinthall, N. A. (1991). Female offenders and their guards: A programme to promote moral and ego development of both groups. *Journal of Moral Education, 20,* 191–203.

Power, F. C., Higgins, A., & Kohlberg, L. (1989). *Lawrence Kohlberg's approach to moral education.* New York: Columbia University Press.

Power, F. C., & Power, M. R. (1992). A raft of hope: Democratic education and the challenge of pluralism. *Journal of Moral Education, 21,* 193–205.

Pratt, A. C., & Brady, S. (1988). Relation of phonological awareness to reading disability in children and adults. *Journal of Educational Psychology, 80,* 319–323.

Pratt, M. W., Boyes, C., Robins, S., & Manchester, J. (1989). Telling tales: Working memory, and the narrative cohesion of story retellings. *Developmental Psychology, 25,* 628–635.

Pratt, M. W., Kerig, P., Cowan, P. A., & Cowan, C. P. (1988). Mothers and fathers teaching 3-year-olds: Authoritative parenting and adult scaffolding of young children's learning. *Developmental Psychology, 24,* 832–839.

Prawat, R. S. (1989). Promoting access to knowledge, strategy, and disposition in students: A research synthesis. *Review of Educational Research, 59,* 1–42.

Prechtl, H. F. R. (1986). New perspectives in early human development. *European Journal of Obstetrics, Gynecology, and Reproductive Biology, 21,* 347–354.

Pressey, S. L. (1926). A simple apparatus which gives tests and scores—and teaches. *School and Society, 23,* 373–376.

Pressey, S. L. (1963). Teaching machine (and learning theory) crisis. *Journal of Applied Psychology, 47,* 1–6.

Pressley, G. M. (1976). Mental imagery helps eight-year-olds remember what they read. *Journal of Educational Psychology, 68,* 355–359.

Pressley, M. (1977). Imagery and children's learning: Putting the picture in developmental perspective. *Review of Educational Research, 47,* 586–622.

Pressley, M. (1979). Increasing children's self-control through cognitive interventions. *Review of Educational Research, 49,* 319–370.

Pressley, M. (1982). Elaboration and memory development. *Child Development, 53,* 296–309.

Pressley, M. (1983). Making meaningful materials easier to learn. In M. Pressley & J. R. Levin (Eds.), *Cognitive strategy research: Educational applications* (pp. 239–266). New York: Springer-Verlag.

Pressley, M. (1986). The relevance of the good strategy user model to the teaching of mathematics. *Educational Psychologist, 21,* 139–161.

Pressley, M. (1990). Four more considerations about self-regulation among mentally retarded persons. *American Journal of Mental Deficiency, 94,* 369–371.

Pressley, M., Borkowski, J. G., & Johnson, C. J. (1987). The development of good strategy use: Imagery and related mnemonic strategies. In M. A. McDaniel & M. Pressley (Eds.), *Imagery and related mnemonic processes: Theories, individual differences, and applications* (pp. 274–301). New York: Springer.

Pressley, M., Borkowski, J. G., & O'Sullivan, J. T. (1984). Memory strategy instruction is made of this: Metamemory and durable strategy use. *Educational Psychologist, 19,* 94–107.

Pressley, M., Borkowski, J. G., & O'Sullivan, J. T. (1985). Children's metamemory and the teaching of memory strategies. In D. L. Forrest-Pressley, G. E. MacKinnon, & T. G. Waller (Eds.), *Metacognition, cognition, and human performance* (pp. 111–153). New York: Academic Press.

Pressley, M., Borkowski, J. G., & Schneider, W. (1987). Cognitive strategies: Good strategy users coordinate metacognition and knowledge. In R. Vasta & G. Whitehurst (Eds.), *Annals of child development,* Vol. 5. (pp. 89–129). Greenwich, CT: JAI Press.

Pressley, M., Borkowski, J. G., & Schneider, W. (1989). Good information processing: What it is and what education can do to promote it. *International Journal of Educational Research, 13,* 857–867.

Pressley, M., & Brewster, M. E. (1990). Imaginal elaboration of illustrations to facilitate fact learning: Creating memories of Prince Edward Island. *Applied Cognitive Psychology, 4,* 359–370.

Pressley, M., Cariglia-Bull, T., Deane, S., & Schneider, W. (1987). Short-term memory, verbal competence, and age as predictors of imagery instructional effectiveness. *Journal of Experimental Child Psychology, 43,* 194–211.

Pressley, M., El-Dinary, P. B., & Brown, R. (1992). Skilled and not-so-skilled reading: Good information processing and not-so-good information processing. In M. Pressley, K. R. Harris, & J. T. Guthrie (Eds.), *Promoting academic competence and literacy: Cognitive research and instructional innovation* (pp. 91–127). San Diego: Academic Press.

Pressley, M., El-Dinary, P. B., & Brown, R. (in press). A transactional strategies instruction Christmas carol. In A. McKeough, J. Lupart, & A. Marini (Eds.), *Teaching for transfer: Fostering generalization in learning.* Hillsdale, NJ: Erlbaum & Associates.

Pressley, M., El-Dinary, P. B., & Brown, R. (1994). Transactional instruction of reading comprehension strategies. In J. Mangieri & C. Collins (Ed.), *Creating powerful thinking in teachers and students: Diverse perspectives.* (pp. 112–139). Fort Worth, TX: Harcourt, Brace.

Pressley, M., El-Dinary, P. B., Gaskins, I., Schuder, T., & Bergman, J. L., Almasi, J., & Brown, R. (1992). Beyond direct explanation: Transactional instruction of reading comprehension strategies. *Elementary School Journal, 92,* 513–556.

Pressley, M., El-Dinary, P. B., Marks, M. B., Brown, R., & Stein, S. (1992). Good strategy instruction is motivating and interesting. In K. A. Renninger, S. Hidi, & A. Krapp (Eds.), *The role of interest in learning and development* (pp. 333–358). Hillsdale, NJ: Erlbaum & Associates.

Pressley, M., & Forrest-Pressley, D. L. (1985). Questions and children's cognitive processing. In A. Graesser & J. Black (Eds.), *Psychology of questions* (pp. 277–296). Hillsdale, NJ: Erlbaum & Associates.

Pressley, M., Forrest-Pressley, D., Elliott-Faust, D. L., & Miller, G. E. (1985). Children's use of cognitive strategies, how to teach them, and what to do if they can't be taught. In M. Pressley & C. J. Brainerd (Eds.), *Cognitive learning and memory in children* (pp. 1–47). New York: Springer-Verlag.

Pressley, M., Gaskins, I. W., Cunicelli, E. A., Burdick, N. J., Schaub-Matt, M., Lee, D. S., & Powell, N. (1991). Strategy instruction at Benchmark School: A faculty interview study. *Learning Disability Quarterly, 14,* 19–48.

Pressley, M., Gaskins, I. W., Wile, D., Cunicelli, B., & Sheridan, J. (1991). Teaching literacy strategies across the curriculum: A case study at Benchmark School. In J. Zutell & S. McCormick (Eds.), *Learner factors/teacher factors: Issues in literacy research and instruction: Fortieth yearbook of the National Reading Conference* (pp. 219–228). Chicago: National Reading Conference.

Pressley, M., & Ghatala, E. S. (1989). Metacognitive benefits of taking a test for children and young adolescents. *Journal of Experimental Child Psychology, 47,* 430–450.

Pressley, M., & Ghatala, E. S. (1990). Self-regulated learning: Monitoring learning from text. *Educational Psychologist, 25,* 19–34.

Pressley, M., Harris, K. R., & Marks, M. B. (1992). But good strategy instructors are constructivists! *Educational Psychology Review, 4,* 3–31.

Pressley, M., Heisel, B. E., McCormick, C. G., & Nakamura, G. V. (1982). Memory strategy instruction with children. In C. J. Brainerd & M. Pressley (Eds.), *Progress in cognitive development research,* Vol. 2, *Verbal processes in children* (pp. 125–159). New York: Springer-Verlag.

Pressley, M., Johnson, C. J., Symons, S., McGoldrick, J. A., & Kurita, J. A. (1989). Strategies that improve children's memory and comprehension of text. *Elementary School Journal, 90,* 3–32.

Pressley, M., & Levin, J. R. (1977a). Developmental differences in subjects' associative learning strategies and performance: Assessing a hypothesis. *Journal of Experimental Child Psychology, 24,* 431–439.

Pressley, M., & Levin, J. R. (1977b). Task parameters affecting the efficacy of a visual imagery learning strategy in younger and older children. *Journal of Experimental Child Psychology, 24,* 53–59.

Pressley, M., & Levin, J. R. (1978). Developmental constraints associated with children's use of the keyword method for foreign language vocabulary learning. *Journal of Experimental Child Psychology, 26,* 359–372.

Pressley, M., Levin, J. R., & Ghatala, E. S. (1984). Memory strategy monitoring in adults and children. *Journal of Verbal Learning and Verbal Behavior, 23,* 270–288.

Pressley, M., Levin, J. R., & Ghatala, E. S. (1988). Strategy-comparison opportunities promote long-term strategy use. *Contemporary Educational Psychology, 13,* 157–168.

Pressley, M., Levin, J. R., Ghatala, E. S., & Ahmad, M. (1987). Test monitoring in young grade-school children. *Journal of Experimental Child Psychology, 43,* 96–111.

Pressley, M., Levin, J. R., & McDaniel, M. A. (1987). Remembering versus inferring what a word means: Mnemonic and contextual approaches. In M. G. McKeown & M. E. Curtis (Eds.), *The nature of vocabulary acquisition* (pp. 107–127). Hillsdale, NJ: Erlbaum & Associates.

Pressley, M., McDaniel, M. A., Turnure, J. E., Wood, E., & Ahmad, M. (1987). Generation and precision of elaboration: Effects on intentional and incidental learning. *Journal of Experimental Psychology: Learning, Memory, and Cognition, 13,* 291–300.

Pressley, M., Ross, K. A., Levin, J. R., & Ghatala, E. S. (1984). The role of strategy utility knowledge in children's strategy decision making. *Journal of Experimental Child Psychology, 38,* 491–504.

Pressley, M., Samuel, J. Hershey, M. M., Bishop, S. L., & Dickinson, D. (1981). Use of a mnemonic technique to teach young children foreign language vocabulary. *Contemporary Educational Psychology, 6,* 110–116.

Pressley, M., Schuder, T., SAIL Faculty and Administration, Bergman, J. L., & El-Dinary, P. B. (1992). A researcher-educator collaborative interview study of transactional comprehension strategies instruction. *Journal of Educational Psychology, 84,* 231–246.

Pressley, M., Snyder, B. L., & Cariglia-Bull, T. (1987). How can good strategy use be taught to children? Evaluation of six approaches. In S. M. Cormier & J. D. Hagman (Eds.), *Transfer of learning: Contemporary research and applications* (pp. 81–120). San Diego: Academic Press.

Pressley, M., Snyder, B. L., Levin, J. R., Murray, H. G., & Ghatala, E. S. (1987). Perceived readiness for examination performance (PREP) produced by initial reading of text and text containing adjunct questions. *Reading Research Quarterly, 22,* 219–236.

Pressley, M., Symons, S., McDaniel, M. A., Snyder, B. L., & Turnure, J. E. (1988). Elaborative interrogation facilitates acquisition of confusing facts. *Journal of Educational Psychology, 80,* 268–278.

Pressley, M., Wood, E., Woloshyn, V. E., Martin, V., King, A., & Menke, D. (1992). Encouraging mindful use of prior knowledge: Attempting to construct explanatory answers facilitates learning. *Educational Psychologist, 27,* 91–110.

Price, J. H., Desmond, S., & Kukulka, G. (1985). *Journal of School Health, 55,* 107–109.

Pritchard, R. (1990). The effects of cultural schemata on reading processing strategies. *Reading Research Quarterly, 25,* 273–295.

Puckering, C., & Rutter, M. (1987). Environmental influences on language development. In W. Yule & M. Rutter (Eds.), *Language development and disorders* (pp. 103–128). Philadelphia: J. B. Lippincott Co.

Purcell-Gates, V. (1991). On the outside looking in: A study of remedial readers' meaning-making while reading literature. *Journal of Reading Behavior, 23,* 235–253.

Purpel, D. E. (1989). *The moral and spiritual crisis in education: A curriculum for justice and compassion in education.* New York: Bergin & Garvey.

Purpel, D., & Ryan, K. (1976). *Moral education . . . it comes with the territory.* Berkeley, CA: McCutchan.

Putnam, R. (1987). Structuring and adjusting content for students: A study of live and simulated tutoring of addition. *American Educational Research Journal, 24,* 13–48.

Putnam, R., Lampert, M., & Peterson, P. L. (1990). Alternative perspectives on knowing mathematics in elementary schools. In C. B. Cazden (Ed.), *Review of Research in Education,* Vol. 16 (pp. 57–150). Washington, DC: American Educational Research Association.

Pylyshen, Z. (1973). What the mind's eye tells the mind's brain: A critique of mental imagery. *Psychological Bulletin, 80,* 1–24.

Rabinowitz, M., Freeman, K., & Cohen, S. (1992). Use and maintenance of strategies: The influence of accessibility on knowledge. *Journal of Educational Psychology, 84,* 211–218.

Rabinowitz, M., & Glaser, R. (1985). Cognitive structure and process in high competent performance. In F. D. Horowitz & M. O'Brien (Eds.), *The gifted and talented: Developmental perspectives* (pp. 75–98). Washington, DC: American Psychological Association.

Rabinowitz, M., & McAuley, R. (1990). Conceptual knowledge processing: An oxymoron? In W. Schneider & F. E. Weinert (Eds.), *Interactions among aptitudes, strategies, and knowledge in cognitive performance* (pp. 117–133). New York: Springer-Verlag.

Rack, J. P., Snowling, M. J., & Olson, R. K. (1992). The nonword reading deficit in developmental dyslexia: A review. *Reading Research Quarterly, 27,* 28–53.

Radford, J. (1990). *Child prodigies and exceptional early achievers.* New York: Free Press.

Radziszewska, B., & Rogoff, B. (1988). Influence of adult and peer collaborators on children's planning skills. *Developmental Psychology, 24,* 840–848.

Ramey, C. T. (1992). High-risk children and IQ: Altering intergenerational patterns. *Intelligence, 16,* 239–256.

Ramey, C. T., & Campbell, F. A. (1987). The Carolina Abecedarian Project: An educational experiment concerning human malleability. In J. J. Gallagher & C. T. Ramey (Eds.), *The malleability of children.* Baltimore: Brooks.

Rand, Y., & Kaniel, S. (1987). Group administration of the LPAD. In C. Lidz (Ed.), *Dynamic assessment* (pp. 196–214). New York: Guilford.

Rand, Y., Tannenbaum, A. J., & Feurstein, R. (1979). Effects of Instrumental Enrichment on the psychoeducational development of low-functioning adolescents. *Journal of Educational Psychology, 71,* 751–763.

Randhawa, B. S., Beamer, J. E., & Lundberg, I. (1993). Role of mathematics self-efficacy in the structural model of mathematics achievement. *Journal of Educational Psychology, 85,* 41–48.

Rao, N., & Moely, B. E. (1989). Producing memory strategy maintenance and generalization by explicit or implicit training of memory knowledge. *Journal of Experimental Child Psychology, 48,* 335–352.

Ravitch, D. (1989). *The schools we deserve.* New York: Basic Books.

Ravitch, D., & Finn. C. (1987). *What do our 17-year-olds know?* New York: Harper & Row.

Rawls, J. (1971). *A theory of justice.* Cambridge, MA: Harvard University Press.

Raymond, C. (1992). Sex differences in gifted math students' achievement. *APS Observer 5, (4),* 5.

Rayner, K. (1988). Word recognition cues in children: The relative use of graphemic cues, orthographic cues, and grapheme-phoneme correspondence rules. *Journal of Educational Psychology, 80,* 473–479.

Rayner, K., Inhoff, A. W., Morrison, R. E., Slowiaczek, M. L., & Bertera, J. H. (1981). Masking of foveal and parafoveal vision during eye fixations in reading. *Journal of Experimental Psychology: Human Perception and Performance, 7,* 167–179.

Rayner, K., & Pollatsek, A. (1989). *The psychology of reading.* Englewood Cliffs, NJ: Prentice-Hall.

Recht, D. R., & Leslie, L. (1988). Effect of prior knowledge on good and poor readers' memory of text. *Journal of Educational Psychology, 80,* 16–20.

Reder, G., McCormick, C. B., & Esselman, E. (1987). Self-referent processing and recall of prose. *Journal of Educational Psychology, 79,* 343–348.

Reder, L. M., Charney, D. H., & Morgan, K. I. (1986). The role of elaborations in learning a skill from instructional text. *Memory and Cognition, 14,* 64–78.

Redfield, D. L., & Rousseau, E. W. (1981). A meta-analysis of experimental research on teacher questioning behavior. *Review of Educational Research, 51,* 237–246.

Reed, S. K. (1972). Pattern recognition and categorization. *Cognitive Psychology, 3,* 382–407.

Reed, S. K. (1989). Constraints on the abstraction of solutions. *Journal of Educational Psychology, 81,* 532–540.

Reed, S. K., Dempster, A., & Ettinger, M. (1985). Usefulness of analogous solutions for solving algebra word problems. *Journal of Experimental Psychology: Learning, Memory, and Cognition, 11,* 106–125.

Reid, M. K., & Borkowski, J. G. (1987). Causal attributions of hyperactive children: Implications for teaching strategies and self-control. *Journal of Educational Psychology, 79,* 296–307.

Reif, F., & Allen, S. (1992). Cognition for interpreting scientific concepts: A study of acceleration. *Cognition and Instruction, 9,* 1–44.

Reisner, E. R., Petry, C. A., & Armitage, M. (1989). *A review of programs involving college students as tutors or mentors in grades K–12.* Washington, DC: Policy Study Associates, Inc.

Renick, M. J., & Harter, S. (1989). Impact of social comparisons on the developing self-perceptions of learning disabled students. *Journal of Educational Psychology, 81,* 631–638.

Renninger, K. A. (1990). Children's play interests, representation, and activity. In R. Fivush & J. Hudson (Eds.), *Knowing and remembering in young children* (pp. 127–165). Cambridge, MA: Cambridge University Press.

Renninger, K. A., & Wozniak, R. H. (1985). Effect of interest on attentional shift, recognition, and recall in young children. *Developmental Psychology, 21,* 624–632.

Renzulli, J. S. (1986). The three-ring conception of giftedness: A developmental model for creative productivity. In R. J. Sternberg & J. E. Davidson (Eds.), *Conceptions of giftedness* (pp. 53–92). Cambridge, UK: Cambridge University Press.

Resnick, D. P. (1991). Historical perspectives on literacy and schooling. In S. R. Graubard (Ed.), *Literacy: An overview by fourteen experts* (pp. 15–32). New York: Noonday Press.

Resnick, L. B. (1983). A developmental theory of number understanding. In H. P. Ginsburg (Ed.), *The development of mathematical thinking* (pp. 109–151). New York: Academic.

Resnick, L. B. (1987). Constructing knowledge in school. In L. S. Liben (Ed.), *Development and learning: Conflict or congruence* (pp. 19–50). Hillsdale, NJ: Erlbaum & Associates.

Resnick, L. B., Levine, J. M., & Teasley, S. D. (Eds.) (1991). *Perspectives on socially shared cognition.* Washington, DC: American Psychological Association.

Rest, J. (1968). *Developmental hierarchy in preference and comprehension of moral judgment.* Unpublished Ph.D. dissertation. University of Chicago, 1968.

Rest, J. (1979). *Development in judging moral issues.* Minneapolis: University of Minnesota Press.

Rest, J. R. (1988). Why does college promote development in moral judgement? *Journal of Moral Education, 17,* 183–194.

Rest, J. R., in collaboration with Barnett, R., Bebeau, M., Deemer, D., Getz, I., Moon, Y., Schlaefli, A., Spickelmier, J., Thoma, S., & Volker, J. (1986). *Moral development: Advances in research and theory.* New York: Praeger.

Reuman, D. A. (1989). How social comparison mediates the relation between ability-grouping practices and students' achievement expectancies in mathematics. *Journal of Educational Psychology, 81,* 178–189.

Reynolds, A. J. (1989). Early schooling of children at risk. *American Educational Research Journal, 28,* 392–422.

Reynolds, A. R., & Walberg, H. J. (1991). A structural model of science achievement. *Journal of Educational Psychology, 83,* 97–107.

Reynolds, C. R., Chastain, R. L., Kaufman, A. S., & McLean, J. E. (1987). Demographic characteristics and IQ among adults: Analysis of the WISC-R standardization sample as a function of the stratification variables. *Journal of School Psychology, 25,* 323–342.

Reynolds, C. R., & Kaiser, S. M. (1990a). Bias in assessment of aptitude. In C. R. Reynolds & R. W. Kamphaus (Eds.), *Handbook of psychological and educational assessment of children: Intelligence & achievement* (pp. 611–653). New York: Guilford Press.

Reynolds, C. R., & Kaiser, S. M. (1990b). Test bias in psychological assessment. In T. B.

Gutkin & C. R. Reynolds (Eds.), *The handbook of school psychology* (pp. 487–525). New York: John Wiley & Sons.

Reynolds, R. E. (1992). Selective attention and prose learning: Theoretical and empirical research. *Educational Psychology Review, 4,* 345–391.

Reynolds, R. E., Shepard, C., Lapan, R., Kreek, C., & Goetz, E. T. (1990). Differences in the use of selective attention by more successful and less successful tenth-grade readers. *Journal of Educational Psychology, 82,* 749–759.

Rice, M. L., Huston, A. C., Truglio, R., & Wright, J. (1990). Words from "Sesame Street": Learning vocabulary from viewing. *Developmental Psychology, 26,* 421–428.

Richardson, A. (1967). Mental practice: A review and discussion. *Research Quarterly, 38,* 95–107, 263–273.

Richardson, S. A., & Koller, H. (1985). Epidemiology. In A. M. Clarke, A. D. B. Clarke, & J. M. Berg (Eds.), *Mental deficiency: The changing outlook,* 4th ed. (pp. 356–400). New York: Free Press.

Richert, E. S. (1991). Rampant problems and promising practices in identification. In N. Colangelo & G. A. Davis (Eds.), *Handbook of gifted education* (pp. 81–96). Boston: Allyn & Bacon.

Rieber, L. P. (1990). Using computer animated graphics in science instruction with children. *Journal of Educational Psychology, 82,* 135–140.

Rieber, L. P. (1991). Animation, incidental learning, and continuing motivation. *Journal of Educational Psychology, 83,* 318–328.

Riesbeck, C. K., & Schank, R. C. (1989). *Inside case-based reasoning.* Hillsdale, NJ: Erlbaum & Associates.

Riley, M. S., & Greeno, J. G. (1988). Developmental analysis of understanding language about quantities and of solving problems. *Cognition and Instruction, 5,* 49–101.

Riley, M. S., Greeno, J. G., & Heller, J. I. (1983). Development of children's problem-solving ability in arithmetic. In H. P. Ginsburg (Ed.), *The development of mathematical thinking* (pp. 153–196). New York: Academic Press.

Rinehart, S. D., Stahl, S. A., & Erickson, L. G. (1986). Some effects of summarization training on reading and studying. *Reading Research Quarterly, 21,* 422–438.

Ringel, B. A., & Springer, C. J. (1980). On knowing how well one is remembering: The persistence of strategy use during transfer. *Journal of Experimental Child Psychology, 29,* 322–333.

Ringness, T. A. (1961). Self concept of children of low, average, and high intelligence. *American Journal of Mental Deficiency, 65,* 453–461.

Rips, L. J., Shoben, E. J., & Smith, E. E. (1973). Semantic distance and the verification of semantic relations. *Journal of Verbal Learning and Verbal Behavior, 12,* 1–20.

Risberg, J. (1986). Regional cerebral blood flow in neuropsychology. *Neuropsychologia, 24,* 135–140.

Rivera v. City of Wichita Falls, 665 F. 2d 531 (1982).

Rizzo, T. A., Corsaro, W. A., & Bates, J. E. (1992).

Ethnographic methods and interpretive analysis: Expanding the methodological options of psychologists. *Developmental Review, 12,* 101–123.

Roberts, B. (1992). The evolution of the young child's concept of *word* as a unit of spoken language. *Reading Research Quarterly, 27,* 124–138.

Roberts, P. (1983). Memory strategy instruction with the elderly: What should memory training be the training of? In M. Pressley & J. R. Levin (Eds.), *Cognitive strategy research: Psychological foundations* (pp. 75–100). New York: Springer-Verlag.

Robertson, E. (1992). Is Dewey's educational vision still viable? In G. Grant (Ed.), *Review of Research in Education,* Vol. 18 (pp. 335–381). Washington, DC: American Educational Research Association.

Robinson, C. S., & Hayes, J. R. (1978). Making inferences about relevance in understanding problems. In R. Revlin & R. E. Mayer (Eds.), *Human reasoning.* Washington, DC: Winston.

Robinson, J. A., & Kingsley, M. E. (1977). Memory and intelligence: Age and ability differences in strategies and organization of recall. *Intelligence, 1,* 318–330.

Rodriguez, O. (1992). Introduction to technical and societal issues in the psychological testing of Hispanics. In K. F. Geisinger (Ed.), *Psychological testing of Hispanics* (pp. 11–16). Washington, DC: American Psychological Association.

Roehler, L. R., & Duffy, G. G. (1984). Direct explanation of comprehension processes. In G. G. Duffy, L. R. Roehler, & J. Mason (Eds.), *Comprehension instruction: Perspectives and suggestions* (pp. 265–280). New York: Longmans.

Rogers, H., & Saklofske, D. H. (1985). Self-concept, locus of control and performance expectations of learning disabled children. *Journal of Learning Disabilities, 18,* 273–278.

Rogoff, B. (1990). *Apprenticeship in thinking: Cognitive development in social context.* New York: Oxford University Press.

Rohman, D. G. (1965). Pre-writing: The stage of discovery in the writing process. *College Composition and Communication, 16,* 106–112.

Rohwer, W. D., Jr. (1980b). How the smart get smarter. *Educational Psychologist, 15,* 34–43.

Rohwer, W. D., Jr., & Litrownik, J. (1983). Age and individual differences in the learning of a memorization procedure. *Journal of Educational Psychology, 75,* 799–810.

Rohwer, W. D., Jr., Raines, J. M., Eoff, J., & Wagner, M. (1977). The development of elaborative propensity during adolescence. *Journal of Experimental Child Psychology, 23,* 472–492.

Romberg, T. A., & Carpenter, T. C. (1986). Research on teaching and learning mathematics: Two disciplines of scientific inquiry. In M. C. Wittrock (Ed.), *Handbook of research on teaching,* 3rd ed., (pp. 850–873). New York: MacMillan.

Rosch, E. (1975). Cognitive representations of semantic categories. *Journal of Experimental Psychology: General, 104,* 192–233.

Rosch, E. (1978). Principles of categorization. In E. Rosch & B. Lloyd (Eds.), *Cognition and cate-*

gorization (pp. 9–31). Hillsdale, NJ: Lawrence Erlbaum Associates.

Rosch, E., & Mervis, C. (1975). Family resemblance studies in the internal structure of categories. *Cognitive Psychology, 7,* 575–605.

Rose, M. (1985). The language of exclusion: Writing instruction in the university. *College English, 47,* 341–359.

Rose, M. (1989). *Lives on the boundary: The struggle and achievements of America's underprepared.* New York: Free Press.

Rose, S. A. (1989). Measuring infant intelligence: New perspectives. In M. H. Bornstein & N. A. Krasnegor (Eds.), *Stability and continuity in mental development* (pp. 171–188). Hillsdale, NJ: Erlbaum & Associates.

Rosen, M. G. (1985). Factors during labor and delivery that influence brain disorders. In J. Freeman (Ed.), *Prenatal and perinatal factors associated with brain disorders* (NIH Publication No. 85–1149). (pp. 237–262). Washington, DC: U.S. Department of Health and Human Services.

Rosenblatt, L. M. (1978). *The reader, the text, the poem: The transactional theory of the literary work.* Carbondale: Southern Illinois University Press.

Rosenblatt, L. M. (1991). Literary theory. In J. Flood, J. M. Jensen, D. Lapp, & J. R. Squire (Eds.), *Handbook of research on teaching the English language arts* (pp. 57–62). New York: MacMillan.

Rosenshine, B. V. (1979). Content, time, and direct instruction. In P. L. Peterson & H. J. Walberg (Eds.), *Research on teaching: Concepts, findings, and implications* (pp. 28–56). Berkeley, CA: McCutchan.

Rosenshine, B., & Chapman, S. (1992, April). *Instructional elements in studies which taught students to generate questions.* Presented at the annual meeting of the American Educational Research Association, San Francisco.

Rosenshine, B., & Meister, C. (1992). *Reciprocal teaching: A review of nineteen experimental studies.* Manuscript submitted for publication consideration. Champaign-Urbana, IL: University of Illinois, Department of Educational Psychology.

Rosenshine, B., & Trapman, S. (1992, April). *Teaching students to generate questions: A review of research.* Presented at the annual meeting of the American Educational Research Association, San Francisco.

Rosenshine, B. V., & Stevens, R. (1984). Classroom instruction in reading. In P. D. Pearson, R. Barr, M. L. Kamil, & P. Mosenthal (Eds.), *Handbook of reading research* (pp. 745–798). New York: Longman.

Rosenthal, R. (1985). From unconscious experimenter bias to teacher expectancy effects. In J. B. Dusek (Ed.), *Teacher expectancies* (pp. 37–65). Hillsdale, NJ: Erlbaum & Associates.

Rosenthal, R., & Jacobson, L. (1968). *Pygmalion in the classroom: Teacher expectation and pupils' intellectual development.* New York: Holt, Rinehart, & Winston.

Rosenthal, T. L., & Zimmerman, B. J. (1978). *Social learning and cognition.* New York: Academic Press.

Roser, N., & Martinez, M. (1985). Roles adults play in preschool responses to literature. *Language Arts, 62,* 485–490.

Ross, A. O. (1981). *Child behavior therapy.* New York: John Wiley & Sons.

Ross, B. H. (1984). Remindings and their effects in learning a cognitive skill. *Cognitive Psychology, 16,* 371–416.

Ross, B. H. (1987). This is like that: The use of earlier problems and the separation of similarity effects. *Journal of Experimental Psychology: Learning, Memory, and Cognition, 13,* 629–639.

Ross, B. H. (1989). Remindings in learning and instruction. In S. Vosniadou & A. Ortony (Eds.), *Similarity and analogical reasoning* (pp. 438–469). Cambridge, UK: Cambridge University Press.

Ross, B. L., & Berg, C. A. (1992). Examining idiosyncrasies in script reports across the lifespan: Distortions or derivations of experience? In R. L. West & J. D. Sinnott (Eds.), *Everyday memory and aging: Current research and methodology* (pp. 39–53). New York: Springer-Verlag.

Ross, H. S., & Balzer, R. H. (1975). Determinants and consequences of children's questions. *Child Development, 46,* 536–539.

Ross, H. S., & Killey, J. C. (1977). The effect of questioning on retention. *Child Development, 48,* 312–314.

Ross, J. A. (1988). Controlling variables: A meta-analysis of training studies. *Review of Educational Research, 58,* 405–437.

Ross, L. E., & Ross, S. M. (1984). Oculomotor functioning and the learning and cognitive processes of the intellectually handicapped. In P. H. Brooks, R. Sperber, & C. McCauley (Eds.), *Learning and cognition in the mentally retarded* (pp. 217–235). Hillsdale, NJ: Erlbaum & Associates.

Ross, S. M., & Ross, L. E. (1976). The conditioning of skeletal and autonomic responses: Normal-retardate stimulus trace differences. In N. R. Ellis (Ed.), *International review of research in mental retardation,* Vol. 8. New York: Academic Press.

Roth, K. J. (1990). Developing meaningful conceptual understanding in science. In B. F. Jones & L. Idol (Eds.), *Dimensions of thinking and cognitive instruction* (pp. 139–175). Hillsdale, NJ: Lawrence Erlbaum Associates.

Roth, K. J. (1991). Reading science texts for conceptual change. In C. M. Santa & D. E. Alvermann (Eds.), *Science learning: Processes and applications* (pp. 48–63). Newark, DE: International Reading Association.

Rothkopf, E. Z. (1966). Learning from written materials: An exploration of the control of inspection of test-like events. *American Educational Research Journal, 3,* 241–249.

Rovet, J. F., Ehrlich, R. M., Czuchta, D., & Akler, M. (1993). Psychoeducational characteristics of children and adolescents with insulin-dependent diabetes mellitus. *Journal of Learning Disabilities, 26,* 7–22.

Rovet, J. F., Ehrlich, R. M., & Hoppe, M. (1988). Specific intellectual deficits in children with early onset diabetes mellitus. *Child Development, 59,* 226–234.

Rowan, B., & Guthrie, L. F. (1989). The quality of Chapter 1 instruction: Results from a study of twenty-four schools. In R. E. Slavin, N. L. Karweit, & N. A. Madden (Eds.), *Effective programs for students at risk.* Boston: Allyn & Bacon.

Royer, J. M., Abranovic, W. A., & Sinatra, G. M. (1987). Using entering reading comprehension performance as a predictor of performance in college classes. *Journal of Educational Psychology, 79,* 19–26.

Royer, J. M., Marchant, H. G. III, Sinatra, G. M., & Lovejoy, D. A. (1990). The prediction of college course performance from reading comprehension performance: Evidence for general and specific prediction factors. *American Educational Research Journal, 27,* 158–179.

Ruff, H. A., Lawson, K. R., Parrinello, R., & Weissberg, R. (1990). Long-term stability of individual differences in sustained attention in the early years. *Child Development, 61,* 60–75.

Rulon, D. (1992). The just community: A method for staff development. *Journal of Moral Education, 21,* 217–224.

Rumelhart, D. E., & McClelland, J. L. (1986). *Parallel distributed processing,* Vol. 1. Cambridge, MA: MIT Press.

Rundus, D. (1971). Analysis of rehearsal processes in free recall. *Journal of Experimental Psychology, 89,* 63–77.

Rushton, J. P. (1992). Life-history comparisons between Orientals and whites at a Canadian university. *Personality and individual differences, 13,* 439–442.

Rushton, J. P., Brainerd, C. J., & Pressley, M. (1983). Behavioral development and construct validity: The principle of aggregation. *Psychological Bulletin, 94,* 18–38.

Russell, T., & Johnston, P. (1988, March). *Teachers learning from experiences of teaching: Analysis based on metaphor and reflection.* Presented at the annual meeting of the American Educational Research Association, New Orleans.

Russow, R. A., & Pressley, M. (1993). *Use of graphing calculators increases students' conceptual understanding of graphing: A quasi-experimental and true experimental evaluation.* Technical Report. College Park, MD: University of Maryland, Department of Human Development (Educational Psychology).

Ruth, L. P. (1991). Who determines policy? Power and politics in English language arts education. In J. Flood, J. M. Jensen, D. Lapp, & J. R. Squire (Eds.), *Handbook of research on teaching the English language arts* (pp. 3–17). New York: MacMillan.

Rutter, M. (1983). School effects of pupil progress: Research findings and policy implications. In L. Shulman & G. Sykes (Eds.), *Handbook of teaching and policy* (pp. 3–41). New York: Longman.

Ryle, G. (1949). *The concept of mind.* New York: Barnes & Noble.

Rynders, J. E., & Horrobin, J. M. (1990). Always trainable? Never educable? Updating educational expectations concerning children with

Down Syndrome. *American Journal of Mental Retardation, 95,* 77–83.

Sabers, D. S., Cushing, K. S., & Berliner, D. C. (1991). Differences among teachers in a task characterized by simultaneity, multidimensionality, and immediacy. *American Educational Research Journal, 28,* 63–88.

Sadoski, M. (1983). An exploratory study of the relationship between reported imagery and the comprehension and recall of a story. *Reading Research Quarterly, 19,* 110–123.

Sadoski, M. (1985). The natural use of imagery in story comprehension and recall: Replication and extension. *Reading Research Quarterly, 20,* 658–667.

Sadoski, M., Goetz, E. T., & Fritz, J. B. (1993a). A causal model of sentence recall: Effects of familiarity, concreteness, comprehensibility, and interestingness. *Journal of Reading Behavior, 25,* 5–16.

Sadoski, M., Goetz, E. T., & Fritz, J. B. (1993b). Impact of concreteness on comprehensibility. *Journal of Educational Psychology, 85,* 291–204.

Sadoski, M., Goetz, E. T., & Kangiser, S. (1988). Imagination in story response: Relationship between imagery, affect, and structural importance. *Reading Research Quarterly, 23,* 320–336.

Sadoski, M., & Quast, Z. (1990). Reader response and long-term recall for journalistic text: The roles of imagery, affect, and importance. *Reading Research Quarterly, 25,* 256–272.

Sagerman, N., & Mayer, R. E. (1987). Forward transfer of different reading strategies evoked by adjunct questions in science text. *Journal of Educational Psychology, 79,* 189–191.

Salomon, G., & Perkins, D. N. (1989). Rocky roads to transfer: Rethinking mechanisms of a neglected phenomenon. *Educational Psychologist, 24,* 113–142.

Salthouse, T. A. (1982). *Adult cognition: An experimental psychology of human aging.* New York: Springer-Verlag.

Salthouse, T. A. (1992). The information-processing perspective on cognitive aging. In R. J. Sternberg & C. A. Berg (Eds.), *Intellectual development* (pp. 261–277). Cambridge, UK: Cambridge University Press.

Salthouse, T. A., & Babcock, R. L. (1991). Decomposing adult age differences in working memory. *Developmental Psychology, 27,* 763–776.

Salthouse, T. A., Kausler, D. H., & Saults, J. S. (1988). Investigation of student status, background variables, and the feasibility of standard tasks in cognitive aging research. *Psychology and Aging, 3,* 29–37.

Saltz, E., Soller, E., & Sigel, I. (1972). The development of natural language concepts. *Child Development, 43,* 1191–1202.

Salvia, J., & Hughes, C. (1990). *Curriculum-based assessment: Testing what is taught.* New York: MacMillan.

Sameroff, A. J. (1975). Early influences on development: Fact or fancy? *Merrill-Palmer Quarterly, 21,* 267–294.

Sameroff, A. J., & Chandler, M. J. (1975). Reproductive risk and the continuum of caretaking casualty. In F. D. Horowitz, M. Hetherington,

S. Scarr-Salapatek, & G. Siegel (Eds.), *Review of child development research,* Vol. 4. (pp. 187–244). Chicago: University of Chicago Press.

Sameroff, A. J., & Fiese, B. H. (1990). Transactional regulation and early intervention. In S. J. Meisels & J. P. Shonkoff (Eds.), *Handbook of early childhood intervention* (pp. 119–149). Cambridge, UK: Cambridge University Press.

Samuels, M. T., Killip, S. M., MacKenzie, H., & Fagan, J. (1992). Evaluating preschool programs: The role of dynamic assessment. In H. C. Haywood & D. Tzuriel (Eds.), *Interactive assessment* (pp. 251–271). New York: Springer-Verlag.

Samuels, M., Tzuriel, D., & Malloy-Miller, T. (1989). Dynamic assessment of children with learning disabilities. In R. T. Brown & M. Chazan (Eds.), *Learning difficulties and emotional problems* (pp. 145–165). Calgary: Detselig Enterprises.

Samuels, S. J. (1970). Effects of pictures on learning to read, comprehension, and attitudes. *Review of Educational Research, 40,* 397–407.

Samuels, S. J., Miller, N., & Eisenberg, P. (1979). Practice effects on the unit of word recognition. *Journal of Educational Psychology, 71,* 514–520.

Samuels, S. J., Schermer, N., & Reinking, D. (1992). Reading fluency: Techniques for making decoding automatic. In S. J. Samuels & A. E. Farstrup (Eds.), *What research has to say about reading instruction* (pp. 124–144). Newark, DE: International Reading Association.

Sandoval, J. H., & Mille, M. P. W. (1980). Accuracy judments of WISC-R items difficulty for minority groups. *Journal of Consulting and Clinical Psychology, 48,* 249–253.

Santa, C. M., & Havens, L. T. (1991). Learning through writing. In C. M. Santa & D. E. Alvermann (Eds.), *Science learning: Processes and applications* (pp. 122–133). Newark, DE: International Reading Association.

Sattler, J. M. (1992). *Assessment of children,* Revised and updated 3rd ed. San Diego: J. M. Sattler.

Sawyer, R. J., Graham, S., & Harris, K. R. (1992). Direct teaching, strategy instruction, and strategy instruction with explicit self-regulation: Effects on composition skills and self-efficacy of students with learning disabilities. *Journal of Educational Psychology, 84,* 340–352.

Saxe, G. B. (1988). The mathematics of child street vendors. *Child Development, 59,* 1415–1425.

Scarborough, H. S. (1989). Prediction of reading disability from familial and individual differences. *Journal of Educational Psychology, 81,* 101–108.

Scarborough, H. S. (1990). Very early language deficits in dyslexic children. *Child Development, 61,* 1728–1743.

Scardamalia, M., & Bereiter, C. (1986). Research on written composition. In M. C. Wittrock (Ed.), *Handbook of research on teaching,* 3rd ed. (pp. 778–803). New York: MacMillan.

Scarr, S. (1992). Developmental theories for the

1990s: Development and individual differences. *Child Development, 63,* 1–19.

Scarr, S., & Kidd, K. K. (1983). Developmental behavior genetics. In M. M. Haith & J. J. Campos (Eds.) & P. H. Mussen (Gen. Ed.), *Handbook of child psychology,* Vol. II, *Infancy and developmental psychobiology* (pp. 345–433). New York: John Wiley & Sons.

Scarr, S., & McCartney, K. (1983). How people make their own environments: A theory of genotype-environment effects. *Child Development, 54,* 424–435.

Scarr, S., & Weinberg, R. A. (1976). IQ test performance of black children adopted by white families. *American Psychologist, 31,* 726–739.

Scarr, S., & Weinberg, R. A. (1983). The Minnesota adoption studies: Genetic differences and malleability. *Child Development, 54,* 260–268.

Schaie, K. W. (1980). Age changes in intelligence. In R. L. Sprott (Ed.), *Age, learning ability, & intelligence* (pp. 41–77). New York: Van Nostrand.

Schaie, K. W., & Labouvie-Vief, G. V. (1974). Generational versus ontogenetic components of change in adult cognitive behavior: A fourteen-year cross-sequential study. *Developmental Psychology, 10,* 305–320.

Schank, R. C., & Abelson, R. P. (1977). *Scripts, plans, goals, and understanding.* Hillsdale, NJ: Erlbaum & Associates.

Schauble, L. (1990). Belief revision in children: The role of prior knowledge and strategies for generating evidence. *Journal of Experimental Child Psychology, 49,* 31–57.

Scheffler, I. (1965). *Conditions of knowledge.* Glenview, IL: Scott, Foresman.

Scheid, K. (1993). *Helping students become strategic learners: Guidelines for teaching and choosing instructional materials.* Cambridge, MA: Brookline Books.

Schloss, P. J. (1992). Special issue: Integrating learners with disabilities in regular education programs. *Elementary School Journal, 92 (3).*

Schmeiser, C. B. (1992). Reactions to technical and societal issues in testing Hispanics. In K. F. Geisinger (Ed.), *Psychological testing of Hispanics* (pp. 79–88). Washington, DC: American Psychological Association.

Schmidt, C. R., Ollendick, T. H., & Stanowicz, L. B. (1988). Developmental changes in the influence of assigned goals on cooperative and competition. *Developmental Psychology, 24,* 574–579.

Schneider, Wa., Dumais, S. T., & Shiffrin, R. M. (1984). Automatic and controlled processing and attention. In R. Parasuraman & D. R. Davies (Eds.), *Varieties of attention* (pp. 1–27). Orlando, FL: Academic Press.

Schneider, Wa., & Graham, D. J. (1992). Introduction to connections models in education. *Educational Psychologist, 27,* 513–530.

Schneider, Wa., & Shiffrin, R. M. (1977). Controlled and automatic processing: Detection, search, and attention. *Psychological Review, 84,* 1–66.

Schneider, W., & Bjorklund, D. F. (1992). Expertise, aptitude, and strategic remembering. *Child Development, 63,* 461–473.

Schneider, W., & Körkel, J. (1989). The knowledge base and text recall: Evidence from a short-term longitudinal study. *Contemporary Educational Psychology, 14,* 382–393.

Schneider, W., Körkel, J., & Weinert, F. E. (1989). Domain-specific knowledge and memory performance: A comparison of high- and low-aptitude children. *Journal of Educational Psychology, 81,* 306–312.

Schneider, W., Körkel, J., & Weinert, F. E. (1990). Expert knowledge, general abilities, and text processing. In W. Schneider & F. E. Weinert (Eds.), *Interactions among aptitudes, strategies, and knowledge in cognitive performance* (pp. 235–251). New York: Springer-Verlag.

Schneider, W., & Pressley, M. (1989). *Memory development between 2 and 20.* New York: Springer-Verlag.

Schoenfeld, A. (1979). Explicit heuristic training as a variable in problem-solving performance. *Journal for Research in Mathematics Education, 10,* 173–187.

Schoenfeld, A. (1985). *Mathematical problem solving.* New York: Academic Press.

Schoenfeld, A. (1987). *Cognitive science and mathematics education.* Hillsdale, NJ: Erlbaum & Associates.

Schoenfeld, A. (1989a). Exploration of students' mathematical beliefs and behavior. *Journal for Research in Mathematics Education, 20,* 338–355.

Schoenfeld, A. (1989b). Teaching mathematical thinking and problem solving. In L. B. Resnick & B. L. Klopfer (Eds.), *Toward the thinking curriculum* (pp. 83–103). *(1989 Yearbook of the Association for Supervision and Curriculum Development).* Washington, DC: ASCD.

Schoenfeld, A. (1992). Learning to think mathematically: Problem solving, metacognition, and sense making in mathematics. In D. A. Grouws (Ed.), *Handbook of research on mathematics teaching and learning* (pp. 334–370). New York: MacMillan.

Schoenfeld, A., & Hermann, D. J. (1982). Problem perception and knowledge structure in expert and novice mathematics problem solvers. *Journal of Experimental Psychology: Learning, Memory, and Cognition, 5,* 484–494.

Schommer, M., Crouse, A., & Rhodes, N. (1992). Epistemological beliefs and mathematical text comprehension: Believing it is simple does not make it so. *Journal of Educational Psychology, 84,* 435–443.

Schön, D. A. (1983). *The reflective practitioner: How professionals think in action.* London: Temple Smith.

Schön, D. A. (1987). *Educating the reflective practitioner.* San Francisco: Jossey-Bass.

Schrage, M. (1990). *Shared minds: The new technologies of collaboration.* New York: Random House.

Schriver, K. A. (1986, April). *Teaching writers to predict readers' comprehension problems with text.* Paper presented at the annual meeting of the American Educational Research Association, San Francisco.

Schroeder, T. L., & Lester, F. K. Jr. (1989). Developing understanding in mathematics via problem solving. In P. R. Trafton & A. P. Schulte (Eds.), *New directions for elementary school mathematics: 1989 yearbook of the National Council of Teachers of Mathematics* (pp. 31–42). Reston, VA: National Council of Teachers of Mathematics.

Schumaker, J. B., & Deshler, D. D. (1992). Validation of learning strategy interventions for students with learning disabilities: Results of a programmatic research effort. In D. Y. L. Wong (Ed.), *Contemporary intervention research in learning disabilities: An international perspective* (pp. 22–46). New York: Springer-Verlag.

Schumaker, J. B., & Lyerla, K. (1991). *The paragraph writing strategy: Instructor's manual.* Lawrence, KS: University of Kansas, Institute for Research in Learning Disabilities.

Schunk, D. H. (1990). Goal setting and self-efficacy during self-regulated learning. *Educational Psychologist, 25,* 71–86.

Schunk, D. H. (1991). Self–efficacy and academic motivation. *Educational Psychologist, 26,* 207–232.

Schunk, D. H., & Cox, P. D. (1986). Strategy training and attributional feedback with learning disabled students. *Journal of Educational Psychology, 78,* 201–209.

Schunk, D. H., Hanson, A. R., & Cox, P. D. (1987). Peer-model attributes and children's achievement behaviors. *Journal of Educational Psychology, 79,* 54–61.

Schuster, D. T. (1990). Fulfillment of potential, life satisfaction, and competence: Comparing four cohorts of gifted women at midlife. *Journal of Educational Psychology, 82,* 471–478.

Schwantes, F. M. (1991). Children's use of semantic and syntactic information for word recognition and determination of sentence meaningfulness. *Journal of Reading Behavior, 23,* 335–350. ·

Schwegler, R. A., & Shamoon, L. K. (1991). Meaning attribution in ambiguous text. In C. Bazerman & J. Paradis (Eds.), *Textual dynamics of the professions: Historical and contemporary studies of writing in professional communities* (pp. 216–233). Madison: University of Wisconsin Press.

Scott, D. T. (1987). Premature infants in later childhood: Some recent followup results. *Seminary Perinatology, 11,* 191–199.

Scott, J. A., & Ehri, L. C. (in press). Sight word reading in prereaders: Use of logographic vs. alphabetic access routes. *Journal of Reading Behavior.*

Scott, T., Cole, M., & Engel, M. (1992). Computers and education: A cultural constructivist perspective. In G. Grant (Ed.), *Review of Research in Education,* Vol. 18 (pp. 191–251). Washington, DC: American Educational Research Association.

Scruggs, T. E., & Mastropieri, M. A. (1989). Reconstructive elaborations: A model for content area learning. *American Educational Research Journal, 26,* 311–327.

Secada, W. G. (1992). Race, ethnicity, social class, language, and achievement in mathematics. In D. A. Grouws (Ed.), *Handbook of research on mathematics teaching and learning* (pp. 623–660). New York: MacMillan.

Secan, K. E., Egel, A. L., & Tilley, C. S. (1989). Acquisition, generalization, and maintenance of question-answering skills in autistic children. *Journal of Applied Behavior Analysis, 22,* 181–196.

Seidel, J. F. (1992). Children with HIV-related developmental difficulties. *Phi Delta Kappan, 74,* 38–40, 56.

Seidenberg, M. S., & McClelland, J. L. (1989). A distributed, developmental model of word recognition and naming. *Psychological Review, 96,* 523–568.

Selfridge, O. G. (1959). Pandemonium: A paradigm for learning. In D. V. Blake & A. M. Uttley (Eds.), *Proceeding of the symposium on the mechanization of thought processes.* London: H.M. Stationery Office.

Seligman, M. E. P., & Hager, J. L. (1972). *Biological boundaries of learning.* New York: Appleton-Century-Crofts.

Semb, G. B., Ellis, J. A., & Araujo, J. (1993). Long-term memory for knowledge learned in school. *Journal of Educational Psychology, 85,* 305–316.

Service, V., Lock, A., & Chandler, P. (1989). Individual differences in early communicative development: A social constructivist perspective. In S. von Tetzchner, L. S. Siegel, & L. Smith (Eds.), *The social and cognitive aspects of normal and atypical language development* (pp. 23–49). New York: Springer-Verlag.

Sexson, S. B., & Madan-Swain, A. (1993). School reentry for the child with chronic illness. *Journal of Learning Disabilities, 26,* 115–126.

Seymour, P. H. K., & Elder, L. (1986). Beginning reading without phonology. *Cognitive Neuropsychology, 3,* 1–36.

Shanahan, T., & Tierney, R. J. (1990). Reading-writing connections: The relations among three perspectives. In J. Zutell & S. McCormick (Eds.), *Literacy theory and research: Analyses from multiple paradigms, Thirty-ninth yearbook of the National Reading Conference* (pp. 13–34). Chicago: National Reading Conference.

Shapiro, E. S. (1990). An integrated model for curriculum-based assessment. *School Psychology Review, 19,* 331–349.

Sharp, A. M. (1987). What is a 'community of inquiry'? *Journal of Moral Education, 16,* 37–45.

Sharp, A. M., & Reed, R. F. (1992). *Studies in philosophy for children: Harry Stottlemeier's discovery.* Philadelphia: Temple University Press.

Sharp, D., Cole, M., & Lave, C. (1979). Education and cognitive development: The evidence from experimental research. *Monographs of the Society for Research in Child Development, 44* (Serial No. 178).

Shaughnesy, M. P. (1977). *Errors and expectations: A guide for the teacher of basic writing.* New York: Oxford University Press.

Shavelson, R. J., Baxter, G. P., & Pine, J. (1992). Performance assessments: Political rhetoric and measurement reality. *Educational Researcher, 21 (4),* 22–27.

Shaywitz, S. E., & Shaywitz, B. A. (1992). Learning disabilities and attention deficits in the school setting. In L. J. Meltzer (Ed.), *Strategy assessment and instruction for students with learning disabilities: From theory to practice* (pp. 221–241). Austin, TX: PRO-ED.

Shell, D. F., Murphy, C. C., & Bruning, R. H. (1989). Self-efficacy and outcome expectancy mechanisms in reading and writing achievement. *Journal of Educational Psychology, 81,* 91–100.

Shepard, L. A. (1989). A review of research on kindergarten retention. In L. A. Shepard & M. L. Smith (Eds.), *Flunking grades: Research and policies on retention* (pp. 64–78). Philadelphia: Falmer Press.

Shephard, L. A. (1993). Evaluating test validity. In L. Darling-Hammond (Ed.), *Review of Research in Education,* Vol. 19 (pp. 405–450). Washington, DC: American Educational Research Association.

Sherman, L. W. (1988). A comparative study of cooperative and competitive achievement in two secondary biology classrooms: The group investigative model versus an individually competitive goal structure. *Journal of Research in Science Teaching, 26,* 55–64.

Sherris, J. (1984). The effects of concept relatedness of instruction and locus of control orientation on the meaningful learning achievements of high school biology students. *Journal of Research in Science Teaching, 41,* 83–89.

Shiffrin, R. M., & Schneider, Wa. (1977). Controlled and automatic human information processing: perceptual learning, automatic attending, and a general theory. *Psychological Review, 84,* 127–190.

Shimron, J. (1975). Imagery and the comprehension of prose by elementary school children. (Doctoral dissertation, University of Pittsburgh, 1974). *Dissertation Abstracts International, 36,* 795-A (University Microfilms No. 75-18, 254).

Shinn, M. R., Rosenfeld, S., & Knutson, N. (1989). Curriculum-based assessment: A comparison of models. *School Psychology Review, 18,* 299–316.

Shirey, L. L., & Reynolds, R. E. (1988). Effect of interest on attention and learning. *Journal of Educational Psychology, 80,* 159–166.

Shochet, I. M. (1992). A dynamic assessment for undergraduate admission: The inverse relationship between modifiability and predictability. In H. C. Haywood & D. Tzuriel (Eds.), *Interactive assessment* (pp. 332–355). New York: Springer-Verlag.

Shonkoff, J. P., & Marshall, P. C. (1990). Biological bases of developmental dysfunction. In S. J. Meisels & J. P. Shonkoff (Eds.), *Handbook of early childhood intervention* (pp. 35–52). Cambridge, UK: Cambridge University Press.

Short, E. J., & Ryan, E. B. (1984). Metacognitive differences between skilled and less skilled readers: Remediating deficits through story grammar and attribution training. *Journal of Educational Psychology, 76,* 225–235.

Shulman, L. (1986). Paradigms and research programs in the study of teaching: A contemporary perspective. In M. C. Wittorck (Ed.),

Handbook of research on teaching, 3rd. ed. (pp. 3–36). New York: MacMillan.

Shulman, L. S., & Keislar, E. R. (Eds.) (1966). *Learning by discovery: A critical appraisal.* Chicago: Rand McNally.

Shurkin, J. N. (1992). *Terman's kids: The groundbreaking study of how the gifted grow up.* Boston: Little Brown & Co.

Siegel, L. S., & Ryan, E. B. (1988). Development of grammatical-sensitivity, phonological, and short-term memory skills in normally achieving and learning disabled children. *Developmental Psychology, 24,* 28–37.

Siegel, L. S., & Ryan, E. B. (1989). The development of working memory in normally achieving and subtypes of learning disabled children. *Child Development, 60,* 973–980.

Siegler, R. S. (1987). The perils of averaging data over strategies: An example from children's addition. *Journal of Experimental Psychology: General, 116,* 1–15.

Siegler, R. S. (1988). Individual differences in strategy choices: Good students, not-so-good students, and perfectionists. *Child Development, 59,* 833–851.

Siegler, R. S. (1989). Hazards of mental chronometry: An example from children's subtraction. *Journal of Educational Psychology, 81,* 497–506.

Siegler, R. S., & Crowley, K. (1991). The microgenetic method: A direct means for studying cognitive development. *American Psychologist, 46,* 606–620.

Siegler, R. S., & Jenkins, E. (1989). *How children discover new strategies.* Hillsdale, NJ: Erlbaum & Associates.

Siegler, R. S., & Shrager, J. (1984). Strategy choices in addition and subtraction: How do children know what to do? In C. Sophian (Ed.), *Origins of cognitive skills* (pp. 229–293). Hillsdale, NJ: Erlbaum & Associates.

Sigman, M., Neumann, C., Jansen, A. A. J., & Bwibo, N. (1989). Cognitive abilities of Kenyan children in relation to nutrition, family characteristics, and education. *Child Development, 60,* 1463–1474.

Silver, E. (Ed.) (1985). *Teaching and learning mathematical problem solving.* Hillsdale, NJ: Erlbaum & Associates.

Silver, E. A. (1987). Foundations of cognitive theory and research for mathematics problem solving instruction. In A. Schoenfeld (Ed.), *Cognitive science and mathematics education* (pp. 33–60). Hillsdale, NJ: Erlbaum & Associates.

Simmons, P. E. (1991). Learning science in software microworlds. In S. M. Glynn, R. H. Yeany, & B. K. Britton (Eds.), *The psychology of learning science* (pp. 241–256). Hillsdale, NJ: Erlbaum & Associates.

Simon, H. A., & Chase, W. G. (1973). Skill in chess. *American Scientist, 61,* 394–403.

Simonton, D. K. (1988). *Scientific genius: A psychology of science.* Cambridge, UK: Cambridge University Press.

Simonton, D. K. (1990). Creativity and wisdom in aging. In J. E. Birren & K. W. Schaie (Eds.), *Handbook of the psychology of aging,* 3rd ed. (pp. 320–329). San Diego: Academic Press.

Simpson, M. L., Hayes, C. G., Stahl, N., Connor, R. T., & Weaver, D. (1988). An initial validation of a study strategy system. *Journal of Reading Behavior, 20,* 149–180.

Sinclair, R. L., & Ghory, W. J. (1987). *Reaching marginal students.* Berkeley, CA: McCutchan.

Singer, J. D., Palfrey, J. S., Butler, J. A., & Walker, D. K. (1989). Variation in special education classification across school districts: How does where you live affect what you are labeled? *American Educational Research Journal, 26,* 261–281.

Singer, R. S. (1972). *The psychomotor domain: Movement behavior.* Philadelphia: Lea & Febiger.

Singley, M. K., & Anderson, J. R. (1989). *Transfer of cognitive skill.* Cambridge, MA: Harvard University Press.

Sizer, T. R. (1984). *Horace's compromise: The dilemma of the American high school.* Boston: Houghton Mifflin.

Skemp, R. R. (1989). *Mathematics in the primary school.* London: Routledge.

Skinner, B. F. (1953). *Science and human behavior.* New York: Free Press.

Skinner, B. F. (1961). Why we need teaching machines. *Harvard Educational Review, 31,* 377–398.

Skinner, B. F. (1977). Corporal punishment. In I. A. Hyman & J. H. Wise (Eds.), *Corporal punishment in American education* (pp. 335–336). Philadelphia: Temple University Press.

Skinner, B. F. (1987). *Upon further reflection.* Englewood Cliffs, NJ: Prentice-Hall.

Skinner, B. F. (1990). Can psychology be a science of mind? *American Psychologist, 45,* 1206–1210.

Skinner, E. A., Wellborn, J. G., & Connell, J. P. (1990). What it takes to do well in school and whether I've got it: A process model of perceived control and children's engagement and achievement in school. *Journal of Educational Psychology, 82,* 22–32.

Slavin, R. E. (1984). Meta-analysis in education: How has it been used? *Educational Researcher, 13,* 6–15.

Slavin, R. (1985a). An introduction to cooperative learning research. In R. Slavin, S. Sharan, S. Kagan, R. H. Lazarowitz, C. Webb, & R. Schmuck (Eds.), *Learning to cooperate, cooperating to learn* (pp. 5–15). New York: Plenum.

Slavin, R. (1985b). Team–assisted individualization: Combining cooperative learning and individualized instruction in mathematics. In R. Slavin, S. Sharan, S. Kagan, R. H. Lazarowitz, C. Webb, & R. Schmuck (Eds.), *Learning to cooperate, cooperating to learn* (pp. 177–209). New York: Plenum.

Slavin, R. E. (1987a). Grouping for instruction in the elementary school. *Educational Psychologist, 22,* 109–128.

Slavin, R. E. (1989). Class size and student achievement: Small effects of small classes. *Educational Psychologist, 24,* 99–110.

Slavin, R. E. (1990a). Achievement effects of ability grouping in secondary schools: A best-evidence synthesis. *Review of Educational Research, 60,* 471–499.

Slavin, R. E. (1990b). Mastery learning re-reconsidered. *Review of Educational Research, 60,* 300–302.

Slavin, R. E., Madden, N. A., Karweit, N. L., Dolan, L., Wasik, B. A., Shaw, A., Mainzer, K. L., & Haxby, B. (1991). Neverstreaming: Prevention and early intervention as an alternative to special education. *Journal of Learning Disabilities, 24,* 373–378.

Slavin, R. E., Madden, N. A., Karweit, N. L., Livermon, B. J., & Dolan, L. (1990). Success for all: First-year outcomes of a comprehensive plan for reforming urban education. *American Educational Research Journal, 27,* 255–278.

Slife, B. D., Weiss, J., & Bell, T. (1985). Separability of metacognition and cognition: Problem solving in learning disabled and regular students. *Journal of Educational Psychology, 77,* 437–445.

Smirnov, A. A. (1973). *Problems of the psychology of memory.* New York: Plenum.

Smith, A., & Sugar, O. (1975). Development of above normal language and intelligence: 21 years after left hemispherectomy. *Neurology, 25,* 813–818.

Smith, C. L. (1979). Children's understanding of natural language categories. *Journal of Experimental Child Psychology, 30,* 191–205.

Smith, E. E., & Medin, D. L. (1981). *Categories and concepts.* Cambridge, MA: Harvard University Press.

Smith, F. (1971). *Understanding reading: A psycholinguistic analysis of reading and learning to read.* New York: Holt, Rinehart, & Winston.

Smith, F. (1986). *Insult to intelligence: The bureaucratic invasion of classrooms.* New York: Arbor House.

Smith, M. L. (1991a). Meanings of test preparation. *American Educational Research Journal, 28,* 521–542.

Smith, M. L. (1991b). Put to the test: The effects of external testing on teachers. *Educational Researcher, 20 (5),* 8–11.

Smith, M. L., & Glass, G. V. (1987). *Research and evaluation in education and the social sciences.* Englewood Cliffs, NJ: Prentice-Hall.

Smith, S. D., Kimberling, W. J., Pennington, B. F., & Lubs, H. A. (1983). Specific reading disability: Identification of an inherited form through linkage analysis. *Science, 219,* 1345–1347.

Smith, S. D., Pennington, B. F., Kimberling, W. J., & Ing, P. S. (1990). Familial dyslexia: Use of genetic linkage to identify subtypes. *Journal of the American Academy of Child and Adolescent Psychiatry, 29,* 204–213.

Smith, S. G., & Jones, L. L. (1988). Images, imagination, and chemical reality. *Journal of Chemical Education, 66,* 8–11.

Sokolov, A. N. (1975). *Inner speech and thought.* New York: Plenum.

Solomon, D., Watson, M. S., Delucchi, K. L., Schaps, E., & Battistich, V. (1988). Enhancing children's prosocial behavior in the classroom. *American Educational Research Journal, 25,* 527–554.

Sommerfeld, M. (1992). "Micro-society" schools

tackle real-world woes. *Education Week, 12, 1,* 14.

Song, M-J., Ginsburg, H. P. (1987). The development of informal and formal mathematical thinking in Korean and U.S. children. *Child Development, 58,* 1286–1296.

Soodak, L. C. (1990). Social behavior and knowledge of social "scripts" among mentally retarded adults. *American Journal of Mental Deficiency, 94,* 515–521.

Sophian, C. (1987). Early developments in children's use of counting to solve quantitative problems. *Cognition and Instruction, 4,* 61–90.

Sostek, A. M., Smith, Y. F., Katz, K. S., & Grant, E. G. (1987). Developmental outcome of preterm infants with intraventricular hemorrhage at one and two years of age. *Child Development, 58,* 779–786.

Sowell, E. J. (1989). Effects of manipulative materials in mathematics instruction. *Journal for Research in Mathematics Education, 20,* 498–505.

Spearman, C. (1904). "General intelligence" objectively determined and measured. *American Journal of Psychology, 15,* 201–293.

Speidel, G. E. & Nelson, K. E. (eds.) (1989). The many faces of imitation in language learning. New York: Springer-Verlag.

Spilich, G. J., Vesonder, G. T., Chiesi, H. L., & Voss, J. F. (1979). Text processing of domain-related information for individuals with high and low domain knowledge. *Journal of Verbal Learning and Verbal Behavior, 18,* 275–290.

Spiro, R. J., Feltovich, P. J., Coulson, R. L., & Anderson, D. K. (1989). Multiple analogies for complex concepts: Antidotes for analogy-induced misconception in advanced knowledge acquisition. In S. Vosniadou & A. Ortony (Eds.), *Similarity and analogical reasoning* (pp. 498–531). Cambridge, UK: Cambridge University Press.

Spitz, H. H. (1986a). *The raising of intelligence: A selected history of attempts to raise retarded intelligence.* Hillsdale, NJ: Erlbaum & Associates.

Spitz, H. H. (1986b). Preventing and curing mental retardation by behavioral intervention: An evaluation of some claims. *Intelligence, 10,* 197–207.

Spivey, N. N., & King, J. R. (1989). Readers as writers composing from sources. *Reading Research Quarterly, 24,* 7–26.

Spreen, O., & Strauss, E. (1991). *A compendium of neuropsychological tests: Administration, norms, and commentary.* New York: Oxford University Press.

Springer, S. P., & Deutsch, G. (1989). *Left brain, right brain,* 3rd ed. New York: W.H. Freeman & Co.

Squire, J. R. (1991). The history of the profession. In J. Flood, J. M. Jensen, D. Lapp, & J. R. Squire (Eds.), *Handbook of research on teaching the English language arts* (pp. 3–17). New York: MacMillan.

Squire, L. R. (1987). *Memory and brain.* Oxford: Oxford University Press.

Stacey, K. (1992). Mathematical problem solving in groups: Are two heads better than one? *Journal of Mathematical Behavior, 11,* 261–275.

Stahl, S. A., & Miller, P. D. (1989). Whole lan-

guage and language experience approaches for beginning reading: A quantitative research synthesis. *Review of Educational Research, 59,* 87–116.

Stallings, J., & Kaskowitz, D. (1974). *Follow Through classroom observation evaluation 1972–73* (SRI Project URU-7370). Stanford, CA: Stanford Research Institute.

Stanovich, K. E. (1980). Toward an interactive compensatory model of individual differences in the development of reading fluency. *Reading Research Quarterly, 16,* 32–71.

Stanovich, K. (1986). Matthew effects in reading: Some consequences of individual differences in the acquisition of literacy. *Reading Research Quarterly, 21,* 360–407.

Stanovich, K. E. (1991). Discrepancy definitions of reading disability: Has intelligence led us astray? *Reading Research Quarterly, 26,* 7–29.

Stanovich, K. E., & Cunningham, A. E. (1993). Where does knowledge come from? Specific associations between print exposure and information acquisition. *Journal of Educational Psychology, 85,* 211–229.

Stanovich, K. E., & West, R. F. (1989). Exposure to print and orthographic processing. *Reading Research Quarterly, 24,* 402–433.

Staver, J. R., & Jacks, T. (1988). The influence of cognitive reasoning level, cognitive restructuring ability, disembedding ability, working memory capacity, and prior knowledge on students' performance on balancing equations by inspection. *Journal of Research in Science Teaching, 25,* 763–775.

Stavy, R. (1991). Using analogy to overcome misconceptions about conservation of matter. *Journal of Research in Science Teaching, 28,* 305–313.

Stedman, L. (1988). The effective schools formula still needs changing: A reply to Brookover. *Phi Delta Kappan, 69 (6),* 439–442.

Stein, B. S., & Bransford, J. D. (1979). Constraints of effective elaboration: Effects on precision and subject generation. *Journal of Verbal Learning and Verbal Behavior, 18,* 769–777.

Stein, B. S., Littlefield, J., Bransford, J. D., & Persampieri, M. (1984). Elaboration and knowledge acquisition. *Memory & Cognition, 12,* 522–529.

Stein, N. L., & Glenn, C. G. (1979). An analysis of story comprehension in elementary school children. In R. O. Freedle (Eds.), *New directions in discourse processing,* Vol. 2. Norwood, NJ: Ablex.

Stein, N. L., & Nezworski, G. (1978). The effects of organization and instructional set on story memory. *Discourse Processes, 1,* 177–193.

Steinberg, E. R., & Anderson, R. C. (1975). Hierarchical semantic organization in 6-year-olds. *Journal of Experimental Child Psychology, 19,* 544–553.

Steinberg, L., & Dornbusch, S. M. (1991). Negative correlates of part-time employment during adolescence: Replication and elaboration. *Developmental Psychology, 27,* 304–313.

Steinberg, L., Fegley, S., & Dornbusch, S. M. (1993). Negative impact of part-time work on adolescent adjustment. *Developmental Psychology, 29*, 171–180.

Stensvold, M. S., & Wilson, J. T. (1990). The interaction of verbal ability with concept mapping in learning from a chemistry laboratory activity. *Science Education, 74*, 473–480.

Stern, J. (1985). Biochemical aspects. In A. M. Clarke, A. D. B. Clarke, & J. M. Berg (Eds.), *Mental deficiency: The changing outlook* (pp. 135–212). New York: The Free Press.

Sternberg, R. J. (1977). *Intelligence, information processing, and analogical reasoning: The componential analysis of human abilities.* Hillsdale, NJ: Erlbaum & Associates.

Sternberg, R. J. (1980). Sketch of a componential subtheory of human intelligence. *Behavioral and Brain Sciences, 3*, 573–584.

Sternberg, R. J. (1981). A componential theory of intellectual giftedness. *Gifted Child Quarterly, 25*, 86–93.

Sternberg, R. J. (1983). Components of human intelligence. *Cognition 15*, 1–48.

Sternberg, R. J. (1985). *Beyond IQ: A triarchic theory of human intelligence.* Cambridge, UK: Cambridge University Press.

Sternberg, R. J. (1986). A triarchic theory of intellectual giftedness. In R. J. Sternberg & J. E. Davidson (Eds.), *Conceptions of giftedness* (pp. 223–243). Cambridge, UK: Cambridge University Press.

Sternberg, R. J. (1991a). Death, taxes, and bad intelligence tests. *Intelligence, 15*, 257–269.

Sternberg, R. J. (1991b). Giftedness according to the triarchic theory of human intelligence. In N. Colangelo & G. A. Davis (Eds.), *Handbook of gifted education* (pp. 45–54) Boston: Allyn & Bacon.

Sternberg, R. J., & Davidson, J. E. (1983). Insight in the gifted. *Educational Psychologist, 18*, 51–57.

Sternberg, R. J., & Wagner, R. K. (1985). *Practical intelligence: Origins of competence in the everyday world.* Cambridge, UK: Cambridge University Press.

Sternberg, S. (1966). High-speed scanning in human memory. *Science, 153*, 652–654.

Sternberg, S. (1969). Memory-scanning: Mental processes revealed by reaction-time experiments. *American Scientist, 57*, 421–457.

Stevens, L. J., & Price, M. (1992). Meeting the challenges of educating children at risk. *Phi Delta Kappan, 74*, 18–23.

Stevens, R. J., Madden, N. A., Slavin, R. E., & Farnish, A. M. (1987). Cooperative Integrated Reading and Composition: Two field experiments. *Reading Research Quarterly, 22*, 433–454.

Stevenson, H. W. (1990). The Asian advantage: The case of mathematics.In J. J. Shields (Ed.), *Japanese schooling: Patterns of socialization, equality, and political control* (pp. 85–95). University Park, PA: Pennsylvania State University Press.

Stevenson, H. W. (1992). Learning from Asian schools. *Scientific American, 267* (6), 70–76.

Stevenson, H. W., Lee, S. Y., Chen, C., Lummis, M., Stigler, J., Fan, L., & Ge, F. (1990a). Mathematics achievement of children in China and the United States. *Child Development, 61*, 1053–1066.

Stevenson, H. W., Lee, S. Y., Chen, C., Stigler, J. W., Hsu, C., & Kitamura, S. (1990b). Contexts of achievement. *Monographs of the Society for Research in Child Development, 55* (1–2, Serial No. 211).

Stevenson, H. W., Lee, S., & Stigler, J. (1986). Mathematics achievement of Chinese, Japanese, and American children. *Science, 231*, 693–699.

Stevenson, H. W., Lummis, M., Lee, S., & Stigler, J. (1990). *Making the grade in mathematics: Chinese, Japanese, and American children.* Reston, VA: National Council of Teachers of Mathematics.

Stevenson, H. W., Parker, T., Wilkinson, A., Bonnevaux, B., & Gonzalez, M. (1978). Schooling, environment, and cognitive development: A cross-cultural study. *Monographs of the Society for Research in Child Development, 43* (Serial No. 175).

Stevenson, J. (1992). Genetics. In N. N. Singh & I. L. Beale (Eds.), *Learning disabilities: Nature, theory, and treatment* (pp. 327–351). New York: Springer-Verlag.

Stewart, L., & Pascual-Leone, J. (1992). Mental capacity constraints and the development of moral reasoning. *Journal of Experimental Child Psychology, 54*, 251–287.

Stigler, J. W. (1984). "Mental abacus": The effect of abacus training on Chinese children's mental calculation. *Cognitive Psychology, 16*, 145–176.

Stigler, J. W., Lee, S., Lucker, G. W., & Stevenson, H. W. (1982). Curriculum and achievement in mathematics: A study of elementary school children in Japan, Taiwan, and the United States. *Journal of Educational Psychology, 74*, 315–322.

Stigler, J. W., Lee, S., & Stevenson, H. W. (1987). Mathematics classrooms in Japan, Taiwan, and the United States. *Child Development, 58*, 1272–1285.

Stigler, J., Lee, S., & Stevenson, H. W. (1990). *Mathematical knowledge of Japanese, Chinese, and American children.* Reston, VA: National Council of Teachers of Mathematics.

Stillings, N. A., Feinstein, M. H., Garfield, J. L., Rissland, E. L., Rosenbaum, D. A., Weisler, S. E., & Baker-Ward, L. (1987). *Cognitive science: An introduction.* Cambridge, MA: MIT Press.

Stipek, D. J., & Daniels, D. H. (1988). Declining perceptions of competence: A consequence of changes in the child or in the educational environment? *Journal of Educational Psychology, 80*, 352–356.

Stipek, D. J., & Hoffman, J. M. (1980). Children's achievement-related expectancies as a function of academic performance histories and sex. *Journal of Educational Psychology, 72*, 861–865.

Stipek, D. J., & Kowalski, P. S. (1989). Learned helplessness in task-orienting versus performance-orienting testing conditions. *Journal of Educational Psychology, 81*, 384–391.

Stipek, D., & MacIver, D. (1989). Developmental change in children's assessment of intellectual competence. *Child Development, 60*, 521–538.

Stodolsky, S. S. (1985). Telling math: Origins of math aversion and anxiety. *Educational Psychologist, 93*, 409–428.

Stokes, T. F., & Baer, D. M. (1977). An implicit technology of generalization. *Journal of Applied Behavior Analysis, 10*, 349–367.

Storfer, M. D. (1990). *Intelligence and giftedness: The contributions of heredity and early environment.* San Francisco: Jossey-Bass.

Strahan, D. B. (1989). How experienced and novice teachers frame their views of instruction: An analysis of semantic ordered trees. *Teaching and Teacher Education, 5*, 53–67.

Strauss, A., & Corbin, J. (1990). *Basics of qualitative research: Grounded theory procedures and techniques.* Newbury Park, CA: Sage.

Streissguth, A. P., Barr, H. M., Sampson, P. D., Darby, B. L., & Martin, D. C. (1989). IQ at age 4 in relation to maternal alcohol use and smoking during pregnancy. *Developmental Psychology, 25*, 3–11.

Stuart, M., & Masterson, J. (1992). Patterns of reading and spelling in 10-year-old children related to prereading phonological abilities. *Journal of Experimental Child Psychology, 54*, 168–187.

Suchman, J. R. (1960). Inquiring training in the elementary school. *Science Teacher, 27*, 42–47.

Sulzby, E. (1985). Children's emergent reading of favorite storybooks: A developmental study. *Reading Research Quarterly, 20*, 458–481.

Sulzby, E. (1988). A study of children's early reading development. In A. D. Pelligrini (Ed.), *Psychological bases for early education* (pp. 39–75). Chichester, UK: John Wiley & Sons.

Sulzby, E., & Teale, W. (1991). Emergent literacy. In R. Barr, M. L. Kamil, P. B. Mosenthal, & P. D. Pearson (Eds.), *Handbook of reading research*, Vol. II (pp. 727–758). New York: Longman.

Summers, M. (1992). Improving primary school teachers' understanding of science concepts—theory into practice. *International Journal of Science Education, 14*, 25–40.

Suppes, P., & Groen, G. J. (1967). Some counting models for first grade performance data on simple addition facts. In J. M. Scandura (Ed.), *Research in mathematics education* (pp. 34–43). Washington, DC: National Council of Teachers of Mathematics.

Sutton, R. E. (1991). Equity and computers in schools: A decade of research. *Review of Educational Research, 61*, 475–504.

Svenson, O., & Hedonborg, M-L. (1979). Strategies used by children when solving simple subtractions. *Acta Psychologica, 43*, 477–489.

Swanson, H. L. (1989). Verbal coding deficits in learning-disabled readers. A multiple stage model. *Educational Psychology Review, 1*, 235–277.

Swanson, H. L. (1990). Influence of metacognitive knowledge and aptitude on problem solving. *Journal of Educational Psychology, 82*, 306–314.

Swanson, H. L. (1992). Generality and modifiability of working memory among skilled and less skilled readers. *Journal of Educational Psychology, 84,* 473–488.

Swanson, H. L., & Cooney, J. B. (1991). Learning disabilities and memory. In B. Y. L. Wong (Ed.), *Learning about learning disabilities* (pp. 104–127). San Diego: Academic Press.

Swanson, H. L., O'Connor, J. E., & Cooney, J. B. (1990). An information processing analysis of expert and novice teachers' problem solving. *American Educational Research Journal, 27,* 533–556.

Sweller, J. (1988). Cognitive load during problem solving: Effects on learning. *Cognitive Science, 12,* 257–285.

Sweller, J. (1989). Cognitive technology: Some procedures for facilitating learning and problem solving in mathematics and science. *Journal of Educational Psychology, 81,* 457–466.

Sweller, J., & Cooper, G. A. (1985). The use of worked examples as a substitute for problem solving in learning algebra. *Cognition and Instruction, 2,* 59–89.

Sweller, J., & Levine, M. (1982). Effects of goal specificity on means-ends analysis and learning. *Journal of Experimental Psychology: Learning, Memory, and Cognition, 8,* 463–474.

Sweller, J., Mawer, R., & Ward, M. (1983). Development of expertise in mathematical problem solving. *Journal of Experimental Psychology: General, 112,* 639–661.

Symons, S., & Pressly, M. (1993). Prior knowledge affects text search success and extraction of information. *Reading Research Quarterly, 28,* 250–261.

Szetala, W., & Nicol, C. (1992). Evaluating problem solving in mathematics. *Educational Leadership, 49* (8), 42–45.

Tangel, D. M., & Blachman, B. A. (1992). Effect of phoneme awareness instruction on kindergarten children's invented spellings. *Journal of Reading Behavior, 24,* 233–261.

Tannenbaum, A. J. (1983). *Gifted children: Psychological and educational perspectives.* New York: MacMillan.

Tannenbaum, A. J. (1986). Giftedness: A psychosocial approach. In R. J. Sternberg & J. E. Davidson (Eds.), *Conceptions of giftedness* (pp. 21–52). Cambridge, UK: Cambridge University Press.

Tarmizi, R. A., & Sweller, J. (1988). Guidance during mathematical problem solving. *Journal of Educational Psychology, 80,* 424–436.

Tarver, S. G., Hallahan, D. P., Cohen, S. B., & Kauffman, J. M. (1977). The development of visual selective attention and verbal rehearsal in learning disabled boys. *Journal of Learning Disabilities, 10,* 26–52.

Tarver, S. G., Hallahan, D. P., Kauffman, J. M., & Ball, D. W. (1976). Verbal rehearsal and selective attention in children with learning disabilities: A developmental lag. *Journal of Experimental Child Psychology, 22,* 375–385.

Tate, B. G. (1972). Case study: Control of chronic self-injurious behavior by conditioning procedures. *Behavior Therapy, 3,* 72–83.

Taub, H. A. (1974). Coding for short-term memory as a function of age. *Journal of Genetic Psychology, 125,* 309–314.

Taylor, A. M., & Turnure, J. E. (1979). Imagery and verbal elaboration with retarded children: Effects on learning and memory. In N. R. Ellis (Ed.), *Handbook of mental deficiency: Psychological theory and research* (pp. 659–697). Hillsdale, NJ: Erlbaum & Associates.

Taylor, B. M. (1982). Text structure and children's comprehension and memory for expository material. *Journal of Educational Psychology, 74,* 323–340.

Taylor, B. M., & Beach, R. W. (1984). The effects of text structure instruction on middle-grade students' comprehension and production of expository text. *Reading Research Quarterly, 19,* 134–146.

Taylor, B. M., Frye, B. J., & Maruyama, G. M. (1990). Time spent reading and reading growth. *American Educational Research Journal, 27,* 351–362.

Taylor, D., & Strickland, D. (1986). *Family storybook reading.* Exeter, NH: Heinemann Educational Books.

Taylor, J. L., & Chiogioji, E. N. (1988). The Holland and Andre study on extracurricular activities: Imbalanced and incomplete. *Review of Educational Research, 58,* 99–105.

Teale, W. (1978). Positive environments for learning to read: What studies of early readers tell us. *Language Arts, 55,* 922–932.

Terman, L. M. (1925). *Genetic studies of genius, mental and physical traits of a thousand gifted children.* Stanford, CA: Stanford University Press.

Terman, L. M., & Childs, H. G. (1912). A tenative revision and extension of the Binet-Simon Measuring Scale of Intelligence. *Journal of Educational Psychology, 3,* 61–74, 133–143, 198–208, 277–289.

Terman, L. M., & Oden, M. H. (1947). *The gifted child grows up: Twenty-five years' followup of a superior group.* Stanford, CA: Stanford University Press.

Terman, L. M., & Oden, M. H. (1959). *The gifted group in midlife: Thirty years, followup of the superior child.* Stanford, CA: Stanford University Press.

Thomas, E. (1990). Filial piety, social change and Singapore youth. *Journal of Moral Education, 19,* 192–206.

Thomas, M. H., & Dieter, J. N. (1987). The positive effect of writing practice on integration of foreign words in memory. *Journal of Educational Psychology, 79,* 249–253.

Thompson, L. A., Fagan, J. F., & Fulker, D. W. (1991). Longitudinal prediction of specific cognitive abilities from infant novelty preference. *Child Development, 62,* 530–538.

Thoreson, C. E. (Ed.) (1972). *Behavior modification in education: The seventy-second yearbook of the National Society for the Study of Education,* Part 1. Chicago: University of Chicago Press.

Thorkildsen, T. A. (1989). Justice in the classroom: The student's view. *Child Development, 60,* 323–334.

Thorkildsen, T. A. (1991). Defining social goods and distributing them fairly: The development of conceptions of fair testing practices. *Child Development, 62,* 852–863.

Thorkildsen, T. A. (1993). Those who can, tutor: High-ability students' conceptions of fair ways to organize learning. *Journal of Educational Psychology, 85,* 182–190.

Thorndike, R. L., Hagen, E. P., & Sattler, J. M. (1986). *Stanford-Binet intelligence scale: Technical manual,* 4th ed. Chicago: Riverside Press.

Thurstone, L. L. (1938). Primary mental abilities. *Psychometric Monographs,* No. 1. Chicago: University of Chicago Press.

Thurstone, L. L. (1947). *Multiple factor analysis.* Chicago: University of Chicago Press.

Tierney, R. J., LaZansky, J., Raphael, T., & Cohen, P. (1987). Author's intentions and readers' interpretation. In R. J. Tierney, P. L. Anders, & J. N. Mitchell (Eds.), *Understanding readers' understanding* (pp. 205–224). Hillsdale, NJ: Erlbaum & Associates.

Tingle, J. B., & Good, R. (1990). Effects of cooperative grouping on stoichiometric problem solving in high school chemistry. *Journal of Research in Science Teaching, 27,* 671–683.

Tipper, S. P., Bourque, T. A., Anderson, S. H., & Brehaut, J. C. (1989). Mechanisms of attention: A developmental study. *Journal of Experimental Child Psychology, 48,* 353–378.

Tippett, L. J. (1992). The generation of visual images: A review of neuropsychological research and theory. *Psychological Bulletin, 112,* 415–432.

Tobias, S. (1979). Anxiety research in educational psychology. *Journal of Educational Psychology, 71,* 573–582.

Tobias, S. (1985). Test anxiety: Interference, defective skills, and cognitive capacity. *Educational Psychologist, 20,* 135–142.

Tobias, S. (1987). Mandatory text review and interaction with student characteristics. *Journal of Educational Psychology, 79,* 154–161.

Tobin, K. (1987). The role of wait time in higher cognitive level learning. *Review of Educational Research, 57,* 69–95.

Tobin, K., & Fraser, B. J. (1990). What does it mean to be an exemplary science teacher? *Journal of Research in Science Teaching, 27,* 3–25.

Todorov, T. (1984). *Mikhail Bakhtin: The dialogical principle.* Minneapolis: University of Minnesota Press.

Tomchin, E. M., & Impara, J. C. (1992). Unraveling teachers' beliefs about grade retention. *American Educational Research Journal, 29,* 199–223.

Tomlinson-Keasey, C., & Little, T. D. (1990). Predicting educational attainment, occupational achievement, intellectual skill, and personal adjustment among gifted men and women. *Journal of Educational Psychology, 82,* 442–455.

Tomporowski, P. D., & Simpson, R. G. (1990). Sustained attention and intelligence. *Intelligence, 14,* 31–42.

Toppino, T. C., Kasserman, J. E., & Mracek, W. A. (1991). The effect of spacing repetitions on the recognition memory of young children and adults. *Journal of Experimental Child Psychology, 51,* 123–138.

Torgesen, J. K. (1975). Problems and prospects in

the study of learning disabilities. In M. Hetherington & J. Hagen (Eds.), *Review of research in child development,* Vol. 5. Chicago: University of Chicago Press.

Torgesen, J. K. (1977). Memorization processes in reading-disabled children. *Journal of Educational Psychology, 69,* 571–578.

Torgesen, J. K. (1979). What shall we do with psychological processes? *Journal of Learning Disabilities, 12,* 16–23.

Torgesen, J. K. (1980). Conceptual and educational implications of the use of efficient task strategies by learning disabled children. *Journal of Learning Disabilities, 13,* 364–371.

Torgesen, J. K. (1991). Learning disabilities: Historical and conceptual issues. In B. Y. L. Wong (Ed.), *Learning about learning disabilities* (pp. 3–37). San Diego: Academic Press.

Torgesen, J. K., & Goldman, T. (1977). Verbal rehearsal and short-term memory in reading disabled children. *Child Development, 48,* 56–60.

Torgesen, J. K., & Houck, D. O. (1980). Processing deficiencies of learning disabled children who perform poorly on the digit span test. *Journal of Educational Psychology, 72,* 141–160.

Torgesen, J. K., Kistner, J. A., & Morgan, S. (1987). Component processes in working memory. In J. G. Borkowski & J. D. Day (Eds.), *Cognition in special children: Comparative approaches to retardation, learning disabilities, and giftedness* (pp. 49–85). Norwood, NJ: Ablex.

Treagust, D. F. (1991). A case study of two exemplary biology teachers. *Journal of Research in Science Teaching, 28,* 329–342.

Treiman, R., & Baron, J. (1983). Phonemic-analysis training helps children benefit from spelling-sound rules. *Memory and Cognition, 11,* 382–389.

Tudge, J. R. H. (1992). Processes and consequences of peer collaboration: A Vygotskian analysis. *Child Development, 63,* 1364–1379.

Tulving, E. (1972). Episodic and semantic memory. In E. Tulving & W. Donaldson (Eds.), *Organization of memory* (pp. 381–403). New York: Academic Press.

Tulving, E. (1983). *Elements of episodic memory.* Oxford, UK: Oxford University Press.

Tunmer, W. E., Herriman, M. L., Nesdale, A. R. (1988). Metalinguistic abilities and beginning reading. *Reading Research Quarterly, 23,* 134–158.

Turnbull, W. W. (1985). *Student change, program change: Why the SAT scores kept falling.* New York: College Entrance Examination Board.

Tyler, R., & Smith, E. (1942). *Appraising and recording student progress.* New York: Harper & Brothers.

Tzuriel, D. (1992). The development of ego identity at adolescence among Israeli Jews and Arabs. *Journal of Youth and Adolescence, 21,* 551–571.

Tzuriel, D., & Feurstein, R. (1992). Dynamic group assessment for prescriptive teaching: Differential effects of treatment. In H. C. Haywood & D. Tzuriel (Eds.), *Interactive assessment* (pp. 187–206). New York: Springer-Verlag.

Ulrich, R., Wolfe, M., & Bluhm, M. (1970). Operant conditioning in the public schools. In R. Ulrich, T. Stachnik, & J. Mabry (Eds.), *Control of human behavior: From cure to prevention* (pp. 334–343). Glenview, IL: Scott, Foresman & Company.

Underwood, B. J. (1966). *Experimental psychology.* New York: Appleton-Century-Crofts.

Underwood, B. J. (1975). Individual differences as a crucible in theory construction. *American Psychologist, 30,* 128–134.

U.S. Department of Education, National Commission on Excellence in Education (1983). *A nation at risk: The imperative for education reform.* Washington, DC: Government Printing Office.

Utley, C. A., Haywood, H. C., & Masters, J. C. (1992). Policy implications of psychological assessment of minority children. In H. C. Haywood & D. Tzuriel (Eds.), *Interactive assessment* (pp. 445–469). New York: Springer-Verlag.

Valdez-Menchaca, M. C., & Whitehurst, G. J. (1992). Accelerating language development through picture book reading: A systematic extension to Mexican day care. *Developmental Psychology, 28,* 1106–1114.

Van der Meer, R., & Valsiner, J. (1988). Lev Vygotsky and Pierre Janet: On the origin of the concept of sociogenesis. *Developmental Review, 8,* 52–65.

van der Meij, H. (1988). Constraints on question asking in classrooms. *Journal of Educational Psychology, 80,* 401–405.

van Dijk, T. A., & Kintsch, W. (1983). *Strategies of discourse comprehension.* New York: Academic Press.

Van Haneghan, J. P. (1990). Third and fifth graders' use of multiple standards of evaluation to detect errors in word problems. *Journal of Educational Psychology, 82,* 352–358.

Van Haneghan, J. P., & Baker, L. (1989). Cognitive monitoring in mathematics. In C. B. McCormick, G. Miller, & M. Pressley (Eds.), *Cognitive strategy research: From basic research to educational applications* (pp. 215–238). New York: Springer-Verlag.

Van Haneghan, J., Barron, L., Young, M., Williams, S., Vye, N., & Bransford, J. (1992). The Jasper series: An experiment with new ways to enhance mathematical thinking. In D. F. Halpern (Ed.), *Enhancing thinking skills in the sciences and mathematics* (pp. 15–38). Hillsdale, NJ: Erlbaum & Associates.

Van Houten, R., & Rolider, A. (1989). An analysis of several variables influencing the efficacy of flash card instruction. *Journal of Applied Behavior Analysis, 22,* 111–118.

van Lehn, K. (1990). *Mind bugs: The origins of procedural misconceptions.* Cambridge, MA: MIT Press.

Vasu, E. S., & Howe, A. C. (1989). The effect of visual and verbal modes of presentation on children's retention of images and words. *Journal of Research in Science Teaching, 26,* 401–407.

Vellutino, F. R. (1979). *Dyslexia: Theory and research.* Cambridge, MA: MIT Press.

Venezky, R. L., & Johnson, D. (1973). The development of two letter-sound patterns in grade 1–3. *Journal of Educational Psychology, 64,* 109–115.

Verhoeven, L. T. (1990). Acquisition of reading in a second language. *Reading Research Quarterly, 25,* 90–114.

Vernon, P. A. (1983). Speed of information processing and intelligence. *Intelligence, 7,* 53–70.

Vernon, P. A. (1985). Individual differences in general cognitive ability. In L. C. Hartlage & C. F. Telzrow (Eds.), *The neuropsychology of individual differences.* New York: Plenum.

Vernon, P. A. (1987). New developments in reaction time research. In P. A. Vernon (Ed.), *Speed of information processing and intelligence* (pp. 1–20). Norwood, NJ: Ablex.

Vernon, P. A. (1990a). An overview of chronometric measures of intelligence. *School Psychology Review, 19,* 309–410.

Vernon, P. A. (1990b). The use of biological measures to estimate behavioral intelligence. *Educational Psychologist, 25,* 293–304.

Vernon, P. A. (1991). Studying intelligence the hard way. *Intelligence, 15,* 389–395.

Vosniadou, S., & Schommer, M. (1988). Explanatory analogies can help children acquire information from expository text. *Journal of Educational Psychology, 80,* 524–536.

Voss, J. F. (1991). Informal reasoning and international relations. In J. F. Voss, D. N. Perkins, & J. W. Segal (Eds.), *Informal reasoning and education* (pp. 37–58). Hillsdale, NJ: Erlbaum & Associates.

Vorhees, C. V., & Mollnow, E. (1987). Behavioral teratogenesis: Long-term influences on behavior from early exposure to environmental agents. In J. D. Osofsky (Ed.), *Handbook of infant development* (pp. 913–971). New York: Wiley.

Voss, J. F., Vesonder, G. T., & Spilich, G. J. (1980). Generation and recall by high-knowledge and low-knowledge individuals. *Journal of Verbal Learning and Verbal Behavior, 19,* 651–667.

Vurpillot, E. (1968). The development of scanning strategies and their relations to visual differentiation. *Journal of Experimental Child Psychology, 6,* 632–650.

Vygotsky, L. S. (1962). *Thought and language.* Cambridge, MA: MIT Press.

Vygotsky, L. S. (1978). *Mind in society: The development of higher psychological processes.* Cambridge, MA: Harvard University Press.

Vygotsky, L. S. (1981). The genesis of higher mental functions. In J. V. Wertsch (Ed.), *The concept of activity in Soviet psychology* (pp. 144–188). Armonk, NY: M.E. Sharpe.

Vygotsky, L. S. (1987). *Thinking and speech* (Edited & Translated by N. Minick). New York: Plenum.

Waddill, P. J., McDaniel, M. A., & Einstein, G. O. (1988). Illustrations as adjuncts to prose: A text-appropriate processing approach. *Journal of Educational Psychology, 80,* 457–464.

Wade, S. E., & Adams, R. B. (1990). Effects of importance and interest on recall of biographic text. *Journal of Reading Behavior, 22,* 331–353.

Wade, S. E., Schraw, G., Buxton, W. M., & Hayes, M. T. (1993). Seduction of the strategic reader: Effects of interest on strategies and recall. *Reading Research Quarterly, 28,* 93–114.

Wade, S. E., Trathen, W., & Schraw, G. (1990). An analysis of spontaneous study strategies. *Reading Research Quarterly, 25,* 147–166.

Wagenaar, W. A. (1986). My memory: A study of autobiographic memory over six years. *Cognitive Psychology, 18,* 225–252.

Wagner, D. A. (1974). The development of short-term and incidental memory: A cross-cultural study. *Child Development, 45,* 389–396.

Wagner, D. A. (1978). Memories of Morocco: The influence of age, schooling, and environment on memory. *Cognitive Psychology, 10,* 1–28.

Walberg, H. J., Harnisch, D., & Tsai, S. L. (1986). Elementary school mathematics productivity in twelve countries. *British Educational Research Journal, 12,* 237–248.

Walczyk, J. J. (1990). Relation among error detection, sentence verification, and low-level reading skills of fourth graders. *Journal of Educational Psychology, 82,* 491–497.

Walczyk, J. J., & Hall, V. C. (1989). Is the failure to monitor comprehension an instance of cognitive impulsivity? *Journal of Educational Psychology, 81,* 294–298.

Walk, R. D., & Gibson, E. J. (1961). A comparative and analytical study of visual depth perception. *Psychological Monographs,* No. 519, *75,* No. 15.

Walker, B. J., & Wilson, P. T. (1991). Using guided imagery to teach science concepts. In C. M. Santa & D. E. Alvermann (Eds.), *Science learning: Processes and applications* (pp. 147–155). Newark, DE: International Reading Association.

Walker, C. H. (1987). Relative importance of domain knowledge and overall aptitude on acquisition of domain-related information. *Cognition and Instruction, 4,* 25–42.

Walker, L. (1984). Sex differences in the development of moral reasoning: A critical review. *Child Development, 55,* 677–691.

Walker, L. J. (1989). A longitudinal study of moral reasoning. *Child Development, 60,* 157–166.

Walker, L. J., & Moran, T. J. (1991). Moral reasoning in a communist Chinese society. *Journal of Moral Education, 20,* 139–155.

Walters, G. C., & Grusec, J. E. (1977). *Punishment.* San Francisco: W.H. Freeman & Co.

Wandersee, J. H. (1988). Ways students read texts. *Journal of Research in Science Teaching, 25,* 69–84.

Wanner, E. (1975). *On remembering, forgetting, and understanding sentences.* The Hague: Mouton.

Ward, M., & Sweller, J. (1990). Structuring effective worked examples. *Cognition and Instruction, 7,* 1–39.

Ward, T. B., Vela, E., & Hass, S. D. (1990). Children and adults learn family-resemblance categories analytically. *Child Development, 61,* 593–605.

Wasik, B. H., Ramey, C. T., Bryant, D. M., & Sparling, J. J. (1990). A longitudinal study of two early intervention strategies: Project CARE. *Child Development, 61,* 1682–1696.

Wasik, B. A., & Slavin, R. E. (1993). Preventing early reading failure with one-to-one tutoring: A review of five programs. *Reading Research Quarterly, 28,* 178–200.

Waterman, A., & Goldman, J. (1976). A longitudinal study of ego identity development in a liberal arts college. *Journal of Youth and Adolescence, 5,* 361–369.

Watson, D. J. (1989). Defining and describing whole language. *Elementary School Journal, 90,* 129–141.

Weaver, C. (1990). *Understanding whole language: From principles to practice.* Portsmouth, NH: Heinemann.

Webb, N. L. (1992). Assessment of students' knowledge of mathematics: Steps toward a theory. In D. A. Grouws (Ed.), *Handbook of research on mathematics teaching and learning* (pp. 661–683). New York: MacMillan.

Webb, N. M. (1984). Sex differences in interaction and achievement in cooperative small groups. *Journal of Educational Psychology, 76,* 33–34.

Webb, N. M. (1989). Peer interaction and learning in small groups. *International Journal of Educational Research, 13,* 21–39.

Webb, N. M. (1991). Task-related verbal interaction and mathematics learning in small groups. *Journal for Research in Mathematics Education, 22,* 366–389.

Wechsler, D. (1939). *The measurement of adult intelligence.* Baltimore: Williams & Wilkins.

Wechsler, D. (1949). *Manual for the Wechsler intelligence scale for children.* San Antonio, TX: Psychological Corporation.

Wechsler, D. (1967). *A manual for the preschool and primary scale of intelligence.* San Antonio, TX: Psychological Corporation.

Wechsler, D. (1981). *WAIS-R: Wechsler Adult Intelligence Scale–Revised.* New York: Psychological Corporation.

Weed, K., Ryan, E. B., & Day, J. (1990). Metamemory and attributions as mediators of strategy use and recall. *Journal of Educational Psychology, 82,* 849–855.

Wegner, D. M. (1987). Transactive memory: A contemporary analysis of the group mind. In B. Mullen & G. Goethals (Eds.), *Theories of group behavior* (pp. 185–208). New York: Springer-Verlag.

Wiederholt, J. L. (1974). Historical perspectives on the education of the learning disabled. In L. Mann & D. Sabatino (Eds.), *The second review of special education* (pp. 103–152). Philadelphia: JSE Press.

Weinberg, R. A., Scarr, S., & Waldman, I. D. (1992). The Minnesota transracial adoption study: A followup of IQ test performance at adolescence. *Intelligence, 16,* 117–135.

Weinberg, R. S. (1982). The relationship between mental preparation strategies and motor performance: A review and critique. *Quest, 33 (2),* 195–213.

Weiner, B. (1979). A theory of motivation for

some classroom experiences. *Journal of Educational Psychology, 71,* 3–25.

Weiner, B. (1990). History of motivational research in education. *Journal of Educational Psychology, 82,* 616–622.

Weinert, F. E., Knopf, M., Körkel, J., Schneider, W., Vogel, K., & Wetzel, M. (1984). Die Entwicklung einiger Gedächtnisleistungen bei Kindern und älternen Erwachsenen in Abhängigkeit von kognitiven, meta kognitiven und motivationalen Einflussfaktoren. In K. E. Grossman & P. Lütkenhaus (Eds.), *Bericht über die sechste Tagung Entwicklung psychologie* (pp. 313–326).

Weinert, F. E., Schneider, W., & Knopf, M. (1988). Individual differences in memory development across the life-span. In P. B. Baltes, D. L. Featherman, & R. M. Lerner (Eds.), *Lifespan development and behavior,* Vol. 9 (pp. 39–85). Hillsdale, NJ: Erlbaum & Associates.

Weinstein, C. F., & Mayer, R. F. (1986). The teaching of learning strategies. In M. C. Wittrock (Ed.), *Handbook of research on teaching,* 3rd ed. (pp. 315–327). New York: MacMillan.

Weizenbaum, J. (1976). *Computer power and human reason: From judgment to calculation.* San Francisco: Freeman.

Welsh, M. C., Pennington, B. F., Ozonoff, S., Rouse, B., & McCabe, E. R. B. (1990). Neuropsychology of early-treated phenylketonuria: Specific executive function deficits. *Child Development, 61,* 1697–1713.

Wentzel, K. R. (1991a). Relations between social competence and academic achievement in early adolescence. *Child Development, 62,* 1966–1078.

Wentzel, K. R. (1991b). Social competence at school: Relation between social responsibility and academic achievement. *Review of Educational Research, 61,* 1–24.

Werner, E. E. (1990). Protective factors and individual resilience. In S. J. Meisels & J. P. Shonkoff (Eds.), *Handbook of early childhood interventions* (pp. 97–116). Cambridge, UK: Cambridge University Press.

Werner, E. E., Bierman, J. M., & French, F. E. (1971). *The children of Kauai.* Honolulu: University of Hawaii Press.

Werner, E. E., & Smith, R. S. (1982). *Vulnerable but invincible: A longitudinal study of resilient children and youth.* New York: McGraw-Hill.

Wertsch, J. V. (1979). From social interaction to higher psychological processes: A clarification and application of Vygotsky's theory. *Human Development, 22,* 1–22.

Wertsch, J. V. (Ed.) (1981). *The concept of activity in Soviet psychology.* Armonk, NY: M. E. Sharpe.

Wertsch, J. V. (1985). *Vygotsky and the social formation of mind.* Cambridge, MA: Harvard University Press.

Wertsch, J. V. (1991). *Voices of the mind.* Cambridge, MA: Harvard University Press.

Wheelock, A. (1992). *Crossing the tracks: How "untracking" can save America's schools.* New York: New Press, Norton.

White, B. Y. (1984). Designing computer games to help physics students understand Newton's laws of motion. *Cognition and Instruction, 1,* 69–108.

White, M. (1987). *The Japanese educational challenge: A commitment to children.* New York: Free Press.

White, R. W. (1959). Motivation reconsidered: The concept of competence. *Psychological Review, 66,* 297–333.

Whitehead, A. (1929). *The aims of education.* New York: MacMillan.

Whitehurst, G. J., Falco, F. L., Lonigan, C. J., Fischel, J. E., DeBaryshe, B. D., Valdez-Menchaca, M. C., & Caulfield, M. (1988). Accelerating language development through picturebook reading. *Developmental Psychology, 24,* 552–559.

Whitehurst, G. J., & Valdez-Menchaca, M. C. (1988). What is the role of reinforcement in early language acquisition? *Child Development, 59,* 430–440.

Whitehurst, G. J., & Vasta, R. (1975). Is language acquired through imitation? *Journal of Psycholinguistic Research, 4,* 37–59.

Whitehurst, G. J., & Zimmerman, B. J. (Eds.). (1979). *The function of language and cognition.* New York: Academic Press.

Whitley, B. E. Jr., McHugh, M. C., & Frieze, I. H. (1986). Assessing the theoretical models for sex differences in causal attributions of success and failure. In J. S. Hyde & M. C. Linn (Eds.), *The psychology of gender: Advances through meta-analysis* (pp. 67–101). Baltimore: Johns Hopkins Press.

Whitman, T. L. (1990). Self-regulation and mental retardation. *American Journal on Mental Retardation, 94,* 347–362.

Whittington, D. (1991). What have 17-year-olds known in the past? *American Educational Research Journal, 28,* 759–780.

Widaman, K. F., Geary, D. C., Cormier, P., & Little, T. D. (1989). A componential model for mental addition. *Journal of Experimental Psychology: Learning, Memory, and Cognition, 15,* 898–919.

Widaman, K. F., Little, T. D., Geary, D. C., & Cormier, P. (1992). Individual differences in the development of skill in mental addition: Internal and external validation of chronometric methods. *Learning and Individual Differences, 4,* 167–214.

Wierda, M., & Brookhuis, K. A. (1991). Analysis of cycling skill: A cognitive approach. *Applied Cognitive Psychology, 5,* 113–122.

Wigfield, A. (1988). Children's attributions for success and failure: Effects of age and attentional focus. *Journal of Educational Psychology, 80,* 76–81.

Wigfield, A., Eccles, J. S., MacIver, D., Reuman, D. A., & Midgley, C. (1991). Transitions during early adolescence: Changes in children's domain-specific self-perceptions and general self-esteem across the transition to junior high school. *Developmental Psychology, 27,* 552–565.

Willerman, L., Schultz, R., Rutledge, J. N., & Bigler, E. D. (1991). *In vivo* brain size and intelligence. *Intelligence, 15,* 223–228.

Willerman, M., & MacHarg, R. A. (1991). The concept map as an advance organizer. *Journal of Research in Science Teaching, 28,* 705–711.

Williams, J. P. (1980). Teaching decoding with an emphasis on phoneme analysis and phoneme blending. *Journal of Educational Psychology, 72,* 1–15.

Williams, J. P. (1993). Comprehension of students with and without learning disabilities: Identification of narrative themes and idiosyncratic text representations. *Journal of Educational Psychology, 85,* 631–641.

Williams, T. M. (Ed.) (1986). *The impact of television: A natural experiment in three communities.* New York: Academic Press.

Willis, S. L. (1985). Towards an educational psychology of the older adult learner: Intellectual and cognitive bases. In J. E. Birren & K. W. Schaie (Eds.), *Handbook of the psychology of aging* (pp. 818–847). New York: Van Nostrand Reinhold Company.

Willis, W. G., Hooper, S. R., & Stone, B. H. (1992). Neuropsychological theories of learning disabilities. In N. H. Singh & I. L. Beale (Eds.), *Learning disabilities: Nature, theory, and treatment* (pp. 201–245). New York: Springer-Verlag.

Wilson, S. (1982). Heritability. *Journal of Applied Problems, 19,* 71–85.

Wineberg, S. S. (1991a). Historical problem solving: A study of the cognitive processes used in the evaluation of documentary and pictorial evidence. *Journal of Educational Psychology, 83,* 73–87.

Wineberg, S. S. (1991b). On the reading of historical texts: Notes on the breach between school and academy. *American Educational Research Journal, 28,* 495–520.

Winer, G. A. (1980). Class-inclusion reasoning in children: A review of the empirical literature. *Child Development, 51,* 309–328.

Winne, P. H., Woodlands, M. H., & Wong, B. Y. L. (1982). Comparability of self-concept among learning disabled, normal, and gifted students. *Journal of Learning Disabilities, 15,* 470–475.

Winter, D., McClelland, D., & Stewart, A. (1981). *A new case for the liberal arts: Assessing institutional goals and student development.* San Francisco: Jossey-Bass.

Wirtz, W. (Chair) (1977). *On further examination: Report of the advisory panel on the Scholastic Aptitude Test score decline.* New York: College Entrance Examination Board.

Wissler, C. (1901). The correlation of mental and physical tests. *Psychological Review, 3* (Monograph Supplement 16).

Witherell, C. S. (Guest Ed.) (1991). Special issue: Narrative and the moral realm: Tales of caring and justice. *Journal of Moral Education, 20, (3).*

Wittrock, M. C. (1966). The learning by discovery hypothesis. In L. S. Shulman & E. R. Keislar (Eds.), *Learning by discovery: A critical appraisal* (pp. 33–75). Chicago: Rand-McNally.

Wittrock, M. C. (1990). Generative processes of comprehension. *Educational Psychologist, 24,* 345–376.

Wittrock, M. C. (1992). Generative learning processes of the brain. *Educational Psychologist, 27,* 531–542.

Wittrock, M. C., & Alesandrini, K. (1990). Gener-

ation of summaries and analogies and analytic and holistic abilities. *American Educational Research Journal, 27,* 489–502.

Wolf, D., Bixby, J., Glenn, John III, & Gardner, H. (1991). To use their minds well: Investigating new forms of student assessment. In G. Grant (Ed.), *Review of research in education* (pp. 31–74). Washington, DC: American Educational Research Association.

Wolff, P., & Levin, J. R. (1972). The role of overt activity in children's imagery production. *Child Development, 43,* 537–547.

Wolff, P., Levin, J. R., & Longobardi, E. T. (1972). Motoric mediation in children's paired-associate learning: Effects of visual and tactile contact. *Journal of Experimental Child Psychology, 14,* 176–183.

Woloshyn, V. E., Paivio, A. U., & Pressley, M. (1994). Use of elaborative interrogation to help students acquire information consistent with prior knowledge and information inconsistent with prior knowledge. *Journal of Educational Psychology, 86,* 79–89.

Woloshyn, V. E., Pressley, M., & Schneider, W. (1992). Elaborative interrogation and prior knowledge effects on learning of facts. *Journal of Educational Psychology, 84,* 115–124.

Woloshyn, V. E., Willoughby, T., Wood, E., & Pressley, M. (1990). Elaborative interrogation facilitates adult learning of factual paragraphs. *Journal of Educational Psychology, 82,* 513–524.

Wolters, G., Beishuizen, M., Broers, G., & Knoppert, W. (1990). Mental arithmetic: Effects of calculation procedure and problem difficulty on solution latency. *Journal of Experimental Child Psychology, 49,* 20–30.

Wood, E., Pressley, M., & Winne, P.H. (1990). Elaborative interrogation effects on children's learning of factual content. *Journal of Educational Psychology, 82,* 741–748.

Wood, R., & Bandura, A. (1989). Impact of conceptions of ability on self-regulatory mechanisms and complex decision-making. *Journal of Personality and Social Psychology, 56,* 407–415.

Wood, S. S., Bruner, J. S., & Ross, G. (1976). The role of tutoring in problem solving. *Journal of Child Psychology and Psychiatry, 17,* 89–100.

Woodruff-Pak, D. S., Logan, C. G., & Thompson, R. F. (1990). Neurobiological substrates of classical conditioning across the life span. In A. Diamond (Ed.), *The developmental and neural bases of higher cognitive functions* (pp. 150–178). New York: New York Academy of Sciences.

Woods, B. T. (1980). The restricted effects of right hemisphere lesions after age one; Wechsler test data. *Neuropsychologia, 18,* 65–70.

Woods, S. S., Resnick, L. B., & Groen, G. J. (1975). Experimental test of five process models for subtraction. *Journal of Educational Psychology, 67,* 17–21.

Wozniak, R. (1972). Verbal regulation of motor behavior: Soviet research and non-Soviet replications. *Human Development, 15,* 13–57.

Wyatt, D., Pressley, M., El-Dinary, P. B., Stein, S., Evans, P., & Brown, R. (1992). *Comprehension strategies, worth and credibility monitoring, and evaluations: Cold and hot cognition when experts read professional articles that are important to them.* Technical Report. College Park, MD: University of Maryland, Department of Human Development.

Wyatt, D., Pressley, M., El-Dinary, P. B., Stein, S., Evans, P., & Brown, R. (1993). Comprehension strategies, worth and credibility monitoring, and evaluations: Cold and hot cognition when experts read professional articles that are important to them. *Learning and Individual Differences, 5,* 49–72.

Wyatt, M. (1992). The past, present, and future need for college reading courses in the U.S. *Journal of Reading, 36,* 10–20.

Yarroch, W. L. (1985). Student understanding of chemical equation balancing. *Journal of Research in Science Teaching, 22,* 449–459.

Yates, F. A. (1966). *The art of memory.* London: Routledge & Kegan Paul.

Yoakum, C. S., & Yerkes, R. M. (1920). *Army mental tests.* New York: Holt.

Yuill, N., & Oakhill, J. (1988). Effects of inference awareness training on poor reading comprehension. *Applied Cognitive Psychology, 2,* 33–45.

Yule, W., Gold, R. D., & Busch, C. (1982). Long-term predictive validity of the WPSSI: An 11-year follow-up study. *Personality and Individual Differences, 3,* 65–71.

Yussen, S. R. (1974). Determinants of visual attention and recall in observational learning by preschoolers and second graders. *Developmental Psychology, 10,* 93–100.

Zaporozhets, A. V. (1965). The development of perception in preschool children. *Monographs of the Society for Research in Children Development, 30* (2, whole No. 100), 82–101.

Zeamon, D., & House, B. J. (1979). A review of attention theory. In N. R. Ellis (Ed.), *Handbook of mental deficiency: Psychological theory and research* (pp. 63–120). Hillsdale, NJ: Erlbaum & Associates.

Zellermayer, M., Salomon, G., Globerson, T., & Givon, H. (1991). Enhancing writing-related metacognitions through a computerized writing partner. *American Educational Research Journal, 28,* 373–391.

Zentall, S. S. (1990). Fact-retrieval automatization and math problem solving by learning disabled, attention-deficit, and normal adolescents. *Journal of Educational Psychology, 82,* 856–865.

Zhu, X., & Simon, H. A. (1987). Learning mathematics from examples and by doing. *Cognition and Instruction, 4,* 137–166.

Zigler, E., & Balla, D. (Eds.) (1982). *Mental retardation: The developmental-difference controversy.* Hillsdale, NJ: Erlbaum & Associates.

Zigler, E., & Hodapp, R. M. (1986). *Understanding mental retardation.* Cambridge, UK: Cambridge University Press.

Zigler, E., & Seitz, V. (1975). "An experimental evaluation of sensorimotor patterning": A critique. *American Journal of Mental Deficiency, 79,* 483–492.

Zimmerman, B. J. (1989a). A social cognitive view of self-regulated academic learning. *Journal of Educational Psychology, 81,* 329–339.

Zimmerman, B. J. (1989b). Models of self-regulated learning and academic achievement. In B. J. Zimmerman & D. H. Schunk (Eds.), *Self-regulated learning and academic achievement* (pp. 1–25). New York: Springer-Verlag.

Zimmerman, B. J. (1990a). Self-regulated learning and academic achievement: An overview. *Educational Psychologist, 25,* 3–18.

Zimmerman, B. J. (1990b). Self-regulating academic learning and achievement: The emergence of a social-cognitive perspective. *Educational Psychology Review, 2,* 173–201.

Zimmerman, B. J., Bandura, A., & Martinez-Pons, M. (1992). Self-motivation for academic attainment: The role of self-efficacy beliefs and personal goal setting. *American Educational Research Journal, 29,* 663–676.

Zimmerman, B. J., & Martinez-Pons, M. (1986). Development of a structured interview for assessing student use of self-regulated learning strategies. *American Educational Research Journal, 23,* 614–628.

Zimmerman, B. J., & Martinez-Pons, M. (1988). Construct validation of a strategy model of student self-regulated learning. *Journal of Educational Psychology, 80,* 284–290.

Zimmerman, B. J., & Martinez-Pons, M. (1990). Student differences in self-regulated learning: Relating grade, sex, and giftedness to self-efficacy and strategy use. *Journal of Educational Psychology, 82,* 51–59.

Zinchenko, P. I. (1981). Involuntary memory and the goal-directed nature of activity. In J. V. Wertsch (Ed.), *The concept of activity in Soviet psychology* (pp. 300–340). Armonk, NY: M.E. Sharpe, Inc.

Zook, K. B. (1991). Effects of analogical processes on learning and misrepresentation. *Educational Psychology Review, 3,* 41–72.

Zook, K. B., & DiVesta, F. J. (1991). Instructional analogies and conceptual misrepresentations. *Journal of Educational Psychology, 83,* 246–252.

Acknowledgments

NOTE: Unless otherwise acknowledged, all photographs are the property of Scott, Foresman and Company. Page abbreviations are as follows: (T) top, (C) center, (B) bottom, (L) left, (R) right.

Page 4: PhotoFest; p. 7: Jean-Claude LeJeune; p. 14: Elizabeth Crews/Stock Boston; p. 37: Jean-Claude LeJeune; p. 44R: S.F. Briggs/National Audobon Society; p. 50: Rohn Engh; p. 58; Courtesy of Alan Paivio; p. 60L and 60R: John Cancalosi/Stock Boston; p. 71: Julian Baum; p. 73L: Mark Richards/Photo Edit; p. 73R: John Maher/Stock Boston; p. 91: Jean-Claude LeJeune; p. 97: Jean-Claude LeJeune; p. 116: Hank Morgan/Rainbow; p. 148: Bill Anderson/Monkmeyer Press Photo Service; p. 156: Courtesy Dr. B. F. Skinner; p. 165: Courtesy of Donald Meichenbaum; p. 168: Chuck Painter/Stanford University; p. 173: Courtesy of Barry Zimmerman; p. 198: Bohdan Hrynewych; p. 201: Harry Wilkes/Stock Boston; p. 208: Harvard News Office; p. 217L: Stacy Pick/Stock Boston; p. 217R: Bob Daemmrich/Stock Boston; p. 218C: Wallowitch; p. 218R: Polk County Democrat, Bartow, Florida; p. 246: Hazel Hankin/Stock Boston; p. 248: Barbara Alper/Stock Boston; p. 255TR: Scott, Foresman; p. 255B: Richard Stromberg; p. 259L: Susie Fitzhugh/Stock Boston; p. 259R: Rob Crandall/Stock Boston; p. 264: Stock Boston; p. 290: Stephen Frisch/Stock Boston; p. 303: Ulrike Welsch/Photo Edit; p. 326: Jean-Claude LeJeune; p. 342: Gary A Conner/Photo Edit; p. 343: Charles Temple, Hobart & William Smith Colleges, Geneva, New York; p. 382: Ulrike Welsch/Photo Edit; p. 432: Freeman/Grishaber/Photo Edit; p. 460: Walter Holt; p. 474L: Ithaca Journal; p. 474C: Scott, Foresman; and p. 474R: Jean-Claude LeJeune.

Name Index

Abdi, H., 321
Abelson, R. P., 50, 55, 61
Aboitz, F., 454
Abraham, M. R., 301
Abrahamsen, A., 41
Abranovic, W. A., 374
Ach, N., 108
Achenbach, T., 452
Achilles, C. M., 264
Ackerman, J., 394–395
Adair, J. G., 11
Adams, M. J., 355, 358–360, 362, 368
Adams, R. B., 100
Adelman, H., 414
Afflerbach, P. P., 351
Ahmad, M., 90, 240, 364
Ahn, W., 56
Aiken, E. G., 246
Ajewole, G. A., 297
Akler, M., 133
Aks, D. J., 5
Alesandrini, K., 365
Alexander, K. L., 258, 342–343
Alexander, P. A., 3, 100, 292
Allen, J. B., 385
Allen, L., 362
Allen, S., 284
Allen, V. L., 262
Allington, R., 362
Allington, R. L., 263
Almasi, J., 18, 370–371
Alvermann, D. E., 85, 198, 293, 373
Amaiwa, S., 337
American Psychological Association, 407, 467

Ames, C., 92–93, 104, 458
Ames, R., 92
Amigues, R., 299
Amsel, E., 301–304
Anastasi, A., 405–407
Anastasiow, N. J., 4, 119, 130
Anderson, B. J., 133
Anderson, C. W., 284, 428–429
Anderson, D. K., 292
Anderson, D. R., 354
Anderson, J. R., 34, 36, 49, 59, 61–62, 247–248, 335
Anderson, L., 428–429
Anderson, L. M., 388–390
Anderson, M. C., 244
Anderson, O. R., 308
Anderson, R., 362
Anderson, R. B., 308
Anderson, R. C., 45, 48, 51–52, 99, 202, 244, 358, 370, 376
Anderson, S. H., 154
Anderson, T. H., 45, 51–52, 99–100, 238–239, 363, 375
Andre, T., 267, 375
Andrews, J., 92
Annett, J., 247–248
Anthony, H. M., 388–390
Apicella, A., 117, 454
Applebee, A., 391–392, 394
Applebee, A. N., 353, 384–385, 391, 393
Araujo, J., 262
Arbitman-Smith, R., 272
Archer, J., 104, 458
Arjmand, O., 462

Armbruster, B. B., 100, 363, 375
Armitage, M., 261
Armour-Thomas, E., 317, 334
Armstrong, D. L., 442
Armstrong, F. D., 131, 133
Arnold, K. D., 210, 214
Artman, L., 25
Artz, A. F., 317, 334
Asarnow, J. R., 30
Ashcraft, M. H., 329–330
Aspinwall, L. G., 183–184, 186
Astin, A. W., 274
Atkinson, R. C., 235
Attannucci, J., 214
Atwell, N., 385
Auble, P. M., 239
Aulls, M. W., 293
Ault, C. S., 294
Ausubel, D. P., 8, 243
Ayabe, C. R., 265

Babad, E. Y., 440
Babcock, R. L., 473
Bach, M. J., 360
Bachicha, D. L., 172
Bacon, G., 133
Baddeley, A., 3
Baer, D. M., 28, 166, 453
Bahrick, H. P., 249–250, 276
Bailey, J., 361
Baird, W., 100
Baker, L., 196, 323, 349–352
Baker, L. A., 116, 420
Baker-Ward, L., 43, 238
Bakhtin, M. M., 4

525

Subject Index